W9-BBB-088

the AMERICANA ANNUAL

1975

AN ENCYCLOPEDIA OF THE EVENTS OF 1974

YEARBOOK OF THE ENCYCLOPEDIA AMERICANA

Library of Congress Catalog Card Number: 23-10041

Standard Book Number: ISBN 0-7172-0206-2

Printed in the United States of America
Lithography by Rand McNally & Company

EDITORIAL STAFF

Editor in Chief
BERNARD S. CAYNE

Executive Editors
JOHN J. SMITH   S. J. FODERARO   JAMES E. CHURCHILL, JR.

Art Director ERIC E. AKERMAN

EDITORIAL

ROBERT S. ANDERSON
JAMES W. CARROLL
JUDITH A. GLICKMAN
EDMUND GREKULINSKI
DAVID T. HOLLAND
ROBERT L. HURTGEN
STEVEN H. MOLL
RICHARD N. MOREHOUSE
EVA E. NEUMANN
NATHAN H. PLETCHER
WESLEY F. STROMBECK
SUSAN C. WINSLOW
MELVIN WOLFSON
DONALD R. YOUNG

Production Editor RUTH M. CHANDLER   **Production Assistant** MARY L. LOCKETT

Indexer VITRUDE DESPAIN   **Editorial Statistician** RUTH N. SKODNICK

Assistant to Editor in Chief ELLEN L. SCHOLZ

Manuscript Typists MATHILDE BURRY, Chief   NILSA JIMENEZ

ART

Picture Research MARGARET L. SKAGGS Head   RICHARD A. GREENE
NATALIE GOLDSTEIN

Art Assistant DORIS E. HUNT

PRODUCTION

Production Supervisor JAMES G. KEARNEY

Assistant Production Supervisor ROCCO A. SUMMA

GROLIER INCORPORATED

Editorial Director
WALLACE S. MURRAY

Editorial Consultant
LOWELL A. MARTIN

Art and Production Coordinator
ELIZABETH CHASE

Editorial Controller
NICHOLAS DEMOS

Manufacturing Director
RAYMOND H. LABOTT

CONTENTS

FEATURE ARTICLES OF THE YEAR

THE ALPHABETICAL SECTION

Articles listed below are in the *Review of the Year* section, which begins on page 73, and are grouped in broad subject categories for the aid of the reader. In addition, separate entries on the continents, the major nations of the world, U. S. states, Canadian provinces, and principal U. S. and Canadian cities will be found under their own alphabetically arranged headings.

ECONOMICS, BUSINESS, AND INDUSTRY

ENTERTAINMENT AND HOBBIES

GOVERNMENT, LAW, AND POLITICS

HUMAN WELFARE

HUMANITIES AND THE ARTS

SCIENCE AND MEDICINE

MISCELLANEOUS

contributors

Following is a complete list of the distinguished authorities who contributed articles to this edition of the annual. Their professional affiliations are shown, together with the titles of their articles.

ADAMS, GEORGE, Legislative Reference Librarian, Connecticut State Library: CONNECTICUT

ADRIAN, CHARLES R., Professor of Political Science, University of California, Riverside: CALIFORNIA; LOS ANGELES

ALEXANDER, ROBERT J., Professor of Economics and Political Science, Rutgers University: GUYANA

ALLER, LAWRENCE H., Professor of Astronomy, University of California, Los Angeles: ASTRONOMY

ALVEY, EDWARD, JR., Professor Emeritus of Education, Mary Washington College: EDUCATION

AMBRE, AGO, Current Business Analysis Division, Bureau of Economic Analysis, U. S. Department of Commerce: INDUSTRIAL REVIEW

AMSPOKER, JOANNE, Associate Professor of History, Oregon College of Education: OREGON

ARMSTRONG, FREDERICK H., Associate Professor of History, University of Western Ontario: TORONTO

BAKER, RICHARD T., Professor of Journalism, Columbia University: PUBLISHING—*Newspapers*

BALLINGER, RONALD B., Professor and Chairman, Department of History, Rhode Island College: SOUTH AFRICA

BANKS, RONALD F., Associate Professor of History, University of Maine: MAINE

BERGEN, DANIEL P., Associate Professor, Graduate Library School, University of Rhode Island: LIBRARIES

BERGER, WOLFGANG H., Assistant Professor of Oceanography, Scripps Institution of Oceanography, University of California, San Diego: OCEANOGRAPHY

BEST, JOHN, Chief, *Canada World News,* Ottawa: NEW BRUNSWICK

BIRD, CAROLINE, Author, *The Invisible Scar, Born Female, Everything a Woman Needs to Know to Get Paid What She's Worth,* and *The Case Against College;* Consulting Editor, *New Woman:* WOMEN'S RIGHTS

BITTON, LIVIA E., Assistant Professor of Hebrew and Jewish Studies, Herbert H. Lehman College, City University of New York: RELIGION—*Judaism*

BLACK, KENNETH, JR., Regents Professor of Insurance, Georgia State University; Coauthor, *Life Insurance* and *Cases in Life Insurance:* INSURANCE

BLAND, WILLIAM F., Editor, *International Oil News:* ENERGY —*Petroleum*

BLANKENSHIP, BENJAMIN R., JR., Economic Research Service, U. S. Department of Agriculture: FOOD—*World Food Supply*

BLOODSWORTH, DAVID R., Acting Director, Labor Relations and Research Center, University of Massachusetts: POSTAL SERVICE

BOULAY, HARVEY, Assistant Professor of Political Science, Boston University: BOSTON; MASSACHUSETTS

BOVEY, JOHN A., Provincial Archivist of Manitoba: MANITOBA

BOWERS, Q. DAVID, Columnist, *Coin World;* Author, *Coins and Collectors, High Profits from Rare Coin Investment,* and *Coin Collecting for Profit:* COIN COLLECTING

BOYLAN, JAMES R., Graduate School of Journalism, Columbia University: PUBLISHING—*Magazines*

BRADDOCK, BILL, Sports Department, *The New York Times:* CONNORS, JIMMY; EVERT, CHRIS; MILLER, JOHNNY; ROBINSON, FRANK; SPORTS

BRAMMER, DANA B., Assistant Director, Bureau of Governmental Research, University of Mississippi: MISSISSIPPI

BRAZDA, JEROME F., Editor, *Washington Report on Medicine & Health:* SOCIAL WELFARE—*Health Care, U. S. Health Insurance*

BRODIN, PIERRE, Director of Studies, Lycée Français de New York: FRENCH LITERATURE

BURDETTE, FRANKLIN L., Professor and Director, Bureau of Governmental Research, University of Maryland: ELECTIONS AND POLITICAL PARTIES; MARYLAND

BURKHEAD, JESSE, Professor of Economics, Syracuse University: TAXATION

BURKS, ARDATH W., Professor of Political Science and Associate Vice President for Academic Affairs, Rutgers University: JAPAN; TANAKA, KAKUEI

BURLINGAME, MERRILL G., Professor of History, Montana State University: MONTANA

BUSTIN, EDOUARD, Professor of Political Science, Boston University: ZAIRE

BUTWELL, RICHARD, Dean of Arts and Sciences, State University of New York College at Fredonia; Author, *Southeast Asia: A Political Introduction, Southeast Asia—Today and Tomorrow,* and *U Nu of Burma:* BURMA; CAMBODIA; LAOS; VIETNAM

CAIRNS, JOHN C., Professor of History, University of Toronto: FRANCE; GISCARD D'ESTAING, VALÉRY; OBITUARIES —*Pompidou, Georges*

CANFIELD, ROBERT L., Associate Professor of Anthropology, Washington University, St. Louis: ETHNIC GROUPS

CANN, STAN, State Editor, *The Forum,* Fargo, N. Dak.: NORTH DAKOTA

CHALMERS, J. W., Faculty of Education, University of Alberta: ALBERTA

CHRIEN, ROBERT E., Senior Physicist, Brookhaven National Laboratory: ENERGY—*Nuclear Energy*

CLARK, C. B., Graduate Assistant in History, University of Oklahoma: OKLAHOMA

CLARK, ROBERT S., Contributing Editor, *Stereo Review:* MUSIC

COCKRUM, E. LENDELL, Professor of Biological Sciences, University of Arizona: ZOOLOGY

COHEN, SIDNEY, Executive Director, Council on Drug and Alcohol Abuse, and Adjunct Professor of Psychiatry, University of California, Los Angeles: DRUG ADDICTION AND ABUSE

COLE, CAROLYN J., Paine, Webber, Jackson & Curtis Inc.: STOCKS AND BONDS

CONDAX, PHILIP L., Curator, Equipment Archives, International Museum of Photography, George Eastman House: PHOTOGRAPHY

COOLEY, JOHN K., Middle East Correspondent, *The Christian Science Monitor;* Radio News Correspondent, ABC News: THE MIDDLE EAST—*The Palestinians*

COPPAGE, NOEL, Contributing Editor, *Stereo Review:* RECORDINGS—*Popular Records*

CORLEW, ROBERT E., Chairman, Department of History, Middle Tennessee State University: TENNESSEE

CORNWELL, ELMER E., JR., Professor of Political Science, Brown University: RHODE ISLAND

CRAINE, DEBRA, News Editor, The Canadian Press, Vancouver: VANCOUVER

CURTIS, L. PERRY, JR., Professor of History, Brown University: IRELAND

DARBY, JOSEPH W., III, Assistant City Editor, *The Times-Picayune,* New Orleans: NEW ORLEANS

DAVIS, PETER G., Recordings Editor, *The New York Times:* RECORDINGS—*Classical Records*

DELZELL, CHARLES F., Professor and Chairman, Department of History, Vanderbilt University: ITALY

DENERSTEIN, ROBERT L., Editor, *African Update,* The African-American Institute: ALGERIA; MOROCCO; SUDAN; TUNISIA

DOBLER, CLIFFORD, Professor of Business Law, University of Idaho: IDAHO

DOLAN, PAUL, Professor of Political Science, University of Delaware: DELAWARE

DONEHOO, PATRICIA A., Fashion and Patterns Editor, *Woman's Day* Magazine: FASHION

DORPALEN, ANDREAS, Professor of History, The Ohio State University: GERMANY; SCHMIDT, HELMUT

DRACHKOVITCH, MILORAD M., Senior Fellow, The Hoover Institution, Stanford University: YUGOSLAVIA

DRIGGS, DON W., Chairman, Department of Political Science, University of Nevada, Reno: NEVADA

DUFF, ERNEST A., Professor of Political Science, Randolph-Macon Woman's College: COLOMBIA

DUPREE, LOUIS, American Universities Field Staff: AFGHANISTAN

DUPREE, NANCY HATCH, American Universities Field Staff: AFGHANISTAN

DURRENCE, J. LARRY, Department of History, Florida Southern College: FLORIDA

ETCHESON, WARREN W., Associate Dean, School of Business Administration, University of Washington: WASHINGTON

ETHERIDGE, ADREN, Assistant City Editor, the Houston *Post:* HOUSTON; TEXAS

EWEGEN, BOB, Staff Writer, The Denver *Post:* COLORADO

FELDBAUM, ELEANOR G., Research Associate, Bureau of Governmental Research, University of Maryland: WASHINGTON, D. C.

FISHER, PAUL, Director, Freedom of Information Center, University of Missouri: CENSORSHIP

FISHER, SIDNEY NETTLETON, Emeritus Professor of History, The Ohio State University: SAUDI ARABIA

FOLTZ, JOHN F., Assistant Professor of Journalism, Pennsylvania State University: PENNSYLVANIA; PHILADELPHIA

GAILEY, HARRY A., Professor of History, San Juan State University: NIGERIA

GEIS, GILBERT, Visiting Professor, Program in Social Ecology, University of California, Irvine; Author, *Man, Crime, and Society:* CRIME

GJESTER, THOR, City Editor, *Norwegian Journal of Commerce and Shipping*, Oslo: NORWAY

GOODMAN, DONALD, John Jay College of Criminal Justice, City University of New York: PRISONS

GORDON, MAYNARD M., Editor, *Motor News Analysis* and *The Imported Car Reports:* AUTOMOBILES

GOUGH, BARRY M., Associate Professor of History, Wilfrid Laurier University, Waterloo, Ont.; Visiting Professor, fall 1974, Duke University: CANADA; TRUDEAU, PIERRE ELLIOTT

GROTH, ALEXANDER J., Professor of Political Science, University of California, Davis: POLAND

GULICK, LEWIS, Staff Consultant, House Foreign Affairs Committee: FOREIGN AID

GUNN, JOHN M., Professor of Radio-TV-Film, State University of New York at Albany: TELEVISION AND RADIO

GUTHERIDGE, GUY G., Director, Polar Information Service Office of Polar Programs, National Science Foundation: POLAR RESEARCH

HAKES, JAY E., Associate Professor of Political Science, University of New Orleans: KENYA; TANZANIA; UGANDA

HALL, FRANCES L., Director, International Trade Analysis Division, Bureau of International Commerce, U. S. Department of Commerce: INTERNATIONAL TRADE

HALVORSEN, DAVID E., Assistant to the Editor, *Chicago Tribune:* CHICAGO; ILLINOIS

HAMAR, HARALDUR J., Editor, *Iceland Review:* ICELAND

HANSON, EARL PARKER, Geographer; Former Consultant to the Puerto Rico Department of State: PUERTO RICO

HARVEY, ROSS M., Chief Publications, Department of Information, Government of Northwest Territories: NORTHWEST TERRITORIES

HAYDEN, DOROTHY, Prairie History Room, Regina Public Library, Sask.: SASKATCHEWAN

HAYES, JOHN D., Rear Admiral, USN (Ret.); U. S. Naval Academy Alumni Association: TRANSPORTATION—*Shipping*

HAYES, KIRBY M., Professor of Food Science, University of Massachusetts: FOOD—*U. S. Food Industry, Nutrition*

HEAD, HOWARD T., Partner, A. D. Ring & Associates, Consulting Radio Engineers: TELEVISION AND RADIO—*Television and Radio Engineering*

HELMREICH, E. C., Thomas B. Reed Professor of History and Political Science, Bowdoin College: AUSTRIA

HELMREICH, PAUL C., Professor and Chairman, Department of History, Wheaton College, Norton, Mass.: SWITZERLAND

HELMS, ANDREA R. C., Assistant Professor, University of Alaska, Fairbanks: ALASKA

HERBERT, WALTER B., Consultant on Canadian Cultural Matters; Fellow of the Royal Society of Arts: CANADA—CULTURAL AFFAIRS

HERRING, RICHARD J., Assistant Professor of Finance, University of Pennsylvania: INTERNATIONAL FINANCE

HERSHKOWITZ, LEO, Professor of History, Queens College, City University of New York: NEW YORK CITY; NEW YORK STATE

HESS, ARTHUR E., Deputy Commissioner, Social Security Administration: SOCIAL WELFARE—*Social Security*

HILLS, THEO L., Department of Geography, McGill University: MONTREAL; QUEBEC

HODGES, RALPH W., Associate Technical Editor, *Stereo Review;* Contributing Editor, *Popular Electronics:* RECORDINGS—*Audio Equipment and Techniques*

HOGGART, SIMON, Political Correspondent, The Manchester *Guardian:* GREAT BRITAIN

HOOVER, HERBERT T., Professor of History, The University of South Dakota: SOUTH DAKOTA

HOPKINS, JAMES F., Professor of History, University of Kentucky: KENTUCKY

HOPKO, THOMAS, St. Vladimir's Orthodox Theological Seminary: RELIGION—*Orthodox Eastern Church*

HOWARD, HARRY N., Adjunct Professor of Middle East Studies, School of International Service, The American University: TURKEY

HUCKSHORN, ROBERT J., Professor and Chairman, Department of Political Science, Florida Atlantic University: THE UNMAKING OF THE PRESIDENT, 1974—*Richard M. Nixon*

JACOBS, WALTER DARNELL, Professor of Government and Politics, University of Maryland: THE UNMAKING OF THE PRESIDENT, 1974—*Gerald R. Ford;* ALBERT, CARL BERT; SCHLESINGER, JAMES R.

JAFFE, HERMAN, Department of Anthropology, Brooklyn College, City University of New York: ANTHROPOLOGY

JOHNSTONE, JOHN K., Professor and Chairman, Department of English, Univ. of Saskatchewan: ENGLISH LITERATURE

JONES, H. G., Curator, North Carolina Collection, University of North Carolina Library: NORTH CAROLINA

KAMINS, ROBERT M., Professor of Economics, University of Hawaii: HAWAII

KARSKI, JAN, Department of Government, Georgetown University: BULGARIA; HUNGARY

KATZ, EUGENE R., Assistant Professor of Biology, State University of New York at Stony Brook: GENETICS

KEE, HERBERT W., Executive Director, Economic Plans and Statistics, Department of Economic Development, British Columbia: BRITISH COLUMBIA

KEHR, ERNEST A., Director, Stamp News Bureau, Executive Chairman, Philatelic Press Club; Stamp News Editor, The Chicago *Daily News:* STAMP COLLECTING

KELLER, EUGENIA, Managing Editor, *Chemistry:* CHEMISTRY

KEMPER, ROBERT V., Assistant Professor of Anthropology, Southern Methodist University: DALLAS

KENNEDY, ROBERT E., JR., Associate Professor and Associate Chairman, Department of Sociology, University of Minnesota: POPULATION

KEYSERLING, MARY DUBLIN, Economic Consultant; President, National Child Day Care Association: SOCIAL WELFARE—*Child Welfare*

KIMBALL, LORENZO K., Associate Professor of Political Science, University of Utah: UTAH

KING, PETER J., Associate Professor of History, Carleton University: ONTARIO; OTTAWA

KLAUSLER, ALFRED P., Editorial Coordinator, *Christian Ministry;* Editor at Large, *Christian Century;* Religion Commentator, Westinghouse Broadcasting Co.: RELIGION—*Protestantism*

KOLEHMAINEN, JOHN I., Chairman, Department of Political Science, Heidelberg College, Tiffin, Ohio: FINLAND

KREITZMAN, STEPHEN N., Professor of Biochemistry, Emory University School of Dentistry: BIOCHEMISTRY

KREPS, CLIFTON H., JR., Wachovia Professor of Banking, University of North Carolina: BANKING

LAI, CHUEN-YAN DAVID, Associate Professor of Geography, University of Victoria, B. C.: HONG KONG

LANDSBERG, H. E., Research Professor, Institute for Fluid Dynamics and Applied Mathematics, University of Maryland: METEOROLOGY

LARSEN, WILLIAM, Professor of History, Radford College: VIRGINIA

LARSON, T. A., Professor of History, University of Wyoming; Author, *History of Wyoming:* WYOMING

LAWRENCE, ROBERT M., Department of Political Science, Colorado State University: ENERGY—*Survey, Coal, Electricity, Gas;* MILITARY FORCES—*World Developments*

LEE, STEWART M., Professor and Chairman, Department of Economics and Business Administration, Geneva College: CONSUMERISM

LEFEVER, ERNEST W., Senior Fellow, Foreign Policy Studies Program, The Brookings Institution: DISARMAMENT AND ARMS CONTROL

LEIDEN, CARL, Professor of Government, University of Texas at Austin: THE MIDDLE EAST—*Review of the Year, Hafez al-Assad, Itzhak Rabin, Anwar el-Sadat;* BANGLADESH; EGYPT; PAKISTAN; THAILAND

LEVIN, RUBEN, Editor, *Labor* Newspaper: LABOR

LEVY, JAMES R., Senior Lecturer, School of Spanish and Latin American Studies, University of New South Wales: ARGENTINA; OBITUARIES—*Perón, Juan*

LEWIS, OSCAR, Author, *San Francisco: Mission to Metropolis, The Big Four,* and other books: SAN FRANCISCO

LINDAHL, MAC, Reporter, Writer, and Translator: DENMARK; SWEDEN

LINDSEY, ROBERT H., Transportation Writer, *The New York Times:* TRANSPORTATION—*Air Transportation*

LITTLER, WILLIAM, Dance Critic, The Toronto *Star:* DANCE

LLOYD, ROBERT M., Director, Research and Management Services, South Carolina Appalachian Council of Governments: CITIES AND URBAN AFFAIRS

LOTT, LEO B., Professor and Chairman, Department of Political Science, University of Montana: PARAGUAY; VENEZUELA

MABRY, DONALD J., Associate Professor of History, Mississippi State University: MEXICO

MACAULAY, NEILL, Associate Professor of History, University of Florida; Author, *The Prestes Column:* BRAZIL; LATIN AMERICA

McCORQUODALE, SUSAN, Assistant Professor of Political Science, Memorial University of Newfoundland: NEWFOUNDLAND

McDOWELL, FRANK, Professor of Surgery, University of Hawaii; Editor, *Plastic & Reconstructive Surgery:* THE SEARCH FOR A 'YOUTHFUL' OLD AGE—*Plastic Surgery*

McKEON, NANCY, *African Update,* The African-American Institute: ALGERIA; MOROCCO; SUDAN; TUNISIA

McLEOD, W. REYNOLDS, Assistant Professor of History, West Virginia University: WEST VIRGINIA

MARCOPOULOS, GEORGE J., Associate Professor of History, Tufts University: CYPRUS Feature; CYPRUS—*Archbishop Makarios III;* GREECE

MARTIN, J. A., JR., Professor of Religion, Columbia University: RELIGION—*General Survey*

MARYLES, DAISY, News Editor, *Publishers Weekly:* PUBLISHING—*Books*

MATHEWS, THOMAS G., Research Professor, Institute of Caribbean Studies, University of Puerto Rico: CARIBBEAN; GRENADA; VIRGIN ISLANDS, U. S.

MEMOLO, MARCELLA M., Public Information Officer, U. S. Agricultural Research Service: AGRICULTURE—*U. S. Agricultural Research*

MESSNER, STEPHEN D., Head, Department of Finance, School of Business Administration, University of Connecticut: HOUSING

MEYER, EDWARD H., Chairman of the Board and President, Grey Advertising Inc.: ADVERTISING

MEYER, RALPH C., Associate Professor of Political Science, Fordham University at Lincoln Center: ASIA

MIESEL, VICTOR H., Professor of the History of Art, University of Michigan; Author, *Voices of German Expressionism:* ART

MILLER, LUTHER S., Editor, *Railway Age:* TRANSPORTATION—*Railroads*

MILLER, NYLE H., Executive Director, Kansas State Historical Society; Coauthor, *Kansas: A Pictorial History:* KANSAS

MILLINGTON, THOMAS M., Associate Professor and Chairman, Department of Political Science, Hobart and William Smith Colleges: BOLIVIA

MILNE, ROBERT SCOTT, Society of American Travel Writers; Coauthor, *Around the World with the Experts:* THEME AMUSEMENT PARKS Feature; TRAVEL

MITCHELL, GARY, Professor of Physics, North Carolina State University at Raleigh: PHYSICS

MONTGOMERY, JAMES D., Vegetation Studies, Ichthyological Associates, Absecon, N. J.: BOTANY

MOORE, CHARLES W., Professor of Architecture, University of California, Los Angeles: ARCHITECTURE

MOSCA, FRANK K., Professor of Russian Studies, New York University: SOVIET LITERATURE; SOLZHENITSYN, A. I.

NEILL, R. F., Associate Professor of Economics, St. Patrick's College, Carleton University: PRINCE EDWARD ISLAND

NEWSOM, DONALD W., Professor and Head, Department of Horticulture, Louisiana State University: GARDENING AND HORTICULTURE

NOGUCHI, TAKEHIKO, Associate Professor of Literature, Kobe University: JAPANESE LITERATURE

NOLAN, WILLIAM C., Associate Professor of Political Science, Southern State College: ARKANSAS

NOWELL, CHARLES E., Professor of History, Emeritus, University of Illinois: GUINEA-BISSAU; PORTUGAL; SPAIN

NUQUIST, ANDREW E., Professor Emeritus of Political Science, University of Vermont: VERMONT

O'HARE, JOSEPH A., S. J., Associate Editor, *America:* PAUL VI, POPE; RELIGION—*Roman Catholicism*

OLIVER, RICHARD B., Architect: ARCHITECTURE

OTT, MARVIN C., Assistant Professor of Political Science, Mount Holyoke College: MALAYSIA; SINGAPORE

PALMER, NORMAN D., Professor of Political Science and South Asian Studies, University of Pennsylvania: GANDHI, INDIRA; INDIA; SRI LANKA

PALMORE, ERDMAN, Professor of Medical Sociology, Duke University; Author, *Normal Aging:* THE SEARCH FOR A 'YOUTHFUL' OLD AGE—*General Survey*

PANO, NICHOLAS C., Assistant Professor of History, Western Illinois University: ALBANIA

PARKER, FRANKLIN, Benedum Professor of Education and Research Associate, Human Resources Institute, West Virginia University: AFRICA; RHODESIA

PARTAN, DANIEL G., Professor of Law, Boston University: LAW—*International Law*

PEARCE, JOHN B., Director, Ecosystems Investigations, Sandy Hook Marine Laboratory, N. J.: MARINE BIOLOGY

PEARSON, NEALE J., Associate Professor of Government, Texas Tech University: CHILE; PERU

PERKINS, KENNETH J., Assistant Professor of History, University of South Carolina: LIBYA; RELIGION—*Islam*

PETERSON, ROBERT L., Director, Center for Inter-American Studies, University of Texas at El Paso: CENTRAL AMERICA

PHEBUS, GEORGE E., JR., Supervisor, Processing Laboratory, Department of Anthropology, National Museum of Natural History, Smithsonian Institution: ARCHAEOLOGY—*Western Hemisphere*

PHILLIPS, JACKSON, Senior Vice President, Moody's Investors Service, Inc.: ECONOMY OF THE U. S.

PIPPIN, LARRY L., Professor of Political Science, Elbert Covell College, University of the Pacific: PANAMA

PLATT, HERMANN K., Associate Professor of History, St. Peter's College, Jersey City: NEW JERSEY

PLISCHKE, ELMER, Professor of Government and Politics, University of Maryland: THE MIDDLE EAST—*Henry A. Kissinger;* UNITED STATES—*Foreign Affairs*

POLK, IRWIN J., Director of Children's Allergy Service, St. Luke's Hospital, New York City: MEDICINE

POPKIN, HENRY, Professor of English, State University of New York at Buffalo; Drama Critic, Westchester-Rockland Newspapers: THEATER

PORTER, J. R., Professor and Chairman, Department of Microbiology, College of Medicine, University of Iowa: MICROBIOLOGY

PRICE, EDWIN W., JR., Managing Editor, *The Morning Advocate,* Baton Rouge, La.: LOUISIANA

PRITCHETT, C. HERMAN, Professor of Political Science, University of California, Santa Barbara: LAW—*Supreme Court;* OBITUARIES—*Warren, Earl*

PUMPHREY, RALPH E., Professor of Social Work, Washington University, St. Louis: SOCIAL WELFARE

QUIRK, WILLIAM H., Editorial Director, *Contractors & Engineers* Magazine: ENGINEERING, CIVIL

RAYMOND, ELLSWORTH, Professor of Politics, New York University; Author, *The Soviet State* and *A Picture History of Eastern Europe:* BREZHNEV, LEONID; KOSYGIN, ALEKSEI; MONGOLIA; UNION OF SOVIET SOCIALIST REPUBLICS

RAYMOND, JACK, Past President and Chief Executive Officer, International Institute for Environmental Affairs; Author, *Power at the Pentagon:* ENVIRONMENT

RICARD, FRANÇOIS, Assistant Professor, Department of French Language and Literature, McGill University: CANADIAN LITERATURE IN FRENCH

RODRIGUEZ, ALFRED, Professor of Spanish, University of New Mexico: SPANISH LITERATURE

ROMAN, JAMES R., JR., Associate Professor of Business Administration, The George Washington University: TRANSPORTATION—*General Survey, Highways, Mass Transit*

ROSE, ERNST, Author, *A History of German Literature;* Professor Emeritus, New York University: GERMAN LITERATURE

ROSS, RUSSELL M., Professor of Political Science, University of Iowa: IOWA

ROWLETT, RALPH M., Associate Professor of Anthropology, University of Missouri—Columbia: ARCHAEOLOGY—*Eastern Hemisphere*

SADLER, LOUIS R., Associate Professor of History, New Mexico State University: CUBA

SALGADO, MARÍA A., Associate Professor of Spanish, University of North Carolina at Chapel Hill: LATIN AMERICAN LITERATURE

SALSINI, PAUL, State Editor, The Milwaukee *Journal:* WISCONSIN

SARRATT, WILLIAM A., Editor, *The Fish Boat,* New Orleans: FISHERIES

SAVAGE, DAVID, Lecturer, Department of English, Simon Fraser University: CANADIAN LITERATURE IN ENGLISH

SCHNEIDERMAN, RONALD A., New York Bureau Manager, *Electronics* Magazine (McGraw-Hill Publications Co.): ELECTRONICS; TELECOMMUNICATIONS

SCHRATZ, PAUL R., Captain, USN (Ret.); Commission on the Organization of the Government for the Conduct of Foreign Policy: MILITARY FORCES—*U. S. Developments*

SCHWAB, PETER, Associate Professor of Political Science, State University of New York at Purchase: ETHIOPIA

SCOTT, EUGENE L. (GENE), Former Member, U. S. Davis Cup Team; Author, *Tennis: Game of Motion;* Publisher, *Tennis Week:* EVERYONE'S PLAYING TENNIS

SCOTT, MARTIN L., Consultant on Technology, International Museum of Photography, George Eastman House, Inc.: PHOTOGRAPHY

SETH, R. P., Chairman, Department of Economics, Mount Saint Vincent University, Halifax: NOVA SCOTIA

SHOCK, N. W., Chief, Gerontology Research Center, Baltimore City Hospital, National Institutes of Health; Editor, *Perspective in Gerontology:* THE SEARCH FOR A 'YOUTHFUL' OLD AGE—*Tips for Successful Aging*

SHOGAN, ROBERT, National Political Correspondent, Washington Bureau, *Los Angeles Times;* Author, *A Question of Judgment: The Fortas Case and the Struggle for the Supreme Court:* THE UNMAKING OF THE PRESIDENT, 1974; UNITED STATES—*Domestic Affairs*

SIMMONS, MARC, Farrier; Author, *Spanish Government in New Mexico* and *The Little Lion of the Southwest:* NEW MEXICO

SINNEN, JEANNE, Senior Editor, University of Minnesota Press: MINNESOTA

SKELDING, FRANK H., Manager, Market Research, Fluor Utah, Inc.: MINING

SLOAN, HENRY S., Associate Editor, *Current Biography:* BIOGRAPHY (in part); OBITUARIES (in part)

SOFAER, ABRAHAM D., Professor of Law, Columbia University: CIVIL LIBERTIES AND CIVIL RIGHTS

SPEIRS, W. BRIAN, Territorial Archivist, Yukon Territory: YUKON TERRITORY

STEHLING, KURT R., Aerospace Consultant, U. S. Government: Space Exploration—*Advances in Space Technology*

STEPHENS, GENE, Assistant to the Dean, School of Urban Life, Georgia State University: ATLANTA; GEORGIA

STERN, JEROME H., Associate Professor of English, Florida State University: AMERICAN LITERATURE

STOKES, W. LEE, Professor of Geology, University of Utah: GEOLOGY

STOUDEMIRE, ROBERT H., Associate Director, Bureau of Governmental Research and Associate Professor of Political Science, University of South Carolina: SOUTH CAROLINA

SYLVESTER, LORNA LUTES, Associate Editor, *Indiana Magazine of History,* Indiana University: INDIANA

TABORSKY, EDWARD, Professor of Government, University of Texas at Austin: CZECHOSLOVAKIA

TAN, CHESTER C., Professor of History, New York University; Author, *The Boxer Catastrophe* and *Chinese Political Thought in the Twentieth Century:* CHINA; CHOU EN-LAI

TAYLOR, PHILIP B., JR., Professor of Political Science and Director of Latin American Studies, University of Houston: ECUADOR; URUGUAY

TAYLOR, ZACK, Boating Editor, *Sports Afield;* Regional Editor, *Waterway Guide:* BOATING

THEISEN, CHARLES W., Assistant City Editor, The Detroit *News:* DETROIT; MICHIGAN

THOMAS, JAMES D., Professor of Political Science, University of Alabama: ALABAMA

THOME, PITT G., Deputy Director for Earth Observations Flight Program, National Aeronautics and Space Administration: SPACE EXPLORATION—*Manned Space Flight, Unmanned Satellites and Space Probes*

TIBBITTS, CLARK, Director, National Clearinghouse on Aging, Office of Human Development, Administration on Aging, Department of Health, Education, and Welfare: OLDER POPULATION

TURNER, ARTHUR CAMPBELL, Professor of Political Science, University of California, Riverside: IRAN; IRAQ; ISRAEL

VALESIO, PAOLO, Professor of Italian and Director of Italian Studies, New York University: ITALIAN LITERATURE

VANDENBOSCH, AMRY, Professor Emeritus of Political Science, University of Kentucky; BELGIUM; INDONESIA; LUXEMBOURG; NETHERLANDS; SUHARTO

WALLACE, BEN J., Professor of Anthropology, Southern Methodist University: DALLAS

WARNER, JOHN W., Administrator, American Revolutionary Bicentennial Administration: UNITED STATES—*Bicentennial*

WEBB, RICHARD E., Former Director, Reference and Library Division, British Information Services, New York: COMMONWEALTH OF NATIONS; UNITED NATIONS; WALDHEIM, KURT

WEEKS, JEANNE G., Author and Lecturer; Director, Advertising and Public Relations, Harvey Probber Inc.; Associate, National Society of Interior Designers: INTERIOR DESIGN

WEISENBURGER, FRANCIS P., Professor of History and University Historian, The Ohio State University: OHIO

WELCH, CLAUDE E., JR., Professor of Political Science, State University of New York at Buffalo: GHANA

WEST, RICHARD G., Former Senior Editor, *Encyclopedia Americana:* NEW HAMPSHIRE; DOAR, JOHN M.; GESELL, GERHARD A.; ROCKEFELLER, NELSON A.; RODINO, PETER W., JR.; ST. CLAIR, JAMES D.; SIRICA, JOHN J.

WESTERN, JOE, Senior Editor, *The National Observer:* AGRICULTURE—*World Agriculture, U. S. Agriculture*

WHITE, JOHN P., Professor of Political Science, Arizona State University: ARIZONA

WHITMAN, ALDEN, Chief Obituary Writer, *The New York Times:* OBITUARIES—*Lindbergh, Charles A.*

WILLARD, F. NICHOLAS, NDEA Title VI Fellow, Department of History, Georgetown University: JORDAN; LEBANON; SYRIA

WILLIS, F. ROY, Professor of History, University of California, Davis: EUROPE

WILLNOW, RONALD D., City Editor, St. Louis *Post-Dispatch:* MISSOURI; SAINT LOUIS

WILSON, JOHN S., Reviewer of Jazz Records, *The New York Times* and *High Fidelity* Magazine; Author, *Jazz: The Transition Years—1940–1960:* OBITUARIES—*Ellington, Edward Kennedy (Duke);* RECORDINGS—*Jazz Records*

WOLF, WILLIAM, Film Critic, *Cue* Magazine; Former Chairman, New York Film Critics: MOTION PICTURES

WOODS, GEORGE A., Children's Books Editor, *The New York Times:* CHILDREN'S LITERATURE

YANG, KEY P., Korean Area Specialist, Orientalia Division, The Library of Congress: KOREA

YOUNGER, R. M., Author, *The Changing World of Australia; Australia and the Australians:* AUSTRALIA; OCEANIA

ZABEL, ORVILLE H., Professor of History, Creighton University: NEBRASKA

ZACEK, JOSEPH F., Professor of History, State University of New York at Albany: RUMANIA

ZAFRA, NICOLAS, Professor Emeritus of History, University of the Philippines: PHILIPPINES

preface

For presidents, prime ministers, and potentates, 1974 was not a good year. Nor, for that matter, was it a particularly happy time for the world's common people.

Through a remarkable series of events, most of the world's major non-Communist nations experienced changes of leadership during the year. New men came forward to take the reins of power, but in many cases they had to grapple—without conspicuous success—with the same old problems that had led to the downfall of their predecessors.

Within two months, the three leading western European countries —Britain, France, and West Germany—had new heads of government. Edward Heath resigned following national elections, Georges Pompidou died in office, and Willy Brandt quit in the wake of a spy scandal. During the same period, a military coup brought an end to nearly a half-century of dictatorship in Portugal, and Israel's Golda Meir, buffeted by domestic discord stemming from the October 1973 war, stepped down.

In July, death claimed Juan Perón, who only last year had returned to power in Argentina after an 18-year exile. Later that month authoritarian rule ended in Greece, and the birthplace of democracy went on to hold its first free elections in a decade. Also in July, Archbishop Makarios was overthrown as president of Cyprus, but he returned before the year was out. Italy underwent one of its frequent cabinet crises in October with the resignation of the country's 36th government since World War II. Another leading power, Japan, lost its premier in November when Kakuei Tanaka bowed out in a controversy involving his personal finances.

To many people, the most poignant departure from the world stage in 1974 was that of Haile Selassie of Ethiopia, who for 58 years had wielded absolute power in his ancient kingdom. In September, the proud Lion of Judah, who traced his ancestry back to King Solomon and the Queen of Sheba, was hauled away from his imperial palace in a Volkswagen and taken to an army barracks.

But the year's most sensational change in leadership occurred in the United States, where, in the early days of August, the end finally came for Richard Nixon's presidency, shortly after he released the last and most damaging of the White House tape recordings. For more than two years he had fought to exonerate himself in the Watergate affair, and now, after admitting he had not told the truth, there was no escape from impeachment except to resign. Shaken by the climax of their long ordeal, Americans turned to a new leader in the knowledge that their revered institutions had withstood their gravest test.

Meanwhile, severe economic dislocations brought on by the soaring price of petroleum raised havoc with the finances of rich and poor nations alike, and in late 1974 a deepening recession was spreading throughout the industrialized world. Coupled with this were apocalyptic warnings of an impending world food crisis that could claim millions of lives in a matter of months. The world's peoples could only hope that their new leaders had some answers to these problems, but at year-end there was no clear indication that these answers were forthcoming.

S. J. FODERARO, *Executive Editor*

DENNIS BRACK, BLACK STAR

Vice President and Mrs. Gerald Ford escort President and Mrs. Richard Nixon to a waiting helicopter as the Nixons leave the White House for the last time as the first family. A short time later Nixon's resignation became official.

CHRONOLOGY 1974

NIXON REJECTS TAPES BID

LEGER TAKES CANADA POST

ISRAEL, EGYPT SIGN PACT

JANUARY

S	M	T	W	T	F	S
		1	2	3	4	5
6	7	8	9	10	11	12
13	14	15	16	17	18	19
20	21	22	23	24	25	26
27	28	29	30	31		

UPI

President Nixon receives ovation from Congress as he arrives to give State of the Union message, January 30.

Jules Léger (*left*) takes the oath of office as the 21st (and fourth native-born) governor-general of Canada, January 14.

UPI

JANUARY

2 To help conserve energy, President Richard Nixon signs into law a bill requiring the states to limit highway speeds to 55 miles per hour in order to continue to receive highway trust funds.

4 In a letter to Sen. Sam J. Ervin, Jr., chairman of the Senate Watergate committee, President Nixon rejects the committee's subpoenas seeking more than 500 tapes and documents. • William B. Saxbe is sworn in as U. S. attorney general. • In Spain, the cabinet of Premier Carlos Arias Navarro is sworn in.

7 Japan's Premier Kakuei Tanaka begins a five-nation tour of Southeast Asia.

13 The Miami Dolphins defeat the Minnesota Vikings, 24–7, to win football's Super Bowl game for the second consecutive time.

14 Canada's Parliament passes a bill limiting wire-tapping and other types of electronic eavesdropping by law enforcement agencies. • Canadian diplomat Jules Léger takes the oath of office as the nation's 21st governor-general.

15 A court-appointed panel of six technical experts reports that an 18½-minute gap on a major Watergate tape was caused by some five separate erasures and rerecordings.

18 Representatives of Israel and Egypt sign an accord on disengaging military forces.

19 France announces that it will permit the franc to float for a six month period. • Five Soviet citizens, including a senior diplomat and two other members of the Soviet Embassy, are expelled from Communist China on espionage charges. • In Belgium, the coalition government of Premier Edmond Leburton resigns.

21 By a 7–2 vote, the U. S. Supreme Court rules that public school systems cannot force female teachers to take extended maternity leaves.

25 In Turkey, Bulent Ecevit, leader of the Republican People's party, becomes premier, heading a new 25-member left-of-center coalition cabinet.

28 In a boxing match between two former heavyweight champions, Muhammad Ali defeats Joe Frazier in a unanimous 12-round decision.

30 In a nationally televised State of the Union message, President Nixon proposes a 10-point plan for "significant progress" in 1974. The President also states that he will not resign and that "one year of Watergate is enough."

FEBRUARY

S	M	T	W	T	F	S
					1	2
3	4	5	6	7	8	9
10	11	12	13	14	15	16
17	18	19	20	21	22	23
24	25	26	27	28		

PATRICIA HEARST KIDNAPPED

HOUSE OK'S NIXON PROBE

USSR OUSTS SOLZHENITSYN

FEBRUARY

1 In São Paulo, Brazil, fire burns through the upper floors of a 25-story bank building, killing 189 persons.

3 Communist China launches a new Cultural Revolution-type campaign, under the leadership of party chairman Mao Tse-tung. • Daniel Oduber Quirós of Costa Rica's National Liberation party (PLN) is elected president.

4 President Nixon proposes a budget of $304.4 billion for fiscal year 1975. • Patricia Hearst, 19-year-old daughter of publisher Randolph A. Hearst, is abducted from her apartment in Berkeley, Calif.

6 By a vote of 410–4, the U. S. House of Representatives grants the House Judiciary Committee the authority to investigate the conduct of President Richard Nixon.

7 The United States and Panama sign an agreement on the principles that would guide the negotiations of a new Panama Canal treaty. • The Caribbean island of Grenada becomes an independent nation.

8 The Skylab 3 astronauts complete a record 84-day spaceflight.

11 A 13-nation energy conference opens in Washington, D. C.

13 Russian author Aleksandr Solzhenitsyn, a Nobelist, is deported by the USSR to West Germany.

19 The Senate Watergate Committee agrees not to hold further public hearings.

21 In Mexico City, Mexico, U. S. Secretary of State Henry Kissinger addresses the opening session of a three-day meeting of Latin American foreign ministers.

22 Pakistan grants diplomatic recognition to Bangladesh, its former eastern wing. • J. Reginald Murphy, editor of *The Atlanta Constitution,* is found unharmed after $700,000 is paid to his kidnappers, members of the self-proclaimed American Revolutionary Army.

23 President Nixon names Vice President Gerald R. Ford head of a special committee to guard citizens' privacy.

25 Herbert W. Kalmbach, President Nixon's personal lawyer, pleads guilty to two violations of federal law regarding campaign funds.

28 Parliamentary elections are held in Britain; neither the ruling Conservative party nor the Labour party wins an overall majority. • The United States and Egypt agree to restore diplomatic relations, suspended since June 1967. • In an attempt to placate mutinous army troops in Ethiopia, Emperor Haile Selassie appoints Endalkachew Makonnen premier and increases army wages. • Canada's Premier Pierre Elliott Trudeau proposes a record spending budget of $22 billion for fiscal year 1975.

WIDE WORLD

Aleksandr Solzhenitsyn, dissident Soviet writer deported from the USSR, gives autographs to the cheering crowd at the Basel, Switzerland, railroad station, February 13. Solzhenitsyn, who won the 1970 Nobel Prize, was en route to his new home, Zürich.

346 DIE IN WORST AIR CRASH

WILSON REGAINS BRITISH POST

ARABS END U.S. OIL EMBARGO

MARCH

S	M	T	W	T	F	S
					1	2
3	4	5	6	7	8	9
10	11	12	13	14	15	16
17	18	19	20	21	22	23
24	25	26	27	28	29	30
31						

MARCH

1 A federal grand jury indicts seven former Nixon aides—John N. Mitchell, H. R. Haldeman, John Ehrlichman, Charles W. Colson, Robert C. Mardian, Kenneth W. Parkinson, and Gordon C. Strachan—on charges of conspiracy regarding the Watergate case.

3 In the worst air disaster in history, a Turkish jumbo jet plunges into a forest northeast of Paris, France, killing all 346 persons aboard.

4 Edward Heath of Britain fails to win the support of the Liberal party and resigns as prime minister. Labor party leader Harold Wilson returns to power.

6 The U. S. Senate sustains the presidential veto of an energy bill, giving the president power to curtail consumption and manage fuel supplies.

7 A federal grand jury indicts six men—Ehrlichman, Colson, G. Gordon Liddy, Bernard L. Barker, Eugenio R. Martinez, and Felipe S. DeDiego—in connection with the 1971 break-in of the office of Dr. Daniel Ellsberg's psychiatrist.

10 A new Israeli cabinet, headed by Premier Golda Meir, takes the oath of office. • Belgium holds parliamentary elections; the moderate Social Christians remain the nation's strongest party.

11 In Britain, the state of emergency, declared on Nov. 13, 1973, is formally ended. (On March 6, striking coal miners and the new government agreed to a wage settlement ending a two-month strike; on March 8 the three-day workweek ended.)

12 Carlos Andres Perez is inaugurated president of Venezuela. • Guatemala's Congress proclaims retired Gen. Kjell Laugerud García the winner of the March 3 presidential election.

14 The White House announces the resignation of Treasury Secretary George P. Schultz, effective in mid-May.

15 Gen. Ernesto Geisel is sworn in as the 28th president of Brazil. • Mariano Rumor takes the oath of office as head of a new coalition government in Italy.

18 The Arab oil countries, except for Libya and Syria, announce that they are ending officially the oil embargo against the United States.

26 George Foreman knocks out Ken Norton in the second round to retain his heavyweight boxing title. • Ion Gheorghe Maurer resigns as premier of Rumania; he is succeeded by Deputy Premier Manea Manescu.

27 U. S. Secretary of State Kissinger concludes three days of talks with Soviet party chairman Leonid Brezhnev in preparation for President Nixon's forthcoming visit to the USSR.

29 A federal grand jury indicts eight former members of the National Guard of Ohio on charges of violating the civil rights of four Kent State University students who were shot to death and nine others who were wounded during a campus demonstration in May 1970.

UPI

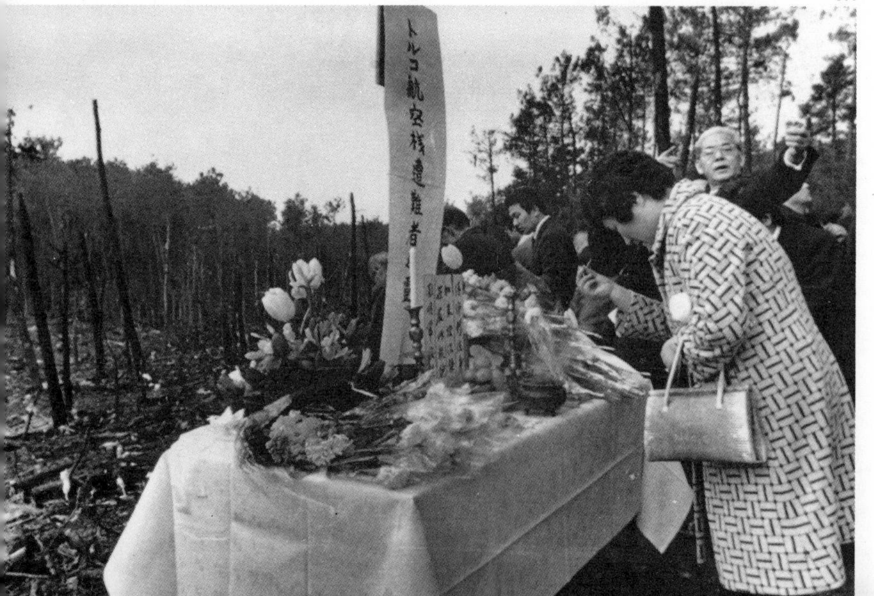

A Japanese woman who lost relatives in the crash of a Turkish jumbo jet near Paris, March 3, prays before an improvised altar at the scene. The crash, which killed 346 persons, was the worst in aviation history.

APRIL

S	M	T	W	T	F	S
	1	2	3	4	5	6
7	8	9	10	11	12	13
14	15	16	17	18	19	20
21	22	23	24	25	26	27
28	29	30				

POMPIDOU DEAD AT 62

AARON BREAKS RUTH'S MARK

MITCHELL, STANS ACQUITTED

APRIL

2 Georges Pompidou, president of France since June 1969, dies in Paris at the age of 62.

3 Alain Poher is proclaimed acting president of France. • The White House announces that President Nixon will pay $432,787.13 in back taxes plus interest. The sum is based on an Internal Revenue Service report that he owed that amount.

6 In Laos, Premier Souvanna Phouma and his new coalition cabinet of neutralists, rightists, and pro-Communist Pathet Lao take a formal oath of religious allegiance.

8 Henry Aaron of the Atlanta Braves hits the 715th home run of his baseball career, surpassing Babe Ruth as the game's leading home-run hitter.

9 India, Pakistan, and Bangladesh sign an agreement to repatriate all Pakistani prisoners of war.

12 In retaliation for an Arab terrorist attack on April 11 that killed 18 persons in Qiryat Shemona, Israel, Israeli forces raid several villages in southern Lebanon.

15 In Niger, the army overthrows the government of President Hamani Diori.

17 President Nixon names William E. Simon to succeed George P. Shultz as secretary of the treasury. John C. Sawhill is nominated to replace Simon as administrator of the Federal Energy Office.

18 Egypt's President Anwar el-Sadat announces that his nation will no longer depend entirely on the Soviet Union for its arms supplies.

21 Alfonso López Michelsen, a 60-year-old law professor, is elected president of Colombia.

22 Israel's Labor party nominates Itzhak Rabin to succeed Premier Golda Meir, who resigned April 10.

25 A group of army officers seizes control of Portugal and announces the end of more than 40 years of authoritarian rule. • In Belgium, a new center-right coalition cabinet, headed by Leo Tindemans, is sworn in.

26 Canadian postal workers return to work, ending a major strike.

28 Former Nixon cabinet officers John N. Mitchell and Maurice H. Stans are acquitted of all charges in their criminal conspiracy trial.

29 President Nixon announces that he will give to the House Judiciary Committee and make public 1,200 pages of transcripts of Watergate conversations.

UPI

Atlanta Braves slugger Henry Aaron hit his 715th career home run on April 8, breaking Babe Ruth's record.

Former Nixon cabinet members Maurice Stans (*left*) and John Mitchell talk to newsmen after acquittal, April 28, on charges of conspiring to defraud the government.

UPI

BRANDT QUITS IN SPY SCANDAL

NEW PRESIDENT IN PORTUGAL

FLYERS CAPTURE HOCKEY CUP

MAY

S	M	T	W	T	F	S
			1	2	3	4
5	6	7	8	9	10	11
12	13	14	15	16	17	18
19	20	21	22	23	24	25
26	27	28	29	30	31	

INGEBORG LIPPMAN

António de Spínola is sworn in as provisional president of Portugal on May 15.

Philadelphia Flyers' Bobby Clarke and Bernie Parent carry hockey's Stanley Cup.

UPI

MAY

1 By a vote of 20–18, the U. S. House Judiciary Committee agrees to inform President Nixon that he has "failed to comply with the committee's subpoena" requesting presidential tapes and documents.

4 Expo '74, a world's fair dedicated to the environment, opens in Spokane, Wash.

6 West German Chancellor Willy Brandt assumes responsibility for the "negligence" in allowing an East German Communist spy to become a member of his staff and resigns from office.

7 James D. St. Clair, President Nixon's chief attorney, announces that the President will not release additional Watergate tapes.

9 Canada schedules parliamentary elections for July 8 after the minority Liberal government of Prime Minister Trudeau is defeated in a House of Commons' vote of confidence over budget policies.

12 The Boston Celtics defeat the Milwaukee Bucks, four games to three, to win the National Basketball Association championship.

13 In a two-day referendum, Italians vote to retain the nation's law permitting divorce.

15 Twenty-five persons, including 21 students, are killed as a result of a raid by three Palestinian guerrillas on a school in Maalot, Israel. • Gen. António de Spínola takes the oath of office as president of Portugal.

16 Helmut Schmidt elected West German chancellor.

17 In Dublin, Ireland, bombs planted in three automobiles explode simultaneously during the rush hour, killing 25 persons.

18 India explodes a nuclear device.

19 Finance Minister Valéry Giscard d'Estaing is elected president of France. • The Philadelphia Flyers win the National Hockey League Stanley Cup.

26 Johnny Rutherford wins the Indianapolis 500.

28 Australia's Prime Minister Gough Whitlam claims victory for his Labor party in parliamentary elections on May 18.

29 A 15-day general strike ends in Northern Ireland. (Because of the strike, the province's coalition government resigned May 28, and Britain temporarily assumed governmental control.)

31 In Geneva, representatives of Israel and Syria sign a troop disengagement agreement.

JUNE

S	M	T	W	T	F	S
						1
2	3	4	5	6	7	8
9	10	11	12	13	14	15
16	17	18	19	20	21	22
23	24	25	26	27	28	29
30						

RABIN NAMED IN ISRAEL

NIXON TOURS MIDDLE EAST

U.S.-SOVIET PACT SIGNED

JUNE

3 The Israeli Knesset (parliament) endorses a new three-party coalition government; Itzhak Rabin is installed as premier.

7 Former Attorney General Richard G. Kleindienst receives a suspended sentence for misleading a Senate committee investigating the ITT case.

8 The United States and Saudi Arabia sign a military and economic cooperation agreement.

10 President Nixon arrives in Salzburg, Austria—his first stop on a tour of Middle East nations.

11 U. S. Secretary of State Kissinger announces that he would resign unless his name is cleared of allegations that he took part in "illegal or shady activity" regarding government wiretapping.

14 In Cairo, Egypt, President Sadat and President Nixon announce that the United States will provide Egypt with nuclear technology for peaceful purposes.

16 In Damascus, Syria, President Hafez al-Assad and President Nixon announce that Syria and the United States have agreed to resume diplomatic relations. ● Hale Irwin wins the U. S. Open golf championship.

17 A communiqué on President Nixon's visit states that the United States and Israel will soon "reach provisional agreement on the further sale of nuclear fuel to Israel." ● China and France conduct separate nuclear tests in the atmosphere. ● Premier Long Boret forms a new cabinet in Cambodia.

19 In Ottawa, Canada, the foreign ministers of the 15 members of the North Atlantic Treaty Organization (NATO) approve a declaration on Atlantic relations. ● En route home from Mideast, President Nixon confers with President Spínola of Portugal.

24 Prime Minister Wilson announces that Britain's first nuclear bomb test in more than nine years occurred "a few weeks ago" in Nevada.

27 President Nixon arrives in Moscow for summit conference with Soviet leaders ● Representatives of France and Iran sign a 10-year development agreement, including provision for the sale of nuclear reactors to Iran.

28 A landslide some 95 miles east of Bogotá, Colombia, kills more than 200 persons.

29 President Nixon and Soviet Secretary Brezhnev sign a 10-year economic agreement.

30 Mrs. Martin Luther King, Sr., mother of the late civil rights leader, is fatally wounded by a gunman in Ebenezer Baptist Church, Atlanta, Ga.

UPI

President Nixon chats with Secretary Brezhnev as he arrives for Moscow talks.

Former Attorney General Kleindienst received a suspended sentence, June 7.

UPI

SOCCER CUP TO WEST GERMANS

TURKS LAUNCH CYPRUS INVASION

COMMITTEE VOTES IMPEACHMENT

JULY

S	M	T	W	T	F	S
	1	2	3	4	5	6
7	8	9	10	11	12	13
14	15	16	17	18	19	20
21	22	23	24	25	26	27
28	29	30	31			

UPI

West German players Gerd Mueller (*left*) and Paul Breitner after West Germany won the world soccer championship, July 7.

Turkish paratroops, supplies, and equipment are dropped on Cyprus, July 20, the first day of an air and sea invasion of the island by the armed forces of mainland Turkey.

UPI

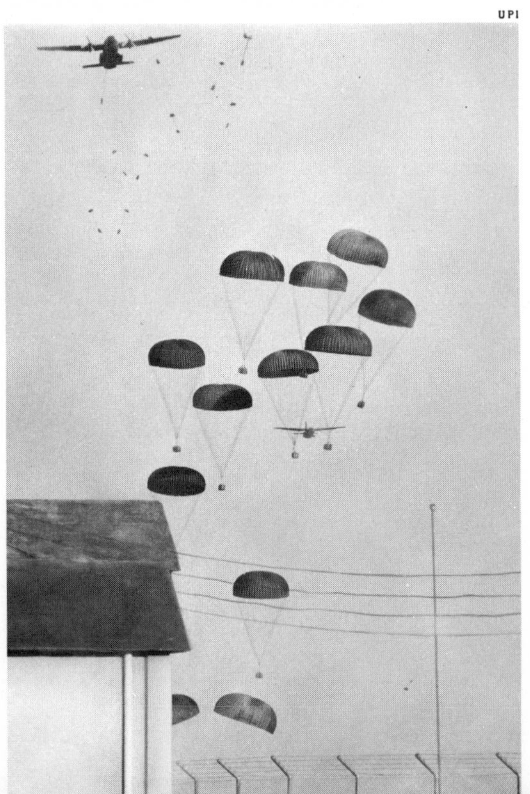

JULY

1 Juan D. Perón dies at the age of 78. Vice President Isabel Perón succeeds her husband as president of Argentina.

3 After signing accords on a limitation of underground nuclear testing and a lower ceiling for defensive missile systems, President Nixon and Soviet party chairman Brezhnev conclude their summit conference in Moscow.

7 West Germany wins the World Cup soccer final, defeating the Netherlands, 2–1.

8 In Canada's parliamentary elections, the Liberal party of Prime Minister Trudeau wins a majority.

15 Cypriot troops overthrow the government of Archbishop Makarios.

17 A new Portuguese cabinet, headed by Col. Vasco dos Santos Gonçalves, is formed.

20 Seeking to overthrow the new Greek-oriented government of Cyprus, Turkish forces invade the island by air and sea. • Two Soviet cosmonauts complete the 15-day Soyuz 14 mission.

22 Michael Imru is appointed premier of Ethiopia.

23 Constantine Caramanlis, the civilian premier of Greece from 1955 to 1963, is sworn in as head of a new government. • Nikos Giorgiades Sampson, the new Cypriot president, resigns and turns the office over to Glafkos Clerides.

24 The U. S. Supreme Court rules that President Nixon must surrender the subpoenaed records of 64 White House conversations for use in the Watergate cover-up trial. The President agrees to comply.

25 In a 5–4 decision, the U. S. Supreme Court all but bans the busing of schoolchildren across school district lines to achieve desegregation.

29 Former U. S. Secretary of the Treasury John B. Connally is indicted by a Watergate grand jury.

30 The U. S. House Judiciary Committee approves its third and final article of impeachment against President Nixon. • Representatives of Greece, Turkey, and Britain sign a declaration in Geneva imposing a new cease-fire in Cyprus.

31 John D. Ehrlichman is sentenced to a prison term of 20 months to 5 years. (The former presidential adviser was convicted on July 12 of conspiring to violate the civil rights of Dr. Daniel Ellsberg's psychiatrist.) • A bill making French the only official language in the Canadian province of Quebec becomes law.

AUGUST

S	M	T	W	T	F	S
				1	2	3
4	5	6	7	8	9	10
11	12	13	14	15	16	17
18	19	20	21	22	23	24
25	26	27	28	29	30	31

NIXON RESIGNS UNDER FIRE

FORD IS 38TH PRESIDENT

ROCKEFELLER NAMED V.P.

AUGUST

2 John W. Dean III, former counsel to President Nixon, is sentenced to one to four years in prison for his admitted role in the Watergate cover-up.

5 President Nixon agrees to release the transcripts of three conversations with H. R. Haldeman taped on June 23, 1972. The President admits "a serious act of omission" in his previous accounts of the Watergate case.

6 The U. S. Senate Foreign Relations Committee votes unanimously to exonerate Secretary of State Kissinger of allegations that he misled the committee concerning his role in government wiretapping.

8 Under severe pressure from congressional and other quarters, Richard Milhous Nixon announces that he will resign as U. S. president, effective at noon August 9.

9 U. S. Vice President Gerald Rudolph Ford is sworn in as the nation's 38th president.

12 Addressing a joint session of Congress, President Ford states that his "first priority" is to work with Congress "to bring inflation under control." • Month-long floods begin to subside in 16 districts of Bangladesh and in seven states of India; the reported death toll reaches 1,200 persons in Bangladesh and 200 in India.

14 Fighting erupts again in Cyprus as peace talks break down in Geneva. • Greece withdraws its armed forces from the North Atlantic Treaty Organization. • Robert L. Stanfield announces that he plans to resign as leader of Canada's Progressive Conservative party.

15 Mrs. Chung Hee Park, wife of South Korea's president, dies from an assassin's bullet. The attack apparently was intended for her husband.

16 Turkish forces complete their military goals of dividing Cyprus into Turkish Cypriot and Greek Cypriot areas and declare a cease-fire.

17 Cease-fire breaks down on Cyprus.

19 Rodger P. Davies, 53-year-old U. S. ambassador to Cyprus, is shot to death during a demonstration of Greek Cypriots at the U. S. embassy.

20 President Ford nominates Nelson A. Rockefeller as the 41st vice president of the United States.

28 Following two days in space, Soyuz 15, a Soviet manned spaceship, returns abruptly to earth. • In Iceland, a coalition cabinet headed by conservative Independent party leader Geir Hallgrimsson takes the oath of office.

UPI

(*Above*) President Nixon goes on nationwide television, August 8, to announce his resignation, effective at noon, August 9. (*Below*) The President comforts daughter Julie on August 7, the day of his decision.

UPI

FORD GRANTS PARDON TO NIXON

HAILE SELASSIE IS DETHRONED

ALGERIAN HEADS UN ASSEMBLY

SEPTEMBER

S	M	T	W	T	F	S
1	2	3	4	5	6	7
8	9	10	11	12	13	14
15	16	17	18	19	20	21
22	23	24	25	26	27	28
29	30					

SEPTEMBER

2 President Ford signs into law the pension reform bill, which seeks to protect the retirement benefits of 23 million U. S. workers.

4 President Ford names George Bush head of the U. S. liaison office in Peking. Mary Louise Smith of Iowa is chosen by the President to succeed Bush as chairman of the Republican National Committee. • The United States and East Germany establish formal diplomatic relations.

6 In New Zealand, Wallace Edward Rowling is named prime minister, succeeding Norman E. Kirk, who died August 31.

7 In Lusaka, Zambia, representatives of Portugal and of the Front for the Liberation of Mozambique (FRELIMO) sign an agreement granting independence to the Portuguese African territory of Mozambique, southeast Africa, in June 1975.

8 President Ford grants Richard M. Nixon an "absolute" pardon for all federal crimes he "committed or may have committed or taken part in" while president of the United States.

9 Jimmy Connors and Billie Jean King win the U. S. Open men's and women's singles tennis titles at Forest Hills, N. Y.

10 Portugal grants independence to the Republic of Guinea-Bissau, formerly Portuguese Guinea.

12 Emperor Haile Selassie, who ruled Ethiopia since 1916, is deposed by the military.

16 President Ford reveals an earned clemency program for Vietnam-era draft evaders and military deserters who agree to work in public service jobs for up to two years. • Gen. Alexander M. Haig, Jr., is appointed supreme commander of the North Atlantic Treaty Organization.

17 The 29th General Assembly of the United Nations opens. Abdelaziz Bouteflika, foreign minister of Algeria, is elected president; and Bangladesh, Grenada, and Guinea-Bissau are admitted as UN members. • The U. S. entry *Courageous* wins the America's Cup yachting race, beating Australia's *Southern Cross.*

19–20 In Honduras, the death toll from hurricane Fifi is estimated at 5,000 persons.

23 Sen. Edward M. Kennedy (D-Mass.) announces "unconditionally" that he will not seek the U. S. presidency in 1976.

28 Closing a national conference on inflation, President Ford announces the creation of an Economic Policy Board, headed by Secretary of the Treasury William E. Simon, and of a White House Labor-Management Committee, coordinated by John T. Dunlop.

30 António de Spínola resigns as president of Portugal and is succeeded by Gen. Francisco da Costa Gomes.

Abdelaziz Bouteflika (*center*) of Algeria is elected president of the UN's 29th General Assembly, September 17.

T. CHEN/UNITED NATIONS

President Ford pardons former President Nixon for crimes Nixon may have committed as president, September 8.

WIDE WORLD

OCTOBER

S	M	T	W	T	F	S
		1	2	3	4	5
6	7	8	9	10	11	12
13	14	15	16	17	18	19
20	21	22	23	24	25	26
27	28	29	30	31		

PALESTINIAN GROUP GETS UN BID

FORD APPEARS BEFORE HOUSE PANEL

OAKLAND A'S WIN WORLD SERIES

OCTOBER

1 The Watergate cover-up trial begins in Washington, D. C.

3 Frank Robinson signs a one-year contract to manage the Cleveland Indians, becoming the first black to be named manager of a major league baseball team.

8 In an address to a joint session of Congress, President Ford outlines 10 proposals to "whip inflation now." • Eisaku Sato, former premier of Japan, and Sean MacBride of Ireland, the UN commissioner for South-West Africa, are named to share the 1974 Nobel Peace Prize.

10 In Britain's second general election of 1974, the Labour party of Prime Minister Wilson wins a three-seat majority.

11 Vice President-designate Nelson Rockefeller provides a list of 20 current and former public officials and aides to whom he had donated over $2 million since 1955.

14 The UN General Assembly approves a draft resolution inviting the Palestine Liberation Organization "to participate in the deliberations of the General Assembly on the question of Palestine." • President Ford signs into law a bill providing for the reform of federal election campaign funding.

15 With racial violence continuing in the public schools of Boston, Massachusetts Gov. Francis Sargent orders the mobilization of National Guardsmen.

17 In a historic appearance before a House subcommittee, President Ford defends his pardon of former President Nixon. • The Oakland A's win their third consecutive World Series by defeating the Los Angeles Dodgers, four games to one.

20 The Swiss electorate rejects a proposal calling for the deportation of half of the nation's 1.1 million foreigners by the end of 1977.

21 During a meeting with President Ford, Mexico's President Luís Echeverría Álvarez confirms that substantial amounts of oil have been found in southeastern Mexico.

26 Henry S. Ruth, Jr., is sworn in as Watergate special prosecutor, succeeding Leon Jaworski who resigned effective October 25.

28 Meeting in Rabat, Morocco, Arab heads of state call for the creation of an independent Palestinian state and recognize the Palestine Liberation Organization as the "sole legitimate representative of the Palestinian people."

30 The United States, Britain, and France veto a Security Council resolution that would expel South Africa from UN membership. • In Kinshasa, Zaire, Muhammad Ali regains the world heavyweight boxing championship by knocking out George Foreman in the eighth round.

GEORGE TAMES/THE NEW YORK TIMES

President Ford defends his pardon of Richard Nixon before a subcommittee of the House Judiciary Committee, October 17. Ford volunteered to testify in order to explain the pardon he granted to his predecessor.

PLO'S ARAFAT ADDRESSES UN

FORD, BREZHNEV SIGN ACCORD

TANAKA QUITS JAPANESE POST

NOVEMBER

S	M	T	W	T	F	S
					1	2
3	4	5	6	7	8	9
10	11	12	13	14	15	16
17	18	19	20	21	22	23
24	25	26	27	28	29	30

NOVEMBER

5 The Democratic party scores major victories in the midterm elections across the United States.

8 U. S. Secretary of the Army Howard H. Callaway announces the parole of former Lt. William L. Calley, Jr., who was convicted of murdering 22 civilians at Mylai in 1968.

12 UN General Assembly votes to suspend South Africa from participating in the remainder of the 1974 session.

13 UN debate on the "question of Palestine" opens with an address by Yasir Arafat, chairman of the Palestine Liberation Organization (PLO).

16 In Rome, the World Food Conference approves a new UN agency, the World Food Council, to supervise antihunger programs.

18 In the first parliamentary elections in Greece since 1964, Premier Constantine Caramanlis and his New Democracy party win a clear mandate.

19 Eduardo Z. Romualdez, the Philippine ambassador to the United States, is released unharmed after being held hostage for some 10 hours by a gunman in Washington, D. C.

20 A German 747 jetliner crashes in Nairobi, Kenya, killing 59 persons.

22 The UN General Assembly approves resolutions declaring that the Palestine people have the right to independence and sovereignty and giving the PLO observer status at the UN.

24 President Ford concludes an eight-day trip to Japan, South Korea, and Vladivostok, USSR. During the trip, the President and Soviet party chairman Brezhnev sign a tentative agreement limiting the number of all offensive strategic nuclear weapons and delivery vehicles through 1985. The pact is subject to further negotiations at Geneva.

25 U Thant, former secretary general of the United Nations (1961–71), dies in New York City.

26 Facing alleged financial scandals, Kakuei Tanaka announces his resignation as prime minister of Japan. ● President Ford signs a six-year, $11.8 billion mass transit bill.

29 A court-appointed panel of three doctors reports that former President Nixon would not be physically able to testify at the Watergate cover-up trial personally before Feb. 16, 1975, and by deposition at his home until January 6.

30 It is officially announced that President Ford will visit China during the second half of 1975. ● India and Pakistan sign a protocol lifting their ban on trade, imposed during the war over Kashmir.

Yasir Arafat, chairman of the Palestine Liberation Organization, addresses the UN on November 13.

CHRISTOPHER LITTLE, CAMERA 5

DECEMBER

S	M	T	W	T	F	S
1	2	3	4	5	6	7
8	9	10	11	12	13	14
15	16	17	18	19	20	21
22	23	24	25	26	27	28
29	30	31				

MAKARIOS RETURNS TO CYPRUS

U.S. UNEMPLOYMENT RISES

ROCKEFELLER IS VICE PRESIDENT

DECEMBER

3 The U. S. Congress overrides President Ford's veto of a bill increasing educational benefits for veterans.

4 Canada's Prime Minister Trudeau discusses matters related to energy with President Ford at the White House.

5 Officials of the United Mine Workers union and the U. S. coal industry sign a new three-year labor contract, ending a 24-day strike by coal miners. • The new government of Premier Aldo Moro receives a vote of confidence from the Italian Senate. • German Chancellor Schmidt meets with President Ford at the White House. • The Most Rev. F. Donald Coggan is sworn in as the 101st Archbishop of Canterbury.

6 The U. S. Department of Labor announces that the nation's unemployment rate reached 6.5% in November—the highest monthly rate since October 1961.

7 Archbishop Makarios, who was ousted as president of Cyprus in a July coup, returns to the Mediterranean island to resume control of the government.

8 In a national referendum, Greek voters decide that Greece will abolish the monarchy and become a republic. • Soyuz 16, a Soviet spacecraft with two cosmonauts aboard, returns to earth, completing a six-day mission.

9 The Japanese parliament formally elects Takeo Miki to succeed Kakuei Tanaka as premier.

11 Rhodesia's Prime Minister Ian Smith announces that his white minority government and black nationalists have agreed to an immediate cease-fire, following prolonged fighting in the north.

14 Attorney General William Saxbe is named U. S. ambassador to India, succeeding Daniel Moynihan.

16 On the Caribbean island of Martinique, President Ford and France's President Giscard d'Estaing agree to coordinate U. S.-French energy policies.

19 Nelson A. Rockefeller is sworn in as the 41st vice president of the United States.

20 The 93d Congress adjourns after approving a foreign trade bill.

25 A cyclone strikes Darwin, Australia, destroying 90% of the city and killing at least 50 persons.

28 An earthquake destroys several villages in northern Pakistan, killing an estimated 5,200 persons.

29 The government of Nicaragua agrees to release 26 political prisoners in exchange for the lives of several persons seized by leftist guerrillas on December 27.

30 President Ford vetoes a bill regulating strip mining of coal.

Archbishop Makarios, who was deposed as president of Cyprus in July, returns to Nicosia on December 7.

CLAUDE SALHANI, SYGMA

The Unmaking of the PRESIDENT, 1974

By Robert Shogan
National Political Correspondent, "Los Angeles Times"

"One year of Watergate is enough," President Nixon declared in a dramatic postscript to his State of the Union address on Jan. 30, 1974. "I believe the time has come to bring that investigation . . . to an end." He called upon Congress to join him "in devoting our full energies to these great issues that I have discussed tonight."

The President spoke with determination and seeming confidence. Though he had already been damaged by the Watergate scandal, he could still fall back upon his celebrated political skills plus the immense prestige of his office. But in the forthcoming months of 1974, events marched on against him with the force of a Greek tragedy. Watergate would culminate in an event unparalleled in U. S. history. Discredited by his own actions, deserted by his allies, Richard Nixon would be forced to quit the office to which he had been overwhelmingly reelected in 1972.

Major Indictments. Even as Nixon spoke in January, the perils facing his presidency were plainly outlined. As the year began, Leon Jaworski, special Watergate prosecutor, reported that the various Watergate grand juries would soon "be prepared to consider the matter of returning indictments in a substantial number of major involvements."

On March 7 two former top White House staffers, John D. Ehrlichman and Charles Colson, were among those indicted for the September 1971 burglary of the office of Dr. Lewis Fielding, psychiatrist to Daniel Ellsberg, the Pentagon Papers defendant. In June, Colson pleaded guilty to trying to obstruct justice; in July, Ehrlichman was convicted of conspiring to violate Dr. Fielding's civil rights and of three counts of perjury.

Another set of indictments, handed down March 1, had even more direct impact on Nixon. These dealt with the conspiracy to cover up the Watergate break-in of June 1972, the core of the scandal that threatened the President. Charged with conspiracy to impede the Watergate investigation were John N. Mitchell, former attorney general and Nixon campaign manager; H. R. Haldeman, former White House chief of staff; Ehrlichman; Colson; Robert C. Mardian, former Nixon campaign official; Kenneth W. Parkinson, lawyer for the Nixon campaign committee; and Gordon C. Strachan, assistant to Haldeman.

Later, it was disclosed that the grand jury had secretly named Nixon as an unindicted co-conspirator in the case. Reportedly it had refrained from indicting the President only because the Constitution shielded him from any action but impeachment while he held office.

Impeachment Inquiry. The cover-up indictments opened the way for the transfer of evidence bearing on the President from the grand jury to the House Judiciary Committee, which was conducting the first inquiry into the possible impeachment of a president in more than a century. That probe had begun the previous October, following the so-called Saturday Night Massacre, when the President ordered the firing of the first Watergate prosecutor, Archibald Cox. The committee had hired a chief counsel, John M. Doar, a Republican and former Justice Department official, and a minority counsel, Albert E. Jenner, Jr., another Republican and a prominent Chicago attorney. It had a $1 million budget and on February 6, by a 410–4 vote of the full House, it had been granted broad subpoena powers.

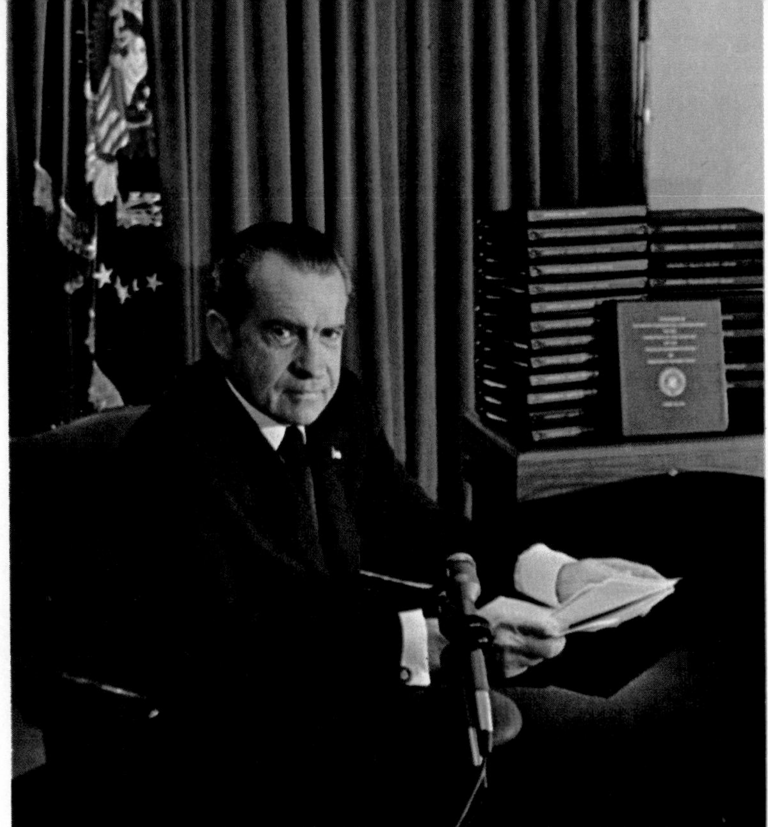

President Richard Nixon goes on nationwide television April 29 to announce that he will release the edited transcripts of Watergate tapes.

NEWSWEEK—WALLY MCNAMEE

Still, the committee moved cautiously. Though the Democrats, with 21 out of 38 members, could dominate proceedings if they wished, Chairman Peter W. Rodino, Jr. (D-N. J.) sought to avoid the appearance of partisanship.

A threshold question facing the committee was what constituted an impeachable offense. In a special report issued February 21 the committee staff argued that the constitutional phrase "high crimes and misdemeanors" should not be interpreted as limited solely to criminal offenses. But Nixon's legal staff, headed by James D. St. Clair, a Boston attorney, took a narrower view: "To argue that the President may be impeached for something less than a criminal offense . . . would be a monumental step backward into all those old English practices that our Constitution sought to eliminate."

Another problem for the committee was getting evidence from the White House, particularly the tapes of recorded presidential conversations, without which the investigations of Nixon might well have collapsed. Though the President promised to cooperate with the committee, he also said he would not do "anything that weakens the office of the President," thus raising the obstacle of executive privilege.

Following the cover-up indictments the committee sought a briefcase of evidence on the case which had been set aside by the grand jury. With the approval of Federal District Judge John J. Sirica, the briefcase and a sealed report from the grand jury were turned over to the committee on March 26.

The committee wanted more information on the case, however, and the White House balked at its requests. Stymied, the committee voted on April 11 to subpoena additional tapes of presidential conversations. Amid warnings from Republican leaders that total defiance of the subpoenas would hasten his impeachment, the President responded dramatically.

Release of Transcripts. On April 29, in a nationally televised address, Nixon announced that he would release to the committee edited transcripts of 46 presidential conversations and also make public more than 1,200 pages of transcripts.

In televised sessions during the summer, the House Judiciary Committee debated whether it should recommend that the full House "adopt articles calling for the impeachment" of President Nixon.

The President acknowledged beforehand that the transcripts would cause him embarrassment. He also said he was troubled about violating the confidentiality of presidential conversations. But, he said, he decided to release the material which would "tell it all" about his involvement in Watergate to establish his innocence. "My actions were directed toward finding the facts and seeing that justice was done fairly and according to the law," he said.

But the reaction to the release of the transcripts on April 30 was sharply different from what the President had hoped for. If the material did not conclusively establish his guilt, it served to darken suspicions about his conduct. Particular attention was focused on a conversation on March 21, 1973, between the President and his then counsel, John W. Dean III, in which Nixon seemed to approve of the idea of paying hush money to the convicted Watergate conspirators.

The overall tone and thrust of the conversations led many people to believe that the President and his closest advisers were far more interested in protecting themselves than in getting at the truth. Senate Republican Leader Hugh Scott of Pennsylvania, hitherto a strong supporter of the President, summed up the impression created by the transcripts as "disgusting, shabby, immoral." Once again, as after the Saturday Night Massacre of the previous October, a hue and cry for Nixon's resignation was raised by leading newspapers and prominent members of his own party.

The President refused to quit, however. In a rare interview on May 14 he told columnist James J. Kilpatrick: "I will never leave this office in a way which resigning would be, or failing to fight impeachment would be, that would make it more difficult for future presidents to make the tough decisions." Democratic congressional leaders also spoke up against resignation, on the grounds that the nation

J. P. LAFFONT—SYGMA

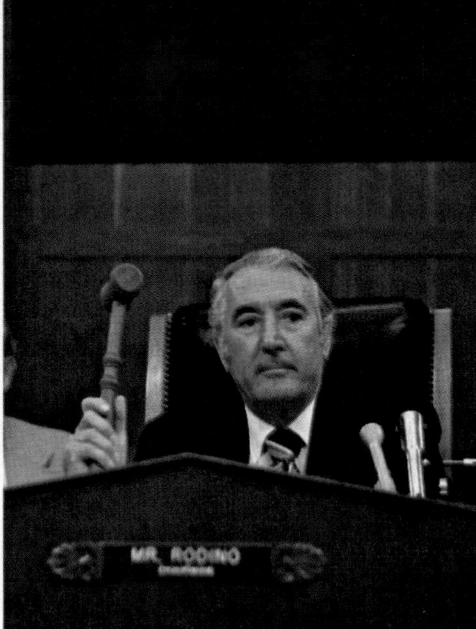

DENNIS BRACK, BLACK STAR

Rep. Peter Rodino (D-N. J.), chairman of the House Judiciary Committee, presided over the impeachment hearings.

would be better served to have the charges against Nixon resolved through the impeachment process.

Struggle over Evidence. Now Nixon dug in for a bitter last-ditch defense. On May 22 he wrote Chairman Rodino that he would not honor further subpoenas from the Judiciary Committee because to do so would "constitute such a massive invasion into the confidentiality of Presidential conversations that the institution of the Presidency itself would be fatally compromised." The committee replied on May 30 that it felt "free to consider whether your refusals warrant the drawing of adverse inferences concerning the substance of the materials, and whether your refusals in and of themselves might constitute a ground for impeachment."

The President was also battling Jaworski over the same issue of disclosure versus confidentiality. On May 20, Judge Sirica ordered the President to turn over the tapes of 64 conversations which Jaworski had subpoenaed on April 18 for use in the trial of the seven cover-up defendants. When White House lawyers said they would appeal, Jaworski asked the Supreme Court to bypass the Court of Appeals and hear the case itself directly. The high court agreed, setting the stage for a constitutional confrontation on executive privilege which would have important consequences not only for Jaworski's investigation but also for the impeachment probe in the House. If the Supreme Court ordered the President to turn over the disputed tapes to Jaworski, the Judiciary Committee could soon expect to get the same material.

With this grave threat impending, the President sought to dramatize the diplomatic achievements of his presidency. In June he traveled first to the Middle East, where Secretary of State Henry Kissinger had negotiated a disengagement of Syrian and Israeli troops, and then to the Soviet Union, with which his administration had fostered improved relations.

The tapes case, *United States* v. *Richard M. Nixon,* came before the Supreme Court for argument on July 8. The basic issue was whether the President was sub-

CHARLON—GAMMA

President Nixon meets with Soviet Chairman Brezhnev in Moscow in early July. Throughout the impeachment debate, Nixon supporters emphasized the President's accomplishments in foreign policy.

ject to the requirements of the law, in this instance the demands of a subpoena. "The President is not above the law," said St. Clair. "But law as to the President has to be applied in a constitutional way which is different from anyone else." Forcing the President to comply with the subpoena, said St. Clair, would make him "an 85 percent President, not a 100 percent President." Besides, by ruling against the President, St. Clair argued, the court would be involving itself in the entirely separate dispute between the President and the Judiciary Committee.

In rebuttal, Jaworski declared: "This nation's . . . form of government is in serious jeopardy if the President . . . is to say that the Constitution means what he says it does. . . . If he is wrong, who is there to tell him so?"

It remained for the Supreme Court to tell him so, which it did by an 8 to 0 vote in a decision handed down on July 24. Chief Justice Warren Burger, whom

EDITORIAL CARTOON BY PAT OLIPHANT, © THE DENVER POST, REPRINTED WITH PERMISSION OF THE LOS ANGELES TIMES SYNDICATE

SUPREME COURT 8
WHITE HOUSE 0

STONEWALLED

Nixon himself had appointed in 1969, declared: "Neither the doctrine of separation of powers, nor the need for confidentiality of high-level communications, without more, can sustain an absolute unqualified presidential privilege of immunity from judicial process under all circumstances." The President, who beforehand had refused to say whether he would comply with the court's order, now announced he would obey and turn over the tapes.

The high court's opinion was in effect the death warrant for the Nixon presidency. It would force the release of evidence which would make clear the President's role in the Watergate cover-up.

Articles of Impeachment. Even before that happened, the President's fortunes had suffered in the House Judiciary Committee, which began its formal debate on impeachment over national television on the same day the high court's ruling was announced. It soon became clear that the advocates of impeachment had support from conservative Southern Democrats and Republicans on the committee.

By July 30, when the committee concluded 35 hours of debate spread over six days, it had voted to send three articles of impeachment to the House floor. Article I, charging the President with obstruction of justice in the Watergate cover-up was approved on July 27 by a 27 to 11 vote. It was supported by all 21 Democrats, including Walter Flowers of Alabama, James R. Mann of South Carolina, and Ray Thornton of Arkansas, and six Republicans—William S. Cohen of Maine, Tom Railsback of Illinois, Hamilton Fish, Jr., of New York, Lawrence J. Hogan of Maryland, M. Caldwell Butler of Virginia, and Harold V. Froehlich of Wisconsin.

Article II accused the President of abuse of power, stemming from his misuse of and interference with government agencies, specifically the Internal Revenue Service, the Secret Service, the FBI, and the CIA. The article was approved by a vote of 28 to 10, with Robert McClory of Illinois joining the six other Republicans for impeachment. The third article, charging Nixon with impeding the impeachment process by defying the Judiciary Committee's subpoenas, was approved by

About to leave office, President Nixon bids farewell to his Cabinet and White House staff as daughter Tricia Cox looks on (*below*). He then left for San Clemente, Calif.

FRED WARD—BLACK STAR

DENNIS BRACK—MAGNUM

DENNIS BRACK—BLACK STAR

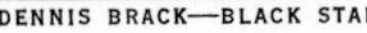

FRED WARD—BLACK STAR

(*Above*) The new President, Gerald Ford, is sworn in by Chief Justice Burger as Mrs. Ford holds the Bible. A member of the House of Representatives for 25 years, President Ford addresses a joint session of Congress three days later (*left*).

21 to 17, with Democrats Flowers and Mann in opposition and only two Republicans, Hogan and McClory, supporting it. Two additional articles of impeachment were rejected by the committee.

Approval of a bill of impeachment by the House now appeared all but certain by the end of August. Nixon's supporters prepared to do battle on the House floor, clinging to the hope that they could prevent a two-thirds majority of the Senate from voting to convict him and remove him from office.

But these hopes were soon dashed. As a result of the Supreme Court order, Nixon was forced to turn over to Sirica tapes that contained evidence contradicting his repeated assertion that he had known nothing of the Watergate cover-up until March 21, 1973. The tapes showed that Nixon, in two conversations with his chief of staff, H. R. Haldeman, on June 23, 1972—only six days after the Watergate break-in—had approved a scheme for thwarting the FBI investigation of the case on the false premise that the Central Intelligence Agency was covertly involved in the affair.

On August 5 the President made public the transcripts of the damaging tapes, conceded that he had withheld knowledge of them from his lawyers and from his supporters on the committee, and acknowledged that his impeachment by the House was "a foregone conclusion." Still, the President insisted that the record did not justify conviction and removal by the Senate.

Few agreed with him. The 10 Republicans on the Judiciary Committee who had held out against impeachment indignantly changed their positions. Demands for resignation came from Republican leaders, and Nixon's own aides in the White House reportedly pressed this course upon him.

Resignation. Unable to withstand this pressure any longer, Nixon privately informed Vice President Gerald R. Ford of his intention to quit, and on August 8 made his public announcement in a televised address.

The President conceded that some of his judgments had been wrong and regretted any injuries he had caused. "To leave office before my term is completed is opposed to every instinct in my body," he said. But he had decided to quit to serve "the interests of America." Nixon did not admit any culpability for the crimes alleged against him.

The resignation became effective on August 9, when Ford took over as president and declared that "our long national nightmare is over."

But the wheels of justice ground on. Five of Nixon's former associates went on trial for their role in the Watergate cover-up. On Jan. 1, 1975, Mitchell, Haldeman, Ehrlichman, and Mardian were convicted; Parkinson was acquitted.

Presidential Pardon. The controversy surrounding Nixon did not end with his departure from the White House. On September 8, just one month after he took office, President Ford granted Nixon a "full, free, and absolute pardon" for all federal crimes that he "committed or may have committed or taken part in" while president. The action took the country by surprise and provoked a storm of protest. Ford defended the pardon by saying the former President had "suffered enough" and that he wished to spare the nation the long ordeal of a Nixon trial. The former President accepted the pardon, admitted "mistakes" in the Watergate case, but did not acknowledge guilt or complicity in any crime.

At the same time the pardon was granted, an agreement was announced giving Nixon control over his presidential papers and tapes, and providing for destruction of the tapes upon his death. Like the pardon, this deal met with widespread opposition, based on the fear that the full story of Watergate might be lost to history if the tapes were not eventually made public. In December, Congress passed a bill requiring that the tapes remain in the possession of the federal government.

BEFORE THE FALL

Nixon's 5½ Years in the White House

By Robert J. Huckshorn
Professor and Chairman, Department of Political Science, Florida Atlantic University

One and one-half years into his second term, President Richard M. Nixon resigned his office on Aug. 9, 1974, when the pressures of the Watergate scandals and related matters brought him to the verge of impeachment and removal from office. He was succeeded by Vice President Gerald R. Ford, who had been appointed to the office upon the forced resignation of Spiro T. Agnew in 1973. Nixon immediately left Washington for retirement at his home in San Clemente, Calif. On September 8, President Ford issued a full pardon to Nixon for any "offenses against the United States which he . . . has committed or may have committed" during his years as president. These unprecedented events ended the political career of Richard Nixon.

In September 1974, Nixon was treated for a recurring phlebitis condition in his left leg in a Long Beach, Calif., hospital. He later reentered the same hospital and went into life-endangering medical shock following surgery to correct the condition.

Foreign Affairs. Richard Nixon's first term (1969–73) was dominated by foreign affairs. He began phased troop withdrawals from Vietnam and ultimately ordered U. S. troops to join South Vietnamese forces in a series of military operations against Communist areas of Cambodia. The saturation bombings of North Vietnam at Christmas 1972 were viewed by critics as barbarous, but the President and his supporters considered the attacks to be a necessary part of American efforts to force the North Vietnamese to the negotiating table. Nixon's four-year effort to de-escalate the long and bloody Vietnam War finally was brought to fruition in January 1973 with the signing of cease-fire agreements.

In 1972, Nixon became the first American president to pay a state visit to the People's Republic of China. The China trip, widely publicized throughout the world, opened communications between the two nations for the first time since 1949.

Shortly after his return from China, President Nixon visited the Soviet Union, the first time an American president had traveled to that country. A series of seven agreements were signed, including pacts on joint space missions, technology, the environment, medical research, incidents at sea, and two treaties limiting stra-

MAGNUM

Nixon and Chinese Premier Chou En-lai at a banquet in Peking during Nixon's historic China trip in 1972.

tegic arms. The latter agreement overshadowed the others by limiting the deployment of antiballistic missiles (ABM's) and by placing a freeze on offensive weaponry. In mid-1974 the President made a second trip to Moscow, where he signed three nuclear pacts generally thought to be of lesser importance.

As 1973 drew to a close the worst outbreak of fighting between Israeli and Arab forces since 1956 developed into a bloody Middle East war. A remarkable performance in "shuttle" diplomacy by Secretary of State Henry Kissinger brought about a cease-fire and a disengagement accord that was widely hailed as a major American diplomatic achievement. In the process, United States relations with Egypt improved to such an extent that formal contacts were reestablished for the first time since 1967. This was followed in June 1974 by a Nixon visit to the Middle East that included stops in Israel, Egypt, Syria, Jordan, and Saudi Arabia.

The Economy. The overriding domestic problem throughout the Nixon presidency was uncontrolled inflation. Nixon and his economic advisers experimented with a tight-money policy and wage, price, and rent controls, as well as devaluation of the dollar, in an effort to bring inflation under control. Nothing appeared to have a lasting effect, and the multitude of economic problems escalated rapidly in 1973–74.

Nixon appeared to vacillate between employing economic controls and extolling the virtues of a free market. He imposed price ceilings on beef, lamb, and pork amidst shoppers' boycotts of those products. He imposed a series of "phased" controls culminating in Phase IV, a selective price-control system. Yet the rate of inflation continued to grow.

The Legislative Record. Because of his preoccupation with foreign affairs during his first term and with Watergate in his second, the Nixon legislative record was somewhat limited. Probably the outstanding administrative initiative in domestic legislation was the State and Local Fiscal Assistance Act of 1972, more commonly known as revenue sharing. Under that act much-needed funds for state and local governments were provided through federal direct payments.

Other important administration bills passed during the Nixon years were the military draft lottery bill, the conversion of the Post Office Department into a government-owned corporation, drug-abuse bills, and several anticrime enactments. A number of environmental laws were passed, but the congressional versions were often stronger than those of the administration. The most significant Nixon initiative rejected by Congress was a far-reaching welfare reform and family-assistance program submitted during the President's first term.

As is often true, some presidential appointments were highly praised while others were condemned as inappropriate and poor. Some of his most controversial appointments stemmed from his efforts to shape the Supreme Court in a more conservative image. He was twice thwarted in his efforts to gain Senate approval of conservative justice nominees from Southern states. Ultimately, he nominated a total of four Supreme Court justices who were confirmed with relative ease.

Politics. After winning one of the closest elections in American history, Nixon was inaugurated in 1969 with a mandate representing only 43.4% of the popular vote. The Democrats retained control of both houses of Congress throughout the entire Nixon administration. In 1972, Nixon won a historic reelection victory over Sen. George McGovern, carrying every state except Massachusetts and the District of Columbia, and receiving 60.8% of the popular vote. The President's popularity peaked in early 1973 during the concluding scenes in the drama of American involvement in Vietnam, then plummeted to an all-time low for any president in the depths of the Watergate scandals.

A serious political setback occurred in October 1973 when Nixon's vice president, Spiro T. Agnew, was forced from office after pleading no contest to a charge of tax evasion. The President was damaged also by charges relating to his personal finances, including questionable tax deductions, limited income tax payments, failure to pay California and District of Columbia income taxes, and improvements to his personal estates at government expense.

OFFICIAL PHOTOGRAPH, THE WHITE HOUSE

The new first family (*left to right*): sons John and Steven; Mrs. Ford; the President; daughter Susan; daughter-in-law Gayle and her husband, Michael.

The 38th President

By Walter Darnell Jacobs
Professor of Government and Politics, University of Maryland

On Aug. 9, 1974, Gerald Rudolph Ford became America's 38th president and the first to have reached that high office as a result of appointment under the terms of the 25th Amendment.

In October 1973, then President Richard Nixon named Ford to succeed Spiro T. Agnew, who had resigned as vice president. Less than a year later Nixon himself resigned under the shadow of the Watergate scandals, and Ford succeeded to the presidency. After being sworn in by Chief Justice Warren Burger, Ford delivered a short speech in which he called for the prayers of the American people and for "a little straight talk among friends."

Although Ford came to the presidency in a novel manner, his accession seemed to be quite popular with the public. His open manner, his plain speaking, his overall simplicity, and his physical ruggedness combined with his political experience to qualify him as "president of all the people." His reputation for integrity and probity motivated public confidence.

Early Years. Ford was born in Omaha, Nebr., on July 14, 1913, as Leslie King, Jr. His mother obtained a divorce from King when Ford was two years old and left Omaha for Grand Rapids, Mich. She remarried and her son took the name of his stepfather, Gerald Ford, a paint manufacturer. It was not until he was a teenager that Gerald, Jr., learned that Gerald, Sr., was not his natural father.

Ford attended South High School in Grand Rapids where he starred as the football center.

OFFICIAL PHOTOGRAPH, THE WHITE HOUSE

President Gerald R. Ford in official portrait.

He was recruited by the University of Michigan, where he played on undefeated teams in 1932 and 1933 and was selected as the most valuable player in 1934. He was graduated in 1935 and entered Yale Law School. At Yale he helped earn his way by assisting the boxing and football coaching staffs. On graduation from Yale in 1941, Ford returned to Grand Rapids and entered private law practice. He enlisted in the Navy shortly after Pearl Harbor and served for 47 months, emerging as a lieutenant commander. He then reentered law practice in Grand Rapids, Mich.

Family. In October 1948, Ford married Elizabeth Bloomer, who had been a professional dancer and model. She had been married to

MARK GODFREY—MAGNUM

As vice president, Ford arrives in Charlotte, N. C. (*above*) to make one of his many speeches in support of President Richard Nixon. (*Below*) Ford, who was an outstanding football player at the University of Michigan, is now an avid golfer.

DOUG BRUCE—CAMERA 5

William Warren of Grand Rapids in 1942 and was divorced five years later.

The Fords have four children—Michael, 24, a divinity student in Massachusetts who is married to Gayle Ann Brumbaugh; John, 22, a student in watershed management at Utah State University; Steven, 18, who works on a Utah cattle ranch; and Susan, 17, a student at a Maryland boarding school. In September 1974, Betty Ford underwent a mastectomy operation for breast cancer.

Career in Congress. In 1948, with the encouragement of Sen. Arthur Vandenberg, Ford ran for Congress from Michigan's 5th District. He won that contest and every subsequent election in which he participated through 1972.

In Congress, Ford generally took the conservative line on issues, a reflection of the nature of his constituency. In foreign affairs, he adopted an internationalist stance. His work with candidates and in support of party positions led to his election as chairman of the House Republican Conference in 1963. Ford served on a number of significant committees and built solid alliances in Congress.

When President Johnson named the Warren Commission to investigate the assassination of President Kennedy, Ford was one of the two representatives selected.

In 1964, when his name was floated as a possible vice-presidential candidate, Ford said, "I would ten times rather be speaker of the House than vice president." He replaced Charles A. Halleck as House minority leader in January 1965, and joined the Senate minority leader, Everett M. Dirksen, in weekly press-conference attacks on the Johnson administration. This gave him some national exposure and a more secure place in the leadership of the Republican congressional party. His rise was thereafter based on solid work. Ford remained a favorite of the broad reach of the GOP and was respected by Democrats as well.

The Presidency. It was probably quite natural that Nixon should select Ford to fill the vacancy in the vice presidency created by Agnew's resignation in 1973. Ford represented most of the moral and political virtues needed at that time—a spotless personal record, a reputation for selfless party service, and a good relationship with members of Congress built up during his 25 years of service in the House. Ford's acceptance speech was marked by modesty—"I am a Ford, not a Lincoln," he said—and quiet confidence.

The Nixon resignation in August 1974 capped a period of national anguish and worry. In such times, the modesty and quiet confidence of Gerald Ford were appropriate.

On assuming the presidency, Ford told America that "our long national nightmare is over" and that a period of national reconciliation was at hand. He said he came into office "indebted to no man" and ready to be "the president of all the people."

Ford's first address to a joint session of Congress emphasized "communication, compromise, and cooperation," and he declared that his would be an open administration. He stressed the need for rapid action against inflation, which he designated Public Enemy Number One. In foreign affairs, Ford made it clear that he would continue the policies originated by Nixon and that he would rely on Henry A. Kissinger as his chief foreign-policy adviser.

One month after entering office, Ford issued a "full, complete, and absolute" pardon to Nixon for any wrongs he committed or may have committed while in the presidency. Some observers thought that concern for Nixon's health may have motivated Ford. Others attacked him for failing to await an indictment and for extending special treatment to the former President. Meanwhile, legal actions against other Watergate defendants proceeded.

The pardon of Nixon aroused strong protests around the country, and in response President Ford made what is believed to be an unprecedented appearance by a president in office before a congressional panel. On October 17, the President told a House Judiciary subcommittee that he had acted in the "best interests" of the country and denied that any deal had been made with his predecessor.

In trying to eliminate the rough edges remaining from the Nixon administration, Ford ordered that the question of amnesty for persons who refused to serve in Vietnam be settled by a program of earned clemency.

To fill the vacancy in the vice presidency created by his move to the presidency, Ford nominated Nelson A. Rockefeller, former governor of New York. Rockefeller was subjected to extensive congressional hearings.

While retaining most of the Nixon cabinet, Ford made sweeping changes in the composition of the White House staff. Donald M. Rumsfeld succeeded Gen. Alexander Haig as chief of staff. Jerald F. terHorst took over for Ronald Ziegler as press secretary and, when terHorst resigned over the handling of the Nixon pardon, was himself replaced by Ron Nessen. Other prominent White House appointees were Robert T. Hartmann, John O. Marsh, Jr., Charles E. Goodell, and William W. Scranton.

Ford's assault on the problems of energy shortages and inflation culminated in an "economic summit" held in Washington in late September. Ford asked Americans to become inflation-fighters and energy-savers. He appointed an Economic Policy Board, headed by Secretary of the Treasury William E. Simon, and a White House Labor-Management Committee, headed by Harvard Professor John T. Dunlop, to begin fighting these problems. Ford promised that there would be no wage and price controls, that government spending would be cut, and that a balanced budget would be produced. He attempted to "jawbone" for a cut in world petroleum prices by convincing the oil-exporting countries of its justice and necessity. He also attempted to have the oil-importing countries adopt a common policy.

The early days of Ford's presidency were marked by an unusual display of affection and respect for a man who had not been elected to that office but who seemed to tave taken to the presidency as if his life had trained him for it. Much of this good feeling undoubtedly resulted from a reaction against the Watergate period. But the "honeymoon" period soon gave way to disputes over the pardon of Nixon, amnesty for Vietnam War resisters, and the economic crisis. For the period of transition of power in a most difficult time, however, Gerald Ford impressed most Americans as competent and confident.

In the 1960's, GOP leaders Ford and Senator Dirksen commented weekly on President Johnson's programs.

WIDE WORLD

CH. SIMONPIETRI—SYGMA

Peacekeeping forces of the United Nations, in the Middle East to supervise the shaky Arab-Israeli truce, move through Egyptian territory.

THE MIDDLE EAST: Walking a Tightrope

By Carl Leiden, Professor of Government, University of Texas at Austin; Coauthor, *The Middle East: Politics and Power*

The year 1974 began in the aftermath of the October war of 1973 between Israel and Syria and Egypt. With assists from U. S. Secretary of State Henry Kissinger, military disengagement took place and the first steps toward a more permanent settlement were made. There were repercussions in Israel, however, with the Meir government collapsing.

World attention was focused increasingly on the Arab states' oil embargo and later on the heavily increased price levels of oil. Attention was thus shifted to the Persian Gulf, the center of petroleum production, as the Arab-Israeli dispute faded in immediate importance. Such a shift seemed doubly appropriate as the year witnessed the clearest indications that the Shah of Iran's ambitions for himself and his country will upset all previous balances of powers in the area. The island of Cyprus in the eastern Mediterranean erupted into violence during the year as well, with Turkish military intervention (see pages 62–67). The United States became heavily involved in Middle Eastern affairs during 1974.

A Strategic Area. The Middle East consists of the Arab world plus the northern tier of Turkey, Iran, Afghanistan, and Pakistan. It also includes Israel and Cyprus. It contains the Turkish Straits and the Suez Canal; it possesses a very large proportion of the world's known petroleum reserves. Much of the area has had a colonial past, and a variety of nationalisms has colored its recent history. Although largely Muslim in religion, it contains Israel, established as an independent nation in 1948. It is an area of turbulence and instability; since 1948 four wars have been fought between Israel and its Arab neighbors. Some of the countries are relatively advanced politically and economically; others are just beginning the modernization process. It still witnesses the competitive efforts of the United States and the Soviet Union.

Peace Accords. In mid-January 1974 a major effort by Kissinger to get the Israelis and Egyptians to agree to disengage from the positions that they had held at the end of the October war culminated in success. The agreement involved the removal of the Israeli spearhead from the western bank of the canal. Indeed all Israeli troops were to move several miles back from the canal with a UN buffer zone separating them from Egyptian forces. Both sides agreed to further negotiations for an even greater resolution of issues between them, but year's end found little progress in this direction. One immediate consequence of the agreement, however, was the possibility of reopening the Suez Canal, closed since the 1967 war. Dredging and clearing operations began immediately; on June 22 the U. S. S. *Barnstable* was the first American naval vessel to move through the canal since the 1967 war.

Two Accords Were Tribute To Kissinger's Diplomacy

With tentative agreement between the Israelis and Egyptians established, Kissinger turned his attention to the Syrian front. It was much more difficult to achieve this disengagement. Despite some dissuasion by Egyptian President Anwar el-Sadat, President Hafez al-Assad of Syria kept up military pressure against the Israelis, including some combat, throughout the spring. It was not until May that Kissinger was able to get the two adversaries to agree. The Israelis withdrew from all territory captured in 1973 plus the town of El Quneitra, which had been held since 1967. Both Israelis and Syrians agreed to further negotiations, but little progress was made during the remainder of the year.

Despite the obvious temporary nature of these agreements and the determination on all sides to maximize their own interests in any future agreements, their existence alone was major testimony to the skill and pertinacity of Kissinger's Middle Eastern diplomacy (see accompanying article). Kissinger, among other things, established a close personal relationship with President Sadat. One result was the reestablishment of diplomatic relations between Egypt and the United States, broken since 1967; another was the successful visit in June of President Nixon. During that visit Nixon promised U. S. support to both Egypt and Israel for the establishment in their countries of nuclear technology for peaceful purposes. A permanent settlement between Israel and its neighbors seems a long way off, but the 1974 achievements were the most promising that have been made in years.

Developments in Israel. Although the Israelis had scored tactical successes in the October war, they had lost it in a strategic sense. Indeed, 1974 was a year of considerable gloom in Israel. A developmental program had been interrupted. Many Israelis were forced to remain on active duty for an extended period; the cost of the war for such a small nation was staggering, with heavy inflation an inevitable result. Considerable bickering developed over whom to blame within Israel for the tactical surprise and for the state of the armed forces. Much of the blame centered on Defense Minister Moshe Dayan, whose political future was perhaps permanently eclipsed by the war.

CH. SIMONPIETRI—SYGMA

While the generals talk peace in Geneva, Israeli soldiers and artillery maintain combat readiness.

SYGMA

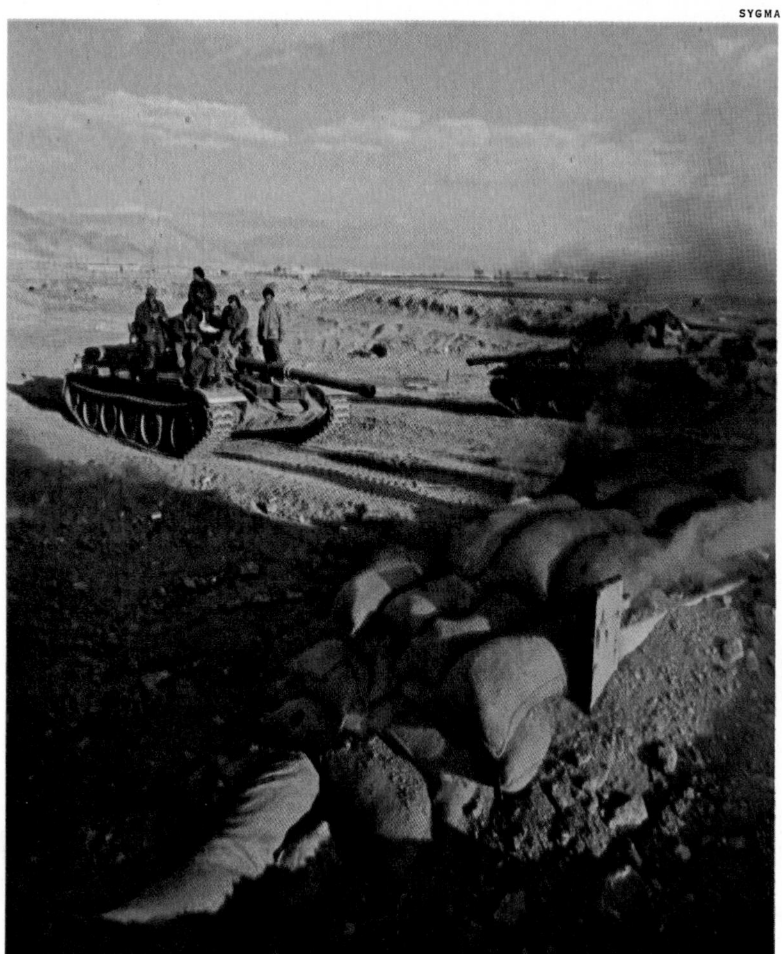

Mechanized units of the Egyptian Third Army pull back from the Sinai front after a disengagement agreement was signed by the Israeli and Egyptian chiefs of staff.

The government of Golda Meir collapsed in the spring, and after much negotiation the Israeli Labor party agreed on Itzhak Rabin as its candidate for premier. A former general officer in the Israeli army and Israeli ambassador to the United States, Rabin won his confidence vote in the Knesset, but his problems at year's end were legion.

Israel must remain on a war footing to a degree, yet the domestic dislocations of that stance must somehow be alleviated. Rabin must eventually reach accommodation with his Arab neighbors, including the Palestinian Arabs, but he must also maintain a viable state, one able to defend its borders. Rabin visited the United States in September and received assurances that American support, including military equipment, would continue to be forthcoming.

"Only a strong Israel which has the capacity to deter aggression and defend herself successfully by her own strengths, has a chance of winning peace."

—Israeli Premier Rabin on being welcomed to the United States, Sept. 10, 1974.

Developments in the Arab World. One of the reasons why the Arabs had achieved strategic success in the October war was that increasing world dependency on Middle Eastern oil had by the fall of 1973 permitted an Arab oil embargo or decreased production to have immediate and deleterious effects throughout the world and certainly the Western world. Although Egypt and Syria were not currently oil producers of any consequence, other Arab states that were—such as Libya and Saudi Arabia—were willing to use their petroleum as a weapon. Kissinger was under great pressure at the end of 1973 to accomplish disengagements somewhat favorable to the Arabs in order to reduce Arab petroleum shortfalls. He in turn applied some of this pressure to the Israelis; some accommodations were the result.

But manipulation of production was not the only factor, as it turned out. The year 1974 saw increased prices at Middle Eastern wellheads, increases of the order of several hundred percent. The resulting impact on balance of payments throughout the world has been catastrophic. Worldwide inflation has resulted, and the collapse of the world financial structure may occur because of the petroleum pricing arrangements. The enormous revenues to countries such as Saudi Arabia are of such size that they cannot be usefully employed domestically; their reinvestment in foreign money markets can, it is feared, be destabilizing. In early fall both U. S. President Ford and Secretary Kissinger warned in vague but unmistakable terms that irresponsible and artificial pricing in the resource and commodity markets would be met with appropriate responses.

Nevertheless, for all the unity displayed during and immediately following the October war, internal politics in the Arab world continued. There is strong evidence that the oil embargo against the United States was not complete; there were leaks. There was and is considerable dissension over future oil pricing and operations. Several Arab leaders—Boumédienne of Algeria, Qaddafi of Libya, Faisal of Saudi Arabia—have attempted to exercise leadership among the oil producers, but none has been successful in dominating the others.

Sheikh Yamani, the Saudi oil minister, continued to argue that production and prices are connected with the Arab-Israeli question, but this argument was not as convincing at year's end as it was in late 1973. Despite the oil problems, Saudi Arabia and the United States continued their close political and military relationship. Overall, the Arab world remained divided at year's end. If the Israelis agree to accommodation, this division may well continue to develop; Israel has long been a catalyst of Arab unity.

U. S. President Nixon and Egyptian President Sadat enjoy a warm reception as their motorcade makes its way through crowded Cairo streets during Nixon's visit to Egypt in June.

MICHEL LAURENT—GAMMA

Developments in Iran. Iran, which is not an Arab state but which lies on the Persian Gulf, is also a major oil producer. Its policy has always been independent of that of the Arab oil producers. For some time the Shah of Iran has nursed ambitions of not only making Iran a modern nation in all the ordinary senses but also of making it the paramount power in the Indian Ocean. Already wealthy with oil, increased prices in 1974 ($23 billion yield) permitted the shah to step up the scale of his ambitions and the timetable for their accomplishment.

The year 1974 was significant in that substantial takeoff in the building of the new empire was finally made possible. The shah is the biggest customer for American military equipment—about $6.5 billion since 1970 on aircraft and naval vessels alone. Incredibly, the shah's goal is to have Iran, by the end of the 1970's, fifth among all nations in terms of conventional armament.

It was announced in July that Iran had acquired 25% interest in the Krupp steel works in West Germany. Later it underwrote a $100 million loan to Grumman Aircraft, the U. S. producer of the F-14 fighter plane. Such equipment is unlikely to shield his nation effectively against the Soviet Union in the case of hostilities, but it will make it possible for Iran to control the Persian Gulf and to extend a dominant influence all the way east to India.

During 1974 minor hostilities broke out between Iraq and Iran; Iran contends that the border drawn between the two countries by the British is inequitable. Iranian troops have been in Oman (in the Arabian Peninsula) for several years, and several islands near the mouth of the gulf were seized in effect from their Arab rulers. Both the Soviet Union and the United States have minor naval stations in the gulf. Although friendly to the United States, the shah argues that he is capable of all necessary peacekeeping functions in the area.

The year saw a distinct shift in the political interest that the world takes in the Middle East. Since 1948 interest in the area has been focused on Israel and the political problems generated by its establishment. Though that issue has by no means vanished, it no longer is so significant. Israel is being forced to make enough concessions to paste together some sort of settlement. With the decline of the Israeli problem, the interest of the world and perhaps the political energies of the area are being shifted to the Persian Gulf.

And in that area—replete with disputes, stagnant societies, oil resources, and ambitious leaders—the focal point of future troubles and altercations can certainly be located. In this context there was no greater development in 1974 than the accelerated aggrandizement of Iran and its leader, the shah. The future politics of the area will be a function of Iranian policies and activities.

Cyprus. The eastern Mediterranean saw its share of difficulty too in 1974. In July regular Greek army officers on the island of Cyprus, inspired by *enosis* (or reunion of Cyprus with Greece), staged a coup against the government of Archbishop Makarios and installed for a brief period Nikos Sampson, a well-known terrorist, as president. Greece and Turkey immediately became involved. Cyprus has about 80% ethnic Greeks and 20% ethnic Turks. The Turks not only threatened war with Greece but quickly invaded Cyprus, only 80 miles off the Turkish coast, and occupied a major portion of the island.

The movements of the U. S. Sixth Fleet in the Cyprus crisis merely underscored the vital importance of the whole region to the United States. U. S. policy in the past has often been chaotic and counterproductive; the series of crises since mid-1973 forced much reorganization of past postures. Secretary Kissinger reestablished personal diplomacy, with considerable short-term success. But in the process of producing disengagement between Israel and its enemies, he found it necessary to articulate American unwillingness to continue the almost total support that Israel has received in the past. This was, although without publicity, a major policy change. American stakes in the oil fields of the Middle East are paramount and obvious. Kissinger has had to formulate a policy with respect to the oil producers flexible enough to apply to Arabs as Arabs, to Israelis with their problems, to NATO partners Greece and Turkey, to a client state such as Saudi Arabia, and the resurgent giant, Iran. It has not been easy; it cannot be totally successful.

American military hardware flows today to the gulf. Both Iran and Saudi Arabia are big purchasers of such equipment. The United States continues its precarious naval station at Bahrain island in the Gulf and was building a bigger installation at Diego Garcia in the Indian Ocean. With the opening of the Suez Canal, Soviet naval vessels will find it easier to make their way into the Indian Ocean and the gulf. The United States continues to be heavily involved in a rapidly changing Middle East whose entire future is quite uncertain. The stakes remain enormous.

THREE PRINCIPAL LEADERS IN THE MIDDLE EAST DISPUTE

CH. SIMONPIETRI—SYGMA

GEN. HAFEZ AL-ASSAD, president of the Syrian Arab Republic, has proved to be the most popular and effective leader Syria has had in the past 20 years. He was born in Latakia province in 1928. He entered a military career as a pilot and gained rapid promotions. Like many Syrian officers, he was active in politics and was identified with the less ideologically Marxist of the two wings of the ruling Baath Socialist party. By the mid-1960's, he was commander of the air force and minister of defense. In 1970 he led a coup against the Marxist-oriented government of Nureddin el-Atassi and became prime minister, and in March 1971 he was elected president. Assad has adhered to the traditional Syrian concern for Arab unity and has made a number of overtures to other Arab countries, particularly Egypt.

Syria, along with Egypt, attacked Israel in October 1973 in order to recover the Israeli-occupied portions of the Golan Heights that had been lost in 1967. The result on the Syrian front was tactically ambiguous for both sides, but Assad gained an immense strategic victory. Moreover, he continued to exert military pressure on the Israelis throughout the spring of 1974. In May 1974, Syria and Israel signed an agreement that called for Israeli withdrawal from all territories captured in 1973, plus the town of Quneitra, taken in 1967. President Assad considered this only an interim solution until all of the Golan is returned.

WIDE WORLD

ITZHAK RABIN, who took office as premier of Israel on June 3, 1974, is the first native-born Israeli, or *sabra,* to hold that post. He was born on March 1, 1922, of Russian immigrants. He took an early interest in farming but joined Haganah (the Jewish defense force) before World War II. After the war, in which he fought as part of the British army, his military career advanced rapidly. He commanded a brigade in the 1948 war and became chief of staff in 1963.

As military chief of Israeli forces during the 1967 war with the Arabs, Rabin received much of the credit for the brilliant conception and execution of that conflict. Just prior to the war he apparently suffered an attack of nervous exhaustion, and in 1974 his political opponents offered this as evidence that he was emotionally unfit for the premiership. Nevertheless, he became one of Israel's authentic military heroes. Retiring from the army, he was appointed ambassador to the United States in 1968. In that post until 1973, he developed close ties with the Nixon administration. Rabin was elected to the Israeli Knesset (parliament) in December 1973 and in March became minister of labor in Golda Meir's last government. When that government fell in April, he became the Labor party's nominee for premier and successfully formed a three-party coalition. In September he went to the United States and received from President Ford assurances of continued American aid to Israel.

WIDE WORLD

ANWAR EL-SADAT, president of Egypt, is no longer merely the successor of Nasser but a major leader in his own right. His popularity and authority in Egypt are great and genuine. He was born in the Nile delta on Dec. 25, 1918. He went into the army as a young man and became associated, along with Nasser and other young officers, with revolutionary groups. He was among the officers who mounted the Egyptian Revolution of 1952. In and out of favor with President Nasser over the years, Sadat was speaker of the National Assembly in 1961–68 and in late 1969 was appointed vice president. He succeeded to the presidency upon Nasser's death in 1970 and was soon elected in his own right.

In July 1972, Sadat expelled the Soviet military advisers and technicians who were in Egypt; at the same time he continued to threaten war against the Israelis. In October 1973 he attacked the Israeli positions across the Suez Canal, simultaneously enlisting the support of the Saudis and other oil-producing Arabs to apply an oil embargo against the United States and other nations. The result of the fighting was a strategic victory of enormous dimensions, although at war's end the Israelis had made tactical gains. After the war Sadat staked his reputation on a rapprochement with the United States. U. S. Secretary of State Kissinger facilitated an agreement in January 1974 by which the Israelis agreed to pull back into Sinai from the canal. President Nixon visited Egypt in June and was given a warm reception. In September, Sadat relinquished the premiership he had held since March 1973 but remained as president.

CARL LEIDEN

WIDE WORLD

Kissinger

Efforts of U.S. Diplomat Helped to Ease Tensions

By Elmer Plischke
Professor of Government and Politics, University of Maryland

U.S. Secretary of State Henry A. Kissinger's intensive negotiations with Israelis and Arabs in the Middle East in 1974 resulted in several widely hailed accomplishments. In January, Egypt and Israel agreed on a Kissinger-mediated troop-disengagement plan along the Suez Canal. A month later, the United States and Egypt resumed diplomatic relations, which had been severed in 1967. In May, his negotiations concluded with a Syrian-Israeli cease-fire and separation of forces agreement. These triumphs of personal diplomacy paved the way for President Nixon's successful visit to the Middle East in June. An immediate result of this visit was the resumption of U.S.-Syrian diplomatic relations. In the fall, Kissinger again traveled to the Middle East and held a series of talks with Arab and Israeli leaders.

Diplomatic Posts. President Nixon appointed Kissinger his assistant for national security affairs in 1969, and four years later Kissinger also was named secretary of state. In the first capacity he has been the President's principal foreign-policy adviser, manager of the National Security Council system, and special diplomatic emissary. In 1973 he also assumed administrative responsibility for the Department of State. After Gerald Ford succeeded Nixon, the new President affirmed his intention to retain Kissinger in his posts.

From his background of teaching (at Harvard), scholarship, and consultantships, Kissinger emerged as a serious-minded, experienced, and dedicated thinker, eager to become a doer, or at least an influencer, in matters of policy and strategy. His competence in rational analysis, his historical perspective, and his ability to penetrate to fundamentals equipped him for appointment to the President's inner foreign-relations team and as his personal envoy.

The Foundation: *Realpolitik*. Much of Kissinger's earlier writing was reflective and negatively critical of American policy, but this changed when he prepared position papers for Republican presidential aspirant Nelson Rockefeller during the 1968 campaign. He formulated a positive, initiatory plan for dealing with the Vietnamese issue, which paved the way for close association with President Nixon and his negotiations to end American participation in the Vietnam War.

During the years prior to presidential appointment, Kissinger framed his ideas, at times by introspection and in part by means of dialogues with himself and with others. He evolved an integrated network of primary and subsidiary principles for contemporary U.S. foreign relations. As a devotee of *Realpolitik* (political realism), he rejected absolutes and looked rather for possibilities and negotiability. Among his basic precepts are that the main goals of the United States should be the preservation of national security and international peace—in accordance with the national interest.

To achieve these goals in a competitive, often adversary, international environment, Kissinger held that the United States must maintain its national capabilities and wield its national power judiciously. Policy must recognize existing realities and be sufficiently flexible to accommodate the goals and interests of other states, and also changes in the international arena. Policies should be carefully planned, should be initiatory as well as reactive, and should be institutionalized, by which he means the devising of a set of principles that possess "a sufficient support among those who have to carry it out, so that continuity within the limits of the changes of the political process is assured."

Holding "absolute national security" as illusory and political domination of equals as untenable, Kissinger regards peace and international stability as best maintainable by a balance of power, which he perceives more as a livable political equilibrium than a military (or nuclear) imbalance in favor of the United States. Thus, he deems it necessary "to construct an international system based on a sense of justice so that its participants would have a stake in maintaining it; with a sufficient balance of power so that no nation or group of nations would be dependent entirely on the goodwill of its neighbors, and based on a sense of participation so that all nations could share in the positive aspirations."

His writings, pronouncements, and actions also provide more precise guidelines, including

J. P. LAFFONT—SYGMA

Henry Kissinger and Nancy Maginnes, an aide to former New York Governor Nelson Rockefeller, were married on March 30.

these points: foreign policy must be planned as a part of overall national strategy; commitments must not exceed capabilities, and overextended assurances must be reduced; diplomacy is the most reliable process for dealing with other nations, including enemies; diplomats must be credible to one another; perfect flexibility in diplomacy is visionary; and confrontation must be avoided, or at least mitigated. He also contends that success in negotiations requires the narrowing of differences between the parties; the method chosen for negotiation should be that which is most likely to bring a settlement; and procedure, as well as substantive policy, is a keystone of the diplomatic process.

Moreover, Kissinger evidences keen awareness of the intellectual dimensions of foreign-relations decision making. He appears to prefer the options analysis system, in which the decision maker personally manages the consideration, examines all reasonable objectives, policies, and procedures, and compares and assesses their advantages, feasibility, and likely consequences in arriving at decisions.

Views on the Middle East. With respect to the Middle East crisis, Kissinger espoused additional, more specific concepts respecting U.S. policy and his mediatory role. It was the American commitment, he maintained, to achieve a peace "that recognizes the security of all countries in the Middle East—as well as the legitimate aspirations of all the peoples in the area." To accomplish this, basic American policy stipulated that the Middle East conflict could not be permitted to escalate into global warfare, that the United States needed to negotiate seriously with all the parties rather than support one of the sides, and that resolution could not be determined primarily by the immediate military situation.

Kissinger regarded the intricate issues involved in the Middle East confrontation as intellectually separable and reduceable to negotiability, although some were more difficult to resolve than others. A viable settlement had to be worked out largely by the parties directly involved, but the important interests of the United States and the Soviet Union had to be recognized. Nevertheless, the great powers could not impose a workable settlement on the parties. Consequently, negotiations had to be conducted by the latter, and success was most likely if they were phased—first a cease-fire to provide disengagement, then a more basic military agreement, and eventually a peace arrangement to resolve underlying political, economic, and territorial issues.

The role of the United States, Kissinger made clear, was not to propose a detailed settlement that might divert both sides to contesting it, but rather to have them formulate their positions and then work to close the gap between them and inject U.S. views to resolve their differences. He also indicated that, at the request of the parties, he was prepared to assist them by his personal diplomacy, largely to convey propositions between the parties, to help engender the trust that is essential for constructive negotiation, and, as the parties establish confidence in each other, to minimize his mediatory role. He served as the principal peacemaker, having gone to the Mideast eight times by October, traveling some 130,000 miles (209,000 km), and spending approximately 90 days in "shuttle diplomacy."

Personal Background. Born in Fürth, Germany, on May 27, 1923, Henry Alfred Kissinger emigrated with his parents to New York City in 1938. He was educated at Harvard University (A.B., M.A., and Ph.D. degrees), where he later served on the faculty (1954–71), both in the department of government and at Harvard's Center for International Affairs. Simultaneously he held several directorships, including that for the Special Studies Project of the Rockefeller Brothers Fund (1956–58). Between 1951 and the time of his appointment by President Nixon, he also held consultantships in various agencies.

Among the most widely read of his half dozen books are *Nuclear Weapons and Foreign Policy* (1957), *The Necessity for Choice* (1961), and *The Troubled Partnership* (1965). He also published more than 40 articles.

Kissinger has two children from his first marriage, which ended in divorce in 1964. He married Nancy Maginnes in March 1974.

F. SAUTEREAU, RAPHO GUILLUMETTE

Palestinian refugees discuss their plight at a camp in Jordan. Some 1.5 million Palestinian refugees live in UN-supervised camps in Jordan, Lebanon, and Syria.

THE PALESTINIANS

New Attention Focuses on the PLO

BY JOHN K. COOLEY, *Middle East Correspondent, "The Christian Science Monitor"*

The future of about 3 million Palestinian Arabs, over one third of whom live under Israeli rule on territory seized by Israel in 1967 or inside Israel's pre-1948 boundaries, is the central and probably the toughest problem in the Middle East conflict. Any Palestinian role in Mideast peace talks in Geneva, therefore, presents the Arab states, Israel, and the big powers with a formidable task in their search for a just settlement.

The Refugee Arabs. Palestinian Arabs, including those individuals who fled or were driven from their homes in the formerly British-mandated territory of Palestine when the new state of Israel defeated its Arab neighbors in 1948, and the children and grandchildren of these refugees, are intellectually and culturally an elite in the Arab world. More than 70,000 Palestinian university graduates, the highest per capita figure of any Arab population, provide a heavy input of trained personnel to top professional and executive posts in those host countries permitting them to do so. But over 1.5 million refugees are cared for on bare subsistence levels in camps in Lebanon, Syria, and Jordan by the United Nations Relief and Works Agency (UNRWA) for Palestine refugees.

The leftist political alignments of this embittered body of people have led conservative Arab governments to regard them as a disruptive social and political force. Simultaneously, guerrilla warfare and terrorism by the armed Palestinian resistance movement, or *fedayeen* (meaning "self-sacrificers"), have brought violent Israeli reprisal raids on their bases and camps in neighboring Arab states.

Attempts at Organization. For the Palestine Liberation Organization (PLO), the central guerrilla body, the main problem was how to cope with the trend toward an Arab political settlement with Israel, launched by the Egypt-Israel and Syria-Israel troop disengagement accords signed in 1974. These were negotiated in January and May, respectively, largely through the efforts of U. S. Secretary of State Henry A. Kissinger.

The PLO's relatively moderate chairman, Yasir Arafat, favored PLO participation in the peace talks being held periodically in Geneva.

WIDE WORLD

Yasir Arafat (*center*) was reelected chairman of the Palestine Liberation Organization (PLO) in June 1974.

YASIR ARAFAT

On Nov. 13, 1974, Yasir Arafat, chairman of the Palestine Liberation Organization (PLO), opened the UN General Assembly debate on the question of Palestine by delivering an address urging the creation of a "democratic" Palestinian state. Earlier the Arab heads of state had recognized the PLO as the "sole legitimate representative of the Palestinian people." Both events were triumphs for Arafat.

Born in Jerusalem in 1929, Arafat and his family fled to Gaza during the Palestine war of 1948. Educated at Cairo University, Arafat worked briefly with an engineering firm in Kuwait. In 1955, he began his commando training with the Egyptian militia. He was one of the first Palestinians to advocate guerrilla attacks against Israel.

A Muslim, Arafat neither drinks nor smokes. He usually wears dark glasses, a desert jacket, and a checkered Arab headdress, the kaffiyeh.

But he was forced to deal with die-hard dissidents who opposed any negotiations or political settlement with the Jewish state. With the support of Iraq, Libya, and some other radical Arab states, these dissidents advocated continuing terrorism against Israel and its Western supporters in order to sabotage the efforts of Kissinger, President Anwar el-Sadat of Egypt, Jordan's King Hussein, and Israeli Prime Minister Itzhak Rabin to reach any permanent peace which did not satisfy Palestinian claims.

The dissidents call for eventual replacement of the state structure of Israel by a secular Jewish-Christian-Muslim state no longer dominated by the doctrine of Zionism. As a first step, the Palestine National Council, a sort of parliament claiming to represent all Palestinians, agreed at a meeting in Cairo on June 1–9, 1974, to organize a Palestinian "national authority" on any of the Palestinian territories—the West Bank of the Jordan River, the Gaza Strip, and the small al-Himma enclave south of Syria's Golan Heights—which might be freed from Israeli control.

At the same time the council agreed not to consider sending a PLO delegation to any peace conference unless UN Security Council Resolution 242 of November 1967, treating the Palestinians only as "refugees," was recast to mention "Palestinian national rights."

Yasir Arafat's own organization, al-Fatah, and two others, the Syrian-backed al-Saiqa (Thunderbolt) led by Zuheir Mohsen, and the leftist Popular Democratic Front for the Liberation of Palestine (PDFLP) of Nayef Hawatmeh, had helped to formulate this platform. They supported it, though with reservations. Opposed were the Popular Front for the Liberation of Palestine (PFLP), led by its secretary general, George Habbash, and the Popular Front—General Command, led by former Syrian Army captain Ahmed Jabril. Both of the latter groups carried out a number of terrorist acts, along with the clandestine Black September group and others not recognized by the PLO.

The Resistance Movement. During 1973 the resistance movement claimed responsibility for 1,251 "military operations" inside Israel or Israeli-occupied territories. According to the PLO, the average number of such operations rose to 15 per day after the October 1973 Arab-Israeli war. Other terrorist operations, not claimed by the PLO, were carried out in areas remote from the Middle East.

On Jan. 31, 1974, two PFLP and two Japanese Red Army (Sekigun) guerrillas together seized a ferry boat and its crew during an unsuccessful attack on the Royal Dutch Shell oil refineries in Singapore. In a related move on February 6, five PFLP and Japanese Red Army terrorists occupied the Japanese embassy in Kuwait and held the entire staff hostage, including the Japanese ambassador. They demanded that Japan fly the four guerrillas in Singapore to Kuwait. The Japanese government complied with the request, and the two guerrilla groups were flown to Aden on February 8.

Meanwhile, on February 2, three Pakistani guerrillas seized the Greek merchant ship *Vori* at Karachi, Pakistan, and demanded the release of two Palestine guerrillas of the Black September organization who had been sentenced to death in Athens for an attack on the Athens airport terminal in August 1973. The Greek government acceded to their demands and subsequently commuted their death sentences, then granted them full pardon and deported them to Libya on May 5. The three Pakistani terrorists were flown to Tripoli, Libya, on February 6.

On April 11, 18 Israelis and three attacking guerrillas were killed in a raid on Kiryat Shemona, Israel, near the Lebanese border, by the Popular Front-General Command group which sought release of Palestinian prisoners in

Israel. On May 15, the PDFLP, in its first such operation, seized about 100 Israeli schoolchildren in the northern Galilee settlement of Maalot. In the Israeli Army's ensuing assault, 22 Israelis (21 of them children) and the three Arab guerrillas were killed, and over 70 Israelis, most of them children, were wounded.

Israel blamed Lebanon for these and other attacks, despite insistence by the guerrillas and the Lebanese government that the attackers came not from Lebanon but from resistance cells inside Israel. Israeli air, land, and sea units struck into Lebanon at intervals throughout the year. Especially severe were Israeli air raids in mid-May, which reputedly killed 53 persons, wounded over 150.

Strengthening of the PLO. After meetings at Alexandria, Egypt, on April 4–6, 1974, King Hussein and President Sadat endorsed an "independent" Palestinian delegation (without mentioning the PLO) to attend future peace talks at Geneva. King Hussein agreed to recognize the PLO only as representing Palestinians outside Jordan. On September 21, Egypt, Syria, and the PLO jointly announced agreement that the PLO was the sole legitimate representative of all Palestinians. King Hussein threatened to take no more active part in negotiations for Israeli withdrawal from the West Bank.

Jordan's opposition to the PLO was a major issue at the summit conference of Arab heads of state at Rabat, Morocco, on October 26–29. There King Hussein was reluctantly persuaded to join the other Arab leaders in unanimously calling for the creation of an independent Palestinian state on such territory as might be "liberated" from Israel (notably the West Bank, Gaza Strip, and El Hamma area of the Golan Heights), under the leadership of the PLO as the "sole legitimate representative of the Palestinian people." The conference further agreed on a massive four-year aid program for Jordan, Egypt, Syria, and the PLO, to be financed by the major oil-producing countries.

Meanwhile, the UN General Assembly in mid-October had voted to invite the PLO to present its case before that body. Accordingly, Yasir Arafat, in a dramatic visit to New York amid the greatest security measures ever taken in that city, opened the Palestine debate in an address to the General Assembly on November 13. His dream, he said, was one of a "democratic state where Christian, Jew, and Muslim live in justice, equality, and fraternity." He had come to the UN "bearing an olive branch and freedom fighter's gun," he said, and urged the UN not to "let the olive branch fall" from his hands. On November 22 the General Assembly approved two resolutions declaring the right of the Palestinian people to independence and sovereignty, and granting the PLO observer status at the United Nations. (See also UNITED NATIONS.)

THE MIDDLE EAST PROBLEM—A CHRONOLOGY

Aug. 29, 1897—Theodor Herzl forms international Zionist Organization in Basel, Switzerland.
Nov. 2, 1917—Britain, in Balfour Declaration, pledges support for a Jewish "national home" in Palestine.
October 1918—Ottoman Empire collapses.
April 24, 1920—Britain is assigned mandate over Palestine, with directive to create a Jewish state.
1929–1930—First major wave of violence by Palestinian Arabs against Jewish immigrants occurs as Jewish population of Palestine approaches 20% of total.
May 1939—Britain imposes regulations restricting Jewish rights in Palestine; immigration is reduced.
March 22, 1945—Arab League is founded to promote cooperation between Arab nations of Middle East.
Nov. 29, 1947—UN General Assembly votes to partition Palestine into Arab, Jewish, and international zones.
May 14, 1948—As British mandate terminates, Palestinian Jews proclaim Israel a sovereign nation; hostilities between Jews and Arabs escalate.
Jan. 7, 1949—First Israeli-Arab war ended by armistice agreement under UN auspices.
July 26, 1956—Egypt nationalizes Suez Canal.
Oct. 29, 1956—Israel invades Sinai Peninsula.
Nov. 1, 1956—French and British troops attack Egypt.
Nov. 6, 1956—Second Israeli-Arab war terminated by a cease-fire, supervised by UN Emergency Force.
Jan. 13–17, 1964—Arab League heads of state resolve to establish a unified military command.
May 18, 1967—UN Emergency Force is withdrawn.
May 22, 1967—Egyptian President Nasser institutes blockade of Gulf of Aqaba against Israeli shipping.
June 5, 1967—Israel again invades Gaza and Sinai areas.
June 10, 1967—UN cease-fire brings Third Israeli-Arab (or "Six-day") war to an end.
Nov. 22, 1967—Swedish diplomat Gunnar Jarring chosen to serve as UN mediator for the Middle East.
June 24–26, 1970—Israeli and Syrian troops on Golan Heights engage in heaviest battle since 1967 war, as clashes in Suez Canal area also increase.
July 31, 1970—U. S.-proposed plan for Israeli-Arab cease-fire and peace negotiations accepted by Israel after approval by Soviet Union and the UAR.
Aug. 7, 1970—Ninety-day cease-fire goes into effect; peace negotiations begin at United Nations.
Sept. 27, 1970—A cease-fire is arranged in Cairo halting a 10-day civil war in Jordan.
March 7, 1971—Arab-Israeli cease-fire, which was extended on Nov. 5, 1970, expires.
June 13, 1972—Israeli and Egyptian planes engage in first air battle since August 1970 cease-fire.
July 18, 1972—Egypt orders the withdrawal of Soviet "military advisers and experts."
Oct. 6, 1973—War breaks out in the Middle East as Israeli forces fight Syrian and Egyptian troops.
Oct. 24, 1973—A cease-fire goes into effect.
Oct. 27, 1973—The UN Security Council approves the establishment of a Middle East peace-keeping force.
Nov. 11, 1973—Egypt and Israel sign a cease-fire pact.
Dec. 21, 1973—Arab-Israeli peace conference opens in Geneva.
Jan. 18, 1974—Israel and Egypt sign an accord on disengaging military forces.
Feb. 28, 1974—The United States and Egypt restore diplomatic relations, suspended since June 1967.
May 31, 1974—Israel and Syria sign a troop disengagement agreement.
June 16, 1974—The United States and Syria agree to reestablish diplomatic relations.
Oct. 28, 1974—Meeting in Rabat, Morocco, Arab heads of state call for the creation of an independent Palestinian state and recognize the Palestine Liberation Organization (PLO) as the "sole legitimate representative of the Palestinian people."
Nov. 13, 1974—UN debate on the "question of Palestine" opens with an address by PLO chairman Arafat.

SIX FLAGS OVER MID-AMERICA

At Six Flags Over Mid-America in Eureka, Mo., two steam locomotives, the Eureka and the Lil' Rock, provide tours of the 200-acre theme park.

THEME Amusement Parks

BY ROBERT SCOTT MILNE

Coauthor, "The Great Escape"; "Around the World with the Experts"

In the early 1950's, Walt Disney started a revolution in the amusement park industry. For it was during these years that Disney conceived of the idea of a theme park—that is, an amusement park whose total character and mood are derived from a definite theme. In July 1955, Disneyland, the world's first modern theme park, opened in Anaheim, Calif. Since that time more than 30 theme parks have sprung up across the United States, and others are being built at a rapid pace. The parks now in existence produce revenue estimated at over $1 billion annually.

The Disney Approach. Disney wanted a theme park that would include the introduction of many attractions that were not found in the conventional amusement park. He believed that a theme or a group of themes with an artistic or architectural connection would be of prime importance for this new type of park, and that

At Walt Disney World in Lake Buena Vista, Fla., visitors cruise on the European Swan Boat past the Cinderella Castle.

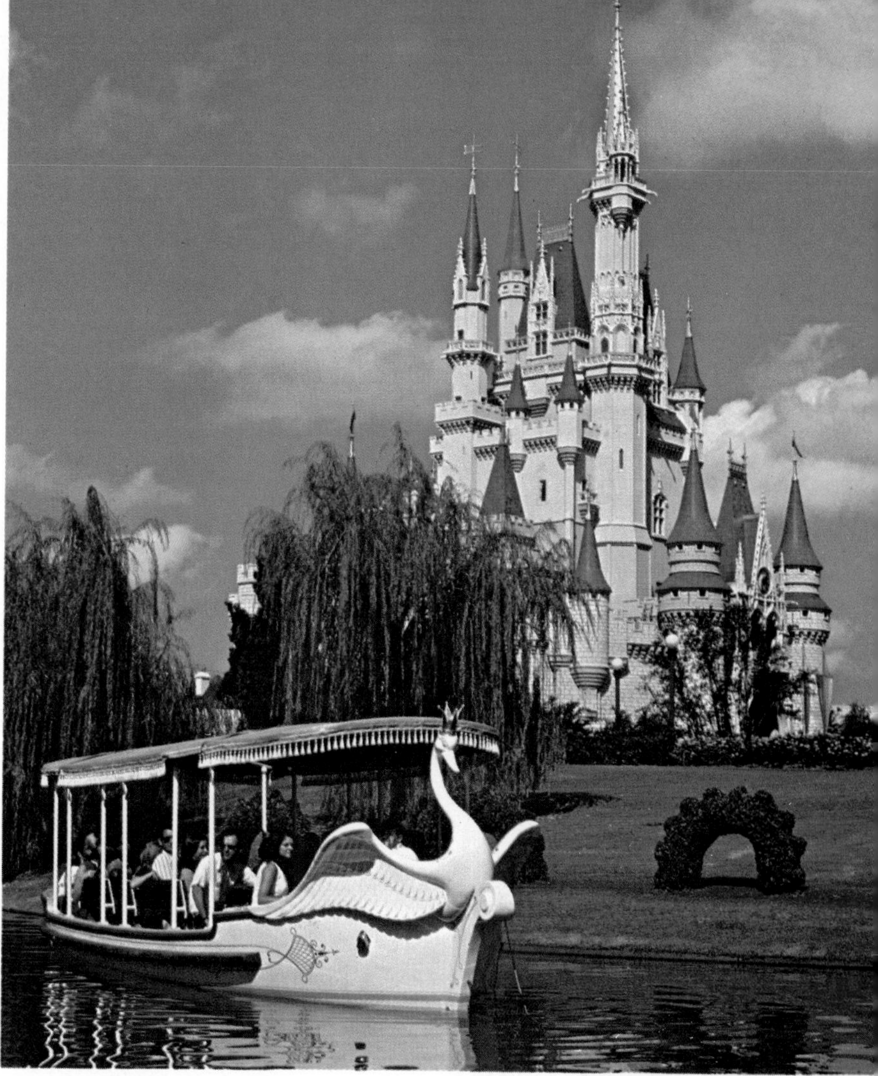

© WALT DISNEY PRODUCTIONS

all attractions in these new parks would be designed to enhance some aspect of the total theme.

In addition, Disney established a set of basic rules to be followed. The rules include: (1) emphasize extreme cleanliness; (2) offer something for all ages; (3) employ as many personable and friendly students as possible; (4) insist that the park's personnel wear clean and neat uniforms; and (5) eliminate the cheap souvenir shop. These rules have been observed by all successful theme-park operators and administrators since.

Located about 30 miles southeast of Los Angeles, Disneyland consists of a number of theme areas—Fantasyland, Tomorrowland, Main Street USA, Adventureland, Frontierland, New Orleans Square, Bear Country, and America Sings. All make use of fantasy. Disney's large organization of theatrical experts developed all kinds of schemes so that the favorite stories of old came to life. This included construction of realistic jungle rivers, castles, and mountains. Fantastic realism is added in the form of automated alligators and tigers who "attack" the guests and are then subdued by brave automated guides. Actors dressed as such characters as Mickey Mouse, Donald Duck, and Snow White and the Seven Dwarfs mingle with the visitors. Since its opening in 1955 the number of attractions at Disneyland has more than doubled. A second Disneyland, Walt Disney World, opened in Lake Buena Vista, Fla., southwest of Orlando, in October 1971.

SEA WORLD OF OHIO

"Shamu," a two-ton performing killer whale, does a balancing act at the aquatic theater at Sea World of Ohio, in Aurora.

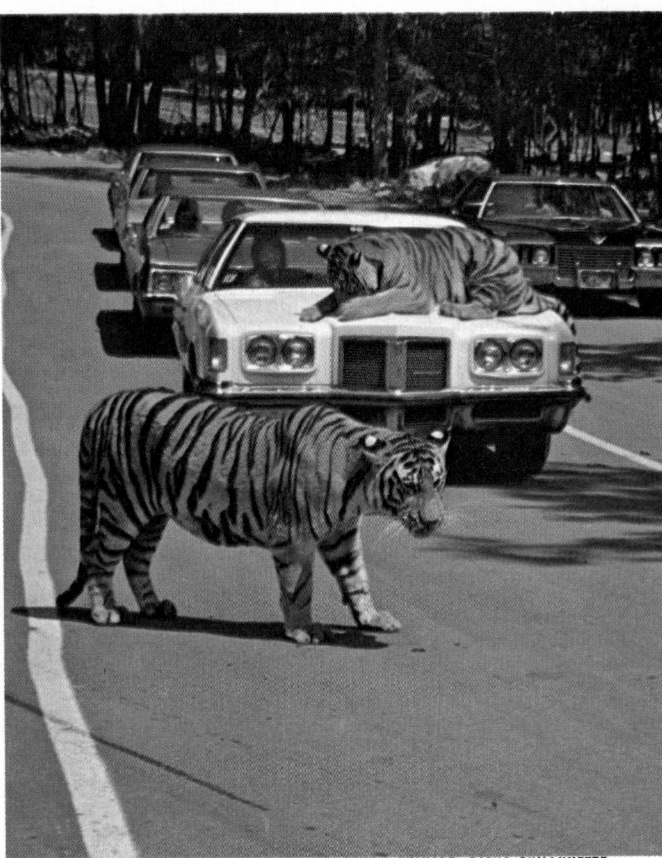

DENNIS YEANDLE, RAPHO GUILLUMETTE

Tigers roam freely and occasionally jump on top of visiting autos at Jungle Habitat, a drive-through zoo in West Milford, N. J.

One of the eleven tigers that perform at Japanese Village, Buena Park, Calif., hurtles through a ring of fire. Animal acts are a leading feature of U. S. theme parks.

JAPANESE VILLAGE, BUENA PARK, CALIF.

Building a Theme Park. Since Disney's death, Randall Duell, an architect and former motion-picture art director, has become the number one force in theme-park architecture. Duell, who has designed most of the nation's theme parks, has a set of basic guidelines for theme-park design. First, Duell investigates the area in which the new park is to be built, and secondly he studies the area's population and the modes of entertainment presently offered in the area. As a result of his findings, Duell establishes a specific theme for the new park.

For example, after being asked to design a theme park to be located in Arlington, Texas, between Dallas and Fort Worth, Duell consulted a state historian who advised him that six flags had flown over the state of Texas. Since Duell's studies showed that Texans would be the largest group attracted to the new park, and that Texans take great pride in their state and its history, the new amusement center was named "Six Flags Over Texas" and was divided into six sections. Each section represents one of the six governments that has ruled Texas—Spain, France, Mexico, the Republic of Texas, the Confederacy, and the United States. Since its opening, the park has been a success.

Animal Parks. With the opening of Busch Gardens in Tampa, Fla., in 1959, the concept of the theme park was changed to include live birds and animals. Originally Busch Gardens was conceived as a lush, tropical garden and bird sanctuary adjacent to an Anheuser-Busch brewery, where people who had visited the brewery could enjoy a free sample of the product in pleasant surroundings. The gardens proved so popular that the original 15 acres were increased to 285 acres.

At first the emphasis was on birds, but then many animals, native to Africa, were brought in and an admission fee was instituted. A monorail was erected so visitors could see the animals in natural settings without disturbing them. The park's theme became "Experience Africa." The park also introduced animal and

(*Below*) Visitors ride in gas-powered antique cars across covered bridges at Six Flags Over Georgia, an Atlanta park with a historic theme. (*Right*) Jazz and blues concerts delight the guests at Nashville's Opryland, U. S. A.

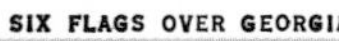
SIX FLAGS OVER GEORGIA

OPRYLAND, U.S.A.

GREAT ADVENTURE/PHOTO BY ALLAN WEITZ

Visitors to Great Adventure, a new theme park in Jackson, N. J., see some of the most romantic buildings of Europe in the Garden of Marvels, a miniature village built to exact scale. The "Big Balloon" (in background) holds a licensed pilot and four passengers.

bird shows, a petting zoo where visitors actually come in direct contact with some of the animals, the Trans-Veldt Railway, live musical shows, and a couple of amusement rides. A second Busch Gardens was opened in Van Nuys, Calif., near Los Angeles, in 1966, and has enjoyed similar success and expansion. A third Busch Gardens, scheduled to open near Williamsburg, Va., in 1975, will emphasize amusement rides, live entertainment, shops, and restaurants.

Ever since the late 1800's, zoos in the United States have been a municipal responsibility, supported primarily with city finances. Then in the late 1960's, Harry Shuster introduced the completely new idea of a jungle park—a privately funded zoo, charging admission, and with the animals roaming semifree in a setting resembling their natural one. Shuster had been impressed by the large number of people who traveled to Africa primarily to visit the game parks and believed that a drive-through zoo would appeal to the American public.

His first venture was Lion Country Safari, which opened in the Everglades near West Palm Beach, Fla., in 1967. It was highly successful, both commercially and zoologically. In this park the animals not only survived but multiplied.

Lion Country Safaris multiplied as well. The second one was introduced in 1970 on 485 acres of the Irvine Ranch, near Disneyland. The park drew 1.2 million visitors its first year. In 1972 two more such zoos opened—one in the Dallas–Fort Worth area and another near Atlanta, Ga. A fourth one opened as a major part of Kings Dominion, near Richmond, Va., in 1974, and a fifth one was planned near Cincinnati, Ohio, to open in 1975. Other similar drive-through zoos have come into existence elsewhere across the United States—including Jungle Habitat in West Milford, N. J.; World Wildlife Safari in Winston, Oreg., and Great Adventure in Jackson, N. J.

From the beginning, directors of the traditional zoo have criticized the new safari zoo. These critics argue that the jungle zoos lack properly trained personnel to care for the many animals, and that the physical and emotional well-being of the animals are sacrificed in favor of financial profit. In defense of the jungle zoo others have pointed out that these parks have hired well-trained animal keepers, including former employees of municipal zoos, and that it is generally recognized that the animals at these parks are treated as well as the animals in the traditional zoo. As evidence of the well-being of the animals, they cite statistics showing that the reproduction rate of the animals at these new commercial parks has been generally good.

Safety in the drive-through zoos is a problem. Despite numerous warnings, visitors insist on leaving their automobiles to take photographs or pet the animals. For this reason, park rangers patrol the parks constantly. Nevertheless several tragic accidents have occurred because of public carelessness.

Amusement Rides. Although in a theme park the amusement ride is simply an extension of the park's total environment, it continues to enjoy immense popularity. The log flume has become a particular favorite at the theme park. On the log flume, passengers in a boat simulating a hollow log float in fast-moving water around a contorted track, and at the end descend so sharply that a curtain of water spray is given off to the delight of all. Since participation is a vital part of the theme park, it is important that each visitor gets a little wet on the flume ride.

In the new theme parks the roller coaster, the most exciting ride in the traditional amusement area, is often disguised under new names—"The Runaway Mine Train," "Sugar Mountain," and the "Rover." "The Great American Scream Ma-

A Roman chariot race thrills the audience in the 6,000-seat arena at Great Adventure.

GREAT ADVENTURE/PHOTO ALLAN WEITZ

SOME MODERN THEME PARKS

ADVENTURELAND, Des Moines, Iowa. Opened 1974. Adventure theme; 10 rides, 10 walk-throughs.

ASTROWORLD USA, Houston, Texas. Opened 1968. Ten themes; 37 rides; 6 stages; musical shows.

BUSCH GARDENS. Van Nuys, Calif. Opened 1966. A total of 79 species of birds; walk-in aviary; performing animals; log-flume ride; monorail tour of brewery.

BUSCH GARDENS, Tampa, Fla. Opened 1959. 285 acres; 3,000 birds and animals of 535 species viewed from Trans-Veldt Railway; monorail, skyride; petting zoo; free-flight cage; animal acts; brewery tour.

BUSCH GARDENS, Williamsburg, Va. Opening scheduled for spring 1975. 300 acres; themed to English, French, and German villages of 1600's; monorail, boat cruise, other rides; performing animals and birds; brewery tour.

CAROWINDS, between North and South Carolina, 10 miles south of Charlotte, N. C. Opened 1973. Carolinas historical themes; 330-foot tower, 30 rides, swimming.

DISNEYLAND, Anaheim, Calif. Opened 1955. Pioneer theme park; themes of adventure, fantasy, history in 54 major attractions.

GREAT ADVENTURE, Jackson, N. J., 65 miles southwest of New York City. Opened 1974. A 1,500 acre, 7-mile drive-through park with 2,000 animals of 48 species.

JAPANESE VILLAGE, Buena Park, Calif., 20 miles southeast of Los Angeles. Opened 1967. Japanese theme; karate, tea ceremony, pearl diving; animal and sea mammal shows; deer park; Japanese musical shows.

JUNGLE HABITAT, West Milford, N. J., 35 miles west of New York City. Opened 1972. 1,000 acres; drive-through zoo with 1,500 animals of 72 species; animal nursery; petting zoo; porpoise show; rides on camels, elephants, and ponies; African dancers.

KINGS ISLAND, Kings Mills, Ohio, 20 miles north of Cincinnati. Opened 1972. Six varied themes; 45 rides; theatrical and musical shows. Adjacent LION COUNTRY SAFARI opened 1974. Animals on 100 acres viewed on 2-mile monorail ride. Hotel and camping.

LION COUNTRY SAFARI, Laguna Hills, Calif, 40 miles south of central Los Angeles. Opened 1970. A 485-acre drive-through African game park; rides; live shows.

LION COUNTRY SAFARI, in the Everglades, 17 miles west of West Palm Beach, Fla. Opened 1967. A 640-acre drive-through African animal preserve.

LION COUNTRY SAFARI, Henry county, Ga., 20 miles south of Atlanta. Opened 1972. Drive-through animal park.

LION COUNTRY SAFARI, Dallas–Fort Worth area, Texas. Opened 1972. Drive-through African animal preserve.

LION COUNTRY SAFARI, Doswell, Va., 20 miles from Richmond. Opened 1974. A 120-acre drive-through animal park; petting zoo; animal nursery; aviary; live shows. This is first unit of King's Dominion, a major theme park scheduled to be completed in 1975.

MAGIC MOUNTAIN, Valencia, Calif., 34 miles northwest of central Los Angeles. Opened 1971. Themed to wizard and trolls; 31 rides; petting farm; famous entertainers.

OPRYLAND USA, Nashville, Tenn. Opened 1974. Developed from famed Grand Ole Opry; theme is American music; 7 musical shows; 15 rides; museum.

RINGLING BROS.–BARNUM & BAILEY CIRCUS WORLD, Barnum City, Fla., near Orlando. Opening planned for 1975. Circus theme.

SEA WORLD OF OHIO, Aurora, Ohio, 20 miles southwest of Cleveland. Opened 1970. Aquatic theater; Japanese pearl divers; zoo.

SEA WORLD OF SAN DIEGO, San Diego, Calif. Opened 1964. Aquatic theme; 5 marine shows; underwater theater; Japanese pearl divers; skyride and hydrofoil boatride.

SIX FLAGS OVER GEORGIA, Atlanta, Ga. Opened 1967. Historical and patriotic themes; 29 rides.

SIX FLAGS OVER MID-AMERICA, Eureka, Mo., 25 miles from St. Louis. Opened 1971. Historical themes; 18 rides, fun house, arcade, and shooting gallery; 4 live shows; picnicking; zoo; name bands.

SIX FLAGS OVER TEXAS, Arlington, Texas, between Fort Worth and Dallas. Opened 1957. Historical themes; 30 rides and 5-story slide; porpoise show; musical revue.

WALT DISNEY WORLD, Lake Buena Vista, Fla., 20 miles southwest of Orlando. Opened 1971. Themes of fantasy, adventure, and history; 36 rides, name bands, fireworks.

WORLDS OF FUN, Kansas City, Mo. Opened 1973. Theme is international areas; 15 rides; artisans; theater and musical shows; dolphin show; bands.

chine" at Six Flags over Georgia in Atlanta is considered one of the world's most exciting roller coasters. The first steep drop is 105 feet (32 meters), turns are sharp, and whipping over the top is breathtaking. Each rider is given a red button as he or she steps off. It says "Red Badge of Courage" and is worn proudly.

Of course, the theme parks offer other amusement rides. What is billed as the world's largest ferris wheel (although the claim is disputed) was introduced at Great Adventure in Jackson, N. J., in 1974, and the famous five-abreast carousel that operated at Chicago's Riverview Park from 1904 to 1967 is now a part of Six Flags Over Georgia. Skyrides with four-passenger gondolas not only give passengers an overall view of the entire theme park but also transport them from one area to another.

Admission Costs. In most of these theme parks there is a single entrance fee at the gate, ranging from about $3.50 to $8.00, which permits the customer to stay in the park and enter the exhibits or enjoy rides as long as he or she desires. Exceptions are the two Disney parks, which charge an admission plus a fee for each ride. Since it has been estimated that the typical customers at these parks consist of a family of four, a visit to a theme park can easily cost $30.00.

In spite of the high cost, the future of the theme park seems quite bright. With the amount of leisure time increasing, the public seems eager to enjoy the freshness, cleanliness, and friendliness of this new type of amusement.

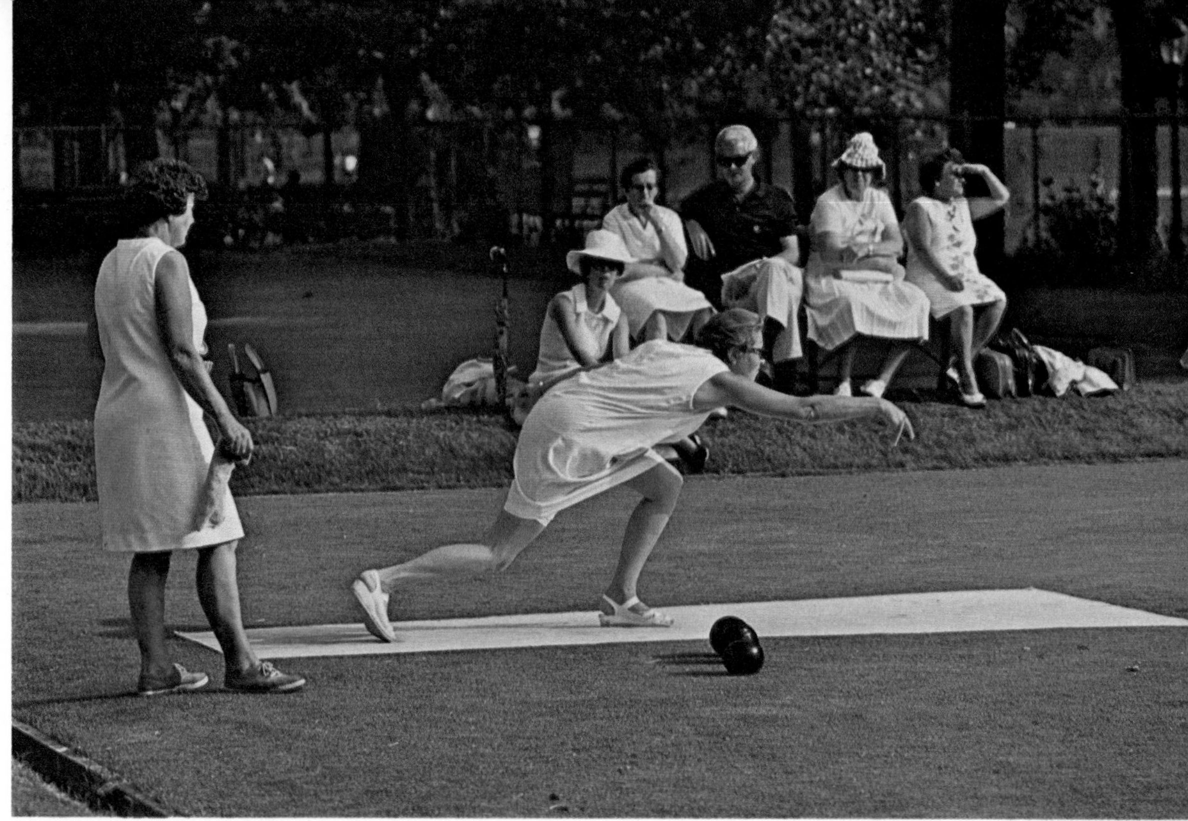

ROGERS-MONKMEYER

Some older people stay youthful and vigorous by engaging in regular exercise, including lawn bowling.

The search for a YOUTHFUL old age

BY ERDMAN PALMORE

Professor of Medical Sociology, Duke University

The search for eternal youth dates from antiquity, but in recent years this search has been accelerated, becoming a worldwide social movement. Americans spend millions of dollars on vitamin E, royal jelly, plastic surgery, and best sellers on how to stay young. In Switzerland, Dr. Walter Michel directs a flourishing cell-therapy clinic in which (for $2,000) seekers of youth are injected with cells scraped from the still-warm flesh of lamb fetuses. According to Dr. Michel's estimate, there are at least 5,000 practitioners of cell therapy in Europe. In Rumania, Dr. Ana Aslan has developed a drug called Gerovital that she claims is effective in the treatment of such symptoms of aging as arthritis, arteriosclerosis, depression, senility, and even white hair.

Most gerontologists (scientists studying the aging processes) dismiss such treatments as fads unsupported by controlled scientific experiments. But the swelling movement to preserve youth and even achieve biological immortality has also spurred the development of a worldwide army of gerontologists dedicated to the study and scientific treatment of old age. A generation ago there were hardly any gerontologists, as such. Now there are over 2,500 members of the Gerontological Society in the United States alone. There is also an International Association for Gerontology whose meetings involve well over 1,000 participants.

This army of professionals is backed up by millions of older persons organized into such groups as the American Association of Retired Persons, the National Retired Teachers Association, the National Council of Senior Citizens, the National Council of the Aging—and even a group called the "Grey Panthers." In addition to pressing for more research on how to "add years to life, and life to years," these persons have become self-conscious members of a minority pressure group, using rallies and other tactics similar to those of racial and other minority groups to achieve their goals. The ideology behind this movement is expressed by such slogans as "It's no sin to be seventy," "We have come of age," "Grey is beautiful," and "You're as young as you feel."

Reasons for the Movement. Several factors have contributed to the rise of this movement. The most basic factor is the increase in longevity and the consequent rise in numbers of older persons. Prior to 1900, there was little or no "old age problem" because few people lived to be over 65 years old. At the turn of the century, the average American baby had a life expectancy of about 50 years. Now that baby has a life expectancy of over 70 years, and many experts predict that this will rise to 90 years or over in the next generation. At the turn of the century, there were only 3 million persons over 65 in the United States. Now there are over 22 million over age 65. This number has been increasing at three times the rate of general population growth.

A second factor is the series of scientific discoveries that promise to extend life and that point the way to a more "youthful" old age in the present. Medical progress has shown that many diseases once thought to be irreversible results of aging (such as arteriosclerosis, senility, and cancer) are largely due to environmental factors (among which are smoking and diet) and often can be cured. The possibilities of slowing or stopping aging processes are discussed below. Social and psychological research has also found that old age need not be as bad as most people fear: surveys have established that most people over 65 in the United States live in their own homes (95%), most are able to carry out their major activities (85%), and most are able to maintain fairly normal physical, psychological, and social functioning until shortly before death.

The Ancient Quest. Despite the obvious and universal fact of death, humans from earliest times down to the present have sought and dreamed of some way to achieve biological immortality, or at least to escape the effects of old age. One of the oldest and most popular legends concerns the fountain of youth. The Greek traveler Pausanias wrote the oldest detailed account of it almost 2,000 years ago. The most famous seeker of the fountain of youth, the Spanish explorer Juan Ponce de León (c. 1460–1521), discovered the present state of Florida in 1513 while searching for the fountain.

Alchemists throughout history have sought not only to transform lead into gold but also to determine the elixir of youth. Chinese alchemists were the first to record their search for the elixir of youth. Emperor Han Wu Ti (died 87 B.C.) was advised that by transmuting cinnabar into gold and using this gold for all his eating and drinking utensils (and by making the proper sacrifices), he could live forever. Another ancient belief is that man can absorb youth from sexual relations or bodily contact with young women. The medieval temples at Khajraho in India with their magnificent carvings are thought to be monuments to this belief.

A more recent series of experiments, related to a belief in semen as a rejuvenator, involves the injection of testicular cells. The distinguished French physiologist C. E. Brown-Séquard was the first to claim rejuvenation by this technique in 1889. He has been followed by many financially successful cell therapists, including Serge Voronoff and Paul Niehans.

Modern Theories. Modern gerontologists discount these earlier attempts at rejuvenation as unsupported by any acceptable scientific theories or controlled experiments. They have developed a new set of theories, however, that many regard as promising enough to warrant testing. One new theory is that *free radicals* (molecule fragments that seek to recombine) cause the aging process through *oxidation,* which inflicts molecular damage, particularly to the cell membranes. Denham Harmon has found that using antioxidation chemicals in the diet of mice lengthened their average life spans by as much as one third.

Vitamin E is one of the antioxidants most widely touted as a rejuvenator. The National Research Council of the National Academy of Sciences recommends 30 milligrams of vitamin E daily. The average person gets only 7 milligrams a day. Proponents of vitamin E claim it cures sterility, impotence, miscarriage, high blood pressure, diabetes, and the general effects of aging. On the other hand, a committee of medical experts for *The Medical Newsletter* stated that, with one minor exception, vitamin E has "no established value in preventing or treating any common human disorder."

A second major theory is that aging is due to increasing *cross-linkage.* Johan Bjorksten discovered that the connective tissue called *collagen* become tougher and less elastic with age because collagen molecules become bound together with chemical links. According to this theory, a chemical that breaks up these cross-linkages could retard the effects of aging.

A third theory is that when a person grows old his immunological system begins to break down and his antibodies, which normally attack foreign matter in the body, begin to attack his own body. Roy Walford found that two drugs that suppress immune responses increased the average life span of short-lived mice by ten weeks.

The theory behind the claims for Gerovital (mentioned earlier) is that while large doses have an anesthetic effect and thus relieve the pain of such disorders as arthritis, smaller doses properly buffered are mild stimulants and thus relieve other symptoms of aging. Gerovital is now being tested in several experiments across the United States.

Another theory is that slowing the *rate of metabolism* can retard aging. It has been demonstrated that reducing calorie intake can extend the life span of rats, and that reducing both diet and the temperature of cold-blooded animals can triple their life spans. Bernard Strehler concludes that a decrease of 3° to 5° Fahrenheit in human body temperature could add 20 to 30 useful years to the life span.

A final biological theory of aging states that it is brought about by failure of cells to reproduce themselves properly because of accumulation of copying errors. If some way could be developed to prevent these errors in cell reproduction, aging could be prevented.

Research on social and psychological factors associated with longevity indicates that the amount and kind of social interaction an older person has, as well as his mental attitudes, are related to how long he will survive. Research at Duke University has shown that the amount of satisfaction an older man derives from his work and activities is a strong predictor of his longevity, while an older woman's overall happiness rating is a strong predictor of her longevity.

When might all this research culminate in a scientific breakthrough that would extend the life span significantly? The average estimates of panels of experts vary from 1993 to 2023.

One thing is certain: society has just begun to face the problems and opportunities that will open up when the search for youth begins to achieve its ancient goal.

JOHN LAUNOIS—BLACK STAR

Woman of Vilcabamba, Ecuador, gathers strands of wool. This mountain village is one of a number of places throughout the world where many inhabitants live exceptionally long lives.

Over 100 Years Old —And Going Strong

In three areas of the world—the Caucasus Mountains of the Soviet Union, the Andean village of Vilcabamba, Ecuador, and the Himalayan state of Hunza, West Pakistan—people have little reason to participate in the search for eternal youth.

For in these three distinct places there is already a high percentage of elderly persons, many over 100 years of age, enjoying life to its fullest. There are some 5,000 persons in the Caucasus region alone who have reached their 100th birthday, and in Vilcabamba, with a total 1971 population of 819 persons, there were nine persons over 100 years old. In comparison, there are only a few thousand 100-year-olds among the 210 million population of the United States.

Scientists and doctors who have studied the elderly people of these regions cite four factors to explain this remarkable longevity:

(1) *Diet.* The diets of the elderly of Vilcabamba and Hunza are remarkably similar and below the minimum recommendations of U. S. health officials. They are not only low in caloric intake but also in animal fats. Protein is supplied mainly by vegetable sources. There are few indications of either obesity or undernutrition in these two regions.

The diet of the elderly of the Caucasus is somewhat different. In fact, the old people here consume 1,700 to 1,900 calories daily, an intake above that generally suggested for this age group. Once again, however, the amount of animal fat is low. Sour milk and cheese (low in fat) are common at all meals. Vegetables, meat, and dairy products are the sources of protein, with bread providing the carbohydrates. No meal is complete without homemade wine. The elderly usually drink two or three glasses daily.

(2) *Physical activity.* In these three regions, the elderly live extremely busy and productive lives. At a very young age, they became accustomed to hard physical labor around the home and in the mountainous countryside, and they work hard all their lives.

The Abkhazians say that "without rest, a man cannot work; without work, the rest may not give you any benefit." In fact, 70% of those over 80 years in the Caucasus are estimated to live active lives, and 60% of this group still work on state collective farms. Retirement is unheard of. Regular exercise, including hiking and swimming, is common.

(3) *Heredity.* Scientists are convinced of the importance of heredity in explaining advanced age, although a single gene accounting for longevity has not yet been isolated. It has been proved, however, that offspring of persons who live beyond their 100th year tend to live long lives too. Almost all of the 100-year-olds of these areas have at least one parent who lived to be more than 100. A 102-year-old resident of Vilcabamba had a sister who lived to be 107 and 12 brothers who lived beyond their 90th year.

(4) *Psychological and emotional factors.* The elderly of these areas feel a strong sense of usefulness and perform vital service to their communities. They are not isolated in special homes or communities for the elderly, but are considered a major part of a close family unit and enjoy special social status because of their advanced age. They spend their advanced years living free lives and doing what they want to do.

Unlike the United States, where a life span of 70 years is expected, the people of the Caucasus region, Vilcabamba, and Hunza consider themselves young until the age of 60 and look forward to their 100th birthday. In addition, the elderly are unconcerned with the strains and problems of today's world. Commenting on life today, one 117-year-old man said simply: "Oh yes, there are a number of things that are not the way I would want them to be, but since I can't change them, I don't worry about them."

JAMES E. CHURCHILL, JR.

JOHN LAUNOIS—BLACK STAR

The Abkhaz ASSR and the state of Hunza, Kashmir, boast inhabitants of remarkable age and vigor, including (*clockwise from upper left*) Khlaf Lasuria, a 130-year-old Abkhazian; 110-year-old Tulah Beg (*with stick*), the oldest person in Hunza; a 95-year-old Abkhazian woman and her 75-year-old son; and Gabriel Chapnian, a 117-year-old Abkhazian.

JOHN LAUNOIS—BLACK STAR

JOHN LAUNOIS—BLACK STAR

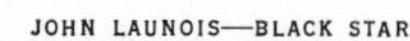

JOHN LAUNOIS—BLACK STAR

Plastic Surgery Can Make You Look Younger

FRANK McDOWELL, M. D.
Professor of Surgery, University of Hawaii; Editor, "Plastic & Reconstructive Surgery"

It has been said about aging—as about the weather—that "everyone talks about it, but no one does anything about it." The plastic surgeon, however, does do something about aging. Patients undergoing operations to alter the effects of age number in the millions. Obviously, a plastic surgeon cannot make anyone younger. But aging is not solely the passing of years: it is also a matter of attitudes, mental acuity and flexibility, spirit, bodily vigor, and appearance. When appearance alone among these factors indicates age, the plastic surgeon can try to make the person look as young as he or she would otherwise seem.

Face-lifting. The best known and the most frequent "youth-restoration" operation is face-lifting (rhytidectomy). In it, the surgeon tries to counteract the excessive stretching, sagging, and drooping of the facial and neck skin that sometimes occurs. Jowls along the jaw line, wattles in the upper neck, and excessive wrinkling may appear at an earlier age in persons with thin skin or a genetic predisposition, from too much exposure to sun and wind over the years, from long use of tobacco, or from overactive muscles of facial expression. Smaller or earlier aging changes may interfere with certain occupations. In any case, the puritanical views of the past are past, and most persons now see nothing wrong with anyone trying to look as young as he or she feels.

The complete face-lift, although a long, major operation, is one of the safest. Most surgeons feel that it should be done in a hospital and that the patient should remain there for several days.

The incision starts, on each side, in the scalp in front and well above the ear, comes down in front of or within the ear, around the earlobe, back up behind the ear into the scalp, and then down the back of the neck within the hair. From the incision, the skin is dissected loose from the face and neck for several inches forward, then pulled taut and the excess cut off—with care taken to tailor the edge perfectly for a precise fit when it is sewed back. For the best result, the surgeon must undermine quite widely and then take out as much of the extra sagging skin as possible, but not enough to cause pulling on the corners of the mouth or the eyelids to produce a "drawn" expression. The distinction requires artistry and fine surgical skill.

Healing requires about two weeks; subsidence of all bruises and swelling takes a bit longer. With a complete face-lift, the improvement is usually substantial, occasionally dramatic, but it varies.

Most plastic surgeons will not do anything less than a complete face-lift, believing that a "minilift" can yield only a "miniresult." The small procedure has been done occasionally by a few surgeons in their offices, usually with disappointing results. It consists of taking small tucks in the temple or behind the ear.

Not infrequently, for the best result, a patient may require some procedure in addition to a complete face-lift—such as removal of excess skin or pouches from the eyelids, abrasion of little vertical wrinkles from the upper lip, or removal of a fat lump under the chin. Often these procedures can be done during the same operation, with a worthwhile additional improvement in appearance.

Chemical face-peeling has received considerable publicity, but it is of limited usefulness. It can remove fine wrinkles by peeling off the outer layers of the skin in a manner that makes the healed skin stiffer, but it does not remove any excess pouches or sags.

Getting the Best Result. To obtain maximum improvement, the prospective face-lift patient should not shop for the *operation* as such—as she or he would shop for a bar of soap or an automobile. Rather, he should try to find the *surgeon* whom he thinks could best remodel his face—in the same way he would seek the artist who could paint the best portrait of him.

However, the choice of a surgeon cannot guarantee the result. The maxim that "the tailor can do no better than his cloth" applies doubly to living tissues, which vary greatly in their health and other characteristics. The patient's full cooperation in every detail is essential. The motivation for the operation is important. It is not a cure for social or emotional problems or for depression. The human face inevitably reflects a person's mental image of the total self.

Other Operations. Sagging breasts can usually be reshaped and put back into place. If they are too large, they can be reduced; if too small, they can be enlarged. These operations are most often done in younger women.

Sagging abdominal walls can be tightened and the excess skin removed, with the scar put down under "the bikini line." This is a rather large operation, requiring considerable hospitalization. One should not attempt to remove fat this way; the fat should be removed first by dieting and exercise. The operation is for tightening muscles and removing excess skin.

Arm-lifts, thigh-lifts, buttock reductions, buttock-lifts, and similar operations have been done by many plastic surgeons for a short time, and by a few for a longer time. Most have found the results generally disappointing. The scars are sometimes not acceptable.

Some Tips for Successful Aging

By N. W. Shock
Chief, Gerontology Research Center,
National Institutes of Health

Although there is no prescription that can guarantee a long and healthy life, an individual can take at least eight steps to increase the probability of achieving long life.

(1) Keep Thin. Mortality statistics show clearly that obese people at any age have a greater probability of developing heart disease, arteriosclerosis (hardening of the arteries), high blood pressure, and diabetes than do those with normal weight. Obesity also shortens the life span. Since physical activity tends to diminish with age, one must reduce total caloric intake to avoid obesity.

(2) Eat Sensibly. There is no evidence that aging is associated with any impairment of food absorption from the gut or that nutritional requirements change significantly with advancing age in adults. Eat a balanced diet that assures an adequate intake of proteins, vitamins, and minerals. As total food intake is reduced to maintain body weight, be sure that protein intake is maintained.

The most effective way to reduce caloric intake is to reduce the amount of fat in your diet. Reducing fat intake has an added advantage of minimizing the development of arteriosclerosis and heart disease. This is especially important in individuals with elevated blood cholesterol levels.

Be sure to maintain an adequate intake of vitamins and minerals, especially thiamine, vitamin B_{12}, vitamin C, iron, and calcium. Although these nutritional requirements can be met by eating a varied diet, it may be desirable to supplement the diet with a multiple vitamin and mineral preparation. There is no evidence that excessive doses of any vitamin contribute to good health or longevity. In fact, excessive intake of some vitamins, such as vitamin D, may actually be deleterious.

(3) Do Not Smoke Cigarettes. The occurrence of lung cancer and heart disease is significantly greater in smokers than in nonsmokers. Studies have also shown that lung function is significantly impaired in smokers as compared with nonsmokers. Furthermore, it has been found that when smoking is stopped, the reduced lung function returns to normal values within 6 to 18 months. The message is: if you smoke cigarettes—stop!

(4) Have an Annual Medical and Dental Checkup. Many diseases that produce major disabilities at advanced ages can be treated effectively if they are found in their early stages. In addition to heart disease, cancer, and diabetes, where early treatment is critical for success, high blood pressure is of special importance. It is a disease that in its early stage produces no symptoms, but it may develop slowly with disastrous results in later life. If detected early, elevated blood pressure can now be treated effectively by a physician. Similarly, glaucoma, which if left untreated will result in blindness, can now be treated effectively if detected before the retina of the eye is permanently damaged.

An annual physical examination benefits the patient only if he follows the physician's recommendations immediately.

(5) Exercise Prudently. The maintenance of physical activity and exercise contributes to feelings of well-being and health. But the levels of exercise must be adjusted to the physiological capacities of the individual. At advanced ages, strenuous exercises, such as tennis or handball, may actually be hazardous unless the individual has engaged in these sports since early youth. On the other hand, less strenuous exercise, such as walking, can well be continued even into advanced ages.

(6) Keep Pitching. One of the keys to successful aging is to maintain and develop a wide range of interests. This is a process that must begin in early maturity and continue over the entire life span. Continued participation in community affairs and the acquisition of new skills and interests are of great importance. Learn something new and challenging. Do not permit your mind (or muscles) to atrophy from disuse. The development of hobbies is especially important, but they must be meaningful to the individual and started during early adult life.

(7) Accept the Facts of Aging. Aging is a normal part of the total life sequence. It is critical for everyone to realize this and to be aware that changes in performance capabilities will occur in the course of normal aging. For example, having difficulty in recalling names or specific items of information is a normal process.

When you encounter evidence of aging in yourself, do not panic. Accept limitations as part of living and make adjustments to compensate for the limitation, like carrying a pocket notebook to jog a failing memory or acquiring a hearing aid to counteract a hearing loss.

(8) Do Not Be a Sucker. View with skepticism claims that a drug or treatment regime can induce rejuvenation or prolong life. Over the years claims have been made that certain drugs, hormones, or treatments will induce rejuvenation or delay aging, but none of them has survived the test of time or the application of adequate scientific tests.

In the early 1900's the injection of extracts made from male sex glands or the transplantation of testicular tissue from young men or animals (goats or monkeys) was supposed to rejuvenate elderly men. Even today, some claim that repeated injections of male and female sex hormones will retard aging. Although such injections of sex hormones have a useful role in the treatment of diagnosed diseases, they are not effective in slowing the general aging process.

CH. SIMONPIETRI—SYGMA

CH. SIMONPIETRI—SYGMA

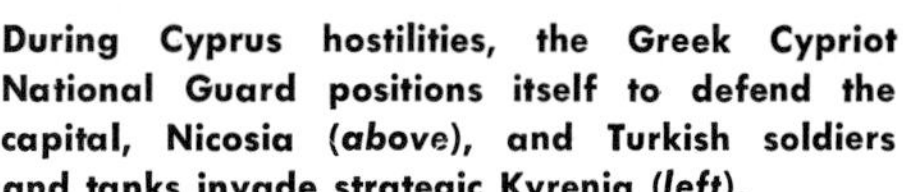

During Cyprus hostilities, the Greek Cypriot National Guard positions itself to defend the capital, Nicosia (*above*), and Turkish soldiers and tanks invade strategic Kyrenia (*left*).

CYPRUS

Long-time Struggle Between Greeks and Turks Reached Tragic Climax in 1974

BY GEORGE J. MARCOPOULOS
Associate Professor of History, Tufts University

Throughout Cyprus' long and troubled history, its strategic position on the sea routes between Europe and Asia has repeatedly made it the scene of conquest and suppression. Even with the attainment of independence in 1960, the island was not to have peace but rather a period of internal conflict between the Greek and Turkish elements. Its basic problem is thus an old one: how to govern itself in a way that is acceptable to both the Greek Cypriot majority and the Turkish Cypriot minority. By 1974 the stage was set for an explosion.

The year therefore was one of momentous and tragic occurrences: the deposition of the president, Archbishop Makarios III; an invasion by Turkey in two major phases, with resultant death and destruction, and the dislocation of

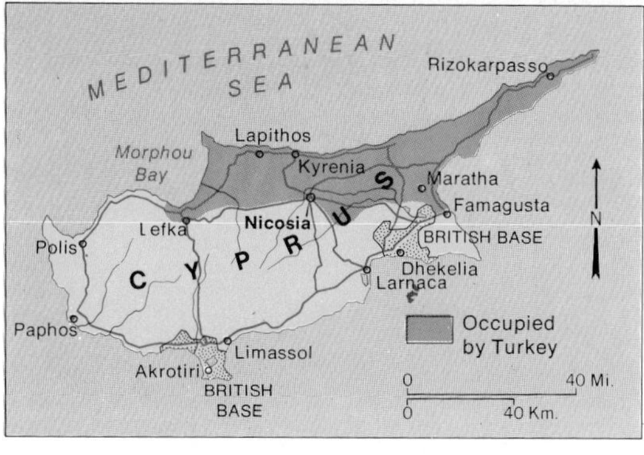

about 200,000 Greek Cypriots; and the killing of the American ambassador during a demonstration by Greek Cypriots in Nicosia.

The *Enosis* Question. In the 1950's, when Cyprus was a British colony, a strong movement for *enosis* (union) with Greece had been led by Archbishop Makarios. This movement was supported by a guerrilla organization, the National Organization of Cypriot Fighters (EOKA), under the Cyprus-born Greek Army officer Col. George Grivas. Fearing domination by the Greek Cypriots, who comprise about 80% of the population, the Turkish Cypriots, representing some 18% of the islanders, opposed *enosis* and instead preferred partition, with part of the country going to Turkey and part to Greece. The Turkish government also was adamant against *enosis*.

Thus in 1959 and 1960 a compromise was worked out by the British, Turkish, and Greek governments, and Archbishop Makarios. Cyprus was to be a unitary, independent state, and an elaborate system to preserve the minority rights of the Turkish Cypriots was incorporated in a new constitution. Provision was made also for the stationing of Greek and Turkish troops on the island, while Britain would retain some military bases. When independence came in August 1960, Makarios assumed the presidency. Still favoring *enosis,* Grivas had left for Greece in 1959.

Within three years of independence the government system began to break down, and the Greek Cypriots complained that the Turkish Cypriots had become obstructionist in government. Following attempts by Makarios to change some of the procedures relating to the political rights of the Turkish Cypriots, a severe outbreak of intercommunal fighting began in December 1963, and in 1964 a Turkish government threat to invade was prevented largely through the efforts of U. S. President Lyndon B. Johnson. Also in 1964 the United Nations dispatched a peace-keeping force to Cyprus. Originally given a six-month mandate, the UN force's term of service has been extended continuously since then.

Although Makarios repeatedly stressed that *enosis* was inopportune because of the attitude of the Turkish Cypriots and the Turkish government, the movement did not subside. Grivas,

KLAUS D. FRANCKE—PETER ARNOLD PHOTO ARCHIVES

Cyprus' agricultural economy: Sheep, raised on the Karpas Peninsula (*above*), provide wool for domestic use and export. With citrus fruits a major product, an orange festival is held near Famagusta (*below*).

KLAUS D. FRANCKE—PETER ARNOLD PHOTO ARCHIVES

KLAUS D. FRANCKE—PETER ARNOLD PHOTO ARCHIVES

The village of Lefkara in the Larnaca district of southwestern Cyprus is in a fertile region of vineyards and olive groves.

having become a lieutenant general in the Greek Army, returned to Cyprus in June 1964 and became head of both the Greek troops on the island and the Cypriot government's military forces. He was removed from these posts and returned to Greece in November 1967 after internal fighting had caused the Turkish government once again to threaten invasion. That action was stopped, as in 1964, primarily through the intervention of President Johnson. In late 1971, Grivas slipped back into the island clandestinely and began underground activities against Makarios. A new, pro-*enosis* guerrilla organization, EOKA-B, was formed and staged terrorist raids which Makarios denounced.

Rift with the Greek Government. General Grivas died at his Cypriot hideout on Jan. 27, 1974. Makarios then offered amnesty to Grivas' followers, but to no avail, and the terrorist activities continued. Despite the unrest, the archbishop in May took a trip to East Asia, during which he met with China's Mao Tse-tung. After his return, Makarios attempted to remove from the Cypriot National Guard elements that were sympathetic to EOKA-B. Early in July he wrote to the president of Greece, Gen. Phaidon Gizikis, to demand the recall of 650 Greek officers who, by contract, were in command of the National Guard.

Makarios' letter was a strong denunciation of these men, whom he characterized as following pro-*enosis* policies. After sending the letter, the archbishop publicly announced that he had proof that the Greek government was planning his overthrow. This culminated a long period of growing estrangement between Makarios and the anti-Communist military regime of Greece, which seemed to distrust its friendly relations with Communist states.

Overthrow of Makarios. During the morning of July 15 the Cypriot National Guard attacked the archbishop's palace. He escaped through the back door, and with the help of the United Nations force he reached a British base from which he was flown to London via Malta. Then he went to New York to plead his cause before the United Nations. On July 15 the National Guard installed as president Nikos Giorgiades Sampson, a terrorist member of the original EOKA and a man whom the Turkish Cypriots distrusted intensely. In obvious reaction, the Turkish government launched a full-scale invasion of Cyprus by sea and air on July 20. This galvanized the feuding Greek Cypriots to resist in unison, but within a few days the Turks had taken Kyrenia and a 10-mile-wide corridor south to the capital, Nicosia. A tentative cease-fire was arranged on July 22.

In Famagusta a group of men gather in the square before the 14th century Gothic Cathedral of St. Nicolas, now a mosque.

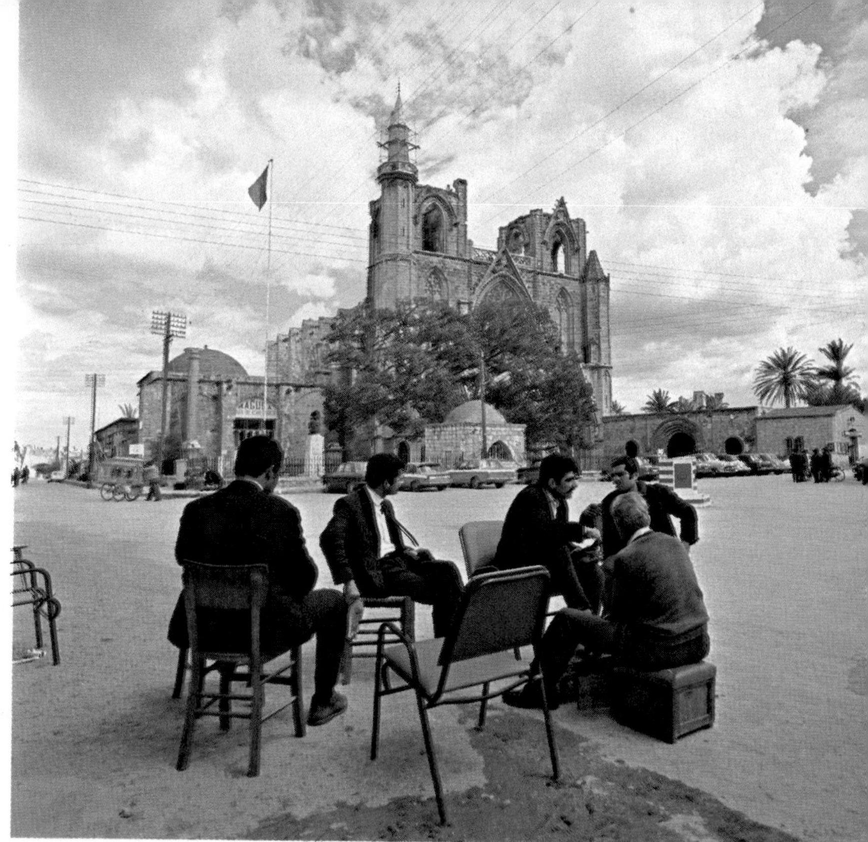

KLAUS D. FRANCKE—PETER ARNOLD PHOTO ARCHIVES

(*Below*) Roman forum in the ruins of Salamis, the main city of ancient Cyprus, near Famagusta. According to tradition, the city was founded just after the Trojan War and named for a Greek island. (*Right*) Typical homes in Kythrea, near Nicosia.

KLAUS D. FRANCKE—PETER ARNOLD PHOTO ARCHIVES

KLAUS D. FRANCKE—PETER ARNOLD PHOTO ARCHIVES

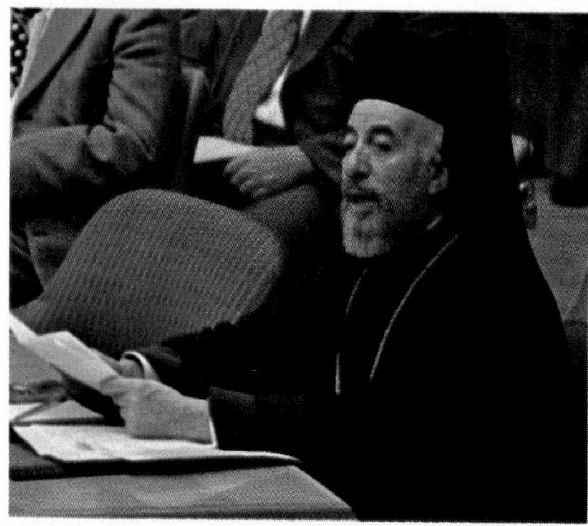

UNITED NATIONS

Archbishop Makarios III, president of Cyprus since 1960, began the year 1974 in an atmosphere of mounting tension. His former colleague in the struggle against the British during the 1950's, Gen. George Grivas, had since 1971 become his chief antagonist by organizing clandestine terrorist operations in favor of *enosis* (union) with Greece. A strong advocate of *enosis* at one time, Makarios came to consider it inopportune because of the intense opposition voiced by the Turkish Cypriot minority and the Turkish government.

After the death of Grivas on Jan. 27, 1974, Makarios offered an amnesty to his followers, but this proved ineffective. On July 3 the archbishop wrote to the president of Greece, Gen. Phaidon Gizikis, demanding the recall of 650 Greek officers in command of the Cypriot National Guard, accused by Makarios of supporting the pro-unionist activities under direction from Athens. On July 15 the National Guard launched an armed attack against the archbishop's palace, from which Makarios barely escaped with his life. Aided by the British, Makarios fled to London and then to New York to address the UN Security Council (July 19). The president returned to Cyprus on December 7.

Background. Makarios was born on Aug. 13, 1913, at Ano Panayia, Cyprus. The son of a shepherd, his given name was Michael Christodoulou Mouskos. After attending the Pancypriam Gymnasium in Nicosia he went to Athens to study theology and law. He was ordained a priest in 1946, and in 1946–48 studied at Boston University's School of Theology. In 1948 he became bishop of Kitium, and in 1950 he was chosen archbishop and primate of the Greek Orthodox Church of Cyprus. Because of his pro-*enosis* activities he was deported by the British in March 1956 to the Seychelles Islands. He returned to Cyprus in 1959 when arrangements had been made to establish an independent republic. Makarios was elected president in December 1959 and took office on Aug. 16, 1960. He was reelected in 1968 and 1973.

GEORGE J. MARCOPOULOS

On July 23 the military regime in Greece resigned and turned the country over to civilian rule under former Premier Constantine Caramanlis. That same day, Sampson resigned as president of Cyprus. He was succeeded by Glafkos Clerides, the respected vice president and speaker of the Cypriot House of Representatives. Clerides had also served as the Greek Cypriot negotiator in intercommunal talks with Rauf Denktas, leader of the Turkish Cypriots. These talks were started in 1968 and carried on at intervals late into 1974 without reaching any basic agreements. On December 7, President Makarios returned to Nicosia after an absence of nearly five months. In an address to a cheering throng, he declared that he would not accept partition of Cyprus between Greeks and Turks.

Danger of a Greek-Turkish War. The Turkish invasion of July 20 raised the possibility of war between Turkey and Greece. Indeed, U. S. Undersecretary of State Joseph J. Sisco was in Ankara discussing Cyprus with the Turks at the moment the invasion was being mounted. War was averted by the Caramanlis government because Greece was unprepared to fight its NATO partner Turkey, which had overwhelming superiority in troops and American-supplied weapons.

Beginning July 25, the Greek government participated in a conference at Geneva with Britain and Turkey as the three original guarantors of Cyprus under the independence settlement of 1959. During the first round of talks, the Turkish government, while ostensibly negotiating, kept pouring troops onto the island and extending its territorial control from Kyrenia in defiance of the cease-fire. The second round of talks broke down on August 14 after the Turkish government had not only presented such far-reaching demands for partition that the Greek government could obviously not accept them, but also had refused to give the Greek representative, George Mavros, 36 hours in which to consult with his government.

That same day, August 14, a second full-scale invasion was mounted by the Turks. By August 16 they had inflicted widespread devastation, conquered the city of Famagusta, and spread out in such a way that they controlled the northeastern corner, or about 40%, of the island from Lefka in the west to Famagusta in the east. Then the Turkish government announced a cease-fire and offered to return to negotiations at Geneva. This was rejected by Greece, which refused to negotiate under Turkish military pressure.

Effects of the Turkish Occupation. The two military campaigns by the Turks left an estimated total of 200,000 Greek Cypriots homeless, while some 20,000 Turkish Cypriots were dislocated. Both sides accused the other of atrocities. Moreover, the tremendous dislocation of the Greek Cypriot population was compounded by the fact that the part of Cyprus occupied by Turkey included about 70% of the vital,

MICHEL LAURENT, GAMMA

Glafkos John Clerides, 55, speaker of the Cyprus House of Representatives, became acting president of Cyprus on July 23, 1974, following the resignation of Nikos G. Sampson. Sampson had served briefly following the ouster of Archbishop Makarios. A man known for his calmness, Clerides is considered a political moderate. He had been the Greek Cypriot negotiator at the prolonged intercommunal talks with representatives of the Turkish Cypriots.

Immediately after taking office, Clerides said that he considered himself only a temporary president. His basic objectives would be to maintain a cease-fire on the island, help minimize friction between the two factions, and prepare the nation for general elections. The elections would determine whether Makarios would be allowed to return to power.

On August 8 the new president named a nine-member cabinet, mainly of men without political experience. For a short period he held the ministries of defense, interior, and foreign affairs for himself. In the fall, President Clerides personally took charge of the negotiations leading to an exchange of prisoners of war with the Turkish Cypriots. Makarios returned to Cyprus on December 7, and he endorsed Clerides as his negotiator at talks between Greek and Turkish Cypriots.

Background. Born April 24, 1919, Clerides was educated at Pancyprian Gymnasium in Nicosia and at the University of London. During World War II he served with the Royal Air Force and was taken prisoner by the Germans. After the war, Clerides returned to Cyprus, where he practiced law and became associated with the National Organization of Cypriot Fighters (EOKA), a guerrilla group. Once independence was granted to Cyprus, he was elected to the House of Representatives in the nation's first general election, and then became speaker of the legislative body. As speaker, he frequently represented Archbishop Makarios during presidential trips abroad.

wealthy segments of the economy, such as farming, shipping, and the tourist industry. Much of this territory had previously been owned by the Greek Cypriots. The result of the occupation, therefore, was that the Turkish Cypriots were strengthened, while the Greek Cypriots were left dejected and bitter.

The bitterness of the ethnic Greeks, however, was not confined to Turkey's activities. The United States government, and particularly Secretary of State Henry A. Kissinger, were denounced for not having used their influence to restrain the Turks, or at least for not having taken a forceful stand against the use of American-made arms by Turkey in Cyprus. Kissinger's policy was compared unfavorably with the forceful actions taken by President Johnson in 1964 and 1967.

On Aug. 19, 1974, a violent anti-American demonstration was held by Greek Cypriots outside the American embassy in Nicosia. Rodger P. Davies, the American ambassador, and Antoinette Varnavas, a Cypriot employed as a secretary at the embassy, were killed in the building as it was being raked by gunfire from automatic weapons. President Clerides condemned the crime and ordered the police to find the killers, but no one was apprehended. By quickly appointing a new ambassador, William R. Crawford, Jr., the American government seemed to affirm that it did not blame all Greek Cypriots for Davies' death.

American Policy Toward Cyprus. Within the U. S. Congress there developed a strong movement of protest against Turkey's invasion of Cyprus. Twice in October, President Gerald R. Ford vetoed legislation aimed at cutting off American military aid to Turkey because he stated vehemently that this would undermine Secretary Kissinger's ability to mediate the fate of the island with the Turks, and would weaken America's NATO defenses. Finally, in mid-October the President reluctantly accepted a compromise by which aid would be cut off by December 10 unless he could attest that progress was being made in negotiations to solve the Cyprus problem and that the Turkish government was adhering strictly to American laws relative to the use of military aid. The compromise legislation provided additionally for an immediate cutoff of aid if the Turks violated the cease-fire, or increased their forces on Cyprus, or sent more American-made instruments of war to the island.

During October, Sen. Edward M. Kennedy, chairman of the Senate Subcommittee on Refugees, accused the Ford administration of having given only paltry assistance to the thousands of Greek Cypriot refugees in order to strengthen Turkey's policies toward the island.

As the year neared its close, it was clear that Cyprus, like so many of its Middle Eastern neighbors, had a long way to go before it could enjoy any real sense of peace and progress.

RONNY JAQUES, PHOTO RESEARCHERS

The 1974 U. S. national championships at Forest Hills were attended by a record number of fans.

everyone's playing TENNIS

By Eugene L. Scott

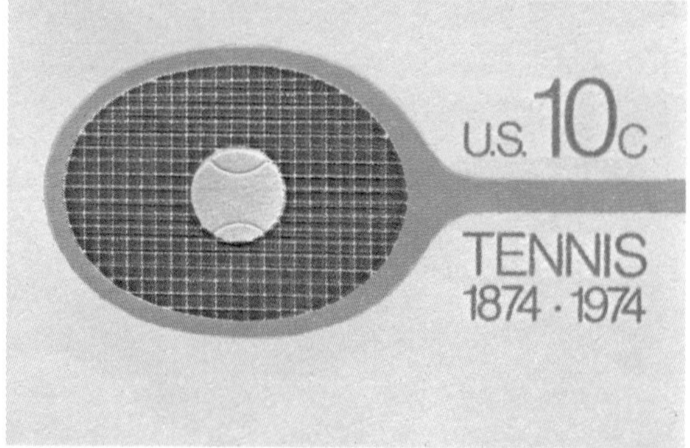

U.S. POSTAL SERVICE

U. S. Postal Service marks 100th anniversary of U. S. tennis with a 10-cent embossed stamped envelope.

In its early days, some 100 years ago, the game of tennis was simply a sleepy pastime for the idle or the rich, or both, and rarely escaped the confines of the country club setting. By 1974, the centennial of the game in the United States, however, the popularity of tennis was accelerating at a rate that would make Wall Street's bluest of chips ecstatic.

Growth of the Sport. The fact that since 1968 professional tennis players have been allowed to compete against amateurs and each other in major world championships provided a rallying point for the sport's boom. Although attendance at Wimbledon, the world's premier tournament, has been constant for the past 20 years, attendance at the annual U. S. national championships at Forest Hills has been rising at the annual rate of 8% to 9%. In fact, the 1974 12-day event at Forest Hills drew a record gate of 153,287 spectators.

About the author: New York City lawyer Eugene L. (Gene) Scott is author of the book Tennis: Game of Motion *and publisher of the new newspaper* Tennis Week. *In addition, he has written tennis articles for such publications as* The New York Times, Sports Illustrated, Newsday, *and* Esquire. *A member of the 1963–65 U. S. Davis Cup team, Gene Scott captured the men's 35 singles tournament at Forest Hills, N. Y., in 1973 and 1974.*

Ironically though, the primary thrust of all the fuss has been in participation, not spectator, tennis. In 1965, only 4.5 million people played tennis in the United States, but by 1970 the number had grown to 8 million. Morever, a Nielsen survey predicted that 16 million Americans would be playing the game by the end of 1975.

Several factors account for the rise in the popularity of participation tennis. In recent years the importance of physical fitness has been emphasized as never before, and the game of tennis provides excellent exercise. Unlike the four or five hours required for a round of golf, tennis can be played in a relatively short period of time and the exercise effect is immediate. This permits many businessmen to play during their lunch hours. Secondly, the elements of the game itself are perfect for mass appeal. Equipment is relatively inexpensive, and the game can be played long after it becomes impossible for a working man to play the team sports enjoyed during high school and college. Thirdly, at the moment, playing tennis is simply an "in" thing to do. It is socially desirable to be seen on the tennis courts.

Results of the Growth. With more Americans playing tennis, interest in learning how to play the game correctly has increased accordingly. Consequently, some 150 tennis camps have sprung up across the United States and attract an estimated 100,000 would-be tennis enthusiasts annually. At some camps, adults spend considerable sums of money for a few days of instructions. In addition, classroom tennis has boomed into a year-round multibillion dollar business. At these schools, which are held in such diverse places as the tops of office buildings and modern bubble-enclosed courts, students are taught the mechanics of the game by the use of ball-throwing devices and other equipment.

Latest tennis fashions: Colorful, terry-cloth warm-up suits (*right*) and comfortable dresses trimmed with color replace the previous all-white dress.

POINT SET

POINT SET

LAVER-EMERSON TENNIS, INC.

A tennis instructor shows the correct techniques when playing at the net.

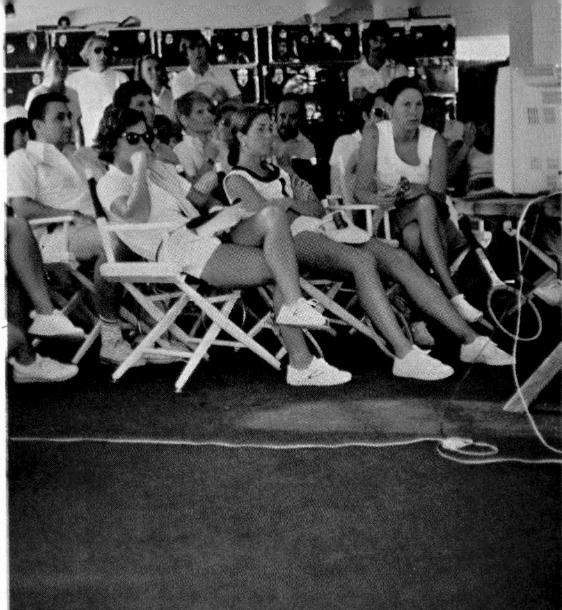

TENNISAMERICA, INC.

Tennis players study themselves on a closed-circuit video system, which enables them to see and correct their mistakes immediately.

LEARNING THE GAME

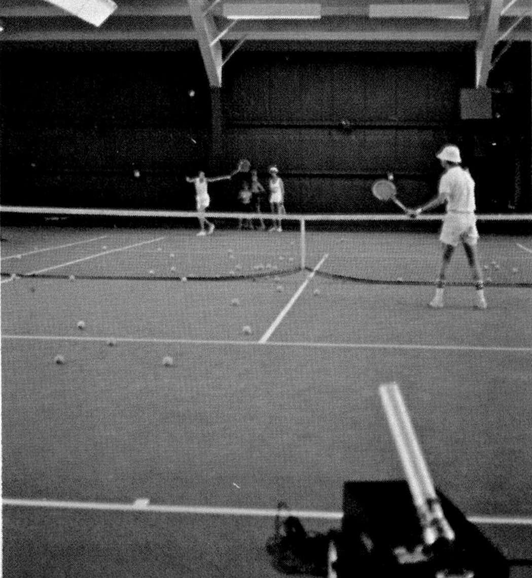

SUNDANCE TENNIS, RUTLAND, VT.

Indoor tennis camp: An enthusiast tries her all-important serve. A ball-throwing device (*lower right*) makes practice easier.

A tennis foursome plays a practice match under the critical eye of their trained instructor.

SUNDANCE TENNIS, RUTLAND, VT.

Because of the sharp increase in play, tennis equipment manufacturers have prospered enormously. In the past, sporting goods companies have not been held in high esteem by either marketing or financial experts. Distribution and advertising techniques of leisure companies were considered primitive. But in response to the new tennis fever, budgets were created for research and product development. The result has been improved materials, design, and style for every piece of equipment used in the game. The modern metal racquet, which first appeared at Forest Hills in 1967, has progressed from steel to aluminum to fiberglass to graphite compositions. Even exotic combinations of each material are now available. The once-clumsy tennis sneaker is now a sleek light slipper, and shorts and shirts are snug-fitting clothes designed for speed and movement. The traditional "all white" costume has given way to a galaxy of pastels, stripes, and bright-colored trims.

New synthetic court surfaces have enabled construction where playing tennis was previously considered impractical or too expensive. Portable carpet-type courts have converted gymnasiums into indoor-tennis facilities, and the building of indoor-tennis complexes has doubled since 1970. In many cases, it has now become necessary for new apartment houses and motel units to offer tennis courts as well as the traditional swimming pool as an attraction for new residents and guests. All of this activity has accelerated tennis to a $350 million business annually.

Each point of activity feeds on itself, and the result is an unbelievable expansion of the base of tennis. Contributing to and at the same time forming a part of this broadening effect is television exposure. In 1967, the only televised tennis event was the U. S. Open at Forest Hills. In 1974 the three major networks, and some syndicated combines as well, were broadcasting tournament action regularly. The mechanics of television coverage need to improve to properly convey the athlete's speed, power, and grace to the viewers. But certainly television is exposing the game to more people than ever before. The high point of the television penetration came in September 1973 when 40 million viewers watched Billie Jean King defeat Bobby Riggs in the "battle of the sexes."

Growing Pains. The game's sudden growth does not mean that there have not been growing pains, particularly for spectator tennis. With the introduction of extravagant prize money, the pros inherited great power, which was often abused in the form of strikes, boycotts, and crude on-court behavior. The game's administrators failed to set a worthy example, as lawsuits and clandestine contracts between associations, player unions, sponsors, and private promoters surfaced regularly.

Another of the game's major face-liftings has been the decline of amateurism. Before 1968, 98% of the major championships were restricted to amateurs, with a handful of pros left to barnstorm in obscure cities before meager crowds. Even if an athlete wanted to turn professional, there was no tour and no place to play. "Closed" tennis was the result of poor pro leadership and fuzzy-thinking amateur rulers of the game who attached an evil stigma to anyone who made a living from sport. Open tennis altered this thinking, but there are some obvious side effects. For example, any talented college player now turns pro after his sophomore year to cash in on the tempting prize money. A college football player, however, inevitably waits until graduation to turn pro, partly because of restrictions by the professional leagues and partly because the college star's price will soar if his college football career is a successful one. Since the tennis pro earns prize-money only on merit, namely victory, he does not require such a publicity buildup.

In no other sport is it as easy to turn professional as in tennis. Unlike golf, there is no school or championship to survive in order to qualify. Easy entry into the business presents problems in the form of instruction. With no prescribed uniform method for teaching, bizarre styles are taught by untutored opportunists eager to capitalize on the boom.

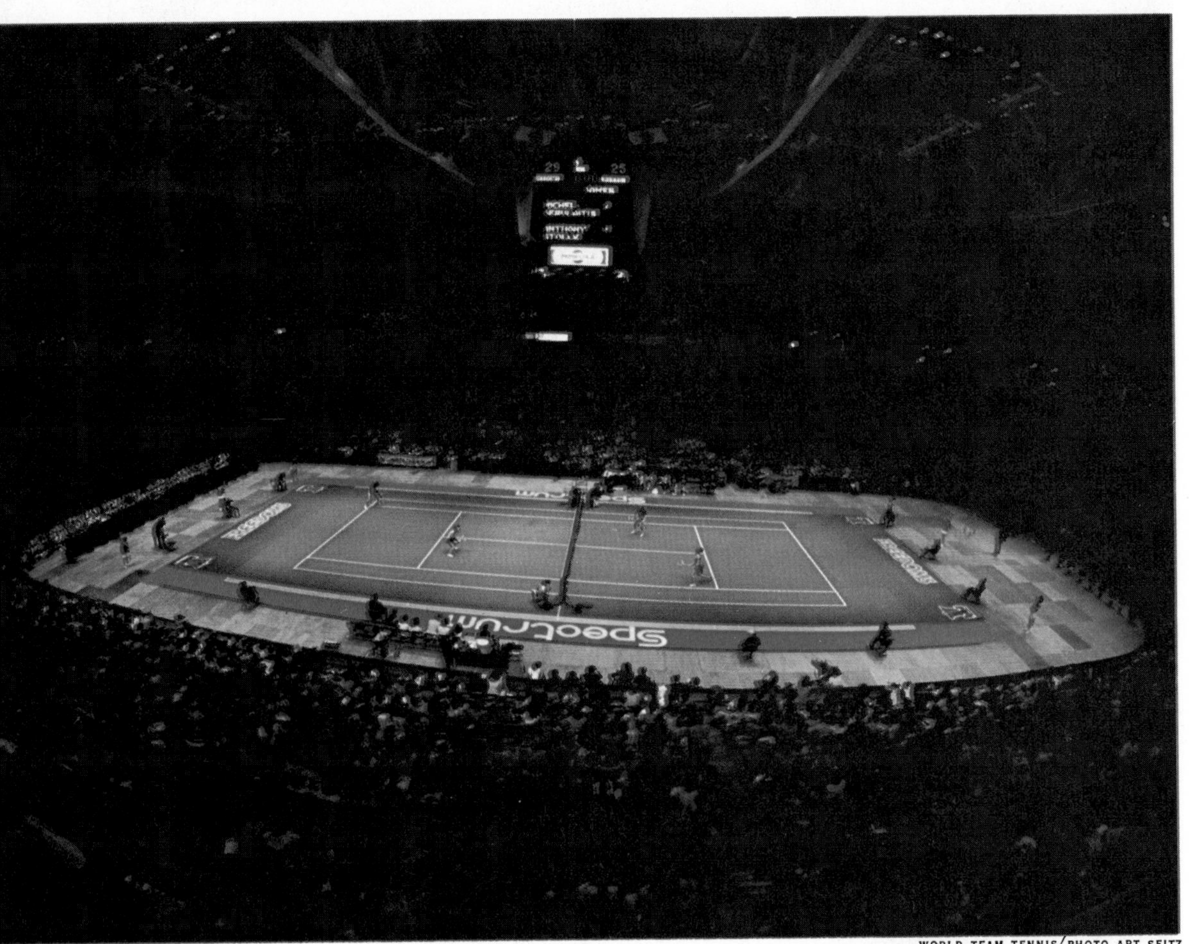

WORLD TEAM TENNIS/PHOTO ART SEITZ

World Team Tennis makes its debut at the Philadelphia Spectrum in May 1974. The new league of 16 teams follows a new scoring system and permits frequent substitution of players.

Professional Changes, Team Tennis. With the game's giant growth, it is not surprising that the traditions have been ravaged. Scoring has undergone an extreme change in the form of "sudden death" tie breakers to end the marathon set and "no ad" games that eliminate deuce and advantage. Both scoring modifications were made with an eye to television coverage, which could not tolerate the unpredictability of long matches.

In 1970, America's five biggest championships were conducted on grass. By 1975 *no* major tournament will be staged on turf—for years a source of player complaint because of bad bounces and irregular footing.

The trend to play big-time events indoors gained momentum with the introduction in 1974 of World Team Tennis, the new intercity league competition. WTT adopted all the scoring changes, uses the synthetic carpet surface, and allows free substitution to streamline the game for mass spectator appeal.

In conclusion, it can be said that tennis has come a long way since a British army officer invented it in 1873, and since Mary Ewing Outerbridge introduced the sport to a U. S. audience at a cricket club on Staten Island, N. Y., the following year. However, as 1974 ended, two questions remained unanswered. One, with the boom, would the new convert to the game be able to find a vacant court in the near future? Two, would the professionals be able to resolve their disagreements and supply the leadership required for the game's success? The answers to both of these questions will have a profound effect on the game's future.

HUBERT LECAMPION, SYGMA

With the world food shortage becoming more acute, particularly in such nations as Bangladesh (*above*), a World Food Conference was held in Rome in November.

REVIEW OF THE YEAR 1974

MANCHETE FROM PICTORIAL

On Feb. 1, 1974, fire sweeps through a 25-story bank building in downtown São Paulo, Brazil, killing at least 189 persons and injuring approximately 300.

ACCIDENTS AND DISASTERS

Accidents and disasters claimed a high toll in 1974. The worst air disaster in history occurred in March, when a Turkish DC-10 crashed near Paris, killing all 346 aboard. The weather was also responsible for terrible losses. Floods in Asia and Latin America, tornadoes in the United States, and Hurricane Fifi in Honduras killed thousands of persons. A list of the year's major disasters follows.

AVIATION

Jan. 31—U. S. jetliner crashes and burns while attempting to land in bad weather at Pago Pago, American Samoa, killing 95 of the 101 persons aboard.

Jan. 26—Turkish jetliner crashes and bursts into flames during take off from Izmir, killing 63 persons.

March 3—Turkish jetliner crashes into forest shortly after take off from Paris, killing all 346 persons aboard.

April 4—Plane carrying gold miners home to Malawi crashes shortly after taking off from Francistown, Botswana, killing 77 of the 83 persons aboard.

April 22—U. S. jetliner crashes in remote, mountainous region of Bali in Indonesia, killing all 107 persons aboard.

Aug. 12—Malian turboprop crashes near Ouagadougou, Upper Volta, killing 47.

Aug. 14—Venezuelan turboprop crashes into a hill on the Caribbean island of Margarita during torrential rain storm, killing 47 of the 48 persons aboard.

Sept. 8—U. S. jetliner crashes in the Ionian Sea off Greece killing all 88 persons aboard.

Sept. 11—U. S. jetliner crashes and burns in the woods while attempting to land at Charlotte, North Carolina, killing 69 of the 82 persons aboard.

Sept. 15—South Vietnamese jetliner, hijacked by a man demanding to be flown to Hanoi, explodes and crashes when hijacker detonates grenades; all 70 persons aboard are killed.

Nov. 20—West German Boeing 747 crashes and burns shortly after taking off from Nairobi, Kenya, killing 59 of the 157 persons aboard; it is the first fatal crash of a 747 jet.

Dec. 1—U. S. jetliner crashes and burns near Washington, D. C., during a rainstorm, killing all 92 persons aboard.

Dec. 4—Dutch charter jetliner carrying Indonesian Muslim pilgrims to Mecca crashes in Sri Lanka, killing all 191 persons aboard; it is the 2d worst air disaster in civil aviation history.

Dec. 22—A Venezuelan airliner crashes shortly after take off from Maturín, 312 miles east of Caracas; all 77 persons aboard are killed.

LAND AND SEA TRANSPORTATION

July 28—Bus and truck collide head-on near Belém, Brazil, killing at least 69.

Aug. 11—Two buses collide in Turkey on the Ankara-Istanbul highway, killing 21 and injuring 41.

Aug. 30—Train crash in the railroad station in Zagreb, Yugoslavia, kills 130 passengers.

Sept. 9—Bus crash in Zambia kills 26.

Sept. 28—Panamanian freighter sinks in heavy seas near Hong Kong during a typhoon; 31 crewmen are lost.

STORMS, FLOODS, AND LANDSLIDES

February—Severe flooding in three northwestern provinces of Argentina leaves at least 60 persons dead and over 100,000 homeless.

March—Floods in Brazil leave 500 persons dead and 65,000 homeless; the heavy rains followed months of drought.

April 3–4—Series of 93 tornadoes slash across 7 states in the South and Middle West of the United States, killing 329 and injuring 6,000; over $1 billion in property damage is caused by the worst tornado disaster since 1925.

April 25—Landslides in Peru, triggered by torrential rains, wipe out two Andean villages; death toll is put at 250 with 500 missing and believed dead.

June 28—Landslide covers a section of the highway east of Bogotá, Colombia, killing at least 200.

July–August—Massive flooding in Bangladesh, following incessant monsoon rains, leaves 2,000 persons dead and two thirds of the country under water; 10 million acres of cropland are ruined.

August—Severe flooding on the island of Luzon in the Philippines, caused by heavy monsoon rains, leaves 78 persons dead and over 1 million homeless.

Sept. 19–20—Hurricane Fifi ravages northern Honduras; floods and landslides wipe out entire communities, leaving 50,000 people homeless; an estimated 5,000 persons are killed and property damage is put at $200 million.

Oct. 6—Landslide buries parts of the small town of Betulia, Colombia, killing at least 30 persons; a week earlier a landslide killed at least 50 in Medellín, Colombia's second largest city.

Dec. 25—A cyclone rips through the port city of Darwin, Australia, damaging 90% of the city and taking more than 50 lives.

FIRES, EXPLOSIONS, AND BUILDING CAVE-INS

Jan. 23—Fire in the dormitory of a Belgian Catholic school kills 23 teenage boys.

Feb. 1—Fire sweeps through the top stories of a 25-story bank building in São Paulo, Brazil, killing at least 189 persons and injuring almost 300; many people, trapped at windows or on the roof, panic and leap to their death.

June 1—Explosion at a chemical plant in the small village of Flixborough, 180 miles north of London, kills 29 and injures 94; 3,000 villagers are temporarily forced from their homes by thick smoke and toxic fumes.

June 17—Fire in a building in downtown Lahore, Pakistan, kills at least 40 persons.

June 30—Smoke from a flash fire kills 24 young patrons and employees of a singles bar astride the New York-Connecticut border.

Nov. 3—Fire sweeps through a crowded discotheque in a hotel in Seoul, South Korea, killing 88.

Dec. 5—The snow-covered roof of the newly enlarged airport in Teheran, Iran, caves in on the main lounge, killing at least 25.

Dec. 27—An explosion and fire tears through a deep shaft of a coal mine in Liévin, northern France, killing 42.

EARTHQUAKES

Oct. 3—An earthquake strikes Lima, Peru, and the surrounding areas, killing 73 persons and injuring some 2,000.

Dec. 28—In Pakistan, several northern villages are destroyed by a devastating earthquake; an estimated 5,200 persons are killed in the disaster.

ADVERTISING

The year 1974 was a stern one for the U. S. advertising industry, squeezed by a "stagflation" economy and facing consumers whose confidence and buying plans sagged lowest in 28 years of monitoring by the Survey Research Center of Michigan University. Many advertisers altered the focus of their advertising to stress direct competitive benefits or to emphasize price, value, and utility.

Total U. S. advertising expenditures in 1974 reached $26.6 billion, up 5.9% from 1973, due largely to rate increases rather than volume growth, and falling far short of the economy's rate of inflation. Regulatory attention again focused on television, while the government itself made growing use of marketing and advertising techniques to enlist support for its programs, ranging from military recruitment to mass transit. The focus of much advertising became increasingly regional and local.

Advertising Copy. Advertising, via the Advertising Council, was officially enlisted to supply the slogan for President Ford's largely voluntary WIN program to "Whip Inflation Now" and to drum up support for energy-conservation measures. The stringent business climate spawned more advertising campaigns, which named competitors in making comparative claims for various products and which resulted in several legal actions.

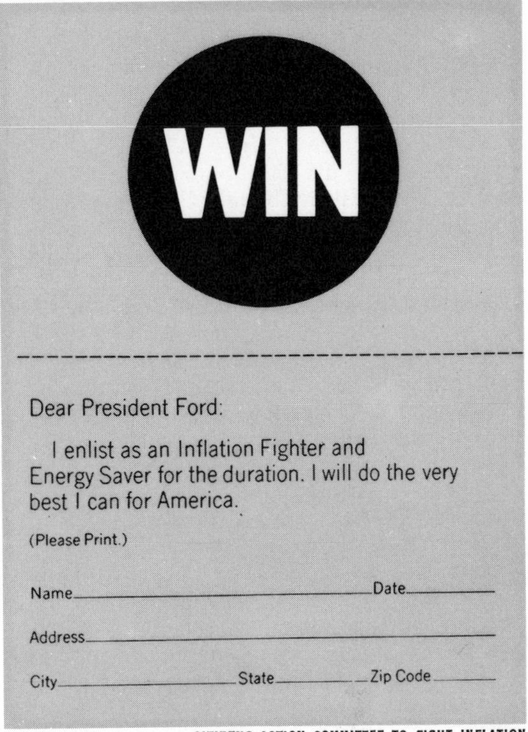

WIN
Dear President Ford:
I enlist as an Inflation Fighter and Energy Saver for the duration. I will do the very best I can for America.
(Please Print.)
Name
Date
Address
City
State
Zip Code

CITIZENS ACTION COMMITTEE TO FIGHT INFLATION

The advertising industry helped drum up support for President Ford's "Whip Inflation Now" (WIN) program.

Media. TV keynotes were improved programming and less advertising aimed at children. The Federal Communications Commission (FCC), ending a four-year study, issued guidelines calling for more educational content in children's programs and fewer commercials (to be reduced 20% by 1976), but avoided the total ad ban sought by consumerists. Networks had already doubled their children's public service programs in 1974, and local stations were beginning to add upgraded material for the young. The Federal Trade Commission (FTC) proposed a ban on premium offers to children, while the FCC moved to extend TV station licenses to five years (from three).

The newspaper attrition trend was reversed, boosted by automated and electronic production technology. Successful new entries included national and local weekly tabloids; New York's first new daily since 1952 was scheduled to appear in 1975. Magazine specialization continued, with successful regional and dozens of city publications reflecting local interest.

Advertising Volume. U. S. advertising revenue in 1974 rose to more than $26.6 billion, a 5.9% increase over the $25.1 billion earned in 1973. Network TV was up by 8%, to $2.1 billion; spot advertising by 4.1%, to $1.5 billion. Radio (net and spot) moved up 5.5%, to $475 million; newspapers, 6.2%, to $1.2 billion; and magazines, 5%, to $1.5 billion. Business publications advanced 9.5%, to $947 million; outdoor advertising, spurred by rate hikes, went ahead by 7.5%, to $2.5 million. All other media (from direct mail to displays) improved by 5%, to $6.7 billion. Local advertising, which had outpaced national in recent years, slowed down for a 4.5% gain, to $11.8 billion, while national advertising increased by 5.7%, to $14.6 billion.

Canada. Another growth year (1974) saw volume up 13%, to $1.6 billion, and local advertising again rising faster than national. Of 300 ad agencies in Canada, the largest now bills $50 million annually.

Although government intervention subsided and self-policing remained effective, moves aimed at lessening U. S. involvement in Canadian communications merit close scrutiny. Legislation was considered to make advertising in U. S.-owned publications in Canada and on border TV stations a nonallowable pretax expense, forcing ad dollars to come from operating profits instead. The Canadian Radio and Television Commission also suggested that by 1977–78, 80% of commercials be produced in Canada.

Cable TV continued its growth; in 1974, 35% of Canadian households (57% in Toronto, 75% in Vancouver) were receiving cable TV. Many cable system owners had begun creating their own commercials.

EDWARD H. MEYER
Chairman of the Board and President, Grey Advertising, Inc.

AFGHANISTAN

The Republic of Afghanistan was alive and well in 1974 as it moved slowly toward the goals that were articulated after a military coup overthrew the monarchy in July 1973.

Politics. In his Republic Day (July 17) speech, President Mohammed Daud intimated that the new constitution being written in 1974 would be built around the concepts of a parliamentary democracy and a two-party system. During 1974, however, Daud held the reins tightly and maintained control through the loyalty of a liberal, professional officer corps. The police force, once noted for its brutality, was transformed into an elite corps by encouraging unemployed high-school graduates to attend the Police Academy.

The left remained quiet, and the only significant internal threat came from the right. Its die-hard monarchist army officers and conservative religious leaders feared a Communist takeover. Some antigovernment leaders were arrested, tried, and executed, but most were imprisoned for allegedly plotting against the state.

A series of laws (presidential decrees) was promulgated in an attempt to define the roles and functions of the various government ministries and other administrative institutions. These laws covered collection of taxes, education policy and reform, and police disciplinary regulations.

Cracks began to appear in the Central Committee. One member was sent to Bulgaria as ambassador, another was expelled for not following the policies and ideals of the republic, and a third was executed. Two Western-trained economists joined the cabinet, thus creating a better balance vis-à-vis nationalization of basic industries and free enterprise in light industry and commercial activities.

At year-end, President Daud was stronger than ever. From a position of consolidated strength, he may soon loosen controls and even permit the free press to function again.

Economy. The republic is attempting to create a mixed, guided economy, and the founding of a central statistics office should help future development planners. For the second straight year, bumper crops of food grains were reported, and the government increased cotton prices by 20% to encourage farmers to grow exportable crops. Sugar is a major import, so sugar-beet prices were also raised by the same percentage to increase local sugar production. The energy crisis passed Afghanistan by, and it continued to import cheap petroleum products from the USSR and Iran. The private sector slowed down considerably because the policy of government toward free enterprise remained rather cloudy, in spite of a new domestic and foreign investments law.

Foreign Affairs. The Soviets stepped up economic assistance. Although the USSR remained Afghanistan's most important trade and aid partner, the republic's foreign policy keystone still is nonalignment. President Daud visited the USSR in June and came home with a long list of 21 proposed projects in agriculture, mining, power generation, and industry. In spite of strictures under new congressional guidelines, the United States continued to offer assistance in education, family planning, administration, demography, agriculture and irrigation, and power. China, at first suspecting a Soviet hand in the 1973 coup, now assists in the development of the textile industry, agriculture, and related projects.

A great increase in Indian economic and cultural assistance occurred, partly in response to continued confrontations with Pakistan by both countries. An Afghan–Indian Joint commission considered a wide range of projects in the fields of agriculture, mines and industries, education, and rural development.

In July, Iran and Afghanistan signed a development agreement that may exceed $1 billion in loans and grants. Among other things, Iran agreed to build a railroad from Kabul to the Iranian border via Kandahar and Herat. Both sides agreed to develop jointly the lower Hilmand Valley, thus eliminating the only outstanding problem between the two countries. Substantial aid was also promised by several Arab countries, including Saudi Arabia, Iraq, and Kuwait.

Relations with Pakistan turned for the worse in the final six months of the year, culminating in Afghan protests over alleged Pakistani violations of its air space.

The problem of the status of the Pushtun and Baluch tribes on both sides of the Durand Line remained unsettled, and the Pakistanis accused the Afghans of training saboteurs. Although the Baluch revolt increased in intensity and frequent explosions rocked Peshawar and other towns in the North-West Frontier Province, the Afghans publicly expressed the desire to settle the problem peacefully.

LOUIS and NANCY HATCH DUPREE
American Universities Field Staff

AFGHANISTAN • Information Highlights

Official Name: Republic of Afghanistan.
Location: Central Asia.
Area: 250,000 square miles (647,497 sq km).
Population (1973 est.): 18,300,000.
Chief Cities (1971 est.): Kabul, the capital, 318,100; Kandahar, 133,800.
Government: *Head of state,* Lt. Gen. Mohammed Daud Khan, president (took office July 1973). *Head of government,* Lt. Gen. Mohammed Daud Khan, prime minister (took office July 1973). *Legislature*—Shura (dissolved July 1973).
Monetary Unit: Afghani (50 afghanis equal U. S.$1, July 1974).
Gross National Product (1972 est.): $1,600,000,000.
Manufacturing (major products): Textiles, cement, processed fruit, refined sugar, carpets.
Major Agricultural Products: Wheat, corn, rice, sugar.
Foreign Trade (1972): Exports, $99,000,000; Imports, $166,000,000.

WIDE WORLD

Before the big fight, Zaire's President Mobutu presents George Foreman (*left*) and Muhammad Ali to Kinshasa stadium crowd.

AFRICA

Africa in 1974 saw historic moves toward the dismantling of Portugal's 500-year-old African empire. Guinea-Bissau became independent and freedom for Mozambique and Angola was set for 1975. Equally historic was the dethronement of Ethiopia's Emperor Haile Selassie after more than a half-century of absolute rule. Deaths from drought continued in the West African Sahel despite rains that brought temporary relief; but military leaders took over the governments in drought-plagued Upper Volta and Niger. Nigeria's stability seemed threatened by census findings that the Muslim north is gaining population faster than the more Westernized south. And the UN General Assembly voted to suspend South Africa from participating in the 1974 session beeause of its racial policies.

INTRA-AFRICAN RELATIONS

Organization of African Unity. William Eteki Mboumoua of Cameroon succeeded Nzo Ekanghaki as secretary general of the 42-nation Organization of African Unity (OAU) at its June meeting of heads of state in Mogadishu, Somalia. Ekanghaki's resignation followed criticism of his pro-Arab stand in the October 1973 Arab-Israeli war and criticism of his failure to consult members about the conduct of OAU business. Specifically, he was criticized for negotiating a contract with a "colonial and racist company" to advise OAU on oil matters. At the meeting, African leaders expressed disappointment over not getting Arab oil at reduced prices. They accepted in principle an Arab offer of a $200 million loan fund to African states at about 1% interest. OAU delegates also urged Angola's three contentious guerrilla groups to collaborate in order to negotiate independence from Portugal. At his first visit to the United Nations, the new Secretary General Mboumoua said on October 10 that the OAU is giving priority to political liberation and is also concerned about the need for economic liberation.

OCAM. Membership in the Afro-Mauritian Common Organization, better known by its French acronym OCAM, has been reduced from 16 nations at its founding in 1965 to these 10: Central African Republic, Dahomey, Gabon, Ivory Coast, Mauritius, Niger, Rwanda, Senegal, Togo, and Upper Volta. At OCAM's annual meeting in August in Bangui, Central African Republic, the presidents of Gabon and Togo threatened to withdraw their countries unless OCAM faces current realities and reorganizes into a stronger association. The French-speaking organization's final report said that it would try to have more contact and collaboration with English-speaking Africa. OCAM's new officers are Regis Franchet of Mauritius as secretary general and Maj. Gen. Juvenal Habyalimana, Rwanda's president, as chairman.

AFRICA IN WORLD AFFAIRS

United Nations. On October 30 the United States, Britain, and France used their vetoes in the 15-member Security Council against the independent black African drive to expel the Republic of South Africa from the UN because of its apartheid racial policy. This first triple veto in the UN's 29-year history came after 12 days of debate. British, French, and Austrian delegates first sought ways to avoid

INFORMATION HIGHLIGHTS ON THE COUNTRIES OF AFRICA

Nation	Population (in millions)[1]	Capital	Area (in sq. miles)	Head of State and/or Government (as of Dec. 1, 1974)
Algeria	15.8	Algiers	919,593	Houari Boumédienne, president
Botswana	.7	Gaborone	231,804	Sir Seretse Khama, president
Burundi	3.9	Bujumbura	10,747	Michel Micombero, president
Cameroon	6.2	Yaoundé	183,569	Ahmadou Ahidjo, president
Central African Republic	1.6	Bangui	240,535	Jean Bedel Bokassa, president
Chad	4.0	N'Djemena (Fort-Lamy)	495,754	Ngarta Tombalbaye, president
Congo	1.0	Brazzaville	132,047	Marien Ngouabi, president Henri Lopès, prime minister
Dahomey	2.9	Porto-Novo	43,483	Mathieu Kerekou, president
Egypt	36.9	Cairo	386,660	Anwar el-Sadat, president Abdul Aziz Hegazi, premier
Equatorial Guinea	.3	Malabo (Santa Isabel)	10,831	Francisco Macias Nguema, president
Ethiopia	26.8	Addis Ababa	471,777	Military Government
Gabon	.5	Libreville	103,346	Albert B. Bongo, president
Gambia, The	.5	Banjul	4,361	Sir Dauda K. Jawara, president
Ghana	9.9	Accra	92,099	I. K. Acheampong, chairman National Redemption Council
Guinea	4.2	Conakry	94,926	Sékou Touré, president Lansana Beavogui, premier
Guinea-Bissau	.5	Bissau	13,948	Luiz de Almeida Cabral, president
Ivory Coast	4.6	Abidjan	124,503	Félix Houphouët-Boigny, president
Kenya	12.5	Nairobi	224,959	Jomo Kenyatta, president
Lesotho	1.1	Maseru	11,720	Moshoeshoe II, king Leabua Jonathan, prime minister
Liberia	1.7	Monrovia	43,000	William R. Tolbert, president
Libya	2.1	Tripoli and Benghazi	679,360	Muammar el-Qaddafi, president Revolutionary Command Council Abdul Salam Jallud, prime minister
Malagasy Republic	7.5	Tananarive	226,657	Gabriel Ramanantsoa, head of government
Malawi	4.8	Zomba	45,747	H. Kamuzu Banda, president
Mali	5.5	Bamako	478,765	Moussa Traoré, president
Mauritania	1.3	Nouakchott	397,954	Mokhtar O. Daddah, president
Mauritius	.9	Port Louis	720	Sir Rawan Osman, governor-general Sir Seewoosagur Ramgoolam, prime minister
Morocco	17.4	Rabat	172,413	Hassan ii, king Ahmed Osman, premier
Niger	4.3	Niamey	489,190	Seyni Kountche, head of military government
Nigeria	79.7	Lagos	356,668	Yakubu Gowon, president Federal Military Government
Rhodesia	5.8	Salisbury	150,803	Clifford W. Dupont, president Ian D. Smith, prime minister
Rwanda	4.0	Kigali	10,169	Juvenal Habyalimana, president
Senegal	4.2	Dakar	75,750	Léopold S. Senghor, president Abdou Diouf, premier
Sierra Leone	2.9	Freetown	27,700	Siaka P. Stevens, president Sorie I. Koroma, prime minister
Somalia	3.0	Mogadishu	246,200	Mohammed Siad Barre, president Supreme Revolutionary Council
South Africa, Rep. of	23.7	Pretoria and Cape Town	471,444	J. J. Fouché, president Balthazar J. Vorster, prime minister
Sudan	17.4	Khartoum	967,497	Jaafar al-Numeiry, president
Swaziland	.5	Mbabane	6,704	Sobhuza II, king Makhosini Dlamini, prime minister
Tanzania	14.4	Dar es Salaam	364,899	Julius K. Nyerere, president
Togo	2.1	Lomé	21,622	Étienne Eyadema, president
Tunisia	5.6	Tunis	63,170	Habib Bourguiba, president Hedi Nouira, premier
Uganda	10.8	Kampala	91,134	Idi Amin, president
Upper Volta	5.7	Ouagadougou	105,869	Sangoulé Lamizana, president
Zaire	23.6	Kinshasa	905,565	Mobutu Sese Seko, president
Zambia	4.7	Lusaka	290,585	Kenneth D. Kaunda, president Mainza Chona, prime minister

[1] Latest estimate

both expulsion and a big-power veto. But the more than 50 pre-vote speeches were mainly by Africans condemning South Africa. The USSR and China were among the ten nations whose representatives voted for expulsion; two countries abstained. British, French, and U. S. delegates condemned South Africa's racial policy but stressed that expulsion would not change that policy. They also pointed out that expulsion would not permit exploration of recent conciliatory statements from South Africa.

The General Assembly acted against South Africa on November 12 when, by a vote of 91 to 22, it voted to suspend that country from the current session. Nineteen countries abstained from voting. The action barred South Africa from taking its seat, participating in debate, or voting in the session that ends in December 1974. The United States, Britain, and other western European nations opposed the suspension.

On October 23, Prime Minister Balthazar John Vorster had indicated South Africa's willingness to change its racial policy and to offer technical aid to black Africa. Zambia's President Kenneth David Kaunda on October 26 expressed hope that Vorster's statement was "the voice of reason for which Africa and the rest of the world have been waiting." On October 28, South African Foreign Minister Hilgaard Muller praised Kaunda's warm response to Vorster's speech as the path to "détente instead of confrontation."

Foreman-Ali Fight. World attention focused on Kinshasa, Zaire (the former Belgian Congo), on October 30 when Muhammad Ali regained the world's heavyweight championship by knocking out titleholder George Foreman in the eighth round. It was the first heavyweight boxing championship to be held in Africa and the first to be used as a national public relations spectacular.

The Zaire government underwrote the event with $12.1 million; each fighter received $5 million. But one report said that the bout would cost the Zaire government about $4 million because receipts were much below expenses. An estimated 60,000 persons saw the fight in person in Kinshasa's soccer stadium. Fight fans from the United States did not travel to Zaire in large numbers, as was hoped, reportedly because tours to the fight were overpriced. Reported mismanagement and a month's delay because of an eye injury to Foreman were also blamed for the low attendance.

Color videotapes of the fight were shown in North American theaters and stadiums at prime viewing time. About 50 million people saw the bout free on home television, mostly in Central and South America and in Japan. President Mobutu was pleased that the much-ballyhooed event had drawn favorable global attention to Zaire.

United States' Africa Policy. Accounts published in October accused the former Nixon administration of following a policy of favoring

UPI

Lt. Gen. Aman Andom, chairman of the Ethiopian provisional military government, was either executed by the junta or died while resisting arrest in November.

white rulers in southern Africa. The accounts were based on an intergovernmental study dated Aug. 15, 1969, which examined the ramifications of five policy options in southern Africa. Sources claimed that former President Nixon approved following the second option, that of partiality toward white power holders in southern Africa, in the belief that constructive change could come about only through the white power structure. This position was seen as a reversal of the pro-black African policies of former Presidents Kennedy and Johnson. State Department officials discredited the charge of pro-white bias. They said that a combination of suggestions had been considered in policy formulations.

DROUGHT

West Africa. Rains which fell between June and mid-September brought some relief to the former French West African countries in Senegal, Mauritania, Mali, Upper Volta, Niger, and Chad, which have suffered from a catastrophic six-year drought. From 1972 to 1974, U. S. aid to the region, the largest single part of the gigantic world relief effort, totaled about 600,000 tons of grain worth over $121 million. Still, tens of thousands of largely nomadic people have died, along with over 3.5 million cattle in 1973 alone, valued at some $400 million. Up to 5 million people are refugees in crowded camps and towns. Although the rains in 1974 brought some relief, millions will have to be fed for some years to come, and the resulting physical and mental illness will doubtless persist for several generations. The drought is attributed partly to a 30-mile-a-year advance southward of the Sahara Desert and mainly to human failures in raising too many animals which overgraze the limited cover crops.

INGEBORG LIPPMANN/THE NEW YORK TIMES

Guerrillas seeking Angolan independence from Portugal drill on a street in an Angolan town. Angola has been a Portuguese colony for nearly 500 years.

Ethiopia. The military rulers who succeeded Emperor Haile Selassie have accused his government of attempting to keep secret that country's tragic drought. They indicated that in 1973 over 100,000 persons starved to death in the drought that still exists in the Wallo and Tigre provinces of northern and central Ethiopia. On August 30 authorities placed the area under a Relief and Rehabilitation Commission.

PORTUGUESE AFRICA

The April 25 military coup in Portugal, which named former Gen. António de Spínola the provisional president, also shook Africa. Spínola, who had led Portuguese troops against African nationalists in Portuguese Guinea (now Guinea-Bissau), warned in his 1973 book *Portugal and the Future* against Portugal's further loss of blood and treasure in military opposition to African rebels' fighting for independence in the Portuguese territories. Before he resigned on September 30, Spínola accomplished a change of direction in Portugal's African policy. He had set in motion meetings that led to agreements to dismantle Portugal's 500-year-old African empire.

Guinea-Bissau's Independence. On September 10, Portugal joined more than 100 countries, including the United States, in recognizing Guinea-Bissau's independence. The tiny West African territory (510,000 population) known formerly as Portuguese Guinea, had unilaterally declared its independence on Sept. 24, 1973. Its new president is 42-year-old Luiz de Almeida Cabral, head of the African Party for the Independence of Portuguese Guinea and the Cape Verde Islands (PAIGC), which since 1956 had fought a guerrilla war against Portuguese troops. Cape Verde Islands will decide later by ballot either to join the new nation of Guinea-Bissau or to remain with Portugal.

Mozambique Self Rule. Portugal's official representatives met frequently with black guerrilla leaders to reach agreement on granting self-rule to Mozambique, its colony in East Africa (over 8 million blacks, 250,000 whites and Asians). The interim government installed in Mozambique on September 20 consists of six ministers from the Mozambique Liberation Front (FRELIMO) and three ministers appointed by the Portuguese. Full independence is scheduled for June 25, 1975.

Clashes occurred between Portuguese soldiers waiting to return home and FRELIMO troops, sometimes over trivial incidents. In September and October over 150 persons died in such clashes, and many more were injured. A steady flow of nonblacks have left Mozambique. One estimate is that about 27,000 whites, Asians, and mixed-blooded people left in the first six months after the April coup in Portugal which heralded that country's withdrawal from control of its African territories.

Angolan Disunity. Factional quarrels among Angola's three separate African nationalist groups delayed until October 7 the formal cease-fire with Portuguese troops. This biggest and richest Portuguese colony on the Atlantic coast of central Africa has 6.1 million people. By referendum in March 1975, Angola will choose either national independence or a loose federation with Portugal. Meanwhile, deaths and injuries resulted from frequent clashes between the rival nationalist groups. Their leaders, in competition for power, are widely separated by ideology as well as by tribal and regional loyalties. Some residents of the oil-rich enclave of Cabinda have begun a separatist movement. Observers fear that the diverse groups are so irreconcilable that partition may become inevitable when Angola attains independence from Portugal.

ETHIOPIA

Emperor Haile Selassie was dethroned by a military group on September 12, ending more than 50 years of his personal rule and possibly ending 2,000 years of the Ethiopian monarchy. Dethronement of the 83-year-old monarch followed a yeaı of unprecedented strikes and unrest in Ethiopia. A military mutiny in February in Asmara, Ethiopia's second-largest city, which forced the cabinet's resignation and the appointment of Endalkachew Makonnen as premier, marked the first time that the emperor had been forced to make major governmental changes.

A general strike in March and continued military and civil unrest led to emerging rule by a military group called the Armed Forces Coordinating Committee in May. Premier Makonnen was ousted and arrested on July 22 and replaced by Michael Imru. Selassie's supporters were arrested, and he was systematically stripped of power. The royal family was denounced publicly for having profited at the people's expense and for having kept the peasant masses in a feudal state. The television showing on September 11 of a film about the famine disaster in Wallo province, whose details Selassie and his government deliberately kept secret, further turned the public against the former emperor and spurred wide demands for his punishment.

Selassie's 58-year-old son, Prince Asfa Wossen, was named royal successor by the armed forces. But because of popular sentiment against his father as well as a severe stroke he suffered in 1972, observers doubted that he would assume the monarchy. In November the ruling military group, composed mostly of junior officers, executed 60 aristocrats and former officials, including two former premiers and a grandson of Haile Selassie. The leader of the military group, Lt. Gen. Aman Michael Andom, was either executed or died resisting arrest.

MILITARY COUPS

Relatively bloodless military coups occurred in the two drought-stricken former French West African countries of Upper Volta and Niger.

Upper Volta. Military officers on February 8 took over without bloodshed the government of Upper Volta, which has a population of over 5.5 million. Gen. Sangoulé Lamizana, who remained as president, said that the military acted because rival civilian leaders had paralyzed government operations since late January. The new cabinet of the drought-stricken country consisted of 11 military men and 4 civilians.

Niger. In neighboring Niger on April 15 another nearly bloodless military coup toppled Hamani Diori, Niger's president since the country gained independence in 1960. Diori's wife was slain in the military takeover. Leader of the coup and Diori's successor as head of state, Army Chief of Staff Lt. Col. Seyni Kountche, charged the old government with "injustice, corruption, selfishness, and indifference." Observers cited the deposed Diori as an admired moderate and a mediator in inter-African disputes. His fall was attributed in part to the 6-year drought that has affected one fourth of Niger's 4 million population. Also, Diori reportedly irritated France, Niger's major benefactor and trading partner, by seeking investments from other countries.

The Niger coup was Africa's 32d military coup since 1952. Niger became the 15th black African country south of the Sahara to fall under military control. More than half of black Africa, about 130 million people, currently live under military governments. Besides Niger, the military-run countries are Burundi, the Central African Republic, the Congo Republic, Dahomey, Ghana, Mali, Nigeria, Rwanda, Somalia, the Sudan, Togo, Uganda, Upper Volta, and Zaire.

NIGERIA'S CENSUS

Nigeria remained Africa's most populous country, according to preliminary findings of the 1973 national census, reported on May 12. The census put the population at 79,760,000 and showed that two thirds of the people live in the six predominantly Muslim northern provinces.

The census is important politically because it determines representation in Nigeria's national assembly. Results of the preceding census, taken in 1963, revealed that most of the population was then also in the Muslim northern states. Fears about regional rivalry are heightened by the fact that after the 1963 census leaders of the dominant Ibo tribe in the East, arguing that they would be slighted, charged that census figures for their region were inaccurately low. This agitation precipitated Biafra's attempted secession and plunged Nigeria into an agonizing civil war.

Again in 1974 a similar pattern emerged. The Christian southern tribes—which the census says have remained static in population—charge inaccuracies in the 1973 census. The government has ordered a review of the census, whose results are still considered provisional. The controversial census caused head of state Gen. Yakubu Gowon to postpone the intended return of Nigeria to civilian rule, originally planned for 1976. Demands for dividing Nigeria into more states were intensifying, and some proposals called for 20 to 24 states instead of the present 12 states.

OLDEST KNOWN HUMAN REMAINS

Human remains believed to be between 3 million and 4 million years old have been found in central Ethiopia near the Awash River by an American-French-Ethiopian anthropological team. These remains place man's origin earlier than the 2.5 million years indicated by the remains found by Richard Leakey in 1972 in nearby Kenya. (See ANTHROPOLOGY.)

FRANKLIN PARKER, *West Virginia University*

INTER-AMERICAN DEVELOPMENT BANK

A farm worker in a palm nursery in the Valley of Aguán, Honduras, prepares to spray African oil palm trees with a pesticide. Palm oil is widely used for food purposes.

agriculture

In 1974 worldwide agriculture production was below the record level of the previous year. Although adverse weather conditions caused U. S. feed crops to fall below the 1973 record, it was generally a good year for U. S. production. This general roundup of 1974 agricultural developments is divided into three sections: (1) World Agriculture; (2) U. S. Agriculture; and (3) U. S. Agricultural Research.

World Agriculture

The specter of widespread hunger began to haunt the world in 1974, especially in the developing lands. So far, the farm surpluses produced in the decades following World War II have kept the planet shielded from large-scale famine. Also, the development and use of higher-yielding varieties of rice and wheat that occurred in the 1960's further put off the time when world population growth would threaten to outpace food and fiber production.

In 1974 world agricultural production failed to match the record output of 1973. Farm experts said that if the output in 1974 equalled that of 1973 then world reserves of food, particularly grain, could be rebuilt. But this did not happen.

"The world food situation, which in these last two years has caused widespread concern and, in places, considerable human suffering, is again deteriorating," declared Addeke H. Boerma, director-general of the Food and Agriculture Organization of the United Nations. "The situation . . . can be saved, but it will require well-planned, rapid collective action by the international community."

Adverse weather conditions mainly were blamed for 1974's disappointing production. Surprisingly, a major trouble spot was the United States where favorable weather is so regular that it is almost taken for granted by farm economists. But in 1974 drought and high temperatures reduced corn, sorghum, and soybean yields. It was the worst U. S. food-producing weather in perhaps 25 years.

The weather also was bad for food output in South Asia and China. Below-normal precipitation in winter and late monsoon rains reduced crops in India. Flooding plagued Bangladesh.

Bad as the year was for food production, the U. S. Department of Agriculture (USDA) insisted that the inhospitable weather struck only a few key producing areas. "This has tended to obscure the fact that conditions over most of the globe have been generally favorable in 1974," the USDA said in its "World Agricultural Situation" report. "The extended drought in the Sahelian countries of Africa appears to have been broken, and most of the other countries of the world were favored with weather which may have posed problems at times in some areas but nevertheless proved in the long run to be advantageous to crop production."

Expert Views. Don Paarlberg, director of agricultural economics of the USDA, elaborated on this theme in a Philadelphia speech in late 1974. He said that for the next decade or so prospects for world food production are better than in the recent past. "During the past 20 years there has been a slight upward trend in average per-capita food supplies, even in less-developed countries," Paarlberg said. "Despite being poorly nourished, the average man in the developing countries of Asia, Africa, and Latin America is better fed than was his father. He is not fed well enough to meet his full bodily needs, nor enough to satisfy his aspirations . . . . It is possible for men to starve while the per capita supply of food is increasing. Improvement in the average . . . should not be allowed to obscure the problems of the many millions that fall below the average . . . . Objectively measured, the world food situation is not worse than it has historically been; it is marginally better . . . ."

Paarlberg noted that per-capita supplies in the past 20 years have trended upward at an annual rate of about 0.4% in the less developed countries and about 1.5% in the developed countries. The gap between the rich and poor nations may be widening in this regard, he said, but in an "absolute sense" both are improving. Both 1972 and 1974 were bad crop years, he said, but he added: "We think they were an aberration, not the beginning of a new trend. We do not think the recent past is the new normal."

Boerma, Paarlberg, and other experts similarly profess optimism about being able to cope with food-supply problems—if widespread concern over food and food prices can be turned into action on curbing future population growth and providing food in times of emergencies. "With respect to food needs in the world," Paarlberg said, "this is the teachable moment. We must not let it pass unperceived or unused."

World Food Conference. For all these reasons, U. S. Secretary of State Henry A. Kissinger called for a UN World Food Conference to be held in late 1974 to discuss ways to maintain adequate food supplies and to orchestrate the efforts of all nations to meet hunger and malnutrition resulting from natural disasters. The UN General Assembly endorsed the idea. The meeting was held in November in Rome, with up to 140 governments sending delegates.

A main focal point of the Conference quickly became how to establish some sort of world food reserve system. One possibility was to set up an international network of national stockpiles, with countries adopting stockpiling policies that conform to internationally agreed-upon principles. But hardly anyone was certain whether the enormous complexities of the problem could be resolved. Who would hold what commodities? How much? How would it be released for use?

The World Food Conference agenda also included two other main subjects—how to increase food production in developing countries and how to improve consumption in all countries.

The Conference Secretariat, in preparing the agenda, issued a 240-page document entitled "The World Food Problem: Proposals for National and International Action." The document set forth 85 proposals for consideration of the conference. For example, to achieve food security for developing lands, food output through 1985 should increase annually by 3.4% in Asia and the Far East, 3.8% in Africa, 3.6% in Latin America, and 4% in the Near East. This would be as much as 50% faster growth than occurred in these regions in the last 10 years. Failure to achieve these objectives, researchers said, would boost food import bills in these countries to $16 billion annually by 1985, roughly triple their already burdensome levels.

The World Food Conference also was asked to consider providing supplementary food to at least one fourth of the 200 million children in the world who suffer malnutrition or undernutrition. The estimated cost was $20 per child per year.

GEORG GERSTER, FROM RAPHO GUILLUMETTE

In the Patagonian region of Argentina, sheep are herded into pens to be sheared. Wool has long been one of Argentina's most important products for export.

WORLD FARM OUTPUT

Worldwide scarcities and high prices of fuel and fertilizer did not significantly affect the productive capacity of agriculture in the developed countries. Governments granted priority allocations of fuel to farm production and to the transportation and processing of agricultural commodities. However, the energy crisis added to production, processing, and marketing costs of farm commodities and resulted in serious shortages and structural dislocations for some commodities.

Crops. The developed countries—even the United States—had a reasonably bountiful harvest in 1974, although well below expectations. Crop prospects in the Northern Hemisphere lands, particularly for grains, deteriorated during the season.

In Canada heavy spring rains forced farmers to plant less wheat. Then high temperatures and low rainfall in mid-July cut wheat production

PAOLO KOCH, FROM RAPHO GUILLUMETTE

GEORG GERSTER, FROM RAPHO GUILLUMETTE

(*Above*) Japanese workers transplant rice from a nursing bed to a paddy field, where it will grow and ripen. (*Left*) In Indonesia, harvested rice is transported to market.

to about 16 million metric tons, down from 17.1 million in 1973.

Much of Western Europe suffered drought in March and June, followed by heavy rain in July. But crop conditions in the Mediterranean countries, particularly Spain, were more favorable than in 1973. Total grain production in western Europe was about 137 million metric tons, nearly 4 million tons more than in 1973.

Japan, after several years of curtailing rice output because of surplus stocks, had expected some production increase in 1974. However, a serious blight affected 40% of the area planted in rice.

Southern Hemisphere countries are in much better condition with regard to grain. Australia produced 12 million metric tons of wheat, third largest crop on record and nearly double the 1973 crop. In South Africa, the corn crop totaled about 11 million metric tons, far more than in 1973.

Livestock. Supplies of livestock products, particularly meat, generally increased in developed countries in 1974. The European Community banned imports of beef, veal, and live cattle because of sharply increased beef supplies, weak consumer demand, and ample supplies of pork and poultry.

In Japan, beef demand slackened as inflation ripped into household budgets. Canadian beef production was on the rise, and most imports of cattle and beef from the United States were banned.

Although livestock producers were experiencing rising costs and declining prices, farmers raising grain crops continued to receive higher prices, allowing profits even though crop-production costs have risen steeply.

Soviet Union. Farm output in 1974 in the USSR was up slightly from the previous year. It was a record high, but short of the 6.4% increase planned. The weather was mostly favorable, especially in the European part of the country, but it was not as good as in 1973. Output of livestock and livestock products was up more than 5% from 1973, but crop production was down 5%.

The total grain output was about 205 million tons, down 8% from 1973. Much rain during harvesting in European sectors and drought in the Asian sectors cut the quality of the grain. The total harvested grain area was about 128 million hectares (315 million acres), the most since 1965.

Eastern Europe. The grain harvest in eastern Europe in 1975 about matched the record 87 million ton crops of the two previous years. Livestock producers, especially in Poland, East Germany, Czechoslovakia, and Hungary, continued to build up herds and flocks through 1973 and into the first half of 1974, expecting increased demand for beef in western Europe. But most west European governments began restricting imports in February. Consequently, some meat exports were shifted to Russia, North Africa, and the Middle East.

People's Republic of China. Farm production in China, always difficult to assess, appeared good but not exceptional in 1974 despite adverse weather. Excessive moisture hampered winter-wheat sowing, and drought hurt growth. Cold spells in southern China in the spring delayed the early rice crop. But if fall-harvested crops had had favorable weather, China's farm production might have reached 1973's record. Experts noted, however, that China recently had purchased large new quantities of wheat from Canada and Australia. Also, imports of food grains in 1974 continued unabated under previously negotiated agreements.

Asia. In non-Communist developing lands of Asia, farm production in 1974 was about 4% less than in 1973. Although most lands showed increases, output fell sharply in India and Bangladesh and slightly in Thailand and Burma.

Excellent crops were harvested in Indonesia, Malaysia, and Pakistan, while smaller upswings were reported in Sri Lanka, South Vietnam, Taiwan, and the Philippines.

The 1974 Asian rice crop was about 103 million tons, down about 2.5% from 1973.

Latin America. Agricultural output in Latin America in 1974 rose about 6% over the 1973 record. Heavy rainfall damaged some early crops in Argentina, Chile, and Brazil, and Mexico's sorghum harvest was reduced by dry weather. General weather conditions improved, however, as almost normal moisture returned to the Caribbean and bordering areas in South America, including Colombia and Venezuela, following a two-year drought. Grain harvests were near-record size in Argentina and Brazil. Coffee production recovered, and the region's production of sugar and oilseeds rose in response to higher prices. Smaller gains were made in the output of bananas and livestock products.

Earnings from exports of petroleum, minerals, and farm products helped offset sharply increased costs of imports in Latin America. Foreign-exchange reserves exceeded December 1973 values in all countries except Costa Rica, Haiti, Chile, Guyana, Peru, and Uruguay.

Africa. African farm production rose significantly in 1974 from the depressed levels of 1973. Record grain crops in South Africa, good grain output in North African countries, improved moisture conditions in West Africa in the Sahelian drought zone, and the reduced scope of East African drought were important factors in the year's improved results.

More coffee, cocoa beans, cotton, and peanuts—major export crops of Africa—were produced in 1974. The production gain in Africa reversed the downward trend in per-capita food output in the past few years.

Middle East. In Middle Eastern lands, the wheat crop failed to meet early expectations. Iran had an average wheat crop, while Turkey's wheat yield was below average size. Large oil earnings by Arabian Peninsula countries, Iraq, and Iran, were being used to import vast new quantities of wheat and rice.

JOE WESTERN
Senior Editor, "The National Observer"

Geneticist Virgil A. Johnson examines new strains of wheat that will be harvested and the seeds used for improving the nutritional value of future winter wheats.

AGRICULTURAL RESEARCH SERVICE, U. S. DEPT. OF AGRICULTURE

U. S. Agriculture

For U. S. agriculture, 1974 was quite a good year for production—but not an outstanding one. Because output fell short of expectations, many farmers and government officials said results were disappointing. Production of the key feed crops—corn, grain sorghums, and soybeans—was down from 1973's record levels because of adverse weather. But because planted acreage expanded, production of some other crops was record high—particularly wheat and rice. Production of meat and meat products was up from 1973 totals. Realized net farm income fell substantially from 1973's record high.

Production. In 1974, U. S. farm output of crops and livestock reached an index number of 109 (1967 = 100), down from the previous record of 112 in 1973. The 1974 production index was the lowest since 1970.

Plantings for harvest totaled 329 million acres (133,141,570 hectares), up 8 million acres (3,237,490 hectares) from 1973, also a year of expansion of plantings. Yields per acre were subpar for most crops. The unfavorable growing weather accounted for much of the decline in per-acre yields, but another reason was that the additional acres planted in crops included much land that was less productive than acreage already in use.

After recovery in 1973 from the generally poor worldwide farm production of 1972, many governments, including the United States, removed almost all planting restrictions in the hope of building reserves of food and fiber. In the United States, the year began hopefully, with farm economists confidently assuming production would be a record.

But spring rains delayed plantings. Drought followed. And then frost in September, earlier than usual, stopped growth of most of the corn crop, the largest of all U. S. crops. The total U. S. crop production index was placed at 110, down from 120 in 1973.

The U. S. Department of Agriculture reported that the corn crop totaled about 4.7 billion bushels, far below the more than 6 billion bushels predicted earlier by government officials.

The 1974 corn crop turned out to be 18% smaller than that of the previous year. Total production of feed grains—the raw materials for meat and milk, namely corn, grain sorghums, oats, and barley—totaled about 165 million tons, down 20% from 1973's outturn. Production of soybeans, source of another key animal feed, was placed at about 1.2 billion bushels, down 20% from 1973. Although disappointing, it was still the third-largest soybean crop of record.

Production of all oilseeds—soybeans, cottonseed, peanuts, and flaxseed—was put at 44.4 million tons, down 18% from 1973.

Nevertheless, production was record high for wheat at 1.8 billion bushels, 4% more than in 1973. Rice output was placed at a record 5.2 million tons, up from 4.2 million tons in 1973. Output of food grains—wheat, rice, and rye—was about 60 million tons, up 5% from 1973.

Other record-high production was achieved for peanuts, dry beans, oranges, lemons, and grapes. The production of oranges climbed to about 234 million boxes, 8% more than in 1973 and 4% more than the previous high in 1972.

Livestock and livestock products reached a production index number of 109, up from 105 in 1973. Cattle slaughter was larger than expected because drought and high feed prices led farmers to cull herds more severely than in recent years. Total slaughter for 1974 was more than 6% larger than in the previous year and may have reached the record kill of 35.8 million head in 1972.

Pork production was up about 7% from 1973, but still 4% below that of 1972. Broiler-chicken output was about the same as in the previous year, but turkey production was up substantially. Milk production was about 1.5% less than the 115.6 billion pounds produced in 1973.

Income. Realized net income for 1974 was about $26.5 billion, down from the previous year's extraordinary record of $32.2 billion. Rising prices for crops more than offset lower prices for many livestock prices. Government payments to farmers, mostly for holding land out of unwanted production, were sharply reduced to encourage farmers to plant more crops, especially grain crops. Government payments totaled only about $600 million, down from $2.6 billion in 1973. Farm net income also was reduced by sharply higher prices paid for fuel and fertilizer.

Retail food prices were about 15% higher than in 1973; prices of vegetable oil end-products, cereal and bakery items, beverages, and sugar products rose more than the average.

Exports. In the fiscal year ended June 30, 1974, U. S. agricultural exports rose to a record of more than $21 billion, 67% more than in the previous 12 months. Most of the gain occurred because prices rose so steeply; export volume increased only 10%.

Largest gains in value sold abroad were for wheat, feed grains, and soybeans. The People's Republic of China showed the largest value increase in buying U. S. food and fiber, although Japan remained the single most important market. Exports to the USSR fell sharply, mostly because of lower Soviet wheat purchases.

The surge in world demand for meat fueled the rapid growth in purchases of U. S. feeds. But that demand is expected to slacken in 1975 because of smaller U. S. feed-grain production, higher prices, larger foreign production, and a slowdown in foreign economic activity.

Exports of animals and animal products rose by one-third in value to $1.8 billion, mostly for live cattle, poultry meat, and inedible tallow.

Consumption. U. S. per capita consumption recovered in 1974 from the previous year's lower intake. Index of per capita consumption in 1974 was placed at a record 103.7 (1967 = 100), up from 102 in 1973. Larger consumption of meat, poultry, fruit, potatoes, cereals, and sweeteners accounted for most of the increase.

Assets and Land Values. Farm real-estate values rose 15% in 1974 to a record $324.2 billion. Average value per acre rose to $310, up $63 from a year earlier. The index of farm real-estate values rose a record 25% for the year ended March 1, 1974. The index reached 187 (1967 = 100). Since 1967 the index has increased at an average annual rate of 9.24%.

JOE WESTERN
Senior Editor, "The National Observer"

U. S. Agricultural Research

The Agricultural Research Service (ARS) of the U. S. Department of Agriculture is the principal agricultural research agency of the federal government. Its chief objective is to carry on a balanced program of agricultural research and development that will provide an ever-increasing population with wholesome, inexpensive food despite limited acres for production; the ravages of insects, diseases, and natural catastrophes; and increasingly complex problems of distribution, marketing, and energy shortages.

Ways to produce more edible protein at a reasonable consuming cost are under constant study. One way to lower production costs and energy inputs is to breed crops resistant to pests and diseases. For example, a strain of corn from South America may provide resistance to corn earworms. Experimental varieties of alfalfa resistant to anthracnose, a disease that damages more than 4 million acres annually, have outyielded several commercial varieties by at least 1 ton per acre in field tests. This is a major breakthrough in incorporating disease resistance in forage crops.

ARS scientists recently developed three breeding lines of wheat that have potential for improving the protein value of future hard red winter wheats. A recent discovery by an ARS plant breeder—a soybean line with the male sterile character—has brought hybrid soybeans one step closer to reality. Although this is not the soybean needed to vitalize commercial production, it does have the male-sterile character needed for developing new plant material.

Long-term beef studies begun in Nebraska in 1957 have shown that crossbreeding improves beef production efficiency. Crossbreeding takes advantage of hybrid vigor, the response in an animal from the cross of parents carrying many unlike genes. In one part of the study, crossbred steers gained 2.9% more than straightbred steers in the feedlot. Crossbreeding generally reduced significantly the age when heifers reached puberty, reduced the interval from calving to first estrus, and advanced the average date of conception. Hereford, Angus, and Shorthorn cattle, with all possible crosses, are being used in this continuing study.

UPI

Iowa farm couple Jim and Mary Peterson look grimly at a field of burned-up corn. A long summer drought scorched the corn and soybean crops throughout the Midwest.

A long-range program to computerize detailed information on the nutrient composition of thousands of foods has begun. The Nutrient Data Bank will provide data useful in nutritional labeling of packaged and processed food.

ARS scientists have developed an appealing, nutritionally balanced and protein-rich candy from corn syrup, nonfat dry milk, and other ingredients.

ARS scientists also have tried making potato chips with the potato peel left on. Consumers found no difference between them and conventional potato chips. The unpeeled variety has the advantages of lowering costs by eliminating a processing step, eliminating a waste-disposal problem, and probably providing greater nutritional value. Commercial development must await further tests.

MARCELLA M. MEMOLO
U. S. Agricultural Research Service

ALABAMA

Alabama experienced the effects of the nationwide energy crisis early in 1974, but as the energy problem abated, the people's attention was drawn to other developments, especially politics and the weather.

Energy Crisis. In Alabama the energy crisis took the form of a shortage of gasoline and other petroleum products during the winter of 1973–74. Problems caused by the fuel shortage were heightened in February by the strike of independent truckers. As a result of the truckers' strike, the gasoline shortage in various localities became particularly acute. The Federal Energy Office provided a measure of relief through allocations of additional quantities of gasoline to Alabama and other states where the shortages were especially severe. By spring, the energy situation had achieved some degree of normalcy, except for the increased price of petroleum products.

Severe Weather. Alabama experienced unusually violent weather in the spring of 1974. On the night of April 3, a series of tornadoes struck a number of Southern and Midwestern states, including Alabama. The tornadoes, which left 73 people dead in Alabama and caused extensive damage to homes and other property, were described as the worst in Alabama in almost 50 years. In such areas as Jasper, Guin, and Huntsville, the storms were especially destructive.

Elections. In the May 7 Democratic primary Gov. George C. Wallace won renomination over several opponents, only one of whom, State Senator Eugene McLain, offered substantial opposition. The most interesting state races were those for lieutenant governor and for a place on the Public Service Commission. In the first primary, incumbent Lt. Gov. Jere Beasley ran second to former gubernatorial candidate Charles Woods. In the race for the seat on the Public Service Commission, a youthful consumer advocate, Jim Zeigler, forced veteran incumbent C. C. Owen into a runoff. In the June 4 second primary, Lt. Gov. Beasley defeated Woods and Zeigler defeated Owen to secure the Democratic nominations. In other notable races, U. S. Sen. James B. Allen won renomination, and a woman, Mrs. Janie Shores, was nominated for a position on the state supreme court.

In the November general election, Wallace was reelected to an unprecedented third term over the Republican candidate, Elvin McCary, whose strength at the polls was minimal. Lt. Gov. Beasley defeated his Republican opponent, Don Collins. Senator Allen, Mrs. Shores, and Zeigler had no Republican opposition in the general election. Allen and Zeigler, who were opposed by candidates of minor parties, were elected with little difficulty. Mrs. Shores was unopposed. In the Sixth Congressional District, incumbent Representative John Buchanan defeated the Democratic nominee, Nina Miglionico, a veteran member of the Birmingham city council, by a surprisingly large margin. In the Seventh Congressional District, Democrat Walter Flowers, who had achieved national prominence as a member of the House Judiciary Committee during its deliberations on the impeachment of President Nixon, was reelected without Republican opposition.

It was thought that the reapportionment of 1972, which became effective at the 1974 legislative election, would have a profound effect on the composition of the state legislature. It was also predicted that the legislative districts created by the reapportionment would cause a great deal of confusion in the legislative election because they crossed conventional voting lines. In general, the predictions of profound change and great difficulty failed to materialize. However, the number of black legislators increased substantially, and the number of inexperienced members of the House seemed relatively high.

Other Developments. The Federal Communications Commission (FCC) tentatively voted in September not to renew the Alabama Educational Television Commission's license to operate the state's public television network. The action was based on charges of racial discrimination in employment and programming during the late 1960's. The indications were that the television commission's operations were now on a satisfactory basis, and efforts were being made to assure the availability of public television throughout the state.

The state government ended its fiscal year (September 30) with substantial surpluses in its two major state funds. The surpluses were generally regarded as reflecting not so much any real growth in the economy as the effects of inflation.

In October the U. S. Supreme Court sustained a state supreme court decision that upheld a 1943 Alabama statute imposing weight limits on trucks operating in the state.

JAMES D. THOMAS
The University of Alabama

ALABAMA • Information Highlights

Area: 51,609 square miles (133,667 sq km).
Population (1973 est.): 3,539,000.
Chief Cities (1970 census): Montgomery, the capital, 133,386; Birmingham, 300,910; Mobile, 190,026.
Government: (1974): *Chief Officers*—governor, George C. Wallace (D); lt. gov., Jere Beasley (D); *Legislature*—Senate, 35 members (35 D); House of Representatives, 106 members (104 D, 2 R).
Education (1973–74): *Enrollment*—public elementary schools, 397,107 pupils; public secondary, 373,632; nonpublic, 52,100; colleges and universities, 125,076 students. *Public school expenditures,* $518,866,000 ($716 per pupil).
State Finances (fiscal year 1973): *Revenues,* $1,889,867,700; *expenditures,* $1,767,650,000.
Personal Income (1973): $13,180,000,000; per capita, $3,724.
Labor Force (July 1974): *Nonagricultural wage and salary earners,* 1,158,700.

ALYESKA PIPELINE SERVICE COMPANY

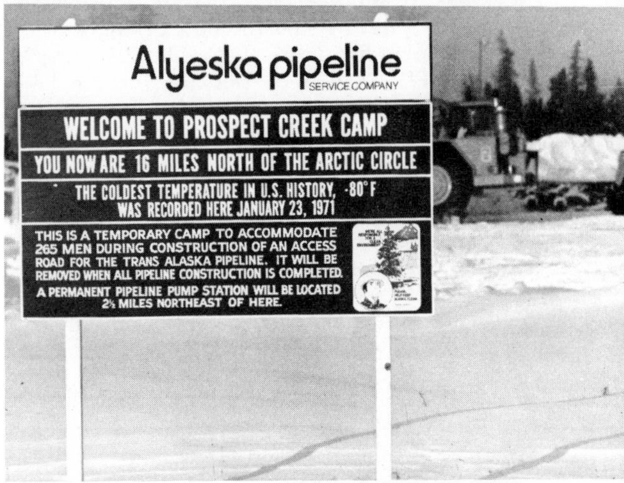

ALYESKA PIPELINE SERVICE COMPANY

Work on the trans-Alaska pipeline. (*Above*) Tractor convoy hauls materials and equipment over a rugged winter trail before the spring thaw makes movement impossible. (*Right*) Entrance to a work camp being built to support construction of the 798-mile (1,284-km) pipeline.

ALASKA

During 1974 the political, social, and economic impact of pipeline construction dominated Alaskan life.

Political Scene. On November 5, Alaskans went to the polls to select a governor, a U. S. senator, a U. S. congressman, and a new state legislature. In an extremely close race, Gov. William Egan (D) lost in his reelection bid to Jay S. Hammond. A colorful state senator with an interest in conservation, Hammond had outpolled Walter J. Hickel, former governor and U. S. secretary of the interior, in the Republican primary. In the Senate race, Mike Gravel (D) gained another term by defeating C. R. Lewis, a national officer of the John Birch Society. State Sen. William L. Hensley was unsuccessful in his attempt to become the first Eskimo to sit in Congress. He lost to Rep. Donald E. Young (R). The new state legislature will be dominated by Democrats.

ALASKA • Information Highlights

Area: 586,412 square miles (1,518,807 sq km).
Population (1973 est.): 330,000.
Chief Cities (1970 census): Juneau, the capital, 6,050; Anchorage, 48,081; Fairbanks, 14,771.
Government (1974): *Chief Officers*—governor, William A. Egan (D); lt. gov., H. A. Boucher (D). *Legislature*—Senate, 20 members (11 R, 9 D); House of Representatives, 40 members (20 D, 19 R, 1 Independent).
Education (1973–74): *Enrollment*—public elementary schools, 48,180 pupils; public secondary schools, 34,325; nonpublic schools, 600; colleges and universities, 14,184 students. *Public school expenditures,* $125,419,000 ($1,597 per pupil).
State Finances (fiscal year 1973): *Revenues,* $466,556,000; *expenditures,* $646,098,000.
Personal Income (1973): $1,852,000,000; per capita, $5,613.
Labor Force (July 1974): *Nonagricultural wage and salary earners,* 127,400.

Also during the primary election, Alaskans voted by a substantial margin to move the state capital from Juneau to a more central location, so that state government would be more accessible to the people of the state. The governor was to appoint a commission to evaluate the move, which could take until 1980. As in many other states, Alaskans approved a conflict-of-interest proposition requiring nearly all officials to report amounts and sources of all income above $100.

The eighth Alaskan Legislature created an Election Campaign Commission to oversee the use of campaign funds by candidates for public office. All candidates are required to submit reports detailing expenditures and the total amount received from contributors. Any contribution of $100 or more must be reported with the name and address of the person making it. Annual contributions of more than $1,000 to one candidate are prohibited.

Social Scene. With construction beginning on the trans-Alaska oil pipeline, Alaskans braced for an influx of people hoping to work in pipeline construction and related areas. Among the anticipated problems were those of increased strain on educational facilities and housing. The latter is already at a premium. Construction of new schools and expansion of existing ones were considered in 1974 and in some cases approved. Rent control legislation, introduced by Senator Hensley, was passed late in the legislative session to limit the soaring costs of housing and to control evictions from rental property. Alaskans approved a $39.5 million bond issue to improve facilities on the campuses of the University of Alaska. Alaska Methodist University prepared to close and sell its property to the University of Alaska.

Concern that the migration of persons seeking employment in Alaska would create increased burdens on the state's social service and law-enforcement agencies gave impetus to attempts to improve the provision of these services. Despite the construction of the pipeline over the next five years, state officials expressed doubt that it would be possible for the labor market to absorb the large numbers of job-seekers from outside Alaska.

Alaskan fisheries suffered throughout the year from foreign competition, especially from the Soviet Union and Japan. Extension of the fishing boundaries to 200 miles off the coast gained widespread support as the fishing industry contemplated a bleak future with catches declining in quality and quantity. In the late summer Governor Egan declared Bristol Bay a disaster area because of the decline in fishing, and requested federal aid for the area.

Pipeline. Construction activities on the trans-Alaskan pipeline began in earnest early in 1974 with the establishment of camps for housing workers along the corridor. On September 29, a 360-mile state road was opened from the Yukon River to Prudhoe Bay. The road will open the Arctic to year-round surface transportation for the first time in history, once a permanent bridge is constructed over the Yukon. Completion date for the Yukon River Bridge is set for December 1975. In the meantime, during the winter an ice bridge will link the north and south banks of the river, and during the summer a combination ferry and ground-effect vehicle will be used.

With the beginning of pipeline construction, debate arose concerning the proper route for a second pipeline to transport natural gas. One proposal was to build the line from the Prudhoe gas fields through the Canadian Mackenzie fields to reenter the United States in the Middle West. The second route proposed was to build in the corridor being used for the oil pipeline. Such a route would allow Alaskan communities to tap into the gas line for local industrial development and construction. Alaskans favor an all-Alaskan route, which would provide additional resources for the state.

ANDREA R. C. HELMS
University of Alaska

ALBANIA

The year 1974 marked the 30th anniversary of the Communist seizure of power in Albania. For the first time since 1960 there were indications of serious policy differences within the inner circle of the Albanian leadership.

Political Developments. At its July 25–26 meeting, the Central Committee of the Albanian Party of Labor (APL) approved a series of measures designed to "further strengthen" the nation's defense capabilities. Following this meeting there were several major leadership changes in the Defense Ministry. The most important of these was the ouster of Defense Minister Beqir Balluku. A member of the APL Politburo from 1948, Balluku had also served as deputy prime minister from the early 1950's. Balluku's removal from his party and state posts apparently stemmed from his opposition to the regime's refusal to moderate its hard-line anti-Soviet policies. Prime Minister Mehmet Shehu assumed the additional duties of the post of defense minister.

In late October, Finance Minister Aleks Verli and Communications Minister Milo Qirko were also dropped from the cabinet. Lefter Goga was appointed finance minister and Luan Babamento was named to the position of communications minister.

According to official returns, only 2 of the 1,248,530 voters who participated in the October 6 parliamentary elections failed to endorse the candidates of the party-dominated Democratic Front.

The Ideological and Cultural Revolution. The cultural crackdown initiated during 1973 continued in high gear. It appears the regime is still not satisfied with the progress being made toward eliminating "all traces of the religious mentality" and other "backward social practices" in the countryside. In the urban areas only modest gains seem to have been made in overcoming worker apathy and student unrest.

The Economy. During 1973, industrial production increased by 10.5% and agricultural output rose by 7%. According to the 1974

ALBANIA • Information Highlights

Official Name: People's Republic of Albania.
Location: Southern Europe, Balkan peninsula.
Area: 11,100 square miles (28,748 sq km).
Population (1973 est.): 2,300,000.
Chief Cities (1970 est.): Tiranë, the capital, 171,300; Shkodër, 55,300; Dürres, 53,800.
Government: *Head of state,* Haxhi Lleshi, president of the Presidium (took office 1953). *Head of government,* Maj. Gen. Mehmet Shehu, premier (took office 1954). *First secretary of the Albanian Party of Labor,* Gen. Enver Hoxha (took office 1941). *Legislature* (unicameral)—People's Assembly.
Monetary Unit: Lek (4 leks equal U. S.$1, July 1974).
Gross National Product (1971 est.): $1,040,000,000.
Manufacturing (major products): Processed foods, textiles, cement, tobacco products.
Major Agricultural Products: Corn, sugar beets, wheat, cotton, tobacco, potatoes.

economic plan, industrial output was expected to be 8% greater and agricultural production was foreseen to be 27% higher than in 1973.

Foreign Relations. On October 3, Enver Hoxha, first secretary of the APL, delivered a major foreign policy address in which he reiterated his determined opposition to rapprochement with the United States and the Soviet Union. Hoxha's remarks on this issue apparently were intended not only for foreign consumption, but also to silence those elements within the Albanian party and leadership that favored a policy of détente with one or both of the "superpowers."

Throughout his speech, Hoxha sought to stress that Albania was not isolated and that its international prestige had never been higher. Perhaps the most surprising aspect of the Hoxha address was his appeal to Greece and Yugoslavia to join with Albania in opposing any aggression against their respective territories. From the tone and content of the Hoxha speech, it was obvious that Albania is concerned about the possibility of Soviet moves against the three Balkan states still outside the Soviet camp.

Albanian-Chinese relations continued to be extremely cordial during 1974. The Chinese retained their position as Albania's chief trading partner and donor of technical assistance, and cultural exchanges between the two nations continued to grow. There was apparently some concern within the Albanian ruling hierarchy regarding the potential impact on the Sino-Albanian relationship of the leadership changes expected to occur in China in the near future. This concern may have caused some Albanian officials, especially in the military sector, to question the regime's policy of almost total dependence on China for military, economic, and diplomatic support.

The APL staunchly opposed the Soviet effort to convene a conference of world Communist parties. It viewed this move as an "ill-disguised maneuver" to formally expel the Albanians and Chinese from the world Communist movement. During the year the APL sought to strengthen its ties with the pro-Peking "Marxist-Leninist" parties of western Europe, and revolutionary organizations in the Middle East, Africa, and Asia.

There was extensive coverage of the Watergate scandal in the Albanian press. The Albanians interpreted President Nixon's forced resignation as a manifestation of the "rottenness and deep crisis" of the U. S. political system. They branded President Ford a "loyal follower of the Nixon-Kissinger imperialist policy" and indicated that the change of administrations would not result in any improvement in Albanian-U. S. relations.

NICHOLAS C. PANO
Western Illinois University

ALBERTA

The year 1974 was one of problems and progress for Alberta, with some labor unrest and agricultural setbacks. The energy crisis caused higher prices but no diminution in fuel supplies in the province.

Industry, Labor, and Agriculture. Labor unrest in both public and private sectors presented difficulties, as did inflation. A wet fall in 1973, followed by extremely heavy snow and a late, wet spring with poor weather thereafter, caused some diminution of grain crops. Rising feed costs and erratic beef prices disturbed the cattle market. However, by the end of 1974, construction, especially in Edmonton and Calgary, was approaching and perhaps surpassing record levels, and unemployment had dropped under 2%, the lowest in Canada.

The labor shortage was particularly acute in the province's oil-sand area, where a second billion-dollar plant was being constructed. Its predecessor, near Fort McMurray, was becoming profitable, after several years' operation, despite some technical problems.

Politics and Government. At the July federal election, Alberta's return of a full slate of 19 Conservative opposition members reflected the continuing federal-provincial controversy over control and taxation of Alberta's publicly owned oil and gas resources.

The province's purchase in August of Pacific Western Airlines, a charter and scheduled airline, Canada's third largest, sparked criticisms; nevertheless Premier Lougheed's Progressive Conservative government appeared to enjoy continued public support. Two popular measures were the province's assumption of almost all education costs, a move made possible by an anticipated billion-dollar budget surplus, and its increased support of cultural activities.

Education. Urban expansion, coupled with declining elementary enrollment, resulted in classroom shortages in some areas and surpluses in others, as well as in unpopular pupil busing.

JOHN W. CHALMERS
University of Alberta

ALBERTA • Information Highlights

Area: 255,285 square miles (661,189 sq km).
Population (1974 est.): 1,709,000.
Chief Cities (1971 census): Edmonton, the capital, 438,152; Calgary, 403,319; Lethbridge, 41,217.
Government (1974): *Chief Officers*—lt. gov., J. W. Grant MacEwan; premier, Peter Lougheed (Progressive Conservative); chief justice, Sidney Bruce Smith. *Legislature*—Legislative Assembly, 75 members (49 P. C.; 24 Social Credit, 1 New Democratic party, 1 Independent).
Education (1972–73): *Enrollment:* public elementary and secondary schools, 434,215 pupils; private, 5,403; Indian (federal) schools, 3,409; colleges and universities, 27,764 students.
Public Finance (fiscal year 1973): *Revenues,* \$1,310,900,000; *expenditures,* \$1,479,200,000.
Personal Income (1972): \$6,217,000,000; average annual income per person, \$3,349.
(All monetary figures are in Canadian dollars.)

ALGERIA

An acknowledged spokesman for the Third World, Algeria in 1974 used the financial windfall occasioned by oil-price increases to strike out on a conservative path of economic planning designed to prepare the nation for the day the oil runs out.

Building the Economy. In the spring, the government of President Houari Boumédienne introduced a new four-year development plan emphasizing small and medium-size industries and agricultural reform. The country used its oil and natural gas to barter for development assistance. Promising Japan up to 100 million tons of crude oil a year, Algeria received in return agreement for Japanese participation in about 20 projects, ranging from petrochemicals to steel and mining. In similar exchanges, West Germany and Spain became partners in Algerian development.

By July, a glut of crude oil on the market had made the resource a slightly less valuable bargaining tool. Algeria was the first member of the Organization of Petroleum Exporting Countries to cut prices in order to hold on to customers who might otherwise stray to other producers. It hoped to avoid a reduction of the flow of revenue necessitated by its ambitious program of industrialization.

About 25% of the Algerian gross national product, estimated at $8.5 billion, was derived from oil and gas. But at the rate the state oil and natural gas concern is expanding, the resources could run out within 15 years. While the oil and gas industries are fairly sophisticated, other segments of the economy—on which Algerians will have to depend when the resources are gone—are not as well organized. Boumédienne has therefore earmarked about $10 million a year to pay U. S. consulting firms to diagnose the managerial and financial ills of the nation's industries and suggest solutions that will jibe with the country's socialist philosophy.

Despite problems of organization, observers from East and West have begun to see Algeria as a model for all Third World countries. There is activity in all segments of the economy, and Algerians are in positions of authority in all areas of political and commercial life. It is a young country, with 60% of the population under age 20, which is somewhat less of a problem now that education has been made compulsory up to age 16.

The Maghreb. Boumédienne visited with Tunisian President Habib Bourguiba soon after the aging Bourguiba had finally rebuffed the political-federation attempts by Libya's Colonel Muammar el-Qaddafi. Algeria's negative reaction to the proposed Arab Islamic Republic had been outspoken, despite Libyan hints that Algeria was to be asked to join. Boumédienne felt Algeria had not been consulted and feared the proposed federation would break up the traditional Maghreb (Algeria, Tunisia, Morocco) by including Libya to the exclusion of Morocco. Another fear, barely articulated but acutely felt, was Boumédienne's reluctance to have at his borders a country dominated by Libya's somewhat impulsive Qaddafi, seen by Algeria as willing to sacrifice Arab unity on the altar of his own Islamic dream.

Foreign Relations. As spokesman for the world's primary producers, Boumédienne called for a special session of the UN General Assembly to discuss the problems of raw-materials producers and economic development. By urging producers of such products as coffee, cacao, and copper to follow the example of the oil producers, Boumédienne pitted himself against U. S. Secretary of State Henry Kissinger, who warned developing nations against such moves.

But if thawing U. S.-Algerian relations remained frosty on this one point, Algeria's dark days with France seemed to be brightening, despite a temporary French ban on Algerian immigrant labor. In effect, Algeria and France were brought together by what they perceived as a new American attempt to dominate not only the producer nations with threats of nonassistance but Europe as well, by asking oil consumers to present a united front.

In other international arenas, the ascendancy of the Algerians was evident. Abdel Aziz Bouteflika, Algerian foreign minister, was elected president of the UN General Assembly in the fall, at a time when Arab diplomatic activity was at an all-time high. Boumédienne was credited with bringing Portuguese and Guinea-Bissau nationalists together in talks that finally brought independence to the former Portuguese territory.

The United States and Algeria reestablished diplomatic relations on November 12, when the two nations exchanged ambassadors for the first time since Algeria broke ties during the 1967 Arab-Israeli war. Diplomatic relations thus mirrored trade relations between the two countries, which have long been healthy.

ROBERT L. DENERSTEIN and NANCY MCKEON
The African-American Institute

ALGERIA • Information Highlights

Official Name: Democratic and Popular Republic of Algeria.
Location: North Africa.
Area: 919,593 square miles (2,381,741 sq km).
Population (1973 est.): 15,800,000.
Chief Cities (1966 census): Algiers, the capital, 943,142; Oran, 328,257; Constantine, 253,649.
Government: *Head of state,* Houari Boumédienne, president (took office June 1965). *Head of government,* Houari Boumédienne.
Monetary Unit: Dinar (4.136 dinars equal U. S.$1, March 1974).
Gross National Product (1974 est.): $8,500,000,000.
Manufacturing (major products): Processed foods, textiles, leather goods, liquefied natural gas, cement, petroleum products.
Major Agricultural Products: Wheat, citrus fruits, wine grapes, cork, olives, dates, figs, tobacco, fish, livestock.
Foreign Trade (1973): *Exports,* $1,900,000,000; *imports,* $2,236,900,000.

SCRIPPS INSTITUTION OF OCEANOGRAPHY, UNIV. OF CALIFORNIA, SAN DIEGO

A 50,000-year-old San Diego Paleo-Indian skull, whose age was determined by a new process, places man's arrival in the New World earlier than once thought.

ANTHROPOLOGY

The 72d annual meeting of the American Anthropological Association (AAA) was held in New Orleans late in 1973, and Ernestine Friedl of Duke University took office as president for 1974. In other developments, Margaret Mead, internationally known anthropologist, was elected president of the American Association for the Advancement of Science, and the 43d annual meeting of the American Association of Physical Anthropologists was held at the University of Massachusetts at Amherst.

Ethiopian Fossil Discovery. In October 1974 it was revealed that hominid jawbone relics found near the Awash River in north central Ethiopia might possibly be 1.5 million years older than the skull and leg bones found by Dr. Richard Leakey in 1972 near Lake Rudolf in Kenya and estimated to be 2.6 million years old. A complete upper jaw and parts of an upper and a lower jaw, all with teeth, were found by an expedition led by Dr. Carl Johanson of Case Western Reserve University and the Cleveland Museum of National History, and by Dr. Maurice Taieb of the French Scientific Research Center. Preliminary dating placed these manlike relics at between 3 and 4 million years old and indicated that the origins of man might well go back over 4 million years. Further tests will be needed to verify both the age of these relics and the fact that they represent ancestors of modern man.

Conference on Early Hominids. Prior to the Ethiopian discovery, a conference on early hominids was held in New York City in January 1974. Sponsored by the Wenner-Gren Foundation for Anthropological Research, the National Science Foundation, and New York University, the organizer of the public sessions, Clifford J. Jolly, said the conference was designed for an overall fresh start in organizing the evidence accumulating from East African sites where new fossils have been found.

Many of the major researchers were present, among them W. W. Bishop, Bedford College, London; Richard Leakey, director of the National Museum, Nairobi, Kenya; Carl Johanson of Case Western Reserve University; and C. K. Brain, curator of the Transvaal Museum, Pretoria, South Africa.

There was general acknowledgment that data from six different sites still left human ancestry obscured. The findings from Olduvai Gorge in Tanzania north to the newly discovered site of Hadar in the Afar Triangle region of Ethiopia show a successful adaptation to the environment. Several speakers referred to the need for more paleoecological studies and more precise dating methods.

New Dating Method. A new method of dating bone has been reported in *Science* (vol. 184, May 17, 1974) by Jeffrey L. Bada, Roy Schroeder (both of Scripps Institution of Oceanography), and George F. Carter (Texas A & M University). The method depends on the gradual change that occurs in amino acids over a period of time. Through the use of this technique, human bones found in a sea cliff near Del Mar, Calif., have been dated at 48,000 years old, indicating that humans have been in North America longer than previously thought. This dating method is considered potentially of major significance because the carbon-14 method is reliable only some 40,000 years into the past.

Other Reports. China has made preparations to begin excavating at Choukoutien, the site where the fossilized bones of Peking man (*Homo erectus*) were found in the 1920's.

The Brazilian Indian Foundation said that a party of ethnologists had made contact with a tribe of fair-skinned, blue-eyed Indians in the Para jungle in northern Amazonia. They are known as the Iixuna after the river that flows through their lands. The foundation believes that they may be descendants of whites kidnapped by the Indians, a common practice.

New Books. New books published in 1974 reflect the growing interest in cultural ecology, the reassessment of women's roles in human society, and the study of urban environments. Major works in these areas were: *Anthropologists in Cities,* by George Foster and Robert V. Kemper; *Urban Anthropology,* edited by Aidan Southall; *Women, Culture and Society,* edited by Michelle Zimbalist Rosaldo and Louise Lamphere; and *Ecology and Change,* by C. Gregory Knight.

HERMAN J. JAFFE
Brooklyn College, City University of New York

UNIVERSITY OF CALIFORNIA, BERKELEY

California Music Professor Richard Crocker plays oldest-known music, worked out from ancient inscriptions by Assyriology Professor Anne Kilmer (*right*), on replica of lyre built by Physics Professor Robert Brown (*center*).

archaeology

Archaeologists are expressing renewed concern over the rate of destruction and despoliation of archaeological resources. With the advent of all-terrain vehicles and the inflationary rise in value of archaeological treasures and art-oriented artifacts, federal officials in the United States are concerned over their inability to effectively monitor access to federally managed public lands and historical sites. Among the areas most affected have been those known for their pictographic art in southern California's Mohave Desert and certain Anasazi ruins in southwestern Colorado.

WESTERN HEMISPHERE

Washington. Excavations continue at the remarkable Ozette village site on the Olympic Peninsula of Washington. This village site has become a "time capsule" of life an estimated 500 years ago. Over 25,000 artifacts have been carefully removed from the debris of the slide-covered village, including elaborately carved whalebone clubs, spruce-root basketry rain hats, anthropomorphic wood bowls, and an abundance of hunting and fishing equipment. The archaeological site is open to visitors by access through the coastal strip of the Olympic National Park.

Ecuador. Archaeologists from the Smithsonian Institution returned in 1974 to the site of an extensive prehistoric cemetery located near Guayaquil on the southwest coast of Ecuador. Earlier excavations had exposed some 250 skeletons, often associated with ceramic urns and identified with the Milagro period (c. 1400–1500 A. D.).

The 1974 excavations revealed an older burial complex of the Jambeli culture dating from 500 B. C. to 0 A. D. Archaeologists found 105 skeletons in a great variety of burial deposition, including cremations, secondary deposits, and practically all manner of flexed and extended body positioning. This was the first excavation of a cemetery of the Jambeli culture, despite evidence of this culture in many occupational sites in the region.

California. California archaeologists and historians now suggest that the long-disputed California landing of Sir Francis Drake in 1579 actually took place at Bolinas Bay in Marin County almost midway between Drake's Bay and San Francisco Bay. Evidence uncovered at Bolinas Bay includes the remnants of a square-shaped fortification and a well, the former disguised through modern use as a duck pond.

Alaska-Siberia. A team of American and Soviet archaeologists jointly funded by the University of Connecticut and two United States foundations has presented evidence that a prehistoric Aleutian population came over a land bridge from Siberia about 10,000 years ago and, even prior to that, may have had its origins in the Gobi Desert in central Asia.

Representatives of the joint archaeological project, sponsored by the U. S. National Academy of Sciences and the Soviet Academy of Sciences, reported that tool blades unearthed on Anangula Island in the Aleutian Island chain were identical with other blades found in Siberia and dated from about 9,000 years.

Additional information suggests that between 7000 B. C. and 6000 B. C. melting glacial deposits caused the prehistoric Aleutian population to abandon one site and remove to a location 100 feet higher above sea level. The Bering land bridge disappeared at that time.

Pennsylvania. A rock-shelter near Avella, Pa., has become the oldest site of prehistoric occupation east of the Mississippi River revealing evidence of man datable to 13,000 B. C. Remarkably, archaeologists from the University of Pittsburgh believe that in 13,000 B. C. the ice front was only 70 miles to the north of the site. They further speculate that the region resembled Alaska climatically.

The rock-shelter has a depth of 16 feet. At the lowest level, archaeologists found three firepits attributable to Ice Age man and, nearby, several blade tools. About 100,000 animal bones have been unearthed plus numerous shells, vegetable remains, and ceramics dating to 1100 B. C. Several examples of Pre-Ceramic Archaic Period basketry also have been unearthed.

Missouri. Archaeological researchers from the University of Missouri report that a small prehistoric village site in the St. Louis area is the only surviving occupational site directly related to the Cahokia Mound Complex, and the first occupational site exhibiting a cultural context temporarily compatible with Cahokia Indian culture.

Experts have long postulated that satellite communities encircling Cahokia acted as intermediaries in the flow of the Cahokia economy, but the village at Sioux Passage County Park along the Missouri River is the first indication that such a regulated trade network actually functioned. Authorities indicate that the village site represents a transition period between the Late Woodland Period and the Mississippian Period, during which nearby Cahokia was to become the largest Indian settlement north of Mexico.

Oregon. South Oregon coast Indians concerned about disappearing traces of their history, have formed the Oregon Coastal Indian Archeological Association. Under the auspices of the Coos, Umpqua, and Siuslaw Indian tribes, it is the first archaeological society to be organized and governed by Indians.

GEORGE E. PHEBUS
Smithsonian Institution

EASTERN HEMISPHERE

In the Eastern Hemisphere some of the most striking advances in archaeology came from experiments in which archaeological hypotheses were tested by duplicating the ancient situations. In other work, field research brought out significant new evidence.

Lyre Test. R. I. Crocker, using a replica of a Sumerian 11-string lyre dating from about 2500 B. C., found that he could sing and play a Hurrian song inscribed in cuneiform writing on a clay tablet unearthed at Ugarit, Syria. The lyrics and musical instructions were deciphered by A. D. Kilmer, although information about note value and pitch was lacking. The three-minute diatonic song seems to be a hymn to the god of love.

Boomerang Test. F. Hess made an exact plywood copy of a flat curved artifact found in an Iron Age (about 400 B. C.) site at Velsen, Netherlands, and found that it would return to him after being thrown. This test clearly proved for the first time that the returning boomerang was known outside Australia, and that it was as useful to the ancient fowlers on the North Sea coast as to the aboriginals of the island continent.

Solar Light Test. Precise measurements by J. Patrick of Dublin University in clear weather in the 1973–74 winter demonstrated the purpose of the "roof window" of the Late Neolithic–Early Bronze Age megalithic tomb "New Grange" in County Meath, Ireland. At the midwinter solstice, the stone-framed window permitted the sun to shine down the full length of the huge monument, thereby illuminating the burial chamber at the back.

Solar Energy Test. For centuries the account of how Archimedes had destroyed the Roman fleet attacking Syracuse about 215–212 B. C. was dismissed by embarrassed classicists. The legend was that he had used mirrors to focus the sun's rays to ignite the Romans' pitch-soaked cedarwood galleys. In a test, Greek engineer I. Sakkis, using only materials available in Archimedes' time, stood 200 flat shield-sized copper rectangles, 5 by 3 feet (1.5 by 0.9 meters), to focus sunlight on a tarred plywood rowboat in Athens harbor. At a range of 55 yards (50 meters), the craft burst into flame in less than two minutes.

Oldest Flake Tools. G. Isaacs has amassed more than 600 flake tools during five years work near Lake Rudolf in Kenya. Found in a deposit dating back 2.6 million years and also containing a rather advanced Australopithecine skull, the tools lay in a ditch with bones of gazelles, waterbucks, pigs, porcupines, and hippopotamuses. While the mostly scraper-like tools—the oldest found so far—seem most useful for flaying, some might have served as knives. All the evidence suggests that the site was a consumption station for the division of mammals taken by hunting.

French Cave Finds. Animal bones from what may be the oldest site in Europe exhibit the teeth and jaws of old, decrepit specimens. Excavated from a cave, Le Trou du Tachou, near the Riviera in southern France by Henry and Marie-Antoinette de Lumley, these remains may be dated to the Günz glaciation 500,000 years ago. No human fossils were found, but pebble and flint choppers and flakes lay among the fragmented residues of elephants, lions, panthers, bears, deer, rhinoceros, seals, whales, and other animals. The cave dwellers left no hearths, so perhaps they did not even make fire.

Sesklo Culture in Greece. At the stratified tell (mound) of Achilleon in Thessaly, Greece, M. Gimbutas has traced the development of the Sesklo culture while amassing a series of radiocarbon dates. Her efforts show that agriculturists who used painted pottery were in Greece by 6500 B. C., a time when the Near East hardly knew more advanced types of settlements. Although not the earliest farming in Europe, this settlement begins with the Sesklo culture, which in its heyday (around 6000–5500 B. C.) produced many female figurines. Perhaps these are mother goddesses, as they are mostly women, often pregnant or holding children.

A number of female masks adorned vases or were detachable but kept on stone or ceramic pillars or phalli. The prevalence of masks reveals an intense theatricality of the Sesklo culture and forces reconsideration of the role of the mask in classical Greece.

City of Jawa in Jordan. Urbanism came early to an unlikely locale at Jawa, Jordan, lying between the primary urban centers of Egypt and Mesopotamia, northeast of Amman in the bleak, black basalt desert. Founded in the late Chalcolithic Period (3800–3350 B. C.)., Jawa stood as an impressive city fortified by a basalt wall 1 kilometer (0.6 mile) long, 5 meters (16 feet) tall, and 4 meters (13 feet) thick. The wall, provided with six main gates and many smaller ones, surrounded a water reservoir comprising about one quarter of the enclosed area of 22 acres (9 hectares). The crowded semi-subterranean houses, containing pottery and flint, were burned when the city was abandoned about 3000 B. C.

Chinese Artifacts. The massively fortified early Shang Bronze (about 1600 B. C.) city at Chengchow, Honan, China, was primarily the abode of royal overlords and their staff. Excavations produced objects of jade, pottery and bronze, and uncovered a bone-tool factory. It utilized human bone as raw material, producing hairpins and other household implements. Also, skullcaps were worked into decorative drinking cups.

Chinese Graves. At Changsha, 1,000 miles (1,600 km) south of Peking, the 2,000-year-old graves of the husband and son of the extremely well-preserved woman found in 1972 were dug intentionally. The man's tomb had leaked, causing everything to decay except for seals indicating his status as the Han Empire's Marquis of Tao. The grave of the 30-year-old son was well preserved, containing maps, silk paintings, more than 300 lacquer boxes, books of Taoist philosophy, scientific treatises on astronomy, and a manual on horse judging.

Bronze-Age Toys? The tell at Daimabad, Maharashtra state, India, yielded four bronze figures mounted on solid wheels depicting an elephant, a buffalo bull, a rhinoceros, and a chariot guided by a handsome driver. The svelte charioteer with coiffure and bangles recalls the dancing-girl figures of the ancient city of Mohenjo-Daro. Dated about 1500 B. C. by S. R. Rao, the four bronze figures may be toys produced by Harappan refugees after the collapse of their urban centers farther north.

RALPH M. ROWLETT, *University of Missouri*

University of Pittsburgh archaeologists unearthed evidence that man occupied this site near Avella, Pa., in 13,000 B. C. Relics of Ice Age man were found.

UNIVERSITY OF PITTSBURGH

architecture

Some of the world's tallest buildings were completed in 1973 and 1974, and yet these years seem not to have been so notable for their skyscrapers as for a trend toward architectural conservation and conservatism, and for a reawakening to the past and the environment.

The Empire State Building in New York City, built in 1930–31, lost its title as the world's tallest building (1,250 feet, 381 meters) after four decades to the World Trade Center (1,350 feet, 412 meters), also in New York. The latter's twin shafts kept the title only a few months, however, before passing it on to the Sears Tower in Chicago (1,454 feet, 442 meters), designed by Skidmore, Owings and Merrill as a bundle of high buildings collected for support and rising to a variety of heights. The world's fourth- and fifth-highest buildings, both in Chicago, are the Standard Oil (Indiana) Building (1,136 feet, 345 meters), completed in 1972, and the John Hancock Center (1,127 feet, 342 meters), completed in 1968.

But where the Empire State Building captured the imagination of a generation, the bland behemoths of the 1970's seemed to receive from architects a bemused or sardonic response. Architectural students returning to their schools from field trips to Chicago were generally unexcited about the Sears Tower and silent about the Standard Oil Building, but ecstatic about their discovery of the Wrigley Building (Graham, Anderson, Probst, and White, 1921).

Discovery of the Past. A hold on the public imagination more powerful than that from progress or mere size came from architectural attempts to connect with the past, and to rediscover the value of existing things found around us. These attempts were partly an outgrowth of the energy crunch, and stemmed from somewhat negative motivations. Inflation, high energy costs, high interest rates, and generally unavailable money made new construction more difficult, and focused attention on the existing environment.

Attempts to connect with the past also had as a positive motivation the desire to save our heritage of notable buildings, so many of which had been lost to redevelopment or to carelessness. In Chicago, the loss of Louis Sullivan's Stock Exchange galvanized people into action. But the city of San Diego, in wanting to restore the Churrigueresque buildings from the Panama-Pacific Exposition of 1915, discovered that historical preservation requires more than simple good intentions. Also necessary are the skills of

The tallest building in the world, the new Sears Tower, designed by Skidmore, Owings & Merrill, dominates the Chicago skyline.

EZRA STOLLER

MITCHELL/GIURGOLA ASSOCIATES ARCHITECTS

The facade of this 1838 building on Independence Square in Philadelphia is being preserved as a free-standing sculpture in the courtyard of the building replacing it.

specially trained artisans and craftsmen, many of whom have disappeared entirely in the 40 years since the ascendancy of modern architecture.

The Contribution of Louis I. Kahn. A major tie to the heroic past was severed on March 17, 1974, when Louis I. Kahn died, at 73, in Pennsylvania Station in New York City. He was on his way home to Philadelphia from India, where work was continuing on his Indian Institute of Management at Ahmedabad, and on the capital buildings of Bangladesh, at Dacca. The bungled and dreary circumstances of his death (his body lay for two days in the New York morgue while his family searched across the world for him) made especially poignant the virtual end of the heroic period of the modern movement in architecture. Now, of all the 20th century giants (Frank Lloyd Wright, Le Corbusier, Mies van der Rohe, Walter Gropius, and others) only Alvar Aalto remained alive and working in Finland.

Kahn's death left some of his major works unfinished, unstarted, or so recently completed that their significance was just beginning to be felt. His Kimball Art Museum in Fort Worth, Texas, whose parallel vaults are formed to admit an almost magical quality of natural light, had been part of the inspiration for his Yale Center for British Art and British studies, under construction in 1974 in New Haven, just across Chapel Street from the Yale Art Gallery (1951), his first major work.

The center is characteristically conservative in shape, fronting, like a Renaissance palazzo, on the street and on an inner courtyard. Its light-seeking upper vaults are hardly visible. Its beautifully crafted concrete frame is exposed, further developing the look of an Italian palace. The familiar shapes are thrown almost (but not quite) into the realm of the surreal by an infill of pewter-colored stainless steel panels, almost randomly fenestrated, and by the surprising provision for commercial space to provide activity along the street front of the institutional building. The center and the art gallery across the street visibly bracket the career of the man who for the past two decades was unquestionably the most potent influence on young architects in the United States.

Architectural Conservatism. The remaining links with the past were more and more carefully nurtured. The renewed interest in architectural conservation gave added impetus to the development of preservation techniques to prevent the further loss of great buildings. The most prominent technique allows the development rights—that is, air rights—to be detached from one site containing a building to be preserved and sold to the developer of another site, so as to make possible the continued existence of important buildings from the past which do not fill out the now allowable development envelope to the satisfaction of their developer-owners.

There is currently a much more unabashed use of fragments from the past. The Penn Mutual Building in Philadelphia, by Mitchell/Giurgola Associates, incorporates the facade of a much smaller, ornate structure already on the site as an integral piece of the new construction. There was a continuing interest in more orthodox forms of historical renewal, as in Savannah, Ga., or at the South Street Seaport, in New York City; and in constructions that recall the past, such as Walt Disney World, or that collect the previously dispersed past in one place or reconstruct it, as at Williamsburg, Va., and Sturbridge Village in Massachusetts. There were also stunning single-building preservations, such as the new headquarters for the Banco de Mexico in the 18th century Iturbide Palace in Mexico City, under the direction of architect Ricardo Legorreta.

Faced with an absence of any exciting new architectural idioms, and seeking new inspiration from past idioms, architects have shown both a much freer spirit in recalling the larger past, and a more doctrinaire attitude in recalling the so-called "modern" past of 50 years ago. Two buildings on Long Island, New York, which reflect the latter are the Weinstein House, by Richard Meier, and the Cogan House, by

Gwathmey-Siegel, both with strong acknowledged connections to Le Corbusier's Villa Savoie in Poissy, France (1929–31).

Buildings with freer connections to the past range from the very polished works of Cesar Pelli, of Gruen Associates, such as the San Bernardino (Calif.) City Hall, which recall what was once called futurism, to the familiarly traditional look of buildings by Venturi and Rauch, such as their classroom building at the State University of New York at Purchase in Westchester county.

In 1974 there was renewed interest in monuments of the recent past. Ada Louise Huxtable wrote a moving article in the New York *Times* on public sculpture in New York City as an important ingredient in urban design, while the Metropolitan Museum of Art simultaneously mounted a major exhibition on the same subject. An article in the *Architectural Record* (April 1974, p. 113) took a new look, some 60 years later, at St. Thomas Church in New York, which upon its completion in 1913 had been billed as the most important parish church in America. The year also saw studies completed or in progress on recycling railroad stations and Midwestern courthouses.

Appreciation of the Environment. The new accommodation to and appreciation of the existing environment was manifested in the effort to find new uses for previously underused or overlooked building sites, instead of opting for the easy approach of further urban decay and suburban sprawl.

A notable example is Waterside, by Davis Brody Associates, a cluster of apartment towers in New York City built on reclaimed land between a freeway and the East River on the east side of Manhattan. Mitchell/Giurgola Associates' design for a building to fit tightly between existing buildings on the Columbia University campus is both a part of this trend and a hint that the heroic period in architecture is over, or nearly so.

Appreciation of the existing environment has led to efforts by citizen groups to protect special pieces of the environment from what people know to be an undesirable future. Most notable have been recent attempts to stop the construction of waterside freeways in Milwaukee, New Orleans, New York, and other cities.

The major architectural monuments of the past decade, therefore, have been not just individual buildings but rather those special pieces of the city and countryside which have been rescued from "progress." A notable example is the development along the river in San Antonio, Texas, which had its start in the days of the Works Progress Administration, but which is continuing, nearly 40 years later, to be extended and enhanced. What is now one of the most pleasant urban waterways in the world once had to be saved from the Corps of Engineers, who wanted to put the river into a pipe.

RONALD THOMAS—WILLIAM MORGAN ARCHITECTS

Florida beach house, designed by William Morgan for his own use, slopes toward the ocean. The six terraces are recessed for protection against frequent strong winds.

Contemporary Design. Some few buildings extensively publicized in 1974 aroused considerable enthusiasm even though they did not actually represent the conserving and conservative trend. James Stirling, of London, added to his continuing independent set of masterpieces a training center for Olivetti at Haslemere, England. It is a building of uncompromisingly clean, smooth plastic surfaces, rounded at the corners, juxtaposed with extensive greenhouses and attached to, though spiritually independent of, an existing manor house.

Clean surfaces and curved lines (this time provided by ducts meant to hold aloft an inflatable structure over a swimming pool) are also in evidence on a fresh and brightly colored building for a swimming center in Wilkes-Barre, Pa., by Bohlin and Powell.

The Civic Center for Thousand Oaks, Calif., designed by Robert Houvener, who had won a national competition for the commission some years before, was completed. The design fulfilled the hopes of the jury that had awarded Houvener the prize for the clarity, simplicity, and giant scale of his scheme.

CHARLES W. MOORE
University of California at Los Angeles
RICHARD B. OLIVER
Architect, New York City

UPI

New Argentine President Isabel Perón (*center*) announces the death of her husband and predecessor, Juan Perón.

ARGENTINA

President Juan Domingo Perón, the dominant figure in Argentine politics since 1945, died on July 1, 1974 (see OBITUARIES). The vice president, his widow, María Estela ("Isabel") Martínez de Perón, succeeded him in the presidency and began to lead Argentina into the post-Perón era.

Political struggle dominated the news in 1974. Within the Peronist movement itself, right- and left-wing factions intensified their bitter conflict, while the guerrillas escalated their activities. Political assassination accounted for about 200 lives; and for the government, control over the guerrillas became the major, perhaps the sole, national issue.

In its attempt to assert authority, the regime moved steadily to the right, and, after the death of Juan Perón, did so without pretense. During the last several months of the year even the populist, reformist rhetoric was dropped while a new rightist terror group, the Argentine Anti-Communist Alliance (AAA), claimed the lives of several prominent leftists. On November 6, President Isabel Perón declared a state of siege in an effort to halt the growing political violence in the nation.

Developments Under Juan Perón. In January, Juan Perón replaced Gen. Jorge Carcagno with Gen. Leandro Anaya as commander-in-chief of the armed forces. Carcagno was known to be a populist not without political ambition or political base. Perón wanted to establish clearly his authority over an army which was deeply divided in its loyalties and ideas about Argentina's future.

Later in the month, both Perón and the army were severely embarrassed by a successful attack on the garrison of Azul, Buenos Aires Province, by the leftist guerrilla organization known as the People's Revolutionary Army (ERP). This led to the forced resignation of the provincial governor, Oscar Bidegaín, a left-wing Peronist, and his subsequent replacement by Victorio Calabro, openly identified with the right.

At the end of February, the police raided the Juventud Trabajadora Peronista (JTP) and shut down the leftist-Peronist daily *El Mundo*. On February 28, Perón looked on passively as a right-wing provincial police chief overthrew the legally elected left-wing Peronist administration of Córdoba Province, headed by Gov. Ricardo Obregón Cano and Deputy Gov. Atilio López. After more than a week, Perón appointed a conservative, Diulio Danilo Brunello, to head the provincial government. Thus the important provinces of Córdoba and Buenos Aires were securely in Perón's rightist camp.

If there were any doubts as to the president's views, he dispelled them in his May Day speech. Discarding his prepared text he savagely attacked the leftists within the movement, particularly the Montoneros, the armed, former guerrilla organization. According to observers, some 60,000 to 80,000 supporters promptly marched out of the Plaza de Mayo where the rally was held.

The Nation Under Isabel. The death of Juan Perón threw the government and the nation into crisis. Isabel Perón succeeded without apparent challenge, but inside the cabinet the long simmering conflict between José López Rega, strongly rightist minister of social security and longtime confidant of Isabel Perón, and José Ber Gelbard, minister of economy, broke into the open.

Just which way the wind was blowing became evident in mid-August when Mrs. Perón accepted the pro-forma resignations of two of her cabinet, Interior Minister Benito Llambi and Education Minister Jorge Taina, both considered moderates. They were replaced by two hard-liners, Alberto Rocamora, in Interior, and the veteran Peronist Oscar Ivanissevich, in Education. Defense Minister Angel Robledo lost his job to Adolfo Savino, ambassador to Rome and former professor in the air force staff college. López Rega won the struggle with his rival; the Montoneros announced that they would return to armed activities; and in mid-October, Gelbard submitted his resignation.

The government did not succeed in controlling the guerrillas. Among their victims during the year were Arturo Mor Roig, interior minister under former President Lanusse; Rogelio Coria, ex-head of the construction workers' union and a right-wing Peronist; Rodolfo Ortega Peña, leftist Peronist lawyer and deputy; Atilio López, leftist Peronist labor leader and deposed vice governor of Córdoba; Father Carlos Mugica, a prominent leader of the Third World movement; and Alberto Villar, federal police chief. And death claimed Gen. Carlos Prats, late of the Chilean military, in a bomb blast in Buenos Aires.

One notable success for the revolutionary ERP was the receipt of $14.2 million as ransom from the Argentine subsidiary of Exxon Corporation for its kidnapped executive Victor Samuelson. With the declaration of the state of siege in November, the government had few impediments in its campaign to stop the leftist guerrillas.

Economy. Increasingly, the government felt the strains of inflation and political conflict. The basic economic policy, the social pact, which is designed to control prices and wages, was under severe threat from unions and the government itself. Gelbard's departure most likely signaled its death knell. Loyal unions were growing restive as inflation eroded salaries despite price controls, while leftist Peronist and Marxist unions, particularly in Córdoba and Tucumán, rejected the pact. In October the militant light and power workers' union of Córdoba, led by Agustín Tosco, was intervened, its headquarters raided, and over 70 members were arrested.

The government's close political alliance with the General Confederation of Labor (CGT) was illustrated when the secretary general, Adelino Romero, died suddenly in July and effective control passed to another loyalist, Lorenzo Miguel. In a major speech on October 17, President Isabel announced the convocation of new commissions to decide on the magnitude of wage and salary increases.

Economically, conventional indicators pointed to reasonable growth. The agricultural and industrial sectors performed well, but inflation eroded much of the economic gain, resulting in a decline in political support for the *pacto social.* In his mid-year report on the economy on national radio and television, Gelbard claimed that for the first half of the year the gross domestic product increased 6.2% over the same period of 1973.

The agricultural sector registered gains of 9.1% in the first quarter and 8.5% in the second. Exports were expected to reach about $3.6 billion in spite of the European Common Market's ban on beef exports, and in the first six months of the year manufactures accounted for $315 million of total exports, about 25% more than in the first half of 1973.

Foreign Relations. Despite the rightward trend in domestic politics, Juan Perón developed important economic and political ties with the USSR, the eastern European countries, Cuba, and the Arab nations, particularly Libya. For example, in February, Argentina and the Soviet Union signed agreements worth some $200 million in trade, technical cooperation, and credit; and in May the Soviets pledged $600 million in credits to develop Argentina's power-generating capacity. In April the government negotiated a $40 million trade agreement with Libya.

But Cuba was the big trading partner as it spent a good part of the billion-dollar credit extended in 1973 principally on automotive equipment, some of which was manufactured by General Motors Argentina. When the U. S. government remonstrated that this violated the Organization of American States' trade embargo on Cuba, Argentina replied tartly that it will determine its own trading partners.

Argentina also emphasized regional cooperation with Bolivia, Paraguay, and Uruguay in such areas as hydroelectric power and river navigation. This cooperation was designed partly to counter the influence of Brazil in the area.

Relations with Chile remained correct. In May, Gen. Augusto Pinochet, the Chilean leader, asked for permission to refuel in Buenos Aires on his return from a visit to Paraguay. Within 1 hour and 40 minutes, Perón, Isabel, and López Rega had lunch with Pinochet at the Morón Air Base and sent him on his way.

JAMES R. LEVY
University of New South Wales, Australia

ARGENTINA • Information Highlights

Official Name: Argentine Republic.
Location: Southern South America.
Area: 1,072,158 square miles (2,776,889 sq km).
Population (1973 est.): 25,300,000.
Chief Cities (1970 census, met. areas): Buenos Aires, the capital, 8,352,900; Rosario, 810,840; Córdoba, 798,663.
Government: *Head of state,* Isabel Perón, president (took office July 1974). *Head of government,* Isabel Perón. *Legislature*—Congress: Senate and Chamber of Deputies.
Monetary Unit: Peso (5 pesos equal U. S.$1, Aug. 1974).
Gross National Product (1973 est.): $27,750,000,000.
Manufacturing (major products): Iron and steel, automobiles, machinery, processed foods, chemicals, petroleum products, meat.
Major Agricultural Products: Wheat, corn, grapes, sugarcane, oats, sunflower seeds, sorghum.
Foreign Trade (1973): *Exports,* $3,266,000,000; *imports,* $2,235,000,000.

ARIZONA

Arizona's continued rapid population growth was accompanied in 1974 by growing unemployment, farm labor troubles, and clashes over environmental controls. In politics, the year saw a resurgence of Democratic party fortunes in the November elections.

Economy. In the four-year period since the 1970 census, the Arizona population grew faster than that of any other state, rising to an estimated 2.15 million. The state's economy, which had demonstrated a remarkable ability to generate new employment to accommodate the population influx, showed some soft spots in 1974. The vital construction industry was seriously depressed because of the shortage of mortgage funds and high interest rates. In the fall there were major layoffs in the electronics industry, a major source of employment in the Phoenix area. By year's end, unemployment rates, which had been significantly below national levels, approached or exceeded them.

Elections. Arizona Democrats made a strong comeback in November, after a series of crushing defeats going back to 1966. In a very close race, Democrat Raul Castro, former U. S. diplomat, became the first Mexican-American governor in the state's history. Democrats also captured most major state offices, and gained control of the state Senate, reversing a previous 18–12 Republican margin. Democrats also gained 5 seats in the 60-member House, but fell short of control by a 33–27 GOP margin.

Republicans were able to maintain their strong control of the state's congressional delegation, reelecting Sen. Barry Goldwater and all three Republican House incumbents, including Rep. John Rhodes, House minority leader. The only Democratic incumbent, Rep. Morris Udall, won easy reelection.

Voters approved a major change in the state constitution by supporting a "Missouri Plan" of judicial selection, replacing the elective system. In the future, all appellate judges and major trial court judges in metropolitan areas will be appointed by the governor on recommendation of a judicial selection commission. At the conclusion of a judge's term, voters will have the opportunity to remove him from office, or to grant him an additional term.

Voters rejected an Arizona version of the so-called Reagan Plan, previously defeated in California, which would have placed a ceiling on state spending at 8.5% of state personal income. Also defeated was another constitutional amendment that would have required a 10% voter turnout in school and other local government bonding elections as a condition of passage.

In what may prove to be a landmark in the state's political history, the largest Indian tribe, the Navajos, gave an impressive demonstration of their potential political power, previously unrealized because of extremely low turnouts. The Navajo vote may have been the decisive factor in Castro's gubernatorial victory. At the same time, Navajos retired a veteran non-Indian Democratic state legislator and replaced him with a Navajo Republican, while reelecting a Navajo Democrat from the same two-member district.

Farm Labor Dispute. The United Farm Workers Union, having suffered major setbacks in grape-growing areas of California, mounted a major organizational effort in the Yuma area, threatening the loss of much of the valuable lemon harvest. UFW pickets attempted to prevent allegedly illegal Mexican entrants from crossing the nearby international border to work in the groves. Growers charged that Cesar Chavez and other UFW leaders were responsible for the harassment and intimidation of nonunion workers.

There was some violence, and these events seemed for a while as if they would pose a threat to the election of Castro as governor, since he was strongly supported by organized labor, though not by the UFW. In the closing days of the campaign, Castro disassociated himself from the UFW drive, and disclaimed any intention to seek repeal of the state's right-to-work law. Even so, normally Democratic Yuma county was carried by Castro's Republican opponent.

Environment. Throughout 1974, state and local political leaders carried on a running battle with the Environmental Protection Agency. The agency had proposed sharp limitations on increases in parking spaces in the Phoenix area as a means of combating air pollution by discouraging the use of automobiles. Opponents of the EPA argued that the proposed rules would have disastrous effects on the economic development of the metropolitan area, and would impose a hardship on residents of an area having little mass transportation. They also maintained that existing state pollution regulations, combined with better anti-emission devices, rendered the EPA proposal unnecessary. In the November election, voters defeated a proposal to make gasoline tax funds available for mass transit.

JOHN P. WHITE, *Arizona State University*

ARIZONA • Information Highlights

Area: 113,909 square miles (295,024 sq km).
Population (1974 est.): 2,150,000. *Density:* 17 per sq mi.
Chief Cities (1970 census): Phoenix, the capital, 581,562; Tucson, 262,933; Scottsdale, 67,823.
Government (1974): *Chief Officers*—governor, Jack Williams (R); secy. of state, Wesley Bolin (D). *Legislature*—Senate, 30 members; House of Representatives, 60 members.
Education (1973–74): *Enrollment*—public elementary schools, 386,858 pupils; public secondary, 154,186; nonpublic, 28,500; colleges and universities, 138,241 students. *Public school expenditures,* $554,740,000 ($1,222 per pupil).
State Finances (fiscal year 1973): *Revenues,* $1,204,886,000; *expenditures,* $1,088,399,000.
Personal Income (1973): $9,268,000,000; per capita, $4,504.
Labor Force (July 1974): *Nonagricultural wage and salary earners,* 720,600; *insured unemployed,* 16,200 (2.8%).

ARKANSAS

In an election year marked by low voter turnout, youthful candidates challenged veteran officeholders and politicians. Reaction to public scandal and inflation was mixed.

Elections. Dale Bumpers, the energetic and progressive governor of the state, decisively defeated J. William Fulbright, 69-year-old chairman of the Senate Foreign Relations Committee, for the Democratic senatorial nomination. During the primary campaign, Bumpers attacked the congressional seniority system and stressed the need for a new direction in state and national politics. Governor Bumpers went on to overwhelm John Harris Jones (R) in the general election.

After the news media publicized reports of alleged illegal contributions to the 1972 abortive presidential campaign of Rep. Wilbur D. Mills and of a public incident involving Mills and a nightclub entertainer and rumors of lavish drinking parties, the chairman of the House Ways and Means Committee was forced for the first time in years to campaign seriously for reelection. His opponent was an attractive 31-year-old woman, Mrs. Judy Chaney Petty (R), who surprisingly polled 41% of the vote. Following the election, criticism of Mills' association with the entertainer increased, and Mills entered the hospital with an undisclosed illness. There were indications that he would not be returned as committee chairman in January 1975.

In the race for a new governor, David H. Pryor, 40-year-old former U. S. congressman, defeated both the 64-year-old former Gov. Orval E. Faubus and Lt. Gov. Bob C. Riley, a World War II veteran, in the Democratic primary and a youthful Ken Coon in the general election. In many state races—including 13 of 18 state Senate seats, 65 of 100 House seats, 12 of 14 circuit judgeships, and 13 of 19 prosecuting attorneys—candidates were unopposed. Although contesting only 12 General Assembly seats, Republicans increased their House membership from 1 to 3 and kept their 1 Senate seat. By a 6 to 1 margin, voters defeated an attempt to repeal the usury law limiting maximum interest rates to 10%.

Legislature. In January the legislature adjourned its 1973 regular session after an unprecedented eight-month recess. Prior to adjournment the House passed a resolution urging the University of Arkansas at Little Rock to fire faculty member Dr. Grant Cooper, self-professed Marxist Progressive Labor party member. Later, in a suit initiated by 23 legislators, a state court stopped his salary. A move to require loyalty oaths for teachers and state employees was tabled until 1975. In a special session the Senate reconsidered its earlier action and expelled a 27-year member, Guy H. (Mutt) Jones, convicted in 1972 for federal income tax evasion. The decision was upheld by the state supreme court. In the same session the General Assembly adopted most of Governor Bumpers' program—including increased retirement benefits and pay for teachers and other state employees and additional revenue for schools.

Judiciary. In several significant cases state courts checked expenditures of state and local governments. A lower state court found unconstitutional a $75 million revenue bond, state capitol office building program proposed by the governor and approved by the Legislative Council. State courts declared illegal allowances to supplement low salaries of legislators and elected county officials, except for actual expenditures. Voters later defeated a constitutional amendment to permit increasing both low legislative and state executive salaries (for example, a $10,000 annual salary for governor), but approved another amendment allowing county salaries to be raised.

Local Government. Voters approved an amendment to replace the antiquated county quorum court, which in Pulaski county had almost 400 members, with a 9- to 15-member county commission and to permit limited county home rule. As inflation cut deeply into the real income of local public employees, some resorted to the tactics of organized labor. Firemen picketed city halls in Texarkana and Little Rock, and garbage workers went on strike in Little Rock. Throughout the state teachers pressed for collective bargaining rights.

Civil Rights. Racial conflict remained a perennial problem. While state colleges and universities presented plans for increasing integration of student bodies and faculties, fighting between races erupted in several high schools.

State prison officials were distressed when the U. S. Eighth Circuit Court reversed a federal district judge by ruling that Arkansas still failed to provide a constitutional and humane environment at the prison farms. After two young inmates drowned, a federal court found a Pulaski county judge guilty of civil contempt for using convict labor to operate the county penal farm in violation of a court order.

WILLIAM C. NOLAN
Southern State College

ARKANSAS • Information Highlights

Area: 53,104 square miles (137,539 sq km).
Population (1973 est.): 2,037,000. *Density:* 38 per sq mi.
Chief Cities (1970 census): Little Rock, the capital, 132,483; Fort Smith, 62,802.
Government (1974): *Chief Officers*—governor, Dale Bumpers (D); lt. gov., Bob C. Riley (D). General Assembly—Senate, 35 members (34 D, 1 R); House of Representatives, 100 members (99 D, 1 R).
Education (1973–74): *Enrollment*—public elementary schools, 240,865 pupils; public secondary, 209,249; nonpublic, 11,600; colleges and universities, 52,212 students. *Public school expenditures,* $317,036,000 ($773 per pupil).
State Finances (fiscal year 1973): *Revenues,* $985,720,000; *expenditures,* $849,770,000.
Personal Income (1973): $7,496,000,000.
Labor Force (July 1974): *Nonagricultural wage and salary earners,* 639,400.

THE J. PAUL GETTY MUSEUM

The J. Paul Getty Museum, Malibu, Calif., opened in 1974. A re-creation of an ancient Roman villa, it has a peristyle courtyard and reflecting pool.

art

In 1974 some critics declared that abstract art was in full retreat, and a few even claimed that all of "modernism" was being repealed, especially by the anecdotal and didactic concerns of new realist and conceptualist artists. Although Europeans showed renewed interest in the abstract expressionism of the 1950's, the international prestige of various kinds of representational and conceptual art continued to increase during the year.

In America and Europe, artists using trompe l'oeil techniques were featured. In a major survey of contemporary art at the Chicago Art Institute, over half the artists used slick illustration and photo-realist techniques. America's most famous realist, Andrew Wyeth, was honored around the world in exhibits in London and Tokyo.

The Eighth Biennale of Young Art in Paris virtually ignored abstract easel painting to concentrate on environments for spectator participation, tableaus, and image series. The latter, sometimes called "story art," presents visual-verbal sequences ranging from intimate and direct expression to highly intellectual and essentially linguistic speculation. Internationally known artists in this area include Victor Burgin (England), Robert Cumming (U. S.), Donald Askevold (Canada), Michael Badura (Germany), and Jean Le Gac (France).

Art and Language. Story art often focuses on the use of language in relation to the perception of objects. Still more radically linguistic is the growing art and language group which emerged during the late 1960's from the same impulses as conceptualism. Through its own publications, rather than conventional gallery shows, it concentrates exclusively on the nature of language and the language of art. Such artists as J. Kosuth, T. Atkinson, M. Ramsden, and T. Smith, convinced that the present condition of art is disastrous, propose a critique of the use of concepts that begin with art but actually are all-encompassing and never-ending.

Body Art. Like the art and language group, body artists are disinterested in and despairing of the traditional formal concerns of abstract art. They also understand their function to be critical and provocative. However, their approach is usually intensely physical, often sensuous and sometimes violent. Inspired by the happenings of the 1950's and the intermedia performances of the 1960's, body art uses the body of the spectator and/or the artist to investigate psychological and sociological issues. A leading exponent of this art form is Joseph Beuys (Germany), whose latest demonstration, "I like America," opened the Rene Block Gallery in New York. Others have used film and video tape to record and intensify their particular investigations.

Machine Art. Interest in visually impressive abstract forms associated with or generated by advanced technological means also declined markedly in 1974. However, a significant number of artists continued to study the ideas and psychological states induced by involvement with such technology. The video art of Nam June Paik, Bruce Nauman, and Vito Acconci provided occasion for thought rather than compelling forms for the eye, but engineers continue to extend the possibilities for richer visual experience. University of Michigan researchers developed a hologram reader and projector capable of producing three-dimensional images with relative ease.

RETROSPECTIVES AND OTHER EXHIBITIONS

Old Masters. Leonardo da Vinci's masterwork *The Mona Lisa* from the Louvre in Paris was exhibited in Tokyo, where it was viewed by over 10 million persons. The Basel Museum, Switzerland, mounted one of the major exhibitions of the year. It was devoted to Lucas Granach. Other important old master exhibits honored 19th century visionary painters Arnold Böcklin (Düsseldorf Museum) and Gustave Moreau (Los Angeles County Museum). Work of the pre-Raphaelites were shown for the first time on the Continent at Baden-Baden; and in the United States, "Late Baroque Art in Florence" had its premiere at an exhibit in the Detroit Institute of Arts.

To celebrate the centenary of impressionism, an exhibition of 130 masterworks, jointly organized by the Louvre and the Metropolitan Museum of Art, was mounted. The National Gallery, Washington, D. C., in association with the Chicago Art Institute, presented 100 drawings by the Rococo master François Boucher. French drawings also were displayed at the Metropolitan and at the Museum of Modern Art, New York.

Modern Masters. A gigantic exhibit honoring Joan Miró on his 80th birthday filled the Grand Palais, Paris. Juan Gris received his first French retrospective at the Musée de l'Orangerie, Paris. In Hamburg two exhibitions celebrated the 90th birthday of the last surviving member of the German expressionist bridge group, Karl Schmidt-Rottluff.

Picasso. The Louvre postponed indefinitely an exhibition of paintings from Picasso's own collection because of doubts about the quality and the authenticity of a number of works. Picasso had insisted that the collection, which contained recognized masterpieces by Cézanne and Matisse, be shown intact.

United States Art. A number of exhibits in New York featured watercolor, among them a group show called "Masters of Watercolor: Ten Americans" (Andrew Crispo Gallery) and many one-man shows, including Charles Burchfield (Kennedy) and Charles Sheeler (Dintenfass). Watercolors, drawings, and small sculptures dating from 1792 to the present under the heading "American Art in Upstate New York" demonstrated the extraordinary collective riches of New York State museums in Albany, Buffalo, Ithaca, Rochester, Syracuse, and Utica. The exhibit opened at the Albright-Knox Art Gallery in Buffalo and then moved to the other cities.

Two exhibitions at the National Portrait Gallery in Washington, D. C., were notable: "Prologue to Revolution, 1760–1774" and "American Self Portraits, 300 Years." At the Whitney Museum, New York, four floors were devoted to a survey of American art from 1906 to the present. Of special interest were shows revealing little-known early works, among them representational paintings by abstract expressionist Hans Hofmann (Emmerich) and painterly experiments by formalist Ad Reinhardt (Marlborough). Pop art was surveyed in depth at the Whitney, where also was held the major retrospective of modern American painting, a showing of the socially conscious work of black artist Jacob Lawrence.

Canadian Art World. Having previously traveled to Paris, London, Vienna, and Stockholm, and subsequently to Washington, D. C., an internationally significant show dominated the season at the Royal Ontario Museum, Toronto. Titled simply "The Chinese Exhibition," it consisted of 385 recently excavated treasures dating from Paleolithic times through the 14th century A. D. The sense of great distances in space and time

A Ming dynasty bottle dating from about 1400 A. D. sold for a record $1 million at a London auction in April.

UPI

THE DETROIT INSTITUTE OF ARTS, GIFT OF THE KRESGE FOUNDATION AND MRS. EDSEL B. FORD

***The Conversion of the Magdalene,* a "lost" work painted in 1598 by Caravaggio, was acquired by the Detroit Institute of Arts during 1974 for $1.1 million.**

evoked by such an exhibit may have had a special appeal for some Canadians. This was the premise in part of *Artscanada,* which devoted an entire issue to maps and mapping and featured such Canadians as Vera Frenkel, who "maps time," and Claude Breeze, who has painted a series of works entitled "Canadian Atlas."

Special Themes. Interest in "outsider art," understood as the art of those working outside of the traditions of fine art, was worldwide in 1974. "Naive art," work by people completely unfamiliar with art school ideas, was celebrated in a huge show at the Haus der Kunst, Munich. In France a specialized museum for Paris and its environs was founded: the Musée d'Art Naif de l'Isle de France. Folk art was given unprecedented aesthetic emphasis at the Whitney Museum, New York, in "The Flowering of American Folk Art, 1776–1876." Kitsch, vulgar pseudo-art, was surveyed at Haus Deutscher Ring, Hamburg; and newspaper cartoons were displayed at the Louvre Museum of Decorative Arts. The largest show of contemporary tapestry ever assembled appeared at the Museum of the Palm Beaches, while the most important exhibit of medieval tapestry to date appeared at the Metropolitan.

At the Guggenheim Museum, New York, a retrospective of Giacometti's sculpture, painting, and drawing was accompanied by a unique exhibition of the paintings of his father Giovanni, his cousin Augusto, and his godfather Cuno Amiet.

Sculpture. Numerous New York gallery exhibits demonstrated the continuing vitality of sculpture, including: Robert Grosvenor (Paula Cooper), Isaac Witkin (Marlborough), Walter de Maria (Heiner Friedrich), Anthony Caro (Emmerich), Lynda Benglis (Paula Cooper), and Louise Nevelson (Pace).

Women in Art. In Philadelphia, 150 exhibitions, films, lectures, and workshops were devoted to women's art, including an exhibition documenting the achievement of women at America's most prestigious school of art: "The Pennsylvania Academy and Its Women, 1850–1920."

Non-Western Art. In addition to the monumental "The Chinese Exhibition," which appeared in Toronto and Washington, D. C., important showings of Oriental art included "Studies in Connoisseurship" at the Princeton Museum of Art. These didactic comparisons of originals with copies and forgeries then traveled to Cleveland, Los Angeles, and New York.

Some 300 Asian art objects valued at between $10 and $15 million, plus funds for a new building, were presented by John D. Rockefeller 3d to the Asia Society in New York. In an unusual intermedia exhibit, the National Gallery, Washington, D. C., presented "African Art in Motion." The show combined masks and other items with film to define a real life context for African art.

MUSEUMS AND COLLECTIONS

Financial Problems. Hit by inflation and the stock market slump, museums in America and abroad suffered in 1974. Museums in Britain decided to charge entry fees for the first time in history. In Italy many museums, including the Brera in Milan and the huge Egyptian Museum in Turin, were closed. Only 20% of the galleries in the Uffizi, Florence, were open regularly. It was feared that New York might lose its world-famous Museum of the American Indian, possessor of the most comprehensive collection in its field.

Thefts. Lack of money for guards was cited in Italy as a major reason for museum art losses, which almost doubled in 1974. An entire museum was emptied by thieves in Minervino Murge. The most spectacular theft occurred in Ireland, where paintings worth $19.2 million

THE METROPOLITAN MUSEUM OF ART, ON LOAN FROM THE LOUVRE MUSEUM

Hopscotch Game and Fruit Picking **is a pastoral tapestry from the Louvre, Paris.**

TAPESTRY SHOW

"Masterpieces of Tapestry from the Fourteenth to the Sixteenth Century," an exhibition of 97 European tapestries at the Metropolitan Museum in New York, was organized by the Metropolitan and French national museums.

THE METROPOLITAN MUSEUM OF ART, ON LOAN FROM THE MUSÉE DE CLUNY, PARIS

Nathan Admonishes David **is from the Cluny Museum's "Story of David" series.**

THE METROPOLITAN MUSEUM OF ART, GIFT OF JOHN D. ROCKEFELLER, JR., 1937—THE CLOISTERS COLLECTION

The Unicorn in Captivity **is from the Metropolitan's own Cloisters collection.**

(including works by Vermeer, Velázquez, and Goya) were stolen on April 26 from a mansion near Dublin. However, they were quickly recovered, undamaged, by the police.

U. S. Museums. The Hirshhorn Museum and Sculpture Garden, containing one of the most comprehensive collections of 20th century art, opened in Washington, D. C., on October 4. A gift to the nation by Joseph H. Hirshhorn, the collection numbers some 4,000 paintings and 2,000 sculptures. In Houston, a $4 million addition, the Brown Pavilion, designed by Mies van der Rohe, significantly enlarged the city's Museum of Fine Arts. A $4 million wing also was added to the Walters Art Gallery in Baltimore. The Neuberger Museum for Modern Art was opened at the State University of New York at Purchase. In addition to the Neuberger collection it houses the uniquely interesting collections of Dada master Hans Richter and contemporary sculptor George Rickey.

Gifts and Purchases. Banker Gerald Cantor has donated 127 sculptures by Rodin to three museums. They will go to Stanford University (where Rodin expert Albert Elsen teaches), the Los Angeles County Museum of Art, and the Museum of Modern Art in New York. In million-dollar-plus purchases, important old master paintings were still being acquired—for example, a Caravaggio by the Detroit Institute of Arts, a Georges de La Tour by the National Gallery,

Alberto Giacometti's bronze *Table* (1933) was part of the Guggenheim Museum's retrospective of the artist's work.

THE SOLOMON R. GUGGENHEIM MUSEUM, FROM THE COLLECTION OF THE MUSÉE D'ART MODERNE, PARIS

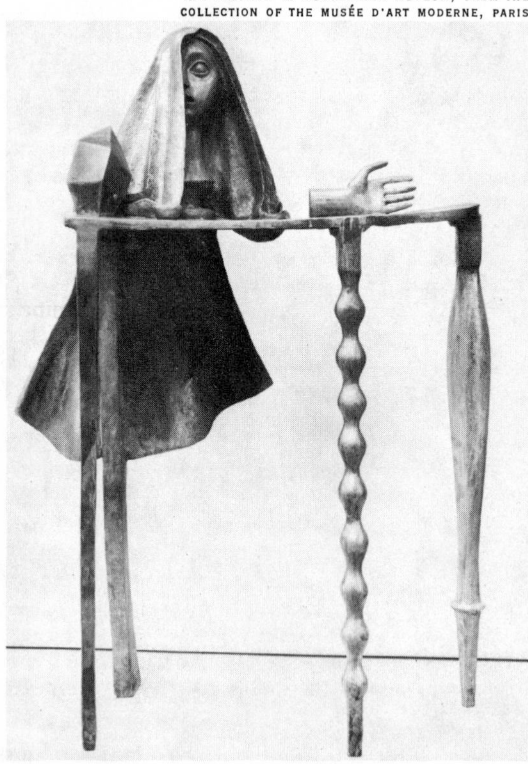

and a Grünewald by the Cleveland Museum of Art. Extremely rare 18th century Syrian house interiors went on display in New York, one at the Metropolitan Museum and one at the Kevorkian Center of Near Eastern Studies. On the occasion of the 50th anniversary of its establishment as a public institution, the Morgan Library put on view an astonishing array of treasures acquired after 1972, including works by Dürer, Tiepolo, Ingres, Blake, Cézanne, and Mondrian.

Museum Cooperation. A rare neo-Sumerian statue will be seen intact for the first time in possibly 4,000 years at the Louvre and the Metropolitan Museum. It was agreed to reassemble the head, owned by the Metropolitan, and the body, which belongs to the Louvre. The figure will be exhibited for three-year periods, first in Paris and then in New York.

Auctions and Sales. A painting by American abstract expressionist Willem de Kooning, *Woman V,* that cost less than $30,000 in 1953, yielded the highest price ever paid for the work of a living artist—$850,000. The previous record ($550,000) was held by a Picasso painting. A record for modern sculpture ($750,000) was set by Brancusi's *Blond Negress II.*

Art, Ethics, and the Law. Clement Greenberg, the important art critic who is also an executor of the estate of one of America's greatest sculptors, David Smith, acknowledged that he had authorized changes in the appearance of some of Smith's works after the artist's death. Among other things, he had ordered the removal of paint from several of Smith's steel pieces. It is known that he disagreed with Smith about the addition of color to sculpture.

Seven sets of lawyers argued over the disposition of 800 paintings left by Mark Rothko, one of the leading abstract expressionists. Involved in multiple suits were the Rothko family, the Marlborough Gallery, the Museum of Modern Art, the Australian National Gallery, the Internal Revenue Service, and executors for the estate. To pay for his share of legal fees, the head of Marlborough Gallery claimed he had sold 35 Rothko paintings for $1.3 million.

Honors and Commissions. German expressionist Oskar Kokoschka's *Crucifixion* became not only his first mosaic but his first religious work to find a place in a church (St. Nikolai, Hamburg). Stained glass designed by Marc Chagall was installed in a chapel at Reims Cathedral. International recognition was awarded U. S. scholar and museum director Alfred Barr by the European Art Dealers Association for his achievements at the Museum of Modern Art, New York.

Obituaries. Among notables in the art world who died in 1974 were Richard Huelsenbeck (82), a leader of the Dada movement; and David Siqueiros (77), one of Mexico's most important painters, on January 6.

VICTOR H. MIESEL
University of Michigan

ALAIN NOGUES/SYGMA

Bangladesh, still staggering from its war for independence, was hit by devastating floods in 1974. This is the area around Dacca, the capital.

ASIA

The year 1974 was one of flux in Asia. India became the world's sixth nuclear power, but the food shortage worsened, the effects of the energy crisis remained widespread, and inflation increased rapidly. The wars in Cambodia and Vietnam continued despite U. S. withdrawal.

THE CHANGING POWER STRUCTURE

India's Nuclear Explosion. The power structure within Asia shifted discernibly to the South and West in 1974. Ten years after China had set off its first nuclear explosion, India ignited a small underground nuclear device that enabled it to become a member of the small nuclear club, the only one not a member of the UN Security Council. The explosion obviously buoyed the morale of the Indian people and the country's foreign supporters. Pakistan was irate. It called off a conference for the further normalization of relations and asked the West for protection under a nuclear umbrella. India insisted that the furor was overdramatic since it intended to use nuclear energy for peaceful purposes only. But in the absence of a clear need for peaceful nuclear explosions, foreign governments generally perceived it as a step toward greater military power.

Iran's Growing Importance. Yet the explosion of India's nuclear device was probably less portentous for the continent's power structure than the huge transfer of wealth to the nations of West Asia (see feature article on Middle East, page 36). Iran produces 6.2 million barrels of oil a day. Its income from oil was over four times that of previous years—around $30 billion, or nearly $1,000 per person. Some of this new-found wealth was invested in petrochemical plants, steel plants, nuclear power stations, oil refineries, and a subway system in Teheran.

To enhance its status as regional power it agreed to purchase six high speed missile landing patrol boats from France and 30 more F-14A Tomcat fighters from the United States. Iran planned to purchase 80 such aircraft in order to counter the MIG 25's that neighboring Iraq had purchased from the Soviet Union. The Shah also talked of building up his country's naval forces, and thus Iran seemed on the way to becoming a major military power in South Asia.

Economic Problems in Japan. Iran expected to increase its gross national product (GNP) 40% in 1974. By contrast, Japan, the dominant economic power in Asia, expected only a slight drop in its GNP, a sharp decline from the 10–11% that was characteristic of the 1960's and early 1970's. Japan's 1974 balance of payments deficit of $6 billion and 25% inflation rate weakened its recently achieved role as Asia's chief banker and economic power.

However, Japan's overseas investment still rose to $10 billion, matching the foreign investment level of West Germany, which ranked third behind the United States and the Soviet Union. Nevertheless the Japanese economy was clearly hurt. The stock market plummeted, and there was widespread fear of a depression for 1975 and beyond.

Cambodia continues to be torn by civil war. Here, government soldiers capture a rebel at Peam Satha, near Phnom Penh.

UPI

(*Below*) An exhausted soldier from a Cambodian government unit on patrol in the area just north of Phnom Penh takes a break at a Buddhist temple along Highway 9.

UPI

China's Progress. China, Asia's other major power, was less affected by the economic turmoil seething throughout the rest of the continent. Relatively self-sufficient in energy, China purchased $1.15 billion of goods from the United States alone and became a U. S. trading partner equal to the Soviet Union.

China's military prowess continued its advance in 1974, and it detonated a 1 megaton nuclear device in June. British observers believed China was spending $10–$12 billion annually on its defense budget. China also continued its diplomatic offensive. It established diplomatic relations with more Latin American and African nations and established relations with Malaysia, an old foe. Taiwan broke relations with all nations that recognized China, but that policy hardly seemed likely to stop the trend.

China won a naval clash with the Republic of Vietnam in the South China Sea and occupied the small Paracel and Spratly islands. Hardly a major victory, it nevertheless indicated China's interest in all surrounding territory. Relations with the Soviet Union continued to be uneven, and no progress was made on settling their border disputes. A Peking-Moscow nonstop air service began in January, but China expelled five Soviet nationals for espionage.

FOOD AND PROSPERITY

The economic well-being and the life chances of the average Asian frequently took a turn for the worse. While overall economic growth still tended to increase in most nations in 1974, most Asians were hurt by increasing rates of inflation. Taiwanese experienced a rate of inflation above 60%; Filipinos and Indonesians, from 40%–50%; citizens of Singapore, around 35%; Indians, Japanese, and South Koreans, from 20%–30%; Iranians, Malaysians, and Sri Lankans, close to 14%.

Food Scarcity. In South Asia there was an obvious shortage of food. There were food riots in Burma and India. Outright starvation occurred there and in Bangladesh and Indonesia. Western nations and West Asian nations were inclined to provide part of the 10 million ton food shortfall, but not all of it. Fertilizer for the next year's crop, if available at all, was frequently too expensive to buy. The condition of perpetual famine in Asia predicted by the experts for the 1980's may have been moved up a decade. Few South and Southeast Asian governments went all out to produce enough food or to control population. Since starvation did not directly affect the governing elites, they appeared fatalistic about the situation.

A World Food Conference, held in Rome in November, produced some long range results in building up a food reserve and in setting up an early warning system, but it did all too little to solve the near-term problems of production and distribution. The UN World Population Conference held in August increased awareness of the problem, but the proposal to set specific targets for reducing births was rejected. No nation was inspired to provide significant economic incentives for the control of births. In fact, President Ne Win of Burma, with an eye to his large neighbors, continued to resist all birth control programs and maintained a ban on the importation of contraceptive devices into his country.

WAR AND PEACE

The wars in Cambodia and Vietnam continued unabated. In neither case did any side win a determining battle. The Vietcong made some inroads in northern South Vietnam, but the South seemed in no serious danger. Fighting was as heavy as it had been in previous years. The government of South Vietnam admitted late in the year that 25,000 of its troops had died and that over 100,000 had been wounded since the celebrated ceasefire in 1973. Casualties were fewer in Cambodia, but 2 million refugees roamed the streets of Phnom Penh. Forces of ousted leader Prince Sihanouk, which had surrounded the capital in December 1973, were forced to withdraw in February 1974. They enjoyed the psychological victory of capturing the provincial capital of Oudang in March, but government forces held all other capitals with frequently isolated garrisons.

Border tension continued between Afghanistan and Pakistan, China and the Soviet Union, and North and South Korea. Japan and South Korea signed a pact dividing mineral rights in the surrounding seas, but Japan protested the trial of a Korean kidnapped from Japanese soil in 1973. The Philippine government was angered by Malaysia's offer to accept Muslim refugees from its war-torn southern islands.

Elsewhere tensions eased somewhat. Relations between Malaysia and Singapore were normalized. India and Sri Lanka signed a territorial water agreement, and India, Pakistan, and Bangladesh exchanged prisoners held since the

UPI

In Saigon, Father Tran Huu Thanh, a Catholic priest, rallies protesters against government corruption.

(*Below*) The new king of Bhutan, 18-year-old Jigme Singye Wangchuk, is the youngest monarch in the world.

UPI

1971 war. Pakistan and Bangladesh established diplomatic relations and resumed trade. Pakistan's president, Zulfikar Ali Bhutto, visited Bangladesh in an attempt to bury the past, but his reluctance to admit any Pakistani responsibility for the earlier clash and his unwillingness to accept any more Biharis prevented further moves toward amicable relations.

AUTHORITARIANIZATION AND SOCIALIZATION

In general, liberal values again lost out to increasing government authority in Asia in 1974. Martial law continued in the Philippines. In Sri Lanka a major independent newspaper chain was shut down by the government. In India the number of persons detained without trial increased, and the noted editor of the Hindustan *Times* was fired, apparently due to the pressure of the prime minister. The press lost even more of its independence in Malayasia.

In Cambodia, President Lon Nol replaced a governing group imposed by the United States with a less representative council more to his liking. In South Korea, President Park decreed that any criticism of the constitution would be a crime. At least 19 persons were sentenced to death and over 100 were imprisoned. The 1973 liberal revolution in Thailand slowed in the absence of any rapid consensus of a new constitution.

One exception to the authoritarian trend may have occurred in tiny Sikkim, where a new constitution sharply curtailed the power of the Chogyal in favor of an elected assembly. However, the shift of power may lead to a less autonomous nation. The constitution allows the Sikkim government to "seek participation and representation for the people of Sikkim in the institutions of India," and the pro-Indian Sikkim Congress party seemed inclined to establish close ties with India.

The trend toward socialization so evident in South Asia in recent years generally continued in 1974. Pakistan nationalized all domestic banks and took over the management of shipping companies, oil distributing concerns, and the vegetable oil industry. However, Bangladesh returned industries taken from one prominent industrialist after the government proved unable to prevent heavy financial losses.

In Seoul, South Korean police repel crowd outside Japanese embassy protesting Japan's refusal to accept responsibility for assassination attempt on Korean president.

UPI

TRANSITION

In June, 18-year-old King Jigme Singye Wangchuk was grandly coronated in Bhutan. In fact, he had been the official ruler for nearly two years, but the year of mourning after his father's death and the advice of astrologers to wait for an auspicious planetary conjunction delayed the ceremony.

Also in June, Premier Yumzhagiyn Tsedenbal was elected Mongolia's new president. In Laos, Prince Souvanna Phouma was again named prime minister of the new coalition government, which now included the Pathet Lao. Prince Souvanouvong, the Pathet Lao leader, did not join the cabinet, but instead became head of the Political Council, which was to advise the government. Burma established itself as a new socialist republic, but kept its ruler of 12 years, Ne Win, who maintained one-party rule.

Elections were held in three Asian states. Sikkim held its first general election, and the Sikkim Congress, a pro-Indian, pro-democratic party won 30 of the 32 seats. The ruling National Front scored an overwhelming victory in Malaysia, winning over three quarters of the seats in Parliament and nearly 90% of state assembly seats. Japan's ruling Liberal Democratic party was reduced to only half the seats in the upper house in elections in July. Nowhere had the energy crisis produced so sharp a political effect as in the nation of Japan. As the end of the year approached, Prime Minister Kakuei Tanaka resigned as a result of the scandals surrounding his personal finances.

China was also facing the possibility of new leaders. Both Mao Tse-tung and Chou En-lai were reported ailing. The question was whether Mao's ideological group, Chou's bureaucratic group, or the army would become dominant. The ideological group promoted an anti-Confucian and anti-Lin Piao campaign in order to keep the other two groups on the defensive.

RALPH C. MEYER
Fordham University at Lincoln Center

JET PROPULSION LABORATORY, CALIFORNIA INSTITUTE OF TECHNOLOGY, NASA

(*Above*) This photo of the planet Mercury was assembled from pictures taken by Mariner 10's TV cameras. (*Right*) In picture of recent heavy activity on the sun, white areas are solar flares, black are filaments of cooler gas.

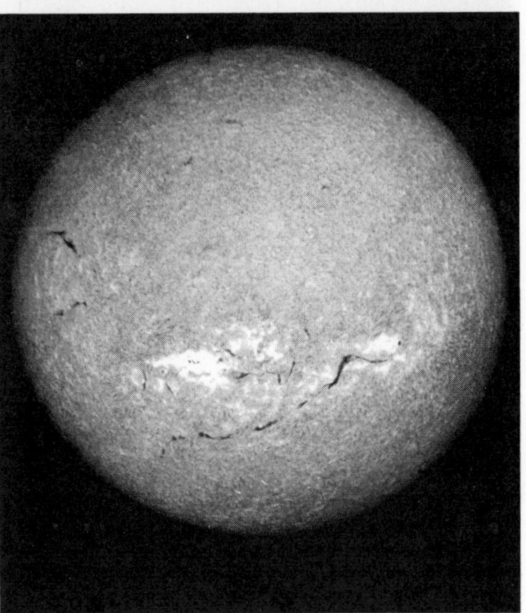

NATIONAL OCEANIC AND ATMOSPHERIC ADMINISTRATION

astronomy

The most exciting developments in astronomy in 1974 pertained to planets in the solar system, although important progress also was made in studies of galaxies, comets, black holes, and quasars.

Mariner 10, which passed near Venus and Mercury, and Pioneer 10, which was sent to Jupiter, have revealed very important data about these various planets. (See also SPACE EXPLORATION.)

Venus. Venus, a disappointing object in visible light, reveals striking cloud formations when observed in ultraviolet light. It has at least two distinct cloud layers, the topmost one being about 60 kilometers (37 miles) above its surface, and the lower layers at heights of 30 to 55 kilometers (19 to 34 miles). The circulation pattern seems to be very orderly, possibly as a consequence of Venus' slow retrograde rotation and the absence of oceans, mountains, and other features. The upper cloud deck appears to move at velocities up to 300 kilometers (about 185 miles) per hour, but the lower, dense atmosphere is probably little disturbed. Not a breath of air blows on the gloomy, oven-hot surface of this desert planet.

Mercury. The planet Mercury, as observed by Mariner 10 in March 1974, showed a lunar-type surface with craters, plains, basins, and ridges. Curiously, there are no rilles but instead ridges that run across plains and craters. This indicates that the surface was subjected not to a tension that would produce cracks, but rather to a compression. There is no evidence for plate tectonics, nor is there evidence that the planet ever had an atmosphere.

Although its high mean density, 5.5 grams per cubic centimeter (343 lbs/cu ft), suggests that Mercury has an iron core, the lunar-type features and reflective properties of the surface layers indicate it has a silicate crust many kilometers thick. Hence, separation of the chemical elements and differentiation of the core from the crust must have occurred before the bombardment of its surface had ceased.

A comparison of the surface features of Mercury, the moon, and Mars indicate that all the inner planets were subjected to heavy bombardment some 3.5 to 4.5 billion years ago. On the earth, all the evidence of early impacts was wiped out by its active geology.

Jupiter. The Pioneer 10 measurements obtained in December 1973 have greatly enhanced our knowledge of Jupiter and its remarkable magnetosphere. Before that date, it was known that the planet radiated more energy than it received from the sun, and that it had a strong magnetic field.

The Pioneer data showed that the Jovian magnetosphere extended sunward at least 100 Jovian radii and had a breadth of perhaps 40 million kilometers (25 million miles), with extremely complicated spatial- and time-dependent variations. Jupiter's magnetic field is directed opposite to that of the earth and is tilted 15° with respect to the vertical.

The average magnetic field intensity is 4 gauss, or about 10 times greater than that of the earth. Thus, as the planet rotates, the inner magnetosphere and its trapped high-energy particles are swept around over Jupiter's inner satellites. The intensity of the radiation—a flux of 4 million protons per square centimeter per second at 3.5 Jovian radii and at energies exceeding 30 MeV—greatly exceeds that in our magnetosphere and poses a hazard to spacecraft.

Jupiter itself seems to embody features of both a planet and a star. It appears to be radiating away internal heat from an interior that may be at a temperature of tens of thousands of degrees. The cloud deck in the atmosphere is at a temperature well below 0°C (32°F), but within 1,000 kilometers (620 miles) below the cloud tops, the gases are compressed to a dense viscous form that resembles a liquid. At a depth of about 25,000 kilometers (15,500 miles) hydrogen is probably compressed to a metallic form, and this form is retained down to the core of the planet. Convection currents in this conducting fluid presumably produce a dynamo effect that causes the strong magnetic field, but one puzzle is why the dynamo is asymmetrical.

On Jupiter, masses of condensates, which would form patchy cloudy areas on a more slowly spinning planet like the earth, are affected by strong Coriolis forces and drawn out into long bands characteristic of this planet. It has been suggested that the Great Red Spot, which has been observed for more than a century, is a Jovian analog of a hurricane that would endure only a few days on earth.

13th Moon of Jupiter. A very small moon of Jupiter was discovered by astronomers in 1974, bringing its total number of known moons to 13.

Complex Molecules in Space. Comets, interstellar molecules, and the origin of life appeared interrelated. Radio astronomers find increasingly complex molecules such as dimethyl ether, $(CH_3)_2O$, methylamine, CH_3NH_2, and ethanol, C_2H_6O, in Orion and other gassy, dusty regions in our galaxy. It now appears likely that the first organic compounds were introduced into the young earth from space rather than being produced on our planet.

Comet Kohoutek yielded a wealth of valuable relevant information while it was observed by well-organized teams using ground-based, satellite, rocket, and Skylab instrumentation. F. L. Whipple's theory that comets are a conglomerate of ice, frozen gases, and silicates that volatilizes as it approaches the sun has been substantiated. A great cloud of hydrogen is developed by a comet as hydrogen-rich parent molecules, many of them similar to those found in interstellar matter, are driven off and dissociated.

Comets are believed to be leftover fragments from the formation of the solar system, and thus they embody the primitive material from which it was formed. The first steps toward life on earth thus may have been taken in the interstellar smog clouds long before the solar system was formed.

Black Holes. Increasing evidence supports the idea that Cygnus X-1 is really a black hole. Additional candidates for black holes were actively being screened. For instance, astronomers at the Center for Astrophysics in Cambridge, Mass., in 1974 said that they may have found a second black hole, the star Circinus X-1.

Quasars. It seems more and more likely that quasars are at cosmological distances—that is, at distances inferred from their red shifts and the Hubble relation. They appear to be cores of unusual far-distant galaxies whose outer portions are very faint as compared with the nucleus. Quasars appear to have occurred more often during the early stages of the development of the universe.

Telescopes. The world's largest radio telescope—the 1,000-foot-diameter (305-meter) dish antenna at the Arecibo Ionospheric Observatory in Puerto Rico—was rebuilt in 1974 by using adjustable aluminum panels in place of the wire mesh of the dish. Wavelengths as short as 7 centimeters can now be used in radar work and passive radio astronomy.

Construction of the Very Large Array (VLA) radio telescope was started on June 25 in New Mexico. The telescope, described as "the single most important project in astronomy for the next decade," will consist of a network of 27 movable 85-foot (26-meter) dish antennas that are maneuverable over a Y shape that stretches over an area 28 miles (45 km) in diameter. The individual antennas will be linked by microwave waveguides to a computer, which can be programmed to assess and interpret the observations. When the system is completed about 1981, it will be possible to observe radio sources with the same angular resolution as that of a 200-inch telescope.

Solar Eclipse. The total solar eclipse of June 30, 1974, passed near the southeast corner of Western Australia, where it was observed by a number of groups.

LAWRENCE H. ALLER
University of California, Los Angeles

ATLANTA

The year 1974 was highlighted in Atlanta by governmental reorganization, a battle for control of the police department, the kidnapping of the editor of *The Atlanta Constitution,* and the slaying of Mrs. Martin Luther King, Sr.

New Mayor. On January 7, Maynard Jackson was sworn in as the first black mayor of the city of Atlanta. Immediately, the new mayor announced the appointment of Jule M. Sugarman, a 22-year veteran of federal and New York City bureaucracy, as his chief administrative officer. Sugarman, former head of the N.Y.C. Human Resources Administration, began the task of reorganizing the city's 26 departments into nine "super" departments, and of transforming governmental operations to comply with the new city charter.

"Superchief." One of the nine "super" departments created under the new charter was the Department of Public Safety, which combined the operations of the Atlanta police, fire, and civil defense departments under one agency. It would be headed by a public safety commissioner—the "superchief," as the position came to be called.

Under normal circumstances Police Chief John Inman would have been in line for the new position, but Mayor Jackson and Inman were at odds over the operations of the police department and over the fact that Atlanta continued in the first quarter of 1974 to hold the title "murder capital of the United States." Atlanta also led the country in numbers of violent crimes (murder, rape, and assault) on a per capita basis.

In May, the mayor suspended the police chief and named former Detective Superintendent Clinton Chafin as "interim chief." Inman refused to relinquish the chief's office, and he and Chafin, both escorted by armed police officers, claimed the chief's job. A lengthy court battle ensued.

Meanwhile, several widely known law enforcers were interviewed for the "superchief" job, but a court-issued restraining order obtained by Inman kept the mayor from hiring anyone for the new post. By the time the Georgia Supreme Court ruled in the mayor's favor—holding the new city charter and its provisions for reorganization to be legal—the candidate list had dwindled. Finally, the mayor named a college classmate, Reginald Eaves, to the post.

Eaves, who had been an administrative assistant to the mayor from the beginning of his term, was formerly director of the Boston Office of Human Rights and served for a time as Boston corrections commissioner. The court suits brought by the police chief were dropped after Inman was named director of police services, a post directly under Eaves.

Eaves began immediately to revamp the police department, a process that involved scores of promotions and demotions. At year's end more patrolmen were on the streets than ever before, and crime had shown a slight decrease.

UPI

The Rev. Calvin Morris comforts a young girl in the Atlanta church where the mother of the slain civil rights leader Martin Luther King, Jr., was shot and killed.

Kidnapping. On February 20, J. Reginald Murphy, editor of *The Atlanta Constitution,* was lured from his home and held for ransom by a man who claimed to be a colonel in the "American Revolutionary Army" which was protesting the "leftist, liberal news media." Murphy was released 46 hours later after his employers paid a $700,000 ransom. Shortly after Murphy's release a self-employed building contractor, William A. Williams, and his wife, Betty, were arrested. The ransom was recovered, and Williams was convicted of extortion. His wife was placed on probation.

Slaying. On June 30, Mrs. Martin Luther King, Sr., was shot to death as she played the organ during Sunday services at Ebenezer Baptist Church. Marcus W. Chenault, 23, of Dayton, Ohio, was convicted of murder in the slaying of the late civil rights leader's mother.

Business. Atlanta moved into third place in the nation in convention business in 1974, behind Chicago and New York. Construction began on five major new downtown hotels—one 70 stories tall—and approval was granted to build a $35 million World Congress Center in downtown Atlanta. Tourism also increased.

GENE STEPHENS
Georgia State University

UPI

Australian Prime Minister and Mrs. Gough Whitlam, arriving in Manila for a four-day state visit, are greeted by Philippine President and Mrs. Marcos.

AUSTRALIA

After a free-spending first quarter, 1974 turned into a year of soaring inflation (over 20%), industrial unrest, and flagging economic activity. By October, unemployment exceeded 3%—the highest level in over 30 years. The flow of settlers from abroad was cut back, moving Australia away from the expansionary approach which had been stimulating development.

Politics. After Prime Minister Gough Whitlam appointed a political opponent, Sen. Vincent Gair, to an ambassadorship in order to open the way for an Australian Labor party (ALP) replacement, the Liberal-Country party coalition combined with the Democratic Labor party (DLP) in April to block various bills in the Senate. This allowed Whitlam to secure a dissolution of both houses of Parliament.

AUSTRALIA • Information Highlights

Location: Southwestern Pacific Ocean.
Area: 2,967,900 square miles (7,686,848 sq km).
Population (1974 est.): 13,340,000.
Chief Cities (1971 census, met. areas): Canberra, the capital, 156,298; Sydney, 2,725,064; Melbourne, 2,394,117.
Government: *Head of state,* Elizabeth II, queen; represented by Sir John Kerr, governor-general (took office July 1974). *Head of government,* Gough Whitlam, prime minister (took office Dec. 1972). *Legislature*—Parliament: Senate and House of Representatives.
Monetary Unit: Australian dollar (0.7686 A. dollar equals U. S.$1, Sept. 1974).
Gross National Product (1973 est.): $53,500,000,000.
Manufacturing (major products): Petroleum products, steel, machinery, chemicals, automobiles, meat.
Major Agricultural Products: Wool, sugarcane, barley, fruit, tobacco, dairy products, sheep.
Foreign Trade (1973): *Exports,* $9,389,000,000; *imports,* $6,802,000,000.

Brushing aside growing public concern about the spiraling cost of living (then rising at about 15% a year), Prime Minister Whitlam claimed inflation was under control and underscored pledges to pursue Labor's social policies. The election of May 18 reduced the ALP majority in the House of Representatives to 5, and left the party in a minority (29–31) in the Senate. It also resulted in the DLP's loss of parliamentary representation. Subsequently a joint session of the two houses carried the six disputed bills.

A running fire of policy disputes and personality clashes continued between the trade union wing and the ALP parliamentary leadership, and parallel strains were apparent within the parliamentary group on many issues. The ensuing trend was toward a growing ascendancy by left-wing elements. Soon after the election, Overseas Trade Minister James Cairns, an activist espousing unorthodox economic views, challenged Defense Minister Lance Barnard, a moderate, for the deputy leadership, and won with the support of the augmented left.

Subsequently the increasing pressure exerted by the caucus majority, and by Cairns as its spokesman, was seen in the government's acceptance of reflationary measures—especially the release of credit to the banking system (from August) and the introduction in September of an expansionary budget "accepting" rather than "restraining" inflation. In November, Whitlam named Cairns to the post of treasurer.

After their electoral failure, the Liberal and Country parties moderated their parliamentary challenges. At the same time their political colleagues in the states stood firmly against further federal encroachment in areas of traditional states' rights. An election in Western Australia resulted in the ALP's overthrow there, and in Queensland the ALP parliamentary minority was further reduced in an election which Premier Joh Bjelke-Petersen declared would undoubtedly "pave the way" for early electoral defeat of the Whitlam government.

Domestic Policy. Adopting a more liberal line toward investment from abroad, the government in November modified its declared objective of blocking further foreign ownership, particularly of uranium, oil, natural gas and coal, and other minerals.

In opening the door again to foreign investment, Whitlam explained the goal as seeking "maximum Australian ownership compatible with Australia's long-term capital requirements and its needs for access to markets, advanced technology and knowhow."

The switch was timed to encourage Japan's involvement in new exploration and development ventures, including uranium. The relaxation was announced in early November at the time of Prime Minister Tanaka's visit to Canberra, during which an understanding was reached to step up Australia's coal exports to Japan from 25 million tons a year to over 40 million tons a year by 1980, and preliminary agreement was reached regarding the building of a uranium-enrichment plant financed by Japan. Australia and Japan undertook also to study plans for a major plant to produce gasoline and other derivatives from coal.

The wider issue of Australia's attitudes as a major trader in minerals was under review. Australia took a leading role in the formation of the International Bauxite Association and at the group's initial meeting came out against a common world-pricing policy for bauxite and alumina. With iron ore, Australia favored informal consultation among exporting countries rather than creation of formalized machinery, and in discussions with other major producing nations stressed the view that consumer countries should be assured of access to supplies of iron ore at fair prices.

The Economy. Wages rose more than 20% in 1974, and prices soared accordingly. For most Australians, 1974 was a year of marginal gains in prosperity, and for many it was a time of grave fears. The rural sector suffered its most severe setback in many years with sharp falls in income from beef and wool. Floods in many areas of southern Australia added to the difficulties caused by higher costs. In the manufacturing and service industries, days lost through strikes were greater than in any year in the nation's history.

A sharp decline in business confidence began about midyear. Plans for even cautious expansion were ended with the tightening of the capital market and unprecedented interest rates (raised 2% in July).

The budget, presupposing a 22.5% inflation rate for 1974–75, featured a massive growth in federal expenditure—up 32.5% over the expanded budget for 1973–74. Education and social services were accorded the biggest increases.

Big increases occurred in the value of Australia's exports of grains, sugar, metal ores, coal, and chemicals, but meat and wool made a poor showing throughout the year. Steep rises in import figures centered around oil, chemicals, plastics, textiles, clothing, machinery, and vehicles, including automobiles.

In the third quarter a record U. S.$786 million balance-of-payments deficit drew international reserves down to approximately U. S.$4 billion. Record imports of U. S.$2.712 billion, up 69% over the third quarter of 1973, overwhelmed record export earnings of U. S.$2.523 billion. The quarter's trade deficit of U. S.$189 million was augmented by outlays of U. S.$646 million on invisibles, while net capital inflow was only U. S.$29 million.

A 12% devaluation of the Australian dollar was made in late September to help stem the drain on reserves, but the deficit continued in the final quarter.

Jim Hardy, skipper of the *Southern Cross*, waves to well-wishers before the America's Cup race. The Australian challenger lost to the American yacht *Courageous*.

UPI

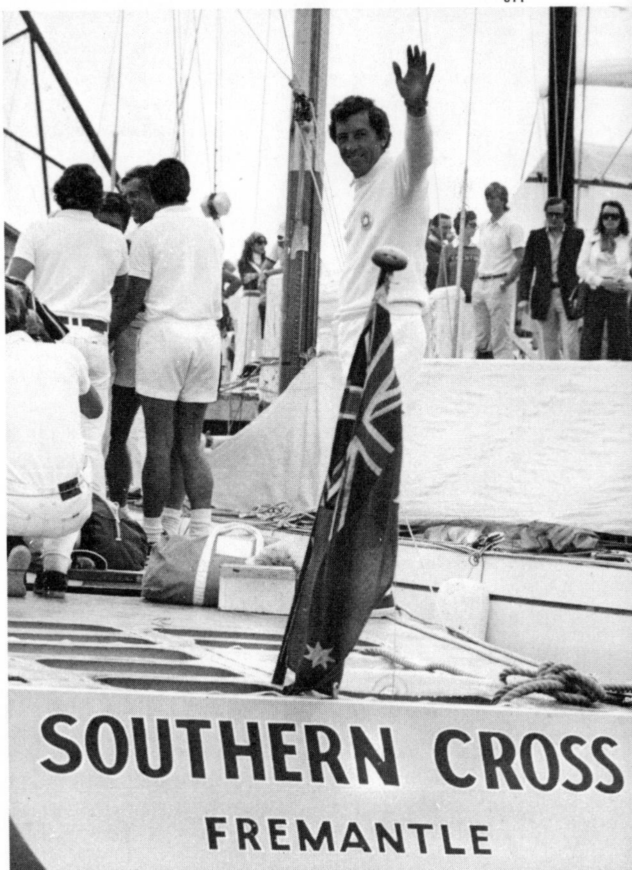

BOB NICOL/AUSTRALIAN INFORMATION SERVICE PHOTO

BOB NICOL/AUSTRALIAN INFORMATION SERVICE PHOTO

Torrential rains in February caused crippling floods in many parts of Australia. These are views of South Brisbane during the worst of the flooding.

In mid-November the government moved to restore confidence by easing the credit squeeze, releasing money for housing, trimming company and personal income taxes, scaling down automobile imports to benefit local manufacture, and removing restrictions on capital inflow. The stock market rose about 10% to end a six-month decline that had cut prices by 50%.

Foreign Affairs. In a year of world economic strains and tensions between resource-consuming and resource-holding nations, relations with Japan took the spotlight among Australia's international policies. The government was at pains to stress the importance attached to maintaining fair and stable trade relationships with Japan, the nation's leading trade partner. Reassurances on access and fair prices were given during the visit to Canberra of Prime Minister Tanaka in early November.

The Whitlam government faced criticism in various quarters (including ethnic groups) for its recognition of the long-existing absorption of Estonia, Latvia, and Lithuania within the Soviet Union.

New Telescope. On October 16, during his visit to Australia, Prince Charles inaugurated the U. S.$21 million Anglo-Australian Telescope, at Coonabarabran, New South Wales. With a 3.9-meter (12.8-foot) mirror, the telescope is the largest optical instrument in the Southern Hemisphere; it is capable of penetrating the southern sky to a distance of a billion light-years. It was built for the Australian Department of Science and the British Science Research Council, and is operated as part of the Australian National University's observatory.

R. M. YOUNGER
Author, "Australia and the Australians"

AUSTRIA

The Austrian economy, in its seventh consecutive year of growth, continued to expand in 1974. In the political realm the most significant event was the death of President Franz Jonas and the election of Rudolf Kirchschläger as his successor.

Political Events. Franz Jonas, a lifelong Socialist and fourth president of the postwar Austrian Republic, was elected president in 1965 and reelected in 1971. Jonas, suffering from cancer, was declared by his doctors on March 27, 1974, to be incapable of fulfilling his duties, and the presidential powers were assumed by Chancellor Bruno Kreisky for no more than a 20-day period. Before this time expired the presidential responsibilities were assumed by the president of the lower chamber and his two deputies. President Jonas died on April 23 and was given a state funeral on April 29.

Largely on the initiative of Chancellor Kreisky, Foreign Minister Rudolf Kirchschläger became the Socialist candidate for president, although some of the party stalwarts opposed his nomination because of his lack of party affiliation. The People's party put forward Alois Lugger, mayor of Innsbruck. The campaign was unexpectedly heated, and both candidates were charged with cooperation with authoritarian right-wing groups before the incorporation of Austria into Germany in 1938. At the election held on June 23, Kirchschläger received 2,392,151 votes to Lugger's 2,238,680.

The new president took office on July 8. He was replaced at the Foreign Office by Erich Bielka-Karltreu, Austrian ambassador to France since 1972. The presidential election was considered to reflect the personal popularity of Chancellor Kreisky and his government. Previous provincial elections, in Salzburg on March 13 and in Lower Austria on June 9, had both shown slight gains for the People's party.

Economic Developments. The Austrian Institute for Economic Research forecast in August a rate of real economic growth in Austria of over 5% for 1974. Exports continued to expand and were expected to surpass the 1973 growth rate.

Inflation continued to plague the economy but to a lesser degree than in most countries. In 1973 the rate of inflation was 7.8%, the same as that of West Germany and below that of the United States (8.8%). It was estimated that the inflation rate would be somewhat higher in 1974, despite efforts by the government to stabilize the economy. Among these efforts was a de facto upward revaluation of the schilling by 3% in May, following the revaluation of 2.25% in March 1973, and 4.8% in July 1973.

On January 29 a U. S. district court ruled that the Austrian concern VOEST owned the patent to the basic oxygen furnace steelmaking process and ordered U. S. steel companies using that process to pay royalties. With its extensive hydroelectric power system and its own oil production, Austria is less dependent on imported oil than most industrialized countries, and the energy crisis of 1973–74 brought no acute problems. The speed limit of 100 km (62 miles) per hour imposed on Nov. 25, 1973, was raised to 120 km (75 miles) per hour in March and to 130 km (81 miles) per hour on May 1.

Foreign Affairs. At the beginning of February, President Luis Echeverría Álvarez of Mexico made a formal state visit to Austria, enlisting the support of the Austrian government for his proposed United Nations charter for economic rights and duties of nations.

Early in June, Chancellor Kreisky paid a visit to Moscow, but was unable to persuade the Soviet leaders to agree that oil exports to Austria should be nearly tripled, to 3 million metric tons, by the end of 1978. The Soviet authorities did offer to increase natural gas deliveries to 4 billion cubic meters (141 billion cubic feet) in the next decade, starting with an increase of 500 million cubic meters (17.7 billion cubic feet) in 1974. The Russians later sent a delegation to Vienna to continue discussions regarding possible joint economic projects with Austria including bilateral cooperation on atomic energy.

On June 10–11, President Nixon stopped off in Salzburg on his trip to the Middle East and met with Chancellor Kreisky.

In September the Austrian government's relocation of the Red Cross Transfer Center for Soviet Jews en route to Israel from Wöllersdorf, south of Vienna, to a heavily guarded building in Vienna's Simmering district aroused considerable protest. It was feared that the transfer center would bring terrorist activity to this residential district. On September 29 the Israeli government ratified a treaty with Austria, settling a 15-year dispute over pension payments by Austria to Austrian Nazi victims now living in Israel.

ERNST C. HELMREICH
Bowdoin College

AUSTRIA • Information Highlights

Official Name: Republic of Austria.
Location: Central Europe.
Area: 32,374 square miles (83,849 sq km).
Population (1973 est.): 7,500,000.
Chief Cities (1971 census): Vienna, the capital, 1,614,841; Graz, 248,500; Linz, 202,874; Salzburg, 128,845.
Government: *Head of state,* Rudolf Kirchschläger, president (took office July 1974). *Head of government,* Bruno Kreisky, chancellor (took office April 1970). *Legislature*—Federal Assembly: Federal Council and National Council.
Monetary Unit: Schilling (18.38 schillings equal U. S.$1, July 1974).
Gross National Product (1973 est.): $24,100,000,000.
Manufacturing (major products): Processed foods, chemicals, textiles, iron, steel, electrical goods, machinery, paper, wood products.
Major Agricultural Products: Rye, wheat, barley, potatoes, sugar beets, oats, forest products.
Foreign Trade (1973): Exports, $5,289,000,000; imports, $7,120,000,000.

New For '75

CHRYSLER MOTORS CORPORATION

Chrysler entered the 1975 "intermediate" car sweepstakes with the Cordoba, a two-door hardtop billed as a "personal luxury automobile designed to reflect the Chrysler name."

GENERAL MOTORS CORPORATION

Among its 1975 models, General Motors brought out the first subcompact to carry the Buick nameplate—the Skyhawk, a four-passenger sports coupe with a six-cylinder engine.

AMERICAN MOTORS CORPORATION

The American Motors' Hornet Sportabout for 1975, the only American-made four-door station wagon in the compact class, features a new electronic ignition system.

FORD MOTOR COMPANY

Ford's 1975 entry in the "intermediate" class, the Granada, has a six-cylinder engine, manual front disc brakes, and fully reclining front bucket seats as standard equipment.

automobiles

The world market for new cars fell sharply during 1974 under pressures from three sources: rising prices and factory costs in the worldwide inflation crisis; the winter-long oil embargo imposed against Western nations and Japan (deemed friendly toward Israel) by the Arab producing nations in mid-October 1973; and increased attention in the United States to improved fuel economy as a new-car buying factor. Only Canada, among the larger new-vehicle market nations, concluded the 1974 model year with increased sales over 1973.

1974 MODEL PRODUCTION

United States auto producers started out 1974-model production at the record pace with which they built over 9 million cars and 3 million trucks and buses during the 1973 model run. But the oil embargo and resulting declines in sales of largest-sized models brought cutbacks and layoffs by December 1973. Sales of compact and subcompact cars improved, but not enough to offset the losses in the standard and intermediate sizes.

Production Figures. Through August 1974, with subcompact lines of 1974 models still coming off the lines at Chevrolet and Ford, 8,067,303 1974-model cars had been built, as compared with a total output of 9,915,803 1973-model cars, a decrease of 22%. The production of trucks for the 1974-model run totaled 2,737,124 units, as compared with 2,950,505 for the 1973-model run.

For the 1974-model run through August 1974, General Motors lost the greatest share of total production—from 5,377,566 cars (54.4% of total U. S. production) in the comparable 1973-model period to 4,017,760 (49.8% of the total). All GM divisions, hurt by the swing away from big cars in the energy crisis, declined substantially: Chevrolet, from 2,417,448 units to 2,100,064; Pontiac, from 894,446 to 560,296; Oldsmobile, from 939,630 to 619,519; Buick, from 821,165 to 495,551; and Cadillac, from 304,839 to 242,330. GM's share-of-output loss allowed other domestic auto makers to increase or stabilize their shares. Ford Motor rose from

25.9% to 28.7%, though production fell from 2,562,625 units to 2,317,387. Chrysler Corporation held even at 16.4% as its output dropped from 1,623,469 to 1,319,885. And American Motors gained from 3.3% to 5.1% on an output increase from 320,786 units to 412,271.

Canada built 975,000 cars and 317,000 trucks in the 1974-model run, up from the previous model year's total of 971,000 cars and 254,200 trucks.

Sales of imported new cars in the United States dropped in the first eight months of 1974 to 969,306 from 1,261,659 in the January–August period of 1973.

Registered Motor Vehicles. Of the world total of 220,051,854 passenger cars in operation at the beginning of 1974, the United States accounted for 96,859,746, of which 10,392,298 were foreign-built. A total of 29,893,739 cars were produced in 1973, of which the United States produced 9,667,156. Japan ranked second in 1973 output, at 4,470,550; West Germany third, at 3,648,880; France fourth, at 3,202,391; and Italy fifth, at 1,823,333. There were 59,177,784 trucks and buses in worldwide use, of which 21,646,117 were in the United States.

THE 1975 MODELS

Fuel Economy and Pollution. The emphasis on "mileage per gallon," first underscored by the oil embargo and gasoline station shortages or shutdowns early in 1974, gained additional significance with adoption of more stringent federal emission standards for 1975-model cars and light trucks. Compliance with the new standards brought an introduction of muffler-like catalytic converters on most domestic 1975 models. This, in turn, ushered in a requirement that 1975 models use lead-free gasoline, because the presence of lead "poisons" or fouls out the platinum/palladium catalyst and makes it ineffectual in reducing pollutant output. Catalytic converters also improved fuel economy because it became possible with 1975 cars to halt installation of several emission-control devices which had worsened mileage-per-gallon ratings on many 1974 models.

The Environmental Protection Agency issued 1975-model mileage data which showed an average increase of 13.5% over the 1974 models. Best rated in mileage per gallon was the Datsun B-210, with 27 miles per gallon in city driving and 39 in highway use. Twelve imported cars were ranked better than the best U. S.-produced car—Chevrolet's Vega, with 22 miles per gallon in city use and 29 on highway tests.

New Models. U. S. manufacturers introduced 10 new models for 1975, all stressing more economical performance features. American Motors, alone in raising its 1974-model output from that of 1973 because of its emphasis on smaller cars, dropped two low-selling, higher-priced models—the intermediate Ambassador and sporty Javelin—and planned to introduce a new subcompact called the Pacer in January 1975. Chrysler Corporation restyled its 1975 intermediates and for the first time offered a middle-sized Chrysler car model—the Cordoba. Chrysler also committed more production capacity to its compact Valiant and Dart lines, which became its top sellers in 1974.

Ford introduced two "luxury compacts" for 1975—the Ford Granada and the Mercury Monarch. Increased attention was being paid to the 112-inch-wheelbase sedan as the "optimum" size for the later 1970's, with six-cylinder and small V-8 engines as options.

General Motors, hardest hit in terms of volume losses during the 1974-model year, introduced a new "economy" car in each of its five divisions in 1975. Chevrolet, Buick, and Oldsmobile offered sporty-type subcompacts called the Monza, Skyhawk, and Starfire, respectively. Pontiac joined its Canadian counterpart in adding a derivative of the subcompact Vega named the Astre. A compact model of the commodious Cadillac, tentatively named the LaSalle, was planned for the spring of 1975. This was to be built on the GM compact body used for the Chevrolet Nova, Pontiac Ventura, Buick Apollo, and Oldsmobile Omega, all of which were redesigned for 1975 as a reaction to economic trends.

A number of Detroit manufacturers modified engines to improve fuel economy, and GM offered a V-6 engine on Buick and Oldsmobile cars which it had discontinued during the 1960's.

MAYNARD M. GORDON
Editor, "Motor News Analysis"

WORLD MOTOR VEHICLE DATA, 1973

Country	Passenger car production	Truck and bus production	Passenger car registrations
Argentina	233,660	77,954	1,825,000
Australia	371,812	82,978	4,461,252
Austria	829	6,399	1,460,163
Belgium	245,933	53,024	2,273,163
Brazil	456,077	273,058	2,984,200
Canada	1,227,432	347,388	7,407,275
Czechoslovakia	165,878	31,927	1,083,582
France	3,202,391	393,788	13,800,000
Germany, East	146,020	32,000	1,400,390
Germany, West	3,648,880	299,185	16,323,997
Hungary	...	11,000	342,920
India	39,071	5,980	729,000
Italy	1,823,333	134,661	12,484,313
Japan	4,470,550	2,612,207	12,531,149
Mexico	200,147	85,366	1,520,144
Netherlands	94,906	12,546	2,900,000
Poland	115,400	75,000	656,900
Portugal	...	432	655,677
Rumania	37,000	53,000	125,730
Spain	706,433	115,527	3,254,801
Sweden	341,503	36,539	2,456,940
Switzerland	143	1,290	1,580,000
USSR	917,000	685,000	1,815,000
United Kingdom	1,747,316	416,625	13,029,760
United States	9,667,156	3,014,361	96,859,746[1]
Yugoslavia	124,993	18,833	996,596
Total	29,983,739[2]	8,933,128	220,051,854[3]

[1]Includes Puerto Rico, 609,634; Canal Zone, 21,949; and Virgin Islands, 27,825. [2]Excludes 1,492,127 cars assembled by 22 countries led by Belgium, 723,331, and South Africa, 224,442. [3]Registration total includes all countries, of which non-producing countries approaching or exceeding 1 million registrations were: Denmark, 1,203,243; Norway, 854,237; New Zealand, 1,000,306; South Africa, 1,660,195; Venezuela, 768,586. Source: Motor Vehicle Manufacturers Association of the United States, Inc.

JEHANGIR GAZDAR—WOODFIN CAMP

Joining hands after settling prisoner issue from 1971 war are *(left to right)* Kamal Hossain of Bangladesh, Swaran Singh of India, and Aziz Ahmed of Pakistan.

BANGLADESH

For Bangladesh, formerly the East Bengal province of Pakistan, 1974 was a year of some recognition and achievement, but the usual natural disasters occurred and the nation sank even deeper into its economic morass.

Foreign Affairs. The year witnessed encouraging progress in the normalization of Bangladesh's relations with its two most important neighbors, Pakistan and India.

On February 22, on the eve of a world Islamic conference being held in Lahore, Prime Minister Zulfikar Ali Bhutto of Pakistan extended recognition to Bangladesh. The next day he welcomed at the airport the arrival of Sheikh Mujibur Rahman, the prime minister of Bangladesh. This recognition, coming nearly three years after Bangladesh was formed, was the product of long negotiation. The key element for Bhutto was that Bangladesh abandon any attempts to try about 200 former Pakistani military officers for atrocities in the 1971 fighting.

On April 5, the foreign ministers of India, Pakistan, and Bangladesh met in New Delhi in the first such joint meeting ever held. On April 10, Pakistan formally apologized for the violence which its troops inflicted on Bangladesh in 1971; in return, Bangladesh agreed to surrender all prisoners of war, including those held for trial for atrocities. The prime ministers of both Pakistan and Bangladesh appealed to the people of Bangladesh to forgive and forget the past and to make a fresh start.

The remaining problem was that of the Biharis, a Muslim refugee group originally from the Indian state of Bihar. They had fled into East Bengal in 1947 when Pakistan and India had received their independence, and in the 1971 civil war in Bangladesh they had supported Pakistan. They number between a half million and a million, and they consider themselves Pakistanis. The disposition of this group was the remaining big issue for the April meeting in New Delhi. Before the New Delhi meeting, Pakistan apparently had agreed to accept 140,000 Bihari immigrants, but in the agreement of April 10 no limitation of numbers was specified.

In late June, Prime Minister Bhutto made an official visit to Bangladesh and was greeted by enormous crowds. Bhutto publicly apologized once again for what he termed the "shameful repression and unspeakable crimes" committed by Pakistan against Bangladesh in 1971. He blamed the former president Gen. Mohammad Yahya Khan for these acts. The visit was not considered a success in Bangladesh, in that no further progress was made on the question of how many Biharis were actually to go to Pakistan. No solution was found for the continuing

—— BANGLADESH • Information Highlights ——

Official Name: People's Republic of Bangladesh.
Location: South Asia.
Area: 55,126 square miles (142,776 sq km).
Population (1974 census): 71,600,000.
Chief Cities (1974 census): Dacca, the capital, 1,310,976; Khulna, 436,000; Chittagong, 416,733.
Government: *Head of state,* Mohammed Ullah, president (took office Jan. 1974). *Head of government,* Mujibur Rahman, prime minister (took office Jan. 1972). *Legislature* (unicameral)—Jatiyo Sangsad (National Assembly).
Monetary Unit: Taka (7.946 takas equal U. S.$1, July 1974).
Gross National Product (1972 est.): $5,300,000,000.
Manufacturing (major products): Jute products, cotton textiles, processed foods, wood products.
Major Agricultural Products: Rice, jute, sugarcane, tea, oilseeds, pulses, fish, forest products.
Foreign Trade (1971): *Exports,* $263,000,000; *imports,* $331,000,000.

problem of an equitable division of the pre-independence Pakistani public debt or the return to Bangladesh of certain assets claimed by it in Pakistan.

In May, Prime Minister Sheikh Mujibur Rahman went to New Delhi for five days of discussions with Indian Prime Minister Indira Gandhi. Minor border rectifications were agreed upon in these talks, and a formula for sharing the Ganges River waters was found. India extended a $50 million credit to Bangladesh for the construction of industrial plants, and agreement was reached on closer trade relations. India and Bangladesh pledged to remain among what they called the "nonaligned" nations, and they called for caution by the United States in its move to create a naval base on Diego Garcia island in the Indian Ocean.

On a trip to the Middle East and Asia in October, U. S. Secretary of State Henry Kissinger visited India, Pakistan, and Bangladesh. His talks with Sheikh Mujibur Rahman and other Bangladesh officials were described as "cordial and warm," and in response to its request for increased economic aid, Bangladesh was reassured of continued American support.

Domestic Affairs and the Economy. In human terms, Bangladesh is in desperate straits; and in economic terms, conditions are worse than those that obtained before the country gained its independence more than three years ago. There was little improvement in 1974.

On January 24 the Jatiyo Sangsad (National Assembly) elected its speaker, Mohammed Ullah, to be president of Bangladesh, succeeding Abu Sayeed Choudhury. The new president took office on January 27.

The year opened with the creation of a five-year plan capitalized at $6 billion. Officials frankly conceded that there could be no turnaround for the economy for several years; meanwhile Bangladesh would remain in what was called "dismal poverty." However, a remarkable rice crop of 12 million tons was harvested, and world jute prices rose during the year. The critical problem is that population continues to grow almost without restriction. Its current annual growth rate of 3% is higher than India's and, if it continues, will result in a doubling of the population of 72 million within 20 years. The five-year plan's objective of 5.5% growth, if realized, will be needed merely to keep pace with population growth. Per capita annual income is approximately $70.

In addition, some natural disaster seems to afflict Bangladesh each year. In 1974 it was the worst floods in 20 years. The Ganges, Meghna, and Brahmaputra rivers rose at the same time in July and August. Nearly 70% of the country was flooded, and 80% of the summer crops was destroyed. About 2,000 people were reportedly killed, and several million were driven from their homes. The result by late fall was widespread starvation throughout the country. The government seemed unable to cope with a situation aggravated by other economic ills. In addition, a cyclone swept through the nation in late November, leaving thousands of people homeless.

At year's end the economic and political prognosis of the country seemed poor.

CARL LEIDEN
The University of Texas at Austin

A mother holds her starving child and an empty bowl in a refugee camp in Bangladesh, where badly needed supplies of food are slow to arrive from the rest of the world.

UPI

BANKING

The term "stagflation" was coined to describe the conditions of inflationary recession that prevailed in the U. S. economy during 1974. Real gross national product declined in each of the year's first three quarters by 7% in the first, 1.6% in the second, and 2.9% in the third. Meanwhile, both prices and unemployment rose drastically; the year's inflation rate was estimated to be 11–12% (for the first year of "double digit" inflation since the 1940's); and the unemployment rate of 6.5% of the civilian labor force in November was expected to reach 7% by the end of the year.

Monetary Policy. The major national economic force attempting to steer the economy between the Scylla of inflation and the Charybdis of recession in 1974 was the Federal Reserve System. Federal Reserve had decided before the end of 1973 that inflation was the lesser of the two evils. That meant that the nation would have to accept whatever unemployment rate was consonant with governmental actions aimed at reducing the inflation rate. Thus, Federal Reserve had begun in 1973 to move forcefully to limit monetary growth, primarily through its open-market operations (the sale of massive amounts of government securities from its portfolio, thereby putting increasing pressure on commercial bank reserve positions), but also through raising member bank reserve requirements against deposits and increasing its discount rate (the rate at which it will lend additional reserves to the commercial banking system).

This policy of severe and increasing monetary restraint continued into 1974, as the real gross national product declined, partly because of the Federal Reserve policy of restraint, but principally because of the direct and indirect effects of the fuel shortage.

The Money Supply, Interest Rates, and Bank Credit. Rapid price inflation during the year raised current-dollar expenditures and sharply increased the book value of inventories, leading to intense business demands for bank credit. Interest rates, which declined somewhat in January and February, began to rise again and rose still faster in April when the Federal Reserve System raised its discount rate from 7.5% to 8%. This action triggered a parallel increase in the commercial banks' prime lending rate—the rate at which they lend to their best business borrowing customers—to 11.75% by the end of June. (This rate later rose to its all-time high of 12%, but began falling back late in the year as Federal Reserve loosened credit conditions slightly.)

Despite rising interest rates and other evidences of severe conditions of monetary restraint, the money supply (privately owned demand deposits and currency) grew at a seasonally adjusted annual rate of 7% in the April-June 1974 period, a rate only slightly below that of the first quarter, and clearly excessive. Commercial banks were enabled to extend huge amounts of credit to their business customers, adding fuel to the inflationary fires.

In the year's third quarter, as Federal Reserve restrictive policies finally began to bite, the money supply grew only 2% (seasonally adjusted annual rate). Member bank borrowings from Federal Reserve nevertheless averaged a record $3.3 billion, but a large part of this reflected lending to the now-defunct Franklin National Bank (see below).

As the year drew toward its close, it became apparent that real gross national product would decline again, for the fourth consecutive quarter, and thus for the year as a whole; that the annualized inflation rate would probably reach 12% in December; and that November's 6.5% unemployment rate would continue to rise during December.

International Aspects. The Nixon administration had devalued the dollar (in terms of gold) in 1973, raising the dollar price of gold from $35 to $44 per fine ounce, and also had made the dollar officially inconvertible into gold. These moves, coupled with the decisions of the major Western trading nations and Japan to "float" their currencies against the dollar, improved the U. S. balance-of-payments position substantially but only temporarily. Following a $776 million surplus in September 1973 on (current) trade and services account, the largest such monthly trade surplus in over eight years, the balance of payments deteriorated substantially, as did the dollar's international position *vis-à-vis* the world's principal remaining "hard" currencies, the German mark and the Swiss franc. (See also ECONOMY OF THE U. S.; INTERNATIONAL FINANCE; INTERNATIONAL TRADE.)

Banking Regulation. The most notable bank-regulatory event of 1974 involved the largest bank failure since World War II—that of the Franklin National Bank of Long Island, New York. Substantial injections of new reserve funds into Franklin by the Federal Reserve Bank of New York proved inadequate to restore the liquidity drained away by exchange speculation by one of Franklin's officers (unauthorized by the bank's management but using the bank's funds) superimposed on an already extended loan position. In the end, the Federal Deposit Insurance Corporation intervened, assuming Franklin's obligation to the New York Federal Reserve Bank plus certain other liabilities, and auctioning off the bank's sound assets to the European-American Bank of New York, which assumed all of Franklin's deposit liabilities. Thus, none of Franklin National's depositors lost anything. There were dismissals in the bank's management, however, and the stockholders lost all their investment.

CLIFTON H. KREPS, JR.
University of North Carolina at Chapel Hill

BELGIUM

For Belgium the year 1974 was characterized by economic prosperity threatened by accelerated inflation and political tension.

Political Events. The year-old Leburton government resigned on January 19 after the failure of negotiations with Iran for the construction of a joint Belgian-Iranian oil refinery. Brussels' delay in approving the project, and the conditions Belgium sought to impose, caused Iran to withdraw. The project had caused dissension in the Belgian cabinet, with the prime minister and the Socialists strongly supporting it and the Christian Social and Liberal members opposing it on the grounds of overextension of the state in the economy. King Baudouin first asked Leo Tindemans, a leader of the Flemish wing of the Christian Social party and deputy prime minister in the outgoing cabinet, to form a ministry. When he failed, the king dissolved Parliament and ordered elections.

Elections for a new Parliament were held on March 10. As for many years, federalism was a leading issue. In the 1971 elections, new parties advocating thoroughgoing federalism made great gains. In the 1974 campaign, the older parties moved toward a federalist position. The Liberals, who in the past few elections had lost heavily to the linguistic federalist parties, took a strong federalist line, while the Christian Socials took a moderate position, and the Socialists, though ready for mild reforms in the state structure, stressed predominantly economic issues.

The election results seem to indicate that federalism along linguistic lines as a political issue has passed its peak. The moderate Christian Social party made the largest gain, capturing 72 seats, an increase of five. On the other hand, the federalist parties, which had made steady gains in the three previous elections, lost one seat but continued to hold a big bloc of seats—a total of 47. The Socialist party emerged with 30 seats, a loss of two, and the Liberals dropped from a total of 31 seats to 30 seats.

King Baudouin on March 21 again asked Leo Tindemans to form a new cabinet. His party, though the largest in Parliament, was far from commanding a majority of votes. Only the Liberals were willing to form a coalition with the Christian Socials. The Socialists and the federationist parties refused to join the coalition. Tindemans' only alternative was to form a minority cabinet (sworn in on April 25) of the Christian Social and Liberal parties, which could count on only 102 of the 212 seats in the Chamber of Deputies. These two parties did better in the elections for the Senate, winning a clear majority of the elective seats.

The coalition government won a confidence vote by 100 to 63 on May 4, but only because the federalist parties abstained. On June 10 the French-speaking federalist party, the Walloon Union, joined the coalition, giving the Tindemans government 12 more seats and a slight majority.

To implement the constitutional changes for more regional autonomy, which were finally approved in 1971, a two-thirds vote is required. Lacking the votes to invest regional councils with legislative power, the Tindemans government had to content itself for the time being with getting approval on July 20 of a measure setting up nonelective regional councils to advise the national Parliament on purely regional matters.

Change from "Flemish" to "Dutch." A royal decree promulgated during the year specified that the people and their language in the northern half of Belgium would officially be referred to as "Dutch," whereas the term "Flemish" would be limited to cases where justified for reasons of history, geography, or folklore.

Foreign Affairs. The special relations between Belgium and Zaire, the former Belgian Congo, have ended. A "treaty of friendship," recognizing "particular relations" between the two countries, was signed in 1970 when King Baudouin visited the Congo. President Mobutu renounced the treaty on May 10, at least in part because of the refusal of the Belgian government to ban a book which claimed that General Mobutu came to power with the aid of the U. S. Central Intelligence Agency.

Economy. The boom of 1973, when the gross national product increased by about 6%, continued into 1974. Production increased in spite of the energy crisis and a marked decline in automobile manufacturing and oil refining, while unemployment declined. In the second half of 1974 the economy came under heavy pressure from accelerated inflation. The rate of inflation was 7.3% in 1973 and continued upward in 1974. The index figure of the price of consumer goods reached 128.27 (1971 = 100) in July 1974, an increase of 13.7 over the same month in 1973.

AMRY VANDENBOSCH
University of Kentucky

BELGIUM • Information Highlights

Official Name: Kingdom of Belgium.
Location: Northwestern Europe.
Area: 11,781 square miles (30,513 sq km).
Population (1973 est.): 9,800,000.
Chief Cities (1971 census): Brussels, the capital, 1,074,726 (met. area): Antwerp, 222,775.
Government: *Head of state,* Baudouin I, king (acceded 1951). *Head of government,* Leo Tindemans, premier (took office 1974). *Legislature*—Parliament: Senate and Chamber of Representatives.
Monetary Unit: Franc (39.35 francs equal U. S.$1, Aug. 1974).
Gross National Product (1973): $41,600,000,000.
Manufacturing (major products): Steel, metals, textiles, cut diamonds, chemicals, glass.
Major Agricultural Products: Sugar beets, potatoes, wheat, oats, barley, flax, hay.
Foreign Trade (Belgium-Luxembourg, 1973): *Exports,* $22,301,000,000; *imports,* $21,925,000,000.

BIOCHEMISTRY

The year 1974 was one of fascinating discovery in the field of biochemistry, particularly in the area of molecular biology.

RNA and DNA. Currently attention is focused on the series of events that results in the protein-synthesizing message coded in the sequence of nucleotides called messenger RNA (m-RNA). The immediate precursor of m-RNA is thought to be a type of RNA, called heterogenous nuclear RNA (HnRNA), that is found in the cell nucleus. Part of the HnRNA is thought to become m-RNA, while the remainder is degraded. Investigators of this critical process have identified markers for following the parts of the HnRNA that are degraded, as well as markers for following the parts converted to m-RNA. This work has helped clarify the role of the strange polyadenylic acid (poly-A) sequences, 200 units long, that are added at the end of the HnRNA molecules before m-RNA is produced. The markers confirm that the poly-A sequences are necessary for the development of m-RNA and that HnRNA is a precursor of m-RNA.

The copying of the genetic message from DNA into the protein-synthesizing message of RNA and the subsequent synthesis of protein require at least three major types of RNA: messenger, ribosomal, and transfer RNA. Considerable progress was made in 1974 toward understanding the mechanism by which the cell regulates the synthesis of the different kinds of RNA in response to different growth conditions. In a study of mouse fibroblasts (predecessors of connective tissue) it was found that ribosomal and transfer RNA start to increase about 11 hours after stimulation of growth and then begin to accumulate in a perfectly coordinated manner. Messenger RNA increases much more rapidly, however, and seems to be a controlling factor in starting protein synthesis and in increasing the efficiency of use of the available ribosomal and transfer RNA.

Cyclic AMP. The cyclic nucleotide AMP is thought to be a messenger mediating the activity of many different hormones. Recent work at two laboratories has studied the control of cell growth by the quantitative relationship between the amount of cyclic AMP and that of another cyclic nucleotide, cyclic GMP. This work shows that cell growth can be regulated by the quantitative balance between cyclic AMP and cyclic GMP. The investigators found that a high ratio of cyclic AMP to GMP in cells is associated with cell proliferation. Other studies have recently shown that increases of cyclic AMP can cause growth inhibition when the increase occurs without a concurrent change in cyclic GMP.

Membranes. Muscle tissue contains a membrane, known as the sarcoplasmic reticulum, that is specialized for the functions of transporting and binding calcium in the muscle tissue. Major progress was made in 1974 in understanding the role played by various proteins in the sarcoplasmic reticulum. It was previously suggested that the protein calsequestrin, which can bind large amounts of calcium, plays a large part in the membrane's calcium binding. It was thought that this protein was located on the inner surface of the membrane and played its part by trapping the calcium that was transferred inside the membrane by calcium-activated adenosine triphosphatase (ATPase).

Most recent biochemical work, however, indicates that calsequestrin is located on the outer surface of the membrane and therefore cannot serve as the internal calcium store. However, the calcium-activated ATPase molecule apparently spans the entire membrane from the outer to the inner surface. Work at several laboratories working independently lends great support to the theory that the ATPase molecule acts both to transfer calcium across the sarcoplasmic reticulum and to store it on the reticulum's inner surface.

Glycoproteins. It has been known for a long time that many proteins (glycoproteins) contain various associated sugars. It was completely unknown, however, whether this was fortuitous or whether the sugars might play a part in the functioning of the proteins. A recent flurry of data has begun to implicate these sugars in the control of biological events, the activity of hormones, the structure of receptor sites for viruses, and the survival of tumor cells. The data appear to indicate that the terminal sugar on a glycoprotein is recognized as functional by the body's cells, but when specific enzymes split off some of the outer sugars and thus expose new sugars, the liver or other defense cells regard the change as a signal to clear the glycoprotein from the blood and break it down.

Antibodies. Antibody molecules are the body's primary defense mechanism against foreign chemicals (antigens) entering the body. The number of possible antigens is virtually unlimited, and—speaking roughly—each antigen can trigger the development of a distinct corresponding antibody. Therefore the question has been raised as to whether the body's original genes could contain the enormous amount of information needed to direct the synthesis of so many antibodies, or whether the information is developed somehow during the course of life in response to specific challenges by antigens. Recent investigations indicate that there is enough genetic information in the body's original genes to direct the synthesis of at least 250 million distinct antibodies. The investigators argue that this is sufficient to account for all of the variability among antibodies, so that it is not necessary to look for mechanisms for forming genes later in life. This indicates that a new phenomenon is not necessary to explain antibody synthesis.

STEPHEN N. KREITZMAN
Emory University

Biography

A selection of biographical sketches of persons prominent in the news during 1974 appears on this and the following pages. The subjects include men and women from many parts of the world, and representing a wide variety of pursuits. The list is confined to living persons; for biographical data on prominent people who died during the year, see OBITUARIES. Unless otherwise indicated, all articles in this section are by Henry S. Sloan, Associate Editor, Current Biography.

ALBERT, Carl Bert

As speaker of the House, Carl Albert stood next in line to succeed to the presidency after Gerald Ford's inauguration on Aug. 9, 1974. Albert had occupied a similar position in 1973 between October 10 when Spiro T. Agnew resigned and December 6 when Ford was sworn in as vice president.

Albert has frequently stated that his highest ambition is to be speaker of the House. He denies presidential ambitions. As a Democrat, and as the highest-ranking elected official in the national government, Albert would have become president should something have happened to Ford before the swearing in of a new vice president.

Albert and Ford, although leaders of rival parties during Ford's service in the House, are good friends. When Ford became president, Albert criticized presidential policies and actions with which he did not agree. In areas of agreement, however, Albert was quick to support Ford and to rally many fellow Democrats behind him. Albert, who is 5 feet 4 inches tall and weighs about 140 pounds, would seem to be an unlikely comrade for Ford, the husky, former football star. In fact, the two men share respect for the congressional function in the government's operation and are vigorous but unspiteful partisans of their political parties.

Background. Albert was born in McAlester, Okla., on May 10, 1908, the oldest of five children. He spent his youth on a cotton farm near Bug Tussle (now Flowery Mound). He graduated from the University of Oklahoma in 1931 and won a Rhodes scholarship. At Oxford he earned degrees in jurisprudence and civil law. He returned to Oklahoma to practice law from 1935 to 1940. In 1941 he enlisted in the Army where he served in the Army Air Corps and with the Judge Advocate General. He won the Bronze Star and was discharged in 1946 as a lieutenant colonel.

Albert established a private law practice but left it in November 1946 to run for Congress. He was elected to the 80th Congress as representative of Oklahoma's 3d District. He has been reelected ever since. In 1955, Albert became the majority whip. He served as majority leader from 1962 to 1971. In 1971, he succeeded John M. McCormack of Massachusetts as speaker of the House. Albert is married to the former Mary Sue Greene Harmon. They have two children, a son at Harvard and a daughter who teaches in Washington, D. C.

WALTER DARNELL JACOBS

ARAFAT, Yasir. See page 46.

ASSAD, Hafez el-. See page 42.

BOUMÉDIENNE, Houari

Algerian President Houari Boumédienne, one of the Arab bloc's most influential statesmen, won increasing recognition in 1974 as a leading spokesman for the developing nations of the Third World. In April, at a special UN General Assembly session on raw materials and world development that had been convened on his initiative, he called on underdeveloped countries to take control of their natural resources from foreign interests and form cartels to market vital raw materials. He also proposed a UN-sponsored assistance program for poor nations.

Earlier in the year, at an Arab summit meeting at Algiers in February, Boumédienne denounced Libya's militant strongman Muammar el-Qaddafi and challenged his claim to "revolutionary leadership" of the Arab world. Boumédienne demonstrated his diplomatic skills as an "honest broker" when he helped to negotiate the agreement that led to the independence of Guinea-Bissau from Portugal in September. His prestige was further enhanced when his foreign minister, Abdel Aziz Bouteflika, was elected president of the UN General Assembly for 1974–75. Speaking at the UN in October, Boumédienne denounced pressure by "certain large industrial countries" to roll back Arab oil prices. Later that month he met with other Arab leaders in a summit conference in Rabat, Morocco, to discuss the Palestinian problem, among other subjects.

Background. Houari Boumédienne, whose original name was Mohammed Ben Brahim Boukharouba, was born on Aug. 23, 1925 (or 1932) in Clauzel, near Guelma, in northeastern Algeria, into a poor family of seven children. After attending Islamic schools in Algeria, he studied at al-Azhar University in Cairo, Egypt. About 1954 he became a member of FLN, the Algerian revolutionary organization, and by 1960 he had become chief of staff of its military forces, with the rank of colonel. In 1962, the year Algeria won its independence from France, Boumédienne became defense minister in the new government, and in 1963 he was also named first vice president. On July 5, 1965, after overthrowing President Ahmed Ben Bella in a bloodless coup, he became president of Algeria's revolutionary council. Over the next few years, Boumédienne—whose ideology is a synthesis of Islam, Algerian nationalism, and socialism—instituted major public works and far-reaching social and economic reforms.

BREZHNEV, Leonid Ilich

Leonid Brezhnev, secretary general of the USSR Communist party, chairman of the party Politburo, and member of the Supreme Soviet Presidium, received more publicity in 1974 than any other Soviet leader. In March a new volume of his collected works was issued. The book contains his speeches of 1954–73 concerning the new grain lands of north central Asia where he was party chief when these steppes were first sown under cereals. The book omits the praise of former Premier Nikita Khrushchev and promises of abundant food which had appeared in the original speeches up to 1964 when Khrushchev was ousted. Also circulating in 1974 was a book by four Soviet newspapermen describing and praising Brezhnev's diplomatic negotiations in the United States in 1973. Despite this publicity he remained head of a USSR "collective leadership" rather than a supreme dictator like Stalin.

As in previous years Brezhnev made several foreign trips in 1974. Early in the year he became the first Soviet party secretary general to visit Cuba, where he received the highest Cuban decoration—the Order of

UPI

Soviet Chairman Brezhnev, here with President Nixon, pursued his goal of détente with the United States.

José Marti. In July he toured Poland, receiving the highest Polish military decoration—the Grand Cross of the Virtuti Military Order. Other brief trips were made to East Germany, Mongolia, and France.

The most important of Brezhnev's personal diplomatic negotiations in 1974 was with U. S. President Nixon during the latter's summer visit to Moscow. This superpower summit meeting resulted in eight U. S.-USSR agreements for: joint housing research, joint energy research, mutual heart disease research, long-time trade, further limitation of antiballistic missiles (ABM's), limitation of the size of nuclear weapons' tests, exchange of information about nuclear test sites, and establishment of new consulates. After Nixon's resignation, Brezhnev continued to seek U. S.-USSR détente, meeting President Ford in Vladivostok in November.

Background. Brezhnev, a Russian of worker parentage, was born in Dneprodzerzhinsk, the Ukraine, on Dec. 19, 1906. Though a college graduate in metallurgical engineering, he has worked as a regional Communist party chief, high-ranking military-political officer, and secretary of the party's central apparatus. In 1960–64 he served as president of the USSR. After helping to oust Khrushchev from power in October 1964, he replaced him as head of the Soviet Communist party. He has now ruled longer than either Lenin or Khrushchev.

ELLSWORTH RAYMOND

BROWN, George S.

In what was described as a major shake-up at the top levels of the U. S. military command, Air Force chief of staff Gen. George S. Brown was named by President Nixon on May 14, 1974, as chairman of the Joint Chiefs of Staff, succeeding Adm. Thomas H. Moorer. He was confirmed by the U. S. Senate on June 5 and continued to serve in the post under the administration of President Ford after Nixon's resignation in August.

Brown had been appointed to the top military post in the Pentagon on recommendation of Defense Secretary James R. Schlesinger, who shares his view of the global military mission of the United States and his analytical approach to defense strategy and planning. A champion of air power, Brown is convinced that U. S. air forces are far superior to those of the USSR and that U. S. Minuteman missile defenses are virtually invulnerable. In military strategy, Brown is expected to favor a multiservice approach, with interdependence of the Army, Navy, and Air Force, but with a primary role for the latter.

In November, General Brown came under fire for remarks derogatory to American Jews that he made at a meeting with Duke University law students. Brown stated that American Jews exerted undue influence in Congress and on foreign policy. President Ford publicly rebuked the chairman of the joint chiefs, and Brown expressed regret over his comments. But there were widespread demands in and out of Congress for his resignation.

Background. George Scratchley Brown was born on Aug. 17, 1918, in Montclair, N. J. He received his high school education in Leavenworth, Kans. and graduated from the U. S. Military Academy in 1941 and from the National War College in 1957. As a bomber pilot in World War II he received the Distinguished Service Cross for heroism after taking command of his decimated group during a raid on the oil refineries of Ploesti, Rumania. In 1952–53 he was director of operations of the 5th Air Force in Korea. Between 1959 and 1963, Brown served as military assistant in the Defense Department, first to Secretary Thomas Gates and then to Secretary Robert S. McNamara. From 1966 to 1968 he was chief assistant to Gen. Earle G. Wheeler, chairman of the Joint Chiefs of Staff. In 1968 he attained the rank of general and was appointed commander of the 7th Air Force with responsibility for all air operations in Southeast Asia, a post he occupied until 1970. As chief of the Air Forces Systems Command from 1970 to 1973, Brown was responsible for the Air Force's multibillion-dollar research projects. He took office as chief of staff of the Air Force in August 1973.

U. S. AIR FORCE

U. S. Air Force Gen. George S. Brown, chairman of the Joint Chiefs of Staff.

BURGER, Warren E.

As the U. S. Supreme Court in 1974 began its sixth year under Chief Justice Warren E. Burger, it continued to steer a moderate course between liberalism and conservatism. As in previous years, Burger voted in most cases with the court's conservative or "strict constructionist" bloc. According to a survey released by the American Jewish Congress in October, analyzing 77 civil liberties cases decided during the preceding 12 months, the court neither extended nor invalidated the liberal decisions enacted under the late Chief Justice Earl Warren in the 1950's and 1960's.

In a continuing effort to define the lengths to which government must go to implement the court's 20-year-old school desegregation decision, the court ruled in a 5–4 opinion, written by Burger, against the "cross-busing" of schoolchildren between Detroit and its 53 suburbs—a ruling that seemed to reflect growing popular sentiment against busing as a means of achieving racial balance.

The court's most significant decision of the year was undoubtedly its 8–0 ruling of July 24 that President Nixon must surrender White House tape recordings and other materials needed in the prosecution of the Watergate cover-up case. Although the decision, written by Burger, recognized the validity of executive privilege in some areas, it affirmed the power of the judiciary to define the limits of such privilege. The ruling was a key factor in the chain of events culminating in Nixon's resignation in August. (For other decisions of the court in 1974, see LAW.)

On October 7, Justice Burger, recovering from injuries sustained in a bicycle accident, presided over the opening of the court's 1974–75 term, during which the justices were expected to rule on capital punishment, sex discrimination, impoundment of government funds, and rights of juveniles, among other matters.

Background. Warren Earl Burger, who is of Swiss-German ancestry, was born in St. Paul, Minn., on Sept. 17, 1907. After attending the University of Minnesota and graduating with honors from the St. Paul College of Law in 1931, he combined teaching with law practice and took an active part in Republican politics. He served as assistant attorney general with the Justice Department's civil division from 1953 until 1956, when he became judge of the U. S. District Court of Appeals in Washington, D. C. On June 23, 1969, he succeeded Earl Warren as U. S. chief justice.

CARAMANLIS, Constantine

Constantine Caramanlis was sworn in on July 24, 1974, as premier of Greece, bringing to an end seven years of military rule in that country. The former conservative premier's return to power after 11 years of self-imposed exile followed in the wake of a serious crisis on the island nation of Cyprus that brought Greece and Turkey to the brink of war. On taking office, Caramanlis replaced the military cabinet with a civilian one; restored freedom of speech and press as guaranteed under the 1952 constitution; proclaimed political amnesty; permitted political parties, including the previously outlawed Communists, to operate freely; promised an early return to democratic government; and took steps to solve Greece's economic problems, including rampant inflation.

In protest against the Turkish invasion of Cyprus and what was considered U. S. favoritism toward Turkey, the Caramanlis government announced in August that it was withdrawing Greek military forces from the North Atlantic Treaty Organization. On September 28, Caramanlis announced the formation of a new, broadly based political party, called the New Democracy, that would "serve the true interests of the nation." He resigned the premiership on October 8 but returned to power the same day as head of a caretaker cabinet of civil servants and technicians. In national elections on November 17, Caramanlis scored an overwhelming victory in Greece's first free elections in a decade.

Background. The son of a tobacco farmer and teacher, Constantine Caramanlis was born on Feb. 23, 1907, in the village of Prote, near Serrai, in Macedonia, which was then under Turkish rule. After graduating from the University of Athens in 1932 he entered law practice, and in 1935 he was elected to parliament as a member of the Populist party. After World War II he served successively as minister of labor, transportation, social welfare, and national defense. As public works minister from 1952 to 1955 he won acclaim as a builder of roads. In 1955 he succeeded Premier Alexander Papagos, becoming the youngest premier in Greek history. His newly established National Radical Union won a parliamentary majority in 1956. As premier, he promoted industrialization, independence for Cyprus, and a pro-Western foreign policy. In 1963, after a dispute with King Paul, Caramanlis resigned as premier and went into exile in France.

CHARLES, Prince

Charles, Prince of Wales and Earl of Chester, the heir apparent to the throne of the United Kingdom of Great Britain and Northern Ireland, delivered his maiden speech in the House of Lords on June 13, 1974. In his 16-minute address—the first made by a member of the royal family in the upper house of Parliament in 90 years—the prince, displaying wit and self-confidence, spoke of the need for government action to promote more recreational facilities for young people.

Among those present was Laura Jo Watkins, the daughter of Rear Adm. James D. Watkins of the U. S. Navy. Charles had met Miss Watkins in March at San Diego, Calif., during a four-month tour of duty in the Pacific with the Royal Navy, and reportedly invited her to visit London. Miss Watkins' presence raised speculation as to the prince's marital plans, although as a Roman Catholic she would be ineligible to marry into the British royal family. In a press interview, Charles had indicated that there was no "essential reason" why he could not marry outside of royalty or aristocracy. Previously, Prince Charles had been seen frequently in the company of Lady Jane Wellesley, the daughter of the eighth Duke of Wellington.

Prince Charles, whose full name is Charles Philip Arthur George Windsor, was born on Nov. 14, 1948, at Buckingham Palace, the oldest of four children of Queen Elizabeth II and Prince Philip, Duke of Edinburgh. Like his father, he received his preparatory schooling at the Cheam School in Headley, Hampshire, and his secondary education at Gordonstoun, Scotland. In 1966 he spent a semester at the Timbertop school in Australia. He entered Trinity College, Cambridge, in 1967, majoring in anthropology and archaeology, and also studied, in 1969, at the University College of Wales. In June 1968 he became a Knight of the Garter, and on July 1, 1969, he was formally invested by the queen as Prince of Wales and Earl of Chester.

Charles, Prince of Wales, shown while on active service with the Royal Navy.

BRITISH INFORMATION SERVICES

In 1970, Prince Charles assumed his seat in the House of Lords. That year, he received his bachelor's degree with honors from Cambridge, becoming the first heir to the British crown to earn a university degree. He entered the Royal Navy in 1971. In recent years, Charles has represented the queen at various functions abroad, including the funeral of President de Gaulle of France and the independence rites of Fiji and the Bahamas.

CHOU EN-LAI

Premier Chou En-lai, known for his vigor and industry, assumed an inactive role in the second half of 1974. "I am not very well," he told foreign visitors, "because of old age." He was later hospitalized, but the nature of his illness was not revealed. Reports from Peking said he had suffered a heart attack.

Chou left the hospital sometime before July 20 when he received a Niger delegation. On August 1 he made his first public appearance in more than two months at the Army Day reception. Looking frail and unsmiling, he seemed to lack the geniality with which he usually greeted his guests and friends. But he remained alert and clear-minded. Early in September, however, his condition turned worse and he entered the hospital again. By September 30 he was out of the hospital and appeared in public at a reception marking the 25th anniversary of Communist rule in China.

His illness forced Premier Chou to reduce his activities considerably, and he relied heavily on Vice Premiers Teng Hsiao-p'ing and Li Hsien-nien to carry out the administrative work of government. Teng, a former general secretary of the Chinese Communist party, had been purged during the 1966–69 Cultural Revolution. His sudden return to leadership reflected the extremely changeable political climate in Communist China.

In the spring of 1974, during the early stage of the ideological campaign to discredit Confucius and the late Lin Piao, Premier Chou was believed to have exerted a restraining influence against extremist tendencies. But the continued attack on Confucius, China's ancient sage who taught moderation and benevolence, seemed to have Chou as the target. It was widely speculated that the premier was losing his political grip while the leftist group headed by Chian Ch'ing, Chairman Mao's wife, was gaining in influence. But to avoid a conflict that might arise over leadership changes, Peking seemed unwilling to replace Chou as premier.

Background. Chou En-lai was born to a gentry family in Shaohing (Shaohsing), Chekiang, in 1898. After graduating from high school in 1917, he studied first in Japan and then in France, where he joined the Chinese Communist party in 1922. Returning to China in 1924, he quickly became a party leader. He was named premier of the Communist government upon its establishment in 1949 and has since held that post. Representing China at various important international conferences, he displayed remarkable diplomatic skills.

Chou supported the Maoists during the Cultural Revolution but at the same time attempted to curb the excesses of the Red Guards. He emerged as a popular leader toward the end of the Cultural Revolution when China's return to political stability needed his moderation and flexibility. Chou played an important role in bringing about the Sino-American détente in 1972.

CHESTER C. TAN

CLERIDES, Glafkos.

See page 67.

COGGAN, F. Donald

On May 14, 1974, the archbishop of York, Dr. F. Donald Coggan, a noted biblical scholar identified with the evangelical wing of the Anglican Church, was named archbishop of Canterbury, effective December 5. He succeeded Dr. Arthur Michael Ramsey, who retired on reaching the age of 70. In accordance with traditional practice, the appointment was made by Queen Elizabeth II on recommendation of Prime Minister Harold Wilson. The archbishop of Canterbury, who also has the title of Primate of All England, is the spiritual leader of the Church of England, with 28 million members, and of the Anglican Communion, which has 45 million members throughout the world, including the 3,500,000 members of the Episcopal Church in the United States.

Although Dr. Coggan condemns the "permissiveness" of contemporary society and calls for a "return to the scale of values introduced by Christ," he often expresses liberal sentiments, advocating, for example, a more compassionate treatment of homosexuals and favoring the admission of women to the priesthood. He is strongly critical of the South African practice of apartheid, and he has indicated that the problems of underdeveloped nations and of the urban poor are among his major concerns. While he does not favor separation of church and state, he has expressed sympathy with those favoring a more democratic selection of bishops.

Background. The son of a prosperous businessman, Frederick Donald Coggan was born in the London suburb of Highgate on Oct. 9, 1909. He attended private school and studied theology and Oriental languages at Cambridge, where he obtained a B. A. in 1931 and an M. A. in 1935. For three years after his ordination in 1934 he was curate at St. Mary's church in the North London working-class district of Islington, where he became an ardent evangelist. From 1937 to 1944 he was professor of New Testament studies at Wycliffe College in Toronto, Canada, which granted him a doctorate of divinity. He served from 1944 to 1951 as principal of the London College of Divinity, and then, for five years, as bishop of Bradford. In 1961 he succeeded Dr. Ramsey as archbishop of York, the second-ranking prelate of the realm.

Coggan is the author of several books, including *The Ministry of the Word* (1945) and *Christian Priorities* (1963). He and his wife, the former Jean Braithwaite Strain, whom he married in 1935, have two daughters, Ruth, a physician, and Anne, a teacher.

CONNORS, Jimmy

A week after his 22d birthday, Jimmy Connors crushed Ken Rosewall in the final of the U. S. Open, 6–1, 6–0, 6–1, at Forest Hills, N. Y., in the most one-sided score ever recorded in the finals of the American tennis championship. Connors, who was not yet born when the 39-year-old Australian first played in major events, had previously throttled Rosewall at Wimbledon in July. After the U. S. triumph, he said, "That is the best I ever played. I didn't miss a ball. From the moment I took the court, I felt I was gliding." Rosewall's assessment of the young man was: "I think he has the game and the style of play to be one of the top players for many, many years. He seems to be able to hit the ball hard whether he's running or standing still or off balance."

Background. James Scott Connors was born in East St. Louis, Ill., on Sept. 22, 1952.

Two of the reasons for the strong game of the 5-foot 10-inch, 155-pound lefthander are his mother, Mrs. Gloria Connors, and his grandmother, Mrs. Bertha Thompson. They were tennis teachers, and Jimmy grew up on the court in their backyard in Belleville, Ill. He was 8 when he played in his first tournament. When he was 17 they took him to Los Angeles and put him under the guidance of Pancho Segura and Pancho Gonzales. From them he learned aggressive play, polished

American tennis star Jimmy Connors after winning the men's singles in the U. S. Open at Forest Hills, N. Y.

UPI

his volleying and overhead, and perfected his all-round strategy.

As a student at UCLA, Connors won the national collegiate title in 1971 and moved into pro competition the following year. He won $90,000 in 1972 and $156,400 in 1973, as well as the U. S. indoor and pro championships. In 1974 he headed the list of prize-winners with a total of $285,490. Connors had planned to marry tennis star Chris Evert but the wedding was called off in late 1974. He also took the Australian Open in 1974 and was ranked No. 1 in the United States.

BILL BRADDOCK

DOAR, John M.

As majority counsel to the House Judiciary Committee, John M. Doar in 1974 directed the staff that assembled the evidence on which the committee based its three-article bill of impeachment against President Nixon. Named to the post on Dec. 20, 1973, Doar worked closely with the minority counsel, Albert E. Jenner, Jr., and for 10 weeks beginning in May presented the evidence to the committee. His methodical exposition, sticking to the law and remaining firmly neutral, was acclaimed by Republicans as well as Democrats on the committee.

On July 19, Doar and Jenner formally recommended that Nixon be impeached on one or more charges. On July 29, Doar gave the committee five sets of proposed impeachment articles and a 306-page summary of the evidence, with a list of 50 "undisputed incidents" which, he said, showed Nixon's implication in the Watergate cover-up.

Doar's impeachment articles centered on four major areas: obstruction of justice in the Watergate cover-up; abuse of presidential power by invading civil rights and privacy and the misuse of federal agencies; contempt of Congress in ignoring committee subpoenas; and income tax fraud and using public funds on personal property. In his summary, Doar mentioned also the burglary of the office of Dr. Lewis J. Fielding, Daniel Ellsberg's psychiatrist; the ITT case; and the milk fund case. Doar put together the 1,228-page report which transmitted to the full House the committee's votes for impeachment in three articles.

When President Ford pardoned Nixon for any federal crimes he might have committed, Doar said he did not feel that his work had been wasted. Nixon's resignation meant that justice was done, he said. Impeachment was a corrective not a punitive process, and he believed that the inquiry had taught the nation the need to preserve a system of government under law.

Background. John Michael Doar was born in Minneapolis, Minn., on Dec. 3, 1921. He graduated from Princeton and the University of California (Berkeley) Law School and practiced law with his father in New Richmond, Wis., until 1960, when he joined the civil rights division of the Department of Justice. Under Presidents Eisenhower, Kennedy, and Johnson, he rendered notable service, especially in defending the rights of blacks in the South. In 1968–69 he was president of the New York City Board of Education. In 1969 he became director of a self-help organization in a Brooklyn ghetto, where he remained until he was named to the House committee position.

RICHARD G. WEST

ECEVIT, Bülent

On July 20, 1974, Turkish Premier Bülent Ecevit ordered his country's military forces to invade Cyprus, following the overthrow of that Mediterranean island nation's elected government by the Greek-led right-wing Cypriot national guard. Although the action, which resulted in Turkish occupation of about one third of the island, was condemned in Greece and in the United States, where Congress voted to cut off military aid to Turkey, it made Ecevit a national hero in his own country. The premier insisted that the action was necessary to safeguard the rights of the Turkish minority on Cyprus, and unlike some of his countrymen, who want outright annexation of the occupied areas, he was willing to accept a federal solution for an independent Cyprus.

When Ecevit took office as premier on Jan. 26, 1974, he immediately took steps to restore democracy after nearly three years of military rule and introduced an amnesty for political dissenters imprisoned by the military. But since his moderately leftist Republican People's party failed to muster a parliamentary majority, he was forced to enter a precarious coalition with the Islamic fundamentalist National Salvation party and was thus unable to form a stable government. Having failed in his bid for early elections that might increase his party's parliamentary strength, Ecevit resigned the premiership in September.

Background. Bülent Ecevit was born in Istanbul on May 28, 1925. His father was a professor, and his mother a noted painter. He graduated in 1944 from the U. S.-sponsored Robert College in Ankara and later studied at London University and at Harvard. He entered parliament in 1957 and served as minister of labor from 1961 to 1965. In 1972 he succeeded Ismet Inönü as chairman of the Republican People's party, which won a parliamentary plurality in October 1973. A poet in his own right, Ecevit has translated the poetry of Rabindranath Tagore, T. S. Eliot, and Ezra Pound into Turkish, and he is the author of several books, including *Atatürk and Revolution* (1970).

ECHEVERRÍA ÁLVAREZ, Luís

During 1974, President Luís Echeverría Álvarez of Mexico was faced by economic instability and increasingly violent polarization between left and right, as he continued in his efforts to alleviate poverty and unemployment and to bring about greater democratization of Mexican society. Internationally he enhanced his role as an articulate spokesman for Latin America and the developing nations of the world.

In February, the Mexican president visited several European countries, including the Vatican, seeking to win support for a UN charter of economic rights and duties of nations that he had proposed two years earlier. As inflation reached a record high, political violence in Mexico steadily increased. Among its victims was José Guadelupe Zuno Hernández, Echeverría's father-in-law, who was abducted by leftist guerrillas in August but released after 10 days. In September, after a general strike threat, the government granted a general wage increase of 22%, and the following month, over objections from business, Echeverría decreed a broad system of price controls. After substantial oil resources were discovered in southeastern Mexico in October, Echeverría declared that these resources would be exploited in a "profoundly nationalist and anti-imperialist" manner. In a meeting with President Ford at the U. S.-Mexican border on October 21, he asserted that the United States would have to pay world market prices for Mexican oil.

Background. Luís Echeverría Álvarez was born in Mexico City on Jan. 17, 1922, the son of a civil servant. A law graduate of the University of Mexico, he joined its faculty in 1947 and became active in Mexico's dominant Institutional Revolutionary party. After serving in a succession of party and government posts he was appointed to the key cabinet post of minister of the interior in 1964. He succeeded Gustavo Díaz Ordaz as president on Dec. 1, 1970, and adopted major social and economic reforms.

EVERT, Chris

At the age of 16, Chris Evert became America's sweetheart, filling a role once held by Mary Pickford and Shirley Temple. The Floridian, who had won a succession of girls' tennis titles, became a heroine in 1971 by winning the decisive match against Britain in

PHOTO © 1974 PETER L. GOULD—KEYSTONE

Chris Evert, U. S. tennis player who captured ten consecutive tournaments in 1974, including Wimbledon.

the Wightman Cup competition. A few weeks later she became the youngest semifinalist ever in the U. S. women's championship but lost to Billie Jean King. The following year she won the national clay courts title and made her first appearance at Wimbledon, where she was stopped in the semifinals by Evonne Goolagong after winning the first set. She again reached the semifinals at Forest Hills.

At the age of 18, Christine Marie Evert, who was born in Fort Lauderdale, Fla., on Dec. 21, 1954, turned pro, won $32,000, and became the sweetheart of Jimmy Connors, who hits his backhand with two hands on the racquet as does Chris. With her mother, Colette, as a chaperone, and her father, Jim, a tennis teacher, acting as her agent, Chris hit the circuit. She reached the Italian, French, and Wimbledon finals in 1973 but was beaten in the semifinals at Forest Hills. She won 90 of 102 matches, losing on grass only to the world's best players. She was almost unbeatable on clay.

In 1974, the precise and proper young woman bettered her net and overhead game, concentrated more on service, and captured 10 straight tournaments by winning 52 straight matches. The biggest of these were the Italian, French, and Wimbledon events. "I never expected to win Wimbledon this year," said the 5-foot 5-inch champion. "I felt I was a little too young to win it especially since Billie Jean clobbered me in the final last year." Miss Goolagong finally stopped Chrissie's winning streak at 56 straight matches in the U. S. Open semifinals. But Chris had her first major title and by November had set a record for season's winnings with a total of $194,157. She also had a racehorse named after her: Chris Evert, a 3-year-old, won the triple crown for fillies.

BILL BRADDOCK

FORD, Betty

Mrs. Betty Ford became the first lady of the United States on Aug. 9, 1974, when Vice President Gerald R. Ford was inaugurated as the nation's 38th president, following the resignation of Richard Nixon. Preparing to move into the White House from the family's Alexandria, Va., residence, Mrs. Ford expressed her satisfaction with the presidential mansion and told reporters that she saw no reason to redecorate. She indicated that as first lady she planned to do volunteer work in the arts and to work with retarded children. More liberal than her husband, Mrs. Ford believes that "it's time for women to step up and take their place," and she has spoken out for day-care centers and liberalized abortion laws. Addressing a consumer conference in Washington in September, she advised housewives on how to cope with rising food prices.

On September 28, Mrs. Ford underwent a radical mastectomy after doctors discovered cancer in her right breast. Returning to the White House after two weeks of hospitalization, she appeared well on her way to recovery from the surgery.

OFFICIAL PHOTOGRAPH, THE WHITE HOUSE

Betty Ford, with her husband, President Gerald Ford, as she recovers from her September 28 breast-cancer surgery.

Background. Mrs. Ford, whose maiden name is Betty Bloomer, was born in Chicago on April 8, 1918, the youngest of the three children, and only daughter, of a moderately prosperous businessman. She grew up in Grand Rapids, Mich., where she attended Central High School. Interested in the modern dance, she attended two summer dance sessions at Bennington College in Vermont. At 20 she went to New York, where she studied at Martha Graham's famous dance school and performed with her professional company. For a time she also worked as a Powers model. On her return to Grand Rapids, she became fashion coordinator for a major department store. Her first marriage, to William C. Warren, a Grand Rapids furniture dealer, ended in divorce in 1947, after five years. She and Gerald R. Ford were married on Oct. 15, 1948, shortly before his election to his first term as a Republican representative from Michigan. Mrs. Ford has taken an active part in her husband's election campaigns, and during his nine years as House minority leader she often accompanied him on speechmaking tours. The President and Mrs. Ford have three sons, Michael, John, and Steven, and a daughter, Susan.

FORD, Gerald R. See page 33.

GANDHI, Indira

For Mrs. Indira Gandhi, as for India, 1974 was the most trying year since she became prime minister in 1966. Increasingly she was blamed for the deteriorating economic situation and for alleged corruption in her Congress party. In two states in particular, Gujarat and Bihar, where food riots and other acts of protest were especially serious, she was unable to find an acceptable formula for restoring law and order and confidence in her and her party.

In February, Mrs. Gandhi faced a political test in her home state, Uttar Pradesh. Her party lost more than 45 seats in elections to the state's Legislative Assembly, but it still held a bare majority of the seats, as it did in similar elections in Orissa. Her firm handling ot a nationwide railway strike in May and the explosion of a nuclear device on May 18—and her indignant reactions to foreign criticism of the test—helped to revive her sagging prestige at home. In August her handpicked candidate for president of India won an overwhelming victory in indirect presidential elections.

During the closing weeks of 1974, with one third of the population living in areas seriously affected by drought and facing the grim prospect of famine conditions, and with food in short supply everywhere and inflation rampant, Mrs. Gandhi's popularity and effectiveness, like the economic situation, steadily deteriorated. But no opposition party was able to take advantage of her declining prestige.

Background. The only daughter of Prime Minister Jawaharlal Nehru, Indira Gandhi was born in Allahabad on Nov. 19, 1917. With her grandfather, father, and mother heavily involved in the independence struggle and often in prison, she led a lonely childhood, an experience which made her "a very private person." She was educated in India and Geneva, and at Oxford. On her return to India in 1941 she took an active part in the independence movement. In 1942–43 she was imprisoned by the British. In 1942 she married a Parsi lawyer, Feroze Gandhi, by whom she had two sons. Gradually she and her husband became estranged, especially after 1947 when she became virtually a full-time hostess for her father.

Mrs. Gandhi was president of the Congress party in 1959–60 and minister of information and broadcasting in 1964–66. In January 1966 she became prime minister. In the fall of 1969 the Congress party split, and her wing of the party gained increasing support. Her decisive victories in the fifth general elections in 1971 and in state assembly elections in 1972, and her firm handling of the crisis with Pakistan in 1971, culminating in the Indo-Pakistan war in December, gave her a commanding position on the Indian political scene. This position has been considerably eroded since 1972.

NORMAN D. PALMER

GESELL, Gerhard A.

Judge Gerhard A. Gesell of the U. S. District Court for the District of Columbia was engaged in 1974 with the trial of the principals in the entry by the White House "plumbers" into the office of Dr. Lewis J. Fielding, Daniel Ellsberg's psychiatrist. Before the trial, he clashed with James D. St. Clair, White House special counsel, over President Nixon's refusal to surrender, on the plea of executive privilege, White House material sought by two of the defendants, John D. Ehrlichman and Charles W. Colson. They contended that the break-in was justified by national security.

Gesell ruled that national security did not legally justify the act. He told St. Clair that by his attitude he might abort the trial, but St. Clair rejoined that Nixon would not yield even if the case were dismissed. Gesell angrily observed that Nixon's position bordered on obstruction of justice.

Colson pleaded guilty in June to plotting to obstruct justice in the case. On June 21, Gesell sentenced him to one to three years in prison and levied a fine of $5,000. On July 12, a jury convicted the other defendants on various charges. On July 31, Gesell sentenced Ehrlichman to 20 months to 5 years for conspiring to violate Dr. Fielding's civil rights and on two counts of perjury. G. Gordon Liddy, leader of the break-in, received one to three years. Gesell suspended the sentences of Bernard L. Barker and Eugenio Martinez, Liddy's partners, and placed them on probation. Ehrlichman remained free on appeal.

Earlier, Gesell had sentenced Egil Krogh, Jr., former chief of the plumbers, to six months for conspiring to violate Dr. Fielding's civil rights, but suspended all but six months. He also had sentenced Dwight L. Chapin, convicted on two perjury counts in the case, to 10 to 30 months. Krogh served his sentence, but Chapin appealed.

Background. Gerhard Alden Gesell was born in Los Angeles on June 16, 1910. His father, Arnold L. Gessell, was a pediatrician with a national reputation for his advice on child-raising. Gerhard graduated from Yale College in 1932 and Yale Law School in 1935. He was admitted to the District of Columbia bar in 1941. After serving five years with the Securities and Exchange Commission, he practiced law in Washington until 1967, when he was named to the federal bench.

RICHARD G. WEST

GISCARD D'ESTAING, Valéry

The early performance of France's new president—elected in May 1974—showed him to be more humane and flexible than his previous record suggested. If Giscard offered no liberal revolution, he seemed likely to inaugurate a new era in the Fifth Republic's domestic and foreign affairs.

Within the "first one hundred days" he raised corporate and personal taxes, proclaimed his liberality on contraception, appointed two women to the cabinet, and lowered the voting age from 21 to 18; and he promised reorganization of the mismanaged and sometimes corrupt state radio and television, and an end to wiretaps, film censorship, and prosecution for defamatory criticism of the president. To the political opposition he gave formal status and policy briefings, especially in foreign affairs. He even spoke of an "alternation" of power.

In foreign affairs, cordial relations with the United States and Germany did not preclude disagreements with those countries and an independent policy for France. The counterpart to "liberalizing French society" was Giscard's call for European economic, monetary, and even political union.

Whatever the appeal of his engaging personal style, relative informality, and attractive family life, Giscard's real test would be the issues of inflation and fiscal justice. In these battles his record under former Presidents de Gaulle and Pompidou had not been brilliant. Now he had the power; he seemed to have the will.

Background. Born in Coblenz, Germany, on Feb. 2, 1926, Giscard comes from a wealthy family. He distinguished himself in the highly competitive education system, passing through two hothouses of France's political, bureaucratic, and business elite—the École Polytechnique and the École Nationale d'Administration—to the prestigious ranks of the Inspection des Finances. In January 1956 he won a National Assembly seat as an Independent for Puy de Dôme. Successful in five subsequent elections, he broke with the Conservative party, rallied to de Gaulle, and served as secretary of state or minister for finance under four prime ministers.

Ultimately de Gaulle found Giscard too ambitious and opportunistic, believing him part of a "cabal" to ease the general into retirement; but Giscard's hold on the Independents had been essential to Gaullist control of parliament. Following Pompidou's death on April 2, 1974, Giscard laid claim to the presidency, trailing the leftist candidate, François Mitterrand, in the first balloting on May 5. In the second vote, on May 19, other candidates having been eliminated, Giscard obtained reluctant Gaullist support to edge past his rival with 50.81% of the vote. Fewer than 400,000 votes separated the two out of a total of more than 27 million votes cast.

This knife-edged victory tempered Giscard's triumph. Perhaps it boded well for that peaceful, pragmatic governance that he offered post-Gaullist France.

JOHN C. CAIRNS

GREENSPAN, Alan

On Sept. 1, 1974, Alan Greenspan, a former consultant to private industry, succeeded Herbert Stein as chairman of the Council of Economic Advisers. A disciple, for more than two decades, of novelist Ayn Rand, Greenspan provoked controversy because of his adherence to Miss Rand's "objectivist" philosophy, which propounds an ethic or "rational selfishness" and unregulated capitalism. Although his position is not a policy-making one, critics believe that as President Ford's chief economic adviser he is certain to have a profound influence on the economic decisions of the Ford Administration.

Greenspan drew fire when he said at an economic conference in September that Wall Street brokers suffered proportionately more from existing inflation than other segments of the economy. In testimony before a congressional committee later that month he asserted that the high levels of government spending and borrowing were the chief causes of inflation, and that a budget cut was essential. Although he foresaw a temporary economic decline and an increase in unemployment, Greenspan said that he saw no ground for pessimism concerning the long-range outlook for the U. S. economy. On September 28, President Ford appointed Greenspan to his top-level Economic Policy Board.

Background. The grandson of a cantor, Alan Greenspan was born in New York City on March 6, 1926. Although he demonstrated an aptitude for economics early in life, his original interest was in music, and in his teens he learned to play the clarinet and saxophone. After attending the Juilliard School of Music he spent about a year playing with the Henry Jerome dance band. Having become interested in banking and finance, he then enrolled in the New York University School of Commerce, from which he graduated summa cum laude with a B. S. degree in 1948 and an M. A. in 1950. He joined the National Industrial Conference Board in 1948 and later taught part-time at N. Y. U. In 1953 he became a partner in Townsend-Greenspan & Co., a leading economic consulting firm which counted among its clients some 100 top U. S. corporations. Greenspan eventually acquired almost sole ownership of the firm, and he served as its president from 1958 until appointed to his present post by President Nixon.

HAIG, Alexander M., Jr.

On Sept. 16, 1974, President Ford named White House chief of staff Gen. Alexander M. Haig, Jr., to succeed retiring Gen. Andrew J. Goodpaster, Jr., as commander in chief of U. S. forces in Europe, effective November 1, and as Supreme Allied Commander Europe, effective December 15. The appointment placed Haig in command of all North Atlantic Treaty Organization forces. On October 15, Haig returned to active duty in the U. S. Army, from which he had resigned in August 1973 after assuming the White House post.

During the final months of the Nixon administration, while the President was preoccupied with Watergate events, Haig was, according to columnist Jack Anderson, in effect "running the country" as acting president. He reportedly played a key role in persuading Nixon to resign in view of the impending release of White House tape recordings implicating the President in the Watergate cover-up, and he was credited with helping to effect an orderly transition of government after Ford's inauguration on August 9. Haig's close relationship with Nixon caused some congressional critics to label him a "political general" and to question his suitability for the sensitive NATO post.

Background. Alexander Meigs Haig, Jr., the son of a lawyer, was born in a Philadelphia suburb on Dec. 2, 1924. He attended Notre Dame University, graduated from the U. S. Military Academy in 1947, and received an M. A. in international relations from Georgetown University in 1961. Haig served as a battalion and brigade commander in Vietnam in 1966–67 and as deputy commandant of West Point in 1967–69. He became military assistant to Henry Kissinger, then Nixon's assistant for national security affairs, in 1969, and was named deputy assistant for national security in 1970. Having been promoted from major general to full general by Nixon, who bypassed 240 officers with greater seniority, Haig was sworn in as army vice chief of staff in January 1973. In May 1973 he became interim White House chief of staff, succeeding H. R. Haldeman, and in August he assumed the post on a permanent basis.

HAILE SELASSIE

Haile Selassie's 58-year reign as emperor of Ethiopia came to an end on Sept. 12, 1974, when he was deposed and placed under house arrest by the Armed Forces Coordinating Committee that had been gradually stripping away his royal prerogatives for several months. Once virtually the absolute ruler of his nation and a respected elder statesman among African leaders, Haile Selassie saw his authority increasingly challenged when his inefficient corruption-ridden government seemed incapable of coping with the starvation and economic chaos that resulted from the severe drought of 1973. Military discontent, accompanied by student and trade union protests against inflation and unemployment, culminated in February 1974 in an uprising by dissident troops.

A constitutional conference, called by Haile Selassie in March, drafted a new constitution that would shift power to parliament and away from the emperor. In July the military rebels, while continuing to profess "unswerving loyalty" to the emperor, persuaded him to grant amnesty to political prisoners, provide for continuing consultations between government and military leaders, and implement promised economic and political reforms. The abolition, in August, of the crown council, court of justice, and military committee stripped the emperor of much of his remaining power.

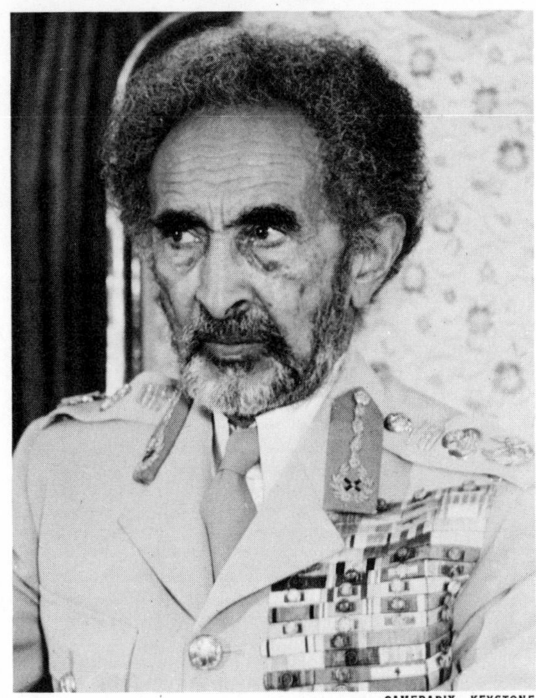

CAMERAPIX, KEYSTONE

Once an absolute monarch, Haile Selassie was deposed as emperor of Ethiopia by a military group in September.

Background. Originally named Tafari Makonnen, Haile Selassie was born in Harar province on July 23, 1892, the son of Ras Makonnen, governor of Harar and a cousin of Emperor Menelik II. Brought up in the Coptic faith and educated at a French mission school, he became governor of Harar in 1910. As a result of a palace coup in 1916, Zauditu, daughter of Menelik, became empress, but Tafari assumed real power as regent and heir to the throne. He was crowned king in 1928 and ascended the throne as Emperor Haile Selassie in 1930. After Italian forces invaded Ethiopia in 1935, Haile Selassie delivered an impassioned plea for help before the League of Nations. In May 1941, after a period of exile, he returned to the throne with British help. In 1955 he granted a constitution that introduced universal adult suffrage, but his efforts at modernization and social reform met with only limited success.

HEARST, Patricia

During much of 1974, news headlines in the United States were dominated by reports of the dramatic kidnapping, and subsequent apparent defection to her captors, of newspaper heiress Patricia Hearst. On February 4 the 19-year-old Miss Hearst, a student at the University of California, was abducted at gunpoint from the Berkeley apartment she was sharing with her fiancé, graduate philosophy student Steven A. Weed, by members of the Symbionese Liberation Army, a multiracial revolutionary group. In a taped message on February 12, SLA spokesmen said that they were holding Miss Hearst as a "prisoner of war" in their struggle in behalf of "oppressed people." Over the next few weeks, in response to SLA demands, Miss Hearst's father, Randolph A. Hearst, president of the San Francisco *Examiner,* initiated a massive food distribution program for the needy.

In another tape recording, received on April 3, Miss Hearst denounced her family and declared that she had been freed by her captors but had chosen to join them and fight for "the freedom of oppressed people." Amid speculation that she might have been brainwashed or drugged, Miss Hearst was reported on April 15 to have taken part in the armed robbery of a San Francisco bank. In early May, Hearst offered a $50,000 reward for his daughter's safe return, while FBI spokesmen admitted that they were "stumped" in their efforts to determine her whereabouts.

After the six key members of the SLA died in a shoot-out with police in Los Angeles on May 17, Patricia Hearst, alias "Tania"—now considered an armed and dangerous fugitive—was reported to be in hiding with surviving SLA members Emily and William Harris. On June 6 a federal grand jury indicted Miss Hearst on charges of armed bank robbery. By year's end, neither the FBI nor her family appeared to have come any closer to determining the whereabouts and fate of Patricia Hearst. Just prior to Christmas her mother published a letter urging Patti to come out of hiding and return home.

Background. Patricia Campbell Hearst, the granddaughter of newspaper magnate William Randolph Hearst, was born in San Francisco on Feb. 20, 1954, and grew up in the exclusive suburb of Hillsborough, where she attended local public schools. She obtained her secondary education at private schools in California and at 17 entered Menlo College, where she achieved top scholastic honors. Having become romantically involved with Steven Weed, who had been her high school tutor, she followed him to Berkeley and enrolled as an art history student at the University of California in early 1973. Friends have described Miss Hearst as essentially nonpolitical, with a "joyous, childlike" and yet strong-willed and somewhat rebellious personality.

JAWORSKI, Leon

On Oct. 12, 1974, Leon Jaworski announced that he was resigning effective October 25 as Watergate special prosecutor, a post he had assumed 11 months earlier. He declared at the time that his task was largely completed, now that the Watergate cover-up trial was in progress. He was succeeded by Henry S. Ruth, Jr., who had been his deputy.

Jaworski had been a central figure in the events leading to President Nixon's resignation in August. Early in the year he persuaded the Watergate grand jury not to indict Nixon, questioning the legality and propriety of such a move, but he accepted the jury's decision to name the President as an "unindicted co-conspirator," and he obtained indictments against eight former White House staff members, three former cabinet members, and others close to Nixon. Dissatisfied with the edited transcripts of presidential conversations that had been released by the White House, Jaworski obtained a subpoena in April for 64 original White House tape recordings and related materials needed in the cover-up trial. The U. S. Supreme Court in July unanimously upheld Jaworski's assertion that Nixon could not invoke executive privilege and withhold the evidence in question.

Although Jaworski's competence as Watergate special prosecutor was widely recognized, he was criticized by some for his occasional resort to plea-bargaining, for his refusal to challenge the legality of President Ford's pardon of Nixon, for his failure to submit to Congress a full report of Nixon's alleged misdeeds and for leaving unsolved the question of illegal campaign contributions and other Watergate-related matters at the time of his resignation.

Background. The son of a Polish-born Evangelical minister, Leon Jaworski was born in Waco, Texas, on Sept. 19, 1905. He received his LL. B. degree from Baylor University in 1925 and his LL. M. from George Washington University the following year. In 1931 he joined the Houston law firm of Fulbright, Crooker, Freeman & Bates, in which he later became a senior partner. During World War II he served in Europe

UPI

Leon Jaworski, the Houston attorney who served as Watergate special prosecutor, resigned in October.

AFP, FROM PICTORIAL

Prince Juan Carlos was Spain's provisional head of state during the hospitalization of Francisco Franco.

as chief of the war crimes trial section of the Judge Advocate General's Corps, with the rank of colonel. As a practicing attorney, as special assistant to the U. S. attorney general from 1962 to 1965, and as president of the American Bar Association in 1971–72, Jaworski was known as a staunch advocate of "law and order." Following Nixon's dismissal of Archibald Cox as Watergate special prosecutor in what became known as the "Saturday night massacre," Jaworski was named his successor. He was sworn in on Nov. 5, 1973.

JUAN CARLOS, Prince

On July 19, 1974, the aging dictator Francisco Franco, stricken by a serious illness, delegated his powers as Spanish chief of state to his chosen successor, Juan Carlos de Borbón, Prince of Asturias and king-designate of Spain. While responsibility for the day-to-day administration of government remained in the hands of Premier Carlos Arias Navarro, Prince Juan Carlos—whose previous duties since his designation as Spain's future king five years earlier had been largely ceremonial—effectively replaced Franco as chief of state for the duration of the Caudillo's illness.

As his first official act on the day he assumed his new role, Juan Carlos signed a joint Spanish-American declaration of principles on mutual defense. On August 9, the prince presided over a special cabinet session which he convened to enable the ministers to dispose of a backlog of some 70 decrees. The prince relinquished his role as interim chief of state in early September, after Franco had recovered sufficiently to reassume his authority.

Background. The son of Don Juan, Count of Barcelona, and the grandson of Alfonso XIII, who vacated the Spanish throne in 1931, Juan Carlos Alfonso Victor María de Borbón y Borbón was born on Jan. 5, 1938, in Rome, Italy, where his family was living in exile. He received his early education in Italy and Switzerland, and at the age of nine he went to Spain, where he later attended the Instituto San Isidro. In 1947, Franco decided on the eventual restoration of the Spanish monarchy, and in 1954 he made an agreement with Don Juan that Juan Carlos was to be groomed as a possible successor to the throne. A graduate of Spain's military, naval, and air academies, the prince holds commissions in all three branches of the service. He also studied at the University of Madrid under the guidance of private tutors. On July 22, 1969, Franco officially designated Juan Carlos as future king. A law providing for his succession as chief of state after Franco's death was passed in July 1972. Juan Carlos was married on May 14, 1962, to Princess Sophia of Greece. They have a son and two daughters.

KELLEY, Clarence M.

In July 1974, veteran law-enforcement official Clarence M. Kelley embarked on his second year as director of the Federal Bureau of Investigation. Since taking office, he has established greater flexibility and a more low-keyed and relaxed atmosphere in the top U. S. law enforcement agency than had prevailed under J. Edgar Hoover, who had headed it for almost half a century before his death in May 1972. Kelley has taken steps to enhance the FBI's public relations, to modernize and professionalize its investigative facilities, and to improve staff morale following the agency's involvement in the Watergate affair, which led to the resignation of acting director L. Patrick Gray 3d in April 1973. He has instituted a "participatory management" program for his 8,500 employees, and he has established closer contacts between FBI headquarters and the 59 field offices.

Among the chief problems concerning the FBI in 1974 were white-collar crime and urban terrorism. Its most publicized case of the year was the kidnaping, in February, of newspaper heiress Patricia Hearst by the terrorist Symbionese Liberation Army. In a show of candor unusual for the FBI, Kelley admitted at a news conference in May that the bureau was "stumped" in its search for Miss Hearst and her abductors. In the months that followed, the FBI continued its relentless search for the missing heiress, who had in the meantime apparently joined her captors voluntarily and was now considered a fugitive. To cope with the rising tide of bomb plots and other terrorist activities, Kelley requested greater wiretapping authority for the FBI.

Background. Clarence Marion Kelley was born in Kansas City, Mo., on Oct. 24, 1911. He graduated from the University of Kansas and the law school of the University of Kansas City. Except for three years of service in the Navy in World War II, he served with the FBI from 1940 to 1961, resigning in the latter year as head of its Memphis, Tenn., bureau to become police chief of Kansas City. Among his innovations there was a computerized police data system and 24-hour helicopter patrols. He was credited with reducing the city's crime rate by 25%, but his relations with the black community brought him some criticism. On July 9, 1973, he became FBI director, succeeding temporary director William D. Ruckelshaus.

KISSINGER, Henry A. See page 43.

KOSYGIN, Aleksei Nikolayevich

Aleksei Kosygin, premier of the USSR and a member of the Politburo of the Soviet Communist party, in 1974 continued to rank second among Soviet leaders only to Leonid Brezhnev, the secretary general of the Communist party. Relations between the two leaders remained harmonious. At the July meeting of the newly elected USSR Supreme Soviet, Brezhnev nominated Kosygin for reappointment as premier, which was confirmed by unanimous vote. Kosygin, in turn, reappointed the members of his entire previous cabinet to their various ministerial posts.

In contrast to previous years, Kosygin made few trips abroad in 1974. In April he visited Poland for a meeting of Warsaw Pact leaders which approved the Soviet policy of détente with the United States. In June he traveled to Bulgaria to participate in a conference of the Council of Mutual Economic Assistance (CMEA, the East European-Soviet-Mongolian-Cuban common market). While there, in honor of his 70th birthday, he received a Bulgarian decoration, the Order of Georgi Dimitrov.

In 1974, Premier Kosygin promulgated three cabinet decrees of great economic importance. One allowed light-industry factories to vary their products according to store-association orders. A second ordered all industrial enterprises to unite in associations similar to Western trusts. The third called for basic improvement in the agricultural output of the wooded steppes of north European USSR, where farming has deteriorated in recent decades. These decrees aimed at better economic efficiency—the major theme of Kosygin's 1974 speeches.

Background. Kosygin was born of worker parentage in St. Petersburg (now Leningrad) on Feb. 20, 1904, and is a graduate of a textile engineering college. Since 1939 he has held such high posts as chairman of the State Planning Committee, USSR vice premier, premier of the Russian Soviet Republic, and head of the ministries for the textile industry, light industry, consumer goods industry, and finance. He was a Politburo member from 1945 to 1952, and has been again since 1957. Following the ouster of Nikita Khrushchev in 1964, Kosygin succeeded him as premier. Although Kosygin is one of the oldest members of the Politburo, there was no sign in 1974 that he planned to retire.

ELLSWORTH RAYMOND

LÓPEZ MICHELSEN, Alfonso

On Aug. 7, 1974, Alfonso López Michelsen, a member of the Liberal party, was sworn in as president of Colombia, succeeding Misael Pastrana Borrero. His inauguration marked the end of an arrangement, initiated in 1958, under which the Liberal and Conservative parties alternated in the presidency every four years. Campaigning as a moderate reformer in an effort to overcome his radical past, López won the election of April 21 by a landslide, with over a million more votes than his nearest opponent, Alvaro Gómez Hurtado, the Conservative candidate.

López has committed his center-left government to the struggle against inflation, unemployment, inequality of income, and official corruption. He announced plans to reorganize the agrarian reform institute on a more efficient basis; to introduce a scheme under which wages, prices, and fiscal policies would be determined jointly by government, management, and labor; and to promote civil marriage and divorce, and equal rights for women. In foreign affairs, he sharply criticized U. S. policies toward Latin America and advocated diplomatic and trade relations with Cuba and China. He pledged to support Latin American integration and to resolve Colombia's boundary dispute with Venezuela.

Background. Born in Bogotá on June 30, 1913, Alfonso López Michelsen is the son of former president Alfonso López Pumarejo. He was educated at private schools in Paris, London, and Brussels and at the Instituto Nuestro Señora del Rosario in Bogotá, and he received his law degree from the University of Chile. While teaching administrative law at the National University of Colombia and other institutions, he practiced as a lawyer in Bogotá, and was for a time editor of the weekly *El Liberal.* In 1959 he founded the Liberal Revolutionary Movement. He was first elected to the Chamber of Deputies in 1960 and made an unsuccessful bid for the presidency in 1962. After joining the Liberal party in 1967 he served until the following year as governor of César department. From 1968 to 1970 he was minister of foreign affairs under Liberal President Carlos Lleras Restrepo.

MAKARIOS, Archbishop. See page 66.

MILLER, Johnny

"It's just ridiculous," said Johnny Miller after winning his eighth victory on the golf tour on Sept. 29, 1974. "I know I'm not that good. I don't know how I've done it." Ridiculous or not, Miller's feats helped him establish a record for a single season's earnings of $353,021, about $32,500 more than Jack Nicklaus'

Johnny Miller, professional golf's player of the year, established a new record for a season's earnings.

WIDE WORLD

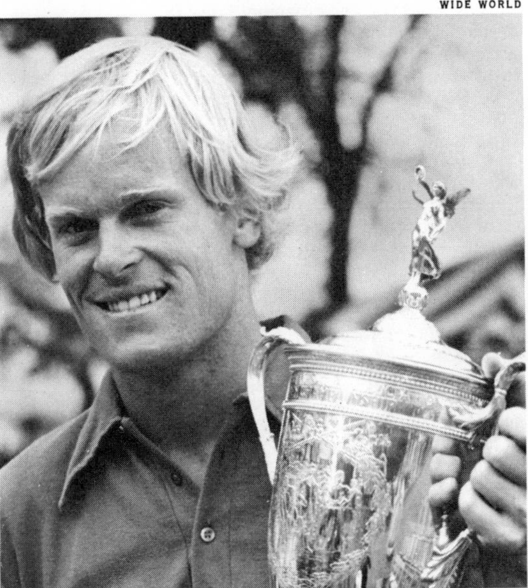

mark in 1972, and in being named the Professional Golfers' Association player of the year.

The 27-year-old Californian won the first three tourneys of the year, an unprecedented feat, but then was sidelined for three weeks because of allergies. By the end of April he had won five times and earned $193,000. He was the defender in the U. S. Open in June but faltered in the first round and never was a factor. From then until late August he played in only two major events. On returning to the tour, he won three of six tournaments. In explaining his play in winning the Westchester Classic, the first of the three, Miller said: "My putting game is outstanding. It's like a machine. If I miss one it is because I read it wrong, not because I mishit."

Background. Miller was born in San Francisco on April 29, 1947. He won the U. S. Junior title in 1964 and joined the pro tour in 1969 after dropping out of Brigham Young University. He is a part-time missionary of the Mormon Church. He had won two tourneys before his 1973 victory in the Open, one each in 1971 and 1972, and earned over $90,000 in each of those years. To win the Open he carded an eight-under-par 63 in the final round to take the title by one stroke. With Nicklaus he won the World Cup for the United States that year, Miller taking individual honors by three strokes over Gary Player. His earnings in 1973 rose to $127,833.

BILL BRADDOCK

NIXON, Richard M. See page 31.

PAUL VI, Pope

During 1974, Paul VI continued his efforts to be a center of unity in a Catholic Church that was rapidly becoming more pluralistic. His style of leadership was described as progressive in content and conservative in style. Despite concerns about his health, the pope, who celebrated his 77th birthday on September 26, presided over the Synod of Bishops meeting in Rome in the fall. He also published two principal documents in 1974: an apostolic exhortation on devotion to the Virgin Mary, and a papal bull proclaiming the Holy Year of 1975 a time for reconciliation. (See special article on the Holy Year in RELIGION.)

In his concluding address to the delegates to the Synod of Bishops on October 26, the pope praised their work but sounded a note of caution on four key themes that had emerged in the month-long discussion: the role of the Church in human liberation; the cultural adaptation of the Christian message; the growth of small Christian communities; and the desire for greater autonomy for local churches. While recognizing the positive value in all of these developments, the pope warned against exaggerations that could either blur the true nature of salvation by excessive political involvement or weaken the central unity of the Church by too much particularism.

On March 21, Pope Paul's apostolic exhortation on Marian devotion (*Marialis Cultus*) was published. It was an attempt to renew devotion to the Mother of God, both affirming the value of certain traditional practices and also calling for the correction of those that were outmoded or overly sentimental. The document attracted public attention because of its comparison of Mary to the modern woman and a description of her in terms of a more recent consciousness of women.

On Ascension Thursday, May 23, the papal bull officially proclaiming the Holy Year of 1975 was read. The bull (*Apostolorum Limina*) recalled the two themes of the year: renewal and reconciliation. In the bull, the pope also expressed the hope that nations would consider the possibility of granting amnesty to prisoners, particularly those "who may have been caught up in political and social upheavals too immense for them to be held fully responsible." This appeal was interpreted to refer in a special way to political prisoners in some of the predominantly Catholic countries of Latin America. In the United States, however, the pertinence of the appeal to the question of draft evaders and war resisters was noted.

Pope Paul VI addressed a special message to Kurt Waldheim, secretary general of the United Nations, on the occasion of the opening of the extraordinary session of the UN General Assembly on April 9. The session had been called to study the problems of the use of the raw materials of the world. Paul VI took the occasion to affirm once again the moral obligation of the richer nations of the world to come to the assistance of the poorer. A more equitable distribution of the world's goods was necessary, the pope said, and should be based on a sense of international social justice and human solidarity.

In March an attack of influenza caused the pontiff to cancel two general papal audiences. The pope recovered sufficiently, however, to participate in the Holy Week public liturgies with only minor restraints.

In late October the Vatican announced the establishment of two new commissions, one to deal with relations between Catholics and Jews and the other to deal with Catholic-Muslim relations.

The visit of a papal emissary to Cuba led to speculation that the Vatican would name a nuncio to Cuba to replace the one recalled over ten years ago.

JOSEPH A. O'HARE, S. J.

PERÓN, Isabel

Following the death of Juan D. Perón on July 1, 1974, his widow and chosen successor, Isabel Perón, was inaugurated president of Argentina, becoming the first woman chief of state in Latin American history. Mrs. Perón had been serving as vice president since Oct. 12, 1973, when Perón reassumed the presidency from which he had been removed 18 years earlier.

As vice president, Mrs. Perón headed the Peronist women's movement, gave speeches defending government policies, received official visitors, presided over occasional senate gatherings and cabinet meetings, assumed executive powers during her husband's visits abroad, and made several political trips, including one to China in 1973. Shortly before Perón's death she had been on a tour of Europe.

Although on taking office Mrs. Perón had received assurances of support from the various segments of society, the semblance of national unity soon broke down as it became evident that she was even less able than her husband had been to cope with Argentina's immense political and economic problems. As guerrilla attacks, assassinations, kidnappings, and bombings became daily occurrences, her government stepped up security precautions. On October 17, she announced plans to "Argentinize" three foreign-owned firms, including a subsidiary of International Telephone and Telegraph Corp.

Background. Mrs. Perón, who adopted the name Isabel at her confirmation, was born María Estela Martínez on Feb. 4, 1931, at La Rioja in northwestern Argentina, where her father was a bank official. In Buenos Aires, where she attended school to the sixth grade, she studied dancing and the piano and later performed in ballet and night club acts. While on tour with a dance troupe in Panama in 1956, she met Perón, who hired her as his secretary. She accompanied him to Spain, where she became his third wife in 1961. After Perón returned from exile and announced his candidacy for the presidency in 1973, his choice of the politically inexperienced Isabel as his running mate was criticized by many, who felt that she lacked the immense appeal of his late second wife, Eva. Although Mrs. Perón had the support of the conservative Peronist trade unionists, she failed to win the loyalty of the younger Peronists of the left. The Peróns were elected with 62% of the vote on Sept. 23, 1973.

RABIN, Itzhak. See page 42.

PARAMOUNT PICTURES

Robert Redford played the glamorous and mysterious title role in *The Great Gatsby*, costarring Mia Farrow.

REDFORD, Robert

Robert Redford's seemingly effortless portrayals of wholesome, athletic, ruggedly individualistic Americans caught between success and failure have made him one of the top motion picture personalities of the 1970's. He typifies the kind of hero popular among female fans, who idolize him as a "sex symbol," and male viewers, who regard him as a projection of their ideal selves.

As the enigmatic hero in Paramount's much-heralded $6,200,000 film version of F. Scott Fitzgerald's Prohibition-era novel *The Great Gatsby,* released in March 1974, Redford fared somewhat better than the production itself, which failed to live up to critics' expectations. He had attained stardom in *Butch Cassidy and the Sundance Kid* (1969), in which he and Paul Newman portray bandits in the old West and South America.

Among Redford's recent hits are *The Candidate* (1972), in which he plays an idealistic lawyer disillusioned by politics; the romantic drama *The Way We Were* (1973), co-starring Barbra Streisand; and *The Sting* (1973), with Redford and Newman as a pair of confidence men. In the forthcoming *The Great Waldo Pepper,* Redford plays a barnstorming stunt pilot. For his own production company, Redford has acquired the film rights to Bob Woodward and Carl Bernstein's *All the President's Men,* an exposé of the Watergate scandals, in which he will appear as the journalist Woodward.

Background. Robert Redford was born in Santa Monica, Calif., on Aug. 18, 1937. He entered the University of Colorado on a baseball scholarship to study art but dropped out and drifted around the United States and Europe, trying to gain acceptance as a serious artist. After studying at the Pratt Institute and the American Academy of Dramatic Arts he began his acting career with minor roles in Broadway plays. On television, he appeared in such programs as *Alfred Hitchcock Presents, The Untouchables,* and *The Virginians* and won critical praise for his performances in the TV dramas *In the Presence of Mine Enemies, The Iceman Cometh,* and *Voice of Charlie Pont.* In 1963 he starred on Broadway in Neil Simon's comedy hit *Barefoot in the Park.* After appearing in several undistinguished films, he re-created his stage success on the screen in 1967. His other films include *Downhill Racer* (1969), *Tell Them Willie Boy Is Here* (1969), *Little Fauss and Big Halsy* (1970), and *Jeremiah Johnson* (1972).

Off screen, Redford prefers the open spaces of Utah, where he owns a ski resort, to the Hollywood scene, and he is active in promoting conservation and the rights of Indians. He and his wife, Lola, who have been married for 16 years, have three children.

ROBINSON, Frank

At the press conference in Cleveland on Oct. 3, 1974, announcing his selection as the Indians' manager, Frank Robinson reiterated his assurance that he was capable of managing a major league club. He had said so in a 1968 autobiography, and he put his self-confidence in focus on October 3 by remarking that the only reason he became the first black manager in baseball was that he had been born black. "I think I've been hired because of my ability." Phil Seghi, the Cleveland general manager, said Robinson was chosen not because he was black or white but because "he has all the qualities necessary to lead a major league club."

Robinson had established himself as a great player and as a leader in 19 years of major league baseball, and he had piloted Santurce in the Puerto Rican winter league for six seasons.

There are two outstanding feats on Robinson's record. He is the only player to be voted most valuable in each major league, and he is one of only nine players to win the triple crown in batting (leading the league in hits, runs batted in, and home runs in one season). Among other accomplishments were his 574 home runs (trailing only Henry Aaron, Babe Ruth, and Willie Mays), and the most valuable rookie award in 1956. He also holds National League records for being hit by pitches.

Background. Frank Robinson was born in Beaumont, Texas, on Aug. 31, 1935, and grew up in Oakland, Calif. He played on a championship American

Frank Robinson, the new Cleveland Indians pilot, is the first black manager in major league baseball.

UPI

UPI

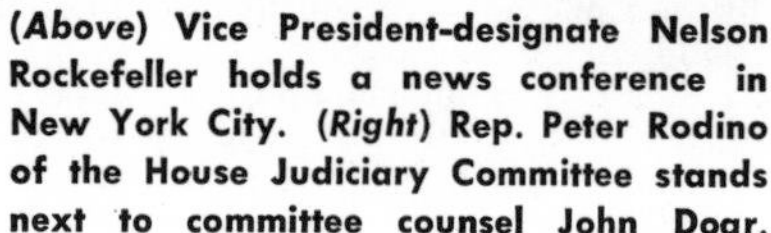

(*Above*) Vice President-designate Nelson Rockefeller holds a news conference in New York City. (*Right*) Rep. Peter Rodino of the House Judiciary Committee stands next to committee counsel John Doar.

UPI

Legion baseball team, and in high school he was a member of a championship basketball team that included Bill Russell. He was signed by Cincinnati on graduation from high school in 1953 and began major league play in 1956 as an outfielder with the Reds. At bat he crowded the plate and twice was seriously injured by being hit in the head. His baserunning was daring and caused numerous spike wounds to himself as well as opposing fielders.

Robinson helped Cincinnati win the pennant in 1961 when he was named most valuable player in the National League. Because he was "an old 30" he was traded to Baltimore after the 1965 season. The following year he won the triple crown and was named most valuable in the American League as the Orioles won the pennant. Baltimore won the championship three more years, 1969–71, with Robinson playing the outfield and first base. In 1972, he was traded to the Los Angeles Dodgers and in 1973 to the California Angels before going to Cleveland at the end of 1974.

BILL BRADDOCK

ROCKEFELLER, Nelson A.

On Aug. 20, 1974, Nelson A. Rockefeller, the 66-year-old former governor of New York, was nominated by President Gerald R. Ford to be the 41st vice president of the United States. Ford, who had been in office only since August 9, when Richard M. Nixon resigned as president, was quoted as saying that he chose Rockefeller as the best qualified of several candidates to assume the presidency in case of emergency.

Largely because of the Rockefeller family wealth and its potential influence, the nomination stirred some controversy. Before a Senate committee, Rockefeller valued his total personal holdings at $218 million, mostly in trusts, and his net worth at $62 million. He disavowed controlling interest in any business, and submitted summaries of his income tax returns for the last 10 years.

Opposition to Rockefeller's confirmation centered chiefly on two issues—the lavish gifts and loans he had made to friends and associates and his role in the publication of a book on his opponent in the 1970 gubernatorial campaign. In October, Rockefeller made public a list of 20 present and former public officials and aides who had received a total of some $2 million in gifts and loans over a 17-year period; the loans were often subsequently forgiven. The book at issue was a biography of Arthur J. Goldberg, Democratic candidate for governor in the race against Rockefeller, and was financed at a cost of $60,000 by Rockefeller's brother Laurance. The biography attacked Goldberg's qualifications for the governorship. Rockefeller admitted its publication was a mistake and apologized for it. But he defended the gifts and loans as being neither illegal nor immoral.

After protracted congressional hearings, Rockefeller finally was confirmed by both houses of Congress and was sworn into office on December 19. He was the third vice president to serve in the four-year presidential term that began on Jan. 20, 1973, when Spiro T. Agnew was elected to serve with Nixon. Agnew had resigned on Oct. 10, 1973, and was succeeded by Ford.

For Rockefeller, who had three times tried to win the Republican nomination for president, his elevation by appointment to the nation's second-highest position, in direct line to succeed to the presidency, was regarded as ironic. He refused to subscribe to this view, remarking that he wished only to serve the country and that he now had a chance to do so.

Background. Nelson Aldrich Rockefeller was born at Bar Harbor, Me., on July 8, 1908, the third of six children of John D. Rockefeller, Jr. Although he was an heir to the immense oil fortune created by his grandfather, he had a strict Baptist upbringing and was taught the importance of thrift and of a sense of responsibility.

He graduated from Dartmouth College in 1930, a member of Phi Beta Kappa. For many years he was identified with Rockefeller family interests, especially Rockefeller Center, the great building complex in New York City.

Public service attracted him; he said that his chief interest was to "solve people's problems." Beginning with President Franklin D. Roosevelt in 1940, he filled an important appointive post in the government under every president through Nixon, ranging from planning foreign policy to forming government agencies. He served as undersecretary of health, education, and welfare in the Eisenhower administration.

Rockefeller's only elective office was that of governor of New York, to which he was elected in 1958 and reelected in 1962, 1966, and 1970. In his administrations, the state budget and taxes went up, but his achievements in social programs and construction projects were noteworthy. He enlarged and strengthened the state university and built a huge mall and state office center in Albany. Many of his policies won praise from liberals, but in his last term they criticized him as turning conservative, especially in his support of tough laws on welfare cheating and drug traffic. His handling of the Attica prison riot in 1971, which claimed 39 lives, also drew fire. He resigned as governor in December 1973 to head the Commission on Critical Choices for America, which he founded to study courses for the nation's future.

Rockefeller's tries for the Republican presidential nomination in 1960 and 1968 were marred by hesitation and indecision in the pre-convention campaigns. At the Republican national convention in 1964, which nominated the conservative Sen. Barry Goldwater, Rockefeller delivered a stalwart defense of liberalism in the face of bitter opposition from the convention floor.

Rockefeller is notable as a philanthropist and an art collector. His collection of 20th century paintings and sculpture and of primitives is world famous.

Family. Rockefeller married Mary Todhunter Clark on June 23, 1930. The marriage produced five children and ended in divorce in 1962. The following year he married Margaretta (Happy) Murphy, shortly after her divorce. He has two sons by his second marriage. In October and November 1974, Mrs. Rockefeller twice underwent surgery for breast cancer.

RICHARD G. WEST

RODINO, Peter W., Jr.

In 1974, Peter W. Rodino, Jr., a rank-and-file Democratic member of the House of Representatives from New Jersey for 25 years, was a center of world attention. As chairman of the House Judiciary Committee, he presided over its inquiry that concluded on July 30 by presenting to the full House a three-article bill of impeachment against President Richard M. Nixon.

Overawed at first by the responsibility of the impeachment inquiry, Rodino grew with its magnitude. He insisted that the proceedings be fair. "What counts," he said, "is that it be done right."

Rodino lived up to his resolve. Facing a committee composed of 20 Democrats besides himself and 17 Republicans, debating a question with a high potential of bitter partisanship, he quietly but firmly kept the debate in balance. By his approval, Nixon's counsel, James D. St. Clair, was allowed a part in the hearings. Rodino's conduct won praise from his colleagues, Republicans and Democrats alike, and favorably impressed the television audience that watched the final sessions.

At an early stage, Rodino agreed with a study by committee counsel that maintained that grounds for impeachment need not be based only on criminal conduct. But during the debates he kept his views to himself, concentrating on sustaining the even pace of the work. On questions requiring a vote, he usually sided with the Democratic majority. He signed subpoenas for material in Nixon's possession, but when the White House did not honor them Rodino did not seek enforcement by the courts.

In the final vote, Rodino supported the three impeachment articles that were passed. He also voted for one—involving Nixon's personal finances—that was defeated. His vote helped to defeat another, concerning the bombing of Cambodia.

The committee's report calling for impeachment was shelved, at least for a time, when Nixon resigned and was pardoned by President Ford for any federal crimes. Rodino did not favor continuing the impeachment debate, as some congressmen proposed. His committee had fulfilled its assignment, and events had passed beyond its scope.

Background. Rodino was born Pellegrino Wallace Rodino, Jr., in Newark, N. J., on June 7, 1909, the son of an immigrant Italian carpenter. He attended the University of Newark, now part of Rutgers University. He wrote poetry and several novels, which were never published. Admitted to the New Jersey bar in 1938, he practiced law in Newark. In World War II he was an Army captain.

Rodino lost a race for Congress from Newark in 1946, but was elected in 1948 and has been reelected 12 times. His career in Congress, in which he compiled a liberal voting record, has not been remarkable. Through seniority, he became chairman of the Judiciary Committee in 1972. In 1973 he presided over the committe's inquiry into the fitness of the vice presidential nominee, Gerald Ford, in which Rodino voted against confirmation.

RICHARD G. WEST

ROUDEBUSH, Richard L.

Former Congressman Richard L. Roudebush was named by President Ford as administrator of veterans affairs on Aug. 19, 1974. The announcement came at the Chicago convention of the Veterans of Foreign Wars (VFW), at which the President also outlined his proposals for granting conditional amnesty to Vietnam draft evaders and deserters. Confirmed by the U. S. Senate on October 1, Roudebush succeeded Donald E. Johnson as head of the mammoth bureaucracy of the Veterans Administration. Johnson had drawn severe criticism from Vietnam veterans for his handling of veterans affairs. An Indiana Republican and a former VFW national commander, Roudebush is a close friend of President Ford. During his 10 years in Congress he established a reputation as a staunch patriot and law-and-order advocate, and as a champion of veterans rights. Since January he had been serving as deputy administrator of veterans affairs.

Background. Born on a farm near Noblesville, Ind., on Jan. 18, 1918, Richard Lowell Roudebush attended the public schools of his native Hamilton county. In 1935 he helped establish the Roudebush Commission Co. in Indianapolis, a livestock business, in which he remained a partner until 1960. After graduating from Butler University with a B. S. degree in business administration in 1941, he enlisted in the U. S. Army and became a demolition specialist. He earned five battle stars in the North African and Italian compaigns.

Discharged from the service in 1944, Roudebush joined the VFW, and over the next few years held various local and state posts in the organization. He served as Indiana state commander in 1953–54 and as national commander in chief in 1957–58. From 1961 to 1971, Roudebush served five terms in the U. S. House of Representatives, running in three different Indiana districts as a result of congressional reapportionment. Among the bills he sponsored was one that would make Flag Day a national holiday. In 1970 he ran for the U. S. Senate but was defeated by Democrat Vance Hartke. He served for three years in the third-ranking post at the Veterans Administration before being appointed deputy administrator.

SADAT, Anwar el-. See page 42.

ST. CLAIR, James D.

James D. St. Clair, a Boston lawyer with a record of winning hard cases by careful preparation of his material and skillful use of legal technicalities, was in 1974 Richard M. Nixon's special counsel for all matters relating to the Watergate affair. Appointed on January 4, he maintained that he presented Nixon as the president and not as an individual.

Much of St. Clair's acumen and energy was employed in implementing Nixon's refusals to release voice tapes and documents sought as evidence by special prosecutor Leon Jaworski, investigating the criminal aspects of Watergate, or by the House Judiciary Committee, considering Nixon's impeachment. By legal tactics, he tried to gain time for Nixon, yielding grudgingly and only partially to subpoenas. In April, when Nixon released a 1,200-page transcript of some White House tapes, St. Clair filed an accompanying brief declaring that "the transcripts affirmed Nixon's innocence."

Beginning in May, by permission of the Judiciary Committee, St. Clair attended the hearings considering the question of impeachment. He was allowed to raise objections during the examination of witnesses and the admission of testimony and to call his own witnesses. On June 27–28, he presented Nixon's defense to the impeachment charges in a closed committee session.

When Nixon went to court to block the release of more tapes subpoenaed by Jaworski, St. Clair argued the case before the U. S. Supreme Court. The court ruled, 8–0, on July 24 that Nixon's claim of executive privilege was invalid, and Nixon directed St. Clair to obey its order to yield the material.

That St. Clair had been filling a difficult role, working on incomplete information, was revealed on August 5 when Nixon released three critical tapes and admitted that he had withheld evidence from his own lawyer and from the committee. It was reported that St. Clair had threatened to resign if these tapes were not made public and had urged Nixon to resign to avoid impeachment, but this was denied by the White House. After President Nixon resigned on August 9, St. Clair resigned also.

Background. James Draper St. Clair was born in Akron, Ohio, on April 14, 1920. He graduated from the University of Illinois in 1941 and, after serving in the Navy in World War II, graduated from Harvard Law School in 1947, joining the Boston law firm of Hale and Dorr. In 1954 he was an associate counsel with Joseph N. Welch, defending the Army against accusations by U. S. Sen. Joseph R. McCarthy.

RICHARD G. WEST

SCHLESINGER, James R.

U. S. Secretary of Defense James R. Schlesinger suggested in 1974 that the U. S. nuclear force be improved so that alternate targeting strategies might be available to the president in the event of enemy attack. Schlesinger asked for a strategic force capable of striking Soviet missile installations in addition to the existing ability to hit Soviet cities. The requests were

James D. St. Clair, President Nixon's Watergate lawyer, arrives at the U. S. Supreme Court Building.

PICTORIAL PARADE

in reaction to the USSR's modernization of its strategic force following SALT (Srategic Arms Limitation Talks) by improvement and augmentation of the existing system. Schlesinger asked for a variety of improvements in U. S. weapons, including the B-1 strategic bomber, the Trident missile-launching submarine, and ICBM's (intercontinental ballistic missiles). The Schlesinger proposals were likely to be debated for some months. With increased costs for weapons systems procurement and some congressional opposition to his ideas, his scheme faced an uncertain future.

Questions of arms control raised a seeming dispute between Schlesinger and Secretary of State Henry A. Kissinger. Kissinger implied that the American and Soviet military establishments were blocking further SALT agreements. Schlesinger replied that the military in the United States was under civilian control. But relations between the two secretaries were calmed, and the dispute went no further.

Schlesinger also faced problems with respect to NATO as developments in Greece, Turkey, and Portugal cooled enthusiasm for the alliance in those member nations.

Background. James Rodney Schlesinger was born in New York City on Feb. 15, 1929. He graduated from Harvard in 1950 with a B. A., summa cum laude, in economics. He traveled about Europe, Asia, and Africa for two years and returned to Harvard to earn the Ph. D. in 1956. In 1955 he joined the faculty of the University of Virginia. He was granted leave to teach at the Naval War College but returned to Virginia in 1958. In 1963 he joined the Rand Corporation as a senior staff member and was director of strategic studies there from 1967 to 1969. In 1969 he became assistant director of the Bureau of the Budget. Two years later he succeeded Glenn T. Seaborg as chairman of the Atomic Energy Commission. In 1973 he was named director of Central Intelligence, serving for only five months before becoming secretary of defense in July.

WALTER DARNELL JACOBS

SCHMIDT, Helmut

Helmut Schmidt, the deputy chairman of the German Social Democratic party (SPD), became chancellor of West Germany on May 16, 1974. He succeeded Willy Brandt, who resigned for having tolerated, for purposes of counterintelligence, the presence of an East German spy, Günter Guillaume, on his personal staff.

Early Life. Schmidt was born in a working-class district of Hamburg on Dec. 23, 1918. His father was a teacher. Helmut attended high school, hoping to become an architect. During that time he was a member of the Hitler Youth, and after graduation he served in the Reich Labor Service. A draftee in the *Wehrmacht* when World War II broke out, Schmidt fought on both the Russian and Western fronts. After his release from internment he studied economics at the University of Hamburg, earning his diploma in 1949. Schmidt is married to a high school friend who until recently was still teaching school in Hamburg. The couple has one daughter.

Political Career. Schmidt joined the SPD in 1946 and the next year was elected national chairman of the Socialist Students League. From 1949 to 1953 he worked in Hamburg's bureau of traffic, soon rose to department head, and in 1952 became the bureau's director. In 1953 he was elected a Bundestag deputy and was reelected in 1957 and 1961. In 1962 he gave up his office to head Hamburg's Department of the Interior. Reelected to the Bundestag in 1965, he became chairman of the SPD's delegation in 1967 and deputy chairman of the party in 1968. In the first Brandt government (1969–72), Schmidt served as minister of defense. In 1972 he became finance minister in Brandt's second cabinet.

The Chancellor. In his first policy statement, Chancellor Schmidt made clear that he would focus his

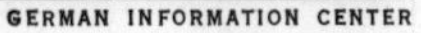

GERMAN INFORMATION CENTER

UPI

Helmut Schmidt (*left*) became the chancellor of West Germany in May. William Simon (*above*) was confirmed as U. S. treasury secretary in April.

attention on financial and economic problems. His main concern was to put a stop to unemployment, which had risen to 2.3% by the latest count—an alarming figure to postwar Germans—without raising the relatively moderate 7% rate of inflation. He proposed cuts in the government's social reform program, but these were to be offset in part by a reduction of taxes for the lower- and middle-income groups. Despite an increase in upper-income tax rates, the tax reform was expected to cut government revenues by $5 billion.

Schmidt knew that West Germany's ability to overcome its economic difficulties depended also on the steps taken by its Common Market partners and by the United States in their respective campaigns against inflation and unemployment. He was concerned that these countries might cut too drastically their purchases from the Federal Republic, thus aggravating the latter's unemployment problem. For this reason the chancellor, in August, granted Italy a $2 billion loan. He also supported a proposed Common Market bond issue that would enable the Market to help members in financial difficulties.

Schmidt did not neglect West German relations with eastern Europe. He managed to avert new crises in the ever-sensitive Berlin situation, but failed, during a visit to Moscow in late October, to secure West Berlin's right to legal representation by West Germany. He did sign, however, some commercial agreements with the Soviet government, among them one on Soviet delivery of natural gas and one, in principle, on West German construction of a nuclear power plant in Kaliningrad.

ANDREAS DORPALEN

SIMON, William E.

On April 17, 1974, William E. Simon, deputy secretary of the treasury and director of the Federal Energy Office, was named by President Nixon to succeed George P. Shultz as secretary of the treasury. He was confirmed on April 30 by unanimous Senate vote.

After his appointment as federal "energy czar" in late 1973, Simon had moved with vigor and efficiency to cope with the fuel shortage brought on by the Arab oil embargo. While instituting an allocation program to ensure sufficient fuel for vital needs, and reluctantly accepting oil-price controls, he resisted outright rationing, preferring to educate the public to exercise voluntary restraint in energy consumption.

After Nixon's resignation in August, President Ford named Simon to a steering committee for an economic summit conference, and in September he appointed him chairman of the new Economic Policy Board to coordinate the administration's domestic and international economic efforts. In October, Simon visited Moscow and reached an agreement regarding the Soviet purchase of U. S. grain.

A staunch defender of free enterprise, Simon is firmly opposed to wage and price controls. He advocates reduction in government spending, fiscal and monetary restraint, and floating rather than fixed exchange rates among currencies. He has defended the Ford administration's proposal for a 5% tax surcharge on above-average incomes, and he has advocated government action against "unjust profits."

Background. The son of an insurance broker, William Edward Simon was born in Paterson, N. J., on Nov. 27, 1927. He graduated from Lafayette College with a B. A. in 1952, and in 1957 he became a vice president of Weeden & Co. In 1964 he joined the Wall Street investment banking firm of Solomon Brothers, where he became a senior partner within a year and acquired a reputation as a leading expert on municipal bonds. Simon was named deputy secretary of the treasury in December 1972. A year later he succeeded John A. Love as director of the five-month-old Federal Energy Office.

SINATRA, Frank

Frank Sinatra, whose unique style of singing romantic ballads caused teen-aged girls to swoon in the 1940's, and who won acclaim as a motion picture actor in the 1950's, proved his continuing popularity when on Oct. 12, 1974, he performed before an enthusiastic audience of more than 20,000 at New York's Madison Square Garden. The one-hour show, entitled *Sinatra—The Main Event,* was broadcast live on ABC-TV. Supported by Woody Herman's band, baritone Sinatra evoked nostalgia with such old-time favorite hits as "Chicago," "I've Got You Under My Skin," "The Lady Is a Tramp," "My Way," and "The House I Live In" and also included some more recent songs, such as "Send in the Clowns."

Early in the year, Sinatra made a triumphant comeback as a nightclub performer with a one-week engagement at Caesar's Palace in Las Vegas. In April he gave his first New York performances since 1965 when he sang to capacity audiences at the Veterans Memorial Coliseum at Uniondale, Long Island, and also gave a benefit concert at Carnegie Hall. His occasional abrasiveness surfaced during a tour of Australia in

WIDE WORLD

Singer Frank Sinatra proves he is as popular as ever by filling New York's Madison Square Garden in October.

July, when following a clash between his bodyguards and TV cameramen he renewed a long-time feud with members of the press. The incident nearly caused a cancellation of the tour when trade unionists threatened to impose a boycott on him.

Background. The son of an Italian immigrant fireman, Francis Albert Sinatra was born in Hoboken, N. J., on Dec. 12, 1917. After high school, where he sang with the band, he worked for a newspaper. Inspired to become a singer after hearing a performance by Bing Crosby in 1936, he appeared on Major Bowes' amateur show and at a New Jersey nightclub before being discovered in 1939 by Harry James, who hired him for his band. Later he sang with Tommy Dorsey's band. He attained the height of his popularity with a solo engagement at New York's Paramount Theatre in the winter of 1942–43 and as soloist with the *Hit Parade* radio program from 1943 to 1945.

In Hollywood, Sinatra appeared in such musicals as *Anchors Aweigh* (1945) and *On the Town* (1949) and won a special Academy Award for the short subject *The House I Live In* (1945). His performance as Maggio in *From Here to Eternity* earned him an Oscar as best supporting actor of 1953. Among his other films are *Man With the Golden Arm* (1956), *The Joker Is Wild* (1957), *A Hole in the Head* (1959), *Come Blow Your Horn* (1963), and *The Detective* (1968). Although he announced his retirement in 1971, he returned to show business the following year. Sinatra, whose marriages to Nancy Barbato, Ava Gardner, and Mia Farrow ended in divorce, is now a grandfather.

SIRICA, John J.

Judge John J. Sirica, judge of the U. S. District Court for the District of Columbia, whose pertinacity launched the Watergate inquiry in 1973, remained a central figure in the case in 1974. In March, the grand jury handed up to him indictments of seven men on various charges in the Watergate cover-up. The trial date was set for September 9. Sirica resigned as chief judge of the court on March 19, his 70th birthday, after assigning himself to preside over the trial.

The grand jury also presented a sealed report, which later was revealed to have named President Nixon as an unindicted co-conspirator in the cover-up. Sirica ordered the report and accompanying evidence given to the House Judiciary Committee's impeachment inquiry.

Nixon, claiming executive privilege, refused to honor a subpoena issued by Sirica on April 18 for tapes of White House conversations sought by special prosecutor Leon Jaworski. But the U. S. Supreme Court ruled, 8–0, on July 24 that Nixon had to comply. The tapes of three conversations whose public release by Nixon on August 5 led to his resignation were among those covered by this subpoena.

Sirica sentenced two Watergate figures who pleaded guilty to various charges: Jeb Stuart Magruder, 10 months to 4 years (on May 21) and John W. Dean III, one to four years (on August 2). Six of those indicted in March remained to be tried in his court; charges against Charles W. Colson had been dropped when he pleaded guilty in the Ellsberg case. Moves to disqualify Sirica as trial judge on the ground that he had shown "prosecutorial bias" failed, and after several postponements the trial began on October 1. The case of Gordon C. Strachan was severed from the others, leaving five defendants as the trial began.

Background. The son of an Italian immigrant barber, John Joseph Sirica was born in Waterbury, Conn., on March 19, 1904. During his early years he lived in Jacksonville, Fla., and New Orleans. He took his law degree at Georgetown University in 1926. After serving as an assistant U. S. attorney in the District of Columbia for four years, he became a partner in a prestigious Washington law firm. President Eisenhower named him to the District Court in 1957, and he came to be regarded as a stern judge. He was named chief judge in 1971.

RICHARD G. WEST

SMITH, Mary Louise

A 25-year veteran of Iowa Republican politics, Mrs. Mary Louise Smith was unanimously elected on Sept. 16, 1974, to succeed George Bush as chairman of the Republican National Committee, becoming the first woman ever to head the national GOP. Nominated for the post earlier that month by President Ford, Mrs. Smith had been serving for about six months as national co-chairman. During the summer of 1974 she traveled some 38,000 miles, seeking to "turn people back on to politics" by means of a series of grass-roots seminars. In her acceptance speech, Mrs. Smith expressed optimism about Republican chances in the

Mary Louise Smith of Iowa is the first woman ever to become chairman of the Republican National Committee.

November election and indicated that she would send staff members of Republican national headquarters into key areas to help in state campaigns. Noting that according to polls only 23 percent of U. S. voters identify themselves as Republicans, she asserted: "It's time... to come to grips with the shape we're in.... Somewhere the Republican party is doing something wrong. Or else we're not doing enough things right."

Background. Mrs. Smith was born Mary Louise Epperson in Eddyville, Iowa, on Oct. 6, 1914. She received a B. A. degree in social work administration from the University of Iowa in 1935. Mrs. Smith became a precinct committeewoman in Eagle Grove in the early 1950's and was named Wright county Republican chairman in 1961.

In 1964, Mrs. Smith was elected Iowa's national committeewoman, and she was reelected in 1968 and 1972. In 1966 she served on a subcommittee on convention reform, and in 1969 and 1971 she was vice chairman of the party's Midwestern regional conference. She served as co-chairman of the Iowa committee to reelect President Nixon in 1972. A "moderate-conservative" and a party loyalist, but "not an ideologue," Mrs. Smith favors the proposed Equal Rights Amendment and liberal abortion laws, and she is a member of Planned Parenthood. She helped convene Iowa's first women's political caucus. She and her husband, Dr. Elmer M. Smith, a physician, to whom she has been married since 1934, make their home in Des Moines. They have three children and five grandchildren.

SOLZHENITSYN, Aleksandr I.

On Feb. 12, 1974, Aleksandr I. Solzhenitsyn, the dissident Russian novelist, was taken by force from his family's apartment in Moscow by secret-police agents and driven to the infamous Lefortovo Prison. There, after an extensive interrogation during which he was given the impression he was to be tried for treason and shot, he was instead taken to the airport and flown to Germany.

Solzhenitsyn's arrest and deportation finally put an end to the enormous suspense and tension that were building up over many years, particularly in 1973 following the publication in the West of his lengthy and devastating indictment of the Soviet slave labor camp system, *The Gulag Archipelago, 1918–1956.* Fully expecting his arrest, he had grown more defiant, capping his rebellion with an open letter to the Presidium in December in which he denounced the leadership and, more importantly, Communist ideology as morally bankrupt and historically anachronistic.

Solzhenitsyn spent a short period at the home of fellow Nobel Prize laureate Heinrich Böll, then settled in Switzerland, where he was joined by his wife and children. At the outset, he showed some displeasure at the persistent curiosity of people, especially the news media, which he termed an infringement on his privacy. But apparently he has grown more comfortable and has settled down to complete a series of projects, including additions to *Gulag.*

Background. Solzhenitsyn was born in Kislovodsk, the northern Caucasus, on Dec. 11, 1918, the son of a czarist officer who died in World War I. He received his education in the Soviet school system, gaining a degree in mathematics and physics as well as one in literature. Solzhenitsyn entered the army at the outset of World War II as a private, and he eventually attained the rank of captain of the artillery. He was arrested in 1945 for having criticized Stalin in a letter to a friend. He spent eight years in prison and exile, coming to prominence only in 1962 when Premier Khrushchev, as part of his anti-Stalinist campaign, allowed the publication of the short novel *One Day in the Life of Ivan Denisovich,* the only major work of Solzhenitsyn to be allowed publication in the Soviet Union. From 1962 until his exile, he produced two lengthy novels about prison life and its aftermath, *The First Circle* and *The Cancer Ward,* and a World War I novel, first of a trilogy, *August 1974.* All were published in the West and established his world reputation. He won the Nobel Prize for literature in 1970.

FRANK K. MOSCA

SPÍNOLA, António de

On April 25, 1974, Gen. António de Spínola, a career army officer, assumed power in Portugal in a coup overthrowing a right-wing dictatorship that had dominated the country for over 40 years—first under Antonio de Oliveira Salazar and then, since 1968, under Marcello Caetano. Although Spínola, who became president on May 15, did not take part in the coup, which had been organized by junior officers, he helped provide the impetus for it with his best-selling book *Portugal and the Future,* published in February, in which he called for eventual self-government for Portugal's African territories as a means of ending the country's debilitating colonial wars and other problems.

After the coup, the new government restored civil liberties, legalized political parties, and freed political prisoners. The heads of the Socialist and Communist parties were offered cabinet posts. Negotiations were begun with rebel leaders in the African territories. But in the months that followed, labor unrest and the activities of extremist groups caused the government to reimpose some press censorship and economic restrictions, and in July the civilian cabinet was replaced by a largely military one.

In the struggle between left and right, Spínola's moderate position was steadily weakened. On September 30 he stepped down as president, yielding power to chief of staff Gen. Francisco da Costa Gomes, who became head of a predominantly leftist regime. In his resignation speech, Spínola warned that the nation was headed toward chaos and "new forms of slavery."

Background. António Sebastião Ribeiro de Spínola, the son of Salazar's inspector general of finance, was born in Estremoz, Portugal, on April 11, 1910. He graduated from the national military academy in 1933. In the Spanish Civil War he headed a detachment of Portuguese volunteers supporting Franco, and during World War II he was an observer with German forces on the Russian front. He commanded a cavalry battalion in Angola from 1961 until 1964, when he became second in command of Portugal's National Republican Guard. As military commander in chief and civil governor of Portuguese Guinea from 1968 to 1972, he combined military action with progressive social and economic measures. In December 1973 he was appointed deputy chief of staff of the armed forces.

SUHARTO

The year 1974 began rather stormily for Indonesian President Suharto and his government. Violent student riots broke out at the time of the visit of Japanese Premier Kakuei Tanaka on January 15 and 16. The disturbances were quickly brought under control but they indicated serious and widespread unrest. Student activists, in a petition to the government, declared that they recognized the president's efforts for socio-economic improvement but they deplored the deepening gap between the rich minority and the poor majority. They called for the elimination of clique and family systems and the eradication of corruption, and appealed to the president to initiate a simple and productive way of life for the rich and to set the example himself.

A statement was issued by parliament deploring the students' resort to violence but also conceding that it could understand the widespread anxiety about prevailing economic and political conditions. It called for an end to corrupt practices, smuggling, and the abuse of power. To promote increased internal security Suharto personally took control of Kopkantib (the Command to Restore Order and Security).

The large amounts of foreign capital which President Suharto has attracted to Indonesia have done much to improve the economy. At the same time the funds have aroused popular resentment against foreign investors and traders, focusing on the Japanese. Foreigners are viewed by these critics as getting rich from Indonesian resources and trade while Indonesians remain poor. To allay this resentment Suharto, on January 22, laid down new guidelines to be followed in foreign investments, including a larger Indonesian share in profits and an accelerated shift to Indonesian control and ownership of the enterprises.

Background. Suharto (his only name) was born in Godean, Java, on June 8, 1921. He began his military career in the Netherlands Indies army, joined the Indonesian revolutionary forces at the end of World War II, and became an officer in the army of the republic. He rose to the rank of general and at the time of the attempted Communist coup, in September 1965, he became the leader in crushing the revolt. By stages he displaced President Sukarno as head of the Indonesian government. He assumed emergency executive powers on behalf of Sukarno in 1966, was named acting president in 1967, and was elected president by the People's Consultative Assembly on March 27, 1968. On March 22, 1973, he was reelected by the Assembly for a five-year term.

AMRY VANDENBOSCH

WIDE WORLD

Pierre Trudeau, prime minister of Canada, whose Liberal party was returned to power with a substantial majority.

TANAKA, Kakuei

Reelected premier by Japan's Diet following elections in 1972, Kakuei Tanaka reshuffled his second cabinet in July 1974 to maintain equilibrium among factions within the majority, business-backed Liberal-Democratic party (LDP). But under growing pressure because of alleged financial irregularities, he resigned as premier on November 26 (see JAPAN).

Personal Diplomacy. The Western Hemisphere was the object of the premier's personal diplomacy when Tanaka visited Mexico (September 12–15), Brazil (September 16–20), and Canada (September 23–26), where he discussed energy, joint economic development, and agricultural aid. On September 21 in Washington, he established personal contact with the new U. S. President, Gerald Ford, and he met with Ford during the President's visit to Japan in November. Earlier, Tanaka had a less successful trip to Southeast Asia (January 7–17), encountering outright hostility in Bangkok and Jakarta. Later in 1974 the premier visited Burma, Australia, and New Zealand.

Japanese Premier Kakuei Tanaka, under fire because of money scandals, announced his resignation November 26.

UPI

Politics. Beginning in late 1973, Premier Tanaka suffered a sharp decline in his popularity because of the impact on Japan of the world energy crisis, a slowdown of the remarkable postwar growth, and deficit trade balances. His domestic political base was badly shaken by the LDP's setback in the (upper) House of Councillors' election, July 7, coupled with the resignations of Finance Minister Takeo Fukuda and Deputy Premier Takeo Miki, powerful LDP faction leaders. In late July, Tanaka shuffled posts in his cabinet to prepare for "total confrontation" with his political opponents. Following his resignation in November, he was succeeded as party leader and premier by Miki.

Background. Tanaka was born on May 4, 1918, into a poor family of Nishiyama, Niigata prefecture. He completed his secondary school education at night in Tokyo while working in the construction business. After a brief stint in the army in Manchuria, he returned to Japan in 1945 to form his own building firm. First elected to the House of Representatives in 1947, he later served in five LDP cabinets and also became secretary general of the party. First elected premier in July 1972, he is the only postwar leader to be drawn from outside Japan's traditional elite of university-trained bureaucrats. Acclaimed for reestablishing relations with the People's Republic of China in 1972, Tanaka is also noted for a national development plan to "remodel the Japanese archipelago."

"Kaku-san," as the press has nicknamed him, is also often called "the computerized bulldozer" because of his vigor and determination. At 56 he is the youngest man to hold the premiership since the end of the war. Tanaka and his wife, Hana, had a son and a daughter, but the son died in 1947. Now his family consists of his wife, daughter Makiko and her husband, and one grandson. Tanaka is very fond of writing, folk songs, recitations (*naniwa-bushi*), horseback riding, and golf (handicap: 18).

ARDATH W. BURKS

TRUDEAU, Pierre Elliott

As leader of Canada's Liberal party, Pierre Elliott Trudeau in 1974 continued to change his image as philosopher-king and became not only a practical politician but a vigorous campaigner on the hustings. The 1972 election had given the Liberals a minority government, held in alliance with the New Democratic party, generally in opposition to the Progressive Conservatives and Social Credit. On May 8, 1974, the government's defeat on a no-confidence vote meant dissolution of the 29th Parliament. For two months Trudeau waged a fighting campaign, and the election of July 8 gave the Liberals a majority in Parliament. Trudeau's public image had improved, but his government still faced pressing economic issues, especially concerning energy, inflation, and unemployment.

In early 1974, Trudeau's government pursued energy policies designed to cut domestic consumption. Because Canada is an oil-exporting nation (though its population east of the Ottawa Valley is dependent on foreign supplies), the federal government applied an export tax on crude oil to cover the widening differential between the domestic price and world market rates. It also established a national petroleum corporation and began plans for extending the national pipeline to include Montreal.

In foreign affairs Trudeau's ministry sought further environmental protection measures with respect to the United States. At the Law of the Sea Conference in Caracas, Canada proposed to extend its seashelf. Canada also worked to promote peace in Cyprus and the Middle East by sending more peace-keeping forces. The results of all these efforts were uncertain. Trudeau's government suspended nuclear aid to India when the latter exploded a nuclear device in May; it had been understood by Canada since 1956 that India would use nuclear production only for peaceful purposes. Trudeau's visit to Paris late in the year aimed at diminishing tensions with France that date back to de Gaulle's *"Vive le Québec libre"* speech in 1967.

Background. Born to a bilingual family in Montreal on Oct. 18, 1919, Trudeau had the best of Canadian preparatory educations and graduated in law from the University of Montreal in 1943. He studied economics, political science, and law at Harvard and in London and Paris, traveled in China, and returned to Quebec to practice law. Interested in labor law and civil liberties, he was regarded as one of Quebec's foremost progressives in the 1950's and 1960's.

Trudeau entered federal politics as economic adviser to the St. Laurent government in 1949–51. He was elected to Parliament as a Liberal for Montreal-Mount Royal in 1965. After serving as parliamentary secretary to Prime Minister Lester B. Pearson in 1966, minister of justice and attorney general in 1967, and leader of the Liberal party in 1968, he became prime minister on April 20, 1968, as a result of the public fervor for him known as "Trudeaumania." He married Margaret Sinclair of Vancouver on March 4, 1971, and on two Christmas Days, in 1971 and 1973, sons were born to the Trudeaus. His most recent books are *Approaches to Politics* (1970) and *Conversation with Canadians* (1972).

BARRY M. GOUGH

TYSON, Cicely

TOMORROW ENTERTAINMENT/GE

Cicely Tyson, winner of 1974 Emmy award as best actress for the TV special *The Autobiography of Miss Jane Pittman.*

For her overwhelming performance in the title role of *The Autobiography of Miss Jane Pittman,* filmed for CBS-TV, Cicely Tyson was named best actress of the year in a television special. The honor came at the 26th annual presentation of Emmy awards on May 28, 1974. Miss Tyson's portrayal of a former slave, from her teens to the age of 110, was described by film critic Judith Crist as "sheer perfection," while critic Rex Reed called it "one of the most brilliant performances . . . by a woman of any color, any age, any season." Earlier, Miss Tyson—who refuses to accept any role that would debase black womanhood—received critical raves for the strength and dignity of her portrayal of Rebecca Morgan, a sharecropper's wife, in the film *Sounder.* That performance earned her the best actress award at the Atlanta Film Festival in 1972 and an Academy Award nomination in 1973.

Background. Cicely Tyson, who is in her 30's, was born in New York's Harlem. Her parents, who had emigrated from the island of Nevis in the Caribbean, were divorced when she was 11. Growing up in poverty, she spent her free time singing and playing the piano and organ at the neighborhood Episcopal church. After graduating from high school she worked as a secretary for the American Red Cross and then became a successful model and cover girl. Later she studied briefly at New York University and attended drama classes at the Actors' Playhouse.

Miss Tyson appeared off Broadway in *The Spectrum* before making her Broadway debut in the revue *Talent '59.* In the early 1960's she won Vernon Rice awards for her performances in Genet's *The Blacks* and in *The Moon on a Rainbow Shawl,* and played in the Broadway production of *Tiger, Tiger, Burning Bright.* In 1966 she was seen on Broadway in *A Hand Is on the Gate,* and in 1968 she took part in *To Be Young, Gifted and Black,* off Broadway. On television she was featured in the series *East Side/West Side* (1963) with George C. Scott. She also appeared in such shows as *Naked City, The Nurses, To Tell the Truth, I Spy,* and the *Bill Cosby Show* and the specials *Americans: A Portrait in Verse, Brown Girl, Brown Stones,* and *Between Yesterday and Today.* Among the motion pictures in which she had featured roles are *Twelve Angry Men* (1957), *Odds Against Tomorrow* (1959), *The Last Angry Man* (1959), *A Man Called Adam* (1966), and *The Heart Is a Lonely Hunter* (1968).

WALDHEIM, Kurt

In 1974, his third year as secretary general of the United Nations, Kurt Waldheim stamped his own imprint even more clearly on the office which he held. Always a firm believer in the UN and its ability to perform a valuable peacekeeping role, Waldheim in 1974 saw the organization increasingly as the forum through which solutions might be found to the world's economic problems as well. Thus, on January 10, he said he felt it was "more necessary then ever for the UN to fulfill its role of harmonizing the political, social, and economic policies of the nations." The same theme underlay his opening and closing statements at the sixth special session of the General Assembly, held from April 9 to May 2, to consider problems of raw materials and development. By the time of his annual report to the General Assembly, published on September 5, the secretary general was warning the world that profound economic and social problems were threatening it with a "crisis of extraordinary dimensions."

As in previous years, Waldheim made a number of visits to various parts of the world. After going to Mexico in early January, he visited 14 African countries in February and March, among them five in the sub-Sahara region stricken by drought (Mali, Mauritania, Senegal, Niger, and Upper Volta). On February 21 at Ouagadougou, Upper Volta, as a result of what he had seen, he appealed again for emergency assistance to the area. Following a tour of eight countries in the Middle East and Africa in June, the secretary general flew direct to Caracas, Venezuela, for the opening of the third UN Conference on the Law of the Sea on June 20, where he urged the 148 nations represented to avoid replacing "old quarrels on land with new quarrels at sea." A further visit was made to Africa to open the Organization of African States' conference at Mogadishu, Somalia, on June 12, and a visit to the Netherlands and Switzerland was combined with his opening of the summer session of the Economic and Social Council (ECOSOC) at Geneva on June 29.

Waldheim's peacekeeping role during the year was demonstrated chiefly by his concern over the Middle East and his talks with its leaders in the course of his visits to the area, and his role in the Cyprus crisis in June, July, and August, in which he was responsible for the renewal of negotiations between the Greek and Turkish Cypriots on June 4. He attended the second phase of the Geneva talks on the Cyprus crisis on August 8–9.

Background. Kurt Waldheim was born near Vienna on Dec. 12, 1918. He was educated at the Consular Academy and the University of Vienna, where he took a law degree. After joining the foreign service in 1945, he led the Austrian observer mission in 1955–56 and headed his country's first delegation to the UN in 1958. From 1964 to 1968 he was Austria's first permanent representative there, a post to which he returned in 1970. He ran unsuccessfully for the presidency of Austria in 1971. Waldheim was elected to a five-year term as UN secretary general by the General Assembly on Dec. 22, 1971, and took office on Jan. 1, 1972.

RICHARD E. WEBB

WHITLAM, Gough

During 1974, Australian Prime Minister Gough Whitlam's Labor government was faced with waning support for its domestic policies. Although Whitlam had won public approval of his "Australia First" policy, which diminished the country's dependence on the United States and Britain while increasing its influence in Asia and the Pacific, his government seemed unable to control mounting inflation, unemployment, industrial unrest, stagnation of business, and rural discontent. The Labor party suffered serious setbacks in state elections, notably in Western Australia where, in March, Whitlam was physically attacked by a crowd of angry farmers.

Since the Liberal-Country opposition had gained control of the Senate by a narrow margin, Whitlam's government was unable to enact such measures as its national health insurance plan. Consequently, he decided to call new national elections midway through his three-year term. But although in popularity polls Whitlam fared far better than opposition leader Billy M. Snedden, the May 18 elections resulted in a stalemate in the Senate and only a slight increase in Labor's margin in the House of Representatives.

Lacking a clear mandate, Whitlam proceeded cautiously in his domestic programs. Beginning in June, he introduced anti-inflationary austerity measures, including cutbacks in government expenditures and in the civil service, that did little to enhance his popularity. In September he announced the third revaluation of Australian currency since he took office, decreasing its value by 12% and ending its ties to the U. S. dollar. In the fall, Whitlam visited the United States and Canada for talks with President Ford and Prime Minister Trudeau.

Background. The son of a Commonwealth crown solicitor general, Edward Gough Whitlam was born on July 11, 1916, in Kew, Victoria, and was educated in private schools. After air force service in World War II he obtained his law degree from Sydney University and entered legal practice. In 1952 he was elected to the House of Representatives as a Labor party candidate, and from 1956 to 1959 he served on the joint parliamentary committee on constitutional review. After his election in 1967 as the Labor party's parliamentary leader, he revitalized the party, divesting it of its ideological orthodoxy. He succeeded William McMahon as prime minister on Dec. 5, 1972, after a hard-fought election that ended the Liberal-Country party coalition's 23-year domination of the Australian government. During his first year in office he instituted major changes in foreign and domestic policies.

WILSON, Harold

After nearly four years in the opposition, Labour party leader Harold Wilson was appointed by Queen Elizabeth II on March 4, 1974, to succeed Conservative Edward Heath as prime minister of Britain. With the 301 seats it had won in the February 28 election, Labour had a plurality but not a majority in the 635-member House of Commons, and thus, after Heath had failed in his effort to form a coalition with the Liberals, Wilson became head of Britain's first minority government in 45 years. During his early weeks in office, Wilson took drastic steps to cope with what has been described as Britain's worst economic crisis since World War II. He settled a crippling coal miners' strike by largely giving in to the strikers' demands. He restored industry, which had been placed on a three-day workweek by Heath, to a full-time work schedule. To ease the effects of inflation—estimated at 17% for the year—on low-income groups, Wilson instituted a freeze on rents and an increase in pensions, placed subsidies on milk and other vital foods, and tightened price controls on some commodities. At the same time he moved to reduce profit margins and restrict mortgage rates, and announced plans for increased taxes on income and property of the wealthy.

In place of the mandatory wage controls introduced by the Heath government, Wilson persuaded the powerful Trades Union Congress to accept a "social contract" designed to promote industrial peace through voluntary wage and price restraints. Although he was moderately successful in his relations with organized labor, the stability of his government continued to be threatened by inflation, unemployment, a vast balance of payments deficit, controversy over Britain's continued membership in the Common Market, and the perennial civil strife in Northern Ireland. Furthermore, his minority government lacked the mandate for carrying out some of his more far-reaching plans. Therefore he decided to call a new election for October 10. The year's second general election gave Labour 319 seats in Parliament, a narrow but clear majority of three.

After final returns were in, Wilson outlined his plans, which included renegotiation of the terms of

British Prime Minister Harold Wilson and his wife, Mary, after his Labour party defeated the incumbent Conservatives in February's general elections.

UPI

British membership in the European Common Market; nationalization of major industries, including recently discovered oil resources in the North Sea; continuation of his voluntary "social contract" program; and taxing the wealthy "until the pips squeak." He told Britons that they faced at least two years of austerity.

Background. The son of an industrial chemist, James Harold Wilson was born in Huddersfield, Yorkshire, on March 11, 1916, and was educated in private schools. After graduating from Oxford University with first-class honors in 1937, he became a lecturer in economics there. During World War II he served in various civil service posts, and in 1945 he won election to Parliament as a Labour party candidate. As president of the Board of Trade from 1947 to 1951, he was the youngest British cabinet member of the century. Originally associated with the left wing of the Labour party, he later adopted a more moderate and pragmatic position. In 1963 he succeeded the late Hugh Gaitskell as leader of the Labour party and of the parliamentary opposition. He became prime minister in 1964 and was returned to office with an increased parliamentary majority two years later. In 1970, following a Conservative election victory, he was succeeded by Edward Heath.

WONDER, Stevie

Singer-musician and composer Stevie Wonder, one of the superstars of contemporary popular music, achieved top honors at the 16th annual Grammy awards ceremony in Hollywood on March 2, 1974. He was named best male pop vocalist for his rendition of his own "You Are the Sunshine of My Life"; his LP *Innervisions* was designated best album of the year; and he was cited both as composer and as vocalist of "Superstition," the best male rhythm and blues recording. On March 25, at New York's Madison Square Garden, he gave his first concert since his nearly fatal automobile accident in August 1973, singing to an enthusiastic audience of 20,000 in his unique style, derived from a variety of sources and transcending musical categories. In September he began a 30-city tour with a concert at the Nassau Coliseum on Long Island.

Wonder, who has been blind since birth, believes that "a handicap isn't a handicap unless you make it one." But although he has been described as "a loose, happy child of music" whose performances are characterized by "innocence and infectious enjoyment," he is profoundly concerned with social and racial justice. "The only people who are really blind," he says, "are those whose eyes are so obscured by hatred and bigotry that they can't see the light of love and justice."

Background. Stevie Wonder was born Steven Judkins (or, according to some sources, Steveland Morris) in Saginaw, Mich., on May 13, 1950. He grew up in Detroit's black ghetto in what he has called "upper-lower-class circumstances." Even as a small child he demonstrated a genius for music, mastering the harmonica, the piano, and the drums. At the age of 12 he was discovered by a Motown Record Corp. executive and given the name Little Stevie Wonder. While attending the Michigan School for the Blind, from which he graduated with honors in 1968, he recorded such Motown hits at "I Call It Pretty Music," "Fingertips," "Uptight," "High Heel Sneakers," "Traveling Man," "My Cherie Amour," and "For Once in My Life."

Wonder became the first Motown artist to tour abroad, including England, France, and Japan; the first to appear in films; and the first to appear on network television programs, including the Ed Sullivan and Mike Douglas shows. His innovative techniques in the use of electronic sound equipment are reflected in his album *Music of My Mind* (1972). By 1974 his recordings had sold 40 million copies.

Stevie Wonder, winner of a number of 1974 Grammy awards, resumed his career after a near-fatal car accident.

MOTOWN

AMF-HATTERAS YACHTS

The queen of the 1974 National Boat Show in New York was the Hatteras 48-foot Yacht Fisherman; price, $162,800.

BOATING

The breaking of two long-standing powerboat and sailboat records, widespread use of a new kind of boat in mid-America, and the introduction of a new super high-strength boating material highlighted boating in 1974.

Racing. Veteran ocean racer Bob Magoon's 40-foot (12-meter) boat *Cigarette,* powered by two 500-hp engines, broke a 10-year record for the 1,257-mile (2,020-km) run from Miami, Fla., to New York City in 1974. Magoon stopped only once to fill his fuel tanks in Morehead City, N. C. His total running time was 22 hours, 41 minutes, and 15 seconds. Despite some rough sea conditions, Magoon averaged 55.4 miles (89.2 km) per hour. The previous record of 31 hours and 27 minutes was set in 1964 by Charles Johnson. The inaugural record was set in 1921 by the legendary Gar Wood. Counting only running time, his trip took 47 hours and 15 minutes.

Ondine, a radical new 79-foot (24-meter) ketch owned by S. A. "Huey" Long, in 1974 topped a Bermuda race record that had stood since 1956. *Ondine* completed the Newport, R. I., to Hamilton, Bermuda, run in 67 hours, 52 minutes, and 22 seconds. The previous mark of 70 hours and 11 minutes was held by the Swedish yacht *Bolero.* On corrected time, a 55-foot (17-meter) aluminum sloop, *Scaramouche,* owned by C. E. Kirch of Sturgis, Mich., was the overall winner of the Bermuda race.

Bassboats. Increasingly popular throughout the South and Midwest are blunt-bowed, low-sided, wide boats designed for one purpose—to help occupants catch bass. Called bassboats, they are about 17 feet (5 meters) long and are powered by the largest outboards. After speeding to the fishing grounds, the gasoline outboard is turned off, and the boats are maneuvered through the fishing waters by powerful and silent electric outboard motors.

Super High-Strength Material. Kevlar is the name DuPont gave to a synthetic material discovered in 1972. Kevlar is destined to replace the steel in steel-belted radial automobile tires because, for the same strength as steel, Kevlar is 80% lighter.

Kevlar has already entered the boating world. Both *Scaramouche,* the Bermuda race winner, and *Courageous,* the America's Cup winner, sailed with Kevlar sails of characteristic honey-yellow color. Kevlar's super strength can be seen in that a one-half-inch (12.7-mm) Nylon line breaks at 6,400 pounds, whereas the same size Kevlar line breaks at 14,300 pounds. Another application for Kevlar threatens to make fiberglass canoes and kayaks obsolete. A plastic 13.5-foot (4-meter) kayak weighs 20 pounds, whereas the kayak weighs only 14 pounds when Kevlar cloth replaces the fiberglass. Yet the lighter boat is 1.8 times stronger. Several firms now offer boats using the new material.

Statistics. Boating accidents and fatalities were up sharply in 1973. Coast Guard statistics showed that 5,322 boats were in accidents, resulting in 1,418 deaths and 1,599 injuries. In 1972, 3,942 boat accidents were reported, with 1,152 fatalities and 829 injuries. Capsizing, operator error, and falling overboard were the chief causes of the accidents.

Boating continued to play an expanding role in recreation in 1973. It was estimated that there was a nationwide fleet of 9,435,000 boats, with about 47,175,000 persons participating in and $4.25 billion spent on the sport. In 1972 about 45 million people sailed in 9 million boats and spent $3.6 billion.

ZACK TAYLOR
Boating Editor, "Sports Afield"

BOLIVIA

Antigovernment protests increased in both rural and urban areas in Bolivia in 1974. The most serious of these occurred in January in Cochabamba, where peasant revolts, spurred by food shortages and price spirals, led to a pitched battle in which 30 peasants were killed and many more taken prisoner by government troops. Incidents between the students, factory workers, and miners on the one hand and government troops on the other occurred sporadically throughout the year. The Bolivian president, Gen. Hugo Banzer Suárez, claimed that these revolts were parts of leftist plots fomented from abroad. In reality, the left-wing revolutionary movement in Bolivia seemed to be marginal in 1974, while antigovernment agitation assumed a broader and more popular base.

Despite some achievements in the export sector, the government was vulnerable to criticism for repression of civil rights, for permitting Brazilian economic penetration of Bolivia, and for mismanagement of the food crisis in early 1974. Since it came to power after the overthrow of Juan José Torres in 1971, the Banzer government has lacked a strong political base outside of the military. As a result of loss of civilian support in 1974, the government became more heavily obligated to the military. Its ability to preside over a process leading to general elections was dubious.

Politics. Political support for President Banzer thinned out considerably in 1974. In July, he threw out a 17-man cabinet of 12 civilians and 5 army officers and replaced them with a cabinet composed only of military men. This change came only one month after a coup by military groups had failed. A low point was reached on August 30, when Banzer "resigned" his office but was persuaded by the military command to stay on pending general elections that now were scheduled for late 1975. The elections originally were scheduled for 1974.

Banzer's political base was weakened most visibly by dissent in the National Revolutionary Movement (MNR), the largest political party in the government coalition. Paz Estensorro, the leader of the MNR and Bolivia's most important politician, went into exile in January because of policy differences with Banzer. Paz sharply criticized Banzer on the postponement of elections and the government's growing economic relations with Brazil. Ciro Humbolt, Paz's successor, fell out with Banzer and was implicated by the government in a plot in June. Banzer cited "inconsistencies" in the MNR as the reason for his "resignation" in August.

Economy. The implementation of the government's Economic Stabilization and Development Act of 1972 continued in 1974. The objectives were to shift resources to increase exports of mineral and agricultural products and to decrease imports by the development of Bolivian substitutes for them.

Bolivia increased its international reserves markedly in 1974. It strengthened its credit position in the International Monetary Fund, and central bank reserves were unprecedentedly high. Foreign exchange holdings, which had reached a low of $21 million in 1971, were at $49 million in July 1974. Petroleum and tin were the main exchange earners.

An acute shortage of food became evident in early 1974. It was produced not only by weather problems but also by contraband food sales outside the country, in which government officials were implicated. The decision of the government to double food prices at home sharpened unrest, especially among the peasant class. Cost-of-living increases were demanded by miners and factory workers, but government wage concessions were too little for the workers and too much for management. In mid-1974, Bolivia was in the grip of a serious inflation, which added fuel to the political attacks on Banzer.

International Affairs. The Chilean military junta made life easier for Banzer by expelling Bolivian left-wing exiles that were operating in Chile. The Argentine government also cooperated with Banzer by arresting Bolivians who were alleged to be plotting against his regime. Generally, diplomatic relations warmed between Bolivia, Chile, Argentina, Uruguay, Paraguay, and Brazil.

Banzer was heavily criticized in 1974 for turning Bolivia into a client of Brazil. For instance, Brazilian investments in Bolivia continued to mount, and fears were expressed over the fact that large tracts of peasant-owned Bolivian land along the border with Brazil were held under mortgage to Brazilian banks. In May, Brazilian president Ernesto Geisel visited Bolivia and signed a major agreement providing for the sale of Bolivian natural gas in exchange for Brazilian technical and financial aid. His visit provoked widespread dissent and allegations of Brazilian penetration of Bolivia.

THOMAS M. MILLINGTON
Hobart and William Smith Colleges

BOLIVIA • Information Highlights

Official Name: Republic of Bolivia.
Location: West-central South America.
Area: 424,163 square miles (1,098,581 sq km).
Population (1973 est.): 5,000,000.
Chief Cities (1969 est.): Sucre, the legal capital, 58,000; La Paz, the actual capital, 525,000; Cochabamba, 157,000.
Government: *Head of state,* Hugo Banzer Suárez, president (took office Aug. 1971). *Head of government,* Hugo Banzer Suárez. *Legislature*—Congress (suspended Sept. 1969): Senate and Chamber of Deputies.
Monetary Unit: Peso (20 pesos equal U. S. $1, July 1974).
Gross National Product (1973 est.): $755,000,000.
Manufacturing (major products): Processed foods, textiles, leather goods, cement.
Major Agricultural Products: Sugar, cotton, corn, potatoes, wheat, rice, coffee, bananas.
Foreign Trade (1972): Exports, $213,000,000; imports, $185,000,000.

UPI

Police escort school buses carrying black students to South Boston, where court-ordered busing for racial integration touched off strong opposition.

BOSTON

A conflict over court-ordered busing to achieve racial balance in the public schools dominated events in Boston in 1974.

School Busing Controversy. Racial segregation in the schools has been an issue in the city ever since 1965, when a state law was passed prohibiting any school in a city or town from being more than 50% black. Although blacks presently comprise 20% of Boston's population, 38% of its 94,000 public school pupils are nonwhite. In the nine years since passage of the law, no resolution of the imbalance problem has been achieved.

As the year opened, suits charging unlawful discrimination in the schools filed by the National Association for the Advancement of Colored People (NAACP) were pending in both state and federal courts. Some 82% of the city's black pupils attended schools that were 50% or more black. The prospect of busing aroused protests, including demonstrations against Boston Mayor Kevin H. White.

On June 12, Federal District Court Judge W. Arthur Garrity, Jr., ruled in the NAACP suit that "racial segregation existed in parts of the Boston School System" and that a state plan requiring the busing of about 20,000 pupils be implemented in September. Amid widespread protest, the city prepared for school opening on September 12.

The first weeks of school were marked by scattered violent incidents, especially in South Boston, where almost no blacks live. Heavy police guards were stationed around South Boston High School, and police convoys escorted buses into and from the area. In other parts of the city there was less violence, but serious incidents did occur at Hyde Park and Boston English high schools. Citywide attendance was estimated at 70% of normal at the end of September. In early October, Mayor White asked Judge Garrity for federal marshals to assist Boston police, but the judge ordered that state police be used first. Over 400 state police were sent into the city on October 10. On October 16, Gov. Francis Sargent ordered an alert of two National Guard military police units. It was widely hoped that incidents in the schools would subside.

In November a referendum to abolish the Boston School Committee, which for a decade has opposed busing and integration, was defeated. (See also EDUCATION.)

Other Events. In April, five Boston doctors were indicted for performing research operations on fetuses obtained from therapeutic abortions. The charges, reflecting widespread antiabortion sentiment in Massachusetts, were decried by the city's large medical community (Boston has over 80 hospitals and research centers).

In August, the federal Environmental Protection Agency moved to implement a plan requiring all employers of 50 or more persons to reduce employee parking by 20% in an effort to limit auto traffic and improve air quality.

HARVEY BOULAY
Boston University

BOTANY

Botanists in 1974 investigated relationships between plants and animals with respect to plant chemistry and pollination.

Tree Rings and Climate. Tree rings are an important source of climatic data for centuries past, since they can be accurately dated and they show differences in response to climatic changes. The most frequently used species is the bristlecone pine, *Pinus aristata,* of the southwestern United States. A record of the last 8,200 years has been compiled using living trees and dead logs and wood. V. C. LaMarche correlated data from the lower elevations at which the tree grows with data from trees at the upper elevation limit. Information was obtained by cross-dating between the two environments, where different factors limit growth and hence the size of the ring.

At lower elevations moisture availability was shown to be the factor that controlled tree ring width; high temperatures had a negative effect by reducing available moisture. At higher elevations, as would be expected, low temperatures were limiting, and so produced narrow rings. Most of the previously reported work, done at upper elevations, gives only an indication of temperature trends. By correlating data from upper and lower elevations, departures from mean growth rates were used to show moisture changes. Thus, a wide ring at both places would indicate a warm, moist growing season, and a narrow ring, a cool dry year.

Variations that persisted over a period of years indicated trends in climate. The period from 800 to 1000 A. D. was indicated as cool and dry, followed by a century of warm and moist conditions, then warm and dry to about 1300 A. D. This was followed by a long cool period lasting nearly to the present century, relatively moist at first, then becoming drier. This century has been warmer, but remained dry.

Plant Chemistry. Alkaloids are nitrogen-containing plant products, many of which have medical significance (such as morphine, codeine, and nicotine). The role of alkaloids in the plant itself has never been established. Many workers have considered that alkaloids are simply useless end products, but there are evolutionary objections to this. T. Robinson has pointed out that alkaloids are actively metabolized by plants and hence cannot be considered dead ends. He reported that the levels of alkaloids vary during plant life cycles and even during a 24-hour period.

The way in which plants make alkaloids, usually from amino acids, is known in many cases. Breakdown products are not as well known. The role of a few alkaloids has been explained in terms of repelling insect predators or excluding other plant competitors. In most cases, however, we do not know the role the alkaloids play, but they are not inert end products.

Another group of plant products are the resins, found, for example, in pines. They are defensive substances. T. Eisner, J. S. Johnessee, and J. Carrel in 1974 reported that the pine sawfly, which eats pine needles, consumes and stores the resin, and emits it to deter such predators as birds and ants.

Pollination. Ants are usually considered of negative value in flower pollination. However, J. C. Hickman reported that in a small annual plant, *Polygonum cascadense,* ants were not only able to pollinate the flowers but actually were necessary for pollination. The flowers were adapted to pollination by ants: they were small, tubular, with sticky pollen, and usually only one was open per plant. The plants, in turn, were small and close together. Ants visited up to six plants per minute. Proof that ants were the chief pollinators was obtained in greenhouse studies, in which ants were excluded, but other insects could visit the flowers. Seed set was markedly reduced. The author proposed that this represents an energy efficient system for both plant and ant.

Insectivorous Plants. The mechanism by which the insectivorous plants, such as Venus' flytrap (*Dionaea*) and the sundews (*Drosera*), are able to capture and digest their prey has fascinated botanists since the time of Charles Darwin. These plants live in bogs and obtain some of their nitrogen by capturing and digesting small insects. The sundews capture their prey on sticky hairs, which bend slowly inward to press the insect against the leaf surface, where it is digested. S. E. Williams has found nervelike signals in these hairs.

The cells in the hairs were found to be able to convert a physical or mechanical stimulus, such as the touch of an insect, into an electrical impulse much like a nerve signal. When the tip of the hair was touched, the message traveled to the base of the hair, but much more slowly than nerve signals travel in animal cells. Very small electrodes were used to measure both rate and direction of travel, and it was found that the message can travel either up or down the hair. This may indicate a way in which the hairs are coordinated.

Fossil Plants. Two separate reports concerning fossil plants appeared in 1974. Evidence was presented by L. A. Nagy for the earliest differentiation of plant cells. Well-preserved fossil blue-green algae, 2.2 billion years old, were found to have large specialized resting cells called skinetes.

J. Gray, S. Laufeld, and A. J. Boucot reported finding land-plant-type spores from Silurian rocks in Gotland, Sweden. These were suggested to indicate an earlier beginning to vascular plants than the late Silurian, as presently accepted by most botanists and other specialists.

James D. Montgomery
Ichthyological Associates

WIDE WORLD

Victims of Brazil's nationwide floods in March wait for food and medicine outside government building. Floods left more than 100,000 homeless.

BRAZIL

Much steam went out of Brazil's economic boom in 1974, as a new administration wrestled with a serious trade deficit, inflation, and natural disasters.

Economy. António Delfim Netto, architect of Brazil's "economic miracle," lost his job as finance minister when the new administration of President Ernesto Geisel took over on March 15. By then Delfim's "miracle" was badly tarnished, and incoming Finance Minister Mário Henrique Simonsen had to find ways to bridge Brazil's widening trade gap, as imports exceeded exports by $1.4 billion in the first four months of 1974.

Simonsen's solutions included encouraging direct foreign investment in Brazilian industry and borrowing money abroad. Brazil's foreign debt, already a record $13.5 billion by mid-1974, mounted as the government reduced the minimum term of foreign loans from 10 to 5 years in September. Despite concern about rising inflation and a slowdown in some Brazilian industries, notably construction and textiles, many foreign investors still considered Brazil a good credit risk. But toward the end of 1974, as the trade deficit exceeded Brazil's foreign exchange reserves ($6.4 billion at the beginning of the year), some observers were warning that the Latin American country was headed for an economic crisis.

The Geisel administration hoped to avert disaster by increasing exports, reducing imports, and maintaining Brazil's extraordinary economic growth rate of recent years. As late as September the government was predicting a rise of 10% in the gross national product for the year, not far below the record 11.4% increase of 1973. With manufactured goods accounting for 20% of the country's exports, Brazil sought financing from the World Bank to continue expansion of its steel industry.

Exports of Brazilian automobiles rose to $250 million during the year, as new markets were found in Africa and the Middle East. Large sums, including $84.5 million from the Inter-American Development Bank, were invested in the development of hydroelectric power during 1974, partly in hopes of lessening Brazil's dependence on imported petroleum as an energy source. Exploration for oil was pushed with great vigor, with some success.

Revitalization of Brazilian agriculture and increased agricultural exports were among the goals announced by President Geisel in March. While agricultural products still comprise more than half of Brazil's exports, agricultural production in recent years has been increasing at less than half the rate of the gross national product. Proclaiming the methods that brought success in industry to be applicable to agriculture, the new administration has favored the interests of large-scale "agribusiness" over those of the small farmer.

The flow of displaced peasants to the cities of Brazil increased noticeably during 1974, but so did production of wheat and soybeans. Coffee production was up also, though not as much as expected. The sugar crop was down slightly from 1973, but sharply higher world prices brought Brazil more than $1 billion for its sugar exports in 1974, almost as much as it received for coffee exports.

As insurance against a world recession, the new government stressed the need to develop Brazil's internal market, which had been relatively neglected since 1964. In March, President Geisel announced that one of the goals of his administration was a fairer distribution of incomes, to check the 10-year decline in the purchasing power of the average Brazilian. But the president's announcement did not affect a slump in production of textiles and some other consumer goods for the domestic market, nor prevent a slackening of internal demand for automobiles. In September the government called on automobile makers to shift their emphasis from passenger cars to more utilitarian vehicles.

Contrary to the professed desire of the government, the gap between the rich few and the impoverished many widened in 1974. Government-imposed controls limited wage increases to 25%, while the cost of living rose more than 35%. Unemployment increased in rural areas and in the cities of the underdeveloped Northeast, where the jobless rate reached 13%.

Social Services. Upon taking office on March 15, President Geisel acknowledged that Brazil's atrocious health conditions required immediate attention. The infant mortality rate in some areas was 168 per 1,000 and rising, the Ministry of Health admitted. The average life expectancy in Brazil was 35 years. Tuberculosis affected nearly half the adult population, while 19 million Brazilians were suffering from hookworm disease, 8 million from schistosomiasis, and 15 million from Chagas' disease. The situation was hardly surprising in a population, already malnourished, that was undergoing a decline in living standards.

Allocations for health—12.6% of the federal budget in 1968—had declined steadily to less than 5% in 1973. The president pledged to reverse the trend, but his promises had no effect on a meningitis epidemic that struck the city of São Paulo (where living conditions of the poor were probably the worst in Brazil) in June. By August the disease had spread to other southern cities and had claimed thousands of victims. An accurate count of meningitis deaths was virtually precluded by government censorship, which suppressed news of the epidemic.

The meningitis epidemic was preceded by devastating floods in southern Brazil. Shortly after President Geisel's inauguration, rampaging rivers caused some 3,000 deaths, left 300,000 homeless, and practically washed away the city of Tubarão. These disasters were followed in July by the defeat of the Brazilian soccer team, defending champions, in the semifinals of the World Cup competition. To superstitious Brazilians (no small portion of the population) Geisel was an "unlucky president," who would bring a succession of calamities.

Trans-Amazon Project. The Amazonian colonization project, much ballyhooed by outgoing President Emílio Garrastazú Médici, came apart as Geisel took office. Soils along the Trans-Amazon highway were not suited for mass colonization by small farmers. In any case, only 5,000 settlers had accepted the government's offer of free homesteads in the vast Amazonian region. The new administration discouraged further movement of settlers into the area and began turning over huge tracts of Amazonian lands to large corporations for cattle raising.

Political Events. Politically, Geisel attempted a policy of "decompression," an easing of the recent police-state repression. Relations between church and state improved somewhat.

Reports of press censorship, mass arrests of opponents of the regime, reports of torture of political prisoners, and mysterious disappearances of critics of military rule continued. Military hardliners unsuccessfully attempted to persuade President Geisel to cancel scheduled congressional and state elections. In the November voting the government party, the National Renewal Alliance (ARENA), was outpolled by nearly 2 to 1 by the only legal opposition party, the Brazilian Democratic Movement (MDB). The MDB, however, did not win enough seats to take control of either house of Congress.

Foreign Relations. Brazilian military maneuvers in the Amazonian border region early in 1974 caused new concern among other South American countries about their "imperialistic" neighbor. Across the Atlantic, Brazil welcomed the new anti-colonialist regime in Portugal. Brazil's close ties with its mother country had hampered Brazilian attempts to establish friendly relations with the oil-rich nations of Africa and the Middle East as long as Portugal was fighting liberation movements in its African colonies. After the March 1974 revolution, as Portugal began liquidating its African empire, Brazil concluded a deal to buy Nigerian petroleum and established diplomatic relations with Libya and Kuwait. Brazil also recognized China, a major purchaser of Brazilian sugar.

NEILL MACAULAY, *University of Florida*

BRAZIL • Information Highlights

Official Name: Federative Republic of Brazil.
Location: Eastern South America.
Area: 3,286,478 square miles (8,511,965 sq km).
Population (1973 est.): 101,700,000.
Chief Cities (1970 census): Brasília, the capital, 272,002; São Paulo, 5,921,796; Rio de Janeiro, 4,252,009; Belo Horizonte, 1,235,001.
Government: *Head of state,* Ernesto Geisel, president (took office March 1974). *Head of government,* Ernesto Geisel. *Legislature*—National Congress: Federal Senate and Chamber of Deputies.
Monetary Unit: Cruzeiro (6.885 cruzeiros equal U. S.$1, July 1974).
Gross National Product (1973 est.): $55,200,000,000.
Manufacturing (major products): Processed foods, chemicals, textiles, automobiles, metals, petroleum products, paper, fertilizers.
Major Agricultural Products: Coffee, soybeans, rice, corn, sugarcane, wheat, oranges, cacao.
Foreign Trade (1973): *Exports,* $6,199,000,000; *imports,* $7,210,000,000.

BRITISH COLUMBIA

On June 20, 1974, the British Columbia Legislature ended the longest session in the history of the province. It was marked by the presentation of Premier David Barrett's "Resource Dividend Budget," which called for expenditures of over $2 billion, and the passage of 106 bills of wide-ranging implications. A brief review of some noteworthy legislation enacted during the session follows.

Mineral Royalties. The new Mineral Royalties Act provides for the collection of royalties on certain minerals produced in British Columbia. There are two levels of royalties, one a fixed percentage charge and the other tied to an average base price of the minerals. The government felt that the previous system of taxing only mining company profits did not return to the province a fair share of the value of its exported resources.

Agriculture. Earlier legislation has been successful in reducing the loss of farm land to other uses. New legislation increases the amount of loans guaranteed by the province, enables the minister of agriculture to undertake directly and pay for projects under the Agriculture and Rural Development Act without first applying for federal approval, and sets up a fund to assist in developing new agriculture-oriented businesses.

Small Business. A small-business development program was established by the British Columbia Development Corporation in an action designed to aid new and imaginative industries in the province. The program will provide loans and other financial assistance.

Housing. Housing for lower-income groups in the province continued to be in short supply during 1974. The Department of Housing is attempting to relieve the situation by providing subsidized housing. The department has purchased Dunhill Development Corporation Ltd., a real estate and development firm.

Economic Development. In the first half of 1974 the province's economy continued to show advances over 1973, although, in some sectors, not at the record pace of 1973. Lumber production was adversely affected by a reduction in United States housing starts. Wages continued to climb, with the average weekly wage in May being $197.64. This represents an increase of $19.84 over May 1973. The employment rate in July equaled that of July 1973, with unemployment at 5.5%.

Compared with July 1973, the labor force was 72,000 greater, including a gain of 68,000 in the number employed and an advance of 4,000 in the number of unemployed. The Vancouver Consumer Price Index increased by 12% from June 1973 to June 1974, with the most notable increase (19.4%) occurring in food.

Farm income continued to increase sharply in response to increased prices for farm produce. Farm cash receipts for the first quarter of 1974 amounted to $98.6 million, a gain of 33.5% over the corresponding months of 1973.

The announcement of the sale of 74.6 million bushels of Prairie wheat worth $350 million to the People's Republic of China meant a continued high level of activity at British Columbia ports.

New Park. A bill establishing the Pacific Rim National Park on the west coast of Vancouver Island was given its final reading in the federal House of Commons on April 4.

HERBERT W. KEE, *Executive Director*
Economic Plans and Statistics
Department of Economic Development

—BRITISH COLUMBIA • Information Highlights—

Area: 366,255 square miles (948,597 sq km).
Population (1974 est.): 2,384,000.
Chief Cities (1973 est.): Metro Victoria, the capital, 211,336; Metro Vancouver, 1,117,040.
Government (1974): *Chief Officers*—lt. gov., Walter S. Owen; premier, David Barrett (New Democratic party); atty. gen., Alexander B. MacDonald (NDP); min. of educ., Eileen Dailly (NDP); chief justice, John L. Farris. *Legislature*—Legislative Assembly, 55 members (38 NDP, 10 Social Credit, 5 Liberal, 2 Progressive Conservative).
Education (Feb. 1974): *Enrollment:* public elementary and secondary schools, 542,270 pupils; private schools, 22,470; Indian (federal) schools, 2,970; colleges and universities, 39,100 full-time students. *Public school expenditures* (1975 est.), $567,822,000.
Public Finance (fiscal year 1974–75): *Revenues,* $2,459,000,000; *expenditures,* $2,457,000,000.
Personal Income (1973 est.): $10,575,000,000; average annual income per person, $4,568.
(All monetary figures are in Canadian dollars.)

BULGARIA

The year 1974 did not bring any important changes in Bulgaria. The political system remained static; the economy remained highly centralized, with low productivity both publicly lamented and well entrenched. The same aging leaders controlled the Communist party, and the unqualified support of the Soviet Union in domestic and foreign policies continued.

Domestic Politics. In September, spectacular celebrations of the 30th anniversary of the Communist take-over were held throughout the country. Appeals to the youth for greater patriotism, self-discipline, and productivity figured prominently in speeches and resolutions. The Academy of Social Sciences and Social Management, established in 1970 and dedicated to ideological and professional cadre training, was frequently praised. Over 80,000 senior activists had been trained there, and some 19,500 were currently enrolled.

In February the party's Central Committee condemned Maoism, right-wing revisionism, and social reformism. The following month the party conference, attended by 15,000 delegates, instructed trade unions to strengthen labor discipline and increase admittedly low individual and collective productivity. In March and July the Communist youth organization, Komsomol, criticized the frequently low level of higher edu-

BULGARIA • Information Highlights

Official Name: People's Republic of Bulgaria.
Location: Southeastern Europe.
Area: 42,823 square miles (110,912 sq km).
Population (1973 est.): 8,700,000.
Chief Cities (1971 est.): Sofia, the capital, 897,949; Plovdiv, 254,548; Varna, 235,177.
Government: *Head of state,* Todor Zhivkov, chairman of the State Council and first secretary of the Communist party (took office July 1971). *Head of government,* Stanko Todorov, chairman of the Council of Ministers (took office July 1971). *Legislature* (unicameral)—National Assembly.
Monetary Unit: Lev (0.94 lev equals U. S.$1, July 1974).
Gross National Product (1973 est.): $12.2 billion.
Manufacturing (major products): Processed foods, machinery, chemicals, steel, tobacco products, petroleum products, clothing.
Major Agricultural Products: Corn, wheat, barley, fruits, tobacco, sugar beets.
Foreign Trade (1973): *Exports,* $3,301,000,000; *imports,* $3,266,000,000.

cation. Apparently some 50% of postgraduate students were found to be unqualified. They collected substantial monthly scholarships "without doing any work sometimes for five, ten, or even more years." No more than 30% were able to complete their studies in time. In April a party-government decree established the National Cultural Complex to lead and control the nation's cultural activities. State agencies, professional associations, the press, radio, television, theaters, and motion pictures, as well as the creativity of individual writers and painters, were to fall under the jurisdiction of this organization.

Economy. In February 1974, new regulations were issued further restricting private artisanship (responsible for 0.3% of the total industrial output) and private retail trade (amounting to no more than 0.07% of the domestic trade). Both were officially labeled as "nonlabor," unduly high-income-producing activities. In August the Council of Ministers passed a decree aimed at saving raw and other materials and reducing widespread labor abuses.

In September the Soviet-Bulgarian pipeline was inaugurated in Vratsa. This pipeline will supply 3 billion cubic meters (105,944 million cubic feet) of Soviet natural gas each year. At approximately the same time inauguration of a nuclear power station in Kozloduy took place. The station, first in the Balkans, was constructed by Soviet specialists. All of its four reactors were to be active by 1978–79. They would produce 11 billion kw-hr, or over 20% of the nation's total electric power production.

The 30th International Fair held in Plovdiv proved to be a success. Forty-one countries participated, with a total of 4,000 individual firms represented.

Ties with the USSR. Of all eastern European countries, Bulgaria continues to rank first in trade with the USSR and last in trade with the West. Approximately half of its trade in 1974 continued to be with the Soviet Union, and over 70% of it with the COMECON countries. Two thirds of the country's imported fuel, minerals, and metals came from the USSR, and 60% of its machine-building products went to the USSR. The USSR had participated in the construction of some 180 heavy industry-related enterprises, and the current five-year plan (1971–75) provides for 150 more. Since the end of World War II, more than 150 million Soviet books have been imported.

Foreign Policy and Trade. In January, Chairman Zhivkov visited East Germany, and in April he went to Iraq. "Identity or similarity of views" as to "imperialist Zionism" were emphasized on both occasions, and measures for economic, political, and cultural cooperation were agreed upon. In May, Rumanian President Nicolae Ceausescu visited Sofia. No meaningful agreements resulted, and the communiqué failed to indicate identity or similarity of views.

In August, Cuban Foreign Minister Raul Roa and Hungarian Premier Jenö Fock visited Sofia. In 1975, trade with Hungary is to be increased by 60%, to 100 million rubles, over the 1970 level.

In May, Italian Foreign Minister Aldo Moro arrived in Sofia; and in June, Bulgarian Premier Stanko Todorov visited Stockholm, Sweden. A 10-year agreement with Italy on scientific and technological cooperation resulted, and trade with Sweden, thus far insignificant, is to be increased.

JAN KARSKI, *Georgetown University*

BURMA

Soaring prices and shortages of many commodities underlay a workers' uprising in June, followed two months later by Burma's worst flood in 100 years. U Ne Win's political leadership was not endangered by either occurrence, however, despite the problems caused for his government by both events.

Politics. Burma held its first election in 14 years in January, following the proclamation of the country's second constitution on January 4. Former General Ne Win became the new "socialist republic's" first president, however, without a direct popular vote. Polling for the 451-seat unicameral People's Assembly, moreover, involved the participation of only the country's single officially recognized party, the Burma Socialist Program Party.

The military-controlled new government, which took over from the dissolved Revolutionary Council on March 2, was unable to deal with the nation's mounting supply and price problems and was almost immediately confronted by the most serious economic demonstrations since independence. Workers seized control of 40 government-operated factories and mills in and near Rangoon in May and early June. As a result, 22 persons were killed and 60 wounded on June 6 when government forces fired on the demonstrators.

Insurrections. The most serious challenge to the Ne Win government continued to come from

BURMA • Information Highlights

Official Name: Socialist Republic of the Union of Burma.
Location: Southeast Asia.
Area: 261,789 square miles (678,033 sq km).
Population (1973 est.): 29,800,000.
Chief Cities (1969 est.): Rangoon, the capital, 1,717,600 (1968 est.); Mandalay, 393,000; Moulmein, 169,000.
Government: *Head of state,* U Ne Win, president (took office March 1974). *Head of government,* U Sein Win, prime minister (took office March 1974). *Legislature* (unicameral)—People's Assembly.
Monetary Unit: Kyat (4.862 kyats equal U. S.$1, July 1974).
Gross National Product (1972 est.): $2,200,000,000.
Manufacturing (major products): Processed foods, textiles, tobacco products, wood products.
Major Agricultural Products: Rice, groundnuts, sesame, tobacco, sugarcane, millet, cotton, forest products.
Foreign Trade (1973): *Exports,* $109,000,000; *imports,* $89,000,000.

China-aided insurgents in the northern part of the country, where Communists and members of various ethnic minorities combined their efforts against the Rangoon regime. Besides this 4,000-man main insurrectionary effort, probably more than 6,000 other Kachin, Shan, Karen, Paoy, and Lahu tribesmen also were involved in separate armed uprisings in other parts of the country. The government sought to woo its rebel foes to lay down their arms through an offer of amnesty, but the deadline expired in June with a minimal response from the insurgents.

Economy. The May-June workers' uprising was prompted largely by rising prices—which increased as much as fourfold for some commodities at one point in late 1973—and widespread shortages of many key items, including various foodstuffs. Part of the problem was the government's policy of buying rice at $60 a ton and selling it to foreign customers for seven times that amount. Farmers, as a result, cut back on the amount of rice they planted (and/or sold to the government) and devoted their efforts to more profitable pursuits, such as raising cattle (which were smuggled out of the country into neighboring Thailand in record numbers). Burmese exports of rice dropped from about 800,000 tons as recently as 1971 to 146,000 tons in 1973.

Record flooding in August, which inundated thousands of villages along the 1,000-mile length of the Irrawaddy River, destroyed much of the 1974 rice crop, as well as other commodities and much property, and left one million persons homeless. The result was an expected further decline in rice exports, new cutbacks in imports, more shortages, and still higher prices.

In May, the economically beseiged Ne Win regime granted contracts to three foreign oil companies to explore offshore on a contractual basis. It also relaxed state domination of domestic trading to relieve shortages and lower prices.

Foreign Affairs. Burma's economic and political difficulties did not prevent Ne Win from leaving the country at the height of the workers' demonstrations in June. His departure reflected the importance he attached to international bridge-building (despite the country's previously isolationist, ultranationalistic foreign policies). On his June trip abroad, Ne Win visited Indonesia, Singapore, Australia, and New Zealand in a bid to improve relations with these Asian and Pacific non-Communist countries. Earlier, in April, as the workers' protest was mounting, he travelled to neighboring India, Pakistan, and Bangladesh for similar fence-mending reasons; and in October he journeyed to eastern Europe.

Besides the oil contracts with three foreign firms, the Rangoon government made a major modification of its previous position respecting vessels that strayed into Burmese coastal waters—reversing an earlier decision and releasing 31 members of a fishery survey vessel of the six-country Southeast Asian Fisheries Development Center. Previously, in February, the government responded to pressure from the United States and various international agencies and issued a new narcotic drugs law prohibiting the cultivation, processing, and sale of the poppies, hemp, and other plants from which the drugs are derived.

RICHARD BUTWELL
State University of New York College at Fredonia

CALIFORNIA

In 1974, California endured a dull election campaign, experienced high unemployment, and found relative calm in matters related to weather and political developments.

Election. Gov. Ronald Reagan kept to his announced intention of not seeking reelection. The Republican primary contest was between conservative Lt. Gov. Ed Reinecke and moderate state Controller Houston I. Flournoy. Before the primary, however, Reinecke was indicted on a charge of perjury before a Senate committee, and he was badly defeated. (He was later convicted, given a suspended sentence, and resigned his office.)

The Democrats had three strong candidates in the June primary, but Edmund G. (Jerry) Brown, son of former Gov. Edmund G. (Pat) Brown, received more than twice as many votes as his nearest competitor, Mayor Joseph Alioto of San Francisco. Brown defeated Flournoy in the general election, but received only 51.51% of the vote and ran next to last on the Democratic slate.

The Democrats won all but one of the statewide offices; Attorney General Evelle J. Younger (R) was reelected. Sen. Alan Cranston (D) was easily reelected over token opposition from state Senator H. L. (Bob) Richardson, a former member of the John Birch Society. State Senator Mervyn M. Dymally became the first black to be elected lieutenant governor. March K. Fong, a Chinese-American woman, was elected secretary of state. Jesse M. Unruh, former powerful speaker of the Assembly, began a political comeback with his election as state treasurer. The Democrats won safe majorities in both houses of the Legislature and gained four Congressional seats.

Ballot Propositions. Nine propositions were voted on in June and 17 in November, about average for the state. Only two were greatly controversial. In June, an enormously complex "political reform" initiative was adopted. Few voters understood even a few of its many details, but the "yes" vote reflected a demand for a political "cleanup." The measure calls for state political campaign finance disclosures, lobby control, expenditure controls on ballot propositions, and restrictions on conflicts of interest. The measure faces many court tests.

In the fall, the most controversial proposal called for prohibiting the construction of a large dam on the Stanislaus River north of San Francisco. Proponents cited environmental concerns. The opposition, however, argued that the hydroelectric power that would be produced was badly needed and that the proponents were mainly interested in preserving a stretch of "whitewater" for rafting and kayaking—upper middle-class activities—while persons of all classes could benefit from the recreational facilities planned for the large lake that would be created behind the dam. The proposal received only 47.11% of the vote.

Legislation. In January, the California Legislature overrode a gubernatorial veto for the first time in 28 years. Significantly, the bill involved the powers of the Legislature. It transferred from the administration to the Legislature the authority to decide whether any of the state's mental hospitals are to be closed or to remain open. In all, the Governor vetoed 198 bills, a high for his years in office. In particular, he killed proposals relative to housing and public-employee benefits. He also made extensive use of the item veto to reduce appropriations.

New substantive legislation included a change in the law limiting testimony in rape trials about the victim's previous sexual experience.

CALIFORNIA • Information Highlights

Area: 158,693 square miles (411,015 sq km).
Population (1973 est.): 20,601,000. *Density:* 131 per sq mi.
Chief Cities (1970 census): Sacramento, the capital, 257,105; Los Angeles, 2,809,596; San Francisco, 715,674.
Government (1974): *Chief Officer*—governor, Ronald Reagan (R). *Legislature*—Senate, 40 members; Assembly, 80 members.
Education (1973–74): *Enrollment*—public elementary schools, 2,699,000 pupils; public secondary schools, 1,736,000; nonpublic schools, 322,200; colleges and universities, 1,467,355 students. *Public school expenditures,* $5,126,438,000 ($1,198 per pupil).
State Finances (fiscal year 1973): *Revenues,* $15,582,635,000; *expenditures,* $13,096,164,000.
Personal Income (1973): $112,038,000,000; per capita, $5,438.
Labor Force (July 1974): *Nonagricultural wage and salary earners,* 7,777,600; *insured unemployed,* 276,100 (4.3%).

UPI

California Lt. Gov. Ed Reinecke and his wife, Jean, leave the U. S. district court after his trial for perjury. Found guilty, he was given a suspended sentence.

The Legislature also passed laws requiring state approval for new power plant sites, authorizing the practice of midwifery, and establishing a new definition of death.

Two San Franciscans, Leo T. McCarthy and Willie L. Brown, Jr., contested for the speakership of the Assembly when Bob Moretti resigned the position after running unsuccessfully for governor in the Democratic primary. McCarthy was chosen in the Democratic caucus.

Economy. The state suffered during the year from above-average increases in the consumer price index in its large cities. Unemployment was also above the national average, reaching 8.4% late in the year.

Education. In October, Charles J. Hitch, president of the University of California, announced his retirement at the end of the academic year. He had been president since 1968.

The Postsecondary Education Commission began operations, although very slowly, and not until December did it fill the position of executive director. The 23-member group was established in 1973 to advise the Legislature and the governor on matters of higher education and the coordination of the various components of public and private education beyond the high schools. Its influence will ultimately depend upon the respect it can earn in the eyes of both legislators and the public.

CHARLES R. ADRIAN
University of California, Riverside

CAMBODIA

The Cambodian war entered its fifth year stalemated in a veritable state of siege and with no apparent indications that the armed struggle between the Lon Nol government and its Communist "Khmer Rouge" adversaries would be ended by early peace negotiations.

The War. The dry-season offensive mounted by the Communists in late 1973 scored initial successes, particularly near the capital city of Phnom Penh, but encountered stiffer resistance from government forces as the months passed by. The advent of the heavy annual rains in July ended the Lon Nol regime's first year without the help of American air bombing (terminated by the U. S. Congress in August 1973). About three quarters of the country and half of the national population remained under Communist control in 1974. Only the major cities and towns remained in government hands.

An average of about 300 persons were killed or wounded in the war each day during 1974—with the four-and-a-half-year death total reaching 80,000 by November (about 35,000 on the government side and an estimated 45,000 Communists). The number of wounded on the two sides probably surpassed 230,000, while more than 310,00 civilians had been slain or wounded since the war's start in March 1970. All such casualties exceeded 600,000 persons—slightly less than 8% of the whole population. Nearly half the surviving population were uprooted refugees of one kind or another as the year 1974 drew to a close.

Peace Prospects. There were recurrent rumors of allegedly imminent peace talks throughout the year, but no such negotiations were known to have taken place. A new U. S. ambassador, John Gunther Dean, supporter of a political settlement in adjacent Laos in his previous diplomatic assignment, was seemingly unable to bring the two Khmer sides together. In July 1974, President Lon Nol eased his own conditions for negotiations, offering to take part in peace discussions "without prior conditions." This bid for an attempt at a political peace was immediately rejected by the opposing Prince (and former chief of state) Norodom Sihanouk, based in Peking, China.

Economy. The economy of once rice-rich Cambodia was stagnated by the persisting war. The capital of Phnom Penh survived largely on U. S.-financed goods flown into the country or transported up the Mekong River from Saigon in neighboring South Vietnam.

Inflation, part of the toll of the insurgent pressure on government-held Phnom Penh, reached an annual rate of nearly 300%. Widespread corruption on the lower levels of the military and civilian bureaucracies continued as in previous years.

Politics. Despite widespread dissatisfaction with the regime of President Lon Nol, even outside the Communist-held areas, the crippled leader apparently strengthened his hold on the government. The High National Council, formed as a result of American pressure in May 1973 and designed to give opposition elements a voice in official decision-making, was dissolved by President Lon Nol on March 31 and was replaced by a lesser four-member advisory group, including the president and the premier. Premier Long Boret resigned on June 13 following a teachers strike and subsequent students demonstration in which the education minister and a former cabinet member were murdered by an apparent infiltrator into the protesters' ranks. On June 17 he formed a new cabinet.

The Communists, meanwhile, consolidated their hold on the countryside, establishing a strong-armed rival government that effectively conscripted young men and women for both military service and work gangs, and was characterized by vigorous political indoctrination and harsh discipline. Meanwhile, Prince Sihanouk, residing in Peking, seemed to be falling out of favor with his Chinese patrons, while pro-Communist Vice Premier and commander-in-chief of resistance forces Khieu Samphan appeared to have increased his role as real leader of the forces whose purpose is to bring down the Lon Nol government.

Foreign Relations. President Nixon sent a letter to Lon Nol in February, pledging that the U. S. government would "provide maximum possible assistance" to the Phnom Penh government. Nixon's later resignation clearly frightened the anti-Communist Cambodian political leadership, which was visibly upset by new U. S. President Ford's expressed desire in his first speech to Congress to see an "early compromise settlement" in the Cambodian war.

American military aid to the Lon Nol regime totaled nearly $650 million during the year. In late August, Prince Sihanouk urged President Ford to stop all American aid to the Lon Nol government.

RICHARD BUTWELL
State University of New York College at Fredonia

CAMBODIA • Information Highlights

Official Name: The Khmer Republic.
Location: Southeast Asia.
Area: 69,898 square miles (181,035 sq km).
Population (1973 est.): 7,643,000.
Chief Cities (1963 census): Phnom Penh, the capital, 393,995; Battambang, 38,780; Kempong Cham, 28,532.
Government: *Head of state,* Gen. Lon Nol, president (took office March 1972). *Head of government,* Long Boret, premier (took office Dec. 1973). *Legislature*—Parliament: Senate and National Assembly.
Monetary Unit: Riel (375 riels equal U. S.$1, May 1974).
Gross National Product (1972 est.): $680,000,000.
Manufacturing (major products): Paper, textiles, tobacco products, sawnwood.
Major Agricultural Products: Rice, corn, rubber, beans, sweet potatoes and yams.
Foreign Trade (1972): *Exports,* $15,000,000; *imports,* $98,000,000.

UPI

CANADA

A member of the Montreal police riot squad stands helplessly before a tenement fire raging out of control during a 2½-day strike of city firemen in November.

On July 8, 1974, Prime Minister Pierre Elliott Trudeau's Liberal party, driven to the brink of defeat in 1972, came back with a majority election victory that cut Progressive Conservative strength and left the New Democratic party (NDP) battered and adrift with a defeated leader. This event, related as it was to inflation and economic dislocation, was the most significant for Canada in 1974.

DOMESTIC AFFAIRS

The Federal Election. Contradicting pollsters and political analysts, the Liberals returned 141 seats in the July election, an increase of 32 over 1972; the Progressive Conservatives 95, a decrease of 12; the New Democrats 16, a loss of 15; and Social Credit 11, a loss of 2. Two independents were elected.

With gains in seven of ten provinces, the victory was a major personal one for Prime Minister Trudeau, as no other Canadian premier has ever fallen to a minority position in Parliament and then captured a majority without being first out of office. In his victory television address from Ottawa, he promised good federal government for all of Canada's regions but expressed disappointment about low Liberal representation from the Prairies, where only 5 of the 45 members of Parliament were Liberals. His principal support remained in Quebec (60 of 74 seats) and Ontario (55 of 88). British Columbia returned only 8 Liberals from 23 constituencies. Progressive Conservatives took 13 seats in British Columbia, 19 seats (a clean sweep) in Alberta, 8 of 13 in Saskatchewan, 9 of 13 in Manitoba, 25 of 88 in Ontario, and only 3 of 74 in Quebec. The Maritimes returned 13 Liberals, 17 Progressive Conservatives, 1 New Democrat, and 1 independent. This lone independent, Leonard Jones, was the former mayor of Moncton, New Brunswick, an opponent of bilingualism who had been rejected by Progressive Conservative party leader Robert Stanfield on this issue.

The election had been called because the NDP on May 8 had decided to vote with the Progressive Conservatives on a nonconfidence resolution on the Liberal budget. In this vote, members of Parliament had been asked if the

CANADA • Information Highlights

Official Name: Canada.
Location: Northern North America.
Area: 3,851,809 square miles (9,976,185 sq km).
Population (1974 est.): 22,450,000.
Chief Cities (1971 census): Ottawa, the capital, 302,341; Montreal, 1,214,352; Toronto, 712,786; Edmonton, 438,152.
Government: *Head of state,* Elizabeth II, queen; represented by Jules Léger, governor general (took office Jan. 1974). *Head of government:* Pierre Elliott Trudeau, prime minister (took office April 1968). *Legislature*—Parliament: Senate and House of Commons.
Monetary Unit: Canadian dollar (0.9858 C. dollar equals U. S.$1, Sept. 1974).
Gross National Product (2d quarter 1974 est.): $137,608,000,000.
Manufacturing (major products): Pulp and paper, petroleum products, iron and steel, motor vehicles, aircraft, machinery, aluminum, chemicals.
Major Agricultural Products: Wheat, barley, oats, rye, potatoes, fish, forest products, livestock, furs.
Foreign Trade (1973): *Exports,* $25,208,000,000; *imports,* $23,314,000,000.

UPI

Prime Minister Pierre Trudeau and his wife, Margaret, after the Liberal party was returned to power in July.

government had failed "to propose any measures to assist pensioners and many other Canadians on low and fixed incomes, to deal with the housing crisis or to remove the glaring inequities in the taxation system."

The vote was 137 to 123 with 106 Conservatives and 31 New Democrats voting against the government. Fifteen Social Credit members sided with the 108 government members. This was the first time in Canadian history that a government suffered a Commons defeat over its budget, and the third time a government was defeated on a nonconfidence vote.

The election setbacks for the Progressive Conservatives and the New Democrats sparked immediate speculation about the future of both Stanfield and David Lewis, NDP leader who had backed Trudeau's minority government before the election. The defeat of Stanfield in the election resulted in his decision to resign eventually as federal Progressive Conservative leader, giving his party an opportunity to find a successor at a forthcoming party meeting, and to leave politics when the next federal election is called. As for Mr. Lewis, his personal defeat, in a Toronto riding, resulted in his decision to retire as party leader. Subsequently 38-year-old Oshawa MP Ed Broadbent was unanimously elected interim leader of the New Democrats in the House of Commons.

A central issue of the 1974 campaign had been inflation and how to control it. Stanfield concentrated on problems resulting in inflation and criticized Trudeau for his "instant policies"—policies announced during the campaign that would protect the credit of low-income, steadily employed wage earners and give home owners protection against unduly high mortgage rates. Stanfield offered, if his party formed a government, a 90-day freeze on wages and prices. He said that this was not a policy that Conservatives could normally agree with, but that he and his party believed that it was the best for the country. He gambled and failed: Ontario's solid swing to the Liberals away from the Progressive Conservatives indicated that that province, which is central to the industrial expansion of the nation, was unprepared for a Stanfield freeze.

The Economy. The debate over inflation during the election reflected the nation's concern with its economy. Statistics Canada reported that there was no real growth in the economy during the second quarter of the year and warned that Canada might be headed for the type of weakness common to industrialized nations of the world.

Declines in volume of exports and business capital investment were the chief factors responsible for the no-growth situation. Though the gross national product grew by 3.6% to an annual rate of $137.6 billion during the second quarter, the entire increase was due to higher prices.

THE CANADIAN MINISTRY

(According to precedence, December 1974)

Pierre Elliott Trudeau, Prime Minister
Mitchell W. Sharp, President of the Queen's Privy Council for Canada
Allan MacEachen, Secretary of State for External Affairs
Charles M. Drury, Minister of State for Science and Technology; Minister of Public Works
Jean Marchand, Minister of Transport
John N. Turner, Minister of Finance
Joseph-Jacques Chrétien, President of Treasury Board
Donald S. Macdonald, Minister of Energy, Mines and Resources
John Carr Munro, Minister of Labor
Gérard Pelletier, Minister of Communications
Stanley R. Basford, Minister of National Revenue
Donald C. Jamieson, Minister of Regional Economic Expansion
Robert Andras, Minister of Manpower and Immigration
James Richardson, Minister of National Defence
Otto E. Lang, Minister of Justice; Attorney-General of Canada
Jean-Pierre Goyer, Minister of Supply and Services; Receiver-General of Canada
Alastair W. Gillespie, Minister of Industry, Trade and Commerce
W. Warren Allmand, Solicitor-General of Canada
James H. Faulkner, Secretary of State
Marc Lalonde, Minister of National Health and Welfare
Dan MacDonald, Minister of Veterans Affairs
André Ouellet, Minister of Consumer and Corporate Affairs
Jeanne Sauvé, Minister of the Environment
Eugene F. Whelan, Minister of Agriculture
Bryce Mackasey, Postmaster-General of Canada
Raymond Perrault, Leader of the Government in the Senate
Barnett Danson, Minister of State for Urban Affairs
Judd Buchanan, Minister of Indian Affairs and Northern Development
Romeo Leblanc, Minister of Fisheries

Estimates of the national income and expenditure accounts indicate that inflation slowed only slightly to a 14.5% annual rate in the second quarter from 15.8% in the first quarter. Until the second quarter the Canadian economy had continued to expand while other industrialized countries recorded slowdowns. In the third and fourth quarters the Canadian economy continued to be hurt by inflation and economic slowdown.

In Canada, the contraction of foreign markets led to a decline of 3.7% in real value of exports in the second quarter. Business capital investment declined 12% in real terms, mainly because of construction strikes in some major cities. Continued strong government spending and a high rate of accumulation in nonfarm business inventories were the sources of strength in the economy during the second quarter. While corporate profits continued to grow strongly in the second quarter, rising at an annual rate of 28%, labor income slowed to a 13.2% annual increase. By early September, analysts in Canada, Britain, and the United States knew that Canada's economic growth was slackening, but that the Canadian record looked good compared with most other Western countries. This was a view that Prime Minister Trudeau had held during the 1974 election campaign. The real growth of the Canadian economy for 1974 approximated 5.5%.

By the close of 1974, various policies or pieces of legislation—on increased food production and home construction, on financial support for small business and regional development, on increased energy supplies, grain exports and job opportunities, and on government restraint on spending—were promised in the Speech from the Throne that opened the new Parliament on September 30. The government's budget, introduced in mid-November, proposed several fiscal reforms or changes designed to combat inflation. A tightening on immigration was intended to stabilize the work force.

On October 30, Prime Minister Trudeau met with Canada's provincial premiers to discuss the economic situation, and particularly inflation, which by that time had reached a 23-year peak (11.6%). The premiers expressed confidence in the economy, advocated the elimination of nonessential government building projects, and looked to expanded housing construction and the possibility of the federal government's making more money available to low-income families for mortgages.

During 1974, energy resource control and a self-sufficient energy policy remained important issues in Canadian policy and federalism. The Arab oil embargo of 1973, which displaced shipments not only from the Middle East but from Venezuela and elsewhere, gave impetus to the idea of petroleum self-sufficiency in Canada. The federal government established a national petroleum corporation and began plans for extending the Trans-Canada Pipeline from Sarnia, Ont., to Montreal. Alberta and Saskatchewan, the oil-producing provinces, were not pleased with Trudeau's centralized policies. In order to keep petroleum reserves high, on October 18 the National Energy Board set the allowable limit for oil exports to the United States at just under a million barrels a day, a slight decrease from a year previous. Total Canadian production in 1974 was estimated at $2 million a day. Canadian domestic requirements were 1.02 million barrels per day.

On November 22, Canada announced plans for further reducing oil exports to the United States starting Jan. 1, 1975, to 800,000 barrels per day, with a view to ending all exports by 1982. In these circumstances, some American senators would continue to regard Canadians as "the blue-eyed Arabs." Ironically, oil production was almost 100% American dominated, though political and economic control of this resource obviously rested with Ottawa.

Race Relations. Another major domestic issue in Canada in 1974 was race relations, this concerned both with the interplay of French and English and the confrontation between Indians and whites. On July 30 the Quebec National Assembly passed the Official Language Act, which made French the sole official language of the province, relegating English to unofficial status and a matter of "individual rights." The provisions gave important preference to French as a language of business and government transactions.

The act brought a flurried response from the rest of Canada. New Brunswick Premier Richard Hatfield asked Prime Minister Trudeau to seek a ruling by the Supreme Court on its

Team Canada's 8-game hockey series with a Russian team, played in Canada and the USSR, was won by the Russians. This game, being played in Quebec city, ended in a tie.

UPI

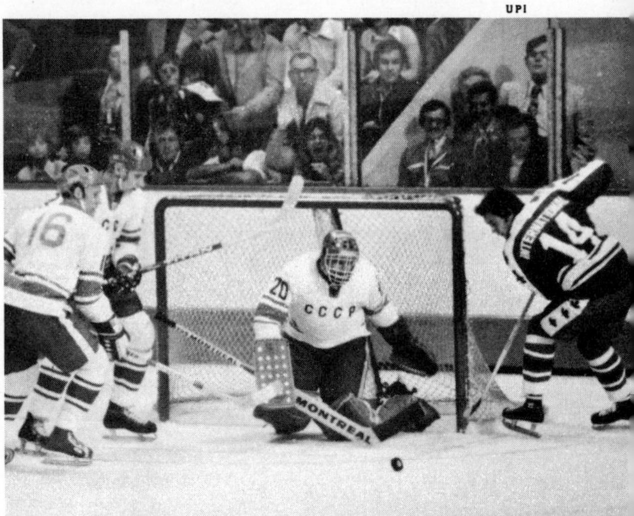

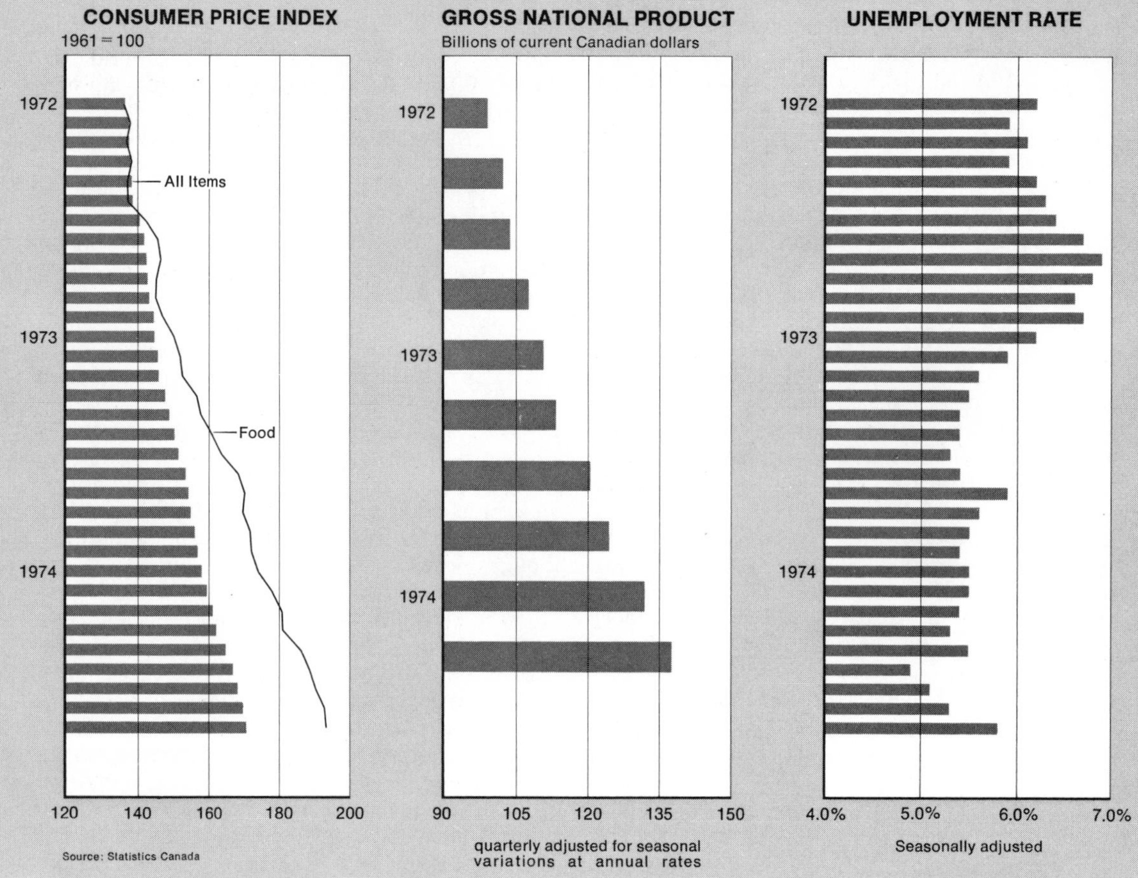

constitutionality on the grounds that it struck at the "spirit of Confederation" and infringed on the language provisions of the British North American Act, Canada's 1867 constitution. Trudeau, who had earlier opposed the bill in principle, replied on October 2 that his government would not contest the act, and that the challenge to its legality ought to be brought by a private individual.

In Indian affairs, Kenora, Ont., and Cache Creek, B. C., were scenes of armed Indian occupation of lands and highways. Negotiations between government officials and Indian leaders in both cases resulted in an end to the occupations by militant Indians. The issues were housing, civil rights, better economic employment opportunities, and treaty rights or benefits. In Quebec, the Indians of Quebec Association demanded (without success) an exemption from all Quebec laws and taxes. The central issue here was Indian rights in the James Bay region, where the Quebec Hydro, a provincial operation, proposed building a vast installation. In February the Indians of Quebec Association rejected a $100 million provincial government offer to end opposition to the project.

In Alberta, Metis (mixed bloods) launched a law suit against the provincial government claiming compensation for natural resource development. In Saskatchewan, British Columbia, and elsewhere, Indian land-claims bureaus continued investigation of native rights and a final settlement of native claims. On September 30, 200 Indians broke through police lines to demonstrate at the opening of Parliament in support of their grievances over land claims, medical care, the Indian Affairs Department, housing, and economic development for Indians.

Other Events. Canada's head of state, Governor General Jules Léger, suffered a heart attack on June 8, and during his convalescence, Supreme Court Judge Bora Laskin assumed all viceregal powers. At the end of March, Pauline McGibbon, chancellor of the University of Toronto, was appointed lieutenant governor of Ontario. This is the first case of a woman's being appointed the Queen's representative of a Canadian province.

The abolition of capital punishment for all murders except those of policemen and prison officers on duty was extended by the Canadian Parliament for a further trial period until December 1977. A cabinet reorganization of August 8 brought extensive changes in the wake of the July 8 federal election results.

In October, Margaret Trudeau, the prime minister's wife, acknowledged that her "severe emotional stress" was due to strain caused by being "first lady"; she also reported that she preferred pizza to political dinners.

In August the United Church of Canada's General Assembly voted in favor of union in principle with the Anglican Church of Canada and indicated its intention toward an ultimate reconciliation with the Roman Catholic Church —further recognition of the strong ecumenical trend in Canada.

INTERNATIONAL AFFAIRS

Canadian government officials in 1974 continued to weigh the merits of contributing to the NATO and NORAD defense forces. Major defense cuts were debated in November, and proposals were made to reduce Canada's military personnel from 80,000 to some 52,000. Withdrawal of NATO forces from Europe is also considered.

European Relations. On April 25, Canada acknowledged that earlier in the year a formal petition for a comprehensive trade agreement with the European Economic Community (EEC) had been made. Ottawa also reported its willingness to work out a "declaration of principles" for Canadian-European relations, but gave top priority to a "concrete trade act." The proposal must be viewed as a major shift in Prime Minister Trudeau's policies for making Canada less dependent on the United States. The Canadian proposal noted that Canada and the Common Market were each other's second largest partner (after the United States).

At Brussels, on October 23–25, Trudeau pressed for trade talks and did not reach a preferential trade agreement with the EEC. On his departure he said "We are telling the Europeans bilaterally and as a community: You may think you will be able to take all our raw materials out. You ain't. . . . We are defining our policies and if you want to get in there you'd better embark on this process of negotiation." He also stressed that Canada was a distinct entity from the United States, with an option of diversifying its economic and political relations in order to reduce its dependence on the United States. The object, he said, was to have relations with Europe, Asia, and Commonwealth countries so that Canada would be more diversified and "less vulnerable to the overwhelming economic presence of the United States."

Trudeau also took measures to reduce tensions between Canada and France. Relations with France had been cool since the late President Charles de Gaulle's 1967 visit to Canada, during which the French leader's call for a "free Quebec" cast a pall over Franco-Canadian relations. Trudeau visited France in October.

His meeting with French President Valéry Giscard d'Estaing was productive. The two countries set a goal of "rapid doubling" of trade. Two study groups were formed to examine closer Canadian-French cooperation, with one panel to study Canadian energy supplies and natural resources, notably uranium, and the other to look into industrial cooperation, particularly surface transportation, aerospace, and marine transportation. It was also announced that Canada would open a fourth consulate in France, at Strasbourg, where the Parliament of the EEC was situated.

Peacekeeping. Canada announced on July 25 that it would increase its United Nations peacekeeping contingent in Cyprus from 486 to 950, and would provide them with improved weapons. This was an attempt to augment the UN force on the war-torn Mediterranean island. A UN Security Council resolution approved on August 2 empowered the force to form a buffer zone between Greek-Cypriot defenders and Turkish forces who invaded the island on July 20.

U. S. Relations. On December 4, Prime Minister Trudeau began three days of talks with President Gerald Ford in Washington. Trudeau's aim was not to solve bilateral trade and environmental problems, but rather to ensure that Ford understands Canadian actions, such as further planned cutbacks in oil exports, import quotas on U. S. beef, and attempts to obtain special arrangements, cited above, with the EEC and the European countries. As noted above, Canada had announced plans on November 22 to reduce oil exports to the United States starting Jan. 1, 1975, from 900,000 barrels per day to 800,000, with a view to ending all exports by 1982. The White House asked Canada to change its mind on this policy, or at least agree to a more gentle phase-out.

Other Foreign Relations. When India became the sixth nuclear power on May 18 on conducting its first nuclear test underground, Canada suspended nuclear aid to India. Since 1956, Canada had been contributing technology and funds for the developing of a nuclear potential for peaceful purposes. The Canadian position as enunciated by the then secretary of state for external affairs, Mitchell Sharp, was that Canada saw no distinction between exploding nuclear devices for peaceful purposes and for military purposes. Though India denied it had other than peaceful uses for the device, Canada remained unconvinced and shocked at India.

On September 23–26, Premier Kakuei Tanaka of Japan visited Ottawa for discussions with Prime Minister Trudeau on the matter of increasing trade between the two countries. On October 4–5, Prime Minister Gough Whitlam of Australia visited Ottawa for personal talks.

At the Law of the Sea Conference in Caracas on July 3, the then environment minister, Jack Davis, called for a restriction on deep-sea salmon fishing, reserving the catch to coastal states controlling an economic zone of up to 200 miles. Although Japan regarded this as unrealistic, the proposal drew some support.

BARRY M. GOUGH, *Duke University*

CANADIAN BROADCASTING CORP.

***The National Dream*, a series about the building of the Canadian Pacific Railway, was called "the best single achievement in . . . Canadian television."**

CANADA: CULTURAL AFFAIRS

In most respects the Canadian cultural scene in 1974 was too placid to be true. There were no artistic rebellions, no angry denunciations, no protest demonstrations, no noteworthy sit-ins at art schools—happenings which have been normal in Canada's artistic world of the past. Some experienced observers attribute the tranquility to "easy money." They say the arts in Canada are becoming a fat cat; and it is not difficult to find reasons for their view. During 1974 about $15 million of subsidy money was pumped into the cultural stream from the public purse; and the private sector, by grants and box-office support, poured additional millions into the cultural pot.

If any single happening on the national scale was outstanding, it was the enthusiastic acceptance of "The French Fact" by Canadian audiences from coast to coast. French Canadian singers, rock groups, and actors literally stole the show in a massive invasion of non-Quebec entertainment places. It was an important development, a bit of serendipity, in Canada's difficult promotion of universal bilingualism.

Theater. During 1974 there was remarkable public interest in the theater throughout Canada. New buildings were started, old buildings were refurbished, props were improved, road trips were multiplied, local playwrights were encouraged, and salaries were upgraded substantially. All this demanded higher admission charges, which the customers took in stride, and larger subsidies from the public purse, which nobody protested.

A notable improvement in theater fare was clearly a result of this substantial financial boost; and better theater attracted greater box-office patronage, with a notable increase in youthful theatergoers. The Canada Council surprised observers when it announced a shift in its policy of aid to theater groups, increasing help for smaller and newer organizations, and, by inference, stabilizing or reducing grants to the well-established theaters. In October, for instance, the council granted $3,100,000 to 41 theater organizations, many of them quite unknown to the average Canadian.

The two Canadian theaters best known to North Americans—the Festival Theatre in Stratford, Ont., and the National Arts Centre Theatre in Ottawa—maintained their leadership in 1974, with top-quality performances and financial success. The Stratford company's home fare included *Love's Labour Lost, Pericles, King John,* and *Le Malade Imaginaire*. Its overseas tour met with generous praise in Australia and New Zealand. The NAC, geared to heavy subsidies from the national treasury, featured an outstanding procession of performances by world-renowned theater groups. Montreal's Théâtre du Nouveau Monde enjoyed its best year ever, both at home and on tour. The Playhouse Theatre in Vancouver, with unprecedented season subscriptions for its 1974–75 program, gained attention by announcing ambitious plans to create a western Canada competitor of the Stratford Festival.

The perpetually successful Neptune Theatre in Halifax, N. S., had a 35% increase in season subscribers for 1974–75. It appointed John

Wood, one of Canada's most experienced theater men, as its new director. The Shaw Festival Company, in its new Niagara-on-the-Lake theater, described public support as "overwhelming" and had to extend its summer season by four weeks. Centaur Theatre in Montreal, which has had a complete house sellout for every performance in the past two years, announced plans to purchase the old Montreal Stock Exchange Building for its permanent home. The Citadel Theatre in Edmonton, Alta., which has been playing in a discarded Salvation Army building for ten years, revealed plans for a multimillion-dollar playhouse complex to open in 1975.

Music. Canadian taste for opera is thriving in the major cities and gaining impetus in the smaller centers, and 1974 proved to be a rewarding year for opera fans and for the emerging corps of Canadian opera singers. Toronto's Canadian Opera Company, the national flagship group, reported ticket sales for home-base performances at 91% of capacity. The company's repertoire for the year consisted of *The Flying Dutchman, Boris Godunov, L'Heure Espagnole, Bluebeard's Castle, La Traviata, Carmen,* and *Faust.*

The Canadian branch of Jeunesses Musicales celebrated its 25th anniversary with concerts in more than 100 communities and a notable summer program at its Mount Orford, Quebec, headquarters. In November the Orford String Quartet was awarded the first prize of 20,000 Swiss francs at an international competition in Stockholm. Thirty-six horses and 43 men of the famed Royal Canadian Mounted Police Musical Ride performed triumphantly in seven European countries during the summer. Another European event which won unstinted praise for Canadian musicians was a 15-concert tour by the Toronto Symphony Orchestra.

Meanwhile, the Montreal Symphony, burdened with a $500,000 deficit, made tortured headway in 1974, encouraged by a $910,000 response to an appeal for public help plus $480,000 contributed by city and provincial governments. Most other big Canadian orchestras had a successful artistic year, despite modest, necessary belt-tightening measures.

Visual Arts. An event of outstanding importance, in October 1974, was the reopening of the Art Gallery of Ontario, in Toronto, after a two-year shutdown for reconstruction. The new $18 million building with its treasures now rates among the top galleries of North America. Of special interest is the gallery's Henry Moore Sculpture Centre, which displays the famous English sculptor's gift of a $15 million collection of his works. In the nearby Royal Ontario Museum, the Exhibition of Archaeological Finds of the People's Republic of China in August-November was a sensational success. On display were nearly 400 artifacts, excavated since 1950, relating to more than 500,000 years of Chinese pre-history and history.

Throughout Canada the growth of public interest in the visual arts has been remarkable during the past five years, and in 1974 participation reached what must be a peak. Painting, sculpture, graphics, fine crafts, and every aspect of applied decor attracted people and money as never before. The evidence was seen in galleries, schools, and auction rooms, in studios and art dealers' shops, and in the proliferation of private collecting.

Dance. In October the Canada Council made grants totaling $1,700,000 to support the 1974–75 programs of eight dance companies. The Big Three ballets in Toronto, Montreal, and Winnipeg received $1,500,000, while modern dance groups in four cities received sums ranging from $25,000 to $70,000 each. Without this help and subsidies from other sources the big companies could not survive, despite the extremely good box-office support they have been receiving. The Royal Winnipeg Ballet, for instance, had a $300,000 deficit from the 1974 season but is going "full tilt ahead"' in 1975, according to the company's general manager.

Toronto's National Ballet Company has been filling the seats at home and on tour by featuring the great international star Rudolf Nureyev as principal male dancer. Les Grands Ballets Canadiens of Montreal had a successful season at home, but the company's real triumph occurred in Paris in June, when it overcame a disastrous first-night performance and won standing ovations before returning home.

While Canada seems officially committed to maintaining its three major ballet organizations, there is evidence that public taste may be turning to the smaller, intimate, and dramatic con-

Nicholas Pennell *(left)* as Pericles and Martha Henry as Thaisa appear in a Stratford Festival production stressing the fairy-tale aspects of Shakespeare's *Pericles.*

THE STRATFORD SHAKESPEAREAN FESTIVAL FOUNDATION OF CANADA, STRATFORD, CANADA

temporary dance groups that are popping up in many cities.

Film. Canadian amateur film buffs, long accustomed to success and glory in international festivals, got the shock of their lives in July when the results of the Fifth Annual Canadian Amateur Film Festival were made known. The top award went to the West German film *G-Moll.* Four categories were won by entries from the United States, while Japan and Austria each topped one category. Not a single important award was won by the Canadian entries. The festival was held in Ottawa and drew 25 entries from 15 countries. However, a bit of chauvinistic relief flowed from the international success of the theatrical film *The Apprenticeship of Duddy Kravitz,* which was written and produced in Montreal by Canadians.

People. Canada's two "grand ladies of the ballet," Celia Franca and Ludmilla Chiriaeff, retired from their artistic director posts in 1974, Miss Franca after 23 years with the National Ballet Company and Miss Chiriaeff after 17 years with Les Grands Ballets Canadiens. Jean Gascon, whose outstanding contributions as actor and director made him a guru of Canadian theater, was awarded the annual Royal Bank Award ($50,000) for 1974. Arnold Edinborough, editor and art critic, was appointed president of the new and important Canadian Council of Business and the Arts.

Composer John Weinzweig of the University of Toronto music faculty was elected president of the Composers, Authors and Publishers Association of Canada, while Dr. Keith Bissell of Toronto became head of the Canadian Music Council for 1974–75. The Diplôme d'Honneur, awarded annually by the Canadian Conference of the Arts, went to Esse Ljung (broadcasting), Erik Bruhn (ballet), Mariette Rousseau-Vermette (tapestry weaving), and Floyd Chalmers (patron).

Obituaries. Widespread sadness was felt when Alexander Young Jackson, most noted of Canada's contemporary painters and formerly the leader of the rebellious and influential Group of Seven, died on April 5 at age 91. Robert Gill, who died in August, served for 20 years as director of Hart House Theatre (University of Toronto). He helped develop Canadian theater.

WALTER B. HERBERT
Consultant on Canadian Cultural Affairs

The Henry Moore Sculpture Centre in the new Art Gallery of Ontario, Toronto, houses the largest collection of Moore's works in the Western Hemisphere.

ART GALLERY OF ONTARIO

UPI

Athlete Alberto Torres lights the flame that signals the opening of the 12th Central American–Caribbean Games in Santo Domingo, Dominican Republic.

CARIBBEAN

Unusual weather patterns and natural disasters marked the year 1974 in the Caribbean. Although elections were held in the Dominican Republic, Cuba, and some of the smaller islands of the Lesser Antilles, there were no major political changes during 1974. Inflation and other related economic problems contributed to a strengthening of regional institutions and furthered economic cooperation in new fields. Civil disorders and politically motivated disturbances generally were at a minimum throughout the Caribbean.

Weather. For the second year in a row, prolonged drought, perhaps aggravated by the smoglike dust from the African Sahara, affected most of the Caribbean. Beginning in January the drought extended in some areas well into the summer months of July and August.

When wetter weather arrived, water deficits were wiped out in a few days and heavy flooding was experienced on several of the larger islands. October and November, usually months with light rainfall, registered above-normal moisture levels. None of the islands was seriously affected by the seven tropical storms which crossed the Caribbean, but some of the lands bordering the sea, especially Honduras, were devastated by high winds and inundated by floods. Hurricane Fifi hit Honduras on September 19–20, leaving an estimated 5,000 dead and 100,000 homeless, with over 180 communities damaged or destroyed.

Early in the morning of October 8 a severe earthquake jolted the Leeward Islands of Antigua, St. Christopher (St. Kitts), Guadeloupe, and Montserrat. The earthquake, which measured 7 on the Richter scale, was the strongest to be felt in the Caribbean since 1946 and the worst to be felt in the Leeward Islands in the last 133 years. In St. John's, the capital of the island of Antigua, the historic cathedral lost its bell tower, and the Parliament building was badly damaged. Some 30 families were left homeless by the tremor.

Agriculture. The adverse weather conditions had some effect on agricultural production in the Caribbean. In the larger islands the cattle and dairy industries felt the lack of rain. In Barbados, weather conditions were blamed for a 16,000-ton drop in sugar production. However, some other islands, such as Puerto Rico, experienced a slight rise in sugar production and were able to take advantage of the high prices being paid for sugar on the world market. The English-speaking communities of the Caribbean, which ship their sugar to the United Kingdom, abruptly halted their exports of sugar until they had negotiated a higher price for the sugar sold to Great Britain, netting an additional 30 million pounds sterling for the islands.

Industry. The worldwide inflation had a very serious effect on the Caribbean nations in 1974, particularly those lacking in any mineral resources and dependent on importing most of their consumer goods. The crisis was met with emergency measures. In the case of Jamaica, these included a Currency Exchange Control Law; and similar measures were adopted in Guyana and Barbados. Soaring fuel and food costs produced severe trade imbalances, forcing governments to restrict drastically the importation of some basic consumer goods and causing shortages of such products as rice, bread, potatoes, and salted fish.

With the precipitous rise in oil and gasoline prices, most of the countries in the Caribbean (with the exception of Trinidad, which has its own oil fields) were faced with an energy crisis and/or a multimillion-dollar trade deficit. With the increased cost of crude petroleum, even such islands as Puerto Rico, St. Croix, Curaçao, and Aruba, which have extensive oil-refining facilities, felt the pinch of the rising cost of energy. Trinidad-Tobago entered into negotiations to increase the role of government in the operations of the private oil companies in that country. Increased oil production was registered from the offshore oil wells around Trinidad. Barbados and St. Lucia increased the exploration for oil and natural gas in the waters off their coasts.

In an effort to counteract the growing trade deficit, those Caribbean nations which contain bauxite deposits—Guyana, Jamaica, Surinam, Haiti, and the Dominican Republic—came together to form with Australia, Yugoslavia, Sierra Leone, and Guinea an International Bauxite Association, which held two meetings in 1974. Since members of the association control only about one third of the world's supply of bauxite, they were not expected to control the price of the ore. However, during 1974, Guyana, Jamaica, and the Dominican Republic extracted significantly higher prices for their ore from the aluminum-producing companies with refineries in the United States and Canada. In the case of Jamaica, the export tax on bauxite was increased 500%.

Guyana, which had previously nationalized the Canadian firm operating in its territory, announced in 1974 its intention to nationalize the United States company which is the only remaining private bauxite operation in that country. Further regional cooperation in this industry was achieved when the governments of Jamaica, Trinidad-Tobago, and Guyana agreed cooperatively to build two aluminum smelters, one in Guyana and the other in Trinidad. In another venture, Guyana and Barbados agreed to build a cement plant in the latter country.

A major crisis in transportation and communication in the English-speaking Lesser Antilles was precipitated by the collapse of a British-based air transport company which served most of the islands between Puerto Rico and Trinidad. Service was continued on an emergency basis through the intervention of the government of Antigua, while a consortium of 11 interested governments negotiated the purchase of the bankrupt airline.

Politics and Government. The Caribbean greeted another independent nation as Grenada was released from British rule on February 7. In September the small nation became the 137th member of the United Nations. The transition to independence was met with strong opposition, general strikes, and violence, which took the lives of three people. (See also GRENADA.)

Civil disturbances also occurred during 1974 on the Dutch side of the island of St. Martin, where a general strike closed the island's services for about a week and a serious fire destroyed the government's offices. A general strike also was staged on the French island of Martinique, where two deaths occurred when workers clashed with armed police.

Crime and lawlessness, which had seriously affected the flow of tourism to such islands as Jamaica, St. Thomas, and St. Croix, declined as a result of vigorous government action. In Jamaica, for example, the government restricted the private use of firearms and undertook an intensive campaign against the traffic in drugs.

Municipal elections were held in certain provinces of Cuba for the first time under the regime of Fidel Castro. In May, Joaquín Balaquer won a third term as president of the Dominican Republic. Elections were held also in the Windward Islands of Dominica and St. Lucia. Patrick John became the premier of Dominica replacing Edward Leblanc; and in St. Lucia, John Compton was returned to power.

One of the more important political events of the year in the Caribbean was the meeting of the presidents of France and the United States on the island of Martinique in the middle of December.

Regional Institutions. Major changes were experienced in the regional economic institutions of the Caribbean. On April 18 the Caribbean Common Market (CARICOM), as was expected when it was created effective Aug. 1, 1973, incorporated six new members—Belize, Dominica, Grenada, Montserrat, St. Lucia, and St. Vincent—into the already existing agreement embraced by the four original members—Trinidad-Tobago, Barbados, Jamaica, and Guyana. Later in 1974, St. Kitts-Nevis and Antigua also joined the Common Market, bringing the total number of members to 12. The resignation of Secretary-General William Demas of CARICOM was reluctantly accepted by the Council of Ministers, and he was succeeded by Alistair McIntyre, professor of economics at the Jamaica campus of the University of the West Indies. Demas then became director of the Caribbean Development Bank, a position vacated by Sir Arthur Lewis in 1973.

The Caribbean Development Bank, which includes such non-English-speaking countries as Colombia and Venezuela, as well as the members of CARICOM, was considering at the end of the year a request for membership by the government of Puerto Rico. If accepted, Puerto Rico would bring a contribution of about $8 million to the reserves of the bank.

THOMAS G. MATHEWS
University of Puerto Rico

CENSORSHIP

The year 1974 saw a unique case of classic censorship when a book, *The CIA and the Cult of Intelligence,* by Victor Marchetti and John A. Marks, was published with deletions demanded by the Central Intelligence Agency and approved in part by a federal district court judge. Publication followed several years of litigation involving Marchetti and the CIA. Such prior restraint of publication by government was never imposed previously in the United States.

The CIA first moved to halt publication by securing a court order to that effect on the grounds that as a condition of employment with the agency Marchetti, years before, had signed an agreement not to disclose any information without prior consent of officials. In line with the court order, the manuscript was submitted to the agency, which first deleted 339 passages. After the publisher, Alfred A. Knopf, Inc., and the authors took steps to sue, 171 passages were reinstated. In a later action a court found that the agency's argument that publication would compromise national security was without merit for all but 27 passages. However, faced with continuing legal appeals by the CIA, the book, published in June 1974, carried notations of 168 deletions.

After the book was published, the director of the CIA went before Congress to ask that tighter sanctions be drawn against those divulging security secrets. At the time of his testimony, Congress was studying proposals which, if enacted, would give the United States its first Official Secrets Act. Sections of a proposed revision of the federal criminal code carry a sweeping plan of press censorship that would include extensive fines and lengthy prison terms for reporters, editors, and sources who release information damaging to national security or to foreign relations.

Censorship at the Source. Since the early 1950's, major concern with censorship in the United States has centered on censorship at the source—the withholding of governmental information by public servants at all levels of government. A major argument for the power to withhold and/or classify information has been the position taken by a series of presidents and their advisers that there is in the executive branch an inherent privilege to keep in confidence from the Congress and the public information that officials consider not in the public interest to release. So broadly worded an exception to the free flow of information essential to a democracy has prompted continuous criticism of its exercise.

Accordingly, when the Supreme Court agreed to hear the case revolving around President Nixon's refusal to deliver tapes on request of the special prosecutor's office as part of its investigation of the Watergate scandal, it was hoped that his plea of executive privilege would be discredited. While ruling that the president is not privileged to withhold information needed in a criminal proceeding, however, the court went on to recognize that there are "constitutional underpinnings" for the exercise of executive privilege where there is a need "to protect military, diplomatic, or sensitive national security secrets." Thus, executive privilege can no longer be viewed as the myth that critics of secrecy in government have long held it to be.

Conceived as a bulwark against censorship at the source, the Freedom of Information Act has become more and more of a disappointment to those who have failed to dislodge information from agencies of the executive branch. Congress substantively rewrote the act to close some loopholes and speed responses that the agencies must make on request for information. The revision was intended to allow judicial review on the complaint of Congress or of a citizen that the executive branch had improperly withheld information. President Fort vetoed the measure, chiefly because of his fear that "military or intelligence secrets and diplomatic relations could be adversely affected by this bill." However, Congress overrode the presidential veto by substantial votes: the House, by 371–31 on November 20; and the Senate, by 65–27 on November 21.

Meanwhile, as it has in every year since its effective date, 1967, the Freedom of Information Act achieved some limited victories over secrecy. For example, the courts held open to public inspection summaries of honor and ethics code adjudications at the U. S. service academies and Internal Revenue Service letter rulings issued at the request of taxpayers seeking advice as to the tax consequences of specific transactions. However, there were also defeats. Under the act's exemption of investigatory files, records of the Department of Health, Education, and Welfare containing reviews of public school segregation and discrimination practices were judged properly withheld from inspection. Although the Justice Department directed that Federal Bureau of Investigation investigatory files over 15 years old be made available to people engaged in historical research, the FBI found cause to withhold such files because of the vagueness of language in the directive.

Censorship and the Courts. Trial court judges throughout the United States enlarged on the practice of issuing restrictive or "gag" orders to reporters covering criminal proceedings. Where these rulings have been challenged in the past, they have consistently been found to be unconstitutional. Occasionally rulings have been broadened to include banning of courtroom sketching. An appeals court has ruled that courtroom artists may ply their trade.

Supreme Court Justice Lewis F. Powell, Jr. stayed an all-inclusive order of a New Orleans court restricting reporting of a murder trial until after the jury was seated and all editorial comment until the trial was concluded. Justice Powell noted that the order "imposes significant prior restraint on media publication" and thus bore "a heavy presumption against its constitutional validity." Hence the stay pending consideration by the full court.

Censorship and Community Standards. In 1973 the Supreme Court promulgated new guidelines (*Miller* v. *California*) to assist states in drawing up legal obscenity statutes. What concerned publishers and motion picture producers most was the court's decision that the "contemporary community standards" by which publications were to be judged would be "local community" standards. The fear was that the thrust of the decision would be to reduce the range of ideas and expression in books and films to conform to limits likely to be imposed by the least tolerant segment of the "community." Disturbed by this, Gov. Milton Shapp of Pennsylvania, in his unsuccessful veto of an obscenity statute establishing the county as the community to make obscenity decisions, noted that the legislation had the effect of conferring on a single county the power to censor books for the entire country since publishers would be economically constrained to produce titles acceptable everywhere without challenge.

Though the issue is still confused, it now appears that the Supreme Court does not intend to allow any and all local censoring of allegedly obscene publications without its review. In *Jenkins* v. *Georgia,* a case involving local censorship of the movie *Carnal Knowledge,* the court ruled it would be a "serious misreading of *Miller*" to conclude that juries have unbridled discretion" for there are "substantive constitutional limitations," deriving from the First Amendment, on the type of material subject to such a determination [of obscenity].

The court notwithstanding, citizen groups in all parts of the United States continued to censor publications through forceful, sometimes irregular, means. Library and school boards in some cases countered, and in others joined in, pressuring groups to remove offending titles from library shelves and school reading lists. The American Library Association reported that "extra-legal pressures and worsening repression" beleaguered local libraries. In Drake, N. Dak., school board members joined the book burners to toss several dozen copies of Kurt Vonnegut, Jr.'s *Slaughterhouse-Five* into a fire. Kanawha County, W. Va. saw a lengthy protest by parents, over school adoption of some "language arts" books that they deemed pornographic, un-Christian, and un-American. After weeks of unrest and violence, a few of the books were removed, but most were reinstated and an uneasy peace ensued. (See also EDUCATION; WEST VIRGINIA.)

In June the Supreme Court agreed to decide whether the Indianapolis, Ind. school board could expel high school students for distributing publications without permission on campus. At issue were thousands of school disciplinary codes permitting censorship of all publications circulated on school grounds. Meanwhile, lower courts continued to deliver blows to censors of school publications. An appellate court ruled that school board regulations prohibiting the distribution in school of literature when this is likely to disrupt the educational process are unconstitutionally vague. Use of the ethics test of the International Rotary Club for the purpose of screening articles for acceptance by a high school paper was being contested.

Censorship: World View. The worldwide trend to increased censorship, evident in recent years in the annual censorship reports of several associations, continued in 1974.

The Inter-American Press Association reported in April 1974 that it had never before in its history had to contend with a greater number of violations of press freedom in the Americas. In the past year a wave of repression has swept over Latin America, where military regimes have become increasingly intolerant of an independent press. Weapons against the press have included increases in newsprint prices, the withholding of governmental advertising, the terrorizing of journalists, and outright banning. Nowhere has censorship been more severe than in Chile, where much of the press has been closed since the military takeover in September 1973. The free press in Uruguay has suffered nearly as much. Guatemala, where journalists who offend officialdom disappear from the streets, practices occasional and violent censorship. Only Colombia and Venezuela possess a freedom of the press approaching that in the United States and most of western Europe.

The International Press Institute's freedom report, issued in January 1974, found "a slight lessening of freedom everywhere." The IPI's concern seemed to parallel concern in the United States with censorship at the source, for the Institute found that it was no longer "press freedom alone but the basic right of the citizen to be informed [that] is undergoing an unprecedented challenge."

The Associated Press' annual survey, issued in January 1974, found press freedom continuing to lose ground, "often falling victim to wars and other upheavals." The difficulty of gathering news abroad was increased by subtle pressures on reporters, the threat of expulsion, and the erosion of a major source of news, an independent local press. However, AP correspondents said that their outgoing dispatches were "almost universally free of outright censorship."

Notable gains in freedom from censorship occurred in Turkey, where several years of martial law ended, and in Greece and Portugal where dictatorships were toppled.

PAUL FISHER
Director, Freedom of Information Center
University of Missouri

UPI

In Honduras, floods spawned by Hurricane Fifi ravage the country in September.

CENTRAL AMERICA

A devastating hurricane, the formation of a banana exporters' union, renewed attempts at regional economic integration, four national elections, and continuing political instability combined to produce an extraordinary series of events within Central America in 1974.

Regional Developments. Throughout the year considerable international attention was focused on what was headlined as "the revolt of the banana republics." Under the leadership of President José Figueres of Costa Rica and Gen. Omar Torrijos of Panama, concrete measures for creating a union of banana producing and exporting nations were taken in early March at a ministerial meeting in Panama. Attending were the seven major exporting nations in Central and South America—Ecuador, Costa Rica, Honduras, Panama, Guatemala, Colombia, and Nicaragua. Accounting for over 70 percent of all banana exports, the countries initially agreed to impose a tax of one dollar a crate. A few weeks later, on March 28, at a conference to organize formally the Unión de Países Exportadores de Banano (UPEB), internal political considerations and external pressures from the multinational banana corporations resulted in the withdrawal of Ecuador from the Union, as well as political controversy within Central America itself. The resulting "banana war" continued unabated throughout the year, with prospects for the success of UPEB diminishing under the combined pressures of the United Brands and Standard Fruit companies and their political-economic allies within the individual countries.

Attempts to revitalize the Central American Common Market (CACM), almost defunct since the 1969 "soccer war" between El Salvador and Honduras, were even less promising than the formation of the banana union. The responsibility for the market now lies in the hands of the High-Level Committee (CAN), which held periodic meetings during the year in an attempt to produce an acceptable agreement to restructure the organization. As in the past, the principal problem deadlocking the market is the Honduran blockade of El Salvador's goods, compounded by increasing nationalism in both of the two countries, sporadic border incidents, and regional trade imbalances. Interestingly, in view of the economic and political problems besieging the economic union, 1973 data showed that trade among the five Central American countries

CENTRAL AMERICA—Information Highlights

Nation	Population (in millions)	Area (in sq mi)	Capital	Head of State and Government
Costa Rica	2.0	19,575	San José	Daniel Oduber Quirós, president
El Salvador	3.9	8,260	San Salvador	Arturo Armando Molina, president
Guatemala	5.6	42,042	Guatemala City	Gen. Kjell Laugerud García, president
Honduras	3.0	43,277	Tegucigalpa	Gen. Oswaldo López Arellano, president
Nicaragua	2.2	50,193	Managua	Anastasio Somoza, president

was the largest ever—$350 million, compared with $305 million in 1972.

Also of general regional concern during 1974 was the recession in coffee prices. Late in the year the presidents of the Central American countries and Venezuela signed an agreement to limit coffee exports in order to raise the price of coffee, which was averaging 62 cents per pound.

Honduras. On Sept. 19–20, 1974, Honduras bore the full impact of Hurricane Fifi. In the wake of the storm came rains, flooding, and landslides that produced large loss of life, considerable property damage, and inestimable human suffering. A provisional report by a mission dispatched by the Organization of American States estimated that between 3,000 and 5,000 persons were dead, and economic losses were put at almost $200 million. Other estimates placed the number of deaths between 6,000 and 8,000 and property damages much higher. The hurricane was the worst natural disaster in the modern history of Honduras and left much of the nation's population in chaos.

The areas hardest hit by the storm were the three major river valleys of the Caribbean Coast —Aguán, Leán, and Sula, all rich agricultural regions. Including the other areas affected by the hurricane, the damage to crops was estimated to be 60% of the banana production, 60% of the sugar harvest, and 10% of the coffee crop, Honduras's major export crops. At least 40% of the nation's cattle were destroyed, and more than 50% of the staple rice and maize crops were lost.

The human and economic problems resulting from the hurricane were compounded by increased political unrest. Early in the year President Oswaldo López Arellano, with the support of the armed forces, instituted a development policy emphasizing internal reform and external nationalism. The program was designed specifically to alleviate the increasingly substandard living conditions of peasants and workers. The principal parts of the plan called for agrarian reform, nationalization of forestry resources, and greater state control of the economy. Conservative opposition among large landowners and businessmen was vehement, with widespread allegations of "socialism" and "communism."

These domestic and foreign pressures mounted after the hurricane and the government's initial attempts at disaster relief. President López Arellano quickly established the Economic and Social Council (CEYS) to administer reconstruction efforts. From its very inception, however, CEYS was plagued by allegations of corruption and maladministration.

Guatemala. Although the March 3 presidential election was considered significant because it marked the third orderly presidential succession in a row, unique in Guatemala's history, the victory of Brig. Gen. Kjell Laugerud García was tainted with charges of fraud and vote rigging. Laugerud was the candidate of the ruling National Coalition. Opposition candidates were Gen. Efraín Ríos Montt of the National Opposition Front and Gen. Ernesto Páis Novales of the Revolutionary party. The official election count gave Laugerud a plurality of some 79,000 votes over Ríos Montt, requiring his formal election by the Guatemalan congress since he did not win an absolute majority.

Economically, Guatemala was beset by shortages of gasoline, sugar, and other commodities and by rapid price increases for food staples such as beans and rice. With a steep rise in the cost of living, the government inaugurated a program of anti-inflationary tax measures. As expected, such tax increases produced strong opposition and, at the end of the year, had failed to curb the problem of inflation.

El Salvador. Despite numerical increases in the Legislative Assembly in the February 3 elections, the regime of Col. Arturo Armando Molina and his ruling Party of National Conciliation was assailed by problems of economic and political instability. Rising unemployment and prices, deterioration of the agricultural sector, and increasing opposition from both Right and Left forced the government into a series of short-term corrective policies both palliative and repressive in nature. Faced, however, with the need for basic socio-economic reform, on the one hand, and the intransigent opposition to reform by the entrenched oligarchy of the country on the other, the administration remained stymied throughout the year.

Nicaragua. To no one's surprise, Gen. Anastasio Somoza emerged victorious in the September 1 elections while his majority Liberal party elected 70 members of the Chamber of Deputies, 30 senators, and a large number of local officials. Although Somoza had earlier said he was retiring from government affairs, this was merely to enable him to run for president under the new Nicaraguan constitution which prohibits the reelection of a president or any of his relatives to the fourth generation.

Costa Rica. The elections of February 3 were enlivened by the presence of several political parties and some political squabbling in the incumbent party. Nevertheless, Daniel Oduber Quirós, President José Figueres' hand-picked successor, won the presidency with approximately 43.5% of the vote. The ruling Party of National Liberation thus broke a 25-year-old tradition that political parties alternate national political control.

Despite the continuity in administration, both Figueres and Oduber were faced with serious problems of inflation, estimated to be approximately 30% in 1973. The government undertook remedial measures in the form of currency devaluation and imposed an export tax of 13% on coffee, meat, cocoa, and sugar.

ROBERT L. PETERSON
University of Texas at El Paso

CHEMISTRY

In 1974, three potential hazards of particular interest to the public were identified. They were the depletion of the ozone layer in the earth's stratosphere, the formation of acid rain, and the release of vinyl chloride used in manufacturing plastics.

Ozone Layer. The ozone layer in the earth's stratosphere filters out lethal ultraviolet rays from the sun, making life possible on earth. Nuclear explosions are a threat to this shield because they produce nitrogen oxides that convert ozone (O_3) to oxygen (O_2) by an irreversible chemical reaction.

High-altitude nuclear explosions were said to be particularly dangerous because of their high yields of nitrogen oxides. At lower levels of the atmosphere, where the ratio of nitrogen to oxygen is high and the energy density is high because the explosion is partially confined by air pressure, many of the nitrogen atoms that are formed can recombine to form molecular nitrogen. But at high altitudes where the air pressure is less and the nitrogen-oxygen ratio is smaller, nitrogen atoms are more likely to react with oxygen to form nitrogen oxides, and these destroy ozone.

Halomethanes, such as $CFCl_2$ and $CFCl_3$ used as refrigerants or as propellants for aerosol spray cans, are another hazard to the earth's ozone shield. In 1974, an estimated 2.5 billion kilograms of halomethanes were produced, making a total of 5 billion kilograms since their use began. In the lower atmosphere halomethanes are inert. But when carried by convection currents into the stratosphere, where ultraviolet rays are more intense, they release chlorine which in turn catalyzes a reaction with ozone, changing the ozone to oxygen.

The halomethanes circulate in the lower atmosphere for long periods, and thus depletion of the ozone layer will continue even if their use were banned. If this were done immediately, depletion of the ozone layer would reach an estimated 5% by 1990. Although little is known about the degree of depletion that would be hazardous to life, one suggestion is that a loss of 50% would make this planet uninhabitable.

Acid Rain. Acid rain mainly is caused by sulfur dioxide in the combustion products from fossil fuels. In the atmosphere this dioxide combines with water to form highly corrosive sulfuric acid, which is washed down by rain and snow. One estimate was that the acidity of rain in the northeastern United States had increased from 100 to 1,000 times. Two reasons given for this increase were the use of emission controls in smokestacks that do not remove gases and the installation of higher stacks that allow pollutants to spread over wide areas. These findings were cited as examples of the hazards of trying to find solutions to world pollution problems by piecemeal efforts.

GEORGE THOMASON, U. S. ARMY PHOTO

A U. S. Army lab technician feeds shredded newspaper and other waste materials into a milling machine, beginning their conversion into ethanol, a gasoline substitute.

Serious damage was predicted for the future. In experiments where acids equivalent to those in an average acid rainfall were sprayed on growing trees and plants, pine needles grew to only half their normal size, birch leaves became spotted and distorted, and tomatoes grew fewer fruits of lesser quality. In Kentucky and southern Indiana, severe damage to growing alfalfa and soybean crops was reported in fields located near coal-burning power plants. Also noted was the increased acidity of lakes in the United States, Canada, and Sweden and the possibility of serious damage to bridges, buildings, and outdoor works of art.

Vinyl Chloride. By 1974, an estimated 2.5 billion kilograms of vinyl chloride, a gas, were being produced annually in the United States. It is used to make polyvinyl chloride, which is made into a host of products, including phonograph records, packaging film, garden hose, and floor tiling. In 1972, vinyl chloride was found to cause a rare and fatal form of liver cancer in rats. As of June 1974, 13 workers in vinyl chloride plants in the United States had died of the disease, which kills about 30 Americans each year. Workers in plastic-product manufacture also were exposed because vinyl chloride fumes can be released during the heating process in molding polyvinyl chloride.

Labor unions demanded that the vinyl chloride in air breathed by workers be at a nondetectable level, but plastics manufacturers said that was impossible because such a standard would put 700,000 workers out of jobs. Hearings were held by the U. S. Department of Labor in October, and the maximum allowable vinyl chloride content in air was set at 1 part per million (ppm).

The Environmental Protection Agency (EPA) found that air samples taken near plants fabricating plastic products contained an average of 0.5 ppm to 1 ppm of vinyl chloride, but 33 ppm in one case. In wastewater leaving plants, the average was 3 ppm, but 20 ppm was found in one case. Nevertheless, the Environmental Protection Agency said that vinyl chloride was not an environmental hazard.

In three Ohio counties where vinyl chloride plants are located, an increase in birth defects was noted. In the Cleveland area, a group of supermarket workers who wrapped meat in vinyl film filed a $285 million suit against two vinyl chloride manufacturers, charging that vinyl chloride fumes inhaled as the film was cut with a hot wire caused skin and throat irritation and may have promoted skeletal deterioration and heart and brain injury.

Element 106. American scientists at the University of California's Lawrence Berkeley Laboratory and Russian scientists at the Joint Institute for Nuclear Research in Dubna claimed to have synthesized chemical element 106. If the claims are true, the number of synthesized elements heavier than uranium was brought to 14. But problems were involved. One was that, according to theory, the new element should decay by spontaneous fission. The Americans found that their element decayed by emission of alpha particles, whereas the Russians said that their element decayed by spontaneous fission just as theory predicted.

The Americans bombarded a target of californium-249 (atomic no. 98) with oxygen ions (atomic no. 8) to form the new element (atomic no. 106). Its half-life is 0.9 second, and it decays by successive alpha emissions to nobelium (atomic no. 102), which is known to occur by this route. The Russians bombarded a lead target (atomic no. 82) with chromium ions (atomic no. 24) to form their new element. Believed to be element 106, it has a half-life of 4 to 10 milliseconds and was believed to decay by spontaneous fission. The Americans think the decay products might be only fragments of lead nuclei shattered by collisions with chromium ions.

Crystals. Crystals up to 12 centimeters (4.7 inches) long were grown on earth, remelted, recrystallized on board the Skylab space station, and then returned to earth. The results, announced in 1974, showed that the space-grown crystals were more nearly perfect than any grown on earth so far. One reason is that in a zero-gravity environment, surface tension prevents the melt from wetting container walls, thereby decreasing contamination. Also, on earth the interference of gravity causes imperfections in the crystal lattice by convection, diffusion, and swirling in the melt, whereas these effects are practically absent in space.

In transistor technology, notably in large integrated circuits for computers and communications systems, the use of crystals is severely limited by smallness and imperfections. Hence, growing crystals on a commercial scale in space and transporting them back to earth seem a future possibility.

Waste Cellulose. A process for converting waste cellulose, such as newspapers, peanut shells, and straw, to the sugar, glucose, was announced by the Army. Conversion is accomplished by an enzyme called cellulase, which is produced by the fungus *Trichoderma viride.*

The products from treated wastes are a syrup containing 2% to 10% glucose and a black sticky residue that dries to a hard cake, chiefly lignin, which can be used as a fuel or as a source of other chemicals. A pilot plant for treating 1,000 pounds of newspapers was designed, with the object of building a demonstration plant having a monthly capacity of 200,000 pounds. It was claimed that the operations could be put on a commercial scale by 1980.

Public Affairs. After nearly a century of being concerned almost entirely with the exchange of scientific information, the American Chemical Society (ACS) began to present its official positions on public issues to the U. S. Congress. This was done because more and more political decisions about pollution and the environment were related to knowledge of chemistry. In 1974 the ACS proposed the establishment of a cabinet-level department of science and technology. Also, it called for emphasis on disarmament of chemical weapons rather than on deterrence, and it proposed that the Geneva Protocol be signed without excluding herbicides and riot-control agents. Another proposal was that production of binary nerve gases be at least delayed. (A binary nerve gas consists of two gases, each nontoxic by itself, that become lethal when mixed in a projectile en route to its target.) One concern was that binary nerve gases might fall into the hands of terrorists because of their simplicity and availability. Another proposal was that vinyl chloride content in air breathed by workers be limited to 1 ppm, a maximum adopted by the government.

New Drugs. The controversy over the use of marihuana triggered considerable study of its active principles, cannabinoids. Results announced in 1974 indicated that, by modifying the chemical structures of these compounds, an entirely new class of drugs acting on the central nervous system was synthesized. Two compounds being tested clinically were said to be nontoxic, sedative, tranquilizing, and pain relieving. Unlike other nervous-system depressants such as narcotics, they do not depress respiration. Also, they are nonaddictive.

EUGENIA KELLER
Managing Editor, "Chemistry" Magazine

WIDE WORLD

Mayor Richard Daley on his return to Chicago City Hall after spending four months recuperating from a stroke.

CHICAGO

U. S. Attorney James Thompson continued in 1974 to successfully prosecute key associates of the powerful Cook county Democratic party machine of Chicago Mayor Richard J. Daley. While the city's political life churned in the depths of scandal, civic pride was lifted with the completion of the Sears Tower, the world's tallest building, and with the contributions of two of the world's noted artists.

Politics. Mayor Daley, 72, entered a Chicago hospital on May 6 following a minor stroke. His illness was not revealed to the public for several days and its seriousness was minimized. However, the mayor underwent surgery to prevent a recurrence and recuperated through the summer. It was his longest absence from city hall since his first election in 1955. Daley returned to a limited work schedule. Late in the year he announced that he would seek reelection in 1975.

At least five candidates, four of them black, announced their intentions to run for the mayoralty. Thompson, a 36-year-old Republican, announced that he would not seek the mayoralty. It came as somewhat of a surprise because political experts thought he would make a strong candidate.

Crime. Three influential associates of Mayor Daley were convicted in the same week. They were Alderman Thomas E. Keane, administration floor leader in the city council and chairman of the important council finance committee; Alderman Paul Wigoda, an influential member of the council zoning committee; and Earl Bush, former press aide to the mayor.

Keane was found guilty in a jury trial of 18 counts of mail fraud and conspiracy in a scheme to buy delinquent property and sell it at a profit to various city-controlled agencies. Wigoda was convicted of failing to report $50,000 in income tax returns. Bush was convicted of conflict of interest for secretly owning a firm that had the billboard advertising at the city's O'Hare International Airport. Keane was sentenced to five years in prison, and Bush received a one-year sentence.

Crime on the streets showed a substantial increase during the year. In one weekend, 23 murders occurred in Chicago, setting off demands for stringent control of handguns. The Cook county coroner reported more drug deaths in the first nine months than in any previous entire year.

The City. Thousands of persons formed in lines to take a quarter-mile elevator ride to the clouds at the 103d floor Sky Walk of the huge downtown tower of Sears, Roebuck & Co. The building actually has 110 floors and a working population of 16,500 persons. There was cultural activity in Chicago's famed Loop. A 70-foot mosaic wall by French artist Marc Chagall was dedicated in the plaza of the First National Bank. A 53-foot stabile, called *Flamingo,* by Alexander Calder was erected in the plaza of the Federal Building complex. In a three-block walk along Dearborn Street, it is possible to view the stabile, the mosaic, and the sculpture by Pablo Picasso in the Civic Center plaza.

Transportation. There was considerable optimism for improved mass transit in the Chicago area when the voters approved in a referendum in March a six-county regional transportation authority (RTA). The vote was close, with the five suburban counties opposed to the RTA. A favorable vote in Cook county, which includes Chicago, was enough for passage. However, RTA got caught in the middle of a political battle between the Chicago Democrats and the suburban Republicans. The suburbs picked four persons to serve on the RTA board and Chicago picked four. The eight members were to select a chairman for a full nine-member board.

The split caused a stalemate in getting the RTA organized. Suburban bus lines were reported near bankruptcy and commuter railroads warned of deteriorating service. Meanwhile, $30 million in RTA money languished in banks while the debate over a chairman continued.

The Dan Ryan Expressway, the major thoroughfare for nearly 2 million persons on Chicago's South Side and south suburbs, underwent major repairs. A cement truck drivers' strike delayed work.

DAVID E. HALVORSEN, *"Chicago Tribune"*

ALAIN KELLER/SYGMA

Students in Santiago, Chile, invite onlookers to join their celebration of the first anniversary, September 11, of the overthrow of Salvador Allende.

CHILE

Events in Chile in 1974 reflected the military government's efforts at restructuring the country's political and economic life. Among the significant events were Gen. Augusto Pinochet Ugarte's assumption of the presidency, friction between the government and the churches and other groups over torture and violations of human rights, and the first surplus in Chile's balance of trade in many years.

Political Events. On June 26, by decree of the military junta, Gen. Augusto Pinochet Ugarte was proclaimed *Jefe Supremo de la Nación* and received the presidential sash from Supreme Court President Enrique Urrutia. Under the decree, Admiral José Toríbio Merino was assigned economic policy; Air Force Gen. Gustavo Leigh, social policy; and *Carabinero* (police) Gen. César Mendoza, agriculture policy.

On July 11, a slightly larger cabinet of 14 military and three civilian men replaced 13 military and two civilians. Before swearing in the new cabinet, President Pinochet signed a decree dividing Chile into 12 regions and a Santiago metropolitan area in place of the existing 25 provinces.

On September 11, the first anniversary of the 1973 coup, President Pinochet indirectly announced that the military planned to stay in office indefinitely by stating that a ban on political activity would continue until a "new generation of Chileans emerges" some time in the next 20 years.

Church-State Friction. In April, Chile's Roman Catholic bishops criticized the ruling junta for its economic policies, political repression, and violations of human rights in a document entitled *Reconciliation in Chile.* In March, Roman Catholic Auxiliary Bishop Msgr. Fernando Ariza Ruiz, Lutheran Bishop Helmut Frenz, and Rabbi Angel Kreiman petitioned a Santiago court on behalf of 131 poor and politically unimportant persons, asking they be released if held without charges being filed.

In a sermon on April 14, Raul Cardinal Silva Henriquez, archbishop of Santiago, said his life had been threatened. The junta asserted the threats came from "leftist extremists." In September, Cardinal Silva was criticized severely in the press for refusing to hold a mass on the anniversary of the coup.

Other Criticism. In a letter to General Pinochet on January 18, Christian Democratic party President Patricio Aylwin and First Vice President Osvaldo Olguin—while not breaking with the military—criticized the junta's social and

CHILE • Information Highlights

Official Name: Republic of Chile.
Location: Southwestern coast of South America.
Area: 292,257 square miles (756,945 sq km).
Population (1973 est.): 10,300,000.
Chief Cities: Santiago, the capital, 2,661,920 (1970 census, met. area); Valparaiso, 292,850 (1970 est.).
Government: *Head of state and of government,* Gen. Augusto Pinochet Ugarte, president (took power Sept. 1973). *Legislature*—Congress (dissolved Sept. 1973).
Monetary Unit: Escudo (800 escudos equal U. S.$1, July 1974).
Gross National Product (1973 est.): $7,500,000,000.
Manufacturing (major products): Iron and steel, petroleum products, pulp and paper, chemicals.
Major Agricultural Products: Wheat, sugar beets, potatoes, corn, grapes, citrus fruits, rapeseed, fish.
Foreign Trade (1971): *Exports,* $962,000,000; *imports,* $980,000,000.

economic policies, as well as the "denial of any real possibility of adequate defense for accused persons."

On March 13, the regime's image was dealt another severe blow when it announced the death of Air Force Gen. Alberto Bachelet, who was to have been the leading defendant in the first public trial of political prisoners since the junta took over. The government said he died of a "heart attack"; others said he died from torture. Two days later, the government announced that former Interior and Defense Minister José Toha González had committed suicide in Santiago's military hospital. Chileans and foreigners alike doubted that Toha—already dying from stomach cancer—was strong enough to hang himself. Cardinal Silva celebrated a requiem mass for Toha in Santiago's Roman Catholic cathedral, a service normally not held for a suicide, and an estimated 3,000 mourners followed the funeral procession.

The two deaths aroused fear for the health of other former cabinet officers and political prisoners previously confined to Dawson Island in the Straits of Magellan and more recently transferred to Santiago hospitals. The island was declared off limits when Roger Gallopin, president of the Executive Committee of the International Red Cross, requested permission to visit it, and later the detention facilities on the island were closed.

Other charges of violations of human rights were made during the year by Amnesty International, the International Commission of Jurists, the UN Human Rights Commission, and the Human Rights Commission of the Organization of American States (OAS).

Although the government faced sporadic economic sabotage and an occasional raid from the Movimiento de la Izquierda Revolucionaria (MIR), President Pinochet felt confident enough on September 11 to promise to release all but a few of the 2,000 political prisoners who wanted to leave the country, and challenged the Soviet Union and Cuba to do likewise.

Foreign Policy. In January, France prohibited the sale of light tanks and electronic equipment to Chile. On April 10, Great Britain's Labour government said it would deliver three remaining warships being built under a 1969 contract with the Frei government, but that it would suspend further arms sales and economic aid. On October 1, the U. S. Senate voted to cut off military aid—currently valued at $15 million annually—in 1975. However, it was disclosed on October 7 that Chile previously had agreed to buy 18 F-5E supersonic fighters and 16 Cessna A-37 attack planes from the United States for $72 million.

General Pinochet attended the March 15 presidential inauguration in Brasília of Gen. Ernesto Geisel. Later, Bolivian papers reported that Geisel had proposed that Chile cede Bolivia a narrow corridor from La Paz to the Pacific Ocean. Peru's President Velasco said Peru would never permit this to happen.

In April, CIA Director William Colby told a closed congressional hearing that the agency had been authorized by a presidential advisory committee to spend $8–11 million to prevent the election in 1970 of late President Salvador Allende Gossens, and to "destabilize" his government afterward. President Ford disclosed in a press conference on September 16 that the money had been used only to "assist the preservation of opposition newspapers and electronic media and to preserve political parties." He thought this was "in the best interests of the people in Chile and . . . in our best interest."

Economic Affairs. After several years of deficits, Chile hoped to register a trade surplus because of high copper prices and increased production over 1973 when the largest mines were affected by strikes. The January-August trade surplus reached $509.4 million but could not be maintained because of falling copper prices in November. On March 25, the U. S. and 11 other nations agreed to refinance 80% of Chile's $750 million foreign debt due before Dec. 31, 1974.

On July 24, 1974, Chile agreed to compensate the Anaconda Copper Co. $253 million for properties nationalized in 1971. In March, Chile had paid the Cerro Corporation $41.9 million in claims.

On July 2, the government said it hoped to hold the 1974 inflation rate to 300%, as compared with 500% for 1973.

NEALE J. PEARSON
Texas Tech University

The members of Chile's military junta are (*left to right*) Gen. César Mendoza; Adm. José Merino; Gen. Augusto Pinochet, chief of state; and Gen. Gustavo Leigh.

UPI

KEYSTONE

Mrs. Ferdinand Marcos, wife of the president of the Philippines, and her son, Ferdinand, Jr., meet in Peking with Mao Tse-tung, chairman of the Chinese Communist party.

CHINA

Two opposing regimes claim to represent China, the world's most populous nation. The Communist government of the People's Republic of China controls the mainland of the country; the Nationalist government of the Republic of China controls the island province of Taiwan.

PEOPLE'S REPUBLIC OF CHINA

Early in 1974 an ideological campaign was launched in the People's Republic against Confucius, the sage of ancient China, and former defense minister Lin Piao, once the designated successor of Chairman Mao Tse-tung. Lin had been reported killed in a plane crash in 1971 after leading an abortive coup. The campaign to criticize Confucius and Lin Piao did not result in widespread violence, but a struggle for power lurked behind it.

China's economic growth slowed down in the first half of 1974. A surge of Sino-American trade placed the United States third among China's trading partners. Stimulated by the world's energy crisis, Peking was establishing definite plans to develop its vast oil resources.

Sino-Soviet antagonism continued during the year. China's political relations with the United States showed no significant progress.

The Communist Party. The active force behind the campaign to discredit Confucius and Lin Piao was the radical faction of the party, which had played a dominant role in the Cultural Revolution of 1966–69. In 1974 its leader, Chiang Ch'ing, the wife of Chairman Mao, was given increasing publicity as a national figure. Premier Chou En-lai, the leader of the moderates, reduced his administrative activities after falling ill. There were indications that his influence had declined, both on account of his health and because of the reemergence of the radical group as a major political force.

The Ideological Campaign. On Feb. 2, 1974, the party newspaper *Jenmin Jih Pao* attacked Confucius and Lin Piao as abettors of individualism and bureaucratism. It called criticism of them "a serious class struggle" and "a declaration of war against feudalism, capitalism, and revisionism." The attack on Confucius was not surprising, for in Communist eyes he was more than an upholder of feudalism: his teachings of moderation and harmony directly contradict the Marxist thesis of class struggle. But the denunciation of Lin Piao as the disciple of Confucius was bewildering, since Lin had never discussed Confucianism in any serious manner.

Mass rallies were held in the various provinces to carry out the campaign of criticism, while wall posters, the main medium for attacking "class enemies" during the turbulent Cultural Revolution, reappeared in the big cities. The drive assumed a moderate tone at the outset, but before long it turned militant. In March, articles in praise of "revolutionary virtues" appeared in the Peking newspapers. Then wall posters in the various provinces attacked officials who were obstructing "the people's revolutionary rebellion" and demanded their dismissal. Disorder was reported in Kiangsi and

— COMMUNIST CHINA • Information Highlights —

Official Name: People's Republic of China.
Location: Central part of eastern Asia.
Area: 3,705,396 square miles (9,596,961 sq km).
Population (1973 est.): 814,300,000.
Chief Cities (1970 est.): Peking, the capital, 7,570,000; Shanghai, 10,820,000; Tientsin, 4,280,000.
Government: *Chairman of the Chinese Communist party,* Mao Tse-tung (took office 1935). *Head of government,* Chou En-lai, premier (took office 1949). *Legislature* (unicameral)—National People's Congress.
Monetary Unit: Yuan (1.96 yuan equal U. S.$1, July 1974).
Gross National Product (1972 est.): $128,000,000,000.
Manufacturing (major products): Iron and steel, machinery, cotton textiles, fertilizers, electronics, pharmaceuticals, instruments, transportation equipment.
Major Agricultural Products: Rice, wheat, sweet potatoes, sorghum, corn, cotton, tobacco, soybeans, barley, tea, fish.
Foreign Trade (1971): *Exports,* $2,200,000,000; *imports,* $2,400,000,000.

Kiangsu provinces, where the government had to organize propaganda teams to serve as arbiters of disputes. The party enjoined officials to support the revolutionary spirit of the masses. At the same time it stressed that the campaign should be conducted under the party's leadership, and it implied that the upper hierarchy was not subject to attack.

Attack on Foreign Influence. The assault on Confucian values was accompanied by a denunciation of foreign influences. Western music was assailed in the Chinese press, which scorned Beethoven as a capitalist composer and Schubert as a petit bourgeois. The attack was the most significant since it came only a few months after the visit of three Western orchestras, including the Philadelphia Orchestra, which had been given glowing reviews at the time of their performances. Similarly, Michelangelo Antonioni, the Italian film director who had been welcomed to China to make a documentary in 1971, was now accused by the government of "deception and forgery" with intent to "smear" the Chinese Revolution.

The Communist Leadership. Chiang Ch'ing, as the leader of the group behind the ideological struggle, assumed an increasingly important role in public affairs. In July, *Jenmin Jih Pao* published two articles to commemorate the tenth anniversary of a speech given by her in 1964 on the reformation of the Peking opera. In doing so, the newspaper accorded her an honor that had been reserved for the major statements of Chairman Mao himself.

Premier Chou En-lai's position in the ideological struggle was a subject of wild speculation. The criticism of classical Western music and the denunciation of Antonioni were believed by some observers to be veiled attacks on Chou, who was a noted advocate of moderation and friendly approaches to the West. The control imposed on the campaign at the initial stage apparently came from the group led by Chou.

The premier's illness, in May, forced him to reduce his official duties. He entered a hospital for treatment but came out shortly before July 20, when he attended a meeting with a Niger delegation that was in Peking to establish diplomatic relations. The nature of his illness was never officially announced, although it was hinted that he had suffered a heart attack. On July 31, Chou made his first public appearance in two months: at a reception on the eve of Army Day, he led a group of Chinese leaders into the banquet chamber of the Great Hall of the People. Thus despite any decline in his influence, outwardly he remained second in the party leadership after Mao.

Restoration of Teng Hsiao-p'ing. The comeback of Teng Hsiao-p'ing, former secretary general of the party who had been purged during the Cultural Revolution, attracted much attention. He had reappeared in 1973 with the title of deputy premier, and in January 1974 he was restored to the Politburo. He was listed now in the leadership rostrum just after members of the standing committee of the Politburo, thereby ranking tenth in the hierarchy of the Chinese communist party.

Teng assumed many of the functions that Premier Chou devolved because of ill health. He represented the premier in welcoming and holding talks with foreign statesmen, including Pakistani Prime Minister Bhutto and former British Prime Minister Heath. Heading the Chinese delegation to a conference of the UN General Assembly, he was given a grand send-off at the Peking airport by top party leaders, including Chou En-lai, Chiang Ch'ing, and Wang Hung-wen.

The rapid rise of Teng Hsiao-p'ing presented a puzzling question. A man denounced as a "renegade" and "revisionist" during the Cultural Revolution was certainly no friend to the radicals, and yet he was chosen to act for Premier Chou. A possible explanation is that the radicals accepted Teng under a temporary arrangement while the various factions jockeyed for an advantageous position in the event of Chairman Mao's death.

Military Reshuffle. The beginning of 1974 saw a sweeping reshuffle of military posts in the various strategic regions. Of the 10 military

The Red Flag Canal brings water to this arid region of Hunan province from a distant river in Shansi province. This section was built by the people of Linhsien county.

UPI

UPI

Workers assemble radios in a factory in Nanking, an ancient city that is now a center for the manufacture of such products as tools and telecommunications equipment.

regions in China, only the commands of Chengtu (Szechwan), Kunming (Yunnan), and Sinkiang regions remained definitely unchanged. The situation in the Tibet region was unclear. Of greatest significance were the transfer of Ch'en Hsi-len, commander of the Shenyang military region in Manchuria, to the command of the Peking region; of Hsu Shih-yu, commander of the Nanking region, to the command of the Canton region; and of Li Teh-sheng, director of the political department of the armed forces, to the command of the Shenyang region. The shifts were attributed to the desire of the party to exert its authority over military leaders who had been too long entrenched in certain areas.

China's celebration of Army Day on August 1 revealed the rehabilitation of 13 high-ranking military officers purged during the Cultural Revolution. The most prominent of them were Yang Ch'eng-wu, acting chief of the general staff from 1966 to 1968, and Yu Li-chin, former political commissioner of the air force.

Economic Development. China's economic policy has been to develop heavy industry while strengthening agriculture and light industry. The program of purchasing new plants from foreign countries, which had involved $1.5 billion in 1973, was continued in 1974.

Economic growth appeared to slow down in the first half of the year. The growth rate in Shanghai during this period was reported to be 6%, compared with 9% for the corresponding months of the previous year. In Shansi province the growth rate was 5%, compared with 12% a year earlier. Some observers attributed the slowing down to the ideological drive, which had brought about disruptions in industrial centers. The need for labor discipline was said to be the reason why the ideological campaign tapered off in the summer.

Despite famine reported in some northern provinces, Peking announced a good summer harvest. Nevertheless China imported 7 million tons of wheat in 1974, including 3 million tons from Canada, 1.1 million tons from Australia, and 1 million tons from Argentina. The United States had contracted to deliver 1.5 million tons, but China rejected three American shipments because the wheat contained fungus.

The surge in Chinese-American trade placed the United States as China's third largest trading partner, after Japan and Hong Kong. This trade was expected to reach $1.25 billion in 1974, an increase of $500 million over the year before. The United States enjoyed an advantage of 10 to 1 in the balance of trade because of China's large importation of American agricultural goods, such as wheat, cotton, corn, and soybeans.

The worldwide energy crisis stimulated China's oil trade in the Far East. Peking was prepared to triple its crude oil exports to Japan in 1974. It also promised diesel oil to Thailand, with which it had no diplomatic relations. China's oil production was moderate: 50 million tons in 1973, according to a statement by Premier Chou En-lai. But reserves were said to be vast—20 billion barrels on shore and more than that offshore, according to one "conservative" estimate. To develop its resources, Peking purchased exploitation equipment from Denmark, Rumania, and Japan. American companies were taking steps to tap the growing Chinese market for these goods.

Foreign Relations—*United States*. Sino-American relations, which had greatly improved since President Nixon's visit to Peking in 1972, cooled off in 1974. David K. E. Bruce, head of the U. S. liaison office in Peking, flew home in January and did not return to China until March. His Chinese counterpart, Huang Chen, stayed away from Washington for an even longer time. Peking was dissatisfied with the continued U. S. support for Taiwan and was particularly unhappy about the appointment of Leonard Unger, a well-known career diplomat, as American ambassador to Nationalist China.

If there was no progress in Chinese-American relations, there were no signs of deterioration either. Contacts between the two countries continued. In May, a group of American state governors was cordially welcomed by the Chinese ministry of foreign affairs. When Sen. Henry M. Jackson visited Peking, he was received by Chou En-lai in the hospital where the premier was recuperating. And to show its good will, the Chinese government promptly released Gerald E. Kosh, a U. S. defense department employee who was captured by Chinese forces in fighting with South Vietnamese troops on the Paracel Islands in the South China Sea.

A congressional delegation led by Sen. J. William Fulbright visited China in September. The Chinese Communists took the occasion to reiterate that full normalization of relations between the two countries depended on the United States severing relations with Nationalist China. On September 4, George Bush, national chairman of the Republican party, was appointed head of the U. S. liaison office in Peking to succeed David Bruce. The move was seen as an effort by President Ford to promote friendly relations with Communist China.

Soviet Union. Antagonism between China and the Soviet Union continued, but no border clashes occurred. In a speech before the UN General Assembly on April 1, Vice Premier Teng Hsiao-p'ing, head of the Chinese delegation, denounced the Soviets as the worst kind of imperialists, "vicious and unscrupulous" in subverting other countries.

Two incidents in 1974 added to the tension in relations between the two countries. On January 19, Peking expelled five members of the Soviet embassy on charges of spying. In reprisal, the Soviet Union ordered the expulsion of a Chinese diplomat on similar charges. Then on March 14, a Soviet army helicopter which had crossed the Chinese border and landed in Sinkiang, was captured by Chinese forces. The Chinese charged that the crew of the reconnaissance plane had been on a spying mission. They dismissed as "lies" the Soviet protest that the plane, assigned to evacuate a sick soldier, had been blown off course in a storm and had made a forced landing.

Sino-Soviet border talks in Peking showed no progress, although the Soviet representative returned to the negotiation table from time to time. On May 23, the Soviet Union announced that unless China recognized Soviet sovereignty over a disputed island at the confluence of two border rivers, the Amur and the Ussuri, Chinese ships would be excluded from using "Soviet inland waterways." In November the Soviet government took a moderate stand toward China, when it stressed "peace and friendship" along the Soviet-Chinese border. But when China expressed interest in a nonaggression pact with a withdrawal of forces along the border, the Soviet Union rejected the Chinese proposal.

Other Countries. After two days of fighting between Chinese and South Vietnamese armed forces, China took possession of the disputed Paracel Islands on January 20. The islands, which are situated in the South China Sea, had attracted the attention of Peking and Saigon because of possible oil deposits offshore.

Malaysia established diplomatic relations with China on May 31. In a joint communiqué issued in Peking, China declared that it considered all Malaysian citizens of Chinese origin to have renounced their Chinese nationality and expected them to abide by Malaysian laws and regulations.

The Malaysian move was expected to pave the way for the other Southeast Asian nations to recognize Peking. An informal trade agreement was concluded between China and the Philippines in September when Imelda Marcos, wife of the Philippine president, visited Peking.

China made vigorous efforts in 1974 to win over the Third World—essentially the developing countries of Asia, Africa, and Latin America. Peking called for the unity of the Third World against Soviet and U. S. "imperialism." On July 2, at the UN Conference on the Law of the Sea held in Caracas, Venezuela, Chai Shu-fan, the chief Chinese delegate, supported the position for 200-nautical-mile maritime rights advanced by the Third World countries. During the year China also upheld the Arab nations' use of oil as a political weapon against "imperialist exploitation."

REPUBLIC OF CHINA

Taiwan managed to trade in 1974 with most of the countries of the world with which it had no diplomatic ties. Economic growth continued, but at a lower rate than the previous year. Faced with the prospect of a large trade deficit, Taiwan had the urgent task of maintaining its competitive position in the world market. The year witnessed a continuance of political stability.

President Chiang's Recovery. On March 25, President and Madame Chiang Kai-shek gave a

Sen. Henry M. Jackson (D-Wash.) and Mrs. Jackson meet Premier Chou En-lai of the People's Republic of China in a Peking hospital. The premier has been in ill health.

WIDE WORLD

farewell reception for U. S. Ambassador Walter P. McConaughly, who was retiring after six years of service in his Taiwan post. It was the first time that the 86-year-old president had appeared in public since he suffered pneumonia in July 1972.

While still in the stage of recuperation, Chiang had limited his administrative activities to the minimum. For some time, even before his illness, his elder son, Premier Chiang Ching-kuo, had practically exercised the powers to govern Taiwan.

The Economy. Taiwan's economy slowed down amid the world oil crisis and shortage of raw materials. Its growth in 1974 was expected to be about 8.5%, compared with 12.3% achieved in 1973. Foreign trade was also affected by adverse developments abroad. Commodity prices rose, not only because of the increased cost of essential imported materials, but also because of a sharp rise in wages.

Taiwan's two-way trade was expected to reach $13.5 billion in 1974 from $8.2 billion a year earlier. But a slowdown in exports was expected to register a trade deficit of about $700 million. The deepening imbalance caused great concern in Taiwan, whose economic strength depended heavily on trade surplus.

To maintain its competitive position in the world market, Taiwan made extensive efforts to cut the increasing costs of production. Anti-inflation measures included constriction of the money supply through high interest rates and the improvement of transportation and distribution facilities.

Members of the Taiwan team are jubilant after winning the Little League World Series in Williamsport, Pa., for the fourth consecutive time and the fifth time in six years.

UPI

—NATIONALIST CHINA • Information Highlights—

Official Name: Republic of China.
Location: Islands off the southeastern coast of mainland China.
Area: 13,885 square miles (35,961 sq km).
Population (1973 est.): 15,000,000.
Chief Cities (1970 est.): Taipei, the capital, 1,740,800; Kaohsiung, 806,300; Tainan, 468,300.
Government: *Head of state,* Chiang Kai-shek, president (elected for 5th 6-year term, 1972). *Head of government,* Chiang Ching-kuo, premier (took office May 1972). *Legislature* (unicameral)—Legislative Yuan.
Monetary Unit: New Taiwan dollar (38.10 NT dollars equal U. S.$1, July 1974).
Gross National Product (1972 est.): $7,690,000,000.
Manufacturing (major products): Petroleum products, processed foods, textiles, electrical machinery, electronics, chemicals, apparel.
Major Agricultural Products: Sugarcane, bananas, mushrooms, pineapples, rice, tea, vegetables, fish.
Foreign Trade (1973): *Exports,* $4,473,000,000; *imports,* $3,791,000,000.

Because of rising wages and rapid industrial development in recent years, Taiwan was shifting its emphasis from labor-intensive industries to technology and capital-intensive industries. The new approach was believed by the Nationalist government to be the path toward achieving the status of a developed nation.

Foreign Relations. Adhering to its determination never to negotiate with the Chinese Communists, Taiwan firmly rejected Peking's propaganda efforts to induce the Nationalists to unite politically with the mainland. The United States was in favor of a reconciliation between Taiwan and Communist China but exerted no pressure on the Nationalists to deal with Peking.

The appointment of Leonard Unger as U. S. ambassador to the Republic of China assured the Nationalists of Washington's continued support. In his first speech in Taiwan on June 22, Ambassador Unger reaffirmed that the United States would keep its commitments and honor its treaty obligations, including that of jointly defending Taiwan. Nevertheless, the United States was taking steps for the withdrawal of combat aircraft from Nationalist China by the year 1975.

Taiwan's relations with Japan suffered a serious setback on April 20 when Japan signed an aviation agreement with Communist China, establishing regular air services between Tokyo and Peking. Taiwan terminated its civil air relations with Japan and announced that necessary action would be taken to bar Japanese planes from its air space. Taiwan had severed diplomatic relations with Japan in 1972, but a growing trade had developed between the two countries.

Taiwan broke off diplomatic relations with Niger and Brazil when those countries officially recognized Communist China. At the end of 1974 Taiwan still had full diplomatic relations with 30-odd states.

CHESTER C. TAN
New York University

Chicago acquires a 53-foot (16-meter) high, bright red stabile, *Flamingo* (*right*), by Alexander Calder, in the Federal Center Plaza, and Marc Chagall's colored stone and glass mosaic, *The Four Seasons* (*below*), in the First National Plaza.

UPI

CITIES AND URBAN AFFAIRS

UPI

In 1970 the noted urbanologist Edward C. Banfield compared the progress of cities in solving their problems to dogs chasing a mechanical rabbit around a racetrack—the rabbit is set to keep just ahead of the dogs no matter how fast they run. If the comparison seemed appropriate when Banfield first made it, it was especially so in 1974. Buffeted first by a critical shortage of energy early in the year and by the effects of inflation throughout the period, urban areas were hit hard. Despite the fact that cities found solutions to some problems, other difficulties arose to take their places and seemingly to negate progress that was being made.

Heading the list of difficulties facing urban centers during 1974 were inflation, together with the inability of urban governments to pay for all goods and services thought to be necessary to maintain an acceptable standard of urban life, and the effects of the energy shortage, especially as they related to transportation and growth policies. But these problems, even more than those that had taken precedence in previous years, were far beyond the control of individual cities and their governments. Acceptable responses to them could not be formulated quickly or by urbanites alone. Indeed, the problems showed observers even more convincingly that external forces have as much to do with the condition of cities as internal ones.

The year began for cities in an atmosphere of increasing urgency. The worldwide shortage of energy brought on largely by an oil trade embargo imposed by Arab nations caused the cities such inconvenience that urban life-styles were altered. Lines of private automobiles assembled for blocks at gasoline stations as motorists attempted to get enough of the precious fuel to ensure a trip to work and back home again after work.

Reductions in power supplies and calls for maintenance of lowered temperatures in homes and businesses and lowered vehicle speeds on the highways added to the impression that the situation was critical. The crisis seemed to fade, however, as the year progressed, and urbanites wondered if there really had been a real energy shortage at all (see also ENERGY).

THE DRAVO CORPORATION

In New York City, a "new town" rises on Roosevelt Island (*right*) in the East River. When completed, the community will house 17,000 persons in 5,000 apartments and have shopping facilities, schools, a hotel, public parks, and office space.

Mass Transit. The energy problem, especially as it related to automobiles, drew more attention to mass transit than environmental concerns ever had. The number of riders on existing rapid rail and bus transit systems rose sharply early in the year, only to drop off when gasoline for automobiles became more plentiful. Still, policymakers grappled with the problem of how to create incentives for city dwellers to leave their private automobiles in favor of mass transit and how to finance the operation of those mass transit systems.

The U. S. Congress deliberated over the question of whether to provide federal funds to subsidize operating as well as capital expenses of transit systems. Even though federal funding for capital and operating expenditures was assured late in November when President Ford signed the $11.8 billion National Mass Transportation Assistance Act, cities still weighed unattractive choices such as raised fares. Los Angeles, Calif., had considered a special sales tax intended to finance mass transit.

The outlook for mass transit was clouded, too, by the operational problems that faced the newest mass transit system in the United States, the long-heralded Bay Area Rapid Transit (BART) in the San Francisco–Oakland, Calif., area. Viewed by its proponents as the best that could be produced in the modern age, BART nonetheless suffered equipment failures, financial deficits, and an altogether inauspicious beginning. Another publicized mass-transit innovation was the so-called "people mover," an experimental system in Morgantown, W. Va., financed by the U. S. Department of Transportation. It also received poor grades because of its high cost and technological difficulties (see also TRANSPORTATION).

Inflation. For cities, the inflation that gripped the economy of the world was especially critical. For years, the costs of providing city services had risen at a much higher rate than the consumer price index, and 1974 was no exception. Among the important factors in the rising costs of city operations was the demand for higher wages and fringe benefits by public employees, themselves strapped by the rising cost of living. As employees demanded more, city officials, caught in the squeeze of meeting many demands with scarce resources, often balked at their requests. In some cases, public employee strikes occurred. Sanitation workers in Baltimore, Md., walked off their jobs during a midsummer heat wave and quickly provided that city's residents with an indication of how unpleasant urban life could be without basic services. But nothing brought the point home quite so forcefully as when most of that city's policemen joined the sanitation workers on the picket line in the first official strike by a big-city police force in the United States since 1919.

Crime. Never far from the minds of many urban dwellers was the spectre of violent crime. While published crime figures indicated a mixed picture for large cities with regard to the problem, there were alarming developments. A study released late in the year by the Law Enforcement Assistance Administration (LEAA) indicated that reported crime accounts for only about one third of actual occurrences. According to the report, the main reason for the discrepancy is that victims believe that little can be done by law enforcement agencies. The revelation buttressed what many law enforcement experts had been saying for years, but confirmation made no one any happier.

Many city officials contended that the root

of crime was the easy availability of handguns. After a particularly violent weekend, Chicago's Mayor Richard Daley called guns the No. 1 problem of the City. Officials in Washington, D. C., where murders occurred at a rate of more than one a day in some months, echoed his words.

Responding to gun crime with a highly publicized program, Baltimore began to pay a bounty to any person who turned in a gun or who gave information that led to confiscation of an illegally held gun. Thousands of firearms were collected, but there was disagreement whether that in itself made the program a success. New Orleans and Kansas City, Mo., began to use computers to chart high-crime incidence areas.

Urban Redevelopment. U. S. city officials continued to be concerned with making life more attractive downtown. Attitude surveys revealed that Americans were increasingly interested in convenience and comfort, and this boded well for those interested in downtown renewal, particularly if they could assure pleasant, functional living areas. Old urban neighborhoods, with interesting architecture and close-in, energy-efficient locations, became more in demand as living areas. Efforts to convert older urban buildings, such as railroad stations and warehouses, to other uses such as restaurants and specialty shops met with increasing success.

A national conference on urban revival with the theme "Back to the City" drew 300 participants in New York City. Speakers warned the gathering that emphasis would have to be on sound housing, services, and employment, not just on historic and architectural restoration.

Seattle, Wash., served as an example of a city where practical and aesthetic goals were not necessarily competing ones. The city established an Office of Urban Conservation, and attempted to build on a record of historic preservation and viable reuse that had already resulted in an increase of over 400% in the tax base and employment in the Pioneer Square area, site of the city's first settlement.

While none of these developments reversed the flow of Americans to the suburbs, the flow seemed to have halted. Suburbanites, particularly those residing in large counties within metropolitan areas, became increasingly aware that their jurisdictions have problems similar to those of large cities. Environmental issues, especially pollution abatement and control of haphazard land use and development, headed the list of concerns of these suburban dwellers.

The U. S. government, too, began to show its awareness that city problems had crossed into the suburbs by passing a major piece of legislation. The Housing and Community Development Act of 1974 automatically provided block grant funds to urban counties as well as cities based on a formula that took account of factors such as population, poverty, and overcrowded housing (see also HOUSING).

The responsibilities the government assumed under the 1974 Housing and Community Development Act added to those already there because of general revenue sharing. The latter, involving the return of a portion of federal taxes to state and local governments for their use, finished its second year in 1974. Already city officials were calling attention to the importance of the program's renewal by Congress in 1975. According to city officials, the improved local fiscal situation that has resulted from revenue sharing has been undermined by inflationary trends and the need of localities to know whether funds would continue to be available.

Housing. The perennial shortage of good urban housing was exacerbated by the difficulty that potential builders and buyers faced in trying to obtain necessary financing. The problem assumed worldwide scope. New construction was cut in the United States, and in Britain the slump was even worse. The U. S. government moved late in the year to loosen the tight financial market and to stimulate demand by releasing billions of dollars in mortgage money.

Meanwhile, the Soviet Union gave no indication that its housing construction was lagging behind the goal set for new construction in the 1971–75 five-year plan. The possibility that Soviet progress might be slow, however, was suggested by the fact that no reference was made to recent specific achievements.

ROBERT M. LLOYD, *South Carolina Appalachian Council of Governments*

In Kansas City, Mo., Hallmark Cards, Inc.'s new Crown Center has a hotel (*foreground*), an office complex (*upper left*), and Hallmark's headquarters (*upper right*).

AUSTIN BEALMER, CROWN CENTER

CIVIL LIBERTIES AND CIVIL RIGHTS

A proper balance of power among the branches of the federal government has always been a necessary condition to civil liberty. It is ironic that although President Nixon (who was forced to resign on Aug. 9, 1974) sought to tip the balance in favor of a stronger presidency, his most enduring legacy is an unprecedented set of judicial and legislative actions limiting the powers he so emphatically asserted.

Perhaps the most significant of these actions in 1974 was the Supreme Court's unanimous ruling that White House tapes relevant to the Watergate conspiracy trial might not be withheld on the mere assertion of executive privilege.

The court recognized the existence of a privilege, applicable even to the confidential communications of presidential advisers. But the President's generalized claim was held subject to judicial review and subordinate to the interest of obtaining evidence for a criminal trial.

While the court rallied to preserve a balance of power in the national government, its record on other civil rights and liberties issues was mixed. (See also LAW.)

Free Speech. Only a year after attempting to limit its role in obscenity cases, the Supreme Court exercised its obligation to ensure adequate protection of First Amendment values; it refused to allow suppression of the film *Carnal Knowledge*. At the same time, the majority reaffirmed its decision to allow "local," rather than state or national, standards to be applied by courts and juries in obscenity cases.

The court reversed the criminal conviction of a man for defacing the American flag by putting a peace symbol on it. On the other hand, it refused to require a city to accept paid advertisements in its transit system, on behalf of candidates for public office.

Government intrusion on freedom of speech was facilitated by the court's ruling that federal agents applying for a wiretap warrant need identify only those telephone users whom the government has probable cause to believe are "committing the offense" under investigation, rather than all likely users. The court also ruled, however, that under the applicable statute, only the attorney general or assistant attorney general may approve requests to apply for wiretaps.

Freedom of the Press. A unanimous Supreme Court defended newspapers against "right-of-reply" laws, noting that increased costs would be imposed by requiring newspapers to accept replies to their statements, but resting ultimately on the fact that such statutes interfered with the essential ingredient of a free press—editorial control and judgment. However, the court significantly limited the protection afforded publishers from state libel laws, announcing it would thereafter allow recoveries without proof of actual knowledge of falsity or reckless disregard of the truth, even though the defamation concerned a matter of public interest.

Freedom of Association. The Supreme Court dealt a severe blow to Americans who need or choose to live in groups, by upholding a village zoning ordinance banning residence in any home by more than two unrelated individuals. The opinion granted sweeping immunity from federal constitutional restraint to efforts by local communities to control their character.

Sex Discrimination. Feminists prevailed in a Supreme Court decision invalidating the Cleveland Board of Education's requirement that pregnant teachers take an unpaid leave from four months prior to the expected birth until the first semester after the child is three months old. The court found that the regulation unduly penalized a teacher's right to bear children, but indicated it would sustain a regulation based on capacity to perform the teaching function. Also significant was the army's decision to amend its rigid policy forcing into retirement any woman who becomes pregnant. Such women may now remain in military service if they can continue as mothers to carry out their assignments.

Women seeking to require public support for pregnancy and childbirth costs were unsuccessful, however. The Supreme Court held that a state may exclude such costs from coverage under its disability insurance program, since the exclusion rationally furthers the interest in keeping the insurance program self-supporting and adequate in coverage while minimizing the employee contribution rate.

The court also indicated that equality for women did not necessarily mean they could be given no special advantages. It upheld a Florida statute giving widows (but not widowers) a $500 property tax exemption, distinguishing its prior rulings indicating that sex might be a suspect classification on the ground that the earlier cases dealt with the denial to women of benefits which were given to men. Rulings of this sort may have to be reexamined if the Equal Rights Amendment is adopted. Three more states ratified the Amendment in 1974, bringing the total ratifications to 33, five short of the number required for adoption.

Equality of Education. In July the Supreme Court, in a sharply divided ruling, refused to sanction the busing of children across Detroit city and suburban school district lines to achieve racial integration in those districts not found to have engaged in racial discrimination, even though the lower courts concluded that such busing was the only effective remedy. The majority opinion held that interdistrict busing should be required only if discrimination in one district produced segregation in the other, or if districts had been drawn with intent to produce racial segregation. The court sent the case back to the lower court with instructions to produce a plan that would get rid of discrimination in Detroit's schools.

On the other hand, the court struck down Montgomery, Alabama's policy of granting segregated private schools and organizations exclusive access to public recreation areas, putting off ruling on the propriety of nonexclusive use of the parks by such schools. And the court held that San Francisco's failure to provide 1,800 Chinese students with English language instruction denied them equal access to the educational system.

Rights of the Poor. The court severely limited an earlier decision protecting debtors from seizure of property without notice, by upholding Louisiana's law authorizing such seizures on the basis of a sworn affidavit of delinquency and necessity, approved by a judge.

In another decision the court majority greatly lessened the utility of class actions by requiring plaintiffs to provide individual notice of the action to all reasonably identifiable class members, regardless of cost. The court also held that persons with small claims could not use the class action to aggregate those claims in order to satisfy the jurisdictional requirement for getting into federal court; each person in the class must have at least a $10,000 interest in the case.

Rights of Suspects and Prisoners. The court narrowed the *Miranda* decision of 1966, which required that suspects be offered counsel before interrogation, by refusing to suppress testimony obtained before the *Miranda* decision, where the violation was "technical." The court also held that some due-process protections apply to prison disciplinary proceedings that could affect an inmate's good-time credit, including notice of charges and a written statement of the evidence relied on and the reasons for any disciplinary actions. The court refused, however, to allow inmates the right to counsel or to cross-examine witnesses.

In two other cases the court held that free speech does not guarantee prisoners the right to be individually designated by media representatives for interviews. The press is not entitled to interview at will within the prison, since the general public has no similar right.

Voting Rights. The court struck down an Indiana law requiring party candidates to swear that their party did not advocate the overthrow of federal, state, or local governments by force. Access to the ballot and the right to associate with political parties cannot, the court held, be limited because a party line includes an abstract belief in violent overthrow, where the party has no program of present or future action.

Texas rules imposing different requirements on minor parties and independents for ballot positions than those imposed on major parties were held constitutional by the Supreme Court.

ABRAHAM D. SOFAER
Columbia University School of Law

COIN COLLECTING

Numismatics had an exciting year in 1974 as coin market activity continued strong in all areas and many price records were set. In a Swiss auction a dekadrachma of Athens sold for $318,000, a world-record price for any numismatic rarity. In the United States an example of the rare (only 14 to 16 pieces are known) MCMVII (1907) double eagle in extremely high relief sold for $200,000 at auction. In a private transaction a specimen of the rare 1804 silver dollar (only 15 specimens are known) changed hands for a reported $225,000. Other numismatic rarities did well also.

Gold Coins. In January the Office of Gold and Silver Operations announced that the import ban on gold coins dated 1934 through 1959 would be lifted. Previously, collectors and dealers could legally hold only gold coins dated prior to 1934, with a few specific exceptions. Later in the year legislation providing for unrestricted holding of gold coins, medals, and gold bullion was passed.

Bicentennial Coin Designs. In January a panel of judges named the 12 semifinalists in the nationwide bicentennial coin design competition. In March the three finalists were announced: Jack L. Ahr, Seth G. Huntington, and Dennis R. Williams, each winning $5,000. The designs for the quarter, half dollar, and silver dollar, each dated 1776–1976, respectively featured a colonial drummer boy, Independence Hall, and the Liberty Bell overlapping the moon.

The annual convention of the American Numismatic Association, the world's largest nonprofit organization devoted to coin collecting, was held in Bal Harbour, Fla., in August. There, Mint Director Mary Brooks unveiled the first striking of the new bicentennial coin design. Bicentennial coins will be available to the general public beginning in 1975.

Cent Shortage. In February rumors swept the country that copper one-cent pieces would soon rise sharply in value. This news was spurred when the Bureau of the Mint asked for authority to substitute aluminum for bronze in one-cent coins. Cents were hoarded in large numbers, with the result that shortages occurred in many places. The situation eased later in the year. No aluminum one-cent pieces were manufactured by the Bureau of the Mint, aside from a few trial strikings.

Production Record. On May 14 the Philadelphia Mint broke a world record by producing more than 25 million coins in a single day to keep up with record coinage demands.

Old Silver Dollars. The General Services Administration continued its mail-bid sales of the remnants of about three million silver dollars left in Treasury vaults since the late 19th century. Included among the items offered were 3,600 specimens of the scarce 1879-CC (Carson City) issue.

ALL: BUREAU OF THE MINT, THE DEPARTMENT OF THE TREASURY

For the first time in history, coins honoring the U. S. bicentennial were struck at the Philadelphia Mint during the summer of 1974.

Eisenhower Dollars. Despite protests from collectors and numismatic publications, the government passed legislation that channeled millions of dollars in sales profits from Eisenhower proof silver dollars into the coffers of Eisenhower College at Seneca, N. Y.

Coin Sets. Worldwide sales of proof coins and other sets to collectors continued actively. The U. S. Mint announced that 2,796,624 proof sets were issued in 1973, down slightly from the 3,267,667 sets produced in 1972. In addition, Bermuda, Canada, Panama, Singapore, South Africa, and Trinidad and Tobago issued sets to collectors as did other countries. Many countries will include gold coins as part of their proof sets in 1975 because U. S. collectors then will be able to hold modern world gold coins legally for the first time since 1933.

Medals. Collector interest in medals continued strong in 1974. The bicentennial of the American Revolution furnished the central theme for many different issuers of medals, including the United States Mint, which announced an 11-piece set with this theme.

Q. DAVID BOWERS
Author of "High Profits from Rare Coin Investment"

COLOMBIA

The 16-year National Front coalition era in Colombian politics came to an end in 1974 when the April presidential elections produced an overwhelming victory for Liberal party candidate Alfonso López Michelsen over his major rival, Conservative Alvaro Gómez Hurtado.

The election also appeared to sound the death knell for the National Popular Alliance (ANAPO), the neo-populist coalition of former dictator Gustavo Rojas Pinilla. ANAPO had barely lost the 1970 election, but this time polled less than 500,000 votes out of a total of more than 5 million. López took office as the new president on August 7, pledged by a series of campaign promises to revamp traditional Colombian social relationships.

Political Affairs. The combined presidential and congressional elections on April 21 marked the official end of the National Front arrangement under which the Liberal and Conservative parties had alternated in the presidency. By special agreement, however, the practice of *paridad* (parity) under which the two parties would share equally in all governmental appointive posts, was to be continued until 1978.

The elections were the first in which Liberals and Conservatives were allowed to campaign freely, and they demonstrated the conclusive and growing preponderance of the Liberal party in Colombian politics. López received over 1 million votes more than Gómez, and the Liberal congressional candidates won overwhelming majorities in both houses of the Colombian congress. In the Senate the Liberals held 66 seats to 37 for the Conservatives, 12 Anapistas, and 2 for the leftist National Opposition Union

COLOMBIA • Information Highlights

Official Name: Republic of Colombia.
Location: Northwest South America.
Area: 439,736 square miles (1,138,914 sq km).
Population (1973 est. census): 23,700,000.
Chief Cities (1972 est.): Bogotá, the capital, 2,680,100; Medellín, 1,091,600.
Government: *Head of state and of government,* Alfonso López Michelsen, president (took office Aug. 7, 1974). *Legislature*—Congress: Senate and House of Representatives.
Monetary Unit: Peso (25.70 pesos equal U. S.$1, June 1974).
Gross National Product (1973 est.): $8,410,000,000.
Manufacturing (major products): Textiles, beverages, iron and steel, petroleum products.
Major Agricultural Products: Coffee, bananas, cotton, sugarcane, tobacco, potatoes, corn.
Foreign Trade (1972): *Exports,* $743,000,000; *imports,* $837,000,000.

(UON). In the House of Representatives the election produced victories for 113 Liberals, 66 Conservatives, 15 Anapistas, and 5 members of the UON.

The new president is a 61-year-old former lawyer and university professor, and son of former president Alfonso López Pumarejo (1934–38). López has been known as the maverick of the Liberal party since 1959, when he founded his own political movement, the Liberal Revolutionary Movement (MRL), which, until its reintegration with the orthodox Liberal party in 1968, was regarded as the left position in Colombian politics.

Although López' campaign rhetoric promised much in the way of reform—specifically in the areas of accelerated agrarian reform, lowering the voting age to 18, legalizing civil marriage and divorce, combating inflation, and moderate tax reform—his initial actions after taking office were cautious.

Perhaps most disappointing to those who wished for more rapid reforms was the makeup of the president's first cabinet, which included several ministers known for their opposition to social reform. Several other ministers, most notably Maria Elena de Crovo in the Labor and Social Security portfolio, may provide balance, but the cabinet was not one that produced cheers on the left or dismay on the right.

Late in September, López made the first significant move of his new administration, when he declared a state of economic emergency under Article 122 of the Constitution. This gave him a period of 45 days in which to issue decree-laws which would remain in force after the emergency unless voted out by Congress. Some of the decrees that were issued were reformist in nature: the tax system was revamped so that the tax burden would be greater on the rich and less on the poor.

By the end of the year, however, no fundamental vested interest had been hurt by López' actions.

Economy. The Colombian economy continued to perform well in 1974. The growth rate for the year surpassed the 7.5% rate of 1973, with exceptionally strong performances in the export sector and in construction. Export earnings were up over 1973, which in turn had shown a 40% increase over 1972. Most of the increase was due to continued high prices for coffee, but also contributing to the happy situation was a record crop of 9.5 million bags for the coffee year (October through September). The construction industry continued to boom in 1974, spurred by the innovative constant-value savings and loan system known as UPAC (under which return on investments is linked to changes in the cost-of-living index).

The most vexing economic problem continued to be inflation. The price index for 1974 rose by over 30%, up from a 23.6% rise in 1973. The food portion of the index rose by more than 40%, and there is some indication that official figures have understated the problem through failure to revise the market basket used in determining the index.

López' initial answer to the inflation problem was to blame it on governmental deficits. The president initiated a governmental austerity program aimed at cutting current expenditures rather than investment, as had been done in the past.

Colombia's foreign trade increased dramatically in 1974, with both exports and imports reflecting substantial increases over 1973 levels. For the first time in the 20th century, Colombia's nontraditional exports surpassed earnings from coffee, fulfilling a major Colombian goal of diversifying its export trade.

ERNEST A. DUFF
Randolph-Macon Woman's College

Celebrating Colombia's 4–1 victory over United States in Davis Cup play, tennis fans in Bogotá hoist Jairo Velasco, a member of the winning squad, to their shoulders.

WIDE WORLD

ATLANTIC RICHFIELD COMPANY/COLONY DEVELOPMENT CORPORATION

A seven-story-high retort unit near Grand Valley, Colo., produces crude oil from local deposits of shale.

COLORADO

Colorado could foresee an economic boom in 1974, but was haunted by doubts of what that boom might do to the spectacular mountain vistas which have fueled both its present prosperity and its reputation for the "good life."

Oil Shale. The state has long been believed to hold, in so-called oil shale deposits, more hydrocarbon fuel reserves than the entire Middle East. However, tremendous development and operating costs limited their use to pilot programs. In the wake of the enormous price increases demanded by the cartel of oil-exporting nations, interest in the shale deposits soared. The first of six federal leases to be let for prototype oil shale development programs brought $210.3 million on January 8 from a consortium of Standard Oil Co. of Indiana and Gulf Oil Corp. The second lease, on March 4, was for $117.5 million from the Atlantic Richfield Co.

While some boosters were joyous, environmentalists feared for the land if strip mining of the deposits begins. Farmers also were uneasy, knowing that the industry would require huge amounts of the state's scarce water supplies. State and local officials worried about the schools, roads, and other services needed to support what could be a huge new industry.

Colorado's postwar boom was in trouble from tight money—and sometimes from shortages of resources such as natural gas that resulted from too rapid growth. In Colorado Springs, once one of the nation's fastest-growing areas, building permits in the first nine months of 1974 were only about a third of the 1973 level.

To balance these concerns, Republican Gov. John Vanderhoof pledged to get a land-use bill, with strong state authority, through the Republican Legislature. Aided by state Rep. Richard Lamm (D-Denver), it passed the House, but the more conservative Senate mangled it badly. Governor Vanderhoof salvaged what he could and signed the bill, while Representative Lamm denounced the compromise as too weak.

Election. Representative Lamm then rode the environmental unrest—and the Watergate scandal—to victory over Governor Vanderhoof in the November 5 election, to end a 12-year Republican lease on the state Capitol. Another liberal Democrat, Gary Hart, defeated Republican Peter Dominick in the U. S. Senate contest. Democrats also took the state House of Representatives 39–26, but the Republicans retained a majority, 19–16, in the Senate.

Liberal Democrat Timothy Wirth defeated five-term Republican Congressman Donald Brotzman to give the Democrats in the U. S. House of Representatives a 3–2 majority in this once-Republican state. Lt. Gov. George Brown became the highest elected black official in Colorado.

Referendums. Voters, in a referred referendum, readopted the death penalty, though its ultimate use depends on federal court rulings.

Worried about Atomic Energy Commission underground nuclear explosions in Colorado designed to stimulate natural gas production, voters passed a referendum requiring future blasts to be submitted to a vote of the people. Two constitutional amendments designed to stop racially mixed Denver from annexing largely white suburban counties also were approved.

Busing. After years of bitter resistance, Denver began court-ordered busing of school children for racial balance. Despite some initial resistance, the city was spared the violence that hit some Eastern cities.

BOB EWEGEN, *The Denver "Post"*

COLORADO • Information Highlights

Area: 104,247 square miles (270,000 sq km).
Population (1973 est.): 2,437,000.
Chief Cities (1970 census): Denver, the capital, 514,678; Colorado Springs, 135,060; Pueblo, 97,453.
Government (1974): *Chief Officers*—governor, John D. Vanderhoof (R); acting lt. gov., Ted L. Strickland (R). *General Assembly*—Senate, 35 members; House of Representatives, 65 members.
Education (1973–74): *Enrollment*—public elementary schools, 305,916 pupils; public secondary, 268,396; nonpublic, 33,800; colleges and universities, 131,189 students. *Public school expenditures,* $572,545,000 ($1,075 per pupil).
State Finances (fiscal year 1973): *Revenues,* $1,450,892,000; *expenditures,* $1,229,856,000.
Personal Income (1973): $12,298,000,000; per capita, $5,046.
Labor Force (July 1974): *Nonagricultural wage and salary earners,* 915,200; *insured unemployed,* 8,200 (1.1%).

COMMONWEALTH OF NATIONS

The Commonwealth of Nations appeared to draw closer together in 1974, largely as a result of the heads of governments meeting held in Ottawa in August 1973.

Commonwealth Relations. Grenada, an associated state since 1967, became the 34th full member of the Commonwealth on achieving independence under Prime Minister Eric Gairy on Feb. 7, 1974. Also, Papua New Guinea announced that it would seek complete independence from Australia.

Relations with Rhodesia showed no improvement during the year. The attitude of Britain's Labour government, elected in February and re-elected in October, was summarized by Prime Minister Harold Wilson on July 4, when he said there would be no consideration of any deal with the Rhodesian regime until the British government knew that Rhodesian government proposals were approved by the majority of the Rhodesian population.

Nor was any progress made with the Ugandan government of Gen. Idi Amin. Exemplifying the situation was another warning from Amin on June 5 that all Britons would be expelled in two days if Britain did not stop disseminating "unfounded propaganda." On June 7, however, Amin said he would give Britain "one more chance," but he nevertheless banned all "imperialist" newspapers, including four London papers and all the Kenyan ones, on June 8.

The recognition of Bangladesh by Pakistan on February 22 opened the way to an agreement between India, Pakistan, and Bangladesh following a meeting of their foreign ministers in Delhi in April. Leading as it did to the repatriation of Pakistani prisoners held in India since 1971, the agreement opened the way to more normal relations between the two countries.

In mid-December, Malta became the 19th republic within the Commonwealth. Governor General Sir Anthony Mamo took office as president.

Colombo Plan. The 23d meeting of the Colombo Plan consultative committee met in Wellington, New Zealand, in late 1973, when Papua New Guinea was admitted as a full member. The committee's report on technical cooperation showed that Australia, Britain, Canada, Japan, New Zealand, and the United States had contributed $1.85 billion between 1950 and early 1973. Under the plan, 87,314 students from southeast Asia had been able to study abroad, and 16,783 experts and advisers and about $600 million in technical equipment had been provided to the area.

Economic Aid. Statistics on Britain's overseas aid in 1972 showed that Commonwealth countries received £217 million ($518,000,000) in aid during that year. New loan commitments totalled £139.3 million ($332,500,000), of which 71% was interest-free.

COMMONWEALTH OF NATIONS

Component	Area (sq mi)	Pop. (mid-1973 estimate)	Status
EUROPE			
Great Britain & islands of British seas[1]	94,526	56,113,000	Sovereign state
Gibraltar	2	27,000	Dependent territory
Malta	122	322,000	Sovereign state
Total in Europe	94,650	56,462,000	
AFRICA			
Botswana	231,804	650,000	Sovereign state
British Indian Ocean Territory	30	2,000	Dependent territory
Gambia	4,361	493,000	Sovereign state
Ghana	92,099	9,360,000	Sovereign state
Kenya	224,959	12,480,000	Sovereign state
Lesotho	11,720	994,000	Sovereign state
Malawi	45,747	4,800,000	Sovereign state
Mauritius (and dependencies)	809	870,000	Sovereign state
Nigeria	356,668	59,600,000	Sovereign state
Rhodesia	150,803	5,900,000	Internally self-governing colony[2]
St. Helena	47	5,000	Dependent territory
Ascension	34	1,000	
Tristan da Cunha	40	300	
Other islands	41	......	
Seychelles	145	60,000	Dependent territory
Sierra Leone	27,700	2,860,000	Sovereign state
Swaziland	6,704	460,000	Sovereign state
Tanzania	364,899	14,400,000	Sovereign state
Uganda	91,134	10,810,000	Sovereign state
Zambia	290,585	4,700,000	Sovereign state
Total in Africa	1,900,329	128,445,300	
AMERICA			
Antigua	171	74,000	West Indies Associated state
Bahamas	5,380	193,000	Sovereign state
Barbados	166	243,000	Sovereign state
Belize (British Honduras)	8,867	132,000	Dependent territory
Bermuda	20	60,000	Dependent territory
British Virgin Islands	59	12,000	Dependent territory
Canada	3,851,809	22,130,000	Sovereign state
Cayman Islands	100	11,000	Dependent territory
Dominica	290	73,000	West Indies Associated state
Falkland Islands (and dependencies)	6,198	2,500	Dependent territory
Grenada	133	100,000	Sovereign state
Guyana	83,000	760,000	Sovereign state
Jamaica	4,232	1,980,000	Sovereign state
Montserrat	38	12,000	Dependent territory
St. Kitts-Nevis-Anguilla	138	70,000	West Indies Associated state
St. Lucia	238	110,000	West Indies Associated state
St. Vincent	150	91,000	West Indies Associated state
Trinidad and Tobago	1,980	1,060,000	Sovereign state
Turks and Caicos	166	6,000	Dependent territory
Total in America	3,963,135	27,119,500	
ASIA			
Bangladesh	55,126	71,620,000	Sovereign state
Brunei	2,226	145,000	Internally self-governing sultanate
Cyprus	3,572	660,000	Sovereign state
Hong Kong	399	4,160,000	Dependent territory
India	1,266,598	574,200,000	Sovereign state
Malaysia	127,316	11,610,000	Sovereign state
Singapore	224	2,190,000	Sovereign state
Sri Lanka (Ceylon)	25,332	13,250,000	Sovereign state
Total in Asia	1,480,793	677,855,000	
OCEANIA			
Australia	2,967,900	13,270,000	Sovereign state
Christmas Island	52	3,000	External territory
Cocos Islands	5	1,000	External territory
Norfolk Island	14	2,000	External territory
Papua New Guinea	178,260	2,563,000	External territory
British Solomon Islands Protectorate	10,983	179,000	Dependent territory
Fiji	7,055	551,000	Sovereign state
Gilbert and Ellice Islands	342	63,000	Dependent territory
Nauru[3]	8	7,000	Sovereign state
New Hebrides	5,700	90,000	Anglo-French condominium
New Zealand	103,736	2,970,000	Sovereign state
Niue Island	100	5,000	Self-governing in association with New Zealand
Tokelau Islands	4	2,000	Dependency
Pitcairn Island	2	100	Dependent territory
Tonga	270	92,000	Sovereign state
Western Samoa	1,097	152,000	Sovereign state
Total in Oceania	3,275,528	19,950,100	
Grand Total[4]	10,714,435	909,831,900	

[1] Includes Northern Ireland, Channel Islands, and Isle of Man. [2] Rhodesia declared its independence Nov. 11, 1965, but technically retains Commonwealth status. [3] Nauru is a special member. [4] Does not include British Antarctic Territory, Australian Antarctic Territory, or Ross Dependency (New Zealand).

Among development loans arranged during 1974 were £33 million ($78,800,000) to India, announced on February 1, and £400,000 ($955,000) toward the construction of the Tarbela Dam in Pakistan, announced in March.

The annual report of the Commonwealth Development Corporation for 1973 showed that the corporation was operating 233 projects in 40 countries, five of them outside the Commonwealth. The corporation's estimated investment commitment at the beginning of 1974 was £243.5 million ($581,300,000), some £41.1 million ($98,100,000) more than at the beginning of 1973.

Commonwealth Meetings. Among the many meetings in 1974 were a meeting of senior officials in London in May; a conference of financial experts in London in June to study a proposal by Kenya and Jamaica for a new financial or investment institution; and a meeting of finance ministers in the Canadian capital of Ottawa in September to increase cooperation in checking the international inflation that threatens disaster for the poorer nations.

Royal Tour. Queen Elizabeth II made a series of visits to the Pacific and Southeast Asia from January 28 to March 23. Included in the tour was Indonesia, to which Queen Elizabeth paid the first state visit ever made by a British monarch.

RICHARD E. WEBB
Former Director, Reference and Library Division, British Information Services, New York

CONNECTICUT

In 1974, Connecticut became the first state in the country to elect a woman as governor in her own right. Ella Grasso led a Democratic sweep in the November elections. Tax cuts, the energy crisis, and election law reform were among Connecticut's major concerns.

Legislature. The General Assembly passed a $1.382 billion budget for fiscal 1974–75. The sales tax was reduced ½% to 6% and eliminated on utility bills, and the elderly were given some tax relief. A $300 bonus was provided for World War I veterans, and tuition was waived entirely at state colleges for veterans and persons over 62. State grants to public schools were increased from $215 to $250 per pupil.

As in many other states following the Watergate scandals, Connecticut enacted campaign financing reforms. Political committees and candidates were required to disclose all campaign contributions and expenditures. Individual campaign contributions were limited to a maximum of $5,000, and cash contributions in excess of $50 were prohibited. Ceilings were placed on campaign expenditures for various state and local offices. Primaries for all state and district offices were consolidated. A State Elections Commission was created to investigate violations of state election laws.

Retail gasoline dealers were prohibited from charging more than the posted price or requiring tie-in purchases. Illegal creation of fuel shortages was forbidden, and an Energy Agency was established and given power to institute civil actions against violators. An Office of Consumer Counsel was established within the Public Utilities Commission.

Elections. Gov. Thomas J. Meskill announced on March 11 that he would not seek reelection. President Nixon recommended him for a judgeship on the United States Court of Appeals for the Second Circuit on August 8. But the appointment was opposed at Senate hearings, and Meskill's confirmation remained uncertain.

The Democratic party united following the July 20 nomination of Congresswoman Ella T. Grasso for governor and Attorney General Robert K. Killian for lieutenant governor. With 69% of the electorate voting, Mrs. Grasso defeated her Republican opponent, Congressman Robert H. Steele, by a 200,000-vote plurality. She will become the first woman governor in the United States in her own right, rather than by succeeding her husband.

U. S. Sen. Abraham Ribicoff (D) was reelected to a third term by a 314,000-vote plurality. The Democrats picked up an additional House seat, with the Connecticut delegation to the new Congress consisting of four Democrats and two Republicans. Among the Democrats elected were Christopher J. Dodd, the son of former Sen. Thomas J. Dodd, and Anthony (Toby) Moffett, former director of the Nader-connected Connecticut Citizen Action Group. The Democrats also regained control of the General Assembly, winning 29 seats to 7 for the Republicans in the State Senate and 118 seats to 33 in the House.

Courts and Corrections. The State Supreme Court on July 23 upheld the Superior Court ruling that Circuit Court sentences exceeding one year were unconstitutional, leading to the release of 140 prisoners. A 1974 reorganization act merged the Circuit Court into the Court of Common Pleas. In November, Connecticut became the first state to adopt United Nations

CONNECTICUT • Information Highlights

Area: 5,009 square miles (12,973 sq km).
Population (1973 est.): 3,076,000. *Density*: 633 per sq mi.
Chief Cities (1970 census): Hartford, the capital, 158,-017; Bridgeport, 156,542; New Haven, 137,707.
Government (1974): *Chief Officers*—governor, Thomas J. Meskill (R); lt. gov., Peter L. Cashman (R). *General Assembly*—Senate, 36 members; House of Representatives, 151 members.
Education (1973–74): *Enrollment*—public elementary schools, 469,720 pupils; public secondary, 196,550; nonpublic, 104,300; colleges and universities, 135,-250 students. *Public school expenditures,* $795,-770,000 ($1,295 per pupil).
State Finances (fiscal year 1973): *Revenues,* $1,926,-301,000; *expenditures,* $1,830,057,000.
Personal Income (1973): $18,114,000,000; per capita, $5,889.
Labor Force (July 1974): *Nonagricultural wage and salary earners,* 1,279,400; *insured unemployed,* 54,-700 (4.5%).

UPI

Ella Grasso, new Democratic governor of Connecticut, is the first woman to be elected governor of a U. S. state without having been preceded in the job by her husband.

standards for humane treatment of prisoners. State police began using .357 magnum revolvers in July. There was criticism of their use and especially of the hollow-point dumdum bullets, which are banned for military use.

Economy. Unemployment stood at 7%, with 101,000 persons out of work in July. The construction industry was hardest hit, having declined 50%. The U. S. Labor Department allotted $6 million to Connecticut to create public service jobs.

Gross state product, however, was at an all time high of $21.7 billion in 1973, and per capita personal income remained first among the states at $5,889. Connecticut ranked third among the states with $2.6 billion in value of prime defense procurement contracts.

Higher Education. Dr. Oakes Ames was inaugurated as the seventh president of Connecticut College, succeeding Charles E. Shain who resigned. Undergraduate professional school enrollment at the University of Connecticut increased 31%, and enrollment at the 12 community colleges in the state increased by 16.5%. The poor economy and lack of jobs were factors in this increase.

Environment. New Haven beaches on Long Island Sound were coated with 42,000 gallons of crude oil when a tanker scraped bottom in New Haven harbor on October 6. A contract was signed for construction of a solid waste recovery system for the Bridgeport area.

GEORGE ADAMS, *Connecticut State Library*

CONSUMERISM

The economy was the principal problem for American consumers in 1974. Although Congress again failed to pass a bill that would establish a consumer protection agency, consumerism continued to be an important governmental concern.

Inflation. The major U. S. consumer problem of 1974 was double-digit inflation, the country's worst inflation since the end of World War II. The Consumer Price Index jumped from 136.6 in October 1973 to 153.2 in October 1974. During that 12-month period prices rose more than 12%.

President Ford declared inflation to be Public Enemy Number One. His WIN (Whip Inflation Now) slogan received wide publicity. Newspapers, magazines, radio, and television gave all kinds of suggestions on how to WIN and how to shop more prudently. A full page ad in a Chicago newspaper stated, "Don't buy sugar." Instead of buying sugar at $.50 a pound, the ad suggested buying sugar substitutes at $.10 to $.15 a pound. Extreme advice to consumers was simply, "Don't buy." From an unknown source came the following advice on how to make ends meet: Waste not; Want not; Use it up; Wear it out; Make it do, or Do without. These last few suggestions were not particularly satisfying or helpful to a society that has grown accustomed to affluency.

Legislative Action. The Consumer Protection Agency bill, also known as the Agency for Consumer Advocacy bill, was the key consumer measure considered by Congress during 1974. After being passed overwhelmingly in the House of Representatives, it was blocked by a filibuster in the Senate. But with the changes in the make-up of the new Congress for 1975, it appeared that this bill or a stronger version would have an excellent chance of passing. The 1974 bill would have created an independent agency to represent consumers in practically all government regulatory proceedings. The new agency would have had the right to prod, if not take to court, governmental agencies that are not fulfilling their responsibilities to consumers in enforcing the laws.

Little significant consumer legislation was passed by Congress in 1974. Many consumer bills were introduced, but practically all failed to pass. President Ford signed a bill that increased the federal insurance protection on accounts in both commercial and thrift (savings and loan) institutions from $20,000 to $40,000. The same law gave consumers greater protection against credit billing errors and credit card mistakes. A major feature of the new law was that it banned bias against women in credit transactions. Consumer reaction against the automobile interlock system, introduced with the 1975 models, was so great that Congress voted to end the requirement for this safety feature.

Federal Regulatory Action. Two important regulations issued by the Federal Trade Commission went into effect in 1974. One regulated door-to-door sales of consumer goods or services costing $25 or more. The customer must be told and given in writing the information that there is a three-day "cooling-off" period during which time the buyer has the right to cancel the contract without penalty or fee by notifying the seller. The other regulation dealt with the "negative option" method of selling by mail such items as books and records through "clubs." This regulation required fuller and more explicit information on promotional material, and gave the "club member" additional protection from abuses.

The Consumer Product Safety Commission (CPSC) issued regulations in 1974 for reporting product defects. The new regulations required manufacturers, distributors, importers, and retailers to notify the commission within 24 hours if they have information that would reasonably support the conclusion that a product defect could create a substantial risk of injury to consumers.

CPSC received a great deal of publicity in the spring when it issued a ban on practically all fireworks. But the ban did not go into effect by the Fourth of July holiday because of a request for hearings that had to be held before the regulation could take effect. It was anticipated that by July 4, 1975, most fireworks that were not banned under the Child Protection Act of 1966 will be banned by CPSC. The commission established a toll-free number to answer inquiries anyone might have about product safety. Concerned consumers should call 1-800-638-2666.

The U. S. Department of Agriculture (USDA) issued regulations on voluntary open-dating of meat and poultry. The date stamped on the product will have to indicate whether it is the "package date," "sell by date," or "use before date." A controversial proposal of USDA would make it possible for slightly leaner beef to qualify for the top grades, make the "eating quality" of beef within each grade more nearly uniform, establish a more restrictive "good" grade, and require that all beef graded for quality also be graded for "yield" (percentage of retail cuts). Consumer advocates were concerned since this proposal would allow more of the former "good" grade to be graded upward to the "choice" grade and be sold at the higher "choice" prices. Thus, the consumer would be paying more for lower quality meat.

Universal Product Code. The introduction of electronic scanners and the use of the Universal Product Code (UPC) at checkout counters in supermarkets has become a major area for discussion and debate among consumers, the business community, and the government. UPC is a series of thin black bars on a label that has ten numbers right below the bars. The first five numbers represent the manufacturer or distributor, and the last five numbers represent the specific product and package which carries that number.

Electronic scanners will be installed at checkout counters in participating stores. These scanners will be able to read the bars and then print out on the tape the name of the product, its price, and any other information that is deemed desirable by the seller. This revolutionary change at checkout counters is being introduced because it will reduce costs, make possible much better control of inventory, be much more accurate, and will avoid both the overcharges and undercharges that happen when prices are rung manually. But the system poses a key problem for the consumer because the price will not appear on the package itself, only on the shelf of the store.

Who Speaks for Consumers? One of the controversies among businesses, consumer advocates, and the government is the question of who speaks for consumers. Do all consumers speak with one voice? The automobile safety interlock system had consumer advocates on both sides. Those whose greatest concern was safety did not want to see the law repealed. Those who were concerned with the added cost and inconvenience of the system wanted the law repealed. Then there were those who believed it was too much of an intrusion by the government into one's private life.

Another clash among consumer advocates and between consumer advocates and businesses focused on a defeated bill that would have required that all new radios be capable of both AM and FM reception. Naturally, the owners of FM radio stations were heartily in favor of this bill. Consumer advocates were on both sides of the bill.

Those in favor said that it was necessary to stimulate FM stations and thereby give consumers a wider selection of stations from which to choose. Also, it would be more economical to produce all radios with both AM and FM reception. Those opposed said that a consumer should have the right to decide whether he wants AM only, FM only, or AM and FM, and that he should not be forced to pay a higher price for something he did not want to buy.

There was little doubt that the debate will continue for many years over what is good for the consumer, what the consumer wants, what consumer advocates think consumers want, what business likes to believe consumers want, and what government thinks consumers want. The basic debate seems to revolve around the question of whether the primary purpose of the marketplace is to serve consumers or to serve the various sellers.

See also ECONOMY OF THE U. S.; INDUSTRIAL REVIEW.

STEWART M. LEE
Geneva College

CRIME

Statistics released in 1974 concerning crime in the United States indicate beyond argument that serious violations of the law will not decrease merely as a consequence of the infusion of vast sums of money into law enforcement efforts. Crime, the statistics strongly suggest, is caused by fundamental characteristics of the society, and will be reduced only when basic changes occur in people's attitudes and in the social structure.

This point is well-documented by the striking contrast between crime rates in Tokyo and those in New York City. The Japanese capital, whose 11.6 million people make it the world's most populous city, had 196 murders in 1973. New York, with a population of about 8 million, recorded 1,680 murders—nearly nine times as many. New York had 3,735 reported rapes, Tokyo 426; and New York's 82,731 reported auto thefts contrasted with 3,550 for Tokyo. Writing in the New York *Times,* Sydney Schanberg offered the following explanations for these different figures:

"The gun control and drug laws in Japan are severe, and they are enforced by an efficient police force. Public respect for law and authority is traditionally strong. Arrest is a deep disgrace both for oneself and for one's family. The level of education is high. Unemployment is low. The country is ethnically and culturally homogeneous." In addition, Schanberg observed, the Japanese people have developed an ability to deal with the stresses associated with dense population, and they have deep respect for the privacy of their neighbors.

Foot patrols are characteristic of police work in Tokyo, and every few city blocks has a *koban,* or police booth, manned by one to a dozen men who patrol the neighborhood constantly. Each *koban* policeman is responsible for about 150 households, and is required to visit each of these households at least twice a year and forward to police headquarters information on the occupants of the household and what they do to earn their living.

Crime in the United States. In the United States, more than $3.2 billion has been pumped into law enforcement efforts through the federal Law Enforcement Assistance Administration (LEAA) since 1968. The failure of these subsidies to reduce crime rates was underscored in a 1974 *Uniform Crime Report,* issued by the Federal Bureau of Investigation. The final figures for 1973, the report noted, showed a 6% increase in serious crimes—the total of all reported homicides, forcible rapes, assaults, burglaries, robberies, larcenies of more than $50, and auto thefts. This 6% rise contrasted with a 4% decrease in 1972, and it included a 16% increase during the last quarter of 1973. In addition, for the first six months of 1974, serious crimes went up another 16%. Commenting on these figures, Attorney General William Saxbe declared them to represent "a failure of substantial dimension—harsh, bitter, and dismaying." The attorney general noted that "we have lost our initiative and are back on the defensive" in the effort to control crime, a situation which he in part blamed on "too many grandiose promises and too much patchwork performance in Washington."

In addition to his observations about crime statistics, Saxbe unloosed a series of attacks on conventional wisdom about crime and its control. In early October, for instance, he described rehabilitation by use of prison, probation, and parole programs as a "myth." "We have been operating on a premise that we can't substantiate," Attorney General Saxbe maintained. His view, the *Wall Street Journal* noted editorially, seemed "as shocking almost as if the Senate chaplain were to pooh-pooh the efficacy of prayer." Nonetheless, the *Journal* noted, "There seems to be growing evidence in support of the Attorney General's iconoclastic opinion," and it argued that "what many well-meaning people overlook is that despite occasional injustices the typical prison inmate is not some erring schoolboy but a hardened criminal who wound up in prison only after repeated violations, usually long after society would have been justified in removing him from the streets." It is time, the *Journal* editorial writer thought, that the individual, rather than society, be held responsible for antisocial conduct.

Saxbe's outspoken views also took in the subject of white-collar crime, a matter of considerable national concern in the wake of the Watergate scandals. In an October 4 speech, the attorney general said that "the white-collar criminal, the price fixer, the income tax evader have something in common—they mock the criminal justice system and they sneer at our most cherished values." Saxbe emphasized that white-collar criminals must be put in prison, that "they are no better than the car thief or the burglar or robber. They are all members of the same fraternity."

President Ford on Crime. The same apparent frustration that led the attorney general to look for new solutions to combat the rising crime rate appeared to be behind President Ford's message on crime in September before the International Association of Chiefs of Police (IACP). Ford stressed that efforts ought not to be concentrated on crime in general but rather on taking "career criminals out of circulation." He suggested that most crime is the work of a limited number of hardened criminals and insisted that it was necessary to make such persons understand that "swift and prolonged punishment will inevitably follow each offense."

Unreported Crime. During his IACP speech, the President also observed that nearly half of the victims of assault and robbery and 80% of

WIDE WORLD

During a shoot-out at a suspected Symbionese Liberation Army hideout in Los Angeles in May, a panic-stricken mother herds her children to safety.

HEARST KIDNAPPING

The kidnapping by the so-called Symbionese Liberation Army of 19-year-old Patricia Hearst of the newspaper publishing family competed for headlines with Watergate in much of 1974. Though her father paid a ransom of $2 million worth of food for the poor of the San Francisco–Oakland area, it appeared that the girl had joined the SLA. She was still missing at year-end.

UPI

(*Left*) Patty Hearst and her fiancé, Steven A. Weed, posed happily in 1972. Both were students at the University of California, Berkeley. (*Below*) The girl's parents, Mr. and Mrs. Randolph Hearst, face newsmen in February.

UPI

the victims of petty larceny fail to report these incidents to the police. Ford's figures were based on a survey conducted in the nation's five largest cities—New York, Los Angeles, Chicago, Detroit, and Philadelphia—by the LEAA and the Census Bureau as part of a continuing $10 million-a-year project to measure levels of crime more precisely. The extent of unreported crime, according to Donald E. Santarelli, at the time the head of LEAA, conveys "a strong message of public apathy . . . bordering on contempt toward criminal justice agencies." The survey was based on questions to 25,000 households and 10,000 businesses. Of those who did not report crime against their persons, 34% said that it was because of lack of proof or because they felt that nothing could be done about the matter. Twenty-eight percent did not consider the crime important enough to report it, while others said that they did not want to be bothered, it was a personal matter, it was too inconvenient, or they were afraid of reprisal.

Among the more surprising findings of the five-city survey was that New York City, which has a reputation as an extremely unsafe place, had less violent crime than any of the other four of the largest American cities. Experts argued that the New York reputation was exaggerated because crime figures in the other cities, most notably in Philadelphia, were, among other things, sometimes falsified for political reasons.

Murder. The surveys of unreported crime did not include the offense of murder because, relatively speaking, few such events occur, and most are presumed to be reported to the police. A survey on murder, completed in April by Arnold Barnett, a mathematician at the Massachusetts Institute of Technology, however, provided ominous conclusions about its incidence. According to Barnett, a male born in 1974 in any of the 50 largest cities in the United States has a 3% chance of being murdered during his lifetime. Barnett noted, for instance, that while approximately 250 residents of Atlanta were murdered in 1973—and that this total seems small compared with the nearly 500,000 persons not murdered—"few persons realize that, if this rate continues, homicide will be the cause of death of roughly one of every 27 Atlantans."

Crime by Women. Crime statistics also indicate a disproportionate increase in serious offenses by women, with a change from traditional illegal acts by females, such as prostitution and shoplifting, to armed robbery, grand larceny, and other so-called "masculine" offenses. In Denver, for instance, the female arrest figures almost doubled between 1967 (2,391 arrests) and 1973 (4,308 arrests). Nationwide, during the past decade, the rate of female arrests for serious crime has increased about 250% compared with a rise of about 90% for men. The increase is most notable in property crimes.

Rising crime among women, Gerald Caplan, director of the National Institute of Law Enforcement and Criminal Justice, has observed, "is the dark side of the women's movement. As women take on an enlarged and equal role in society as a whole it's not surprising that they show up more frequently on police blotters."

Crime Abroad. Statistics indicate that an increase in crime is a worldwide phenomenon, though few countries have the kinds of rates recorded in the United States. A report from Australia by Paul Wilson, a sociologist at the University of Queensland, published in the *Current Affairs Bulletin* in June, notes that "the most disturbing trend in major crime in Australia over the past few years has been the increase in a most frightening form of violence—motiveless assaults and street bashing." Wilson also reports a doubling of the number of serious assaults in Australia over the past decade.

In France, Michel Poniatowski, the minister of the interior, in June began extensive street spot-checks on identity cards in a program labeled "Operation Fist." The effort was initiated in the face of an increase in holdups of 28 times over the past ten years. "Criminals in 1974," the minister noted, "have all the sources of modern technology, efficient arms, fast cars, and radios. They don't hesitate to take hostages to murder and torture." Most French citizens approved of Operation Fist, a survey by *Le Point,* a weekly newsmagazine, indicated, with 89% saying that the inconvenience to law-abiding citizens was either negligible or acceptable.

In the People's Republic of China, according to a Washington *Post* report from Peking, an upswing in "hooliganism," apparently caused by resentment among youngsters regarding forced work in rural areas, has led to street patrols by groups of men and women "carrying menacing-looking nightsticks and flashlights, doing their best to combat a burgeoning wave of street crime."

Crime in the News. By far the most sensational criminal event of the year (aside from the Watergate scandals) centered about the activities of the Symbionese Liberation Army, a terrorist organization operating in California. On February 4, SLA members kidnapped Patricia Hearst, the 19-year-old daughter of Randolph A. Hearst, a multimillionaire newspaper owner. While the police and her parents sought to obtain her release, Miss Hearst was apparently persuaded by her abductors to join with them in the daylight robbery on April 15 of a Hibernia Bank branch office in San Francisco. On May 17, six of the SLA members died during a shoot-out with the Los Angeles police and federal law enforcement officers after they were discovered hiding out in a house in Los Angeles. Miss Hearst was not among those in the house, and at year's end she and Emily and William Harris, who were apparently with her in Los Angeles, continued to evade continued police attempts to capture them.

GILBERT GEIS
University of California, Irvine

UPI

Cuban Prime Minister Fidel Castro is flanked by U. S. Senators Claiborne Pell (*left*) and Jacob Javits during the lawmakers' brief visit to Havana in September.

CUBA

The year 1974 was an auspicious one for the Cuban government of Premier Fidel Castro as limited moves were made toward rapprochement with the United States, new diplomatic and economic ties with other Latin American nations further loosened the island nation's isolation, and increased sugar production brought substantially increased revenues.

Sugar. In 1974 the production of sugar, the island's largest export, was estimated at approximately 6 million tons, an increase of more than 1 million tons from the previous year. With the world price of sugar exceeding 40 cents per pound in the latter part of the year, Cuba was expected to reap some $1.5 billion from sales to other nations (after shipping half of its crop to the Soviet Union).

Foreign Relations. On the diplomatic scene, the most important development in 1974 concerned the United States. Reports from Havana suggested that Soviet leader Leonid Brezhnev, in a visit to Havana, January 28 to February 3, had proposed to Castro that the Cuban government should improve relations with the United States, although Soviet spokesmen later issued denials.

On June 29, the staff director of the U. S. Senate Foreign Relations Committee, Pat Holt, arrived in Havana for a 10-day visit, during which Premier Castro reportedly told him that he would be willing to meet with Secretary of State Kissinger. Diplomatic sources reported that U. S. and Cuban officials had met secretly in Switzerland to work out differences between the two nations, but Washington did not confirm this. On September 27, U. S. Senators Jacob Javits and Claiborne Pell flew to Havana for a three-day stay during which they held "frank, warm and friendly" discussions with Castro. As a goodwill gesture, Castro subsequently freed four Americans who had been held in jail in Cuba.

Cuba also strengthened its ties with other Latin American nations when Panama in August became the seventh country in the Latin bloc to restore diplomatic relations. However, on November 12 the Western Hemisphere foreign ministers at a meeting of the Organization of American States failed by a two-vote margin to end the economic and diplomatic sanctions voted against Cuba in 1964. The United States abstained, as did five other countries.

Economy. Economically, Cuba continued to make progress in 1974. Argentine-Cuban trade reached the $600 million level, leading to a reluctant agreement by the United States government to allow Argentine subsidiaries of American automobile companies to sell more than 40,000 vehicles to Cuba, a breach of the United States trade embargo of the island. In March, a Canadian corporation partially owned by an American firm agreed to sell $17.9 million of locomotives to Cuba.

Elections. Cuba held its first elections in more than 15 years, but only in the province of Matanzas. More than 4,000 candidates, so-called "delegates to popular power assemblies," were selected in late June, according to Cuban officials. Subsequent elections are reportedly to be held to elect regional executive committees, which would govern the province. Government spokesmen state that if the Matanzas experiment is successful, elections will be held throughout the island.

LOUIS R. SADLER
New Mexico State University

CUBA • Information Highlights

Official Name: Republic of Cuba.
Location: Caribbean Sea.
Area: 44,218 square miles (114,524 sq km).
Population (1973 est.): 8,900,000.
Chief Cities (1970 census): Havana, the capital, 1,755,400; Santiago de Cuba, 276,000; Camagüey, 196,900.
Government: *Head of state,* Osvaldo Dorticos Torrade, president (took office July 1959). *Head of government,* Fidel Castro Ruz, premier (took office Feb. 1959).
Monetary Unit: Peso (0.80 peso equals U. S.$1, Sept. 1974).
Gross National Product (1970 est.): $4,500,000,000.
Manufacturing (major products): Sugar products, tobacco products.
Major Agricultural Products: Sugarcane, tobacco, rice, oranges and tangerines, sweet potatoes and yams.
Foreign Trade (1972): *Exports,* $803,000,000; *imports,* $1,292,000,000.

CYPRUS. See special feature on pages 62–67.

CZECHOSLOVAKIA

The year 1974 was a relatively uneventful one for Czechoslovakia, both in domestic and foreign affairs. While the Prague regime continued to adhere to Soviet-style orthodoxy at home, it persevered in its efforts to improve relations with the West and thus to gain better access to Western markets and technology.

Party and Government. A minor change occurred in the central government in December 1973 when the Ministry of Metallurgy and Engineering was divided into two ministries, one for metallurgy and heavy engineering, headed by Josef Šimon, and one for general engineering, headed by Pavel Bahyl. A reshuffle took place in the Ministry of Finance where Leopold Leer replaced Rudolf Rohlíček, who became deputy premier and permanent representative to COMECON.

In March, Ludvík Svoboda became too ill to perform his duties as president of Czechoslovakia. The possibility of his death presented the party leadership with a delicate issue of succession. Svoboda's partial recovery permitted the regime to sidestep the thorny problem for the time being.

Economy. By mid-1974 the following percentage increases over the corresponding period of 1973 were registered in Czechoslovakia's economy: industrial production, 6.2% (with the highest increment of 9% in metallurgy and engineering goods); consumer goods, 4.9%; food industry, 3.9%; construction, 7.3%; freight transportation, 2.8%; cattle, 1.5%, and pigs, 7.8%; retail trade, 8.3%; exports, 20.4% (10% to socialist and 35% to nonsocialist countries); imports, 32.9% (19% from socialist and 52.7% from nonsocialist countries); labor productivity in industry, 5.4%, and in construction, 5.5%; and monetary income of the population, 4.7%.

While these results were characterized as being satisfactory, a "substantial number" of enterprises were criticized by the government for "unevenness" in their performance and other shortcomings. As usual, the worst results were attained in the field of residential construction, which fulfilled its goals by only 39% by mid-1974.

EASTFOTO

In March the aging Ludvík Svoboda became too ill to perform his duties as president of Czechoslovakia. By the end of the year he had only partially recovered.

Foreign Affairs. The improvement in United States-Czechoslovak relations that began in 1973 continued in 1974. Under an agreement initialed on July 5, 1974, Czechoslovakia agreed to pay compensation for U. S. property nationalized following the 1948 Communist coup and for the defaulted Czechoslovak government debt. The United States, in turn, promised to compensate Czechoslovakia for an undelivered steel mill paid for in advance and to release 18,400 kilograms of gold belonging to Czechoslovakia as its share of the gold seized by the Nazis in eastern Europe during World War II and recovered by the Allies. The gold is worth about $80 million on the free market.

On July 19, the Czechoslovak-West German treaty on the nullification of the Munich agreement came into force with the solemn exchange of ratification documents in Bonn.

Prague's University of Seventeenth November, founded in 1961 for the education of students from developing countries, closed at the end of its 1973–74 academic year.

EDWARD TABORSKY
The University of Texas at Austin

— CZECHOSLOVAKIA • Information Highlights —

Location: East central Europe.
Area: 49,370 square miles (127,869 sq km).
Population (1973 est.): 15,000,000.
Chief Cities (1970 census): Prague, the capital, 1,078,096; Brno, 335,918; Bratislava, 283,539.
Government: *Head of state,* Ludvík Svoboda, president (took office 1968). *Head of government,* Lubomir Strougal, premier (took office 1970). *Communist party secretary general,* Gustav Husak (took office 1969). *Legislature*—Federal Assembly: Chamber of Nations and Chamber of the People.
Monetary Unit: Koruna (5.2 koruny equal U. S.$1, July 1974).
Gross National Product (1973 est.): $35,300,000,000.
Manufacturing (major products): Machinery, chemicals, petroleum products, glass, textiles, iron, steel.
Major Agricultural Products: Rye, oats, sugar beets.
Foreign Trade (1973): *Exports,* $6,569,000,000; *imports,* $6,449,000,000.

DALLAS

Dallas and its region continued to grow and prosper in 1974. The city population passed 900,000, and the county had nearly 1,400,000 residents. The recently created Dallas–Fort Worth standard metropolitan statistical area, with an estimated population of nearly 2,500,000 persons, moved up to 10th largest in the nation from its previous 12th position.

Economy. The Dallas unemployment rate fluctuated between 2.6% and 3.0%, less than half the national norm and only a third that of many large U. S. cities. The local cost-of-living index climbed 10.6% during the year—a rate lower than the national average. The fuel crisis of the winter and spring affected Dallas less than other major cities.

The July opening of the World Trade Center was the highlight of another busy year of commercial and residential construction. This seven-story, 1.4 million-square-foot edifice, dedicated by then Vice President Gerald Ford, established the Dallas Market Center as the largest single-site facility in the world.

The Dallas World Trade Center is dedicated in the building's seven-story atrium. The center is the world's largest wholesale merchandise mart on a single site.

DALLAS CHAMBER OF COMMERCE

Airport. The much-heralded Dallas–Fort Worth Regional Airport opened to passenger and cargo service in January. Early difficulties with the people-mover system, known as Airtrans, were resolved by mid-year, but unfavorable publicity still lingered on. The airport served an estimated 8 million passengers in its first year of operations. The number of flights per day reached 423, with Braniff and American the most important airlines.

Arts and Literature. The U. S. A. film festival, held March 25–31 at Southern Methodist University, honored Joseph Mankiewicz as the great American director of the year. The October debut of a professional Dallas Civic Ballet was a signal event in the city's development as a cultural center in the Southwest. However, in March the 74-year-old Dallas Symphony Orchestra suspended performances for an indefinite period because of a financial crisis.

The inauguration of *D, The Magazine of Dallas,* brings Dallas into that elite group of American cities with high-quality monthlies dedicated to local affairs. The final significant publishing event of the year was the appearance of Stanley Marcus' *Minding the Store,* an intimate history of Nieman-Marcus, a world-famous Dallas institution.

Sports. The Texas Rangers baseball team emerged as a vigorous and popular pennant contender in 1974, eventually finishing second to Oakland in the Western Division of the American League. Nearly 1,200,000 fans attended their games at Arlington Stadium—an increase of more than half a million over the 1973 season.

Meawhile, Southern Methodist University (SMU) saw its athletic fortunes decline. The National Collegiate Athletic Association placed its football and basketball teams on probation for rule violations regarding payments to athletes. And home attendance plummeted to abysmal levels—less than 15,000 spectators saw the SMU Mustangs football team play their 1974 home opener in the vast Cotton Bowl.

On the professional level, the Dallas Cowboys did not enjoy the success in 1974 that they had in 1973. In October, quarterback Craig Morton was traded to the New York Giants for a future draft choice.

SMU President Resigns. In the wake of these athletic problems and the transfer of the prestigious Southwestern Legal Foundation to the University of Texas at Dallas, Paul Hardin was forced to resign in June as president of Southern Methodist University. He had come to SMU in 1972 with a liberal image and had faced many problems during his short term of office. His "resignation" called into question not only the goals of Southern Methodist University, but also the power of certain prominent businessmen in Dallas life.

ROBERT V. KEMPER and BEN J. WALLACE
Southern Methodist University

MARTHA SWOPE

Frank Augustyn and Karen Kain of the National Ballet of Canada appear in Tchaikovsky's *Sleeping Beauty*.

dance

Politics, economics, and art make strange bedfellows, but they kept frequent company during the 1974 dance year—a year which saw the collapse of one of America's major ballet companies, the defection of one of the Soviet Union's greatest dancers, and the arrival in Israel of Valery and Galina Panov.

Soviet Dancers. Valery Panov, a Jew and a soloist with Leningrad's Kirov Ballet, had applied for permission to emigrate to Israel. He was not only denied exit but was dismissed from his company and prevented from practicing his art. Ultimately granted the visa in June, following a two-year global campaign waged on his behalf, during which the Soviet government cancelled the Kirov Ballet's 1974 tour of America, Panov and his dancer-wife, Galina Ragozina, made their home in Tel Aviv. Their North American debut, originally scheduled for December 10 in Philadelphia, was postponed until 1975.

Another Kirov dancer, Mikhail Baryshnikov, defected to the West in June while appearing as a guest artist with the Bolshoi Ballet in Toronto. Widely regarded as the Soviet Union's finest male classical stylist, Baryshnikov was quickly engaged for guest appearances by the American Ballet Theatre, making his debut on July 27 in New York as Albrecht in *Giselle,* opposite Natalia Makarova, who had defected from the same company four years earlier.

Ballet. Aside from engaging Baryshnikov, the American Ballet Theatre (ABT) appointed Antony Tudor, one of its founding members and choreographers, as associate director to share all future artistic decisions with codirectors Lucia Chase and Oliver Smith. Since ABT's debut in 1940 there has been no season without at least one Tudor ballet; and the 1974 summer season included three: *Jardin aux Lilas, Pillar of Fire,* and *Undertow.*

Other major productions included the first U. S. staging of the *Kingdom of the Shades* from *La Bayadère,* marking Natalia Makarova's debut as an ABT producer, and the third act of *Sleeping Beauty,* mounted by David Blair with sets and costumes by Oliver Smith and Miles White.

The New York City Ballet, suffering from the aftereffects of a recent strike and more than its share of injuries, began the year 1974 on the brink of financial ruin, only to be rescued by an $800,000 conditional grant from the New York State Arts Council on the eve of the season's most controversial new production, Jerome Robbins' *Dybbuk,* with music by Leonard Bernstein. Based on a Hasidic tale of exorcism, *Dybbuk* divided the critics as much as did George Balanchine's *Variations pour une porte et un soupir,* a duet between a female door and a male sigh.

Balanchine also collaborated with Alexandra Danilova on a new staging of *Coppélia,* with the first two acts based on Danilova's remembrances of the Marius Petipa version and the third embracing new Balanchine dances. As in *Dybbuk,* the lead roles were interpreted by Patricia McBride and Helgi Tomassen.

For the first time in its history, the City Center Joffrey Ballet produced no new works during its spring season, injuries and financial difficulties having dictated caution. By fall the company had four new productions: Massine's *Pulcinella,* Gerald Arpino's *The Relativity of*

Icarus, Jonathan Watts' *Evening Dialogues,* and Frederick Ashton's *Monotones.*

The Harkness Ballet also boasted its share of exciting new dancers, but unlike the Joffrey, could not surmount its financial problems. After inaugurating the Rebekah Harkness Theatre on Broadway with a season involving six premieres, it suspended activities. Unless $1 million could be raised by March 31, 1975, the company reportedly would have to disband.

Though the continued existence of the Harkness Ballet remains in doubt, that of the National Ballet of Washington, D. C., is now a matter of history. Codirectors Frederic Franklin and Ben Stevenson, after fighting a long battle to remain solvent, decided to dissolve the company, with Stevenson subsequently signing a three-year contract as director of Ruth Page's Chicago Ballet.

Amid so many reports of near and total collapse, the season was brightened by the birth of an important new company, the Eliot Feld Ballet, which opened its inaugural season on May 28 at the New York Shakespeare Festival Public Theatre with a roster of 18 dancers and a repertory of six Feld ballets, two of them new —*The Tzaddik* and *Sephardic Song.* Acclaimed one of America's most important choreographic talents, Feld was so warmly greeted by the public that his three-week season had to be extended to five. Another season followed in December, introducing yet another Feld ballet, *The Real McCoy.*

Modern Dance. Although Martha Graham provided two new works for her Broadway season, *Chronique* and *Holy Jungle,* 1974 went down in the records primarily as the year in which the 80-year-old first lady of modern dance once again took full charge of her company, revitalizing its dancing.

That other fountainhead of modern dance, Merce Cunningham, spent February and March presenting a series of "events" at various New York locations. Titled *Events 83–115,* these presentations comprised sections of Cunningham dances combined in unannounced ways.

The Brooklyn Academy of Music's hospitality accommodated a number of other choreographers, from Rudy Perez to Paul Taylor, who introduced his first full-length work, *American Genesis,* in March. Taylor's company also presented a season at New York's Alvin Theatre, highlighted by the appearance of the ubiquitous Rudolf Nureyev in *Taylor's Aureola.*

Black Dance. The phenomenon of all or mostly black companies continued to grow, with the Alvin Ailey Dance Company remaining in the forefront in 1974, including new or revived works by two black women choreographers, Janet Colins and Pearl Primus, in its repertoire. Pearl Primus was also decorated with the Star of Africa by the Liberian government.

Arthur Mitchell's Dance Theatre of Harlem, after presenting its first New York season in April, turned out to be a runaway success during its August visit to London.

Visiting Companies. Although the Kirov Ballet's projected tour was cancelled, the Soviet Union did send three units of the Bolshoi Ballet abroad—to England, to Canada, and to the United States—with all of them receiving highly critical reviews and the American-bound stars of the Bolshoi troupe depending heavily on the presence of Maya Plissetskaya.

Britain's Royal Ballet received a much warmer summer reception, if not for Kenneth MacMillan's latest full-length ballet, *Manon,* then certainly for its dancing, including Nureyev's.

Nureyev also headed the cast when the National Ballet of Canada presented John Neumeier's *Don Juan* at the Metropolitan Opera House in a season that saw Erik Bruhn return to the stage in the mime role of the witch Madge in his own production of *La Sylphide.*

Once again the parade of visiting folk or ethnic companies featured Russia's Moiseyev Dance Company, which brought its staging of the dances from *Prince Igor* to America for the first time. In addition to such familiar names as the Royal Swedish Ballet, the Ballet Folklorico of Mexico, Poland's Slask, and the Jamaican Dance Theatre, audiences encountered the Soviet Georgian Dancers and Armenian State Dance Ensemble, both making their North American debuts, as well as the dancers of the Ivory Coast and the Royal Tahitian Dance Company.

Special Events. The tireless Margot Fonteyn, unofficial prima ballerina of British ballet, became the first woman and the first dancer to receive the Benjamin Franklin Medal, awarded by the Royal Society of Arts each year to a citizen of Britain or the United States who has made a notable contribution to the cause of Anglo-American understanding in the fields of arts, industry, or commerce.

Dame Ninette de Valois and Maurice Béjart were jointly awarded the Erasmus Prize by Prince Bernhardt of the Netherlands for their contribution of European culture.

Miscellaneous. In the field of dance journalism, the major event was the first North American Dance Critics Conference, in New York City in June. The largest gathering of dance writers ever assembled, with more than 100 present, the conference voted the Dance Critics Association into being, with William Littler of the Toronto *Star* as founding chairman.

Among the dance figures who died during the year were Lydia Sokolova, the first English dancer to become a soloist with Diaghilev's Ballets Russes; Sonia Gaskell, founder of the Dutch National Ballet; and Sol Hurok, the impresario who was called the King of Ballet for bringing Anna Pavlova, the Sadler's Wells, Kirov, Bolshoi, and Royal Ballets to America.

WILLIAM LITTLER
Dance Critic, The Toronto "Star"

DELAWARE

The 1974 political scene was concerned primarily with events leading up the November elections, as a result of which Pierre S. duPont IV (R) was elected to the state's single seat in the federal House of Representatives, and all 41 state House members were selected (25 Democrats, 16 Republicans), as were 10 Senate seats (7 Democrats, 3 Republicans). The state Senate in 1975 will consist of 13 Democrats and 8 Republicans.

Constitution. The chief controversy in the General Assembly revolved around the proposed new state constitution. After weeks of bitter infighting, opponents of the proposal succeeded in defeating it, at least until 1975.

Taxes. Gov. Sherman Tribbitt appointed a committee to look into modification of the state's tax structure. Proponents of a general sales tax have been rebuffed repeatedly, but the question of how to provide increased funds, especially for welfare and education, remains. Suggestions for higher income taxes arouse opposition from middle and higher income groups.

Unemployment. Unemployment continued to climb in 1974, reaching 7.6% in August, with prospects for further increases, especially in the auto and building trades. Farm marketing receipts totaled $23.7 million in August 1974 ($28.9 million a year earlier).

Legislation. Enactments of the 1974 General Assembly included an election campaign law requiring candidates to report all contributions and expenditures, a "no-fault" divorce law, establishment of a state lottery, and restoration of the death penalty for certain crimes.

Wilmington. The state's largest city continued to have severe financial problems, with over one fourth of the city budget allocated to education. An attempt to increase the unpopular city wage tax failed. The city became involved in a suit seeking busing of city students (86% of them nonwhite) to suburban areas but no decision had been reached by fall.

PAUL DOLAN
University of Delaware

DELAWARE • Information Highlights

Area: 2,057 square miles (5,328 sq km).
Population (1973 est.): 576,000.
Chief Cities (1970 census): Dover, the capital, 17,488; Wilmington, 80,386; Newark, 21,078.
Government (1974): *Chief Officers*—governor, Sherman W. Tribbitt (D); lt. gov., Eugene D. Bookhammer (R). *General Assembly*—Senate, 21 members; House of Representatives, 41 members.
Education (1973–74): *Enrollment*—public elementary schools, 69,558 pupils; public secondary schools, 63,386; nonpublic schools, 17,800; colleges and universities, 28,841 students. *Public school expenditures,* $169,870,000 ($1,388 per pupil).
State Finances (fiscal year 1973): *Revenues,* $442,173,-000; *Expenditures,* $492,742,000.
Personal Income (1973): $3,191,000,000; per capita, $5,-540.
Labor Force (June 1974): *Nonagricultural wage and salary earners,* 236,600.

DENMARK

Denmark has experienced a half-century of economic change and expansion. It has been said by its own economists, however, that Denmark has constantly "eaten off tomorrow's loaf." Salaries and wages have left productivity far behind, and the public sector has grown enormously. Prime Minister Poul Hartling of the Moderate Liberal party, formerly minister of foreign affairs, as head of a minority government thus took the reins of a nation in dire economic straits when he began his tenure after elections in December 1973.

Economy. In his statement at the opening of the Folketing (Parliament) on Oct. 1, 1974, Prime Minister Hartling stated that a firm working basis had already been achieved in the first nine months of 1974 by the government's efforts to restore stability to the Danish economy. He referred above all to the reduction in state income taxes, enacted a few days earlier, and the attendant reform of government expenditure. Denmark's balance of payments position, he noted, was weak even before the energy crisis had made itself felt. A deficit in the balance of payments in 1974 of approximately 7 billion kroner (Dkr) ($1,170,000,000) would have to be expected. Increases in the prices of oil were particularly upsetting, since Denmark must import more than 80% of its oil.

A noticeable growth in the unemployment rate was met in the latter part of 1974 by the lifting ahead of schedule of the freeze on local government construction and civil engineering. Regulation of private housing construction was rescinded, and the freeze on starts of state projects expired on October 1. The financing of long-term export credits was improved.

Cost of Living. Inflation in Denmark slowed down somewhat in 1974, the rate reaching 15%. Rising taxes rather than price increases, according to the Danish Confederation of Employers, took most of the real wage increase given to workers during the ten years from 1963 to 1973. Gross wages almost trebled in that period, while taxes increased by 480%. The cost of living rose by 85%, while the increase in real wages over the period was 17%.

The new government's plan for a tax reform will become effective on Jan. 1, 1975, and it is hoped that it will contribute significantly to a stabilization of the economy. According to the plan, the direct tax will be cut by about 10 billion Dkr ($1,670,000,000), and the value added tax will be increased from 15% to 20%. This would provide some 5 billion Dkr ($835,000,-000), and government expenditures would be reduced by nearly the same amount.

Common Market. In a 1972 referendum, the Danish people had approved Denmark's membership in the European Economic Community (EEC), or Common Market, by 57–33%, with 10% abstaining. However, inflation and rising

DENMARK • Information Highlights

Official Name: Kingdom of Denmark.
Location: Northwest Europe.
Area: 16,629 square miles (43,069 sq km).
Population (1973 est. census): 5,100,000.
Chief Cities (1971 est.): Copenhagen, the capital, 618,-900; Aarhus, 241,300, Odense, 166,700.
Government: *Head of state,* Margrethe II, queen (acceded Jan. 1972). *Head of government,* Poul Hartling, prime minister (took office Dec. 1973). *Legislature* (unicameral)—Folketing.
Monetary Unit: Krone (5.980 kroner equal U. S.$1, July 1974).
Gross National Product (1973 est.): $24,400,000,000.
Manufacturing (major products): Beverages, processed foods, machinery, ships, chemicals, furniture.
Major Agricultural Products: Barley, oats, sugar beets, dairy products, cattle, hogs, fish.
Foreign Trade (1973): Exports, $6,242,000,000; imports, $7,791,000,000.

food prices have turned many Danes against the EEC, and in October several thousand persons demonstrated in Copenhagen against the Common Market.

Environmental Activity. Denmark's new Environmental Protection Act went into force on Oct. 1, 1974, and Prime Minister Hartling asserted that the government would enforce new antipollution measures with great vigilance. To begin with, Denmark will invest more than 1 billion Dkr ($167,000,000) during the coming five years in order to cleanse its sewage outlets, mainly those emptying into Öresund, the sound between Denmark and Sweden. The most important project will be a purification plant near Copenhagen, which will cost 700 million Dkr ($117,000,000) and will be supervised by a joint Danish-Swedish commission.

The Faroe Islands. The local government of the Faroe Islands, the self-governing group of islands within the Danish kingdom, early in 1974 obtained approval of a motion stating that membership in the EEC could not be recommended. After some very detailed negotiations, however, a trade agreement was concluded between the EEC and the islands. It entered into force on September 1, and put nearly all Faroese export goods on a par with other Danish export goods in relation to the Common Market.

China Visit. Premier Hartling visited Communist China for nine days beginning October 18, and was received by Chairman Mao Tse-tung and Premier Chou En-lai.

Greenland. Greenland's locally elected politicians met in Holsteinsborg at the end of June to formulate their wishes for home rule for their island, which at present has the constitutional status of a Danish county. It was agreed that the desirable status for Greenland should be modeled on the Faroese home rule system. In the meantime, the Danish government promised a continuation of its development policy in Greenland, aimed at increasing local influence on domestic affairs and on trade, labor, and education.

MAC LINDAHL
Reporter, Writer, and Translator

DETROIT

Detroit's first black mayor, Coleman A. Young, who assumed office on January 1, was confronted with a host of difficult problems during 1974.

Police. City administration moves to reorganize the city's police department aroused the opposition of the Detroit Police Officers Association and the Lieutenants and Sergeants Association. The two groups went to court to stop an "affirmative action" promotion policy from being put into effect. The policy allowed the promotion of blacks and women to supervisory positions over white males with higher scores on qualifying exams. Promotions were frozen pending the outcome of the suit.

The two police groups unsuccessfully opposed plans to establish 55 mini-stations in storefront locations to give the police a "more visible presence" in neighborhoods. The mini-stations, first opened in the spring, were staffed by 1,000 officers reassigned from special bureaus to precinct duty.

Housing. The City Council engaged in a running battle with the U. S. Department of Housing and Urban Development, which had acquired 8,000 houses and 4,100 vacant lots in Detroit by late 1974. The council attempted to get federal authorities to adopt programs to rehabilitate and resell the properties. A proposal to sell the houses to the city for $1 each for resale to Detroiters failed.

Schools. On July 25, the U. S. Supreme Court overturned, by a 5–4 vote, a lower court decision ordering massive cross-district busing of schoolchildren between Detroit and 52 suburban school districts. The court returned the case to the federal District Court in Detroit with orders to find another solution to the segregation found to exist in city schools. The NAACP, which had filed the original suit, proceeded to seek a Detroit-only desegregation plan. But Judge Stephen J. Roth, who had presided over more than three years of hearings culminating in the Supreme Court decision, died two weeks before the verdict. The need to name a new judge to oversee hearings was expected to delay proceedings.

Clubs. Nearly seven years of legal fighting ended in October when the Detroit Yacht Club and Detroit Boat Club, private clubs renting city-owned parkland for $1 a year each, agreed to increase their black membership.

Auto Industry. Faced with slumping sales and declining profits, the automobile industry undertook drastic cost-cutting measures. Almost 52,000 auto workers were unemployed in late October. Chrysler Corp. confirmed it was considering the shutdown of its Jefferson Avenue assembly plant, which employed 5,875 workers in Detroit.

CHARLES W. THEISEN
Assistant City Editor, The Detroit "News"

DISARMAMENT AND ARMS CONTROL

The underground explosion of a nuclear device in India on May 18, 1974, making that country the sixth to conduct a successful atomic test, focused renewed attention on the risks and problems of rapidly spreading nuclear technology. The Indian government's claim that the test was "peaceful" and that it had "no intention of developing nuclear weapons" was met with skepticism by the governments and press of many countries.

Canada, the United States, France, and the Federal Republic of Germany had provided nuclear technology or fuel (natural or enriched uranium) to India with the clear understanding that no fuel would be used for military purposes. Most observers assumed that this first nuclear explosion in ten years by a non-nuclear state meant that India would press ahead to develop nuclear weapons.

The NPT Treaty. The Nuclear Non-Proliferation Treaty (NPT), which entered into force on March 5, 1970, prohibited "the diversion of nuclear energy from peaceful uses to nuclear weapons or other nuclear explosive devices."

The Indian explosion has prompted a new effort to persuade more governments to adhere to the NPT. As of December 1974, 106 governments had signed the treaty and 83 had become full parties to it. Conspicuous among nuclear states that had not signed were France and China; and among states assumed to be capable of conducting a nuclear explosion in the next five to ten years, Iran, Israel, Argentina, and Brazil.

All signatories to the NPT pledge to accept certain safeguards designed to monitor compliance or noncompliance with an agreement not to divert nuclear energy to military purposes. These safeguards are administered by the International Atomic Energy Agency (IAEA), with headquarters in Vienna, Austria. The system involves on-site inspection of nuclear records, facilities, and processes by IAEA representatives and the right to report any infractions to the UN Security Council.

Of the 104 member governments in the IAEA, only 40 have nuclear facilities. Consequently, IAEA safeguards are applied to all such facilities in the 24 states adhering to the NPT and to some or all such facilities in 16 others.

The Moscow Summit. The meeting between President Richard Nixon and Chairman Leonid Brezhnev in Moscow, June 27–July 3, 1974, resulted in agreements on four partial arms control measures:

(1) A treaty banning underground nuclear tests with a yield above 150 kilotons (equivalent to 150,000 tons of TNT), to become effective on March 31, 1975.

(2) An agreement to limit to one site the defensive missile launchers (ABM's) of each side. The 1972 ABM treaty permitted two sites.

(3) An agreement on procedures for dismantling or destroying older land- or sea-based missile launchers and ABM launchers in excess of treaty limits.

(4) A joint statement agreeing to confer further on methods "to overcome the dangers" of "environmental modification techniques for military purposes" and on ways to deal "with the most dangerous, lethal means of chemical warfare."

The Vladivostok Declaration. The long stalemate in the Strategic Arms Limitation Talks (SALT 2) was broken by the accord reached by President Gerald Ford and Chairman Brezhnev in Vladivostok, Nov. 24–25, 1974, to limit the numbers of all offensive strategic weapons and delivery systems through 1985. The two governments hoped to translate the accord into a formal agreement in 1975.

The accord places a ceiling of 2,400 for each side on the total number of strategic delivery vehicles (intercontinental ballistic missiles, submarine-launched missiles, and heavy bombers) and limits to 1,320 the number of permitted missiles that can be armed with multiple warheads (MIRV's) on each side.

President Ford said the accord can prevent "an arms race with all its terror, instability, warbreeding tension, and economic waste." However, two chief criticisms arose: (1) the accord confers an advantage on the Soviet Union; and (2) it fails to dampen the arms race, and indeed may stimulate it.

The SALT 1 accord allowed the Soviet Union 2,358 strategic missiles to 1,710 for the United States. Within this limit Moscow has deployed much larger missiles than Washington, achieving a throw-weight advantage of approximately three to one. The United States has retained the lead in deliverable warheads because of its advanced MIRV technology, but the USSR is adding multiple warheads to some of its large missiles.

A major criticism was stated in a *New York Times* editorial (Dec. 4, 1974), which emphasized that the accord "legitimizes a further buildup" by both sides. On the Russian side, for example, it "authorizes the Soviet Union to replace 1,320 of its existing inaccurate single-warhead ICBM's with new, more accurate MIRV missiles carrying an estimated 6,600 hydrogen warheads of a megaton or larger." Several analysts noted that the quantitative limit on missile launchers may well stimulate a qualitative missile race between the two superpowers.

Chemical and Biological Weapons. On Dec. 16, 1974, the U. S. Senate ended a 50-year deadlock and ratified, by a vote of 90 to 0, the 1925 Geneva protocol prohibiting chemical and biological warfare. The Senate also approved the 1972 treaty banning the production and stockpiling of biological weapons.

ERNEST W. LEFEVER
The Brookings Institution

DRUG ADDICTION AND ABUSE

Although the global nature of the drug-abuse problem tends to be disregarded because of concern with local issues, the current upsurge in drug abuse is in fact worldwide. Modern technology facilitates the dissemination of information and of drug-abuse epidemics; and tourist travel, migrations, wars, and urbanization have introduced drugs and drug-using customs into previously uninvolved populations.

Universal Trends. Adolescent alcohol abuse is a growing problem on every continent. Because alcohol is relatively inexpensive, easily obtained, and effective in providing a variety of other-than-sober states, its penetration into almost every culture is the most impressive single trend in drug-abuse activities today.

Multiple-drug abuse is now a common practice, with alcohol and marihuana generally the basic intoxicants. Sedatives, stimulants, hallucinogens, and narcotics are used simultaneously, depending on the occasion and availability of drugs.

The misuse of prescription-type and over-the-counter drugs by adults is seen in all developed countries. Sleeping pills, tranquilizers, amphetamines, and other legal stimulants are being used without supervision or particular knowledge of the hazards involved.

Heroin addiction, at one time seen only in the metropolitan centers of the West, has spread to small communities and to countries where previously it had been unknown.

United States. A steady liberalization of laws against the sale, possession, and use of marihuana was noted in 1974. Several cities and states revised their laws to make marihuana possession a misdemeanor rather than a felony, and efforts to discover and halt sales of the drug were relaxed. Among some segments of the population, use of marihuana became an accepted custom, even though its use remained officially illegal.

In June the federal government reported an increase in the flow of heroin into the country, notably from Mexico. It was feared that Turkey's partial lifting of the ban on growing opium poppies in 1975 might increase further the illicit supply. In New York City, where some 33,500 heroin addicts were undergoing methadone treatment, it was found that the death rate from methadone was twice that from heroin, presumably stemming from black market sales of methadone. The overall death rate from narcotics of all types showed a definite decline in the city, from 924 in 1972 to 745 in 1973.

Canada. Canada's drug problems are similar to those of the United States, but in miniature. The country is believed to have about 15,000 narcotic addicts, many of them in Vancouver. Heroin supply lines mingle with those of the United States, and Vancouver and Montreal serve as drug entry points from abroad.

The final report of the Commission of Inquiry into the Non-Medical Use of Drugs (the so-called LeDain Commission) recommended the legalization of marihuana under a system similar to that which regulates alcohol. While the legislation may not be enacted nationally, it is possible that provincial action may be taken.

Mexico. The unusual number of hallucinogenic drugs indigenous to Mexico makes their usage there fairly predictable. Peyote cactus, Psilocybe mushrooms, and psychedelic morning glory seeds are consumed by part of the rural population. Marihuana is also widely cultivated and used. Heroin from native opium and transshipped material of Asian and European manufacture has begun to appear in the larger cities. The Drug Enforcement Administration has estimated that as much as 50% of the heroin entering the United States may come over the Mexican border.

Sweden. Some 10,000 intravenous injectors of amphetamines and Preludin are reported to live in Stockholm and other large cities. Authorities have tightened the controls over stimulants to the extent that Sweden now has the most restrictive laws governing these agents.

Iron Curtain Countries. Little information is available, but the major drug problem clearly is alcoholism. Stringent laws and severe penalties are not producing a notable decrease in chronic inebriation. Although drug abuse officially does not exist in the Soviet Union, very stringent penalties governing drug use were announced by the government in 1974.

Turkey. A large part of North America's illegal heroin supply originated in the opium poppy fields of Anatolia until 1972, when cultivation was banned and alternative crops were subsidized. For the 1975 season, however, the government has authorized a limited planting. Turkey has only a minimal opium and heroin problem.

India. India has made the use of strong cannabis preparations illegal, although the weaker bhang (equivalent to marihuana) is widely used as a popular tea. The stronger forms, charas (hashish) and ganja, are frequently used by low-income groups, while middle-class youths have become increasingly involved with charas and alcohol.

Japan. Japan had a serious methamphetamine-abuse problem after World War II (by 1954 over 550,000 people were dependent on that stimulant), but with the introduction of compulsory hospitalization of addicts and stricter law enforcement, the number of dependent users decreased rapidly. During the last decade, however, the number of users had begun to rise again. Analgesics, solvents, and sleeping pills have become popular, and marihuana is being used in increasing amounts.

SIDNEY COHEN, M. D.
Executive Director, Council on Drug and Alcohol Abuse, University of California, Los Angeles

UPI

With a record 120-day supply of unsold cars in its new car storage lots, Chrysler Corporation announced the closing of five of six U. S. assembly plants.

ECONOMY OF THE U. S.

In 1974 the American economy produced the highest rate of inflation in decades at the same time it was drifting off into what might be one of the nation's severest postwar recessions. There was the paradox of material shortages in some areas of the economy and underutilization of capacity in others. Crosscurrents of strong business spending and weakening consumer demand occurred simultaneously.

The economy grappled with the long-term implications of worldwide food and energy problems and was buffeted by global inflation. Seeking to adjust to the new high price of energy, parts of the economy overcompensated, while others cut back output levels sharply and sent shock waves through related areas of business. In brief, the attempt to deal with inflation and the fuel shortage led to maladjustments and to a deepening business recession.

Gross National Product. As the year opened, the economy was still reacting sharply to the November 1973 oil embargo by the Arab producers. After a sluggish first quarter, general activity improved moderately but inflation stepped up sharply. Having registered strong annual rates of gain of nearly 10% in 1972 and nearly 12% in 1973, the gross national product (GNP) was down to a little over 8% for most of 1974, each quarter showing lessened strength as compared with the preceding year. Even measured in current prices, which includes the inflation factor, economic activity was lacking the zip which had characterized recent years. As the year ended, it was clear that the energy problem was a lasting new dimension and that its associated complications were to be an added consideration in this and future cyclical fluctuations of business.

Real growth in the economy was reversed. By the third quarter of 1974, GNP in constant prices stood at an $822.7 billion seasonally adjusted annual rate. This represented a cumulative decline of 2.2% from a year earlier and of 2.7% from the fourth quarter of 1973. Each quarter in the year declined from the one preceding it, and this appeared to qualify the trend as recessionary after three years of real growth. A considerable body of opinion developed, however, that with production levels remaining high and business capital spending strong, inflation remained the No. 1 problem and the emerging recession was not yet troublesome. The ambivalence in governmental policy contributed to the worsening of both inflation and recession.

Prices. What was not in doubt early in the year was that inflation was becoming more severe. The implicit price deflator for GNP, which is the broadest measure of price change in the economy, rose at an annual rate of about 12.5% in the first quarter, dropped off to gain 9.5% in the second, and rose to 11.5% in the third. Double-digit inflation, as it came to be known, confirmed what housewives and consumers had recognized for several years, that the United States was in the grip of an upward price spiral whose consequences were debilitating.

THE U.S. ECONOMY IN 1974

Some Key Indicators Turn Sour

GROSS NATIONAL PRODUCT

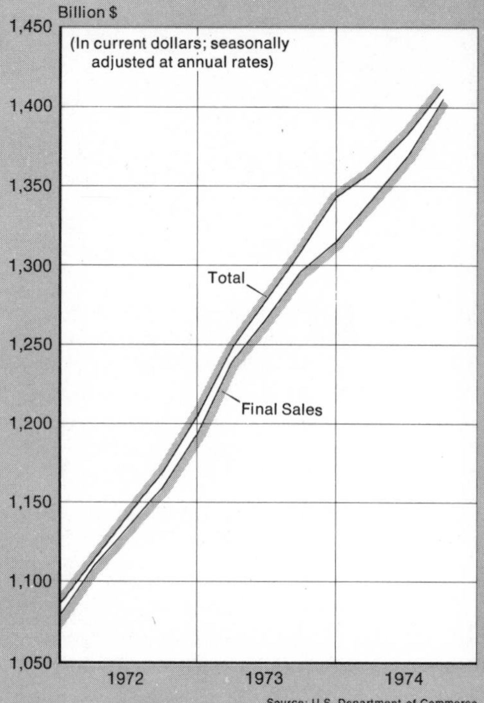

UNEMPLOYMENT RATE

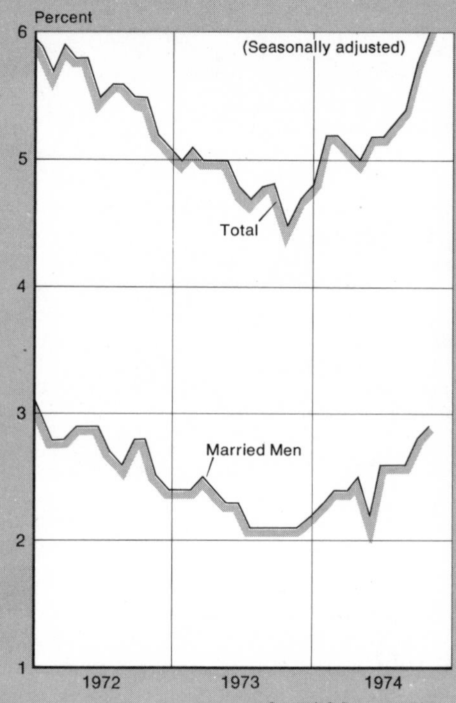

INDUSTRIAL PRODUCTION

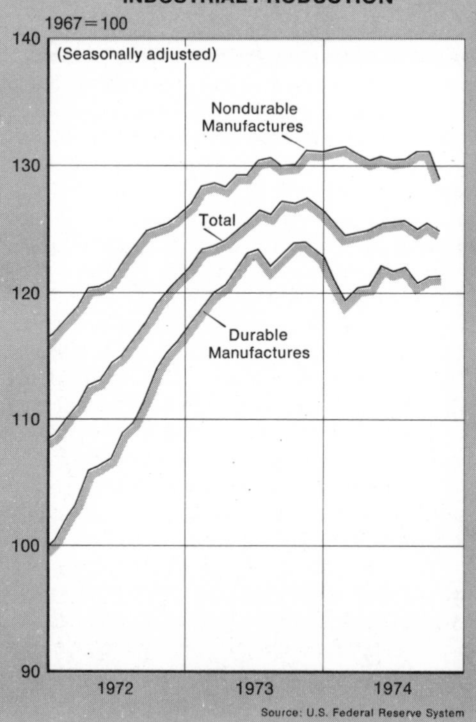

CONSUMER PRICE INDEX

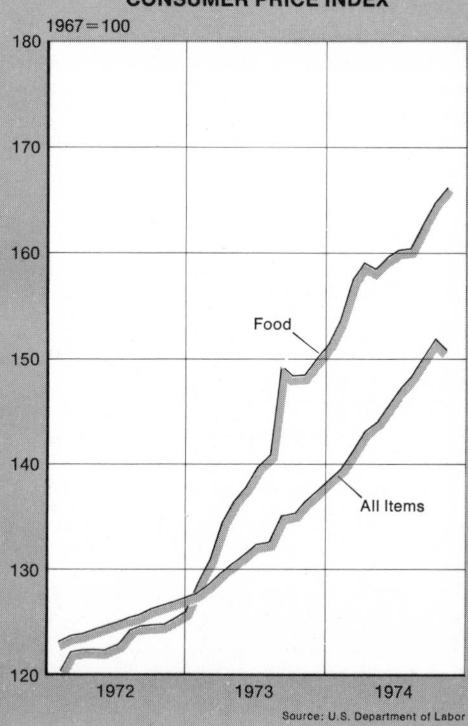

The consumer price index seemed certain to top the 1973 levels by 11%, putting the cost of all consumer items at least 50% higher than they had been in 1967. Food and energy prices accelerated fastest initially, but as they slowed down in rate of gain other prices accelerated. Wholesale prices, too, continued to surge ahead during the year, with the index (1967 = 100) reaching 170 by October, although there was some slowdown in the rate of increase toward the end of the year.

Industrial Production. One development that made observers reluctant to talk about recession was the continued high level of production and its failure to show any significant decline. The Federal Reserve Board's index of industrial production (1967 = 100) had registered 125.6 for all of 1973, and there was little departure, up or down, from that level through the first three quarters of 1974. But in the fourth quarter the index began to decline, depressed in part by a coal strike but also by cuts in production on a broad front. Consumer durables other than autos, business equipment, and industrial materials all declined from previous output levels.

When the index reached 122 in November, it was noted that it was down 5.5 from the previous peak in November 1973 and that the magnitude of the decline was already half the drop experienced in the two previous recessions. Further declines were expected in the months following, as widespread layoffs were announced in the industrial sector.

The production of automobiles was predictably a weak spot in the economy throughout the year, sales having begun to drop sharply in the last two months of 1973. For all of 1974, it appeared that about 7.8 million new automobiles would be produced, representing a drop of 20% from the all-time record output of 9.7 million in 1973.

The level of auto production, while down sharply, varied over the year. At the start, gloom was widespread as severe gasoline shortages gripped many local areas and several regions of the nation. Auto producers reacted by cutting output 30% in the first half of the year and in some cases by shifting production to smaller cars. With the return of adequate but higher-priced supplies of fuel, output was increased, small car demand fell off, and producers were looking to a return to previous patterns of production. At year-end, however, the automakers' gloom was again prevalent, now increased by the consumers' weakened position in the market.

The steel industry continued its strong performance in 1974, shading off only slightly from its 1973 records and illustrating the paradoxical behavior of the economy. Steel output began to surge in 1972 and final 1973 results saw 150.8 million tons produced, surpassing the previous record set in 1969 by 7%. In 1974 domestic steel output was unable to keep pace with the 1973 record because of strained plant capacity and some materials shortages, but with world prices rising even faster than those in the United States and with demand remaining firm, the 1974 showing was expected to be second only to the record year.

Sales and Profits. Business generally showed strength in the first half of the year where measured by dollar values. This was generally interpreted as a case of demand factors having stabilized as compared with preceding periods but with dollar volume pushed up by inflation. Profits continued to advance through the third quarter, although it was argued that this was illusory as the gains reflected the impact of inflation on inventory and goods in process.

Dollar volume of sales by all business on a seasonally adjusted monthly average basis advanced during the first three quarters of the year and then edged down a bit as retail sales weakened. At the same time inventories relative to manufacturers' shipments continued to creep upward but were viewed with caution as new orders weakened. Retailers' gloom increased as the year wore on.

Capital Spending. Aided by strength in some sectors of the economy, businesses maintained a record level of capital outlays for expansion, despite high interest rates. Actual capital spending by all business in 1973 totaled $99.7 billion, and it was anticipated that this figure would rise to average $111.9 billion for all of 1974. However, by the third quarter businesses were trimming capital spending plans for the first time in four years. There was even the expectation that in real terms, after accounting for inflation, there would be a decline, despite the stimulus of energy-related industry such as electric utilities and pipelines, which had to expand to meet the growth that was forecast.

In this area, perhaps more clearly than others, could be seen the elements which if continued, as now seemed possible, could eventually lead to a leveling off or even a decline in the general standard of living, reversing what had come to be expected of the American economy. As public utilities faced future expansion requirements, clearly called for by past standards, they were trimming previously planned capital outlays under pressure of high interest rates, credit weakening, and inflated costs.

Personal Income and Employment. Consumers showed little enthusiasm over the year as inflation wiped out any purchasing-power gains in income, scarcities and threatened scarcities reminded them of general economic dislocations, and unemployment materialized as a distinct threat to income security. While total personal income continued to rise at a swift rate, tax payments and price rises absorbed the gains and ate into previous levels of income and purchasing power. From the high of $2,952 per capita, disposable personal income in constant dollars declined as each quarter passed, and was down 3.7% after midyear.

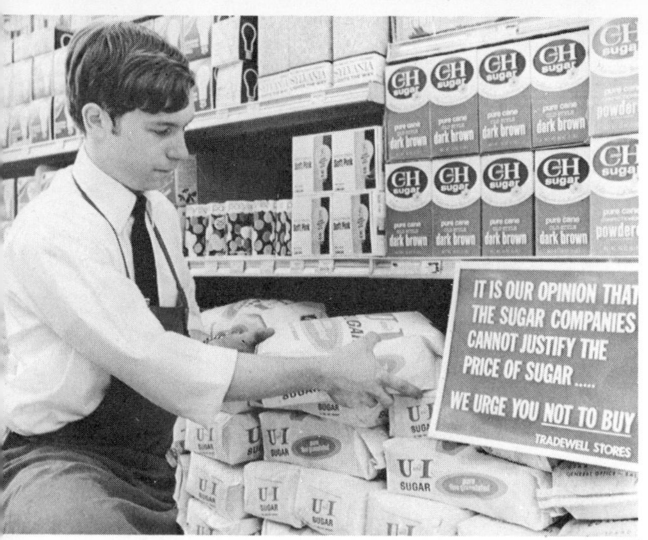

UPI

Retail grocery chains post signs urging customers not to buy sugar at prices they feel cannot be justified by the sugar companies. Sugar quadrupled in price in one year.

The consumer could not help but feel he was getting nowhere. With the added high cost of borrowing and the ever-present threat of energy shortages, the consumer showed little zest for expansion of durable goods purchases. Toward the end of the year unemployment rose rapidly, and at 7.1% in December was at the highest level in 13 years.

Housing. Housing lagged under the impact of high mortgage costs and general uncertainty despite high rates of new family formation. The result was to push total construction spending below 1973 levels and to depress the construction industry generally, the problem being compounded by omnipresent inflation. From a high of nearly 2.4 million new private housing starts in 1972, the total dropped precipitously to around the 1.5 million level in 1974 and little hope for improvement was held out for 1975.

Housing construction, dependent on borrowed money, was again a victim of high-cost money pursued as a policy by some branches of the federal government in the fight on inflation. This time, however, there was a feeling that the problem was being aggravated by uncertainties connected with the economy and by future transportation and energy problems.

Government Finances. In the government sector, federal receipts were increasing as higher dollar incomes put individuals in higher tax brackets and pushed up the amounts of taxes withheld. High levels of corporate profits also contributed to gains in federal receipts. Outlays by the federal government did not advance as fast, and as a consequence the federal deficit dropped to $3.5 billion in the 1973–74 fiscal year, as compared with $14.3 billion in 1972–73. Indications were, however, that the deficit would widen again in 1974–75 as the federal government turned its attention to the oncoming recession and away from the restrictions imposed by inflation. Already, corrective measures for rising unemployment were indicated as proposals were made for federal outlays to provide jobs, increase jobless benefits, and generally stimulate consumer purchasing power. Similarly stimulative tax measures to encourage investment by businesses were readied in anticipation of worsening economic developments.

In the area of state and local government finance, inflation was pushing up costs, and business-related tax revenue systems were producing sluggishly.

Financial Markets. The financial structure of the nation was shaken by the general turmoil in the economy. Common stock prices plunged downward over the year, reacting to unfavorable developments and wiping out savings. Bond prices also declined to record low levels, reflecting the tight money policies being pursued by Washington as well as the fixed-income investors' antipathy to high rates of inflation. A consequence was a closing of the door to the money market for marginal borrowers and weak financial performers.

The failure of the nation's largest public utility to pay a quarterly common stock dividend in the midst of a liquidity crisis of its own spread a chill throughout the financial world and virtually closed the money market to it as well as raising doubts about all other utilities. The failure of a major bank contributed further to the general apprehension, and liquidity problems permeated other areas of American business.

As a symbolic gesture, the United States again legalized the holding of gold by individuals, and as the year closed some individuals were preparing to place their assets in the ancient symbol of wealth, while others were ready to join the worldwide speculation that had been going on in the commodity for several years.

The Outlook. The major areas of weakness in the nation's economy in 1974 were in housing, auto production, loss of consumer confidence, and the financial sphere—all compounded by inflation and the energy problem. Toward the end of the year it became clear that the nation was headed into a continuing recession that could become quite severe.

The more optimistic forecasts saw a recovery beginning in the last half of 1975, while the gloomier ones could not locate a turning point in the trough ahead. But it was widely expected that unemployment would rise to 7% or 8% in 1975 while inflation was being reduced to a level of 7.5% to 8%.

(See also INTERNATIONAL FINANCE; INTERNATIONAL TRADE; LABOR; STOCKS AND BONDS; UNITED STATES. For economic developments in other nations, see articles on the individual countries.)

JACKSON PHILLIPS, *Senior Vice President*
Moody's Investors Service, Inc.

ECUADOR

The military government of Gen. Guillermo Rodríguez Lara, which came into power in February 1972, remained in control throughout 1974. In July it reaffirmed earlier statements that elections are a "luxury" not possible for at least five years, and in September the special courts established in 1972 to stamp out corruption were abolished.

Political Affairs. Partisanship is much restrained in Ecuador, but the government tolerates supportive behavior. Thus in August the Communist party, which supports the government, received a fraternal visit by a Soviet delegation, and President Rodríguez received the visitors. Earlier, the spokesman for the principal conservative landowners' association was jailed briefly for criticism of the government's agrarian policy, and the president warned that the prestige of the armed forces was committed to upholding that policy.

A basic change was under way in 1974, however, with the tripling of official income from oil revenues. Government policies imply sweeping socioeconomic changes concerning land use and ownership, export-import patterns, and financial roles, to offer examples. Quito may supplant Guayaquil as the economic center as a result of these changes. At the same time, membership in the Andean Common Market implies major changes in industry and foreign trade. Inflation has added to the insecurity of the lower and middle classes as the classic case of too much money and too few goods occurs.

Petroleum and the Five-Year Plan. The Integral Plan for Transformation and Development has been dubbed (as in Venezuela) the "sowing of the petroleum." Oil revenues alone are expected to contribute $3 billion to the economy in 1974. Ecuador became a full member of the Organization of Petroleum Exporting Countries (OPEC) in November 1973; it supports policies that have raised the world price to over $10 per barrel—triple the 1972 price.

In July 1974, Ecuador received $8.50 per barrel in taxes, licenses, royalties, and shares, partly through the official state corporation, CEPE, on exports of 210,000 barrels per day (bpd), down from 225,000 bpd by official order to conserve reserves and maintain world prices. In June, CEPE purchased a 25% share of the properties of the Texaco-Gulf consortium; and in October it announced its plan to increase its share to a majority. In July, of 35 potential bidders, only official Argentine and Polish companies were given contracts for exploration of areas east of the Andes mountains. Through self-financing, CEPE will exercise a monopoly of all internal marketing by 1976, including the 50,000-bpd Japanese-built petroleum refinery at Esmeraldas.

Petroleum income is expected to play a part in direct government investment in 541 projects proposed by the National Planning Council. In September, 337 of these, costing $648 million, were under way; the overall total is expected to be $1.8 billion. The Basic Electrification Law of October 1973 assigns 47% of all state oil revenue to power projects and to subsidies for small electricity users.

The Land Use Law of the same month will force owners to put land in commercial and productive use or sell to the government for collective farm communities. Severe food shortages in 1972 and 1973 gave impetus to this policy. Port facilities, especially at Guayaquil, will be doubled in anticipation of import and export needs as industrial diversification proceeds. Vocational as well as academic educational facilities are being enlarged. The Andean market assigns Ecuador special advantages in the form of tariff preferences and some industrial development monopolies.

Government budget plans call for a 21% increase in central administration costs, to $457 million in 1974. Substantial prepayment of foreign debts is occurring, and pay-as-you-go policies are developing. Major investments in irrigation, cattle improvement and disease eradication, and food supply, warehousing, and marketing are under way. The armed forces also are using new funds for cash purchases of weapons in Europe and the United States.

International Affairs. Ecuador has shown increasing independence in its foreign policy since 1972. It has joined OPEC in forcing higher oil prices despite protests from major consumer states. At the 15th Meeting of Consultation of OAS Foreign Ministers at Quito in November, it pressed the United States to renew Cuban relations. CEPE sought much of its technical advice from Rumanian and other Soviet-bloc contract personnel, and accepted Japanese participation in its developmental plans.

The "tuna war" with U. S. companies over offshore fishing has been settled on Ecuadorian terms, to the chagrin of American opponents of Ecuador's 200-mile territorial waters claim.

PHILIP B. TAYLOR, JR.
University of Houston

ECUADOR • Information Highlights

Official Name: Republic of Ecuador.
Location: Northwest South America.
Area: 109,483 square miles (283,561 sq km).
Population (1973 est.): 6,700,000.
Chief Cities (1972 est.): Quito, the capital, 564,900; Guayaquil, 860,600.
Government: *Head of state,* Guillermo Rodríguez Lara, president (took office Feb. 1972). *Head of government,* Guillermo Rodríguez Lara. *Legislature*—Congress (suspended June 1970).
Monetary Unit: Sucre (25.25 sucres equal U. S.$1, July 1974).
Gross National Product (1973 est.): $2,255,000,000.
Manufacturing (major products): Processed foods, textiles, petroleum products.
Major Agricultural Products: Bananas, coffee, cacao, rice, potatoes, sugarcane, cotton, fish, forest products.
Foreign Trade (1973): *Exports,* $567,000,000; *imports,* $517,000,000.

UPI

At Marine Park, South Boston, some 8,000 demonstrators stage a peaceful rally protesting the busing of about 18,200 of the city's 94,000 public school pupils.

education

The busing of schoolchildren to achieve racial balance in individual schools continued to be a highly controversial issue throughout the year 1974. While decided progress in integration has been made by this means in many Southern cities, the court-ordered program in some Northern cities has met with prolonged and determined resistance.

BUSING AND INTEGRATION

Violence in Boston. Prior to 1974 there had been little integration in the city of Boston, where 82% of the black pupils in the nation's oldest public school system were in black-majority schools.

In June 1974, U. S. District Judge W. Arthur Garrity, Jr., charged that the Boston School Committee had "intentionally segregated schools at all levels," and there was in effect a separate school system for the 36,000 nonwhite students. The judge ordered an integration plan, to take effect in September, that involved busing of about 18,200 of the city's 94,000 public school pupils.

Opposition to the plan centered in the closely knit white neighborhoods of South Boston and Hyde Park. White parents warned that they would resist the effort tc bus black pupils into their neighborhood schools and would boycott the black schools to which their children had been assigned.

When schools opened in South Boston, buses carrying black students were greeted by jeering crowds and rock throwing. Mayor Kevin H. White banned street gatherings in South Boston and ordered police escorts for buses transporting black students to the troubled areas.

Six hundred state and local police were assigned to special duty. A request to send federal marshals to maintain order was denied by Judge Garrity, but regular Army paratroopers at Fort Bragg, N. C., were alerted for two days. Beatings and a stabbing at Hyde Park High School prompted Gov. Francis Sargent to call up 450 National Guardsmen, who were stationed, without arms, in armories in the event local police needed help.

As authorities sought ways to make the integration plan work, parents in South Boston continued their defiance. After five weeks of required busing, citywide school attendance climbed to 74%. Attendance at most schools was back to normal, but the situation in the troubled areas remained tense.

In fact, in mid-December some 6,000 whites staged a protest on the Commons against busing for school desegregation. The demonstration came one day after a coalition of civil-rights groups held a pro-busing rally.

Restrictions on Busing. On Aug. 21, 1974, President Ford signed a $25 billion education bill, which, after extended and at times bitter congressional arguments over restrictions on busing, prohibits the federal courts from ordering the busing of a child beyond the closest or next-closest school to his home to achieve desegregation unless it is necessary to protect the constitutional rights of minority children. The bill also prohibits busing across district lines or altering district lines unless, as a result of discriminatory action in both school districts, the lines caused segregation.

President Ford said in signing the bill that he generally opposed forced busing of school children. He characterized the new curbs on busing as "reasonable and equitable restrictions." However, he criticized what he called double standards between districts already operating busing plans and those districts that would be affected by the new law.

Detroit Decison. Court action to achieve racial balance by requiring the busing of white pupils from suburban school districts into heavily black city schools has been sought in a number of cities, including Detroit, Richmond, Atlanta, Cleveland, Indianapolis, and others.

On July 25, 1974, the U. S. Supreme Court, in a 5-to-4 vote, overturned lower-court orders that would have required the cross-busing of an estimated 78,000 children between the Detroit city school system and 53 suburban school districts outside the city limits.

The court declared that desegregation "does not require any particular balance in each 'school, grade, or classroom.' " Suits to require city-suburban busing across school district lines in a number of other cities were directly affected by the Detroit ruling.

The decision was widely hailed as a "curb on racial busing" and characterized as a "historic reversal." The National Association for the Advancement of Colored People (NAACP) called it the most important school case since the Brown decision in 1954. Opponents of busing were gratified by the decision. Some observers felt it would accelerate the flight of whites from the cities to the suburbs.

Justice Thurgood Marshall, the only black member of the court, described the ruling as "a giant step backward." He feared that metropolitan areas would become divided into separate cities—one white and one black. The decision does not change the "racial balancing" that exists in a number of cities, mostly in the South. Nor does it apply to the Boston ruling, where busing is not across school district lines. (See also CIVIL LIBERTIES; ETHNIC GROUPS.)

Educational Gains by Blacks. Educational gains by blacks since 1970 have been impressive. In its 1974 survey of the social and economic status of blacks in America, the Bureau of the Census reports increases in the number graduating from high school and in those attending college.

In the 20- to 24-year-old group, 70% of the black men and 72% of the black women were high school graduates in 1973, as compared with 62% and 67%, respectively, three years earlier. In comparison, 85% of the white men and women in the 20-to-24-age group in 1973 had finished high school, a 2% gain since 1970.

Black college students numbered 684,000 in 1973, a 31% increase over the 1970 figure and 41% over 1967. There is still a disparity in percentage of the black population enrolled, as compared with white students, despite extensive scholarship grants and loans specifically designated for black students.

ENROLLMENTS, COSTS, AND FEDERAL AID

School Enrollments. Enrollments are expected to drop and expenses to rise in U. S. schools and colleges during the 1974–75 school year, according to Office of Education estimates.

The decrease in elementary school enrollment, a reflection of the declining birthrate, accounts for the loss in total school enrollment that began in 1971. In 1974–75, enrollment in kindergarten through the eighth grade is expected to drop by 2.1%, to 34.4 million. Public elementary schools will have more than 600,000 fewer students, while private schools will lose about 100,000.

High school enrollment is expected to continue to increase, from 15,365,000 in 1973–74 to 15,610,000 in 1974–75. Private high school enrollment is expected to remain constant at 1,200,000; the entire gain is in public schools. The high school graduating class of 1975 is expected to exceed the 1974 figure of 3.1 million, which would set a new record.

Rising Educational Costs. Expenditures for education at all levels in 1974–75 are expected to total $108 billion, an increase of about $11 billion over the previous year. Funds from local, state, and federal sources during 1973–74 totaled $97 billion. Education expenses now represent nearly 8% of the gross national product. Virtually everything is more expensive, and further increases in taxes seem inevitable.

According to statistics compiled by the National Education Association, the federal government supplied 7.5% of the revenue for public elementary and secondary schools in 1972–73, while state governments supplied 43% and local sources supplied the remaining 49.5%.

Increased Federal Aid. In August 1974, after a long debate over busing, Congress passed an omnibus education bill extending and amending the Elementary and Secondary Education Act of 1965 and authorizing appropriations of more than $25 billion through fiscal 1978. The bill was regarded as a victory for advocates of federal assistance under existing programs rather than the educational revenue-sharing plan favored by former President Nixon.

Among its many provisions, the act authorized increased appropriations totaling $585 million in fiscal 1975–78 for bilingual education assistance, and established an Office of Bilingual Education within the U. S. Office of Education.

The Educating the Handicapped Act was extended through fiscal 1977, and authorized appropriations were increased greatly from an annual $47.5 million available previously to $746 million in fiscal 1975, $252 million in fiscal 1976, and $266 million in fiscal 1977. Each state was required to establish a goal of providing equal educational opportunity to all its handicapped

UPI

Few children are at their desks as Kanawha county, W. Va., parents boycott the schools in an attempt to remove textbooks they consider un-American or un-Christian.

children. Appropriations to the states totaling $413.5 million for fiscal 1975–78 were authorized for a new reading-improvement assistance program.

Among the miscellaneous provisions of the act are one authorizing the president to convene a White House Conference on Education in 1977 and another directing the secretary of health, education, and welfare to study the incidence of crime and violence in schools and to report his findings to the U. S. Congress by Dec. 1, 1976.

Surplus of Teachers. The number of new teaching positions has decreased as school enrollments have leveled off or even decreased in the elementary grades in most areas. At the same time, teachers are tending to hold the jobs that they have, making things even tougher for recent graduates.

According to National Education Association estimates, there were 290,200 college graduates in 1974 who had prepared specifically for teaching. Only 118,830 beginning teachers were employed in public schools. Some 171,000 of what is regarded as the best-prepared group of prospective teachers in years were unable to obtain teaching positions.

Tenure regulations provide older teachers with job security. Where declining enrollments result in laying off teachers, the younger ones are the first to go. Some school systems have experimented with financial inducements to encourage veteran teachers to retire earlier.

HIGHER EDUCATION

Enrollment Trends. Enrollment in U. S. colleges and universities is expected to rise only about 1.3%, from 8.5 million degree-credit students in 1973–74 to 8.6 million in 1974–75, according to U. S. Office of Education estimates. Virtually all of the increase is expected to occur in public institutions.

Private colleges are experiencing acute difficulties. Rising costs of operation have necessitated annual increases in tuition and fees, which have further depleted enrollments that were already shrinking in many private institutions. College costs rose about 40% between 1970 and 1973. Heavily dependent on student fees, many of the small private colleges are operating in the red.

There is now what has been described as a buyer's market in higher education. It is estimated that there were a half-million empty places in the nation's 2,686 colleges and universities as the 1974 fall term began. This is a dramatic reversal of the situation a decade ago when colleges were inundated with applications, and students applied to at least three colleges in hopes of acceptance at one.

Faculty Employment. For several years graduate schools have been graduating Ph. D.'s at a rate exceeding the demand. There is now keen competition among qualified applicants for academic job openings. The situation has been aggravated by the pruning of faculty rolls in many institutions in the face of escalating costs and declining enrollments. Jobs of untenured instructors and assistant professors are being terminated in the budget squeeze, with a resulting erosion of faculty morale. Even the positions of tenured faculty are in jeopardy. To the traditional reasons for dismissal for gross negligence or moral turpitude has been added a third cause: financial exigency.

The Stock Market and Higher Education. Foundations and universities that depend on endowments and gifts for much of their income are feeling the effects of the plummeting stock market, according to the Washington *Star-News* (Oct. 3, 1974). The market value of stock portfolios has declined sharply. Assets of the Ford Foundation, the largest in the United States, dropped from $3 billion to $2 billion in less than a year. The foundation is considering a substantial cutback in its spending.

In October 1974, Harvard University, which has the largest U. S. endowment, figured the market value of its investments at $1.5 billion, a loss of $200 million in less than a year.

While dividend earnings have not been materially affected as yet, a continuing slump could affect both company earnings and donations by the wealthy. More than 75% of the $2.2 billion given to higher education in 1972–73 came from gifts of $5,000 or more, many of them in the form of donations of stock.

OTHER DEVELOPMENTS

Sex Equality in Education. New rules to end sex discrimination in schools and colleges were proposed by the U. S. Department of Health, Education, and Welfare on June 18, 1974. Actually, the new directives, to take effect in the 1974–75 session, implement congressional action taken two years previously as Guidelines for

Landmark Decision

The 'Brown' Case — 20 Years Later

On May 17, 1954, the U. S. Supreme Court, in the case of *Brown* v. *Board of Education of Topeka,* ruled unanimously that racial segregation in the public schools of the United States is unconstitutional. Chief Justice Earl Warren declared: "In the field of public education the doctrine of 'separate but equal' has no place. Separate educational facilities are inherently unequal. . . ." Thus ended the "separate but equal" doctrine laid down by the court in 1896 permitting segregated public schools.

Early Opposition. In 1954 about 40% of U. S. public school pupils were in areas where laws required segregation. Seventeen states and the District of Columbia required it, while local option prevailed in four other states.

The new decision was met with defiance by many Southern leaders. Others counseled restraint and patience pending further orders from the Supreme Court. These came on May 31, 1955, when the court decided unanimously to give the job of ending segregation to lower federal courts and local school authorities. It set no deadline, but ordered desegregation to proceed "with all deliberate speed."

In most of the border states and in St. Louis, Baltimore, and Washington, desegregation began promptly and with little incident. However, there was violent opposition in some areas. Opposition increased in many Southern states where legislatures passed laws cutting off state money to integrated schools. "Massive resistance" was advocated. Enforcement reached a showdown in Virginia, where the entire public school system was threatened as schools were closed down in four areas. When it was apparent that appeals for further delay were useless, the inevitability of desegregation was accepted, and a trickle of black pupils began attending previously all-white schools in the South.

Progress in Desegregation. Progress was slow. By 1960 only 768 of the 6,676 school districts in the Southern and border states were desegregated, many in a token manner. Scarcely 1% of the black children were in school with whites. However, a steady process of acceptance was beginning.

Finally, ten years after the Brown decision, the Civil Rights Act of 1964 gave the federal government the authority to withhold funds from segregated school districts. The Departments of Justice and of Health, Education, and Welfare aided in drawing up compliance plans to end racial discrimination.

WIDE WORLD

Black children attend Fort Myer, Va., class in 1954 following Supreme Court ruling against segregation.

In the past decade the progress of desegregation in the South has been dramatic. Now schools in the Deep South are more thoroughly integrated than are those in the North.

Statistics compiled by the Office of Civil Rights, Department of Health, Education, and Welfare, revealed that in 1972, 46% of the black children in the 11 states which once comprised the Confederacy were in predominantly white schools. On the other hand, only 26% of the blacks in the Northern and Western states were attending white schools.

In the Southern states only 25% of the black children were enrolled in schools that were 90% or more black; in the Northern and Western states, 49% of the black children were in such schools; in the border states, 53% were in predominantly black schools.

De facto segregation in the North tends to offset gains in the South. For example, Muscogee County, Ga. (the Columbus area), is better integrated than Boston, according to the New York *Times* (May 12, 1974). Both systems are about one third black. In Columbus, three out of four black children were in majority-white schools, while in Boston, 82% were in majority-black schools.

The Busing Problem. The flight of whites to the suburbs has made it difficult to maintain racial balance in many large cities. Extensive busing has been employed to transport children from predominantly black areas to white-majority schools and vice versa.

In July 1974, the U. S. Supreme Court overturned lower court orders that would have required extensive busing across school district lines in the Detroit area. The $25 billion education bill signed by President Ford in August 1974 contained a number of restrictions on court-ordered busing to achieve desegregation.

EDWARD ALVEY, JR.

Title IX, Education Amendments Act of 1972, which authorized the withdrawal of federal funds for institutions shown to be discriminating against women.

The broad coverage includes "all aspects of all education programs or activities of a school district, institution of higher education, or other entity" which receives federal aid. Only military institutions and certain church-run programs are exempt.

Sex discrimination in admissions by separate rankings or sex-based quotas, or the use of marital, parental, or pregnancy data are forbidden, except in the traditionally single-sex institutions. Housing and other facilities must be available to both men and women without discrimination in fees, hours, or rules. Separate housing quarters, locker-room facilities, toilets, and showers are permitted as long as they are comparable in quality.

In general, equal treatment of sexes applies to staff members, full-time or part-time. Pregnant employees are to get the same leave and benefits as other temporarily disabled employees. Sex bias in all extracurricular activities except revenue-producing sports is prohibited. All physical education programs must make equal provision for men and women.

The new rules were to be evaluated during the fall of 1974, appropriate changes made, and the entire program submitted to the White House for approval.

To help them with drill and review work, these fourth graders in the Bronx, N. Y., have a robot named Leachim, created by their teacher Gail Freeman's husband, Michael.

UPI

Confidentiality of School Records. Among the provisions of the omnibus education bill of 1974 is a section withholding federal funds from any educational institution or agency that refuses to permit parents to inspect and review any and all official records and files containing information about their children. The measure also gives parents the opportunity for a hearing to correct or remove inaccurate, misleading, or "inappropriate" data.

The act also prohibits schools from releasing records or files regarding identifiable children or parents without the written consent of the parents except for certain specified educational purposes.

Textbook Protests. In September 1974, dissension over the use of certain textbooks in public schools erupted in Kanawha county, West Virginia, and spread to neighboring counties. Classes were boycotted and coal mines were picketed. At one point, 6,000 miners were off their jobs in the Charleston area, and classes were suspended for about 44,000 students.

At issue was the right of educators to choose what they believe to be the best textbooks for their classes. A coalition of ministers and parents opposed the use of a series of supplementary texts in junior and senior high school English classes, which contained readings described by the protesters as "anti-American, anti-Christian, and immoral."

Finally, a compromise settlement was reached and certain selections eliminated. Demonstrators dispersed and miners returned to work, although occasional acts of nighttime sabotage continued. Elsewhere it has been suggested that parents and other citizens from outside the education profession be included on textbook-evaluation committees.

Vandalism. Vandalism and its prevention cost American schools an estimated $500,000,000 in 1972–73—$260 million for vandalism damage, arson losses, and destruction of property, and $250 million for security personnel and equipment. Security and patrol forces have been strengthened, and sound- and motion-detecting devices have been installed.

Such measures are having some effect. New York City school officials reported that vandalism losses in 1972–73 were down 21% from the previous year, to $3.8 million. In Los Angeles, damage from vandalism has leveled off at about $2 million a year since alarm systems were installed. Miami and Dallas have also cut losses by this means. Houston has assigned armed guards to its school buildings at night.

While most officials urge a firm stand and various safeguards against vandalism, some propose investigating possible internal causes of malicious incidents, which may be due to poor pupil-staff relationships, pupil frustration, or alienation by failure to achieve.

EDWARD ALVEY, JR.
Mary Washington College

EGYPT

At the conclusion of the 1973 October war, Israeli troops had established positions along the Cairo Road on the west bank of the Suez Canal. Israel agreed to withdraw from both banks of the Suez in January and the military forces of the belligerents were separated. This led, with the support of Egyptian President Anwar el-Sadat, to the lifting in March of the oil embargo by the Arab states. It also led to the beginning of efforts to clear the Suez Canal, which had been closed since 1967.

Negotiations with Israel for further Israeli withdrawal did not make much progress during the rest of the year. U. S. Secretary of State Henry Kissinger made several trips to Egypt and the Middle East in 1974. But by November, Egyptian enthusiasm for him was somewhat tarnished. There was at year's end renewed talk in Egypt of more hostilities with Israel if further concessions were not made.

Diplomatic relations with the United States, broken since 1967, were renewed in February. In June, President Nixon visited Egypt and was received with great warmth. He had earlier in April asked Congress for $250 million in aid for Egypt. He announced during his trip that the United States would provide a nuclear reactor to Egypt. Secretary of the Treasury Simon visited Cairo in July. In the same month four big American banks obtained permission to open Egyptian branches. In August, 100,000 tons of U. S. wheat were pledged to the Egyptians. Relations between the countries were better than they had been in perhaps 20 years.

Relations with the Soviet Union remained ambiguous during 1974. In April, President Sadat announced that Egypt would no longer rely on the Soviet Union for arms; later, however, Sadat assured the Soviet Union that the latter should play an active role in the process of achieving settlement of the Middle East dispute. In September, Sadat reported that Egypt would continue to receive arms from the Soviet Union.

Egypt and its president, Anwar el-Sadat, continued their roles of leadership in the Arab world. Sadat strongly influenced the Syrians in their disengagement with the Israelis in May; earlier, he had played a significant part in the lifting of the oil embargo by the Arab states. At year's end he was active in working out some role for the Palestinians in any eventual Middle East settlement with the Israelis.

UPI

During a state visit to Cairo in June, President Nixon is entertained by a belly dancer. Nixon is flanked by Secretary of State Kissinger and Egyptian President Sadat.

Domestic Affairs. In January, Sadat felt secure enough to release from jail a number of formerly powerful military and press figures. In February, however, Mohammed Hassanein Heykal, who had criticized aspects of Sadat's foreign policy, was ousted as chief editor of the newspaper *Al-Ahram*. Most censorship was lifted at the same time. Press editorships were again shaken up in May. On May 15 some 8 million Egyptians voted in a referendum that approved a government program calling for new and liberal changes in both government and the economy.

In late April a coup was attempted, apparently by fanatical religious forces. Egypt accused President Muammar el-Qaddafi of Libya of fomenting this trouble. In August, Qaddafi went to Cairo to attempt to resolve his differences with President Sadat.

Although 1974 saw a number of significant gains for Egypt and for Sadat personally, there continued to be economic ills at home, including major food shortages. And permanent peace with Israel was not yet in sight.

CARL LEIDEN
University of Texas at Austin

EGYPT • Information Highlights

Official Name: Arab Republic of Egypt.
Location: Northeastern Africa.
Area: 386,660 square miles (1,001,449 sq km).
Population (1973 est.): 36,900,000.
Chief Cities (1970 est.): Cairo, the capital, 4,961,000; Alexandria, 2,032,000; Giza, 712,000; Port Said, 313,000.
Government: *Head of state,* Anwar el-Sadat, president (took office Oct. 1970). *Head of government,* Abdul Aziz Hegazi, premier (took office Sept. 1974). *Legislature* (unicameral)—People's Assembly.
Monetary Unit: Pound (0.3906 pound equals U. S.$1, July 1974).
Gross National Product (1972 est.): $8,270,000,000.
Manufacturing (major products): Cotton textiles, processed foods, fertilizer, iron and steel.
Major Agricultural Products: Cotton, forage plants (berseem), rice, wheat, sugarcane, millet, corn, fish.
Foreign Trade (1973): *Exports,* $1,117,000,000; *imports,* $906,000,000.

UPI

Governor-elect Edmund G. Brown, Jr., of California waves to Democratic supporters on election night. On his left are his parents, former Governor and Mrs. "Pat" Brown.

ELECTIONS AND POLITICAL PARTIES

With the electorate in a grim and frustrated mood, Democrats won substantial new victories in U. S. elections in 1974. Rampant inflation, growing unemployment, shortages of consumer supplies, high taxes, and unease about the stability of America's international relations all alarmed the voters. They were also highly indignant or distressed about revelations that led to the resignation of President Nixon on August 9 and over his pardon by President Ford.

The political outcome, foreshadowed by polls and by Democratic successes earlier in the year in six of seven special elections for congressional seats, was a severe blow to conservative Republicans. In the general elections on November 5, voters tended to reward moderate liberals in both parties while giving Democrats a resounding victory. A low turnout, about 38% of voters of eligible age, reflected public disenchantment.

Congress. Democrats increased their majorities in Congress, particularly in the House. Democrats controlled the Senate in the new 94th Congress by 61 to 38 (the New Hampshire race was undecided at year-end) and the House by 291 to 143 (a special election was to be held in January in Louisiana's 6th Congressional District). (The 93rd Congress ended with the Democrats in control, 58 to 42 in the Senate and 248 to 187 in the House.)

Forty incumbents in the House met defeat in the election, 36 of them Republicans and 4 Democrats. Two Republican senators were defeated: Marlow W. Cook by Gov. Wendell H. Ford in Kentucky, and Peter Dominick, Colorado, by Gary W. Hart, a manager of George McGovern's 1972 presidential campaign. Membership in both the new House and Senate is

WIDE WORLD

"V" for victory is signaled by Democrats George Wallace (*above*), elected to an unprecedented third term in Alabama, and John Glenn, the new U. S. senator from Ohio.

WIDE WORLD

younger and more liberal. Six new women members won election to the House, raising the total from 16 to 18. Reelection of every black incumbent plus another member from Tennessee brought the total of blacks in the House to 17.

All incumbent Democratic senators running in the election were successful. Among them were Birch Bayh, Indiana; Alan Cranston, California; Thomas F. Eagleton, Missouri; Daniel K. Inouye, Hawaii; George S. McGovern, South Dakota; Warren G. Magnuson, Washington; Gaylord Nelson, Wisconsin; Abraham A. Ribicoff, Connecticut; Adlai E. Stevenson 3d, Illinois; and Herman E. Talmadge, Georgia. Among other Democrats elected to the Senate were Gov. Dale Bumpers, Arkansas, who defeated Sen. J. William Fulbright in the primary, and John H. Glenn, Jr., former astronaut, who won an impressive victory in Ohio.

Among Republican senators reelected were conservative Barry Goldwater, Arizona; Jacob K. Javits, a liberal successful in his three-way race in New York; and moderate liberals Charles McC. Mathias, Jr., Maryland, Robert Packwood, Oregon, and Richard S. Schweiker, Pennsylvania.

State Elections. Democrats also made gains in state offices that provide them with new opportunities for influence in the 1976 elections. In 35 races for governor, they won 27, the Republicans 7. In Maine, James B. Longley was elected as an independent in an antipolitics campaign, defeating nominees of both political parties. The results gave the Democrats 36 governorships and the Republicans 13, with one independent.

Of the ten Democratic victories overturning Republican governorships, those in New York, Connecticut, Massachusetts, and Oregon produced the widest margins. In New York, Hugh L. Carey of Brooklyn won 58% of the vote, highest in this century. Connecticut elected Ella T. Grasso, the first woman governor in the country whose husband had not preceded her in that office. Liberal Michael S. Dukakis, in defeating Republican incumbent Francis W. Sargent in Massachusetts, led a Democratic upsurge. In Oregon, Democrat Robert W. Straub won with the support of labor and of retiring Republican Gov. Tom McCall. By a margin smaller than expected, California voters chose Democrat Edmund G. Brown, Jr., son of a former governor, to succeed retiring Republican Gov. Ronald Reagan. Democrats also wrested governorships from Republican control in Arizona, Colorado, Tennessee, and Wyoming.

The most important Republican victories in races for governor were in Michigan, with reelection of William G. Milliken, and in Ohio. In the latter state former Gov. James A. Rhodes barely toppled incumbent John J. Gilligan, who was vulnerable because of Ohio's first income tax. Republicans also overturned Democratic regimes in Kansas and South Carolina. Democrats reversed Republican control of both houses of legislatures in six states, including Connecticut, Illinois, and New Jersey and gained one house in each of ten other states, New York among them.

WIDE WORLD

UPI

New faces in Congress will include Dale Bumpers of Arkansas (*above, with his wife*), who succeeds veteran Sen. William Fulbright, and Mrs. Helen Meyner, who joins the New Jersey contingent in the House.

Party Developments. President Ford named Mary Louise Smith of Iowa as chairman of the Republican National Committee. She became the first woman to hold that post. Democratic Sen. Edward M. Kennedy's announcement, September 23, that he would not be a candidate for president left his party without a front-runner. Gov. George C. Wallace of Alabama, later overwhelmingly reelected, stood next in the polls but was not expected to gain liberal support. Senators Henry M. Jackson and Lloyd M. Bentsen were openly campaigning, but Sen. Walter F. Mondale announced he would not run. In November, Representative Morris K. Udall of Arizona became the first Democrat officially to declare his candidacy. President Ford announced on November 15 that he would seek the Republican nomination in 1976.

FRANKLIN L. BURDETTE, *University of Maryland*

ELECTRONICS

With total United States sales nearing the $38 billion mark, the electronics industry is contributing a more significant share of the nation's gross national product.

Integrated Circuits. The driving force behind much of the industry's growth is the advances being made in integrated circuit technology by semiconductor makers. The declining average cost and steadily increasing capacity of electronic functions in integrated circuits are broadening their use into such rapidly growing areas as calculators, electronic cash registers, automotive devices and subsystems, instrumentation, and telecommunications, where electromechanical devices previously had been the predominant technology.

U. S. factory sales of integrated circuits in 1974 increased about 35%, to $1.5 billion. U. S. factories produced an estimated 2 billion integrated circuits during the year, or more than the semiconductor industry turned out in the decade through 1972.

Foreign Trade. What may prove to be one of the more significant developments during the year was the position taken in July by semiconductor companies on trade and technology transfer with the Soviet Union and its allies. Basically, the semiconductor makers told a Senate subcommittee that there seems to be little reason why they should make their technical know-how available to Communist countries. C. Lester Hogan, vice chairman of Fairchild Camera & Instrument Corp., a leading semiconductor producer, told the Senate group that: "It takes a great deal of gullibility to believe that a Communist country, once it has the know-how to produce integrated circuits, for example, will not increase its capacity enough to fill its own needs. Furthermore, Communist nations use this 'come on' as another opportunity to 'whipsaw' one company against another and one country against another." According to Dr. Hogan, the potential market within the Soviet Union and eastern European countries may prove to be very small, and its loss would probably not cause financial problems for U. S. companies.

Minicalculators. The drop in the retail price of minicalculators to as low as $20 helped boost the worldwide market for these products from under 3 million units in 1971 to about 26 million in 1974. Currently there are some 50 suppliers of calculators, but this number will shrink as more semiconductor companies—which produce the major components for calculators, including the circuitry, digital display, and keyboard—enter the field and gain almost immediate consumer recognition with their aggressive marketing tactics. By cutting their suggested retail prices several times during the year, these companies placed considerable pressure on calculator suppliers, who had to rely on the semiconductor firms for their parts. It also became apparent during the year that the under-$100.00 calculator market was becoming a seasonal business with sales picking up rapidly at tax time, Father's Day, the opening of school, and Christmastime. Despite these trends, some nonelectronics-oriented companies made plans to enter the field with private-labeled models.

Digital Watches. The electronic digital watch has gained public acceptance faster than any other innovation in timekeeping technology. The U. S. market in 1974 exceeded 1 million units. End-of-year patterns indicated that unit sales might double in 1975 as more digital watches enter the market, and as prices decline and new features are added.

Television Costs. A study sponsored by the National Science Foundation, conducted by the Massachusetts Institute of Technology's Center for Policy Alternatives in association with the Charles Stark Draper Laboratory, Inc., determined that servicing charges account for 35% of the total expenditure on a color television set during its useful life, while the purchase price and electrical power costs account for 53% and 12%, respectively. This means that the owner of a $400 color TV can expect to spend another $400 during its useful life. The study group stated that while color TV accounted for 40% of all TV set failures in 1970, the percentage was expected to increase to about 67% by 1980.

Also, TV carry-in service is expected to rise from 57% of all service in 1970 to 74% in 1980. In sum, productivity of TV service is not expected to change much in the future, and the television service business in 1980 will be somewhat smaller, leaning heavily toward color TV and carry-in service, the latter due to the smaller sets and modularization. While the need for technicians is expected to decline, other home electronics products such as cable TV and videotape systems may take up the slack.

Marine Electronics. The U. S. Coast Guard announced in 1974 that Loran-C (for long-range navigation) will replace Loran-A systems to improve marine vessel traffic safety in U. S. harbors, estuaries, and along the entire coastline from Maine to Alaska.

The Coast Guard explained that the growing volume of vessel traffic and the expected increase in the number of fixed structures, such as off-shore drilling platforms, demand precise and accurate navigation by the mariner. With Loran-C, a vessel's position can be plotted to within one-quarter nautical mile (500 yards). Loran-A, the system developed during World War II and currently in wide commercial use, is accurate only to between one-half mile and two miles. A transition period of five years will be provided before any continental U. S. Loran-A stations are closed down.

RONALD A. SCHNEIDERMAN
"Electronics" Magazine

WIDE WORLD

As President Ford signs a bill creating a new energy agency, Sen. Charles Percy (R-Ill.) hands a ceremonial pen to Rep. Frank Horton (R-N. Y.) across Sen. Abraham Ribicoff (D-Conn.).

energy

Energy developments in 1974 are reviewed in this article under the following headings: (1) Survey; (2) Coal; (3) Electricity; (4) Gas; (5) Nuclear Energy; and (6) Petroleum.

Survey

The United States and much of the rest of the world faced a number of serious problems associated with the so-called energy crisis. Heading the list of energy-related problems is the high cost of petroleum sold by the oil-rich nations that form the Organization of Petroleum Exporting Countries (OPEC).

Impact of Oil Costs. The continued high cost of OPEC oil was seen by Western industrialized nations as being one of the prime reasons for inflation, which remained unchecked. Poor nations, which are attempting to industrialize to improve the lives of their citizens, viewed the high oil prices as constituting an almost insurmountable obstacle to their development plans because without energy a nation cannot build an industrial base.

To make matters worse, much of the agricultural activities in both the Western industrialized nations and the poor developing countries depend on chemical fertilizers, many of which are derived from petroleum. Thus, the cost of oil resulted in increased prices for fertilizer. While U. S. farmers generally could pay higher prices, farmers in the poor nations often could not. This situation was particularly serious because many poor nations depend on hybrid crops to produce the large yields necessary to feed growing populations, and such crops produce well only with heavy applications of chemical fertilizers.

Another basic problem occasioned by the price paid for oil to the OPEC nations was the fear by the Western industrialized nations that the revenues earned by the oil nations would seriously undercut international monetary stability if caution and restraint were not used in their investment. In 1974 alone, it was estimated that the consuming nations paid $60 billion for oil.

Oil-Fed Arms Buildup. A special problem related to the high price of oil is the amount of oil revenues that are earmarked or spent by the Arab petroleum nations as they continue their confrontation with Israel. In October an Arab summit conference in Rabat, Morocco, concluded with a pledge to the Arab neighbors of Israel that more than $2 billion will be provided from oil revenues to finance the anti-Israel campaign. Most of the funding will go to Egypt and Syria, with lesser amounts for Jordan and the Palestine Liberation Organization. The immediate objective of the Arab states is to establish an independent Palestinian state on the west bank of the Jordan River. The area has been held by Israel since it was occupied during the 1967 war.

As the Arab states used their oil wealth to arm for another conflict with Israel, fears were expressed in the West that the Arabs might again cut off oil shipments to pressure Western nations to cease selling military equipment to Israel. With the increasing dependence of Western countries on Arab oil such action could

AMERICAN TELEPHONE AND TELEGRAPH COMPANY

This heat recovery system is used by AT&T to recycle heat from central office equipment to warm offices and thus reduce the consumption of energy.

have serious consequences for Israel, which does not produce much of the advanced military hardware needed by its armed forces.

U. S. Energy Policy. By the end of 1974 it was widely accepted, in and out of government, that the optimistic expectations that the United States could become independent of foreign energy imports by 1980 had been seriously in error. Thus, the objective of Project Independence, as the effort to become self-sufficient in energy had been called by President Nixon, became under the Ford administration an effort to keep dependence on foreign oil to less than 35% of U. S. needs. The problem was that new sources of energy could not be developed and put into commercial operation as soon as originally hoped.

Addressing the United Nations in September, President Ford sought to link the world's food and energy problems when he said, "The food and oil crises demonstrate the extent of our interdependence. Many developing nations need the food surplus of a few developed nations. And many industrialized nations need the oil production of a few developing nations." Whether or not the world could solve the twin crises harmoniously became the subject of considerable speculation, and some pessimism.

Chinese and Soviet Energy Policy. As the United States and its allies assessed their oil-related problems, it was no solace to know that the Soviet Union and the People's Republic of China appear to be self-sufficient in energy. This fact was often interpreted to mean that the two largest Communist nations could be expected to make use of their favorable position relative to the energy-deficient status of their capitalistic competitors.

Coal

Coal is by far the most abundant of the fossil fuels being extracted from the earth in the United States today. However, it ranks third, at approximately 20%, behind petroleum and natural gas in terms of the total U. S. energy usage. Because of its abundance, coal is viewed by many as a likely replacement for oil and natural gas. However, serious environmental problems may limit the degree to which the use of coal can be expected in the future.

Coal in the western states is relatively low in sulfur content, and hence, when it is burned in power plants, it creates less sulfur-dioxide air pollution than coal from the eastern United States. However, environmentalists object to the burning of even low-sulfur coal in the relatively clear atmosphere found in the western United States.

Western coal is found close to the surface of the earth in Wyoming, Montana, Utah, Colorado, New Mexico, and Arizona. Economic considerations encourage the strip-mining of this coal, leaving open pits from which the covering soil has been removed prior to the digging out of the coal. Environmentalists object strenuously to this method of coal removal because of the resulting scars on the land, which cannot be easily revegetated because of the poor soil and lack of rainfall.

In contrast, eastern coal is often deep mined, which means that the environmental damage associated with strip-mining is avoided. However, eastern coal use involves certain disadvantages. These include the danger to miners working in deep mines, and the higher dollar costs associated with deep mining operations. Furthermore, when burned in power plants, eastern coal frequently violates the air pollution standards of eastern cities.

For these reasons coal was something of a problem in terms of the part it would play in future U. S. energy plans—there is a great deal of coal in the United States, but it often appears to be a less than satisfactory energy source.

U. S. coal production was on an upward trend in the mid-1970's, following a 20-year downward trend. U. S. coal production in 1974 was estimated at about 650 million tons, up from about 590 million tons in 1973. The United States exported about 10% of its coal production, mainly to Japan, which is poor in coal, oil, and natural gas resources.

Electricity

Electricity is a popular type of energy for Americans, and the growth in its usage continued in 1974. In a curious fashion the high demand for electricity added to the problems facing the electric generating industry. In times past the industry would have been pleased with the necessity to construct new power plants. In today's world, however, the demand for new generating plants brought headaches to the utility companies.

A difficulty in meeting demand for more electric power is that generating plants take several years to construct, and they are becoming increasingly expensive. The scarcity of capital for new construction of power plants, the high interest electric utilities must pay for funds borrowed for construction, and the rapidly increasing cost of fuel for generating plants all added to the fiscal squeeze on the electric generating industry.

Other problems facing the electric utilities were the opposition to new plant siting expressed by local residents afraid of various environmental hazards and by environmental groups particularly concerned about the expanded construction of nuclear power plants.

Because of the uncertainty of oil supplies from the Middle East it was difficult to guarantee adequate fuel stocks for oil-fired power plants. In an effort to reduce dependence on Middle East oil and to make more petroleum available for processing into gasoline, the government asked that coal be substituted for oil in power plants where that substitution could be made. In order to make such substitution it was necessary, at least temporarily, to lower the air pollution standards that had been established previously by the government.

As was the case with other forms of energy, President Ford made the request that citizens voluntarily contribute to the national effort to conserve energy by carefully husbanding the electricity they used. The government expressed the hope that voluntary conservation would eliminate the need for various types of mandatory controls on energy usage.

Worldwide electric generating capacity has been approximately doubling every decade since 1910. The leading producers of electric energy now are the United States, the USSR, Japan, the United Kingdom, West Germany, Canada, France, and Italy. Since hydroelectric power, nuclear power, and geothermal power now play small or negligible roles in these countries, they are critically dependent on adequate supplies of coal, oil, or gas for their electric power plants, at least into the near future.

WORLDWIDE PRODUCTION OF NATURAL GAS

Country	1971 (millions of cubic meters[1])	1972
United States	636,931	638,030
USSR	212,398	221,386
Canada	70,765	82,503
Netherlands	43,742	58,385
United Kingdom	18,462	26,571
Rumania	25,251	26,212
Mexico	18,220	18,694
Iran	14,423	17,185
West Germany	15,142	16,924
Italy	13,380	14,142
Venezuela	9,365	9,468
Libya	465	7,800
France	7,149	7,517
Argentina	6,447	6,183
Poland	5,164	5,823

[1] One cubic meter equals 35.31 cubic feet. Source: 1973 UN Statistical Yearbook.

Gas

Of the various fossil fuels, natural gas creates the least environmental impact when it is burned. Furthermore, because of government-imposed low prices, natural gas has been one of the best energy bargains in the nation. Unfortunately this premier fuel is dwindling in supply, and the United States is not able to produce all the natural gas it consumes.

Several alternative sources for natural gas are under study. One possibility is to increase imports of natural gas from North Africa. Another alternative would be to advance U. S. capital to the Soviet Union to assist in the development of vast gas fields, from which supplies could be imported to the United States. Neither option is attractive because of the increased dependence on foreign energy sources each would involve.

Still another option is to convert coal to synthetic natural gas. Several processes for doing this are either developed or under examination. As noted above, there are vast coal deposits in the United States that could be used for gas conversion. However, in order to obtain the coal for conversion the same problems arise as in regard to obtaining coal for power plants. Furthermore, the gas-conversion processes require large amounts of water, which could be a problem in the water-short West. Offsetting these disadvantages is the fact that once produced, synthetic natural gas, like natural gas, produces essentially no air pollution when burned. Although consid-

WORLDWIDE PRODUCTION OF ELECTRIC ENERGY

Country	1971 (millions of kilowatt hours)	1972
United States	1,717,521	1,853,390
USSR	800,360	857,435
Japan	385,612	428,577
West Germany	259,633	274,769
United Kingdom	256,587	263,681
Canada	216,472	237,627
France	148,998	163,412
Italy	124,860	134,930
Poland	69,887	76,475
East Germany	69,421	72,828
Sweden	66,550	71,682
India	66,385	....
Spain	62,516	68,910
Norway	63,564	67,793
Australia	57,974	61,020

Source: 1973 UN Statistical Yearbook.

MICHAEL EVANS/THE NEW YORK TIMES

Keeping a watchful eye on the consumption of energy throughout New York City, these employees of Consolidated Edison man the utility's control center.

erable interest has been shown in developing commercial coal-conversion plants, it appears that at least several more years will elapse before any substantial quantities of synthetic natural gas will be available to alleviate the energy problems in the United States.

Natural gas accounts for about 35% of the total U. S. energy usage, but proved reserves of U. S. natural gas have been declining since 1967. The leading producers of natural gas are the United States, the USSR, Canada, and the Netherlands. According to a Soviet specialist in energy resources, the USSR has about half of the world's total known natural-gas resources. It has huge natural-gas deposits in Siberia. The United States and Canada have large untapped deposits in Arctic lands.

ROBERT M. LAWRENCE
Colorado State University

Nuclear Energy

After over 28 years of service to the American people, the oft-praised and oft-criticized Atomic Energy Commission (AEC) was formally disbanded in 1974. This move was the single most important development for U. S. nuclear energy in 1974.

Reorganization. President Ford signed into law on Oct. 11, 1974, a bill replacing the AEC with a Nuclear Regulatory Commission. The bill had received near unanimous support in the House and Senate. Significantly, the bill also created a new entity—the Energy Research and Development Administration (ERDA)—designed to assume the research and development functions of the old AEC. The move is expected to strengthen government control over nuclear-energy electrical production and other peaceful applications of nuclear energy.

The nuclear regulatory body would be required to limit its membership to no more than three members from any one political party. It would also establish penalties to ensure reporting of operational defects that pose substantial safety hazards. The three regulatory offices of the new commission—reactors, materials, safeguards, and research—would be directly responsible to the commissioners.

The newly formed ERDA will not be restricted to nuclear energy alone, but will assume responsibility for a full range of energy problems. Separate research offices are to be established for energy conservation, safety and environment, nuclear energy, fossil fuels, and advanced energy systems, including solar and geothermal energy. Energy research formerly done by the Atomic Energy Commission, the Department of Interior, the Environmental Protection Agency, and the National Science Foundation will be transferred to ERDA.

The ERDA will provisionally assume responsibility for nuclear weapons development until it and the Secretary of Defense decide whether the weapons program is to be transferred to the Department of Defense.

President Ford appointed Robert Seamans, former Secretary of the Air Force, to be the first administrator of the ERDA. Dixie Lee Ray, chairperson of the abolished AEC, moved over to the Department of State to become an assistance secretary in charge of energy. William Anders, a former astronaut, was nominated to be the first head of the Nuclear Regulatory Commission.

Curtailment of Nuclear Expansion. Rapidly rising costs and decreases in the growth of electrical power usage combined to cause the nation's electrical power industry to curtail sharply plans for nuclear expansion. An independent survey showed that approximately one half of planned nuclear generating capacity was abandoned in 1974. Also, out of a total of $88.1 billion in expected construction through 1978, utilities have cancelled about $16.1 billion for fossil-fueled and nuclear plants. The reductions amount to 132,500 megawatts (MW), of which 89,300 MW are in nuclear-fueled plants. Prior to 1974 about 175,900 MW of nuclear power were slated to be added. These cutbacks will seriously jeopardize the goal of reaching national self-sufficiency in the production of energy. Earlier AEC estimates had predicted that 15% of the U. S. electrical generating capacity would be nuclear by 1980, compared with 7.4% in 1974.

While U. S. nuclear growth slowed in 1974, the impact of nuclear power production in alleviating oil imports already was quite significant. Up to mid-1974, U. S. nuclear reactors had generated a cumulative total of more than 270 million megawatt-hours of energy, or the equivalent of 490 million barrels of oil.

Safety. Continuing concern for public safety was evident in 1974 as intervenors in nuclear-plant licensing hearings questioned AEC safety standards. Public concern prompted the AEC to undertake a monumental study of the safety of nuclear plants. A 3,300-page report was issued in August after two years of effort by 60 scientists and engineers headed by Norman C. Rasmussen of the Massachusetts Institute of Technology. The exhaustive analysis indicates public fatality safety risk from nuclear reactor accidents is very small—about 3 parts per billion per year. Such a fatality rate is small compared with motor-vehicle fatalities (3 parts in ten thousand), air travel (9 parts in one million), or tornados and hurricanes (4 parts in 10 million). However, the report also indicated a probability of 6 parts in 100,000 per reactor-year for a core meltdown, which would occur in a loss-of-coolant accident. Various groups of environmentalists, intervenors, and independent scientists indicated that the report would be subjected to searching examination by their organizations.

Nuclear Plants Abroad. Elsewhere in the world significant plans for nuclear-energy plants continued to be made. In Canada, Ontario Hydro announced its intention to build 8,000 MW of capacity over the next 10 years. The Canadian-developed CANDU reactors at Ontario's Pickering plant have excellent operating records, reporting a net capacity factor of over 82% through April 1974. CANDU plants are also operating in Pakistan and India.

After an extensive debate on national nuclear policy in 1974, the United Kingdom decided on a program of building steam-generating heavy-water reactors (SGHWR) in preference to the U. S.-developed pressurized-water reactor (PWR). The SGHWR concept is similar in principle to the Canadian CANDU reactor, which uses ordinary uranium fuel and heavy water (D_2O) as a moderator. The British design differs, however, in the use of light water (H_2O) for steam generation and the use of fuel slightly enriched in U-235. Britain plans to add about 4,000 MW of electrical capacity in the next four years by building several reactors in the 600-MW range.

Even in the oil-rich Middle East, nuclear building plans were laid in 1974. While the U. S. plans for reactors for the Israelis and Arabs were debated, oil-rich Iran quietly arranged to invest heavily in a nuclear-reactor program. A French company has contracted to build five 1,000-MW light-water reactors at a cost of $1.2 billion. Iran will also cooperate with France in studies of breeder reactors and nuclear shipbuilding. France will also help to build a nuclear research center near Teheran.

In Japan, nuclear energy received unfavorable publicity as its new nuclear frigate, the *Mutsu,* ran into difficulties. During low-power testing, a small defect in the radiation shielding of the frigate's reactor was uncovered. Because of protests by the fishermen of Honshu, who feared contamination of their scallop beds, the ship was kept out of its home port of Ominato. The Japanese government, which spent $30 million to develop the port, has promised to transfer the ship to a new port. The incident was regarded as having a negative effect on Japan's efforts to accelerate nuclear-power programs as an answer to its oil shortage.

Breeder Reactors. A landmark in breeder reactor history occurred in August when the experimental breeder reactor EBR-2 at the National Reactor Testing Station (NRTS), Idaho Falls, Idaho, completed 10 years of operation as an experimental power producer. EBR-2, a sodium-cooled fast breeder, has demonstrated the feasibility of the liquid-metal cooled, fast breeder reactor (LMFBR) concept for electrical power production.

In 1973–74 several important breeders either commenced operations or entered the start-up phase. These are the French Phenix, a 250-MW demonstration power station; the British 250-MW Prototype Fast Reactor; the Russian BOR-60; and the Russian BR-350, a 350-MW power reactor and water desalting unit. The Russians are also constructing the BN-600, a 600-MW power reactor. While several foreign prototypes are in operation, the United States has not produced a successor to EBR-2 in the past decade. In the planning stage is the Clinch River breeder reactor (CRBR), jointly sponsored by the AEC and the utility industry. The CRBR is expected to be completed by 1982.

Nuclear Fusion. The AEC supports two programs aimed at electric power production by nuclear fusion. One controlled fusion research program, carried out at four AEC laboratories, studies magnetically confined fuel plasmas. The primary types of magnetic bottles being studied are the low-plasma-density tokamak devices and the high-density thetapinch devices. The laser fusion research program, under way at three AEC laboratories, emphasizes the use of high energy, short-pulse laser beams focused on thermonuclear pellets to heat, compress, and ignite this fuel. For lasers and for magnetic confinement, a plasma temperature of 100 million degrees is required to achieve self-sustaining fusion.

The United States and the Soviet Union have developed an exchange of scientific personnel on nuclear fusion research. The first of 12 scientific exchanges started in October 1974 with the arrival of four Soviet scientists. In both countries more than 50% of the research efforts involve the tokamak, a doughnut-shaped fusion device invented in the USSR and adopted by the United States.

Nuclear Tests. India surprised the world by detonating an underground nuclear explosive device on May 18, 1974, thereby becoming the world's sixth nuclear power. Official statements from the Indian AEC stressed that the tests were staged for peaceful applications, such as earth excavations.

Meanwhile, France continued an extensive series of atmospheric nuclear tests in the South Pacific. France and Communist China are the only nuclear powers that continue to test in the atmosphere. France uses a testing area in the Polynesian area of the Pacific Ocean, while the Chinese use the Lop Nor nuclear test area in northwest China. Both the United States and the Soviet Union continue to conduct underground nuclear detonations.

Sections of pipe for the trans-Alaska oil pipeline are stacked in this storage yard in Fairbanks, Alaska.

ALYESKA PIPELINE SERVICE COMPANY

Research. Recent laboratory experiments in Israel and the United States have indicated that laser beams can be used to separate the isotopes of uranium. Researchers at the AEC's Lawrence Livermore Laboratory have aimed a laser beam and an ultraviolet light through a thin beam of uranium vapor at 2100° C. The laser selectively excites the electronic structure of U-235 atoms so they are ionized by the ultraviolet radiation. The U-235 atoms can then be electrically separated from the vapor. If this process can be duplicated on a large scale, U-235 separation for nuclear fuels could be made simpler and cheaper than by the present thermal diffusion process.

In other energy research, Soviet authorities claimed a breakthrough in the direct conversion of nuclear-reactor heat to electricity without the use of generators or turbines. In a direct-conversion device one side of a silicon-germanium alloy is heated in a reactor, while the other side is cooled. The resulting electrical current can be transmitted to an external circuit. The Soviet reactors provide a steady output of 10 kilowatts and can be used in remote power applications.

ROBERT E. CHRIEN, *Senior Physicist*
Brookhaven National Laboratory

Petroleum

A sharp increase in the price of crude oil highlighted petroleum developments in 1974. By year-end, foreign crude oil was selling for about $10.25 a barrel, compared with about $2.50 a barrel at the start of 1973.

Another major development was the shift in the ownership of oil-company operations. The major oil-exporting countries generally increased their participation in the international oil companies' operations within their borders to 65% ownership, with some countries looking toward 100% ownership. As a result, the role of the oil companies was in a state of flux.

Production. Crude-oil production worldwide was 55,656,500 barrels a day (b/d) in 1973, up 9.7% from 1972. In 1974, however, fairly firm figures for the first ten months indicated that production was down about 1.7% from 1973, with no likelihood that the downward trend would be reversed by year-end. The 1974 decline was attributed to several interrelated factors: the Middle East oil embargo which began in October 1973 and generally continued through the first quarter of 1974, greatly increased prices for oil, and a slackening in demand.

Exploration. Spurred by higher oil prices, drilling activity showed a sharp upsurge in 1974, particularly in the United States, where 32,000 wells were expected to be completed, up 23% from 1973 and more than in any year since 1967. Canadian drilling declined over 17% in 1974 to an estimated 3,800 wells. Worldwide, excluding Eastern Europe and China, total well completions were estimated at 41,600, up 17.5% from 1973. Outside the United States and Canada, major areas of drilling activity were Argentina, Indonesia, Mexico, Nigeria, Saudi Arabia, Venezuela, and the North Sea.

Reserves. Proved recoverable reserves of crude oil in the world at the end of 1973 were estimated to be 546.4 billion barrels, an increase of 4.3% over proved reserves of 523.7 billion barrels at the end of 1972. Over half the increase was accounted for by new discoveries in the North Sea and Nigeria, which continued to be active areas in 1974. These reserves figures do not include liquid hydrocarbons recoverable from natural gas.

Transportation. As of mid-1974, there were 3,443 oil tankers of 10,000 deadweight tons (dwt) or larger in operation, with a total capacity of 232 million dwt. At the same time, 1,202 tankers totaling 195 million dwt were on order for delivery by 1979. Of these, 181 (25 million dwt) were due for delivery in the second half of 1974, and 383 (54 million dwt) were scheduled for 1975 delivery—with some indications that about 25% of this capacity might be delayed. With prospects that the Suez Canal would be opened to tanker traffic during the first half of 1975, the general expectation was that the trend toward building larger tankers (a 476,000 tonner entered service in 1974) might be reversed.

Consumption. Major oil-consuming countries, faced with higher prices, were making efforts to reduce consumption. In the United States, use of oil products averaged 16.5 million b/d in the first 10 months of 1974, down 3.7% from the same period in 1973. Demand in Europe for the first half of 1974 was down even more —14.3% in West Germany, 8.9% in the United Kingdom, 5.7% in France, and 4.3% in Italy.

Refining. Worldwide crude-oil refining capacity totaled 63,578,000 b/d at the start of 1974, with over 20 million b/d of new capacity expected to be built and in operation by the end of 1976. The United States, with 13,383,000 b/d of capacity, had 21% of the total. Japan, with 5,410,000 b/d of capacity, was the next largest crude refiner. Four European countries—France, Italy, the United Kingdom, and West Germany—accounted for 12,472,000 b/d. However, the important refining areas could very well change in the next ten years as the major oil-producing countries strive to upgrade their domestic resources and build their own refineries so that they can export higher-value products and petrochemicals instead of raw crude oil.

WILLIAM F. BLAND
Editor, "International Oil News"

WORLD CRUDE OIL PRODUCTION
(Thousands of barrels daily)

	1970	1971	1972	1973
North America				
Canada*	1,263.5	1,347.5	1,531.9	1,974.0
United States*	9,636.8	9,462.8	9,440.9	9,187.3
Totals	10,900.3	10,810.3	10,972.8	11,161.3
Latin America				
Argentina	392.9	423.3	433.0	418.1
Bolivia	24.2	36.2	43.6	47.2
Brazil	156.2	174.0	166.9	170.8
Chile	34.0	35.3	34.2	30.5
Colombia	209.0	214.0	195.8	184.7
Ecuador	4.0	4.5	78.1	208.8
Mexico	428.8	427.1	440.8	519.5
Peru	72.0	61.9	64.6	68.2
Trinidad & Tobago	139.8	129.2	141.3	166.0
Venezuela	3,708.0	3,549.1	3,219.9	3,366.0
Others	4.7	2.2	2.2	3.3
Totals	5,173.7	5,056.8	4,820.4	5,183.1
Western Europe				
Austria	52.0	48.3	47.4	47.2
France	47.2	37.4	29.6	25.8
Germany, West	146.2	146.8	140.2	132.7
Italy	28.1	24.1	21.4	19.0
Netherlands	35.9	32.1	29.8	29.0
Norway	....	6.0	33.2	37.5
Spain	4.0	2.4	2.9	20.6
Turkey	69.1	65.8	64.5	58.9
United Kingdom	1.7	4.1	7.2	8.0
Yugoslavia	55.0	58.0	64.8	71.0
Others	....	....	1.7	1.8
Totals	439.2	425.0	442.7	451.5
Eastern Europe				
Albania	24.0	27.0	28.7	30.0
Bulgaria	6.0	6.3	4.9	5.0
Hungary	40.0	41.0	41.8	42.0
Poland	8.4	8.0	8.2	8.5
Rumania	271.0	280.0	287.7	295.0
USSR	7,030.0	7,400.0	7,912.6	8,450.0
Others	9.6	6.0	9.8	10.0
Totals	7,389.0	7,778.3	8,293.7	8,840.5

	1970	1971	1972	1973
Middle East				
Bahrain	76.6	75.3	69.7	63.2
Iran	3,829.0	4,539.5	5,023.1	5,860.9
Iraq	1,548.6	1,694.1	1,465.5	2,018.1
Kuwait	2,989.6	3,196.7	3,283.0	3,020.4
Oman	265.5	294.3	281.8	295.0
Qatar	362.4	430.7	482.4	570.3
Saudi Arabia	3,799.3	4,769.1	6,012.5	7,601.2
Syria	80.4	103.0	123.5	85.6
United Arab Emirates	779.6	1,059.5	1,202.7	1,532.6
Others	87.1	120.0	120.0	100.0
Totals	13,818.1	16,282.2	18,064.2	21,147.3
Africa				
Algeria	1,029.1	785.6	1,062.3	1,097.3
Angola	98.0	113.1	139.1	154.5
Congo (Brazzaville)	0.4	0.8	6.4	33.8
Egypt	326.7	293.9	202.6	165.7
Gabon	108.8	114.6	125.2	150.2
Libya	3,318.0	2,760.8	2,239.4	2,174.9
Nigeria	1,083.1	1,531.2	1,815.7	2,054.3
Tunisia	88.3	87.3	83.0	95.0
Others	0.9	0.5	0.6	0.7
Totals	6,053.3	5,687.6	5,674.3	5,892.6
Asia & Far East				
Brunei & Malaysia	160.0	192.1	275.9	325.7
Burma	18.0	19.0	20.3	20.0
China	402.0	510.0	525.0	720.0
India	144.1	142.7	155.6	161.0
Indonesia	853.6	892.1	1,078.7	1,336.9
Japan	15.5	15.1	14.6	14.2
Pakistan	9.2	8.2	8.2	9.9
Others	0.5	0.5	2.5	2.0
Totals	1,602.9	1,779.7	2,080.8	2,589.7
Oceania	179.9	311.6	393.9	390.5
World Totals	45,556.4	48,131.5	50,742.8	55,656.5

* Does not include synthetic crude or natural gas liquids, but does include lease condensate. Source: Annual Statistical Bulletin, 1973, Organization of Petroleum Exporting Countries.

Note: Due to rounding, totals may not add exactly.

UPI

Already nicknamed the "Golden Gate of Hamburg," the new Koehlbrand Bridge over the Elbe in Hamburg, West Germany, links the city with its harbor area.

ENGINEERING, CIVIL

In 1974 noteworthy civil engineering projects were under construction throughout the world.

BRIDGES

Notable bridges under construction or completed in 1974 included several in the United States and Brazil.

United States. The 3,000-foot (914-meter) New River Gorge Bridge under construction near Fayetteville, W. Va., will be the world's longest steel arch bridge. It will exceed by some 25 feet (7.6 meters) the arch on the former record holder, the Kill van Kull Bridge at Bayonne, N. J. Its main arch span measures 1,700 feet (518 meters) in length, and is 876 feet (267 meters) above New River.

Expected to be opened in 1976, the four-lane highway bridge will be a major link in the state's Appalachian expressway system, which is designed to provide area residents with direct access to Interstate Highways 77 and 79. The bridge will not require painting. It is constructed of 22,000 tons of high-strength, corrosion-resistant steel that oxidizes with age.

Another first of its type in the United States was the bridge completed in 1974 to carry Interstate Highway 8 across Pine Valley Creek Canyon, about 40 miles (64 km) east of San Diego, Calif. The $10 million structure is the first segmental prestressed cast-in-place concrete box-girder bridge built in the United States by the cantilever method. The 1,716-foot (525-meter) span is 450 feet (137 meters) above the creek bed. Its two main piers stand about 370 feet (113 meters) high.

A long-span highway bridge was built also in 1974 over the James River west of Newport News, Va. Nearly 4.5 miles (7.2 km) of concrete structure was completed in less than 1½ years by using a marine assembly line technique. In a $16 million operation, major structural elements, such as precast and prestressed composite girder and deck slab sections, were fabricated on shore, shipped to the site on barges, and positioned between the pile bents by floating cranes. Bents are on 75-foot (23-meter) centers. The two-lane bridge will eventually replace an existing two-lane parallel crossing.

One of two major crossings of the Ohio River in northern Kentucky was completed in 1974. Part of the Interstate 275 belt route around Cincinnati, the 1,758-foot (536-meter) steel structure carries four lanes of traffic across the river to a point just north of Lawrenceburg, Ind. The three-span bridge consists of a 750-foot (229-meter) continuous tied-arch-truss span over the main channel, and 504-foot (154-meter) truss-anchor spans to either side, with 68 feet (21 meters) between the truss centerlines. The other major crossing will carry Interstate 471 from Newport, Ky., to Cincinnati, and is scheduled for completion in 1975.

Brazil. In March 1974, Brazil opened the 6.8-mile (11-km) Rio-Niterói Bridge across Guanabara Bay, connecting Rio de Janiero and the bayside city of Niterói. About 5½ miles (9 km) of the structure are over water. It replaces a ferry line.

Designed by U. S. consulting engineers, the six-lane highway bridge was built by a joint venture of British and Brazilian contractors. It is the world's fifth-longest structure, and includes

BUREAU OF RECLAMATION, PHOTO BY J. TODD

Pueblo Dam on the Arkansas River near Pueblo, Colo., will provide household and irrigation water for downstream communities by 1975.

the longest unstayed steel box girder. The superstructure for most of the crossing is of concrete box design. The three center spans, however, totaling 2,493 feet (760 meters), are of unstayed steel box girder design to provide 197 feet (60 meters) vertical clearance. The center span provides 984 feet (300 meters) horizontal clearance.

CANALS

War and politics heavily influenced canal development in 1974.

Egypt. The Suez Canal is expected to be reopened in the summer of 1975. The 103-mile (166-km) canal has been closed since the 1967 Middle East war. Extensive clearing operations and dredging are restoring the 300-foot (91-meter) width and the 38-foot (12-meter) depth to the 106-year-old channel. Eventually Egypt hopes to widen and deepen the canal.

United States. The Cross-Florida Barge Canal has come into the news again with President Nixon's resignation. The former President halted construction on the 107-mile (172-km) waterway in 1971, but a federal judge since ruled that only Congress could stop the project. Environmental problems in the area and possible alternate routes for the canal are being studied.

DAMS

Public benefit continued to be the prime consideration for the construction of dams in 1974.

United States. Building Pueblo Dam on the Arkansas River near Pueblo, Colo., meant constructing two barriers: a massive head-buttress-type concrete structure (the first of its kind in the United States) and a 10 million-cubic-yard (7.65 million-cu-meter) earthfill structure that

Cutting a two-hour trip to 15 minutes, the Rio-Niterói Bridge over Guanabara Bay connects Rio de Janeiro and the bayside city of Niterói. It opened in March.

BRITISH STEEL CORPORATION

wraps around both ends of the concrete section. The central 180-foot (55-meter) high, 550-foot (168-meter) long section of the 1,750-foot (533-meter) concrete dam is an ungated overflow spillway. The earth embankments make up most of the 2-mile (3.2-km) length of the structure. The dam is an element in the U. S. Bureau of Reclamation's trans-basin Fryingpan-Arkansas project, and will provide domestic and irrigation water for downstream communities in 1975.

The Bureau of Reclamation is also building multipurpose Teton Dam on the Teton River near St. Anthony, Idaho, for flood control, power, irrigation, recreation, and wildlife conservation. An earth and rockfill structure, scheduled for completion in 1976, the embankment will be 305 feet (93 meters) above the foundation and have a crest length of 3,050 feet (930 meters). It will contain 9.5 million cubic yards (7.3 million cu meters) of material. Eventually a power plant at the site will have a total capacity of 20,000 kw.

The U. S. Corps of Engineers in 1974 completed two earth and rock dams, 10 miles (16 km) apart on two tributaries of the San Joaquin River, California. Buchanan Dam on the Chowchilla River is a rockfill structure with impervious earth core. It rises 202 feet (62 meters) above its foundation, and contains 2.3 million cubic yards (1.76 million cu meters) of material. Hidden Dam on the Fresno River is an earthfill structure 163 feet (50 meters) high, and 5,730 feet (1,747 meters) long, containing about 6 million cubic yards (4.6 million cu meters) of material. Both reservoirs will provide flood protection to downstream areas, supply additional irrigation water, and enhance the area's fish and wildlife habitat. Together the dams cost about $30 million to build. Another Corps of Engineers project, scheduled for completion in 1976, is Clinton Dam on the Wakarusa River near Lawrence, Kans. The earthfill dam, now under construction, will be 9,250 feet (2,820 meters) long, with a maximum height of 114 feet (35 meters).

Japan. Takase Dam, the largest rockfill dam in Japan, will form the upper pool for the Takase River pumped-storage hydroelectric peaking plant. Nestled in the mountains of the Japanese Alps, the dam rises to a height of 577 feet (176 meters). Nanakura Dam, forming the lower pool of the system, is somewhat smaller, rising 410 feet (125 meters). The entire system is scheduled to start up in 1977.

TUNNELS

Tunnels were being dug in many parts of the world in 1974 for new subways, for water supply, for opening new mines, and for other purposes.

United States. In New York City, work is moving slowly on the 14.3-mile (23 km) Second Avenue subway line. Construction on the two-track line started in 1972, and is expected to take 10 to 15 years at a cost of $2 billion. It will run from Whitehall and Water streets in the financial district of Manhattan to East 180th Street in the Bronx, near the Bronx Zoo.

Washington, D. C. is building a $4 billion, 98-mile (158-km) rapid-transit rail system, of which 43 miles (69 km) will be surface lines. The first section, 4.6 miles (7.4 km) in tunnel, including six stations, is expected to be opened in August 1975. It will serve downtown shopping and office areas and Union Station. The construction includes twin 4,000-foot (1,219-meter) tunnels under the Potomac River.

Henderson Tunnel in the Rocky Mountains in Colorado is somewhat unusual in that it is being driven on a straight west-to-east downgrade of 3% for its 10-mile (16-km) length. The drilling and blasting method is used to excavate. When completed in 1977, it will connect

PHOTO BY CARLTON READ, DELAWARE RIVER PORT AUTHORITY

Replacing the ferry service between Chester, Pa., and Bridgeport, N. J., Commodore John Barry Bridge over the Delaware River is the largest highway cantilever bridge in the world.

WASHINGTON METROPOLITAN AREA TRANSIT AUTHORITY

The new subway system in Washington, D. C., is scheduled to open in 1975. (*Above*) The stations have waffle-like walls and ceilings to muffle noise and frustrate grafitti artists. (*Right*) The massive mechanical "mole" is used to excavate the tunnels.

MORRISON-KNUDSEN COMPANY

an underground molybdenum mine east of the Continental Divide, with an ore-processing mill being constructed on the west side. The west portal is at an elevation of 8,950 feet (2,728 meters). The tunnel section is horseshoe-shaped, 15 feet 2 inches (4.62 meters) high by 16 feet 6 inches (5.03 meters) wide.

In a hard rock tunnel in Rochester, N. Y., a tunnel boring machine is used to drive the 5.7-mile (9.2-km) Cross Irondequoit sanitary interceptor sewer at depths of 80 to 200 feet (24 to 61 meters). Its circular cross section has an 18.3-foot (5.6-meter) diameter, and will be lined with concrete to a finished 16-foot (4.9-meter) diameter. The project will cost $37.4 million.

Canada. Montreal is adding 31 miles (49.9 km) of track to its Metro subway system under a $665 million, seven-year program. The present network of three lines is 14 miles (22.5 km) long. The initial section of new trackage is scheduled for completion by the end of 1975. Metro tunnels are 27 feet (8.2 meters) wide by 19 feet (5.8 meters) high.

Japan. Nippon Kokan, a steel producer, is completing a 1-mile (1.6-km) long undersea tunnel linking its new Ogishima Island iron- and steel-making complex in Tokyo Bay with the company's Keihin Works in Yokohama. Construction of the sunken tube-type tunnel began in October 1971, and was scheduled to be opened to traffic in January 1975. Each of the six tunnel sections is 361 feet (110 meters) long, 71 feet (21.6 meters) wide, and 23 feet (7 meters) high. Each section weighs 17,000 tons. The total length of the tunnel is 5,052 feet (1,540 meters), including the 2,165-foot (660-meter) submerged portion and approaches. The tunnel has four traffic lanes for transporting personnel, materials, and steel products between Ogishima Island and the Keihin Works. In addition, water and gas pipelines and electric cable conduits are carried through the center of the tunnel.

Tokyo's seven subway lines total 96 miles (154.5 km) in length—the fourth largest among world leaders in subway systems (London, 240 miles, or 386 km; New York, 239 miles, or 385 km; Paris, 144 miles, or 232 km; and Moscow, 88 miles, or 142 km). Four new subway lines under construction in Tokyo in 1974 will contribute an additional 29.3 miles (47.2 km) when completed in 1977.

WILLIAM H. QUIRK
"Contractors & Engineers" Magazine

GARY GUISINGER/THE NEW YORK TIMES

Strip mining in Gillette, Wyo., is expected to triple the town's population and create massive problems with respect to water supply and sanitation.

ENVIRONMENT

The oil crisis and three major conferences in 1974 underscored the linkage between population, food, and housing problems in the world's environment concerns. The oil crisis, while it created a new consciousness of the need for increasing international cooperation, nevertheless served to put in question certain environmentalist goals. However, the United Nations Environmental Program (UNEP) continued its planning at its Nairobi, Kenya, headquarters, for rational global environmental protection measures.

The three conferences of global environmental import were the Law of the Sea Conference in Caracas, Venezuela, the World Population Conference in Bucharest, Rumania, and the World Food Conference in Rome, Italy.

Law of the Sea. The second United Nations Conference on Law of the Sea (UNCLOS) in Caracas, Venezuela, June 20 to August 29, was marked by seemingly fruitless confrontation between the developed and developing countries. However, the issues regarding uses of the ocean, the development of its food and energy resources, and the protection of the marine environment were more clearly defined.

One issue, which remained undecided but apparently was due ultimately to be settled in its favor, is whether a 12-mile territorial sea and a 200-mile economic zone should become the law of the sea. The issue was important to environmentalists because it affected proposals to place shared responsibility for ocean pollution control in independent states, regional and global international organizations, and the proposed Seabed Authority of UNEP. Hope was expressed that the third conference, scheduled for Geneva in June 1975, would indeed produce a world "law."

Population Control. The World Population Conference, sponsored by the United Nations and held in Bucharest in August, ended with mixed reviews. Advocates of population control were rebuffed insofar as birth control devices and other family planning measures on a personal scale were concerned. But there was a general consensus recognizing the need to cope with population growth as a societal and economic phenomenon.

Significantly, although problems of population growth had been purposely excluded from the UN Conference on the Human Environment in Stockholm in 1972, Maurice Strong, director of the UNEP, addressed the Population Conference in Bucharest. He observed that "the main risks" of environmental damage on a global scale came from the population growth and economic activities of rich rather than poor countries. "A citizen of an advanced industrialized nation consumes in six months the energy and raw materials that have to last the citizen of a developing country his entire lifetime," Strong noted. (See also POPULATION.)

Food Conference. The World Food Conference in Rome in November took place against a backdrop of reports of imminent mass starvation in many parts of the world. In addition to unusual efforts at food and grain allocation, the conference gave special attention to such environmental concerns as use of dangerous insecticides, damage to fishing areas, and climate and weather controls. It also approved a World Food Council, associated with the Food and Agriculture Organization, and with headquarters in Rome, to improve the world food supply, particularly for the developing nations. (See also FOOD).

United Nations Environmental Program. The 58-member Governing Council of UNEP met in Nairobi in March 1974 and swept through its agenda with remarkable harmony and a sense of common purpose. The Council authorized a Global Environmental Monitoring System (GEMS) that would trace at least 15 specific pollutants throughout the world—in effect an "early warning system."

The members urged the highest priority be given to research in arid lands and to the development of medium and long-term programs for preventing desertification, not only in Africa but in Asia and Latin America as well. The other area of special emphasis was "human settlements," an inescapable preoccupation of the developing world.

The Council confirmed its participation in Habitat: Conference on Human Settlements, scheduled for the spring of 1976 in Vancouver, and authorized a contribution of as much as $1.5 million for the financing of the exposition itself. Enrique Peñalosa, of Colombia, is secretary general of Habitat.

Some 180 projects were financed by UNEP. Subjects included the food situation in developing countries, the use of pesticides rather than natural fertilizers, drought, aspects of marine pollution, aquatic mammals, patterns of energy use and production (in consultation with the industrial sector of the United States and Europe), industry guidelines for insertion in national legislation, standards of global environmental protection to be incorporated in national law, and aspects of weather modification. (The Soviet Union has presented a draft resolution to the United Nations General Assembly prohibiting weather modification for military purposes).

Ocean Pollution. Seventy-one nations in the International Maritime Consultative Organization, a United Nations agency, agreed on measures designed to reduce pollution from ocean-going ships, although two to five years will elapse before all the provisions of the agreement go into effect.

The new Convention for the Prevention of Pollution from Ships prohibits the dumping of plastics and places limits on the discharge of other trash and garbage; prohibits the discharge of the most harmful chemical substances and regulates the discharge of others; forbids the discharge of oil within 50 miles of land; calls for the construction of facilities for the reception of waste oil and chemicals at all major ports; stipulates that within three years of the convention's coming into force (after ratification by at least 15 nations collectively having not less than half of the world's shipping tonnage) all tankers, whether old or new, shall be equipped to retain oily ballast waste on board rather than washing it directly into the sea; requires that all tankers of more than 70,000 tons built after 1975 be equipped with segregated ballast tanks; and provides for compulsory arbitration of disputes.

As usual, the major weakness of the convention is enforcement. Unless an offense is committed within an area of "national jurisdiction," prosecution can be brought only by the state whose flag the offending ship flies. Observers were not sanguine on that likelihood. (See also OCEANOGRAPHY.)

Oil Industry Group. To present the views of the international oil industry to UNEP and other international agencies concerned with environmental protection, the International Petroleum Industry Environmental Conservation Association (IPIECS) was formed by some 20 oil companies and associations. The organization will be based in London, England. By late 1974 the Soviet Union had not become a member.

Progress in China. Maurice Strong, UNEP director, and his deputy director, Mustafa Yamal Tolba, an Egyptian microbiologist, visited China in September. Strong reported consider-

The Monsanto Company's "Landgard" waste-disposal and resource-recovery system being tested in St. Louis, Mo., shreds 35 tons of waste daily, recovering useful items.

MONSANTO COMPANY

In Tel Aviv, Israel, young people wear gas masks to protest the smell coming from a river into whose waters industrial wastes are being dumped.

UPI

able success there in reclaiming semiarid regions, especially in the western part of Liaoning Province. He also reported that the Chinese had shown considerable care in locating industrial plants to avoid pollution problems and to utilize waste products efficiently. Dr. Tolba praised the Chinese progress in coping with the parasitic disease schistosomiasis. The disease is known to infect the banks of canals and rivers, especially in Africa, the Middle East, and Latin America. Chinese scientists have developed a technique for diverting the silt and burying the snails that carry the parasitic disease.

Propellant Sprays. Worldwide use of chemical sprays is estimated at half a million tons annually, at least half of which is used in the United States. The most dangerous gases in question are chlorfluoromethanes—known as fluorocarbons. Some international alarm has developed because of evidence that, while these gases are normally inert, they break down under the glare of ultraviolet light, releasing chlorine that then breaks down ozone. It was reported that continued use of such sprays could increase the incidence of skin cancer by 10% or more and might affect crops throughout the world.

Paris Conference. The danger from propellant sprays constituted perhaps the main theme of a five-day conference in Paris in October on "The Latest Progress in Evaluating the Effects of Environmental Pollution on Health." Organized by the Commission of the European Communities, the World Health Organization, and the U. S. Environmental Protection Agency, the conference was attended by 700 specialists from 50 countries. A principal objective of the 160 papers, round-table discussions, and debates was to help the commission "fix reference levels which will enable it to harmonize the environmental policies of the nine member states of the community."

Baltic Sea. The first cooperative study of the condition of and causes of pollution in the Baltic Sea was said to be making substantial progress, now that all the littoral nations were participating. Seven nations—the USSR, Poland, Finland, Sweden, Denmark, and the two Germanys—signed a convention in December 1973 to protect the Baltic's fish resources. These seven nations signed a pact in Finland in March to prevent further pollution of the Baltic Sea.

Malaysia. The Malaysian Parliament passed a bill creating an Environmental Quality Council and a federal department headed by a director general to administer the council. The measure also provided for government licensing of all waste-producing establishments and the imposition of license fees according to type of industry, its location, and the kind and quantity of pollutants discharged.

South Africa. South Africa's Air Pollution Appeal Board refused the state-owned Iron and Steel Corporation permission to expand its plant. It was the first finding of its kind under the country's Atmospheric Pollution Act of 1965. The board ruled that the planned $100 million extension would increase pollution, and that the site was probably the worst that could have been chosen, in that oil spills in the ocean might sink to the bottom or be caused to do so as a means of "cleaning up."

Rhine River. France again refused to stop dumping salts into the Rhine River from its potassium mines. At a ministerial meeting in Bonn, the French managed to frustrate any significant progress in cleaning up the river. The best the conference of six riparian nations could do was produce a statement that the dumping of mercury, certain organic chemicals, and known cancer-causing substances would be reduced "as much as possible."

Mediterranean Sea. The pollution of the Mediterranean is "extremely grave" according to two members of the French Parliament, who conducted a four-month investigation. Raw sewage from Marseille, "red muds" (titanium oxide) from Corsica, and other pollutants are causing affected areas of the sea to die, they reported.

Part of the UNEP program for 1975 includes an examination of the Mediterranean. A meeting of the coastal states and United Nations agencies was scheduled for early 1975 in Barcelona to discuss protection and management of the Mediterranean. The program was to include legal strictures on pollution, monitoring of the Mediterranean as part of GEMS, and collection of data from existing specialized industrial plants, ships, and fisheries.

United States. The Ford administration followed up a policy initiated by the Nixon administration to reduce spending on environmental protection and to ease strictures on pollution, especially the use of high-sulfur coal and oil, as a consequence of shortages and high costs precipitated by the Arab oil embargo and price manipulation.

The impact of these environmental policy impediments was still unclear by the end of 1974 as they had little effect on existing laws and directives. In addition, continued popularity of environmental protection efforts was reflected in the November elections across the United States. Politicians favored by environmentalists won wherever environmentalism constituted an issue.

Energy Programs. Catalytic converters on automobiles were first in use in 1974. These devices were expected to reduce the levels of auto exhaust pollutants by 50%. However, the Clean Air Act of 1970 was amended to give automobile manufacturers more time to comply with the next stage of clean air standards. Intended to reduce the level of pollutants by 90% from 1968 levels, the law was amended to permit extensions from 1976–77 to 1977–78. Auto manufacturers could request further extensions up to a year.

In addition, a study released by three leading universities—Harvard, Columbia, and Massachusetts Institute of Technology—proposed that the federal deadline for a 90% reduction in air pollutants emitted by new automobiles should be relaxed until 1980. The study said that forcing the auto companies to adopt the catalytic converter now, because it is the only immediately feasible technology to control exhaust fumes, is an "unwise gamble." (See also AUTOMOBILES.)

A strong conservation effort, including mandatory federal standards for energy requirements of automobiles, appliances, and buildings was reported to have been suggested in the administration's Project Independence, a study on ways of achieving energy self-sufficiency for the United States. The unpublished study was said to favor drilling for oil and natural gas in the Atlantic Ocean according to a key government official, while taking an unenthusiastic view of costly crash programs to tap new energy sources, such as shale oil and solar heat. This prompted immediate warnings of environmentalist opposition.

The Energy Policy Project of the Ford Foundation, the most comprehensive study of energy ever undertaken in the United States, reported that the country could put off for 10 years "massive new commitments" to offshore drilling, oil imports, nuclear power, or development of coal and shale in arid areas of the West. The report recommended enactment of pollution taxes, among other measures.

Drinking Water Peril. After a study of water-treatment plants by the Environmental Protection Agency (EPA) had indicated that New Orleans and nearby communities were using drinking water from the Mississippi River that showed a high percentage of potentially cancer-producing contamination by industrial chemicals, the EPA in November ordered a nationwide study. Some of the chemicals appeared to be carcinogenic in animals, and the conditions in the New Orleans area appeared to be symptomatic of other areas. The study was due to be completed by June 1975.

The chlorination of drinking water is also under study, after preliminary reports that chlorination may be a factor in producing cancer. From Cleveland in October, and from New Orleans in November, it was announced that the carcinogenic factors seemed to point to chlorination. The EPA planned other studies on a nationwide basis to determine whether other materials in water (such as fertilizer and pesticides) may be the culprit.

Other Measures. A land-use bill, sponsored by Rep. Morris Udall (D-Ariz.), would have given $100 million a year for eight years to states willing to start planning to control the ugly spread of highways, gas stations, and real estate developments. However, the House of Representatives decided in June not even to debate the question. Administration support had been garnered for the bill, but this was suddenly withdrawn.

The ban on DDT remained in effect, with minor exceptions. The U. S. Forest Service was allowed to use DDT to control the spread of tussock moths that eat pine needles and may eventually kill the trees. EPA has allowed the use of DDT for pharmaceutical needs where there is no other solution for the protection of human health.

President Ford refused to sign a strip-mining bill approved by Congress in mid-December. Environmentalists favored the banning of strip mining, while industry wished to minimize reclamation activities. In question were mining rights in Western states where there is a large amount of low-sulfur coal.

JACK RAYMOND, *Past President*
International Institute for Environmental Affairs

ETHIOPIA

In 1974, Ethiopia was rocked by internal political disorder that culminated in the ouster of Emperor Haile Selassie after 58 years of rule.

Political Change. In the wake of civil disturbances reflecting public concern over unemployment, increasing prices, soaring inflation, and a spreading famine, dissident military forces took over Asmara in late February and a few days later surrounded all public buildings in Ethiopia's capital, Addis Ababa. Calling for military pay raises, land-reform programs, and the dismissal of the premier and cabinet, the enlisted men who appeared to have organized the revolt forced Haile Selassie to submit to their demands.

A new premier, Endalkachew Makonnen, took office on February 28. He agreed to the pay raises, appointed a new cabinet that included military figures, and promised to embark on a land-reform program. Former Premier Aklilu Habte Wold and many in his cabinet were placed under arrest pending an investigation into charges that they had enriched themselves at public expense. By mid-April the rebels had given control of Asmara back to civilian authorities and had removed their troops from the streets of Addis Ababa.

On March 7 and 8 a general strike was led by the Confederation of Ethiopian Labor Unions. The settlement gave 100,000 workers a minimum wage of E.$1.50 a day. Yet, as more and more of the demands of military and civilians were met by the emperor, more demands were generated, and shooting and violence continued into May.

On March 5 and April 14, Haile Selassie made two major moves in an effort to quell the growing disorders and threats to his authority. On March 5 he called for a 30-member constitutional convention to bring about political reforms. The convention would bring into being Ethiopia's third constitution. On April 14 he named his 21-year-old grandson, Prince Zara Yacob, as his successor. The prince, a student at Oxford University, formerly attended Eton and McGill University.

ETHIOPIA • Information Highlights

Official Name: Empire of Ethiopia.
Location: Eastern Africa.
Area: 471,777 square miles (1,221,900 sq km).
Population (1973 est.): 26,800,000.
Chief City (1971 est.): Addis Ababa, the capital, 881,400.
Monetary Unit: Ethiopian dollar (2.07 E. dollars equal U. S.$1, July 1974).
Gross National Product (1972 est.): $2,265,000,000.
Manufacturing (major products): Processed foods, textiles, cement, leather and shoes.
Major Agricultural Products: Coffee, cotton, sugarcane, corn, millet and sorghum, oilseeds, pulses, cattle, sheep.
Foreign Trade (1973): *Exports,* $237,000,000; *imports,* $213,000,000.

The armed forces arrested additional officials of the former government of Aklilou Habte Wold on June 29, claiming they were conspiring to obstruct the administration of the new premier. Although the military pledged its loyalty to Haile Selassie, it demanded that political and social reforms proceed rapidly. On July 22, unhappy over the slow pace of change, the Armed Forces Coordinating Committee placed Premier Endalkachew Makonnen under arrest and forced the emperor to appoint the "liberal" 44-year-old Michael Imru to the post.

By early August, the new premier announced the completion of the draft constitution, which required approval by parliament. It would make the emperor a constitutional monarch.

Finally, on September 12, the military moved decisively against Haile Selassie and toppled the 82-year-old monarch from his throne. A military decree announced that he had been deposed from office, and the emperor was removed from his sumptuous palace and taken to army headquarters. The Armed Forces Coordinating Committee did not abolish the monarchy but asked instead that Crown Prince Asfa Wossen, who was in Switzerland recovering from a stroke that left him partly paralyzed, become a figurehead king.

The committee also dissolved parliament, banned strikes and demonstrations, and named Lt. Gen. Aman Michael Andom, armed forces chief, to head a 120-man military council. However, on November 24 the military government announced that General Aman, together with former premiers Endalkachew Makonnen and Aklilou Habte Wold and a grandson of Haile Selassie, Rear Adm. Alexander Desta, had been executed, along with 56 others. Four days later, as a threat of insurrection grew in Eritrea and the military council began rushing troops into that province, Brig. Gen. Tafari Banti was elected chairman of the 120-man council. On December 20 the military council announced that Ethiopia would become a one-party "socialist" country.

Famine. In late 1973, famine, caused by a lack of rainfall, hit Wallo, Tigre, and Shoa provinces. Thousands died of starvation. In 1974 the famine spread south into Gamu-Gofa, Sidamo, Bale, and Harar provinces and devastated much of the area. The government initiated plans to feed some 2 million people with 200,000 tons of food donated by relief agencies and governments. At least 250,000 persons were said to have died as a result of the famine.

Foreign Affairs. As a consequence of the 1973 Arab-Israeli war, Ethiopia broke diplomatic relations with Israel in late 1973. The United States in 1974 was nearing completion of its new military base on the island of Diego Garcia in the Indian Ocean. Many of the U. S. troops formerly stationed at Kagnew base, Asmara, were transferred to Diego Garcia.

PETER SCHWAB
State University of New York at Purchase

American Indian Movement (AIM) leaders Russell Means (*left*) and Dennis Banks join hands in a victory gesture after a judge dismisses charges against them in connection with their occupation in 1973 of Wounded Knee, South Dakota.

UPI

ETHNIC GROUPS

The year 1974 marked the 20th anniversary of the landmark Supreme Court decision outlawing racial segregation in U. S. public schools, but the Department of Health, Education, and Welfare (HEW) noted that racial discrimination in public schools persists. Many schools in Topeka, Kans., a defendant in the 1954 decision, still had a disproportionate number of minority students, and most junior high and elementary schools serving minority students had inferior facilities. HEW data compiled in late 1972 showed that 11.2% of American black students were in all-black schools.

Educational Desegregation. HEW acted to enforce desegregation in public schools, but was criticized for failing to use its powers with vigor. It cut off integration-aid funds to the Pasadena (Calif.) School Board because the board had not complied with a court-ordered desegregation plan. HEW had already threatened to stop federal funds to several state college systems if suitable plans for racial desegregation were not developed, and in 1974 it accepted the plans of eight states. But because the state of Louisiana would not comply, HEW requested the Justice Department to file its first suit against an entire state college system. HEW claimed that the integration of Louisiana state universities had been only technical, and that the state had in fact been expanding a dual network of campuses to keep black and white students apart. The state of Mississippi will also be sued for noncompliance.

Criticism of HEW came from the U. S. Commission on Civil Rights, which claimed HEW had not cut off funds from school districts discriminating against Chicanos (Mexican-Americans). The commission argued that because public schools were not responding to Chicano needs, only 60% of Chicano children graduated from high school, compared with 90% of white students. The commission recommended programs in bilingual education, recruitment of Chicano teachers, and better representation of Chicanos on school boards.

HEW was also criticized by the Center for National Policy Review for failing to push for desegregation of schools in the North and West. The center pointed out that desegregation had been more effective in the South than in the North and West: in the South the proportion of black students in all-black schools fell from 97% in 1964 to 9% in 1972, but in the North and West, 57% of the black students were still in predominantly black schools.

Caspar W. Weinberger, secretary of HEW, defended the policies of HEW, arguing that extreme measures were sometimes unwise, and noting that public opposition to school desegregation in the North has been "fierce," while the South has been "much more willing to accept desegregation."

In 1974 the federal courts softened some previous rulings on school integration, and especially those on the busing of students to attain desegregation. Earlier in the year, U. S. District Court Judge Jack B. Weinstein ordered city, state, and federal agencies in New York to cooperate in altering housing and social patterns to effect desegregation of a junior high school in Brooklyn. Judge Weinstein ordered these agencies to propose plans that would induce white middle-class families to move into the area and stabilize its population.

The plans ordered by the judge were to include temporary busing of students to balance the school enrollment, police protection of children, and development of parks. But in July, Judge Weinstein modified his final order, allowing the city school board until 1977 to raise the number of white students in the school to 70% and suggesting that the junior high school be

FITZGERALD PUBLISHING COMPANY

FITZGERALD PUBLISHING COMPANY

***Golden Legacy*, a new illustrated magazine designed to present black history to black children, uses an easy-to-read, comic-book format that appeals to youngsters.**

made a school for gifted children to attract students from throughout the district.

In other desegregation cases the courts manifested a greater tractability. For example, the Supreme Court ruled in favor of a desegregation plan for Knoxville (Tenn.) schools, even though 9 schools were allowed to have 64% or more black students. The court supported a Memphis (Tenn.) school desegregation plan, even though, to save money and limit student busing, it retained 25 all-black schools.

The most important court decision on busing concerned the previously court-ordered busing of students between the mostly black Detroit school district and 53 predominantly white neighboring school districts. In a 5–4 decision the Supreme Court effectively struck down attempts to achieve desegregation by busing children across school district lines. The majority opinion, written by Chief Justice Warren E. Burger, emphasized that school boundary lines could not be casually ignored as mere administrative conveniences, for locally based school districts are essential to the continuance of community involvement in public schools; moreover, consolidating 54 school districts would create large problems in financing and administration. Justice Thurgood Marshall dissented, complaining that this decision provided "no remedy at all, ... thereby guaranteeing that Negro children in Detroit will receive the same separate and inherently unequal education in the future as they have been unconstitutionally afforded in the past."

Within school districts, busing was required in some cases. A federal judge ordered the Denver schools to integrate by fall. He required school boundaries to be redrawn so that black, Spanish-American, and white students would share classrooms. The plan involved busing about 23,000 students.

Court-ordered busing broke into violence in one Northern city. Ruling against a proposed referendum to use large-scale busing to integrate Boston schools, the Supreme Court of Massachusetts suggested that an "opinion poll" might be allowed. In an unusually low turnout, Boston voters rejected assigning children to particular schools to achieve racial balance without parental consent. But in June a U. S. district court judge ruled that Boston had deliberately maintained segregation in its public schools. He ordered the state to devise a temporary plan for racial balance in Boston to be implemented by fall.

The state plan reduced, but did not abolish, black-majority schools, and required the busing of at least 6,000 students, black and white. When school opened in September there was violence and schools were boycotted, especially in the predominantly Irish area of South Boston. Buses carrying either black or white students were stoned as they left school.

On October 4, 5,000 white demonstrators, led by many city officials, marched through South Boston protesting the forced busing. On October 9 at least 38 persons were injured in various incidents. In the Roxbury district hundreds of black students pulled fire alarms and stoned passing cars; and in South Boston a white mob attacked a black man. On October 15, in a clash between black and white students at a South Boston high school, one white student was stabbed. Gov. Francis Sargent called out 450 National Guardsmen and asked President Ford to send in federal troops, but the President refused. Sporadic violence continued and school attendance in Roxbury and South Boston remained low.

Meanwhile, Congress struggled to limit busing requirements to achieve racial integration. On a bill to aid elementary and secondary education, the House included provisions prohibiting all busing to achieve desegregation except when other attempts had been proved ineffective, and then only to a school "closest or next closest" to a student's home. It took the Senate a week of debate, mainly on busing, to pass a similar education bill. Its version allowed the court under extenuating circumstances to overcome racial segregation by busing students beyond the "next closest" school. The bill worked out in conference favored the Senate version. (See also EDUCATION.)

Living Standards and Employment. The need to integrate the white suburbs of large cities was pointed out by the U. S. Commission on Civil Rights. It urged that federal, state, and local reforms be instituted to overcome the "white nooses" of affluent suburbs around the black and poor communities in the urban centers.

But if discrimination against ethnic minorities exists in the suburbs, it exists also in the U. S. Congress, where 20 congressional offices were found to have placed discriminatory restrictions, such as "white only," on requests for staff employees.

In September the first national black economic conference, attended by more than 50 black leaders, was held in Washington. Members of the conference called on the administration to start a public works program to provide a million jobs for blacks suffering a "depression." Economic conditions of blacks and other minorities indeed seemed depressed. The unemployment rate among blacks and other minorities rose to well above 9%, almost double the national average. A Census Bureau report showed that in 1973 the median income of a black family was $7,269, barely more than half the $12,595 earned by a comparable white family. The difference had widened by 1% over the previous year, the median income for blacks having increased 5.9%, as against 9.1% for whites. The report showed that about 31% of blacks (compared with 8% of whites) live in poverty, including 40% of all black children.

Government agencies worked to rectify unjust hiring and wage practices. For example, under government pressure the El Paso Natural Gas Co. agreed to provide back pay and salary increases for underpaid minority employees (women as well as ethnic groups) and for the next seven years to hire specific percentages of minority groups. The Georgia Power Co. was forced to pay almost $2.1 million in retroactive wages and pension benefits to blacks deprived of equal employment; the company was also required to increase employment of blacks to 17% of its employees within five years.

Nine major steel companies agreed to pay back salaries totaling $30.9 million to about 34,000 minority employees hired before 1968; they also agreed to set timetables for filling openings in trade and craft positions with minority persons. Seven major trucking companies adopted goals for hiring blacks and Spanish-surnamed persons, agreeing to fill 50% of their job vacancies with minority group members in areas where minorities constituted more than 25% of the work force, and 33⅓% in areas where the minorities made up less than 25%.

Elections. The national elections of 1974 brought few gains for blacks and other minorities. Of 50 blacks who sought congressional seats, 17 won, one more than in the previous election. But in Colorado and California, blacks were elected to state lieutenant governorships. Several more blacks were elected to state legislatures in the South. Jerry Apodaca became the first governor of New Mexico since 1921 to have a Spanish surname.

Indian Affairs. The trial of two militant Indian leaders, Dennis Banks and Russell Means, for their part in occupying Wounded Knee, S. Dak., in 1973 was dismissed by a federal district court judge on September 16. The judge severely criticized the government for its conduct of the case. He accused the chief prosecutor and the Federal Bureau of Investigation of deceiving the court, and the Justice Department of indifference to justice.

Among the Indians themselves the militants seemed to have declined in influence. A moderate leader successfully prevailed over Russell Means, militant leader of the American Indian Movement (AIM), in an election for president of the Oglala Sioux.

The Justice Department for the first time sued to protect voting rights of Indians. It charged that a plan to redistrict one county in Arizona discriminated against Indian voters on a Navajo reservation. Government hearings on treatment of Indians in the Southwest revealed that Indians were being victimized in many ways, from cheating in business to murder. (See also CIVIL LIBERTIES.)

ROBERT L. CANFIELD
Washington University, St. Louis

UPI

Chicano businessman Ronaldo Terrazas (*right*) and assistant in Oakland, Calif., factory-workshop he founded with the financial assistance of a Chicano community development corporation.

UPI

EUROPE

Leaders of the nine European Economic Community countries gather in Paris in December. Following a two-day conference, a declaration on oil diplomacy and terms of British membership was issued.

The full dimension of the economic stresses to which the four-fold increase in the price of oil would expose their industry and agriculture became painfully clear to the European powers in 1974. Europe's attention shifted from the progress of détente, which had begun dramatically in 1972–73 with military and political agreements between the Western and Communist blocs, to each nation's internal problems.

Battered by inflation, which was further stimulated by price rises imposed by suppliers of raw materials and foodstuffs, the European countries were unable to respond with similar united measures. The European Economic Community (EEC) came under attack, especially from Britain, as contributing to the economic distress.

Efforts to restrain inflation by restriction of private and public spending, combined with a decline in the expansion of world trade, reduced the real economic growth of most European countries and threatened imminent recession. Partly as a result of their economic difficulties, two right-wing governments, in Portugal and Greece, were replaced by reforming regimes. Italy failed to form a coherent governing majority, and Britain held two elections in an effort to form a viable government. By the end of the year, even France's popular new president, Valéry Giscard d'Estaing, faced nationwide strikes.

Détente's Slow Progress. After the rapid progress achieved in 1972–73 in normalization of relations between West Germany and its Communist neighbors, there was little improvement of relations between the Communist and non-Communist blocs. West German Chancellor Willy Brandt resigned in May, following discovery that his personal aide was a Soviet spy. This incident left many Europeans in doubt as to the sincerity of Soviet gestures of détente.

More concrete doubts were raised by the North Atlantic Treaty Organization (NATO) experts who warned that the Warsaw Pact forces were increasing in relation to those of the West, in ground troops, tactical aircraft, and tanks. Above all, the great expansion of the Soviet navy, both in size and technology, appeared to challenge NATO's Mediterranean flank, which was weakened by the Turkish-Greek quarrel over Cyprus.

In spite of discussions between members of NATO and the Warsaw Pact in Vienna and a 35-nation Security Conference in Geneva, no significant breakthrough was made toward an agreement of force reductions or for a greater exchange of information and movement of people. Partly for that reason, the strategic arms limitation agreement in Vladivostok in November between President Gerald Ford and Soviet Communist party leader Leonid Brezhnev was welcomed in Europe as reviving the momentum of détente.

Consequences of the Oil Crisis. The reduction in oil supplies to Europe announced by Arab producers in late 1973 affected Europe only slightly, and by March 1974 rationing and bans on Sunday driving had been dropped. Even the

Netherlands, placed under embargo for its pro-Israeli stance, was receiving supplies from non-Arab sources. Europeans therefore resisted U. S. efforts at a Washington energy conference in February to create a unified Western policy for sharing energy supplies and to pressure Arab countries into lowering prices. They agreed only to study methods of coordination. The French set the example of seeking unilaterally to conclude agreements with oil-producing states; in July, for example, they agreed to supply Iran with nuclear power plants and other industrial equipment valued at $5 billion in return for guaranteed oil supplies.

As supply difficulties eased, the quadrupling of the oil price caused disruption. Italy, whose exports were already slumping, faced a payments deficit of $9 billion, and was forced to use part of its gold reserves to secure a $2 billion loan from West Germany. Great Britain, with a deficit of approximately $10 billion, and France, with a deficit of $6 billion, both sought loans from Iran.

Moreover, the accumulation of vast financial reserves by the oil-exporting powers, expected to reach $60 billion by the end of 1974, threatened disruption of the European financial system. Part of these reserves could be absorbed by the purchase of industrial or other assets; Iran, for example, purchased a 25% share in the Krupp steel company and Kuwait a 14% share of the Daimler-Benz automobile company. Oil revenues also could be placed in government securities. But the major proportion of the reserves, especially of the Arab countries, were invested in short-term deposits in a small number of large banks.

Linked to the existing balance of $40 billion in Euro-dollars, these monetary reserves caused instability. They could be shifted from currency to currency to profit from expected revaluations. Shifting of deposits caused rapid fluctuations in national interest rates. Currency alignments were difficult to maintain.

The inflation fed by the oil crisis was accelerated by the rise in world commodity prices. Europe's dependence on foreign suppliers for industrial raw materials and foodstuffs made it especially vulnerable to world inflation due to increased demand, speculation, action by producers, and poor harvests.

By the middle of the year, inflation varied from West Germany's relatively low 7% to intolerable levels of 15% in France, 17% in Britain, and almost 20% in Italy.

Problems Within the EEC. The economic crisis delayed movement in the EEC toward achievement of the goal of economic, monetary, and political union by 1980. "Action programs" for social, industrial, scientific, and technological policy were approved. But disputes among member governments prevented the strengthening of the powers of the European Parliament. The worst blow to Community unity was, however, the demand of Britain's Labour government that the terms of its membership, particularly its financial contribution to the organization and the working of the common agricultural policy, be renegotiated.

The government heads of the Community held a two-day summit meeting in Paris in December. The deadlock over Britain's demand that it contribute less to the EEC was broken by an agreement to reduce the financial contribution of countries in economic difficulties. They agreed to establish a regional fund of $1.56 billion to aid underdeveloped areas of the Community, especially in Ireland and Italy. Finally, at French insistence, they agreed to limit to exceptionally important matters the right of veto by each individual government.

Political Repercussions of Economic Distress. The energy crisis and payments deficits halted the economic resurgence in Britain and Italy that began in 1973 as a result of expansionist monetary and fiscal policies. In Britain, Conservative Prime Minister Edward Heath placed industry on a 3-day workweek in late 1973 in an attempt to force striking coal miners to reduce their wage demands. Heath, however, failed to win a majority in Parliament, after calling for a mandate in elections in February to resist the miners' claims. His successor, Labour party leader Harold Wilson, settled the dispute on the miners' terms.

During a strike by London teachers, youngsters join adults in a march from Hyde Park to House of Commons to dramatize strikers' demand for a £350 increase.

KEYSTONE

Although Wilson won a slight overall majority in new elections in October, social unrest remained strong. Unions threatened greater wage demands, while businessmen opposed the Labour government's plans for further nationalization and for major ownership by the state of North Sea oil operations.

In Italy, social and economic breakdown increased political unrest. Mail service was months delayed. Housing shortages in the cities were so great that squatters in Rome began to seize new apartment buildings. The probity of the Chamber of Deputies was impugned by reports of payoffs from oil companies to politicians, and support for the ruling Christian Democrats was eroded by the party's support of the unsuccessful attempt to repeal the 1970 divorce law. In June and again in October, Premier Mariano Rumor was compelled to resign after disagreements with the minor partners of his coalition government over steps to meet the economic crisis.

Europe's Move to the Left. The most immediate political gains from Europe's economic difficulties were reaped by the Communist parties. In Britain, Communists occupied key positions in several unions and played a role in planning union strategy during the miners' strike. In France, following the death of President Georges Pompidou in April, the Communist party threw its support to the Socialist candidate, François Mitterand, who was only narrowly defeated by the Independent Republican Valéry Giscard d'Estaing. Giscard had defeated the right-wing Gaullist candidate on the first ballot.

The new president promised to close the gap between the privileged and depressed segments of French society, and incidentally to reduce the appeal of communism, by educational reforms, changes in the tax structure, and minimum wage increases. When he was compelled to attack inflation by cutting government spending and raising taxes, his program was challenged in December by widespread strikes.

The move to the left was more pronounced in Portugal and Greece. Portugal had been governed since 1926 by an authoritarian regime primarily representing the interests of a small group of wealthy banking and industrial families. Discontent at the disparities in living standards was repressed by a powerful secret police. In April, a group of young army officers overthrew the government of Premier Caetano. The new government, led by Gen. Antonio de Spínola, wanted to force a change in the costly, unsuccessful attempts to defeat liberation movements in the Portuguese African colonies of Angola, Mozambique, and Guinea-Bissau.

Although Spínola admitted both Communists and Socialists to his government, his cautious, conservative approach to decolonization and economic reform was insufficiently reformist for the Armed Forces Movement. He was forced to resign in October. The new president, Costa Gomes, and Premier Vasco Gonçalves affirmed the right to independence of the Portuguese colonies. But with inflation reaching 30% and production endangered by a year of intermittent strikes, pressure on the regime for more rapid social change remained strong.

In Greece, the military dictatorship established in 1967 had been reorganized on more repressive lines in 1973 under President Phaedon Gizikis and Brig. Gen. Dimitrios Ioannidis, the head of the military police. The government attempted to shift attention from its economic failures by fomenting a crisis on Cyprus, supporting the overthrow of President Archbishop Makarios, apparently with the ultimate intention of uniting the island to Greece. When Turkey responded with an invasion of Cyprus, the conservative faction in the Greek army forced Gizikis to call a former premier, Constantine Caramanlis, back from exile to form a civilian government.

PUBLIFOTO, KEYSTONE

In October a mass demonstration is held in Piazza Solferino, Turin, Italy, to protest a reduction in the workweek for 73,000 Fiat auto workers. Following the cut, Italy's unemployment rate soared to 5.8% of the labor force.

UPI

With municipal workers on strike in Paris, French servicemen collect the city's accumulating garbage.

Caramanlis, a respected conservative and brilliant administrator, restored civil liberties, and was returned to power in elections in November in which his New Democracy party won 52% of the vote. As in Portugal, however, the threatening economic situation, especially an inflation rate of over 30%, persuaded one-quarter of the voters to support either the Socialist or Communist party. In December, the Greek people overwhelmingly voted an end to the monarchy and establishment of a republic.

National or Religious Minorities. The Cyprus crisis dramatized one of Europe's potentially disruptive problems, the clash between national or religious minorities and the dominant majority in many states. In Cyprus, the Turkish minority, comprising 18% of the total population, had been withdrawing into its own territorial enclaves as a result of clashes with the Greek majority. Power-sharing in the executive and legislature and the presence of 2,000 UN troops had failed to bring cooperation between the two communities. The invading Turkish army seemed determined to bring about a settlement by taking possession of one-third of the island. Internationally sponsored negotiations appeared to have made little progress by the end of the year.

Northern Ireland remained torn by the conflict between its Protestant majority and Catholic minority. Protestant extremists destroyed the feeble hope that the new power-sharing executive formed in 1973 by Unionist party leader Brian Faulkner would be able to persuade the two religious communities to cooperate politically. Through a general strike that paralyzed the province, the Ulster Workers Council compelled Faulkner to resign, thus reestablishing direct rule by the British government. The terrorists of the Irish Republican Army (IRA), whose goal was to unite Ulster to the Republic of Ireland, responded by extending their terrorist campaign to Britain itself. In December, after bombs in Birmingham had killed 20 people, the British government outlawed the IRA and began a nationwide search for its terrorist members.

In other parts of Europe, protests by national minorities took a variety of forms. Basque separatists in Spain assassinated Premier Luis Carrerò Blanco in December 1973, to dramatize their demands for the independence of the country's four Basque provinces. In Scotland and Wales, nationalist parties ran candidates in Britain's parliamentary elections. In October, the Welsh nationalists won three seats in Parliament, while the Scottish nationalists, emphasizing Scotland's right to control the finds of North Sea oil around its shores, won 11 parliamentary seats and 30% of Scotland's vote.

Thus, many Europeans regarded the events of 1974 as merely the first evidence of vast changes that were beginning to transform the society they had created after World War II. The changes were characterized especially by a challenge to the nation-state, growing demands for an end to economic disparities between classes and regions, and a decline in Europe's share of the world's wealth.

See also special feature on CYPRUS, pages 62–67, and articles on the individual countries of Europe.

F. ROY WILLIS
University of California, Davis

FASHION

Perhaps 1974 will be known as the beginning of another great upheaval in the way women dress. The year may represent a sudden departure from a more quiet, settled period in fashion when classic clothes of understated elegance, expensive materials, and excellent workmanship were favored by the fashionable cognoscenti, and thus became the standard to which all aspired. And perhaps not.

Possibly the Big Look or The Droop, introduced in Paris and subtly rendered by Seventh Avenue clothing manufacturers, would be so timidly endorsed by American women that by 1975 it would leave scarcely a ripple on the fashion scene. Certainly after the terrible lesson of the midi—that sudden lowering of hemlines after an ebullient period of thigh-high miniskirts, and so resoundingly rejected by the American woman—clothing manufacturers were not about to risk so soon a plunge into radical new clothing design.

WOMEN'S CLOTHES

A Fluid Look, Full of Motion. Nevertheless, what was being offered in the fall of 1974 was significantly different. It was an extension of the soft easy look that had prevailed during the previous few years but was now being given a lively fluidity and volume, an even more gently softened line and a much looser silhouette. Clothes remained easy and free—there was no return to constructed clothes. Where clothes had previously conformed to the body they now moved away with a dramatic swinging motion. Full flaring skirts were topped with bulky sweater sets, loose jackets, and then voluminous capes. Several scarves were wrapped loosely around the wearer's neck. Women tried out the new look, testing it for comfort and attractiveness, and assessing where the new things would fit into their existing wardrobes. For 1974 was a year of runaway inflation, and the public was not about to cast aside the clothes they already had.

Wardrobe Extenders. Women wanted good value for their money, longer lasting pieces, fewer clothes but of better quality. The concept of "wardrobe extenders" became an established way of merchandising. Fashion recycling became firmly established.

It was perfectly all right, even chic, to wear your old turtleneck with a new skirt, an old jacket over a new softer blouse, and a new loose Russian tunic top over classic pants or skirts. Bonnie Cashin had begun the "wardrobe extenders" idea years ago by designing clothes that could be added to clothes she had designed the previous season. Yves St. Laurent followed the same principle in his Rive Gauche Boutiques

(*Opposite*) Sweaters played a prominent role in fashion in 1974. Fur-collared sweaters replaced blazers and were worn with full-length and below-the-knee bigskirts for casual and formal occasions.
COURTESY SAKS FIFTH AVENUE, NEW YORK

VOGUE, © 1974, THE CONDE NAST PUBLICATIONS INC.

Multipurpose clothes were popular in 1974. (*Above*) Stephen Burrows' robe over wide pants was worn at home or for a night out. (*Below*) Bikinis with matching sarongs by Diane von Furstenberg (*left*) and Mirella (*right*) were fine for beach and leisure wear.

VOGUE, © 1974, THE CONDE NAST PUBLICATIONS INC.

in 1974. Many other designers were moving in the same direction as they realized that women were hunting specifically for new clothes that would go with the old ones.

A Fresh Response to Fashion Needs. Smart designers and retailers started taking their cues from the public. Women had called a halt to fashion dictation with their rejection of the midi and forced Seventh Avenue to cater to their tastes. Even established American couture designers recognized the change in attitude; people like Bill Blass now sought out their customers in stores in an effort to find out what kinds of clothes were needed and wanted at what particular prices.

Hemlines Cease to Matter. Hemlines, about which so much fuss had been made in previous years, stabilized at just below the knee for most women. Women had become accustomed to doing their own thing. They no longer followed the dictates of any one fashion authority. No longer did they really care much whether their hems were high or low. They seemed to have become free to decide for themselves how long their skirts would be and judged each skirt, dress, or coat according to its overall design and the use to which it would be put. Skirts, meanwhile, presented all the new subtle fashion changes in an acceptable, not-too-expensive form. They came in all kinds of loose, gathered, pocketed, flared, and gored styles, and as easy to wear as pants.

A New Chemise. In addition there was excitement over a new chemise silhouette. It was not the old narrow unbelted sheath, but a full, soft, feminine dress that often had several deep gathered tiers and ended in a sweeping lowered hemline.

Sweaters Everywhere. Sweaters, having reached significant fashion importance in 1973 as coats and jackets in addition to the favorite turtleneck and sweater sets, continued to be developed. Designers created new designs, new shapes, and new knitted textures. Pointelle open work, tweed bulkies, stripes and intarsia (mosaic) motifs, sporty designs, cables and Aran knits plus delicate crochet work were among the variations endorsed. As the sweater replaced the blazer, it took on elaborate collars, including luscious furs, and showed up in the evening as an elegant cover-up for the most formal occasions.

The return of the cape was a natural event, given the new bulkier clothes. Women who had been waiting for something interesting in the coat departments were eagerly trying capes. They noted with surprise that many were unlined, floaty, lightweight tent and smock silhouettes that exemplified the new relaxed fashions. Thick woolen fabrics, linings, and interlinings became unnecessary as sweaters took over the job of keeping bodies warm.

Loungewear Steps Out. Multipurpose clothes attained a new significance especially in the light of soaring prices. If one item of clothing could be made to serve several purposes, it was prized. Loungewear that had previously been confined to the bedroom moved into the living room in the form of classy, clingy pajama outfits or great swirling floor-length smocks and tunics. It then moved right out the front door into society.

John Kloss may have started it all with his slinky nightgowns that had been avidly adopted by young women who looked great in their sleek outlines, and found that the under-$20 price made them a reasonable purchase.

Complementary Colors Prevail. Fashion colors have always had great importance for any one year or season. Certain shades were selected by the major fabric manufacturers to look distinctly different from the colors of the previous year or season. In 1974, however, there was an attempt to choose a fall range of colors that actually complemented those of the previous spring. Thus it was possible to put together a smart outfit by coordinating a new fall skirt with last spring's sweater.

Boots. Boots became the important foot fashion in 1974, possibly because they paired off so well with the voluminous capes and skirts. This new boot was quite different from the slim, delicate ones that had made their entrances with the ill-fated midi a few years earlier. The sweaters, scarves, and capes demanded a more substantial underpinning. The new riding-type boots with their wider outlines and soft crushed ankles provided just the right note.

In contrast, the real shoe grew daintier than ever, and the pump returned in many varieties. T-straps and ankle straps with delicate little details were everywhere. Heels were high and slimmer. The platform sole that had dominated shoe fashions for several years became very thin or was phased out completely.

Homemades—A New Chic. The need for individuality that has always been a driving force behind the urge to buy new clothes made itself felt in a new appreciation of handmade, one-of-a-kind things. Dorothy Bis' handknit coats, capes and sweaters, and shoulderbags were quickly bought up faster than they could be produced. Even Bill Blass included some handcrafted items in his fall collection. For such unique items the customer was willing to pay. Women's magazines recognized the increased demand for handcrafted clothing and included special designs for their readers who knit or crochet.

Accessories. Accessories became an important fashion in themselves. Hats, belts, scarves, and jewelry attained individuality and were frequently coordinated into fashion looks. The St. Laurent rolled-brim knit cap was so sought after that it was copied at every price. Scarves also took on importance. There were long fringed woolen mufflers, fragile chiffon prints, and handkerchief squares.

Jewelry designers effected a striking simplicity. Silver, after years of subordination to gold, reached a new status.

Jeans. Jeans dressing continued in 1974 as an established fashion for every age group. Perhaps the everyday nature of work clothes had something to do with the ultrafeminine clothes women chose to wear at night. However, such ultrafeminine clothes never precluded pants. Pants remained the favorite feminine fashion for most women, more basic than the traditional dresses.

MEN'S WEAR

Coordinates. At long last men's wear designers latched on to an idea that women had known about for years—that coordinated outfits consisting of a number of color-related pants that could be mixed and matched provided the wearer with a multipurpose wardrobe of great versatility. Once introduced, the man's suit wardrobe caught on fast. It was known variously as the mixed suit, trios, weekenders (four pieces), and fashion fivers. The basic concept was to combine jackets and pants with other items such as vests and the new, varied sweater fashions such as turtlenecks, sleeveless pullovers, and cardigans. The jacket could be worn with matching slacks and vest for a formal affair, for instance, or paired with contrasting slacks for a more casual look.

Classic patterns and plaids were often integrated with heather tones and flannels in garments made in year-round weights. Knit sweaters picked up the color of jackets. Woven fabrics and knits were being engineered to go nicely together.

At-Ease Clothes. Even more significant in its implications was the more relaxed attitude toward fashion reflected in the new at-ease collections of leisure suits. These designs attempted to depart even more seriously from the classic man's uniform, the business suit. The leisure suit still conformed to the tailored construction of serious suits but took on a sportswear styling. At the same time sportswear designers were making all sorts of innovative designs—jean suits, battle jacket sets, and other matching tops and bottoms of unconventional cut.

Sweaters and Sweater Jackets. Sweaters also attained a new importance for men, probably as a result of the new ease in clothes. Traditionally men's sweaters had been associated with weekends or sportswear, but now they began to be worn interchangeably with the new unconstructed jackets. They even ventured out on the town along with color-coordinated slacks for a new "suit" look.

Fashionable shirts were toned down considerably so that they would blend with their coordinates. Dress shirts were muted or in fancy solids and off-whites. The Western shirt was interpreted in corduroy, chambray, and wool as well as the ever-popular denim.

The year's bulkier clothes brought a return of the cape. Yves St. Laurent's popular cape was worn over a velvet skirt with braid trim. Cossack suede and leather boots and a felt fedora complete the outfit.

COURTESY BLOOMINGDALE'S, N. Y.

Shoes. Shoes were saner and more comfortable than they had been since the advent of the platform sole. Ghillies and wing-tip ties came back and wafer thin platforms supplanted the deep-dish Dogwood sole. Gucci-like moccasin shoes had become a classic for both formal and casual wear. Sleek pants-boots were worn with slacks, and high Western styles were favored with jeans.

As in previous years, jeans persisted as the most popular dress for the young, and as middle-aged businessmen discovered their comfort and attractiveness jeans became the off-hours uniform for all ages.

PATRICIA A. DONEHOO
Fashion and Patterns Editor, "Woman's Day"

FINLAND

The worldwide oil crisis adversely affected Finland's economy in 1974, but developments in domestic politics and foreign affairs were favorable.

Energy Situation. Two thirds of Finland's crude oil imports (6.5 million tons in 1974) came from the Soviet bloc (chiefly from the USSR), along with oil products, solid fuels, and natural gas. While there were no serious shortages (the opening of a new natural gas pipeline on January 9 brought an additional 500 million cubic meters, or 7.7 billion cubic feet, from the USSR), prices rose steeply, equivalent to 5% of the gross national product. The Communist countries' share of Finnish foreign trade went up from 15% in 1973 to 20% in 1974. Meanwhile, Finland's atomic energy program remained far behind schedule.

The Economy. Among the major problems facing Finland in 1974 were inflation, foreign trade imbalance, and a drop in foreign-exchange reserves. Despite labor agreements, anti-inflationary measures, and price freezes on 67% to 97% of the cost-of-living index items, the inflation rate for the year ending July 1974 reached 16.4%.

By early July, the first phases of an anti-inflation program were announced by the government. Price controls (scheduled to have been eased by September) were continued, an import price control office was set up, and savings and housing-aid programs were encouraged. Proceeds from an export tax on forest products would be channeled into various projects aimed at stimulating the economy.

In the first eight months of 1974, imports rose 58% and exports 49%, leaving a trade deficit of 3,202 million Fmk (Finnish marks), more than double that of the same period in 1973. On May 31, 1974, foreign exchange holdings totaled 1,802 Fmk, down 455 million Fmk from the end of 1973.

Expected growth in the gross national product in 1974 was 3% to 4%, the same as that of industrial production. The unemployment rate was about 2.3%. Continuing bright spots in the economy were shipbuilding and the metals-engineering industries. Agricultural production grew 7.2% annually in 1970–73. Over 500,000 hectares (1,236,000 acres) of farmland were diverted to other uses in 1962–72.

The preliminary 1975 budget totaled 21.7 billion Fmk, a 26% increase over that for 1974. The foreign debt reached 11.4 billion Fmk, a fourfold increase in 10 years.

During the year, two large joint Finnish-Soviet enterprises were announced: a new cellulose factory at Svetogorsk, and a copper-nickel smelting plant at Norilsk, both in the USSR. A trade agreement with the European Economic Community came into force on Jan. 1, 1974, and became the model for agreements completed or under negotiation during the year with Bulgaria, Hungary, Poland, and Czechoslovakia.

The Presidency. On March 1, 1974, Urho K. Kekkonen was sworn in for a fourth term (to expire in 1978). His election by the legislature (Eduskunta) early in 1973 was the fifth in Finland's history that circumvented the normal electoral college. A 250-page committee report in March urged restrictions on the presidency: a two-term limit; selection by the legislature of cabinet members; and a diminished role in military-foreign affairs.

Political Parties. Finland had 13 registered parties in 1974, of which 10 were represented in the 200-member Eduskunta, led by the Social Democrats (SDP), 56; Finnish People's Democratic League (SKDL), 37; Center, 35; and Conservatives, 32. Although often challenged, the four-party coalition cabinet of Prime Minister Kalevi Sorsa (SDP), with a six-vote majority, remained in office (it assumed power on Sept. 4, 1972).

International Environmental Protection. On Feb. 20, 1974, Finland joined its Nordic neighbors in a pact (effective mid-1975) aimed at reducing pollution and permitting citizens of one country to bring anti-pollution suits in the others. The Seven-Nation Baltic Sea Convention, in the creation of which Finland played a leading role, was signed on March 22. It established a commission and a secretariat at Helsinki.

Miscellaneous. There was considerable popular opposition to the military coup in Chile in 1973; and during 1974, Finland's aid to Chile was terminated. Meanwhile, the International Commission of Inquiry into the Crimes of the Military Junta in Chile held a conference in Helsinki on March 21–24, with representatives from some 30 countries.

Sibelius' Järvenpää home was opened to the public late in June. A new model city, rivaling Tapiola, was planned at Kivenlahti, near Helsinki; it was designed to combine "the great elements of nature" with the advantages of urban living.

JOHN I. KOLEHMAINEN
Heidelberg College, Ohio

FINLAND • Information Highlights

Official Name: Republic of Finland.
Location: Northern Europe.
Area: 130,120 square miles (377,009 sq km).
Population (1973 est.): 4,800,000.
Chief Cities (1971 est.): Helsinki, the capital, 528,800; Tampere, 157,810; Turku, 156,900.
Government: *Head of state,* Urho Kaleva Kekkonen, president (took office March 1974 for 4th term, to expire in 1978). *Head of government,* Kalevi Sorsa, prime minister (took office Sept. 1972). *Legislature* (unicameral)—Eduskunta.
Monetary Unit: Markka, or Finnish mark (3.71 markkas equal U. S.$1, July 1974).
Gross National Product (1973 est.): $14,800,000,000.
Manufacturing (major products): Wood and paper products, ships, machinery, chemicals, metals, textiles, cement.
Major Agricultural Products: Oats, potatoes, sugar beets, barley, rye, wheat, forest products.
Foreign Trade (1973): Exports, $3,724,000,000; imports, $4,210,000,000.

FISHERIES

In common with industry in general, U. S. commercial fishing reeled under economic adversities in 1974. Operating costs skyrocketed, with the price of trawl cable, netting, and other gear in some cases more than doubling within a year's time. Most crucial of all, the spiraling cost of diesel fuel made much fishing a profitless or money-losing activity.

Industry Trends. Particularly hard hit was the nation's most important fishery, shrimping. The shrimpers were caught in a squeeze between inflationary operating costs and a depressed market for shrimp. For over a decade it had appeared that there was no saturation point to the demand for shrimp, and prices continually moved higher. But by the beginning of 1974, buyer resistance was firmly established, and cold-storage holdings were alarmingly high. Processors and wholesalers suffered from selling shrimp at lower prices than they had paid to fishermen, and the year saw some major processors closing their doors.

Fishermen's groups turned to the federal government for help in fighting the cost-price squeeze, asking that it buy surpluses for school lunch programs, the Food for Peace program, and the like. New legislation made fishermen eligible for Small Business Administration loans.

Despite the economic situation, boat-building for the commercial fisheries continued to boom in 1974. The generally healthy tuna fishery—the market for the largest and most sophisticated vessels in the U. S. fisheries—continued to add superseiners to its fleet. Also, the crisis in the shrimp fishery notwithstanding, South Atlantic and Gulf of Mexico yards specializing in shrimp trawler construction kept busy, with an increasing amount of their business coming from abroad, notably from Japan, Korea, and Central America.

During 1974 the long-troubled fisheries of New England found no respite from the ills of fleet obsolescence and competition from foreign vessels on traditional fishing grounds.

200-Mile Limit. The year brought intensified pressure from New England fishery and legislative leaders, who called for the United States to declare a 200-mile (322-km) limit for U. S. fishing grounds, replacing the present 12-mile (19.3-km) fishing limit. The 200-mile limit is also supported by Pacific Northwest fishermen, but it is bitterly opposed by the California tuna fishery, which operates off the South American coast. Nor do Gulf Coast shrimp fishermen want a 200-mile limit.

International Negotiations. The United States had been more or less marking time in the area of international negotiations, awaiting the outcome of the Law of the Sea Conference in Caracas, Venezuela, in the summer of 1974. The conference ended with delegates agreed on nothing except to meet in Geneva in March 1975 to attempt to work out a treaty and then to reconvene in Caracas at a later unspecified date and, it was hoped, sign it.

LEADING FISHING COUNTRIES
(In millions of metric tons)

Country	1968	1969	1970	1971	1972
Japan	8.7	8.6	9.3	9.9	10.2
USSR	6.1	6.5	7.3	7.4	7.8
China (Communist)	5.4	5.5	6.3	6.9	7.6
Peru	10.6	9.2	12.6	10.6	4.8
Norway	2.9	2.5	3.0	3.0	3.1
United States	2.5	2.5	2.8	2.8	2.6
Six-nation total	36.2	34.8	41.3	40.6	36.1
Other countries	27.7	27.8	28.3	29.1	29.5
World catch	63.9	62.6	69.6	69.7	65.6

The United States entered the Caracas meeting committed to the 3-mile (4.8-km) territorial sea limit and to a 12-mile (19.3-km) fishing limit, as did the Soviet Union. However, during the course of the conference both dropped their opposition to a 200-mile territorial sea concept, provided that the zones would be open to other nations for fishing and scientific research.

World Catch. The UN Food and Agricultural Organization reported a sharp decline in world fisheries production in 1972, the last year for which production figures were available (see table).

WILLIAM A. SARRATT
Editor, "The Fish Boat," New Orleans

FLORIDA

Floridians were shocked by political scandals in high places in 1974, but these did not obscure major ecological, economic, and social issues.

Politics. Florida's Republican party suffered a serious setback when Edward Gurney, Florida's first Republican U. S. senator since Reconstruction and a member of the Senate Watergate Committee, was charged with violating state election laws. A county grand jury in April indicted him on that charge, but the indictment was dismissed. In July, a federal grand jury indicted Gurney and six others for influence-peddling and extortion, alleging that at least $223,000 had been raised for the senator from real estate developers and contractors. Gurney canceled plans for a reelection campaign.

Democrats found little opportunity to rejoice, however, since three Democratic members of the state cabinet, Education Commissioner Floyd Christian, Treasurer Thomas O'Malley, and Comptroller Fred Dickinson were indicted for illegally accepting funds from groups seeking to influence state policies.

These scandals provoked the Legislature to enact a weak financial disclosure law, but their impact on the November elections was more difficult to assess. Democrats made a clean sweep of the top state offices, with the popular Reubin Askew heading the ballot and winning a second term as governor by defeating Jerry Thomas. In the U. S. Senate race, Democrat

Richard Stone won a narrow victory over Republican Jack Eckerd because a little-known American party candidate, Dr. John Grady, ran a surprisingly strong race, carrying conservative votes that otherwise would have gone to Eckerd. The Republican party's weakness in general was revealed when Thomas O'Malley, at the time under investigation for perjury and accepting kickbacks, handily defeated the Republican challenger in the state treasurer's race. Republicans also lost seats in the state Legislature.

One milestone was achieved with the appointment of Dorothy W. Glisson to replace the secretary of state, who became a candidate for the U. S. Senate. She is the first woman ever to serve in the cabinet.

Economy. Since Floridians derive approximately $5.5 billion annually from tourism, the national fuel shortage adversely affected the economy. Tourism declined by up to 20% during the early months of the year. The related national strike by truckers forced many farmers and growers to watch in dismay as fruits and vegetables rotted because there was no means of transporting them to market. The easing of the fuel crisis led to normalization of the state's economy by midyear; however, the national recession hit the state by late fall. The economic slowdown caused the state unemployment rate to reach 7%. It also reduced tax revenues, generally, forcing local governments to institute budget cuts of up to 10%.

The incumbent governor of Florida, Democrat Reubin Askew (*right*), and his running mate, Lt. Gov. Jim Williams, share the podium at their victory party on election night.

UPI

FLORIDA • Information Highlights

Area: 58,560 square miles (151,670 sq km).
Population (1973 est.): 7,678,000. *Density:* 134 per sq mi.
Chief Cities (1970 census): Tallahassee, the capital, 72,586; Jacksonville, 528,865; Miami, 334,859; Tampa, 277,767.
Government (1974): *Chief Officers*—governor, Reubin O'D. Askew (D); lt. gov., Tom Adams (D). *Legislature*—Senate, 40 members; House of Representatives, 120 members.
Education (1973–74): *Enrollment*—public elementary schools, 773,020 pupils; public secondary, 674,580; nonpublic, 107,600; colleges and universities, 281,394 students. *Public school expenditures,* $1,478,879,000 ($962 per pupil).
State Finances (fiscal year 1973): *Revenues,* $3,882,857,000; *expenditures,* $3,449,745,000.
Personal Income (1973): $35,680,000,000; per capita, $4,647.
Labor Force (July 1974): *Nonagricultural wage and salary earners,* 2,734,500; *insured unemployed,* 49,900 (2.1%).

Education. New laws were enacted to encourage quality education and educational facilities. One of the more important requires that students be tested in the areas of reading, writing, and mathematics to determine the level of achievement in relation to the national average. The results are to be used as a guide for future planning. Another law imposed a uniform building code and greater state supervision of school construction. The Legislature also added a consumer education course to the curriculum of secondary schools.

Environment. As Florida's population continues to mushroom, much attention remains focused on protecting the environment, especially the precious sources of water. The U. S. Congress appropriated $116 million to supplement the $40 million state appropriation to purchase Big Cypress Swamp, the source of water for much of south Florida. Other endangered lands also have been recommended for purchase. It is becoming apparent, however, that state acquisition of all the endangered recharge areas, rivers, bays, and estuaries is not feasible, and that land-use regulations must be implemented to help some of the problems.

The petroleum shortage caused some setbacks for state environmentalists. Following complaints by oil companies, the Legislature greatly reduced the penalties imposed under the state oil-spill law, previously the nation's toughest. Exploratory oil drilling in the Gulf of Mexico was also authorized, although the state is organizing a special commission to oversee the operations. The oil shortage also influenced the decision to review the status of the Barge Canal which had been killed by President Nixon, much to the relief of state environmentalists. The Federal Environmental Protection Agency was conducting an environmental impact study which, along with a cost-benefit ratio study, will undoubtedly influence the final decision regarding construction.

J. LARRY DURRENCE
Florida Southern College

MANITOBA DEPARTMENT OF INDUSTRY AND COMMERCE

A bumper crop of wheat is harvested in Manitoba, Canada, though worldwide wheat production declined sharply in 1974.

FOOD

In the face of a growing world population and diminishing reserves of food, the United Nations sponsored two major conferences in 1974: a World Population Conference, held in Bucharest in August, and a World Food Conference, held in Rome in November. The latter conference approved creation of a World Food Council, associated with the Food and Agriculture Organization and based in Rome, to find ways of improving the world food supply, especially to developing nations.

With the population of the earth increasing by 2%—over 70 million persons—each year, the world population total of 4 billion would double in about 35 years, provided the present rate continues. At the same time, there is general agreement among experts that food production cannot be increased rapidly enough, and distribution systems improved substantially enough, to keep pace with such population growth, let alone to improve the nutritional standards of millions of people existing on substandard diets. That is the prospect for the long term. For the shorter-range future, improvements are possible.

WORLD FOOD SUPPLY

The Danger Signals. The weather, after being favorable for crops in 1973 and helping world food production to reach a record level, turned capricious again in 1974.

Such production reverses ordinarily would not be cause for great concern. But with world grain reserves depleted, the concern is both great and legitimate. Even though food production per person in 1974 was still very large in comparison with that of most recent years, it was below the record 1973 levels. And the depleted reserve stocks meant that the food-short areas of the world could not rely, as they had in past crises, on large food shipments from areas of surplus production.

It was claimed at the World Population Conference in August that the world's reserve of food had shrunk to 27 days' supply—an insufficient amount to meet a major disaster. Although this calculation did not include current crop production or consider the record numbers of livestock being raised, it did point up the seriousness of the problem.

Great concern over the situation was also expressed through the various proposals advanced during the World Food Conference in November. A concrete manifestation of the problem was the decision by the United States in October 1974 to cancel a grain sale to the Soviet Union, arranged previously with private companies, when it became uncertain whether there was enough grain to supply traditional overseas customers until the 1975 harvests begin. Subsequently, a U. S.-Soviet agreement was reached for smaller shipments than originally had been intended, and for the shipments to be made over the course of several months.

By late 1974, many developed countries of the world were still expecting reasonably bountiful harvests. But crop prospects for Northern Hemisphere countries, particularly for grains, generally deteriorated.

Soviet agricultural production in 1974 probably was larger than in 1973, but short of the planned increase. Production in eastern Europe was close to the record crops of the past two years. In China, the harvest of early crops was good, although not exceptional.

Sharp decreases in India and Bangladesh pulled down agricultural production in developing Asia. A generally good harvest was expected in Latin America despite some weather damage to early crops. African agricultural production rose significantly because of record crops in South Africa and northern African countries and improved rainfall in the formerly parched Mediterranean coastal areas of Algeria and Tunisia and parts of East Africa.

The Grain Supply. On a worldwide basis, sharp declines in wheat and coarse grain production, coupled with a smaller decrease in rice production, pulled total grain production down to about 1,121 million metric tons, or 56 million tons below the record volume of the previous year. Estimates of world demand, adjusted to reflect the limiting effect of short supplies and high prices, nevertheless exceed expected production for the third straight year.

Even with wheat, rice, and coarse grain stocks drawn down some 8 to 9 million tons, world grain use per capita is still falling short of the 1973 average. Most of the decrease is seen occurring in the developed grain-feeding countries, including the Soviet Union and eastern Europe. Consumption may actually increase in most developing countries except India and Bangladesh.

World wheat production in 1974 was expected to total about 348 million tons, or 19 million below the 1973 crop. Continued tight supplies and high prices will reduce use by 16 million tons, down to about 351 million. Despite this decline, stocks on hand prior to new harvests may shrink a million or so tons to a new low of about 50 million tons.

For coarse grains—such as corn, sorghums, and oats—the supply and demand situation is even more precarious than that for wheat. World production in 1974 is estimated at 563 million tons, 37 million below the record volume produced a year earlier. Despite a drop of some 30 million tons, demand for coarse grains will still total perhaps 572 million tons, slightly above production for the third consecutive year.

World output of milled rice in 1974 probably fell at least 1 million tons from the 211 million-ton-crop of the year before. Since rice stocks were drastically reduced in 1973, demand can be expected to continue pressing on supply at current prices. Rice consumption requirements increase at least 2.5% a year, in line with population growth and without allowing for any increased demand due to rising incomes of consumers. The reduced world production of rice in 1974 implies a drop in availability per person from 55 to 54 kilograms (121 to 119 pounds) for the year.

Smaller U. S. soybean production in 1974 was reducing world edible oil and meal potential output in an otherwise improved year elsewhere. The 7 million-ton decline in the 1974 U. S. soybean crop was equal to about 5 million tons of meal, or about 7% of world output. On the other hand, meal production in the rest of the world was expected to rise by 2 million tons, so the net decrease was small. Stocks, rebuilt during 1974, also added to world supplies. For soybean oil, production in the United States fell about 1 million tons, or 4% of world production. But world edible oil production was expected to show only a half-million-ton decline.

Meat and Dairy Products. World commercial meat production increased in 1974, reversing the sharp drop in 1973. The economic boom experienced in major developed countries in 1971 to mid-1973 pushed up prices of meat, especially beef, and encouraged farmers to build up their herds and flocks. But the decline in world economic growth since mid-1973, helped along by the energy crisis and the sharp rise in feed prices, caused consumer demand to slacken and livestock slaughtering rates to increase.

World cattle in January 1974 numbered a record 1.3 billion, up nearly 2% from the preceding year. Also, there were more hogs and

AID

Sorghum from the United States is brought by camel to nomads of drought-stricken sub-Saharan Africa through the Agency for International Development.

sheep—up 3% and over 1%, respectively. Poultry flocks also increased sharply.

Slaughter rates for beef, which had dropped in recent years, rose in most major producing countries in 1974. Pork production also increased sharply, while broiler chicken production rose early in 1974 but fell later.

Not only did the demand for meat decrease in many areas of the world, but the costs of raising livestock, particularly feed costs, shot up. At the same time, farmers' prices for livestock and livestock products either fell or failed to keep up with costs.

Milk production generally showed gains in the world's major dairy regions in 1974. These increases and the continued downtrends in per capita consumption of butter are again producing surpluses of butter stocks, especially in the European Economic Community. Demand for cheese and nonfat dry milk remains strong.

The Role of the United States. With the world facing a third consecutive year of real uncertainty over food availabilities and costs, the focus shifts to the situation in the United States. This leading world producer had a fourth less farm production for export in the fiscal year ending in June 1975 because of bad weather during the crop growing season.

Of immediate concern in the United States is the question of how much of its food production should be allocated to domestic and to foreign buyers. Another concern is the capacity and responsibility of the United States to provide food to needy countries around the world.

Food price inflation within the United States in 1974 led to efforts to legislate reserve policies. And as a consequence of the cancellation, then elimination, of the sale of grain to the USSR in the fall of 1974, a voluntary system of keeping tabs on U. S. food exports was established. Sales contracts above a certain limit became subject to prior government approval.

Such moves necessarily affect the levels of U. S. food aid abroad. Food aid shipments have been valued at about $1 billion annually for the past several years. Because of price inflation, however, the volume of food that could be bought with that amount of money is less than in previous years. But President Ford, in a speech to the UN General Assembly on Sept. 18, 1974, urged all nations to cooperate in a "global strategy for food and energy" and promised: "To make certain that the more immediate needs for food are met this year, the United States will not only maintain the amount it spends for food shipments to nations in need, but it will increase this amount."

The Long-Range Picture. Problems surrounding the level of U. S. food aid abroad and the prospects for export controls, as well as the depleted reserve stocks, are all of pressing and immediate concern. However, they tend to obscure the long-range progress in world food production over the past two decades.

From 1954 to 1973, food production had declined only once on a global basis—in 1972. Over this period, production increased at an average annual rate of 2.8%, outpacing the population growth rate of 2.0%. Food production increased at about the same rate in both the developed and developing groups of countries, but because of differing population growth rates the amount of food production per person rose only 0.5% a year in poorer countries.

Understandably, most of the current concern about the world food situation thus focuses on the problems of the developing countries. An assessment report prepared by the United Nations for the World Food Conference in Rome stated: "The central problem needing attention is how to expand food production more rapidly in the developing countries."

Another United Nations document prepared for the conference listed three major reasons why greater food production in the developing countries is vital. First, the larger production of food, especially by small and subsistence farmers, will improve the nutrition of their families, many of whom are malnourished. Second, an increase in output will increase farm incomes, leading to increased economic activity in rural areas. And finally, an increase in food output will contribute to progress in national development, either through lessening needs for food imports or expanding the volume of food exports, thus saving or generating essential foreign exchange reserves.

What are the longer-term prospects for world food production, particularly for the developing regions? Three organizations—the UN Food and Agricultural Organization, the U. S. Department of Agriculture, and Iowa State University—have prepared economic projections of the world food situation 10 and 15 years in the future, analyzing world production, use, and trade in agricultural commodities. These studies suggest that the world will be able to produce enough food to keep ahead of population growth, but that the developed grain-exporting countries may have to supply even more to the developing importing countries than they have in the past.

Meanwhile, there are the immediate problems at hand. There is concern, for example, that the drought in the midwestern United States in the summer of 1974 might recur in 1975. As a result of that drought, corn yields in 1974 were reduced to an average of 74 bushels per acre—the lowest average since the blight-reduced crop of 1970, and sharply below the 97-bushel-per-acre average of 1972 and 1973. And there is the problem of obtaining sufficient fertilizer for producing bumper crops. Fertilizer production continues upward, but at higher prices and not in pace with demand. Prices for both fertilizer and crops generally have risen the most in North America, with crop prices showing somewhat the greater increase. Other developed

UNIVERSITY PATENTS, INC.

(*Left to right*) Scientists L. S. Wei, A. I. Nelson, and M. P. Steinberg of the University of Illinois sample new foods they created from soybeans, including butter, milk, and ice cream.

countries have experienced lesser inflationary price hikes.

In his concluding remarks to the UN General Assembly in September, President Ford said: "As new economic forces alter and reshape today's complex world, no nation can be expected to feed all the world's hungry people. Fortunately, however, many nations are increasingly able to help. And I call on them to join with us . . . in the struggle to provide more food at lower prices for the hungry and, in general, a better life for the needy of this world." (See also POPULATION.)

BENJAMIN R. BLANKENSHIP, JR.
U. S. Department of Agriculture

U. S. FOOD INDUSTRY

The food industry was occupied with problems of shortages, rising prices, governmental actions, consumerism, and natural disasters in 1974. Nonetheless, it provided an abundant food supply to the United States and other nations.

Shortages and Rising Costs. Rising costs and shortages of goods were universal within the food industry. The skyrocketing cost of sugar, which more than doubled in price in 1974, particularly affected the beverage, baking, and processed fruit industries. Raw products dependent on the weather were spotty in supply, with soybeans, corn, and wheat falling below predicted harvest levels. Export demands and contract cancellations created havoc in the marketplace, and prices for processed foods generally moved upward later in the year. Shortages of fertilizer throughout the world added uncertainty to future harvests and prices.

With regard to food ingredients, allocations of supplies or shortages forced an increasing search for adequate substitutes. For example, gum arabic, a widely used food thickener in short supply for several years, can now be replaced by a substitute that took over five years to develop. Besides such costs for research, the rising cost of food in 1974 also was boosted by increased costs of containers, packaging, energy, chemicals, equipment, labor, and money, as well as increased pressure from consumer and regulatory groups.

Consumer Reaction. In 1974, the consumer was both frustrated and concerned. His frustration stemmed from spiraling inflation, up a minimum of 12% in 1974, which caused consumers to limit food choices to lower priced items. After beef shortages in 1973, the consumer raised his purchases by an estimated 2.5 pounds per capita as beef production was at near-record levels. The U. S. Department of Agriculture (USDA) and Congress were studying a proposal by the meat industry to combine the yield and quality grading systems into a single grading system. Such a system would encourage production of beef containing less excess fat and would reduce the amounts of costly feed grain used in fattening cattle for market. This plan might result in lower beef prices at the retail level.

Consumer attitudes and concern were creating changes within the food industry. The industry and government conducted consumer surveys that showed: (1) increased concern by consumers over the safety of canned foods and the use of food additives; (2) greater demand for food expiration dates, nutritional labeling, and nutritional information for shopping; and (3) changes in buying and eating habits, such as a rise in canned vegetable consumption.

Requests by consumer groups resulted in changes within the food industry. For instance, many large retail chains and processors have created separate nutrition groups to ensure accurate information in labels, pamphlets, and direct-mail replies. Other changes included a USDA requirement that the voluntary calendar dating system on meat or poultry labels include a statement explaining what the date means.

Federal and State Actions. Many actions affecting various segments of the food industry occurred in 1974. At the state level, California passed a law that required food processors to list all ingredients of foods on the label, whether or not a product is standardized. A standardized food is one for which there is a Food and Drug Administration (FDA) Standard of Identity that specifies allowed ingredients that need not be declared on the label.

In federal actions, the primary effort was pointed at food quality and food safety. The Consumer Product Safety Commission, created in May 1973, has been deeply involved in studying potential hazards in different types of packaging and foodstuffs. Its primary thrust has been to ensure that hazardous or unsafe packaging or food products are upgraded to a safe user level.

In other action, the FDA expanded guidelines on nutritional labeling, issued regulations on food ingredient definitions, set up defect limits for canned and frozen fruits and vegetables, and delineated regulations for fortification, the size of uniform servings, microbiological standards, and recommended daily allowances (RDA) for infants. In a new program of retail sampling of low-acid canned foods, the FDA found that more than 35,000 cans showed no evidence of underprocessing or excess residues. This program and others have increased food plant inspections to 20,000 per year. The USDA ordered the redesign of glass jar caps for meat and poultry products.

Industry Advances. The FDA approved the use of aspartame, a synthetic product, as a sweetener for certain foods. Aspartame, the first sugar substitute approved since cyclamates were banned in 1971, is 180 times sweeter than sugar. Containing four calories per gram (the same as sugar), it may be used as a free-flowing sugar substitute, in tablets for hot beverages, in cold breakfast cereals, in chewing gum, and in certain dry bases for beverages and puddings.

As of June 30, food processors had signed 60 Cooperative Quality Assurance Program agreements with the FDA. This program, which is designed to make processors self-inspecting, provides the FDA with assurance that safe, wholesome, and nutritious food is being produced.

Fabricated foods, which account for about 6.5% of all food sales, were expected to reach sales of 7.8%, or $23 billion, in 1980. It was expected that vegetable protein products serving as meat substitutes will increase at an even faster rate.

KIRBY M. HAYES
University of Massachusetts

NUTRITION

Rising food costs and increasing consumer interest in the quality and safety of all foods dominated the field of nutrition in 1974.

Consumer Attitudes. The safety of food supplies was questioned by many consumers. A Louis Harris poll showed that more than 60% of the consumers were concerned about the safety of canned foods, as compared with 48% in 1971. Concern over artificial additives rose from 64% to 68%. The results indicated interviewees felt that not enough was being done.

A U. S. Food and Drug Administration (FDA) survey showed that nutrition and economical food were the most important factors named by shoppers, with 80% stating that nutritional labeling is of more interest than recipes.

Other surveys have shown cost-conscious consumers changing eating and buying habits. U. S. Department of Agriculture (USDA) figures showed an increase in vegetable consumption, with canned vegetables rising the fastest. Concurrently, meat consumption was being reduced or shifted to lower grades. Overall food purchases were down, with slightly more than 16% of disposable income being used for food. Another study showed many consumers planned to grow and preserve their own food to cut costs.

The use of nutritional labeling and unit-pricing information is not widespread. To offset this, the FDA initiated an extensive educational campaign on nutritional labeling.

Food Programs. In mid-1974, President Nixon signed into law several amendments to the various food programs. Most dealt with cost increases in existing programs or raised appropriations in areas such as food-stamp program administrative costs. A new effort, the Special Supplemental Food Program for Women, Infants, and Children, was inaugurated in January. This program provides cash grants to make nutritious foods available to new and expectant mothers, infants, and children up to four years of age.

The scope of food programs under the USDA and other agencies has risen rapidly in the past few years and includes such activities as meals for the elderly and summer feeding support in day-care centers, where 1.7 million children were fed in the summer of 1974. The USDA requested $5.9 billion for food programs in 1975, including food stamps, child nutrition programs, supplementary family feeding programs, and nutrition education.

Food Quality. In June, the FDA established 18 areas relating to food labeling, the most important establishing the general principles governing the addition of nutrients to food. In California the legislature passed a law requiring California food processors to declare all ingredients of foods on the label.

KIRBY M. HAYES
University of Massachusetts

FOREIGN AID

The massive international economic upheaval of 1974 seriously affected many poor countries which, with foreign aid and self-help, had been progressing economically in recent years. World-wide inflation, soaring oil prices, higher food and fertilizer costs, and recession in industrialized nations had an especially severe impact on those developing countries lacking oil and mineral resources. The World Bank reported that while the annual GNP growth of developing countries as a whole exceeded 6% in 1968–72, prospects for growth of the poorest lands—with per capita incomes under $200 a year, comprising 800 million people—now appear negligible for the rest of this decade unless there is an immense increase in external assistance.

International Conferences. The plight of the poor nations was the focus of several major international meetings during the year. A special session of the UN General Assembly, proposed by Algeria, was convened in April to discuss raw materials and world development. A World Population Conference, meeting in Bucharest in August, stressed the relationship between socio-economic development and slowing the rapid population rise in poor countries. A World Food Conference, held in Rome in November, adopted a wide range of recommendations for an international campaign to wipe out hunger. (See UNITED NATIONS.)

U. S. relief grain is distributed in a town in Niger, one of the countries most seriously affected by the widespread drought on the African continent just below the Sahara.

CARL PURCELL/AID

Multilateral Aid. The World Bank Group—the International Bank for Reconstruction and Development, the International Development Association, and the International Finance Corporation—again expanded its financial and technical assistance to developing countries, with commitments totaling $4,517 million in fiscal 1974, a $962 million increase over the previous year. The largest amounts went for projects in the fields of transportation, agriculture, and electric power. The United Nations Development Program was projected at $447 million for 1975, up from $379 million in 1974.

Industrialized Nations' Assistance. The 16-nation Development Assistance Committee, whose members account for nearly all economic aid from non-Communist industrialized nations, reported a nominal increase of 9%, from $8.7 billion in 1972 to $9.4 billion in 1973, in Official Development Assistance (ODA) to developing countries. ODA consists of grants and loans provided by governments on concessional terms. The real-term value of this ODA actually declined by some 6% between the two years, however, because of deterioration from exchange rates and inflation. While the $9.4 billion marked a statistical high for ODA in one year, its per-capita equivalent of about $4.80 in developing countries amounted to a decline of about 30% in real terms from the ODA of a decade ago and a record low of 0.3% of the collective gross national product of the industrialized nations.

U. S. Aid. Foreign assistance measures again encountered rough going in Congress. A bill to authorize the $1.5 billion U. S. share of replenishment of International Development Association funds was defeated by the House on January 23. Under White House pressure, and with the addition of a popular provision allowing private ownership of gold by U. S. citizens, the House reversed itself on July 2 with a 225–140 vote for the IDA contribution.

The Senate voted, 41–39, on October 2 to recommit the annual omnibus foreign assistance authorization bill for fiscal 1975, but then passed a revised version on December 4 by a one-vote margin, 46–45. The bill, as finally sent to the White House shortly before Congress' year-end adjournment, authorized $2.69 billion, about $555 million less than the presidential request. It featured large-scale assistance to Israel and its Arab neighbors, a sharp cutback in aid to Indochina, and a compromise provision to allow military aid to Turkey through Feb. 5, 1975, pending negotiations on the Cyprus issue.

Communist Aid. The Development Assistance Committee reported that the USSR reduced its aid to developing countries from $870 million in 1970 to $750 million in 1973. China was estimated to have increased its aid from $300 million in 1970 to over $500 million in 1973.

LEWIS GULICK, *Staff Consultant*
House Foreign Affairs Committee

UPI

Valéry Giscard d'Estaing, the new president of France, waves to the crowds lining the Champs Élysées in Paris as he walks to the Élysée Palace for his inauguration.

FRANCE

In 1974 the French apparently bade a final farewell to Gaullism. They chose a comparatively young president, but the new regime could not shield them from the growing world economic crisis. As the year ended, it was clear that even intelligence and a certain goodwill were unable to make headway against France's intractable problems.

DOMESTIC AFFAIRS

Politics. President Georges Pompidou's government had been under attack since the March 1973 elections. The lackluster performance of Premier Pierre Messmer's bickering cabinet and rumors about the obviously deteriorating health of Pompidou caused restlessness. Instead of resigning, the president had Messmer resign on February 27, then reappointed him to form a smaller cabinet with a "new program" for social justice, energy conservation, and restraints on inflation.

Pompidou died on April 2. The public, which had been given only scraps of information about his failing health, was deeply shocked by his death. Pompidou had revealed his approaching fate only to his immediate circle, and to three journalists in March 1973: "To each his troubles: Nixon has Watergate, and as for me, I am going to die." Courageously he had tried to fulfill his reduced schedule, and he had even flown to a Black Sea meeting with the Soviet leader Leonid Brezhnev in February. He met his ministers almost to the last day. No announcement was made about the cause of death, but it was believed that he died of bone marrow cancer. He was buried in the village churchyard at Orvilliers, 31 miles (50 km) west of Paris, on April 4. Two days later, 7,000 persons, including 70 chiefs of state or government or their representatives, gathered in Notre Dame de Paris for a requiem mass. It was a momentary pause in the almost indecent scramble for the succession (see OBITUARIES).

The leading contenders were liberal Gaullist Jacques Chaban-Delmas, 59, former premier; Independent Valéry Giscard d'Estaing, 48, long-

FRANCE • Information Highlights

Official Name: French Republic.
Location: Western Europe.
Area: 211,207 square miles (547,026 sq km).
Population (1974 est.): 52,450,000.
Chief Cities (1968 census): Paris, the capital, 2,590,771; Marseille, 889,029; Lyon, 527,800; Toulouse, 370,796.
Government: *Head of state,* Valéry Giscard d'Estaing, president (took office May 1974). *Chief minister,* Jacques Chirac, premier (took office May 1974). *Legislature*—Parliament: Senate and National Assembly.
Monetary Unit: Franc (4.741 francs equal U. S.$1, Sept. 1974).
Gross National Product (1973 est.): $231,100,000,000.
Manufacturing (major products): Steel, machinery, metals, chemicals, automobiles, airplanes, processed foods, beverages, clothing, textiles.
Major Agricultural Products: Wheat, barley, oats, sugar beets, vegetables, apples, grapes, cattle, fish.
Foreign Trade (1973): *Exports,* $35,565,000,000; *imports,* $36,987,000,000.

AEROPORT DE PARIS

Aerial view of the new Charles de Gaulle airport in Roissy, near Paris, showing the main terminal surrounded by seven satellite terminals.

time minister of the economy and finance; Socialist Francois Mitterrand, 57, many times a minister under the Fourth Republic; Premier Pierre Messmer, and an army of hopefuls. Only Chaban, Giscard, and Mitterrand seemed serious candidates. With anti-Gaullist Senate president Alain Poher as acting president of the Republic, the election was set for May 5 and 19.

Backed by the Gaullist Union of Democrats for the Republic (UDR), despite orthodox Gaullist hostility, Chaban, mayor of Bordeaux, was the favored challenger to Mitterrand, leader of a coalition of Socialists, Communists, and trade-unionists. Mitterrand had forced Charles de Gaulle into the second round of balloting in 1965. Beaten then, he had been defeated by Pompidou in 1969. Leader of the small Independent party supporting Gaullism, Giscard claimed to be Pompidou's choice; his chance seemed to lie in the failure of Chaban or Mitterrand to win on the first ballot. Chaban drew strength from the withdrawal of Messmer and other Gaullists opposing him, but Gaullist rifts increased when post office minister Jean Royer entered to unite the right and the lower middle class on a law and order platform. Mitterrand's chances in the first ballot were judged good.

As usual, Gaullists prophesied Mitterrand's election would introduce a Communist "hell." The anarchy produced by Gaullist rivalries was illustrated by Interior Minister Jacques Chirac assailing Chaban (to whom Pompidou had been hostile). By April 13 ministers and deputies were issuing a "last appeal" to Chaban to step down for the sake of Gaullist unity. The polls forecast Mitterrand would be ahead on the first ballot, then would lose to Chaban or Giscard on the second, neither one of whom would withdraw. They were old enemies: publication of Chaban's embarrassing tax returns in 1972 was attributed to Finance Minister Giscard. The only light moments were provided by eccentric dark horses. "They have one aim," commented *Le Monde:* "to see their names published twice in the press: when they announce their candidacy and when they withdraw."

As the election approached, Mitterrand's chances for victory on May 5 faded. Giscard overtook Chaban and seemed likely to win on May 19. Televised debates confirmed Giscard's growing strength. Chaban, outspending both, attacked his principal opponents vitriolically. Mitterrand was helped by the Communists and trade-unionists keeping a low profile. All the candidates appealed to women and to youth. They journeyed incessantly by car, plane, and helicopter. Some had rotten fruit, eggs, and obscenities hurled at them.

On May 5, with 12 candidates still running, Mitterrand took 43.4% of the vote; Giscard 32.9%; Chaban 14%. In the final battle between the two front-runners, the humiliated Gaullists gave Giscard their endorsement; Mitterrand may have gathered some liberal Gaullist votes. Both candidates now wooed the center. They were evenly matched in television debate. Enjoying last minute support from Radical leader Jean Jacques Servan-Schreiber, and assisted by his own attractive family, Giscard worked to alter his austere conservative image, blithely advocating social reforms that had been anathema to him weeks before. On their side, George Marchais and the Communists said modestly that they expected only 6 or 7 cabinet posts from Mitterrand, and would not ask for the critical interior, defense, and foreign ministry posts. This battle for the moderates ended May 19. In an unprecedentedly high turnout, Giscard received 50.18% of the vote to Mitterrand's 49.19%.

Following an informal inauguration on May 27, Giscard named Jacques Chirac premier. The cabinet included only three holdovers; less than half was Gaullist; many were technicians; two were women. Both the centrist leader, Jean Lecanuet, and Jean Jacques Servan-Schreiber were rewarded for their support, the former at justice, the latter in a new ministry of reforms. Giscard's friend Michel Poniatowski went to interior. Ambassador Jean Sauvagnargues became foreign minister. Giscard intended to have a disciplined ministry and fired Servan-Schreiber June 9 for publicly criticizing continued nuclear testing. Nevertheless, Servan-Schreiber regrouped his Radicals on September 30 into a new reform party to protect the regime's left flank.

"I'm a traditionalist," Giscard said at his first press conference, July 25, "who likes change." Minimum wages, pensions, and family allowances were raised on July 1. The government, employers, and unions signed an agreement in October guaranteeing 20 million workers one year's wages should they be laid off because of recession. Initially funded by the government (employers would then provide 80%, workers 20%), the plan evidently outstripped labor legislation anywhere else in the world.

On another front, the government worked to refurbish the police image, concentrating more on crime prevention than on maintenance of order. The notorious wiretapping of the Gaullist era was to be halted. The scandal-ridden government radio and TV monopoly was to be decentralized and competition introduced to improve its quality. This worthy aim was in doubt after Chirac fired a radio station director for refusing him air time.

Election promises were made good by lowering the voting age from 21 to 18. The government decreed a "pause" in office building construction in Paris, the restoration of old quarters of the city, a ban on urban highway construction, and an increase in park and public transit development.

Journalist Françoise Giroud was appointed on July 16 secretary of state for the condition of women. After years of public debate, the National Assembly on June 28 approved Health Minister Simone Veil's legislation for the distribution of contraceptives under the social security system. Even more remarkable for this Roman Catholic country was the passage of a bill on November 29 by the National Assembly that legalized abortion during the first 10 weeks of pregnancy. Sponsored by the health minister, it was passed by a wide margin.

The power struggle among Gaullist leaders reached a climax on December 14 when Premier Chirac took over control of the Gaullist party. His election to the secretary general's post was denounced by Mitterand as a "mini coup d'état," and some leaders threatened to quit.

Strikes. Industrial unrest continued. Shutdowns involved the post office, banks, shipyards, gas, and electricity; strikes were also held by

UPI

Interim French President Alain Poher (*center, foreground*) leads world leaders at memorial mass for the late President Pompidou.

UPI

Libyan Premier Abdal Sellam Jalloud (*left*) and French Prime Minister Pierre Messmer sign an agreement in Paris to exchange Libyan oil for French industrial assistance.

textile and railway workers, coal miners, printers, broadcasters, autoworkers, and garbage collectors. Troops were used to collect Paris garbage in November. A general strike on November 19 was only partially successful. More happily, the Lip watch company affair was peacefully resolved: workers, who had seized the factory in June 1973 and carried on production and sales until their expulsion in August 1973, obtained a settlement promising full employment by January 1975, thanks to the intervention of progressive industrialists. The episode encouraged both militancy among workers believing themselves victims of poor management and responsible action by the National Employers Federation to prevent unnecessary shutdowns or to ensure alternative employment.

Scandals. Government agents, it was revealed in January, had bugged not only the satirical weekly *Le Canard Enchaîné* but also the homes of François Mitterrand, senior civil servants, the prefect of Paris, and the head of the narcotics squad. For trying to obstruct judicial inquiry into the *Canard* case, Henry Biard was removed as director of the counterespionage agency.

Scandal also plagued the Bordeaux wine merchants. A trial was held between October 28 and November 8 of 18 prominent Bordeaux wine merchants, some from the house of Cruse. Convicted of massive adulteration of vintage wines and of fraud, Lionel and Ivan Cruse were given one-year (suspended) prison sentences, fined $5,400, and ordered to pay more than $12 million in back taxes. A wine broker, Pierre Bert, received a one-year jail sentence. Faced with costs of $20 million in civil suits, the defendants were evidently ruined by the affair. The Bordeaux industry as a whole was severely damaged.

Economy. The economy declined in 1974. With foreign reserves dropping, the franc was floated on January 20, effectively devaluing it by 5%. Giscard set a 51 billion franc ($10,625,000,000) ceiling on 1975 oil imports as the balance of payments deficit rose. Higher corporation and income taxes, higher interest rates to curb borrowing, and restriction on foreign worker entry into France elicited criticism from employers and workers. Thousands of small businesses closed. The Citroën autoworks sought merger with the state-owned Renault corporation. Unemployment rose above 500,000 for the first time since 1945.

Accused of hiding the truth from the public, Giscard told his October 24 press conference that demographic, resource, and financial indicators showed "disaster" ahead. He urged austerity and conservation.

Defense. In spite of international criticism, France conducted its eighth and last series of nuclear tests in the atmosphere around Mururoa atoll between June 17 and September 15. The next tests, in 1975, were to be underground.

The battle against U. S. manufacturers for the multibillion dollar NATO fighter-plane contract caused something like national hysteria when Gen. Paul Stehlin, a former chief of air staff, and a vice president of the National Assembly, sent a 30-page memorandum to Giscard claiming that the U. S. planes being considered were cheaper and better-tested than the Breguet-Dassault Mirage F-1. Stehlin was known to have business connections with a Howard Hughes subsidiary. In the parliamentary tempest that followed, Stehlin resigned his vice presidency, after what he called an "odious, despicable and unjustified" one-day debate. Shots were fired at his car, wounding his son.

FOREIGN AFFAIRS

Neither President Pompidou nor his successor advanced the cause of a united Europe. Pompidou and Foreign Minister Michel Jobert refused to cooperate with other West European nations in the February oil crisis. When James Callaghan, Britain's chancellor of the exchequer, on April 1 demanded renegotiation of its Common Market (EEC) membership, Jobert termed this "unacceptable." But at the Common Market summit in Paris in December, Giscard granted the financial concessions which Britain's deepening economic crisis seemed to demand if it was to remain in the organization.

Relations with West Germany apparently improved with the advent of Giscard and Chancellor Helmut Schmidt, two former ministers of finance. In a series of meetings in Paris and Bonn, May 31–June 1 and July 8–9, they agreed to work for EEC unity by 1980. But by the end of the year Schmidt seemed to have lost some of his confidence in Giscard.

Relations with the Soviet Union were cordial. Despite his painful final illness, Pompidou held talks with Brezhnev on March 12–13 near Sochi on the Black Sea. Displeased by Russian failure to include France in the negotiations to end the Yom Kippur War of 1973, Pompidou withheld support for Brezhnev's haste to convene the European Security Conference. During a three-day visit to Paris in December, Brezhnev reached agreement with Giscard on a wide range of issues. He won French backing for a 35-nation summit meeting in 1975 to conclude the European conference, and the two leaders signed a five-year trade agreement.

In the Middle East oil crisis, Pompidou dealt directly with the Arab states. But by March 21, Jobert was warning the Arabs to treat Europeans equally, which indicated that the special consideration he had expected from the Arabs had not been fully realized. Giscard indicated greater readiness to cooperate with the Common Market and the United States. He lifted the arms embargo on sales to the Middle East countries, including Israel, but he backed the UN call for Israeli evacuation of Arab lands. He and his predecessor supported the massive 10-year development accord concluded with Iran. France would sell Iran five giant reactors and otherwise develop Iranian industry and supply arms in return for oil.

Relations with the United States remained cool. Jobert's public and private collisions with U. S. Secretary of State Henry Kissinger were well publicized. Amid a series of trans-Altantic rows, President Richard Nixon's scheduled visit to Europe in April was cancelled. His brief appearance in Paris that month for Pompidou's funeral was marked and marred by a bizarre flurry of personal diplomacy. His immediate congratulations by telephone to Giscard on May 19 did not clear the atmosphere. Giscard was quick to comment on President Gerald Ford's failure to mention Europe in his address to Congress, saying this demonstrated that Europe would have to look after itself.

UPI

Angry farmers block the main Paris-Chantilly road with dozens of tractors as part of a European community-wide protest against sagging farm prices.

An accord on the thorny issue of energy policy came at a meeting of Giscard and Ford on the French island of Martinique, December 15–16. The United States agreed to a French-proposed conference of oil-consuming and -exporting countries at an early date, while France accepted the American view that consuming nations should seek a unified position.

Relations with Canada seemed improved. France, however, would not permit a special Canadian economic relationship with the Common Market, as Prime Minister Pierre Trudeau learned during his October state visit.

JOHN C. CAIRNS, *University of Toronto*

PICTORIAL PARADE

At Le Havre, the *France*, the largest ocean liner in the world still on active service, ends its career because of high operating costs. With the crew on strike in protest against the move, the passengers are removed and taken ashore.

GRANT HEILMAN

Skyrocketing supermarket prices encourage more and more Americans to grow their own vegetables in home gardens.

GARDENING AND HORTICULTURE

Interest in home gardening, inspired largely by spiraling food prices, increased rapidly in 1974. Also, the energy crisis—notably the shortage of petroleum supplies and the higher cost of petroleum derivatives—created serious shortages in plastic pots and other materials, fertilizers, pesticides, and fuel. These two factors moved legislators to ask for more funds for agricultural research.

The Need for Research. Sen. Lloyd Bentsen (D-Texas), addressing the U. S. Senate, stated that "at a time when the demand for food and fiber has been increasing dramatically, our agricultural research and development effort has been slipping miserably. When we need increased production desperately, we do not have the proper research dollars or the manpower to produce that productivity." The Senator pointed out that whereas in 1955, 10.7% of the U. S. Department of Agriculture's budget went for agricultural research and development, in 1973 only 2.5% of the budget was marked for research. Reduced financial support for agricultural research has been the trend over the past several years at both the national and the state levels. This in turn has contributed to food shortages, balance-of-payments problems, and increased food prices.

All-America Selections. Roses in all three of the major classes shared All-America Awards for 1975: the hybrid tea Oregold, the grandiflora Arizona, and the floribunda Rose Parade.

Oregold is the only deep yellow in any rose classification to win an All-America Award since King's Ransom in 1962. The blooms consist of 35 to 40 sturdy petals usually borne singly on 8- to 14-inch stems, with the distinctly opulent form of Peace. With good lasting quality, long stems, a delicate hybrid tea fragrance, and graceful bud shape, this rose is ideal as a cut flower. Although no more hardy than other hybrid teas, Oregold is a vigorous grower and blooms continuously through the growing season.

Arizona, the award-winning grandiflora, is unusual in its Arizona sunset color combinations of bronze and copper with various shadings of yellow, red, pink, and orange. The classic buds of the Arizona open to blooms up to 4½ inches across, with a total of 26 to 32 petals. The blooms last extremely well when cut, and the color holds throughout the life of the flower. Arizona is a vigorous grower with sturdy stems, each carrying several blossoms in a neat candelabrum effect above the tall plants.

Rose Parade is a compact floribunda thickly set with light coralum pink 2½-inch flowers, delicately highlighted with shadings of peach. The clusters of buds, borne continuously, open slowly into perfectly formed, full, richly fragrant blooms that contrast beautifully with the abundant dark green foliage. This variety has a true floribunda growth habit—compact, symmetrical, of medium height, and with heavy, glossy foliage. The flowers last well, fade slowly, and drop cleanly when the blooming period is over.

The dahlia Redskin and the pansy Imperial Blue were the only All-America Award winners among the flowering annuals. Two vegetables—broccoli Premium Crop and cauliflower Snow Crown—also won All-America Awards.

New Books. *Food and the Consumer,* by Amihud Kramer, may be of particular interest to consumers during this period of high food costs. In the area of ecology, *The Living Year,* by Mary Q. Steele, and *A Walk Through the Marsh,* by C. William Harrison were of interest. Also, a second edition of Robert W. Schery's *Plants for Man* was published.

Books on herbs included *Herb Magic and Garden Craft,* by Louise Evans Doole, and *Herbs,* by H. L. V. Fletcher. The latter also had published *Popular Flowering Shrubs.*

Other subjects of general interest to gardeners were *House Plants,* by Joan Compton; *Foliage Plants,* by Frederick A. Boddy; *Terrariums,* by John Hoke; *Dictionary of Annual Plants,* by H. G. Witham Fogg; *The Complete Book of Garden Ornaments, Complements, and Accessories,* by Daniel J. Foley; and *The Complete Rosarian,* by Norman Young. For travelers in Europe, *Flowers of Europe: A Field Guide,* by Oleg Polunin, should prove to be helpful.

DONALD W. NEWSOM
Louisiana State University

GENETICS

Excitement in genetics during 1974 arose from the possibility of transplanting genes from higher organisms to bacteria and from advances in the understanding of the make-up of chromosome structure.

Gene Transplantation. In May 1974, Stanley Cohen and co-workers at Stanford University reported an experiment in which they transplanted a toad gene into a bacterium. In doing this, they took advantage of several biochemical and genetic techniques that have been developed in the last several years.

To begin the transplantation they prepared the gene by treating the toad genetic material, deoxyribonucleic acid (DNA), with an enzyme called endonuclease, which cleaved the DNA to gene-size pieces. At the same time they used the same enzyme to treat the DNA from a bacterial plasmid. (A bacterial plasmid is a small piece of DNA containing only a few genes, and it is normally found inside a bacterial cell.) The enzyme-treated toad DNA and plasmid DNA were then mixed and joined together by another enzyme called a ligase. The hybrid DNA was then able to enter a bacterial cell where, like a normal plasmid, it replicated many times. It was also able to express its genes inside the bacterium.

Cohen and his co-workers were able to show conclusively that the toad gene was being expressed. They reported that their methods could be readily adapted to the transplantation of many other kinds of genes into bacteria—a prospect that is very exciting to geneticists.

The potential practical applications of these transplantation methods are also very exciting. For instance, if the human genes for insulin could be transplanted to a bacterium, the expression of these genes might lead to insulin-producing bacteria. Since enormous quantities of bacteria can be grown very easily, this transplantation could lead to unlimited supplies of human insulin that could be prepared very cheaply.

As with many great advances in science, this breakthrough is somewhat double-edged because the potential dangers perhaps outweigh the benefits. In fact, in a letter to two major scientific publications in July 1974, a group of leading biologists proposed a six-month ban on most research in this area so that scientists could have an opportunity to better evaluate the hazards of gene transplantation.

Their primary concern was to halt two types of transplantation experiments—those that put genes from one kind of bacterium into another, and those that put genes from an animal virus into a bacterium. The potential danger in the bacterium-to-bacterium transplant is the accidental transfer of antibiotic resistance or toxin-producing genes to a bacterial strain that normally does not contain them. The spread of these bacteria could be a major health hazard. The danger in the animal virus to bacterium transplant arises because animal viruses are known to cause a variety of diseases, including cancer. The transplantation of genes from these viruses and the possible subsequent dissemination of these genes through the human population via the bacterial recipient could also present a great health hazard.

Chromosome Structure. In the 1970's, molecular geneticists have turned their attention to gene regulation in higher organisms and found things considerably more complicated than what had previously been found in bacteria.

One complication—and indeed a puzzle—was the amount of DNA contained in the chromosomes of higher organisms. One would expect higher organisms to have more genes than bacteria, but even the most generous estimates of the number of extra genes higher organisms would need does not account for all the DNA they contain. Several years ago the use of a technique called molecular hybridization enabled researchers to estimate the number of times each gene was present in a cell. Although most genes were found to be present only once (single-copy DNA), a small percentage was found to be present in as many as several thousand copies (repetitive DNA). The discovery of repetitive DNA provided an explanation for the excess DNA but raised new questions, since the function of the repetitive DNA remains unknown to scientists.

Another feature of higher-organism gene organization and regulation not found in bacteria is the appearance of a sequence of about 150 adenylic acid residues (poly A) on the end of the primary gene product, the messenger RNA. As with the repetitive DNA, the function of the poly A is unknown.

In a recent series of papers, Harvey Lodish, Allan Jacobson, and Richard Firtel of the Massachusetts Institute of Technology examined the organization of the genome of a fungal-like organism called a cellular slime mold and proposed a model for the structure of the DNA of the slime mold. In their view the active genes (structural genes) are present in the single-copy DNA sequences. Adjacent to each structural gene is a sequence of repetitive DNA that may have a role in gene regulation. When the messenger RNA for the gene is copied from the DNA, both the repetitive and single-copy DNA appear to be transcribed. In addition, a sequence of about 25 adenylic acid residues is also copied. The remaining part of the poly A seems to be added after the transcription.

There is great hope that these advances in the understanding of the structural arrangement of the DNA in a higher-organism chromosome will lead to a clearer understanding of gene regulation.

EUGENE R. KATZ
State University of New York at Stony Brook

GEOLOGY

Advances were made on many fronts in earth and planetary geology during 1974. Work continued on lunar samples, and important data on Mercury, Venus, Mars, and Jupiter were obtained by instrumented flybys. Sampling and sounding of the ocean basins continued on an expanded international scale. And geologists became more involved with problems of conservation and shortages, and with hazards of life on earth generally.

Astrogeology. Mariner 10 spacecraft passed Venus on Feb. 5, 1974, and was in instrumental contact with Mercury in April and again in September. Pioneer 10 had passed Jupiter on Dec. 4, 1973. Information gained about the planets Jupiter and Venus during the year pertained mainly to their atmospheres, radiation belts, and force fields.

Excellent photographs of the surface of Mercury revealed an outer layer of lightweight material on which moonlike features, mainly craters, abound. But the planet has high density (5.5 times that of water), which would require a core at least as heavy as iron. This unusual combination raises the question of when and how the planet became differentiated in this way. Was it layered from its origin, or did it melt and stratify later, as the earth is thought to have done? No substantial atmospheric erosion or crustal activity is evident, but a few lava flows indicate heat sources within.

Scientists continue to study the 850 pounds of samples and miles of data tapes brought back by the moon missions. The feeling grows that, although the surface material is heterogeneous, it is rather uniformly so. A few samples over 4 billion years old have been found, and considerable interest attaches to the question of whether any material from really deep sources has turned up. The great impact craters, contrary to expectations, may not have thrown out material from deeper than about 6 miles (10 km), and deep-seated basalts may not have been sampled.

Plate Tectonics. The concept of the earth's outer rigid shell (lithosphere) as being fragmented into a half-dozen major plates 30–60 miles (50–100 km) thick and a few hundred to a few thousand km broad, moving horizontally with respect to each other, is now almost universally accepted.

A major continental break-up commencing about 200 million years ago eventually created the present Atlantic Ocean, and there is good evidence for an early Paleozoic proto-Atlantic that was closed by collision of Europe-Africa and North America about 350 million years ago. Debate continues over the question of how plate movements relate to mountain building and inundations of the continents. Evidently plates maintain their mutual relations and motions for relatively long periods and then undergo rapid reorganizations, including splitting along new fractures and shifts in the direction of motion. It is difficult to distinguish motion of individual plates from possible motion of the lithosphere as a whole. Which of the two possible motions explains evidence for polar ice caps in equatorial regions and coal forests in polar regions is not yet clear.

Ocean Basins. The Deep Sea Drilling Project continued, with the research vessel *Glomar Challenger* drilling sites between Hawaii and Tahiti (5 holes), near the Galápagos Islands and off the coast of Peru (6 holes), northwest of Antarctica in the Southeast Pacific Basin (4 holes), the submerged Falkland Plateau between the capes of South America and Africa (10 holes), and near the Mid-Atlantic Rift southwest of the Azores (4 holes).

Important discoveries at these sites include evidence that volcanoes of the Line Islands chain erupted at about the same time, rather than in sequence, as some theories held; unusual concentrations of metals near the Galápagos Islands; confirmation of 20 million years of glaciation of Antarctica; and evidence of the inception of strong circumpolar currents beginning 5 million years ago in the Southeast Pacific Basin. Continental rocks 600 million years old were taken from the Falkland Plateau, which proved to be a sunken fragment fitting between Africa and South America. Its presence is strong evidence for the opening of the Atlantic about 200 million years ago.

Finally, the penetration of 1,910 feet (582 meters) of igneous (basement) rocks, chiefly basalt, beneath the oceanic sediments near the Mid-Atlantic Rift was a technological achievement favorable to future deep-sea drilling of all types.

Project FAMOUS (Franco-American Mid-Ocean Undersea Study) is conducting an intensive survey of the Mid-Atlantic Rift about 350 miles southwest of the Azores. Observational geology made possible by use of three manned submersible vessels is being stressed. Sampling, photography, and direct observation of the sea bottom strongly support the idea that new crustal material in the form of basalt is being extruded in a ribbon-like belt along the center of the trench, and that successively older belts occur outward on the ridge. Much interest attaches to the discovery of mineral-rich submarine springs of warm water around which deposits high in manganese and iron oxides, with minor quantities of copper and other metals, are being slowly built up.

Economic Geology. The so-called "bright-spot" method of locating potential hydrocarbon deposits (primarily natural gas, secondarily petroleum), which had been quietly developing, was finally given wide publicity. The method is geophysical and is named for the appearance of certain anomalous areas on cross-sectional records of the subsurface. The bright spot represents a greater-than-average return of seismic echos (sound waves) from areas of porous rock in which natural gas may be trapped. The method works best in relatively young and unconsolidated sedimentary beds less than 10,000 feet (3 km) deep, such as those predominating in many fringing near-shore continental shelves. As many as 60% to 80% of wells drilled into bright spots are successful.

Of great potential in alleviating certain metal shortages is the steadily growing body of knowledge and technology applicable to mining the ocean floor. Metal-rich, potato-sized nodules are estimated to be concentrated on no less than 1.5 million square miles (nearly 4 million sq km) of the northern Pacific Ocean bottom, mostly at depths of 12,000 to 20,000 feet (3.7 to 6.1 km). Other large tracts are known, but relatively few are in the Atlantic. The nodules "grow" in place, accumulating manganese, nickel, copper, cobalt, and traces of two dozen other metals from the seawater. Concentrations vary with area, an average assay being 27–30% manganese, 1.1–1.4% nickel, 1.0–1.3% copper, and 0.2–0.4% cobalt. American, Japanese, French, and German interests are actively participating in developments.

PHOTO BY B. J. NIXON, DEEPSEA VENTURES INC.

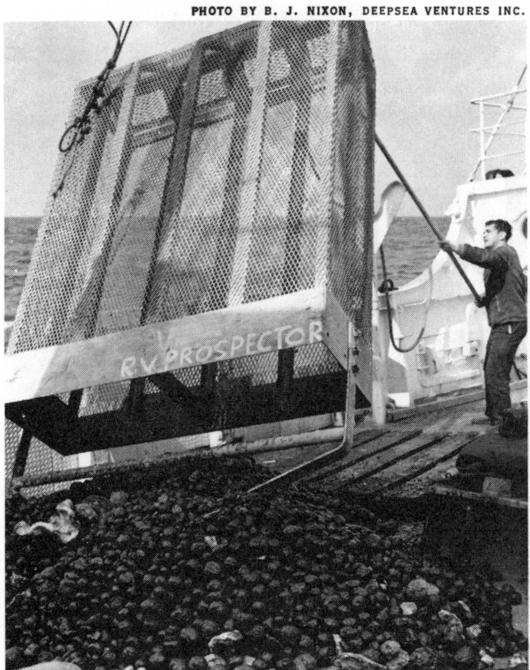

Earthquake Prediction. Capability of predicting earthquakes continued to develop rapidly. Two earthquakes, one in New York and one in California, were successfully predicted during the year.

International. Unprecedented cooperative projects were under way in 1974. They included those of the International Union of Geological Sciences (concerned chiefly with continental igneous and sedimentary rocks); the Geodynamics Project (earth movements and forces); the Deep Sea Drilling Project, scheduled to become the International Program of Ocean Drilling in 1975; and the International Decade of Ocean Exploration (seabed, water masses, and economic resources). Publication of a colorful geologic map of China represented an international breakthrough of great interest to geologists.

W. LEE STOKES
University of Utah

(*Left*) A dredge basket filled with samples of manganese nodules from the sea floor are unloaded on the deck of a barge. (*Below*) The nodules are processed in a pilot plant to extract copper, cobalt, nickel, and manganese.

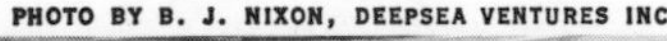

PHOTO BY B. J. NIXON, DEEPSEA VENTURES INC.

GEORGIA

The apparent end of the political career of former Gov. Lester Maddox was the major event in Georgia, overshadowing the battle for control of the state's $1.7 billion budget and the plans of outgoing Gov. Jimmy Carter to campaign for the presidency.

Maddox. Lt. Gov. Lester Maddox, former governor-restauranteur-entrepreneur and self-styled segregationist, was defeated in the Democratic primary in his bid for a second term as governor. House Majority Leader George Busbee of Albany collected about 60% of the vote in winning a runoff election with Maddox by more than 200,000 votes. Busbee went on to defeat the Republican nominee, Mayor Ronnie Thompson of Macon, to win the governorship. Democrat Zell Miller, former executive secretary to then Governor Maddox, won the race to succeed Maddox as lieutenant governor. After leaving the Maddox fold, Miller had served as executive secretary of the Georgia Democratic party, where he considerably broadened his political base. In another statewide race U. S. Sen. Herman Talmadge, who served on the Senate Watergate Committee, easily won reelection.

Maddox, who ran for office regularly for more than two decades, gained national attention in the mid-1960's when he stood in the door of his Pickrick restaurant and turned back potential black patrons with harsh words. Finally, Maddox closed the restaurant rather than comply with civil rights laws.

In the midst of civil-rights turmoil in 1966, Maddox captured the Democratic nomination for governor of Georgia. In the general election, Republican nominee Howard "Bo" Callaway (now secretary of the Army) captured more votes than Maddox but failed to gain a majority because of the write-in campaign for former Democratic Gov. Ellis Arnall. The decision as to whom should be governor, in the absence of a clear majority vote, was left to the Democratic legislature, which chose Maddox.

After a stormy four-year term, Maddox—prohibited by law from succeeding himself as governor—easily won the lieutenant governorship. In this office he presided over the Georgia State Senate, which constantly combated the programs of Governor Carter for four years. It was from this base that Maddox sought his second term as governor. After his defeat, Maddox emotionally admitted that he probably would not run again for public office.

Maddox announced plans to reopen a Pickrick-type cafeteria, this time in a night-club area —Underground Atlanta—and this time in compliance with the civil rights laws.

Budget Battle. The 1974 Georgia General Assembly was marked by a lengthy battle between Governor Carter and the legislature for control of the state's record-setting $1.7 billion budget. Georgia has traditionally had an "executive budget," prepared by the governor and sent as a package to the General Assembly for expected quick approval. Beginning with the Maddox years in 1967, the Assembly has moved toward independence from the governor and toward closer scrutiny of the budget.

In 1974, a group of legislators led by House Speaker Tom Murphy and House Appropriations Committee Chairman James H. Floyd demanded that the governor provide a "line item" budget, with detailed explanations of each line. The governor, backed by administrative department heads, refused, saying it would not provide the flexibility needed to operate state government. The legislators threatened to make wholesale changes in the budget, and the governor threatened to dissolve the Assembly. Finally, a compromise was reached.

Legislation. Major legislation passed by the 1974 Assembly included a no-fault automobile insurance plan to lower insurance rates; a campaign ethics bill requiring all candidates for public office to report the sources of all contributions of $100 or more; and a $50 million tax rebate, which was vetoed by the governor. The Assembly also passed a measure to allow Georgia counties to vote individually to exempt themselves from the state's "blue laws." In addition, the legislature removed 38 categories of business from the required Sunday closing law but retained the statewide prohibition on beer and liquor sales on Sunday.

The legislature created the Georgia Residential Finance Agency to offer housing loans to families in the $7,000 to $15,000 annual income range, and the lawmakers passed an omnibus education measure calling for statewide kindergartens, lower pupil-teacher ratios, and greater emphasis on special and vocational education. No funds were provided for fiscal 1975 for the housing or education legislation.

Carter. Outgoing Governor Carter, who did not run for office in 1974 but instead coordinated the national Democratic congressional election campaign, announced plans to campaign for the presidency in 1976.

GENE STEPHENS, *Georgia State University*

GEORGIA • Information Highlights

Area: 58,876 square miles (152,489 sq km).
Population (1973 est.): 4,786,000. *Density:* 81 per sq. mi.
Chief Cities (1970 census): Atlanta, the capital, 497,421; Columbus, 155,028; Macon, 122,423.
Government (1974): *Chief Officers*—governor, Jimmy Carter (D); lt. gov., Lester D. Maddox (D); atty. gen., Arthur K. Bolton (D); supt. of schools, Jack P. Nix (D); chief justice, Benning M. Grice. *General Assembly*—Senate, 56 members; House of Representatives, 180 members.
Education (1973–74): *Enrollment*—public elementary schools, 683,354 pupils; public secondary, 402,527; nonpublic, 31,600; colleges and universities, 146,356 students.
State Finances (fiscal year 1973): *Revenues,* $2,514,-318,000; *Expenditures,* $2,344,539,000.
Personal Income (1973): $20,307,000,000.
Labor Force (June 1974): *Nonagricultural wage and salary earners,* 1,808,600.

(*Right*) **Helmut Schmidt takes the oath of office as West German chancellor, replacing Willy Brandt (*below*). Brandt had resigned when it became known that one of his personal aides was an East German agent.**

GERMAN INFORMATION CENTER

GERMANY

The geographical area of Germany is divided into two separate states. The Federal Republic of Germany (West Germany) is a democratic, parliamentary republic and a member of such Western organizations as the North Atlantic Treaty Organization (NATO), the European Coal and Steel Community, and the European Economic Community (Common Market). The German Democratic Republic (East Germany), also known as DDR from its German-language initials, is, in effect, a Communist one-party state. It is affiliated with the Warsaw Pact and the Council for Mutual Economic Assistance (COMECON), the Eastern counterparts of NATO and EEC.

Between these two states, West Berlin, a Western outpost within East Germany, maintains its precarious existence. Economically and culturally it is tied closely to West Germany, but politically and militarily it has a separate status.

D. P. A., PICTORIAL PARADE

FEDERAL REPUBLIC OF GERMANY (West Germany)

The most dramatic event of the year was the resignation, on May 6, of Chancellor Willy Brandt. It was triggered by the arrest of a member of Brandt's personal staff, Günter Guillaume, as an East German spy. Brandt had known that Guillaume was under suspicion, but he had kept him on as an aide on the advice of the West German intelligence service, which thus hoped to observe Guillaume more easily. It was learned, however, that despite surveillance he had had access to sensitive information.

Brandt's departure had become almost inevitable in any event. After nearly five years as chancellor, Brandt was tired and unable to cope with the country's economic difficulties. Looking back, he could take credit, however, for improved relations with eastern Europe and especially with East Germany.

New Government. Brandt's successor was Helmut Schmidt, deputy chairman of the German Social Democratic party (SPD) and finance minister in the last cabinet. Schmidt made some changes in the government; the most important was the replacement of Vice Chancellor and Foreign Minister Walter Scheel by Minister of the Interior Hans-Dietrich Genscher, Scheel's successor also as chairman of the Free Democratic party (FDP), the SPD's partner in the government coalition. Scheel was elected president of the Federal Republic and succeeded President Gustav Heinemann on July 1.

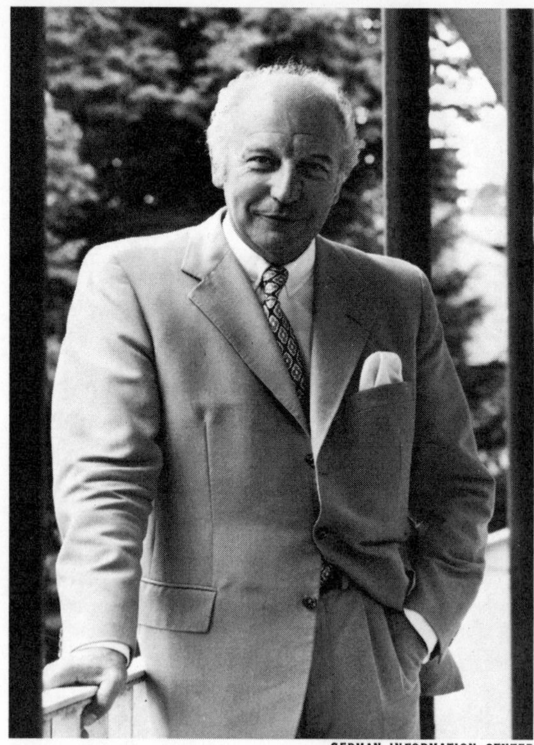

GERMAN INFORMATION CENTER

Walter Scheel, the new president of West Germany, had been the foreign minister in the Brandt government.

In his policies Schmidt assigned top priority to the country's economic problems. A substantial tax cut, to take effect on Jan. 1, 1975, was to prime the ailing economy. Social reforms that had been proposed by his predecessor were shelved on the other hand as too costly. Aid to underdeveloped countries also was cut.

Political Parties. The problems of inflation and unemployment with which both the Brandt and Schmidt governments were faced were reflected in the election returns. In state and communal elections the SPD kept suffering setbacks. Inevitably, as the SPD's junior partner, the FDP, too, lost ground. The SPD also had internal problems. Its left wing, composed mostly of younger members, protested against the party's increasing conservatism and called for an aggressive social reform program, including the socialization of major industries. Despite the rejection of their demands by both Brandt and Schmidt, the Young Socialists frightened off some earlier supporters of the SPD.

Yet the opposition party, the Christian Democratic Union, was not able either to develop a plausible policy to ward off the impending recession. Its chairman, Helmut Kohl, seemed, moreover, too colorless to make an attractive candidate for chancellor.

Anniversary. On May 23 the Federal Republic was 25 years old. This was not considered an occasion for jubilant celebrations. For the state that had been established provisionally in 1949, pending the reunification of East and West Germany, had evidently become a permanent one. There was some serious soul-searching in books, speeches, and editorials. On the positive side, the consolidation of the democratic-parliamentary order was welcomed. But there was concern, too, that the republic had not yet fully realized the constitutional goals of legal and social security for everyone.

Economy. Unlike the other major industrial powers of the West, West Germany's rate of inflation remained stable at a comparatively moderate rate of 6.9%, due to extremely high interest rates. Unemployment, by the latest account, did not exceed 2.7% since the export boom continued throughout 1974. Yet the economy was clearly suffering; car sales dropped by 25%, compared with 1973, and sales of other non-essentials also declined.

The government, which had so far been more concerned with fighting inflation, turned its attention to unemployment. Apart from the tax cut, interest rates were lowered to encourage new construction and other investments. On the other hand, no reduction was planned in the foreign labor force, still numbering 2.5 million. (No additional workers may be recruited, however, outside the Common Market.) There is a manpower shortage in the areas in which most of them work—mining, food processing, sanitation, and hotels and restaurants. Many Germans shy away from these kinds of work.

Inevitably inflation prompted demands for higher wages. Public service employees led the way with a strike in February that disrupted mail and rail service. The ensuing wage increases in public and private industries did not accelerate the inflation, but did endanger the competitiveness of some export industries. They reinforced the inclination of some industries to set up plants in foreign countries rather than export to them, thus increasing the threat of domestic unemployment. Narrowing profit margins also affected the accumulation of capital for investment. A major steel producer, Krupp, solved this problem by selling 25% of its stock to the government of Iran.

WEST GERMANY • Information Highlights

Official Name: Federal Republic of Germany.
Location: North central Europe.
Area: 95,790 square miles (248,096 sq km). West Berlin, 186 square miles (481 sq km).
Population (1973 est.): 59,800,000; West Berlin, 2,100,000.
Chief Cities (1970 census): Bonn, the capital, 274,528; Hamburg, 1,793,823; Munich, 1,293,590.
Government: *Head of state,* Walter Scheel, president (took office July 1974). *Head of government,* Helmut Schmidt, federal chancellor (took office May 1974). *Legislature*—Parliament: Bundesrat and Bundestag.
Monetary Unit: Deutsche Mark (2.653 D. Marks equal U.S.$1, Sept. 1974).
Gross National Product (1973 est.): $301,100,000,000.
Manufacturing (major products): Mechanical engineering products, automobiles, chemicals, iron and steel.
Major Agricultural Products: Rye, oats, wheat, barley, potatoes, sugar beets, hops, forest products, fish.
Foreign Trade (1973): *Exports,* $67,468,000,000; *imports,* $54,503,000,000.

Foreign Policy. With Schmidt as chancellor, West Germany's "Eastern policy" no longer received the special attention it had been given by Brandt. Nevertheless, by August the resumption of diplomatic relations with all Soviet-bloc countries had been completed. Chancellor Schmidt, though more concerned with the West, sought to strengthen economic relations with Moscow on a visit in late October. Agreements were signed concerning the supply of Soviet natural gas to the Federal Republic and the construction of a nuclear power plant by West German firms in Kaliningrad.

Relations with the United States were temporarily troubled in March when Washington objected to plans of the Common Market countries to pursue policies of their own toward the oil-producing countries. Concerned that an angered United States might reduce or withdraw its armed forces from Europe, Bonn proposed regular prior consultation with Washington before the Common Market made any important decisions. It also agreed to contribute $2.4 billion to the maintenance of American troops in West Germany for two years. The amount was to be credited to West German arms purchases in the United States, thus easing American balance-of-payments difficulties. In August, in turn, Bonn asked to be consulted on any deflationary measures the United States might wish to take, fearful lest a resulting recession would reduce American imports and thus have a serious effect on other economies, especially West Germany's.

The ties between Germany and France were strengthened when Schmidt became chancellor. Schmidt and French President Valéry Giscard d'Estaing share similar political and economic views; personally close, they work well together. A minor crisis arose when Bonn vetoed a French-sponsored increase by 5% of guaranteed agricultural prices in the Common Market. It withdrew its veto, however, in return for the promise of a review next spring of the Market's agricultural policies.

In September the Federal Republic agreed to assist Italy in solving its financial difficulties by granting it a $2 billion credit.

GERMAN DEMOCRATIC REPUBLIC (East Germany)

For the German Democratic Republic (DDR), the 25th anniversary of its founding, on October 7, constituted the most momentous event of the year. The occasion was celebrated with marches and meetings, military and torchlight parades, street entertainment and fireworks. Speakers pointed proudly to the achievements of the first quarter-century—recognition by practically every country in the world, full employment and stable prices, a fivefold increase of per capita income since 1950, wide-ranging educational and social services, and the ascent to the position of the ninth largest industrial country in the world.

The anniversary was also the occasion of several significant amendments to the East German constitution. Described until then as a "socialist state of German nationality," the DDR became now a "socialist state of workers and peasants." All references to reunification were deleted; instead, a statement was inserted, noting that "the people of the DDR . . . have realized their right to socio-economic, state, and national self-determination." Similarly, the term "German" was dropped from many official designations; the "German Academy of Sciences thus became the "Academy of Sciences of the DDR." There was also a reference to the "DDR's lawful march into the Communist future," suggesting that social rather than national developments would determine the shape of the future. In the same vein speakers kept emphasizing the close association of the DDR with the other Communist countries.

A further amendment lowered the minimum age of a member of parliament from 21 to 18 years. The term of parliament was extended from four to five years to coincide with the DDR's economic five-year plans.

Economy. Special attention was paid to consumer needs. New apartment complexes were constructed in increasing numbers, and for the first time systematic efforts were made to repair

West Germany's new Berlin-Tegel airport, officially inaugurated on October 23, began limited operations in November. Finishing touches were still to be added.

GERMAN INFORMATION CENTER

and improve older residential structures. One out of five families now owned a car. Fresh fruits and vegetables, so far often in short supply, were more readily available.

This latter advance, however, may suffer setbacks again. Almost half of the fruit was grown by amateur gardeners in their spare time on small plots they leased; such small-scale gardening also accounted for a large part of the vegetables, eggs, chickens, and rabbits that were sold, through cooperatives, in open-air markets in all towns and cities. Much of this leisure-time farming took place in urban areas, often on land that had not been built up again after World War II. The new building activities, however, have already driven some of the gardeners from their plots; since residential construction is to be greatly expanded in order to meet housing needs by 1990, urban gardening doubtless will be curtailed.

Foreign Affairs. The establishment of diplomatic relations with the United States put the finishing touch on the DDR's recognition as a separate sovereign state. On December 3 the first U. S. ambassador took up his duties in East Berlin. As part of the accord, the DDR government agreed to consider compensation claims of Nazi victims and of American citizens and business concerns. This was in keeping with the more flexible attitude that the DDR had assumed toward other Western countries as well. Earlier it had rejected such claims on various legal and ideological grounds.

East Germany's relationship to the Common Market was challenged by several Market members. They objected to the continued treatment of East Germany as part of a fictitious "Germany" in its dealings with the Market. This fiction enabled the DDR to export its goods duty-free to West Germany and in effect to other Market members as well. It also allowed for cheaper agricultural imports from Market countries, thus further complicating the Market's controversial agricultural policies. The loss of these advantages may be the price the DDR will have to pay for its insistence on complete separateness from West Germany.

In East Berlin, a huge Soviet-made rocket is displayed at a massive military parade on October 7, the 25th anniversary of the founding of the East German state.

UPI

EAST-WEST GERMAN RELATIONS

In June the permanent representatives of East and West Germany assumed their posts in Bonn and East Berlin, respectively. In accordance with Bonn's view of the special nature of the East-West German relationship, the DDR envoy was accredited to the West German chancellery, while his West German counterpart was to deal with East Berlin's foreign ministry, as the representative of a foreign country.

In non-political areas, too, the DDR insisted on its wholly separate status. At the Leipzig Book Fair, Deputy Minister of Culture Klaus Hoepcke expressed his pleasure at the interest East German literature had aroused in West Germany. Yet he also warned the West Germans not to claim these works as part of an overall "German" literature. His concern may have been justified in regard to older West Germans. Younger ones, as letters to the West German weekly *Die Zeit* revealed, tend to feel closer to Britain and France than to East Germany.

New Agreements. The Guillaume espionage affair had no visible impact on the relations between the two states. A number of agreements, supplementing the Basic Treaty of 1973 that "normalized" East-West German relations, were signed during the year. One concerned cooperation in medical and public health matters. Negotiations concerning the improvement of rail and barge traffic across the DDR, the building of a new *Autobahn* connecting Hamburg and West Berlin, and the laying of power transmission lines from the USSR across East Germany to the Federal Republic are continuing.

Travel. From January to July 1974 almost 590,000 East German pensioners visited the Federal Republic. This constituted an increase of 14% over the same period in 1973. On the other hand, only 20,000 DDR citizens under 60 were allowed to go to West Germany for urgent family reasons, as they are entitled to under the Basic Treaty. This represented a drop of almost 7%. Some 780,000 West Germans came to the DDR during the first six months of 1974, 23% less than in 1973. The decrease was due largely to the doubling of the amount of money each visitor was expected to spend in the DDR. In November this increase was reduced by two-thirds.

The Escape Issue. Attempts of DDR citizens to escape to the West continued, but were less frequent. More effective surveillance of the

UPI

On September 4, in Washington, D. C., the United States and East Germany formally establish diplomatic relations.

transit routes between West Berlin and West Germany and to the Scandinavian and East European countries made escapes even more hazardous than before. DDR agents also managed to infiltrate organizations arranging escapes. Of attempts made with such outside help, only one in five was successful. Stiff penalties imposed on commercial escape helpers deterred many from further activity. Over 200 of them have been arrested on the *Autobahn* between West Germany and West Berlin since June 1972, when East German controls were ended. While amateurs who were caught smuggling out a friend or a relative received prison terms of 2 to 3 years, professional escape helpers were given terms of at least 5 years and in case of repeated offenses up to 15 years. So as not to jeopardize the transit arrangements, the Federal Republic, too, began prosecuting persons involved commercially in escapes. However, those caught and prosecuted in West Germany, generally on charges of fraud or forgery, got away with fines or suspended sentences.

WEST BERLIN

The legal status of West Berlin as a "separate political entity" continued to be the source of serious disputes between East and West. In January the Bonn government proceeded to set up an environmental protection agency in West Berlin. The Soviet Union protested on the grounds that according to the Four-Power Berlin Agreement of 1971 no new federal office could be established in West Berlin. The protest was reinforced by repeated curbs on *Autobahn* traffic between West Berlin and West Germany. West Germany, backed by the Western Powers, insisted that the new agency had no political or governmental authority, but was merely engaged in research and hence admissible, according to the Berlin Agreement. This argument was weakened, however, by the statement of the then Minister of the Interior Genscher that the establishment of the office was also a "political demonstration." The West won out, but is unlikely to make any further attempt to thus strengthen the ties between West Berlin and West Germany.

Diplomatic Status. Another bitterly fought-over issue concerned the diplomatic representation of West Berlin by West Germany. The Berlin Agreement authorized Bonn to represent West Berlin's permanent residents, but said nothing about corporations and institutions. The countries of the Soviet bloc therefore denied West German consuls the right to act for the latter. The matter has not yet been resolved. On the other hand, Chancellor Schmidt succeeded in having West Berlin included in the trade agreements concluded with Moscow.

Social Conditions. Nearly 10% of West Berlin's two-million population are foreigners. Most of those who do not speak German are concentrated in three of the city's districts. To halt this trend, the city government prohibited the influx into these districts of additional foreigners (except for German-speaking ones or citizens of Common Market countries.

ANDREAS DORPALEN
The Ohio State University

EAST GERMANY • Information Highlights

Official Name: German Democratic Republic.
Location: North central Europe.
Area: 41,768 square miles (108,178 sq km).
Population (1973 est.): 17,400,000.
Chief Cities (1971 census): East Berlin, the capital, 1,086,374; Leipzig, 583,885; Dresden, 502,432.
Government: *Head of state,* Willi Stoph, chairman of the Council of State (took office 1973). *Head of government,* Horst Sindermann, minister-president (took office in 1973). *First secretary of the Socialist Unity (Communist) party,* Erich Honecker (took office 1971). *Legislature* (unicameral)—Volkskammer (People's Chamber).
Monetary Unit: Ostmark (1.78 Ostmarks equal U. S.$1, Sept. 1974).
Gross National Product (1973 est.): $38,200,000,000.
Manufacturing (major products): Iron and steel, machinery, chemicals, transport equipment, electronics.
Major Agricultural Products: Rye, potatoes, sugar beets, wheat, oats, barley, livestock.
Foreign Trade (1973): *Exports,* $7,521,000,000; *imports,* $7,854,000,000.

GHANA

Ghana's military junta maintained its tight grip on power in 1974, allowing civilians only a minimal role in governing.

Politics. The so-called National Redemption Council (NRC) remained under the chairmanship of Col. Ignatius K. Acheampong, who first seized power in a bloodless coup in January 1972. Of the 14 NRC members, only two were civilians in 1974. Military officers filled the major policymaking positions.

Acheampong frequently rejected suggestions for a return to civilian rule. He indicated that power would not be restored to an elected government until economic stability was attained, and he appealed to politicians to "give us time to put things right." However, rumbles of discontent mounted not only among students and former politicians but also in the economically disadvantaged Volta Region.

In February all three universities in Ghana were closed for a month following demonstrations protesting the beating of a student by an army officer. A government-appointed committee of inquiry reported that excessive force had been used by the officer, but this finding was rejected by the NRC.

Late in 1973 the government brought six prominent Ghanaians to trial before a special military tribunal for alleged conspiracy and subversion. Four were sentenced to death, a penalty subsequently commuted to life imprisonment. Those initially given the death sentence included Kojo Botsio (former foreign minister), John Tettegah (former minister of labor), Imoru Ayarna (former leader of the People's Action party), and John Alex-Hammah (a former trade union official). Col. Robert Kotei, commander of the First Brigade and chief prosecution witness, was awarded the country's Grand Medal for having "resisted attempts to corrupt him by selfish, disgruntled, and power-seeking politicians." Kotei also was named to the NRC as commissioner for works and housing.

Agitation flared during 1974 in the Volta Region, which is inhabited largely by members of the Ewe tribe. For several years, Ewe leaders pressed for unification within a single political system since the tribe is divided between Ghana and Togo. Colonel Acheampong warned in March that "under no circumstances" would Ghana surrender a portion of its territory. In particular, he denounced the self-styled liberation movement in the region inhabited by the Ewes.

To broaden its popular support during 1974, the NRC created several advisory groups. The most important of these was a 36-member Consultative Advisory Committee, whose members were drawn from major Ghanaian institutions such as the civil service, police, Council of Churches, Trades Union Congress, and National House of Chiefs. Also, a 12-man national committee was created to propagate the charter issued by the NRC on the first anniversary of the coup; a National Youth Council was established; and a military advisory board was set up.

Economy. Despite record world prices for cocoa—the London market topped £1,000 (about $2,400) per ton early in the year—Ghana's share of international production continued to slump. Poor rainfall cut the 1973 crop to 340,000 tons, the second lowest in a decade. Experts estimated that the 1974 real earnings of cocoa farmers were half what they had been in 1951. Shortages of tools and limited replanting further reduced production.

Ghana, like other developing countries, was severely affected by inflation and the escalation of oil prices. Because of the heavy fiscal burdens imposed, the NRC was forced to suspend subsidies on basic commodities in June. These subsidies had been provided by the NRC since 1972 at a total cost of nearly $30 million for food alone. The elimination of subsidies meant a near tripling of prices for some foods.

The government appointed a salary review committee, which recommended an increase in the daily minimum wage of nearly 36%. However, the NRC ordered an even greater rise, hiking the minimum from 1.29 new cedis to 2.0 new cedis per day. The cost to the government alone was estimated at over $30 million.

In May the Ghana government signed a letter of intent with Kaiser Aluminum regarding development of bauxite resources at Kibi. The cost is estimated at $160 million, which would permit the annual production of 600,000 tons of alumina from Kibi bauxite. Half of this output would be exported.

Education and Health. The government proposed an educational reorganization in April that would lead to free and compulsory primary and junior secondary education for a total of nine years. The World Bank announced plans for a 20-year, $120 million campaign against river blindness disease in the Volta River basin, covering most of Ghana.

CLAUDE E. WELCH, JR.
State University of New York at Buffalo

GHANA • Information Highlights

Official Name: Republic of Ghana.
Location: West Africa.
Area: 92,099 square miles (238,537 sq km).
Population (1973 est.): 9,900,000.
Chief Cities (1970 census): Accra, the capital, 633,880; Kumasi, 342,986.
Government: *Head of state,* Col. I. K. Acheampong, chairman of National Redemption Council (took office Jan. 1972). *Legislature*—National Assembly (dissolved Jan. 1972).
Monetary Unit: New cedi (1.1494 new cedis equal U. S.$1, July 1974).
Gross National Product (1972 est.): $2,572,000,000.
Manufacturing (major products): Processed agricultural products, wood products, cement.
Major Agricultural Products: Cocoa, corn, cassava, groundnuts, sweet potatoes, forest products.
Foreign Trade (1973): *Exports* $530,000,000; *imports* $573,000,000.

LONDON DAILY EXPRESS

Ignoring the smoking roof of the bomb-blasted Parliament building in the background, Londoners make their way to work through a light drizzle. They seem more concerned with staying dry.

GREAT BRITAIN

Britain had an exceptionally difficult year in 1974, marked by a worsening economic crisis, two general elections, and a frightening increase in terrorist violence on the mainland.

Miners' Strike. The year opened with most of Britain's industrial workers on a three-day week as a result of the threatened miners' strike, and ended with the nation in its most perilous economic situation since the war.

The three-day week began in January, imposed by a Conservative government fearful that the slowdown and threatened strike would so deplete the nation's energy stocks that essential services could not be maintained. The miners were asking for pay raises which went far above the Phase III prices-and-incomes policy. The government feared that a concession would wreck its anti-inflation policy, and refused to give way.

The First Election. In the face of the miners' demands, the government decided to assert its authority by calling a general election and winning a new mandate. This was announced on February 7, and the first surprise was the withdrawal of Prime Minister Heath's bitterest enemy, Enoch Powell, a right-wing Conservative with a strong popular following. He announced that he would vote Labour because of his opposition to the European Economic Community (EEC), and this decision undoubtedly affected the voting.

Conservatives fought the campaign almost entirely on the single issue of union power, but added that the miners could expect a substantial wage raise after the election. Labour argued that a prices-and-incomes policy was bound to fail, especially when opposed by a group as powerful as the miners. They promised a swift return to work after the election.

The Conservatives lost the election on February 28 by a narrow margin. They won 296

GREAT BRITAIN • Information Highlights

Official Name: United Kingdom of Great Britain and Northern Ireland.
Area: 94,226 square miles (244,046 sq km).
Population (1973 est.): 57,000,000.
Chief Cities (1972 est.): London, the capital, 7,353,810; Birmingham, 1,006,760; Glasgow, 861,900; Liverpool, 588,600.
Government: *Head of state,* Elizabeth II, queen (acceded Feb. 1952). *Head of government,* Harold Wilson, prime minister (took office March 1974). *Legislature*—Parliament: House of Lords and House of Commons.
Monetary Unit: Pound (0.4288 pound equals U. S.$1, Sept. 1974).
Gross National Product (1973 est.): $159,900,000,000.
Manufacturing (major products): Iron and steel, motor vehicles, aircraft, textiles, chemicals.
Major Agricultural Products: Barley, oats, sugar beets, potatoes, wheat.
Foreign Trade (1973): *Exports,* $30,549,000,000; *imports,* $38,920,000,000.

UPI

Prime Minister Harold Wilson, with his wife, Mary, waves to the crowd in front of No. 10 Downing Street after the Labour party's victory in the October elections.

parliamentary seats, against 301 to Labour, 14 to the Liberals, 7 to the Scottish National party, 2 to the Welsh Nationalists (Plaid Cymru), and 11 to the United Ulster Unionist Coalition from Northern Ireland.

Prime Minister Heath, however, refused to acknowledge defeat, and spent three fruitless days trying to reach a coalition with the Liberals. After Heath's failure, Harold Wilson, as Labour leader, was named prime minister and formed the first minority government since World War II.

Minority Government. Prime Minister Wilson managed to get through most of his planned legislation, in spite of his failure to win a majority. Conservatives, realizing that public opinion was with the government, were fearful of precipitating an election, and on several occasions encouraged their members not to vote on crucial matters. In summer, when it had become clear that the next election would not be called until fall, they did challenge the government, winning a number of votes concerned with industrial relations.

On its return, the government took immediate steps to improve the economy. The miners were given a slightly higher pay raise than they had demanded, and the three-day workweek ended within a week. They took steps to abolish wage controls, although retaining price controls, and started to demolish the controversial Industrial Relations Act.

The powers of the Prices Board were increased, leading to complaints from industry that profit margins were becoming dangerously low. Rents were frozen until the end of the year, and a system of food subsidies began to bring down the price of bread, butter, milk, flour, and cheese, in order to protect poorer families.

The Economy. The worst sign of Britain's desperate economic state was the trade deficit. Though the government managed to reduce the non-oil deficit to around £80 million ($187 million) a month, the figure for oil was around £240 million ($560 million) each month, giving Britain the worst trading position it had ever had. There were two slight consolations: for most of the year the pound stayed fairly steady against the U. S. dollar, falling only 0.2 cent in 11 months; and in July, Chancellor of the Exchequer Denis Healey was able to announce a $1,200 million line of credit negotiated with the government of Iran.

Nevertheless, the slump in industrial confidence and investment, caused by fears of the general situation and of nationalization plans by the new government, led to a drop in share prices throughout the year. The index fell from 340 to 185 in 11 months. Chancellor Healey adopted a policy of mild reflation, making it clear that his first job was to avoid unemployment as much as possible. In the course of no less than three budgets, he made a modest increase in income tax, increased gasoline taxes by 12½ pence ($0.29) per gallon, but reduced the value-added tax from 10% to 8%, in the hope of increasing demand.

After increasing the corporation tax in his first budget from 50% to 52%, Chancellor Healey in November took steps to add £1.5 billion ($3.5 billion) to corporate liquidity, following the collapse or near collapse of several of Britain's largest firms, including the Ferranti defense and engineering company and the massive Court Line holiday firm.

The Social Contract. The government pinned all its hopes of keeping wages down on this "contract," in fact an unwritten agreement between ministers and the Trades Union Congress. Its basis was that wages would not rise higher than the cost of living, and would be renegotiated no more often than annually. Although it had some slight success early in the year, the contract was in grave danger by November, having been overstepped by Rolls Royce workers, Ford car workers, and most significantly of all by the miners, who rejected a productivity deal and announced their intention of winning a wage raise near £30 ($70) a week.

North Sea Oil. Britain's only real ray of economic hope was the prospect of obtaining oil from the North Sea. The government estimated that Britain would be self-sufficient in oil by 1980 with production at 1 million to 1.4 million tons per year.

In July it took steps to get greater public benefit from the oil, publishing a white paper in which it said it would take majority participation in all new fields, would negotiate with the oil companies to take a majority holding in existing fields, and would impose a new tax on profits. The oil companies said that the net effect could be to halve their necessary return on investment.

State Intervention. A system of planning agreements and state control was announced in August by Anthony Benn, secretary for industry. Large firms would be invited to join the government in planning their futures for the good of the economy as a whole, and a National Enterprise Board would offer capital to firms in distress, taking part of the equity stock in exchange. In both cases it was threatened that failure to cooperate could lead to a state takeover. The plans were vigorously opposed by both industry and the opposition.

Devolution. The startling success of the Scottish National party in the February election led the government to produce plans for devolving some power from London to Scotland and Wales. The Scottish Labour party reversed its earlier opposition in summer, and it was announced that Scotland would have its own legislative assembly, and Wales an advisory assembly. The exact plans were to be made known during the year 1975. Devolution was seen as an essential means to reduce secessionist feeling in Scotland, which could threaten Britain's offshore oil supplies.

The EEC. The Labour government was returned with a promise to consult the electorate about Britain's future membership in the EEC. An urgent series of negotiations with the other eight EEC members began, centering chiefly on Britain's contribution to the Regional Fund, a revision of the Common Agricultural Policy, and Britain's freedom to purchase food supplies from outside the EEC.

Britain's demands for a reduction in its contribution to the EEC budget came under discussion at a meeting of Common Market leaders in Paris on December 9–10. The British desire for easier terms was strongly opposed by France. The meeting produced a compromise on the issue under which the market's executive commission was instructed to devise a new formula for payments by countries that find themselves in economic difficulties. (See also EUROPE.)

Scandals. The government suffered from two scandals in the period between elections. First it was revealed that Anthony Field, a brother of Prime Minister Wilson's chief political adviser, Mrs. Marcia Williams, had been involved in a profitable deal involving the sale of a slag heap in Lancashire. Since the Labour party had made its opposition to "speculators" a key part of its election campaign, the revelation was damaging, particularly when one newspaper published a letter "signed" by Wilson indicating involvement in the sale. The letter proved to be forged, and a solicitor from Wolverhampton was given a three-year jail sentence. Mrs. Williams was elevated to the peerage by Wilson.

Shortly afterward it was alleged that the Labour deputy leader, Edward Short, had received £250 ($580) for assistance from a corrupt Newcastle businessman, T. Dan Smith, also sent to jail. Short admitted taking the money but said it was for legitimate expenses. In spite of massive publicity, neither of these two events appeared to harm the reputation of either the Labour party or its leaders.

The Second Election. The second general election was called by Wilson in October, in an attempt to win an overall majority for the government. Labour fought on the need for a majority Parliament, and said that it would in no circumstances join a coalition. The Conservatives, who had changed their policies fairly radically over the months since February, fought on a policy of national unity, and offered cabinet seats to other parties. They offered cheap mortgage rates for house buyers, and accused the government of trying to hide the seriousness of the economic situation.

CENTRAL PRESS

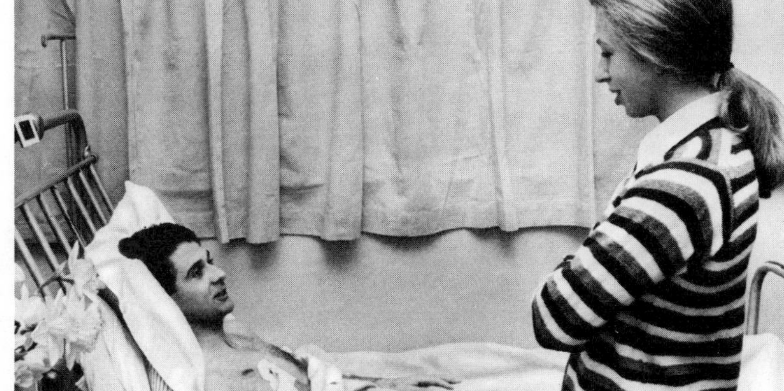

Princess Anne visits the hospital bedside of Inspector James Beaton, the bodyguard wounded in the kidnapping attempt against her and her husband, Capt. Mark Phillips, in March.

In the October 10 election, Labour managed to get their majority over all other parties—by three seats. They took 319 seats, the Conservatives 276, the Liberals 13, the Scottish Nationalists 11, the Welsh 3, and the Ulster Unionists 10. The government's first main act was not, however, the red-blooded socialism which the opposition had threatened, but a moderate budget designed to increase industrial confidence and investment. In turn this created greater anger in the left wing of the Labour party, which announced its intention in November to create its own economic policy.

Northern Ireland. The year ended with the province of Northern Ireland seemingly as far away from a settlement as ever. The power-sharing Executive, in which government posts were held by both Protestants and Catholics, collapsed in May, and at the end of the year Ulster people were waiting for a constitutional convention, which some thought would be Britain's last attempt to solve the crisis.

In January the chief executive, Brian Faulkner, was forced to resign as leader of the Unionist party because he had been a signatory to the Sunningdale agreement. This agreement, which was never ratified, included among its provisions a Council of Ireland, a joint north-south body to discuss matters of mutual interest. To many Protestants this looked suspiciously like the beginning of a united Ireland—their chief dread—and their mounting opposition was the root of the political collapse.

In the February general election the right-wing loyalist parties managed to win 11 of Northern Ireland's 12 Westminster seats, fighting on a platform of total opposition to Sunningdale. In spite of this the power-sharing Executive soldiered on until May, when a group named the Ulster Workers' Council called a provincewide strike.

The British government underestimated support for the strike, and the secretary of state for Northern Ireland, Merlyn Rees, refused to negotiate with its leaders. However, the stoppage rapidly gained mass support, with electricity almost cut off, gasoline almost unobtainable, and food becoming dangerously in short supply. At a cabinet meeting on May 23, the government decided to use troops to break the gasoline blockade, but their use four days later merely intensified support for the strikers. The Executive and the British government postponed ratification of Sunningdale, but this was not enough; one day later, the Protestant members of the Executive decided they would resign, thus bringing the power-sharing experiment to an end.

In July, after the province had been returned to direct rule from London, the government announced that it would set up an elected "constitutional convention" to allow the Ulster people to decide their own future. This will be formed in 1975, and will have a wide range of choices. But it must decide on some form of power sharing if its plans are to be ratified by the Westminster Parliament.

The strength of the local police force (the RUC) was steadily increased through the year, and the number of British troops was reduced to 15,000. An attempt was made to reduce the number of detainees—suspected terrorists held without trial—though by the end of the year the number of net releases was only just over 100. The task was made more difficult by a series of prison riots in mid-October, including one in which the Maze, Ulster's largest prison camp, was virtually burned to the ground. A committee under Lord Gardiner was set up to review detention and to see if alternatives actually existed.

Terrorism in Great Britain. The Northern Ireland problem resulted in a new wave of terrorism on the British mainland, thought by police to be almost entirely the work of the Provisional IRA. More than 40 persons were killed in 1974.

One of the worst attacks was an explosion in the back of a bus carrying soldiers and their families through Yorkshire on February 4. Twelve persons died, including an entire family of four. Later a 25-year-old English girl with Irish connections, Judith Teresa Ward, was jailed for life.

On July 17 a woman died and 37 persons, including many children and tourists, were injured when a bomb exploded in the Tower of London, Britain's most popular tourist attraction. A month before that, some damage was caused when Westminster Hall in the Houses of Parliament was bombed. In October five teenagers were killed in Guildford, Surrey, during an attack on public houses used by soldiers.

The most serious attack occurred on November 21, when two pubs in Birmingham were bombed, resulting in 20 persons killed and over 180 wounded. The police had only slight success in tracing these and other bombers, but the government took immediate action. On November 29, rigorous new laws went into effect, outlawing the IRA and providing police with unprecedented powers to search and detain suspected persons and to limit travel between England and Ireland.

For the first time this century, the royal family was involved in a shooting incident, though unconnected with Northern Ireland. On March 20, a young man named Ian Ball attempted to kidnap the newly married Princess Anne, daughter of the Queen, by forcing her official car to halt in the Mall, the main road to Buckingham Palace. In the gun battle which followed, four persons—two policemen, a driver, and a bystander—were injured. Princess Anne and her husband, Capt. Mark Phillips, were unhurt, and Ball was committed to a prison for the criminally insane.

SIMON HOGGART
The Manchester "Guardian"

GREECE

The collapse of the Greek military dictatorship, the rejection of the monarchic system by the electorate, and a dispute with Turkey over Cyprus dominated 1974 events in Greece.

Dictatorial Rule. The year started with the Greek military in control of the government, as it had been since April 21, 1967, when a coup had eliminated the parliamentary system. However, within the military the leadership had changed. In November 1973, George Papadopoulos, who had dominated the government since April 1967, was ousted by another coup and replaced as president by Gen. Phaidon Gizikis. Real power was considered to rest with Brig. Gen. Dimitrios Ioannidis, chief of the military police, although a civilian, Adamantios Androutsopoulos, was premier.

Beset by a rapidly rising rate of inflation and other serious economic problems, the regime maintained repressive policies against the press and treated political opponents severely. Typical of its desire to control all aspects of Greek life was the government's high-handed actions in selecting a new primate for Greece's Orthodox Church. That post was vacant because Archbishop Ieronymos of Athens had been forced to resign in December 1973. The government declared that Ieronymos had been improperly elected and barred all bishops associated with him from voting for his successor. On January 12, 28 bishops voted, and only 20 votes were cast for Metropolitan Seraphim of Ioannina, a friend of Gizikis. The president designated Seraphim as the new primate.

Greek-Turkish Relations. The discovery of oil deposits in the waters off the Greek island of Thassos raised the possibility of more oil finds near other Greek islands in the Aegean Sea. The Turkish government, whose shoreline on the Aegean is very close to many Greek islands, claimed for itself oil rights that conflicted with Greek claims. The dispute became so acrimonious that in late May it seemed possible the two countries might go to war.

The Cyprus Imbroglio. Relations with Turkey were seriously embittered by events in Cyprus. In early July the Cypriot president, Archbishop Makarios, demanded the recall of 650 Greek officers who had been placed in charge of the Cypriot National Guard. Makarios claimed they were planning his overthrow in favor of elements seeking *enosis* (union) of the island with Greece. He also publicly accused the Greek government of plotting against him.

On July 15 the Cypriot National Guard deposed Makarios, and five days later Turkey invaded Cyprus. Reports abounded that the coup against Makarios had been directed from Athens by Ioannidis, thus confirming the archbishop's earlier allegations. Although the Greek government mobilized its forces in the wake of the Turkish invasion, it was obvious that Turkey's army was overwhelmingly superior.

Democracy Reestablished. The disastrous intermixing in Cypriot affairs helped destroy the Greek dictatorship. Military leaders, including President Gizikis, removed Ioannidis from power. On July 23 it was announced that the government would be turned over to civilian rule under Constantine Caramanlis, who had been premier from 1955 to 1963. He swiftly returned from Paris where he had lived, and on July 24 he took the oath as premier. Gizikis retained the presidency until December 15.

Foreign Policy of Caramanlis. Since Greece, Turkey, and Britain were guarantors of Cyprus' independence by prior agreements, the three countries met at Geneva in July and early August to seek an accommodation. The talks were broken off on August 14 when the Turkish representative refused to give the Greek representa-

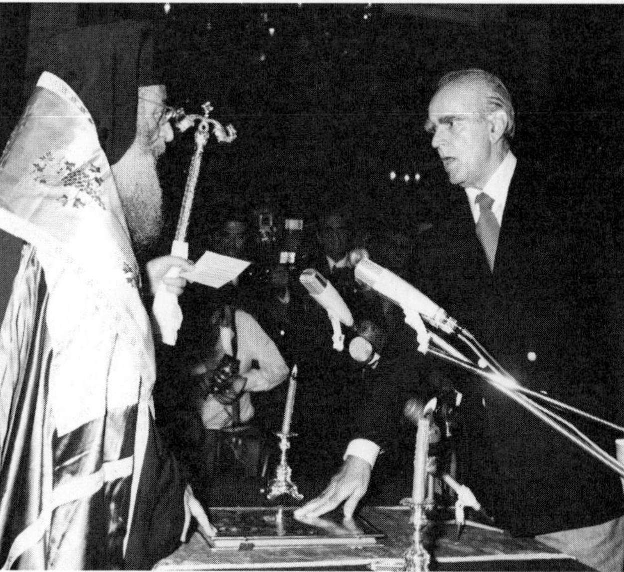

GREEK PHOTO AGENCY/KEYSTONE

Constantine Caramanlis (*right*) is sworn in as the Greek prime minister. After ten years in exile, Caramanlis was called back by the military junta to form a government.

GREECE • Information Highlights

Official Name: Hellenic Republic.
Location: Southeastern Europe.
Area: 50,944 square miles (131,944 sq km).
Population (1973 census): 9,100,000.
Chief Cities (1971 census): Athens, the capital, 867,023; Salonika, 345,799; Piraeus, 187,458.
Government: *Head of state,* Michael Stassinopoulos, acting president (took office Dec. 1974). *Head of government,* Constantine Caramanlis, premier (took office July 1974). *Legislature*—Parliament.
Monetary Unit: Drachma (30 drachmas equal U. S.$1, Aug. 1974).
Gross National Product (1973 est.): $13,800,000,000.
Manufacturing (major products): Construction materials, textiles, chemicals, petroleum products, processed foods, metals, ships.
Major Agricultural Products: Tobacco, grapes, cotton, wheat, olives, citrus fruits, tomatoes, raisins.
Foreign Trade (1973): *Exports,* $1,454,000,000; *imports,* $3,473,000,000.

tive time to discuss Turkish demands with his government. That same day the Turks resumed their invasion of Cyprus, gaining control of the entire northeastern portion of the island. They then offered to reopen negotiations, but the Caramanlis government refused to do so under military threat.

The August 14 Turkish offensive led to a severe outbreak of anti-American sentiment in Greece. Many Greeks felt that the United States government, and particularly Secretary of State Henry Kissinger, could have restrained the Turks. Moreover, there were widespread allegations that the United States had been willing to give friendly assistance to the hated Greek dictatorship, while the democratically-minded Caramanlis was given no such support. Caramanlis, in turn, pulled Greece's forces out of NATO.

Restoration of the Constitution. The constitution of 1952, which had fallen victim to the 1967 coup, was restored to force on Aug. 1, 1974, by the Caramanlis government. Although that constitution called for a "crowned democracy," all provisions relating to the monarchy were left in suspension until a referendum would decide the form of government. Prior to the referendum, parliamentary elections were held on November 17. Premier Caramanlis won an overwhelming victory. His New Democratic party received 54.37% of the vote and gained 220 out of 300 parliamentary seats.

Rejection of the Monarchy. In a referendum on December 8 only 30.8% of the Greeks voted for a "crowned democracy," while 69.2% voted against. Thus the electorate repudiated King Constantine II, who had lived outside Greece since 1967, and his dynasty, the House of Glucksburg. On December 9, Greece was proclaimed a republic; Michael Stassinopoulos was named interim president on December 18.

GEORGE J. MARCOPOULOS, *Tufts University*

GRENADA

Grenada, smallest and most densely populated of the Windward Islands, was granted independence by Great Britain on Feb. 7, 1974.

Prime Minister Eric Matthew Gairy, whose United Labor party won 13 of the 15 seats in the island's House of Representatives in the 1972 election, persuaded the British government to grant the colony complete independence. But as the promised date for independence approached, the opposition grew, drawing support from the Chamber of Commerce, most religious groups, some labor unions, and a radical socialist group known as the New Jewel Movement, led by Maurice Bishop.

Three prolonged general strikes were staged during the final months of 1973 and the early months of 1974. Violence occurred as opposition leaders were beaten, and three persons were killed as mass demonstrations were met by riot squads and armed secret police.

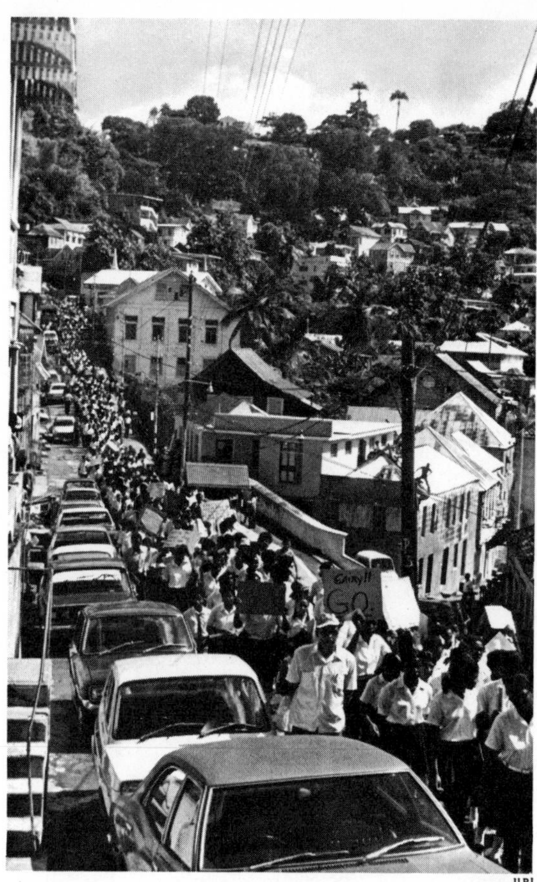

UPI

Antigovernment demonstrators march in newly independent Grenada, which was crippled by a general strike called to oppose the Caribbean island's strong man, Eric M. Gairy.

Independence Day found Grenada a bitterly divided island, suffering from an estimated loss of $100 million from the general strikes. Months afterward the docks remained closed and the island was without electricity. Some normal operations were resumed in April as Prime Minister Gairy agreed to disband his secret police and a panel of West Indian jurists investigated the civil disorders of the past two years. On September 17, Grenada was admitted to membership in the United Nations.

THOMAS G. MATHEWS
University of Puerto Rico

GRENADA • Information Highlights

Official Name: Grenada.
Location: Eastern Caribbean Sea.
Area (including Carriacou and other dependent islands in the southern Grenadines): 133 square miles (344 sq km).
Population (1973 est.): 100,000.
Chief City (1973 est.): St. George's, the capital, 7,000.
Government: *Head of state,* Elizabeth II, queen, represented by Leo de Gale, governor-general (took office Feb. 1974). *Head of government,* Eric M. Gairy, prime minister (took office Feb. 1974). *Legislature*—Parliament: Senate and House of Representatives.
Monetary Unit: East Caribbean dollar (2.01 E. C. dollars equal U. S.$1, Oct. 1974).

GUINEA-BISSAU

The former colony of Portuguese Guinea, in revolt for 13 years, became an independent nation on Sept. 10, 1974, following negotiations in London and Algiers between Portuguese Foreign Minister Mario Soares and representatives of the revolutionary party. An informal cease-fire had been observed for months.

The New Country. Guinea-Bissau is a small West-African coastal enclave of 13,948 square miles and a population of about 510,000. The 2,200 Portuguese colonists began a general exodus from Portuguese Guinea once independence became certain. The principal native stocks are Balanta, Fula, and Mandingo, many of whom are Muslim. They include over 30 tribes and subtribes, and the *lingua franca* is a Portuguese creole dialect brought from the Cape Verde Islands. The country is a humid, swampy area dependent on small crops of rice, millet, peanuts, and palm oil. Guinea-Bissau has no railroad and almost no paved roads.

Independence. An independence movement began in the early 1950's and was organized in 1954 with the formation of the African Party for the Independence of Guinea and Cape Verde (PAIGC), led by Amílcar Cabral, a Cape Verdean. In 1961 this party began military action, largely directed from nearby Conakry, Guinea, and Dakar, Senegal, and aided by arms from the Soviet Union and China.

Cabral was assassinated on Jan. 20, 1973, and Portuguese authorities were widely accused of the killing but denied any complicity. By then the Portuguese had 30,000 white troops in Guinea, besides an estimated 9,000 black auxiliaries, in an unavailing effort to suppress the rebels, who held most of the interior outside Portuguese garrison points.

When Gen. António de Spinola overthrew the Portuguese Caetano regime in April 1974, he hoped for a referendum in Guinea that would make the country an autonomous part of a Portuguese commonwealth. The PAIGC leaders rejected such a solution, and in August, Portugal consented to outright independence, with legal transfer of authority to take place on September 10 and Portuguese troops, with limited exceptions, to leave by the end of October.

The presidency of Guinea-Bissau, as the country was now named, was assumed by Luíz de Almeida Cabral, brother of the dead Amílcar. Cabral and his associates demanded that the Cape Verde Islands, birthplace of most of the independence leaders, be included in the new republic. Portugal declined to grant this, but indicated that there might be a referendum on the question there in the future.

In August, before the legal transfer of authority, Portugal proposed Guinea-Bissau for membership in the United Nations, whose Communist and Third World members had already granted recognition. The Security Council adopted the proposal, but the procedure displeased the new republic's leaders, as it implied Portuguese "concession" of an independence already won.

Foreign observers anticipated friction in Guinea-Bissau between the largely illiterate indigenous element and the generally better-educated and more sophisticated leaders from the Cape Verdes, whose presence promised to be particularly important as the small white business class, hitherto in control of commerce, returned to Portugal.

CHARLES E. NOWELL
University of Illinois

GUINEA-BISSAU • Information Highlights

Official Name: Republic of Guinea-Bissau.
Location: West African Coast.
Area: 13,948 square miles (36,125 sq km).
Population (1973 est.): 510,000.
Chief City (1950 census): Bissau, the capital, 18,309.
Government: *Head of state,* Luíz de Almeida Cabral, president (took office Sept. 1974). *Head of government,* Luíz Cabral.
Monetary Unit: Portuguese escudo (26.02 escudos equal U. S.$1, Aug. 1974).
Major Agricultural Products: Groundnuts, rice, millet, coconuts, palm oil.

Portugal recognized the independence of Guinea-Bissau in September. Here, Portuguese troops lower their national flag preparatory to leaving the former Portuguese Guinea.

DIX/SYGMA

GUYANA

The most important developments in Guyana during 1974 centered on the bauxite industry. Most spectacular was the announcement by Prime Minister Forbes Burnham in late July that his government would nationalize the mining operations of the Reynolds Metals Company as of Dec. 31, 1974. This company produces about one fifth of Guyana's output of bauxite. Meanwhile, the government imposed a substantial increase in export taxes on Reynolds, amounting to about $7 million for the year. The company protested, offering to pay $4 million in additional taxes, an offer Burnham rejected. When payment of the first half of the tax increase came due, the company refused to pay.

Two important international initiatives concerning bauxite and involving Guyana also took place. One was the establishment in April of the International Bauxite Association (IBA), based on the model of the very successful oil cartel, OPEC, and like it, designed to defend the price of the mineral involved. Guyana became a founding member of IBA.

In late July a joint announcement was made by Guyana, Trinidad, and Jamaica of plans to establish two aluminum refineries. The first, to be set up in Trinidad, is due to be completed by 1977; the second, in Guyana, has a completion date of 1980.

Political Developments. Politics during the year were marked by growing bitterness between the government of Burnham's People's National Congress (PNC) and various opposition parties. Throughout the year the largest opposition party, People's Progressive party (PPP), headed by former Premier Cheddi Jagan, refused to allow its elected members to participate in parliament, as they had done since the last election in July 1973.

The only opposition group participating in parliament was the United Force. In April, Marcellus Felden Singh, leader of United Force, assumed the official post of leader of the opposition. Meanwhile, virtually all other opposition parties, headed by the PPP, formed a united front and held a series of joint meetings.

ROBERT J. ALEXANDER, *Rutgers University*

GUYANA • Information Highlights

Official Name: Republic of Guyana.
Location: Northeast coast of South America.
Area: 83,000 square miles (214,970 sq km).
Population (1973 est.): 800,000.
Chief City (1970 census): Georgetown, the capital, 167,068 (metro. area).
Government: *Head of state,* Arthur Chung, president (took office March 1970). *Head of government,* Forbes Burnham, prime minister (Dec. 1964). *Legislature* (unicameral): National Assembly.
Monetary Unit: Guyana dollar (225 G. dollars equal U. S.$1, Aug. 1974).
Gross National Product (1972 est.): $272,000,000.
Major Agricultural Products: Sugarcane, rice, corn.
Foreign Trade (1972): *Exports,* $150,000,000; *imports,* $145,000,000.

HAWAII

The year 1974 in Hawaii was one of political continuity and economic uncertainty. Reelected to the national Congress were Sen. Daniel K. Inouye and Congressmen Patsy Takemoto Mink and Spark M. Matsunaga, all Democrats, while George Ariyoshi, former lieutenant governor, defeated Republican Randolph Crossley to become the first person of Oriental ancestry to serve as the chief executive of any state in the Union. Mr. Ariyoshi was the victor in a closely contested Democratic primary over Mayor Frank Fasi of Honolulu and Thomas Gill, former lieutenant governor. He succeeds Jack Burns, the three-term governor who was the chief architect of the party locally. Nelson Doi (D) was elected lieutenant governor.

Race Relations. In midsummer, Fujio Matsuda was appointed the first non-Caucasian president of the University of Hawaii, an event widely hailed as symbolizing the attainment of full participation in the state's variegated society by its Americans of Japanese ancestry.

With former immigrant groups achieving greater recognition, the burden of discontent passes to Hawaii's original population, the descendants of the Polynesian people. Under the perhaps sardonic acronym of ALOHA (Aboriginal Lands of Hawaiian Ancestry), a recently organized group of Hawaiians sought indemnities from the national government for the loss of their lands, much as the Indians of Alaska have done successfully. A bill to provide payment of a billion dollars was introduced before the U. S. Congress, backed by Hawaii's delegation. A new militancy was shown in the temporary "occupation" by Hawaiian squatters of leased government land on the island of Hawaii. In a trespass suit, the judge held for the Hawaiians. In other actions, groups of young Hawaiians demonstrated against land reclassification on Oahu which would convert land they are farming to subdivisions and tourist areas.

Economy. Economically, 1974 was a year of pause and reconsideration. Tourism, the chief source of income after federal military expenditures, continued to rise (to an indicated total of 2.8 million visitors in a state of 830,000 population), but hotel employment was down. Indeed, overall unemployment stood at 7% or higher during most of 1974, with increasing indications that the national recession was being experienced locally. Tight money held down construction, though less than was the case nationally. Sugar and pineapple prices and profits rose sharply, bolstering hope for these declining industries.

The state's economy became increasingly internationalized in 1974 with the purchase by Tokyo financier Kenji Osano of three major hotels for $104 million, making Osano the largest hotel owner in Waikiki. The matter of Japanese ownership of Hawaii real estate and other

HAWAII • Information Highlights

Area: 6,450 square miles (16,706 sq km).
Population (1973 est.): 832,000. *Density:* 126 per sq mi.
Chief Cities (1970 census): Honolulu, the capital, 324,871; Kailua, 33,783; Kaneohe, 29,903; Hilo, 26,353.
Government (1974): *Chief Officers*—governor, John A. Burns (D); lt. gov., George R. Ariyoshi (D). *Legislature*—Senate, 25 members (17 D, 8 R); House of Representatives, 52 members (35 D, 16 R).
Education (1973–74): *Enrollment*—public elementary schools, 95,300 pupils; public secondary schools, 82,500; nonpublic schools, 20,900; colleges and universities, 42,717 students. *Public school expenditures,* $170,021,000 ($1,027 per pupil).
State Finances (fiscal year 1973): *Revenues,* $870,396,000; *Expenditures,* $957,608,000.
Personal Income (1973): $4,391,000,000; per capita, $5,309.
Labor Force (June 1974): *Nonagricultural wage and salary earners,* 342,000; *insured unemployed,* 13,700 (4.6%).

enterprises was an issue in the 1974 elections, but not a major one.

Energy. Regarded as more threatening by most people was the action of the Arab oil-producing nations in reducing the fuel supply early in 1974—though for several weeks Hawaii escaped the full effects of the embargo. Hawaii's virtually complete dependence on oil stimulated a search for indigenous energy sources—power from solar heat, from the trade winds, from the conversion of biodegradable materials, and from geothermal sources on the island of Hawaii, which is active volcanically.

ROBERT M. KAMINS
University of Hawaii

CHARLES LUCKMAN ASSOCIATES

Oahu Stadium near Honolulu, Hawaii (*architect's rendering*) features grandstands that move on a cushion of air, making it possible to adjust the seating to the sport offered. The 50,000-seat arena is to be completed in 1975.

HONG KONG

Trade and inflation continued to increase, but stock values continued to decline in 1974. English, written Chinese, and spoken Cantonese were declared Hong Kong's official languages.

Economy. The stock market continued its downward drift in 1974, with the Hang Seng Index dipping to 205.61 on October 4, the lowest since March 29, 1971. Increases in the cost of storage, transport, rents, and wages led to the rise in the consumer price index from 170 in July 1973 to 193 in July 1974, representing an increase of 13.5% in the cost of living.

Trade climbed to a record $11 billion in 1973, with increases of 22.8% in imports, 28.2% in exports, and 57% in re-exports, as compared with 1972. The United States, Britain, and West Germany continued the main buyers, but the fastest growth in purchases was registered by eastern European countries, to which exports were valued at $7 million, an increase of 219% over 1972. After abolition of regulations on gold and diamonds, and on the movement of currency in January 1974, Hong Kong became a marketplace for free-market gold.

Nearly 1.3 million tourists came to Hong Kong in 1973. The largest group was Japanese. In January–September 1974, over 25,000 immigrants entered Hong Kong legally, and 5,675 illegal immigrants from China were arrested.

Transportation. The double-tracking of the railway between Hung Hom and Sha Tin was expected to be completed in 1976 when Sha Tin New Town would have about 106,000 people. Construction of a six-lane highway between Tsuen Wan and Tuen Mun new towns was begun in October 1974.

Relationship with China. Hong Kong's new coaxial cable system to Canton, which will have a capacity of 300 telephone circuits, was opened in April 1974. The China Resources Co. secured from China the allocation of about 300,000 tons of various oil products for Hong Kong, representing about 7% of the colony's oil needs in 1974. Arrangements were made to increase the supply of water from China from 15 billion to 18.5 billion gallons per year.

CHUEN-YAN DAVID LAI
University of Victoria, B. C.

HONG KONG • Information Highlights

Location: Southeastern coast of China.
Area: 398 square miles (1,034 sq km).
Population (1973 est.): 4,219,000.
Chief City (1971): Victoria, the capital, 521,612.
Government: *Head of state,* Elizabeth II, queen (acceded Feb. 1952). *Head of government,* Sir Murray MacLehose, governor (took office 1971).
Monetary Unit: Hong Kong dollar (5.08 H. K. dollars equal U. S.$1, July 1974).
Gross Domestic Product (1972 est.): $4,493,000,000.
Manufacturing (major products): Textiles, clothing, furniture, jewelry, electronic components.
Foreign Trade (1973): *Exports,* $5,051,000,000; *imports,* $5,631,000,000.

UNIVERSITY OF DELAWARE

The sun provides heat and electricity for "Solar One," an experimental solar house at the University of Delaware.

HOUSING

Runaway inflation, high interest rates, and severe shortages of funds for home builders and buyers have brought about a housing depression in a large portion of the world's housing market. Housing problems were further exacerbated in 1974 by the worldwide energy crisis. While the general level of economic activity was depressed in most countries in Europe, Latin America, and the Far East, those countries that are particularly dependent on imported energy resources have been hardest hit.

Housing in the United States

New U. S. housing starts in 1974 plummeted, continuing the trend downward which began in 1973. During the first half of 1973, some 1,154,000 new private housing units were recorded, while in the same period in 1974, the number fell to less than 800,000 units. By August, housing starts had slipped to a four-year low, and analysts saw little help in sight.

Inflation. The general economy continued to be plagued by record rates of inflation accompanied by increasing unemployment. As the Federal Reserve Board utilized traditional tight-money policies to fight inflation, the home-building industry was hit quickly and dramatically by the lack of credit for both home builders and buyers. This lack of credit contributed to relatively high rates of bankruptcy among home builders, unemployment rates well above 10% for the nation's construction workers, soaring land and material costs, and mortgage money with a cost of 10% or more for most borrowers.

Housing costs have moved upward steadily over the past few years, but 1974 marked exceptional price rises. Over the past two and one-half years, the median price of new one-family homes has increased over 40%, and in 1974 median prices moved up over $41,000. Although increases in the prices of land, financing, labor, and building materials have all been responsible for the increased cost of new construction, environmental curbs have also added to the price of many new homes.

Apartments—Short Supply and High Rents. The pronounced drop in housing construction, accompanied by inflationary pressures on apartment operating costs, has resulted in a relative shortage in the supply of rental apartment units, with a sharp increase in rental prices. Many prospective home buyers, particularly young couples, have been frustrated by high housing prices, larger down-payment requirements, and the general lack of mortgage money, and have turned increasingly to rental apartments.

Condominium apartments continue to capture an increasing share of new-home construction, even though the general housing market is depressed. In 1973, condominiums accounted for over 11% of the total units constructed, but this form of housing will probably make up over 15% of the new-home starts in 1974.

On the negative side, condominium apartments received much adverse publicity in 1974 when the government announced an investigation of possible unfair or deceptive industry practices. In addition, there was a significant inventory of unsold condominiums in various market areas of the United States.

Government Programs to Combat the Housing Depression. The primary effort being made by the federal government to fight the housing slump is in the area of mortgage financing. Cooperation among the major secondary mortgage market institutions—the Federal Home Loan Mortgage Corporation ("Freddie Mac"), the Federal National Mortgage Association ("Fannie Mae"), and the Government National Mortgage Association ("Ginnie Mae")—has been the most effective means of providing mortgage funds when traditional sources were lacking.

In March 1974, "Fannie Mae" accepted $1.5 billion in commitments to buy future mortgages, and the year's total was expected to top the 1973 record of $6.1 billion. On a smaller scale, "Freddie Mac" operates to purchase existing loans from savings and loans, and 1974 was expected to establish a record high purchase total. Finally, "Ginnie May" has been more active than ever before, particularly in the area of "pass-through" securities where "Ginnie" guarantees securities issued by lenders that represent loans in which the net principal and interest on the mortgage loan are passed through to investors each month.

Public housing in 1974 experienced no significant change over the recent past. Continued concern over the crisis in private housing starts and the mortgage market has drawn attention from the long-standing issues related to public housing. While successive housing and urban development enactments in the United States have promised much, relatively little has been done to improve the status of public housing. However lofty the goals of public housing, the program continues to be plagued with operational problems and ineffective results.

The most recent innovation has been the idea of "urban homesteading." The basic concept, which originated in Wilmington, Del., involves the reoccupation of abandoned housing in inner-city areas. Essentially, qualified individuals are allowed to rehabilitate abandoned housing and assume full equity ownership when the building is officially approved by building inspection authorities. This approach to providing public housing resulted in the enactment of the 1973 federal "Urban Homestead Act" and the spread of the concept to numerous other cities during 1974.

The Housing and Community Development Act of 1974. On Aug. 22, 1974, President Ford signed the first major piece of housing legislation in four years. The most dramatic impact of the Housing and Community Development Act is through the establishment of a block grant system which replaces such programs as Model Cities and Urban Renewal. This system is designed to shift a major portion of the decision-making responsibility to state and local levels. The new approach has been funded $8.4 billion over a three-year period. (See also CITIES AND URBAN AFFAIRS.)

In addition to the implementation of the block grant system, this new act is also intended to help provide improved conditions in the mortgage market. The new law raises to $55,000 the limit for lending on single-family homes by federal saving and loan associations, establishes a new line of credit authority for construction loans, and allows savings and loan associations to lend up to $10,000 on home-improvement loans.

As 1974 ended, the picture for housing was neither clear nor optimistic. There was, however, general agreement that inflation—the real problem—must be slowed or halted before any effective solution can be found for U. S. housing ills.

Housing in Canada

Canada fared better than many countries in the first half of 1974, but experienced a pronounced slowdown in new housing starts in the latter half of the year. During the first half of 1974, housing starts were at the same approximate production level of 1973, but the second half of the year saw a 28% decline over the same period in 1973. As in other countries, soaring mortgage interest rates have been labeled as the prime deterrent to new construction activity in the residential market. The rising housing costs seen in 1973 continued in 1974, having a further dampening effect on housing construction.

In Toronto, Canada's second-largest city, concern over the environment has resulted in legislation placing special restrictions on the construction of all high-rise structures, including apartments. Although the intent of such building limitations is an improved urban environment, the broader impact is likely to be even fewer dwelling units than would have otherwise been built by the declining construction sector. Single-family housing prices in Toronto reflect the highest rises in the country, with an increase in the average housing price of $21,360 in 1966 to $57,461 by the middle of 1974.

Housing in Other Countries

Great Britain. Since 1930, housing in the British economy has been one of its strongest and steadiest sectors. Many economists feel, however, that 1974 marks a low point in housing construction from which Britain may never completely recover. Runaway inflation, with rising home prices, prompted a great housing boom in Britain that peaked in 1973, when the high inflow of capital into the country's building societies began to decrease. Inflationary policies instituted by the Conservative government drove interest rates up to a point where the societies could no longer compete effectively with other borrowers. Interest rates rose from 6% in the late 1960's to over 11% by the beginning of 1974. In early 1974 the societies found themselves in a position of experiencing net outflows of capital, when only a few months earlier they had average monthly inflows approaching $500 million.

The building industry of Great Britain had over 100,000 unemployed workers during 1974. By August 1974 there were some 50,000 completed but unsold private homes in inventory, and housing starts for the year were down nearly 30% from 1973. Prospects for the future depend on the British government's ability to cope with inflation and help the mortgage lenders.

Japan. With one of the world's highest inflation rates, Japan faces a housing slump similar to that being experienced in most other areas of the world. Japan's special problem is

J. PAVLOVSKY, SYGMA

These apartment buildings nearing completion in Creteil, northeast of Paris, have been dubbed "les choux de Creteil" ("the cabbages of Creteil").

that it has long suffered from a serious shortage of land for development. As a result, residential construction must increasingly go "up" rather than "out." Although more intensive construction is quite efficient in terms of land utilization, this type of construction has significantly higher per-unit construction costs.

With persistent monetary restraint slowing housing loans and pushing interest rates up, a dramatic downturn in housing starts in Japan began in October 1973 and continued through 1974. It was estimated that housing starts during 1974 declined over 30% from 1973 production levels.

Other Countries. Perhaps the only countries not hampered by substantial reductions in housing starts are those which have had a long history of housing shortages or have managed to overcome the deleterious effects of inflation (such as the major oil-producing countries). Poland, for instance, has barely replaced the housing units it lost during World War II, and the demand for additional housing is so strong that, inflation or not, the government has placed a high priority on housing construction well into the foreseeable future. The immense economic benefits of oil exports have prompted many of the Middle Eastern countries to accelerate greatly their domestic spending on housing production. Kuwait, for example, has increased the capital base of its Home Mortgage Bank from $117 to $350 million as an indication of the nation's desire to spur new housing starts.

In general, the world housing market is suffering from the ill effects of sagging housing starts in the private market brought on by constantly rising prices and the resultant lack of mortgage and construction funds at attainable interest rates.

Public Housing. Even public housing felt the effects of inflation and tight money in 1974. The significance of these effects had varying impacts according to the proportion which public housing occupied in the total housing picture, but the overall impact was, nonetheless, negative for 1974. In Britain, approximately 35% of all housing is public or publicly assisted in one form or another. France, while its present stock is perhaps 14–15% public, currently produces one unit of public housing for every two privately developed units. In West Germany, about a third of all housing is public. Israel, with its large in-migration problem, must rely on public auspices for over 50% of its housing starts. The USSR produces all of its multi-unit housing under government programs.

Attempts to bolster private housing starts by increasing public housing construction did not have a significant impact on housing starts in 1974. In Britain public housing starts plummeted by 50,000 units in 1974—a drop of over 40% from 1973. Japan, faced with rising land prices, spiraling material costs, and other inflation-related economic realities, sharply curtailed its public housing starts.

STEPHEN D. MESSNER
University of Connecticut

HOUSTON

Change in the city and the school system administrations, a strike by bus drivers, and a railroad disaster dominated events in Houston in 1974.

New Mayor. On January 2, Fred Hofheinz took the mayoral reins from Louie Welch, who chose not to run for reelection after 10 years as the city's chief executive. Assuming the office at the age of 35, Fred Hofheinz was the second generation of his family to become mayor of Houston. His father, Roy Hofheinz, served in the office before acquiring ownership of the Houston Astros baseball team and becoming the driving force behind the construction of the Astrodome.

Fred Hofheinz took a politically unpopular action soon after his inauguration by pushing through substantial water and sewer rate increases. Although the increases were met with disfavor by many homeowners, they were applauded by the Texas Water Quality Board, which said the rate hikes were an indication that the city was beginning to show good faith in upgrading its inadequate sewer system.

In early September, Hofheinz and the city council had to deal with a three-day sickout in the fire department. It stemmed from an administrative dispute between the firefighting and ambulance divisions of the department and ended after a district judge issued a temporary restraining order compelling the "sick" firemen to return to work.

Bus Strike. One of the first actions of the Hofheinz administration was the purchase of the privately owned city bus system. In early November, the city had another labor dispute on its hands when the bus drivers struck over wages. Christmas shopping was affected as the strike continued into December.

New School Administrator. The Houston Independent School District—the nation's sixth largest—also got a new chief administrator in 1974. Billy R. Reagan, a former regional commissioner of the U. S. Office of Education, was appointed general superintendent in May. He replaced George G. Garver, who was fired by the school board in February. Garver's dismissal came after a conservative majority gained control of the board in the 1973 school election.

Railroad Disaster. On September 21 the northeastern part of Houston was rocked by an explosion that killed one person and caused an estimated $14 million in property damage. It occurred at a rail yard owned by the Southern Pacific Transportation Company when butadiene gas leaking from a tank car ignited during a coupling operation. About 80 persons were taken to hospitals, most with minor injuries. The railroad company paid damage claims on property within a 20-block area of the rail yard.

ADREN ETHERIDGE
Assistant City Editor, The Houston "Post"

EASTFOTO

Hungarian Communist party leader János Kádár (*right*) greets visiting Polish Prime Minister Piotr Jaroszewicz at Communist party headquarters in Budapest.

HUNGARY

The economic reforms introduced in 1968, known as the "New Economic Mechanism," were still in effect in 1974, and Communist Party Secretary János Kádár's slogan, "He who is not against us is with us," still represented official policy.

Domestic Politics. A new law aimed at greater protection of marriage, women, and children was passed in April. The law was prompted by extremely high divorce and abortion rates and the resulting zero population growth.

In June, over 150 localities actively participated in the government-sponsored Book Week. In the previous 12 months some 2 million books had been distributed or sold. Two thirds of the books by foreign authors came from the Soviet Union. The best-sellers included Kádár's speeches and the writings of Marx and Lenin.

To offset "decadent Western influences," a vigorous campaign was launched against rock music bands. Although the performers received exorbitant pay, 98% of them had less than college education.

In May the Council of Ministers imposed severely progressive taxes on privately owned homes, vacation cottages, and water craft exceeding in size or luxury "socially acceptable" norms. Taxes on substandard dwellings were

HUNGARY • Information Highlights

Official Name: Hungarian People's Republic.
Location: Southeast central Europe.
Area: 35,919 square miles (93,030 sq km).
Population (1973 est.): 10,400,000.
Chief Cities (1971 est.): Budapest, the capital, 2,027,-300; Miskolc, 186,600; Debrecen, 168,300.
Government: *Head of state,* Pál Losonczi, chairman of the presidential council (took office 1967). *Head of government,* Jenö Fock, premier (took office 1967). *First secretary of the Hungarian Socialist Workers' (Communist) party,* János Kádár (took office 1956). *Legislature* (unicameral)—Parliament.
Monetary Unit: Forint (9.39 forints equal U. S.$1, Aug. 1974).
Gross National Product (1973 est.): $16,900,000,000.
Manufacturing (major products): Machinery and tools, vehicles, chemicals, pharmaceuticals.
Major Agricultural Products: Corn, wheat, potatoes.
Foreign Trade (1973): *Exports,* $4,479,000,000; *imports,* $3,856,000,000.

reduced. As of July 1, the working hours for some 400,000 persons engaged in trade and the catering industry were reduced to 44 hours per week. It was planned that by 1978 a 44-hour workweek would be extended to all fields of the national economy.

Economy. The budget for 1973 closed with an unexpectedly small deficit amounting to less than 1% of national income. The state enterprises produced 12% more than planned. Exports increased by 14% over 1972, while imports rose only 4%, resulting in a stable foreign trade balance. The net value of industrial production rose more than 7%. Real industrial wages increased 5.5%. Only housing was behind schedule, with some 2,000 units below the planned output.

Some 4.5 million tons of wheat was produced in 1974. Almost 1 million tons was exported, bringing in approximately $150 million of hard currencies. In order to increase production of vegetables, the small individual vegetable producers were accorded special tax benefits. Small farmers continued to be more efficient than the big cooperatives: 1 million of them, owning some 17% of the total arable land, produced more than 34% of all agricultural output, including over 50% of all vegetables.

As a result of a 300% increase in the world price of soybeans, the government introduced a crash program to produce home-grown soybeans. While in 1973 only 2,000 hectares (4,940 acres) were used, by the end of 1974 some 15,000 hectares (37,065 acres) were sown to soybeans, and the plan provided for 100,000 hectares (247,100 acres) by 1980.

In the first six months of 1974 over 2,500,000 foreigners visited Hungary—a 100% increase over the same period in 1973. The traditional Budapest International Fair was split into two parts: a spring fair devoted to investment opportunities, and a fall fair for consumer goods. The spring fair opened in May with some 630 Hungarian and 800 foreign firms from 25 countries displaying their products. In August the fourth World Congress of Economists, attended by 1,600 experts from 70 countries, was held in Budapest.

Foreign Trade. Hungary's dependence on foreign trade continued to be heavy. In the first six months of 1974 both imports and exports increased 33.7% and 20.1%, respectively, as against the same period of 1973. Some 45% of the imports came from nonsocialist countries. The trade balance with the COMECON countries continued to be positive, and by the end of 1974, Hungary had accumulated foreign exchange credits of over 5,300 million forints ($564 million).

Beef cattle exports, valued at $140 million in 1973, suffered losses due to severe import restrictions in Italy, the largest single importer of Hungarian beef. Hungary's positive trade balance with Italy has more than tripled since 1970: from $45 million to almost $155 million.

In April, an Iranian trade delegation signed agreements in Budapest increasing trade between the two countries by 25%, from $37 million in 1973 to $46 million in 1974. In May, a West German–Hungarian joint company (with Hungarians in control of 51% of the stock) was created to service various enterprises. Soon afterward the Swedish firm Volvo entered into a similar kind of agreement whereby some 200 jeep-type cross-country vehicles will be produced by 1975, and 1,200 vehicles annually thereafter.

In June the Hungarian National Bank signed a $100 million loan agreement with 20 American and Canadian banks. The loan, to be paid in 8 years, at a so-called "floating interest rate," would help to modernize production and increase Hungary's export capacity. Soon afterward Hungarian and American chambers of commerce signed an agreement providing for an increase in trade. By the end of 1974, Hungary's yearly exports to the United States, consisting mostly of foods, amounted to $20 million, while imports from the United States, principally machinery and agricultural equipment, amounted to $74 million.

Foreign Relations. In April, President Tito of Yugoslavia paid a "friendly working visit" to Hungary. His visit was followed by several agreements. Trade between both countries, based on a convertible currency basis, was to be increased. It had reached $170 million in 1973, with exports and imports in balance. Subsequently the foreign ministers of West Germany and Italy visited Budapest, and cooperation in the scientific, cultural, sports, and health fields was pledged on each occasion.

Relations with the United States improved markedly in 1974. Cultural exchange and cooperation was agreed upon; restrictions on movements of respective diplomats were lifted; and negotiations aimed at according Hungary a most-favored-nation status were initiated. Rumors spread that soon the St. Stephen crown, symbol of Magyar tradition, held by the United States since World War II, might be returned to Hungary.

JAN KARSKI, *Georgetown University*

ICELAND

Following the fall of the left-wing government, general elections were held in the summer of 1974 and a new coalition government, led by the right-wing Independent party, took office.

Elections and Foreign Affairs. The three-year-old left-wing government, known for its policy of aiming at closing down the country's only defenses—the U. S. naval air base at Keflavík—did not last the full term. The main issue of the elections on June 30 was foreign policy, which was a subject of heated discussions during all these three years and a matter of great concern to Iceland's NATO allies, due to the constantly increasing strength of the Soviet Navy in the North Atlantic.

Iceland's largest political party, the Independence party, which opposed closing the base, won with almost 43% of the vote. After two months of negotiations, a new coalition government was formed under the leadership of this party but with the participation of the Progressive party, which had led the outgoing government. The new premier, Geir Hallgrímsson, took office on August 28.

A fundamental change was thus made in foreign policy. The aim of the new government was to cooperate with the United States so that the necessary defenses of the country would be guaranteed by the presence of U. S. forces. Accordingly, an agreement was reached to maintain the U. S. defense base, but some technical reorganization will take place.

Economy and Foreign Trade. With an annual inflation rate of over 30%, Iceland faced great economic problems in 1974. Foreign trade has been showing an increasingly unfavorable balance, due mainly to declining fish catches, despite increasing efforts, and sinking world market prices for Iceland's most important export, fish products. Skyrocketing oil prices have also affected Iceland, and an increased effort is planned to utilize further the country's energy resources.

Due to the economic difficulties, the new government devalued the currency (Icelandic króna) by 17% in August, shortly after it took office. This came on top of another 17% gradual "devaluation" of the króna against the U. S. dollar since the beginning of the year, while the currency had been "floating."

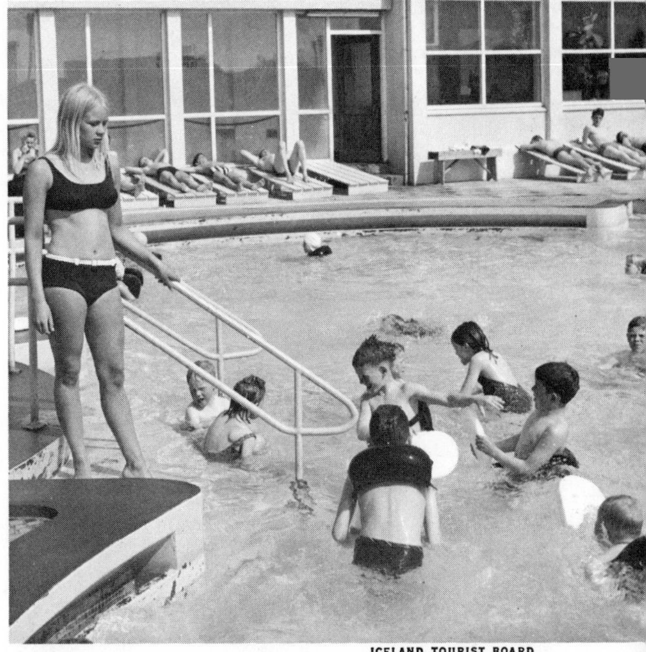

ICELAND TOURIST BOARD

Children romp in one of Iceland's many open-air swimming pools filled with water heated geothermally. Geothermal energy heats many Iceland homes in winter.

It is still to be seen whether the new government will be able to overcome the economic difficulties. Although it is strong in parliament (together the two parties got 67.7% of the total vote in the elections and 42 seats out of 60 in parliament), various factors beyond the control of Icelanders—primarily, fish catches and foreign market prices for fish products—are going to affect the economy in the future.

Fishery Limits. With the economy dependent to a large extent on the fisheries, Iceland will continue trying to preserve the fishing banks against over-exploitation. The extension of the fishing limits to 50 miles in 1972 was a step in this direction. To protect the interests of the country, the government has announced that in 1975 the fisheries limits will be extended finally to 200 miles. Although the Conference on the Law of the Sea, held in Caracas in 1974, did not provide a firm basis in international law for 200-mile fishing limits, the debates at the conference reflected, in the opinion of the Icelandic government, overwhelming support for the cause of coastal states depending on harvesting the sea.

HARALDUR J. HAMAR
Editor, "Iceland Review"

ICELAND • Information Highlights

Official Name: Republic of Iceland.
Location: North Atlantic Ocean.
Area: 39,768 square miles (103,000 sq km).
Population (1973 est.): 210,000.
Chief City (1971 est.): Reykjavík, the capital, 82,900.
Government: *Head of state,* Kristján Eldjárn, president (took office for 2d 4-year term Aug. 1972). *Head of government,* Geir Hallgrímsson, prime minister (took office Aug. 1974). *Legislature*—Althing: Upper House and Lower House.
Monetary Unit: Króna (95 krónur equal U. S.$1, June 1974).
Gross National Product (1973 est.): $700,000,000.
Manufacturing (major products): Fish products, clothing, shoes, chemicals, fertilizers.
Major Agricultural Products: Potatoes, hay, dairy products, fish, sheep.
Foreign Trade (1973): *Exports,* $291,000,000; *imports,* $362,000,000.

UPI

Evel Knievel takes off in rocket-powered Sky-Cycle in unsuccessful attempt to leap Snake River Canyon, Idaho.

IDAHO

Elections and legislative activities dominated the news in Idaho in 1974.

Elections. Gov. Cecil Andrus (D) won reelection with 71% of the votes. Sen. Frank Church (D) and Rep. Steve Symms (R) kept their seats, while George Hansen (R) unseated Rep. Orval Hansen (R). John Evans (D) captured the lieutenant governor post; Wayne Kidwell (R) unseated Attorney General Tony Park.

Democrats gained eight seats in the House, reducing their deficit to 27 to 43, and two seats in the Senate, leaving them down 14 to 21. Women members increased from six to ten.

Legislation. Two legislative highlights were the reorganization of the executive branch and the televising of proceedings on the bill to fund public schools. A record $12.8 million increase for schools raised the amount to $70.6 million. Higher education rose from $31.8 million to $42 million, and the general fund spending rose from $153.6 million to $199.4 million.

Tax relief was granted to the elderly poor by a measure that helped those with income below $6,000 by reducing real property taxes for homeowners. A $15 per person income tax deduction to offset sales taxes on food was made permanent.

In other actions, the legislature passed a reapportionment plan that met court approval, raised maximum interest rates on credit cards to 18%, imposed a 2% surcharge on liquor to fund a program to "crack down" on drunk driving, made parents and guardians liable for goods shoplifted by their children, permitted doctors to dispense birth control information, required local governmental agencies to hold open meetings, and made possession of three ounces or more of marihuana a major felony.

Legislators refused to pass a "Sunshine Law" to force office seekers to disclose contributions and expenses and require lobbyists to reveal who pays them and what bills they are supporting. However, the measure was placed on the November ballot as an initiative and passed overwhelmingly.

Environment and Natural Resources. A heavy winter snowfall provided ample water for irrigation and electric power production. Scant rainfall from June through October left nonirrigated areas in drought conditions.

The fall steelhead run was so reduced by nitrogen poisoning as a result of flood waters falling over dams and by commercial and Indian fishing that Idaho closed its sport fishing. Idaho brought suit against Oregon and Washington to force them to give Idaho a vote on fishery management on the lower Columbia River.

The Forest Service was granted special permission by the Environmental Protection Agency to spray DDT on about 80,000 acres of forest infested with the Douglas-fir tussock moth. Experimental spraying with Sevin, a less polluting chemical, showed promise, but the kill was not as good as with DDT.

A September survey released by the Department of Health and Welfare revealed serious lead poisoning in children living near the Bunker Hill and Sullivan smelter at Kellogg.

Damage Suit. The families involved in the Sunshine Mine disaster that killed 91 people in May 1972 filed damage actions against the company totaling $11 billion.

Rocket Stunt. In September about 15,000 spectators saw Evel Knievel fail in his attempt to rocket across the Snake River Canyon.

CLIFFORD DOBLER, *University of Idaho*

IDAHO • Information Highlights

Area: 83,557 square miles (216,413 sq km).
Population (1973 est.): 770,000. *Density:* 9 per sq mi.
Chief Cities (1970 census): Boise, the capital, 74,990; Pocatello, 40,036; Idaho Falls, 35,776.
Government (1974): *Chief Officers*—governor, Cecil D. Andrus (D); lt. gov., Jack M. Murphy (R). *Legislature*—Senate, 35 members (23 R, 12 D); House of Representatives, 70 members (51 R, 19 D).
Education (1973–74): *Enrollment*—public elementary schools, 90,550 pupils; public secondary schools, 94,250; nonpublic schools, 5,900; colleges and universities, 35,198 students. *Public school expenditures,* $143,500,000 ($812 per pupil).
State Finances (fiscal year 1973): *Revenues,* $473,122,000; *expenditures,* $435,110,000.
Personal Income (1973): $3,329,000,000; per capita, $4,323.
Labor Force (July 1974): *Nonagricultural wage and salary earners,* 262,200.

ILLINOIS

The year 1974 was a difficult one in Illinois for many. Farmers reported poor crops, the state shared in the national problems of inflation and unemployment, and the politicians hassled in what many called the least productive legislative session in years.

Economy. Farmers were optimistic in the spring for record crops of soybeans and corn. But a midsummer drought hurt farmers in the broad prairie farms of the central sector of the state, and a record early frost in September caused even more damage. Commerce remained generally healthy during the year, with some Illinois companies reporting good earnings.

Politics. So bitter were the battles between the governor and the legislature that few meaningful bills were enacted. Daniel Walker, an independent Democrat, was in his second year as governor. His relationship with Mayor Richard Daley of Chicago, an organization Democrat, was cool. The result was that Daley's legislative supporters were often at odds with Walker. Predictably, Walker had strong opposition from the Republicans, who controlled the Senate and the House by one seat each.

There was even a feud between the two legislative chambers. Walker had to order the Senate back for a special session to approve appropriation bills to guarantee pay for state employees. This came after the state representatives balked at the Senate dumping a score of bills on them the last day of the regular session. Even Walker and his lieutenant governor, Neil Hartigan, had a cool relationship. Though both are Democrats, Hartigan has close ties with Mayor Daley.

The equal rights amendment to the U. S. Constitution failed in the legislature, where it needed a three-fifths vote. Attempts to dismantle the six-county Regional Transportation Authority (RTA) around Chicago failed, but legislators agreed on minor changes that made the RTA more acceptable to the suburbs.

A bill to let legislators, judges, and state employees collect their pensions even though convicted of a felony whistled through the legislature before opponents saw its evils. It came at a time when the U. S. Justice Department was investigating the activities of some of the legislators. Walker vetoed the bill.

Walker used his amendatory veto powers to reduce an increase in public welfare payments from 10% to 5%. He was sharply criticized for this action.

There were some legislative accomplishments. Funding of education was increased, and a campaign ethics bill requiring candidates to report all contributions and campaign spending of $150 or more was passed. Tougher regulations were enacted to curb unscrupulous collection agencies, and a $70 million bond program was passed to promote coal development.

ILLINOIS • Information Highlights

Area: 56,400 square miles (146,076 sq km).
Population (1973 est.): 11,236,000. *Density:* 202 per sq mi.
Chief Cities (1970 census): Springfield, the capital, 91,753; Chicago, 3,369,359; Rockford, 147,370.
Government (1974): *Chief Officers*—governor, Daniel Walker (D); lt. gov., Neil F. Hartigan (D). *General Assembly*—Senate, 59 members; House of Representatives, 177 members.
Education (1973–74): *Enrollment*—public elementary schools, 1,442,295 pupils; public secondary, 876,950; nonpublic, 423,900; colleges and universities, 494,859 students. *Public school expenditures,* $2,543,051,000 ($1,228 per pupil).
State Finances (fiscal year 1973): *Revenues,* $6,432,161,000; *expenditures,* $6,034,221,000.
Personal Income (1973): $64,639,000,000; per capita, $5,753.
Labor Force (July 1974): *Nonagricultural wage and salary earners,* 4,453,800; *insured unemployed,* 93,500 (2.5%).

Political observers said the legislative session was so unproductive that there were no victors. The lawmakers had little to take home to convince the electorate that they should be returned to office in the November election.

Election. The election was far more devastating for the Republicans than the Democrats. For the first time in 36 years the Democrats gained control of both houses in the legislature. Furthermore, they attained substantial working majorities in both houses.

In the two statewide races, Adlai Stevenson easily was reelected to the U. S. Senate, and Allen Dixon was reelected state treasurer. Both are Democrats. The Republicans had controlled the Illinois congressional delegation by 14 to 10, but after the election the Democrats had the edge, 13 to 11.

Suburban counties around Chicago, traditionally Republican strongholds, elected a few Democrats to county offices. Other Democrats made strong challenges to Republicans in the outlying counties. Heavily Democratic Chicago gave Democrats easy victories for major Cook county offices.

Disaster. Seven persons were killed and 150 injured when five jumbo tank cars containing propane gas exploded in a rail yard in Decatur in July. A major fire ensued, and the damage was estimated at $17 million. The accident occurred when the tank cars rammed a standing boxcar.

Environment. Illinois had its first statewide ozone alerts in the summer. Ozone is a reactive combination of oxygen atoms formed by the effect of sunlight on automobile and industrial air pollutants. Yellow alerts were announced, primarily for the industrial northeast corner of the state. No major illnesses were reported, but there were complaints of discomfort from persons with respiratory ailments. Environmentalists debated whether Illinois had proper standards for ozone pollution. Some contended the state did not react fast enough, while others argued the pollution was not serious enough to warrant an alert.

DAVID E. HALVORSEN, *"Chicago Tribune"*

UPI

In New Delhi, India, "junior doctors" (internes), who earn about 50 U. S. dollars a month, go on strike to protest against poor service and other conditions in hospitals.

INDIA

In almost every respect, 1974 was the worst year India has experienced since independence. Vastly higher prices for imported fuel and food, disastrous droughts and floods, and governmental floundering led to a staggering rate of inflation and food shortages that in more than one-third of the states produced famine or near-famine conditions. Strikes and protest movements, often involving an unusually high incidence of violence, were almost daily occurrences. In February, elections were held in four states, and in August, Fakhruddin Ali Ahmed was elected president of India. On May 18, India became the sixth member of the "nuclear club," the most highly publicized event of 1974.

DOMESTIC AFFAIRS

Violence and Protest Movements. In two states, Gujarat and Bihar, the political situation was unusually unstable and the level of violence and unrest unusually high. In January and early February, large-scale rioting, led by student activists, erupted in Gujarat, formerly a relatively stable and peaceful state. It began as a protest against high food prices and turned into an uprising against an allegedly corrupt state government. By January 27, when the army was called in, at least 37 persons had been killed. On February 9 the chief minister, Chimambhai Patel, resigned, and president's rule was proclaimed. Fresh waves of violence took place in late February and early March, and intermittently throughout the remainder of the year.

The situation in Bihar, one of the most underdeveloped and worst governed states, was even more chaotic. Acts of violence, arson, and sabotage disrupted normal activity. In March police forces were used against student demonstrators in Patna, the capital. In October a three-day *bandh* (strike) again paralyzed Patna. Over 2,500 persons were arrested. The protest movements in Bihar gained additional strength and support when Jayaprakash Narayan, a 72-year-old apostle of non-violence who had a reputation for devotion to the people and complete incorruptibility, gave it his endorsement and actively participated in it. His criticisms of the existing state of affairs, in Bihar and in the country as a whole, put Prime Minister Indira Gandhi in a difficult position. A meeting in late October failed to resolve the differences between them.

Elections. During the second half of February, important elections were held in four states and one Union Territory, involving more than 50 million voters. In Uttar Pradesh, Mrs. Gandhi's home state, the Congress' prospects appeared to be very poor, but they improved somewhat as a result of Mrs. Gandhi's indefatigable campaigning. The Congress lost 58 seats in the state legislative assembly, but it retained a bare majority of the seats and with the help of the CPI (Communist Party of India) was able to continue in power. In Orissa, a Congress-CPI alliance showed unexpected strength in spite of the formation of a united front of

INDIA • Information Highlights

Official Name: Republic of India.
Location: South Asia.
Area: 1,266,598 square miles (3,280,483 sq km).
Population (1973 est.): 600,400,000.
Chief Cities (1971 census): New Delhi, the capital, 301,-801; Bombay, 5,970,575; Delhi, 3,287,883; Calcutta, 3,148,746.
Government: *Head of state,* Fakhruddin Ali Ahmed, president (took office Aug. 1974). *Head of government,* Mrs. Indira Gandhi, prime minister (took office Jan. 1966). *Legislature*—Parliament: Rajya (Council of States) and Lok Sabha (House of the People).
Monetary Unit: Rupee (8.045 rupees equal U. S.$1, Aug. 1974).
Gross National Product (1972 est.): $58,250,000,000.
Manufacturing (major products): Iron and steel, industrial machinery and equipment, chemicals.
Major Agricultural Products: Rice, wheat, groundnuts, barley, sesame, sugarcane, corn, rubber.
Foreign Trade (1973): *Exports,* $2,940,000,000; *imports,* $3,066,000,000.

most opposition parties, and Congress rule continued in that state, on a rather unstable basis. In Nagaland the United Democratic Front, which was identified with the underground resistance movement, barely defeated the Nagaland National Organization, which had been in power since the state was formed. In Manipur, local parties, as usual, proved to be stronger than the Congress. In the Union Territory of Pondicherry the Congress won only 7 of the 30 seats, whereas the Anna DMK, a local party based in the neighboring state of Tamil Nadu, won 12 seats.

Elections for a new president and vice president, based on a complicated indirect system of proportional representation, were held in August. Mrs. Gandhi decided not to endorse the incumbent president, V. V. Giri, for reelection, and instead chose a member of her cabinet, Fakhruddin Ali Ahmed, a prominent Muslim. He was elected by an overwhelming majority, as was the Congress selection for vice president, B. D. Jatti, who had been governor of Orissa.

A New Political Party. In April, leaders of eight opposition parties decided to merge to form a new political party, which later took the name of the Bharatiya Lok Dal (BLD; People's Party of India). The new party was officially launched on August 29, with Charan Singh of the BKD as president. It emphasized a Gandhian approach, and claimed to offer "a viable national alternative" to the Congress party; but it was doubtful whether such a weak coalition of such disparate elements could gain widespread support.

Cabinet Reshuffle. On October 10, Mrs. Gandhi made her most extensive cabinet reorganization since she became prime minister in 1966. Two cabinet ministers, one minister of state, and three deputy ministers, were dropped. The significant changes were the transfer of Jagjivan Ram from defense to agriculture, Swaran Singh from foreign affairs to defense, Y. B. Chavan from finance to foreign affairs, and C. Subramaniam from agriculture to finance. On November 17, D. P. Dhar, a close associate of Mrs. Gandhi who had been under criticism for alleged failure to develop a realistic economic program, resigned as planning minister.

India Joins the Nuclear Club. On May 18 India gained world headlines by exploding its first "nuclear device." This was an underground explosion in a desert area of Rajasthan, apparently of somewhat less than the explosive power of the atomic bomb dropped on Nagasaki in 1945. It was officially described as "a peaceful nuclear explosion experiment." Mrs. Gandhi and other Indian spokesmen repeatedly pledged that India would use its nuclear power solely for peaceful purposes, and they often reacted indignantly to expressions of skepticism and criticism from abroad. These expressions were particularly strong in Pakistan, whose leaders stated that Pakistan might be forced to follow the Indian example; in Japan, where aversion to any nuclear tests is understandably great; in Canada, which charged that India had violated the agreement under which Canada was providing assistance in the nuclear field; and in the United States, where criticisms were voiced that a poor nation like India could hardly afford to invest scarce resources in expensive nuclear explosions and that India had opened up a "Pandora's box" by being the first country to force its way into the "nuclear club" since the signing of the nonproliferation treaty (to which India has consistently refused to adhere). In spite of the criticism abroad, the nuclear explosion was widely acclaimed in India and gave a considerable boost to the sagging morale of Mrs. Gandhi's government and the nation as a whole.

Sikkim. The first general elections in Sikkim were held in April, under Indian supervision. It resulted in a landslide victory for the pro-

Indian Prime Minister Indira Gandhi applauds as President Tito of Yugoslavia receives the Jawaharlal Nehru Award for Peace and Understanding in New Delhi ceremonies.

UPI

Fakhruddin Ali Ahmed, the new president of India.

India and Nepali-dominated Sikkim Congress, which in June passed the Government of Sikkim Act, reducing the position of the *chogyal* (king) to that of a mere figurehead, and giving an Indian administrator overriding control over all aspects of the government. In September, allegedly at the request of the Sikkim Assembly, the Constitution (36th Amendment) Act, adopted by the Lok Sabha on September 3, changed the status of Sikkim from that of protectorate to that of an "associate" in the Indian Union. This action was widely hailed in India, but it provoked strong protests by the *chogyal* and by China, and produced anti-Indian demonstrations in Nepal.

THE ECONOMY

India was one of the developing countries most adversely affected by the sudden tremendous increases in the costs of fuel, food, and fertilizers. Its normally heavy dependence on outside sources for all of these essentials was increased by unusually serious shortages—amounting to nearly 10 million tons of foodgrains—because of intermittent monsoon rains, drought conditions in several states and floods in others, strikes and other labor tie-ups, industrial stagnation, inefficient governmental policies, and a host of other natural and man-made reverses. Although the value of exports went up by 25%, the foreign exchange gap was more than $900 million. In September, Finance Minister Y. B. Chavan said that India would have to use nearly 80% of its export earnings for imports of oil, fertilizers, and food.

The high and escalating rate of inflation, amounting to at least 25% overall and to much higher rates for many basic commodities, and shortages of fertilizers and power seriously affected almost the entire population and created problems of human survival in those parts of the country, embracing nine states and perhaps 200 million people, that were most adversely affected by droughts and floods. In many of these affected areas near-famine or famine conditions developed.

Vital areas of India's industrial and transportation system were crippled by prolonged strikes. Most serious were a 33-day strike in the jute industry in West Bengal, a 41-day strike in the textile mills in Bombay, and, above all, a month-long nationwide strike of railway workers. The railway strike involved a large number of railway unions, coordinated by a national labor organization led by socialist labor leader George Fernandes. Fernandes and hundreds of other union members were arrested even before the strike was declared in early May. While making some concessions to their demands, the government stood firm, and the workers abandoned the strike without realizing their major goals.

Under these depressing conditions the government's annual budget and the fifth Five-Year Plan set targets that soon proved to be impossible of realization. The annual budget, introduced in the Lok Sabha by the finance minister on February 28, included provisions for $280 million in additional taxation, but it still estimated a budget deficit of about $170 million. By September the estimated deficit had risen to $875 million.

The fifth Five-Year Plan (1974–79) officially entered into effect on April 1. Its overall objectives, to remove poverty and achieve "economic self-reliance" by the end of the Plan period, seemed quite unrealistic in the light of the crisis that the Indian economy was facing at the time of its inauguration. It provided for a total expenditure over five years of about $70 billion, nearly 70% in the public sector, and for an annual growth rate of 5.5%. Since the growth rate in 1974 was less than 1%, the Plan target seemed to be another impossible goal.

To assist India in obtaining needed imports and in meeting its financial needs, the Aid-India Consortium, under the aegis of the World Bank, voted to sanction financial assistance totaling approximately $1.4 billion in 1974 (an amount that would be forthcoming only if the donor nations agreed). India received some assistance by the postponement of about half of its debt payments of nearly $500 million, by credits on easy terms or other concessional assistance from the International Development Association, the European Economic Community, Iran and other oil-producing nations, the Soviet Union, the United States, and several other countries.

FOREIGN AFFAIRS

On April 8 a historic agreement was signed in New Delhi by the foreign ministers of India, Pakistan, and Bangladesh, providing for the repatriation of all Pakistani prisoners of war in India, including the 195 whom Bangladesh had previously insisted must be tried as war crim-

NIK WHEELER/SYGMA

Some of New Delhi's orphans and unwanted children are given food by the Bengal Society, a charitable organization.

inals. On May 16, India and Bangladesh signed an agreement on economic and political cooperation. Relations between India and Pakistan showed some improvement. On September 19, they agreed to resume postal, telecommunications, and travel facalities, and in November they agreed to end their 10-year ban on trade.

The two major issues in dispute between India and Sri Lanka, regarding the status of some 150,000 persons of Indian origin in Sri Lanka whose future had not been settled previously, and the demarcation of the boundaries in the waters from Adam's Bridge to the Palk Strait, were "finally" settled in agreements concluded in January and June, respectively.

On September 24, India and Portugal decided to take steps for the reestablishment of diplomatic relations, severed since 1950, following recognition by Portugal of India's full sovereignty over Goa and other former Portuguese holdings in India.

Mrs. Gandhi made several official visits to other countries during the year, including Iran, Sri Lanka, and the USSR.

Relations between India and the United States seemed to improve considerably in 1974. On February 18, an agreement for the disposition of PL-480 and other U. S. funds in India was signed in New Delhi. From October 27 to 30 the U. S. Secretary of State, Henry Kissinger, made an official visit to India. In an important address in New Delhi on October 28 he declared that "the United States accepts nonalignment," and that "the American people want to be helpful, while avoiding the dependence we both reject." On the same day he and the new Indian Foreign Minister, Y. B. Chavan, signed an important agreement to establish a joint commission on economic, commercial, technological, educational, and cultural cooperation.

NORMAN D. PALMER
University of Pennsylvania

NIK WHEELER/SYGMA

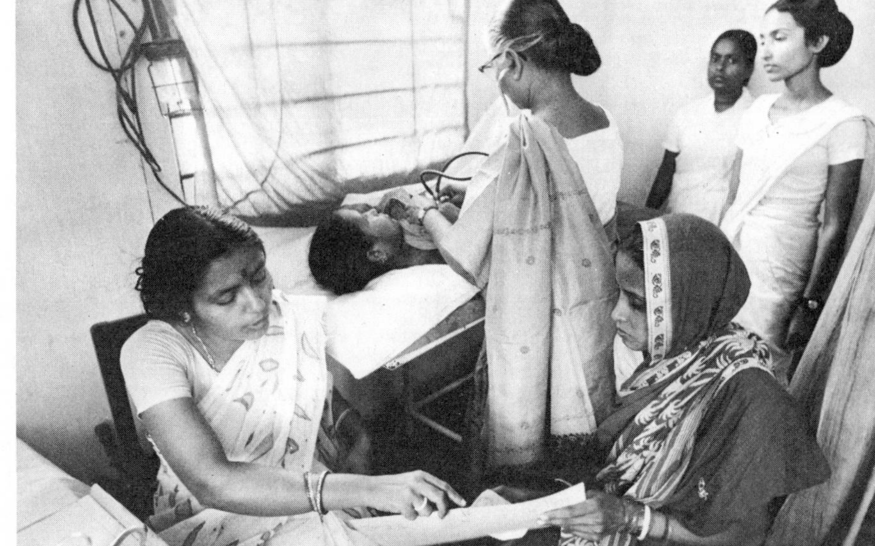

In one of many planned parenthood clinics in New Delhi, women are treated and advised in an attempt to reduce India's 13-million-per-year birthrate.

INDIANA

Democrats scored strong gains in the off-year elections in Indiana in 1974. Energy, the economy, and the weather also made headlines during the year.

Elections. A fairly substantial voter turnout disproved predictions of voter apathy in the November elections. Democrats swept to their biggest statewide victory since 1964 and their best off-year election triumph since 1958. Democratic candidates captured 9 of Indiana's 11 congressional seats, a larger number than they had held since 1936 and a reversal of the previous 7-to-4 ratio in favor of the Republicans.

The most stunning victories were those of Indianapolis schoolteacher David Evans, a Democrat, over the 12-term GOP veteran William G. Bray and of Floyd Fithian over Republican Earl Landgrebe in a district that last went Democratic in 1932. Democrats also retained all four state offices on the ballot, gained control of the lower house of the General Assembly for the first time since 1964, and substantially reduced the Republican plurality in the state Senate.

In a contest significant nationally because of the prominence of both candidates, incumbent Democratic U. S. Sen. Birch E. Bayh, Jr., narrowly defeated Indianapolis Mayor Richard G. Lugar. Don Lee, the American party candidate for the U. S. Senate, polled 2.4% of the votes cast, the best showing for a third-party candidate for that office since 1946.

Energy Crisis. In compliance with federal guidelines relating to the energy crisis, the Indiana General Assembly passed legislation reducing the state's top speed limit to 55 mph, effective March 1, 1974. Although designed to cut down the consumption of gasoline, the lower speed limit also reduced the number of highway deaths in the state by approximately 33% in the rural areas compared with 1973. The General Assembly passed several other energy-related measures during its short 30-day session, including the creation and funding of the State Office of Petroleum Allocation.

INDIANA • Information Highlights

Area: 36,291 square miles (93,994 sq km).
Population (1973 est.): 5,316,000. *Density:* 147 per sq mi.
Chief Cities (1970 census): Indianapolis, the capital, 744,743; Fort Wayne, 178,021; Gary, 175,415; Evansville, 138,764.
Government (1974): *Chief Officers*—governor, Otis R. Bowen (R); lt. gov., Robert D. Orr (R). *General Assembly*—Senate, 50 members; House of Representatives, 100 members.
Education (1973–74): *Enrollment*—public elementary schools, 639,000 pupils; public secondary, 568,000; nonpublic, 102,300; colleges and universities, 198,457 students. *Public school expenditures,* $970,000,000 ($890 per pupil).
State Finances (fiscal year 1973): *Revenues,* $2,213,911,000; *expenditures,* $2,072,690,000.
Personal Income (1973): $26,091,000,000; per capita, $4,908.
Labor Force (July 1974): *Nonagricultural wage and salary earners,* 2,037,100.

Legislation. Additional legislation included an ethics bill which requires members of the legislature, elected state officers, and candidates for these positions to file statements of financial disclosure. Deleted from the measure and weakening it were sanctions defining criminal penalties for violation of the act and preventing legislators from voting on bills that affect their nonlegislative incomes. The General Assembly approved and funded a plan to complete Indiana's interstate highway system within 4 years rather than the 10 or 12 years previously expected. It also enacted legislation clamping down on convicted rapists. Defeated were bills providing for a state lottery, pari-mutuel betting, and repeal of a ban on household use of laundry detergents containing phosphates.

Budget. The legislature approved a $33.5 million supplemental budget for 1974–75. Of this amount $13.2 million was appropriated to upgrade and modernize Indiana's system of state parks, including $3 million to begin work on the state's newest park, Wyandotte Woods in the Harrison-Crawford State Forest. Legislators allotted $2.1 million for further work on the Clark Maritime Center, a new port facility being planned for the Ohio River near Jeffersonville. Completion of this facility and the Southwind Maritime Center near Evansville will provide Indiana with two river ports that can probably be used throughout the year.

Economy. Further curtailment of railroad freight service in the state adversely affected the economic development of several Indiana communities. A $25,000 legislative appropriation provided funds for a study of the impact on the state of this reduction of rail service. Although unemployment rose substantially from 1973, diversified manufacturing continued to dominate Indiana's economy.

Heavy spring rains combined with the worst summer drought in several decades and early killing frosts severely damaged the state's corn and soybean crops. A county-by-county assessment of farm losses was initiated in lieu of Gov. Otis R. Bowen's unsuccessful attempt to have the entire state declared a federal agricultural disaster area.

Tornadoes. On the afternoon of April 3, 1974, five bands of tornadoes devastated scattered communities in both northern and southern Indiana. Hardest hit were Madison and Hanover and historic Hanover College in Jefferson county in the southern part of the state and Monticello and Rochester, county seats of White and Fulton counties, respectively, in the north central region. Deaths numbered approximately 48; at least 1,000 were injured; and property damage totaled in excess of $200 million. The state was declared a federal disaster area, and tornado victims became eligible for loans through the Federal Disaster Relief Agency.

LORNA LUTES SYLVESTER
Indiana University

INDONESIA

Indonesia continued to make slow but steady economic progress in 1974, but there were signs of growing student and popular impatience with the prolonged austerity demanded by the development program. There was also bitterness over the corruption and luxurious living by people at the top, and the affluence of foreigners exploiting Indonesian resources.

Student Riots. Grave unrest came to the surface on the eve of Japanese Premier Kakuei Tanaka's visit to Jakarta (Djakarta). Student activists, in a petition presented to the government on January 5, complained that there were ambitious people in superior positions who were seeking personal or group benefit, and they appealed for the elimination of clique and family systems and of corruption.

The rising student unrest was a serious but delicate matter for Suharto's government to deal with. Student support had been of tremendous help in getting rid of the Sukarno regime, and students were regarded by large sections of the population as their spokesmen. The government proceeded cautiously with the students, but also firmly, lest popular impatience give way to disorder and revolution. Only a short time before, students in Bangkok had overthrown the Thai government.

There had been rising resentment against Japanese "colonialism" and "economic imperialism." Indonesians complained of Japanese arrogance. A practice which especially offended Indonesians was the taking of ethnic Chinese instead of Indonesians as partners in joint enterprises to satisfy the legal requirements. The visit of Prime Minister Tanaka led Indonesians to focus their resentments and frustrations on the Japanese.

Prime Minister Tanaka was greeted by student demonstrators when he arrived at Jakarta on January 14. Some of the students broke through the police lines as the motorcade of the Japanese political leader and the Indonesian president moved from the airport to the city, but there was no serious incident. During the two days of Tanaka's visit there were violent demonstrations in which 11 persons died, 40 were injured, several shopping centers were damaged, destroyed, burned, or looted, and about 250 Japanese-made automobiles were burned or otherwise destroyed. The prime minister's engagements outside the presidential compound were cancelled. By decisive police action, order was restored in a few days.

Government Reaction. The army occupied the campus of the University of Indonesia, and several hundred students were jailed and their leaders arrested. Suharto personally took over the control of the Command to Restore Order and Security, the highest agency for internal security. A National Board of Political Stabilization and National Security, under the chairmanship of the president, replaced the president's special aides—the so-called palace guard. Suharto requested officials not to engage in private business, give gifts and parties at government expense, or receive gifts in any form.

INDONESIA • Information Highlights

Official Name: Republic of Indonesia.
Location: Southeast Asia.
Area: 735,269 square miles (1,904,345 sq km).
Population (1973 est.): 132,500,000.
Chief Cities (1971 census): Jakarta (formerly spelled Djakarta), the capital, 4,576,009; Surabaja, 1,556,255; Bandung, 1,201,730.
Government: *Head of state and of government,* Suharto, president (took office for second 5-year term March 1973). *Legislature* (unicameral)—Dewan Perwakilan Rakyat (House of Representatives).
Monetary Unit: Rupiah (374 rupiahs equal U. S.$1, July 1974).
Gross National Product (1972 est.): $10,620,000,000.
Manufacturing (major products): Processed agricultural products, petroleum products, mineral products, cotton textiles, tires, cement.
Major Agricultural Products: Rice, rubber, sweet potatoes, cassava, copra, sugarcane, coffee.
Foreign Trade (1973): *Exports,* $3,211,000,000; *imports,* $2,346,000,000.

Foreign Affairs. During the visits of a number of important government officials in 1974, the Indonesian government pursued its foreign policy objectives in several significant matters. In a joint statement, Premier Tanaka declared that in its relations with the peoples of Southeast Asia his country's basic principle was to respect their wishes and to contribute to their development without impeding their economic self-reliance, while President Suharto expressed the hope that foreign private investment would create substantially more employment opportunities, enhance the managerial proficiency of Indonesian entrepreneurs, and train personnel for responsible positions.

U. S. Deputy Secretary of State Kenneth Rush, on a visit to Jakarta, March 3–5, assured President Suharto and Foreign Minister Adam Malik that the United States was not planning to set up a military base on Diego Garcia in the Indian Ocean, but that, on the contrary, U. S. policy was to reduce its military forces abroad and to cut the size of its navy. Malik stated that Indonesia had no objection to an American harbor in Diego Garcia, but that it did not want to see a superpower confrontation in the Indian Ocean.

Economy. As an important producer of petroleum, Indonesia has benefited from the rise in the price of oil. Production was 1.4 million barrels per day in 1973, and is scheduled to rise to 2 million barrels per day by 1976. The government is pressuring the oil companies for new contracts to increase its share of the profits. Oil exports earned nearly $1 billion in 1973—about half of the country's export earnings—and about $1.5 billion in 1974. The oil industry provides the government with nearly half of its tax receipts.

AMRY VANDENBOSCH
University of Kentucky

BETHLEHEM STEEL CORPORATION

Molten iron from a blast furnace enters a new "basic oxygen" furnace, where it will be mixed with scrap iron to make steel. Generally, 1974 was a good year for steel production.

INDUSTRIAL REVIEW

Industrial production showed a decline in major countries around the world in 1974, reflecting the recessionary climate and problems caused by soaring petroleum prices.

United States

U. S. industrial production held up fairly well in 1974, considering the energy crisis and weakening in economic activity in general. The brunt of the energy crisis was borne by the automobile industry. Most of the other industries fared better, thanks to the decision to favor the industrial fuel demand at the expense of consumers, especially the motoring public.

The coal strike and a very sharp drop in auto production at year-end suggested that final figures would show a decline of nearly 1% in the industrial production index rather than the 0.6% lag suggested by preliminary data for the first 11 months of 1974.

The industrial production index, prepared monthly by the Board of Governors of the Federal Reserve System, measures the physical volume of production by U. S. factories, mines, and utilities. It covers about two fifths of the nation's total output of goods and services and reflects current trends in the economy.

The decline in manufacturing output was centered in durable goods, especially transportation equipment, which was dragged down by the precipitous decline in auto production and a 3.5% drop in the production of the lumber, clay, and glass products group. The curtailed output in the latter reflected to a large extent the depressed situation in homebuilding.

Although producers of nondurable goods as a whole avoided a decline, the relatively strong showing was due to gains by chemicals, rubber and plastics, and food producers. There was a 5% drop in the output of the textile, apparel, and leather group. Most of that decrease was accounted for by apparel manufacturers. Tobacco products showed an output decline of 3%.

Metals. The steel industry operated at high levels through most of 1974, with output slackening in the last quarter of the year from the coal strike and the drop in auto production. Raw steel production reached a record 150.8 million short tons in 1973, and the tonnage poured during the first 11 months of 1974 was about 2% below the comparable 1973 period, indicating a total of 147 million tons for the year. The slackening steel demand in the second half of 1974 gave the producers a much-needed breather for maintenance and repair.

Steel mills shipped a record 111 million tons in 1973, greatly reducing their inventories. Shipments totaling 107 million tons were indicated for 1974. Since steel prices abroad were generally higher than in the United States, exports rose from 2.9 million tons in 1973 to about 6 million tons in 1974. Steel imports dropped from 15.2 million tons in 1973 to about 12 million tons in 1974.

Among nonferrous primary metals, aluminum output gained 8% and copper production dropped 15% from 1973. The nonferrous mill products output declined by 2%. Copper mill products dropped by 10%, while the output of aluminum mill products rose by 3%.

Automobiles. The automobile industry reeled from the twin blows of the energy crisis and the weakening economy in 1974, with production dropping by 25%. Passenger car production had reached an all-time high of 9.7 million units in 1973, but output for all of 1974 amounted to about 7.3 million. Higher prices heralded for 1975 models helped to sell the 1974 models but severely depressed the 1975 model run. In addition, many would-be auto buyers were wary of the catalytic converters requiring unleaded gasoline and were afraid that fuel for the 1975 models would be difficult to find in some areas. Truck production in 1974 reached 2.7 million units, down 10% from 1973.

Foods and Chemicals. Despite the national concern about energy, production of domestic fuels did not expand in 1974. Extraction of crude oil and natural gas declined in volume by about 3%. Production of bituminous coal had been running higher than in 1973 when 591.7 million short tons were produced, but the miners' strike that began on November 12 dashed any hope of sustaining the 7% output gain that had been maintained that far. Output of anthracite continued its long-term decline, with tonnage down from the previous year by 10%.

The production of chemicals and synthetic materials advanced 4% during 1974, thanks partly to efforts made to avoid serious shortages in feedstocks. Rubber and plastic products output also gained, by 1%. Petroleum refining dropped 3%. The only fuel to register an increase was residual fuel oil, used to fire heavy boilers, which showed a production gain of 8%.

Consumer Goods. In terms of final markets, consumer goods generally held up well, with an overall decline limited to a little over 2%. There was an almost 7% decline in consumer durables output. In addition to the sharp drop in automobile production, there were declines among home goods as well. The output of appliances and air-conditioning declined by about 7%, largely due to a lackluster housing market. Output of carpeting and furniture advanced by about 3%.

Consumers cut their fuel and lighting demand, aided by generally mild weather conditions, and brought about minor declines in the output of residential utilities. Clothing output dropped by nearly 6%. Production of consumer chemical products rose 3%. There was a small gain in the output of consumer paper products. In contrast to durables, the production of consumer softgoods generally remained level during the year.

Capital Spending. Manufacturing activity was buoyed by a 12% increase in business spending on plant and equipment, which rose to $112 billion in 1974. Capital spending growth was spearheaded by manufacturing industries, which hiked their outlays by 20%. Among durables producers, spending grew rapidly by aircraft manufacturers (45%) and by primary metals producers (40%). The highest spending increase in capital outlays by nondurables manufacturers was by paper producers (42%) and by petroleum firms (43%). Capital spending by the nonmanufacturing sector rose about 7% in 1974. Large outlays for the Alaska pipeline boosted the capital expenditures for the "other transportation group" by 34%. Railroads increased their outlays by 27%, while airlines cut their capital spending by 18%.

A new measure of capital expenditures for air and water pollution abatement was prepared by the Bureau of Economic Analysis in 1974. According to BEA, nonfarm business spent $4.9 billion in 1973 for new plant and equipment to combat air and water pollution, with $6.9 billion earmarked for similar 1974 outlays. About two thirds of antipollution spending goes for improving air quality.

Benefiting from the strength in capital outlays, production of business equipment advanced more than 6%. Especially strong was the gain in the output of building and mining equipment, which grew by 13%. Manufacturing equipment production increased by 8%. Commercial and farm equipment output also advanced strongly. Gains in the production of power and transit equipment were fractional. Defense and space equipment production increased by 2%, but amounted to only 82% of the 1967 level.

Other Statistics. Manufacturing industries employed 19 million workers in 1972, according to the 1972 Census of Manufactures released by the Bureau of the Census in May 1974. That was 556,000 more than in 1971. Manufacturing industries' payrolls amounted to $173 billion, an 11% increase over the preceding year.

Value added by manufacture reached $353 billion, almost $38 billion or 12% higher than in 1971. "Value added" is the difference between the value of shipments and the value of materials, supplies, etc., used in production.

The Federal Reserve Board's measure of capacity utilization by producers of major materials reached a record 93.3 during the year. The index held steady at 90.2 through the first half of 1974 and dropped to 88.3 in the third quarter. The capacity utilization rate for durables receded from 91.8 in 1973 to 85.6 in the third quarter of 1974, after hovering around 90 in the first half. The rate for nondurables was a record 93.9 in 1973, but slackened to 89.2 in the third quarter of 1974.

AGO AMBRE, *Current Business Analysis Division, Bureau of Economic Analysis, U. S. Department of Commerce*

UPI

Two 45,000-ton cargo ships are built simultaneously in the Ponto do Caju dockyard in Rio de Janeiro, Brazil, the Western Hemisphere's largest dockyard.

World Developments

World industrial production slowed down considerably throughout 1974, as the United States and West Germany experienced a decline in overall economic activity and Japan, the United Kingdom, and Canada registered very substantial slowdowns in their growth rates. In France and Italy, overall economic growth slowed substantially during the year.

The average annual growth rates for industrial production at the end of 1974 show the following picture for developed countries in comparison with a year earlier: United States —4.3%; Japan, —9.5%; West Germany, —3.8%; France, 4%; United Kingdom, —1.6%; Italy, —5.2%; and Canada, 5.3%.

These rates of change compare unfavorably with the average growth rates these countries experienced since 1970, which were 3.8% for the United States, 5.2% for Japan, 2.4% for West Germany, 6.2% for France, 2.2% for the United Kingdom, 4% for Italy, and 5.8% tor Canada.

Durable Goods. The production of durable goods rose generally worldwide in 1974, as the long-term outlook was strong for such items as engines and turbines, electrical equipment, railway equipment, aircraft and parts, and ships. Since a push was underway to develop energy, the demand was strong for oil-drilling equipment.

Hit hard by the high cost of oil and weakening consumer demand were consumer durables, notably automobiles. Auto production dropped 25% in the United States, about 20% in West Germany, and more than 10% in the United Kingdom. The French auto industry experienced its worst crisis in the post-World War II period, and Italian auto output also was severely curtailed toward year-end. Complicating the auto outlook was the Japanese export drive, which is especially irritating to Europeans who note with dismay that Japan sold 15 times more autos in Europe in 1973 than it bought from European manufacturers.

Nondurable Goods. Consumer softgoods production was sluggish. This was reflected in the output of man-made fibers, which declined in 1974, with weakness showing up first in Europe and Asia around the middle of the year and spreading to the United States toward year-end. There was a worldwide tightness in the supply of raw materials, but with some major producers cutting production by approximately 30% the supply situation loosened up in the second half of the year.

Prices. The slowing world industrial production was accompanied by some price declines in industrial commodities, but inflation still remained rampant. Industrial wholesale prices increased almost 30% from a year earlier in the United States, Japan, and France. Italian prices rose almost 50%. Canada and the United Kingdom saw their price indexes for industrial commodities rise by over one fourth. West Germany, with an over-the-year boost of less than 20%, had the best price performance among the large industrial market economies.

Steel Capacity. Expansion of production capacity of basic industry received considerable emphasis in 1974. The steel industry's capacity increased 9% worldwide, to 835 million tons. Ranking highest in production capacity in 1974 was the United States, with about 160 million tons. That represented a 6½% increase in capacity, considerably below the worldwide gain. The Soviet Union raised its steel production capacity to nearly 153 million tons, up 5.3% from 1973. Japan's raw steel capacity increased 10.5%, to 145 million tons. West Germany added fastest to capacity in 1974—11%—and brought its capacity to over 60 million tons.

Japan. The "miracle growth" of Japan was severely set back in 1974. Industrial production in Japan was about 7% below year-earlier levels in September 1974. The country imports all its oil, and one reaction to the precipitous rise in oil prices was a concerted export drive that helped stem the slide in industrial production. For example, although domestic passenger car sales dropped more than one third in 1974, unit output declined little more than 10%. But overseas markets were not readily absorbing the influx. Thus shipments of Japanese cars to the United States for most of the year ran some 40% ahead of actual sales.

In addition to automakers, other industries hit hard by the Japanese recession were textiles and plywood. The slackening industrial demand spurred producers of such basic metals as copper, lead, zinc, and steel to redouble their export efforts, but even so some major producers announced output cuts of over 10% as the year drew to a close.

Soviet Union. Industrial production in the Soviet Union is projected to grow 8% per year during the current 5-year plan, which covers the 1971–75 period. The growth in 1974 was about 8.3%, compared with 7.4% in 1973.

The purpose of Soviet economic planning is to coordinate the activities of the thousands of economic units to do the job that market mechanisms accomplish in Western countries, and to set the directions and growth rates of economic development.

Thus the Soviet 5-year plans reflect investment strategy, general guidelines, and a fairly narrow range of choices for the annual plans. The annual plans take into account problems and shortages of the immediate past, and adjustments are made that may change the original goals of the 5-year plan.

An example of such plan modification is the huge Kama River Automotive Factory, a prime example of planning on a grandiose scale. Original plans called for the immense complex, capable of turning out 150,000 trucks and 250,000 diesel engines a year, to go into production in 1974. But cranking in more than $1 billion in Western technology and equipment involved design and delivery problems, which on top of admitted Soviet management inadequacies and low productivity have combined to push back plant completion at least two years.

The current Soviet plan specifies highest production growth in machinery and chemicals (11.5% per year). In machinery, goals are especially high for passenger cars, agricultural machinery, instruments, and consumer durables. The targets for chemicals are high for fertilizers, plastics, man-made fibers, and synthetic rubber. Soviet fuel supplies are ample; crude oil production reached about 460 million metric tons in 1974, putting it slightly ahead of the U. S. crude oil output.

The Soviet Union is increasingly looking to Western technology in order to meet its goals. It placed a huge order with West German firms for equipment and technology for a direct reduction steel plant. Large orders were placed in the United States for mining machinery, tractors and bulldozers, and canning machinery. Orders for equipment for the Kama River truck plant have been placed in almost all major industrial countries. Soviet industry is highly interested in importing production know-how for high-technology products, especially for such strategic items as wide-bodied jets, computers, and integrated circuitry.

Soviet plans also rely on productivity increases to fulfill production goals. Early reports indicate labor productivity rose more than 6%, thus lending credence to the 7.5% increase in the production of consumer goods slated for 1974.

Oil Producers. Industrial production was the focus of interest in oil-rich countries, especially Iran, Venezuela, Nigeria, Indonesia, and Malaysia. Iran, with an infrastructure and basic

Quality control is one key to the popularity of products made in Japan. Here a project engineer checks the adjustment on a color television set in a Yokohama factory.

WIDE WORLD

TASS, FROM SOVFOTO

Tractors from the Minsk, USSR, Tractor Works stand in a storage yard, awaiting shipment all over the world.

industry more or less in place, is force-feeding its industrial development, buying into such basic firms as West Germany's Krupp, and looking forward to obtaining five nuclear reactors from France as part of a 10-year development agreement involving a total of $4 billion. The Middle East idea is to extract Arab oil, to have it refined in Arab refineries, and to have the feedstocks processed by Arab petrochemical industry. Such ambitions will keep the durables manufacturers in the industrialized countries of the world busy filling and competing for orders.

The impact of the quadrupling of oil prices shocked such countries as India, which had been hoping to expand their production of fertilizers. These countries had built substantial fertilizer production capacity, but much of their effort seems to have been wasted in view of the fact that the basic raw material, petroleum, has been priced out of reach. As a case in point, India is spending about $100 million a year out of its meager resources to support oil exploration.

Oil companies have undertaken enormous exploration commitments in Southeast Asia, as the pressure grows to discover petroleum reserves outside the Middle East.

Manufacturing in Asia. The industrialization of southeast Asia is proceeding apace. The Philippines and Indonesia have joined Hong Kong, Taiwan, South Korea, Malaysia, and Singapore as attractive manufacturing areas. For example, Singapore has attracted more than 100 factories from international manufacturers over the past five years, representing an investment of about $1.2 billion, about half of it coming from U. S. corporations. Well over 400 American corporations now have operations in Singapore.

It is the low wages—the average pay in manufacturing in Singapore is about one fifth of that in the United States—that give the products assembled in Asia a sharp competitive edge. This is especially true of electronic products, from television sets to computers, that carry nameplates known the world over. These products contain parts and circuits that have been assembled, wired, and soldered by Asian women.

The Developing Countries. Industrial development in the developing countries of the world continued to shift emphasis from exporting basically raw materials to processing them into exportable semiprocessed and finished goods. This has meant growth in labor-intensive industries such as electronics, apparel, furniture, and canned goods.

Mining. Inspired by the effective cartel of the oil-producing countries, which succeeded in quadrupling the world price of crude oil, countries producing bauxite, iron ore, and copper sought to increase revenues from their commodities. Thus Jamaica increased ninefold the tax that U. S. aluminum companies pay on the Jamaican bauxite they mine.

International resource firms were increasingly faced with demands for more local participation and outright nationalization. But the efforts of major copper producers—Chile, Zaire, Peru, and Zambia—which control two thirds of the world's copper trade, fell apart in the face of market forces. Manufacturers all over the world took large inventory losses as the price broke on the metal they had stocked up on at the peak of the market. Indeed, no major commodity agreement except the one for oil has survived the price cycle of 1973–74.

AGO AMBRE, *Current Business Analysis Division, Bureau of Economic Analysis U. S. Department of Commerce*

INSURANCE

The insurance business in the United States continued in 1974 to adjust to a changing social and economic environment. Consumerism, inflation, and competition all were catalysts in the process.

PROPERTY AND LIABILITY INSURANCE

There was a significant deterioration in underwriting results, producing a net underwriting gain of approximately $5.76 million (down from $1.1 billion in 1972) for the property-liability insurance business in 1973, according to the Insurance Information Institute. This dip in underwriting profits came as a result of governmental controls holding insurance rates stable at the same time that inflation was pushing up the costs of items and services for which insurance pays.

Premium volume increased about 7%, from $39.3 billion in 1972 to just over $42 billion in 1973. Net investment income also increased to $3.2 billion in 1973, almost 18.7% higher than in 1972.

Automobile Insurance. More state legislatures have evidenced interest in proposals for change from the traditional third-party liability system of automobile insurance to a principally first-party system under which a person who suffers a loss is compensated by his own insurance company. Six more states adopted auto insurance reform laws providing motorists with benefits covering medical bills, loss of wages, and loss of services on a no-fault basis, while limiting the right to sue another driver for damages. A seventh state passed a law that requires that motorists be offered first-party benefits but does not restrict the right to sue. As of July 31, 24 states had laws that mandate or require the offer of first-party benefits (5 of these states enacted such legislation during the first seven months of 1974).

While reduced speed limits and other restrictions on the use of automobiles resulted in improvements in the traffic accident toll, an industry study committee found that an accelerated rate of increase in claim costs had offset a decline in claims frequency. Traffic fatalities dropped from 56,600 in 1972 to 55,800, but injuries and the number of accidents increased during 1973. Resulting dollar losses were estimated at $30.4 billion.

Other Developments. Fire losses in the United States in 1973 exceeded $2 billion for the fourth consecutive year, reaching a record of $2.64 billion, but nevertheless were slightly lower for the second consecutive year. A record number of tornadoes (1,109) was the main ingredient in pushing insured catastrophic losses during 1973 to some $293 million, up from $210 million in 1972.

Federal legislation to broaden the national flood-insurance program contributed to a sharp rise in the number of homes and businesses across the United States insured against flood damage.

LIFE INSURANCE

The average insured family in the United States had $28,800 worth of life insurance at the start of 1974. This amounted to more than 2¼ years of that family's disposable personal income.

Purchases and Payments. New life insurance purchases in the United States amounted to $234 billion in 1973. Of this sum, $170 billion represented individually purchased ordinary and industrial life insurance. New purchases of group life insurance totaled $64 billion. During 1973, life insurance companies paid $20 billion in benefits to policyholders, annuitants, and other beneficiaries.

Investments. Assets of the 1,815 legal reserve life insurance companies totaled over $252 billion on Jan. 1, 1974. Corporate securities accounted for 46.7% and mortgages for 32.2% of these investment holdings. Loans to policyholders reached 8.0% of the total assets of insurance companies. The net pretax earning rate on life insurance company investments in 1972 was 5.88%.

Private Pension System. The life insurance business supported the passage of legislation designed to improve and strengthen the private pension system. The elements supported included mandatory minimum vesting, mandatory minimum funding standards, increased disclosure of important information to participants in the plans, and higher standards of accountability for those handling the pension funds.

The so-called Pension Reform Bill, which was signed into law Sept. 2, 1974, will have a major impact on the United States private pension system. The life insurance business should benefit from this legislation, since it represents general congressional agreement that private pension plans should be encouraged. A massive overhaul of something like 1.8 million existing plans will be required.

HEALTH INSURANCE

A record 182 million persons had health insurance through private organizations in the United States at the start of 1974. Private health insurance policyholders received $22.9 billion in benefit payments in 1973. The coverage was provided by insurance companies, Blue Cross-Blue Shield organizations, other plans approved by medical societies, and independent plans.

Since life insurance companies provide much of the nation's health insurance, they were deeply involved in the growing debate over various national health care proposals. (For a discussion of these proposals, see SOCIAL WELFARE: Health Insurance.)

KENNETH BLACK, JR.
Georgia State University

STEVE LEVIN, COURTESY PARAMOUNT THEATRE OF THE ARTS

An old movie palace becomes a community cultural center, as the Paramount Theatre in Oakland, Calif., is restored to its 1920's Art Deco grandeur.

INTERIOR DESIGN

"Interiors worth saving are far too numerous and diverse to be saved, except in a fragmentary way, by laws alone; and the strategies of adaptive reuse and historic enshrinement can salvage only a few more pieces. Preserving a large portion of this heritage—really intact—is a matter of broader public policy; it demands maintaining the circumstances that keep such spaces active and raising public awareness of their quality." (John Morris Dixon, *Progressive Architecture,* December 1973.)

Restoration and rehabilitation of old buildings are not new. The old city of Paris, for example, is one large restoration. But there is an increasing awareness today that in the rebuilding of our cities something worth saving is being lost. Perhaps modern architecture has gone too far in dictating the way we should live. Perhaps the idea of disposability has gone too far. Perhaps we should recycle what we have instead of demanding something new.

In any event, many old buildings are being recreated for contemporary uses. This is not just restoration in the true sense; rather, it is rehabilitation. Fortunately the interiors of the buildings are often changed only superficially, with reconstruction accommodating such concessions as elevators, plumbing, and air-conditioning. The architecture and materials of these old buildings are emphatic, and those who recreate show great responsiveness toward the old.

The interior architecture, usually stripped of unnecessary ornamentation, becomes the surrounding. It sets the stage for new furnishings, which are generally sparse and, whether old or new, are honestly designed, their texture blending with the textures of the old spaces.

The creative mind has found new functions for buildings originally designed for other purposes, as shown in the following examples.

Universities. A crumbling 17th century convent in Urbino, Italy, has been given a new life to function as a law school, thanks to the foresight and sensitivity of architect Giancarlo deCarlo, who has created a facility of great beauty. Shaving the interiors down to the structural bare wooden bones and ancient bricks of the high Romanesque arches and walls, and without superimposing any new architectural feature, deCarlo has created a thoroughly modern series of spaces. Furnishings, classic modern in style, are sparse, and their simple profiles punctuate the serene spaces as sculptural forms.

Reconversion of old buildings for schools, rather than the building of new ones, is gaining some advocacy in the United States. Reconversion not only solves the problem of acquiring new sites where land is scarce but also prevents the decay of inner-city buildings. Such was the case in Baltimore, where the Mount Royal railroad station (1896) was adapted by architects Cochran, Stephenson and Donkervoet into the library, cafeteria, sculpture studio, and gallery of the Maryland Institute College of Art. The old high-vaulted interior created an impressive background, and the aged floor-to-ceiling windows give ample light (resulting in a decided savings in fuel costs). Unlike the cubicles allotted in new facilities, these rooms provide ample space for group movement and personal activity. The furnishings are functional and minimal.

Concert Hall. The charismatic essence of Hollywood may be found in those great emporia dedicated to the film—the Paramount theaters. Many of these old palaces are in ruins, and many have been torn down, but one (dating from 1931) has been saved in all its extravagant Art Deco glory: the Paramount Theatre of the Arts in Oakland, Calif., which was opened on Sept. 22, 1973. Various architects, designers, and consultants have made the building responsive to the needs of a concert hall. Every embossed lacquer and gilt wall panel was reburnished, lighting fixtures were cleaned, carpets and mohair fabrics were recreated, and furniture was restored. It was hoped that the old Wurlitzer organ, found in a pizza parlor, might be reinstalled.

Museum. In Cuenca, Spain, an old castle has been converted into a museum. The Andalusian brass-studded doors, the beams, arched doorways, and curvilinear stairways are architectural considerations balanced with the wall-hung modern paintings.

Residences. It is not extraordinary to find families searching out old buildings that can be converted into residences. Those who choose to live the modern life in small architectural gems of great age may travel throughout the world to find them.

On the small island of Elba, off the west coast of Italy, the German architect Edgar Jeuch has rehabilitated a charming 17th century cluster-house as a residence. In the Cotswolds in England, architect Anthony Cloughly and interior designers Tom Parr and David Hicks have restored an 18th century manor house to its former glory, for use as both a residence and a factory for Peter Saunders.

In Winston-Salem, N. C., Eldridge Hanes has restored an 18th century missionary-horticulturist's house, and the Rauschenburg family has converted a tiny tailor's workshop into a permanent home. Both buildings are on the outskirts of Old Salem, an 18th century Moravian village that has been completely restored by local Moravian residents.

What each of these conversions has in common with the general trend is the excitement of discovering dispirited architectural gems, rehabilitating them, and spending years of active life refining the interior furnishings to enhance or relate to the beautiful old architecture.

JEANNE WEEKS
Associate, National Society of Interior Designers

An old railroad station in Baltimore, Md., is redesigned for use by an art school. The entrance court is below, and the library is on the second level.

GEORGE CSERNA, COURTESY COCHRAN, STEPHENSON & DONKERVOET

UPI

Saudi Arabia's delegation attends meeting of the Organization of the Petroleum Exporting Countries, which discussed lifting the oil embargo against the United States.

international finance

At the start of 1974 members of the Organization of Petroleum Exporting Countries (OPEC) raised petroleum prices fourfold. Thus, overnight, they delivered the largest single shock to the world economy since World War II. This increase in the price of oil placed enormous pressures on the international financial system.

During 1974 alone, the deficit of all oil-importing countries vis-à-vis OPEC was expected to increase by $45 to $65 billion. By the end of 1985 accumulated OPEC reserves were forecast to rise above $375 billion.

RECYCLING OIL REVENUES

The immediate problem was that of financing the higher cost of oil imports. To the extent that the oil-exporting countries increase their oil revenues faster than their imports of goods and services—thus preventing the rest of the world from paying for the increased cost of oil imports with increased exports—they must lend or invest their surplus in the oil-importing countries. Thus, at a global level, there is necessarily sufficient credit available from OPEC to finance the aggregate oil deficit. The principal financial problem arises from the fact that, while the global totals must balance, the distribution of oil deficits among importing countries may differ substantially from the distribution of OPEC investments. The process of rechanneling the surplus revenues of the oil-exporting countries to countries where they are needed to finance oil deficits is known as "recycling."

Efforts to recycle oil revenues were quite successful during 1974; no major country was unable to pay for the increased cost of its oil imports. Recycling was accomplished through direct lending from OPEC and through the intermediation of private and official financial institutions.

A substantial amount of financing took the form of produced credits, inasmuch as oil payments did not increase until four months after the increase in oil prices. In addition, several OPEC members lent directly to some of the poorest nations.

But most of the flow of funds between OPEC and the oil importers has occurred through the banking system. The Eurodollar market, the offshore market in dollar deposits, proved remarkably adaptable as both borrowers from oil-importing countries and lenders from oil-exporting countries sharply stepped up their demands on the market.

Early in the year official and semiofficial borrowers in the United Kingdom, Italy, and France obtained loan commitments totaling $10 billion in anticipation of mounting oil deficits. Developing countries also increased borrowings sharply, as did public-sector institutions in Spain and Greece. In addition, banks in the United States substantially increased their loans to foreigners. Toward year-end, however, the pace of new lending slowed markedly both in the Eurodollar market and in the United States as banks found themselves in an increasingly risky position with respect to both their loans and deposits.

Official international financial institutions played a comparatively minor role in recycling oil revenues during 1974. In September the International Monetary Fund (IMF) announced the first drawing from its special oil facility, which was funded with $3.5 billion provided largely by the oil-exporting countries. By year-end more than 26 countries had made drawings which nearly depleted the facility. During the year there were several proposals to increase official involvement in the recycling of oil revenues.

EXCHANGE RATE MOVEMENTS AND PAYMENTS ADJUSTMENTS

The economic impact of higher oil prices dominated events in the foreign exchange markets and balance of payments developments, exacerbating the difficulties policymakers faced in most industrial countries as they attempted to slow the rate of inflation without halting economic growth.

United States. During the last quarter of 1973 the outbreak of fighting in the Middle East and the rationing of petroleum exports by the Arabs led to an appreciation of the dollar relative to the yen and European currencies, principally because the United States is relatively less dependent on external supplies of petroleum. By early January 1974, the dollar had risen against some currencies to levels which prevailed before the second devaluation of the dollar in February 1973, thus reversing the substantial depreciation of the first half of 1973.

This appreciation of the dollar and the shift of U. S. trade and payments balances into surplus during the last half of 1973 led U. S. officials to move ahead of their announced schedule in abolishing controls on capital outflows. In a coordinated announcement on January 29, the Federal Reserve Board, the Commerce Department, and the Treasury announced the termination of the capital controls programs which they had administered. These capital control programs had been imposed in stages since 1963 in an attempt to improve the U. S. balance of payments position.

Both in response to this relaxation of capital controls and in response to an easing of U. S. interest rates relative to those abroad, there were substantial capital outflows from February through May, and dollar rates fell steadily against most European currencies. By mid-May the dollar had fallen 21% below its January high against the mark. The subsequent recovery of the dollar in late spring and throughout the summer was accompanied by generally favorable trends in the U. S. trade balance excluding petroleum, an increase in U. S. interest rates relative to those abroad, and a shift of OPEC funds into U. S. credit markets as the capacity of European banks to handle short-term placements became saturated.

During the first three quarters of the year 1974, the U. S. trade balance was in deficit $2.3 billion. This figure, however, concealed a substantial strengthening of the surplus on non-petroleum trade relative to the early 1970's. Petroleum imports accounted for about one fourth of the value of U. S. imports even though their quantity declined during the year relative to the previous year, in which they accounted for roughly one tenth of the value of the nation's total imports.

Canada. Because Canada is largely self-sufficient in oil, its trade balance was not much affected by the sharp rise in oil prices. Moreover, as a major exporter of raw materials and industrial commodities, Canada continued to benefit from historically high commodity prices. Throughout 1974 the Canadian dollar was relatively steady against the U. S. dollar, although the average level of the exchange rate was somewhat higher than during 1973.

Italy. The steep rise in oil prices had especially grave implications for Italy, which depends on oil for nearly 80% of its energy needs and which, apart from the oil problem, began the year with a substantial balance-of-trade deficit. In addition, Italy was beset with serious political and social problems that impeded efforts to initiate effective policies to restore external balance.

Throughout much of the year the Bank of Italy intervened in the exchange market to support the lira. This intervention was financed primarily with borrowing from Italy's Common Market partners and with medium-term borrowing in the Eurodollar market.

In an effort to reduce the payments deficit, the Italian authorities tightened monetary policy, raised taxes, imposed a 50% import-deposit requirement, and attempted to reduce government expenditures. Nevertheless, the current account deficit was expected to total almost $10 billion, which, along with that of Britain, would rank as the largest deficit among industrial countries.

West Germany. Despite the impact of higher oil prices and the appreciation of the mark relative to most other major currencies over the past four years, the German trade surplus increased to nearly $14 billion in the first three quarters of 1974, twice the $7 billion surplus in the same period of 1973. Although this development was in part a result of the *relative* success of German policymakers in combating inflation, the magnitude of the German surplus placed considerable pressure on other industrialized countries already burdened with enormous oil deficits.

The dollar/mark exchange rate displayed considerable variability. At several points during the year both the Federal Reserve and the Bundesbank intervened in the dollar/mark exchange market in order to moderate day-to-day fluctuations in the exchange rate.

INTERNATIONAL FINANCIAL CONDITIONS

Gold. Gold prices were quite volatile although generally higher than during the previous year. During the year President Ford signed a bill, effective Dec. 31, 1974, which permits U. S. citizens to own gold, thus ending a 41-year ban. Later the Treasury announced that almost 1% of its 276 million-ounce gold stock would be sold at auction early in 1975 to mitigate the balance of payments impact of gold purchases by U. S. residents.

In December, President Ford and French President Valéry Giscard d'Estaing agreed that "it would be appropriate for any government that wished to do so to adopt current market prices as the basis of valuation of its gold holdings," rather than the official price of $42.22 an ounce. Each of these events had significant impact on the market price of gold.

Interest Rates. Central bank discount rates were at or near record levels in most major industrial countries as governments continued to tighten monetary policy in order to combat inflation. Interest rates in the Eurodollar market rose to record levels as borrowers sought to finance the higher cost of oil imports. New issues of Eurobonds decreased markedly.

In late spring and early summer news of substantial losses in foreign exchange trading in several large banks and the closing of Bankhaus Herstatt in Germany led to significant dislocations in financial markets and to a reduction in flows to all but the most prestigious banks. This exacerbated the already difficult problem of recycling oil revenues and threatened the liquidity of banks in several nations. Central banks took several measures to insure bank liquidity and monitor foreign exchange trading in an effort to shore up confidence in the international banking system.

Mrs. Mary Brooks, director of the mint, is surrounded by gold bars in Fort Knox. On Dec. 31, 1974, U. S. residents were allowed to buy gold for the first time in 41 years.

UPI

INTERNATIONAL MONETARY REFORM

Attempts to reform the international monetary system were forestalled by the necessity of dealing with the immediate consequences of higher oil prices. The IMF Committee of Twenty, which had been given the responsibility of drawing the blueprint for a new world monetary system, produced instead a set of interim arrangements to deal with current international monetary difficulties.

The package of interim measures included: the establishment of an oil facility within the IMF in order to help finance oil deficits; the establishment of guidelines for the management of floating exchange rates in order to prevent competitive depreciations; and an agreement to value the SDR (Special Drawing Right) in terms of a "basket" of 16 currencies and to increase the interest rate on the SDR to 5% in order to enhance its usefulness in settling payments imbalances.

Although the international financial system proved remarkably resilient during 1974, by year-end there were signs of strain. Trade deficits in several countries had deepened, the rate of bank lending had slowed, and borrowers in many oil-importing countries found it increasingly difficult to obtain financing.

As oil-importing countries encounter greater difficulties in obtaining additional funds and as they become more reluctant to accumulate further debt, there is an increasing likelihood that some countries will take unilateral measures to shift the burden of their oil deficit to their trade partners. While it is possible for one oil-importing country to reduce its overall deficit by depreciating its exchange rate, deflating its economy, or imposing direct controls on trade or capital flows, the oil-importing countries as a group cannot reduce their oil deficit unless they can increase their exports to (or reduce their imports from) the Organization of Petroleum Exporting Countries.

Because the capacity of OPEC members to absorb additional goods and services is quite limited in the short run, unilateral attempts to reduce individual deficits are likely to lead to a proliferation of trade barriers and capital controls with a consequent decline in world trade and investment. Thus it is of utmost importance that the oil-importing nations continue to seek mutually satisfactory means of dealing with the oil deficit.

RICHARD J. HERRING
University of Pennsylvania

UPI

New Japanese automobiles on a Yokohama dock await shipment to the United States. During the 1973–74 gasoline shortage, the U. S. market for small cars jumped dramatically.

international trade

Inflation and oil prices were the chief determinants of international trade in 1974. World exports were expected to total $750 billion, 35% above the 1973 level of $518 billion. If price increases are taken into consideration, however, that total represented a "real" increase of no more than 5% over the preceding year. A sizable share of the inflation in trade values stemmed from the explosive increase in the price of crude petroleum that came into effect at the end of 1973.

U. S. trade, which had moved into surplus through the first half of the year, shifted to a deficit again as a result of the rise in oil prices. Most nations not exporting oil experienced imbalances in their trade for this (as well as for other) reasons—the notable exceptions being Germany and, by the third quarter, Japan.

In its final action under the 93d Congress, the Senate passed the Trade Act of 1974, which had been enacted by the House of Representatives in 1973. President Ford signed the bill in a special White House ceremony on Jan. 3, 1975.

TRADE TRENDS

Despite widespread economic recession in Europe, Japan, and the United States, world trade values grew to peak levels, fed by inflation. With few exceptions, prices of industrial materials, which had jumped in 1973 because of shortages in the face of a worldwide economic boom, continued to rise, at least through the first nine months. Food prices soared, partly as a result of poor harvest in certain key producing and consuming countries, and partly as a result of rising world demand. But the major inflationary price shock resulted from the nearly four-fold increase in the price of oil, most of which occurred abruptly on January 1. Faced with few immediate alternatives other than reduced consumption, countries had to cope with enormous increases in import bills, which had to be paid from new earnings, borrowings, or reductions in reserves.

In an effort to prevent destructive trade action among the industrial countries as they tried to bring their international payments back into balance, the United States urged the 24-member Organization for Economic Cooperation and Development to adopt a trade-standstill declaration. This statement, agreed at the May 29–30 ministerial meeting, was an expression of political intention and was not legally binding. The member countries expressed their determination, in dealing with the economic situation arising from the oil crisis in the year ahead, to avoid restrictive measures on imports and new programs to stimulate exports.

United States. Inflationary pressures had a strong impact on U. S. foreign trade in 1974. Three-fourths of the 35% rise in the value of exports through September was accounted for by price increases alone, while all of the 42% import advance resulted from this cause. In the first nine months exports totalled $95.4 billion at an annual rate. Imports exceeded exports by $3.1 billion to reach $98.6 billion. Thus, trade moved again into deficit after recording a $1.3 billion surplus in the previous year.

U. S. Exports. Exports grew much more slowly in "real" terms than in 1973 because of the slowing in economic growth in most of the major industrial nations that form the country's principal markets. Despite this, machinery sales showed sizable gains as investment in plant and equipment abroad remained strong and demand for U. S. technically sophisticated equipment continued. Exports of industrial goods also gained, but most of the advance stemmed from price increases. For example, coal and steel sales doubled in value, but the quantity increases were small.

Following a boom year in 1973, agricultural exports jumped again, rising to $16.5 billion in the first nine months. This total represented a 33% increase over the preceding year, but no change in the quantity of products shipped. Prices were pushed upward as a result of the tight world supply situation, the reduction of grain stocks to the lowest level in many years, and, by autumn, the disappointing level of the 1974 harvest—especially for corn and soybeans.

U. S. Imports. The huge jump in the price of petroleum was the major factor causing imports to rise so sharply in value. Though the quantity of imports of petroleum and petroleum products dropped by 3%, the value of these imports shot up to $17.9 billion in January–September compared with $5.1 billion in the same months of 1973. Higher prices—not so spectacular as those for oil—were also the main cause of increased values for imports of most metals, paper products, and chemicals.

Among consumer products, foreign automobiles arrived in much greater numbers than in 1973, but as sales were lower, inventories began to build up by midyear. Many other such imports, including TV's, radios, footwear, and clothing, for years on a strongly rising import trend, changed little. Food entries were about one-fourth higher in value, as prices of sugar, coffee, meat, and fish advanced.

The U. S. trade balance improved with every major area of the world except the oil-exporting developing countries and the socialist nations. Imports from the oil countries through September rose by $10.3 billion, while exports increased only $2.2 billion. The balance with the developing areas shifted by $4 billion, from a deficit to a $2 billion surplus.

U. S. Balance of Payments. Measured by the basic balance, U. S. international transactions were in deficit in the first six months by $1 billion. This was a deterioration from the $1.3 billion surplus in the preceding half, but it was a considerable improvement over the first half of 1973.

In January–June, the trade position on a payment basis moved to a sharply negative position. In contrast, the surplus in the services account rose sharply, mostly reflecting larger petroleum company earnings overseas and higher foreign interest rates. Government grants climbed to $4 billion, three times the level in either half of 1973. This growth was largely due to a grant to India, used by that country to repay loans made over many years by the United States for economic assistance. Net outflows of private capital increased to reflect greater lending by U. S. banks.

The official reserve transactions balance, the overall payments measure which includes volatile short-term capital flows and errors and omissions, was in deficit by $3.5 billion through June, a major shift from the $4.6 billion surplus in the last half of 1973. The large outflow was related to loans to other nations, so they could pay their higher oil bills.

Canada. Canada's imports in the first nine months of the year advanced at a faster pace than exports. Though its surplus in foreign trade was reduced, it remained positive. Through September, exports, with a value of Canadian $23.2 billion, were 28% above exports in the same months of 1973, while imports rose by 35.5% to C$22.7 billion.

Canadian export prices rose very sharply in 1974, influenced by higher prices for petroleum and agricultural products. When account is taken of the 37% price rise, the actual volume of goods sold is found to have dropped from the preceding year by 6%. Especially strong were increases in the price charged for petroleum. Canada levied a large export tax in order to match world prices. These world prices had to be paid by the eastern Canadian provinces that imported oil. Import prices rose slightly less than those for exports, resulting in a small 5% increase in the volume of imports.

Major gains in Canadian exports over the previous year were reported for petroleum, wheat, woodpulp, and newsprint, all largely due to price changes. Among imports, Canada paid out much more not only for petroleum, but also for sugar, coal, and steel. For all these products, prices were higher than in 1973.

The Canadian balance of payments deficit on current account totalled C$1.0 billion in the first half of the year. Although various service items —particularly Canadian travel expenditures and development assistance contributions—accounted for the deficit in the first quarter, a decline in the trade account was mainly responsible in the second quarter. A net capital inflow of C$1.3 billion in the first half offset the current account imbalance and produced an increase in Canada's official monetary assets of about C$350 million.

Western Europe. Despite the slowdown in the economic growth of most of West Europe's major trading partners, West European exports continued to soar in value in the first half at the same high 36% rate as in the boom year of 1973. In most European countries, however, inflation was running at higher levels than the year before, and the increase in real exports accounted for only a fraction of that advance.

Many of the nations were also in balance of payments difficulties as a result of the large price increases for oil. Heavily dependent on such imports, the nations found that these changes had a severe effect on their net outflows of funds. Many took steps to reduce consumption in order to alleviate somewhat this sudden sharp imbalance.

Moving contrary to the general trend was the economy of the Federal Republic of Germany. In that country, general prosperity and a low rate of inflation and unemployment accompanied soaring exports and a modest import increase. Exports at an annual rate of $88 billion in the first nine months exceeded imports by $20 billion.

It was anticipated that net export earnings for the year would be close to double the 1973 surplus, despite some slowing down in sales after midyear. The West German economy itself was growing at less than half its normal rate, which accounted for the fact that import volume through September was 3.7% below the same period of 1973. The strength and buoyancy of the economy was in fact almost entirely led by exports, as demand for West German goods soared throughout the world.

Almost the only bright side to the British economic picture was the strength of export demand. Through September, that country's sales to foreign countries climbed in value by 28% to $26.5 billion. Even this growth represented only a 4% increase in quantity over January–September 1973. Exports of machinery and chemicals were especially buoyant. Road vehicle sales, reflecting the sluggish worldwide car market, were up only modestly, and those of textiles, another large British export, advanced little over the preceding year. As in other industrialized countries, fuel showed the largest import increase. On a net basis, fuel import costs rose from an average of £29 million per month in 1973 to £340 per month through August, with only marginal increases in quantities.

To stem France's high rate of inflation and redress its deteriorating trade position, the French government instituted new programs to reduce domestic demand. A restrictive monetary limitation was placed on imports of oil in an emergency bill passed in October. Through July, the French trade deficit had already reached $2.3 billion, largely as a result of price increases on imported oil.

TARIFFS AND TRADE REGULATIONS

Of the nearly 700 trade and related bills introduced in the 93d Congress, the one with the most potential impact on the majority of citizens was HR 10710—the Trade Act of 1974. The new act, passed after 20 months of congressional deliberations, authorizes the president to enter into agreements with foreign countries for five years to reduce tariffs by 60% on items with present rates of duty over 5%, and to eliminate tariffs on items with duties of 5% or less. He may also negotiate agreements to harmonize, reduce, or eliminate nontariff barriers affecting U. S. exports.

The president is further empowered to extend nondiscriminatory, most-favored-nation tariff treatment to countries not now receiving such treatment, in return for appropriate benefits to the United States. A nonmarket economy country is ineligible to receive such treatment, however, unless the president determines that it does not deny its citizens the right to emigrate. Development of a compromise on this provision was largely responsible for the long delay in Senate passage of the act. Authority also is granted for the president to give tariff preferences to imports from developing countries for ten years. Finally, criteria providing for relief from import injury are significantly liberalized.

In spite of delays in passage of this act, work proceeded during the year on the organization of the seventh round of multilateral negotiations under the General Agreement on Tariffs and Trade (GATT). When the bill became law, it was expected that substantive negotiations would get under way with 100 countries by mid-February 1975.

The Senate followed the House of Representatives in the autumn in passing HR 15977 to extend the life of the Export-Import Bank for four years and to provide increases in its commitment authority. Differences between the amendments attached by the two houses had to be resolved in conferences.

After lengthy negotiations, an agreement was reached in May between the United States and the European Economic Community (EEC) on compensation due this country as a result of the enlargement of the Community in 1973 to include the United Kingdom, Ireland, and Denmark. The U. S. claim for damages arose from the increase in tariffs necessitated in some cases by the new members' adoption of the common external tariff of the EEC. Reductions in duties were agreed to on some two dozen industrial and agricultural items of interest to U. S. exporters.

Frances L. Hall
Director, International Trade Analysis Division
U. S. Department of Commerce

IOWA

Democrats and farmers had a good year in Iowa in 1974.

Legislation. Two thirds of Gov. Robert Ray's 44-point legislative program was enacted into law. The sales tax was removed from food and prescription drugs, state employees were granted a 7.5% salary increase, collective bargaining rights for all public employees was passed effective in 1975, a department of transportation was established, interest rates charged on loans and installment sales were allowed to reach a high of 18%, and a $5.5 million coal research mining program was authorized.

Economy. In spite of adverse weather and below-record crops, the higher than normal prices of corn and soybeans yielded record cash values. The 1974 corn crop of 964 million bushels had a cash value of $3.18 billion, and the 198-million-bushel soybean harvest had a cash value of $1.58 billion.

Unlike much of the industrial part of the United States, unemployment in Iowa continued to average less than 3%.

Elections. In the 1974 elections, Iowans elected former Democratic Congressman John Culver to the U. S. Senate to replace Harold Hughes, who was not a candidate. Culver defeated state Rep. David Stanley by a vote of 460,792 to 420,501. In the six congressional races, Democrat Edward Mezvinsky, Democrat Michael Blouin, Republican Charles Grassley, Democrat Neal Smith, Democrat Tom Harkin, and Democrat Berkley Bedell won, giving the Democrats a 5-to-1 margin in the U. S. House delegation from Iowa.

The Republicans maintained their hold on the state administrative offices. They reelected Robert Ray for an unprecedented fourth term as governor and reelected Arthur Neu as lieutenant governor. Both will serve terms expiring in January 1979.

In the state legislative races, the Democrats won control of the House, 60 to 40, and the Senate, 26 to 24.

RUSSELL M. ROSS, *University of Iowa*

IOWA • Information Highlights

Area: 56,290 square miles (145,791 sq km).
Population (1973 est.): 2,904,000. *Density:* 52 per sq mi.
Chief Cities (1970 census): Des Moines, the capital, 201,404; Cedar Rapids, 110,642; Davenport, 98,469.
Government (1974): *Chief Officers*—governor, Robert D. Ray (R); lt. gov., Arthur A. Neu (R). *General Assembly*—Senate, 50 members; House of Representatives, 100 members.
Education (1973–74): *Enrollment*—public elementary schools, 349,800 pupils; public secondary schools, 290,000; nonpublic schools, 68,200; colleges and universities, 109,118 students. *Public school expenditures,* $667,800,000 ($1,116 per pupil).
State Finances (fiscal year 1973): *Revenues,* $1,554,-028,000; *expenditures,* $1,416,285,000.
Personal Income (1973): $14,139,000,000; per capita, $4,869.
Labor Force (July 1974): *Nonagricultural wage and salary earners,* 1,010,800; *insured unemployed,* 8,500 (1.1%).

IRAN

Iran in 1974 continued to enjoy political stability and rapid economic development, under the firm but benevolent autocracy of Shah Mohammed Reza Pahlavi. Both domestic and foreign policy are shaped by the fact that Iran receives vast revenues from its oil fields, revenues that were enormously increased in 1974 because of the sharp rise in oil prices.

Domestic Developments. Existing Iranian oil wells have generally been estimated to have a shorter productive life before them than those in other parts of the Middle East. There was therefore great significance in the announcement, made on July 31 by the state-owned National Iranian Oil Co., that "gigantic" new oil reserves had been found near Ahwaz in southwest Iran. Also the discovery of a major natural-gas deposit in the Persian Gulf containing an estimated 70–100 trillion cubic feet (2–2.8 trillion cubic meters) was made by a Japanese firm, Nissho-Iwaii and Co. On July 30, National Iranian Oil signed contracts with the West German Deminex group for oil exploration and development near Shiraz and Abadan.

On August 4 the Shah announced a revision of the fifth five-year plan (1973–78), which more than doubled—to $69.6 million—the original allocation of funds and envisaged an annual growth rate of 25.9%. Oil payments from consumer states now cascade into Iran at the rate of more than $1 billion a month; they are the basis for the Shah's determination that within a quarter of a century Iran will become as developed as any West European country.

Problems. The new money and the policy of development have attendant disadvantages: they have underscored and aggravated problems posed by rising inflation and a lack of trained manpower. Prices for some goods have doubled within the past year. The government is attempting to meet the skilled manpower shortage by setting up training programs for industrial workers and by financing study abroad for all who agree to government approval of their programs and official posting to assignments on their return.

The importance and extent of a radical opposition to the government within Iran are difficult to estimate. However, the sentencing to death on January 9 by a military court in Teheran of seven persons—for plotting to assassinate the Shah and kidnap members of his family—was typical of the government's energetic measures against radical terrorism.

Economic Agreements. The Shah's government, though anxious to secure the maximum prices for its oil, is basically pro-Western and has no wish to ruin the nations on whom it depends for technical expertise. The result in 1974 was a series of bilateral economic accords between Iran and West European states. The most impressive was that with France, signed

IRAN • Information Highlights

Official Name: Empire of Iran.
Location: Southwest Asia.
Area: 636,294 square miles (1,648,000 sq km).
Population (1973 est.): 31,100,000.
Chief Cities (1971 est.): Teheran, the capital, 3,639,000; Isfahan, 546,200; Meshed, 530,500; Tabriz, 475,600.
Government: *Head of state,* Mohammed Reza Pahlavi, shah (acceded Sept. 1941; crowned Oct. 1967). *Head of government,* Amir Abbas Hoveida, premier (took office Jan. 1965). *Legislature*—Parliament: Senate and Majlis (Lower House).
Monetary Unit: Rial (67.62 rials equal U. S.$1, July 1974).
Gross National Product (1972 est.): $17,400,000,000.
Manufacturing (major products): Petroleum products, iron, steel, textiles, carpets, food products.
Major Agricultural Products: Wheat, rice, barley, cotton, tobacco, almonds, fruits, fish (caviar).
Foreign Trade (1973): *Exports,* $6,966,000,000; *imports,* $3,440,000,000.

in Paris (February 9), and amplified by further agreements made during an official visit to France by the Shah, June 24–26. It provided for the placing of orders in France worth some $4 to $5 billion over the next ten years. Iran made a $1 billion advance payment. Among other projects, France is to build in Iran five nuclear reactors and a steel plant and construct a subway for Teheran. Iran undertook to increase its oil shipments to France.

In May, West German firms and Iran signed preliminary agreements for more than $2.2 billion of industrial projects, while Iran acquired a 25% holding in Krupp Steel. An agreement with Italy in June envisaged the building of a steel works at Bandar Abbas on the Persian Gulf. An agreement with Britain in January looked to the augmenting of mutual trade, and Iran extended to Britain in July a $1.2 billion line of credit.

Arms Buildup. The Shah accelerated his spending of enormous sums on modern weapons in support of his aim to make Iran the predominant military power in the Persian Gulf area. Most, though not all, of this sophisticated weaponry was being sold to Iran by the United States. U. S. arms sales to Iran in 1974, including transport planes, ships, tanks and personnel carriers, total an estimated $4 billion.

Foreign Relations. Despite resumption of diplomatic relations between Iran and Iraq in October 1973, Iraq's radical Baath regime and the Shah's government continued to be less than friendly. A series of clashes on the border between Iraqi and Iranian troops took place during the first three months of 1974.

For several years Iran has given military aid to the sultan of Oman against attacks coming from South Yemen. Oman commands the entry to the Persian Gulf, and in Zürich in February the Shah vigorously justified his policy, describing the Persian Gulf as Iran's "jugular vein," and saying that his country could not survive the presence of any "forces of subversion" close to the entrance to the Gulf.

ARTHUR CAMPBELL TURNER
University of California, Riverside

IRAQ

There were in one sense no important changes in Iraq in 1974. The country continued to be ruled by the radical and authoritarian Baath party, which had seized power in 1968. Since the summer of 1973 the party has based its power on a "National Progressive Front" in which the Communist party participates. Policy remained in the hands of President Ahmed Hassan al-Bakr and the Revolutionary Command Council, and their grasp of power increased in tenacity. However, they were engaged throughout the year in trying to cope with a major internal problem in the shape of a full-scale revolt among the Kurds.

Armed Revolt in Kurdistan. The Kurds, who number in all perhaps 5 to 7 million, are an ethnic minority constituting 15–20%—that is, 1.5 to 2 million—of the Iraqi population. Living principally in the northeast region of Iraq, they are racially akin to the Iranians. They are to be found in similar numbers in northwest Iran and southeast Turkey. They are a nation without a country. The Treaty of Sèvres (1920) envisaged that they should have their own national state, but this did not happen. The Kurds, however, have experienced much more difficulty in coexisting with the rest of the population in Iraq than in Turkey or Iran.

After an armed struggle against the Iraqi government lasting nine years, a peace agreement was signed (March 1970) which guaranteed Kurdish autonomy. Apparently the terms of the agreement were not fully carried out. Additional friction has arisen over the question of whether the oil-rich Kirkuk region should be included within autonomous Kurdistan. Since 1971 relations between the Kurds and the Iraqi government have steadily deteriorated.

New negotiations began on Jan. 16, 1974, between the vice-president of Iraq (Mr. Takriti) and the Democratic Party of Kurdistan (DPK). There was a wide gap between the two negotiating positions. The government wished to exclude Kirkuk from the Kurdish zone, whose boundaries it proposed to draw on the basis of the 1957 census. That census gave the number

IRAQ • Information Highlights

Official Name: Republic of Iraq.
Location: Southwest Asia.
Area: 167,925 square miles (434,924 sq km).
Population (1973 est.): 10,800,000.
Chief Cities (1970 est.): Baghdad, the capital, 2,183,800 (met. area); Basra, 370,900; Mosul, 293,100.
Government: *Head of state,* Ahmed Hassan al-Bakr, president (took office July 1968). *Head of government,* Ahmed Hassan al-Bakr.
Monetary Unit: Dinar (0.2961 dinar equals U. S.$1, July 1974).
Gross National Product (1972 est.): $4,650,000,000.
Manufacturing (major products): Petroleum products, processed foods, textiles, cigarettes, cement.
Major Agricultural Products: Barley, wheat, dates, rice, cotton, tobacco.
Foreign Trade (1973): *Exports,* $2,292,000,000; *imports,* $898,000,000.

of Kurds in Iraq as 800,000. The DPK claims that the present figure is 2,300,000. The DPK wished to see the adoption of a constitution granting full democratic rights to all Iraqis—a request unlikely to be granted by the present government in Baghdad. The government regarded the DPK proposals as tantamount to a demand for secession. Negotiations broke down at the end of February.

The government then produced its own proposals for Kurdish autonomy, which were approved on March 4 by the Baathist-Communist National Progressive Front. One of the proposals was that the DPK should join the Front. Over DPK protests the government's proposals were promulgated on March 11. The DPK viewed this as a declaration of war, and there immediately followed a full-scale armed revolt and a mass migration to Kurdistan by Kurds living in other parts of Iraq.

Fighting broke out on March 12 and continued during the rest of the year, though its scale dwindled in the fall as the government forces—comprising most of Iraq's 90,000-man army—reduced the area under control of the DPK leader, Mulla Mustafa Barzani, and of the DPK militia. By the end of the year over 100,000 Kurds had taken refuge in Iran.

It seemed clear in the latter part of the year that the government was being assisted against the Kurds by Russian pilots flying Soviet-built fighter-bombers. For its part the Iraqi government claimed Kurdish resistance was being bolstered by aid from Turkey, Israel, Iran, and the United States. The only truth in these claims appeared to be that the Kurds were receiving some arms from Iran and possibly financial assistance from Israel.

Border Clashes with Iran. Although diplomatic relations with Iran, broken in 1971, had been restored (Oct. 6, 1973), border violence between the two states, a regular occurrence in recent years, continued in 1974 and occasioned several protests to the United Nations by both sides. This led to the appointment in March by UN Secretary-General Kurt Waldheim of Luis Muñoz, Mexico's ambassador in Bonn, to investigate the situation. An agreement was signed on March 19 but sporadic trouble continued, exacerbated by the Shah's sympathy for the Kurds and his unconcealed dislike for the leftist regime in Baghdad, which in turn regards as "imperialist" the Shah's intention to dominate the Persian Gulf area.

Other Foreign Relations. Iraq, a difficult neighbor for Iran, Turkey, and Kuwait, differs on policy matters even with other Arab states, and there were reported clashes at Arab summit meetings. Iraq's warmest diplomatic relations were with the Soviet Union, symbolized by the visit (March 23–26) to Baghdad of Soviet Marshal Andrei Grechko.

Since Iraq ranks fifth among Middle East oil producers, it is in a strong position in dealing with oil-consuming nations. Michel Jobert, French foreign minister, visited Baghdad (February 6–8), and plans were made for increased economic cooperation based on the 10-year agreement of June 1972. In a major pact signed on January 17, Japan and Iraq traded the promise of large Japanese loans for industrial projects and increased oil supplies for Japan.

Diplomatic relations between Britain and Iraq, ruptured in 1971 by Iraq, were resumed.

ARTHUR CAMPBELL TURNER
University of California, Riverside

Kurdish guerrillas in training. The Kurds seek an independent nation ("Kurdistan") in northern Iraq.

SVEN SIMON/KATHERINE YOUNG

IRELAND

For most Irishmen, 1974 was the year when the proverbial light failed to materialize at the end of the tunnel. In political terms, the prolonged and bitter conflict over Northern Ireland came no closer to settlement, while the depressed state of the economy showed that the country could not escape those forces of inflation, unemployment, and energy shortages afflicting the rest of the world.

As the year neared its end, the country was saddened by the death on November 17 of President Erskine Childers, in Dublin, at the age of 68. He was succeeded by Cearbhall Ó Dálaigh, a judge of the European Court.

Continued Conflict with the North. During January the chances for conciliation over the northern question looked bright, as Prime Minister (Taoiseach) Liam Cosgrave's coalition ministry joined with British and Northern Irish leaders to implement their agreement of Dec. 9, 1973, at Sunningdale, Berkshire, England, to create a Council of Ireland that would bridge some of the political, religious, and social divisions which had torn apart the people of Northern Ireland. Underlying this agreement was a consensus that Protestants in Northern Ireland had to share political power with the Roman Catholic minority there.

Hopes were shattered, however, by a general strike of Protestant workers in the north during late May. The powerful Ulster Workers Council called this strike to protest the principle of power sharing. Disrupting all the essential services in the north, the strikers toppled Brian Faulkner's ministry and managed to wreck the Sunningdale agreement.

Against this background of crumbling moderation, the gunmen and bombers of extremist groups continued to take their toll of life, limb, and property. Violence and counterviolence could not be confined to Belfast or Londonderry any more than it could be contained within the six counties of the north. Conflicts between Irish Republican Army (IRA) members and British soldiers turned sections of the border into small-scale combat zones. Protestant extremists made occasional forays into the Republic in order to "punish" those who gave food and shelter to the IRA.

On May 17 three car bombs exploded in downtown Dublin during the evening rush hour. A fourth bomb blast caused casualties on the same day in the town of Monaghan. A total of 30 people were killed in these explosions, while 150 were wounded. Protestant terrorists were suspected of causing this atrocity, but no arrests ensued.

Other Crimes. Several sensational crimes broke up the grim routine of sectarian violence. On the night of April 26, thieves entered the country house of Sir Alfred Beit in County Wicklow and stole 19 paintings valued at $19.2 million. The police considered this a political crime, as the stolen works of art were to be used as leverage to force the British government to transfer four convicted IRA terrorists from an English to a Northern Irish jail. The thieves also demanded ransom in excess of $2 million. On May 6 the stolen paintings were discovered in a cottage near Glandore, County Cork, where the police arrested Bridget Rose Dugdale, who was well known for her commitment to radical causes. In a special criminal court in Dublin, Dugdale was found guilty of receiving stolen goods and was sentenced to nine years in prison.

On June 4, masked gunmen kidnapped two prominent aristocrats, the Earl and Countess of Donoughmore, from their house near Clonmel in County Tipperary. Again, the motive was political, as the kidnappers hoped to use their captives as hostages in order to force British officials to treat more leniently IRA prisoners who had been on a hunger strike. After the British home secretary agreed to transfer several of these terrorists to prison in Northern Ireland, the kidnappers released Lord and Lady Donoughmore on June 9.

Among the less fortunate victims of the guerrillas was Protestant Fine Gael Senator Billy Fox, who was found shot to death on March 12, near his home in Clones, County Monaghan. Five members of the IRA were eventually convicted of this crime and sentenced to life imprisonment, but several of these men joined in a mass escape from Portlaois prison in August and eluded a massive search by both the police and military.

The Economy. The Irish economy provided no sensational headlines, but it exuded a sense of gloom for most of the year. The discovery of "significant" deposits of natural gas and oil off the Old Head of Kinsale in County Cork failed to arouse much optimism among consumers trying to cope with spiraling costs of food and durables. Between July 1973 and July 1974, the rate of inflation soared to 16.2%, compared with an average of 5.4% for the entire decade 1961–71.

L. PERRY CURTIS, JR., *Brown University*

IRELAND • Information Highlights

Official Name: Ireland
Location: Island in the eastern North Atlantic Ocean.
Area: 27,136 square miles (70,283 sq km).
Population (1973 est.): 3,000,000.
Chief Cities (1971 census): Dublin, the capital, 566,034; Cork, 128,235.
Government: *Head of state,* Cearbhall Ó Dálaigh, president (took office Dec. 19, 1974). *Head of government, Liam Cosgrave,* prime minister (taoiseach) (took office March 1973). *Legislature*—Parliament; House of Representatives (Dáil Éireann) and Senate (Seanad Éireann).
Monetary Unit: Pound (0.4315 pound equals U.S.$1, Aug. 1974).
Gross National Product (1973 est.): $5,900,000,000.
Manufacturing (major products): Processed foods, clothing, textiles, paper products.
Major Agricultural Products: Wheat, potatoes, sugar beets.
Foreign Trade (1973): *Exports,* $2,131,000,000; *imports,* $2,776,000,000.

UPI

Israeli artillerymen fire a self-propelled cannon at Syrian positions during ground and air skirmishes in Israeli-occupied Syria in April.

ISRAEL

The year 1974 was a clouded and uncertain one in Israel, perhaps the most stressful of any since the foundation of the state a quarter of a century before. The whole year was passed in the aftermath of the Arab-Israeli war of October 1973. That indecisive war, halted in midcourse, left a legacy of unresolved questions which, as 1974 passed, seemed on the whole to be receding further from possible solution. The frontiers of Israel were fixed merely by ceasefire and disengagement agreements. Israel was exceedingly isolated in the international arena. Nor was all well even within its boundaries, where dissension and a lack of political cohesion were manifest.

Formation of Government. The general election of Dec. 31, 1973, produced a prolonged internal crisis which really did not reach its eventual resolution in a new prime minister and a new government until the year was almost half over. The election was held on Israel's proportional representation system and contested by the record number of 22 parties and splinter groups.

Premier Golda Meir's ruling Labor Alignment won 51 of the 120 Knesset seats (a loss of five). The parties of the right-wing Likud bloc gained seven more seats for a total of 39. The National Religious party, Labor's former coalition partner, lost one of its 11 seats. Another former Labor partner, the Independent Liberals, were steady at four seats.

Mrs. Meir was asked by President Ephraim Katzir on January 30 to form a new government. Negotiations between Mrs. Meir and the National Religious party broke down on February 13, however, when the NRP refused to serve any longer in a coalition with the Labor and Independent Liberal parties. The dispute turned on the long-vexed question of the Law of Return and the legal definition of a Jew, on which the NRP has rigid Orthodox views.

Mrs. Meir then announced her intention to form a minority government which would command only 58 of the Knesset's 120 seats. Her attempts to form such a government failed, however, and on March 3 she gave up the task and walked out of a meeting of the Labor party's central committee. The next day Mrs. Meir retracted her decision, and on March 5 she was given an overwhelming vote of confidence by the Labor party, while the NRP reversed its previous decision on rejoining the coalition. On March 6 the new government was announced, and it was given a 62–46 vote of confidence four days later.

Change in Premiership. Mrs. Meir's new government was short-lived. Just a month later (April 10) the premier, who was 76, announced her "irrevocable" decision to resign her post. Mrs. Meir remained in office in a caretaker capacity pending the creation of a new government. The Labor party's central committee on April 22 chose Gen. Itzhak Rabin as prime minister-designate to succeed Mrs. Meir, and Rabin's new administration was announced on May 28. The cabinet included Yigal Allon as deputy premier and foreign minister and Shimon Peres as defense minister.

The new prime minister, who took office on June 3, has a reputation for solid and unostentatious ability. His selection was noteworthy on several grounds. Israel's youngest premier at 52, he was the first *Sabra* (native-born Israeli) to hold the post; all four of his predecessors were born in Tsarist Russia. Before becoming premier, Rabin had held cabinet office for exactly one month and had played no part in politics before the 1973 election. He was chief of staff at the time of the June 1967 war. From 1968 to 1973 he was ambassador in Washington.

Premier Rabin's cabinet had to be constructed without the NRP; and, resting on a coalition of the Labor Alignment, the Independent Liberals, and the small Civil Rights group, it controlled 61 Knesset seats and thus had a slim majority of two. In October the NRP voted to join the coalition government.

Military Post-Mortems. The fact that Israel was totally surprised by the Arab launching of war in October 1973 has been the source of much subsequent controversy and recrimination. Defense Minister Dayan was the target of hostile demonstrations in February as the presumably responsible cabinet minister. Other critics of Mrs. Meir's government held that the whole cabinet must accept joint responsibility.

In its interim report on April 2, the five-man commission of inquiry set up to investigate the initial military reverses exonerated Mrs. Meir and Dayan and placed the major blame on the chief of staff, Gen. David Elazar. Elazar resigned immediately, protesting the commission's findings, and was replaced by Gen. Mordecai Gur, who had been in charge of the Northern Command.

Other Domestic Events. A record budget of $8.4 billion for the fiscal year starting April 1 was announced on March 14. It included $3.5 billion for defense, twice the previous amount. Finance Minister Pinhas Sapir said that the 1973 war had cost Israel $7.2 billion. A program of increased taxes and compulsory loans testified to Israel's current financial difficulties, which are serious. The cabinet on July 2 enacted a series of drastic measures to curb the nation's increasing inflation and offset the war-caused deficits.

Zalman Shazar, president of Israel from 1963 to 1973, died on October 5, one day before his 85th birthday.

An Israeli court on December 10 convicted the Greek Catholic Archbishop of Jerusalem, Hilarion Capudji, of smuggling weapons into Israel from Lebanon for Palestinian guerrillas and sentenced him to 12 years in prison; but it seemed likely he would in fact be deported.

The Cease-Fires. Israel's freedom from outright war in 1974 rested on the fragile basis of the two cease-fires for the northern and southern fronts, respectively. Israel and Egypt, with the strong assistance of the U. S. government, reached agreement on the disengagement and separation of their forces in an agreement signed on January 18.

A similar disengagement agreement with Syria proved much harder to achieve, and it was not until May 31 that, as a result of U. S. Secretary of State Henry Kissinger's untiring diplomacy, the Israeli-Syrian agreement was signed in Geneva.

Terrorist Activity. The cessation of organized formal hostilities was not paralleled by any letup in the Arab terrorist attacks on Israelis, some 60 of whom became victims of terrorism in the course of the year. These attacks were frequently followed by Israeli retaliatory strikes by ground or air forces on terrorist havens in Lebanon. The most serious terrorist attacks were those at Kiryat Shemona (April 11), in which 18 persons, including eight children and five women, were murdered; and at the Maalot high school (May 15), which led to 25 deaths.

International Isolation. Israel's international standing grew steadily worse as the UN majority adopted intransigent anti-Israeli policies. The reception given to Yasir Arafat, leader of the Palestine Liberation Organization, when he addressed the UN General Assembly in November and the UN recognition of the PLO as the only spokesman for the Palestinians were severe blows to Israel, as well as to hopes of a negotiated settlement in general, since Arafat has proclaimed his objective as being the destruction of Israel. The ostracizing of Israel by UNESCO on November 20 and the restrictions imposed on it in the Palestinian debate were similar if less serious steps.

(See also special report on the Middle East, page 36.)

ARTHUR CAMPBELL TURNER
University of California, Riverside

ISRAEL • Information Highlights

Official Name: State of Israel.
Location: Southwest Asia.
Area: 7,992 square miles (20,700 sq km).
Population (1974 est.): 3,400,000.
Chief Cities (1972 census): Jerusalem, the capital, 304,500; Tel Aviv–Jaffa, 362,200; Haifa, 217,400.
Government: *Head of state,* Ephraim Katzir, president (took office May 1973). *Head of government,* Itzhak Rabin, prime minister (took office June 1974). *Legislature* (unicameral)—Knesset.
Monetary Unit: Pound (4.6 pounds equal U. S.$1, Nov. 1974).
Gross National Product (1973 est.): $8,700,000,000.
Manufacturing (major products): Polished diamonds, processed foods, chemicals, petroleum products, aircraft, electric and electronic equipment, textiles, clothing.
Major Agricultural Products: Citrus fruits, vegetables, cotton, eggs.
Foreign Trade (1973): *Exports,* $1,382,000,000; *imports,* $2,944,000,000.

UPI

Workers in Milan gather in the Piazza del Duomo during a four-hour strike on October 17 called to protest rising unemployment.

ITALY

Italy, the scene of an "economic miracle" in 1960, was Europe's "sick man" in 1974.

ECONOMICS

Violent shock waves ripped through the country when the oil-producing states quadrupled the price of petroleum late in 1973.

Trade Deficit. The higher prices had a devastating impact on Italy's international balance of payments. Whereas in 1973 the trade deficit totaled $5 billion, the 1974 adverse balance was expected to reach at least $8.75 billion. Some $6 billion of this was accounted for by the increased price of oil.

Government efforts during the last half of 1974 to squeeze credit and augment taxes led some observers to think that the non-oil portion of the trade deficit might be eliminated by the end of 1975. Much of this portion of the deficit was attributed to Italy's growing taste for beef, Scotch whisky, and other expensive imported items. The nation used to produce 90% of its food needs; now it produces only 60%. The collapse of Italy's agriculture was an unfortunate concomitant of its quick industrialization since World War II.

Inflation. Inflation accelerated at an alarming pace. In 1973 the annual rate was 12.4%; early in 1974 it approached 20%; by year's end it was 24%. The worsening situation reached crisis stage in June. Guido Carli, governor of the Bank of Italy, called for "shock treatment" in the form of higher taxes and a freeze on escalator clauses in wage agreements. At the same time Italy urgently sought a loan of more than $2 billion from West Germany or the United States, offering as collateral its 2,500 tons of gold reserves. Valued at the official rate, this gold was worth nearly $3.5 billion; but if valued at prevailing prices on the free market (as the International Monetary Fund permitted in June), it was worth more than $14 billion.

In the previous two years Italy had borrowed $10.5 billion from abroad and was paying $700 million in interest annually. The country's credit was almost exhausted. Before additional loans could be negotiated, Italy had to show that it was raising some $5 billion annually in new taxes. Thus at the end of June the Italian government authorized higher taxes on gasoline (by about 20 cents per gallon), automobiles, motorcycles, pleasure boats, and private airplanes. A

ITALY • Information Highlights

Official Name: Italian Republic.
Location: Southern Europe.
Area: 116,303 square miles (301,225 sq km).
Population (1974 est. census): 55,300,000.
Chief Cities (1971 census): Rome, the capital, 2,799,-836; Milan, 1,724,173; Naples, 1,232,877; Turin, 1,177,939.
Government: *Head of state,* Giovanni Leone, president (took office Dec. 1971). *Head of government,* Aldo Moro, premier (took office Nov. 1974). *Legislature*—Parliament: Senate and Chamber of Deputies.
Monetary Unit: Lira (660.45 lire equal U.S.$1, Sept. 1974).
Gross National Product (1973 est.): $128,400,000,000.
Manufacturing (major products): Automobiles, petroleum products, machinery, processed foods, chemicals.
Major Agricultural Products: Wheat, grapes, tomatoes, citrus fruits, rice, vegetables, olives, nuts.
Foreign Trade (1973): *Exports,* $22,224,000,000; *imports,* $27,797,000,000.

value-added tax on beef and other imported consumer items was raised from 6% to 18%. It was expected that such additional taxes would result in a 5% cut in national consumption during the year.

In mid-July the European Economic Community promised Italy a loan in various forms of $1.82 billion and gave it three more years to repay a loan that initially fell due that summer. On August 31, after two days of talks with Premier Mariano Rumor at Bellagio, Chancellor Helmut Schmidt of West Germany revealed that his country would extend Italy $2 billion credit, accepting its gold reserve as collateral.

Unemployment. Despite the loan from West Germany, Italy's economic situation continued to deteriorate. In October the Fiat Motor Company in Turin announced it was cutting production by 200,000 cars. One third of its 200,000 employees were placed on a three-day workweek. Repercussions were felt everywhere. Unemployment mounted to about 1 million, or 5.8% of the nation's labor force. The situation was further complicated by the return of thousands of Italian workers from northern Europe, where layoffs also were increasing.

In spite of the grim news, some Italian analysts predicted that, paradoxically, the gross national product might rise by 4% in 1974. They noted that Italy, unlike northern Europe, is still a developing country and needs continued economic growth. So long as the "economic pie" can be made to grow, they suggested, social upheaval is unlikely. Many foreign observers were less hopeful.

POLITICS

Italy entered 1974 under a center-left coalition government formed by Mariano Rumor, a Christian Democrat, in July 1973. It consisted also of Social Democrats, Socialists, and Republicans. Rumor's government promised vigorous steps to fight inflation and revive the economy, as well as reforms in education, housing, and health care. The important treasury and budget ministries were held, respectively, by Ugo La Malfa (Republican) and Antonio Giolitti (Socialist). The resignation of La Malfa on February 28 in a dispute over ways to tackle inflation led to the fall of the government on March 2. La Malfa had called for austerity in order for Italy to qualify for a large loan from the International Monetary Fund. His policy was opposed by the Socialists, who favored more governmental spending to halt further stagnation and unemployment.

Rumor's Fifth Government. On March 15, Premier Rumor formed a new government—his fifth and Italy's 36th since the end of World War II. The new cabinet, sworn in on March 15, was a slightly revised, slimmed-down version of its predecessor. It consisted of a coalition of Christian Democrats, Socialists, and Social Democrats. The Republicans were not included, but pledged to support it in Parliament. Calling for austerity, Rumor won a 343–231 vote of confidence in the Chamber of Deputies on March 23.

Referendum on Divorce Law. Public interest next turned to the May 12 referendum to consider repeal of the three-year-old divorce law. Legalization of divorce was bitterly opposed by the Catholic Church and had split the center-left coalition. The Christian Democrats were the only government party to favor repeal. They had embarrassing support from the neo-Fascist Italian Social Movement–National Right Wing. The Socialists, Social Democrats, and Republicans all favored continuation of the existing divorce law. They were supported by two parties outside the government—the Communists and the Liberals.

Voters in the referendum rejected by a 3 to 2 margin the proposed repeal. The results were a kind of vote of no confidence in the Christian Democrats and produced new strains in the center-left coalition, the Socialists feeling encouraged to resist the Christian Democrats' austerity program.

Roman demonstrators, some carrying red flags and singing the Italian Communist party anthem, mark the defeat of a Vatican-backed attempt to repeal Italy's divorce law.

UPI

Public Financing of Parties. In April, Italy enacted a law that introduced public financing of campaigns by the major political parties. It provided $75 million a year to be divided among the parties, with another $25 million for each general election.

Political Violence. The nation was plagued by violence throughout the year, especially on the part of conspiratorial groups of neo-Fascists and military officers, whose strategy was to create so much chaos that the army would have to take over the government. The most violent groups were the National Vanguard, New Order (outlawed in November 1973), and Black Order. These were dissident, pro-Nazi offshoots of the neo-Fascist Italian Social Movement–National Right Wing, which enjoyed legal status and had attracted 8.7% of the vote in the 1972 parliamentary elections. Early in 1974 numerous army officers were arrested on charges of participating in the "Compass Rome" conspiracy to seize control of the government and execute 1,617 people.

On May 28 a high-explosive time bomb exploded in Brescia during an anti-Fascist rally, killing six and injuring 94. The blast occurred during an official inquiry into activity by the Black Order in that region. President Leone declared that the massacre provided "clear evidence" of an attempt by "tiny and squalid terrorist minorities to throw the state and nation into chaos." On May 29 a four-hour general strike was called throughout Italy. Thousands held anti-Fascist rallies in Turin, Rome, and Milan, while in Naples leftists attacked neo-Fascist headquarters. On May 31 both President Leone and Premier Rumor attended the funeral services in Brescia.

On August 5 the Rome-Munich express train was bombed by the Black Order, killing 12 and injuring 48 persons.

In October the government revealed that a serious rightist plot had been uncovered in August. Conspirators had planned to arrest President Leone, dissolve Parliament, and pollute Rome's aqueduct. The government arrested Andrea Mario Piaggio, a wealthy industrialist, who was accused of giving $470,000 to a subversive group known as "Rose of the Winds." Gen. Vito Miceli, formerly head of Italy's intelligence service, also was implicated.

In November five more bombings occurred, this time in Savona. One person was killed.

New Governmental Crisis. On June 10, Premier Rumor's three-month-old government submitted its resignation to President Leone. After three days of consultations he formally rejected the resignation, a most unusual constitutional action. Meanwhile, Enrico Berlinguer, head of the Communist party, let it be known that his party wanted a voice in high-level decision-making. The Socialists—but not the Social Democrats—supported this move for a so-called "democratic turn" in Italy's governance.

Politicians marked time until after the Sardinian elections of June 16 for a 75-seat regional assembly. These resulted in a new setback for the Christian Democrats, who polled only 38.3% of the vote, compared with 40.9% in 1972. Neo-Fascists also suffered a loss—7.5% instead of the 11.3% they enjoyed in 1972. Socialists, on the other hand, rose from 8.1% to 11.7%, while the Communists increased from 25.3% to 26.8% of the popular vote. Many observers believed the Sardinian results reflected a nationwide trend.

Late in June, Rumor was able to patch up a new center-left government, his sixth. He asked Parliament to raise $5 billion annually in new taxes and announced a lottery-style system of random audits to catch tax evaders. On June 28 he obtained a 326–225 vote of confidence in the Chamber of Deputies.

But on October 3, Rumor's shaky government fell, once again because of disagreement over how to handle the economic crisis and the rising Communist demand for a voice in governmental decision-making. Amintore Fanfani, secretary of the Christian Democratic party, tried in vain for three weeks to organize a new center-left coalition. Fanfani's prestige had been greatly lowered as a result of his effort to repeal the divorce law.

Moro's Government. President Leone then turned to Aldo Moro, another Christian Democratic leader. At last on November 23 (seven weeks after Rumor's resignation) Moro formed a minority government of Christian Democrats and Republicans, with support from the other center-left parties, but few expected it to endure. Many observers blamed the crisis on the United States, which, they asserted, wanted Italy to hold parliamentary elections now instead of waiting until 1977. The Communists were expected to make a renewed push to enter the government in the spring of 1975.

On December 4 some 14 million Italians (75% of the labor force) went on strike for higher wages.

FOREIGN RELATIONS

Italy's foreign relations in 1974 were concerned mainly with seeking aid to cope with the oil crisis and adverse balance of payments.

U. S. Secretary of State Kissinger was in Rome in July to brief the Italian government and the Vatican on President Nixon's summit talks at Moscow with Chairman Brezhnev. He was in Rome again in November to help launch the World Food Conference.

From September 25 to 29, President Leone was in the United States on a state visit. He also addressed the UN General Assembly on September 27. The Socialist party voiced concern that Leone might approve more U. S. naval bases in Italy in the wake of the Cyprus crisis, but Italy's government denied this possibility.

CHARLES F. DELZELL, *Vanderbilt University*

UPI

Members of Japan's lower house of Parliament applaud after Takeo Miki (*standing*) is elected premier on December 9. He succeeded Kakuei Tanaka, who resigned.

JAPAN

After two years and five months as premier of Japan, Kakuei Tanaka resigned in November 1974. The event caused little surprise, for his steady loss of public support represented the sharpest setback borne by any postwar Japanese head of government. Tanaka's majority Liberal-Democratic party (LDP) continued in power under Takeo Miki, who was named premier by a consensus of its leading members.

The Tanaka government, despite an auspicious start in July 1972, had seen its popular support fall below 30% during the energy crisis of 1973. In 1974 the Premier's political base was further eroded by public concern over environmental disruption and new blows to the economy. Japan had the highest inflation rate among the 10 leading industrial nations of the world, and in the April–June quarter its economic growth dropped to zero for the first time since World War II. According to a poll taken in October, only 18.8% of the voting public supported the Premier. This survey was made before an unusual exposé of Tanaka's interlocking personal wealth and political power.

The visit of Gerald Ford to Japan in November was the first by an American president in office. After talks with Premier Tanaka and other Japanese officials, Ford met with Soviet leader Leonid Brezhnev in Vladivostok. The Tokyo meetings, clouded by Tanaka's political troubles, served mainly to emphasize the importance of U. S.-Japanese relations. The talks were further complicated by Japan's "nuclear allergy," which had been aroused by the testimony of a retired American admiral. The latter claimed that, without consulting the Japanese, U. S. forces had carried nuclear arms in and out of Japanese ports. Ford's visit was therefore conducted with Tokyo's tightest security

A large sign welcomes U. S. President Ford to an exhibition by Japanese athletes. The President visited Japan in November.

© ORION PRESS, KATHERINE YOUNG

JAPAN • Information Highlights

Official Name: Japan.
Location: East Asia.
Area: 143,689 square miles (372,154 sq km).
Population (1973 est.): 108,300,000.
Chief Cities (1971 est.): Tokyo, the capital, 8,830,000; Osaka, 2,939,000; Yokohama, 2,342,000; Nagoya, 2,052,000.
Government: *Head of state,* Hirohito, emperor (acceded 1926). *Head of government,* Takeo Miki, premier (took office December 1974). *Legislature*—Diet: House of Councillors and House of Representatives.
Monetary Unit: Yen (298.5 yen equal U. S.$1, Sept. 1974).
Gross National Product (1973 est.): $415,000,000,000.
Manufacturing (major products): Ships, automobiles, electronic components, textiles, iron, steel, petrochemicals, machinery, electrical appliances, processed foods.
Major Agricultural Products: Rice, wheat, barley, potatoes, vegetables, fruits, tobacco, tea, fish.
Foreign Trade (1973): *Exports,* $36,971,000,000; *imports,* $38,321,000,000.

measures, to prevent demonstrations like those mounted in 1960 when President Eisenhower had to cancel a trip to Japan.

INTERNATIONAL AFFAIRS

Despite difficulties, Premier Tanaka and President Ford presided over a Japanese-U. S. dialogue still buttressed by a bilateral security treaty. Their two countries enjoyed a trans-Pacific exchange that represented the largest cross-ocean volume of trade in history. But Japan's close relationship with the United States was set in the general context of need for a balanced foreign policy. During 1974, Premier Tanaka conducted personal diplomacy in Southeast Asia (January), in South Korea (August), in the Western Hemisphere (September), and in the South Pacific (October–November).

Relations with the United States. Late in 1973, Ambassador Robert S. Ingersoll had left Tokyo to become an assistant secretary of state in Washington. Thomas P. Shoesmith acted as chargé d'affaires in Tokyo until Ambassador James D. Hodgson, a former Lockheed Aircraft officer, arrived on July 15. In mid-August, Foreign Minister Toshio Kimura told the Japanese public that the Tokyo-Washington relationship would remain unchanged under the new Ford administration, especially with Secretary of State Henry Kissinger staying on. In Tokyo, Ambassador Hodgson gave reassurances that President Ford's new economic program contained no demands or requests unfavorable to Japan.

Premier Tanaka rearranged his trip to Latin America and Canada so as to work in a visit to Washington on September 21 and establish a personal contact with the new president. At that time, President Ford announced his plans to visit Japan in November.

On October 21 some 300,000 students, trade unionists, and representatives of opposition parties rallied throughout Japan on the occasion of International Antiwar Day. The mass rally in Meiji Park, Tokyo, specifically protested the alleged government approval of American forces bringing nuclear arms into Japan. What caused the rallies and unrest was doubt about the rigor with which Tokyo had been enforcing the "prior consultation" provisions of the 1960 mutual security treaty. The pact required the United States to consult with Japan before making major changes of U. S. forces or their equipment in Japan. Successive cabinets, including that of Premier Tanaka, had reassured the public on Japan's three principles of nuclear policy: not to possess nuclear arms, not to import them, and not to allow them to be imported.

Nonetheless, retired Admiral Gene LaRocque had testified before the U. S. Congress that American ships regularly entered and left Japanese ports with nuclear weapons aboard. On October 15, Washington informed Tokyo that these were the entirely unofficial views of a

UPI

Kakuei Tanaka addresses a luncheon meeting of The Foreign Correspondents Club of Japan on October 22. It was one of his last meetings with members of the press as premier.

"private citizen" but did not directly deny the testimony. Premier Tanaka and Foreign Minister Kimura found it necessary to stress that the commitments of the security treaty were fulfilled and, further, that Japan would flatly reject any U. S. request to transit nuclear arms through the country. Newspapers and the Japanese public were still uneasy, for it seemed to them that nuclear arms could have been introduced without consultation.

President Ford's visit to Tokyo and Kyoto on November 18–22 produced no major demonstrations or hostile incidents. Because of the tight security arrangements, Ford was isolated from the Japanese public. The President and Premier Tanaka agreed to strengthen U. S.-Japanese economic cooperation, but the official communiqué avoided reference to the issue of U. S. nuclear arms in Japan.

Relations with China. The establishment of normal relations between Tokyo and Peking in 1972 had profited both parties. In the first nine months of 1974, bilateral trade between Japan and mainland China totaled over $2 billion, surpassing the figure for all of 1973. In the same period, Japan's exports to China were up 80% over the previous year.

On September 29, the two countries inaugurated reciprocal scheduled air service. Japan Air Lines (JAL) sent a DC-8 from Tokyo via Osaka to Peking, while the Civil Aviation Administration of China (CAAC) dispatched a goodwill mission to Tokyo aboard a Boeing 707. Conservatives in Premier Tanaka's party opposed the agreement to the bitter end. The Republic of China (Taiwan) cut off Japanese air service to Taipei, but foreign carriers continued the Japan-Taiwan connection.

Relations with the USSR. Japan's relations with the Soviet Union remained clouded. The two countries had established diplomatic ties in 1956 but without concluding a peace treaty settling issues left over from World War II. Late in 1973, Tanaka had visited Moscow and stubbornly reminded Soviet leaders of obstacles in the way of a peace treaty and cooperation in the joint development of Siberia. These were continued Soviet occupation of the "northern territories" (the lower Kuril Islands, claimed by Japan) and disputes over fishing rights in the North Pacific. Foreign Minister Kimura did informally accept an invitation to visit Moscow in December 1974 or January 1975, in order to fulfill the governments' agreement to launch full-scale negotiations toward a peace treaty. The visit was postponed following the change in government.

Meanwhile, Japan signed an agreement with the Soviet Union to import over 100 million tons of coking coal against a Japanese loan of $450 million. The Soviets and Japanese continued to discuss other Siberian development projects, involving oil, natural gas, wood, pulp, and paper.

WIDE WORLD

At the Imperial Palace, Emperor Hirohito and Empress Nagako enjoy the family photo album. The couple celebrated their golden wedding anniversary in 1974.

Relations with Korea. Historically sensitive relations between Japanese and Koreans were even more strained by a dramatic incident in Seoul, capital of the Republic of Korea. On August 15 a Korean named Mun Se Kwang, resident in Japan, killed the wife of President Park Chung Hee in an attempt on the President's life. Premier Tanaka personally attended the funeral and offered official condolences. But on September 6 a Korean mob broke into the Japanese embassy, seized its flag, and set fire to official vehicles. After a firm protest, Tokyo sent special envoy Etsusaburo Shiina to Seoul to promise restrictions on illegal acts in Japan aimed at the South Korean government.

DOMESTIC AFFAIRS

In a news conference on November 26, Premier Tanaka took responsibility for the domestic political crisis and announced his resignation. On December 9, after LDP leaders had informally consulted, Takeo Miki was formally selected by the Diet (parliament) to be the new premier. He promptly formed a caretaker cabinet, including Tanaka's party foe Takeo Fukuda, pending the party presidential election scheduled for 1975 and a general election sometime in the future.

Tanaka's Fall. On the eve of President Ford's visit, Premier Tanaka had reshuffled his cabinet and the LDP executive lineup. This move was

Representatives of China and Japan wave to crowd at Tokyo airport, September 29, as the two nations mark the second anniversary of diplomatic relations by establishing direct air service between their capitals, Peking and Tokyo.

UPI

a futile attempt to ride out the political storm that had just reached its height. On October 10 the respected magazine *Bungei Shunju* published results of its investigative reporting on Tanaka's financial background, covering also his 28-year career as a politician. It was a story of immense wealth—a "family" of companies, as well as "ghost" companies; a 1973 declared income of 78 million yen ($260,000); a luxurious residence in Tokyo and three villas in Karuizawa, in addition to the official residence. According to the magazine, Tanaka had made large contributions to LDP candidates running for the Diet. On November 11 the Premier declared in a news conference: "I've done nothing illegal." He promised a report to the nation "in due course."

Nevertheless, LDP party leaders forced Tanaka to resign, charging that he had parlayed great wealth into political power, practically buying votes in elections; and then used that power to amass additional wealth. Despite the original image projected of a man of decision and action, Tanaka had done little to solve the energy crisis of 1973, galloping inflation of 1974, and threatened depression in 1975.

Elections. Miki had left the cabinet on July 12 to protest against Tanaka's leadership and the LDP's campaign style in the election of July 7. There had been widespread criticism of Tanaka's alleged attempt, and failure, to "buy" victory in the upper house election.

The election was for seats in the House of Councillors, the upper chamber of the Diet. LDP strength was reduced from a majority to 126 seats—exactly half of the total—with the remaining seats split among opposition parties and independents. In local elections held in April the LDP did much better, except for the Kyoto governor's race, which was won again by the Communist-backed Torazo Ninagawa.

There was no election for the all-important House of Representatives, or lower chamber of the Diet. The LDP held a safe majority of 279 of its 491 seats at the end of the ordinary session in June.

The Economy. In December 1973, Japan's wholesale price index had shown an annual increase of almost 30%. In January 1974, the consumer price index in Tokyo registered a 4% rise over that of the previous month, or an annual rise of almost 21%, the highest increase in over 20 years. Only slight rises marked the midyear, but by September the Tokyo index was back up to a 22% annual inflation rate. The consumer index for Tokyo's 23 wards stood at 149.8 (1970 = 100). As a result, business was in a slump: textile plants were running 35% below capacity; auto sales were down 30%; and in August, color TV production dipped 33% from the year before. The annual rate of economic growth (discounted for inflation) had been about 11% in 1973. By the end of March 1974 it was about 5%; and by the end of June, only 0.6%, according to the Economic Planning Agency (EPA).

Nonetheless, the economy was still strong. In 1973, according to EPA, the gross national product passed the $400 billion mark for the first time. Per capita income was over $3,000. In May 1974, Japan's monthly exports exceeded $5 billion for the first time. After a dip at the end of 1973, foreign-exchange reserves rose to a total of $13.2 billion on June 1, according to the finance ministry.

Inflation, of course, had direct effects on politics and the society. In March the Diet

CULTURED PEARL ASSOCIATION

Pearl-bearing oysters are kept in wire baskets suspended from rafts on pearl farms in southwestern Japan. In 1974 the USSR agreed to resume purchasing large amounts of Japan's cultured pearls, giving the industry hope for an improvement in its export business.

began investigations of the major trading houses —for hoarding, price fixing, and excess profits. An association of oil producers, which included the largest refining firms, was indicted for limiting production, as were the companies' executives. In November, Japan indicated to the United States its willingness to participate in a five-nation conference on oil consumption. Beginning with organized labor's spring offensive, trade unions pressed the legislature to deal with inflation. During the year, the Diet passed a land bill with price ceilings and a special corporate tax.

Social Unrest. Opposition parties accused the Tanaka government of "oppression" when, in June, leaders of the Japan Teachers Union were arrested for leading a strike of some 400,000 public school teachers. They were protesting stricter government control of school organization and Premier Tanaka's plan to reintroduce a curriculum in "ethics," banned just after the war.

During President Ford's visit, most Japanese saw only television broadcasts of the ceremonies. Many people were far more concerned with the nationwide public transportation strike occurring at the time.

On August 30 and October 14, Tokyo, which had been proud of its reputation as one of the safest cities in the world, suffered two serious bomb explosions. They killed 8 Japanese and injured over 100. Targets were the Mitsubishi and Mitsui combines, which handle defense contracts.

The Post-Industrial Society. When Kakuei Tanaka first became premier in 1972, he received wide publicity for his plan to build a "new Japan" (based on his best-seller *Remodeling the Japanese Archipelago*). Implementation of the plan in 1973, however, brought criticism on the grounds that it would alter the nation's landscape, increase pollution, and spread urban blight throughout the country. Moreover, landowner supporters of the LDP had made windfall profits on properties in areas where industry was to be relocated.

In June 1974, Tanaka announced his intention of improving the tarnished image of his earlier scheme. Japan, he stated, was moving toward a "post-industrial society"—that is, an "information-oriented society," in which citizens would seek a different kind of affluence. Slowdown of economic growth would help Japan to face the "advancing global menace of pollution."

Tanaka's new design was embraced in a 10-point program submitted to government advisory councils. It was to be applied over the period 1976–1985. The major goal of "remodeling" continued to be industrial relocation so that the value of factory shipments from the crowded Pacific coastal belt would decline from 73% to 50% by 1985. Sophisticated transportation networks would be vital both to relocation and the building of knowledge-intensive industries in regional centers. Thus every point in Japan was to be put within one day's surface journey from any other point. Regulation of land use—and restriction on property speculation—was central to the program. Finally, the Premier proposed, there would have to be a conversion of the present "horizontal" urban sprawl into "vertical" high-rise cities. The plan was likely to be continued under Miki, since the decline in growth itself dictated a shift in domestic priorities.

ARDATH W. BURKS, *Rutgers University*

JORDAN

The year 1974 began with the possibility that Jordan's King Hussein would emerge from the diplomatic isolation plaguing his position in Arab politics since 1970. Evidenced by the resumption of diplomatic ties with Syria and Egypt and the return of Kuwait's annual $40 million subsidy, the benefits of Hussein's belated participation in the October 1973 Arab-Israeli war appeared to assure his return to a position of influence in Arab affairs. However, during negotiations between Israel and the Arabs, Hussein's claim to be the legitimate negotiating agent for the return of the formerly Jordanian-occupied West Bank of the Jordan River came under direct attack in the wake of calls for the establishment of an independent Palestinian state.

Inter-Arab Politics. It was not the establishment of the Palestinian entity but rather the issue of who would represent West Bank Palestinians in negotiations with Israel that proved to be Hussein's thorniest problem. In the aftermath of the October war, the Palestine Liberation Organization (PLO)—the guerrilla organ that had advocated Hussein's overthrow since 1970—advanced its claim to be the sole spokesman for Palestinian interests. To Hussein's discomfort, the PLO's claim won considerable currency in the Third World.

With Saudi Arabia's King Faisal and Egypt's President Sadat attending, the Second Islamic Summit Conference at Lahore, Pakistan, passed a resolution on February 23 naming the PLO as the sole legitimate spokesman for the restoration of Palestinian rights and territories. Hussein, during a two-week stay in the United States, announced on March 15 that he favored the PLO's presence at the Geneva peace conference on the Middle East but, with regard to the future of the West Bank and a Palestinian state, that decision was the West Bank Palestinians' alone. He would support them in whatever course they chose in a referendum he would hold when the West Bank was returned to his sovereignty.

Following King Hussein's visit to Egypt, Syria, and Saudi Arabia during the week of April 4–11, Jordan's position underwent a critical modification: on May 1, Hussein announced that if it was the unanimous will of other Arab states to give the PLO sole responsibility for the restoration of Palestinian territory, he had no alternative but to respect their decision, considering it to relieve him of any responsibility to attend the Arab-Israeli peace talks at Geneva.

Even though Hussein received a July 18 endorsement from Egypt's Sadat following an Israeli refusal to negotiate with the PLO, Jordan was not invited to a September 21–22 meeting of Egypt, Syria, and the PLO to discuss strategy prior to the Arab summit conference that resulted in a joint Syrian-Egyptian endorsement of the PLO's position.

It was at the October 26–29 Arab summit conference in Rabat, Morocco, that Hussein received what may have been the most severe diplomatic defeat of his life. On October 25, Arab foreign ministers voted 19–1 to endorse the PLO. On October 28, Hussein acquiesced in the face of Arab unanimity and a pledge of an annual $300 million subsidy from Saudi Arabia: the 20 kings and presidents of the Arab League issued a communiqué unanimously declaring the PLO to be the sole legitimate spokesman of the Palestinian people on any Palestinian land that is liberated.

Constitutional Shake-up. In November, Hussein supported enabling legislation that would reorganize Jordan to reflect the change in status of West Bank Palestinians as a result of the decisions taken at Rabat. The new parliamentary and constitutional elections that were being considered would strip West Bank Palestinians of half of the seats in Parliament and half of the cabinet posts reserved for them. Hussein announced that Jordan would no longer pay for the civilian administration of the Israeli-occupied West Bank. In short, the initiatives appeared to be designed to make it difficult for West Bankers to side with the PLO.

Internal Problems. Economic dependence proved to be heavier than expected when announcements in January and May, respectively, revealed a $70 million budget deficit and a $350 million trade deficit. The United States pledge of $65 million for 1974–75, the Kuwaiti $40 million subsidy, and the prospect of Saudi Arabia's massive aid will help Jordan temporarily, but self-sufficiency is not on the immediate horizon.

Politically, King Hussein had to cut short a trip to Great Britain when army units called for the resignation of Prime Minister Zaid al-Rifai and higher pay scales on February 6, the aftermath of which was the forced retirement of 10 senior military officers. In January, two Amman dailies were seized as press censorship was reimposed for the first time since the October war of 1973.

F. NICHOLAS WILLARD
Georgetown University

JORDAN • Information Highlights

Official Name: Hashemite Kingdom of Jordan.
Location: Southwest Asia.
Area: 37,738 square miles (97,740 sq km).
Population (1973 est.): 2,600,000.
Chief Cities (1971 est.): Amman, the capital, 520,700; Zarqa, 225,000; Irbid, 115,000.
Government: *Head of state,* Hussein ibn Talal, king (acceded Aug. 1952). *Head of government,* Zaid al-Rifai, premier (took office May 1973). *Legislature*—National Assembly: Senate and House of Representatives.
Monetary Unit: Dinar (0.3289 dinar equals U. S.$1, July 1974).
Gross National Product (1972 est.): $686,000,000.
Manufacturing (major products): Cement, petroleum products, cigarettes, vegetable oil, flour.
Major Agricultural Products: Wheat, tomatoes, barley, fruits, corn, olives, sorghum, grapes, tobacco.
Foreign Trade (1973): *Exports,* $56,000,000; *imports,* $328,000,000.

KANSAS

Although a killer tornado struck a portion of Emporia on June 8, 1974, followed by a less-than-record farm crop year, Kansans could remain unruffled and cast their heavy mandate in the November elections for the right to play bingo, leaving major political candidates to worry through contests that were undecided until the final hours of counting.

Agriculture. Wheat production in Kansas in 1974, estimated at some 319 million bushels, was 17% below the record crop of 1973. July's precipitation, less than one-fourth normal, also sharply reduced the state's row crop prospects. Increased moisture in August halted the slide toward disaster, but damage had been done, and the year ended with these 1974 crop estimates—below the 1973 production by the following percentages: corn, 112 million bushels, off 27%; sorghum grain, 127 million bushels, down 42%; and soybeans, 20 million bushels, off 24%. Better was the sugar beet estimate of 595,000 tons, only 2% below 1973.

Weather. A tornado that hit Emporia on June 8 dealt heavy damage to a shopping center, an apartment complex, and nearby residences and trailer homes. Six deaths and more than 100 injuries resulted, with property damage estimated at $25 to $30 million. On August 17 thunderstorms, with hail and hurricane-force winds up to 100 mph, swept 20 eastern and central Kansas counties. Damages from these storms were estimated at up to $100 million.

Legislation. The 1974 session of the Kansas Legislature approved appropriations and spending authority for a budget of $1.28 billion. A new ethics code was approved to control financing of political campaigns and establish standards of conduct for state officers, employees, candidates for state or legislative office, and lobbyists; and conflict-of-interest laws also were tightened.

Increased funding was provided for elementary and secondary education, junior colleges, special education, post-high school vocational education, and community-based mental health centers and retardation programs. A due-process law was enacted for teachers.

Other acts included the revision of the workmen's compensation law to allow for greatly expanded benefits for workers injured on the job; increased pay for faculties of state colleges and most officers and employees of the state and counties; and the reduction of residency requirement for divorce to 60 days.

Among several proposed constitutional amendments receiving legislative approval for submission to the voters, one would allow certain nonprofit organizations to conduct games of bingo. The voters of Kansas approved the measure overwhelmingly.

Election. The majority of Kansas voters demonstrated in the November 5 election that they were not averse to switching parties to secure candidates of their choice. In the two highest and hottest races, Republicans squeaked through. U. S. Sen. Robert Dole, former Republican national chairman, won a hard-fought battle against his Democratic challenger, Dr. William R. Roy, to retain his seat in the Senate. Roy, who chose to give up an apparently secure seat in the U. S. House of Representatives, trailed by some 13,000 votes. The House seat he vacated was won by Democrat Mrs. Martha Keys of Manhattan. Her opponent was a young Republican state legislator, John Peterson of Topeka. Kansas' other seats in the U. S. House were retained handily by Republican incumbents Keith Sebelius, Garner Shriver, Joe Skubitz, and Larry Winn, Jr.

Democrat Robert B. Docking, after eight years as governor, chose not to run again. A change in the law now requires candidates for governor and lieutenant governor to run as teams, and for four-year terms instead of two. The Republican nominee for governor was Robert F. Bennett of Overland Park, president of the state Senate, and he chose as his running mate Kansas House member Shelby Smith of Wichita. Democratic candidates were Attorney General Vern Miller of Wichita for governor and state Sen. Jack Steineger of Kansas City for lieutenant governor. The Bennett-Smith team won by 3,677 votes.

The vacated seat of attorney general was won by Democrat Curt Schneider of Coffeyville over Treasurer Tom Van Sickle, and the treasurer's position was filled by Mrs. Joan Finney, a Democrat of Topeka. Other state officers reelected, all Republicans, were Mrs. Elwill Shanahan, secretary of state; Fletcher Bell, commissioner of insurance; and Robert Sanders, state printer.

In legislative races the Democrats gained one seat in the Senate, filling an unexpired term, and scored a net gain of eight seats in the House. But Republicans remained in control in the Senate, 26–14, and in the House, 72–53.

NYLE H. MILLER
Kansas State Historical Society

KANSAS • Information Highlights

Area: 82,264 square miles (213,064 sq km).
Population (1973 est.): 2,279,000. *Density:* 28 per sq mi.
Chief Cities (1970 census): Topeka, the capital, 125,011; Wichita, 276,554; Kansas City, 168,213; Overland Park, 79,034.
Government (1974): *Chief Officers*—governor, Robert Docking (D); lt. gov., David C. Owen (R). *Legislature*—Senate, 40 members (27 R, 13 D); House of Representatives, 125 members (80 R, 45 D).
Education (1973–74): *Enrollment*—public elementary schools, 269,434 pupils; public secondary schools, 207,552; nonpublic schools, 33,300; colleges and universities, 107,986 students. *Public school expenditures,* $449,902,000 ($1,037 per pupil).
State Finances (fiscal year 1973): *Revenues,* $1,144,418,000; *expenditures,* $978,090,000.
Personal Income (1973): $11,525,000,000; per capita, $5,057.
Labor Force (July 1974): *Nonagricultural wage and salary earners,* 768,200; *insured unemployed,* 8,800 (1.5%).

WIDE WORLD

Democratic Governor Wendell Ford of Kentucky is elated after winning the Senate seat of Republican Marlow Cook.

KENTUCKY

A somewhat controversial legislative session, the weather, the fall elections, and the coal boom made the year 1974 memorable in Kentucky.

The General Assembly. The biennial session, though criticized for lack of leadership and subjection to special influences, enacted some 400 laws, including some measures of real consequence. Gov. Wendell H. Ford's reorganization of the executive agencies of state government, begun in 1973 and completed on Jan. 1, 1974, with the creation of a Consumer Protection and Regulation Cabinet, received legislative approval, as did his record-shattering budget of $4.4 billion for the next two fiscal years—about $1 billion more than the figure for the last biennium.

Other enactments provided for compilation of a new penal code, for equal rights for women in the areas of credit and insurance, for amending Kentucky Revised Statutes in order to eliminate discrimination on the basis of sex, and for optional no-fault auto insurance; prohibit strip-mining under the old broad-form deeds without consent of the land owner; permit abortion at the mother's discretion during the first three months of pregnancy; and place restrictions on electioneering and on campaign financing.

The Weather. In less than a week, beginning March 29, a destructive wind and rain storm swept through central Kentucky. A tornado wiped out the business section of Campbellsburg on April 1, leaving one person dead; and two days later, 18 tornadoes hit widely dispersed areas, causing 71 deaths, razing Brandenburg, Stamping Ground, and parts of Louisville, Frankfort, and other towns, and damaging farms, killing livestock, and destroying timber. By presidential proclamation, 40 counties were declared disaster areas. Heavy rains caused flash floods in eastern Kentucky in June and, three months later, in Barren County and the Red River valley. Unusually early frosts damaged some crops, including tobacco, not yet housed.

Politics. In November, Governor Ford defeated incumbent Republican Marlow Cook in the U. S. Senate race, giving Kentucky for the first time in almost two decades two Democrats in the upper house. The party division of the state's delegation to the U. S. House of Representatives remained unchanged at 5 Democrats and 2 Republicans. Without prior announcement Senator Cook resigned his office on December 27. Ford then resigned from the governorship, Lt. Gov. Julian Carroll was sworn in as Kentucky's 50th governor, and Ford was appointed to the Senate seat vacated by Marlow Cook.

Coal. Kentucky experienced a boom in the coalfields in 1974. Soaring prices brought feverish activity in both strip and underground mining, especially to the eastern mountains. County governments in coal-producing areas enjoyed unaccustomed revenue from the severance tax, a part of which, by action of the General Assembly, was returned to them. After 13 months the strike at Eastover Mining Company's Brookside mine ended with a United Mine Workers union victory, but coalfield labor troubles were far from general settlement.

Under Governor Ford's leadership, and with legislative approval, the state launched a $50 million research program in the conversion of coal to gas and in liquefaction of coal. On November 1, the Federal Office of Coal Research announced the choice of Catlettsburg as the site of a test plant for liquefying coal.

JAMES F. HOPKINS, *University of Kentucky*

KENTUCKY • Information Highlights

Area: 40,395 square miles (104,623 sq km).
Population (1973 est.): 3,342,000. *Density:* 83 per sq mi.
Chief Cities (1970 census): Frankfort, the capital, 21,902; Louisville, 361,958; Lexington, 108,137; Covington, 52,535.
Government (1974): *Chief Officers*—governor, Wendell H. Ford (D); lt. gov., Julian M. Carroll (D). *General Assembly*—Senate, 38 members (29 D, 9 R); House of Representatives, 100 members (80 D, 20 R).
Education (1973–74): *Enrollment*—public elementary schools, 447,000 pupils; public secondary, 263,000; nonpublic, 60,200; colleges and universities, 110,611 students. *Public school expenditures,* $474,000,000 ($727 per pupil).
State Finances (fiscal year 1973): *Revenues,* $1,914,060,000; *Expenditures,* $1,782,288,000.
Personal Income (1973): $13,259,000,000; per capita, $3,967.
Labor Force (July 1974): *Nonagricultural wage and salary earners,* 1,064,700; *Insured unemployed,* 18,400 (2.2%).

KENYA

Kenya held parliamentary elections in October 1974, the second since independence in 1963. As in the 1969 polling, the leadership of President Jomo Kenyatta was not threatened, and few changes in the government's policy were expected.

Election Results. The Kenya African National Union (KANU) is Kenya's ruling and only political party. Although opposition parties are not legally banned outright, such groups must be registered by the government, and none has secured such registration since the banning of the Kenya People's Union (KPU) and the detention of its leaders in 1969.

Oginga Odinga, former president of KPU and former vice president of Kenya, sought permission to run in the 1974 elections. Although he had rejoined KANU after being released from detention in 1971, Odinga was not allowed to become a candidate.

Despite the absence of opposition parties, Kenyan elections provide the voters with some, though carefully limited, choices. In 1974 over 700 KANU candidates ran for the 158 constituency seats in parliament. They faced an electorate expanded by a constitutional amendment in April to include 18-year-olds.

As in 1969, less than half of the incumbent members of parliament won reelection. The circulation of parliamentary membership enables voters to express their discontent and new voices to be heard in the National Assembly.

Since cabinet members, including the president, must first be elected as members of parliament, voters can even affect changes at high levels. President Kenyatta and Vice President Daniel arap Moi ran unopposed. However, several members of the cabinet, including Foreign Minister Njoroge Mungai, were defeated. Mungai was a close associate of Kenyatta and was considered a possible successor to him. Mungai's defeat solidifies Vice President Moi's position as leading contender for the presidency after Kenyatta. Mungai was replaced as foreign minister by Munyua Waiyaki, former deputy speaker of the National Assembly.

Other cabinet members defeated were Minister for Tourism and Wildlife Juxon Shako, Minister for Labor E. Ngala Mwendwa, and Minister for Natural Resources William Odongo Omamo, who had represented Odinga's old constituency. The political establishment is frequently criticized in parliament for the uneven distribution of wealth and development in the country. A number of outspoken critics of the government, such as M. J. Seroney and J. M. Kariuki, were reelected, so lively debates were expected to continue in 1975.

The new parliament will conduct its business in Swahili, since Swahili replaced English as the national language in July. According to Attorney General Charles Njonjo, English will continue to play a major role in the country's legal system.

KENYA • Information Highlights

Official Name: Republic of Kenya.
Location: East coast of Africa.
Area: 244,959 square miles (582,644 sq km).
Population (1973 est.): 12,500,000.
Chief Cities (1970 est.): Nairobi, the capital, 535,200; Mombasa, 255,400.
Government: *Head of state,* Jomo Kenyatta, president (took office Dec. 1964). *Head of government,* Jomo Kenyatta. *Legislature* (unicameral)—National Assembly.
Monetary Unit: Kenya shilling (7.143 shillings equal U.S.$1, July 1974).
Gross National Product (1972 est.): $1,964,000,000.
Manufacturing (major products): Construction materials, processed agricultural products, petroleum products.
Major Agricultural Products: Coffee, tea, sugarcane, sisal, corn, cassava, pyrethrum, fruits, livestock.
Foreign Trade (1973): *Exports,* $351,000,000; *imports,* $593,000,000.

The Economy. Critics of Kenya's economic development have concentrated on the wide gap between the rich and the poor rather than rates of aggregate growth. The economy continued to grow at a rapid pace in 1974. Reports indicated that exports in 1973 had increased by 37% over 1972, considerably greater than the 16% rise in imports.

Despite gradual industrialization, agriculture continues to be the mainstay of Kenya's economy, and coffee was the main reason for the improved balance of trade position in 1973. Production of coffee was up 15%, while the average price rose 22%.

However, 1974 saw a drought-caused downturn in food production. The problem was far less severe than that in neighboring Ethiopia or other affected areas of Africa, and the government announced that it had enough grain in storage to avert any crisis. Nonetheless, the government strictly limited exports of domestically consumed grains, such as maize and rice.

The government announced several new policies to spread economic development. These announcements were prompted, in part, by an earlier report of the International Labour Organization that asserted that economic gains in Kenya were too limited to the elite. The changes included abolishing school fees for the first four years of education, launching a new 40,000-acre (16,190-hectare) irrigation program on the Tana River banks, establishing a goal of providing land for all citizens by 1980, and improving amenities such as water supplies and health clinics.

University Closed. The University of Nairobi was shut down and its 5,000 students sent home twice during the year. The closures followed students protests and boycotts.

It was announced in April that Canada would provide Kenya with $9,400,000 in grants and loans to build and staff a technical teachers' training college in Nairobi. The program will also provide training in Canada for Kenyan teachers.

JAY E. HAKES
University of New Orleans

WIDE WORLD

Mrs. Park Chung Hee, wife of South Korea's president, is shown campaigning with her husband. She was killed in August during an assassination attempt on the President.

KOREA

Relations between the South and North seemed to reach a point of no return in 1974. Disparaging and slanderous propaganda reached its extreme; even the presidents of both sides attacked each other for the first time since July 1972, when they had agreed to eliminate their differences. It was also the year that South Korea experienced a most tragic event, the death of the first lady by an assassin's bullet; and the year that those who questioned the rule of President Park Chung Hee drew long prison terms or death sentences.

North Korea, on the other hand, heightened its vigilance of South Korea, intensified its revolutionary fervor, and called for the fulfillment of the 6-year economic plan (1971–76) by October 1975—one year earlier than scheduled under a new slogan of "speed battle."

SOUTH KOREA

Political Turmoil. As early as January 8, President Park issued two emergency decrees to quell mounting demonstrations for the restoration of democracy that had been nullified by the new 1972 constitution, which gave him total and permanent rule. The first set a maximum penalty of 15 years for those criticizing the constitution; and the second set up emergency courts-martial to try anyone violating the first decree. The promulgations were justified by the claim of a threatened Communist takeover.

To pacify the general populace, President Park issued decree No. 3 on January 14, exempting low-income citizens from taxes. These three measures, however, were insufficient to quiet the opposition, especially mounting unrest among college students. On April 3, decree No. 4 was promulgated, making it a capital offense to oppose the regime and to refuse to attend classes.

A score of political dissidents, especially young students and social-conscious Christian leaders, were arrested and court-martialed. Some received death sentences, others were given long prison terms. A notable aspect was the opposition to the regime by the Christian sector, which traditionally had been silent on political issues.

Notable opponents given prison terms were the only living former president, 76-year-old Yun Po-son, and Catholic Bishop Daniel Chi, on charges of aiding and instigating the overthrow of the government; and Kim Chi-ha, the renowned poet, for his stinging satirical poems depicting the endemic corruption among high officials in the government. His death sentence was commuted to life imprisonment. The harsh, repressive, and intimidating measures taken by the South Korean Central Intelligence Agency stirred international protests, and the U. S. Congress voiced its displeasure by cutting Korean aid funds.

In a move to placate his opponents, President Park lifted decrees Nos. 1 and 4, effective August 23, thus relaxing government activities against the political opposition and antigovernment campus organizations. This action did not affect those who were already convicted under the decrees and whose cases were pending. Sporadic demonstrations erupting in mid-September became so serious by October that Premier Kim Jong Pil warned of the possible restoration of the repealed decrees. As a result lectures were suspended and major colleges closed.

—— SOUTH KOREA • Information Highlights ——

Official Name: Republic of Korea.
Location: Northeastern Asia.
Area: 38,022 square miles (98,477 sq km).
Population (1974 est.): 33,300,000.
Chief Cities (1970 census): Seoul, the capital, 5,536,-377; Pusan, 1,880,710; Taegu, 1,082,750; Inchon, 646,013.
Government: *Head of state,* Park Chung Hee, president (took office Dec. 1963). *Head of government,* Kim Jong Pil, premier (took office June 1971). *Legislature* (unicameral)—National Assembly.
Monetary Unit: Won (399 won equal U. S.$1, Aug. 1974).
Gross National Product (1972 est.): $9,720,000,000.
Manufacturing (major products): Textiles, electronic equipment, petrochemicals, clothing, plywood, hair products, processed foods, metal products, furniture, ships.
Major Agricultural Products: Rice, barley, wheat, soybeans, sweet potatoes and yams, fish.
Foreign Trade (1973): *Exports,* $3,221,000,000; *imports,* $4,218,000,000.

A young standard-bearer of the opposition New Democratic party, Kim Yong-sam, 47, was unanimously elected on August 23 to succeed the late president of the party, Yu Chin-san, who died on March 28. Kim pledged in his inauguration speech to restore political liberties and to fight to restore democracy by annulling the new constitution.

Death of the First Lady. The volatile political situation reached a climax on August 15 when an assassin named Mun Se Kwang (later sentenced to death on October 15), a Korean resident in Japan, accidentally shot and killed the first lady, Yuk Yosa (Madame Yuk—Mrs. Park's maiden name, as a married woman is called according to Korean custom). The shot narrowly missed President Park as he delivered a Liberation Day speech in the National Theater. This tragedy exacerbated the already shaky diplomatic relations with Japan, since the assassin was a legal permanent resident of Japan. The Japanese government at first refused to accept any moral responsibility for the incident. Angry mobs stormed the Japanese embassy in Seoul, an act apparently approved by the government. Subsequently, Japan yielded and made a formal apology to the Korean government by sending a special envoy to Seoul.

Other Developments. President Park's New Community Movement (SAEMAUL undong) is well under way, effecting noticeable improvements in rural communities. The export free zone expected to be completed in 1978 was inaugurated in Iri, North Cholla province. It was inspired by one successful operation in Masan.

U. S. President Ford paid a one-day visit to South Korea on November 22 as part of his Far East journey. Ford reportedly told President Park that continued U. S. military aid would depend upon approval of funds by Congress, which has been critical of Park's repressive policies.

NORTH KOREA

North Korea's foreign policy took a new turn in 1974 with a surprise appeal for a bilateral peace agreement with the United States. At the 3d session of the 5th Supreme People's Assembly, North Korea on March 25 adopted a letter to be sent to the U. S. Congress. The action was a potentially important move toward a bilateral peace agreement, seeking to remove the existing state of military confrontation. A similar appeal had been sent to the U. S. Congress in April 1973.

Seoul denounced this Pyongyang bid as a "preposterous proposal" and a propaganda gambit intended to hasten the withdrawal of the 40,000 U. S. troops in the South. Although the U. S. State Department reacted coolly to the North Korean appeal, Rep. Michael Harrington (D-Mass.) declared that in view of the potential explosiveness of the situation on the Korean peninsula, both the executive and legislative branches of the U. S. government should look into the proposal.

NORTH KOREA • Information Highlights

Official Name: Democratic People's Republic of Korea.
Location: Northeastern Asia.
Area: 46,540 square miles (120,538 sq km).
Population (1973 est.): 15,100,000.
Chief Cities (1967 est.): Pyongyang, the capital, 840,000.
Government: *Head of state,* Kim Il Sung, president and secretary general of the Korean Workers' (Communist) party (took office Dec. 1972). *Head of government,* Kim Il, premier (took office Dec. 1972). *Legislature* (unicameral)—Supreme People's Assembly.
Monetary Unit: Won (0.961 won equals U. S.$1, Aug. 1974).
Gross National Product (1972 est.): $3,500,000,000.
Manufacturing (major products): Cement, metallurgical coke, pig iron and ferroalloys, textiles.
Major Agricultural Products: Rice, sweet potatoes and yams, soybeans, livestock, fish.
Foreign Trade: *Chief exports*—metals, farm products; *chief imports*—machinery.

In the fall, North Korea introduced to the 29th UN General Assembly a resolution calling for the withdrawal of all foreign troops stationed in South Korea under the flag of the United Nations. South Korea countered this move by proposing to continue their dialogue in the spirit of the previous year's UN resolution under which the UN omitted debate on the Korean question. The United Nations, through an East-West compromise, refused to take up the Korean question in 1974, returning the matter to the hands of the South Koreans and North Koreans to shape their own destiny.

Despite all these ruptures, the two Koreas maintained contact through a number of international events. Both sides participated in the 7th Asian Games held at Teheran, Iran, September 1–16, and in the annual meeting of the Inter-Parliamentary Union held in Tokyo, Japan, during October.

Economic Developments. At the 3d session of the 5th Supreme People's Assembly, held in March, a resolution was adopted to speed up completion of the 6-year economic plan (1971–76) by one year. The new deadline is Oct. 15, 1975, the 30th anniversary of the founding of the Korean Workers' party. It was also decided to complete abolition of taxes effective April 1, 1975, making North Korea possibly the first tax-free country in the world.

During Indonesian Foreign Minister Adam Malik's visit to Pyongyang in October 1974, North Korea contracted with Indonesia to sell 200,000 tons of rice. This marked the second Indonesian purchase of rice from North Korea. A first order for 100,000 tons was placed during the previous year.

North Korean geologists discovered new deposits of iron ore of rich content. The find, estimated at hundreds of millions of tons, is in the northeastern region. A new gigantic People's Palace of Culture, with 500 rooms and a meeting hall of 3,000 seats, was dedicated in Pyongyang on April 13.

KEY P. YANG
Korean Area Specialist
The Library of Congress

WIDE WORLD

National Guardsman watches trucks on Pennsylvania highway as drivers attempt to impede traffic in protest against fuel costs and speed limits during energy crisis.

LABOR

For labor, as for other segments of society, 1974 was a painful year in nearly all industrialized nations. Inflation rose in most countries to the double-digit level, or higher, and strikes surged as unions struggled to keep abreast of inflation. At the same time, recession deepened and widened, and unemployment mounted, forcing many governments to switch emphasis from anti-inflation to anti-recession programs.

U. S. Labor Developments

Labor in the United States grappled with the worst of all possible worlds in 1974—an inflation rate that rose to 12% and a deepening recession. Labor sought to meet the inflation impact at the bargaining table and the recession impact by the legislative route.

Wage Trends and Unemployment. Collective bargaining in major industries produced wage-fringe benefits considerably higher than in 1973. In that year, with controls still in effect, the real wages of workers, in terms of buying power, fell more than 5% below 1972.

After all controls expired on April 30, 1974, a pent-up wage explosion followed. By the third quarter of 1974, first-year wage increases in newly negotiated union-management contracts averaged 11.1%, compared with 5.8% for the year 1973. Most of the contracts also carried cost-of-living escalator clauses designed to protect the purchasing power of covered workers during the life of the contracts, generally two to three years.

On the recession side of the picture, the unemployment rate jumped to 6.5% in November, the highest level since October 1961, up from 4.7% in November 1973. Meanwhile, additional layoffs by the thousands were being announced by auto manufacturers, appliance makers, and many other branches of industry. Also, some companies eliminated overtime work or put their forces on reduced workweeks. In numbers, the jobless total rose to just under 6 million in November, up 1.1 million in three months.

Further, the U. S. Department of Labor reported that the number of part-time workers who desired full-time jobs mounted by 100,000 in October to 2.9 million. The department estimated that if this group was considered as unemployed, the October unemployment rate would have been 6.5%.

The Administration's Program. Late in the year the administration was still giving priority to the fight on inflation, rather than to the recession. President Ford submitted to Congress a program calculated to meet the problem, a highlight of which was a proposed 5% tax surcharge on income above $7,500 for individuals and $15,000 for families, with a similar 5% surcharge on corporate profits. This program met a chilly reception in Congress and even a chillier reception in the labor movement.

Instead, Congress, by an overwhelming vote, authorized a $5.5 billion program of extended unemployment insurance benefits, public service jobs for the idle, and job-creating public works projects.

The AFL-CIO. On the heels of the November 5 election, which resulted in victory for a record number of liberal, labor-endorsed congressional candidates, the AFL-CIO pressed for changes in government laws and policies to combat the recession and "turn the economy around towards expanding sales, production, buying power, and employment."

The AFL-CIO Executive Council warned that the economy is "perilously close to disaster" and it proposed a series of steps to revive the stagnating economy, such as lower interest rates, mandatory allocation of credit to priority needs, public service jobs on a large scale, curbs on exports of scarce commodities, action to spur housing construction, and other measures.

The AFL-CIO and unions outside the federation opposed reinstitution of wage-price controls, as urged by some, unless the controls were applied equitably across the board on prices, dividends, profits, and other elements of the economy. Past controls, the AFL-CIO charged, held down wages while prices and profits soared.

Prices and Production. Statistically, the Consumer Price Index rose 0.9% in October, following a 1.2% rise in September, to a rate 12.2% above a year earlier and 53.2% above the 1967 base period. Big new wholesale price increases presaged further rises in the CPI during the months immediately ahead.

Meantime, the gross national product, the measure of the nation's total output of goods and services, fell in the July–September period for the third quarter in a row. Such a drop for three consecutive quarters has been normally accepted as evidence of a recession. Federal officials at first declined to characterize the situation as a recession, but some, including the president, did so later.

Strikes. Strikes increased as labor fought for larger settlements to keep pace with inflation. These walkouts affected iron ore mining and processing, copper mining and processing, some airlines, part of the telephone industry, many local governmental units, the coal mines, and numerous other operations. The Labor Department reported that during the first nine months of 1974, man-days of idleness in labor disputes reached 38 million, the highest level since 1970. This amounted to 0.26% of total working time put in, nearly double the 0.14% rate for the first nine months of 1973.

Health and Safety. Unions stepped up efforts to improve health and safety conditions in the workplace. They pressed the Labor Department to conduct more effective enforcement of the previously passed Occupational Health & Safety Act. Some of them also won contract provisions for company-paid health research to reduce workplace hazards and for monitoring such hazards by union stewards. Greater safety was also a major objective of the United Mine Workers in that union's hard-fought dispute with mine operators.

Pensions. After a seven-year struggle, Congress in August passed a broad pension-reform bill aimed at correcting gaps and abuses in the supplemental pension plans prevailing in much of private industry. The law aims to insure that the 23 million workers presently covered by such plans will actually receive the benefits they expect when they retire. Known as the Employee Benefit Security Act of 1974, the legislation grew out of disclosures that "hookers" in many of the pension plans left workers without some or any of the benefits they had counted on upon retirement.

Insurance. Prepaid legal insurance has become a growing fringe benefit in union-management agreements as an aftermath of action by Congress in 1973, lifting a Taft-Hartley Act ban against employer payments to funds for such purposes. Scores of unions have negotiated such plans, financed by employers alone or equally by both sides. Under these plans, specified legal services, up to a maximum cost per year, become available to covered workers.

White Collar Employment. The shift toward white collar employment continued during the year. Within the labor movement, white collar unions registered impressive gains among employees in federal, state and local government, also among teachers and professional employees. Strikes rose sharply in state and local governmental units as the unions fought for recognition and for wage increases adequate to overcome the inflationary spiral.

These work stoppages occurred during the year despite their illegality in most U. S. states. Also, the unions are pressing Congress for federal legislation which would establish full collective bargaining rights, including the right to strike, in some circumstances, for state and local government workers.

Typographical Agreements. Landmark agreements were reached by the International Typographical Union with the *New York Times* and New York *Daily News*—and with two Washington (D. C.) dailies, the *Post* and *Star-News,* giving the printers lifetime job guarantees and other benefits in return for a free hand to the employers to modernize and automate their printing processes. Similar settlements are anticipated throughout the industry, and the result is expected to be a slow but steady long-range erosion of the typographer craft in its present form as new devices displace the venerable Linotype.

RUBEN LEVIN
Editor, "Labor" Newspaper

With jobs increasingly hard to find, a resourceful New York girl carries a sign proclaiming her skills.

UPI

WIDE WORLD

Striking Japanese railroad workers block the tracks as Japan comes to a virtual halt on April 13, the beginning of a general strike by transportation workers.

World Labor Developments

Labor's struggle with inflation and recession in Canada, Japan, western Europe, and Latin America during the year 1974 was much like that in the United States.

Canada. Retail prices in November 1974 increased to a level 12% above those of a year earlier. Organized workers in major settlements kept ahead of the price level, with wage increases averaging over 12%. Unemployment approached 6%, and in November the government shifted ground from an anti-inflation policy to a federal budget calling for cuts in personal taxes, and for measures to expand the economy and create more jobs.

Major strikes of the year were mainly in the public sector. Toronto's big bus, streetcar, and subway system was shut down by a strike in late August. It was ended by special provincial legislation which gave the employees 23% in wage increases over two years, with remaining issues left to binding arbitration. Also, Montreal firefighters struck for two days in November. They settled for a $750 cost-of-living bonus covering 1974, while agreeing to continue negotiations for a 1975 contract. Some fires flared uncontrolled during the strike.

For a change, a peaceful settlement was reached on Canada's railroads, averting the customary strikes and slowdowns of recent past years. The railroad unions won a $350 cost-of-living bonus for 1974, on top of a 9% wage increase secured earlier in the year, plus a wage package totaling 15% for 1975.

There were mixed developments on the nationalism issue in Canadian labor. The paperworkers formed a separate Canadian union and the broadcast technicians split into Canadian and U. S. unions, while retaining a joint advisory council for liaison purposes. However, delegates of the big steelworkers union, at a national conference, voted overwhelmingly against breaking away from their international union.

Japan. Inflation flared in 1974, in part because of soaring oil prices. As a result the annual spring "shunto," or wage offensive, proved more militant than usual, bringing a spurt of strikes and ending with record wage increases averaging nearly 33%, compared with 20% in 1973. Much of that gain was eaten up by later retail price increases. By October the price index was 26% above a year earlier.

Meanwhile, as the Japanese government sought to restrain inflation, the economy slowed down, and job layoffs grew, raising Japan's hitherto marginal unemployment rate to almost 2%. The layoffs jarred industry's "lifetime employment" tradition, under which most workers are guaranteed jobs regardless of the economy. However, many of those laid off for three to six months received 90% of their normal pay.

Changes occurred in Japan's unique system of retirement at age 55. In a growing number of firms the retirement age was raised to the high 50's, or to 60, or even to 65.

As in past years, transportation strikes and work-to-rule slowdowns, precipitated by a variety of issues and grievances, paralyzed the railroads at intervals during the year.

Western Europe. Inflation and recession spread through western Europe in 1974. Consumer price rises ranged from 7% in West Germany to over 20% in Italy. Unemployment kept mounting. Among labor and economic highlights in the major countries were these:

Great Britain. The year began with escalation of a dispute involving coal miners—a dispute that led to toppling of the Conservative government and elevation of a Labour party government at a special election. This government granted the miners their demand for a 35% wage increase, thus ending the strike and an accompanying national emergency that had been marked by three-day workweeks in coal-starved plants. Late in the year the Labour government faced a new coal mine strike threat. Meanwhile, the British retail price index rose in November to 18.3% above a year earlier, but basic wage rates increased over 20% on the average. Unemployment climbed to 3% of the total work force in November.

West Germany. West Germany was pictured as the "miracle nation" of Europe for holding its inflation rate below 7%. However, as unemployment kept rising—to a rate of 3.5% in November—the German government began shifting from a fight against inflation to one against recession. During the year, unions in wage negotiations secured wage increases averaging between 10% and 12%.

France. Industrial strife escalated late in the year as unions fought the economic austerity and wage restraint programs of France's new government under President Giscard d'Estaing. In November the two big labor confederations called a one-day general strike throughout France, though its effectiveness was limited.

Also the French nation was hit hard by the longest postal strike in history, and by numerous short strikes in the railroad industry, urban transport, telephone and telegraph, coal mining, gas and electricity, garbage collection, and other fields. Meanwhile, the inflation rate reached 15%.

Italy. This country was plagued by strikes as workers struggled to keep ahead of fast-rising prices. The consumer price index mounted to 24% above 1973 levels. Unemployment climbed to nearly 6% as the government pressed austerity programs and as economic chaos spread throughout the country.

Latin America. In most Latin countries, inflation in 1974 was quite severe, and labor unrest was widespread, even in lands ruled by military juntas.

Argentina. Left- and right-wing Peronists in the labor movement engaged in violence. Union leaders in both camps were shot and killed during the year. A "social pact" among the General Labor Confederation, the government, and Peronist industrialists was arranged early in the year, providing for wage-price restraints, but its effectiveness was diminished after President Juan Perón died on July 1, and as retail prices escalated by over 15%.

Mexico. A major labor-management agreement reached in September raised wages by 22%, about equal to the officially stated rise in the consumer price index, thereby averting a threatened nationwide strike.

Chile. Under military rule, an anti-inflation program pared consumer price increases from an annual rate of 800% under the Allende regime to an estimated 300% in 1974. The unemployment rate went up to 12%.

Brazil. A widely publicized "indexing system," designed to keep prices and wages in tandem, showed signs of faltering. Retail prices, after being held in check, began rising at a rate of 3% a month.

Venezuela. Surging oil revenues brought a new burst of prosperity, with higher wages and a record per capita income. Real economic growth in 1974 was calculated at 12%, but the nation's unemployment and underemployment were estimated at 2.3 million, nearly a third of the labor force.

RUBEN LEVIN
Editor, "Labor" Newspaper

British coal miners walk off the job over a wage dispute after the failure of a government appeal to postpone the strike, which it feared would cripple Britain's economy.

UPI

LAOS

Taking office in April 1974, the third coalition government to be established in Laos since 1957 joined in a single regime anti-Communist and Communist battle foes of more than 10 years. The new administration fulfilled the political terms of the February 1973 peace agreement between the U. S.-supported Souvanna Phouma government and the North Vietnam–aided Pathet Lao insurgents. In the summer, however, Premier Souvanna suffered a heart attack and went abroad for treatment, raising doubts about the country's newfound stability and its future political orientation.

Military Situation. During 1974 there was virtually no fighting between the two chief Laotian political-military factions. However, the country remained divided territorially. Pathet Lao troops shared patrol duties with anti-Communist forces in the administrative and royal capitals of Vientiane and Luang Prabang, but the three-quarters of the land in Pathet hands when the 1973 peace pact was signed remained under Communist military and political control. In addition, traffic continued to be heavy along the Ho Chi Minh Trail in eastern Pathet Lao territory—North Vietnamese supplies still flowing down the artery into South Vietnam.

Politics. Portfolios in the 12-member coalition government were shared equally between Pathet Lao and pro-American "neutralists." The 73-year old Prince Souvanna Phouma continued as premier, but his younger half-brother, titular Pathet Lao leader Prince Souphanouvong, headed the Joint National Political Council, a 42-member policy advisory body. In early post-coalition political jockeying, the council gained ascendancy over the rightist-dominated National Assembly, which it first prevented from opening officially and then caused to stop sitting altogether.

Souvanna Phouma's strategy after inauguration of the coalition government was to play a reconciling role rather than continue as leader of the anti-Communist faction. This left a gap in anti-Communist ranks that no other personality was able to fill through 1974. As a result, the Communist Souphanouvong emerged as the strongest partisan political figure in the new coalition regime, and the Pathet Lao clearly the dominant faction.

The heart attack suffered by Premier Souvanna Phouma on July 12 removed from the political scene, if only temporarily, the country's one real national leader. Foreign Minister Phoumi Vongvichit of the Pathet Lao faction was designated acting premier by Souvanna during his absence for medical treatment in France, but the government, which made no major decisions during this period, seemed less pro-Communist under Phoumi than before Souvanna's heart attack. Souvanna returned to the country in November but did not immediately resume its political leadership.

Economy. The Laotian countryside and economy were not as disrupted by ten years of warfare as neighboring South Vietnam's, but damage was nonetheless widespread. Whole villages in Communist-held territory had been destroyed by U. S. bombing, and rehabilitation was slow and inadequate. Inhabitants of refugee camps in non-Communist territory numbered 160,000 officially, but as many as 700,000 persons—over a fifth of the national population—were believed to be uprooted from their homes.

Laos, once self-sufficient in rice, had to import that staple and other foodstuffs. The nation's trade imbalance grew in 1974, with American-financed imports maintaining the country's standard of living. U. S. aid in the fiscal year that ended in June totaled $110 million. Only one third of the $35 million worth of imports, however, were essential goods, the vast majority of imported products being luxury items for the country's still high-living conservative economic elite.

Foreign Affairs. The maneuvering for influence in Laos among outside powers continued in 1974, though on a reduced scale. By June, all American and Thai troops had left Laos, but 25,000 to 30,000 North Vietnamese troops remained, contrary to terms of the 1973 peace settlement. However, in November, at least some of these troops were reported to have been withdrawn, and most of those remaining were said to be performing nonmilitary duties.

Although the United States otherwise disengaged militarily from Laos, American reconnaissance planes based in Thailand continued to observe the North Vietnamese forces in Laos. An official American study, released in June, revealed, moreover, that U. S. economic and military aid was still being channeled to agencies controlled by anti-Communist leaders.

China also largely disengaged from Laos, withdrawing most of the military personnel and antiaircraft gunnery it had in the north.

RICHARD BUTWELL
State University of New York College at Fredonia

LAOS • Information Highlights

Official Name: Kingdom of Laos.
Location: Southeast Asia.
Area: 91,429 square miles (236,800 sq km).
Population (1973 est.): 3,200,000.
Chief Cities (1970 est.): Vientiane, the capital, 150,000; Luang Prabang, the royal capital, 25,000.
Government: *Head of state,* Savang Vatthana, king (acceded Nov. 1959). *Head of government,* Prince Souvanna Phouma, premier (took office June 1962). *Legislature* (unicameral)—National Assembly.
Monetary Unit: Kip (600 kips equal U. S.$1, July 1974).
Gross National Product (1972 est.): $202,000,000.
Manufacturing (major products): Cigarettes, textiles.
Major Agricultural Products: Rice, corn, coffee, cotton, tobacco, cardamom, vegetables, forest products.
Foreign Trade (1972): *Exports,* $3,000,000; *imports,* $44,000,000.

UPI

(*Above*) The shrouded coffin of Argentine President Juan Perón is wheeled through the streets of Buenos Aires. (*Right*) A soldier prevents a youth from rushing to the coffin as it passes by the grieving crowd, some of whom make the Perónist "V" salute or wave handkerchiefs.

UPI

LATIN AMERICA

The year 1974 was a relatively quiet one in Latin America. María Estela "Isabel" de Perón succeeded her deceased husband, Juan Perón, as president of Argentina, becoming the first woman president in Latin America. Significant developments included the discovery of new oil fields in Mexico, which promise to bolster that country's faltering economy, and the growing economic strength of Venezuela, Latin America's leading petroleum exporter.

Venezuela's Growing Wealth. Under its new president, Carlos Andrés Pérez, Venezuela continued to press for the nationalization of all oil operations within its borders before 1983, when the leases held by foreign companies begin to expire. Venezuelan government revenues mounted, as a result of the increasingly profitable operations of the oil companies.

Promising to share the economic windfall with its partners in the Andean Group (Colombia, Ecuador, Peru, Bolivia, Chile), Venezuela pledged $60 million to the Group's lending agency, the Andean Development Corporation (ADC), enabling the ADC to increase its authorized capital to $400 million. Outside the Andean Group, Venezuelan aid was extended to Guyana ($17 million) and Honduras ($5 million) in the form of no-interest loans. Venezuela also promised to contribute to the development funds of the World Bank and the Inter-American Development Bank (IADB).

Development Loans. The IADB celebrated its 10th anniversary in 1974, making loans to Brazil for hydroelectric power development ($84.5 million) and highway construction ($36 million), and to Colombia for hydroelectric power ($48.5 million). Argentina began drawing on a $756 million package, approved in December 1973, for urban improvements and for aiding small and medium industries, exporters of capital goods, farmers and ranchers. Other countries favored with IADB loans in 1974 included Uruguay ($21.4 million), El Salvador ($18.4 million), Panama ($8 million), and Trinidad and Tobago ($2.4 million).

The World Bank, for the first time since 1962, granted a loan to Haiti, $10 million for highway repair. Mexico remained at the top of the list of World Bank borrowers in Latin America ($1.8 billion to date), receiving $214 million for road improvements and irrigation. The World Bank lent Brazil $60 million to improve its cattle industry.

Common Market. There was some dissension in the Andean Group, Latin America's most successful common market. Chile argued for a relaxation of restrictions on foreign investment in member countries, while Venezuela and Peru insisted on strict adherence to the established schedule for the nationalization of foreign firms operating in the region. The rightist government in Santiago claimed that the Group's nationalistic regulations were impeding Chile's flow of foreign capital, which it saw as essential to the reconstruction of the country's economy, still wracked by Latin America's highest inflation rate. Although Chile unilaterally suspended some of the Group's rules on foreign investment, there was no serious move to expel it from the community. In fact, the Andean Development Corporation lent Chile $20 million for government-run small and medium industry.

Venezuela announced plans to nationalize its steel industry, which it promised to develop in accordance with Andean Group policies. Colombia decided against selling large quantities of coal to Brazil, reserving the resource for its Andean partners, particularly Venezuela.

The Caribbean Common Market (CARICOM), composed of former British colonies, received its first membership application from a non-English-speaking country, Haiti. The Dutch colony of Surinam, due to become independent in 1975, also expressed interest in joining CARICOM. Together with Haiti, Surinam, and the Dominican Republic, the CARICOM countries produce 42% of the world's bauxite. Inspired by the success of the Organization of Petroleum Exporting Countries (OPEC) in controlling the production and marketing of oil, Prime Minister Michael Manley of Jamaica took the lead in forming the International Bauxite Association (IBA). The IBA called for a 12% increase in government royalties, negotiations leading to the expropriation of land owned by transnational aluminum companies, and government acquisition of a 51% interest in each company.

Lingering hostility between Honduras and El Salvador prevented a revival of the moribund Central American Common Market (CACOM). But a new international organization was launched in the region in 1974 as Honduras, Costa Rica, and Panama joined in the Union of Banana Exporting Countries (UBEC). UBEC's plans for collecting a $1 per crate export tax on bananas were thwarted by the refusal of Ecuador and Guatemala to join the cartel, the resistance of the Standard Fruit Company and United Brands (formerly United Fruit), and the destruction of much of Honduras' banana crop by hurricane Fifi.

The OAS and Cuba. The new, democratically elected governments of Venezuela, Colombia, and Costa Rica took the lead in urging repeal of the diplomatic and commercial sanctions imposed against Cuba by the Organization of American States (OAS). The repeal resolution was not openly opposed by the United States, but, to the surprise of many, it failed to receive the necessary two-thirds vote at a November meeting of OAS foreign ministers in Quito, Ecuador. Only Chile, Paraguay, and Uruguay voted against repeal, but abstentions by the United States, Brazil, Guatemala, Bolivia, Nicaragua, and Haiti left the pro-Cuba forces two votes short of the required 14. The fact that the sanctions were opposed by a majority of OAS members was expected to prompt other countries to join the seven already violating them and establish normal diplomatic and trade relations with Havana.

The U. S. and Latin America. U. S. Secretary of State Henry Kissinger was conspicuous by his absence from the OAS meeting in Quito, where the United States was represented by Undersecretary of State Robert Ingersoll. Kissinger had met in February with Latin American foreign ministers in Mexico City, where he argued, with little effect, for hemispheric solidarity in dealing with overseas oil suppliers.

Also in February, Kissinger made a five-hour visit to Panama and signed an "agreement on basic principles for negotiations" with Panamanian strongman Gen. Omar Torrijos. The agreement cleared the way for amicable discussions on ways of attaining the stated objectives of phasing out U. S. jurisdiction over the Canal Zone and granting a "fair and equitable" share of the Canal's proceeds to Panama.

Revelations that Kissinger had approved the clandestine use of U. S. funds to "destabilize" the Marxist government of the late Chilean President Salvador Allende caused consternation among many Latin Americans.

The resignation in August of President Richard Nixon, who was believed to have a personal antipathy for Premier Fidel Castro, was seen as opening the possibility of a new U. S. policy toward Cuba and, perhaps, toward Latin America as a whole. While President Gerald Ford has no record of interest in Latin America, the man he designated as his vice president, Nelson Rockefeller, is a long-time advocate of closer ties with the area.

Problems and Promise for Mexico. Gerald Ford's first visit to Latin America as president was a one-day border crossing into Mexico in October. Like most Latin American countries, Mexico faced a mounting balance of payments

UPI

New president of Venezuela Carlos Andrés Pérez and his wife, Blanquita, wave to inauguration day crowd in Caracas.

deficit, a sharp rise in the cost of living, and a slowing of its rate of economic growth in 1974. Rising popular dissatisfaction was reflected in increased rural and urban guerrilla activity. In one of a series of spectacular kidnappings, rebels abducted the father-in-law of President Luis Echeverría. The 83-year-old victim was released after he expressed agreement with the revolutionary aims of his captors.

President Echeverría's fortunes improved with the announcement in October of the discovery of a vast new petroleum field in southern Mexico, which put him in a fairly strong position when he met with President Ford. Echeverría indicated that his country would gladly sell any surplus oil to the United States, at world market prices.

Brazil. Important petroleum reserves were discovered off the coast of Brazil. Announcement of the find came at the end of a year in which the increased costs of oil imports had contributed to an inflation surge, which was especially hard on Brazil's working people, whose wages were held down by government decree. Despite widespread discontent with the inflation and deteriorating living conditions, there was no recrudescence of the large-scale protest demonstrations and revolutionary terrorism that marked the late 1960's.

Brazil's new president, Ernesto Geisel, found the time propitious for easing up on the policies of political repression instituted by his predecessors. Against the advice of hard-liners in his government, he permitted Congressional and state elections in November, which resulted in stunning victories for Brazil's only legal opposition party.

Peronist Argentina. Guerrilla violence continued to plague Argentina after the death in July of President Juan Perón, who was succeeded by his vice president and widow, Isabel Perón. Latin America's first woman president, a former nightclub performer, she pursued a steady rightward course, inviting a showdown with leftist guerrillas. In October she replaced the last important Left Peronist in her cabinet, Finance Minister José Ber Gelbard, with the conservative Alfredo Gómez Morales. Later she acceded to a Left Peronist demand that the body of Eva Perón, her late husband's charismatic second wife, be repatriated from Spain. But the Montoneros, Left Peronist guerrillas, were not mollified, and in November they assassinated the head of the federal police.

Other Developments. Bolivia also experienced political violence in 1974, as President Hugo Banzer survived two coup attempts, in June and November. In Peru, there were riots in Lima when President Juan Velasco Alvarado's left-wing military government expropriated the last of the country's major newspapers. Elsewhere in South America the scene was relatively peaceful. Right-wing military dictatorships in Chile and Uruguay intrenched themselves, while Colombians went to the polls and elected as their president the candidate of the opposition Liberal party, Alfonso López Michelsen.

In Central America, Costa Ricans broke a 25-year tradition and elected the government-party candidate, Daniel Oduber, as their president. Military strongman Anastasio Somoza Debayle was again elected president of Nicaragua, while Gen. Kjell Laugerud García, the candidate of the outgoing military president of Guatemala, was declared the winner in an election that many observers felt his opponent had won. In the Dominican Republic, President Joaquin Balaguer easily won reelection.

NEILL MACAULAY
University of Florida

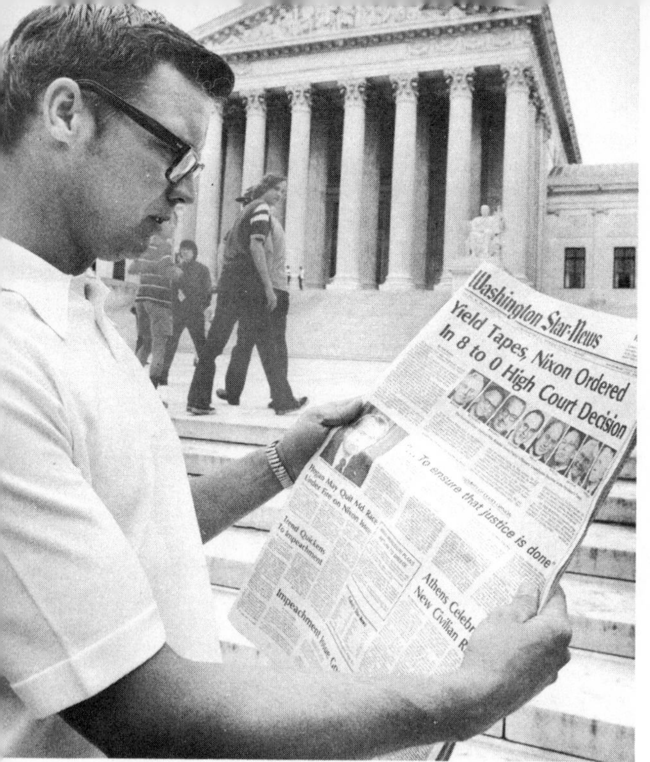

UPI

In front of the Supreme Court Building in Washington, D. C., a visitor reads of court's ruling on Nixon tapes.

Law

Major developments of 1974 in the chief areas of law, in the United States and among nations, are surveyed under the headings (1) U. S. Supreme Court, and (2) International Law.

Other legal developments are reviewed in the special feature on the U. S. presidency, beginning on page 24, and in the articles CIVIL LIBERTIES AND CIVIL RIGHTS; CRIME; DISARMAMENT; PRISONS; and UNITED NATIONS.

U. S. Supreme Court

The U. S. Supreme Court took the two most important actions of its 1973–74 terms a month after the term would normally have ended. On July 24, 1974, the court decided the historic case of *United States* v. *Richard M. Nixon,* holding that the President must turn over to Watergate special prosecutor Leon Jaworski 64 tapes of presidential conversations that Jaworski had subpoenaed for use in the "Watergate cover-up" trial of former Attorney General John Mitchell and five other former Nixon aides or campaign officials. The case, requiring the court for the first time in its history to rule on the claim of "executive privilege"—that is, the right of the President to withhold information or evidence from the courts or Congress—had been argued on July 8 by Jaworski and the President's counsel, James D. St. Clair.

Chief Justice Warren E. Burger's opinion for the unanimous court (Justice William H. Rehnquist not participating) recognized that executive privilege, though not mentioned in the Constitution, may legitimately be claimed by the President under some circumstances, particularly where national security is involved. But here there was no such claim, and the court ruled that the President had no right to withhold evidence needed in a criminal trial.

The court had also agreed to consider a second issue—whether the action of the Watergate grand jury in naming President Nixon as an unindicted co-conspirator in the Watergate cover-up—was unconstitutional. But finding that this issue was irrelevant to a decision on turning over the tapes, the court declined to rule on it.

The following day the court, divided 5 to 4 in *Milliken* v. *Bradley,* voted against further racial integration in education for the first time since the original desegregation ruling in 1954. In a decision almost certain to slow school desegregation in the North, the court ruled that white suburban school districts outside Detroit should not be forced to integrate the city's predominantly black schools by court-ordered busing across city-county boundaries.

There was no change in the membership of the court, and the structure of opinion remained much the same as in the previous term. The four Nixon appointees—Chief Justice Burger and Justices Harry A. Blackmun, Lewis F. Powell, Jr., and Rehnquist—formed a conservative bloc, opposed by the liberal trio of William O. Douglas, William J. Brennan, and Thurgood Marshall. The two remaining justices, Potter Stewart and Byron White, were thus in a strategic position, with one or both joining the conservative group in most opinions.

The court handed down 140 signed opinions, of which only 43 (31%) were unanimous. In the preceding term the output was also 140 signed opinions, of which 34 (24%) were unanimous. The court also issued 30 per curiam opinions, 14 of them unanimous. The four conservatives voted together in 130 of the 170 cases and the three liberals were together in 133 cases.

EQUAL PROTECTION

The Supreme Court avoided a ruling in what had been expected to be one of the most significant cases of the term, *DeFunis* v. *Odegaard.* The University of Washington Law School, seeking to remedy the imbalance in minority lawyers, gave certain advantages to minority applicants for admission. Marco DeFunis, Jr., a white, who was refused admission though his grades and scores on admission tests were higher than nearly all of the minority applicants admitted, brought suit and the state trial court ordered his admission. The state supreme court reversed, but Justice Douglas stayed that decision pending Supreme Court review. By the time the court was ready to decide the case, DeFunis was in his last semester, assured of graduation, so the court declared his case moot, 5–4.

The federal Civil Rights Act of 1964 was interpreted to require the San Francisco school system to provide bilingual education for Chinese-speaking children (*Lau* v. *Nichols*). Giving Indians employment preference in the federal Bureau of Indian Affairs was held not to constitute prohibited racial discrimination (*Morton* v. *Mancari*).

The court continued its concern about equal protection for women. It struck down (7–2) arbitrary dates for the start of mandatory maternity leave for public school teachers (*Cleveland Board of Education* v. *LaFleur*), and held (5–3) that under the 1963 federal Equal Pay Act pay scales for men and women must be equal even though the men worked different shifts (*Corning Glass Works* v. *Brennan*).

But the court refused to regard classifications based on sex as automatically invalid. *Geduldig* v. *Aiello* held (6–3) that states with disability insurance programs need not pay benefits for normal pregnancy, and *Kahn* v. *Shevin* approved (6–3) a Florida law giving widows, but not widowers, a $500 property tax exemption. The court left standing a decision allowing a New Orleans hotel to refuse to serve women in its men's grill (*Millenson* v. *New Hotel Monteleone*).

FIRST AMENDMENT

An unusual issue in press freedom was presented in *Miami Herald* v. *Tornillo* by a Florida law that required a newspaper criticizing a political candidate to publish the candidate's reply without charge. While recognizing that news monopolies might use their press freedom unfairly, the court unanimously invalidated this statute on the ground that it usurped editorial judgment and amounted to a legislative order of what to print. But the court upheld (5–4) a libel judgment secured by a Chicago lawyer against a John Birch Society magazine in an opinion that restored to private citizens protection against libelous statements that recent court decisions had seemed to limit (*Gertz* v. *Welch*).

In *Miller* v. *California* and other 1973 decisions the court had revised its rulings on obscenity to apply to "patently offensive" material, and permitted the fact of offensiveness to be judged against local, not national, community standards. A Georgia jury took advantage of this freedom to convict a theater manager for showing the film *Carnal Knowledge*. In *Jenkins* v. *Georgia* the court reversed the conviction, holding that *Miller* did not mean to give juries unbridled discretion in determining what is patently offensive. Yet in apparent contradiction the court continued to assert that juries could base their determinations as to obscenity on the prevailing moral standards of their communities. In *Hamling* v. *U. S.* the court approved (5–4) the use of local standards even in a federal prosecution for distributing through the mails a brochure advertising an illustrated version of a government report on pornography.

On the issue of aid to religious education, *Wheeler* v. *Barrera* avoided deciding whether the federal Education Act of 1965 required employment of teachers for private schools if such services were provided for public schools, or whether such a requirement, if it existed, would violate the First Amendment. But the court did invalidate a New Jersey program that proposed to reimburse parents up to $20 a year for secular textbooks used in parochial schools (*Marburger* v. *Public Funds*).

The court invalidated (6–3) as too broad an ordinance making it unlawful to curse a policeman (*Lewis* v. *New Orleans*). A conviction of a youth who wore a U. S. flag on the seat of his pants was reversed (6–3) because the statute forbidding "contemptuous" treatment of the flag was too vague (*Smith* v. *Goguen*).

A city transit system that denied a political candidate advertising space on its buses was upheld (5–4) on the ground that a bus is not a First Amendment forum (*Lehman* v. *City of Shaker Heights*). *Arnett* v. *Kennedy* held (5–4) that a federal employee had not been denied his right of free speech when he was fired after publicly charging his supervisor with attempted bribery.

CRIMINAL LAW

The court continued to take a rather hard line in construing the constitutional rights of persons accused of crime. It upheld (6–3) broad powers of the police to search motorists arrested for violating traffic laws (*Gustafson* v. *Florida*, *U. S.* v. *Robinson*). *Cardwell* v. *Lewis* ruled (5–4) that Ohio police did not need a search warrant to take incriminating paint samples and tire impressions from an auto in a public parking lot. In *Michigan* v. *Tucker* the court upheld (8–1) the admission of evidence in violation of the *Miranda* rules against a rape suspect who had been told by the police that he had a right to remain silent and to have counsel, but not that the state must provide counsel if he could not afford to hire one.

The Justice Department was dealt a severe blow when the court ruled unanimously in *U. S.* v. *Giordano* that former Attorney General Mitchell had violated the 1968 wiretapping law in some 60 narcotics and gambling cases by failing to sign the wiretap applications personally or to designate an assistant to act for him. The wiretaps were consequently unlawful, and the cases, involving a total of 626 persons, had to be dismissed.

Fuller v. *Oregon* upheld (7–2) a law requiring indigent criminal defendants, as a condition of parole, to repay the cost of court-approved lawyers once their finances improved. The court also ruled (6–3) that states need not furnish free attorneys to indigent defendants wanting to appeal their convictions to the highest court in the state and even to the U. S. Supreme Court (*Roff* v. *Moffitt*).

Several decisions dealt with the rights of prison inmates, usually adversely. The court did grant that prisoners were not wholly stripped of constitutional protections, and *Procunier* v. *Martinez* unanimously invalidated regulations allowing prison officials wide power to censor letters to or from inmates and barring interviews between prisoners and law students working with lawyers representing inmates. But *Pell* v. *Procunier* and *Saxbe* v. *Washington Post* ruled (5–4) that prison officials can bar a journalist from interviewing specific inmates without violating rights of either free speech or free press. *Wolff* v. *McDonnell* denied (6–3) inmates the right to counsel and to cross-examine witnesses at prison disciplinary hearings, but did hold that they must be given notice of the charges against them and the right to present evidence. Finally, the court upheld (6–3) a state law depriving convicted felons of the right to vote, even after they had served their prison sentences and completed satisfactorily their paroles (*Richardson* v. *Ramirez*).

Parker v. *Levy* upheld (5–3) the court-martial conviction of an army doctor who had opposed the Vietnam war and encouraged similar opposition. The majority rejected arguments that the provisions of the Code of Military Justice invoked were so vague as to be unconstitutional, and took the same position in *Secretary of the Navy* v. *Avrech*.

CLASS SUITS AND STANDING

Class actions, in which individuals with relatively small or similar claims join to seek relief in court, particularly in consumer and environmental problems, were limited in two cases. *Eisen* v. *Carlisle and Jacquelin*, brought on behalf of all odd-lot purchasers of stock on the New York Stock Exchange over a 4-year period, held (6–3) that persons initiating a federal class suit must notify, at their expense, all other persons in the class. When class suits are brought in federal courts under diversity of citizenship, the court ruled (6–3) that each party must meet the statutory requirement of $10,000 in damages (*Zahn* v. *International Paper Co.*).

The court rejected (5–4) a taxpayers' suit seeking to force disclosure of the CIA budget, which is now known only to a few key members of Congress (*U. S.* v. *Richardson*). By a 6 to 3 vote the court rejected for lack of standing a class suit seeking to forbid members of Congress from serving in the armed forces reserves (*Schlesinger* v. *Reservists Committee*). But in *Scheuer* v. *Rhodes* the court upheld without dissent the right of parents of students killed at Kent State in 1970 to sue the governor of Ohio and other officials who sent the National Guard onto the campus.

ELECTIONS

Lubin v. *Panish* held that a state cannot use mandatory high filing fees to keep poor people from running for public office. The court ruled unconstitutional (7–2) as a restriction on free political association an Illinois law prohibiting a person from voting in one party's primary if he had voted in the primary of another party any time within the previous 23 months (*Kusper* v. *Pontikes*).

The court unanimously voided a law, challenged by the Communist party, which required minor parties to file a loyalty oath in order to get on the ballot (*Communist Party of Indiana* v. *Whitcomb*). But in two cases the court upheld state laws that handicapped minority parties and independent candidates from winning a place on the ballot (*American Party* v. *White*, *Storer* v. *Brown*).

The court encouraged campaign reform laws by declining to review a Washington state statute requiring disclosure of the incomes of public officials and candidates, spending by lobbyists, and details of campaign finance (*Simmons* v. *Gorton*).

BUSINESS REGULATION AND TAXATION

The Bank Secrecy Act of 1970, adopted by Congress to curb violation of federal laws by use of secret foreign bank accounts and foreign financial transactions, was upheld (6–3) in *California Bankers Assn.* v. *Shultz*. Under the act, banks are required to make microfilm copies of all checks over $100, and to report to tax officials all domestic transactions over $10,000 and foreign transactions over $5,000.

Use of the zoning power by towns and villages to restrict land use to one-family dwellings, thereby barring boarding houses, fraternity houses, and communes, was upheld (7–2) in *Belle Terre* v. *Boraas*. The court ruled unanimously that cities may levy a high tax on downtown parking lots and garages in order to reduce urban congestion (*Pittsburgh* v. *Alco Parking Corp.*).

Reversing a 1972 decision guaranteeing installment buyers notice and hearing before their purchases were repossessed for nonpayment, *Mitchell* v. *W. T. Grant Co.* upheld (5–4) a Louisiana law allowing the court to take custody of property over which there is a dispute concerning payment.

In two cases nonprofit institutions that had been denied tax-exempt status by the Bureau of Internal Revenue were told that an 1867 act forbade the granting of injunctions against such rulings. Their remedy was to sue in the Tax Court or to seek refunds. Meanwhile, their fund-raising ability would be seriously compromised (*Bob Jones University* v. *Simon, Commissioner* v. *Americans United*).

C. HERMAN PRITCHETT
University of California, Santa Barbara

International Law

Significant developments in international law during 1974 concerned three important areas: law of the sea, fisheries jurisdiction, and arms control.

Law of the Sea. Ten weeks of discussion by nearly 150 governments at the third UN Conference on the Law of the Sea achieved consensus on some major issues and framed others in precise alternative texts that focus them for decision at a final negotiating session scheduled for Geneva in 1975. The 1974 conference was held at Caracas, Venezuela, from June 20 to August 24. The central concept to emerge at Caracas was a 12-mile territorial sea coupled with a 200-mile economic zone, which would give coastal states vastly expanded jurisdiction over both living and nonliving resources of the oceans subject to as yet undetermined international supervision and reserved rights of noncoastal states.

The chief remaining issues are a right of free transit through, under, and over international straits brought within national jurisdiction by the 12-mile territorial sea, and the obligation of coastal states to accept certain limitations on their control of the 200-mile zone. The latter includes a duty to permit full utilization of coastal fishery resources, the exemption of highly migratory species from national control, rights to unimpeded navigation and overflight, freedom for scientific research, coastal state acceptance of international pollution protection standards, and an obligation to share a portion of seabed revenues with landlocked or shelf-locked states and with the international community.

As to the seabed beyond national jurisdiction, the Caracas meeting proceeded on the understanding that an International Seabed Authority would exercise control over seabed mining, but achieved little progress on the precise design or the specific functions and powers of the new agency. Unresolved issues include whether the authority should itself engage in exploitation activities or be limited to licensing exploitation by firms and governments, whether and how price and production controls might be established, how the proceeds are to be divided, and who is to control a voting majority of the Seabed Authority.

Fisheries Jurisdiction. On July 25 the International Court of Justice (World Court) handed down final decisions in cases begun in 1972 by the United Kingdom and the Federal Republic of Germany (West Germany) to challenge the extension by Iceland of its exclusive fisheries jurisdiction from 12 to 50 miles. Although Iceland refused to respond in either case, the court found the cases properly brought under existing agreements, and held by a vote of 10 to 4 that the Icelandic extension could not be maintained as against either Britain or Germany. But it said that both applicant and respondent "are under mutual obligations to undertake negotiations in good faith for the equitable solution of their differences concerning their respective fishery rights."

The court took the cases on the basis of the applicants' traditional fishing practices in the contested waters, tempered by its recognition of Iceland's preferential rights in those resources as a state specially dependent on fisheries in adjacent waters. The court's decision clearly strikes down Iceland's unilateral exclusion of British and German fishing, but does not rule the 50-mile limit unlawful for all purposes. The decision also imposes on Britain and Germany the obligation of reviewing, together with Iceland, measures necessary for conservation, development, and exploitation of the contested fisheries in the light of Iceland's right to "a preferential share to the extent of the special dependence of its people upon the fisheries in the seas around its coasts for their livelihood and economic development."

Although the immediate impact of the decision is to protect the applicants' traditional fishing rights, the emphasis placed upon the preferential rights of the coastal state is not likely to be confined to the special circumstances of Iceland. The net impact over time may be to strengthen coastal state control over fishery resources.

Arms Control. Agreements reached at two U. S.–Soviet summit meetings during 1974 may accelerate rather than limit the arms race between the superpowers.

On July 3, President Nixon and Secretary Brezhnev signed a treaty at Moscow banning underground nuclear weapons tests above a yield of 150 kilotons beginning March 31, 1976. Critics point out that the high threshold permits continued testing of most weapons that either side might wish to develop, which contradicts previous commitments to work for a total nuclear test ban. Furthermore, since the agreement does not cover tests for "peaceful purposes," even the threshold limit can be avoided in much the same way that India acquired nuclear capability. Thus the threshold agreement does not restrict weapons development, and undercuts efforts to halt the spread of nuclear weapons.

On November 24, President Ford and Secretary Brezhnev agreed at Vladivostok to limit strategic offensive missiles and bomber forces to 2,400 delivery vehicles for each side, of which 1,320 may be missiles equipped with MIRV multiple warheads. Although the agreement thus places an upper limit on such weapons, it places no limit on weapons development or on the number of warheads built into a single MIRV missile. It thus legitimizes, and may stimulate, both qualitative improvements and a buildup by both sides to the high numbers set in the agreement. (See also DISARMAMENT.)

DANIEL G. PARTAN
Boston University

LEBANON

A severe inflation and constant labor unrest would have been sufficient to bring about the fall of Premier Takieddin Solh's 15-month-old government on Sept. 25, 1974. However, the key to the month-long cabinet crisis leading to his fall was the continued presence of Palestinian commandos on Lebanese soil. The security of the republic was seriously threatened as the Israelis sent reprisal raids into Lebanon because of guerrilla operations against Israel allegedly originating in Lebanon. Furthermore, the country suffered as tension grew between the Palestinians and their Lebanese hosts.

Economy. A spiraling inflation forced desperate government countermeasures in the face of massive strikes and a greater general strike called by the General Labor Federation. Demands for higher wages and better working conditions were partially met to avert a general strike scheduled for February 6: wages were increased by 10% on January 23, and a price control council was established on January 28 to limit prices of commodities and costs of services.

Strikes and demonstrations in March in preparation for another general strike set for April 2 forced the government to reform the Labor Laws by liberalizing regulations governing family allowances, sick leave, and dismissals. A mid-July proposal by Minister of Economy Nazih Bizri to empower the government to fix profit margins was unanimously rejected in an August 7 meeting of 900 businessmen representing 18 employer associations.

Threats to Internal Security. Although Palestinian guerrilla leaders assured the government on at least four occasions that no attacks on Israel would originate from Lebanon, Israel held Lebanon responsible for guerrilla operations in northern Israel. Following major commando operations at Qiryat Shemona on April 11, Maalot on May 15, and the Shamir kibbutz on June 17, Israel launched massive air and sea strikes on both Palestinian refugee camps and Lebanese villages that left over 150 dead and 500 wounded.

In the wake of these attacks and the almost daily shelling of southern Lebanon, Premier Solh faced constant criticism for the lack of an effective defense policy. Appeals to international public opinion and to Lebanon's Arab neighbors brought the country both vocal support and offers of military assistance. Following the June 18–19 attacks, Egypt's President Anwar el-Sadat offered units of his air force to Lebanon. But the offer was rejected in the face of an Israeli threat to turn Lebanon into a full-scale theater of war should Egyptian aircraft or missiles be stationed in Lebanon. In addition, President Suleiman Franjieh rejected on July 11 reported offers of arms from the Soviet Union.

Lebanon's inability to defend itself led to civilian self-help remedies and resentment toward the guerrillas. The major right-wing Christian parties—former president Camille Chamoun's National Liberal Party and Pierre Geyemal's Falange—formed heavily armed, private militias, numbering 1,000 and 5,000 men, respectively, ostensibly to counterbalance the presence of 10,000 armed Palestinians in Lebanon. Frequent critics, led by Progressive Socialist Party leader Kemal Jumblatt, charged that the purpose of the militias was to provoke an armed confrontation between the military and the commandos, similar to that of May 1973. For the most part, however, the militias fought among themselves: in one clash in the Beirut suburb of Dekwaneh, 16 were killed and more than 40 wounded.

Government Crisis. Premier Solh's resignation on September 25 was precipitated by a series of ministerial resignations and a massive campaign by various parliamentary blocs to bring down the government over the issues of inflation and the growing threat to internal security of a confrontation between the militias and the guerrillas. The government crisis began on September 17 when Jumblatt withdrew his party's two ministers, citing the government's lack of seriousness on the law and order issue: Jumblatt alleged that the government had failed to react when a huge shipment of arms intended for the militias was landed on the coast north of Beirut.

The resignation was temporarily stayed on September 18 when the cabinet revoked the right to private ownership of firearms. However, when Economic Minister Bizri resigned on September 22 and another clash between the militias took place on the 23d, President Suleiman Franjieh was compelled to accept Premier Solh's resignation.

The government crisis lasted until October 30 when Rashid Solh was successful in forming an 18-member cabinet. Solh, a cousin of Takieddin Solh, was an independent member of parliament. His new cabinet, which was approved by parliament, included five ministers from the previous government.

F. NICHOLAS WILLARD
Georgetown University

LEBANON • Information Highlights

Official Name: Republic of Lebanon.
Location: Southwest Asia.
Area: 4,015 square miles (10,400 sq km).
Population (1973 est.): 3,100,000.
Chief Cities: Beirut, the capital, 938,990 (met. area; 1970 est.): Tripoli, 127,600 (1964 est.).
Government: *Head of state,* Suleiman Franjieh, president (took office Sept. 1970). *Head of government,* Rashid Solh, premier (took office Oct. 1974). *Legislature* (unicameral)—Chamber of Deputies.
Monetary Unit: Lebanese pound (2.28 pounds equal U. S.$1, July 1974).
Gross National Product (1972 est.): $2,312,000,000.
Manufacturing (major products): Processed foods, textiles, petroleum products, cement, tobacco products.
Major Agricultural Products: Cereals, fruits, vegetables, tobacco, wheat.
Foreign Trade (1972): *Exports,* $351,000,000; *imports,* $849,000,000.

AL LE CLAIRE, NIAGARA FALLS PUBLIC LIBRARY

The new Earl W. Brydges Public Library in Niagara Falls, N. Y., opened in March. On the main floor are a children's library, audio-visual areas, and main reading room (*right*).

AL LE CLAIRE, NIAGARA FALLS PUBLIC LIBRARY

libraries

Two specters—declining governmental support and economic inflation—hung hauntingly over the American library scene in 1974. Just how poorly libraries have fared under the federal government's program of general revenue sharing was indicated in March when the Office of Revenue Sharing of the U. S. Department of the Treasury released a brief document titled *Revenue Sharing: The First Actual Use Reports.* It revealed that libraries received less than 1% of the $1.9 billion in general revenue sharing funds expended by state and local governments between January 1972 and June 1973.

Although there are eight priority categories in general revenue sharing, including libraries, over 60% of such funds went to but three of them: education, public safety, and public transportation. Of the $18.5 million received by libraries, nearly 92%, or $17 million, was used to support existing programs and services. More direct forms of federal aid to libraries, under existing but at present poorly funded legislation, authorize considerably more money for innovation and the expansion of presently available library services.

Because local authorities often view cultural services, including those of the library, as marginal, a program of funding which is as indirect and vaguely categorical as general revenue sharing may force libraries into fiercer competition for dollars with noncultural services than might be the case were the allocation of monies determined at the national level.

Research Libraries Group. In late March 1974, the libraries of Harvard, Yale, and Columbia universities, along with the New York Public Library, formed the Research Libraries Group, a consortium dedicated to the selective purchase and systematic sharing of library materials. Confronted with rising costs and radically curtailed budgets, these libraries plan to share the contents of expensive books and infrequently consulted journals through an exchange of photocopies within the limits imposed by "fair use" as defined in copyright law. Such sharing will reduce the costs of acquiring, housing, and maintaining these materials in each of the four libraries, but the substantial expense of their bibliographic control will remain for each library to assume.

The cooperating libraries plan to reduce the cost of providing access to expensive, low-use, unnecessarily duplicated publications by centrally cataloging them with the help of a computer.

While only one of the four libraries will acquire a particular item of this kind, users of the other three will have satisfactory intellectual and physical access to it at reduced cost all around. Whether other scholarly libraries will associate themselves with the Research Libraries Group is a matter of some concern to the authors and publishers of those specialized materials for which such libraries form the major market. An enlarged consortium could mean, in the absence of some compensatory scheme, a reduction in sales for book publishers and in royalties for authors.

Although revision of the Copyright Act of 1909 is not expected until some time in 1975, the Senate Judiciary Committee defined "fair use" of copyrighted material in amendments reported in early July 1974. In its section on library photocopying, this revision prohibits libraries from systematically reproducing copyrighted materials for other libraries or groups of users with which they have formal or informal agreements.

"Fair use" of copyrighted work for teaching and research is defined as no more than a single copy for replacement or archival purposes. The committee urged authors and publishers to meet with librarians and educators for the purpose of developing a licensing arrangement whereby the reproduction of multiple copies of the same material would be permitted.

The realization of significant economies within groups of cooperating libraries seems dependent on the right to reproduce more than the single copy permitted in the committee's amendments for normal interlibrary loan activity. In the meantime, an early ruling by the U. S. Supreme Court was expected on whether systematic copying by libraries actually deprives authors and publishers of right to property under copyright.

In another development, the Graduate Library School at Indiana University received a $117,000 grant from the National Science Foundation in 1974 for a study aimed at resolving the differences between publishers and librarians as they relate to the production and use of scholarly journals.

Personnel. *Library Manpower: A Study of Requirements and Supply,* a report issued by the Bureau of Labor Statistics of the U. S. Department of Labor in early 1974, predicted that library employment would increase by 41%, from 115,000 to 167,000, between 1970 and 1985. In the 1960's, less than 50% of all library job openings in the United States were created by retirement, death, or departure from the profession. In the period 1970–85, about 75% of all employment openings are expected to be of that variety.

While job opportunities will vary from field to field within librarianship on account of the change in population structure over the 15-year span, only about 20% of each year's job openings will be available to other than new graduates of programs in library education. New graduates will have to be more mobile and more versatile in their job capacities in order to obtain satisfactory positions.

Between 1970 and 1985, there will be an accelerating demand for library technical assistants and other paraprofessional personnel, as well as for individuals prepared to organize community information or outreach programs, to work as information scientists, and to handle media of communication other than print.

National Planning. In late summer 1974, the National Commission on Libraries and Information Science issued the second draft of its *National Programs of Library and Information Service.* The first version, released in October 1973, had emphasized the design and creation of a national library and information network and had paid less attention to the improvement of local library services. The later draft corrected that imbalance to some extent. It stressed the importance of local and state library services and the need to focus more sharply on the library and information needs of special groups, ethnic minorities, and the institutionalized, as well as the handicapped and those who are presently unserved.

Finally, the commission discussed the role of the Library of Congress as the crown of the network and a "National Lending Library of final resort." For the immediate future, the commission recommended that the Library of Congress include in its machine-readable cataloging project materials in foreign languages, and that it take steps to ensure that such cataloging data are rapidly and comprehensively diffused to the libraries of the nation via an electronic, on-line system of communication.

Federal Legislation. President Gerald Ford's proposed Library Partnership Act, sent to the Senate on Aug. 22, 1974, recommends authorization of $15 million in the 1975 fiscal year for the demonstration, in public and private agencies and institutions, of "exemplary and innovative library and information services." Such services would include networking and other cooperative arrangements; the extension of library services to handicapped, institutionalized, and economically disadvantaged persons; the creation of nontraditional community information centers; the integration of library service and basic education; and the improvement of library administration and fiscal control.

Library Partnership Act funds would be distributed to public and private institutions in the form of individual grants and contracts and at the discretion of the secretary of health, education, and welfare. Present library legislation limits this kind of discretion on the part of an administration. A substantial part of library appropriations to academic and public libraries must now be released to them regardless of the position of the administration. The new legislation permits an administration to avoid spending appropriated money at its discretion and without resorting to the legally questionable tactic of impoundment.

New Library of Congress Building. During the summer of 1974, nearly 230 members of the House of Representatives petitioned the speaker of that body, urging that a portion of the $90 million James Madison Memorial Building of the Library of Congress, then under construction, be converted to House office space. If the House has its way (and there is strong Senate opposition) the library will be unable to centralize, in the new building, staff and collections now dispersed in eight different locations in the District of Columbia, Maryland, and Virginia. When the building is completed in late 1976 or 1977, it will contain about 2 million square feet of floor space.

Library Education. The number of graduate library schools accredited by the American Library Association increased to 60 in 1974 with the approval of master's degree programs offered by the Graduate Library School, University of Arizona, and the Graduate School of Library and Information Science, University of Tennessee (Knoxville).

The 1974 Beta Phi Mu Award for distinguished service to education for librarianship went to Martha Boaz, dean of the School of Library Science at the University of Southern California.

National Library Week. The two themes of National Library Week, April 21–27, were "Grow with Books" and "Get It All Together—At Your Library." The 17th annual event was again sponsored by the National Book Committee in cooperation with the American Library Association.

ALA Conference. The 93d Annual Conference of the American Library Association was held in New York City, July 7–13, 1974. Its theme was "The Nature of the Profession," and some 1,140 sessions were attended by over 14,000 librarians and others. Edward G. Holley became president of ALA, and Allie Beth Martin, director of the Tulsa (Okla.) City-County Library System, was elected first vice president and president-elect.

Awards. The year's major library awards included the following:

The Newbery Medal for the most outstanding children's book went to Paula Fox for her novel *Slave Dancer;* and the Caldecott Medal for most distinguished picture book went to Margot Zemach for her illustrations in *Duffy and the Devil.*

The Melvil Dewey Award for creative professional achievement of a high order was given to Robert B. Downs, dean of library administration at the University of Illinois. The Joseph W. Lippincott Award for distinguished service in the library profession was received by Jerrold Orne, professor in the School of Library Science at the University of North Carolina, Chapel Hill.

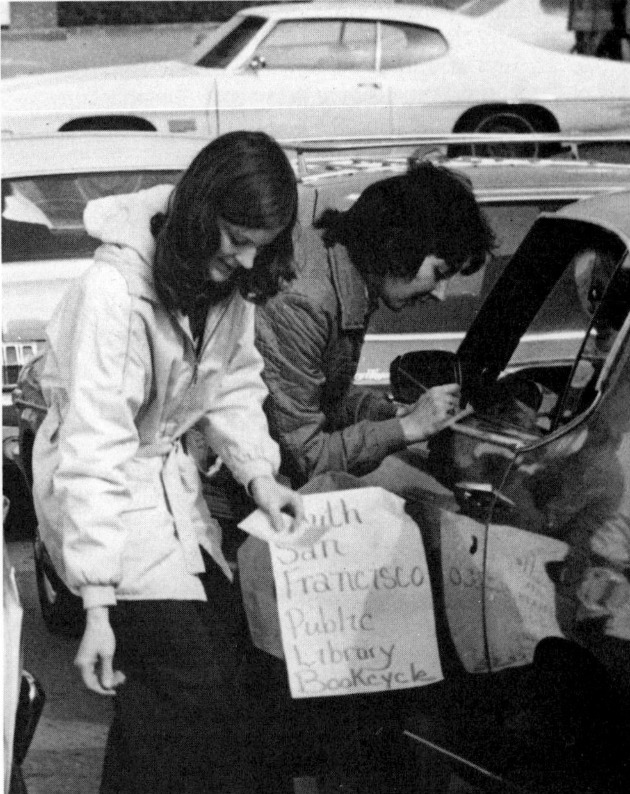

JOHN GUSSMAN, ENTERPRISE JOURNAL

Two South San Francisco library aides bring paperback books and magazines to drivers waiting in long gas lines.

Frederick G. Kilgour, director of the Ohio College Library Center, was awarded the Margaret Mann Citation for outstanding contribution in cataloging and classification.

To Florence E. Blakely, head of the Duke University Library Reference Department, went the Isadore Gilbert Mudge Citation for distinguished contributions to reference librarianship. Regina U. Minudri, director of professional services at the Alameda (Calif.) County Library, received the Grolier Award for achievement in guiding and stimulating the reading of children and young people.

International Library Activities. The International Federation of Library Associations (IFLA) held its first United States conference in Washington, D. C., Nov. 16–23, 1974. Its theme, like that of the International Conference on Planning of National Overall Documentation, Library and Archives Infrastructures held by UNESCO in Paris in late September, was "National and International Planning."

Meanwhile, the Cuban government declared it illegal for a man to become a librarian. On account of a shortage of manpower in Cuba, librarianship was among over 30 occupations designated "woman's work."

DAN BERGEN
University of Rhode Island, Kingston

LIBYA

Early in 1974, Libya proposed a merger with its western neighbor, Tunisia. On the country's eastern border, however, its relations with Egypt worsened steadily. The duties of President Muammar el-Qaddafi, the country's ruler since September 1969, were redefined in April, but no major shifts in governmental policy ensued. The country continued to utilize its vast oil resources in political bargaining.

Abortive Merger. On January 12, after several meetings between Qaddafi and Tunisian President Habib Bourguiba, the leaders announced the projected union of their countries. A communiqué heralded the formation of an Islamic Arab Republic, with a single president, constitution, army, and flag. A plebiscite on the merger was scheduled in each country for January 18. However, facing mounting opposition from Morocco and Algeria, Tunisia at first postponed, and later cancelled, the vote. Qaddafi, angered by another failure to fulfill his ambition to create a greater Muslim state, denounced leaders who paid lip service to unity while consistently blocking its implementation.

Administrative Change. On April 6 the Revolutionary Command Council relieved Qaddafi of some of his powers. He retained control of the armed forces, but was to devote himself to matters of popular organization and ideology. Abdul Salam Jallud, the premier, assumed the president's ceremonial, political, and administrative functions. It soon became evident, however, Qaddafi remained the prime mover in Libyan politics.

Cold War with Egypt. Relations with Egypt, already strained by Qaddafi's attacks on that nation's policies toward Israel and the Palestinians, continued to deteriorate. The Egyptian government accused Libya of instigating an attack against its Military Technical College in Cairo in April. Egypt claimed that Libya had supported the Islamic Liberation Organization, the group responsible for the attack, in an effort to disrupt moderate Arab governments. Libya strenuously denied the charge. Nevertheless, amid major changes in the Egyptian cabinet the following week, the Ministry for Libyan Affairs was eliminated. Charges and countercharges were exchanged, with Qaddafi accusing President Sadat of Egypt of lacking moral rectitude.

The cold war between the two nations intensified through the summer. Libya restricted Egyptian shipping and imposed rigorous customs checks on all Egyptians entering the country. Egypt terminated all shipping to Libya, precipitating more anti-Egyptian statements from Qaddafi. In August, Sadat implicated the Libyan government in a plot to assassinate him. Libya responded by demanding the return of military aircraft recently loaned to Egypt and by accusing Sadat of sabotaging the now virtually defunct Federation of Arab Republics (Egypt, Syria, and Libya). Egypt withdrew its advisers from Libya and banned its citizens from working in the country. At the urging of other Arab leaders, however, the two heads of state met in Alexandria on August 17 and 18, and a temporary thaw in Libyan-Egyptian relations resulted.

The troubles with Egypt spawned difficulties in other areas as well. In late spring, the Sudanese government thwarted an attack similar to the one perpetrated in Cairo. Libya was again alleged to be behind the plot. Later, France, disturbed by the disclosure that planes that it had sold to Libya with the proviso that they not leave the country had done so, threatened to end all arms sales.

Oil and Trade Developments. As world energy problems persisted, Libya assumed a greater control over the disposal of its petroleum resources. In February, three American oil firms (Texaco and subsidiaries of Standard Oil of California and Atlantic-Richfield) were nationalized, as the government carried out the provisions of a 1973 law designed to ensure 51% Libyan control of all foreign operations. A fourth company, Shell Oil, was nationalized in March. In that same month, when seven major Arab oil exporters ended their boycott of the United States, Libya refused to resume shipments to the American market. Qaddafi proposed a four-tier pricing system for oil, according to which the commodity would be sold at the lowest price to Islamic nations, at a slightly higher rate to other developing nations, at a still higher rate to industrialized nations that rendered technical assistance to Libya, and at the highest rate to the remaining industrial countries.

During the year Libya signed compacts with numerous countries. Relations with the Soviet Union improved, and joint committees were created to explore aid and trade. Libya also established diplomatic relations with Rumania. Reciprocal agreements centering on the supply of oil in exchange for technical assistance were completed between Libya and Argentina, France, Italy, Sweden, and Peru.

KENNETH J. PERKINS
University of South Carolina

LIBYA • Information Highlights

Official Name: Libyan Arab Republic.
Location: North Africa.
Area: 679,360 square miles (1,759,540 sq km).
Population (1973 est.): 2,100,000.
Chief Cities (1970 est.): Tripoli, joint capital, 264,000; Benghazi, joint capital, 170,000.
Government: *Head of state,* Muammar el-Qaddafi, president, Revolutionary Command Council (took office 1969). *Head of government,* Abdul Salam Jallud, premier (took office 1972).
Monetary Unit: Dinar (0.2959 dinar equals U. S.$1, July 1974).
Gross National Product (1972 est.): $4,583,000,000.
Manufacturing (major products): Petroleum products, processed foods.
Major Agricultural Products: Wheat, barley, tomatoes, dates, olives, peanuts, vegetables.
Foreign Trade (1973): *Exports,* $3,596,000,000; *imports,* $1,903,000,000.

LITERATURE

It is interesting to note that in the United States books dealing with the year's major news stories—Watergate and increasing inflation—made the best-seller list. Included were Carl Bernstein's and Bob Woodward's *All the President's Men* and Harry Browne's *You Can Profit from a Monetary Crisis.*

In October the Swedish Academy awarded the 1974 Nobel Prize in literature to Swedish writers Eyvind Johnson and Harry Edward Martinson, both very popular in Sweden (see PRIZES AND AWARDS).

Reviews of the year's developments in the various major literatures follow.

JILL KREMENTZ

In 1974, Joseph Heller published *Something Happened,* his first novel since his 1961 comic masterpiece *Catch-22.* The dust jacket of *Catch-22* shows the young Heller.

American Literature

Rising costs presented serious problems in 1974, but the publishing industry still proved responsive to its readers. How-to books, such as Harry Browne's *You Can Profit from a Monetary Crisis,* appeared on the best-seller lists. Watergate precipitated a flood of books only weeks behind the fast-breaking news stories themselves. Of more permanent interest were an unusually large number of important biographies and some serious new interpretations of American history. In fiction and poetry, interesting work appeared, but it was Robert Pirsig's rather unclassifiable opus which generated the most excitement.

Awards. The normally staid National Book Awards ceremony was enlivened by controversy. The prize for fiction, Thomas Pynchon's provocative *Gravity's Rainbow,* was accepted by a nightclub comedian impersonating Pynchon. The award was shared with Isaac Bashevis Singer for his short story collection, *A Crown of Feathers.*

The shared poetry prizes, to Allen Ginsberg for *The Fall of America* and to Adrienne Rich for *Diving into the Wreck,* were fiercely received. Peter Orlovsky, accepting for Ginsberg, sharply criticized American political policies, and Adrienne Rich announced that she was sharing her award with her sister nominees, Audre Lord and Alice Walker.

The arts and letters prize went to Pauline Kael for *Deeper into Movies,* and Douglas Day received the biography award for *Malcolm Lowry.* Murray Kempton's account of a black Panther trial in New York, *The Briar Patch,* won in contemporary affairs; John Clive's *Macaulay* in history; Maurice Natanson's *Edmund Husserl* in philosophy; and S. E. Luria's *Life, The Unfinished Experiment* in science.

Gravity's Rainbow also made the news when its "obscenity" and "obscurity" were cited as reasons by the Pulitzer Prize Committee for denying it the fiction award despite the unanimous recommendation of the three distinguished judges. The prize for poetry went to Robert Lowell for *The Dolphin.* Louis Scheaffer received the biography award for *O'Neill, Son and Artist,* which completed his two-volume life of O'Neill. Daniel Boorstin's *The Americans: The Democratic Experience* gained him the history prize. In general nonfiction, Ernest Becker was recognized for *The Denial of Death.*

Novels. This was an interesting year for novels, not so much because new ground was broken but because "traditional" themes and forms were found to be still viable. Joseph Heller's first novel since *Catch-22* appeared 13 years ago, *Something Happened,* deals with a subject we associate most with the 1950's: a middle-class man's unsatisfactory relationships. The main character, Robert Slocum, is a sad man living a bleak life and, according to Heller, "the most contemptible character in literature."

Philip Roth, whose experiments with the fantastic had gained limited critical approval, recalled his earlier style with *My Life as a Man,* the story of the unhappy marriage of a successful young writer.

A novel about social and domestic discord on a college campus would also seem a burnt-out subject, yet Alison Lurie's fifth novel, *The War Between the Tates,* was widely praised.

Exciting too was Ishmael Reed's *The Last Days of Louisiana Red,* a wildly satiric novel. A much gentler but still serious vein continues to be worked by Richard Brautigan in his "gothic Western," *The Hawkline Monster.* Robert F. Jones' *Blood Sport* and R. H. W. Dillard's *The Book of Changes* fracture time, space, and logic.

COURTESY RANDOM HOUSE

Daniel Boorstin won the 1974 Pulitzer Prize in history for *The Americans: The Democratic Experience.*

Many established writers published in 1974. Vladimir Nabokov produced the ingeniously autobiographical *Look at the Harlequins.* John Updike puzzled critics with *Buchanan Dying,* a curious dramatization of the life of one of the most obscure U. S. presidents. Gore Vidal followed up *Myra Breckinridge* with an equally outrageous sequel, *Myron.* James Baldwin attempted a new but not entirely successful approach in *If Beale Street Could Talk,* a story told from the point of view of a 19-year-old girl whose lover is unjustly sent to prison.

John Hersey expressed his concern about overpopulation in a science fiction novel, *My Petition for More Space.* Leslie Fiedler's *The Messengers Will Come No More* is also science fiction. Bruce Jay Friedman wrote *About Harry Towns* and John Knowles produced *Spreading Fires.*

George Higgins, a writer whose formal achievements have yet to be recognized, brought out another novel of underworld life, *Cogan's Trade.* John Hawkes, who has been writing intense novels since 1949, published the strange *Death, Sleep and the Traveler.*

Some younger writers who attracted attention were Richard Price for *The Wanderers,* a story of adolescent gang life in the Bronx; Albert Murray for *Train Whistle Guitar,* on growing up black in Alabama in the 1920's; and Toni Morrison for her second novel, *Sula.* Jeff Fields produced a fine first novel, *A Cry of Angels.*

Short Fiction. The difficulties in marketing collections of short fiction left the field largely to authors of established reputation. Tennessee Williams' *Eight Mortal Ladies Possessed,* his first collection of short stories in 10 years, demonstrated his delicate sensibility. *Good Samaritan* gathered stories published by John O'Hara during the last 10 years of his life. Joyce Carol Oates brought out *The Hungry Ghosts,* a coruscating group of short stories satirizing the internecine politics of the literary world.

A number of writers associated with *The New Yorker* published their works. Maeve Brennan's *Christmas Eve* was drawn from 20 years of writing; Brendan Gill's *Ways of Loving* gathered two novellas and 18 stories. Grace Paley was widely praised for her urbane *Enormous Changes at the Last Minute.* Donald Barthelme collected his parodies, fables, and political satires in *Guilty Pleasures.* John L'Heureux's realistic and touching *Family Affairs* and John Gardner's *The King's Indian* are also worthy of note.

Poetry. Anne Sexton's latest volume, *The Death Notebooks,* testified again to that fascination with personal death which had run through all her poetry. When she was found dead on Oct. 4, 1974, apparently by her own hand, she joined the tragically large number of contemporary poets who have died prematurely and left American poetry curiously adrift.

William Everson published his first collection since leaving the Dominican Order in 1969, *Man-Fate: The Swan-Song of Brother Antoninus.* John Beecher attested to the continued vitality of the idealistic proletarian tradition in his *Collected Poems 1924–1974.* Other volumes worthy of note are Richard Howard's *Two-Part Inventions;* John Hollander's long poem, *The Head of the Bed;* Alan Dugan's *Poems 4;* and X. J. Kennedy's *Emily Dickinson in Southern California.* Michael Ryan's *Threats Instead of Trees* was the Yale Series of Younger Poets selection. May Sarton's *Collected Poems 1930–1973* and the *Selected Poems of Robert Watson* were notable. Helen Vendler drew attention to some vigorous young poetry in her *New York Times Book Review* essay, *Good Black Poets One by One,* by discussing the publications of Dudley Randall's Broadside Press.

Literary History and Criticism. The most eagerly awaited literary biography of the year was Joseph Blotner's *Faulkner.* An exhaustive two-volume work, it was widely criticized for its excessive detail and its inability to catch the spirit of its subject. However, it was only the latest in a series of literary biographies intended as source books for scholars. A different problem was posed by T. S. Matthews' *Great Tom.* T. S. Eliot wanted no biography; attempts to do his life must necessarily be fragmentary. Richard Ellman discussed such problems for biographers in his collection of literary essays, *Golden Codgers.* William M. Chace's *The Political Identities of Ezra Pound and T. S. Eliot* was a valuable discussion of a difficult subject.

Robert Frost is affectionately remembered by his friend Kathleen Morrison in the profusely illustrated *Freedom in Departure.* Another pictorial biography is *The Romantic Egoists,* derived from the scrapbooks of F. Scott and Zelda Fitzgerald by their daughter, Scottie Fitzgerald Smith. Continued interest in writers of the 1920's is reflected in James R. Mellow's *Charmed Circle: Gertrude Stein and Company.*

Some interesting biographies were devoted to relatively minor literary figures. John Leggett's *Ross and Tom* told the stories of Ross Lockridge, author of *Raintree County,* and Thomas Heggen, who wrote *Mr. Roberts.* Both writers achieved sudden fame and wealth with these first novels, and both committed suicide before writing another. Robert Conrow's *Field Days* reveals the seamier side of the life of the poet, Eugene Field. Justin Kaplan's fine *Lincoln Steffens* is about the muckraker who exerted a major influence on modern journalism.

Louis Auchincloss wrote an engaging memoir, *A Writer's Capital.* The fifth volume of *The Diary of Anaïs Nin* covered 1947–1955. *Wampeters, Foma & Grandfalloons* is a collection of pieces by Kurt Vonnegut. Allen Ginsberg's lectures were edited by Gordon Ball in *Allen Verbatim.* Selden Rodman's *Tongues of Fallen Angels* is a collection of conversations with various contemporary writers.

Charles Kadushin's *The American Intellectual Elite* seemed to prove that serious thinking was invariably associated with a small group of journals, especially the *New York Review of Books.* But Philip Nobile's *Intellectual Skywriting* implicitly demonstrated the insularity of the New York literary establishment. The history of *Harper's* is touched upon in Wallace Stegner's *The Uneasy Chair,* a portrait of Bernard DeVoto.

Particularly interesting works of criticism include Joyce Carol Oates' *New Heaven, New Earth: The Visionary Experience in Literature,* an insightful discussion of the spiritual affirmation of several modern writers often seen as basically pessimistic. Ground was broken by David Ketterer with his imaginative *New Worlds for Old: The Apocalyptic Imagination, Science Fiction, and American Literature.* Richard Slotkin's outstanding *Regeneration through Violence: The Mythology of the American Frontier 1600–1860* provided insights into all our forms of cultural expression.

History and Biography. A radical revision of ideas on American slavery was called for by Robert William Fogel and Stanley L. Engerman in their *Time on the Cross: The Economics of American Negro Slavery.* This new breed of historian, "cliometricians" as they are called, compiles masses of data and subjects them to statistical analyses. Their conclusions argue that slavery was an efficient and profitable economic system, and that the *Uncle Tom's Cabin* view was unsupported by fact. The authors, conscious of the charge that they are apologists for slavery, published a companion volume explaining their research techniques, *Time on the Cross: Evidence and Methods.*

Another major work was Eugene D. Genovese's *Roll, Jordan, Roll: The World the Slaves Made.* The Marxist historian sees the paternalism inherent in American slavery as a variety of feudalism. He compassionately explores the effects of the slave system on both black and white society.

Fawn Brodie's *Thomas Jefferson: An Intimate History* argued that Jefferson had a longtime Negro mistress. Less lively was *Jefferson the President: Second Term 1805–1809,* the fifth volume of Dumas Malone's huge biography.

Thomas Paine was the subject of two biographies, Samuel Edwards' *Rebel!* and David Freeman Hawke's well received *Paine.* Hawke is judicious in explaining the virtues and vices of the notoriously provocative and difficult Paine. Another significant figure in American Revolutionary history was reexamined in *The Ordeal of Thomas Hutchinson* by Bernard Bailyn.

Two works on the World War II period achieved both critical and popular success. Cornelius Ryan's *A Bridge Too Far* was a vivid account of the Allies' disastrous attempt to cross the Rhine at Arnhem in September 1944. Merle Miller gave us the pungent *Plain Speaking: An Oral Biography of Harry S. Truman.*

Most striking of all was to see the almost simultaneous making and recording of history

COURTESY WILLIAM MORROW & CO.

Perhaps the most unusual book title of 1974 was *Zen and the Art of Motorcycle Maintenance.* Author Robert Pirsig, shown at right with his motorcycle, tells of a motorcycle trip he and his young son took from Minnesota to the Pacific Coast.

COURTESY WILLIAM MORROW & CO.

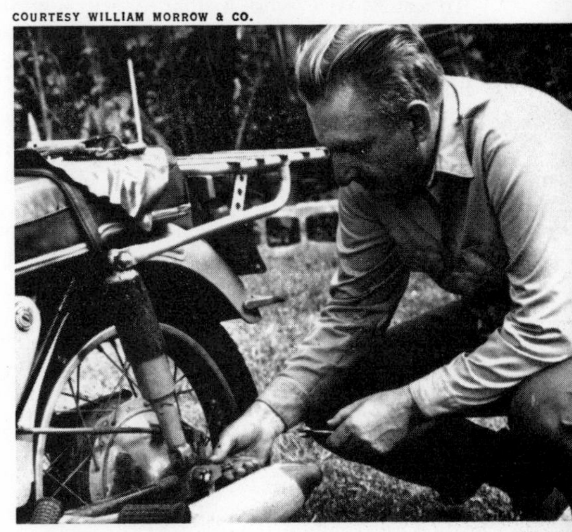

FROM DUFFY AND THE DEVIL BY HARVE ZEMACH ILLUSTRATED BY MARGOT ZEMACH COPYRIGHT © 1973 BY FARRAR STRAUSS & GIROUX

Margot Zemach won the 1974 Caldecott Medal for her illustrations in *Duffy and the Devil* by husband Harve.

that surrounded Watergate. Of the many books that appeared in 1974, some likely to remain of interest are *All the President's Men* by Carl Bernstein and Bob Woodward, the reporters who broke the case; Mary McCarthy's description of the Judiciary Committee proceedings, *The Mask of State;* defendant Jeb Stuart Magruder's apologia, *An American Life: One Man's Road to Watergate.*

Other Nonfiction. There were important contributions to feminist literature. Kate Millett came out with her extremely candid autobiography, *Flying.* Ti-Grace Atkinson's *Amazon Odyssey* and Jill Johnston's *Gullible's Travels* spoke for radical feminism. Elizabeth Janeway's *Between Myth and Morning: Women Awakening* in a collection of her essays. Elizabeth Hardwick dealt with women in literature in her penetrating book, *Seduction and Betrayal.*

Cities and the people who create them were the subjects of a number of books. Most notable was Laura Woods Roper's *F.L.O., A Biography of Frederick Law Olmstead,* the pioneer landscape architect who designed New York's Central Park. Also focused on New York was Robert A. Caro's *The Power Broker,* a study of Robert Moses, who brilliantly foresaw that the modern city would have to change for the automobile but could not envision what the automobile would do to the city. That story is included in Emma Rothschild's *Paradise Lost: The Decline of the Auto-Industrial Age.* Robert Conot's notable *American Odyssey* in a history of Detroit since 1701.

Among the less conventional nonfiction published during the year 1974, the most stunning was Robert M. Pirsig's *Zen and the Art of Motorcycle Maintenance: An Inquiry into Values.* This narrative, of a father and son motorcycling from Minnesota to San Francisco, is interspersed with monologues in which the father beautifully and powerfully dramatizes his gropings for peace and sanity.

JEROME H. STERN
Florida State University

Children's Literature

Beginning in mid-1974, children's publishing was beset by economic woes. Spiraling costs for paper, ink, printing, and distribution made a $6.95 price tag for a hardcover book not uncommon. Several large publishers instituted staff reductions which, coupled with a declining birth rate, presaged significant future cuts in title output for the industry. Early estimates of 1974 production indicated a drop of several hundred titles from the previous year's 2,000 titles. Paperback publishing increased in significance, with over 300 new releases during the year.

Awards. The major awards presented in 1974 for children's books published the previous year were as follows: The American Library Association's John Newbery Medal for the most distinguished contribution to American literature for children went to Paula Fox for her novel *The Slave Dancer,* the story of a 13-year-old white boy shanghaied aboard a slave ship. The ALA's Randolph Caldecott Medal for the most distinguished picture book was given to Margot Zemach for her illustrations in *Duffy and the Devil,* a retelling of a 19th century Cornish play based on the Rumpelstiltskin story.

Doris Buchanan Smith received the 32d annual award of the Child Study Association of America for *A Taste of Blackberries,* a realistic story about the death of a young boy's friend. The National Book Award for children's books was won by Eleanor Cameron for *The Court of the Stone Children,* an elegant story of a modern-day girl communing with a ghost child from Napoleon's time.

Noteworthy Publications. Emphasis during the year was on ecological themes, on cookbooks, handicrafts, early childhood education, biographies of sports personalities, magic, mysticism, demonology, and, in obvious preparation for the Bicentennial, books on the American Revolution. No one book stood out. The best picture books for the 4–7 age group were: Uri Shulevitz's *Dawn,* an evocative depiction of early morning through its many stages; Edna Mitchell Preston's *Squawk to the Moon, Little Goose,* a beguiling fable illustrated by Barbara Cooney; and Charlotte Pomerantz's *The Piggy in the Puddle,* a nonsense chant exuberantly illustrated by James Marshall.

For ages 6 to 10 the most outstanding titles were: *Arthur's Honey Bear,* written and illustrated by Lillian Hoban, a beginning-to-read book about a chimp; *When the Whale Came to My Town* by Jim Young, about the death of a whale stranded on a beach; *Over the River and Through the Woods,* Lydia Maria Child's traditional Thanksgiving song, with art work by Brinton Turkle; and *Allumette,* Tomi Ungerer's witty tale of a modern-day Little Match Girl.

Worthy of note for readers 9 years old and up were: M. J. Gladstone's *A Carrot for a Nose,* a handsome treasury of American folk sculpture; Elinor Lander Horwitz's *Mountain People, Mountain Crafts,* which visits the folk artisans of the southern Appalachians; Shel Silverstein's *Where the Sidewalk Ends,* a rollicking collection of rhymes and chants; William Kurelek's *Lumberjack,* illustrated with virility; and David McCaulay's *City,* a detailed presentation of the construction of a Roman town.

The three best books for the teenage audience were Robert Cormier's *The Chocolate War,* a powerful, sometimes sadistic novel about the misuse of power; Scott O'Dell's *Child of Fire,* about a Chicano gang leader; and Virginia Hamilton's *M. C. Higgins, the Great,* an almost experimental novel about a young black boy living in Southern strip-mining hill country.

Other books worthy of note for teenagers were: Joan Aiken's *Midnight Is a Place,* a tongue-in-cheek Dickensian novel about two orphans in 1840 industrial England; Patricia Wrightson's *The Nargun and the Stars,* a fantasy set on an Australian sheep farm with a primordial mass creeping ever closer; and Bette Greene's *Philip Hall Likes Me: I Reckon Maybe,* a novel set in rural Arkansas, exemplifying the joy-despair of an 11-year-old girl's first crush.

GEORGE A. WOODS
Editor, Children's Books
"The New York Times"

Canadian Literature in English

Canadian books in 1974 reflected two main trends. The first is a desire to know Canada and all its resources, both human and inanimate. The second is strong criticism of what Canadians have done and are doing to those resources.

Typical of these trends are two remarkably handsome books. Art critic Paul Duval's magnificently illustrated *High Realism in Canada* is about an art style that is especially popular in Canada. Leading novelist Hugh MacLennan presents some of his best writing in *Rivers of Canada,* which has brilliant photography by John De Visser. MacLennan not only lovingly describes the major rivers that have flowed through Canada's history but also worries about their future.

Public Affairs. The Canadian Environmental Law Association's *Environment on Trial,* edited by David Estrin and John Swaigen, describes the laws Canada has, and the laws Canada needs, on environment. *The Mackenzie Pipeline,* edited by economist Peter Pearse, examines the economics of the energy resources in Canada's north and the decisions that must be made about these resources.

The Asbestos Strike, edited by Pierre Elliott Trudeau and translated by James Boake, tells of the violent 1949 strike by 2,000 asbestos workers in Asbestos, Quebec. At that time, the nation's present prime minister was an editor and lawyer. The book appeared in French in 1956.

MIMI FORSYTH, THE BRADBURY PRESS

Paula Fox *(left)* received the 1974 Newbery Medal for *The Slave Dancer,* a story of a slave ship.

THE BRADBURY PRESS

Cultural Sovereignty: The Time and Reader's Digest Case in Canada, by Isaiah Litvak and Christopher Maile, traces the history of the Canadian magazine industry, and the effect on it of the special status of *Time* and *Reader's Digest.* The Canadian government ruled that the Canadian editions of these two were Canadian magazines and thus exempt from the tax on Canadian advertising in foreign magazines. Paul Weiler's *In the Last Resort* criticizes the Supreme Court of Canada and suggests reforms.

Desmond Morton's *NDP: The Dream of Power* follows the fortunes of the New Democratic party through 13 years, until just before the 1974 federal election. Canadian diplomat Chester Ronning draws on his lengthy experience in China for *A Memoir of China in Revolution: From the Boxer Rebellion to the People's Republic. The Politics of the Canadian Public School,* edited by George Martell, deals mainly with school politics in eastern Canada. George Manuel and Michael Posluns plead the case of Canada's native Indians in *The Fourth World.*

Poetry. Two of Canada's most influential poets, E. J. Pratt and Earle Birney, are each the subject of a scholarly volume. Sandra Djwa's *E. J. Pratt* describes Pratt's response to the 19th-century conflict between Christianity and Darwinism. Bruce Nesbitt's *Earle Birney* provides an authoritative introduction to Birney's poetry.

Timelight by Robin Skelton maintains this poet's high standard. Skelton now has written more than 50 books of poetry and prose. Alden Nowlan's fourth collection of poetry, *I'm a Stranger Here Myself,* bears his hallmarks of feeling and clarity. Prolific George Bowering enhances his reputation with *In the Flesh,* a collection of early short verse.

Susan Musgrave's *Grave-Dirt and Selected Strawberries* shows some promise, as do Tom Wayman's *For and Against the Moon,* his second volume, and Dale Sullivan's *HE: A Short Biography of HIM,* a poetic self-observation. Patrick Lane's *Beware of the Months of Fire* is his ninth volume of poetry. In *A Choice of Dreams,* Joyce Kogawa gives the experiences and feelings of a Japanese Canadian. Two poets, Douglas Lochhead and Raymond Souster, edit *100 Poems of Nineteenth Century Canada,* which displays a period in Canadian poetry that is often heavily discounted. *Ninety Seasons,* edited by Robert Gibbs and Robert Cockburn, is an anthology of contemporary poetry of the Maritime Provinces.

Fiction. Margaret Laurence, perhaps the finest novelist in Canada, strengthens her reputation with *The Diviners,* which shows clarity of writing and rare insight. The novel is set in her familiar fictional town of Manawaka.

Ray Smith's *Lord Nelson Tavern* is an accomplished and witty story of student life. Clarke Blais' impressive *Tribal Justice,* a collection of short stories, contains some of Canada's best current writing. Equally good is Alice Munro's *Something I've Been Meaning to Tell You,* with stories set in rural Ontario.

Matt Cohen's third novel, *The Disinherited,* deals with an Ontario farmer disinherited from his past by illness and the spread of the city. R. L. Gordon's *The River Gets Wider* asks if the fictional chief justice of the Supreme Court of Canada is guilty of manslaughter in the death of his alcoholic wife. The reader decides. Nicholas Meyer's *The Seven-Per-Cent Solution* brings Sherlock Holmes back to fictional life. Surprisingly, Sigmund Freud is brought back to life, too, as a friend and helper of Holmes.

DAVID SAVAGE, *Simon Fraser University*

Canadian Literature in French

Two special events affected intellectual and literary life in Quebec in 1974. One was the founding of the Montreal daily *Le Jour,* the first specifically (*indépendantiste*) newspaper. The other was the appearance of a new publishing house. Named Aurore, it is directed by the novelist V. L. Beaulieu, the uncontested leader of the school called "joual" (for the French-Canadian dialect).

Fiction. The strongest category of important works appearing during the year was the novel. André Major's admirable *Épouvantail* was strikingly successful with both critics and the general public. It recounts the turbulent adventures of Momo Boulanger, a former prisoner seeking his lost happiness but hunted on all sides by the underworld and also his fellow villagers.

Also noteworthy was the fifth novel of André Langevin, *Une Chaine dans le parc,* a tender, serious story of an orphan in the Montreal of the 1940's. Among the newcomers, Yves Beauchemin made a strong impression with *L'Enfirouapé,* a tragic and yet burlesque reconstruction of October 1970 events in Quebec.

Poetry. Nicole Brossard's three books (*Sold out; Mécanique jongleuse; French kiss*) exemplify literature that is resolutely modern, artificial, and also fascinating. But the major names to note are those of Gilbert Langevin, who, after *Novembre,* published *La Douche ou la seringue,* and of Michel Garneau, who, with *Moments,* establishes himself as one of the most authentic poets of his generation.

Theater. Marcel Dubé published two more plays, *Virginie* and *L'Impromptu de Quebec,* the latter work the first comedy written by this author of *Zone* (prix David 1973). Among the new authors, Roland Lepage, already known in theater circles, presented the general public with his best works: *La Complainte des hivers rouges* and *Le Temps d'une vie.*

Literary Criticism. André Brochu enriched this field in 1974 with his *Hugo—Amour/Crime/Révolution,* an essay on *Les Misérables,* as well as with *L'Instance critique,* a collection of his pieces written between 1961 and 1973.

FRANÇOIS RICARD
McGill University

English Literature

The year 1974 was a prosperous one for fiction, poetry, and literary studies in Britain. Several well-known novelists published new books, while the quality and variety of novels by newer writers augured well for fiction in the future. There was an unusual number of substantial books of poetry and a good selection of important critical works and biographies.

Fiction. C. P. Snow's *The Onlookers* (British title: *In Their Wisdom*) was regarded by some reviewers as one of his best novels. The plot, which concerns a legal struggle over a will, is old-fashioned, but it enables Snow to examine closely a group of characters engaged in a battle for money. His conclusions about human nature are unflattering. The "onlookers" of the title are peers of the House of Lords, who regret the passing of the world they knew and of the power many of them once had.

Lawrence Durrell's *Monsieur, or The Prince of Devils* is more complex, though not less pessimistic than Snow's work. A gnostic belief that the Prince of Devils, rather than God, must rule the world is held by Akkad, an Egyptian banker. Piers de Nogaret, perhaps in accordance with this view, has committed suicide. His sister is in an insane asylum. The main narrator, Bruce, who loved them both, returns to the old de Nogaret chateau at Avignon and recalls a trip he took with them on the Nile. Another narrator, Rob Sutcliffe, writes about the relationship of these three. We later find that yet another writer has written Sutcliffe's memoirs. The gnostic trinity is echoed by the three narrators and the three major characters.

In *The Sacred and Profane Love Machine,* Iris Murdoch continued her consideration of the complexities of human relationships and of moral questions. Blaise Gavender, a psychotherapist, has a wife and a mistress, a legitimate and an illegitimate son. When his wife Harriet and her son discover their counterparts, Harriet charitably accepts them. The mistress is less generous. Blaise vacillates between the two. There are stark scenes. The Gavenders' neighbor killed his dying wife; Blaise is attacked by Harriet's dogs; Harriet is killed in an airport massacre, and the mistress comes to live in her house. Murdoch's main concern, however, is the moral condition of her characters which those events dramatize.

In *The Abbess of Crewe: a Modern Morality Tale,* Muriel Spark is also concerned with moral questions, this time in a convent where the election of an abbess is held. The right-wing candidate wins with the help of electronic "bugs" used to oppose what she sees as corruption.

Anthony Burgess published two novels, *The Clockwork Testament, or Enderby's End* and *Napoleon Symphony*. In the first, F. X. Enderby is a visiting professor at the University of Manhattan—not unlike his creator, who recently filled a similar position at Columbia University. The book is a lively, if dyspeptic, satire. *Napoleon Symphony* is freely based both on the life of Napoleon and on the *Eroica* Symphony, which Beethoven had once intended to dedicate to that warrior. Napoleon is treated irreverently, Beethoven with respect, in what is perhaps the most skillful imitation of music in fiction since Joyce wrote the Sirens episode of *Ulysses*.

As his father did before him, Martin Amis won the Somerset Maugham Award for fiction, for *The Rachel Papers,* a novel about a youth on the verge of manhood. In *Ending Up,* his father, Kingsley Amis, writes brilliantly and compassionately about five aged characters who are near death.

Other outstanding novels were Thomas Hinde's *Agent;* Stanley Middleton's *Holiday;* Jennifer Johnston's *How Many Miles to Babylon?;* J. G. Ballard's *Concrete Island;* Susan Hill's *In the Springtime of the Year;* Beryl Bainbridge's *The Bottle Factory Outing;* and Penelope Mortimer's *Long Distance.*

Fine collections of short stories were Edna O'Brien's *A Scandalous Woman and Other Stories;* Julia O'Faolain's *Man in the Cellar;* Angela Carter's *Fireworks;* V. S. Pritchett's *The Camberwell Beauty and Other Stories;* and John Fowles' *The Ebony Tower.*

Nonfiction. It was not a vintage year for autobiographies. However, in *Another Part of the Wood,* Kenneth Clark, who is perhaps best known for his television series *Civilisation* and *The Romantic Rebellion,* recounted the first 35 years of his life, which include his Edwardian childhood and his appointments as curator of the Ashmolean Museum, the National Gallery, and the Royal Collection at Windsor. A more homely, but not less pleasing, memoir was Dannie Abse's *A Poet in the Family,* which evokes incidents and scenes from the 1930's through the 1950's with vivid good humor.

Lady Gregory's decorous autobiography, completed in typescript in 1923, was published as part of the Coole edition of her works. Another posthumous work was the second volume of Lady Ottoline Morrell's memoirs, *Ottoline at Garsington,* which describes her encounters with some of the greatest writers and thinkers of her age at her country home, Garsington. In *Nancy Astor and Her Friends,* Elizabeth Langhorne wrote of a more politically inclined group at another country home, Cliveden. David Gadd described Virginia Woolf and her friends in *The Loving Friends: A Portrait of Bloomsbury.*

The subject of Graham Greene's *Lord Rochester's Monkey,* written years ago but published in 1974, was the brilliant, dissolute Restoration rake, John Wilmot, 2d Earl of Rochester. Audrey Williamson's *Wilkes* is a life of the notorious but effective 18th century politician and reformer John Wilkes. Barbara Stoney wrote *Enid Blyton,* a biography of the prolific writer of children's stories. Claire Tomalin produced a timely life of an 18th century feminist, Mary Wollstonecraft. Margaret Drabble paid tribute to the character and skill of a fellow novelist in *Arnold Bennett.* In *Ivy When Young,* Hilary Spurling shed welcome light on the early life of the novelist Ivy Compton-Burnett. Glen Cavaliero studied the works of Powys in *John Cowper Powys, Novelist,* and Anthony Curtis analyzed Somerset Maugham's fiction in *The Pattern of Maugham.*

Poetry. Five important poetry collections were published in 1974: Andrew Young's *Complete Poems;* William Plomer's *Collected Poems;* Austin Clarke's *Collected Poems;* C. H. Sisson's *In Trojan Ditch;* and R. S. Thomas' *Selected Poems.* The first four volumes contain the work of poets recently deceased. Young is a lyrical nature poet, sharply observant, and fond of conceits. Plomer is equally alert, but chillier, more worldly, and more critical of mankind than Young. Clarke's poetry was at first influenced by the Irish revival of the early 20th century. He then turned to personal poems which examined moral questions, and finally to narrative poetry that at its best is both entertaining and intense. Sisson cultivated a plain, disciplined style and chose religious and quietly patriotic subjects. Thomas' poems are spare, direct, drawing their materials from the Welsh countryside in which he lives and reflecting an outlook that is free of illusions about the universe, man, or modern technology.

Several other collections of verse appeared in 1974. Philip Larkins' *High Windows* contains skillful poems of urbane disillusionment. John Fuller's *Epistles to Several Persons* masquerades as light verse, but is weighted with encyclopedic, and sometimes private, references. Anthony Thwaite's *New Confessions* reflects upon a North African setting. Jon Silkin's *The Principle of Water* consists of poems set in a coal-mining district in Durham and a verse play, *The People.*

Finally, W. H. Auden's posthumous volume, *Thank You, Fog,* should be mentioned. The title poem is about his return to England from the United States in 1972. *A Thanksgiving* pays tribute to those from whom Auden learned.

J. K. JOHNSTONE
University of Saskatchewan

French Literature

Two eminent French writers, both members of the French Academy, died during 1974. Marcel Pagnol (1895–1974) was known mainly for his theater trilogy *Marius-Fanny-César.* Marcel Achard (1899–1974), loved for the tender humor of his plays, especially *Jean de la lune* and *Patate,* was a particularly popular dramatist.

Two surviving elders—and leaders—of French literature, Louis Aragon and André Malraux, each published a work in 1973–74: Aragon's *Théâtre-roman, le poète et la mort* is a species of inventory, meditation, and testament. Malraux's *La Tête d'obsidienne* is a short, brilliant essay concerned with Picasso, art, and eternity.

Poet Henri Michaux published *Par la Voie des rythmes,* a 120-page album in which he crystallizes his phantasms and obsessions—no longer with words alone but with the help of pictures in juxtaposed linear series.

Poetry. Two interesting original collections appeared during the year: *Répétitions sur les amas* by Alain Veinstein and *Le Discours du chameau* by Tahar Ben Jelloun. Veinstein, a disciple of René Char, like him has a gift for creating tight-knit poetry charged with meaning. *Le Discours du chameau* is a tender and shattering poem inspired by the tragedy at the Munich Olympics.

Three remarkable anthologies were published. Pierre Seghers' *Le Résistance et ses poètes* assembles a number of "clandestine" patriotic, anti-Hitler poems written between 1940 and 1945. Bernard Delvaille's *La Nouvelle Poésie française* presents 600 pages of poetry written by a hundred or so young poets. *Dada,* by Ribemont-Dessaignes, a militant in the "dadaist" movement, contains his manifestos, articles, and poems.

Novels. Although certain avant-garde critics condemn it, this form continues to proliferate. One of the best-selling novels of 1974 was *Les Noisettes sauvages* by Robert Sabatier. A sequel to two earlier works, it continues the story of a Montmartre orphan's life. Another highly successful work was *Au Plaisir de dieu,* by Jean d'Ormesson.

Several other novels published by writers already known and loved by the public should be noted. *Les Hommes protégés* by Robert Merle is a kind of "politics-fiction" work set in a world of the future dominated by women. *Adios,* by Kléber Haedens, is the portrait of a prewar adolescent; *Le Bateau du courrier,* an ironic and compassionate work by Geneviève Dormann, is the most accomplished performance to date by this author of best sellers. *Un Profil perdu,* by Françoise Sagan, a slight work but not devoid of charm, centers on a young woman who avoids the trap of a second marriage to a rich man and chooses the love of a young veterinarian. In *Mardi à l'aube,* Lucie Faure shows the loneliness and disintegration of an apparently happy, adored, and privileged man. Two American girls go to France in search of happiness in Michel Mohrt's *Deux Indiennes à Paris.* Emmanuel Robles based his semiautobiographical *Saison violente* on his youth in Oran.

Interesting novels from fledgling or little-known authors included *Les Armoires vides* by Annie Ernaux; its heroine is a café-keeper's daughter caught up in a cultural struggle. *La Rage au cœur,* by Gérard Guégan, is a fiercely ironic leftist caricature of the ways of thought of the last decade's leftist intellectuals.

Memoirs and Chronicles. The year 1973–74 was particularly fertile in memoirs. Among the most important is *Jeunesse,* the fourth volume of Julien Green's autobiography. Covering the years 1922–26, it describes the awakening of the young Franco-American puritan to the world of the senses and of literature. Other titles are *La Boîte à couleurs,* in which André Roussin, playwright and member of the Académie Française, recreates a happy childhood spent in Marseille and Aix-en-Provence; *Dans la Salle des pas perdus,* the first volume of memoirs of the 1920's by playwright Armand Salacrou; *Le Temps immobile* by Claude Mauriac; and *La Vie est un film* by the famous movie director Jean Renoir.

In this category but transcending it in every way is *Souvenirs pieux* by Marguerite Yourcenar. The author, writing as both poet and historian, narrates the lives of her forebears—immediate and distant—and, through this description, presents a 19th century sociology as well as information about herself and her work.

History. One of the finest works of the year is *Le Vent d'Amérique* by Claude Manceron, an unconventional historian in the fine tradition of Jules Michelet. It is the second volume of a huge fresco that began brilliantly with *Les Vingt Ans du roi.*

Theater. Foreign plays and reruns dominated the French theatrical scene in 1974. But with *Ce Formidable Bordel,* Eugène Ionesco presented a significant and powerful play. And Victor Haim's *Abraham et Samuel* won a prize.

PIERRE BRODIN
Lycée Français de New York

German Literature

As in past years, German literature in 1974 continued on a predominantly conservative path. No new figures of importance emerged in 1974, but an old giant, Erich Kästner, died. A brilliant wit and satirist, he leaves a great gap in the fabric of German literary life.

Nonfiction. The phenomenal success of Joachim C. Fest's biography *Hitler* was accompanied by the minor successes of Richard Friedenthal's biography of Jan Hus, *Ketzer und Rebell;* Fritz J. Raddatz's biography *Marx;* and Jürgen Thorwald's study of the Wlassow-army, Hitler's ineffective Russian auxiliary, *Die Illusion.* Konrad Lorenz triumphed in the scientific field with his criticism of behaviorism in *Die Rückseite des Spiegels.* Robert Jungk's *Der Jahrtausendmensch* tried to outline the psychological problems of the future. In the reference book area three new multi-volume encyclopedias were brought out in 1974.

Fiction. The more noteworthy works of fiction included Dieter Kühn's novel *Die Präsidentin,* about the life of an unscrupulous stock manipulator, and Joseph Breitbach's story collection *Die Rabenschlacht,* which described capitalistic and imperialistic excesses. In *Albissers Grund,* the Swiss author Adolf Muschg portrayed fashionable anarchism in a rather dubious light. Sigrid Brunk treated the problem of unmarried motherhood in *Ledig, ein Kind,* while the male view of it was ably presented in Rudolf Hagelstange's novel *Der General und das Kind.* An apolitical work was Hans J. Fröhlich's account of the divergent development of two brothers, *Anhand meines Bruders.* Ernst von Salomon's novel *Die Kette der tausend Kraniche* was published posthumously.

Frankly autobiographical works of fiction included Margarete Moses' *Daniel,* a treatment of the problem of Jewish integration in pre-Hitler Germany, and Max Frisch's *Dienstbüchlein,* an account of Swiss army life. Hilde Domin's autobiographical notes, *Von der Natur nicht vorgesehen,* tried to bridge the generation gap.

Poetry. Among the few outstanding collections of poetry were Dieter Schmidt's *Schattenveränderung;* Walter Neumann's unsentimental reminiscences *Grenzen;* and Richard Gerlach's nature poems *Glanz über dem Bodensee.* Prose poetry was represented by Erhart Kästner's sad Byzantine reminiscences *Aufstand der Dinge.*

Drama. Ambitious new plays by Rolf Hochhuth, Peter Handke, and Thomas Bernhard met with mixed reactions. Revivals of older plays, including Hanns Eisler's *Johann Faustus* (1952) and Marieluise Fleissner's *Der starke Stamm* (1950), were better received.

East German Literature. Reliable information on East German writers can now be gleaned from West German author Fritz J. Raddatz's critical review in *Traditionen und Tendenzen* (1972). In fiction, Anna Segher's *Sonderbare Begegnungen* was the top best seller. Christa and Gerhard Wolf's *Till Eulenspiegel* presented an interesting modernization of the medieval jokester's life. In *Walther von der Vogelweide,* Eberhard Hilsch also chose a medieval hero for his stylistic experiments.

Orthodox critics felt somewhat uncomfortable with Rolf Schneider's novel *Die Reise nach Jaroslaw,* about a young girl denied the education she desired by the regime. Günter Kunert caused a stir at home by his visits to England and, most recently, the United States, on which he reported in *Der andere Planet.* His poetic collection *Ausgang* managed to stay on safe Marxist territory. Another noteworthy collection of lyrics was Sarah Kirsh's *Zaubersprüche.*

The simultaneous publication in both East and West Germany of Stefan Heyne's controversial book about the quelling of an East German workers' revolt by Soviet tanks in June 1953, was a memorable event.

Obituary. Erich Kästner, internationally known for his biting pacifistic verses and his children's classic *Emil und die Detektive,* died on July 29, 1974.

ERNST ROSE
Author of "A History of German Literature"

GIULIO EINAUDI PUBLISHERS, TORINO

Elsa Morante, author of *La storia*, the 1974 literary sensation and the most successful Italian book in years.

Italian Literature

In 1974, Italian writers maintained an uneasy relationship with the society around them. While they revealed a lively interest in current cultural and social problems, they displayed a tendency to express this interest in muddled language and to defuse potentially explosive issues by projecting them back into history. Thus, for example, the laudable concern with the revived threat of fascism in various new forms in Italy today often turned into a nostalgic celebration of the Resistance period, and the new feminist awareness frequently became the pretext for generic dissertations or for an equally generic renewal of interest in women writers as such. In addition, there was a persistent tendency on the part of critics and writers to mistake opacity of language for concern with scientific and current speech.

Fiction. Among the works that dealt with the Fascism-Resistance nexus were Arrigo Benedetti's *Rosso al vento;* Felice Chilanti's *Gli ultimi giorni dell'età del pane;* Mario Spinella's *Memoria della Resistenza;* and Guglielmo Petroni's *La morte del fiume,* winner of the Strega Prize. But the most effective novel of this type was *La storia* by Elsa Morante. Launched at midyear in a paperback edition, the novel caught the attention of a vast mass of readers (100,000 copies were sold just in the first month). Set in Rome between 1941 and 1947, and told in a consciously straightforward style (a stark contrast with recent experimental novels), the novel contrasts an innocent world of simple souls with the alien world of political reality.

Other writers concentrated on psychological exploration. Among them were Carlo Cassola with *Gisella;* Stefano Terra with *Alessandra* (winner of the Campiello Prize); and Clotilde Marghieri with *Amati enigme* (winner of the Viareggio Prize).

Oh, Serafina! by Giuseppe Berto, about the utopian idyll between an old-fashioned small industrialist and a flower girl, won the Bancarella Prize. The utopian theme was even more effectively developed by Umberto Simonetta in *Lo svergognato,* in which nudists win political power, and (with a realistic reference) by Francesco Leonetti in *Irati e sereni,* about the struggles of extra-parliamentary leftist groups in Milan.

Psychological analysis was the dominant element in several short story collections in 1974. The seven stories in *Le labrene* by Tommaso Landolfi describe obsessive, bizarre episodes in an elegant and cultured style. Bizarre is also the tone in Luigi Compagnone's short stories *Città di mare con abitanti,* set in Naples. In his collection *Uomini chiari,* Renzo Rosso ranged in settings from ancient Egypt to the modern world.

Poetry and Drama. Rossana Ombres won the Viareggio Prize with her collection of poems, *Bestiario d'amore,* a series of subtle descriptions, drawn in an atmosphere of myth and sometimes of horror, and based on an erudite background of medieval images derived from Hebrew literature and other sources. Pier Paolo Pasolini drew upon Calderón de la Barca's classic, *La vida es sueño,* as the inspiration for his *Calderón,* a verse drama that details the successive re-awakenings of a young woman in a variety of historical periods from Renaissance Spain to the world of modern capitalism.

Nonfiction. The great ideological debates that brought international renown to Italy in the 1940's were evoked with the publication, 20 years after his death, of selected letters of the Christian Democratic leader Alcide De Gasperi. The published letters were written from prison in the period from 1927 to 1928. More significant writings of another political figure, the communist leader Palmiro Togliatti (d. 1964), were collected in *Opere scelte, 1923–1964.* This work is part of the ongoing project by the publishers, Editori Riuniti, to bring out all his writings. In his *Linguaggio d'Italia,* Giacomo Devoto, the doyen of Italian linguists, reworked much of his earlier research in a rich profile of linguistic and cultural history.

Obituaries. Italy lost a number of major intellectual figures in 1974. Among them were Vito Pandolfi, one of the leading theater historians in Italy, best known for his six-volume collection of texts from the *Commedia dell'Arte;* the literary critic Enrico Falqui, the prolific symbol of empirical, commonsensical criticism of modern Italian literature; the novelist Guido Piovene, author of *Lettere di una novizia* (1942), who was also an urbane essayist; and the masterful poet and novelist Aldo Palazzeschi (pseudonym of Aldo Giurlani). Born in 1885, Palazzeschi, especially known for his novel *Sorelle Materassi* (1934), was probably the best representative of that early 20th century style that combined neoclassic restraint with a taste for merry recklessness.

PAOLO VALESIO
New York University

Japanese Literature

During 1974, several writers who were born just prior to World War II and whose boyhoods coincided with the war years seemed to attain a new maturity. These writers are all extremely conscious of the enormous gap they perceive between the obsession with death and the end of the world instilled in them by the experience of war, and the peace of daily life in the postwar world. Their search for identity in the midst of both the petty details of their present lives and their memories of the war has led this "fourth generation" of postwar writers to be termed the "generation of introversion."

Fiction. The most remarkable work of 1974 was the voluminous novel *Kōzui wa Waga Tamashii ni Oyobi* (*The Waters Have Reached Unto My Soul*) by Kenzaburō Ôe, who is still in his thirties and has been writing professionally for the past 15 years. The leading character, to protect his idiot son from the ravages of a nuclear war that he believes to be inevitable, lives as a recluse, associating only with a group of young men who, frustrated with their political impotence, likewise seek to flee from society. In the final chapter, a gun battle with riot police, the father dies, entrusting the future to his son. The conclusion of Ôe's pessimistic panorama of Japan's thwarted radicalism, its ecological crisis and spiritual prostration, implies an almost religious hope for salvation.

Employing an image reminiscent of Gogol, Meisei Gotō's *Hasamiuchi* (*Outflanked*) portrays a groping for identity in the form of a search for an overcoat lost during the leading character's student days. Similarly, Hiroshi Sakagami's account of his experience as a wartime evacuee, *Wara no Otoshiana* (*Trap of Straw*), and Senji Kuroiwa's tale of a boy who stole flowers, *Hanabasami o Motsu Kodomo* (*A Boy with Pruning Shears*), reveal a tendency to search for a positive sense of self among memories of the past rather than in a contemporary social world that can only destroy that sense. Yoshikichi Furui's *Kushi no Hi* (*The Burning Comb*) treats essentially the same theme in an erotic context. It is one of the more noteworthy pieces of this writer, whose work has been influenced by his extensive reading in modern German literature.

A unique and active branch of contemporary fiction is the work of several Korean writers who live in Japan and write in Japanese. In Seikihan Kin's *Yoru no Koe* (*A Voice from Night*), Kakuei Kin's *Kamen* (*A Mask*), and Kaisei Ri's *Tsuihō to Jiyū* (*The Exile and the Freedom*), the central problem is one of establishing a racial identity as a minority group in an alien environment.

Criticism. The so-called *Fonii Ronso* (*Dispute on Phoniness*), a series of articles by Jun Etō and Tokuyoshi Hiraoka, drew much attention. Etō's criticism of several currently popular writers as "phoney" sparked this exercise in mudslinging, which, in fact, was inextricably connected with the problem of defining critical standards for all of modern Japanese literature. It posed the fundamental question of how the reality of the Japanese sense of life is to be expressed, using the techniques of modern fiction —a Western literary invention.

Highly relevant to this issue was Saiichi Maruya's monthly critical column in the *Asahi Shinbun* newspaper, which discussed recent works of fiction in the broad contexts of the Japanese classical tradition and of world literature. Also noteworthy was Shōichi Saeki's *Nipponjin no Jiden* (*Autobiographies of Japanese*), which shed new light on the formation of self-awareness in Japan.

Drama. Kunio Shimizu won the Kishida Drama Prize with *Bokura ga Hijō no Kawa o Kudaru Toki* (*When We Go Down the Cold-Blooded River*), which treats the disillusionment of young Japanese radicals in the 1970's. Minoru Betsuyaku's *Isu to Densetsu* (*Of Chairs and Legends*) is noteworthy for its daring use of nonsense Japanese to express the absurd.

Poetry. Ryūichi Tamura's *Shinnen no Tegami* (*New Year's Letter*), Sachiko Yoshihara's *Ondînu* (*Ondine*), and Mikirô Sasaki's *Suichū Kasai* (*Fire in the Water*) were among the more outstanding collections. All reveal a self-conscious pondering of the limits of avant-gardism while seeking an affirmative lyricism in the midst of alienation.

TAKEHIKO NOGUCHI
Kobe University

Latin American Literature

Several outstanding books by well-known authors were published in 1974, and, as a result, Latin American literature may be said to have had another good year.

Fiction. Significant prize-winning writers were Juan Carlos Martelli of Mexico (International Prize "America Latina") for *Los tigres de la memoria;* Agustín Yáñez of Mexico (Mexico's Premio Internacional de Letras); and Jorge Luis Borges of Argentina (Mexico's International Prize "Alfonso Reyes").

Three successful Argentinian novelists published in 1974. In *En la ardiente oscuridad,* Eduardo Mallea probed the mystery of human existence. Ernesto Sábato wrote *Abaddón el exterminador,* the last of a trilogy in which the author becomes a character, revealing his soul to the reader. With *El laberinto,* Manuel Mujic Láinez also completed a trilogy.

WIDE WORLD

Miguel Angel Asturias, Guatemalan writer and diplomat who won 1967 Nobel Prize for literature, died in June.

Two novelists wrote about one of Latin America's prototypes, the figure of the dictator: Alejo Carpentier of Cuba, *El recurso del método,* and Augusto Roa Bastos of Paraguay, *!Yo, el supremo!.* Juan Carlos Onetti of Uruguay published *Tiempo de abrazar.* In *El presidente,* Manuel del Cabral of the Dominican Republic presented a black U. S. president as a protagonist.

Other important novels published in 1974 were *Lázaro,* the posthumous work of Ciro Alegría of Peru; *Las vueltas del tiempo* by Agustín Yáñez, *Mal don* by Silvina Bullrich of Argentina; *Los pies de barro* by Salvador Garmendia of Venezuela; *El tañido de una flauta* by Sergio Pitol of Mexico; and *Los desheredados* by Héctor Sánchez of Colombia.

The field of short fiction was enriched with several works. In *Octaedro,* Julio Cortázar of Argentina presented eight fantastic stories on the theme of the search for identity; Gabriel García Márquez of Colombia published a collection of early tales, *Ojos de perro azul;* Alfredo Bryce Echenique of Peru turned out a collection of caustic tales entitled *La felicidad, ja, ja;* and José Donoso of Chile portrayed the artificial life of Barcelona's upper middle-class in *Tres novelitas burguesas.* The Mexican Enrique Jaramillo Levy published *Duplicaciones.*

Nonfiction. One of the most interesting nonfiction works of 1974 was Pablo Neruda's *Confieso que he vivido,* his posthumous memoirs. They were put together from an unfinished manuscript by his widow and the Venezuelan novelist Miguel Otero Silva. The Argentinian Héctor A. Murena confronted basic artistic problems with religious principles in *La metáfora y lo sagrado.* In *Cuaderno cubano,* Mario Benedetti of Uruguay evaluated the experience of his visits to Cuba.

The Mexican poet Octavio Paz expanded his literary theories in *Los hijos del limo.* In *La apariencia desnuda* (a study of Marcel Duchamp), he explored the relationship between the artist and life. He also collaborated with Julian Ríos in *Solo a dos voces,* conversations on writers and literature. Violeta Luna did a fine analysis of representative Ecuadorian poets in *La lírica ecuatoriana actual.* In *Cortázar y Carpentier,* Mercedes Rein studied two of Latin America's best novelists.

Poetry. There were many reprints and studies of the works of the late Nobel Prize-winner Pablo Neruda. Several posthumous books by Neruda were published: *Arte de pájaros; La rosa separada; Todo el amor; El corazón amarillo; El mar y las campanas; Libros de las preguntas; Jardín de invierno; Defectos escogidos;* and *Las vidas de un poeta.*

Octavio Paz published *Versiones y diversiones* and Mario Benedetti brought out a collection of militant prose and poetry, *Letras de emergencia.* The year also saw the appearance of the first volume of César Vellejo's *Obras completas* and Stefan Baciu's *Antología de la poesía surrealista latinoamericana.*

Theater. In Mexico, much interest was generated by two plays dealing with the life of the Inquisitor Torquemada: the Mexican Hugo Argüello's *El gran inquisidor,* a study of power and an indictment of fanaticism, and the Brazilian Augusto Boal's *Torquemada.* In Argentina a great success was *El gran soñador,* a demythification of Charles Chaplin.

Obituaries. Mexico lost three leading writers, Salvador Novo, recipient of the "Premio Nacional de Letras"; the poet Jaime Torres Bodet; and Rosario Castellanos. Guatemala lost the Nobel Prize-winning novelist Miguel Angel Asturias.

MARÍA A. SALGADO
University of North Carolina at Chapel Hill

Soviet Literature

The year 1974 in Soviet literature began with the arrest and exile of Aleksandr Solzhenitsyn. This traumatic event powerfully dramatized the chief conflict of Soviet literature—freedom for the individual writer versus state dictated guidelines. The pages of *Pravda,* January 14 and 24, and *Literaturnaya gazeta,* January 16 and 23, were filled with denunciations of Solzhenitsyn's work *The Gulag Archipelago* by many main-line Soviet writers despite the fact that it and the bulk of his other works have never been published in the Soviet Union. This case as well as the cases of the many underground Samizdat works illustrate again that a great deal more is being written and read in the Soviet Union than is officially published there.

In the province of literary criticism, a struggle between "conservative" and "liberal" tendencies continues to be strongly felt, even on the official level. The bulk of literary criticism, including the space devoted to this subject in leading periodicals such as *Voprosy literatury,* defends the "socialist realist" stance as essentially the only legitimate credo. January 1974 was the second anniversary of the Central Committee's Declaration on Literature and, during the year, repeated reference was made again to the need to follow the party's directions faithfully in the drive to build a truly international socialist culture.

However, there are individual critics who feel that contemporary Soviet literature often fails to fulfill the needs of the general readership to see real people involved in basic human problems and situations. In the opening number of *Novyi mir* in 1974, F. Kuznetsov wrote of the need to come to grips with the "Dostoyevskian" enigma concerning the meaning of a life without God. The shape of Kuznetsov's defensive polemics reveals the extent to which pre-Soviet and emigré writers and thinkers, such as N. Berdyaev, have become a source of inspiration for many more liberally disposed critics. This tendency is severely criticized in official literary circles.

Also at the core of this controversy is the question of the aesthetic worth of official literary criticism, which recognizes only educative content as valid. The opposition, loyal and otherwise, has generally been severely criticized for differing views.

Prose Fiction. Fiction dominated the Soviet literary scene again in 1974 if for no other reason than its sheer quantity. Unfortunately, the quality of much Soviet fiction continued to be mediocre. Many novels had as their goal the enlightenment of Soviet youth—offering a moral education through the adherence of their heroes to the paradigms of Soviet reality. K. Kovaldzhi's novel *Five Points on a Map* was one such work, depicting the vicissitudes and eventual triumph of students coming from great distances to study in Moscow.

Women were the central characters of numerous novels, such as Y. Avdeyenko's *Wild Hops,* in which a woman worker rises from a rank and file position to be section leader in a factory. While many stories, such as I. Lazutin's family, worker chronicle, *The Karetnikov's,* had an urban, industrial setting, quite a few

Attack on dissident Soviet writer Aleksandr Solzhenitsyn amuses passersby in Moscow. The musical group in the poster is labeled "The Anti-Soviet Orchestra."

UPI

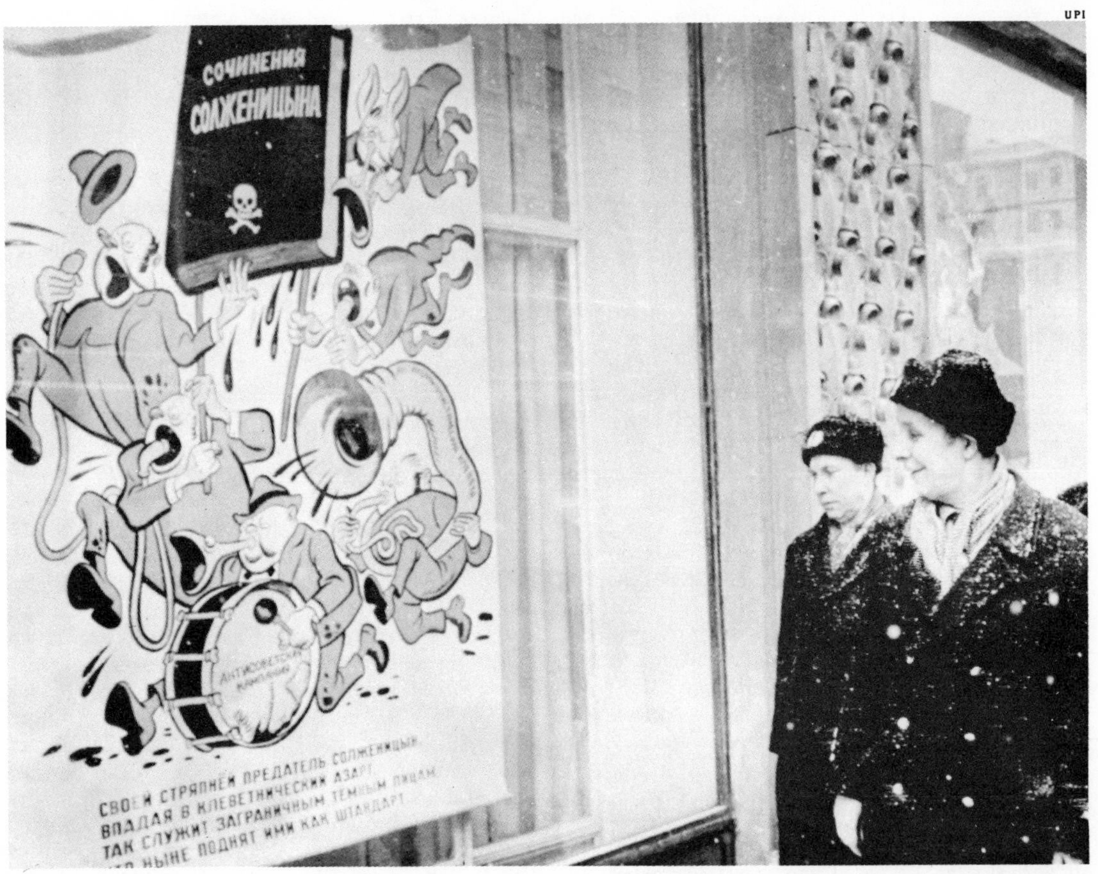

works were set in a rural background. Some authors feel perhaps that the ambience of nature allows an attempt at freer, less dogmatic portraits of individual heroes. One work which falls into this category is I. Chernev's *The Family,* a survey of the impact of revolution and Soviet life on a remote Old Believer settlement. Novels about World War II were plentiful. A typical one was *The Astrologers,* A. Marshenko's rather standard paean to soldiers, officers, and chekists. There was also historical fiction published on such figures as the poet Mikhail Lermontov.

Poetry. Poetry continued to generate great vitality. A group of poems by Andrei Voznesensky appeared in Vol. 1 of *Novyi mir* and poems by Bella Akhmadulina were published in Vol. 6 of the same journal. Yevgeni Yevtushenko published a selection of poems of reminiscences in the February 8 issue of *Literaturnaya rossiya.* Part of Yevtushenko's epic about Siberian construction, known as the *Kam Az* cycle, appeared in *Literaturnaya gazeta* of May 22.

The year 1974 marks the 175th anniversary of Aleksandr Pushkin's birth. The event was celebrated by articles about him in leading journals, as well as by publication of selected pieces of his prose and poetry.

FRANK K. MOSCA, *New York University*

Spanish Literature

The year 1974 saw no significant change from the incomplete liberalization of publishing criteria that was achieved some time ago. The failure to complete the liberalization process continued to hamper the creative efforts of Spanish writers.

Fiction. Ramón Sender, now past 70, and the last of Spain's major pre-Civil War novelists, published *Nancy, doctora en gitanería,* the sequel to an earlier work. Among the major contemporary novelists who published were Camilo José Cela with *Officio de tinieblas 5* and Miguel Delibes with *El príncipe destronado.*

Some major prizes became extinct. The Alfaguara Prize was the first to end. The Barral Prize, also cancelled, was first rejected by the poet José María Caballero Bonald, who was granted its last award for *Agata ojo de gato.* Other important prizes seemed healthy. Carlos Rojas' *Azaña* took the Planeta Prize, and Rodrigo Royo's *Todavía . . . ,* a naked focus on the Civil War, received the Ateneo de Sevilla award. Well-received novels from established writers included Ramón Solis' *Mónica, corazón dormido;* Carmen Martín Gaite's *Retahilas;* Manuel Barrios' *Retablo de picardías;* Domingo Manfredi Cano's *Juan el negro,* about a black American's experience in the Spanish Civil War; Jorge Perrer-Vidal's *Te emplazo, padre, te exijo que respondas;* Héctor Vázquez-Azpiri's *Corrido de Valo Otero;* and José Asenjo Sedano's *Crónica.*

Short fiction of significance appeared mostly in anthologies. Two of the more important of these were *Historias del 36,* dealing with the Civil War and including such authors as Max Aub and Luis Romero, and *Doce relatos,* by Valencian writers. Outstanding individual collections were Manuel Barrios' *La guerra ha terminado* and María Angeles Arazo's *Obsesión.* La Felguera Prize was awarded to Luis Fernández Roces' *Sobre este cadáver de cenizas.*

Nonfiction. Important scholarly publications included Francisco Ayala's *La novela: Galdós y Unamuno* and *Cervantes y Quevedo;* Segundo Serrano Poncela's *Formas simbólicas de la imaginación;* Manuel Muñoz Berberán's *La máscara de Tordesillas;* Pablo Corbalán's *Poesía surrealista en España;* Miguel Oliver's *La literatura del desastre;* and Jesús Castañón's *La crítica literaria en la prensa española del siglo dieciccho.*

Significant publications in the field of the essay included Ignacio Agusti's *Ganas de hablar,* memoir-like commentaries by the famed novelist; Medardo Fraile's *La penúltima Inglaterra;* Miguel Pérez Ferrero's *Tertulias y grupos literarios;* the late Gaspar Gómez de la Serna's *Los viajeros de la ilustración;* and Rafael Sánchez Ferlosio's long-awaited new work *Las semanas del jardín.*

Poetry. Major prizes went to Ramón Pedro's *Los cuatro nocturnos y una lenta iluminación sobre Cherbourg* (Leopoldo Panero Prize); Carlos Sahagún's *Estar contigo* (Juan Ramón Jiménez Prize); and the veteran José García Nieto's *Revelaciones y sonetos de Madrid* (Francisco de Quevedo Prize). Works published by master poets included Vicente Aleixandre's *Diálogos del conocimiento* and Luis Rosales' *Como el corte hace sangre.* Major works by established poets were Concha Lagos' *Fragmentos en espiral desde el pozo;* Pureza Canelo's *El barco de agua,* and Eduardo Chicharro's *Música celestial y otros poemas,* containing much of the late poet's previously unpublished work. Two important compilations were Enrique Badosa's *Poesías, 1956–1971,* and Vicente Gaos' *Poesías completas, 1958–1973.*

Outstanding publications by younger poets included Gonzalo Vázquez Dodero's *Mundo, demonio y carne;* Antonio Leandro Souza's *Caín muere en la cruz;* and Clara Janés' *Límite humano.*

Theater. The highlight of the theatrical season was Antonio Buero Vallejo's *La fundación,* a great box-office success and, critics seem to believe, one of the better efforts of Spain's major living playwright. Other established dramatists who staged new works were Lauro Olmo (*Historia de un pechicidio*) and Jaime Salom (*Nuevo brindis por un rey*). Promising theatrical entertainment by younger playwrights included Eduardo Fernández Fournier's *Teólogos,* based on the life of Bartolomé de Las Casas, and Jesús Campos García's *Siete mil gallinas y un camello.*

ALFRED RODRIGUEZ
The University of New Mexico

LOS ANGELES

Los Angeles felt the effects during 1974 of national inflation, recession, and political reform sentiment. The year was relatively free of natural disasters. A threatened fuel shortage in the Department of Water and Power did not materialize, although charges for electrical energy were raised considerably as a result of increased fuel costs.

Bus Strike. One result of inflation was a 59-day strike in the autumn by drivers and mechanics of the Southern California Rapid Transit District, demanding higher wages. A settlement was finally negotiated, but the result was a decline in public confidence in mass-transportation systems. For a while there was serious talk of turning the bus system over to the county, whose employees are forbidden by state law to strike. A proposal on the November ballot to reserve taxpayers' funds toward a rapid-transit rail system was defeated.

Political Irregularities and Proposed Reforms. Throughout the year the Los Angeles County Board of Supervisors was involved in a number of disputes over administrative reorganization and in investigating charges of irregularities in various agencies, including the civil service commission and the sheriff's department. Late in the year, the board dismissed the county's chief probation officer, charging him with numerous administrative failures.

After Congress adopted a plan for public financing of presidential contests, the City Council gave serious consideration to a method of financing campaigns of Council members, the mayor, and other elective officers by a voucher system from public funds. On a tie vote, the Council failed to approve the method even for a trial basis. This was the first such public financing plan voted on by a city council anywhere in the nation.

In suburban Long Beach, a federal grand jury began an investigation of various allegations of fraud and corruption in Los Angeles' largest suburb. The investigation involved charges of illegal gambling, bribery, conspiracy, the solicitation of payoffs, and irregularities in the conversion of the *Queen Mary* into a tourist attraction.

The Philharmonic. The Los Angeles Philharmonic Orchestra, which in recent years has toured Japan, Israel, and elsewhere, enjoyed a highly successful tour of Europe in the early fall. Zubin Mehta, the orchestra's outstanding conductor, signed a long-term contract to stay with the organization.

Crime. One of the most bizarre criminal episodes in California history began on the evening of February 4, when Patricia Hearst, then 19, daughter of the editor of the *San Francisco Examiner,* was kidnapped from her Berkeley apartment by a group calling itself the Symbionese Liberation Army (SLA). The SLA demanded that millions of dollars worth of food be distributed to the state's needy. Much of it was wasted or stolen, and Patricia Hearst was still not released. In April, the group, including Miss Hearst, was identified as having held up a San Francisco bank. Later she dramatically announced that she was joining the SLA. The group fled to Los Angeles and on May 17, six members died in a gunfight with Los Angeles police. Only two known members of the SLA and Patricia Hearst remained at large. At year's end, they were still being sought.

Sports. The great UCLA basketball dynasty finally came to an end. After 88 straight wins, the team suffered a one-point loss to Notre Dame, then two in the conference. UCLA took the conference championship, but lost in the NCAA semifinals. The team had won 38 consecutive NCAA tournament games, an all-time record.

The Los Angeles Lakers gained the NBA playoffs after winning the Pacific title, but lost in the championship series. Later in the year, Jerry West, the team's great playmaker, retired.

The Los Angeles Dodgers, with a well-balanced young team and the league's most valuable player, relief pitcher Mike Marshall, defeated Pittsburgh in the National League playoffs. The team then lost to Oakland, four games to one, in the World Series.

CHARLES R. ADRIAN
University of California, Riverside

LOUISIANA

Louisiana was fortunate in many ways in 1974, with general racial harmony and few natural disasters to mar the life of its citizens. The state began preparations for a new government era, ushered in with 1975, as a new constitution replaced the cumbersome document previously in effect since 1922.

New Constitution. Gov. Edwin Edwards and the Legislature, working with a commission of legal experts and constitutional convention delegates, drafted year-end legislation to transfer hundreds of provisions formerly in the constitution into statutory law. A brief November spe-

LOUISIANA • Information Highlights

Area: 48,523 square miles (125,675 sq km).
Population (1973 est.): 3,764,000. *Density:* 83 per sq mi.
Chief Cities (1970 census): Baton Rouge, the capital, 165,963; New Orleans, 593,471; Shreveport, 182,064.
Government (1974): *Chief Officers*—governor, Edwin W. Edwards (D); lt. gov., James E. Fitzmorris, Jr. (D). *Legislature*—Senate, 39 members; House of Representatives, 105 members.
Education (1973–74): *Enrollment*—public elementary schools, 508,840 pupils; public secondary schools, 333,610; nonpublic schools, 135,100; colleges and universities, 135,247 students. *Public school expenditures,* $730,800,000 ($949 per pupil).
State Finances (fiscal year 1973): *Revenues,* $2,321,105,000; *expenditures,* $2,230,123,000.
Personal Income (1973): $14,397,000,000; per capita, $3,825.
Labor Force (Aug. 1974): *Nonagricultural wage and salary earners,* 1,168,000; *insured unemployed,* 26,500 (2.7%).

cial session enacted some new criminal code laws to conform with the new Bill of Rights, hailed as one of the most liberal and protective of individual rights in the nation. Voters approved the new document on April 20 by a generous majority, making it clear they expect substantive governmental reform, including consolidation of all state agencies into 20 major departments.

Economy. The state faced economic woes in 1974, many of them anticipated rather than actual. However some major industries announced brief December layoffs or extended "holidays," and strikes halted construction in the Baton Rouge area for several weeks. The shrimping industry is in such an economic slump that the Legislature was forced to enact laws to guarantee loans to shrimpers under certain conditions.

A single hurricane swept the southwestern part of the state, but principal harm was to the sugarcane crop, eventually adding to the national rise in the price of sugar.

Despite the unstable economic conditions, the state government sailed through the year with a surplus, thanks largely to a doubled severance tax on oil and gas. But raises for state employees, particularly schoolteachers, remained a top priority for 1975.

New mineral exploration and increased production helped bolster state income. Governor Edwards continued to battle for some modification of Federal Power Commission rules which set low prices for gas and oil shipped out of the state. Edwards, who has made several appearances in the East and on national television, has been very blunt in his contention that other areas should begin offshore oil exploration and try to provide their own energy sources.

Elections. Politically, it was a strange year. While much of the nation veered away from the two-party system and elected a heavily Democratic Congress, Louisiana returned its lone Republican, David Treen, to Congress by a substantial majority. Another race, in the Sixth District (including the capital city of Baton Rouge), ended with the Republican candidate, Henson Moore, holding a five-vote lead over the Democrat, Jeff LaCaze, a 29-year-old former television sportscaster, who deposed incumbent Rep. John Rarick in the primary. A new election was scheduled for early 1975.

The Louisiana Supreme Court retained its 4–3 "liberal" majority with the reelection of Pascal Calogero, former law partner of New Orleans Mayor Moon Landrieu. He was bitterly opposed by "law and order" forces who regard recent court rulings as too lenient.

Superdome. Completion date for the New Orleans Superdome has now been moved up to June 1975, and investigations into numerous contracts for the structure are continuing.

EDWIN W. PRICE, JR.
"Morning Advocate," Baton Rouge

LUXEMBOURG

As a result of the parliamentary elections held on May 26, 1974, a new coalition government came to power in Luxembourg. The ministry, headed by Gaston Thorn, leader of the Democratic party (generally known as the Liberal party), was sworn in by Grand Duke Jean on June 18. A coalition of Liberals and Socialists replaced the government of Christian Social and Democratic parties under Pierre Werner.

The Election. The Christian Social party, which had been the dominant force in the country's politics for about half a century, fared badly in the election. Its representation in the Chamber of Deputies declined from 21 to 18, while that of the Democratic party increased from 11 to 14. The Socialists did even better, gaining 5 seats for a total of 17 in the new Chamber. As a result of its setback in the election, the Christian Social party, which had been a member of every ministry since 1926, and Pierre Werner, its leader since 1959, dropped out of the government. The number of seats held by the Communist party and a splinter Socialist party declined from 6 to 5 each.

Persons between 18 and 21 years of age voted for the first time in this election, which may have been a factor in the political shift. The issues in the election campaign were inflation, liberalization of the abortion law, and women's rights. Premier Thorn continued also as foreign minister.

Economy. A general strike in October 1973 was settled by a substantial wage increase. The strikers also demanded worker participation in management decisions. Luxembourg is one of the few countries in the world enjoying excellent industrial conditions. Production has improved steadily since the end of 1973. Crude steel production in 1974 was running about 10% higher than in 1973, and in March 1974 reached 554,000 tons, the highest for any month on record. Luxembourg's rate of inflation is the second lowest in the Common Market; it was only 6% in 1973, and rose moderately in 1974.

AMRY VANDENBOSCH
University of Kentucky

LUXEMBOURG • Information Highlights

Official Name: Grand Duchy of Luxembourg.
Area: 999 square miles (2,586 sq km).
Population (1973 est.): 400,000.
Chief Cities (1970 census): Luxembourg, the capital, 76,143; Esch-sur-Alzette, 27,575; Differdange, 17,963.
Government: *Head of state,* Jean, grand duke (acceded 1964). *Head of government,* Gaston Thorn, premier (took office June 18, 1974). *Legislature* (unicameral) —Chamber of Deputies.
Monetary Unit: Franc (39.35 francs equal U. S.$1, Aug. 1974).
Gross National Product (1973 est.): $1,500,000,000.
Manufacturing (major products): Iron and steel, chemicals, fertilizer, textiles, nonferrous metals.
Major Agricultural Products: Barley, wheat, oats, grapes, potatoes.
Foreign Trade (Luxembourg-Belgium, 1973): *Exports,* $22,301,000,000; *imports,* $21,925,000,000.

MAINE

The major events of 1974 in Maine were the November election and the inflation explosion, particularly as related to the energy crisis.

The Election. In a stunning upset on November 5, James Longley, running as an independent, was elected governor by a 9,000-vote margin. Longley, a Lewiston insurance man and chairman in 1972 of the Maine Management and Cost Survey, a group of businessmen charged by the governor to explore ways to bring great efficiencies to state government, made the issues of economy and efficiency the major thrust of his gubernatorial campaign.

In defeating Republican James Irwin and Democrat George Mitchell, Longley became the first independent since 1880 to win the governorship. Observers attributed his success to the burdens of inflation and to his post-Watergate insistence that Maine needed a businessman as its chief executive.

In another upset, voters chose Rockland Republican David Emery over incumbent Peter Kyros, a Democrat, in the 1st Congressional District. In the 2d District, Republican William Cohen won a second term in Congress over Mark Gartley, a Democrat and former prisoner of war in North Vietnam. Cohen had gained national stature as a member of the House Judiciary Committee, which voted for the impeachment of President Nixon in August.

Maine voters also elected a Democratic-controlled House and a Republican-controlled Senate in legislative contents. Democrats filled all seven positions on the Executive Council, as well as the positions of attorney general and secretary of state when Maine's state government was organized in January 1975.

Several referendum questions were also disposed of by the electorate. Bond issues were approved for highway and school construction. Defeated was an act permitting trucks to substantially increase their weight.

Economy. Galloping inflation came to Maine in 1974, with fuel oil prices doubling and gasoline, food, and other commodities increasing dramatically in price. Particularly hard hit were homeowners, whose fuel costs skyrocketed, and the tourist industry, which slumped because of gasoline prices and shortages. As the full impact of inflation passed through the economy, political leaders indicated that an unprecedented revenue gap would face the next session of the legislature.

One of the fortunate results of the worldwide demand for food and fiber was the announcement that Maine's pulp and paper industry had embarked on a $500 million plant-expansion program, the largest program of industrial expansion in Maine's history.

Environment. Maine continued in 1974 as a major battleground between the friends and foes of oil refineries. The Environmental Improvement Commission in August announced that the Pittston Company had failed to meet all requirements for a permit to construct a refinery at Eastport.

UPI

The only Independent candidate in 1974 to win a governorship, James Longley of Maine embraces his wife.

Hearings were scheduled by the Department of Environmental Protection on the application of the New England Energy Company for a refinery at Sanford.

Criticism was voiced by environmentalists at the decision of the Congress to revive the Dickey-Lincoln hydroelectric project on the upper St. John River. Proponents successfully obtained $800,000 in planning funds.

RONALD F. BANKS
University of Maine

MAINE • Information Highlights

Area: 33,215 square miles (86,027 sq km).
Population (1973 est.): 1,028,000. *Density:* 33 per sq mi.
Chief Cities (1970 census): Augusta, the capital, 21,945; Portland, 65,116; Lewiston, 41,779; Bangor, 33,168.
Government (1974): *Chief Officers*—governor, Kenneth M. Curtis (D); secy. of state, Joseph T. Edgar (R). *Legislature*—Senate, 33 members (22 R, 11 D); House of Representatives, 151 members (78 R, 73 D).
Education (1973–74): *Enrollment*—public elementary schools, 174,566 pupils; public secondary schools, 70,901; nonpublic schools, 19,000; colleges and universities, 36,122 students. *Public school expenditures,* $204,100,000 ($884 per pupil).
State Finances (fiscal year 1973): *Revenues,* $639,694,-000; *expenditures,* $624,766,000.
Personal Income (1973): $4,054,000,000; per capita, $3,944.
Labor Force (July 1974): *Nonagricultural wage and salary earners,* 365,400; *insured unemployed,* 15,200 (5.4%).

MALAYSIA

The Malaysian government registered some notable political, economic, and diplomatic achievements during 1974.

Political Events. The political strength of the ruling National Front coalition was graphically demonstrated by the outcome of the general elections in August, the first since the communal violence of 1969. Led by the United Malays National Organization (UMNO), the nine parties comprising the multiracial National Front captured 135 out of 154 parliamentary seats and gained control of all state legislatures. No state election was held in Sabah.

The victory was widely regarded as an impressive endorsement of the leadership and moderate politics of the prime minister and leader of UMNO, Tun Abdul Razak. Some observers saw reason for caution in the fact that the Front actually obtained only 59% of the ballots cast. Furthermore, the one opposition party to effectively withstand the Front sweep by winning nine seats and 20% of the vote is a militant voice for Chinese communal interests—the Democratic Action party.

The Economy. Following a year of economic boom, fueled by rising world market prices for Malaysian raw material exports and increased government expenditures, preliminary indications were that 1974 would witness a slowdown of growth, continued inflation, and a balance of trade deficit. In April, the government announced a number of anti-inflation measures, including steps to ease the impact of price rises on low-income groups by subsidizing food and other essential commodities.

With over 50% of the gross national product derived from external trade, Malaysia remains vulnerable to imported inflation and an economic downturn in the industrialized West, the principal market for Malaysian goods. Nevertheless, there were indications of the economy's basic vitality: continued growth in output, strong prices in international markets for Malaysian commodity exports, foreign exchange reserves equal to eight months of retained imports, and a currency characterized by the *Financial Times* as the world's second strongest.

The picture was further brightened by announcements of commercially promising oil strikes off both the east and west coasts of Malaya. With a current production of 100,000 barrels daily of high-quality sulfur-free crude, the federation has already become an oil exporter. Projections call for production to grow to 500,000 barrels daily by 1978, and to one million by 1980. With petroleum emerging as a major factor in the Malaysian economy, the government announced the establishment of a state-owned oil company, Petroleum Nasional Berhad (PETRONAS), under the supervision of the prime minister.

Security. The year 1974 was marked by one notable success in the government's protracted conflict with various Communist insurgents. In March, it was revealed that the principal leader of some 700 guerrillas in Sarawak had previously surrendered with 481 of his followers to the state government in response to a virtual amnesty offered by the chief minister. This brought near to conclusion a 12-year conflict to which the government had committed seven battalions and an average annual expenditure of $20 million.

Similar progress was not recorded in the even more durable struggle waged by Malayan Communist Party (MCP) guerrillas in the jungles of northern Malaya. In fact, 1974 saw an increase in the number and geographical extent of MCP terrorist actions, culminating in a bold daylight assassination of the inspector general of police in downtown Kuala Lumpur.

Foreign Affairs. In terms of foreign policy, 1974 was the year of China. After two years of cautious negotiation, China and Malaysia decided to establish diplomatic relations, a step formalized when Prime Minister Razak visited Peking from May 28 to June 2. Malaysia acknowledged that Taiwan was an "inalienable part of China" and agreed to sever all governmental ties with the Nationalist Chinese government. In return, Communist China renounced any claim on Malaysian Chinese who chose Malaysian citizenship, and apparently disavowed any interest in the MCP guerrillas to whom Peking previously had extended at least moral and political support. The status of 220,000 stateless Chinese in Malaysia would be negotiated after an exchange of ambassadors.

Other foreign policy concerns included strained relations with the Philippines, resulting from Manila's charge of Malaysian support, through Sabah, for the Muslim rebellion in Sulu and Mindanao—an accusation denied by Kuala Lumpur. Similar, but less serious, tensions arose between Malaysia and Thailand concerning Muslim separatists active in the Southern Thai provinces bordering Malaysia.

MARVIN C. OTT
Mount Holyoke College

MALAYSIA • Information Highlights

Official Name: Malaysia.
Location: Southeast Asia.
Area: 127,316 square miles (329,749 sq km).
Population (1973 est.): 11,800,000.
Chief Cities (1970 census): Kuala Lumpur, the capital, 451,728; Pinang, 270,019; Ipoh, 247,689.
Government: *Head of state,* Sultan Tunku Abdul Halim Mu'adzam (took office 1971). *Head of government,* Tun Abdul Razak, prime minister (1970). *Legislature*—Parliament: Dewan Negara (Senate) and Dewan Ra'ayat (House of Representatives).
Monetary Unit: Malaysian dollar (2.40 M. dollars equal U. S.$1, Aug. 1974).
Gross National Product (1972 est.): $5,191,000,000.
Manufacturing (major products): Petroleum products, refined sugar, rubber goods, steel, lumber.
Major Agricultural Products: Rubber, rice, palm oil and kernels, tea, pepper, coconuts, spices.
Foreign Trade (1973): *Exports,* $3,213,000,000; *imports,* $2,617,000,000.

MANITOBA

The year 1974 was a relatively quiet and stable one for Manitoba, but marked by a growing apprehension about economic prosperity.

Economy. The unemployment rate fell to 2.1% of the labor force in October, but some skilled trades had difficulty finding sufficient trained workers. Grain prices were high, with crop yields low and the quality poor. The effects of inflation were widespread.

Politics. The province continued to vote one way provincially and another federally. In the July 8 federal election 9 Progressive Conservative, 2 Liberal, and 2 New Democratic party (NDP) candidates were returned to the House of Commons. The NDP lost one seat to the Progressive Conservatives. In 1973 the voters had given the provincial NDP and its program of social democracy one of the largest popular votes in Manitoba's history.

Churchill Forest Industries. The Churchill Forest Industries (CFI) complex at The Pas continued to be the subject of controversy. It was begun in 1966 by European entrepreneurs who came to the province at the invitation of the Progressive Conservative government. In 1971 the NDP government placed the company in receivership, seized all its assets, and appointed a Commission of Enquiry to investigate its operations. In October 1974 the commission finally published its report, and almost everybody involved in the project was criticized. Criminal charges were brought against the founders of the complex, and the CFI affair seemed likely to cast a continuing cloud on government subsidization of resource development.

Guaranteed Annual Income. The launching of a guaranteed annual income project in Manitoba was announced in February. Up to 2,500 families will participate in the $17 million program, which was founded by the federal and provincial governments to determine the impact of a guaranteed annual income on the willingness of the participants to work.

JOHN A. BOVEY
Provincial Archivist of Manitoba

MANITOBA • Information Highlights

Area: 251,000 square miles (650,090 sq km).
Population (1974 est.): 1,008,000.
Chief Cities (1971 census): Winnipeg, the capital, 246,246; St. James-Assiniboia, 71,431.
Government (1974): *Chief Officers*—lt. gov., W. J. McKeag; premier, Edward Schreyer (New Democratic party); atty. gen., Howard R. Pawley (NDP); min. of educ., Ben Hanuschak (NDP); chief justice, Samuel Freedman. *Legislature*—Legislative Assembly, 57 members (31 NDP, 21 Progressive Conservative, 5 Liberal).
Education (1972–73): *Enrollment:* public elementary and secondary schools, 252,634 pupils; private schools, 7,224; Indian (federal) schools, 6,376; colleges and universities, 17,023 students. *Public school expenditures* (1972), $180,600,000.
Public Finance (fiscal year 1974–75 est.): *Revenues,* $1,012,000,000; *expenditures,* $1,133,000,000.
Personal Income (1972): $3,551,000,000; average annual income per person, $3,557.
(All monetary figures given in Canadian dollars.)

MARINE BIOLOGY

Whales and other marine mammals are increasingly recognized as endangered species. Consequently, many marine biologists have turned their attention to studies of the normal behavior, physiology, and biology of these unique animals. Research and fishery biologists are seeking new ways to attach instruments to the bodies of whales, porpoises, and seals so that the temperature, heart rate, depth of dives, migration patterns, and other phenomena can be measured. The urgency of these studies, required to manage marine mammals wisely, has resulted in increased cooperation between marine biologists and the engineers and technologists who design the scientific apparatus.

Kelp Research. As the need for new supplies of nutrients and other resources necessary to sustain mankind has become evident, scientists have increasingly turned their attention to underutilized species of marine organisms which might fill these various needs. In 1974, for instance, marine biologists studied for the tenth consecutive year the giant kelp forests in waters off the southern California coast. These large algae are presently used in pharmaceuticals and a variety of industrial products, and have many other potential uses as well.

Research scientists have been interested in restoring kelp habitats which have been affected through overgrazing by sea urchins, storms, and pollution. To do this, they have had to study the reproduction of kelps, as well as the interaction between the kelps, their environment, and a particularly damaging predator, the sea urchin. These interests have led the researchers into detailed studies of the ecology of the urchins and their reproduction—a perfect example of the importance of the multidisciplinary, basic research needed to solve a single, practical problem involving environmental management.

Octopus Research. Although many marine biologists have been content to understand marine organisms in their natural environment, the technology of aquaculture is increasingly drawing the attention of scientists and bioengineers toward the rearing and maintenance of marine species in artificial aquatic environments. The biology of species such as the common octopus is being studied in detail so that the various life stages can be manipulated to accommodate it to a highly artificial environment. While marine ecologists are studying the behavior of the octopus in its underwater cave habitat (or in a flowerpot substituted to duplicate a natural den) other biologists are examining the development of the octopus egg with the electron microscope. Again, both lines of research, and many others, are essential to understanding the octopus and the development of rearing facilities suitable for the mass culturing of this species.

Immunology Studies. As more has been learned about the physiology and biochemistry of marine organisms, increasing numbers of medical physiologists and mammalian biologists have diverted their attention to marine organisms. For instance, very recent investigations in the field of immunology indicate that immune systems, those responses of organisms which internally protect them from foreign proteins or disease-causing microorganisms, are well developed in flounders and other marine fish. Marine invertebrate animals are now being studied to determine at what point in evolutionary history these complex immune systems became established in living systems.

Other Biomedical Research. Other biomedical researchers have recently isolated apparent anticancer drugs from a variety of marine organisms, including the lowly sponges and clams. Another group has developed techniques for the study of insulin, a well-known hormone, using marine finfish. The anatomy of the pancreas of the goosefish lends itself particularly well to this research.

New Environment. At the same time that marine scientists are studying data and preparing reports based on their investigations in the laboratory and coastal zone, marine biogeographers are investigating the recruitment of marine species in areas previously uncolonized. The sudden appearance of new volcanic islands provide exciting opportunities to study the movement of animals and plants onto new sediments, never before utilized by marine life. In certain instances the parent populations which contribute their spawn to the colonization are located only a few meters or kilometers away, but often a species may be carried thousands of kilometers before colonizing a new environment. Archipelagoes, such as the Galápagos chain off South America, are favorite sites for the study of animal migration or transport. Marine biogeographers have known for some time that such island chains are habituated by unique groups of animals which have evolved over unusually long periods of time in almost complete isolation from the larger continental landmasses.

Marine scientists now recognize that the swift transportation systems developed by man will greatly accelerate movement. Surface vessels, submarines, and seaplanes pick up water containing marine eggs and larvae in one area and discharge them as bilge or ballast water in an environment thousands of miles removed from the original. Species of crabs have been carried in a saltatory fashion from North America to Hawaii and thence to the Orient. Studies of the success of colonization and adaptation to new marine environments by introduced organisms have the potential to greatly expand our understanding of the evolutionary processes in aquatic ecosystems.

JOHN B. PEARCE
Ecosystems Investigations
Sandy Hook Marine Laboratory, N. J.

WIDE WORLD

Gov. Marvin Mandel (*right*) and Attorney General Francis Burch enjoy the news of their reelection in the Democratic sweep of Maryland on November 5.

MARYLAND

Like other states, Maryland felt the frustrations of inflation, unemployment, shortages of consumer supplies, and threatening pressures on public budgets. New investigations and charges against local officials and contractors added to the pall of unease that lingered from the revelations of 1973 involving Spiro Agnew and his associates while the former vice president served in county and state offices. On August 2, the U. S. Court of Appeals in Washington overturned the 1972 conviction of former U. S. Sen. Daniel B. Brewster, charged with accepting a bribe while in office, and ordered a new trial.

MARYLAND • Information Highlights

Area: 10,577 square miles (27,394 sq km).
Population (1973 est.): 4,070,000. *Density:* 410 per sq mi.
Chief Cities (1970 census): Annapolis, the capital, 30,095; Baltimore, 905,759; Dundalk, 85,377; Towson, 77,799.
Government (1974): *Chief Officers*—governor, Marvin Mandel (D); lt. gov., Blair Lee III (D). *General Assembly*—Senate, 43 members; House of Delegates, 142 members.
Education (1973–74): *Enrollment*—public elementary schools, 491,463 pupils; public secondary, 419,786; nonpublic, 111,200; colleges and universities, 177,166 students. *Public school expenditures,* $1,091,781,000 ($1,322 per pupil).
State Finances (fiscal year 1973): *Revenues,* $2,514,083,000; *expenditures,* $2,556,241,000.
Personal Income (1973): $21,697,000,000; per capita, $5,331.
Labor Force (July 1974): *Nonagricultural wage and salary earners,* 1,462,700; *insured unemployed,* 28,000 (2.5%).

Legislation. The General Assembly approved a record operating budget of $2.77 billion, exclusive of substantial construction authorization. Special projects included $50 million for sewage plants, $5 million for reclamation of solid waste, and $500,000 for community mental health centers. State school construction accounted for $212 million, and aid for facilities in 16 private colleges increased from $3.4 million to $5.9 million. Salary increases for 60,000 state employees averaged 6.8%.

To revitalize a stagnated housing market, a new law increased for two years the permissible annual mortgage rate from 8% to 10%. A controversial land-use program authorized state and local officials to designate critical areas for rigid development controls, locally enforced. State health officials now have stronger powers over noise control.

Horse racing at three one-mile tracks will increase, under new legislation, by 48 days from the customary 180 days. Another 18 days will be added to the 24 days of half-mile racing at Timonium. A daily lottery will supplement the present weekly lottery by 1975 and the state will spend $225,000 in bonuses to encourage businesses to sell more tickets.

Elections. Democratic Gov. Marvin Mandel, running on a record of holding firm the state tax rate, won reelection on November 5 with 63% of the vote. He defeated former ambassador Louise Gore, who unexpectedly won the Republican nomination on September 10 over Congressman Lawrence J. Hogan, who had been the first Republican on the House Judiciary Committee to announce an intention to vote for impeachment of President Nixon. The voter turnout for the election was 54%, a drop of 7% from the 1970 election. Other statewide officers, all Democrats, were reelected. Republican U. S. Sen. Charles McC. Mathias, Jr., a moderate liberal, obtained a second term with 57% of the votes. He defeated Barbara Mikulski of Baltimore. Incumbents who sought reelection to Congress, four Democrats and three Republicans, were successful; but Democrat Gladys N. Spellman won the seat vacated by Hogan. Congressman Gilbert Gude, Republican of Montgomery County, won a fifth term with 66% of the vote.

The election brought a majority of new members to the state legislature. Republicans lost a net of two seats in the state Senate and six in the House of Delegates, leaving them with eight senators and 15 delegates.

State voters approved 12 constitutional amendments, including provisions to remove officers upon conviction of felony and to tighten discipline in the judiciary. They rejected by referendum legislation to provide state aid for students in nonpublic schools. A proposal to increase the annual salary of the governor was also rejected.

FRANKLIN L. BURDETTE
University of Maryland

UPI

Employees picket the Baltimore city jail after walking off their jobs on July 8, joining other municipal workers in a strike for higher pay. The dispute was settled a week later.

MASSACHUSETTS

Gasoline shortages, Sen. Edward Kennedy's withdrawal from the 1976 presidential race, and election results highlighted the news in Massachusetts in 1974.

Energy Crisis. Early in 1974 Massachusetts struggled with shortages of gasoline and heating oil. Gov. Francis W. Sargent announced a voluntary gasoline rationing system beginning January 14. Drivers of cars with odd-numbered license plates were urged to buy fuel only on odd-numbered days, and drivers with even-numbered plates to buy on even-numbered days. The program was called highly effective in the first two months of the year. By mid-March, the gasoline shortage had eased somewhat, and the voluntary system slowly went out of use.

The state's energy problems also led to demands for the construction of a refinery in the area (there now are none in all of New England) and the promotion of offshore drilling. Proposals to locate a refinery on one of two sites north of Boston met with opposition from area residents and from environmental groups. Both environmentalists and fishermen opposed offshore drilling as potentially harmful. The issues remained unresolved at year-end.

New Kennedy Library Plans. In early June new plans were announced for the John F. Kennedy Memorial Library. The new version by architect I. M. Pei was considerably scaled down from earlier plans due to rapidly rising construction costs and fears about the impact of the library complex on the already congested Harvard Square area of Cambridge, Mass.

Kennedy Withdrawal. On September 23, Edward M. Kennedy, the state's senior senator, announced that he would not be a candidate for the 1976 presidential nomination under any terms. Kennedy's move was seen as stemming from family considerations as well as from lingering doubts about his role in the July 1969 automobile accident on Chappaquiddick Island in which Mary Jo Kopechne was drowned.

Elections. Electoral contests dominated political events from midyear onward. With neither of the state's Senate seats—held by Senator Kennedy and Sen. Edward W. Brooke (R)—up for election in 1974, interest centered on the battle for the governor's chair. Republican incumbent Francis Sargent was seeking a second full term. Sargent became governor in 1969 when Republican John A. Volpe resigned to become secretary of transportation in President Nixon's administration. Governor Sargent had won a decisive victory in 1970, but was opposed for the Republican nomination in 1974 by state Rep. Carroll Sheean, who was supported by many conservative state Republican party leaders. On the Democratic side, Attorney General Robert H. Quinn faced 41-year old liberal Democrat Michael Dukakis. In the primary, Sargent and Dukakis easily defeated their opponents.

The newly elected governor of Massachusetts, Democrat Michael S. Dukakis, and his wife celebrate in Boston on election night. He defeated Francis Sargent.

WIDE WORLD

—MASSACHUSETTS • Information Highlights—

Area: 8,257 square miles (21,386 sq km).
Population (1973 est.): 5,818,000. *Density:* 740 per sq mi.
Chief Cities (1970 census): Boston, the capital, 641,071; Worcester, 176,572; Springfield, 163,905.
Government (1974): *Chief Officers*—governor, Francis W. Sargent (R); lt. gov., Donald R. Dwight (R). *General Court*—Senate, 40 members; House of Representatives, 240 members.
Education (1973–74): *Enrollment*—public elementary schools, 675,000 pupils; public secondary, 547,000; nonpublic, 191,200; colleges and universities, 329,693 students. *Public school expenditures,* $1,326,000,000 ($1,136 per pupil).
State Finances (fiscal year 1973): *Revenues,* $3,745,822,000; *expenditures,* $3,868,186,000.
Personal Income (1973): $30,444,000,000; per capita, $5,233.
Labor Force (July 1974): *Nonagricultural wage and salary earners,* 2,357,500; *insured unemployed,* 105,100 (5.3%).

In the November election, the strong Democratic party tide observed nationally was also evident in the state. Sargent and his running mate, Lt. Gov. Donald Dwight, were defeated by Dukakis and Thomas P. O'Neill III, the son of the U. S. House majority leader. In other statewide contests former Lt. Gov. Francis X. Bellotti was elected attorney general over Josiah Spaulding (R). For secretary of state, Paul H. Guzzi, who had defeated incumbent John F. X. Davoren in the Democratic primary, outpolled his Republican opponent John M. Quinlan.

Democrats won all but two of the state's 12 House seats. In the first district, Republican Silvio Conte easily won a ninth term. Democrat Edward Boland was unopposed in the second district. The third district race was a three-way match between Republican David Lionette, Independent Douglas Rowe, and Democrat Joseph Early, with Early the victor. Congressman Robert Drinan, a Jesuit priest, won election to a third term in the fourth district in another three-way race. The fifth district contest was an upset, with Democrat Paul Tsongas overwhelming first-term incumbent Paul Cronin to win the seat for the Democrats for the first time in this century. Liberal Democrat Michael Harrington was unopposed in the sixth district, and Democrat Torbert MacDonald faced only token opposition in the seventh. House Majority Leader Thomas P. "Tip" O'Neill was opposed only by minor party candidates in the eighth district, as was incumbent John Moakley in the ninth. Incumbent Republican Margaret Heckler won in the tenth district, and Democrat James Burke was unopposed in the eleventh. In the twelfth district, the first-term incumbent, G. E. Studds (D), won reelection.

Democrats increased their control of the state legislature with the largest majority in history. The new legislature will have 32 Democrats and 8 Republicans in the Senate and 191 Democrats, 46 Republicans, and 3 independents in the House of Representatives.

HARVEY BOULAY
Boston University

medicine

Breast cancer dominated the medical news in 1974 after it was reported that the disease had struck Betty Ford, wife of the President, and Happy Rockefeller, wife of the vice president-designate.

Breast Cancer. Cancer of the breast is the leading killer of women between 40 and 44 years of age and is the leading cause of cancer deaths among women of all ages, occurring in one woman out of every 15. By the end of 1974, the diagnosis of breast cancer will have been made for about 90,000 women, and another 33,000 will die from the disease. Breast cancer also occurs in men, but it is 150 times more common in women.

The exact cause of breast cancer is not known, but some factors seem important. For example, breast cancer is more common in countries where people consume large amounts of animal fat. Viruses have been associated with the production of breast cancer in experimental animals but not in man, although virus particles have been detected in the milk of patients who have breast cancer as well as in the milk of patients who do not. Neither injuries to the breast nor the use of birth control pills have been shown to be related to the development of cancer of the breast. Nursing seems neither to be causative of nor protective against cancer.

Breast Examination. Since the breast is on the outside of the body proper, it can be examined easily and effectively by many methods. Self-examination for lumps in the breast is the easiest method for finding a suspicious lump. Examination by a doctor may be more thorough and may be supplemented by several laboratory techniques. One simple but effective method of looking for cancer of the breast makes use of the fact that breast tumors seem to generate more heat than normal tissue. Skin temperature can be measured simply by a skin-temperature thermometer or more precisely by thermal or infrared scanning devices. Simple X-ray procedures are often helpful in finding breast cancer. So is a new technique called xerography, which uses a charged electric plate and a photoelectric system to build an image on paper.

Despite the sophisticated techniques that are available for finding breast cancer, self-examination remains the technique by which 95% of such tumors are discovered. But in more than half these cases, cancerous cells have already reached the lymph nodes that drain the breast area. If the cancer is found before it has spread to the lymph nodes, the patient has at least an 85% chance of surviving five years after her treatment. If the cancer has spread to the lymph nodes, the survival rate is cut in half. Consequently, it is essential that breast cancer be found early.

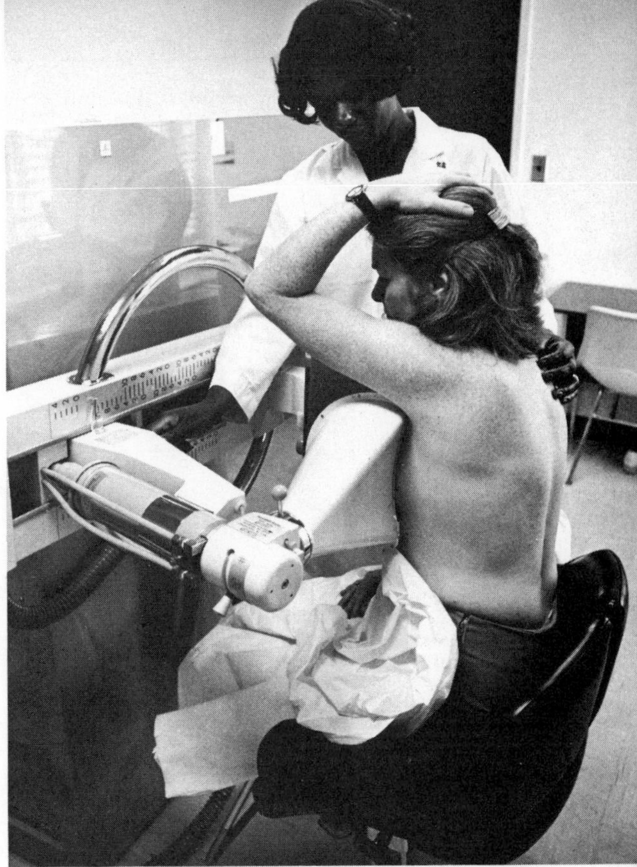

AMERICAN CANCER SOCIETY

A woman is checked for breast cancer by mammography as part of a regular periodic examination to detect the disease early when it can be most successfully treated.

Breast Cancer Treatment. Removal of the tumor, the organ in which it arises, and the lymph nodes and connecting lymphoid vessels is the usual approach to the treatment of cancer. Treatment for breast cancer has not changed much in the past century. For treatment of breast cancer, surgical management includes removal of the involved breast, muscle, and other tissue under the skin as far as the armpit and the lymph nodes of the armpit. This operation is called a radical mastectomy. Developed by an English surgeon in 1850, it continues to be the mainstay of treatment for breast cancer today.

A report from the Breast Cancer Task Force of the National Cancer Institute offers some alternatives. Simple mastectomy—surgical removal of the breast only—followed by X-ray treatments of the area is another procedure that has been used for many years. Lately, mastectomy has been followed by treatment with drugs such as L-phenylalanine mustard (L-PAM). Other drugs under study for breast cancer treatment include several used for treatment of leukemia, such as 5-fluorouracil, methotrexate, and cytoxan. But it should be stressed that while there are various kinds of treatment for breast cancer, the major factor in the outcome of treatment is early diagnosis. This can be accomplished by frequent, careful self-examination.

Cancer Survey. The National Cancer Institute has organized a survey of cancer data that is believed to be the largest and most detailed program of its kind ever undertaken in the United States. The cancer survey, which will cover regions having a total population of more than 20 million, will cost about $3.5 million annually. The program will provide information on trends in the incidence of various forms of cancer, variations in the occurrence of cancer in different population groups and geographic areas, and the results of treatment for cancer patients.

Heart-Attack Care. Emergency medical care by laymen for a patient with an acute and severe heart attack was the topic of a national conference held in May 1973 under the joint sponsorship of the American Heart Association and the National Academy of Sciences' National Research Council. It has been estimated that more than a million Americans each year have heart attacks. More than 650,000 die from heart attacks each year. But 350,000 of these deaths occur outside the hospital, usually within two hours after the onset of the symptoms. Thus, sudden death from heart attack is the most important medical emergency today.

It seems probable that many lives can be saved by prompt and proper use of techniques that can be performed by trained members of the general public. Thus, the recommendations developed by the national conference are aimed at training the lay public in emergency cardiac care as a means of reducing the number of deaths from heart attacks that occur outside the hospital.

Emergency Heart Care. Emergency cardiac care (ECC) is conceived as an integral part of a total, community-wide comprehensive system of emergency medical services. It includes four major elements: (1) recognizing early warning signs of heart attacks, preventing complications, reassuring the victim, and moving him to a unit where basic life-support procedures are available; (2) providing immediate basic life support at the scene, when needed; (3) providing advanced life support as quickly as possible; and (4) transferring the victim for continued cardiac care when his condition has stabilized.

Basic life support is an emergency first-aid procedure that includes recognition of airway obstruction, respiratory arrest, and cardiac arrest, and the proper application of cardiopulmonary resuscitation (CPR). In turn, CPR means opening and maintaining the airway, providing artificial ventilation by means of rescue breathing, and providing artificial circulation by means of external cardiac compression. Advanced life support also includes the use of electrical and mechanical equipment, intravenous fluids, and drugs as needed for complete emergency care.

The greatest risk from heart attack is in the first two hours after it begins. Thus, the potential victim must be educated to recognize the signs and symptoms—persistent pain in the chest, shoulder, or arm; sweating; and nausea. Also, the patient must know how to get access to medical care. Medical care, including CPR and ECC, must be available when called on.

Training in Cardiopulmonary Resuscitation. CPR training programs are already under way in such places as Seattle, Grand Rapids, and Boston. Trainees are taught the ABC method: keep *a*irways open, *b*reathing restored, and *c*irculation maintained. Trainees must be at least in the eighth grade since smaller children are not considered strong enough to maintain effective CPR.

CPR seems to be helping to reduce the death rate from sudden heart attacks. In Seattle, where more than 100,000 people have been taught the CPR procedures, a third of the heart-attack victims who develop irregular heartbeat now reach the hospital alive, and some of these eventually go home. Before the training program was begun, virtually none of these patients were alive when they reached the hospital.

Childhood Diseases. The Reye syndrome, a rare but often fatal childhood disease, caused near-panic among parents in Chicago, Pittsburgh, and Milwaukee. The disease, which may have been related to recent outbreaks of type B influenza, has never been reported in adults.

The illness usually occurs in a child who has had a recent upper-respiratory infection or a viral disease such as influenza or chicken pox. The first sign of trouble is often vomiting for as long as 24 hours, followed by a lethargy that is sometimes broken by spells of unusual aggression or hyperactivity. Finally, the child may lapse into coma and may ultimately die.

The disorder seems to be the result of an inability of the liver cells to metabolize ammonia. Consequently, the amount of ammonia in the blood increases, as does the amount of ammonia in the brain. The immediate cause of death is swelling of the brain associated with the high ammonia content there. No specific treatment is available, but measures are taken to lower the ammonia content of the blood by techniques including hemodialysis. However, there is little help to be offered to patients who sustain severe brain or liver damage. The Reye syndrome, although it develops after an acute infection, is neither contagious nor likely to occur in true epidemic fashion.

Common Childhood Diseases. There also was renewed interest in the common infectious diseases of childhood. Reports of an upsurge in childhood diphtheria, measles, and polio led to the proclaiming of October as Immunization Action Month by several medical and health associations in an attempt to encourage parents to have immunizations begun or updated to assure protection against childhood diseases.

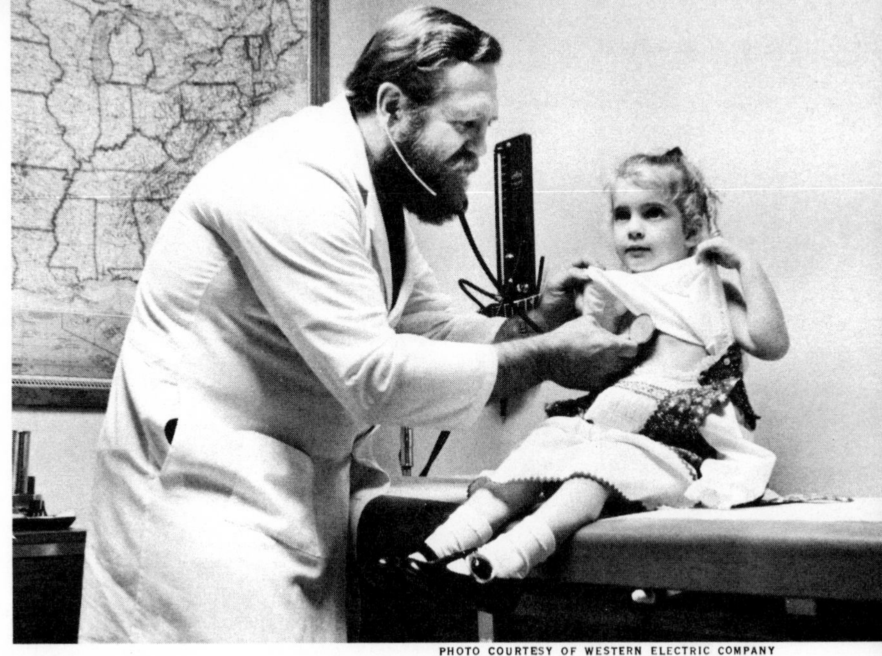

A doctor examines a child who is enrolled in a Health Maintenance Organization (HMO), a program of prepaid medical care designed to deal with people before they become sick. HMO's pay for many items not covered in other health insurance plans, such as examinations for eyeglasses, tests for allergies, inoculations, and the like.

PHOTO COURTESY OF WESTERN ELECTRIC COMPANY

Cholera and Plague. Cholera and plague, two infectious diseases usually considered no longer dangerous, made a reappearance in the United States in 1974. Cholera was reported in one isolated case in Texas, where the patient responded promptly to treatment with antibiotics and supportive fluid replacement.

Plague is caused by a bacterium called *Pasteurella pestis,* which lives in and infects rodents, including rats, mice, squirrels, and gerbils. The germs may be passed from such pets to people, who develop fever and large, swollen, tender, hot lymph nodes called buboes. Plague is also passed as a respiratory-tract infection in droplets shed from the nose and throat. This respiratory-tract transmission results in a severe pneumonia that can rapidly be fatal.

Plague germs respond readily to treatment with certain antibiotics such as tetracycline and streptomycin. Such treatment is uniformly successful provided that it is begun within the first 15 hours of the onset of symptoms. Plague was reported in just a few patients in New Mexico and Utah in 1974.

Gallstones. Recent work using oral medicine to dissolve gallstones has been reported by the Mayo Clinic. Gallstones are actual stones that accumulate in the gallbladder. This organ, which lies just below the liver, stores and concentrates the bile that is produced by the liver. Bile contains salts, sugars, a pigment called bilirubin, steroid hormones, and enzymes. The gallbladder absorbs water and salt from bile, concentrating it in the process. As bile is concentrated, sometimes bile salts settle out of solution and produce gallstones.

Gallstones cause trouble because they sometimes move into the nearby bile ducts or pancreas and cause obstructions. Also, the occurrence of gallstones is associated with a high incidence of inflammation and infection as well as with the development of cancer of the gallbladder and liver. Therefore, it is important to find gallstones and remove them when they occur. Until recently, the only possible means of removing gallstones has been surgery. Thus, the operation to remove the gallbladder, cholecystectomy, has become a commonplace operation.

Treatment for Dissolving Gallstones. Studies aimed at dissolving rather than removing gallstones were begun at the Mayo Clinic as early as 1967. It was known that most gallstones were made of cholesterol, a fatty substance that circulates in the blood. About 75% of all gallstones consist of cholesterol and other substances, while 10% of the gallstones are pure cholesterol. The remaining 15% of the gallstones contain no cholesterol but consist largely of bile pigments.

Early work explored the possibility of using some of the normal components of bile to dissolve gallstones. Only one of those substances proved useful in dissolving gallstones. It is a chemical called chenodeoxycholic acid, or cheno for short. Cheno has been used in a small number of patients at the Mayo Clinic, where experts have shown that the medicine dissolves or decreases the size of gallstones in more than half of the patients. So far, the treatment seems safe since the side effects are mild and minor.

The next part of the gallstone investigation will be under the direction of the National Institutes of Health and financed by a grant from the government. Plans call for a series of 900 patients to be treated with chenodeoxycholic acid at ten centers throughout the country. Patients to be given the medicine will be chosen in 1975, after which they will be treated for two years with the drug. Another year will be taken for analyses of data, so it will not be before 1980 at the earliest that chenodeoxycholic acid

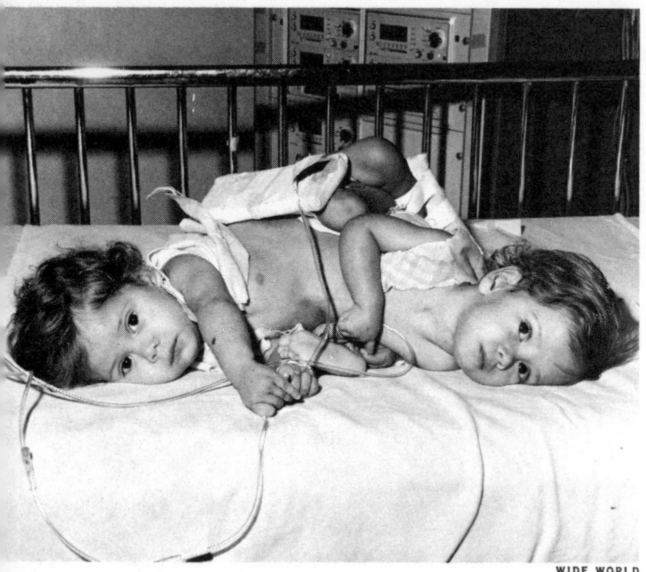

WIDE WORLD

(*Above*) The Rodriguez Siamese twins before they were separated September 18 at Children's Hospital, Philadelphia. (*Below*) After the successful separation, Mrs. Rodriguez holds Clara, and Mr. Rodriguez holds Alta.

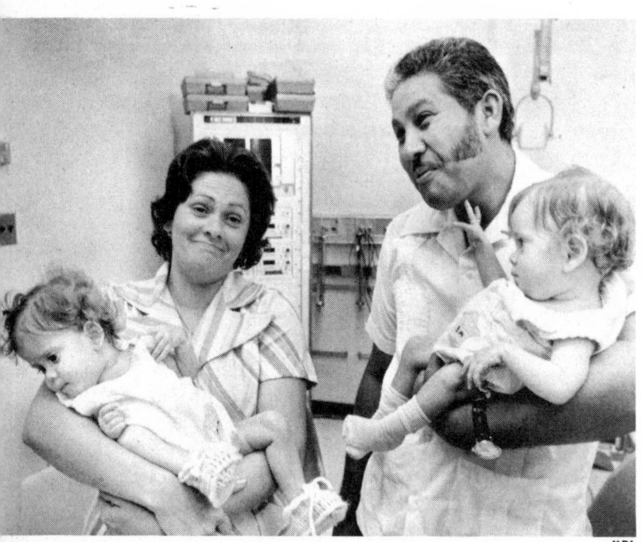

UPI

will be available by prescription for treatment of gallstones.

Ultrasound for Diagnosis. Ultrasound is now being used to fight sickness. A system using ultrasound to provide pictures of the internal soft tissues of the body has received much attention lately. It may prove to be as important an advance in diagnostic equipment as X rays were.

Ultrasound is simply high-frequency waves that have a frequency above the upper audible range of the human ear. These waves are nonionizing at the energy levels and exposure times used for diagnosis. Under the controlled conditions in which it is used, ultrasound does not alter the physiology of the tissues, but it can provide a description of parts of the patient's body as small as 0.1 millimeter (0.004 inch) in size.

Ultrasound has been used to find tumors in soft body tissues as well as to find foreign bodies. It can also be used to measure parts of the body with remarkable accuracy and thereby enable the doctor to judge the relationship of one part to another.

Using the ultrasonic device is a painless and safe procedure. Unlike X rays, which require special precautions to prevent damage to healthy tissue, there is no harm from use of the ultrasound technique. The small, portable units can be carried anywhere, and they can be used in the hospital, at the doctor's office, or at the bedside at home.

How Ultrasonic Diagnosis Works. Ultrasonic examination is carried out by coating the skin with any fluid agent that is capable of transmitting sound and excluding air. Mineral oil is the substance most often used for this purpose, but there are some preparations designed especially for use with ultrasonic devices.

In the next step, a small transducer is placed over the area to be examined and moved back and forth over that area. The transducer is simply a device that changes electrical energy into sound energy, or sound energy into electrical energy. The sound energy that is produced by the transducer is reflected by the tissues underneath and reconverted into an electrical signal by the same transducer. Then the sound energy pattern is amplified electronically and displayed on a cathode-ray tube like a television image. A photograph is then taken of this image, and this photograph is used for permanent record and analysis.

Uses for Ultrasonic Diagnosis. There are many specific uses for ultrasound in diagnosis. The part of the body around the eye provides a good example of the usefulness of this technique. Tumors in the skull around the eye can be identified and measured, and the path of the optic nerve can be examined. Also, the inside of the eyeball can be checked for cataracts, hemorrhages, and other abnormalities.

Ultrasound also is quite useful for an examination of the heart. The mitral valve has been extensively studied, and it has been possible to recognize many anatomic and functional abnormalities there. The size of the heart and of each of its chambers can be measured with ultrasound, which therefore is an important tool in the study of congenital heart disease.

In obstetrics, the fetus, placenta, and position of the abdominal organs of the mother can be identified ultrasonically in complete safety. This is most important because the ionizing radiations of X rays make it undesirable to use that technique in the early months of pregnancy. But with ultrasound, pregnancies can be detected as early as the fifth week.

In addition to the use of ultrasound to obtain cross-sectional views of the body, there is another possibility. Using the Doppler principle, ultrasound can show the direction of blood flow within the body. The Doppler principle states that the pitch of sound approaching the observer increases, and the pitch of a sound moving away from the observer decreases. In this way it is possible to tell which way blood is traveling within the blood vessel walls by noting an increase or decrease in the frequency of the ultrasound recording.

On the horizon are uses of ultrasound for examining for breast tumors or for tumors of such internal organs as the liver, kidney, and spleen. Ultrasound recordings, often known as echograms, are an important new diagnostic tool for medical science.

Surgery. There were new developments in surgery during 1974. Further investigation and practice of cardiac surgery resulted in little change in technique but many advances in operative detail. Mechanical ventilation, optimal oxygenation, and humidification were described.

There was considerable interest shown in studies of acute myocardial infarction, and there was a suggestion that hydrocortisone protected against heart-cell death during heart attack. Also, there was evidence that surgery to reestablish the blood flow to the heart muscle, if done within a few hours after a heart attack, resulted in lessening of damage to the heart muscle.

Interest in abdominal surgery in 1974 centered on basic physiology. Among the new techniques used for the study of the digestive process is one involving radio immunoassay of polypeptide hormones. Using this method, a hormone, gastrin, produced by the stomach has been carefully located, and along with it, two larger gastrin molecules.

Orthopedic Surgery. Clinical interest in orthopedic surgery mainly centered on operations to replace joints completely. By using plastic materials and cement, reliable replacements for the hip, knee, shoulder, and ankle joints have been used. Most of the clinical data to date have been concerned with the hip joint.

Apparently, prostheses can be emplaced that will work satisfactorily at the forementioned joints. Some concern has been expressed about the safety of an acrylic bone cement that is used to connect the bone to the plastic prostheses. But in several large series of patients, most of whom had a hip-joint replacement, no problem has arisen.

Intravenous Feeding. Special attention has been called to the use of intravenous feeding to meet the complete nutritional requirements of patients of all age groups. This technique involves using fluids containing amino acids, fats, carbohydrates, vitamins, and minerals according to the requirements of the individual patient. It has been particularly helpful after surgery and in putting the bowel to rest in such diseases as regional ileitis. Called hyperalimentation, the intravenous feeding technique has been used successfully on newborn infants and small children.

Gynecology and Obstetrics. There were no dramatic breakthroughs in gynecology and obstetrics in 1974. Nevertheless, monitoring of the heart of the fetus before and during labor and delivery became more widespread. The ultimate goal is to provide simultaneous monitoring of the fetal heart and uterine contractions for all women throughout labor in an attempt to identify and alleviate fetal distress.

In the field of contraception, the controversy regarding the role of oral contraception in causing the formation of blood clots (thrombi) continued. The conclusion seems to be that oral contraceptives can indeed cause thrombi and stroke, but the incidence of these complications is small. "Mini pills" containing a small dosage of progestin or a small dosage of both estrogen and progesterone have been used to minimize the likelihood of clotting. These pills have the disadvantage of lowered success in preventing pregnancy.

Intrauterine contraceptive devices releasing about 10 milligrams of copper a year were introduced. They seem to work on the basis that increased levels of copper in uterine secretions impair the survival of sperm and the onset of pregnancy. Although attention was given to chemical methods of male contraception, there is no immediate prospect of an acceptable pill for men.

Estrogens for Youthfulness. A recent report from the conference on "Menopause and Aging," sponsored by the National Institute of Child Health and Human Development, covers the question of whether or not women should receive estrogens to retain their youthful vigor and appearance in their later years. There is no evidence that estrogens can prevent any of the diseases of aging. Disadvantages of the use of estrogens include increasing the amount of fat in the blood, impairment of liver function, and impairment of glucose tolerance. The major indications for an advantageous use of estrogens in menopause are hot flashes and atrophic changes in the sex organs. There is little or no risk to the patient if low dosages of estrogens are used.

(See feature article on THE SEARCH FOR A 'YOUTHFUL' OLD AGE, page 55.)

Women in Medicine. Data from the Association of American Medical Colleges and from the Journal of the American Medical Association show that the percentage of women students in U. S. medical schools has been rising for the past decade, increasing from about 7% in 1963–64 to about 16% in 1973–74. Medical men and women foresee a number of changes in the medical profession as a result of this increase.

IRWIN J. POLK, M. D.
St. Luke's Hospital, New York City

meteorology

A massive international effort in the study of tropical weather conditions highlighted meteorology in 1974.

Atlantic Tropical Experiment. The first part of the internationally sponsored Global Atmospheric Research Program (GARP)—the GARP Atlantic Tropical Experiment (GATE)—was conducted from June 15 to Sept. 23, 1974, with 4,000 scientists from 72 countries participating. The main objectives of the project were to study the origin and development of tropical storms and to collect weather data relevant to the droughts in Africa. An area of 20 million square miles (52 million sq km) extending from Africa to South America was studied with the support of an unprecedented array of equipment, including 38 research vessels, 13 instrumented aircraft, and six weather satellites. The main targets of the investigation were cloud clusters. They form over the tropical waters and carry heat aloft that later drives tropical storms or is transferred to higher latitudes. This heat is one of the principal energy sources of the atmosphere.

Both atmospheric and oceanic profiles were obtained to study the interaction between the atmosphere and the ocean. Already, some interesting results have been obtained from the new observations. For instance, African squall lines have come under study and can be better forecast. Also, freezing nuclei that induce rainfall were found to be about ten times more abundant than in the western portion of the United States.

Weather Satellites. The first synchronous meteorological satellite, SMS-1, was launched into orbit from the Kennedy Space Center on May 17, 1974. SMS-1 is the first of five synchronous satellites that will observe the earth from 60° N to 60° S latitude. Placed at various longitudes, they will provide a complete circle of weather eyes around the globe. SMS-1, which is about 23,000 miles (37,000 km) above a point off the coast of Brazil, covers the longitudes from 10° E in Africa to 140° W in North America. Its cloud pictures, which resolve objects as small as 0.5 mile (0.8 km) in diameter, are the sharpest ever obtained by weather satellites.

Tornado Warning Systems. The tornado is still the main target for early discovery and warning after a record-breaking year in 1973 when 1,107 twisters hit in 47 of the 50 states. They included some monster storms with long tracks of 135 miles (215 km) in Alabama and 160 miles (255 km) in Kansas and Nebraska. Although the death toll was only 87 in 1973, the April storms of 1974 caused 329 deaths, indicating the difficulty and urgency of identifying the cyclones that spawn the twisters.

Radio and radar systems now are used to locate and track tornadoes. For instance, about 20 systems have been installed in danger spots in the South and Midwest.

Pollutants in the Atmosphere. A balloon-borne sampling system developed by the National Center for Atmospheric Research is used to measure trace gases, especially oxides of nitrogen, up to 92,000 feet (28,000 meters) in the atmosphere. Monitoring of the oxides of nitrogen is very important because they disturb the earth's ozone layer, which shields the earth from lethal ultraviolet radiation. Only 4 parts per billion have been measured to be naturally present in the ozone layer, but close monitoring is required because high-flying aircraft release oxides of nitrogen into the upper atmosphere.

Pollutants in the lower atmosphere continued to be of concern, partly because they reduce solar radiation at the earth's surface. In St. Louis, Mo., particles in the atmosphere weaken sunshine in the city by 2% to 3% and weaken ultraviolet wavelengths by more than 4%. In many parts of the country washout of various pollutants has led to acidic rains, which can have serious ecological consequences such as affecting forest growth.

The aerosol content of the atmosphere has remained a debatable problem. Some scientists believe that the atmospheric dust from man-made sources is a menace to the stability of the climate and anticipate a doubling of the dust load in two decades. Others believe that there has been an improvement due to control measures.

Weather Modification. Deliberate weather modification acquired political overtones in 1974 when the U. S. Department of Defense finally admitted that attempts to increase rainfall had been made in Southeast Asia to hamper North Vietnamese logistics from 1967 to 1972. In 2,600 sorties, more than 47,000 seeding projectiles were used. In Senate hearings, rainfall increases were variously assessed at 5% to 30% more than would have fallen naturally. As a tactical weapon the operations probably had very little effect.

Scientists from the University of Washington reported success in redistributing snowfall by cloud seeding over the Cascade mountains. In the Soviet Union experimenters used large jet engines to produce updrafts in order to induce clouds and rain. They succeeded only in creating clouds, but trials with more powerful engines were envisioned.

The U. S. National Oceanic and Atmospheric Administration has been investigating the feasibility of creating high-level clouds in order to intercept sun rays and thereby reduce high surface temperatures that could promote severe local storms. Such schemes may be rapidly put to a test in view of the evidence that squall lines with heavy thunderstorms do not develop in areas where natural clouds provide shielding from intense morning sunshine.

H. E. LANDSBERG, *University of Maryland*

BILL GARLOW, JOURNAL HERALD, DAYTON, OHIO

DISASTER IN XENIA

(*Above*) Half of Xenia, Ohio, was destroyed and 35 of its inhabitants were killed in April when tornadoes ripped through seven states in the South and Middle West. A total of 329 persons were killed in the disaster, and damage was estimated at $1 billion. (*Below*) One of the injured in Xenia is removed from the wreckage.

WALT KLEINE, JOURNAL HERALD, DAYTON, OHIO

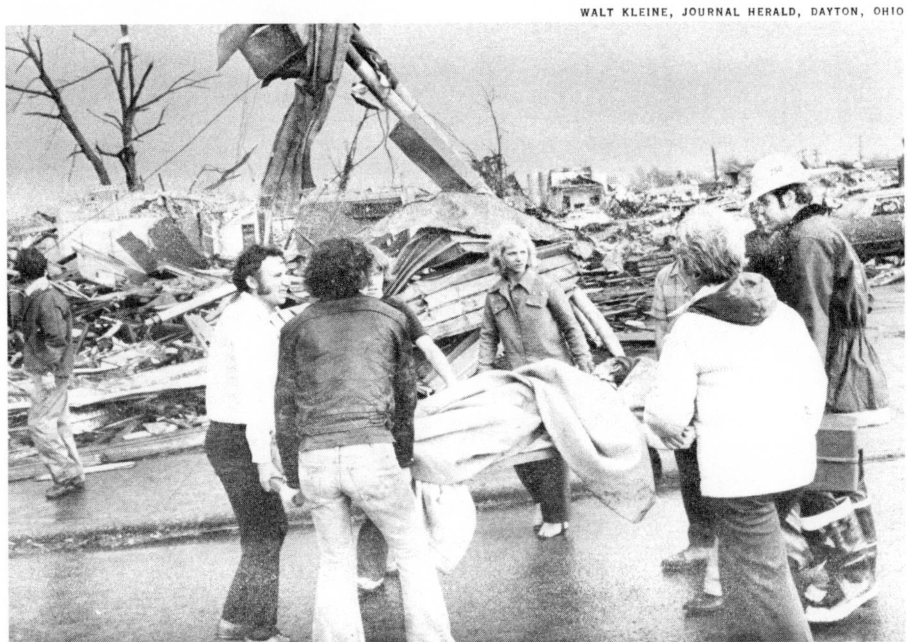

Killer Storm Struck Honduras

The weather in 1974 made tragic headlines because of tornadoes and drought in the United States and a devastating hurricane in Central America.

December 1973–February 1974. Compared with other winters this season was quite tame. It was mild west of the Rockies, in Texas, and in the East, a welcome circumstance in a time of fuel shortage. Only western Colorado and eastern Utah were cold, with temperatures of over 6° F below average. The Great Plains were moderately cool. Precipitation was heterogenous, with the Oregon coast, Colorado, the Great Lakes region, and the Gulf States receiving more than one and a half or even twice their average amounts. Southern Arizona, New Mexico, southwest Texas, and South Dakota had less than half of their average amounts, and, as a bad foreboding, northeastern Kansas had the driest February on record.

Abroad, western Russia and central Finland had an unusually warm late winter, almost 15° F above average. In the Antarctic, summer brought a "heat wave" for that particular environment, sending the temperature at the Soviet East Antarctic Base Mirny above the freezing point for an unprecedented period.

Catastrophic weather events were comparatively few. They included unusual December tornadoes in South Carolina, Georgia, Tennessee, and Florida. Tropical storms affected Bangladesh and the Fiji Islands with many casualties. In January, eastern Australia was struck by floods leaving eight towns and a million square miles (2,590,000 sq km) under water.

In the second week of January the British coasts were struck by 100-mph gales causing deaths and damages. At the same time severe storms raged in the Pacific Northwest, dumping 5 to 8 inches of rain in 24 hours, causing the worst flooding in Washington, Idaho, Oregon, and northern California since 1964, and inflicting 16 deaths and $100 million damage. Jerusalem had a rare snowfall in the middle of January that left 4 to 6 inches on the ground in the Holy City. At the end of that month the middle and lower Mississippi was at or above flood stage as a result of heavy rain and early snow melt.

March–May. Most of the nation, including Alaska and Hawaii, was warmer than average, with excesses up to 6° F in the southern Great Plains. Precipitation was excessive in the Pacific Northwest coastal areas, but drought prevailed in much of New Mexico, Colorado, and central Texas.

Unfortunately, the season was packed with weather disasters, including many tornadoes. A series of them hit Georgia, Alabama, and Louisiana on March 22, leaving 6 dead. This was the prelude to the worst tornado catastrophe in the United States since 1925 when, on April 3 and 4, a series of 93 twisters hit Alabama, Georgia, Kentucky, Tennessee, Indiana, Ohio, Illinois, and West Virginia. The twisters, which were associated with a giant storm system, left 329 dead, 6,142 injured, and 13,458 dwellings destroyed or severely damaged. Floods drove 10,000 from their homes in Mississippi in mid-April, and the North Platte River in northwestern Missouri flooded several communities and caused 2 deaths in mid-May.

In other countries, floods struck Ethiopia's Wallo province, the site of the 1973 drought, killing livestock and destroying crops in March. At the end of that month nine states of Brazil suffered from floods with a death toll of 500 and 65,000 homeless. At the end of May the worst storm in 20 years hit the coast of New South Wales (Australia), leaving 7 dead and causing $20 million damage. Sweden suffered severe crop damage from drought, experiencing an interval of 60 days without rain.

June–August. Summer on the whole was about 2° F warmer than average in the western half of the United States and, except for New England, 2° to 4° F cooler than average in the central, eastern, and southern states. Precipitation was not far from average east of the Mississippi but quite deficient from North Texas northward in the Great Plains and the Midwest toward the Great Lakes. July was a particularly unfavorable month in that region, with many areas receiving less than 20% of average rainfall and temperature excesses of 4° to 6° F. This had a very unfavorable influence on the U. S. corn and soybean crops, with losses exceeding $1 billion. In June tornadoes and severe storms plagued 15 states. Oklahoma, Kansas, Arkansas, Iowa, and Illinois were most affected, with scores of fatalities and multimillion dollar damages.

The Mexican State of Sonora suffered from drought which killed large numbers of cattle. In Africa, the long-lasting Sahelian drought was broken by above-average rainfall. The drought in China was also considerably relieved. On the whole, floods were widespread in the world, affecting the Indian states of Assam and Bihar, central Honshu in Japan, and the island of Luzon in the Philippines, where seven provinces were badly affected and parts of Manila were under 5 feet (1.5 meters) of water. The worst disaster, however, struck Bangladesh, where two thirds of the country was under water, affecting 32 million people. Ten million acres of cropland were ruined, 500,000 homes were damaged, and deaths were conservatively estimated at 2,500.

September–November. The harvest season was not too kind in North America. Early sharp cold snaps with freezing temperatures in September and October set harvest prospects further back in the corn belt, which earlier had suffered from the summer drought. That crop was down 1 million bushels or about 18% from the previous year. The soybean crop was also 300,000 bushels below the 1973 crop, and other feed grains were deficient. The overall world food reserves were down to less than a month's needs, because of a combination of bad weather and strong demand. In several areas of the world sugar beet and sugarcane plantations were also hit by unfavorable weather. Excessive rains during the season caused floods in Oklahoma, central Texas, and Nome, Alaska.

In the North Atlantic and the Caribbean an average number of hurricanes occurred. But one of these, Hurricane Fifi, brought widespread death and destruction to Honduras in Central America. Striking on September 19 and 20, the storm not only took a terrible toll in lives but dealt a crippling blow to the Honduran economy. Estimates of fatalities ranged from 3,000 to 10,000, and losses to property were estimated at $200 million to $500 million. A U. S. Agency for International Development mission reported that 600,000 people, or 20% of the population, had been directly affected by the hurricane, which represented the worst natural disaster in modern Honduran history. Damage to the country's export crops was severe; about two thirds of banana production was destroyed, as well as large percentages of the sugar, coffee, rice, and maize crops and the livestock herd. A large-scale disaster relief effort was mounted by the United States and several other countries, but a government spokesman said that Honduras would need at least two years to recover from the devastation wrought by the storm.

Elsewhere, Hurricane Carmen, with 150-mile-per-hour winds in the Gulf of Mexico, caused appreciable damage in Yucatan. The Pacific had an active typhoon season. In October alone four of them—Bess, Carmen, Della, Elaine—hit the Philippines in rapid succession, causing scores of deaths and leaving several hundred thousand persons homeless. Carmen later hit Hong Kong with furious 100-mile-per-hour winds, causing casualties and widespread damage. The Philippines were again hard hit at the end of November.

H. E. LANDSBERG

WIDE WORLD

President Ford receives a warm welcome in Magdalena, Mexico, in October as he strolls with Mexico's President Echeverría Álvarez and Mayor Alicia Arellano.

MEXICO

Inflation, petroleum, and social reform dominated Mexican news during 1974. President Echeverría reaffirmed his intentions of reforming Mexican society in the face of economic difficulties and criticisms from the political right. Although terrorist acts continued, the government's tough stance paid dividends.

Political Changes. Women's liberation, statehood, and minority party representation altered the political scene. In a major departure in this male-dominated country, President Echeverría attacked discrimination against women and submitted a constitutional amendment and appropriate bills to Congress, where they received prompt attention. Congress approved legislation granting statehood to the territories of Quintana Roo and Baja California Sur. When ratified, Mexico will have 31 states and a federal district. The party deputy system, which guarantees representation to minority parties, was extended to half of the state legislatures. Previously, minority parties found it almost impossible to obtain a voice in state government.

Terrorists. President Echeverría refused to deal with terrorists, even though his father-in-law, J. Guadalupe Zuno Hernández, was one victim. He characterized the terrorists as criminals, cowards, counterrevolutionaries, and victims of family discord who are easily manipulated by covert domestic and foreign political forces. He warned that Mexico would not tolerate attempts to forestall socioeconomic reform nor allow a repetition of the mid-1840's divisiveness that cost Mexico half its territory in the war with the United States.

A few days after this speech, Zuno was returned safely, and the Guerrero senator and gubernatorial nominee Rubén Figueroa, who had been kidnapped on May 30, was rescued by the Mexican army. Other victims were not so fortunate, including U. S. Vice Consul John Patterson, who disappeared in March, apparently for non-political reasons, and whose body was found in the desert in July.

Economy. Inflation continued to be the most serious economic problem, but the government took decisive steps to cut the rate and mitigate the effects on the average citizen. Prices were increasing at a rate of 22% during most of the year. In January, minimum wages were raised an average of 13%. As prices continued to zoom, organized labor began threatening a nationwide strike unless demands for a 35% wage hike were met. Employer resistance to these demands crumbled when Echeverría announced his full support of the right to strike, castigated employers for refusing the just demands of labor and for raising prices beyond cost increases, and announced that all federal employees would receive a 22% pay hike, effective September 1. Shortly thereafter, employers and workers agreed to the same average increase. The government set up machinery to require cost of living escalator clauses in all labor contracts to avoid such confrontations in the future.

Other measures were adopted during the year to aid the average citizen. In October, the list of commodities put under price controls in June was extended. CONASUPO, which subsidizes basic commodities for the poor, almost doubled its budget during the year.

In further steps to control inflation, stimulate investment, and reverse the outflow of investment capital, the government reduced real government deficit spending by raising taxes on luxury items and public utilities, raised interest rates, and directed spending to increase production.

Despite its problems, however, the Mexican economy remained strong. The real increase in the gross national product was expected to be almost 6%, less than in previous years but close to the average for the last 35 years. Agricultural production rose to 62 billion pesos ($4,964,000,000) and agricultural exports exceeded imports by 5.3 billion pesos ($425,000,000). Manufacturing sales doubled in the first quarter and demand remained strong for the remainder of the year. Tourism continued to increase, earning 25 billion pesos ($2,000,000,000). New copper strikes promised to increase production by 400%.

Petroleum. Mexico's termination of its longstanding cheap energy policy paid handsome returns in 1974. Petroleum price increases offset the government oil monopoly (PEMEX) deficit and provided capital for exploration. By June new fields in Chiapas and Tabasco states had made the country an oil-exporter again. Although the size of the fields is a secret, initial crude oil production was averaging 76 million barrels yearly. In addition, the discovery of large fields of natural gas will reduce Mexico's dependence on imports. Although encouraged by domestic politicians and by other oil-producing nations, Mexico did not join the international oil cartel (OPEC), but did announce that its oil would be sold at world prices.

MEXICO • Information Highlights

Official Name: United Mexican States.
Location: Southern North America.
Area: 761,602 square miles (1,972,546 sq km).
Population (1973 est.): 56,200,000.
Chief Cities (1970 census): Mexico City, the capital, 6,874,165 (federal district); Guadalajara, 1,193,601; Monterey, 858,107.
Government: *Head of state,* Luis Echeverría Álvarez, president (took office Dec. 1970). *Head of government,* Luis Echeverría Álvarez, *Legislature*—Congress: Senate and Chamber of Deputies.
Monetary Unit: Peso (12.49 pesos equal U. S.$1, Aug. 1974).
Gross National Product (1973 est.): $44,000,000,000.
Manufacturing (major products): Petroleum products, iron, steel, chemicals, transport equipment, aluminum, pharmaceuticals, cement.
Major Agricultural Products: Corn, cotton, sugarcane, wheat, vegetables, citrus fruits, fish.
Foreign Trade (1973): *Exports,* $2,452,000,000; *imports,* $4,146,000,000.

Government Planning. The government reaffirmed its agricultural and industrial development plans combined with programs in favor of the average citizen. Direct federal expenditures were expected to reach at least 235 billion pesos ($18,800,000,000), up 16%, but their inflationary effects were dampened by higher tax receipts. Public investment (40% of all investment) was directed toward increasing agricultural and livestock production and strengthening transportation and marketing systems. Support prices were raised on a number of commodities. Distribution of land continued, while titles to urban squatter settlements were regularized.

Capitalist confidence in the government and the economy was demonstrated by the private sector's decision to boost production investment by 11% to 77.5 billion pesos ($6,205,000,000) and by increases in foreign investment and loans from the United States, Western Europe, and Japan.

Social Policy. President Echeverría increased government spending on social programs during the year.

Education, housing, and health received major attention. Subsidies for the national university and the national polytechnical institute were increased 41% and 46% respectively. The government planned to spend 20 billion pesos ($1,600,000,000) on education and sent 67% of the newly contracted teachers to rural areas. Low and middle income housing was built at an increased rate by various governmental agencies. Medical facilities were expanded and the national program for family planning promoted birth control with free contraceptives.

Foreign Affairs. Mexico continued its policies of seeking Latin American unity and Third World leadership, and of expanding trade and foreign investment. Diplomatic relations were established with the Bahamas, Hungary, Malaysia, Bulgaria, and Cyprus. Relations with Canada were strengthened when Canada agreed to import Mexican farm labor (*braceros*).

United States-Mexican relations deteriorated as Mexico attacked American domination of the Organization of American States, sought to organize Latin America independently of the United States, supported Panamanian claims to sovereignty over the Canal, supported normalization of relations with Cuba, fostered the Charter of Rights and Duties of Nations (the Echeverría Charter), which favored small and underdeveloped nations, and criticized positions taken by the great powers on maritime rights.

On October 21, Echeverría and President Gerald Ford met in Arizona and the Mexican state of Sonora to discuss a variety of common issues, including Mexican *braceros,* Mexicans illegally in the United States, and oil. No substantive agreements were reached.

DONALD J. MABRY
Mississippi State University

MICHIGAN

Election results highlighted events in Michigan in 1974.

Election Results. Gov. William G. Milliken scored an immense personal victory in November when he won a second term in the face of a Democratic tide that changed the face of Michigan politics. The win propelled Milliken into the national limelight as one of only a few Republican governors able to withstand a Democratic sweep. Governor Milliken defeated his opponent, Sander M. Levin (D), by more than 100,000 votes.

Democrat Richard Austin won reelection as secretary of state and Frank J. Kelley was reelected attorney general, both by margins of more than two to one. Five incumbent Republican state senators were unseated. Democrat Richard F. VanderVeen of Grand Rapids retained the congressional seat once held by President Ford.

Two presidents visited the state during the year. President Ford campaigned in October in Grand Rapids on behalf of Paul G. Goebel, a Republican seeking election to the seat once held by Ford. Richard M. Nixon toured small towns in the state's thumb area in April, campaigning for James M. Sparling, Jr., who was seeking election to a vacant seat. Both Republican candidates subsequently were defeated.

The state sales tax of 4% on food and 2% on prescription drugs was repealed by voters in the November election. Governor Milliken, who opposed the repeal, proposed a variety of budget cuts to absorb the estimated $80 million loss of revenue expected by the end of the fiscal year, June 31, 1975. The amendment to the state constitution was the result of a petition drive by a group called the Michigan Citizens Lobby. Also approved by voters in the November election was a bonus for veterans who served in the Armed Forces during the Vietnam war. Proposals for a $1.1 billion bond issue to improve transportation facilities and to restrict use of the state gasoline tax were rejected.

Doctors' Complaints. In October a group of 600 doctors, who organized the Physicians Crisis Committee, petitioned the state Supreme Court to restrict "clearly excessive" legal fees charged by lawyers handling medical malpractice suits. The group also asked the Michigan Medical Practices Board to take strong action to lift the licenses of doctors found to be incompetent. The committee said it was alarmed by an increase in the number of medical malpractice lawsuits, the damages awarded, and the soaring cost of physicians' malpractice insurance.

Lottery. The success of the state's 50-cent lottery prompted a $1 game in addition, first on a test basis and then, effective Oct. 1, 1974, as a permanent feature. In November the state announced the 15th winner of the top $1 million prize since the lottery was started.

MICHIGAN • Information Highlights

Area: 58,216 square miles (150,779 sq km).
Population (1973 est.): 9,044,000. *Density:* 160 per sq mi.
Chief Cities (1970 census): Lansing, the capital, 131,546; Detroit, 1,513,601.
Government (1974): *Chief Officers*—governor, William G. Milliken (R); lt. gov., James H. Brickley (R). *Legislature*—Senate, 38 members; House of Representatives, 110 members.
Education (1973–74): *Enrollment*—public elementary schools, 1,146,390 pupils; public secondary, 1,016,610; nonpublic, 254,800; colleges and universities, 426,126 students. *Public school expenditures,* $2,460,125,000 ($1,260 per pupil).
State Finances (fiscal year 1973): *Revenues,* $6,503,617,000; *expenditures,* $5,830,839,000.
Personal Income (1973): $49,190,000,000; per capita, $5,439.
Labor Force (July 1974): *Nonagricultural wage and salary earners,* 3,221,200.

Fishing Rights of Indians. In October, the Michigan Court of Appeals ruled the state could not ban Chippewa Indians from fishing in state waters because their rights were guaranteed by an 1836 treaty. But the court also held that Indians are subject to state regulations on how many fish could be taken. Nearly 50 cases involving Indians accused of violating state fishing laws were pending in the courts as the year drew to a close.

Lake Dikes. The Army Corps of Engineers, which had undertaken an extensive program of diking to prevent damage to shore property on Lakes Erie, St. Clair and Huron, claimed success in 1974. Property damage, estimated in the millions of dollars in 1972 and 1973, was sharply reduced during the winter of 1973–74 and the fall of 1974. Lake levels peaked in April 1974, and then began to fall.

Contamination of Animal Feeds. The Michigan Department of Agriculture supervised the destruction of more than 10,000 beef and dairy cattle that had been fed a poisonous bromine compound that contaminated their meat and milk. The feed was sold by the Michigan Farm Bureau Services, Inc. Claims totaling millions of dollars were filed against the Farm Bureau Services and a chemical company that had delivered a bromide compound used in fire extinguishers instead of a magnesium-oxide feed supplement. Also destroyed were 2,200 swine, 1.2 million chickens, 4.4 million eggs, 100,000 pounds of cheese, and 3,000 pounds of butter.

Censure of Smeekens. State Rep. John P. Smeekens, a controversial Coldwater Republican, was censured on a 96-to-5 vote by the House of Representatives on September 19 for improper conduct in office. Smeekens had failed in the August primary to win nomination for reelection after the state attorney general accused him of conflict of interest. Smeekens was charged with appearing on behalf of the Hillsdale Foundry Co., of Hillsdale, before the state Air Pollution Control Commission without revealing he was employed by the firm.

CHARLES W. THEISEN
The Detroit "News"

MICROBIOLOGY

Studies of microorganisms led to significant advances in 1974, and some of these may soon have considerable impact on the world food supply and world health.

Agricultural and Soil Microbiology. Efforts are being made to expand agricultural production because of shortages of plant and animal proteins in the world. The nitrogen required for this increased production must come from the soil or from the reservoir of atmospheric nitrogen. Because certain microorganisms are the only known forms of life capable of converting atmospheric nitrogen to compounds that can be utilized by plants, great emphasis is being placed on understanding ways to improve microbial nitrogen fixation.

Breakthroughs in research in 1974 were highly significant. In particular, it was found that the genes controlling nitrogen fixation in certain bacteria can be transferred to other species of bacteria that ordinarily are incapable of fixing nitrogen from the atmosphere. This may mean that the capability of nitrogen fixation can be transferred artificially to many types of soil bacteria, leading to an increase in the amount of nitrogen for plant growth in the soil. This scientific finding could help to avoid a world food crisis.

Microbial Physiology, Genetics, and Enzymology. A recent review shows that nearly 5,000 metabolic products are produced by microorganisms. These include not only simple acids, alcohols, and carbohydrates, but also antibiotics, enzymes, toxins, and other complex substances. About 75 of these products are of sufficient importance that they are now produced commercially, including new ones that were added to the list in 1974.

Scientists have recently made interesting and important discoveries about microbial enzymes. With certain techniques scientists now can manipulate microorganisms in such a way that they form specific enzymes, proteins, or other products in larger amounts than are normally produced. Also, the genetic material that controls the formation of such substances can be transferred from one bacterium to another unrelated species that normally does not synthesize the material. For instance, the antibiotic resistance of an organism, its ability to produce diphtheria toxin, its ability to fix atmospheric nitrogen, or its ability to cause disease can be transferred among bacteria almost at will in the laboratory. In a similar manner chromosomal material that controls the enzymatic synthesis of fruit-fly protein or silkworm protein can be transferred to bacteria in such a way that the progeny synthesize these proteins. Likewise, the genes that are responsible for skin proteins in frogs can be transferred to bacteria in such a way that the progeny synthesize the proteins. Such methods have led to the expansion of a field called "enzyme engineering," which has great scientific and technical potentials.

Food Microbiology. Advances were made in preventing microbial deterioration of certain foods and in increasing microbial production of amino acids and vitamins. But the most important progress came in the use of microorganisms as a source of protein for animal feed supplements and in the commercial production of microbial polysaccharides as hydrocolloids for the preparation of certain foods.

The possibility of using microorganisms as a source of food protein has been considered noncompetitive with conventional sources. But with the world shortage of protein and the energy crisis, microbial proteins are gaining significance. At least six processes, using algae, bacteria, and yeasts, have now been developed to a pilot-plant scale or to large-scale production (50,000 metric tons per year).

When certain bacteria are cultivated in sucrose or other sugar solutions they form complex polysaccharides, or gums. By isolating and purifying these substances it has been found that they have many uses in the food industry, pharmacy, and medicine. A new gum called xanthan was developed on a commercial scale in 1974. In the food industry it serves as an emulsion stabilizer in salad dressings and enhances certain starch products. When xanthan is used in gluten-free bread dough, it is possible to enrich the product with soybean protein, thereby greatly increasing the nutritional qualities of the bread.

Pathogenic Microbiology. Even though many microbial animal and human diseases in the world were fairly well under control in 1974, there were serious outbreaks of smallpox in India, and anthrax occurred in cattle in various countries, including the United States. Plant diseases continued to be a problem in many places in the world. However, significant discoveries were made about some of the lesser known but serious diseases.

A virus responsible for infant diarrhea, which is a major cause of illness and death of babies throughout the world, was isolated and identified in 1974.

Research has been done in an effort to untangle the relationship among the so-called slow viruses that are thought to cause kuru and multiple sclerosis in human beings, scrapie in sheep and goats, encephalopathy in mink, and spindle tuber disease in the potato. A theory has been advanced that some plants and insects serve as a reservoir for viruses that are pathogenic for animals and human beings.

Much research was done in 1974 on the parasites responsible for malaria, trypanosomiasis (Chagas' disease), toxoplasmosis, and amebiasis in hopes of improving the health of millions of persons in the world who suffer from these diseases.

J. R. PORTER, *The University of Iowa*

NATO INFORMATION SERVICE

The North Atlantic Treaty Organization (NATO) celebrates the 25th anniversary of its founding in ceremonies at NATO headquarters in Brussels, Belgium, April 4.

MILITARY FORCES

The detonation of a nuclear device by India and heavy arms acquisitions by Middle Eastern countries highlighted ominous military developments in 1974. Among the superpowers, the United States and the USSR maintained an uneasy détente, while Communist China continued to build its nuclear arms capabilities.

WORLD DEVELOPMENTS

Although the level of conflict in Southeast Asia and the Middle East was much less in 1974 than in previous years, there were a number of important developments regarding military forces around the world. Perhaps the most important were the ostensible efforts of the United States and the USSR to hold down the deployment of strategic nuclear weapons systems while simultaneously increasing research and development of new weapons for possible deployment later in the 1970's.

The detonation of a nuclear device by India, coupled with closely watched developments in other "near-nuclear" countries, increased fears that the spread of nuclear weapons could not be halted. A violent dispute between NATO members Greece and Turkey, the necessity for Western nations to obtain Middle Eastern oil, and increasing racial tensions south of the Sahara led to significant alterations in the flow of conventional armaments. While criticizing the United States and the Soviet Union for stockpiling arms, the People's Republic of China continued to increase its conventional and nuclear armaments, as did France. Among nuclear weapons states only Britain was content with its existing military forces.

U. S.-USSR Arms Competition. The two superpowers were seriously engaged in research and development of new strategic nuclear weapons while claiming to be searching for ways to limit the nuclear arms race. In the West the rationale for the extensive Soviet research and development program remained something of a mystery. However, many were starting to agree with Secretary of Defense James R. Schlesinger, who suggested that the Soviet Union appeared to be preparing for a major new round of strategic nuclear weapons deployment after 1977 when the Interim Agreement on the Limitation of Offensive Weapons expires.

Regarding the purpose of the U. S. research and development effort concerning strategic nuclear weapons, Secretary Schlesinger said: "I repeat, we are eager to begin a reduction of the strategic forces by mutual agreement and on terms of parity. This is our first preference. We would be quite content if both the United States and the Soviet Union avoided the acquisition of major counterforce capabilities. But we are troubled by Soviet weapons momentum, and we simply cannot ignore the prospect of a growing disparity between the two major nuclear powers. We do not propose to let an opponent threaten a major component of our forces without our being able to pose a comparable threat."

In Vladivostok, USSR, in late November, President Ford and Soviet Chairman Brezhnev reached a tentative agreement limiting the number of strategic offensive nuclear weapons and delivery vehicles (see also DISARMAMENT).

Soviet Armament. The Soviet research and development that most disturbed Secretary Schlesinger was the continuing work on four new intercontinental ballistic missiles (ICBMs), designated the SS-16, SS-17, SS-18, and SS-19, and a new submarine-launched ballistic missile (SLBM).

The tempo of Soviet naval expansion did not slacken in 1974. As a concern to the United States, this activity was second only to the research and development in strategic nuclear missiles. The Soviet navy operates the world's largest submarine force. Two hundred and fifty craft are designed for the traditional submarine role of attacking surface vessels and, in some instances, for attacking other submarines. More than 40 Soviet submarines are nuclear-powered ones that carry SLBMs.

In terms of surface vessels, the Soviet navy is second only to the United States. This force consists of approximately 220 ships, including 2 guided-missile helicopter carriers, 17 missile cruisers, 14 gun cruisers, 40 missile destroyers, 37 gun destroyers, and some 100 escort ships.

A worrisome characteristic of the Soviet naval forces was the rise in the number of ships equipped with surface-to-surface antiship missiles or surface-to-air antiaircraft missiles. The percentage of such ships to 1970 was estimated to be 23%, but by 1977 it was expected that half of the Soviet surface fleet will be equipped with missiles.

In addition to the two helicopter carriers, one aircraft carrier designed to carry V/STOL (vertical/short-take-off and landing) aircraft has been launched, and another is under construction. Augmenting the submarine and surface ship forces is the naval aviation component, with some 500 land-based bombers comprising this force. These aircraft generally are equipped with air-to-surface antiship missiles. Some of the naval aviation planes are very-long-range reconnaissance craft used to track U. S. naval forces in the oceans of the world.

For some years the Soviet long-range bomber force has remained relatively constant in numbers at approximately 200 planes. Three fourths are bombers, and about 50 are tankers used in aerial refueling of the bombers. A possible future addition to the bomber forces is the recently developed Backfire bomber. This craft is a swept-wing supersonic jet that is twice the size of the U. S. FB-111 and about two thirds the size of the B-1, the new American strategic bomber under development.

The Soviet Union, like the United States, is limited by the 1972 Antiballistic Missile (ABM) Treaty to 100 ABMs around its capital city and a second 100 about an ICBM installation. To date the Soviets have placed only the defense missiles about Moscow.

In other important but less spectacular armament developments, the Soviet Union continued the modernization of its ground forces, which number about 2.2 million men. The Soviets maintain about 160 combat divisions. A quarter of these are stationed along the Chinese border, about 80 divisions are assigned to the area fronting the North Atlantic Treaty Organization (NATO) countries, and the rest are scattered about the Soviet Union.

Civilians employed in a chemical plant in Kansu province, the People's Republic of China, man antiaircraft guns as part of the factory's "air defense exercise."

UPI

People's Republic of China. In the fall of 1964 the People's Republic of China became the fifth nation to develop nuclear weapons. Since that time the Chinese have demonstrated steady progress as they have developed atomic and thermonuclear weapons and the missiles with which to deliver them. One Western estimate is that the Chinese have 200 to 300 nuclear weapons.

According to estimates by the Institute for Strategic Studies, the Chinese now possess about 25 intermediate-range missiles with ranges in the neighborhood of 1,600 miles (2,600 km). These missiles have sufficient range to hit targets in the Asiatic portion of the Soviet Union, as well as much of the rest of Asia. The Chinese have flight tested an ICBM and are expected by Pentagon experts to be capable of deploying several dozen before the end of the decade. Such missiles, with a 5,000- to 6,000-mile (8,050–9,650 km) range, could strike all of the Soviet Union and the United States.

The F-1 Mirage is the French entry in the low-cost fighter aircraft competition. At stake are billions of dollars worth of sales to members of NATO.

AVIONS MARCEL DASSAULT—BREGUET AVIATION

France. The French government continued its thermonuclear weapons tests in the atmosphere over the Southwest Pacific during 1974 in spite of sharp objections by Australia and New Zealand.

At home, the French launched their fourth SLBM-carrying nuclear-powered submarine, the *L' Indomptable,* and deployed their first tactical nuclear weapon, a guided missile called the Pluton, which has a 75- to 100-mile (120–160 km) range. Previously, the French had stationed 18 medium-range ballistic missiles in mountainous terrain in southern France. These missiles are capable of hitting targets in the Soviet Union. For some years the French have operated Mirage medium-range jet bombers, which can carry nuclear bombs to Russia. In numbers and types of nuclear weapons deployed, the French have moved far beyond the British, America's other nuclear-armed ally.

The Middle East. Three to five billion dollars worth of modern arms and extremely sophisticated arms poured into the Middle East in 1974 or was ordered for delivery in 1975. The major recipients of Soviet arms, possibly including MIG-23 and MIG-25 jet fighters, were Syria and Iraq. Israel obtained substantial resupply of equipment from the United States to replace that lost in the October 1973 war with the Arab states.

Three oil-rich Persian Gulf states—Kuwait, Iran, and Saudi Arabia—used their oil revenues to purchase immense amounts of military equipment. For example, Iran placed orders for the F-14, an advanced U. S. jet fighter that would be added to its force of U. S. Phantom jets. Saudi Arabia negotiated for aircraft, naval vessels, and missiles from the United States and France. Kuwait sought American and French aircraft and missiles.

The arms acquisitions in the Middle East were fueled by a number of rivalries. In addition to the long-standing Israeli-Arab confrontation, there was a developing rivalry in the Persian Gulf between Saudi Arabia and Iran. Kuwait was concerned about military incursions from its much larger northern neighbor, Iraq. Within Iraq, a seething civil war was in progress between the central government and Kurdish tribesmen who sought to establish an autonomous Kurdish state. In tiny Oman the forces of the sultan, with British and Iranian assistance, were battling guerrillas.

In summary, the Middle East became one of the world's most rapidly militarized areas, with no end in sight for the continuing arms acquisitions by contending nations and groups.

NATO. While American arms were flowing into the Middle East, there was a curtailment in arms supplies from Washington to Turkey, a NATO ally. This reduction in arms was forced upon a reluctant President Ford by a Congress angered over the alleged use of U. S. equipment by Turkey in its invasion of the island of Cyprus. In Washington some worried whether the arms cutoff ordered by the Congress for the end of 1974 would substantially weaken the eastern terminus of the NATO alliance.

The United States also encountered military problems with Greece. The difficulty grew over the desire of the United States to station portions of the Sixth Fleet in Greek ports. After the overthrow of the military junta led by Col. George Papadopoulos in 1973, the new Greek government wanted more aid and weapons than Washington wanted to provide. A more difficult problem was the possibility that hostilities between Greeks and Turks on Cyprus might resume, with the result that Greece might expel the U. S. Navy forces if the United States appeared to tilt toward Turkey.

Indian Ocean. In spite of efforts by nations bordering the Indian Ocean to prevent arms competition in the area, events in 1974 strongly pointed toward a new arms competition building up between the United States and the USSR. The most visible aspect of the rivalry was the island of Diego Garcia, where the United States plans to increase the capabilities of the island to handle heavy jet bombers and naval forces. The

United States claimed it had to increase the strength of its Indian Ocean forces as a prudent response to the alleged presence of Soviet ships and submarines in the area. A second reason given by Washington was the possibility that a U. S. naval facility on the island of Bahrain in the Persian Gulf might be ordered closed by a local sheikh because of U. S. support of Israel, thus forcing the American naval units to find other bases.

Africa South of the Sahara. The change of government in Portugal led to establishment of black rule in Angola and Mozambique. Arms and money that previously had supported anti-Portuguese guerrilla warfare in the two colonies were believed to have been shifted to the support of preparations to attack the white minority government of Rhodesia, and possibly later the much stronger forces of the Republic of South Africa.

In the fall, after the Portuguese forces left Mozambique, reports were circulating that Communist-made weapons were entering Mozambique and that guerrilla war training was in progress. Some observers doubted whether the whites in Rhodesia could long withstand guerrilla warfare within their nation and armed attacks across their border, should both types of assault be mounted in the future. Although the army of Rhodesia is small, it is well equipped with Western armaments.

Taking the lead against possible violence, the government of the Republic of South Africa took measures to increase spending for defense forces and called up some reservists for active duty. These new troops were generally added to the armed forces stationed along the nearly 400-mile (645 km) border with Mozambique. It is widely believed by Western military experts that the South African government has the fiscal and technological capabilities to produce nuclear weapons if the decision is ever taken to do so. The army and air force of South Africa are well equipped with Western arms, as well as some of local manufacture.

Proliferation of Nuclear Weapons. On May 18, India detonated a nuclear device underground. The explosion came as something of a shock to many. It served to warn nations supporting the Nuclear Nonproliferation Treaty, such as the United States, the Soviet Union, and Britain, that greater efforts might be required if additional states were not to acquire nuclear weapons. What those efforts should be became the central point of discussion as the supporters of the treaty prepared for the 1975 Nonproliferation Treaty Review Conference.

The Indian explosion demonstrated that a so-called developing nation can have the technical ability to operate a nuclear reactor in which plutonium is produced, separate the plutonium from the reactor residue, fabricate the plutonium into an explosive device, and detonate the nuclear explosive with roughly the same force as that of the two American nuclear bombs dropped on Japan in World War II. The fact that the reactor from which the plutonium was taken for the Indian explosion was built with the help of Canadian technicians was of little solace to those concerned about stopping nuclear proliferation. This was because the Indians are operating other reactors that they built themselves, which is the case with other nations as well.

Prime Minister Indira Gandhi assured the world that her government did not plan to develop nuclear weapons from their "peaceful nuclear explosive." However, some Indian strategic analysts suggested that New Delhi should threaten to develop nuclear weapons unless the United States and the Soviet Union showed substantial progress in reducing their stockpiles of nuclear weapons.

Several other nations, some considerably more technically advanced than India and some much wealthier, are generally considered possible candidates to develop nuclear weapons. Among them are Israel, Japan, South Africa, West Germany, Brazil, Argentina, Pakistan, and Iran. Some believe that Israel already has developed nuclear weapons as a hedge against being left without allies should the Arabs again use the threat of cutting off oil to deter Western military aid and assistance to Israel. The theory is that the Israelis have developed nuclear weapons in secret. It is suggested there have been no Israeli nuclear tests not only because the Israelis are confident that the weapons will work but also because nuclear weapons tests would cause political problems with the United States and with the governments of other generally pro-Israeli nations.

A particularly sinister aspect of the nuclear weapons proliferation problem is the possibility that criminal or terrorist groups might be able to steal nuclear weapons or manufacture them. In the latter case the weapons would be primitive in comparison with the advanced ones in the arsenals of the two superpowers. Still, a crude atomic bomb could wreak havoc in a sizable portion of a city. Such weapons in the hands of terrorist bands—similar to those that have killed diplomats, blown up airplanes, and shot innocent bystanders—pose a difficult problem to the security of most urban areas.

To date little has been done by the world community to combat this type of nuclear weapon danger other than to tighten security of nuclear weapons in national arsenals and more closely guard fissionable material from which weapons could be fabricated. The latter task will become considerably more difficult as time passes and more nuclear reactors are built around the world to produce electricity because plutonium, a basic ingredient of a particular kind of atomic bomb, is a by-product of nuclear power plants.

ROBERT M. LAWRENCE
Colorado State University

GENERAL DYNAMICS

NORTHROP CORPORATION

American candidates for NATO fighter plane sales are General Dynamics' YF-16 (*top*) and Northrop Aviation's YF-17 (*bottom*).

U. S. DEVELOPMENTS

In 1974, U. S. defense policy focused on problems of fiscal management that were aggravated by serious challenges at home and abroad. Abroad, new Soviet missiles appeared, and modern naval task forces carried the hammer and sickle increasingly on the seven seas. At home, U. S. defenses were severely limited by the first peacetime budget in a decade and sharply increased inflation, both presenting Secretary of Defense James R. Schlesinger with unprecedented challenges to his managerial skills.

Budget. In terms of purchasing power, the approved fiscal year 1975 budget of $82.6 billion was the lowest since 1950. Also, the defense share of the gross national product declined over a seven-year period from 9.5% to 5.6%, the smallest since the days of post-World War II demobilization. Inflation cost $11 billion in defense purchasing power, emphasizing the need for a maximum capability of smaller force levels that can be achieved by modernizing, exploiting technology, and maintaining austere inventories.

High-Low Mix. A new "high-low mix" policy on procurement seeks a small number of high-performance sophisticated weapons capable of countering the maximum enemy threat and a larger number of less sophisticated weapons to counter lesser threats. A reasoned choice between sophisticated and less sophisticated weapons is required; for example, choosing between a sophisticated aircraft carrier and a less capable and less costly Sea Control Ship. Congress, however, denied fiscal 1975 funds for the Sea Control Ship and required all major ships to be nuclear powered.

HUGHES AIRCRAFT COMPANY

The U. S. Army's TOW antitank missile, here being launched from a ground tripod, has a maximum range of almost 2 miles (3 km). It can also be launched from ground vehicles or helicopters.

All-Volunteer Services. After a full year without a draft law, the armed services entered the fiscal 1975 year at or near the programmed strength of 2.162 million men and women. Voluntary enlistments and reenlistments were better than expected, 50% for first-term personnel and 80% for careerists. The Air Force was in the best shape, meeting its 643,000-man force, getting more recruits than needed, and maintaining a high level of technical skills with 92% high-school graduates. The Navy met recruitment goals for its 551,000-man strength, but the Marine Corps was about 6,000 persons short of the planned 196,000 force. The Army had some difficulty stemming from too many high-school dropouts and low intelligence scorers.

Early results looked promising, but estimates of the success of the volunteer service must guard against premature optimism. However, wage scales in the military have increased personnel costs from 35% to 55% of the budget, and a stagnant national economy and 18% unemployment among teenagers made military service unusually attractive.

Arms Control Negotiations. Two significant arms limitation agreements were negotiated in Moscow in July 1974. The first defers construction of the additional ballistic missile defense site authorized in the SALT I treaty. The second agreement, a Threshold Test Ban, prevents both sides from tests of nuclear weapons with yields in excess of 150 kilotons. If ratified by both sides, the ban will go into effect on March 31, 1976.

Defense Strategy and Weaponry. Secretary Schlesinger announced that small new warheads and high-precision delivery techniques allow a new nuclear targeting strategy that concentrates on enemy forces rather than on cities. Neither so novel nor controversial as may have been advertised, the aims of the new procedures are to attain "essential equivalence" in the nuclear balance, to provide the president with more flexibility in possible responses to a nuclear challenge, and to prevent massive destruction even in the cataclysmic circumstances of nuclear war.

Increases in the capability of the Soviet navy required modifications of U. S. naval policy. Increased attention was being given to protection of sea lanes, to a vigorous naval modernization program, and to increased airlift and sealift capabilities. The U. S. naval presence in the Indian Ocean was slated to become more prominent through the planned $29 million expansion of facilities on the island of Diego Garcia in the center of the Indian Ocean.

Rapid advances in weapons technology demonstrated in the 1973 Middle East war were being incorporated into a major modernization program for U. S. land forces in 1974. Accurate and lethal antitank missiles and small antitank mines and bombs strongly influence new policies on tank warfare and the role of the infantryman. Air-defense improvements were being based on mobile, short-range antiaircraft weapons.

Airplane-Launched ICBM. In October the Air Force made the first successful test of an airplane-launched ICBM. The missile, dropped from a transport plane, was held aloft by parachutes until its engines had fired. The test was part of an Air Force program to develop a missile that can be launched from an airplane, a railroad car, or an underground silo.

SR-71 Transatlantic Flight. A U. S. Air Force SR-71 reconnaissance plane crossed the Atlantic from New York to London in 1 hour and 56 minutes, surpassing the previous record of 4 hours and 46 minutes for the 3,490-mile (5,615 km) flight. Its average speed was approximately 1,800 miles (2,900 km) per hour.

Command. On July 1, 1974, the Chairman of the Joint Chiefs of Staff, Adm. Thomas H. Moorer, was relieved by Gen. George S. Brown. In turn, Brown was relieved as Chief of Staff, U. S. Air Force, by Gen. David C. Jones. Adm. Elmo R. Zumwalt was relieved as Chief of Naval Operations by Adm. James L. Holloway III. On Sept. 4, 1974, Gen. Creighton W. Abrams, Chief of Staff, U. S. Army, died in office. He was succeeded by Gen. Frederick C. Weyand on Oct. 7, 1974. Gen. Andrew J. Goodpaster, U. S. Commander-in-Chief, Europe and Supreme Allied Commander Europe, was relieved on Dec. 1, 1974, by Gen. Alexander M. Haig, Jr., former chief of staff to Presidents Nixon and Ford.

PAUL R. SCHRATZ, *Captain, USN, Retired*
Commission on the Organization of the Government for the Conduct of Foreign Policy

Surface Effect Ship (*artist's conception*), which is being developed by Textron's Bell Aerospace Division for the U. S. Navy, rides on a cushion of air like a hovercraft.

TEXTRON, BELL AEROSPACE DIVISION, NEW ORLEANS

UPI

Pennsylvania's first women coal miners enter the elevator that will take them into a Bethlehem mine at Ebensburg.

MINING

As expected in 1973, the latest year for which complete production figures are available, there was a significant increase in world mineral output. Gains averaging 7.5% were recorded for 58 mineral commodities, ranging from 0.2% for magnesite to 54.5% for columbium/tantalite. Production of 19 minerals fell an average 3.8%, from less than 0.1% for industrial diamond to 12.6% for monazite. Excluding coal, more than 90% of this output was attributable to 1,069 large mines owned and operated by 106 mining companies producing 22 major minerals.

Despite the energy crisis, high rates of inflation, and spreading recession later in the year, world mineral production continued strong through most of 1974. Declines appeared in a few sectors, especially copper and aluminum late in 1974 in response to less consumer demand. This cycle is familiar to the mineral industries; but in other respects, 1974 was not an easy year for mineral producers, consumers, or governments.

Economic Nationalism. The inflationary need for more government revenue, particularly in the developing nations, strengthened the trend to nationalization in 1974. Early in the year Togo took over its only operating mine (phosphate) and Mauritania followed suit in November. Venezuela announced plans to nationalize its U. S.-owned iron mines by year-end.

The classic pattern of nationalization appeared to be changing, however, as governments became more innovative and sophisticated. Outright expropriation is giving way to a mixture of majority ownership and greatly increased taxes and royalties designed to increase revenue and control of national mineral resources. Some of these plans are workable.

In 1974, Jamaica unilaterally increased taxes greatly on the six U. S.-owned bauxite producers, the nation's only significant mining activity and its major source of income. It is also taking over majority ownership of the mines. Further, Jamaica has been purchasing stock in at least two of the parent companies, Kaiser and Reynolds, in order to secure a place on the boards of directors and participate in corporate policy decisions. Finally, Jamaica and Mexico reached an agreement to mine bauxite and produce alumina in Jamaica for smelting in Mexico and open-market sale.

In Canada, on the other hand, Manitoba's proposed mineral taxation and royalty bill proved wholly unworkable and was withdrawn. British Columbia had to grant exceptions to its 1974 tax legislation, which has already virtually halted mineral exploration, stopped the development of several new mining projects, and is expected to bankrupt several operating mines. Ontario, too, had to reconsider its hastily passed mineral tax bill, because of adverse impact on the industry. Yet unresolved is the plan of the federal government not to permit the deduction of provincial taxes from federal taxes owed by the miners.

Commodity Cartels. High prices and demand for minerals encouraged a number of mining countries to emulate the oil producers by forming cartels for which partial or complete nationalization of mineral resources is the first step.

WORLD PRODUCTION OF MAJOR MINERALS*

Aluminum (thousands of metric tons)

	1972	1973
United States	3,740	4,109
USSR[e]	1,250	1,360
Japan	1,015	1,103
Canada	925	934
Norway	548	620
West Germany	445	533
France	394	360
United Kingdom	171	252
Australia	206	207
Netherlands	166	190
Italy	122	184
Spain	140	168
India	179	[e]154
Ghana	144	152
China[e]	140	150
Greece	131	142
Rumania	122	141
Brazil	97	113
New Zealand	88	[e]110
Bahrain	78	103
Poland	102	102
Sweden	78	83
Total (est.)	11,004	12,117

Antimony (metric tons)

	1972	1973
South Africa	14,571	[e]15,694
Bolivia[a]	13,128	14,933
China[e]	11,793	11,793
USSR[e]	6,985	7,076
Thailand	4,724	[e]3,401
Turkey	2,705	3,353
Mexico	2,975	2,387
Yugoslavia	1,975	[e]1,724
Australia	1,364	1,499
Italy	1,201	1,370
Morocco	832	1,133
Guatemala	890	961
Canada[b]	308	859
Peru	799	816
Czechoslovakia[e]	599	599
Austria	501	577
United States	443	493
Total (est.)	66,459	69,320

Asbestos (thousands of metric tons)

	1972	1973
Canada	1,530.4	1,790.8
USSR[e]	1,220.0	1,280.0
South Africa	323.1	325.0
China[e]	200.0	210.0
Italy	132.1	149.3
United States	119.4	136.1
Rhodesia[e]	80.0	80.0
Brazil	33.0	40.0
Australia	17.3	32.0
Total (est.)	3,774.4	4,171.1

Barite (thousands of metric tons)

	1972	1973
United States	821.9	1,001.5
West Germany	368.3	326.5
USSR[e]	310.2	322.9
Mexico	261.4	255.2
Ireland	233.5	[e]249.9
Peru	205.0	215.0
Italy	181.8	[e]166.5
China[e]	155.1	165.1
Spain	132	[e]149.7
North Korea[e]	119.7	119.7
India	46.1	116.6
Rumania	116.1	116.1
France	[e]99.7	[e]109.7
Greece	100.3	[e]109.7
Morocco	93.2	102.6
Total (est.)	3,956.7	4,318.8

Bauxite (thousands of metric tons)

	1972	1973
Australia	14,437	17,816
Jamaica	12,542	13,600
Surinam	7,777	8,100
USSR[e]	4,200	4,300
Guyana	3,344	3,201
France	3,254	3,133
Guinea	2,050	3,050
Greece	2,436	2,600
Hungary	2,358	2,600
Yugoslavia	2,197	2,167
United States	1,841	1,909
India	1,684	1,270
Malaysia	1,076	1,220
Indonesia	1,277	1,219
Dominican Republic	[a]1,035	1,145
Haiti	687	[e]700
Sierra Leone	694	663
Brazil[e]	606	[e]650
China[e]	580	600
Ghana	362	310
Total (est.)	65,114	70,694

Cement (millions of metric tons)

	1972	1973
USSR[e]	104.29	109.50
United States	76.71	79.38
Japan	66.33	78.02
West Germany	43.14	40.86
Italy	33.45	36.25
France	30.24	30.72
China[e]	20.87	22.68
Spain	19.50	22.24

Cement (cont'd) (millions of metric tons)

	1972	1973
United Kingdom	18.04	19.99
Poland	13.98	15.55
India	15.70	15.00
Brazil	11.37	13.34
East Germany	8.86	11.00
Canada	9.05	9.87
Rumania	9.20	9.85
Mexico	8.60	9.79
Turkey	8.42	8.95
Czechoslovakia	8.04	8.38
South Korea	6.49	8.17
Belgium	7.09	7.04
South Africa	6.11	6.86
Greece	6.34	6.46
Austria	6.36	6.26
Total (est.)	653.50	669.86

Chromite (thousands of metric tons)

	1972	1973
USSR[e]	1,850.6	1,905.1
South Africa	1,483.2	1,649.2
Albania	[e]571.5	[e]653.1
Turkey[e]	644.0	617.9
Rhodesia[e]	544.3	544.3
India	294.8	267.6
Iran[e]	179.6	[e]181.4
Malagasy Republic	111.6	156.9
Finland	97.0	[e]117.9
Greece	97.0	[e]117.9
Total (est.)	6,329.3	6,810.2

Coal[i] (millions of metric tons)

	1972	1973
USSR	655.2	667.7
United States	540.1	536.8
China[e]	381.0	408.2
East Germany	249.3	247.0
West Germany	210.9	209.6
Poland	188.9	195.8
United Kingdom	116.4	127.6
Czechoslovakia	113.4	109.0
Australia	83.3	85.4
India	77.8	80.3
South Africa	57.1	60.9
Yugoslavia	30.8	32.5
Hungary	25.2	26.8
Bulgaria	26.6	26.6
Japan	28.2	22.5
France	24.2	21.5
North Korea	6.7	7.2
Total (est.)	2,930.4	2,983.3

Copper (mine) (thousands of metric tons)

	1972	1973
United States	1,510.0	1,558.5
Canada	719.7	816.0
Chile	725.7	740.8
Zambia	717.7	706.6
USSR[e,b]	664.9	700.0
Zaire[k]	428.9	488.3
Philippines	213.7	221.2
Peru	225.0	218.8
Australia	186.8	218.5
Papua, New Guinea	123.9	182.8
South Africa	161.9	175.8
Poland[e]	135.0	155.0
Yugoslavia	103.1	147.7
China[e]	100.0	100.0
Japan	112.1	91.2
Mexico	78.7	80.5
Rumania	35.0	42.0
Rhodesia[e]	38.3	41.8
Bulgaria	38.0	[e]40.0
Indonesia	5.0	37.9
Finland	29.1	37.4
Turkey	24.7	33.5
Sweden	30.6	32.4
Spain	36.1	30.3
Norway	25.4	28.4
Total (est.)	6,649.4	7,122.7

Diamonds (thousands of carats)

	1972	1973
Zaire[k]	13,390	12,940
USSR[e]	9,200	9,500
South Africa	7,395	7,420
Ghana	2,659	[e]2,700
Botswana	2,403	2,416
Angola	2,155	2,125
Sierra Leone	1,800	[a,e]1,670
South West Africa	1,596	1,600
Liberia[a]	[e]764	[e]820
Venezuela	456	788
Tanzania	[a]651	[e]580
Central African Republic	524	380
Brazil	310	320
Total (est.)	43,810	4,578.1

Fluorspar (thousands of metric tons)

	1972	1973
Mexico	1,042.4	1,085.9
Spain	491.3	471.7
USSR[e]	426.4	444.5
Thailand	395.1	398.0
France[e]	290.3	299.4
China[e]	254.0	254.0
Italy	277.5	235.5
United States	227.1	225.5
South Africa	210.8	210.3

Fluorspar (cont'd) (thousands of metric tons)

	1972	1973
United Kingdom	198.9	[e]199.6
Canada	163.0	136.9
Total (est.)	4,589.9	4,578.1

Gas, natural (billions of cubic feet)

	1972	1973
United States	24,016.1	24,067.2
USSR[e]	8,200.0	8,800.0
Canada	3,316.1	3,587.0
Netherlands	2,063.1	2,501.5
Venezuela	1,625.2	1,745.7
Iran	1,469.7	1,698.7
Saudi Arabia	1,127.0	[e]1,140.0
Rumania	978.7	1,032.5
United Kingdom	942.8	[e]980.0
Mexico	660.2	676.8
West Germany	643.2	[e]660.0
Total (est.)	52,037.7	54,948.9

Gold (millions of troy ounces)

	1972	1973
South Africa	29.25	27.49
USSR[e]	6.90	7.10
Canada	2.08	1.93
United States	1.45	1.18
Australia	0.75	0.94
Ghana	0.72	0.72
Philippines	0.61	0.57
New Guinea	0.41	0.57
Rhodesia	[e]0.50	[e]0.50
Colombia	0.19	0.22
Japan	0.24	0.19
Brazil	0.17	0.16
North Korea	0.16	0.16
Zaire[k]	0.08	0.13
Mexico	0.15	0.13
India	0.11	0.11
Total (est.)	44.71	43.07

Graphite (thousands of metric tons)

	1972	1973
USSR[e]	81.6	81.6
North Korea[e]	77.1	77.1
Mexico	55.1	[e]58.9
China[e]	29.9	29.9
Malagasy	18.3	[e]18.1
Austria	18.7	17.2
Norway	8.2	6.9
Rumania	5.9	5.9
Italy	0.7	[e]3.9
Total (est.)	357.8	NA

Gypsum (thousands of metric tons

	1972	1973
United States	11,183.77	12,299.5
Canada	7,347.3	7,544.1
France	6,192	6,323.0
USSR[e]	4,717.3	4,717.3
Spain	4,100.4	4,100.4
United Kingdom	4,163.9	3,688.5
Italy[e]	3,501.7	3,501.7
Iran	2,400.4	[e]2,449.4
West Germany	1,788.0	1,713.6
Niger	1,650.2	1,650.2
Mexico	1,497.7	1,514.0
Australia	931.7	997.9
India	1,104.9	883.5
Austria	760.2	875.4
Poland	[e]850	850
China[e]	599.6	599.6
Czechoslovakia	500.7	519.8
Argentina	508	508
Japan	465.4	378.2
Total (est.)	60,002.7	60,810.1

Iron Ore (millions of metric tons)

	1972	1973
USSR	208.1	215.9
United States	76.6	89.0
Australia	63.8	84.7
China[e]	59.9	66.0
Brazil[e]	42.1	57.9
France	54.3	54.2
Canada	40.2	49.7
India	35.5	35.4
Sweden	33.1	34.8
Venezuela	18.4	22.0
Total (est.)	779.8	862.9

Iron, pig[g] (millions of metric tons)

	1972	1973
USSR[e]	91.30	94.88
United States	80.62	91.56
Japan	72.05	90.00
West Germany[m]	31.68	36.46
China[n]	29.93	32.66
France	18.55	19.76
United Kingdom	15.33	16.68
Belgium	11.77	12.63
Italy	9.41	10.03
Canada	8.49	9.54
Czechoslovakia[o]	8.36	[e]8.52
Poland	7.29	[e]7.71
Australia	6.49	7.65
India	7.20	[e]7.53
Spain	5.92	6.27
Rumania	4.89	[e]5.53
Brazil	5.30	5.47
Luxembourg	4.67	5.09
Netherlands	4.29	4.71
South Africa	4.41	[e]4.45
Austria	2.85	3.00

WORLD PRODUCTION OF MAJOR MINERALS* (Continued)

Iron, pig (cont'd) (millions of metric tons)	1972	1973
Mexico	2.67	2.77
Sweden	2.70	2.75
North Korea[n]	2.63	2.72
East Germany	2.15	2.20
Hungary	2.04	[e]2.09
Bulgaria	1.53	[e]1.63
Total (est.)	456.10	504.26

Lead, smelter (thousands of metric tons)	1972	1973
United States[g]	624.7	623.9
USSR[e]	462.6	471.7
Australia[g]	348.0	370.4
Japan[g,p]	223.2	228.0
Canada[g]	186.9	183.7
Mexico[g]	155.8	172.9
France	136.1	129.0
China, Communist[e]	99.8	99.8
Bulgaria[p]	102.0	[e]99.8
Spain	100.7	99.3
Yugoslavia[g,p]	87.5	98.0
Belgium[p]	92.8	97.7
West Germany	102.0	86.4
Peru[g]	85.5	82.9
North Korea[e]	75.3	79.8
Poland[g,p]	65.3	65.0
South West Africa	63.9	63.6
Sweden[g]	47.6	[e]49.9
Rumania[e]	36.3	39.0
Argentina	39.5	37.8
Italy	50.6	35.1
Morocco	25.0	34.8
United Kingdom (Great Britain)	25.0	30.3
Tunisia	25.1	26.0
East Germany[e]	21.9	25.3
Zambia[g]	25.8	25.0
Total (est.)	3,397.1	3,448.0

Magnesium (thousands of metric tons)	1972	1973
United States	109.60	111.06
USSR[e]	54.43	57.15
Norway	36.49	[e]37.01
Japan	10.89	11.20
Italy	7.56	[e]7.17
France	6.85	6.99
Canada	5.37	5.29
Total (est.)	232.20	236.87

Manganese Ore (thousands of metric tons)	1972	1973
USSR[e]	7,819.0	7,999.5
South Africa	3,271.4	4,175.6
Brazil	2,057.4	2,157.3
Gabon	1,936.6	1,918.8
India	1,641.9	1,534.9
Australia	1,167.9	1,522.4
China[e]	1,000.0	1,000.0
Mexico	295.6	364.0
Zaire[k]	369.4	334.0
Ghana	498.3	318.2
Japan	260.7	188.8
Hungary	187.5	188.0
Morocco	96.0	146.4
Bulgaria	29.9	[e]29.9
Italy	25.6	25.5
Total (est.)	20,855.6	22,035.7

Mercury (thousands of flasks)	1972	1973
Spain	53.99	60.77
USSR[e]	50.00	52.00
Italy	41.80	32.31
Mexico	22.51	28.00
China[e]	26.00	26.00
Yugoslavia	16.42	15.60
Algeria	13.36	14.00
Canada[r]	14.60	12.50
Turkey	7.96	8.43
Czechoslovakia	6.61	7.00
Japan	5.17	3.74
United States	7.33	2.17
Total (est.)	279.58	276.20

Molybdenum (thousands of metric tons)	1972	1973
United States	50.9	52.6
Canada	11.1	12.5
USSR[e]	8.2	8.5
Chile	5.9	5.9
China[e]	1.5	1.5
Total (est.)	79.1	82.2

Nickel (mine) (thousands of metric tons)	1972	1973
Canada	234.9	243.9
USSR[e]	127.0	136.0
New Caledonia[q]	88.9	98.9
Australia	35.8	40.1
Cuba[e]	31.7	31.7
Indonesia	22.4	20.8
Dominican Republic	17.4	20.8
United States	15.3	16.6
Greece	11.3	12.6
Southern Rhodesia	11.9	11.9
South Africa	11.7	[e]10.4
Total (est.)	633.1	658.6

Petroleum (crude) (millions of barrels)	1972	1973
United States	3,455.4	3,360.9
USSR	2,895.9	3,094.4
Saudi Arabia	2,202.0	2,772.7
Iran	1,838.9	2,139.2
Venezuela	1,178.5	1,228.6
Kuwait	1,201.3	1,100.4
Libya	819.6	794.1
Nigeria	665.3	749.8
Iraq	529.4	736.6
Canada	560.7	648.3
Indonesia	395.6	488.5
Abu Dhabi	384.2	479.2
Algeria	384.9	390.7
China[e]	216.1	365.0
Qatar	176.5	208.2
Mexico	185.0	191.5
Argentina	158.5	153.5
Australia	119.5	142.3
Oman	103.1	106.9
Rumania	105.3	106.6
Syrian Arab Republic	45.2	38.2
Total (est.)	18,600.5	20,357.2

Phosphate Rock (thousands of metric tons)	1972	1973
United States	37,041	38,226
USSR	19,731	21,228
Morocco	14,971	16,564
Tunisia	3,387	3,473
China[e]	2,630	2,994
Nauru Island[a]	1,337	2,323
Togo	1,927	2,292
Senegal	1,416	[e]1,693
Christmas Island[a]	1,151	1,538
South Africa	1,252	1,365
Jordan	694	1,106
Israel	873	633
Egypt	562	550
North Vietnam[e]	281	499
Total (est.)	89,794	98,030

Potash[c] (thousands of metric tons)	1972	1973
USSR	5,433.1	5,715.2
Canada	3,494.5	4,020.6
West Germany	2,844.9	2,993.7
East Germany	2,457.6	[e]2,639.9
United States	2,412.2	2,361.4
France	1,759.9	2,262.5
Total (est.)	20,408.8	21,964.6

Pyrite[h] (thousands of metric tons)	1972	1973
USSR[e]	7,213	[e]7,315
Spain	2,140	2,187
China[e]	2,032	2,032
Japan	1,580	1,275
Italy	1,382	1,169
Rumania[e]	843	874
Norway	795	792
Finland	856	777
Sweden	487	680
United States	753	568
South Africa	439	551
Portugal	553	532
Total (est.)	23,148	22,391

Salt (millions of metric tons)	1972	1973
United States	40.86	39.86
China[e]	17.96	18.14
USSR[e]	12.16	12.16
West Germany	8.46	9.46
United Kingdom	9.73	9.25
India	6.52	7.00
France	5.21	[e]5.48
Canada	4.91	4.83
Mexico	4.56	[e]4.63
Italy	4.02	4.43
Australia	4.00	4.00
Rumania	3.15	3.27
Poland	3.01	3.08
Netherlands	2.80	3.04
East Germany	2.18	2.18
Total (est.)	147.81	150.16

Silver (millions of troy ounces)	1972	1973
Canada	44.79	48.16
Peru	40.19	42.02
USSR[e]	40.00	41.00
Mexico	37.48	38.79
United States	37.23	37.83
Australia	22.80	23.20
Japan	10.02	8.86
East Germany[e]	5.00	7.00
Bolivia	5.58	5.71
Chile	4.69	5.04
Sweden	4.26	[e]4.50
Yugoslavia	3.58	4.30
France	3.29	4.18
South Africa	3.29	3.65
Morocco	3.38	3.52
Honduras	3.60	3.15
Argentina	2.12	[e]2.50
Spain[b]	[e]1.64	2.25
Zaire[k]	2.08	2.00
Philippines	1.85	1.89
Ireland	1.55	1.83
Korea	1.77	1.49
West Germany	1.74	1.38
Italy	2.17	1.35
Czechoslovakia	1.10	1.10
Rumania	1.00	1.10
Total (est.)	290.56	350.92

Sulfur (elemental) (millions of metric tons)	1972	1973
United States (all forms)	9.39	10.18
Canada (recovered)	6.95	7.40
USSR (all forms)[e]	3.89	4.15
Poland (Frasch, ore)	2.93	3.54
France (recovered)	1.73	1.80
Mexico (all forms)	.94	1.61
Total (all forms) (est.)	28.66	32.06

Tin (mine) (thousands of long tons)	1972	1973
Malaysia	75.6	71.1
Bolivia	31.1	29.8
USSR[e]	28.5	29.0
Indonesia	21.0	22.1
Thailand	21.7	20.2
China[e]	20.0	20.0
Australia	12.0	10.4
Nigeria	6.6	5.7
Zaire[k]	5.8	5.5
Total (est.)	239.6	232.4

Titanium (thousands of metric tons)	1972	1973
(Ilmenite)		
United States	618.4	729.7
Norway	608.5	729.0
Australia	708.8	709.0
Finland	149.5	159.0
Malaysia[a]	152.1	152.2
Total (est.)	2,420.6	2,666.4
(Rutile)		
Australia	317.4	327.9
India	3.06	4.3
Total (est.)	323.4	333.6

Tungsten[d] (metric tons)	1972	1973
China[e]	7,484	7,983
USSR[e]	7,212	7,394
United States	3,696	3,436
Thailand	3,343	2,601
South Korea	1,984	2,252
Bolivia	2,233	2,184
North Korea[e]	2,150	2,155
Canada	1,600	2,084
Portugal	1,403	1,512
Australia	1,529	1,220
Brazil	1,141	951
Japan	897	940
Peru	856	795
Total (est.)	38,316	38,701

Uranium Oxide (U_3O_8) (metric tons)	1972	1973
United States	11,703	12,006
Canada	4,432	4,354
South Africa	3,628	3,094
France	1,760	1,769
Niger	867	948
Gabon	523	645
Total (est.)[f]	23,246	23,120

Zinc (smelter) (thousands of metric tons)	1972	1973
Japan	804.7	842.7
USSR[e]	650.4	671.3
Canada	476.2	532.5
United States	574.4	491.1
Australia	294.7	297.2
Belgium	257.4	281.1
France	261.5	257.8
West Germany	213.6	240.9
Poland	228.0	235.0
Italy	155.9	190.1
North Korea[e]	119.7	129.7
Spain	99.7	106.9
China[e]	99.8	99.8
United Kingdom	73.8	83.8
Norway	73.3	80.5
Finland	81.1	80.1
Bulgaria	80.0	80.0
Mexico	79.4	67.2
Total (est.)	5,121.2	5,257.4

* Output of countries not individually listed and estimates are included in world totals. [a] Exports. [b] Smelter. [c] Marketable in equivalent K_2O. [d] Contained tungsten (W basis). [e] Estimated. [f] Excludes all Socialist bloc countries. [g] Refined. [h] Gross weight. [i] Combined bituminous and lignite. [k] Formerly Congo, Kinshasa. NA—Not available. [m] Includes blast furnace ferroalloys except ferromanganese and spiegeleisen. [n] Includes ferroalloys. [o] Includes blast furnace ferroalloys. [p] Includes secondary. [q] Includes alloys. [r] Output of Cominco, excludes production (if any) by minor producers.

In March 1974, Jamaica, Australia, Guyana, Surinam, Guinea, and Yugoslavia formed the International Bauxite Association (IBA) to control the production and price of bauxite, the ore of aluminum. These countries account for more than 80% of the Free World's bauxite production, but only 3% of aluminum output, one reason for forming the group. The IBA had its organizational meeting in the fall, at which the Dominican Republic, Ghana, and Haiti were admitted as members.

An organization of iron-exporting countries was proposed, but its creation was uncertain without the support of Brazil and Sweden. Cartels for other metals are under consideration, including tungsten, zinc, and silver.

Inflation, Recession, and Prices. High consumer demand for minerals in 1973–74, together with various international monetary uncertainties and inflation, resulted in record high prices for many minerals in 1974. On April 1, for example, copper was $1.52 per pound on the London Metal Exchange (LME); however, by late September it fell briefly below $0.60.

With some fluctuation, gold prices reached several highs during the year, among them $190.50 per ounce on November 18. U. S. producer's price for aluminum ingot rose to $0.39 per pound in September, but by late November there were reports of producer discounts of 1 to 2 cents per pound. Phosphate prices were more than tripled by major producers to over $70 per ton. Mineral prices began to weaken toward the end of 1974 as demand slackened in response to the recession.

Meanwhile, inflation had its impact on mining. All production cost components rose alarmingly throughout the world with predictable impact on mineral prices. Worse, new mining projects under construction found their costs soaring. Heavy equipment, which requires a manufacturing lead time of up to two years, was being sold, with price to be set at the time of delivery. Under these conditions, the cost of a large new copper project (mine, concentrator, smelter) in a remote location, for example, has doubled or more in the last two years. At least three such projects are now expected to cost about $1 billion each.

Precious Metals. Despite the increased price of gold, 1973 production declined 3.7%. By late 1974, however, many new, mostly small mines were under development. The gold price has revived the South African mines, but they are experiencing the onset of a serious labor shortage which will necessitate an expensive program of mechanization. Silver production increased 20% in 1973, and 1974 prices (Handy & Harman) ranged from $3.22 per ounce in January to a year-end figure of about $4.20 (it peaked at $6.70 in February). Platinum production increased slightly and evaluation of a promising platinum prospect began in the western United States in 1974.

Ferrous Metals and Ores. Notwithstanding increased 1973–74 output of iron ore, pig iron and steel (about 10% each in 1973), a serious shortage of steel developed in 1973 and did not begin to abate until late in 1974 as the recession reduced consumption. Development of several large new iron ore projects in the Ivory Coast, Angola, Brazil, and Venezuela was initiated in 1974, with completion planned for late in the decade.

More projects are contemplated for 1975, especially in Australia. Demand for nickel remained strong in the face of tight supplies which raised the producers' cathode price from $1.62 to $1.85 per pound in May. At year-end, Falconbridge instigated another rise to $2.05. Several new nickel mines are being constructed. Molybdenum output rose in 1973, and demand apparently continued strong through 1974, if the more or less steady rise in price, partially affected by inflation, is any guide.

Nonferrous Metals. Copper production, strong in 1973, was cut back toward the end of 1974 as demand and prices fell. Worldwide exploration and the development of major new mines—as in Zaire, Mexico, Poland, and Peru—continued in recognition of long-term demand and the need to diversify sources to lessen the impact of local political disturbances. Completion in 1974–75 of Zambia's nationalization program, for example, is expected to greatly reduce output there.

Zinc was in moderately short supply during 1974 until recession weakened demand at year end. Average monthly zinc prices on the LME declined to about 34–36 cents per pound from 79 cents in March, while the U. S. producer price rose through the year from about 31 cents to 37–39 cents by December. Worldwide exploration for zinc continues strong.

Aluminum, too, was in short supply through most of 1973–74, and although demand fell late in 1974, plans to expand world production continues. Creation of the IBA is strengthening the development of alternative ores to bauxite, and several pilot plants came into production during 1974.

For the second year, tin consumption outstripped production, and the average monthly LME cash price ranged from over $4 per pound to about $3.30–$3.40 at year end after beginning low in January 1974.

Miscellaneous. After several years of oversupply, demand for phosphate and potash reached a point that started the development of new mines in 1974. A new worldwide uranium boom is rapidly developing, and the spot price for uranium oxide (U_3O_8) rose from $6 per pound early in 1973 to over $14 late in 1974. Several new uranium mines were under construction or commissioned in 1974, and more are planned for 1975–76.

FRANK H. SKELDING
Manager, Market Research, Fluor Utah, Inc.

MINNESOTA

Following the national trend, Minnesota voters gave overwhelming support to the Democratic party in the November election. They were registering not only disapproval of the Republicans in the wake of the scandals that rocked the Republican administration in Washington but distress over inflation and the depressed economy, especially in the hard-hit agricultural sector. The election results reflected as well the strength of the state Democratic-Farmer-Labor organization (DFL), led by Gov. Wendell R. Anderson and U. S. Senators Hubert H. Humphrey and Walter F. Mondale.

Elections. Incumbent Governor Anderson garnered a record 65% of the vote on November 5. Swept into office with him were all the DFL candidates for state constitutional office and a lopsided majority, 104–30, in the state House of Representatives. Five of the eight U. S. congressmen elected are DFLers; Senators Humphrey and Mondale were not up for reelection. Earlier, on April 30, DFL Mayor Lawrence Cohen was returned for a second term in St. Paul; all seven City Council seats also went to members of the Democratic-Farmer-Labor organization.

Economy. A late spring, floods, a month-long drought in June, and a severe frost early in September made the 1974 growing season in Minnesota one of the worst in memory. Frost damage alone was estimated at $500 million. Shortages of fertilizer and low farm prices together with the abbreviated crop season led to predictions of a disaster year for Minnesota agriculture; the economic loss to the state was likely to total $1 billion. On November 4 cattlemen in Pillager dramatized their protest against federal price policies by slaughtering and burying calves.

At the Port of Duluth there was a 56% decline in the tonnage of international cargo handled, in comparison with the 1973 level, owing to increased fuel costs and labor unrest, climaxed by a strike of grain handlers in September and October.

Courts. On August 23, after a 388-day trial, Federal District Judge Miles Lord declared the evidence on the merits of the Reserve Mining Company case closed; jurisdiction in this important environmental lawsuit thus passed to the 8th Circuit Court of Appeals, with an ultimate appeal to the U. S. Supreme Court almost certain. In April, Judge Lord had ruled that Reserve's discharge of taconite tailings into Lake Superior created an immediately serious public health hazard and closed the company's plant at Silver Bay. But a three-judge panel of the 8th Circuit, while agreeing that pollution existed, did not find the danger to area residents imminent and permitted Reserve to reopen and continue dumping tailings into the lake. It ordered the company to prepare plans for on-land disposal of the refuse.

In another U. S. District Court chamber in the Twin Cities, the emotion-fraught "Wounded Knee" trial attracted national attention during its eight-month course. The defendants, Russell Means and Dennis Banks, had in 1973 led the forces of the American Indian Movement that occupied the South Dakota reservation village of Wounded Knee. Their attorney, activist William Kunstler, presented them as rebel-heroes of a social movement who were protesting against government abuse of Indian rights; the prosecution charged them with conspiracy and larceny. In an abrupt conclusion to the trial, Judge Fred Nicol dismissed all charges against the two, citing gross misconduct by the government.

Educational-Cultural Scene. In October three major architectural complexes were dedicated in the state. The Minneapolis Society of Fine Arts Park, a $26-million facility designed by Kenzo Tange, encompasses the remodeled Minneapolis Institute of Arts building and new buildings for the Minneapolis College of Art and Design and the Children's Theatre Company and School. The Minnesota Orchestra settled into its new home in the $10-million Orchestra Hall in Minneapolis. In Rochester a $25-million, two-building addition to the Mayo Clinic was opened, housing an extensive diagnostic laboratory and a Center for Research in Human Behavior, as well as other units.

On November 26, C. Peter McGrath was inaugurated as 11th president of the University of Minnesota, where the student enrollment of 51,834 was the highest in the school's history.

1974 Legislative Session. The legislature appropriated $28 million to supplement the $3.5 billion appropriated in 1973 for the 1973–75 biennium. The largest sums of the new funds were allocated to assist school districts and welfare agencies in meeting spiraling costs and to support development of mass transit. Among the major actions of the session were a modified no-fault insurance law to take effect in 1975, and a campaign ethics law providing for partial public funding of political campaigns and requiring disclosure of contributions.

JEANNE SINNEN, *University of Minnesota Press*

MINNESOTA • Information Highlights

Area: 84,068 square miles (217,736 sq km).
Population (1973 est.): 3,897,000. *Density:* 49 per sq mi.
Chief Cities (1970 census): St. Paul, the capital, 309,828; Minneapolis, 434,400.
Government (1974): *Chief Officers*—governor, Wendell R. Anderson (Democratic-Farmer-Labor); lt. gov., Rudy Perpich (DFL). *Legislature*—Senate, 67 members; House of Representatives, 134 members.
Education (1973–74): *Enrollment*—public elementary schools, 460,000 pupils; public secondary, 445,000; nonpublic, 111,900; colleges and universities, 163,781 students. *Public school expenditures,* $1,035,135,000 ($1,201 per pupil).
State Finances (fiscal year 1973): *Revenues,* $2,747,783,000; *expenditures,* $2,591,532,000.
Personal Income (1973): $19,175,000,000; per capita, $4,921.
Labor Force (July 1974): *Nonagricultural wage and salary earners,* 1,493,100.

MISSISSIPPI

The energy crisis, inflation, and other economic problems troubled Mississippians throughout 1974. Proving especially bothersome were periodic gasoline shortages and the soaring cost of food and utilities, particularly electricity. The 1974 legislative session was productive, if not imaginative, and congressional elections were less than exciting.

The Legislature. The 1974 legislative session began with third-year governor William L. Waller showing renewed strength in his efforts to wrest power from an increasingly dominant legislature but ended with lawmakers overriding 4 gubernatorial vetoes. This action marked the first time since 1942 that a veto had been set aside.

In other actions the legislature adopted a record general fund budget without any increase in taxes; enacted a number of county government "reforms," including mandatory centralized purchasing; authorized an increase in general interest rates from 8% to 10%; and restored the death penalty for specified murder cases, air piracy, and rape of a child under 12. Also approved during the 90-day session were bills reorganizing the penitentiary under a strong superintendent–weak board arrangement, combining mental health services under a new agency, and granting university status to 5 colleges.

Congressional Elections. All 5 incumbent congressmen won reelection on November 5. The state's 2 long-term Democratic congressmen, Jamie Whitten (1st Dist.) and G. V. Montgomery (3d Dist.), were nominated without opposition and reelected without a Republican challenge. The 3 freshmen congressmen—David Bowen (D, 2d Dist.), Thad Cochran (R, 4th Dist.), and Trent Lott (R, 5th Dist.)—faced opposition in both the June primaries and the November election. While the congressional campaign generated only limited voter interest, it did bring Vice President Ford to Mississippi in August.

James Meredith, perhaps best known as the first black student to enroll at the University of Mississippi (1962), led a 5-man field in the 4th District Democratic primary but withdrew from the runoff in order to run as an independent in the general election. Upon denial of his qualifying petition by the state Board of Election Commissioners, and affirmation of that denial by the Mississippi Supreme Court, Meredith turned to the federal courts. In late October a three-judge federal panel rejected Meredith's bid for a place on the ballot.

Judicial Actions. A three-judge federal panel on February 7 made permanent a 1971 injunction against the use of Mississippi's 1970 Open Primary Law and denied a motion for rehearing. Final death for the law came on April 26 when it was rejected by U. S. Attorney General William Saxbe.

In other court actions, U. S. District Judge William C. Keady ruled that the Mississippi Cooperative Extension Service had discriminated against black employees and must give priority in future promotions to former Negro county agents and home demonstration agents. On June 17, the U. S. Supreme Court refused to stay a 5th Circuit Court of Appeals order calling for further desegregation of the Mississippi Highway Safety Patrol.

Teacher Protest. Angered because the Legislature voted pay raises for future lawmakers but failed to increase teachers salaries, several hundred public schoolteachers staged a one-day walkout in mid-April. Governor Waller promised a special legislative session to consider pay raises and other education needs, but only if state finances supported such a session. Speculation about the session ended in August with the governor's announcement that funds were not sufficient to warrant a meeting.

Other Events. In late March and early April, Mississippi poultrymen were forced to destroy several million market-ready chickens after they were found to contain excessive amounts of Dieldrin pesticide. Measures to compensate chicken farmers for their losses were introduced in Congress but failed to gain approval.

On April 25, President Richard M. Nixon addressed the 25th annual meeting of the Mississippi Economic Council in Jackson.

The U. S. Department of Health, Education, and Welfare in June labeled Mississippi's desegregation plan for senior colleges "an acceptable component" but rejected the overall plan because it failed to include junior colleges. A federal suit was averted when the 16 independent junior colleges agreed to submit a coordinated plan.

Mid-April floods in 34 southern Mississippi counties accounted for at least 9 deaths, forced nearly 10,000 persons from their homes, and produced an estimated $50 million in property damage.

DANA B. BRAMMER
University of Mississippi

MISSISSIPPI • Information Highlights

Area: 47,716 square miles (123,584 sq km).
Population (1973 est.): 2,281,000. *Density:* 48 per sq mi.
Chief Cities (1970 census): Jackson, the capital, 153,968; Biloxi, 48,486; Meridian, 45,083.
Government (1974): *Chief Officers*—governor, William L. Waller (D); lt. gov., William Winter (D). *Legislature*—Senate, 52 members (50 D, 2 R); House of Representatives, 122 members (119 D, 2 R, 1 Independent).
Education (1973–74): *Enrollment*—public elementary schools, 293,416 pupils; public secondary, 226,370; nonpublic, 65,300; colleges and universities, 82,255 students. *Public school expenditures,* $381,659,000 ($787 per pupil).
State Finances (fiscal year 1973): *Revenues,* $1,348,448,000; *expenditures,* $1,217,098,000.
Personal Income (1973): $7,864,000,000.
Labor Force (June 1974): *Nonagricultural wage and salary earners,* 691,200; *insured unemployed,* 8,900 (1.7%).

MISSOURI

Democrats overwhelmed Republicans in most elections in Missouri in 1974. Sen. Thomas F. Eagleton, aided by a sympathy vote for his removal from the Democratic national ticket in 1972, warded off a determined challenge by former Congressman Thomas B. Curtis to win by nearly 250,000 votes. The state's nine Democratic congressmen all were reelected in landslides, but the lone Republican congressman, Gene Taylor, narrowly edged his Democratic challenger in heavily Republican southwest Missouri. Democrats also unseated Republican John D. Ashcroft as state auditor, putting Jackson County (Kansas City) executive George W. Lehr in his place. The General Assembly, already heavily Democratic, had its Democratic strength increased in both houses.

State Government. A special legislative session called by Gov. Christopher S. Bond early in the year succeeded where previous sessions had failed in fulfilling a voter mandate to reorganize the state government. The reorganization, which took place July 1, converted 87 state agencies into 14 new departments. The reorganization was a compromise between what Republican Bond and Democratic legislative leaders were seeking. Bond's efforts to replace patronage in the Department of Revenue and a few other state departments with a merit system was turned down by the legislature, however. The special legislative session also reduced the state's speed limit to 55 mph to conserve gasoline.

Campaign Reform. Democrats were blaming Republicans and Republicans were blaming Democrats for the failure to approve a campaign financing reform in the regular legislative session. A group of citizens and legislators, however, was not accepting the excuses and promptly gathered more than 100,000 signatures to put the Watergate-inspired reform on the November ballot. The proposition carried the state by more than a 3-to-1 margin, thus setting limits on campaign giving and spending, requiring full disclosure of contributions and outside interests, and establishing a commission to enforce it.

Legislation. The elimination of the intangible tax on interest on bank accounts and the personal property tax on household goods was approved by the General Assembly in 1974, following the adoption of a 1973 constitutional amendment that authorized the change. The legislature also wrote a new law attempting to regulate abortions after the U. S. Supreme Court ruled the state's previous law was invalid. The new law was immediately challenged in court. Also, an effort to reinstate the death penalty failed.

A special legislative session was called for late in the year to attempt to eliminate the 8% ceiling on home mortgage loans. Leaders and builders contended this ceiling was making it impossible to sell real estate in the state.

Investigations. A federal grand jury probe into alleged influence peddling in the administration (1965–73) of former Gov. Warren E. Hearnes centered around Delton L. Houtchens, a Clinton lawyer and Democratic state chairman for all eight years Hearnes was in office. It was revealed that Houtchens had received more than $400,000 in public relations retainers in the late 1960's. The retainers were generally found to be contingent on the receipt of state business. Among those placing Houtchens on retainer were an Indiana firm that makes the state's driver license cards, banks that received interest-free state deposits, individuals seeking bank charters, architects with sizable state contracts, as well as state fair concessionaires.

An investigation by the state insurance division and the St. Louis *Globe-Democrat* revealed that many insurance firms and employers were being cheated by doctors, insurance agents, and others who falsified accident reports or sick-leave vouchers. A state welfare investigation was begun late in the year into alleged abuses in the food-stamp program.

In another investigation, Missouri legislators lambasted the state Agriculture Department's lease of the state fairgrounds for a rock music festival. More than 100,000 showed up for the festival in July and, according to some legislators, they caused extensive damage to the fairgrounds. Five persons were indicted by a state grand jury for their roles in the festival.

Court Decisions. The Missouri constitution's strict provisions on the separation of church and state were upheld by state and federal supreme courts in decisions prohibiting state-financed busing of parochial school children and nullifying a state law providing free textbooks to private-school children. The U. S. Supreme Court held, however, that federal funds for special remedial work must be made available to parochial school students.

RONALD D. WILLNOW
St. Louis "Post-Dispatch"

MISSOURI • Information Highlights

Area: 69,686 square miles (180,487 sq km).
Population (1973 est.): 4,757,000. *Density:* 69 per sq mi.
Chief Cities (1970 census): Jefferson City, the capital, 32,407; St. Louis, 622,236.
Government (1974): *Chief Officers*—governor, Christopher S. Bond (R); lt. gov., William C. Phelps (R). *General Assembly*—Senate, 34 members (21 D, 13 R); House of Representatives, 163 members (97 D, 65 R, 1 vacancy).
Education (1973–74): *Enrollment*—public elementary schools, 700,674 pupils; public secondary, 319,129; nonpublic, 99,400; colleges and universities, 191,749 students. *Public school expenditures,* $871,996,000 ($963 per pupil).
State Finances (fiscal year 1973): *Revenues,* $2,086,447,000; *expenditures,* $1,848,756,000.
Personal Income (1973): $22,227,000,000.
Labor Force (July 1974): *Nonagricultural wage and salary earners,* 1,754,900; *insured unemployed,* 34,100 (2.4%).

MONGOLIA • Information Highlights

Official Name: Mongolian People's Republic.
Location: East central Asia.
Area: 604,248 square miles (1,565,000 sq km).
Population (1974 est.): 1,377,900.
Chief Cities (1969 census): Ulan Bator, the capital, 267,400; Darkhan, 22,800.
Monetary Unit: Tugrik (3.20 tugriks equal U. S.$1, July 1974).
Gross National Product (1973 est.): $840,000,000.
Manufacturing (major products): Processed foods, leather goods.
Major Agricultural Products: Livestock, wheat.

MONGOLIA

In June 1974, Yumzhagiyn Tsedenbal became president, relinquishing the premiership to 48-year-old Jambyn Batmounkh, an economist and former professor.

Mongolia in 1974 achieved a 9.8% gain over 1973 in industrial output and exceeded the economic plan in crop acreage and meat production. Much of the economy was administered by joint Soviet-Mongolian companies engaged in nonferrous metallurgy, mining, mineral prospecting, transport, trade, and construction. In Moscow in July, Tsedenbal signed a treaty providing more Soviet technical aid to Mongolia.

With recognition by West Germany in January, Mongolia in 1974 maintained diplomatic relations with 64 foreign governments. Relations with Communist China remained tense during the year, particularly after a Chinese nuclear test explosion occurred near the Mongolian border.

ELLSWORTH RAYMOND
New York University

MONTANA

Broad well-researched legislation, innovative experiment in government structure, unrest in state agencies, and continued progress in environmental and agricultural affairs marked the year 1974 in Montana.

Legislation. An annual legislative session, decreed in the 1972 constitution, was continued by the second session of the 43rd Assembly. It considered 300 measures held over from the first session, including a controversial gambling bill. Compromise produced a mild law giving final decision on limited options to city and county governments.

A 55-mile per hour highway speed limit was passed to meet a federal request and safeguard highway funding. The proposed Equal Rights Amendment to the federal constitution was ratified, a state educational TV system was initiated, abortion was legalized, a uniform probate code was adopted, and personal and household property was exempted from taxation.

Government Structure. Prolonged direct attack against the 1972 constitution ceased when the U. S. Supreme Court refused an appeal. Under provisions of the constitution, governmental review commissions were chosen in the November elections in every city, town, and county (182 in all). The commissions are to formulate an alternative form of government for possible choice in 1976. Similar procedures will take place every ten years.

A Democratic landslide in the November elections replaced Republican Congressman Richard Shoup with Democrat Max Baucus. The election also approved an initiative providing for a biennial legislative session of 90 days to replace the present annual 60-day session.

State Agencies. A financial surplus of some $27 million was partially used by the legislature to assist custodial institutions and the university system, and salaries were increased for the state's lower paid workers.

Environment. Environmental action centered on the future of coal strip-mining in eastern Montana. The legislature declared a moratorium on water developments on the Yellowstone River pending further study concerning needs for proposed electric power and coal gasification plants, also held in abeyance by legislative act. A controversial shipment of a trainload of coal to Japan for testing resulted in Japan's decision not to purchase large quantities of Montana coal.

Additional legislation was enacted to restrict permanent building on floodplains and establish adequate planning and zoning for rural lands against unwise housing developments.

Agriculture. Despite a hot dry summer and declining livestock prices, Montana farms and ranches yielded a record $1.14 billion income. The legislature funded a continuing study to determine causes and remedies for large amounts of productive lands being ruined by saline seep. A movement to increase the sales of Montana's agricultural products in international markets led to the shipment of trainload lots of grain to West Coast ports. It also led to the establishment of the Port of Butte, where goods were cleared through customs for shipment in large quantities direct to foreign ports.

MERRILL G. BURLINGAME
Montana State University

MONTANA • Information Highlights

Area: 147,138 square miles (381,087 sq. km.).
Population (1973 est.): 721,000. *Density:* 5 per sq. mi.
Chief Cities: Billings, 61,581; Great Falls, 60,091.
Government (1974): *Chief Officers*—governor, Thomas L. Judge (D); lt. gov., William E. Christiansen (D). *Legislative Assembly*—Senate, 50 members; House of Representatives, 100 members.
Education (1973–74): *Enrollment*—public elementary schools, 113,900 pupils; public secondary, 56,100; nonpublic, 10,500; colleges and universities, 27,269 students. *Public school expenditures,* $160,326,000 ($1,015 per pupil).
State Finances (fiscal year 1973): *Revenues,* $499,593,-000; *Expenditures,* $439,600,000.
Personal Income (1973): $3,186,000,000; per capita, $4,418.
Labor Force (June 1974): *Nonagricultural wage and salary earners,* 244,400; *Insured unemployed,* 5,300 (3.3%).

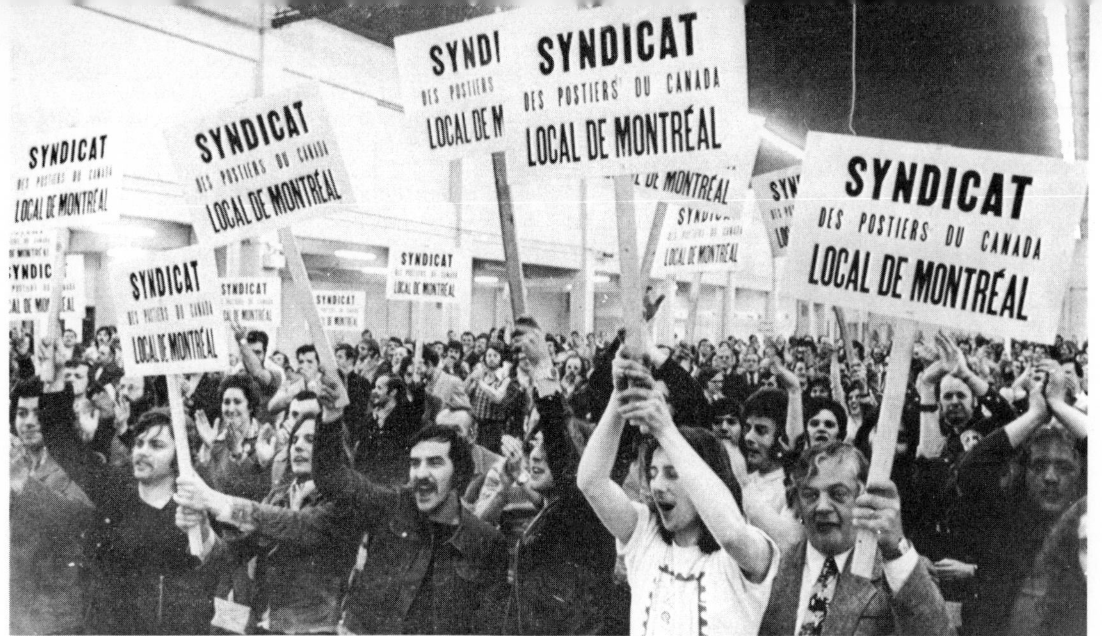

UPI

Montreal postal workers hail an agreement ending a nationwide strike against the postal service in April.

MONTREAL

Preparations for the 1976 Summer Olympic Games, mayoralty and council elections, and a six-week strike of maintenance workers of the bus and metro services dominated news in the city of Montreal in 1974. The city was particularly affected by Provincial Bill 22, which made French the official language of Quebec.

Elections. Undoubtedly the biggest news of the year in Montreal was the rise of an opposition in the City Council. At the mayoralty and council elections of November 10, a new party, the Montreal Citizens Movement (MCM), won 17 of the 60 seats. This new party, led by Jacques Couture, a Jesuit priest and social worker, appealed to Montrealers on the grounds that there had been no effective opposition in City Hall for over a decade, that housing construction and renewal were being given a very low priority by the city administration, that the city had performed poorly in handling labor relations, and that the Council Executive Committee was being extremely secretive about the details of the city budget for the 1976 Olympic Games. They also drew attention to the fact that city services had generally deteriorated in the last year or two, in order to economize, as they suggested, for the Olympics, in spite of Mayor Jean Drapeau's denials.

Only 35% of the voters turned out at the polls, but this number was sufficient to indicate considerable dissatisfaction. Most members of the ruling Civic party who were returned to office, including Mayor Drapeau, had their support reduced by 25% to 40%. The MCM members were elected primarily in those electorates dominated by either low-income groups and/or the English-speaking population of the city.

Transportation Strike. The transportation strike that ran from August 7 to September 19 was due primarily to the fact that the city would not pay the Metro maintenance workers a cost-of-living allowance of $750 for 1974. The strike was finally settled with such a payment, but not before there was considerable dissatisfaction on the part of residents, not only with the lack of public transportation (though some buses did run), but also with the dangerous level of pollution due to the increased number of automobiles entering the city daily. Montreal at the best of times has a serious pollution problem, and it was greatly aggravated by the transportation strike.

Plans for the Olympic Games. The residents of Montreal remain uneasy about the financing of the Olympic Games. Progress in construction has been slow, but it appeared that all amenities would be completed on time. Revenue from a special lottery, and from the sale of stamps and coins, lived up to expectations. Throughout the first half of 1974 the financing of the Olympic Village remained uncertain, but eventually it was stated that the funds were secure and construction of this controversial village proceeded. All final plans were approved by the International Olympic Committee.

Effects of Bill 22. Largely because Montreal is the chief focus of the English-speaking community of the province of Quebec, it was there that one heard most of the objections to Bill 22, the Official Languages Act, which made French the official language of the province. However, it was too early to forecast the result of these objections.

See also QUEBEC.

THEO L. HILLS
McGill University

MOROCCO

For Morocco, 1974 was marked by stunning economic gains, thanks to a dramatic upsurge in world demand for phosphates, and by a flaring of tensions between Madrid and Rabat, as King Hassan II vociferously laid claim to the tiny, phosphate-rich territory of Spanish Sahara. Between the buoyant economy and preoccupation with Spain, the executive-style monarch continued to consolidate his authority, shrewdly mixing liberalization with intolerance to opposition.

Political Events. King Hassan's continuing attempt in 1974 to secure his reign, after years of attempts on his life and attacks on his government, meant a continuation of intrigues that have become symptomatic of Moroccan political life. The year began inauspiciously when a young Moroccan was arrested at Britain's Heathrow airport, alleged to be a member of a group that was planning to assassinate or kidnap Morocco's ambassador to London in order to force Hassan to change his domestic policies. It soon became clear, however, that the period of stability, albeit tenuous, that analysts had forecast for Morocco had indeed begun.

During the year, political trials continued with hundreds facing charges from an uprising among the Atlas Mountain and Saharan peoples in March 1973. Although press reports vary, it seems clear that more than 140 persons were condemned to death, 84 of them in absentia. Among the fugitives was thrice-condemned Mohammad Basri, leader of the outlawed Socialist opposition party, Union Nationale des Forces Populaires (UNFP).

Mass trials were seen as an attempt finally to wipe out UNFP, as Hassan kept the heat on his political foes. It is reported that there are between 3,000 and 4,000 political prisoners in Morocco, most of them not charged or tried. Meanwhile, Hassan was making concessions to his critics, mostly in the form of a promise to establish Parliament, disbanded in 1965, and to institute judicial reform. On the surface, these pledges seemed to be quieting the traditional opposition party, Istiqlal, or at least moving it into more of a loyal opposition role than it had been playing.

Foreign Relations. As the year 1974 drew to a close, it seemed as if Morocco was leaning toward a diplomatic solution to the problem of who should control Spanish Sahara, now under Spain's authority and the source of a recently discovered phosphate deposit thought to be the world's richest. After Moroccan troops had amassed on the Spanish Sahara frontier, King Hassan backed away from his saber-rattling and called for settlement of the issue through a World Court decision. Earlier, he had staunchly pledged to free the sparsely populated territory, by force if necessary.

Spain has promised a 1975 referendum to allow the territory's population to decide its future. Hassan even hinted that the referendum might be acceptable if Spanish troops are withdrawn from the territory and refugees are allowed to return. Morocco has argued that a referendum under present conditions would favor the Spanish, since most of the country's nonnomadic residents (likely voters in any election) are of Spanish stock.

A flurry of diplomacy during the year indicated that Hassan was seeking support from the French, who still are pressing him for settlement of claims of French settlers whose property was seized in a recent nationalization move. Hassan's diplomacy did not appear to have added any pressure to Spain. Even the Organization for African Unity tended to veer toward separate independence for the tiny territory, which is also considered by Mauritania to be part of its national boundary.

The Economy. Clearly, Morocco's claims to Spanish Sahara are, at least in part, based on that territory's rich phosphate supply, and if any mineral is important to Rabat, it is phosphates. Morocco is the world's third-largest producer of phosphates (after the United States and Soviet Union), but is the world's top exporter of the mineral, which accounts for 30% of all Moroccan exports. Annexation of Spanish Sahara could eliminate potential competition, as well as bolster Morocco's supplies.

Hassan has used phosphates to become one of the few African nations, without oil, to experience economic boom. During 1974, Rabat boosted the price of phosphates threefold, from $14 to $63 a ton. Annual phosphate earnings are expected to top $1.5 billion, as demand for the mineral increases as an ingredient of chemical fertilizers. Morocco's gross national product growth was expected to climb back to around 10% in 1974, as compared with 2.5% in the year 1973. It is estimated that more than 80% of the country's capital investment under its current five-year plan (1973–77) can now be financed out of earnings from natural resources.

ROBERT L. DENERSTEIN and NANCY MCKEON
The African-American Institute

MOROCCO • Information Highlights

Official Name: Kingdom of Morocco.
Location: Northwest Africa.
Area: 172,413 square miles (446,550 sq km).
Population (1973 est.): 17,400,000.
Chief Cities (1971 census): Rabat, the capital, 435,510 (Rabat-Sale); Casablanca, 1,371,330; Marrakesh, 330,400; Fez, 321,460.
Government: *Head of state,* Hassan II, king (acceded 1961). *Head of government,* Ahmed Osman, premier (took office 1972).
Monetary Unit: Dirham (4.39 dirhams equal U. S.$1, May 1974).
Gross National Product (1972 est.): $4,844,000,000.
Manufacturing (major products): Processed foods, metals, textiles, wine, cement, leather goods, chemicals and pharmaceuticals.
Major Agricultural Products: Barley, wheat, citrus fruits, vegetables, sugar beets, almonds, tomatoes, grapes, sheep, wool.
Foreign Trade (1973): *Exports,* $822,000,000; *imports,* $1,016,000,000.

© DINO DE LAURENTIS CORP. 1974

In *Death Wish,* Charles Bronson avenges the savage mugging of his family by killing attackers in New York's Central Park.

Motion Pictures

Some years are known for an abundance of film disasters, but 1974 may be remembered in part for its disaster films. With the world sinking into the mire of inflation and other traumas, some Hollywood-oriented producers were convinced that the public was ready to be diverted with thrillers of threatened and actual doom. *Airport 1975* places stewardess Karen Black in the cockpit of a 747 crippled by a hole ripped through it, with gallant Charlton Heston being dropped inside by helicopter to take the controls. A subway train in New York is hijacked and passengers held hostage at threat of death in *The Taking of Pelham One Two Three.* In England, director Richard Lester made *Juggernaut,* in which a passenger ship is hijacked and about to be blown up with passengers and crew. For the showing of *Earthquake,* theaters were rigged with electronic systems that created a rumbling sensation to give audiences the feeling of being in danger themselves. *The Towering Inferno* was another star-studded exercise in terror, this one about a high-rise building that catches fire.

Foreign Films. In a more serious vein, a respectable number of films fitting the designation of American product reached levels of distinction, artistic or charismatic. But the best of the year's releases, the films most likely to excite the buffs and endure as major works, were dominated by pictures from Europe. Despite the economic difficulties of the European film indus-

© 1974 BY LONG ROAD PRODUCTIONS (PARAMOUNT)

(*Above*) Jack Nicholson and Faye Dunaway in *Chinatown.* (*Below*) Liv Ullman and Erland Josephson in Bergman's *Scenes from a Marriage.*

CINEMA 5

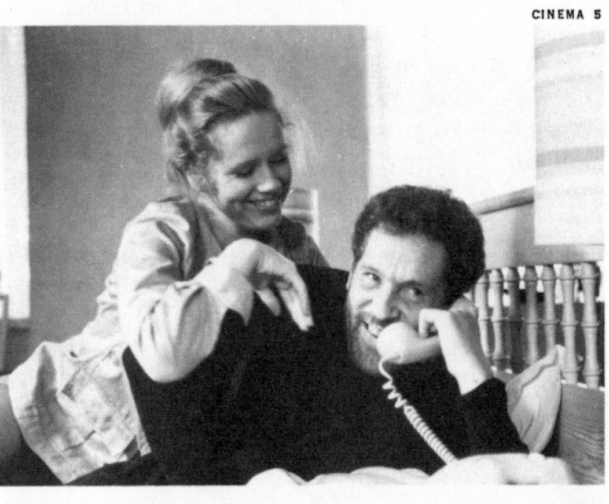

tries, major achievements evoked considerable excitement.

Veteran filmmaker Luis Buñuel again came through with a dazzler, *Le Fantôme de la Liberté.* Italian master Federico Fellini unveiled *Amarcord,* a sensitive and flamboyant recollection of Italy during the Mussolini years. The genius of Ingmar Bergman was present again with *Scenes from a Marriage,* originally made for Swedish television and reshaped by Bergman for theatrical distribution. The incisive probing of a relationship offered a showcase for what some consider Liv Ullmann's greatest performance.

Consider other riches. Louis Malle's *Lacombe, Lucien,* about a blank-faced, amoral youth who collaborates with the Nazis, impressively explores the banality of evil. Alain Resnais, true to his ability to master the visual and intellectual approach, made the beautifully crafted *Stavisky,* based on a scandal that rocked France in the 1930's. Several pictures of exceptional merit came from Germany. *A Free Woman* proved one of the deepest explorations of the plight of a woman who wants to break out of society's mold. A penetrating performance by Margarethe von Trotta was abetted by the deft direction of Volker Schlöndorff. Actor-turned-director Maximillian Schell made a superb film, *The Pedestrian,* about the exposure of a Nazi war criminal. Rainer Werner Fassbinder's *Fear Eats the Soul-Ali* is an unusual drama about love and prejudice and further cemented the director's growing reputation.

Two women directors gained considerable attention. Lina Wertmuller, who works in Italy, was increasingly lauded after the international release of her films *Love and Anarchy* and *The Seduction of Mimi,* both showing a special strength in style and tragicomic content. Liliana Cavani, also based in Italy, sent out shock waves with *The Night Porter,* starring Dirk Bogarde and Charlotte Rampling in a sadomasochistic binge amid Nazi trappings. In France, Bernard Blier's *Going Places* earned much admiration from more youthful audiences and the hostility of many of the older generation for its tale of hell-bent youth both sympathetic and viciously destructive. Veteran Claude Chabrol was back with a drama of lust and murder, *Wedding in Blood,* and celebrated Jean Renoir received a respectful but mixed reception with his satirical *Le Petit Théâtre de Jean Renoir.*

Canada was the source of one of the year's finest films, *The Apprenticeship of Duddy Kravitz,* starring American performer Richard Dreyfuss as a frenetic, grasping young man on the make. Ted Kotcheff directed. There was some activity in the budding film industry of Latin America, but nothing very distinguished achieved release. Ambitious Sergio Ricardo's *The Night of the Scarecrow,* a Brazilian picture which found its way into the New York Film Festival, was a daring but pretentious attempt to mix folk legend, revolution, comedy, tragedy, and music into an epic.

U. S. Films. The high quality of many foreign films was at variance with the continued depletion of the market for foreign-language films among American audiences. The overwhelming bulk of the public was opting for English-language attractions, mostly home produced. *The Sting,* which opened late in 1973, took the lion's share of Oscars at the Academy Awards event and piled up a huge gross. Of the new films, *Chinatown* was immensely popular and renewed the drawing power of star Jack Nicholson, also a standout in *The Last Detail.* Director Robert Altman won acclaim for *Thieves Like Us* and *California Split,* the latter a look at gambling fever, having more audience appeal. Comedy got a lift from Mel Brooks' satirical Western *Blazing Saddles,* and Brooks followed with *Young Frankenstein,* another spoof.

Nostalgia was still a major commodity, with *That's Entertainment,* a compilation of clips from MGM musicals, achieving enormous popularity. But another effort to tap the well of nostalgia, *The Great Gatsby,* met with little critical success despite extensive hoopla. Nostalgia king Peter Bogdanovich fizzled with *Daisy Miller,* based on the Henry James story.

The year was also marked by the feature film debuts of directors Terrence Malick, who did *Badlands,* story of a youthful crime spree, and Steven Spielberg who showed considerable promise with *Sugarland Express.* Francis Ford Coppola's *The Conversation* laid bare the dangers of wiretapping. Director Joseph Strick made a strong but underrated film about truckers, *Road Movie.* Art Carney, known primarily as a comedian, proved he could act by playing an elderly man exploring life in *Harry and Tonto.* Dustin Hoffman was back with a highly praised performance as Lenny Bruce in *Lenny.* The public was given *Godfather II,* and individualistic director John Cassavetes released his latest, *A Woman Under the Influence,* which turned out to be the only American film in the New York Film Festival.

Documentaries with special strength were *Attica,* an exposé of the revolt at the New York prison in 1971; *Promised Lands,* critic and filmmaker Susan Sontag's personal, contemplative look at the tragic Middle East situation; and *Antonia: A Portrait of the Woman,* a moving biography of orchestra conductor Antonia Brico.

Exploitation continued to be a major factor in the film business. Violence was a prime selling point, although there was an apparent drop-off in the making of black-oriented films touting such violence. Some effort to make more serious statements about the life of blacks could be noted, as in the appealing *Claudine.* One picture that drew sharp criticism was *Death Wish,* a skillful film starring Charles Bronson as a vigilante in New York who takes to killing muggers. The film had audiences cheering him each time

Mariangela Melato and Giancarlo Giannini try to avoid bigamy charges in *The Seduction of Mimi*.

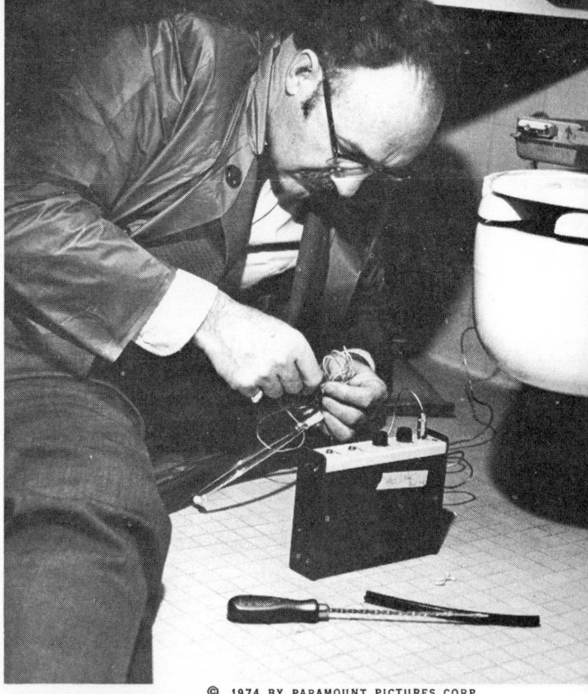

Gene Hackman installs a "bug" in a men's room in Francis Ford Coppola's *The Conversation*.

Richard Dreyfuss as Duddy in *The Apprenticeship of Duddy Kravitz* is determined to be "somebody" no matter what it costs those around him.

Elliott Gould (*left*) and George Segal are the compulsive gamblers of Robert Altman's *California Split*.

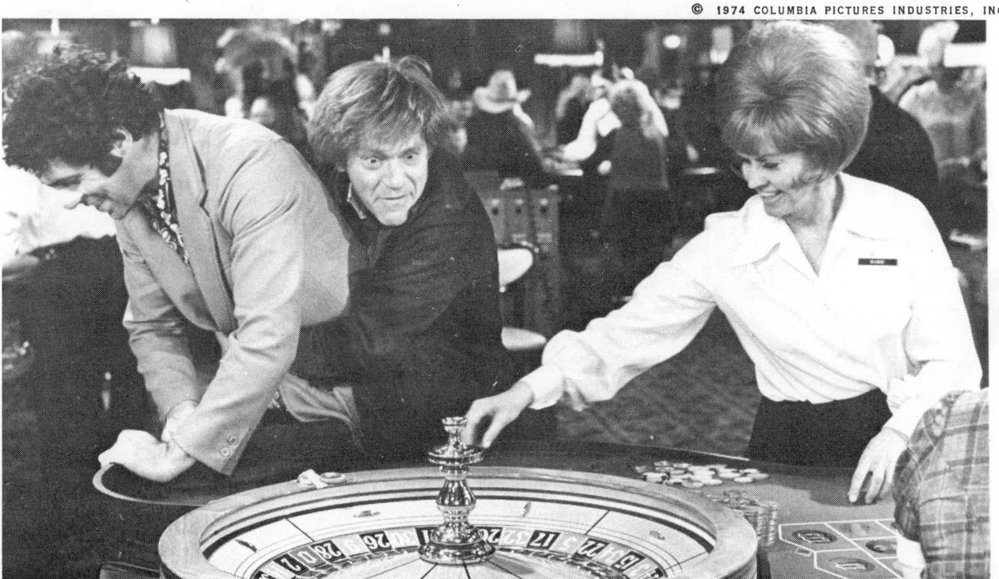

NOTABLE MOTION PICTURES OF 1974

The following list of films released in the United States in 1974 presents a cross section of the most popular, most typical, or most widely discussed motion pictures of the year.

Airport 1975. Director, Jack Smight; screenplay, Don Ingalls. With Charlton Heston, Karen Black, Gloria Swanson, Myrna Loy.

Amarcord. Director, Federico Fellini; screenplay, Fellini, Tonino Guerra. With Magali Noel, Bruno Zanin, Pupella Maggio, Armando Brancia.

Andy Warhol's Frankenstein. Director, Paul Morrissey; screenplay, Morrissey. With Joe Dallesandro, Monique Van Vooren, Udo Kier.

Antonia: A Portrait of the Woman. Directors, Judy Collins, Jill Godmilow; documentary. With Antonia Brico.

The Apprenticeship of Duddy Kravitz. Director, Ted Kotcheff; screenplay, Mordecai Richler from his own novel. With Richard Dreyfuss, Jack Warden, Joe Silver, Micheline Lanctôt, Denholm Elliot, Randy Quaid.

Attica. Director, Cinda Firestone; documentary. With the prisoners and guards of Attica prison.

Badlands. Director, Terrence Malick; screenplay, Malick. With Martin Sheen, Sissy Spacek.

Blazing Saddles. Director, Mel Brooks. Screenplay, Brooks, Norman Steinberg, Andrew Bergman, Richard Pryor, Alan Uger. With Cleavon Little, Gene Wilder, Harvey Korman, Madeline Kahn, Mel Brooks.

California Split. Director, Robert Altman; screenplay, Joseph Walsh. With Elliott Gould, George Segal.

Chinatown. Director, Roman Polanski; screenplay, Robert Towne. With Jack Nicholson, Faye Dunaway, John Huston.

Claudine. Director, John Berry; screenplay, Lester and Tina Pine. With Diahann Carroll, James Earl Jones.

The Conversation. Director Francis Ford Coppola; screenplay, Coppola. With Gene Hackman, Allen Garfield.

Daisy Miller. Director, Peter Bogdanovich; screenplay, Frederic Raphael from story by Henry James. With Cybill Shepherd, Barry Brown, Mildred Natwick, Cloris Leachman, Eileen Brennan.

Death Wish. Director, Michael Winner; screenplay, Wendell Mayes from Brian Garfield novel. With Charles Bronson, Vincent Gardenia, Hope Lange.

Earthquake. Director, Mark Robson; screenplay, George Fox, Mario Puzo. With Charlton Heston, Ava Gardner, George Kennedy, Genevieve Bujold.

Escape to Nowhere. Director, Claude Pinoteau; screenplay, Jean-Loup Dabadie. With Lino Ventura, Lea Massari.

Le Fantôme de la Liberté. Director, Luis Buñuel; screenplay, Buñuel, Jean-Claude Carriere from story by Gustavo A. Becquier. With Michel Piccoli, Monica Vitti, Jean-Claude Brialy, Michael Lonsdale, Adriana Asti.

Fear Eats the Soul-Ali. Director, Rainer Werner Fassbinder; screenplay, Fassbinder. With Brigitte Mira, El Hedi Ben Salem.

A Free Woman. Director, Volker Schlöndorff; screenplay, Schlöndorff, Margarethe von Trotta. With Margarethe von Trotta, Friedhelm Ptok.

The Front Page. Director, Billy Wilder; screenplay, Wilder, I. A. L. Diamond from the play by Ben Hecht and Charles MacArthur. With Jack Lemmon, Walter Matthau, Carol Burnett, Vincent Gardenia, David Wayne.

The Gambler. Director, Karel Reisz; screenplay, James Toback. With James Caan, Paul Sorvino, Lauren Hutton.

Godfather II. Director, Francis Ford Coppola; screenplay, Mario Puzo, Coppola. With Al Pacino, Diane Keaton, Robert Duval, Robert De Niro.

Going Places. Director, Bertrand Blier; screenplay, Philippe Dumarcay. With Gerard Depardieu, Patrick Dewaere, Miou-Miou, Jeanne Moreau.

The Great Gatsby. Director, Jack Clayton; screenplay, Francis Ford Coppola from novel by F. Scott Fitzgerald. With Robert Redford, Mia Farrow.

Harry and Tonto. Director, Paul Mazursky; screenplay, Josh Greenfeld, Mazursky. With Art Carney, Ellen Burstyn, Geraldine Fitzgerald, Joshua Mostel.

Juggernaut. Director, Richard Lester; screenplay, Richard Dekoker. With Richard Harris, Omar Sharif.

Lacombe, Lucien. Director, Louis Malle; screenplay, Malle, Patrick Modiano. With Pierre Blaise, Aurore Clément, Holger Lowenadler, Therese Giehse.

The Last Detail. Director, Hal Ashby; screenplay, Robert Towne. With Jack Nicholson, Otis Young.

Law and Disorder. Director, Ivan Passer; screenplay, Passer, William Richert, Kenneth Fishman. With Carroll O'Connor, Ernest Borgnine, Karen Black.

Lenny. Director, Bob Fosse; screenplay, Julian Barry from his own play. With Dustin Hoffman, Valerie Perrine.

The Little Prince. Director, Stanley Donen; screenplay and lyrics, Alan Jay Lerner from story by Antoine de Saint-Exupéry; music, Frederick Loewe. With Richard Kiley, Bob Fosse, Steven Warner, Gene Wilder.

Love and Anarchy. Director, Lina Wertmuller; screenplay, Wertmuller. With Giancarlo Giannini, Mariangela Melato, Lina Polito, Eros Pagni.

The Mother and the Whore. Director, Jean Eustache; screenplay, Eustache. With Bernadette Lafont, Jean-Pierre Léaud, Françoise Lebrun.

Murder on the Orient Express. Director, Sidney Lumet; screenplay, Paul Dehn from the book by Agatha Christie. With Albert Finney, Lauren Bacall, Martin Balsam, Jean-Pierre Cassel, John Gielgud, Anthony Perkins.

The Night Porter. Director, Liliana Cavani; screenplay, Cavani, Italo Moscati, from story by Cavani, Barbara Alberti, Amedeo Pagani. With Dirk Bogarde, Charlotte Rampling.

The Odessa File. Director, Ronald Neame; screenplay, Kenneth Ross, George Markstein from novel by Frederick Forsyth. With Jon Voight, Maximilian Schell, Mary Tamm.

The Parallax View. Director, Alan J. Pakula; screenplay, David Giler and Lorenzo Semple, Jr. With Warren Beatty, Hume Cronyn.

The Pedestrian. Director, Maximilian Schell; screenplay, Schell. With Maximilian Schell, Gustav Rudolf Sellner, Peter Hall.

Le Petit Théâtre de Jean Renoir. Director, Jean Renoir; screenplay, Renoir. With Jean Renoir, Jeanne Moreau, Pierre Olaf.

Promised Lands. Director, Susan Sontag; documentary.

Road Movie. Director, Joseph Strick; screenplay, Judith Raskin. With Robert Drivas, Barry Bostwick, Regina Baff.

The Savage is Loose. Director, George C. Scott; screenplay, Frank De Felitta, Max Ehrlich. With George C. Scott, Trish Van Devere, John David Carson, Lee H. Montgomery.

Scenes from a Marriage. Director, Ingmar Bergman; screenplay, Bergman. With Liv Ullmann, Erland Josephson, Bibi Andersson, Jan Malmsjo.

The Seduction of Mimi. Director, Lina Wertmuller; screenplay, Wertmuller. With Giancarlo Giannini, Mariangelo Melato.

Stavisky. Director, Alain Resnais; screenplay, Jorge Semprun. With Jean-Paul Belmondo, Anny Duperey, Charles Boyer, François Périer.

Sugarland Express. Director, Steven Spielberg; screenplay, Hal Barwood, Matthew Robbins. With Goldie Hawn, William Atherton, Michael Sacks, Ben Johnson.

That's Entertainment! Directed and written by Jack Haley, Jr. With Fred Astaire, Judy Garland, Gene Kelly, Frank Sinatra, Liza Minelli.

Thieves Like Us. Director, Robert Altman; screenplay, Calder Willingham, Joan Tewkesbury, Altman. With Keith Carradine, Shelley Duvall.

The Three Musketeers. Director, Richard Lester; screenplay, George MacDonald Fraser, suggested by the Alexandre Dumas novel. With Michael York, Oliver Reed, Raquel Welch, Richard Chamberlain.

The Towering Inferno. Director, John Guillermin; screenplay, Stirling Silliphant from the novels *The Tower* by Richard Martin Stern and *The Glass Inferno* by Thomas N. Scortia and Frank M. Robinson. With Steve McQueen, Paul Newman, William Holden, Faye Dunaway.

Wedding in Blood. Director, Claude Chabrol; screenplay Chabrol. With Michel Piccoli, Stephane Audran.

A Woman Under the Influence. Director, John Cassavetes; screenplay, Cassavetes. With Gena Rowlands, Peter Falk.

Young Frankenstein. Director, Mel Brooks; screenplay, Gene Wilder, Brooks, suggested by the Mary Wollstonecraft Shelley novel. With Gene Wilder, Peter Boyle, Madeline Kahn, Marty Feldman.

he killed, with the implication that this was an answer to the crime problem. The same problem was approached in a more responsible way in *Law and Disorder,* also set in New York. Directed by Czech filmmaker Ivan Passer, it viewed the tragedy, comedy, and ineptness of a group of citizens trying to take the law into their own hands. Violence was exploited for kicks in two campy films, *Andy Warhol's Frankenstein* and *Andy Warhol's Dracula,* both directed by Warhol's associate Paul Morrissey. The former was in 3-D. The films mixed satire with bloodbaths.

Censorship. The U. S. Supreme Court threw the motion picture industry into a panic in 1973 with what seemed like opening the path to widespread censorship. The court decreed that community standards were to prevail. The decision gave rise to widespread rewriting of state censorship laws and much litigation. Some fears as to how far this might go were allayed in 1974 when the court upset the banning of *Carnal Knowledge* in Georgia, thereby serving notice that pictures could not be frivolously censored as obscene. But by the end of 1974 the situation was still a maze of uncertainty. Hard-core pornography was under attack, with many films being seized. But pornography continued to be made and shown even while particular pictures were banned, and the entire definition of what is a community—state, county, city, town, neighborhood?—had yet to be defined by the court. Filmmakers noted a trend toward playing it safe and steering clear of questionable scenes in movies meant for general distribution (see also CENSORSHIP).

Economics. Shake-ups within the film industry and economic uncertainty persisted as the norm. Moviegoing attendance was on the increase, and a few of the veteran companies counted successes, while others were hard pressed. The major trend to be noted was the searching for new methods of distribution capable of yielding greater opportunities and profits. One method gaining popularity was "four-walling," the system under which a producer or distributor rents a theater for a flat fee. The theater owner has his guarantee, and should the picture prove a smash attraction the theater owner does not share in the windfall, which goes to the producer or distributor.

George C. Scott, now also a producer and director, tried another gambit with *The Savage Is Loose.* He sold prints to theaters, which in turn could keep the prints for showings beyond the initial run. The American Film Theater policy of filming plays and selling tickets on a subscription basis proved successful enough to spawn plans for a 1975 season. AFT is also making children's films for a similar subscription series.

Film Festivals. Cannes still reigns as the chief attraction. *The Conversation* was the 1974 grand prize-winner. The special jury prize went to Pier Paolo Pasolini for *A Thousand and One Nights.* The jury prize went to Spanish director Carlos Saura for *La Prima Angelica* and in recognition of his body of films to date. The New York Film Festival, which does not award prizes, was nearly totally dominated by films from outside the United States. The major Hollywood companies shunned the festival, judged not to be helpful in getting the promotion mileage which the companies demand.

Women in Films. The mushrooming of the fight for women's rights has yielded efforts to change patterns in the film industry. Outspoken critics have demanded roles on screen that more accurately reflect the lives of women and get away from the traditional image of women as sexual playthings. Particular hostility has been aimed at the recent tendency toward the "buddy" films that team male stars and freeze out women —Newman and Redford, McQueen and Hoffman, and similar casting. Emphasis has also been placed on getting more women into positions of directing, producing, and screenwriting and including them on technical crews. Progress has been slow.

WILLIAM WOLF
Film Critic, "Cue" Magazine

Randy Quaid (*in handcuffs*) is a young seaman who has an unexpectedly good time being taken to prison by Otis Young (*center*) and Jack Nicholson in *The Last Detail.*

© BETH BERGMAN 1974

(*Above*) British tenor Peter Pears sings the role of Aschenbach and dancer Bryan Pitts plays the nonsinging part of Tadzio in the Metropolitan's production of Britten's *Death in Venice*. (*Below*) The new Orchestra Hall in Minneapolis uses plastic cubes to enhance acoustical effects.

MINNESOTA ORCHESTRA

Music

Amid the deepening worldwide recession that cut off traditional funding sources for the arts, and the runaway inflation that raised costs, the musical world in 1974 hailed two major 20th century composers: America's Charles Ives and Austria's Arnold Schoenberg.

Schoenberg and Ives. Principal attention centered on Schoenberg's native city, Vienna, which paid tribute to him with a memorial exhibition. Included were autograph manuscripts of his works and many of his paintings, the composer's chief avocation. The International Schoenberg Society set aside the house on the Bernhardgasse, where Schoenberg formulated the 12-tone system, for archives devoted to the composer. The climax of the summer congress, to which musical scholars came from all over the world, was the reinterment of Schoenberg and his wife Gertrud in Vienna's Zentralfriedhof, near the Mozart, Beethoven, and Schubert memorials. The highlight of the tributes to the composer was the Italian pianist Maurizio Pollini's playing of the Piano Concerto, sponsored by the Gesellschaft der Musikfreunde.

In September, on the hundredth anniversary of the composer's birth, the University of Southern California (Los Angeles) dedicated the future location of an Arnold Schoenberg Institute in the university's new $12 million School for the Performing Arts complex. The institute will house a collection of letters, documents, paintings, and original scores donated by the composer's sons and daughter. After fleeing Austria in the 1930's, Schoenberg had made Los Angeles his adopted home.

Charles Ives' hometown was the site of a Fourth of July concert led by Leonard Bernstein and Michael Tilson Thomas in honor of the hundredth anniversary of Ives' birth. In a bandshell on the Danbury (Conn.) State Fair Ground, Bernstein conducted the American Symphony Orchestra in the Second Symphony, and Thomas led *Three Places in New England, From the Steeples and the Mountains,* and a group of choral pieces. An exhibition of Ives memorabilia was on view in Danbury.

In October, Brooklyn College and Yale University jointly sponsored a five-day festival-conference that included performances of Ives' choral, chamber, band, and organ music in New York and New Haven. Also in October, Avery Fisher Hall and the Juilliard Theater in New York were the scenes of a "Mini-Festival Around Ives." Pierre Boulez, the New York Philharmonic, and the Chamber Music Society of Lincoln Center offered works of Ives, Copland, Ruggles, Cowell, and other modern American and European composers. The climax was the Philharmonic's performance of Ives' multilayered Fourth Symphony, conducted by Boulez.

In Washington, D. C., the Kennedy Center presented a series of free concerts honoring Schoenberg and Ives, with ensembles from six American universities. In London, in October, the Park Lane Group gave a week of free Ives chamber concerts, and the London Philharmonic Orchestra performed the Fourth Symphony under José Serebrier at Festival Hall.

The American Academy of Arts and Letters and the National Institute of Arts and Letters also paid homage: the Charles E. Ives Society received a grant to compile a definitive edition of his complete works.

New Facilities. Music of Ives was on the program as the Minnesota Orchestra inaugurated its first permanent home in October. Orchestra Hall in Minneapolis, a $10 million structure that seats 2,570, received unanimous praise for its acoustics. Stanislaw Skrowacewski, the orchestra's conductor, also led works by Stravinsky and Beethoven in the dedicatory concert.

In Lewiston, N. Y., north of Niagara Falls, a state park devoted to the arts was christened in July. On Artpark's 172 acres is a 2,500-seat theater for the creative and performing arts. The opening program, featuring the Buffalo Philharmonic and soloists in a 19th century musicale evening, launched a two-month season that included appearances by orchestras, theater and ballet troupes, and rock bands.

In Birmingham, Ala., two new sections of the city's civic center, a 3,000-seat concert hall and an 800-seat theater, were unveiled in October. At the concert hall's opening, Van Cliburn played Tchaikovsky's Piano Concerto, and later the Birmingham Symphony Orchestra and the Civic Chorus, led by Amerigo Marino, offered Beethoven's Ninth Symphony. A chamber group drawn from the orchestra inaugurated the theater with a concert of Schoenberg, Willaert, and Mendelssohn.

Concert Life. The New York Philharmonic made a five-week tour of the Pacific in late summer, performing 18 times in New Zealand, Australia, and Japan. The ten concerts in the first two countries were conducted by Leonard Bernstein, who presented the premiere of an orchestral suite from his new ballet *Dybbuk.*

In New York, two widely different artists made important appearances in halls usually given to other kinds of music. Virgil Fox drew a capacity crowd to Carnegie Hall for a concert of music by Bach, Dupré, Vierne, and Franck to dedicate the new $200,000 Rodgers electronic organ. And in November, Vladimir Horowitz made his first appearance in the city in six years, choosing the Metropolitan Opera House as the scene of his performances of Clementi, Schumann, Chopin, and Scriabin. The proceeds went to the Metropolitan Opera, as did those from two equally extraordinary artists who made the first of several benefit appearances at Carnegie Hall in the spring: Maria Callas and Giuseppe di Stefano.

Opera. The Metropolitan Opera completed an impressive spring program and began its 90th season in September in spite of unprecedented financial shortages and internal conflicts. In February, Rafael Kubelik resigned in his first season as music director, citing financial restrictions on his plans. But also behind the resignation were Kubelik's absences from the house to pursue his career as conductor, and differences of opinion about casting policy with Schuyler Chapin, general manager of the house, and the board of directors.

Still, the spring saw, in addition to the repetition of the major success of the fall, Berlioz' *Les Troyens,* an imaginatively staged and well-sung premiere of Verdi's *I Vespri Siciliani* with Montserrat Caballé, Nicolai Gedda, and Sherrill Milnes, James Levine conducting. Musically impressive too was a revival of Wagner's *Tristan und Isolde,* in which an unheralded soprano from Brooklyn, Klara Barlow, made a strong debut on short notice when the Isolde for the first performance fell ill. At a later date Birgit Nilsson and Jon Vickers teamed up for a triumphant evening. Other successes were Verdi's *Otello,* which introduced the Maori soprano Kiri Te Kanawa to Met audiences, and Mozart's *Don Giovanni* with Sherrill Milnes.

In the fall the house mounted the American premiere of Benjamin Britten's *Death in Venice,* based on the Thomas Mann story; Peter Pears made his Met debut as the protagonist, and Steuart Bedford conducted. The Czech composer Leos Janáček's *Jenufa,* sung in English, was another triumph; Teresa Kubiak, Jon Vick-

UPI

Schuyler G. Chapin, the Metropolitan Opera's general manager, now is responsible for artistic matters only.

ers, and Astrid Varnay headed the excellent cast. A new production of Moussorgsky's *Boris Godunov* in December saw the initial U. S. appearance of Finnish bass Martti Talvela.

Boris Godunov had been heard earlier at the Cincinnati Summer Opera and at the Saratoga (N. Y.) Festival, in an English translation, with Norman Treigle as Boris, Richard Dufallo conducting. Another Cincinnati highlight was Puccini's *Manon Lescaut* in a production by the film director Luchino Visconti, imported from the Spoleto Festival. Nancy Shade and Harry Theyard were believable young lovers, and Thomas Schippers conducted ably.

Early opera enjoyed unaccustomed attention in 1974. In January, the Opera Society of Washington (D. C.) presented Monteverdi's *Il Ritorno di Ulisse in Patria* at the Kennedy Center. The realization by the English musicologist Raymond Leppard was used, and Frederica von Stade as Penelope and Richard Stilwell as Ulysses were outstanding. Alexander Gibson conducted. The Philadelphia Musical Academy staged Antonio Salieri's *Falstaff* (1799) in March, the work's North American premiere. And at the Santa Fe Opera's summer season audiences saw the first staging of Francesco Cavalli's *L'Egisto,* again in a realization by Leppard.

Newer opera was not neglected. In Houston, the Grand Opera mounted the world premiere of *The Seagull,* with music by Thomas Pasatieri and a libretto by Kenward Elmslie, based on the Chekhov play. The cast included Frederica von Stade, Evelyn Lear, John Reardon, and Richard Stilwell, and Charles Rosekrans conducted. In Boston, Sarah Caldwell staged and conducted Sergei Prokofiev's gargantuan Tolstoy opera *War and Peace* in its entirety. The four-and-a-half-hour epic work was sparked by Donald Gramm's portrayal of General Kutusov. And the pathbreaking St. Paul Opera presented the American premiere of German composer Werner Egk's *Engagement in Santo Domingo* (1963), with a libretto based on a Kleist story.

The New York City Opera's fall program was marked by Beverly Sills' first appearance in a single season in all three Donizetti "English queen" operas: *Maria Stuarda, Roberto Devereux,* and *Anna Bolena.* The house also revived its production of Gilbert and Sullivan's *Mikado,* and gave the podium assignment to Judith Somogi, the first woman to become a member of the company's conducting staff.

The Paris Opera prospered under Rolf Liebermann's stewardship. Three new mountings were on view in 1974: Massenet's *Don Quichotte,* in a staging by Peter Ustinov; Jean-Pierre Ponnelle's production of Mozart's *Così fan tutte,* led by Serge Baudo; and Strauss' *Elektra,* with a first-rate cast of Birgit Nilsson, Leonie Rysanek, Christa Ludwig, and Tom Krause, conducted by Karl Böhm.

In February, at East Berlin's German State Opera House on Unter den Linden, Paul Dessau's *Einstein,* an opera utilizing the famous scientist's career for an anti-American morality play, received its world premiere.

Festivals. The Berkshire Festival at Tanglewood celebrated the centenary of the birth of its founder, the conductor Serge Koussevitzky, with an orchestral marathon. The Boston University Young Artists Orchestra initiated five concerts played one after the other on Koussevitzky's birth date; next was the World Youth Orchestra, led by Leonard Bernstein, followed by the Berkshire Music Center Orchestra, first under Gunther Schuller and then under Bernstein for his own *Age of Anxiety;* and finally, the Boston Symphony Orchestra, which Koussevitzky had led for 25 years.

Washington (D. C.) was the site of a three-week Mozart Festival in May, organized by Julius Rudel, the Kennedy Center's musical director. Local churches presented sacred music, the Smithsonian Institution lent authentic instruments for chamber concerts in its auditorium, and the Kennedy Center played host to Alexander Schneider, Isaac Stern, Jaime Laredo, and others in works of the Viennese master. At the festival's end, the Kennedy Center Opera House saw Gerald Freedman's production of the opera seria *Idomeneo* in a new performing edition by Daniel Heartz of the University of California. The cast, including Elly Ameling, Maralin Niska, and Leo Goeke, was generally praised, but the production was called overbearing and tasteless.

At Spoleto, Italy, the film director Roman Polanski staged his first opera, Alban Berg's

Lulu. Christopher Keene, the young American conductor in his first year as co-musical director with Thomas Schippers, led a worthy performance. *Tamu-Tamu,* the latest opera of the festival's founder, Gian Carlo Menotti, was also given, and *Manon Lescaut* was repeated.

The Salzburg Festival paid homage to its reason for being, the music of Mozart, with Giorgio Strehler's new staging of *The Magic Flute* under Herbert von Karajan. Also in the repertoire were *The Marriage of Figaro* and a new production of Strauss' *Die Frau ohne Schatten* with Karl Böhm conducting and Leonie Rysanek, James King, Walter Berry, and Ursula Schröder-Feinen in the cast. At Bayreuth, the highlight of the Wagner festival was a new *Tristan und Isolde* directed by August Everding and designed by Josef Svoboda. Led by Carlos Kleiber, the cast included Helge Brilieth, Yvonne Minton, and Caterina Ligendza.

Awards and Appointments. The Tchaikovsky competition in Moscow, for violinists and pianists, threw the spotlight on two young American artists. In the first, the 24-year-old Eugene Fodor of Colorado shared second prize with two Soviet violinists, and on his return to the United States played before President and Mrs. Ford at the White House. The pianist was 21-year-old Myung-Whun Chung, an adopted New Yorker from Korea, who took second place.

After Rafael Kubelik's resignation, the Metropolitan Opera announced the appointment of John Dexter, the British stage director, as production supervisor. Daniel Barenboim, the 31-year-old Israeli-born pianist and conductor, was named to succeed Sir Georg Solti as chief conductor of the Orchestre de Paris, effective in 1975. George Semkow will become music director of the St. Louis Symphony beginning with the 1975–76 season, and Maurice Peress assumed the post of music director of the Kansas City (Mo.) Philharmonic for a three-year term. Antal Dorati, music director of the National Symphony, will leave his second post as chief conductor of the Stockholm Philharmonic in 1975 to become senior conductor of the Royal Philharmonic of London.

POPULAR MUSIC

Though 1974 felt the loss of one of the longest-lived and most prolific of America's musical giants, Duke Ellington, who died on May 24 at the age of 75, the year seemed to belong to perennial figures. One was George Wein, whose Newport Jazz Festival flourished in its third year of transplantation to New York City, and featured such staple attractions of the pop-music scene as Ella Fitzgerald, Lionel Hampton, Eubie Blake, and Dizzy Gillespie. Another was Bob Dylan, who refurbished his mystique in a tour of 21 cities that began in Chicago in January and peaked in New York's Madison Square Garden. The four artists who made up the superstar rock group—Crosby, Stills, Nash, and Young—tried a reunion for a summer tour that began in California.

And there was Frank Sinatra, recently out of retirement, who started over again in Las Vegas in January and landed at Madison Square Garden in October. But the hardiest bloom in America's musical garden proved to be country and western music, which sent its own ambassador, with the blessing of the U. S. State Department, to the Soviet Union. George Hamilton IV took the Nashville sound to Moscow's Palace of Culture of the Railway Workers in March after four concerts in Prague that drew audiences of 28,000. (See also RECORDINGS.)

ROBERT S. CLARK
Contributing Editor, "Stereo Review"

Folk-rock singer Bob Dylan (*center*), surrounded by The Band, makes one of his rare public appearances as he performs in Chicago during a cross-country tour.

CHUCK PULIN

NEBRASKA

The year 1974 in Nebraska was characterized by a legislative session with considerable controversy, reelection of a Democrat as governor—but election of Republicans to other major offices—stable state taxes, poor crops, increased energy production, and educational issues.

Legislation. The legislature's 60-day election-year session produced both some important legislation and the expected controversies with Gov. J. James Exon. Significant legislation included state aid for watershed financing, creation of the Metropolitan Technical College Area around Omaha, a state-aid-to-schools act (later repealed by referendum), and addition of troopers to the state patrol's drug force. A prison reform bill fell to a veto, but seven of the governor's 22 other vetoes were overridden.

Elections. In May, voters defeated constitutional amendments aimed at increasing the pay of state senators and changing the duties of the lieutenant governor. In November, Nebraska reelected Democratic Gov. J. James Exon, while Republicans handily won other major state offices. In the three congressional races, Republicans Charles Thone and John McCollister were reelected, while a Republican newcomer, Mrs. Haven Smith, narrowly defeated her opponent. Voters approved student representation on the state university's Board of Regents.

Budget and Taxes. The total approved budget for the 1974–75 fiscal year is $712.7 million. The general fund will provide a larger part of the state budget than in the preceding year. Defeat of the state-aid-to-schools proposal in the November 1974 referendum prevented raising state sales taxes from 2½%; and income taxes dropped from 11% to 10% of the federal tax.

Agriculture. In spite of high grain prices and an excellent wheat crop, 1974 was a poor year for many Nebraska farmers. A summer-long Great Plains drought and early frosts reduced production of corn 35%, soybeans 27%, and grain sorghum 54% as compared with 1973. Grain farmers also faced high fuel and fertilizer prices, and meat, poultry, and dairy producers received comparatively low returns for their products while feed costs rose.

Energy. The Fort Calhoun nuclear power plant reached its 455,000 kilowatt capacity, and the Cooper Nuclear Station at Brownville began production of electricity. The latter, the largest nuclear generating plant between the Mississippi and the West Coast, has a designed capacity of 788,000 kilowatts. Construction on a new fossil fuel power plant at Sutherland was halted by legal action of environmentalists.

Education. While Omaha worked on school integration with a policy based on transfer of students, the state's most controversial education issue in 1974 was a state-aid-to-schools act passed over the governor's veto after being successfully vetoed in each of the last three legislative sessions. Aimed at equalizing education statewide, the act provided for shifting half of school costs from real-estate taxes to income and sales taxes. Opponents, by petition, brought the issue to a referendum in November, and it was soundly defeated. Proponents vow to continue working to change the method of financing public schools.

The Nebraska Supreme Court held that a property tax providing funds to technical colleges was unconstitutional, and a 1972 law allowing grants for students attending private colleges was also declared unconstitutional.

ORVILLE H. ZABEL
Creighton University

NEBRASKA • Information Highlights

Area: 77,227 square miles (200,018 sq km).
Population (1973 est.): 1,542,000. *Density:* 20 per sq mi.
Chief Cities (1970 census): Lincoln, the capital, 149,518; Omaha, 346,929; Grand Island, 31,269; Hastings, 23,580.
Government (1974): *Chief Officers*—governor, J. James Exon (D); lt. gov., Frank Marsh (R). *Legislature* (unicameral)—49 members (nonpartisan).
Education (1973–74): *Enrollment*—public elementary schools, 176,000 pupils; public secondary, 149,225; nonpublic, 42,900; colleges and universities, 65,788 students. *Public school expenditures,* $293,600,000 ($957 per pupil).
State Finances (fiscal year 1973): *Revenues,* $689,545,000; *expenditures,* $616,116,000.
Personal Income (1973): $7,444,000,000; per capita, $4,827.
Labor Force (July 1974): *Nonagricultural wage and salary earners,* 556,500; *insured unemployed,* 6,900 (1.6%).

NETHERLANDS

The Arab oil embargo was the dominant concern of the Netherlands during the first half of 1974. Fear that the embargo might accelerate inflation led to drastic and quite successful measures to control the economy. The left-center government also moved toward basic political reforms.

Economy. The Netherlands economy was not as adversely affected by the embargo of the Arab oil producing countries as had been feared. Gasoline rationing was imposed January 12 but was ended February 4 and replaced by a ban on Sunday pleasure driving every other week. Consumption of petroleum and its products, which had been increasing at the rate of 5% to 8% annually, declined 15%. In spite of the embargo the Netherlands received substantial supplies of oil. When the embargo was lifted on July 10, Rotterdam harbor, Western Europe's most important crude oil terminal, was operating at 80% of normal.

Under a Special Powers Act, approved by parliament on January 8, 1974, the ministry was given extensive powers to control wages, prices, rents, dividends, and income and to reduce central and local government expenses. When unions and employers failed to reach agreement on wages, the government intervened to set the

KEYSTONE

Farmers all over the Netherlands blocked roads with their agricultural machinery to protest against increased expenses and lower prices for their products.

rates. Businesses were required to give prior notice of planned price increases. In addition to tightening price controls, the government has increased annual personal income tax exemptions and granted more generous tax write-offs. The annual rate of inflation for the 12 months through July was 9.6%, which was the second lowest in the European Economic Community. Though unemployment was increasing, the economic outlook for the country was regarded as favorable.

Politics. For several decades the Dutch had talked of a thorough revision of their constitution. The government of Prime Minister Joop den Uyl regards the need for revision as urgent, and in the early months of 1974 it informed parliament of its intention to submit a complete revision of the basic law. To curb the multiplication of parties—a glaring weakness of the Dutch system of proportional representation—the ministry proposed to introduce a limited district system and to raise the quota required for election. If the thinking of the den Uyl ministry were to prevail, the power and functions of the First Chamber would be greatly reduced and its composition and manner of election changed. Another interesting proposal was the popular designation, at the same time as the election of members of the Second Chamber, of the person to form a new cabinet. Unless a candidate were to receive an absolute majority of the votes, however, the crown would be free, as under the present system, to appoint this official.

In the provincial elections held on March 2 the Labor party, the largest in the den Uyl coalition, increased its share of the votes by 2% to 27.9%. The opposition Liberal party gained by 4½%, and its 18.9% share makes it the second largest party in the country. The Radical party also made gains, while the Catholic Peoples party and the Anti-Revolutionary party suffered slight losses and the Democrats 66 lost heavily.

Foreign Affairs. When the Netherlands government began to formalize its plan to carry out the promise Prime Minister den Uyl made to the parliament May 28, 1973, to reduce military expenditures, the other NATO allies became alarmed. The plans called for cutting about

NETHERLANDS • Information Highlights

Official Name: Kingdom of the Netherlands.
Location: Northwestern Europe.
Area: 15,770 square miles (40,844 sq km).
Population (1973 est.): 13,500,000.
Chief Cities (1972 est.): Amsterdam, the capital, 807,742; Rotterdam, 670,060; The Hague, 525,368.
Government: *Head of state,* Juliana, queen (acceded Sept. 1948). *Head of government,* Joop den Uyl, prime minister (took office May 1973). *Legislature*—Staten General: First Chamber and Second Chamber.
Monetary Unit: Guilder (2.714 guilders equal U.S.$1, Aug. 1974).
Gross National Product (1973 est.): $52,500,000,000.
Manufacturing (major products): Metals, processed foods, petroleum products, chemicals, textiles, machinery, electrical appliances, clothing.
Major Agricultural Products: Sugar beets, potatoes, wheat, barley, rye, oats, flax.
Foreign Trade (1973): *Exports,* $24,058,000,000; *imports,* $23,835,000,000.

20,000 men from the 112,000-man armed forces. The Netherlands at first yielded to the pressure of its NATO allies and on June 13 agreed not to make immediate cuts in its armed forces. On July 9, however, it revealed its intention to proceed with extensive cuts in men and equipment. The NATO Council, meeting in Brussels on July 9, declared that the proposed Dutch action would seriously weaken NATO defenses and urged the Netherlands to reconsider. The economic situation and competitive claims on public resources were the same in other countries, the council asserted, and the Dutch action would place a heavier burden on its allies. A high official in the Netherlands defense ministry was reported as having said that his government took the action in order to shock NATO "to achieve greater unification of the equipment of all NATO partners."

Surinam and the Antilles. At a conference between Prime Minister den Uyl and the political leaders of the former Netherlands colonies, now autonomous states under the Dutch crown, it was agreed that Surinam would become completely independent at the end of 1975 and the Antilles at the end of 1980. In anticipation of restrictions on immigration after independence, some 500 Surinamese are flying to the Netherlands each week. Already there are about 80,000 Surinamese in the country, with one-fourth of them unemployed.

AMRY VANDENBOSCH, *University of Kentucky*

NEVADA

Despite the energy crisis during the winter of 1973–74, tourism continued to thrive in Nevada, and the state treasury had a healthy surplus at the end of 1974.

Elections. Former Gov. Paul Laxalt was the only Republican in the nation to win a U. S. Senate seat held by a Democrat in 1974, winning a narrow, hard-fought victory over 34-year-old Lt. Gov. Harry Reid. Laxalt will succeed Sen. Alan Bible, who had not sought reelection. Former District Judge James Santini survived a bitter challenge in the Democratic primary from a fellow Las Vegan to defeat Republican Congressman David Towell by over 30,000 votes.

Mike O'Callaghan, the popular Democratic governor, was reelected with the highest percentage of votes for a gubernatorial candidate in Nevada history. He easily defeated Shirley Crumpler, the first woman in the state's history to be nominated for governor. Robert Rose, the 34-year-old Democratic district attorney of Washoe County, easily defeated State Sen. William Raggio for the post of lieutenant governor, whereas Republican Attorney General Robert List barely won reelection after a strong challenge from State Sen. Richard Bryan.

The 1975 Nevada Legislature will have the most lopsided party majority in the 20th century, with the Democrats holding 17 of the 20 seats in the Senate and 31 of the 40 seats in the Assembly. Beverly Harrell, the madam of a bordello in Esmeralda County, received nationwide publicity when she finished first in a field of seven candidates in the primary election for her Assembly district. However, she was defeated in the November general election in a very close race.

NEVADA • Information Highlights

Area: 110,540 square miles (286,299 sq km).
Population (1973 est.): 548,000. *Density:* 5 per sq mi.
Chief Cities (1970 census): Carson City, the capital, 15,468; Las Vegas, 125,787; Reno, 72,863.
Government (1974): *Chief Officers*—governor, Mike O'Callaghan (D); lt. gov., Harry M. Reid (D). *Legislature*—Senate, 20 members (14 D, 6 R); Assembly, 40 members (25 D, 15 R).
Education (1973–74): *Enrollment*—public elementary schools, 72,900 pupils, public secondary, 62,100; nonpublic, 2,800; colleges and universities, 20,044 students. *Public school expenditures,* $129,000,000 ($1,032 per pupil).
State Finances (fiscal year 1973): *Revenues,* $442,489,-000; *expenditures,* $382,151,000.
Personal Income (1973): $3,047,000,000; per capita, $5,650.
Labor Force (July 1974): *Nonagricultural wage and salary earners,* 261,100; *insured unemployed,* 9,100 (4.5%).

Economy. The large hotel-casinos in Las Vegas, Reno, and Lake Tahoe responded to gasoline shortages in the winter of 1973–1974 by increasing advertising and arranging for additional bus and plane excursions for California residents. The added expenditures reduced the net profits of some casinos, but the state gambling tax is assessed on gross revenues. Thus with the opening of several large new hotels, Nevada's income from the gambling tax for the 1973–1974 fiscal year was up 19.5% over the previous year. Sales tax revenues also showed a healthy 15.8% increase. On the negative side, unemployment in the state reached a high of 7.9% in August.

Environment. The major environmental issue in Nevada in 1974 involved the proposed construction of two new high-rise hotel-casinos on the Nevada side of Lake Tahoe. Construction was started, but California obtained an injunction to halt work, and the case was still in the courts at year's end.

Education. Nevada schoolteachers continued to do well in collective bargaining under the compulsory arbitration provision of the state law. Some school boards were calling for the 1975 Legislature to make changes in the collective bargaining statute. The new community colleges in Las Vegas and Carson City–Reno had a spectacular 62% increase in full-time-equivalent student enrollment in the fall term of 1974. The University of Nevada campuses at Las Vegas and Reno registered increases of 9% and 4%, respectively. The centennial of the university was marked on October 12 by a special convocation and appropriate activities on the Reno campus.

DON W. DRIGGS
University of Nevada

NEW BRUNSWICK

The year 1974 was an unusually active one politically, as voters went to the polls twice in general elections: the federal election on July 8, and the provincial general election on November 18.

Politics. In the November provincial election, Premier Richard Hatfield led his Progressive Conservative party back into office with 33 seats, as compared with 32 when the legislature was dissolved. The opposition Liberals elected 25, one fewer than before, in the 58-seat Legislative Assembly. The premier said that the first priority in his second term would be economic development and improvement of New Brunswickers' living standards.

The five-week election campaign was a quiet one, with no single issue predominating. Liberal leader Robert Higgins conducted a low-key campaign, much to the disappointment of many of his followers, who felt he should be attacking the government's record more vigorously.

In the summer federal election, New Brunswick voted with the national trend. The Liberals won six of New Brunswick's 10 House of Commons seats to the Conservatives' four. In 1972, each major party had elected five members.

Combines. K. C. Irving Ltd. of Saint John, and three associated publishing companies, were convicted on January 24 of forming a monopoly of New Brunswick's five English-language daily newspapers. Mr. Justice Albany Robichaud, who had presided at the long trial under the Combines Investigation Act in late 1972, levied fines totaling $150,000 against Irving; New Brunswick Publishing Co. Ltd., Saint John; Moncton Publishing Co. Ltd.; and University Press of New Brunswick Ltd., Fredericton.

Languages. Education Minister Lorne McGuigan (later defeated in the provincial election) announced on April 16 that separate English- and French-language instruction divisions would be established. Two pilot programs under the planned new system were begun late in 1974, with implementation of the full, provincewide system set to begin in 1976.

— NEW BRUNSWICK • Information Highlights —

Area: 28,354 square miles (73,437 sq km).
Population (April 1974 est.): 660,000.
Chief Cities (1971 census): Fredericton, the capital, 24,254; St. John, 89,039; Moncton, 47,891.
Government (1974): *Chief Officers*—lt. gov., Hedard Robichaud; premier, Richard B. Hatfield (Progressive Conservative); prov. secy., Omer Leger (PC); min. of educ., J. Lorne McGuigan (PC); chief justice, C. J. A Hughes. *Legislature*—Legislative Assembly, 58 members (33 PC, 25 Liberal).
Education (1972–73): *Enrollment:* public elementary and secondary schools, 175,191 pupils; private schools, 636; Indian (federal) schools, 704; colleges and universities, 10,229 students. *Public school expenditures* (1972), $150,200,000.
Public Finance (fiscal year 1974–75 est.): *Revenues,* $742,000,000; *expenditures,* $791,000,000.
Personal Income (1972): $1,793,000,000; average annual income per person, $2,810.
(All monetary figures are in Canadian dollars.)

On May 23, a preliminary draft of the revised statutes of New Brunswick, translated into French for the first time, was tabled in the provincial legislature. New Brunswick is the first predominantly English-speaking province to draft its statutes in both of Canada's official languages.

Premier Hatfield on August 9 entered the controversy over Quebec's much-disputed Bill 22, making French that province's official language. He wrote Prime Minister Trudeau arguing that sections of the bill appeared unconstitutional, and urging that the federal government refer it to the Supreme Court of Canada. Trudeau replied on September 4, promising to consider the premier's suggestion, but he later told the Commons that his government would not oppose Bill 22 in the courts.

Nuclear Power. A point of land jutting into the Bay of Fundy south of Saint John, called Point Lepreau, was chosen as the site for a $900 million nuclear power plant to be built by the New Brunswick Power Commission. The twin-reactor plant will produce a total of 1,200 megawatts.

Strike. A six-week, provincewide strike by 430 New Brunswick Telephone Co. operators ended October 30. The settlement provided for a 35.7% wage increase over two years, bringing experienced operators up to $153 weekly.

JOHN BEST
Chief, Canada World News, Ottawa

NEW HAMPSHIRE

A constitutional convention, a special session of the legislature, and the November elections, particularly the U. S. Senate race, dominated New Hampshire affairs in 1974.

Constitutional Convention. The first such meeting in 10 years, the constitutional convention avoided major controversial issues, rejecting several proposed reforms that have been persistently advanced by liberal elements. These included prohibiting the death penalty, reducing the size of the 400-member House of Representatives, extending the governor's term to four years, and removing the prohibition against an income tax. A proposal by Gov. Meldrim Thomson, Jr., to limit future state spending to the growth in state personal income also was defeated.

The convention approved 27 constitutional amendments, to be submitted to the voters over a period of years. In 1976, voters will pass on amendments that would end the pocket veto, permit the legislature to call itself into special session, and pay legislators the per diem rate for the lowest grade of classified state employees rather than $200 per biennium. Others would provide that a member of the elected State Executive Council would succeed to the governor's office if it became vacant, and guarantee the public's right to examine public documents and attend government meetings.

ARTHUR GRACE/THE NEW YORK TIMES

Townspeople of Durham, N. H., vote against permitting Aristotle Onassis to build an oil refinery there.

A proposal on the 1978 ballot would place the state court system under administrative control of the state Supreme Court, and one on the 1980 ballot would lower to 18 the minimum age for a candidate for governor, state senator, or the State Executive Council.

Legislature. A special session called by Governor Thomson to complete 1973 business imposed a 5-cent-per-barrel tax on refined petroleum products produced in the state, formed a commission to study energy facilities, and provided that sites for all refineries be approved by local option. No refinery now exists in the state. On March 7, the House of Representatives rejected legislation that, in effect, would have enabled Aristotle Onassis to build a $600 million refinery in Durham, where the townspeople had voted against the project, 8 to 1.

The legislature approved a capital improvement budget of $27.4 million and supplemental appropriations of $1.4 million for fiscal 1975. The improvements budget provides for funding for new university buildings and 30-year financing bonds for various projects. The supplemental appropriations met deficits in department budgets caused by the energy crisis. A cost-of-living increase for retired state employees and a $520 raise for state employees were passed.

NEW HAMPSHIRE • Information Highlights

Area: 9,304 square miles (24,097 sq km).
Population (1973 est.): 791,000. *Density:* 85 per sq. mi.
Chief Cities (1970 census): Concord, the capital, 30,022; Manchester, 87,754; Nashua, 55,820; Portsmouth, 25,717.
Government (1974): *Chief Officers*—governor, Meldrim Thomson, Jr. (R); secy. of state, Robert L. Stark (R). *General Court*—Senate, 24 members; House of Representatives, 400 members.
Education (1973–74): *Enrollment*—public elementary schools, 102,135 pupils; public secondary, 69,287; nonpublic, 26,600; colleges and universities, 32,924 students. *Public school expenditures,* $144,413,000 ($909 per pupil).
State Finances (fiscal year 1973): *Revenues,* $453,584,000; *Expenditures,* $419,830,000.
Personal Income (1973): $3,621,000,000; per capita, $4,578.
Labor Force (July 1974): *Nonagricultural wage and salary earners,* 318,200; *insured unemployed,* 8,800 (3.4%).

Election. Governor Thomson (R) won a second term over Richard W. Leonard (D); both candidates opposed new taxes. For the U. S. Senate seat vacated by retiring Norris Cotton (R), Rep. Louis C. Wyman (R) edged John Durkin (D) by 452 votes out of 220,000 cast. In a recount, the State Ballot Law Commission declared Wyman the winner by a mere 2 votes. Wyman felt there should be a runoff election, and at year's end the result remained in doubt, with indications that a ruling might come from the Senate. Wyman's vacated seat in Congress was won by a Democrat, Norman D'Amours.

Three constitutional amendments were passed, affirming equal rights for all, providing for a presession organizational meeting of the legislature, and lowering the voting age to 18.

RICHARD G. WEST
Former Senior Editor
"Encyclopedia Americana"

NEW JERSEY

Political reform and the recurring theme of corruption in government were prominent in New Jersey in 1974.

Reform. The reform impetus stemmed largely from Gov. Brendan T. Byrne, decisive winner in the gubernatorial election of 1973, who entered office in January with a pledge to end corruption in the state. Under his leadership the legislature enacted a law requiring public financing of gubernatorial election campaigns, thus making New Jersey the first state in the nation to have legislation of this kind. Private contributions would be limited to $600 per person, with a candidate eligible to receive public funds after raising $40,000.

Byrne was not as successful with other important initiatives. Like his predecessors, William Cahill and Richard Hughes, he included an income tax plan in his first message to the legislature. At a special session in July, by a vote of 41 to 38, the Assembly approved a graduated income tax of 1.5% to 8%, designed to raise

NEW JERSEY • Information Highlights

Area: 7,836 square miles (20,295 sq km).
Population (1973 est.): 7,361,000. *Density:* 980 per sq. mi.
Chief Cities (1970 census): Trenton, the capital, 104,638; Newark, 382,288; Jersey City, 260,545.
Government (1974): *Chief Officers*—governor, Brendan T. Byrne (D); secy. of state, J. Edward Crabiel. *Legislature*—Senate, 40 members (29 D, 10 R, 1 Independent). General Assembly, 80 members (66 D, 14 R).
Education (1973–74): *Enrollment*—public elementary schools, 967,200 pupils; public secondary, 520,800; nonpublic, 249,600; colleges and universities, 255,314 students. *Public school expenditures,* $2,053,000,000 ($1,432 per pupil).
State Finances (fiscal year 1973): *Revenues,* $4,111,999,000; *expenditures,* $3,800,271,000.
Personal Income (1973): $42,389,000,000; per capita, $5,759.
Labor Force (July 1974): *Nonagricultural wage and salary earners,* 2,808,900.

$950 million in revenue. This was the first time that either house had ever voted in favor of an income tax. However, opposition in the Senate was insurmountable, and on July 24 it was decided that the tax reform bill would not be brought to the floor for a final vote.

Rejection of the tax plan threw the sizable Democratic legislative majorities into disarray. In order to combat a large projected deficit for 1975, existing taxes would have to be raised considerably, which was not a popular move in a state hard hit by inflation and unemployment.

The income tax defeat raised the problem of how to comply with the state Supreme Court's ruling barring the property tax as a constitutional means to finance public education. The Legislature failed to meet the court's Dec. 31, 1974, deadline to produce an alternate plan.

Corruption. In late March it was revealed that Secretary of State Edward J. Crabiel, a key figure in the Byrne administration, was being investigated by a grand jury on charges that he accepted kickbacks while president of a highway construction company. Byrne refused to defend him publicly, yet resisted pressures to force his resignation. In July, Crabiel was indicted on charges of rigging highway construction bids. He was the third successive secretary of state to be indicted on corruption charges.

Former state Republican chairman Nelson Gross was convicted on March 29 on five counts of perjury and advising tax evasion while serving as Governor Cahill's campaign manager. On December 11, former state Treasurer Joseph McCrane, Jr., was convicted on four counts of assisting corporations to file false records in an attempt to cover up contributions to the 1969 campaign of Governor Cahill.

Elections. A generally dull campaign was enlivened by one emotional issue, that of whether to permit casino gambling. Those in favor of the proposal contended that legalized casino gambling would revitalize the economy of the Jersey Shore, especially Atlantic City, while the opposition, led by church groups, pointed out that it would encourage organized crime and make the state an eastern Las Vegas. The proposal was defeated in a November referendum.

In balloting for congressional races, Democrats scored their biggest victory in years. Four of seven Republican seats were lost as the Democrats gained a 12–3 margin in the House delegation. Among those defeated were Representatives Charles W. Sandman, Jr., and Joseph J. Maraziti, who had gained nationwide attention for their staunch defense of President Nixon in the House impeachment hearings.

Other Events. In October a confrontation developed between the state and the New York-New Jersey Port Authority over the Authority's threat to deny funds for a PATH extension to Newark. Governor Byrne threatened to withhold approval of a PATH route to Kennedy International Airport.

Congressman Peter Rodino of Newark, chairman of the House Judiciary Committee, gained a national reputation for his fair-minded handling of the Nixon impeachment inquiry. (See BIOGRAPHY.)

HERMANN K. PLATT
St. Peter's College, Jersey City

TOM HERDE/NEW JERSEY NEWSPHOTOS

Gov. Brendan T. Byrne delivers a controversial tax-reform message to a joint session of the New Jersey Legislature.

NEW MEXICO

In 1974 many New Mexicans developed a profound sense of unease about the future. Because their state is an energy exporter, they suffered less from the fuel crises than most other sections of the country, and political scandals in Washington seemed remote. But these national problems, together with inflation, contributed to the attitude of gloom.

Politics. On November 5, New Mexico voters elected state Sen. Jerry Apodaca, Democrat from Las Cruces, to succeed retiring governor Bruce King. Apodaca is the first Spanish-surnamed person to win this office since 1918.

Indians. Indian leaders from throughout New Mexico gathered at San Juan Pueblo in late July to discuss land problems, needed school facilities, a juvenile detention home, and other issues involving tribal governments. Morris Thompson, Commissioner of Indian Affairs for the U. S. Department of Interior, attended and advised the representatives.

In early summer, militant Navajos associated with the Coalition for Navajo Liberation staged a series of protest marches in Farmington to call attention to alleged discrimination by the community. The coalition also charged that an excessive number of bars near Farmington contributed directly to the acute problem of alcoholism among Indians.

Crime. The FBI Crime Index, released in August, showed that in 1973 Albuquerque dropped from first place to tenth place on the list of U. S. cities with high crime rates per population. Santa Fe, the capital, showed a slight decline in overall crime statistics, but burglaries soared by 200%. Much of this increase was due to major thefts of Indian crafts and artifacts from commercial businesses, museums, and private collectors. In a public address, Sen. Joseph Montoya scored the heavy increase in juvenile crime and urged the creation of community task forces to study the problem.

Environment and Energy. A national celebration was held in Silver City on June 2 to commemorate the 50th anniversary of the National Wilderness Preservation System of the Department of Agriculture. The nearby Gila Wilderness, the first designated wilderness area, was created on June 3, 1924.

On May 23, New Mexico Citizens for Clean Air and Water and the Sierra Club filed a lawsuit in U. S. District Court against Phelps-Dodge Corporation's new Hidalgo copper smelter in the southwestern corner of the state. Contending that the plant will emit about 90 tons per day of sulfur dioxide into what is now a clean area, the plaintiffs emphasized that they sought only to force the use of modern, proven antipollution equipment.

State executives meeting in Albuquerque at the Western Governors Conference expressed concern that rapid energy resource exploitation in sparsely populated regions of the West might lead to urban blight and haphazard sprawl.

New Mexico, a leading energy-producing state, is rich not only in uranium, oil, natural gas, and low-sulfur coal, but also in solar energy, wind power, and geothermal energy. Interested citizens in 1974 formed the New Mexico Solar Energy Association, and New Mexico State University at Las Cruces announced plans to construct the largest building in the nation to be both heated and cooled by solar energy. Meanwhile, scientists at Los Alamos Scientific Laboratory continued research on several geothermal projects.

MARC SIMMONS, *Author and Historian*

NEW MEXICO • Information Highlights

Area: 121,666 square miles (315,115 sq km).
Population (1973 est.): 1,106,000. *Density:* 9 per sq mi.
Chief Cities (1970 census): Santa Fe, the capital, 41,167; Albuquerque, 243,751; Las Cruces, 37,857; Roswell, 33,908.
Government (1974): *Chief Officers*—governor, Bruce King (D); lt. gov., Robert A. Mondragon (D). *Legislature*—Senate, 42 members (30 D, 12 R); House of Representatives, 70 members (50 D, 20 R).
Education (1973–74): *Enrollment*—public elementary schools, 140,114 pupils; public secondary schools, 138,718; nonpublic schools, 13,100; colleges and universities, 48,636 students. *Public school expenditures,* $247,347,000 ($939 per pupil).
State Finances (fiscal year 1973): *Revenues,* $819,589,000; *expenditures,* $715,930,000.
Personal Income (1973): $4,163,000,000; per capita, $3,764.
Labor Force (July 1974): *Nonagricultural wage and salary earners,* 361,700; *insured unemployed,* 8,600 (3.5%).

NEW ORLEANS

Like most of the rest of the country, New Orleans suffered from inflation and a sluggish economy in 1974. Unemployment rose to 7.0% late in the year, and the value of construction contracts and housing starts was down sharply.

Construction. A huge multimillion-dollar hotel-and-office-building complex near the Mississippi River was postponed indefinitely by the Pan American Life Insurance Company, which cited economic uncertainties as the reason for the delay. However, construction began on the $60 million Poydras Plaza office-apartment-hotel complex adjacent to the domed stadium.

Meanwhile, work on the stadium itself plodded on. Originally scheduled for use in the 1974 football season, the mammoth structure is now scheduled for completion in mid-1975. Additionally, a state legislative investigating committee uncovered claims of political favoritism in dispensing stadium contracts.

Another huge project, a proposed new bridge across the Mississippi River, also crept toward reality. After months of study, state and local agencies appeared to agree upon a site just downriver from and parallel to the existing Greater New Orleans Bridge. Officials hope to obtain a federal building permit for the new span sometime in early 1975. The project is estimated to cost $200 to $300 million.

Politics. Politically it was a relatively quiet year in New Orleans. Perhaps the biggest news was the political demise of former District Attorney Jim Garrison, who gained national attention several years ago when he claimed he had solved the murder of President John F. Kennedy. Garrison, who was unseated as district attorney at the end of 1973, finished third in a three-man race for a seat on the state supreme court. But Garrison wasn't the only "old pro" to be defeated. Early in the year a new group of candidates ousted the "ins" from several parish (county) positions, including those of the sheriff and the clerks of the criminal and civil courts. Also, New Orleans elected its first black man, Sidney Barthelemy, to the state senate since Reconstruction days.

Redistricting. City Council members sat beyond their normal terms, which should have ended in May 1974, because of legal disputes over the council's redistricting of itself. A federal court ruled the redistricting was racially discriminatory, but the U. S. Supreme Court will review that decision early in 1975.

JOSEPH W. DARBY III
"The Times-Picayune," New Orleans

WIDE WORLD

A section of the Lake Pontchartrain Causeway, the world's longest bridge and the main commuter artery in New Orleans, collapses after being struck by four barges.

NEW YORK

Watergate and crime control, the state of the economy including the energy crisis, and the gubernatorial contest were uppermost in the minds of New Yorkers in 1974.

Budget and Finances. Gov. Malcolm Wilson's $9.38 billion budget was submitted to the Legislature on January 22. Although $772 million more than the previous year, the new budget offered few new spending programs and stressed economy in government. The Governor requested an end to the 2.5% personal income tax surcharge, but asked that the so-called "hotdog" tax on meals of less than $1 be kept. The legislators suspended, but did not repeal outright, the surcharge.

Assailed by Democrats who wanted increases in public services, especially for New York City, a trimmed budget of $9.2 billion was passed. Legislators also voted themselves and other state officials and judges large salary increases. New York City's 35-cent bus and subway fare was temporarily maintained by the granting of a $100 million state subsidy.

Education. An additional $307 million in state aid to local schools was voted by the Legislature for a total state expenditure of $2.767 billion, producing significant increases for suburban school districts. Also approved was a controversial $8.2 million to reimburse parochial schools for the costs of mandated state programs. The state ended community college expansion. There were 38 such institutions as 1974 ended.

Other Legislation. Continuing his often expressed war on crime, Governor Wilson signed a bill restoring a limited death penalty. It mandated execution for the willful murder of a police officer in the performance of his duty or an employee of a local or state correctional institution. Wilson also signed a bill placing restrictions on the state's four-year-old abortion law. Pregnancy after 12 weeks could be terminated only in hospitals and only on an in-patient basis. Both the death penalty and abortion bills were victories for the state's conservative elements.

NEW YORK • Information Highlights

Area: 49,576 square miles (128,402 sq km).
Population (1973 est.): 18,265,000. *Density:* 384 per sq mi.
Chief Cities (1970 census): Albany, the capital, 115,781; New York, 7,895,563; Buffalo, 462,768; Rochester, 296,233.
Government (1974): *Chief Officers*—governor, Malcolm Wilson (R); lt. gov., vacancy. *Legislature*—Senate, 60 members (37 R, 21 D, 2 vacancies); Assembly, 150 members (79 R, 69 D, 2 vacancies).
Education (1973–74): *Enrollment*—public elementary schools, 1,829,150 pupils; public secondary schools, 1,644,550; nonpublic schools, 713,500; colleges and universities, 895,400 students. *Public school expenditures,* $5,620,800,000 ($1,809 per pupil).
State Finances (fiscal year 1973): *Revenues,* $15,694,079,000; *expenditures,* $14,396,384,000.
Personal Income (1973): $103,429,000,000; per capita, $5,663.
Labor Force (Aug. 1974): *Nonagricultural wage and salary earners,* 7,135,100; *insured unemployed,* 229,600 (3.8%).

UPI

Democrat Hugh Carey, who was elected governor of New York, leaves the polling station in Brooklyn. A widower, he is accompanied by nine of his 12 children.

Consumer protection also received a share of support from the Legislature. All auto repair shops are now required to register with the Department of Motor Vehicles, and this registration may be revoked or suspended if fraudulent or negligent practices are found. In addition, auto mechanics must now be certified. Lending institutions are now required to pay a minimum of 2% interest on monies in their mortgage escrow accounts.

Politics. Politics received early attention, as district lines for legislative and congressional seats were redrawn for Brooklyn and Manhattan, under orders from the Justice Department, to give greater opportunity for minority group representation. The state primary election was set forward to September 10, and the political conventions were moved forward to the month of June.

While crime and the state's economy were prime issues, voter interest centered around personalities. Governor Wilson and Sen. Jacob K. Javits headed the Republican party ticket. Louis Lefkowitz once again received the Republican party's nomination for attorney general. There was little party discord.

Democrats, however, provided excitement in a hotly contested primary race. Rep. Hugh L. Carey of Brooklyn easily defeated the choice of the Democratic State Committee, Howard J. Samuels, for the gubernatorial nomination, while reformer Ramsey Clark, former U. S. attorney general, defeated the party choice Mayor Lee Alexander of Syracuse for the U. S. Senate nomination. Bronx Borough President Robert Abrams won a landslide victory over party candidate Robert R. Meehan for the attorney general nomination. Mary Anne Krupsak became the first woman candidate for lieutenant governor, easily defeating two male opponents in the primary. Arthur Levitt's nomination by the State Committee for state controller was the only statewide seat not contested in the primary.

Wilson and his running mate Ralph G. Caso, Nassau County executive, hurt by Watergate and disclosures in Senate hearings on Nelson Rockefeller's nomination for vice president, as well as the economy and inflation, fell easily to Carey and Krupsak 2,669,157 to 1,841,480. Democrats gained impressively, winning control of the state Assembly, additional congressional seats, and many new local positions.

Senator Javits won reelection, as did Louis Lefkowitz, but by greatly reduced margins. A number of prominent Republicans were toppled, including 12-year veteran District Attorney William Cahn of Nassau County, who lost convincingly to Democrat Denis Dillon. In an interesting race for a seat on the Court of Appeals, Democrat Jacob Fuchsberg, despite vehement opposition from state bar associations, swept by his closest rival, Harold Stevens.

LEO HERSHKOWITZ
Queens College, City University of New York

NEW YORK CITY

Even with a new chief executive in office, New Yorkers in 1974 faced old budgetary problems, labor unrest, and crime. The growing exodus of major corporations and the effects of inflation and recession intensified the city's financial crises.

Budget and Financing. Mayor Abraham D. Beame, an accountant and former city controller, presented early in the year a capital budget of "fiscal prudence and responsibility" amounting to $1.7 billion for the fiscal year 1974–75, about $800 million less than the previous budget. The chief cuts were in transportation, schools, and the fire department.

The mayor won a signal victory when the City Council and Board of Estimate adopted virtually unchanged his $11.1 billion expense budget, and the Council approved the taxes needed to balance it. To meet the new budget, the state passed legislation permitting the city to raise its sales tax by 1 cent to 8 cents per $1.00, and to impose a $15 auto use tax to be collected by the State Motor Vehicle Bureau when a vehicle is reregistered. The Council also set a new real estate tax of $7.35 for every $100 of assessed valuation, a raise of 46.4 cents. In addition, the state increased aid to the city by $87 million and granted advance payments from the 1975–76 budget of some $114 million.

Nevertheless, it was still necessary to reduce staff positions and curtail expenditures in lower priority programs. Inflation obviously hit hard at city finances. It also affected clean-air goals as the federal government relaxed its pressure on the city to achieve healthful air standards. At the end of the year the city faced a budget deficit estimated by the mayor to be $430 million and by Controller Harrison J. Goldin at $650 million. Consequently, the mayor announced the dismissal of 3,725 city employees.

Earlier in the year, a financial storm occurred when Controller Goldin "discovered" that $5.4 million in securities was missing from city vaults. He implied that his predecessor in office, the present mayor, as official in charge bore the responsibility for either the theft or a gross error in bookkeeping. Bitter charges and countercharges followed, as did audits and investigations. The affair ended quickly with an announcement by investigators from the District Attorney's and Investigation Commissioner's offices that the millions "missing" from the vaults were never lost; the discrepancy was due to poor bookkeeping in the controller's office. A rift between the mayor and controller was obvious.

Labor. In early January, strikes by the school system's 6,000 boiler room and maintenance workers forced 730 schools to close. Almost 900,000 students, or two-thirds of the enrollment, were without classes for several days. Strikers returned to work after receiving a three-year contract providing for wage increases of $1.38 per hour.

In April, a threatened strike of 37,000 bus and subway workers was averted when Dr. William Ronan, head of the Metropolitan Transit Authority, agreed to a $135 million package of raises tied to increases in the cost of living. A newspaper strike was also averted when labor mediator Theodore Kheel announced that an agreement had been reached giving newspaper publishers the right to use automated processes in the printing of their papers, and guaranteeing employees lifetime job security. A taxicab strike was also avoided in August when union drivers working for the taxi fleets received a pay increase from $3.75 to $4.60 per hour. Taxi fares went up several months later. Firemen received a raise in pay effective by 1976, from $15,250 to $18,000 per year.

Building. After nearly a decade of planning and controversy, ground was finally broken for the first of 16,000 apartments scheduled to rise in Battery Park City, a 100-acre, $1.1 billion development to be built on a mile-long strip of Hudson River landfill in lower Manhattan. First occupants are expected by July 4, 1976. This "new town," will be larger than many cities in the country, and is seen as a sign of the continued resiliency of the city.

Crime. Crime remained a major problem, particularly teen and pre-teen age crime, as a number of eight- and nine-year-olds were accused of murder. In an effort to make subway riding safer, the mayor issued an edict in July closing the rear half of subway trains between the hours of 8 P.M. and 4 A.M.

Elections. Politics produced little that was new. The city remained solidly Democratic in 1974. Robert Morgenthau defeated Richard Kuh in the Democratic primary for district attorney for New York County and also heavily outpolled him in the November election, when Kuh ran on the Republican ticket. Kuh had been appointed district attorney by Gov. Malcolm Wilson following the resignation of Frank Hogan, shortly before his death in March, after 32 years in office.

Democrats won 24 of the 27 state Senate seats from the city, and 56 of the city's 65 Assembly seats. The 23-member delegation to Congress from the city was entirely Democratic. Two members of the House Judiciary Committee, Charles Rangel and Elizabeth Holtzman, who early called for President Richard Nixon's impeachment, were reelected to the House of Representatives overwhelmingly. In the race for governor, Hugh L. Carey of Brooklyn received 1,207,478 votes on the Democratic-Liberal lines in the city to Republican-Conservative incumbent Malcolm Wilson's 532,239 votes, thus carrying the city by a margin of better than two to one.

LEO HERSHKOWITZ
Queens College, City University of New York

NEW ZEALAND

The sudden death of Prime Minister Norman Kirk at the age of 51 on August 31 overshadowed all other public events in New Zealand in 1974. His death came after less than two years in office and several months of poor health. Britain's Prince Charles represented Queen Elizabeth at his state funeral.

Politics. As a result of the reorganization of the Labour administration following Kirk's death, Finance Minister Wallace Edward Rowling, 46, became the nation's youngest prime minister in the 20th century. Robert J. Tizard, 50, was chosen as deputy prime minister and took the finance portfolio. A minor cabinet reshuffle followed. In a subsequent by-election, John Kirk, son of the late prime minister, easily won election to the seat formerly held by his father.

In July former Prime Minister Jack Marshall retired as leader of the Opposition and parliamentary head of the National party. He was replaced by deputy party leader Robert Muldoon, who in turn was succeeded by Brian Talboys, a former minister of agriculture. Public opinion polls indicated that the Labour government's popularity was holding up remarkably well, and a September poll showed a 10% lead over the National party.

However, at the triennial nationwide local body elections held in October, the Labour party's bid to win control of large cities was repulsed. Sir Dove-Myer Robinson was reelected mayor of Auckland City for an unprecedented fifth term.

The Economy. Serious inflation posed a continuing threat to the stability of the economy. Prices maintained an upward spiral, due in part to a radical increase in petroleum costs (benzene was up by 9 cents a gallon in April) and a 9% devaluation of the New Zealand dollar in September. The devaluation was designed to preserve trading competitiveness with Australia and lift declining farm income. The annual accounts had revealed that the yield from income tax exceeded by almost 30% that of the previous year, while expenditure was up 17%. As the year progressed, an acute shortage of loan financing became apparent, and agricultural exports sagged.

Contrary to predictions, both direct and indirect taxes were left untouched by the budget presented in May. Instead, social security benefits were raised and building controls reintroduced at the same time that housing finance was boosted. Much reliance was placed on increased production to contain inflation. Rowling saw the need for "steadying the economy and ensuring that the demand for growth is in line with available resources." To combat a 50% increase in import payments, the government in October announced a temporary compulsory savings scheme, collected through a 9% increase in tax deductions.

Domestic Affairs. The 10th Commonwealth Games, were held in Christchurch from January 24 to February 2. Thirty-nine nations participated. Queen Elizabeth and the Duke of Edinburgh opened the games.

The state-owned New Zealand Shipping Line commenced operations with two cargo ships on the New Zealand-Britain run in February.

In April the Accident Compensation Act, providing personal insurance for everyone involved in any sort of accident, came into being. Almost 48,000 claims were lodged and $6,900,000 paid out during the first six months of its operation.

The Most Reverend Reginald Delargey, Roman Catholic bishop of Auckland, was appointed archbishop of Wellington in May.

Dr. William B. Sutch, an eminent economist and former secretary of industry and commerce, was arrested and charged under the Official Secrets Act of 1951 with obtaining information which could be useful to an enemy. He was committed to the Supreme Court for trial.

The 3-year-old racing prodigy, Noodlum, electrified the light-harness world. He broke the New Zealand trotting record by winning his 11th consecutive race in September.

Sir James Fletcher, perhaps New Zealand's most dynamic industrialist, died in August at the age of 88. After building up an empire in construction and related fields, he became the first commissioner of works in 1944. Later he instigated a thriving newsprint, paper, and pulp industry. Sir Leslie Munro, New Zealand diplomat, journalist, and jurist, died on February 12.

Foreign Affairs. In Washington, D. C., on February 27, Prime Minister Kirk and U. S. Deputy Secretary of State Kenneth Rush signed an agreement increasing scientific and technological cooperation.

New Zealand issued a strong protest against French nuclear testing in the Pacific Ocean.

The Shah of Iran and President Julius K. Nyerere of Tanzania were among heads of state who visited New Zealand during the year.

G. W. A. BUSH
The University of Auckland

NEW ZEALAND • Information Highlights

Official Name: New Zealand.
Location: South Pacific Ocean.
Area: 103,736 square miles (268,675 sq km).
Population (1973 est.): 3,000,000.
Chief Cities (1973 est.): Wellington, the capital, 140,000; Christchurch, 168,800.
Government: *Head of state,* Elizabeth II, queen, represented by Sir Denis Blundell, governor-general (took office Sept. 1972). *Head of government,* Wallace E. Rowling, prime minister (took office Sept. 1974). *Legislature* (unicameral)—House of Representatives.
Monetary Unit: New Zealand dollar (0.7692 N. Z. dollar equals U. S.$1, Sept. 1974).
Gross National Product (1972 est.): $9,740,000,000.
Manufacturing (major products): Processed foods, meat, wood products, cement, fertilizers.
Major Agricultural Products: Wheat, potatoes, dairy products, sheep, wool, forest products.
Foreign Trade (1973): *Exports,* $2,579,000,000; *imports,* $2,190,000,000.

NEWFOUNDLAND

In 1974, Newfoundland celebrated 25 years of confederation with Canada. By and large the people took the event calmly, aware of the benefits which come from union, but not overwhelmed by or with Canadian nationalism. In October, Joseph R. Smallwood (premier in 1949–72) appeared at a Liberal Party Leadership Convention. Smallwood had emerged from retirement at the age of 73 to challenge the incumbent, Ed Roberts, but the convention rejected him on a second ballot, 298 to 402.

Labrador. In March, the provincial government announced that it had successfully negotiated the purchase, at a price of $160 million, of all the hydroelectric development rights held by Brinco Corporation. The province, with help from the federal government, hopes to build a billion-dollar hydroelectric complex at the Lower Churchill Falls site and transmit the power to the island part of the province. In May 1974 the Royal Commission on Labrador under Chairman D. Snowden made public its six-volume report, which contained 288 recommendations covering virtually all aspects of Labrador life. By late 1974 the provincial government had not made public its reaction to these recommendations.

In September, Eastcan Exploration Ltd. confirmed that it had found a promising field of natural gas offshore of Labrador. There was uncertainty as to the size and value of the find and the difficulties of exploitation, but the possibilities of future wealth have intensified the competition between provincial and federal authorities as to which government is responsible for the regulation of the field. The province threatened to lay the matter before the Supreme Court of Canada.

Provincial Government. In April the minister of finance brought down a budget characterized by conservative fiscal management. Expenditures rose by 15% to a total of $750 million. At the same time the sales tax was increased to 8% and personal income tax was raised from 36% to 40% of the basic federal tax.

— NEWFOUNDLAND • Information Highlights —

Area: 156,185 square miles (404,520 sq km).
Population (1974 est.): 541,000.
Chief Cities (1971 census): St. John's, the capital, 88,102; Corner Brook, 26,309.
Government (1974): *Chief Officers*—lt. gov., E. John A. Harnum; premier, F. D. Moores (Progressive Conservative); min. of justice, T. A. Hickman (PC); min. of educ., G. R. Ottenheimer (PC); chief justice, Robert S. Furlong. *Legislature*—Legislative Assembly, 43 members (32 PC, 8 Liberal, 1 New Labrador party, 1 vacancy).
Education (1972–73): *Enrollment:* public elementary and secondary schools, 162,700 pupils; private schools, 843; colleges and universities, 7,309 students. *Public school expenditures* (1972), $124,700,000.
Public Finance (fiscal year 1974–75 est.): *Revenues*, $661,000,000; *expenditures*, $750,000,000.
Personal Income (1972): $1,310,000,000; average annual income per person, $2,477.
(All monetary figures are in Canadian dollars.)

Natural Resources. In line with its investment in the Stephenville linerboard mill and a general awareness of the need to protect and enhance the province's control over natural resources, the government announced in January that it would manage forest resources more actively. In addition, it established a Royal Commission on Mineral Revenue to investigate the complex issue of the management of mines. As for the fisheries, that oldest of Newfoundland's natural resources, 1974 was the worst year in living memory. Ice conditions were very bad until late in the season, and then, when the fishery did open, the fish were not there. The province is urging the federal government to declare a 200-mile zone of management to protect what seems to be a rapidly depleting resource.

SUSAN MCCORQUODALE
Memorial University of Newfoundland

NIGERIA

The stability of the military government and ever-increasing revenues from petroleum enabled Nigeria to continue its development program in 1974 despite inflation and drought.

Domestic Developments. During 1974 there were few challenges to the military. The most serious were student demonstrations on the third anniversary (February 1) of student disorders. On February 4 the police used tear gas on the demonstrators at Ibadan. Soon afterward there were disturbances at Lagos, Ife, Ahmadu Bello, and in some of the polytechnic schools. Hundreds of students were arrested, and four of the six universities were closed in February for three weeks.

In April, 3,000 nurses in the West, complaining about inflation and inadequate salaries, went on a brief work slowdown. During the following month, train services were almost halted by similar protests on the part of railway workers. However, no group in Nigeria had sufficient popular support to affect the central government authority and its 200,000-man army.

Census data for 1973, released at midyear, indicated that Nigeria had a total population of 79,760,000. There were startling increases in the population of the North since the 1963 census. North-East state had increased by 97%, Kwara by 93%, and Kano by 88%, while the Western and the Eastern states had lost population. A National Data Review Committee was formed to recheck the census.

In 1970, the president, Maj. Gen. Yakubu Gowon, had hinted at a return to civilian government by 1976. During 1974 there was much public speculation on the subject. Practically every major political and military figure had discussed civilian rule, and the press had speculated about it. Even the probable number of states in a reorganized Nigeria had been debated in all areas of the country. But all such hopes were dashed by Gowon on Independence

Day, when he stated that there would be no return to "cutthroat politics that once led the nation into serious crisis." The ban on political activity was continued.

Economy. The most important factor in Nigeria's economy continued to be petroleum, exports of which were valued at 2,227 million naira ($3,600 million) in 1973. Nigeria was the world's seventh largest producer of petroleum, which earned over 80% of its foreign exchange moneys. The Ministry of Mines and Power, in a decree dated April 1, announced the country's intention to assume controlling (55%) interest in five oil companies (including the U. S. companies Gulf Oil and Mobil Oil) engaged in exploration there. This, combined with the rise in the price per barrel from $4.80 in October 1973 to $14.96 during the first quarter of 1974, meant even greater capital accumulation.

The petroleum picture, however, masked problem areas. The peanut crop was a fraction of normal; palm oil production has never recovered from the civil war; and the 1974 cocoa crop promised to be 20% less than in 1972. Major developments, such as road building, also were hurt by inflation. Unemployment in the cities and towns remained very high. Per capita earnings of Nigerians remained low, the same as that of Gambians (about $140).

Despite these problems, Nigeria continued to develop its industrial sector in 1974. Automobile assembly plants at Kaduna and Lagos were being constructed, Japan was fabricating new railroad equipment, a new refinery was under construction at Warri, and cement factories were being erected in Lagos and the North-East state. With an estimated gross domestic product of 4,705 million naira ($7,622 million) and an annual growth rate of 10%, Nigeria has one of the healthier economies in Africa.

Drought. The areas in the northern states that had been declared disaster areas in January 1973 continued to be hard hit in 1974. An estimated 4 million persons have been affected by the drought. Kano state alone spent 600,000 naira ($972,000) on relief. Dikwa Emirate of the North-East was further devastated by bush rat and locust invasions, which ended hopes of a harvest there. Shrinkage in the size of Lake Chad affected not only fishing but also livestock raising and farming in the area. Throughout the north the slaughter of livestock continued and crushing mills were shut down by July because of peanut shortages. Schools in the affected areas were forced to close. The drought was felt also in the Western state, and there was damaging erosion in parts of the East-Central state.

Long-range plans to ward off future disasters were focused on the development of water supplies. The most dramatic plan begun in 1974 was the Sokoto-Rima Basin scheme, which called for a major dam at Bakolori to bring 75,000 acres of marginal land under cultivation.

Foreign Affairs. General Gowon continued as a major spokesman for sub-Saharan Africa. Many times he voiced Nigeria's opposition to the white regimes of southern Africa and called for specific action against them by Britain and the Organization of African Unity (OAU). He paid state visits to Guinea in February and Libya in June, and made a week-long official tour of the Soviet Union in May.

Difficulties with Cameroon over land and sea boundaries were exacerbated by the potential riches of petroleum in the disputed area. A joint Nigerian and Cameroon commission was appointed to study the delimitation question.

HARRY A. GAILEY, *San Jose State University*

NIGERIA • Information Highlights

Official Name: Federal Republic of Nigeria.
Location: West Africa.
Area: 356,668 square miles (923,768 sq km).
Population (1973 census): 79,760,000.
Chief Cities (1971 est.): Lagos, the capital, 901,000; Ibadan, 758,000; Ogbomosho, 387,000; Kano, 357,000.
Government: *Head of state and of government,* Gen. Yakubu Gowon, president (assumed power Aug. 1966).
Monetary Unit: Naira (0.6173 naira equals U. S.$1, June 1974).
Gross National Product (1972 est.): $8,650,000,000.
Manufacturing (major products): Processed foods, cotton textiles, cement, petroleum products.
Major Agricultural Products: Groundnuts, palm kernels, cacao, rubber, cotton, sweet potatoes and yams, forest products, fish.
Foreign Trade (1973): *Exports,* $3,385,000,000; *imports,* $1,877,000,000.

NORTH CAROLINA

Politics, sports, and the fuel shortage were the leading stories of 1974 in North Carolina.

Elections. In the November 5 elections, Democrat Robert Morgan defeated Republican William Stevens for the U. S. Senate. Rufus Edmisten, who worked for Senator Sam Ervin on the Watergate committee, defeated Republican James Carson in a bitter race for attorney general. The Democratic tide swept from office two Republican congressmen (Earl Ruth and Wilmer Mizell) and reduced the Republican membership in the General Assembly to only 10 out of 170.

The Administration. The accelerated replacement of career employees by Republicans, many of them not natives of the state, led some Democrats to allude darkly to "the second coming of the carpetbaggers." Even the state personnel director was fired. Of the 21 appointees to the Sir Walter Raleigh Commission, none was a member of a statewide historical organization.

The Legislature. The Democrat-controlled General Assembly, however, meeting for the first time this century in an annual rather than biennial session, approved most of Gov. James E. Holshouser's programs. Together with 1973 appropriations, the budget totaled nearly $6 billion, as compared with $4.4 billion in the previous biennium.

UPI

North Carolina's new U. S. senator, Democrat Robert B. Morgan, with his wife, Katie, on election night. Morgan succeeds Sen. Sam J. Ervin, Jr., who is retiring.

Record appropriations were made for kindergartens, occupational education, and programs for exceptional children. Three previously approved state historic sites were funded. The controversy over the location of the new state art museum continued. The General Assembly voted $7.5 million for expansion of the medical education program at East Carolina University, and funds were provided for the establishment of area health centers. In addition to increasing funds for the correctional institutions, the Assembly abolished capital punishment except for first-degree murder and first-degree rape.

Environmentalists failed to push through a strong land-use law, but a weak Coastal Area Management Law, affecting 20 eastern counties, was passed. The 8% ceiling on home loans was repealed, and the Utilities Commission was empowered to consider projected future economic conditions in fixing utilities rates.

The Economy. An expanding economy was indicated by increased state revenue—up 9.9% during the 1973–74 fiscal year—but the unemployment rate rose to 4.6% in June 1974, up from 3.5% a year before. Concern for road improvements developed as gasoline revenue dropped at a time when a report revealed 40% of the rural roads to be substandard. In order to cope with the gasoline crisis early in the year, a voluntary alternate-day purchasing plan was instituted and worked fairly well.

People in the News. Death came on March 15 to former U. S. Senator B. Everett Jordan, and on October 6 to former Secretary of Commerce Luther H. Hodges. Sen. Sam Ervin, Jr., chose not to run for reelection despite his popularity gained as chairman of the Senate Watergate investigating committee.

Sports. North Carolina State University's basketball team dethroned UCLA as NCAA champions; and UNC's Tony Waldrop ran a record nine consecutive sub-four-minute miles. The USSR defeated the United States in a track and field competition at Duke University.

H. G. JONES
University of North Carolina

— NORTH CAROLINA • Information Highlights —

Area: 52,586 square miles (136,198 sq km).
Population (1973 est.): 5,273,000. *Density:* 107 per sq mi.
Chief Cities (1970 census): Raleigh, the capital, 123,793; Charlotte, 241,178; Greensboro, 144,076.
Government (1974): *Chief Officers*—governor, James E. Holshouser, Jr. (R); lt. gov., James B. Hunt, Jr. (D). *General Assembly*—Senate, 50 members (35 D, 15 R); House of Representatives, 120 members (85 D, 35 R).
Education (1973–74): *Enrollment*—public elementary schools, 786,697 pupils; public secondary schools, 358,984; nonpublic schools, 27,200; colleges and universities, 204,080 students. *Public school expenditures,* $958,195,000 ($900 per pupil).
State Finances (fiscal year 1973): *Revenues,* $2,873,534,000; *expenditures,* $2,472,679,000.
Personal Income (1973): $21,726,000,000; per capita, $4,120.
Labor Force (July 1974): *Nonagricultural wage and salary earners,* 2,013,000; *insured unemployed,* 28,900 (1.7%).

NORTH DAKOTA

North Dakota granted its first water permit for coal gasification in 1974, opening its western grain and grazing lands to future development of vast lignite reserves to meet the nation's energy needs. That act became a major issue in a bitter political campaign, sent land values soaring, stepped up leasing of coal-bearing sites, and increased demands from natural gas and electric generating companies for a share of the state's water. Coupled with gasification and onsite power generation, strip mining—now a minor economic activity—could eventually equal agriculture as a source of state wealth.

Politics. In the Senate race, incumbent Sen. Milton R. Young (R) defeated former Gov. William L. Guy (D) by so slim a margin that a recount was inevitable. An independent third candidate, environmentalist James Jungroth, was a factor in the outcome. He attracted votes away from both candidates. Congressman Mark Andrews (R) was reelected, as was Public Service Commissioner Ben Wolf, a Republican. Democrats made impressive gains in the legislature but fell short of majorities in both chambers.

Voters approved two constitutional amendments pairing the governor and lieutenant governor as a ballot team and providing for retirement or removal of judges. Rejected by the voters were measures earmarking funds to give

NORTH DAKOTA • Information Highlights

Area: 70,665 square miles (183,022 sq km).
Population (1973 est.): 640,000. *Density:* 9 per sq mi.
Chief Cities (1970 census): Bismarck, the capital, 34,703; Fargo, 53,365; Grand Forks, 39,008; Minot, 32,290.
Government (1974): *Chief Officers*—governor, Arthur A. Link (D); lt. gov., Wayne G. Sanstead (D). *Legislative Assembly*—Senate, 51 members (40 R, 11 D); House of Representatives, 102 members (76 R, 26 D).
Education (1973–74): Enrollment—public elementary schools, 90,351 pupils; public secondary schools, 47,951; nonpublic schools, 11,600; colleges and universities, 29,189 students. *Public school expenditures,* $126,000,000 ($947 per pupil).
State Finances (fiscal year 1973): *Revenues,* $420,146,000; *expenditures,* $379,909,000.
Personal Income (1973): $3,061,000,000; per capita, $4,782.
Labor Force (July 1974): *Nonagricultural wage and salary earners,* 191,100; *insured unemployed,* 1,900 (1.4%).

summer employment to youth and to permit family units to form farming corporations.

The U. S. Supreme Court agreed to hear an appeal from a federal court panel's legislative reapportionment plan. At issue were multiple Senate districts in major cities and arbitrary election district boundaries.

Agriculture. In a year of rising prices, when farmers hoped to increase their acreage, spring floods and heavy rain delayed start of farming operations. The growing season was hot and dry, and it was shortened by early frost. Although wheat growers harvested the fourth largest crop in 10 years, adverse weather conditions cut the value of the crop by more than $180 million.

Other grain and row-crop production continued strong, and farm prices remained high except for livestock. Ranchers suffered losses from soaring feed-grain costs and a 40% drop in feeder-cattle prices. The first sugar beet crop processed by grower-owned cooperatives in their new refineries was sweetened by skyrocketing sugar prices.

Industry. Water-use permits were issued to two power cooperatives building a lignite-fired electric-generating facility. A request by a private utility for water to operate a four-plant complex is pending, as are permits for 11 gasification plants. Construction started in 1974 on a huge electric generating unit and on additions to two existing plants. Six coal-fed generating facilities now export electric energy out of the state along 9,400 miles of transmission lines.

Environment. Conditions to safeguard the environment were attached to permits issued to the energy-producing industry. Citizen groups urged additional legislation regulating strip mining and establishing reclamation standards. The 1975 legislature probably will create a department of natural resources. Environmentalists challenged the gigantic Garrison Dam diversion project, which some day will irrigate much of the state with water from Lake Sakakawea, and enlisted help of the Canadian government to fight continuation of construction.

STAN CANN, *"The Forum," Fargo*

NORTHWEST TERRITORIES

The Canadian Parliament approved significant legislation in 1974 for the political development of the Northwest Territories.

Amendments to the Northwest Territories Act increased the number of elected members of the Territorial Council from 10 to 15 and eliminated appointed members. Elections will be held in March 1975 for the first entirely elected council. The new council will select its own speaker from among its members; previously the commissioner of the Northwest Territories was the presiding officer.

Legislation. The government of the Northwest Territories has begun handling many of the affairs that are handled by a regular provincial government, with the exception of natural resources, which are administered by the federal government. The council passed a $150 million budget for 1974, up about $110 million since 1969, reflecting the territorial government's increased responsibility over the five-year period. Other legislation passed included a complete revision of the Worker's Compensation Ordinance establishing a Worker's Compensation Board. The minimum wage was increased to $2.50 an hour.

Mackenzie Valley Pipeline. A consortium of 27 companies, mostly foreign controlled, applied on March 21 for permission to build a $5.7 billion pipeline to carry natural gas from the Arctic, through the Mackenzie Valley, to Canadian and U. S. markets. Preliminary hearings were held by Justice Thomas Berger, who indicated that he would consider all aspects related to construction of the pipeline, including its economic, environmental, and social implications. Northern native groups have indicated that aboriginal rights will be an issue.

The government of the Northwest Territories has been planning for the possibility of a pipeline. It wants to ensure that if the pipeline is built the region's population will get the maximum economic benefit and that efforts will be taken to minimize social disruption.

ROSS M. HARVEY, *Chief of Publications*
Government of the Northwest Territories

NORTHWEST TERRITORIES • Information Highlights

Area: 1,304,903 square miles (3,379,699 sq km).
Population (1974 est.): 38,000.
Chief Cities (1974 est.): Yellowknife, the capital, 8,000.
Government (1974): *Chief Officers*—commissioner, Stuart M. Hodgson; deputy commissioner, John H. Parker; dir. of educ., N. J. Macpherson; judge of the Supreme Court, William G. Morrow. *Legislature*—Territorial Council, 14 members, 10 elected, 4 appointed; (projected 1975) 15 elected members.
Education (Sept. 1974): *Enrollment:* elementary and secondary schools, 12,803 pupils, including 4,951 Eskimos, 1,921 Indians. *Public school expenditures* (1973–74), $31,243,200.
Public Finance (fiscal year 1974–75 est.): *Revenues,* $109,000,000; *expenditures,* $141,000,000.
Mining (1973 est.): Production value, $164,777,000.
(All monetary figures are in Canadian dollars.)

NORWAY

Norway's economy continued to prosper through 1974, despite the worldwide economic downturn caused largely by the energy crisis. Employment was maintained at a very high level, and foreign demand remained strong for most of the country's main export goods. Inflation was kept under better control in Norway than in most other Western industrial countries. The minority Labor government achieved this by extensive use of subsidies for food and other essentials and by keeping a tight rein on credit. According to the Economic Cooperation and Development Organization (OECD), consumer prices in Norway rose by only 9.9% in the 12 months ending Aug. 31, 1974, while the average for Western Europe was 14%.

Labor. New two-year wage contracts for most of the country's industrial workers were negotiated, industry by industry, through the months of the spring and summer of 1974. Bargaining was tough, partly because the high wages being paid by companies involved in the offshore oil boom tended to inflate the demands of workers in other industries. In a few cases employers and unions failed to reach agreement, so that strikes ensued. Norsk Hydro, the industrial combine in which the state has a controlling interest, suffered a two-week strike in July. The stoppage ended when the government ordered compulsory arbitration. Compulsory arbitration also was used to settle a dispute between farmers and the government over farm product prices and agricultural subsidies. During the dispute the farmers called a six-day producers' strike, and for several days milk was unobtainable in most food stores throughout the country.

Negotiation of the new wage contracts would doubtless have been even more difficult if the government had not given wage earners a "package" of tax cuts, increased subsidies, and higher social security benefits just prior to the bargaining. The package, announced in March, was financed by borrowing against future revenues from offshore oil and gas.

The Oil and Gas Industry. The prospect of future oil revenues also was used to justify a deficit budget in the autumn, when the government handed out further substantial tax concessions. At the same time it was announced that very large balance-of-payments deficits were expected in both 1974 and 1975, partly a result of the government's expansionary economic policies.

There was much public debate, during the year, about the danger of disrupting Norway's economy through a too-rapid development of off-shore petroleum resources. A white paper published by the Ministry of Finance in February promised that the pace of development on the continental shelf would be kept under tight control, mainly by limiting the number of new search licenses granted, but also by postponing exploitation of finds made. Allocation of new licenses, originally expected for the spring, was repeatedly postponed during the year.

There were signs, however, that the oil boom could prove difficult to keep under control. Only a few months after the government's promises of cautious development, a new oil and gas field was discovered in Norwegian waters with reserves apparently even larger than those of the giant Ekofisk structure. The new field, called Statfjord, was declared commercial at the end of August. Exploitation rights were held by a consortium in which the state oil company, Statoil, had a half share. Statoil was believed to favor rapid development of the field, in order to give the company the resources it needed to become a fully integrated oil concern, with interests in refining, petrochemicals, and marketing. Under pressure from its own state oil company, the government might find it hard to enforce its suggested future production ceiling of 90 million tons per year, from Norway's continental shelf.

The Fishing Industry. The question of Norwegian fishing boundaries was much in the news during the year. Norwegian fishermen wanted fishing limits extended, but the government was reluctant to act unilaterally. It hoped the UN Law of the Sea conference in Caracas during the summer would vote to give coastal states rights over resources in a 200-mile "economic zone" off their shores. When the conference ended without definite results, the fishermen increased their pressure on the government. In September it announced it would seek first to create "no trawling" zones outside the existing 12-mile limit, in areas where foreign trawlers had often destroyed local fishermen's lines and nets. Soon after, it would extend fishing limits to 50 miles, along the northern part of the coast, pending international agreement on the "economic zone" proposal. It promised, however, to consult with the various countries affected about both of the measures before putting them into effect.

THOR GJESTER, *"Norwegian Journal of Commerce and Shipping," Oslo*

NORWAY • Information Highlights

Official Name: Kingdom of Norway.
Location: Northern Europe.
Area: 125,181 square miles (324,219 sq km).
Population (1973 est.): 4,000,000.
Chief Cities (1973 est.): Oslo, the capital, 472,500; Bergen, 213,700; Trondheim, 131,300.
Government: *Head of state,* Olav V, king (acceded Sept. 1957). *Head of government,* Trygve Bratteli, prime minister (took office Oct. 1973). *Legislature*—Storting: Lagting and Odelsting.
Monetary Unit: Krone (5.53 kroner equal U.S.$1, July 1974).
Gross National Product (1973 est.): $16,600,000,000.
Manufacturing (major products): Metals, pulp and paper, chemicals, ships, fish products.
Major Agricultural Products: Potatoes, barley, apples, pears, dairy products, livestock.
Foreign Trade (1973): *Exports,* $4,688,000,000; *imports,* $6,233,000,000.

NOVA SCOTIA

Nova Scotians in 1974 were concerned with the provincial election, the enactment of some significant legislative measures, the publication of the Royal Commission Report on Education and Public Services, oil exploration on the Scotia Shelf, and rising food prices.

Legislature and Government. In April 1974, the Liberal party of Nova Scotia was returned to power with a substantially improved majority. The newly elected legislature, which remained in session from May 23 to June 28, enacted 90 bills of 98 proposed, including amendments to the Health Services and Insurance Act, the Property Tax Bill, the Gasoline Licensing Act, and a bill setting up a Nova Scotia Police Commission.

Whereas under the Health Act the government for the first time introduced a "pharmacare" program for supplying free drugs to 74,000 senior citizens of Nova Scotia, the Gasoline Act enabled Nova Scotia to become the first province in Canada to control wholesale fuel prices and the use of its products in times of shortages. The Property Tax Bill authorized municipalities to give a 25% property tax rebate on all residential properties, and made it mandatory for all landlords to pass the tax reductions on to their tenants. One controversial bill which could not find its way through the House would have established collective bargaining rights for teachers.

After more than three years of investigation, the Royal Commission on Education and Public Services, acting under the chairmanship of J. F. Graham, published its findings in a 7,000-page report. This report suggests a complete reorganization of the boundaries of municipal government, drastic changes in financing and managing public education, and in the machinery for handling municipal-provincial relationships. These changes, when implemented, will have a far-reaching effect on the economic, social, and cultural life of Nova Scotians.

NOVA SCOTIA • Information Highlights

Area: 21,425 square miles (55,490 sq km).
Chief Cities (1971 census): Halifax, the capital, 122,035; Dartmouth, 64,770; Sydney, 33,230.
Government (1974): *Chief Officers*—lt. gov., Dr. Clarence Gosse; premier, Gerald A. Regan (Liberal); atty. gen., Allan E. Sullivan (L); min. of educ., J. William Gillis (L); chief justice, Ian M. McKeigan. *Legislature*—Legislative Assembly, 46 members (31 Liberal, 12 Progressive Conservative, 3 New Democratic).
Education (1973): *Enrollment:* public elementary and secondary schools, 220,380 pupils; private schools, 1,394; colleges and universities, 16,095 students. *Public school expenditures* (1972–73), $177,077,806.
Public Finance (fiscal year 1974–75 est.): *Revenues,* $642,978,200; *Expenditures,* $766,195,700.
Personal Income (1973): $2,682,000,000.
(All monetary figures are in Canadian dollars.)

Economy. The provincial economy, after having reached its peak during the major part of 1973, started to slow down. The overall increase in capital investment was expected to have slowed down as 1974 neared a close. The unprecedented building boom experienced by the provincial economy during 1973 seems to be tapering off, indicating a slowdown in the construction industry by the end of the year. In spite of this cooling, the economy, through its capacity to absorb the labor market entrants, was able to keep the level of unemployment low. Average weekly wages and salaries increased, but with the rate of inflation touching the 10% mark and the food prices component of the consumer price index recording 15.6% increase, almost all of this increase was absorbed by escalating prices.

Oil Exploration. Oil exploration on the Scotia Shelf has made further progress. The oil companies were expected to complete the drilling of eight additional wells in 1974. Encouraging quantities of hydrocarbons have been found, ranging in volume from 10 to 17 million cubic feet of natural gas and up to 1,050 barrels of crude oil per day.

R. P. SETH
Mount Saint Vincent University, Halifax

MOBIL OIL CANADA LTD.

A helicopter lifts off from an oil-drilling rig near Sable Island in the Atlantic Ocean, about 250 miles (400 km) east of Halifax, Nova Scotia. Oil and natural gas finds below the Scotia Shelf are encouraging drillers to face risks in Canada's stormy "Iceberg Alley."

SVEN SIMON FROM KATHERINE YOUNG

DUKE ELLINGTON (1899–1974)
Elegance at an early age.

ELLINGTON, Edward Kennedy (Duke)

American composer, jazz pianist, and orchestra leader: b. Washington, D. C., April 29, 1899; d. New York City, May 24, 1974.

Duke Ellington was the most complete American musician of the 20th century. He was a composer whose work was based on his Afro-American heritage rather than the European musical styles that were the source for most of his contemporaries among "serious" American composers. His compositions encompassed almost all forms of American music—jazz, popular songs, concert works, theater scores, ballet music, film scores, sacred music. As a pianist and orchestra leader, his work was as much at home in a nightclub or dance hall as it was in a concert hall or the world's greatest churches.

Ellington composed jazz pieces that are part of the basic jazz repertory—"Mood Indigo," "The Mooche," "Black and Tan Fantasy." He wrote popular songs that have become standards —"Solitude," "Sophisticated Lady." He explored new areas of extended composition with "Black, Brown and Beige," "Night Creature," and "Such Sweet Thunder." By 1974 he was developing a highly individual repertory of sacred music.

Early Years. Unlike many black jazz musicians, Duke Ellington did not use music as a means of escaping poverty. He was born in Washington, D. C., on April 29, 1899, to a family of moderately comfortable means. His father was a blueprint maker for the Navy Department who also worked occasionally as a butler.

Young Duke, who got his nickname at the age of eight from a friend because of the elegance of manner that he had cultivated even then, was initially torn between music and art. He won a scholarship to study art when he was 19 but rejected it in favor of music. In 1914, at the age of 15, he wrote his first piece of music, "Soda Fountain Rag." By the time he was 20, he was earning $150 a week leading his own small band which included Sonny Greer, a drummer who continued to work with Ellington for 32 years. Ellington and Greer moved to New York in 1923 to join Elmer Snowden's band. Snowden left the group a year later, and Ellington succeeded to the leadership.

Musical Style. The Ellington orchestral style began to emerge during the next two years through the "growl" and "wah-wah" sounds produced by trumpeter Bubber Miley and trombonist Joe (Tricky Sam) Nanton. These were the basic elements in the so-called "jungle" style for which the Ellington band became known when it started a long engagement at the Cotton Club in Harlem in 1927. In that same year, a 17-year-old saxophonist, Harry Carney, joined the band and was still with it 47 years later when Ellington died. In the next few years, a number of other musicians with very individual musical styles and sounds came into the band—Johnny Hodges, Barney Bigard, Cootie Williams, Lawrence Brown. Ellington used their musical colorations as elements in his compositions to create an effect unlike that of any contemporary orchestra.

Career. In 1943 the Ellington band gave the first of a series of concerts at Carnegie Hall in New York City for which the Duke composed a 50-minute work, "Black, Brown and Beige," a pioneering effort in a field in which most compositions ran for only three or four minutes. In the years that followed, Ellington composed one or two concert works every year, most of them of 15 or 20 minutes duration.

During the 1940's, he wrote scores for two musicals—*Jump for Joy* (1941) and *Beggar's Holiday* (1947). In the 1950's, Ellington works were commissioned by the Symphony of the Air and the NBC Symphony, and the Duke also wrote and narrated a television production, *A Drum Is a Woman.* In 1963 he composed a musical panorama of black history, "My People," which was presented in Chicago, and in 1965 he introduced his first Concert of Sacred Music at Grace Cathedral in San Francisco. His Second Concert of Sacred Music was premiered in 1968 at the Cathedral of St. John the Divine in New York City. A third Sacred Concert, first performed in Westminster Abbey in 1973, was never given in America before Ellington's death.

JOHN S. WILSON
Author, Jazz: The Transition Years—1940–1960

UPI

CHARLES A. LINDBERGH (1902–1974)
Flight into history.

LINDBERGH, Charles A.

American aviator and conservationist: b. Detroit, Mich., Feb. 4, 1902; d. Kipahulu, Maui, Hawaii, Aug. 26, 1974.

Charles A Lindbergh made the first solo nonstop flight from New York to Paris, landing there on May 21, 1927. He flew his fragile monoplane, *Spirit of St. Louis,* about 3,600 miles (5,800 km) across the Atlantic on a 33½-hour journey, winning the $25,000 Orteig Prize and becoming an instant world celebrity.

Young, tall, and slim, and a clean-living bachelor with an engaging grin and a modest demeanor, Lindbergh was engulfed in publicity that soon revolted him and from which he spent a lifetime trying to escape. The fame and adulation, for which he was ill-equipped psychologically, led to the kidnapping and murder of his first child and impelled him, by complex circumstances, to oppose U. S. entry into World War II. Because his stand mirrored many Nazi views, his name was sullied for many years, but it was much redeemed in later life by his active work for conservation.

Life and Work. Charles Augustus Lindbergh was the son of Charles A. Lindbergh, a prosperous Little Falls, Minn., lawyer and liberal Republican congressman of Swedish descent, and his second wife, Evangeline Lodge Land. He was an imaginative, inventive child, who, upon seeing a plane, wished he could "fly up there among those clouds." The farmboy graduated from high school in 1918 and entered the University of Wisconsin in 1920 to study engineering, but left because of low grades. He learned to fly in 1922 and barnstormed the West as a stunt flier. In 1924 he joined the Army and graduated first in his class at flying school in 1925. The next year he was chief pilot on the St. Louis–Chicago mail run, his first and last regular job.

After Lindbergh's Atlantic trip, he received the U. S. Medal of Honor, the Distinguished Flying Cross, and hundreds of other awards. He visited every state in his monoplane, and then married Anne Spencer Morrow, daughter of diplomat and banker Dwight Morrow, on May 27, 1929. In the 1930's, he was a consultant in laying out Latin American, Atlantic, and Pacific air routes, worked with Nobel Prize winner Alexis Carrel in devising a tissue-perfusion pump, and gave encouragement and support to Robert Goddard, the rocket pioneer.

His first son, Charles Jr., born in 1930, was kidnapped and slain in 1932, a crime for which Bruno Hauptmann, a carpenter, was arrested in 1934 after a bizarre hunt. Following Hauptmann's sensational trial in 1935, Lindbergh, his wife, and a second son, Jon, went into exile in Europe, where he was befriended by Nazi leaders, among others.

Lindbergh returned to the United States in 1939, and, speaking for the America First Committee, opposed intervention in the war. His remarks offended most Jews, but he denied being anti-Semitic or pro-Nazi. President Roosevelt suggested, however, that he was disloyal, and Lindbergh resigned his colonelcy. After Pearl Harbor, he went to the Pacific in 1944 to study warplanes under combat conditions and as a civilian flew 50 missions against the Japanese. This experience was recounted in *The Wartime Journals of Charles A. Lindbergh* (1970), one of his four books. The others were *We* (1927), *Of Flight and Life* (1948), and *The Spirit of St. Louis* (1953), which won a Pulitzer Prize for biography.

After the war he was a consultant to Pan American World Airways until his death and a company director until 1972. He also was a consultant for the U. S. aerospace program. In 1964, becoming acutely aware of threats to the global ecosystem, he began to devote most of his energy to conservation and in 1968 emerged from a self-imposed privacy to speak publicly for environmental action. He is credited with saving the humpback and blue whales and other imperiled species and with having helped to block U. S. development of commercial supersonic planes.

The Lindberghs—his wife is a noted writer—had six children. Besides Charles, they are Jon, Land, Anne, Reeve, and Scott.

ALDEN WHITMAN, *"The New York Times"*

PERÓN, Juan Domingo

President of Argentina: b. Lobos, Argentina, Oct. 8, 1895; d. Buenos Aires, July 1, 1974.

Perón was one of the remarkable leaders of the 20th century. His political career spanned 30 turbulent years, ending just in time to preserve his image among most Argentines as the great social reformer, protector of the poor, and the nation's defender from economic domination by foreigners.

Military Career. He moved with his family to Buenos Aires in 1904 and attended schools there. In 1913 he graduated from the Colegio Militar as sublieutenant in the infantry. For the next 30 years, he climbed steadily up the military ladder, combining assignments in Argentina with missions abroad. In 1930, he dabbled in politics briefly as a participant in the coup that overthrew President Yrigoyen.

Rise to Leadership. In 1943, Perón emerged as a political leader when he led a secret group of officers called the GOU in a revolution against President Ramón Castillo. He became undersecretary of war and head of the National Department of Labor so as to develop contacts with the labor movement. In this he was aided by his attractive and intelligent mistress, Eva Duarte. Soon thereafter came appointment as minister of war, and, on June 7, 1944, appointment as vice president.

On Oct. 13, 1945, as a result of his growing power, Perón was detained and flown to the prison island of Martín García. In response, Eva Duarte and his allies in the labor movement organized a gigantic demonstration in downtown Buenos Aires. His enemies backed off, and that night he addressed the crowd as the new leader of Argentina. In February 1946 he was elected president.

From 1945 to his downfall 10 years later, Perón transformed the country, skillfully combining nationalism with reform. He was the first Argentine political leader to undertake a meaningful redistribution of income. With Eva, whom he married in 1945, he encouraged the organization of labor, increased wages, and gave the masses the feeling that the government had responsibilities to them.

In 1952, Eva Perón died of cancer (she was Perón's second wife) just three weeks after his second term began. The pace of economic growth also slowed, due largely to the failure of agriculture, and increasingly Perón combined repression with demagogy to retain power. Finally, landholders, foreign investors, and professional groups—with decisive aid from the Catholic Church and sectors within the armed forces—mounted a successful revolt against Perón in September 1955.

Exile. From Buenos Aires, Perón fled to Paraguay and then to Panama where he met his future and third wife, María Estela Martínez, known as Isabel, who became his secretary. Perón's travels took him from Panama back to Caracas and then on to the Dominican Republic, which he left for Spain in 1960. Perón's years in the wilderness of right-wing regimes did not destroy his appeal in Argentina. From Madrid, he manipulated his followers and through their numbers, his enemies. Clearly, there was to be no stability without Perón.

UPI

JUAN PERÓN (1895–1974)
Death preserved the myth.

Return to Power. Reluctantly, the armed forces accepted the return of the exile on Nov. 17, 1972, and arranged for elections. Still barred from the presidency itself, Perón returned briefly to Spain while his handpicked candidate, Dr. Héctor Cámpora, led the now-legal Peronists to electoral victory. Cámpora resigned soon thereafter to allow new elections. This time Perón, with his wife as vice presidential candidate, swept to an easy victory.

On Oct. 12, 1973, the fantastic story of Juan Perón reached its climax when he donned the presidential sash again after 18 years. But Argentina was vastly different—the social divisions were deeper, the guerrillas more daring, the Peronists bitterly divided. Before he could preside over the destruction of his own myth, the ailing Perón died of heart disease at the age of 78 and was succeeded in the presidency by his wife. As Argentina collectively mourned his death, the legend grew.

JAMES R. LEVY
University of New South Wales, Australia

UPI

GEORGES POMPIDOU (1911–1974)
He followed de Gaulle to the height of power.

POMPIDOU, Georges

President of the French Republic: b. Montboudif, France, July 5, 1911; d. Paris, April 2, 1974.

Georges Pompidou, teacher, author, and politician, owed his public career to Charles de Gaulle, but his success to his talents. He almost accidentally took service with the general in 1944. Surprisingly, he was named prime minister in 1962, and as abruptly dismissed in 1968. Following de Gaulle's resignation, he was elected president of France on June 15, 1969, causing schisms in Gaullism.

Early Life. Born on July 5, 1911, in an obscure Auvergne village, he was the grandson of a peasant and the son of a schoolteacher. Exceptional qualities won him a first-class education. In 1935 he married Claude Cahour, by whom he had one son.

Pompidou taught literature in Marseille and Paris for ten years, interrupted by military service in the disastrous campaign of 1939–40. Joining de Gaulle's staff in a literary secretarial capacity, he was appointed to the Council of State and remained an adviser to de Gaulle after his resignation in January 1946.

Socially active in the literary and artistic world, he joined the Rothschild investment bank in 1954, but continued to help de Gaulle. When the general returned to power in 1958, Pompidou became his chief of staff. He went back to the bank after de Gaulle's election to the presidency of the Fifth Republic. In 1962, however, Pompidou succeeded Michael Debré as prime minister.

Prime Ministership. Since Pompidou had never held public office, his appointment was an extraordinary one. He proved to be a formidable party manager, adviser, and executant of his master's will. He built up the Gaullist organization, assisted in reshaping the 1958 constitution against opposition, and helped General de Gaulle to win a second seven-year presidential term in 1965.

The testing came in the spring of 1968 with the worst outbreak of social violence since 1945. In May and June the capital was paralyzed, and industry shut down. Momentarily de Gaulle seemed lost. Pompidou was blamed for permitting student protest to escalate into street warfare and a national crisis, but it was he who devised the strategy that ended the troubles. For his criticized initial advice, or for the prestige won in successfully handling these troubles, Pompidou was fired on July 10, 1968, ten days after the Gaullist election triumph he helped organize. He had become a political force on his own.

Presidency. When the April 1969 referendum failed, de Gaulle resigned immediately, and Pompidou won the ensuing presidential election. After de Gaulle's death in 1970, many of the party's old guard resigned. Pompidou was accused of betraying the legacy by devaluing the franc and by permitting Britain to enter the Common Market.

In fact, however, his domestic, defense, and foreign policies were only variations of the general's. Lacking de Gaulle's mystique and authority, he was the administrator of a national enterprise based on a healthy economy and a newly assured world situation. He believed in modernization, some degree of European coherence, and East-West accommodation. He knew little of the world at first hand, spoke no foreign languages, did not care much for Americans or Englishmen, nor greatly trusted the Russians. Still, he journeyed widely.

He was less remote than de Gaulle. He ignored protests against government wiretapping and French nuclear testing. He accepted tax and other scandals with apparent equanimity. Demonstrations, strikes, and occasional violence punctuated long periods of quiet. No new society emerged; social justice remained distant; parliament was moribund.

By 1973 rumors were rife that Pompidou was seriously ill. Public appearances revealed his sufferings. No detailed medical bulletin was ever issued, but the consensus was that he had cancer of the bone marrow. Forced to cancel many engagements, he continued stoically to the end. He died suddenly on April 2, 1974, in his Paris apartment. Following a private requiem Mass, he was buried near his country home at Orvilliers, west of the capital. On April 6 emissaries from more than 70 nations attended a memorial Mass in Notre Dame Cathedral, in Paris.

JOHN C. CAIRNS
University of Toronto

WARREN, Earl

Chief Justice of the U. S. Supreme Court: b. Los Angeles, March 19, 1891; d. Washington, D.C., July 9, 1974.

Earl Warren, 14th chief justice of the United States, and generally regarded as second in importance only to John Marshall, died on July 9, 1974, at the age of 83. During his years as chief justice (1953–1969) the court had been in the vanguard of social change, handing down historic decisions on racial discrimination, equal representation, criminal justice, and civil liberties. His efforts to make the Supreme Court a "people's court" won him worldwide acclaim but also aroused a campaign to "impeach Earl Warren."

Early Career. Warren was a popular three-time governor of California, Republican nominee for vice president with Thomas E. Dewey in 1948, and unsuccessful candidate for the Republican presidential nomination in 1952. President Eisenhower appointed him chief justice on Sept. 30, 1953, following the death of Fred H. Vinson. While Eisenhower had intended to offer a Supreme Court seat to Warren, he was reluctant to name Warren chief justice because of his lack of judicial experience. However, Warren let it be known that he would accept nothing less. The recess appointment was confirmed by the Senate on March 1, 1954.

A big, fair-haired, genial man who wore double-breasted blue serge suits, Warren had begun his political career as a conservative. He was a hard-hitting district attorney of Alameda county. As California attorney general (1939–43) he favored the compulsory flag salute in schools and outlawry of the Communist party. As governor he supported placing California Japanese in concentration camps. But his thinking gradually liberalized, and at his nomination hearings several right-wing spokesmen testified against him. While the Warren appointment may well have been the most momentous act of his administration, Eisenhower was unhappy with the liberal position Warren took on the court and was reported to have said that the appointment was "the biggest damned-fool mistake I ever made."

Supreme Court Years. Warren's best-known action came in his first year on the court, when he wrote the opinion in *Brown* v. *Board of Education,* holding racial segregation in the public schools unconstitutional. The achievement of unanimity on this explosive issue was a tribute to Warren's diplomacy and tact.

Warren himself regarded the legislative apportionment cases of the 1960's as more important than *Brown.* He wrote the opinion in *Reynolds* v. *Sims* (1964) holding that both houses of a state legislature must be elected on the basis of "one person, one vote." His opinion pointed out that "legislators represent people."

UPI

EARL WARREN (1891–1974)
Leader of a "people's court."

When he first came on the court, Warren was hesitant to impose stricter constitutional standards on state criminal prosecutions, but as a judge he came to see things in a different light. He supported Justice Hugo Black's campaign to make all of the procedural protections of the Bill of Rights effective in state prosecutions. In 1966 he wrote a code of conduct (*Miranda* v. *Arizona*) to control the procedures of law enforcement officers in their interrogation and arrest of suspects.

During the Eisenhower years, Warren was often in a liberal minority. But as the Kennedy and Johnson appointees joined the court, he headed a strong liberal majority which sometimes went further than he liked.

At the request of President Johnson, Warren in November 1963 assumed the chairmanship of the commission to investigate the assassination of President Kennedy. Warren offered his resignation to Johnson in 1968, but because of the refusal of the Senate to confirm Abe Fortas as his successor, he continued as chief justice until June 1969.

Background. Warren was born in Los Angeles on March 19, 1891. His parents were Scandinavian, his father a railway worker. He earned his way through the University of California law school. After service in World War I, he became deputy city attorney of Oakland.

C. Herman Pritchett
University of California, Santa Barbara

obituaries · 1974

The following is a selected list of over 200 prominent persons who died in 1974. Separate articles on major figures appear on the preceding pages.

Abbott, Bud (William A.) (78), U. S. comedian: b. Asbury Park, N. J., Oct. 2, 1895; d. Woodland Hills, Calif., Apr. 24, 1974. As the hawk-like, fast-talking "wise guy" straight man to Lou Costello's roly-poly childlike buffoon, he helped make the comedy team of Abbott and Costello one of the most popular show-business attractions. After stints as a seaman, a traveling burlesque-show manager, and cashier in a Brooklyn theater, he teamed up with Costello in 1931, and together they toured the vaudeville circuits for eight years. They received their first major break in 1938, when they appeared at Loew's State in New York and on the Kate Smith radio show, and in 1939 they had their own Broadway revue, *Streets of Paris*. They made their motion picture debut in *One Night in the Tropics* (1940), and for a decade they were among Hollywood's top ten money-makers. Their 35 films include *Buck Privates* (1941), *In the Navy* (1941), *Abbott and Costello in Hollywood* (1945), and *Jack and the Beanstalk* (1952). Their famous skit "Who's on First?" is inscribed on a plaque in Baseball's Hall of Fame. After dissolving his partnership with Costello in 1957, Abbott continued to make occasional television and stage appearances.

Abrams, Creighton W(illiams, Jr.) (59), general of the U. S. Army: b. Springfield, Mass., Sept. 15, 1914; d. Washington, D. C., Sept. 4, 1974. The son of a railroad mechanic, he graduated from West Point in 1936. As commander of the 37th Tank Battalion in the latter stages of World War II, he led his forces through German lines to relieve airborne forces in Bastogne during the Battle of the Bulge. In the Korean war he served as chief of staff of four combat corps, and in the early 1960's he commanded federal troops sent to Mississippi and Alabama to ease racial tensions. From 1964 to 1967 he was Army vice chief of staff. As commander of the U. S. Military Assistance Command in Vietnam from 1968 to 1972, he supervised the gradual disengagement of U. S. forces there and trained Vietnamese to assume responsibility for their own defenses. He was confirmed as Army chief of staff in October 1972 and supervised transition of a largely conscript army into an all-volunteer force.

Ace, Jane (74), U. S. radio personality who with her husband, Goodman Ace, had a popular comedy show in the 1930's and 1940's; noted for such malapropisms as "a thumbnose description": d. New York City, Nov. 11.

Achard, Marcel (75), French dramatist; wrote popular comedies for 50 years; elected to French Academy in 1959: d. Paris, Sept. 4.

Aldrich, Winthrop W(illiams) (88), U. S. banker and diplomat: b. Providence, R. I., Nov. 2, 1885; d. New York, N. Y., Feb. 25, 1974. A member of the Rockefeller clan through marriage, he headed Rockefeller banking interests for a number of years and served as U. S. ambassador to Britain from 1953 to 1957. The son of a noted banker and U. S. senator, he graduated from Harvard Law School in 1910 and served in the U. S. Navy in World War I. From 1922 to 1930 he was chief counsel for the Rockefeller controlled Equitable Trust Co. As president of the Chase National (now Chase Manhattan) Bank from 1930 to 1933 and as its board chairman from 1933 to 1953, he proposed a number of banking reforms. A champion of liberal Republicanism, he was an early supporter of Dwight D. Eisenhower's presidential candidacy in 1952. During his years at the Court of St. James's he worked for the strengthening of U. S.-British relations. He was also noted as a philanthropist and yachtsman.

Alsop, Stewart (Johnnot Oliver) (60), U. S. journalist: b. Avon, Conn., May 17, 1914; d. Bethesda, Md., May 26, 1974. With his older brother, Joseph Alsop, and later on his own, he reported authoritatively and in a colorful style on national and international politics for nearly three decades. A member of a prominent New England family, he was educated at Groton and Yale, where he graduated in 1936. During World War II he served in the British army and worked with the French underground as a member of the U. S. Office of Strategic Services. From 1946 to 1958, Stewart and Joseph Alsop wrote their syndicated column "Matter of Fact." Based on careful research, the column, described as a "blending of political and economic punditry, forecast, and crusades," earned its authors Overseas Press Club Awards in 1950 and 1952. From 1958 to 1968 Stewart Alsop was with the *Saturday Evening Post*, and from 1968 he wrote a weekly column for *Newsweek*. Representing a moderately liberal viewpoint, he was critical of the McCarthy era witchhunts, the Vietnam War, and the draft. His books include *Nixon and Rockefeller; A Double Image* (1960). He also wrote of his own final struggle with a rare form of leukemia in his book *Stay of Execution* (1973).

Apgar, Virginia (65), U. S. physician; developed a widely recognized test—the Apgar Score—for determining the physical state of newborn infants: d. New York City, Aug. 7.

Arquette, Cliff (68), U. S. comic actor in vaudeville and on radio and television; created the Charley Weaver character on television: d. Los Angeles, Sept. 23.

Asturias, Miguel Angel (74), Guatemalan writer: b. Guatemala City, Oct. 19, 1899; d. Madrid, Spain, June 9, 1974. For his "highly colored writings, rooted in a national individuality and Indian traditions" he was awarded the 1967 Nobel Prize in literature. The son of a supreme court magistrate, he began his literary career as a student at the University of San Carlos, from which he graduated in 1923 with a law degree. After a decade in Paris, where he studied Latin American culture at the Sorbonne, he practiced journalism, served in the Guatemalan congress, and held several diplomatic posts. With the advent of a right-wing government in 1954 he went into exile. From 1966 to 1970 he was Guatemala's ambassador to France. His concern with the national tradition and Indian heritage, and his compassion for the underdog, are reflected in his ten novels, including *El Señor Presidente* (1946) and *Mulata* (1963), and in his poems, stories, and plays. He received the 1966 Lenin Peace Prize for his trilogy of novels, *Viento Fuerte* (1950), *El Papa Verde* (1953), and *Los Ojos de los Enterrados* (1960), in which he attacked U. S. economic domination of Latin America.

Ayub Khan, Mohammad (66), Pakistani statesman and army officer: b. Rehana, British India, May 14, 1907; d. near Islamabad, Pakistan, April 19, 1974. A career military man, he came to power in Pakistan in a bloodless coup in 1958 and served as president until he was forced to resign in 1969. While maintaining what amounted to a military dictatorship, he also instituted reforms that brought benefits to the poor and stabilized the economy. The son of a cavalry officer, he attended the British Royal Military Academy at Sandhurst and was commissioned in 1928. After Pakistan became independent in 1947, he became Commander-in-Chief of the Pakistani army. In 1954–55 he served as defense minister, and in 1958 he proclaimed himself president. In 1962 he introduced a constitution but retained strong presidential powers. His foreign policy was oriented toward China and the third world and away from the Western camp. In 1969 he stepped down in the wake of popular unrest that culminated in 1971 in the establishment of East Pakistan as the independent nation of Bangladesh and the accession of his chief opponent, Zulfikar Ali Bhutto, to the presidency.

Bates, Marston (67), U. S. naturalist; did research on mosquitoes and yellow fever; taught for 20 years at the University of Michigan; wrote popular books including the influential *The Forest and the Sea* (1960): d. Ann Arbor, Mich., April 3.

Beirne, Joseph A. (63), U. S. labor organizer; president of the Communications Workers of America from its founding in 1947 until 1974: d. Washington, Sept. 2.

Benny, Jack (80), U. S. comedian: b. Chicago, Ill., Feb. 14, 1894; d. Beverly Hills, Calif., Dec. 26, 1974. Master of the delayed response and the hurt look, he developed a comedy style that brought him fame and a devoted following for his radio broadcasts, TV shows, and movies. Throughout his long career, he portrayed himself as a pompous miser—quite the opposite of his real character—who reflected the most common human foibles and who remained permanently at age 39. "Never laugh at the other fellow," he is reported to have said, "but let him laugh at you." He was born Benjamin Kubelsky, the son of a Russian Jewish immigrant, who gave him a violin at the age of eight. The violin thus became his constant prop, and his hallmark was an unfinished and poorly played version of *Love in Bloom*. At an early age he moved to Waukegan, Ill., where his father had a shop, and which he later claimed as his birthplace in comedy routines. He left school in the ninth grade and began making vaudeville appearances with the violin as a comedy prop. In World War I he was assigned to a road show in the Navy, and there he further developed his talent for comedy. His first Broadway appearance, in *The Great Temptations*, came in 1926, and by 1932 he had his own NBC radio show, based in Hollywood. He had been married in 1927 to Sadie Marks, who became Mary Livingstone on his shows. In 1948 he transferred his broadcasts to the CBS network, where his show remained one of the country's most popular Sunday night programs until 1955. Meanwhile, in October 1950 he had his first TV broadcast. Gradually his TV shows appeared more regularly, becoming weekly in 1960–65. Thereafter he appeared in many special telecasts, as well as in nightclubs and in frequent benefit performances for charitable causes. He also appeared in more than a dozen movies, beginning with *Hollywood Review of 1929* and including *Artists and Models, Buck Benny Rides Again, Charley's Aunt,* and *The Horn Blows at Midnight.*

Bickel, Alexander Mordecai (49), U. S. authority on constitutional law: b. Bucharest, Rumania, Dec. 17, 1924; d. New Haven, Conn., Nov. 7, 1974. Politically a liberal Democrat, he was known for his conservative interpretations of constitutional law. He achieved fame for his successful defense of *The New York Times* in publishing the so-called Pentagon Papers in 1971 over the government's objections on grounds of national security. He moved from Bucharest to New York City with his family at the age of 14 and attended City College there before going on to Harvard (LL. B. degree in 1949). He was admitted to the Massachusetts bar in 1950, then went to Washington as law officer in the State Department and law clerk to Supreme Court Justice Felix Frankfurter. In 1956, Bickel joined the Yale Law School faculty, advancing through various professorships to Sterling Professor of Law. He wrote several books, including *The Supreme Court and the Idea of Progress* (1970).

Blackett, Lord (Patrick Maynard Stuart Blackett) (76), British scientist; served as a chief military adviser during World War II; won the Nobel Prize in physics (1948) for his studies of cosmic rays; president, Royal Society (1965–70): d. London, July 13.

Bohlen, Charles E(ustis) (69), U. S. diplomat: b. Clayton, N. Y., Aug. 30, 1904; d. Washington, D. C., Jan. 1, 1974. A career diplomat and a top expert on all aspects of Soviet affairs, he played a key role in U. S.-Soviet relations for over three decades and served as U. S. ambassador to Moscow during the crucial period from 1953 to 1957. A graduate of Harvard, "Chip" Bohlen entered the U. S. Foreign Service in 1928 and joined the staff of the newly established U. S. embassy in Moscow as a consular official in 1934. As a State Department official during World War II he served as presidential interpreter, and sometimes adviser, at top-level international conferences, including those at Teheran, Yalta, and Potsdam. After the war he counseled secretaries of state on Soviet affairs. As ambassador to Moscow he established rapport with Kremlin officials but was skeptical as to any long-term rapprochement between the U. S. and the USSR and urged the U. S. to maintain strong defenses. He served as U. S. ambassador to the Philippines from 1957 to 1959 and to France from 1962 to 1968. He retired as undersecretary of state for political affairs in 1969. His memoirs, *Witness to History, 1929–1969,* were published in 1973.

Borghese, Prince Junio Valerio (68), Italian naval hero of World War II, called the "Black Prince" because of the black-shirt Fascist uniform; led postwar neo-Fascist and ultrarightist movements; fled to Spain in 1971: d. Cádiz, Aug. 26.

Creighton W. Abrams

U. S. ARMY

Samuel Goldwyn

SAMUEL GOLDWYN PRODUCTIONS

UPI

Jack Benny

Boyle, Hal (Harold Vincent) (63), U. S. journalist: b. Kansas City, Mo., Feb. 21, 1911; d. New York, N. Y., Apr. 1, 1974. During three decades as a correspondent and columnist for the Associated Press, noted for his folksy, informal style and his human interest stories, he became that wire service's top byliner. He joined the A. P. as a copyboy in 1928 and received a degree in journalism from the University of Missouri in 1932. After working for several midwestern A. P. offices he was assigned to the New York bureau as night editor in 1937. Sent to North Africa as a war correspondent in 1942, he also covered World War II campaigns in the European and Pacific theaters and wrote a highly acclaimed column, "Leaves From a War Correspondent's Notebook." In 1945 he won a Pulitzer Prize for distinguished war correspondence. Later he covered the Korean and Vietnamese conflicts. His assignments over the years took him to some 70 countries.

Braddock, James J. (68), U. S. boxer; on June 13, 1935, he won a unanimous decision over Max Baer in 15 rounds to become the world heavyweight champion in a historic upset; on June 22, 1937, Joe Louis knocked him out in the 8th round, taking the title; Braddock fought a total of 84 bouts, scoring 52 victories (28 knockouts): d. North Bergen, N. J., Nov. 29.

Branzell, Karin (83), Swedish-born singer; for 21 seasons, beginning in 1924, a leading contralto with the Metropolitan Opera in New York City, noted for Wagnerian roles: d. Altadena, Calif., Dec. 15.

Brennan, Walter (80), U. S. movie and television actor; many of his more than 100 movies were Westerns; won 3 Academy Awards: d. Oxnard, Calif., Sept. 21.

Britton, Pamela (50), U. S. actress; starred on Broadway in the musical *Brigadoon* and in the television series *Blondie*: d. Arlington Heights, Ill., June 17.

Bronowski, Jacob (66), Polish-born, English-educated popularizer of science and its philosophical bases; since 1964 a resident fellow of the Salk Institute of La Jolla, Calif.: d. East Hampton, N. Y., Aug. 22.

Brown, Eddy (78), U. S. violin prodigy who made his debut at the age of 10 in Berlin; in the 1920's he made recordings and later worked in radio and taught: d. Abano, Italy, June 14.

Brown, Ivor (82), English author and critic and former editor of *The Observer;* his essays on words were perhaps his best-known works; he also wrote several books on Shakespeare: d. London, April 22.

Brown, Johnny Mack (70), U. S. college football player and star of Western movies; All-American player for the University of Alabama and hero of 1926 Rose Bowl; made hundreds of Westerns between 1930 and the mid-1950's: d. Woodland Hills, Calif., Nov. 14.

Brunis, Georg (74), U. S. jazz trombonist, identified with the "tailgate" style and early Dixieland; born in New Orleans, made his name in Chicago and New York from the 1920's onward: d. Chicago, Nov. 19.

Bush, Vannevar (84), U. S. electrical engineer and administrator: b. Everett, Mass., Mar. 11, 1890; d. Belmont, Mass., June 28, 1974. One of the foremost scientific minds of the 20th century, he was a pioneer in the development of the electronic computer and played a key role in mobilizing U. S. scientific and technological resources during World War II. The son of a Universalist minister, he graduated from Tufts University and obtained his doctorate under a joint Harvard-MIT program. He joined the MIT faculty in 1919 and served as its dean of engineering from 1932 to 1938 and as MIT Corporation chairman from 1955 to 1959. From 1939 to 1955 he was president of the Carnegie Institution. As director of the Office of Scientific Research and Development from 1941 to 1947, he coordinated the work of some 30,000 scientists and supervised, among other projects, the early stages of the atomic bomb program. His many innovations included a prototype of the modern analogue computer. He helped found several successful enterprises, including the forerunner of Raytheon Manufacturing Co. His books include *Modern Arms and Free Men* (1949) and the autobiographical *Pieces of the Action* (1970).

Caffery, Jefferson (87), U. S. diplomat, who had served as chief of mission for more years than any other Foreign Service officer when he retired in 1955; was ambassador to France from 1944 to 1949: d. Lafayette, La., April 13.

Chadwick, Sir James (82), British physicist; won 1935 Nobel Prize in physics for discovering the neutron: d. Cambridge, England, July 24.

Chenery, William L. (90), U. S. newspaperman and editor; for 25 years (1925–49) directed *Colliers* magazine, recruiting many famous contributors: d. Monterey, Calif., Aug. 18.

Childers, Erskine (68), president of Ireland; English-born son of a prominent Protestant Republican who was executed in 1922; succeeded the venerable Éamon de Valéra in June 1973: d. Dublin, Nov. 17.

Chotiner, Murray M. (64), U. S. lawyer and politician; adviser and aide to Richard M. Nixon since 1946; special counsel to the President (1970–71): d. Washington, D. C., Jan. 30.

Coldwell, Major James William (85), Canadian political leader; headed the socialistic Co-operative Commonwealth Federation (CCF) from 1942 to 1960; became honorary president of CCF's successor, the New Democratic party, in 1961: d. Ottawa, Aug. 25.

Cole, Jack (59), U. S. choreographer; danced in the Ziegfeld Follies; choreographed such Broadway shows and movies as *Man of La Mancha, Gentlemen Prefer Blondes,* and *The Jolson Story*: d. Los Angeles, Feb. 17.

Condon, E(dward) U(hler) (72), U. S. physicist: b. Alamogordo, N. Mex., Mar. 2, 1902; d. Boulder, Colo., Mar. 26, 1974. As associate director of research of Westinghouse Electric Company during World War II, he made important contributions to the development of equipment for the isolation of uranium, and he worked with Dr. J. Robert Oppenheimer and others in developing the atom bomb. In the 1920's he helped to formulate important principles in theoretical physics, especially quantum mechanics. The son of a civil engineer, he obtained his doctorate at the University of California. After additional study in Germany he worked for Bell Telephone Laboratories and then taught at Columbia and Princeton. From 1937 to 1945 he was associated with Westinghouse, and from 1945 to 1951 he was director of the National Bureau of Standards. In 1948 he was attacked as a security risk by the House Un-American Activities Committee. Although President Truman defended his loyalty, Condon lost his security clearance in 1954 and had to leave the post of research director with the Corning Glass Works. His clearance was later restored, however. He was professor of physics at Washington University in St. Louis from 1956 to 1963 and at the University of Colorado from 1963 on.

Connolly, Cyril (71), British literary critic and author; founded and edited (1939–50) the influential English literary monthly *Horizon;* his best-known book is *The Unquiet Grave* (1944): d. London, Nov. 26.

Cooley, Harold D. (76), U. S. congressman; member, U. S. House of Representatives (D-N. C., 1935–67); chairman, House Agriculture Committee for 18 years: d. Wilson, N. C., Jan. 15.

Cornell, Katharine (81), U. S. actress: b. Berlin, Germany, Feb. 16, 1893; d. Vineyard Haven, Mass., June 9, 1974. Described as the "first lady of the theater" or the "American Duse," she ranked with Lynn Fontanne and Helen Hayes as one of the reigning feminine stars of the Broadway stage in the second quarter of the 20th century. In her ability to captivate audiences with her sensitive performances in romantic roles—notably in *The Barretts of Wimpole Street, Candida,* and *Romeo and Juliet*—she was without peer. The daughter of a physician who was studying in Germany at the time of her birth, she grew up in Buffalo, N. Y. She made her Broadway debut in 1921 in *Nice People,* directed by Guthrie McClintic, whom she married that year, and who directed most of her subsequent plays. She was clearly established as a star with her performance in *The Green Hat* (1925). In 1931 she established her own production company, Katharine Cornell Presents, which toured 77 U. S. cities in 1933–34. Its first production, the highly successful *The Barretts of Wimpole Street,* marked Miss Cornell, in the role of Elizabeth, as a great romantic actress. Other plays in which she gave memorable performances over the years include *Saint Joan, The Doctor's Dilemma, Antigone,* and *The Three Sisters.*

Cowan, Clyde (54), U. S. physicist; codiscoverer of the neutrino (1956); taught at Catholic University (1958–74): d. Washington, D. C., May 24.

Craig, Lyman C. (68), U. S. chemist; taught at Rockefeller University for 41 years; his research made possible new techniques for purifying drugs, penicillins, proteins, and hormones: d. Glen Rock, N. J., July 7.

Crisp, Donald (93), U. S. actor; won an Academy Award for supporting actor in *How Green Was My Valley* (1941): d. Van Nuys, Calif., May 25.

Crossman, Richard (66), British left-wing Labour party leader; entered Parliament in 1946; served in cabinet: d. Banbury, Oxfordshire, April 5.

Cruickshank, Allan D. (67), U. S. ornithologist, author, and teacher; on staff of the National Audubon Society for 37 years; his books include *Wings in the Wilderness*: d. Gainesville, Fla., Oct. 11.

Daley, Arthur (69), U. S. sportswriter; joined *The New York Times* in 1926; won Pulitzer Prize (1956): d. New York City, Jan. 3.

Darvas, Lili (72), U. S. and European stage and motion-picture actress: d. New York City, July 22.

Das, Durga (73), Indian journalist; career spanned 50 years of turbulent Indian history; edited New Delhi's *Hindustan Times*: d. New Delhi, May 17.

Davis, Adelle (70), U. S. nutritionist: b. Lizton, Ind., Feb. 25, 1904; d. Palos Verdes Estates, Calif., May 31, 1974. A leading authority on natural foods and vitamins, she extolled their virtues as prerequisites for good health in her lectures and television appearances, and in her best-selling books, *Let's Cook it Right* (1947), *Let's Have Healthy Children* (1951), *Let's Eat Right to Keep Fit* (1954), and *Let's Get Well* (1965). She graduated from the University of California with a B. A. in dietetics in 1927 and obtained an M. S. in biochemistry from the University of Southern California in 1939. For a number of years she worked as a consulting nutritionist for schools and hospitals and in private practice. Concerned about the poor diet to which most Americans are subjected from early childhood, she criticized the food additives, pesticides, and "empty calories" present in many popular foods.

Davison, F. Trubee (78), U. S. aviation pioneer and public official; flew in World War I and survived a crash; assistant secretary of war for air (1926–32) and president of the American Museum of Natural History (1933–51): d. Locust Valley, N. Y., Nov. 14.

Dean, Dizzy (Jay Hanna) (63), U. S. baseball player: b. Lucas, Ark., Jan. 16, 1911; d. Reno, Nev., July 17, 1974. The star pitcher of the St. Louis Cardinals "Gashouse Gang" in the 1930's, he was known for his blazing fastball and his colorful, often ungrammatical prose. A sharecropper's son, he dropped out of school in the second grade and joined the U. S. Army at 16. Discovered by a scout in a Texas sandlot in 1929, he played briefly for the Cardinals and spent some time in the minor leagues before being brought up by Branch Rickey as a full-fledged member of the St. Louis team in 1932. He reached the height of his pitching career in 1934, when his 30 victories, and the 19 won by his brother Paul, brought the Cardinals the National League pennant. The brothers went on to pitch the team to the World Series championship, winning two games each. That year, Dizzy Dean was named the league's most valuable player. An injury in 1937 resulted in damage to his right arm and a weakening of his pitching delivery. Sold to the Chicago Cubs in 1938, he helped them win the pennant that year. After his retirement from the game in 1941, with a career record of 150 wins and 83 losses, he became a baseball announcer on radio and television. He was elected to the Baseball Hall of Fame in 1953.

De Seversky, Alexander P. (80), Russian-born U. S. aviator and aeronautical engineer; his inventions—including an automatic bombsight, an all-metal trainer, and a high-speed fighter plane—contributed significantly to the development of flying; in 1931 founded company that later became Republic Aviation; an energetic promoter of strategic air power, he wrote *Victory Through Air Power* (1942): d. New York City, Aug. 24.

De Sica, Vittorio (73), Italian screen star and director; popular romantic movie actor in the 1930's; after World War II directed such classic "neo-realistic" films as *The Bicycle Thief* (1949), which won him the first of his five Oscars: d. Paris, Nov. 13.

Dewey, Bradley (87), U. S. chemical engineer, inventor, and a cofounder of Dewey & Almy Chemical Co.; contributed to development of gas masks, sealants for metal cans, and plastic film: d. New London, N. H., Oct. 14.

De Wolfe, Billy (67), U. S. comedian-actor; beginning as a dancer, he later appeared in movies (including *Call Me Madam*), on Broadway in reviews, and on TV: d. Los Angeles, March 5.

Douglas, Lewis W. (79), U. S. businessman, envoy, and public official; member, U. S. House of Representatives (D-Ariz., 1927–33); director, U. S. Bureau of the Budget (1933–34); U. S. ambassador to Britain (1947–50); former president and chairman, Mutual Life Insurance Company of New York: d. Tucson, Ariz., March 7.

Draper, William H., Jr. (80), U. S. government official and population expert: b. New York, N. Y., Aug. 10, 1894; d. Naples, Fla., Dec. 26, 1974. His many-faceted career included service as head of the economics division of the American Military Government in Germany after World War II, undersecretary of war and of the Army, President Truman's special ambassador in Europe, honorary vice chairman of the Planned Parenthood Federation of America, member of the governing body of the International Planned Parenthood Federation, and U. S. delegate to the UN Population Commission. He had also held several important banking positions.

Dumaine, Alexandre (78), master French chef; for nearly 30 years his restaurant in Saulieu, eastern France, was ranked at the top: d. Saulieu, April 22.

Dunn, Leslie C. (80), U. S. geneticist; member of Columbia University's faculty (1928–62); author, *Heredity and Evolution in Human Populations* (1958); editor, *The American Naturalist*: d. North Tarrytown, N. Y., March 19.

Dutra, Eurico Gaspar (89), marshal and former president of Brazil; war minister under dictator Getulio Vargas (1936–45) and president from 1946 to 1951, when Vargas succeeded him: d. Rio de Janeiro, June 11.

Dutt, R. Palme (79), British Marxist; a founder in 1920 of the British Communist party, he was its foremost theoretician; wrote prolifically: d. London, Dec. 20.

Ellington, Edward (Duke). See separate article preceding this section.

Elliot, "Mama" Cass (33), U. S. popular singer; star of the folk-rock group the Mamas and the Papas (1965–68); began a solo career in 1968: d. London, July 29.

Ewing, (William) Maurice (67), U. S. geophysicist: b. Lockney, Texas, May 12, 1906; d. Galveston, Texas, May 4, 1974. An international authority on the earth sciences, he founded the Lamont-Doherty Observatory at Columbia University and served as its director from 1949 to 1972. As a research associate at the Woods Hole Oceanographic Institution from 1940 to 1945, Ewing pioneered in the exploration of ocean floors through the use of seismic waves. During World War II he developed the SOFAR underwater communications system, using depth charges to transmit sound waves for great distances. His work at the Lamont-Doherty Observatory was central to the recent revolution in the earth sciences, notably the discovery of evidence supporting the theory of continental drift. He also designed a lunar seismograph for the U. S. space program. In 1972 he joined the Marine Biomedical Institute of the University of Texas.

Feldman, Gladys (82), U. S. stage actress; appeared in the Ziegfeld Follies and on Broadway in *The Great Gatsby* and *Baby Pompadour*: d. New York City, Feb. 12.

Fitzhugh, Louise (46), U. S. author and illustrator of children's books; probably best known for *Harriet the Spy* (1964): d. New Milford, Conn., Nov. 19.

Flynn, F. M. ("Jack") (71), U. S. newspaper executive; former publisher (1955–1973) and chairman (1970 until his death) of the New York *Daily News*: d. New York City, Nov. 15.

Flynn, Joe (49), U. S. actor; portrayed the commander of a PT boat base in the television series *McHale's Navy*: d. Hollywood, Calif., July 18.

Fok, Vladimir Aleksandrovich (76), Soviet physicist, did work chiefly in fields of quantum electrodynamics, electromagnetic propagation and diffraction, and theory of relativity: d. Leningrad, USSR, (announced) Dec. 28.

Fouchet, Christian (63), French politician; joined Gen. de Gaulle's Free French movement in London in 1940; wrote the Fouchet Plan for European political unity; served in various Gaullist cabinet positions during the 1960's: d. Geneva, Aug. 11.

Frazier, George (63), U. S. journalist and commentator noted for his preoccupation with style in prose and behavior; wrote for *Life*, *Esquire*, and other publications: d. Cambridge, Mass., June 13.

Freed, Fred (53), U. S. broadcast journalist; won seven Emmy Awards as television producer and documentary news writer for the National Broadcasting Company: d. New York City, March 31.

Friesell, William H. (Red), Jr. (80), U. S. football referee; in the 1940 Cornell-Dartmouth game made a "fifth-down" officiating error (reversed days later) that permitted Cornell to win: d. Pittsburgh, June 23.

Furtseva, Yekaterina (63), Soviet Communist party official and minister of culture (1960–74); served (1957–61) as the only woman member ever of the party's elite ruling body, the Presidium (now called the Politburo): d. Moscow, Oct. 25.

Gambling, John B. (77), British-born U. S. radio personality; pioneered the cheerful, chatty-type early-morning show on station WOR in New York City from 1925 to 1958: d. Palm Beach, Fla., Nov. 21.

Gerber, Daniel F. (75), food manufacturer; in 1929 introduced strained baby foods to millions of Americans; president and chairman of Gerber Products Company: d. Fremont, Mich., March 16.

Germi, Pietro (60), Italian film director; gained international fame for *Divorce, Italian Style*, which won an Oscar in 1962: d. Rome, Dec. 5.

Giegengack, Augustus E. (84), U. S. official; as public printer of the United States, headed the Government Printing Office from 1934 to 1948, a period of significant expansion: d. Bethesda, Md., June 21.

Gloucester, Duke of (74), member of British royal family; last surviving son of King George V; uncle of Queen Elizabeth II; served in military for many years: d. Barnwell Manor, Northamptonshire, England, June 10.

Goldsmith, Alfred N. (85), U. S. electronics scientist, engineer, and inventor; through his research came the first commercial radio with two control knobs and a built-in speaker; created first commercial radio-phonograph; helped develop the color-television tube: d. St. Petersburg, Fla., July 2.

Goldwyn, Samuel (91), U. S. motion picture producer: b. Warsaw, Poland, Aug. 27, 1882; d. Los Angeles, Calif., Jan. 31, 1974. One of the last of Hollywood's pioneer motion picture tycoons, he produced over 70 films during a career that spanned more than half a century. His elaborately staged productions were noted for their quality and taste. The son of poor parents, he went to the United States at 13 and worked his way up in the business world. In 1913 he formed a film company with Jesse I. Lasky and Cecil B. DeMille, and its first production, *The Squaw Man*, was a major success. A few years later he helped found the company that eventually evolved into Metro-Goldwyn-Mayer. In 1922 he became an independent producer, and from 1926 to 1941 he was associated with United Artists. Recruiting top writers, directors, and other talent, he applied his standards of perfection to such hits as *Wuthering Heights* (1939), *Hans Christian Andersen* (1952), *Guys and Dolls* (1955), the Academy Award-winning *The Best Years of Our Lives* (1946), and his last film, *Porgy and Bess* (1959). Among the stars he introduced to the public were Gary Cooper, Tallulah Bankhead, and Danny Kaye. One of Hollywood's most colorful personalities, he enriched the American vernacular with such "Goldwynisms" as "Include me out!"

Golenpaul, Dan (73), radio producer and publisher; created the radio quiz show *Information Please;* began publishing *Information Please Almanac, Atlas and Yearbook* in 1947: d. New York City, Feb. 13.

Gordon, Kitty (96), U. S. actress in musicals and early films; Victor Herbert composed *The Enchantress* (1911) for her: d. Brentwood, N. Y., May 26.

Gottlieb, Adolph (70), U. S. artist: b. New York, N. Y., March 14, 1903; d. there, March 4, 1974. With Jackson Pollock, William de Kooning, and Mark Rothko he founded the New York school of abstract expressionist painting in protest against the dominant social realism of the 1940's. The son of Hungarian immigrants, he studied at the Art Students League, at Cooper Union, and in Paris and had his first exhibition in 1930. During the Depression he was associated with a group of expressionists known as "The Ten." In the 1940's he painted abstract expressionist, gridlike "pictographs," with designs inspired in part by Freudian symbolism. His "Burst" series, begun in the 1950's, depict sunlike spheres, suspended over exploding red and black horizons. He also created decorations, inspired by religious iconography, for New York synagogues.

Grant, Frederick Clifton (83), U. S. theologian and biblical scholar; ordained an Episcopal priest (1913); was Edward Robinson Professor Emeritus of Biblical Theology, Union Theological Seminary; helped prepare the Revised Standard Version of the New Testament (1946): d. Gwynedd, Pa., July 11.

Griffis, Stanton (87), U. S. financier and diplomat under Presidents Roosevelt and Truman; served as ambassador to Poland, Egypt, Argentina, and Spain: d. New York City, Aug. 29.

Griffith, Paul Howard (77), U. S. businessman and former government official; served as national commander of the American Legion, 1946–47, assistant secretary of defense, 1949–50, and in various Selective Service System posts: d. Washington, D. C., Dec. 29.

Grivas, George (75), Greek-Cypriot general; helped lead Cyprus to independence (1960); leader of the underground guerrilla movement to unite Cyprus with Greece: d. Limassol, Cyprus, Jan. 27.

Gruening, Ernest (87), U. S. journalist and politician; former newspaperman and editor (*The Nation*); territorial governor of Alaska (1939–53); provisional U. S. senator (1956–58); lobbied for Alaskan statehood; U. S. senator (D-Alaska, 1959–69); early critic of U. S. involvement in Vietnam: d. Washington, D. C., June 26.

Guttmacher, Alan F(rank) (75), U. S. physician and family-planning crusader: b. Baltimore, Md., May 19, 1898; d. New York, N. Y., March 18, 1974. As president of the Planned Parenthood Federation of America since 1962, he advocated unlimited access to birth-control information and liberal abortion laws, as well as individual freedom of choice in the bearing of children. The son of a rabbi, he obtained his medical degree at Johns Hopkins Medical School in 1923 and later taught there as professor of obstetrics. He also taught at Columbia and Harvard, and from 1952 to 1962 he was director of the department of obstetrics and gynecology at Mount Sinai Hospital in New York. In behalf of Planned Parenthood, Guttmacher traveled extensively, lecturing, raising funds, and testifying before legislative committees. He was especially concerned that the poor should have adequate birth-control information. His books include *Pregnancy and Birth* (1957) and *Planning Your Family* (1964).

Hahn, Kurt (88), German educator; founded the Salem School near Lake Constance in 1920; expelled by the Nazis, he established (1933) the Gordonstoun School in Scotland: d. Hermannsberg, West Germany, Dec. 15.

Hale, William Harlan (63), U. S. editor and writer; served with the Office of War Information during World War II; later associated with *The Reporter* and *Horizon* magazines: d. White Plains, N. Y., June 30.

Harris, Seymour E. (77), U. S. economist who advised Presidents Kennedy and Johnson; taught at Harvard for more than 40 years; championed theories of British economist J. M. Keynes: d. La Jolla, Calif., Oct. 27.

Hathaway, Sibyl (90), the Dame (in fact, ruler) of Sark, a tiny British island in the English Channel; inherited the "feudal domain" in 1927: d. Sark, July 14.

Hearst, Millicent (92), U. S. society figure, widow of publishing magnate William Randolph Hearst; worked for patriotic and charitable causes: d. New York City, Dec. 5.

Hershfield, Harry (89), U. S. humorist; a cartoonist, toastmaster, columnist, and raconteur, he was featured on the radio show *Can You Top This?* in the 1940's: d. New York City, Dec. 15.

Heyer, Georgette (71), English novelist admired particularly for her accounts of Regency England; her books include *Bath Tangle, The Spanish Bride,* and *An Infamous Army*: d. London, July 4.

Hodges, Luther H. (76), U. S. textile executive and public official; entered public service at the age of 52 after success in business; served as governor of North Carolina (1954–60) and as U. S. secretary of commerce (1961–64): d. Chapel Hill, N. C., Oct. 6.

Hoffman, Paul Gray (83), U. S. industrialist and public official: b. Western Springs, Ill., April 26, 1891; d. New York, N. Y. Oct. 8, 1974. In a career that took him well past normal retirement age, he achieved fame at home as an automobile executive and abroad as administrator of Marshall Plan and United Nations programs for aid to war-torn and underdeveloped countries. He attended the University of Chicago for a year, but left for financial reasons and became a car salesman near Chicago. He moved to Los Angeles in 1911 and by 1915 had become manager of the Studebaker division there. After Army service in World War I, he returned to Los Angeles and purchased the Studebaker retail branch in 1919. His successful record soon caused him to be named vice president of the parent company in South Bend, Ind., in charge of sales. Although the company went into receivership in 1933, it emerged two years later with Hoffman as president until 1948. In 1942–48 he was board chairman of the Committee for Economic Development. In the latter year, President Truman appointed him administrator of the Economic Cooperation Administration to supervise Marshall Plan aid to war-devastated Europe, and in the next two and one-half years he administered the expenditure of $10 billion. In 1950 he became president of the Ford Foundation, and in 1954 he returned to Studebaker-Packard as chairman of the board. He served as a member of the U. S. delegation to the UN General Assembly in 1956–57, and in 1959–66 was managing director of the UN Special Fund. After 1966 he administered the UN Development Programme. Hoffman was awarded the Medal of Freedom in 1951 for his Marshall Plan work. His books include *Seven Roads to Safety* (1939), *Peace Can Be Won* (1951), and *World Without Want* (1962).

Hogan, Frank S. (72), U. S. lawyer; Manhattan district attorney (1942–73): d. New York City, April 2.

Hooper, Harry (87), U. S. baseball player, with the Boston Red Sox for 11 years (1909–20) and then the Chicago White Sox for 5 years; elected to the Baseball Hall of Fame in 1971: d. Santa Cruz, Calif., Dec. 17.

Hopson, Sir Donald C. (59), British diplomat; headed the British mission in Peking (1965–68); in 1967, Red Guards burned the mission and he was detained for nearly a year: d. Buenos Aires, Argentina, Aug. 27.

Hull, Warren (71), U. S. radio and television personality; acted in movies as well as on radio; probably best known as master of ceremonies on the 1950's radio-television show *Strike It Rich*: d. Waterbury, Conn., Sept. 14.

Hunt, H. L. (85), U. S. oilman-billionaire; of modest birth, he left home at 16, later had a few months of college; in 1921 he began to trade in oil leases—the foundation of his huge fortune, later multiplied by other enterprises, the total extent and value of which remained unknown; he was noted for his ultraconservative political stance: d. Dallas, Nov. 29.

Huntley, Chet (Chester Robert) (62), U. S. news commentator: b. Cardwell, Mont., Dec. 10, 1911; d. Bozeman, Mont., March 20, 1974. As the solemn-voiced partner of NBC-TV's popular nightly *Huntley-Brinkley Reports* for nearly 15 years, he elevated the standards of news broadcasting with his intelligent analyses of controversial topics. He grew up on his family's Montana sheep ranch. While a student at the University of Washington, he began his broadcasting career with a Seattle radio station in 1934. After working in Los Angeles as a radio newscaster with the CBS network from 1939 to 1951 and with ABC from 1951 to 1955, he joined NBC in New York. A year later, he and David Brinkley were chosen as anchormen for the political conventions. Over the next few years, their *Huntley-Brinkley Reports,* covering serious news events as well as contemporary fads and foibles, attained top ratings. Huntley, who won several national broadcasting awards, came into conflict with right-wing forces because of his attacks on Sen. Joseph McCarthy in the 1950's; with organized labor because of his refusal to honor a picket line at NBC in 1967; and with conservationists because of his development of the Big Sky recreational complex in Montana, to which he devoted himself after retiring from broadcasting in 1970.

Hurok, Sol (85), U. S. impresario: b. Pogar, Russia, April 9, 1888; d. New York, N. Y., March 5, 1974. For over 50 years, Sol Hurok was the leading importer of foreign musical, dance, and theatrical groups into the United States. After emigrating to the United States from Russia in 1906, he became a U. S. citizen in 1914. The following year he became manager of weekly concerts in the Hippodrome in New York City. He later managed such famous artists as Anna Pavlova and Isadora Duncan. A major proponent of the ballet, Hurok introduced the Bolshoi company to the U. S. public in 1959. He defined the role of the impresario as one who "discovers talent, who promotes it, who presents it, and who puts up the money and takes the risk." His memoirs *Impresario* and *S. Hurok Presents* were published in 1946 and 1953, respectively.

Husseini, Haj Amin el- (80), Arab leader and former Grand Mufti of Jerusalem; though in exile, championed Palestinian cause against Israel to the end: d. Beirut, Lebanon, July 4.

Ismail, Ahmed (57), Egyptian field marshal; served with the British in World War II; named minister of war and commander in chief of military forces in 1972; led Egyptian forces in the October 1973 Arab-Israeli war: d. London, Dec. 25.

James, Frankie (72), U. S. Ziegfeld Follies star; appeared in *45 Minutes from Broadway;* also in Broadway musical *Big Boy* opposite Al Jolson: d. Beverly Hills, Calif., Feb. 13.

Johnson, Earl J. (73), U. S. newspaperman; editor of United Press International and its predecessor, the United Press, for 30 years: d. Tucson, Ariz., Jan. 3.

Jonas, Franz (74), president of Austria since 1965; a lifelong Socialist: d. Vienna, April 23.

Jordan, B. Everett (77), U. S. politician; U. S. senator (D-N. C., 1958–73); as chairman of Senate Rules Committee led 1964 investigation of Senate aide Bobby Baker: d. Saxapahaw, N. C., March 15.

Kahn, Louis I. (73), U. S. architect: b. Oesel, Estonia, Feb. 20, 1901; d. New York, N. Y., March 17, 1974. His unorthodox philosophy, attributing an almost human vitality to architecture and assuming that space, light, and construction materials had a "will" to take on particular forms, made him one of the most influential contemporary architects and is reflected in his strong, simple, yet gracefully designed buildings. He was brought to the United States in 1905, settling with his family in Philadelphia, where he lived most of his life, and graduated in 1924 from the University of Pennsylvania School of Fine Arts. Trained in the Beaux Arts tradition, he rejected both the organic school of architecture of Frank Lloyd Wright and the pure European modernism of Le Corbusier. His first major project was the design of the Yale Art Gallery, completed in 1953, in which he began to develop the concept of "servant" and "served" areas. Among his other important buildings are the Alfred Newton Richards Memorial Research Building at the University of Pennsylvania, the Jonas Salk Institute in California, the Kimbell Art Museum at Fort Worth, Texas, a management institute at Ahmedabad, India, and government buildings at Dacca, Bangladesh. From 1957 until his death, Kahn was professor of architecture at the University of Pennsylvania.

Kelly, George E. (87), U. S. vaudeville actor and playwright, uncle of Princess Grace of Monaco; won a Pulitzer Prize for his play *Craig's Wife* (1925): d. Bryn Mawr, Pa., June 18.

King, Alberta (69), mother of the slain U. S. civil-rights leader Dr. Martin Luther King, Jr., and wife of the Rev. Martin Luther King, Sr.; fatally wounded by gunman as she played the organ in church: d. Atlanta, Ga., June 30.

Kirk, Norman E. (51), New Zealand statesman: b. Waimate, New Zealand, Jan. 2, 1923; d. Wellington, New Zealand, Aug. 31, 1974. As prime minister of New Zealand from December 1972, he headed that country's first Labor government in 12 years. The son of a cabinetmaker, he dropped out of school at 12. Before entering politics he worked at various manual labor jobs and as a railroad engineer. He served as mayor of the township of Kaiapoi from 1953 until 1957, when he was elected to parliament from the Lyttleton constituency. Elected president of the New Zealand Labor party in 1964, he served as leader of its parliamentary faction from 1965 to 1969. As prime minister, "Big Norm" Kirk promoted regional development and industrial harmony. He ended his country's involvement in Vietnam, established relations with mainland China, and forged unity within the divided Labor party.

Kleberg, Robert J., Jr. (78), U. S. rancher, president of the King Ranch, Inc., which owns the country's largest ranch, in Texas, with lucrative gas and oil fields, and 11.5 million ranching acres abroad; developed first U. S. breed of cattle, the Santa Gertrudis; raced thoroughbreds: d. Houston, Oct. 13.

Klein, Anne (Hannah Golofski) (51), U. S. fashion designer: b. Brooklyn, N. Y., 1923?; d. New York, N. Y., March 19, 1974. A leader in the U. S. fashion industry, she won international recognition for the "all-American look" with her casual, yet elegantly tailored and sophisticated women's sportswear. She studied at the Traphagen School of Fashion and began her career at 15 as a free-lance fashion illustrator. In 1948 she formed Junior Sophisticates with her first husband, Ben Klein, and her early designs, injecting the sophisticated look into junior-size clothes, brought her into prominence. Her manufacturing company, Anne Klein & Co., established in 1968, has distributed her collections to some 800 stores in the United States and entered the international market in 1973. Miss Klein was named to the Coty American Fashion Awards Hall of Fame in 1971.

Knowland, William F. (65), U. S. politician and newspaper executive; U. S. senator (R-Calif., 1945–59); Senate majority leader (1953–54) and minority leader (1955–58); publisher and editor, *Oakland Tribune* (1966–74): d. Guerneville, Calif., Feb. 23.

Krips, Josef (72), Austrian conductor: b. Vienna, Austria, April 8, 1902; d. Geneva, Switzerland, Oct. 12, 1974. Renowned for more than half a century as conductor of some of the world's most famous orchestras, he was especially honored for his interpretations of Mozart and Beethoven. He made his debut as first violinist with the Vienna Volksoper at the age of 15, and became choirmaster and assistant conductor there at 19. Thereafter he served as music director at the Staatstheater in Karlsruhe, Germany (1926–33) and as conductor of the Vienna State Opera Company (1933–38, and conductor in chief, 1945–50), London Symphony (1950–54), Buffalo (N. Y.) Philharmonic (1954–63), and San Francisco Symphony (1963–70). In 1938, when Austria was occupied by the Nazis, he was assigned briefly to work in a pickle factory, but he soon became conductor of the Belgrade Opera and Philharmonic (1938–39). His last years were spent in retirement in Montreux, Switzerland, except for guest appearances.

Krishna Menon, V(engalil) K(rishnan) (77), Indian political official: b. Calicut, Kerala, India, May 3, 1897; d. New Delhi, India, Oct. 6, 1974. One of India's most controversial public figures, he was closely allied with Prime Minister Jawaharlal Nehru in a number of important posts at home and abroad. After attending Presidency College in Madras, and Madras Law College, he went to London, where he studied at the London School of Economics (B. S., 1927; M. Sc., 1934) and University College (M. A., 1930). In 1934 he was admitted to the bar at the Middle Temple, and until 1947, as secretary of the India League, he worked tirelessly for Indian independence. He also became a member of the Borough Council in the St. Pancras district of London. By 1947, when India became independent, he had become a close friend of Nehru, who appointed him India's first high commissioner (ambassador) in London. Scandals over his exorbitant purchases there led Nehru to send him to the United Nations in New York to assist Mme. Pandit, Nehru's sister, who headed the Indian delegation. In 1956 he was recalled to serve in Nehru's cabinet without portfolio, and in 1957 he was appointed defense minister. In October 1962, when Communist China invaded India's northern border, Krishna Menon's "trust-the-Chinese" policy caused Nehru to relieve him as defense minister.

Krock, Arthur (87), U. S. journalist: b. Glasgow, Ky., Nov. 16, 1886; d. Washington, D. C., April 12, 1974. During a career that spanned six decades, including nearly 40 years with the New York *Times,* he won recognition as one of the most distinguished personalities in U. S. journalism. After studying at Princeton and at the Lewis Institute in Chicago, he obtained the first of a succession of newspaper jobs about 1907. As editorial manager for two Louisville, Ky., papers, he covered the post-World War I Paris peace conference. From 1919 to 1923 he was chief editor of the Louisville *Times,* and from 1923 to 1927 he served as assistant to New York *World* publisher Ralph Pulitzer. He joined the New York *Times* in 1927 as an editorial writer and headed its Washington bureau from 1932 to 1953. A pioneer of the modern newspaper column, he wrote his penetrating editorial page column "In the Nation" for the *Times* from 1933 until his retirement in 1966. He received Pulitzer prizes in 1935 and 1938—the latter for his exclusive interview with Franklin D. Roosevelt—and special Pulitzer awards in 1950 and 1955. His books include *In the Nation* (1966) and *Memoirs: Sixty Years on the Firing Line* (1968). A conservative in his political, economic, and social views, Krock looked with regret on the passing of what he considered a more genteel and civilized era.

Chet Huntley

UPI

Sol Hurok

HUROK CONCERTS

WILLIAM SAURO/THE NEW YORK TIMES

Walter Lippmann

NBC

Frank McGee

Kruger, Otto (89), U. S. stage, screen, radio, and television actor: d. Los Angeles, Sept. 6.

Lagerkvist, Pär (Fabian) (83), Swedish author: b. Växjö, Sweden, May 23, 1891; d. Stockholm, July 11, 1974. His "artistic power and deep-rooted independence" in his search for "an answer to the eternal questions of humanity" won him the 1951 Nobel Prize in literature. Self-described as a "religious atheist," he was recognized as Sweden's most distinguished and representative man of letters of his era. During his lifetime he published more than 30 books, including fiction, poetry, plays, and essays. The son of a railroad stationmaster of Lutheran peasant stock, he rebelled early against his conservative background. He studied at Uppsala university, published his first poems in 1912, and was profoundly influenced by Cubist and Fauvist artists in pre-World War I Paris. His early writings were of a strongly expressionist and pessimistic nature. Later he adopted a more realistic style and propounded a humanist and idealistic philosophy. His plays, including *The Last Man* (1917), caused him to be recognized as a successor to Strindberg. Internationally he was best known for his novels *The Dwarf* (1945) and *Barabbas* (1951). He was named to the Swedish Academy of Literature in 1940.

Lane, Rosemary (61), U. S. singer and actress, one of the four singing Lane sisters; gained prominence with Fred Waring's band in the 1930's; appeared in numerous movies and starred in the Broadway musical *Best Foot Forward*: d. Hollywood, Nov. 25.

Leech, Margaret (80), U. S. historian; twice winner of Pulitzer Prize (for *Reveille in Washington,* 1942, and *In the Days of McKinley,* 1960): d. New York City, Feb. 24.

Lengyel, Melchior (95), Hungarian playwright; gained international fame in 1910 with *Typhoon;* screen versions of his plays included *Ninotchka* with Greta Garbo: d. Budapest, Oct. 25.

Leslie, Kenneth (81), Canadian poet; won the Governor-General's Medal for *By Stubborn Stars* (1938): d. Halifax, Nova Scotia, Oct. 7.

Levy, Robert L. (86), U. S. physician, an early specialist in cardiology; he taught at Johns Hopkins, Harvard, and Columbia: d. New York City, Nov. 23.

Lindbergh, Charles A. See separate article preceding this section.

Linklater, Eric (75), Scottish writer; a prolific author, he produced novels (including *Private Angelo,* 1946), short stories, plays, biographies, travel books, and histories: d. Aberdeen, Scotland, Nov. 7.

Lippmann, Walter (85), American journalist and political analyst: b. New York, N. Y., Sept. 23, 1889; d. New York, N. Y., Dec. 14, 1974. Often called the dean of American political journalists, he produced 26 books and more than 4,000 columns in a career that spanned six decades. Lippmann attended private school in New York City and graduated with honors from Harvard University in 1910. At Harvard he became interested in Fabian socialism, and met such intellectuals as Graham Wallas, William James, and George Santayana. During his last year in college he worked as assistant to Santayana, and in 1910 he began writing for Ralph Albertson's journal, *The Boston Common.* Later (in 1917) he was to marry Albertson's daughter Faye. He soon began assisting Lincoln Steffens in New York as a reporter of the Wall Street scene for *Everybody's Magazine,* and within a year had become a member of the editorial board. By 1912 his zeal for Socialist reforms led him to serve for a few months as executive secretary to the Rev. George R. Lunn, Socialist mayor of Schenectady, N. Y. However, he soon concluded that socialism was a sterile cause, and in 1914 he embarked on a somewhat more conservative phase of his career in helping to launch *The New Republic.* World War I saw him in various government posts, including assistant to the secretary of war and a member of the staff of Col. Edward M. House, adviser to President Woodrow Wilson, at the Paris Peace Conference. He returned briefly to *The New Republic* after the war, then moved to the New York *World* in 1921, serving as editor from 1929 to 1931, when the newspaper ceased publication. In the latter year he was invited to prepare a column for the New York *Herald-Tribune.* The result was his famous column "Today and Tomorrow," which was widely syndicated until he discontinued it in 1967. Meanwhile, his first marriage having ended in divorce, he was married in 1938 to Helen Byrne Armstrong and moved to Washington, D. C., where he developed the style of astute political analysis and philosophical observation of the world scene that brought him the respect of political leaders throughout the world and the devoted attention of millions of readers of both his columns and his books. He retired in 1967 and returned to New York City, but continued writing an occasional column for *Newsweek* magazine until 1971. Liberal in many of his political theories and archly conservative in others, but always an independent thinker, he supported presidential candidates ranging from Thomas E. Dewey to John F. Kennedy, from Dwight D. Eisenhower to Lyndon B. Johnson. His many awards included the Pulitzer Prize in 1957 and 1962, the Medal of Freedom in 1964, the Gold Medal of the National Institute of Arts and Letters in 1965, and decorations from Belgium, Norway, and the Netherlands. His books included *A Preface to Politics* (1913), *The Stakes of Diplomacy* (1915), *Public Opinion* (1922), *Men of Destiny* (1927), *A Preface to Morals* (1929), *The Method of Freedom* (1934), *The Good Society* (1937), *The Public Philosophy* (1955). and *Western Unity and the Common Market* (1962).

Litvak, Anatole (72), Russian-born U. S. film director; in 45 years, he worked in Russia, France, Germany, Britain, and the United States; among his best-known films was *The Snake Pit*: d. Paris, Dec. 15.

Liu Shao-ch'i, Chinese Communist leader, born in 1898 or 1899; succeeded Mao Tse-tung as chief of state (chairman) of the People's Republic in 1959; strongly attacked as a "revisionist" during Cultural Revolution in 1966–67; removed from all posts in 1968, he disappeared from public view; on Oct. 31, 1974, a Communist newspaper in Hong Kong revealed that he was dead, but no details of date or circumstances were given.

Long, Lois (73), U. S. fashion editor, on the staff of *The New Yorker* magazine; pioneered in the field of fashion criticism: d. Saratoga, N. Y., July 29.

Lovejoy, Clarence E. (79), U. S. newspaperman and educational consultant; boating editor, *The New York Times* (1934–62); founded series of school and college guides bearing his name: d. Red Bank, N. J., Jan. 16.

Lunn, Sir Arnold (86), British ski expert; invented the slalom and in 1922 established first modern slalom course, in Switzerland; prominent Catholic layman, wrote books on the faith: d. London, June 2.

McCafferty, Don (53), U. S. football coach; head coach, Baltimore Colts (1970–72) and Detroit Lions (1973–74): d. Pontiac Mich., July 28.

McGee, Frank (52), U. S. news commentator: b. Monroe, La., Sept. 12, 1921; d. New York, N. Y., Apr. 17, 1974. One of the most highly rated newscasters of the NBC network, he was noted for his crisp, flawless delivery and incisive analyses of news events and his well-informed narration of documentaries. Reared in Oklahoma, he studied at the universities of California and Oklahoma under the G.I. Bill before entering the broadcasting field. In 1957, while working for a Montgomery, Ala., TV station, he impressed NBC officials with his coverage of racial strife and was hired for the network's Washington staff. For a number of years he served as anchorman of NBC radio's weekend *Monitor* program and NBC-TV's nightly *Sixth Hour News,* and he gained nationwide popularity for his impromptu coverage of such events as political conventions, space shots, and the John F. Kennedy assassination. In 1970 he became co-anchorman with David Brinkley and John Chancellor of the *NBC Evening News.* From 1971 until his death he was co-host of the popular *Today* show.

McGuigan, James Cardinal (79), Canadian prelate, former archbishop of Toronto: d. Toronto, April 8.

McKeldin, Theodore R. (73), U. S. public official, "Mr. Republican" of Maryland and two-term governor (1951–59); twice elected mayor of Baltimore (1943 and 1963); opposed racial segregation: d. Baltimore, Aug. 10.

Malone, Ross L. (63), U. S. lawyer; held private, public, and corporate legal posts; served as U. S. deputy attorney general, and also two terms as American Bar Association president: d. Roswell, N. Mex., Aug. 13.

Manning, Harry (77), U. S. vice admiral; commanded the liner *United States* on her record-breaking maiden voyage across the Atlantic Ocean in 1952: d. Saddle River, N. J., Aug. 1.

Marie, André (76), French official; held many cabinet posts, beginning in 1933; deported and imprisoned by Germans in World War II; served briefly as premier in 1948; d. Rouen, Normandy, June 12.

Massey, Ilona (62), Hungarian-born U. S. actress in films (*Balalaika,* 1939), on Broadway, and on radio and television: d. Bethesda, Md., Aug. 20.

Meyer, Karl F. (89), Swiss-born U. S. veterinarian scientist; made numerous contributions to public health, including saving canning industry from botulism threat and discovering two encephalitis viruses: d. San Francisco, April 27.

Milhaud, Darius (81), French composer: b. Aix-en-Provence, France, Sept. 4, 1892; d. Geneva, Switzerland, June 22, 1974. A pioneer of polytonality, he ranked with Debussy and Ravel among the most important personalities in modern music. His more than 400 compositions include ballets, operas, symphonies, concertos, string quartets, and incidental music for the theater and motion pictures, and drew from virtually every musical idiom, including Jewish liturgical music, New Orleans jazz, and Brazilian folk songs. A member of a prosperous French Jewish family, he studied at the Paris Conservatoire. In 1917 he went to Rio de Janeiro as secretary to the French poet and ambassador to Brazil Paul Claudel, with whom he collaborated on several compositions. During the 1920's, in Paris, he was a member of the influential avant-garde Groupe des Six, a loosely knit group of composers in revolt against the strong influence of impressionism on French music. Milhaud's major works include *Six Little Symphonies* (1917–23); the ballets *Le Boeuf sur le Toit* (1919) and *La Création du Monde* (1923); the operas *Christophe Colomb* (1928) and *David* (1954); the piano suite *Scaramouche* (1939); and the oratorio *Pacem in Terris* (1963). From about 1940 until his retirement in 1972, he taught composition alternately at Mills College in Oakland, Calif., and at the Paris Conservatoire.

Miró Cardona, José (71), Cuban official; served briefly in 1959 as Fidel Castro's first premier, then as Cuban ambassador to Spain; defected to the United States in 1961: d. San Juan, P. R., Aug. 10.

Mirsky, Alfred E. (73), U. S. biochemist; joined Rockefeller Institute (now University) in 1927; in 1940's developed methods for isolating the genetic material of animal cells for study: d. New York City, June 19.

Molyneux, Capt. Edward H. (79), British fashion designer; after distinguished service in World War I, opened a design house in Paris; scored great success there and in London: d. Monte Carlo, March 22.

Moore, Arthur J. (85), U. S. evangelist and bishop of the United Methodist Church; a compelling orator, he had many missions abroad: d. Atlanta, Ga., June 30.

Moorehead, Agnes (67), U. S. actress; five times nominated for an Academy Award; portrayed Endora on the television series *Bewitched*: d. Rochester, Minn., April 30.

Morse, Wayne (Lyman) (73), U. S. senator: b. Madison, Wis., Oct. 20, 1900; d. Portland, Oreg., July 22, 1974. A maverick, who considered principle more important than party labels, he represented Oregon in the U. S. Senate for 24 years, first as a liberal Republican, then as an independent, and finally as a Democrat. He consistently championed civil rights and the interests of farmers and organized labor, and he steadfastly opposed U. S. military involvement in Vietnam. In 1964 he and Ernest Gruening (D-Alaska) were the only senators to vote against the Gulf of Tonkin resolution. A Wisconsin farmer's son who was inspired in his political views by progressive Republican Sen. Robert La Follette, he obtained law degrees at Minnesota and Columbia universities and became dean of the University of Oregon law school at the age of 30. After two years on the War Labor Board, he entered the Senate in 1945. Differences with President-elect Eisenhower caused him to break with the Republican party in 1953, and after three years as an independent he became a Democrat. He lost his Senate seat by a narrow margin to Robert Packwood in the 1968 election but was actively campaigning to regain it at the time of his death.

Muilenburg, James (77), U. S. theologian and biblical scholar; worked on the Revised Standard Version of the Bible (1952); taught at Union Theological Seminary (1945–63): d. Claremont, Calif., May 10.

Mundt, Karl E. (74), U. S. public official; congressman (R-S. Dak., 1939–1948) and senator (1948–1973); he was staunchly anti-Communist in the post-World War II years: d. Washington, Aug. 16.

Munro, Sir Leslie (72), New Zealand diplomat and politician; president, UN General Assembly (1957–58); member, New Zealand parliament (1963–74): d. Hamilton, New Zealand, Feb. 13.

Niarchos, Tina (45), Greek-born international figure; first and third husbands were Greek shipowners Aristotle Onassis and Stavros Niarchos; second husband was British, the Marquess of Blandford—now duke of Marlborough: d. Paris, Oct. 10.

Nilsson, Anna Q. (85), Swedish-born actress; first of the Swedish blondes to become a Hollywood star; portrayed herself in *Sunset Boulevard* (1950): d. Hemet, Calif., Feb. 12.

Nourse, Edwin G. (90), U. S. economist; first chairman of the President's Council of Economic Advisers, appointed by Truman in 1946: d. Bethesda, Md., April 7.

O'Brien, Kate (76), Irish novelist and playwright; won two literary prizes for first novel, *Without My Cloak* (1931): d. near Faversham, Kent, England, Aug. 13.

Odría, Manuel A. (77), Peruvian official; president of Peru (1948–56): d. Lima, Peru, Feb. 18.

Oistrakh, David Fyodorovich (65), Russian violinist: b. Odessa, Ukraine, Oct. 30, 1908; d. Amsterdam, the Netherlands, Oct. 24, 1974. One of the world's greatest living musicians, he attended the Odessa Conservatory and made his debut at the age of 12. He played in concerts throughout Russia, became a professor at the Moscow Conservatory, and in 1942 was awarded the Stalin Prize. His first U. S. appearance was at Carnegie Hall in New York, on Nov. 20, 1955. One month later he appeared with the N. Y. Philharmonic, and thereafter he frequently was soloist with that orchestra. Although he was Jewish, he was a member of the Communist party and came under attack occasionally because of the USSR's anti-Jewish policies. His son Igor also is an accomplished violinist.

Pagnol, Marcel (79), French movie director and playwright; widely admired for his *Fanny* trilogy, about ordinary waterfront people in Marseille: d. Paris, April 18.

Partch, Harry (73), U. S. composer; based his microtonal compositions on his own 43-interval octave; also devised and constructed his own extraordinary instruments, including a 72-string kithara and the bloboys, built of bellows, three organ pipes, and an auto exhaust; achieved critical and institutional recognition, although the general public had little opportunity to hear his works: d. San Diego, Calif., Sept. 3.

Pellizza, Pierre (56), French tennis player; won French national championship in 1939, 1946, and 1947; later became U. S. citizen: d. Louisville, Ky., June 7.

Perón, Juan. See separate article preceding this section.

Pierce, Billie (67), U. S. jazz pianist; with her horn-playing husband, De De Pierce, led the Preservation Hall Jazz Band in the 1960's; also performed with several rock groups: d. New Orleans, Oct. 1.

Pincherle, Marc (86), French musical historian; probably best known for cataloging the works of Vivaldi: d. Paris, June 20.

Pollet, Howie (53), U. S. baseball player; helped pitch the St. Louis Cardinals to a World Series victory in 1946: d. Houston, Aug. 8.

Pompidou, Georges. See separate article preceding this section.

Protitch, Dragoslav (72), Yugoslav-born UN official; after service as a Yugoslav diplomat, he joined the United Nations in 1945, becoming an undersecretary in 1954; retired in 1969: d. Wolfboro, N.H., Dec. 21.

Quayle, Oliver A., 3d (52), U. S. public-opinion pollster: d. Hanover, N. H., April 14.

Ransom, John Crowe (86), U. S. poet; b. Pulaski, Tenn., April 30, 1888; d. Gambier, Ohio, July 3, 1974. Described by Allen Tate as "one of the first poets in any language," he produced a small body of eloquent verse, much of it extolling the rural South while rejecting both romanticism and the machine age. As Carnegie professor from 1937 to 1958, and then as professor emeritus at Kenyon College, Ohio, he inspired several younger poets. He expounded his "new criticism," holding that art is the best form of knowledge, in the prestigious *Kenyon Review,* which he founded in 1939 and edited until 1958. The son of an itinerant Methodist minister, he graduated from Vanderbilt University in 1907. After studying at Oxford as a Rhodes scholar, he taught at Vanderbilt for 23 years. His early interest in mysticism was reflected in his *Poems About God* (1919) and in his leading role in the literary group around the magazine *The Fugitive* (1922–25). He turned to fundamentalist Christianity in *God Without*

Thunder (1930), which inspired his short-lived "Agrarian" movement. His later concerns were largely with aesthetics. Among his honors are a Bollingen Prize, a Fellowship Prize, and a National Book Award.

Revson, Peter (35), top U. S. road-racing driver; killed in a crash during a practice run: d. Johannesburg, South Africa, March 22.

Rice, Sam (84), U. S. baseball player, a member of the Baseball Hall of Fame; in a 20-year career (1915–1934) collected 2,987 hits and had a .322 lifetime batting average: d. Rossmor, Md., Oct. 13.

Ritter, Woodward Maurice ("Tex") (67), U. S. singing cowboy star; famous for recording of *I've Got Spurs that Jingle Jangle Jingle;* ran unsuccessfully for U. S. Senate and Tennessee governorship: d. Nashville, Tenn., Jan. 2.

Rosay, Françoise (82), French actress; during a 61-year career appeared in over 100 French, British, American, and German films: d. Paris, March 28.

Rounseville, Robert (60), U. S. singer and actor; most widely known as an operatic tenor: d. New York City, Aug. 6.

Ruby, Harry (79), U. S. popular-song composer; collaborated with lyricist Bert Kalmar for more than 30 years; wrote such hits as *Three Little Words, Who's Sorry Now?, I Wanna Be Loved by You*: d. Woodland, Calif., Feb. 23.

Ryan, Cornelius John (54), U. S. author: b. Dublin, Ireland, June 5, 1920; d. New York, N. Y., Nov. 23, 1974. He was best known for three narratives of battles in World War II: *The Longest Day* (1959), *The Last Battle* (1965), and *A Bridge Too Far* (1974), all best sellers. In 1943 he became a war correspondent for the London *Daily Telegraph,* and two years later he opened that newspaper's office in Tokyo. Moving to New York in 1947, he began a series of writing assignments for *Time, Newsweek, Collier's* and *Reader's Digest* magazines, and also produced six books, including two on space subjects in collaboration with Wernher von Braun. *The Longest Day* was made into a very successful movie. His wife, the former Kathryn Ann Morgan, is a novelist.

Saillant, Louis (73), French labor leader; for 24 years (1945–69) directed the Communist-oriented World Federation of Trade Unions, from headquarters in Prague (after 1948): d. Paris, Oct. 28.

Santos, Eduardo (86), Latin American journalist and politician; president of Colombia (1938–42); founder of the liberal newspaper *El Tiempo*: d. Bogotá, March 27.

Seaton, Fred(erick) A. (64), U. S. newspaper publisher and government official; U. S. senator (R-Neb., 1951–53); adviser to President Eisenhower; secretary of the interior (1956–61); owned a Midwest network of newspapers, radio, and television stations: d. Minneapolis, Minn., Jan. 16.

Secunda, Sholom (79), Russian-born U. S. musician; gained fame as an 8-year-old cantor; later wrote about 60 operettas and 1,000 songs (*Bei Mir Bist du Schoen, Donna, Donna*); also active as a conductor, producer, and music critic: d. New York City, June 13.

Seeley, Blossom (82), U. S. vaudevillian; began performing as a child; for many years teamed with her third husband, Benny Fields: d. New York City, April 17.

Sessions, Almira (85), U. S. stage, film, and television actress; her career spanned some 65 years: d. Los Angeles, Aug. 3.

Sexton, Anne Harvey (45), U. S. poet: b. Newton, Mass., Nov. 9, 1928; d. Weston, Mass., Oct. 4, 1974. From an early age she contributed poetry to magazines and received several grants and fellowships for her writing. She served on the faculties of Boston University (1970–72) and Colgate University (1972), and in 1967 won the Pulitzer Prize for *Live or Die.* Her other books of poetry included *To Bedlam and Part Way Back* (1960), *All My Pretty Ones* (1962), *Love Poems* (1969), *The Book of Folly* (1972), and *The Death Notebooks* (1974). *Mercy Street,* a play, appeared in 1969.

Shaw, Clay L. (60), U. S. businessman who was acquitted in 1969 of plotting to assassinate President John F. Kennedy: d. New Orleans, Aug. 15.

Shazar, Zalman (84), the third president of Israel (1963–73); born in Russia, he was a life-long activist in the Jewish national movement, particularly in cultural, journalistic, and educational activities; also a leader of the Labor party: d. Jerusalem, Oct. 5.

Simonds, Guy Granville (71), Canadian general; a foremost Canadian field commander in Europe during World War II; at age 39 became dominion's youngest general: d. Toronto, May 15.

Siqueiros, David Alfaro (77), Mexican muralist, easel painter, and political activist: b. Chihuahua, Mexico, Dec. 29, 1896; d. Cuernavaca, Mexico, Jan. 6, 1974. Together with Diego Rivera and José Clemente Orozco, Siqueiros is considered in the top rank of Mexican muralists. His art, demonstrating genuine social protest, is characterized by a dynamic realism. It utilizes a color range that depends on strong contrasts of light and dark. Siqueiros' largest and most ambitious work, *The March of Humanity,* took 10 years to complete and cost an estimated $1 million. Occupying almost 2 acres in the gardens of the Hotel de Mexico, Mexico City, it spans the exterior and interior of an octagonal structure called the Polyforum. Other Siqueiros murals are located in the Palace of Fine Arts, Mexico City, the universities of Mexico and Morelia, and Warsaw's Sports Stadium in Poland. Several of his paintings are part of the permanent collection of New York City's Museum of Modern Art. A political activist since his youth and a Communist since the 1920's, Siqueiros spent the years 1960–64 in prison in Mexico for his part in organizing antigovernment student demonstrations.

Slocum, Bill (62), U. S. newsman, radio reporter, and columnist; began his career as a sports writer, turned to broadcasting, then became a newspaper columnist: d. Somerville, Mass., Nov. 26.

Smith, Howard Leland (80), U. S. architect; designed early Manhattan skyscrapers and bridges; chief architect, Federal Housing Administration (1935–50): d. Canandaigua, N. Y., March 19.

Snyder, Marty (61), U. S. restaurateur; served as Gen. Dwight D. Eisenhower's mess sergeant in World War II; later ran a New York City restaurant and a food-packaging concern: d. Nyack, N. Y., June 30.

Soyer, Moses (74), Russian-born U. S. painter; his representational portraits hang in leading U. S. museums: d. New York City, Sept. 2.

Spaatz, Carl A(ndrew) (83), U. S. Air Force general and military aviation pioneer: b. Boyertown, Pa., June 28, 1891; d. Washington, D. C., July 14, 1974. The son of a state senator of Pennsylvania Dutch background, "Tooey" Spaatz graduated from West Point in 1914 and from the Army's Command and General Staff School in 1936. He served as a combat pilot in Europe in World War I. In 1929 he helped to set a refueling-endurance flight record, remaining aloft 151 hours. During World War II he commanded the Eighth Air Force in Europe, then took command of Allied air forces in the North African and Italian campaigns. In 1944 he became chief of the Strategic Air Force in Europe, and in 1945, as commander of the Strategic Air Force in the Western Pacific, he supervised air strikes against Japan, including the atomic bombings of Hiroshima and Nagasaki. When the Air Force became a separate branch of the service in 1947 he was named its first chief of staff. After his retirement from the service in 1948 he became chairman of the Civil Air Patrol.

Spottswood, Stephen Gill (77), U. S. churchman and civil-rights leader, a retired bishop of the African Methodist Episcopal Zion Church; served as board chairman of the National Association for the Advancement of Colored People from 1961: d. Washington, D. C., Dec. 1.

Strasser, Otto (76), German Nazi theoretician; formulated party's "Bamberg Program" in 1925; expelled from party in 1930: d. Munich, Aug. 27.

Strauss, Lewis L. (77), former U. S. government official: b. Charleston, W. Va., Jan. 31, 1896; d. Brandy Station, Va., Jan. 22, 1974. A banker by profession, Lewis Strauss possessed an excellent knowledge of physics for someone not trained in the field. He served with the U. S. Navy during World War II, rising to the rank of rear admiral in the reserve. A member of the Atomic Energy Commission (1946–50) and its chairman (1953–58), he played a key role in the development of U. S. thermonuclear policy. Following the explosion of an atomic bomb by the USSR in 1949–50, Strauss advocated the immediate development of the hydrogen bomb. President Truman accepted Strauss' views, and the first hydrogen device was exploded on Nov. 1, 1952. Strauss' dealings with Congress, however, were not always smooth, and the Senate rejected his appointment as secretary of commerce in 1959. He then returned to private life, devoting much time to philanthropy.

Sullivan, Edward Vincent (73), U. S. columnist and television host: b. New York, N. Y., Sept. 28, 1901; d. New York, N. Y., Oct. 13, 1974. He achieved fame first as a Broadway columnist for New York newspapers, then as master of ceremonies of his TV variety show. He attended high school in Port Chester, N. Y., then held a long series of newspaper jobs in New York and Philadelphia before becoming Broadway columnist for the N. Y. *Evening Graphic* in 1929 and for the N. Y. *Daily News* in 1932. From 1948 until 1971 he was master of ceremonies of his TV show, the *Ed Sullivan Show* (originally called *Toast of the Town*), on which many famous entertainers made their debut.

BANTAM BOOKS

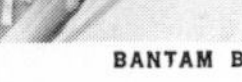

Jacqueline Susann

SULLIVAN PRODUCTIONS, FROM CBS

Ed Sullivan

Sullivan, Elliott (66), U. S. actor; appeared in many stage, screen, and television productions: d. Los Angeles, June 2.

Susann, Jacqueline (53), U. S. actress and writer; her book *Valley of the Dolls* (1966) became the world's best-selling novel: d. New York City, Sept. 21.

Sutherland, Earl W., Jr. (58), biomedical scientist; winner of 1971 Nobel Prize in medicine and physiology for "his discoveries concerning the mechanisms of the actions of hormones": d. Miami, Fla., March 9.

Tabbert, William (53), U. S. singer and actor; originated role of Lt. Joseph Cable in *South Pacific;* appeared in other Broadway musicals, in concerts, in nightclubs, and on television: d. New York City, Oct. 19.

Tanaka, (Paul Francis) Kotaro (83), Japanese purist; chief justice of the Supreme Court of Japan (1950–61); judge of the International Court of Justice (1961–70): d. Tokyo, March 1.

Thant, U (65), Burmese statesman: b. Pantanaw, Burma, Jan. 22, 1909; d. New York, N. Y., Nov. 25, 1974. Elected the third secretary general of the United Nations in 1962, he held that post until 1971, longer than any other person. U Thant (the "U" is a form of Burmese address, somewhat akin to "Uncle" or "Mister") attended University College, Rangoon, where he met U Nu, who later became premier and remained a close friend throughout his life. He taught high school in Pantanaw, Burma, and during the Japanese occupation in World War II was active in educational work. When U Nu became premier of independent Burma in 1948, U Thant (who had become press director in 1947) was made director of broadcasting and then minister of information. In 1952 he was sent to the United Nations as an alternate member of the Burmese delegation, and in 1957 he became Burma's chief delegate. In November 1961, after Dag Hammarskjöld's death, the UN General Assembly elected him acting secretary general; and on Nov. 30, 1962, he was elected secretary general. In that post he proved a firm but gentle influence in the peaceful settlement of disputes, most notably in the Cuban missile crisis of 1962, the Congo revolution, and the Kashmir dispute. His concept of his role as an impartial but vigorous secretary general often brought him into conflict with the great powers, but he never lost their respect. He retired as of Jan 1, 1972, and settled in Harrison, N. Y., where he completed the first draft of his memoirs shortly before his death from cancer.

Thompson, Helen M. (66), U. S. orchestra manager and lobbyist; headed the American Symphony Orchestra League for 20 years (1950–70) and then managed the New York Philharmonic (1970–73): d. Carmel, Calif., June 25.

Topping, Dan(iel Reid) (61), U. S. sports executive; part-owner, New York Yankee baseball club for 22 years; d. Miami, Fla., May 18.

Trochta, Stepan Cardinal (68), Czech prelate; named to the College of Cardinals "in secret" by Pope Paul VI in 1969 after spending many years in Nazi concentration camps and Czech Communist jails: d. Litomerice, Czechoslovakia, April 6.

Troisgros, Jean Baptiste (77), French restaurateur; his three-star restaurant in Roanne, Burgundy, was considered the greatest in the world by a number of discerning diners: d. French Riviera, Oct. 23.

Vanderbilt, Amy (66), U. S. columnist and authority on etiquette: b. July 22, 1908; d. New York, N. Y. (fell from her apartment window), Dec. 27, 1974. The successor to Emily Post as America's arbiter of social manners and etiquette, she was a student of home economics at the Heubi Institute in Lausanne, Switzerland, and of journalism at New York University. She spent some years in public relations and advertising work, and as a newspaper columnist, before publishing *Amy Vanderbilt's Complete Book of Etiquette* in 1952. The book sold millions of copies in its original and revised editions. Other books and many columns on etiquette appeared afterward, and she was a frequent guest on radio and television shows. She was married four times, most recently to Curtis B. Kellar.

Vanderbilt, Cornelius, Jr. (76), U. S. author and journalist, member of the wealthy New York family; published three tabloids that failed: d. Miami Beach, Fla., July 7.

Wahl, Jean (88), French existentialist philosopher and poet; influential teacher at the Sorbonne since 1936; among his students was Jean Paul Sartre; writings include *The Philosopher's Way*: d. Paris, June 19.

Warren, Earl. See separate article preceding this section.

Watson, Arthur K(ittredge) (55), U. S. corporation executive and diplomat: b. Summit, N. J., April 23, 1919; d. Norwalk, Conn., July 26, 1974. The younger of the two sons of Thomas J. Watson, Sr., founder of International Business Machines Corp., he built the IBM World Trade Corp. from a new IBM subsidiary in 1949 into an international enterprise with revenues of over $2.5 billion in 1970. A Yale graduate, he promoted the concept of "World peace through world trade" while serving the IBM World Trade Corp. as vice president from 1949 to 1953, as president from 1954 to 1963, and as board chairman from 1963 to 1970. As U. S. ambassador to France from 1970 to 1972 he took part in the effort to combat international narcotics traffic, and helped establish first contacts between the U. S. and Communist China.

Webb, Del (75), U. S. construction and real-estate millionaire; part-owner of the New York Yankees from 1945 to 1964: d. Rochester, Minn., July 4.

Whitney, Richard (86), U. S. financier; credited with halting the stock panic of Oct. 24, 1929, through his generous bids; served five years as president of the New York Stock Exchange; later imprisoned for embezzlement: d. Far Hills, N. J., Dec. 5.

Wickwire, Nancy (48), U. S. actress; performed on Broadway and on television and, most conspicuously, in major repertory companies: d. San Francisco, July 10.

Wightman, Hazel Hotchkiss (87), U. S. tennis champion, member of the Tennis Hall of Fame and donor of the Wightman Cup in women's tennis; won her 44th national title at the age of 68: d. Chestnut Hill, Mass., Dec. 5.

Wolfson, Harry A. (86), Russian-born U. S. philosopher and a foremost scholar of comparative religion; in 1915 joined the faculty of Harvard, remaining there the rest of his life; his books include *The Philosophy of the Church Fathers* (1956): d. Cambridge, Mass., Sept. 19.

Young, Rodney S. (67), U. S. archaeologist; since 1950 the director of excavations at Gordium, Turkey, sponsored by the museum of the University of Pennsylvania, where he taught; among his finds was a palace believed to have been inhabited by King Midas: d. Chester Springs, Pa., Oct. 25.

Yurka, Blanche (86), U. S. stage and screen actress; achieved stardom in 1925 as Gina in Ibsen's *The Wild Duck*; last New York appearance was in 1970: d. New York City, June 6.

Zhukov, Georgy K(onstantinovich) (77), Soviet military commander: b. Strelkovka, Russia, December 1896: d. Moscow, USSR, June 18, 1974. The Soviet Union's greatest military commander of World War II, he turned German forces back from Moscow in 1941, engineered the defense of Stalingrad and the lifting of the siege of Leningrad, and led his forces to victory in Berlin in 1945. The son of a peasant, he switched from the Czarist army to the Red army in 1918 and became a Communist party member in 1919. Trained in armored warfare at Frunze military academy, he rose through military ranks, surviving Stalin's purge of 1937, and was an observer in the Spanish Civil War. In 1939–40 he served on the Manchurian frontier and then in the Finnish campaign. Although his World War II triumphs made him a great popular hero, he was relegated to the status of a "nonperson" by Stalin, who apparently feared his influence. Rehabilitated after Stalin's death, he became deputy defense minister in 1953, defense minister in 1955, and a member of the Communist party presidium in 1957. Premier Khrushchev again relegated him to obscurity for some eight years, but in 1965, after Khrushchev's fall from power, Zhukov was fully rehabilitated.

OCEANIA

Within the South Pacific's island nations and territories, inflation—stemming from higher costs of imported food and fuel—produced uncertainty and shaded economic progress.

The long-standing distinction between the South Pacific Commission and the South Pacific Conference ended with the merger of the two organizations. The Commission was reconstituted as a Conference committee empowered to decide the administrative program.

Although official protests were voiced against nuclear testing in the atmosphere over French Polynesia, the issue faded following assurances by Paris that the 1974 series would be the last in France's atmospheric test program.

During an extended visit to Oceania, Britain's Queen Elizabeth received a warm welcome. With the Queen were Prince Philip, Princess Anne and her husband, Capt. Mark Phillips, and Lord Louis Mountbatten. Thousands of Cook Islands warriors greeted the Queen and bore her aloft on a portable throne before she officially opened Rarotonga's new jetport.

Fiji-based Air Pacific was strengthened as a result of Fiji's determination to give the airline, jointly owned by the area's national and territorial governments, a pivotal role. At the South Pacific Forum, held in March, Fiji's Prime Minister Ratu Sir Kamisese Mara called for solidarity on civil aviation. Following withdrawal of American Airlines from the South Pacific, Air Pacific secured landing rights at American Samoa, becoming the sole operator between Pago Pago and Nadi.

Political Developments and Regional Cooperation. Papua New Guinea was caught up in major political disputation, and plans to make Dec. 1, 1974, the date of independence were canceled. Fractionalism and differences on such fundamental issues as the degree of centralized authority the government should enjoy and the powers of the parliamentary leader were among the underlying causes of friction.

PNG's Chief Minister Michael Somare stood against the majority report of the constitution planning committee, which produced long and detailed proposals in a draft constitution. A provision to prevent direct transition from chief minister to prime minister was included in the draft. Somare placed his own proposals before the House of Assembly in the form of a simplified constitution.

Australia voted PNG $300 million in aid. In October the PNG government announced that no formal alliance would be entered into with Australia but that PNG and Australia wanted a "continuing close relationship" following independence. It was also announced that the PNG government would take over the running of its defense force from December 1; full defense responsibilities would follow with independence.

The 100-square-mile coral island of Niue gained independence from New Zealand on October 19, although close ties remained with New Zealand, and the islanders retained their New Zealand citizenship.

The Gilbert and Ellice Islands also moved closer to self government. Debate centered on whether the islands should become one nation or whether the Ellice people, outnumbered 6 to 1 by the Gilbertese, should set up their own administration. The House of Assembly chose 36-year-old Naboua Ratieta as the colony's first chief minister.

In the British Solomon Islands Protectorate, self-government was advanced with the introduction of the ministerial system. However, the legislature decided to form a one-party government; the United Solomon Islands party's elected representatives dropped their party label in favor of a parliamentary group.

In the Condominium of New Hebrides, political groups were active. The National party (founded in 1971) drew together a fragmented leadership, and the party's conference voted in favor of tighter immigration laws, education reform, and nationalization of all former patriot-held land as well as citizenship for New Hebrideans. Two planter-based parties opposing radical change in land ownership were organized.

In November the British and French governments agreed to set up an elective Assembly in 1975 to replace the advisory Council and to drop the triform legal system (British, French and "local") in favor of a uniform legal code. Passports in the name of New Hebrides were to be issued.

Economic Change. Rising prices of imports and escalating local wages shook the economic stability of most island communities. Fiji, Tonga, New Hebrides, New Caledonia, and French Polynesia were the hardest hit. Buoyant prices for sugar and copra, and, for phosphate rock in Nauru, helped moderate balance-of-payments difficulties. Papua New Guinea had gains from the working of the great copper-gold mine on Bougainville. After the announcement of Bougainville Mining's profit, running at over $250 million a year, the PNG government moved to increase the government's tax share.

Fiji abolished its preferential tariff rates on goods from Commonwealth countries and overhauled its income-tax system. A turnover tax on hotel charges was introduced; it and higher company taxes helped boost revenue to meet increased expenditure for social services, education, and medical care.

French Polynesia's predominantly Gaullist Territorial Assembly supported a greatly expanded budget designed to inject new life into the economy. France provided loan funds, and customs duties and local taxes were increased.

R. M. YOUNGER
Author, "Australia and the Australians"

CNEXO PHOTO

The French bathyscaphe *Archimède* teamed with other deep-submersible vessels in a joint French-American exploration of the mid-Atlantic rift valley.

OCEANOGRAPHY

In 1974 the trend toward large cooperative efforts in oceanography continued although funds for research remained tight.

The International Conference on the Law of the Sea, held in Caracas in 1974, has clarified the positions of the participating nations. It appears that national control over exploration and exploitation of coastal areas eventually will be extended to 200 miles (320 km) offshore. About 35% of all ocean beds are involved in this expansion of national jurisdiction. The fundamental issue is that most of the world's fish resources and virtually all of its marine petroleum and gas resources occur in the coastal zone. Also, the right to mine deep-sea minerals remains under discussion.

Ocean Resources. Exploration of continental margins by scientists from oceanographic institutions and the U. S. Geological Survey continued, largely as a part of the International Decade of Ocean Exploration (IDOE). These surveys are advancing knowledge of the structure and history of continental margins, where hydrocarbon reserves are yet to be discovered.

A large-scale effort within IDOE is directed toward mapping and analyzing manganese nodules on the sea floor. The mode and rate of growth of these nodules, which are rich in copper, zinc, and nickel, is still a mystery.

Deep-sea mining for ores and offshore drilling for hydrocarbons pose severe engineering problems. Research is being conducted on the environmental impact of such operations as well as on accident prevention and response.

During the last 20 years, the harvest of marine finfish and shellfish has tripled, and marine products now supply about one seventh of the world's human food protein. The major portion of the harvest is used for animal feed.

An understanding of the processes affecting the survival rate of fish broods is important to the technology of fishery. In particular, the effects of temperature, salinity, food density, food quality, and predators on larval growth and survival are being studied.

The effects of human fishing on fish population dynamics also must be assessed if fishery resources are to be managed intelligently. Recent studies of fossil fish scales in deposits off California showed that the fish population has fluctuated considerably over the last 1,000 years, even without human exploitation.

Deep-Sea Circulation. Studies of the dynamics of ocean circulation and of the global distribution of water properties continued in 1974. Much effort was devoted to analyzing field data collected by MODE (Mid Ocean Dynamics Experiment). The long-term objective of the MODE program is to provide information about medium-scale (100-mile) eddy processes in the ocean that can be related to mathematical models of the general circulation of the ocean.

Large computers are being used to simulate the dynamics of flow in ocean basins, with emphasis on the interaction between the eddies and the basin-sized components of water motion. Ultimately, the program is expected to lead to a better understanding of the relationship between quasi-geostrophic currents and eddy dynamics. Such understanding is necessary for the construction of ocean models in forecasting climate.

The Geochemical Ocean Sections Study (GEOSECS) applies chemical methods to the problems of large-scale circulation and mixing in the ocean. The program obtained detailed measurements of oceanic constituents at all depths in profiles from the Arctic to the Antarctic. The second phase of GEOSECS ended in June 1974 after R/V *Melville* had logged 35,000 miles during a ten-month expedition from Antarctica to the Bering Sea.

In addition to obtaining greatly improved detail on hydrographic parameters such as temperature, salinity, and oxygen, GEOSECS provided an impressive store of data on the distribution of stable and radioactive isotopes, rare gases, and suspended particulate matter.

Environmental Forecasting. In a world where food production is insufficient to satisfy all needs, any fluctuation in climate produces hardship. Climatic change is a result of many factors, an important one being the energy exchange between ocean and atmosphere.

Research in 1974 focused on several aspects of the air-sea interaction, making use of field studies, laboratory experiments, historical reconstruction, mathematical modeling, and computer simulation. One major study was the total heat exchange across the air-sea interface on scales ranging from months to days and smaller. Also, there was a program to monitor the extent of sea ice, another important factor in controlling climate.

A large-scale field program is being conducted in the North Pacific Experiment (NORPAX). The major objective of this study is to describe and explain the mechanisms responsible for the large-scale oceanic and atmospheric fluctuations that occur in the mid-latitudes of the North Pacific Ocean. During the winter of 1974, NORPAX commenced a series of observations on how temperature anomalies form in ocean surface waters. *Flip,* a stable floating platform with a very long submerged pipelike hull, was used in making direct measurements of air-sea fluxes and ocean currents.

Climatic developments are being followed on scales of years, decades, centuries, and millennia. The short-term climatic variations are described in expedition reports, while the long-term fluctuations are determined from an analysis of sediments. A major effort is underway by a group within IDOE to reconstruct the extreme glacial mode of operation of the ocean-atmosphere system. One striking discovery in 1974 was that there seems to be a lag of several millennia in the response of the bottom-water circulation to changed conditions at the surface.

Chemistry and Fertility. Research on the chemistry of seawater is being focused on an improvement in the understanding of ionic equilibria and the formation of biological species in seawater, and the determination of sources, sinks, and pathways of chemical species in the ocean.

Knowledge of the physical chemistry of seawater is being refined by experiment; for example, by accurate measurements of freezing point and osmotic pressure under various conditions. Combined with theoretical studies, such experiments provide insights into the energy of interaction between water molecules and between ions and water molecules in the complex medium that is seawater.

Major and minor elements within seawater spend various amounts of time in different phases and in different water masses. The cycling from solid to solute and back has been a subject of major interest because these processes of precipitation and redissolution control the chemistry of the ocean and its fertility.

Coastal Environment. Demands on the coastal waters for recreation, sewage disposal, oil exploitation, and cooling for power plants are rising exponentially. Research in 1974 concentrated on three major aspects: coastal upwelling, near-shore dynamics, and coastal pollution.

The major upwelling areas in the ocean occur along the western coasts of the continents. Fishing yields from these areas exceed those from other regions by vast amounts. The Coastal Upwelling Ecosystem Analysis (CUEA) program, which is part of IDOE, continued field work and theoretical studies to provide models for predicting the characteristics of upwelling in particular locations. Several research vessels are involved in collecting field data. Observations were made off northwest Africa and off the northwest coast of the United States.

Studies of near-shore and estuarine dynamics have acquired a new urgency in view of man's impact on these environments. An important aspect is a better understanding of how a continuously injected pollutant or tracer behaves within the near-shore circulation cells and associated long-shore movements. The cells, consisting of incoming wave movements and outgoing rip currents, produce a continuous interchange between the waters of the surf zone and those of the off-shore zone, and this prevents free mixing of tracers into the open ocean. Instead, such a tracer tends to travel along the shore within the long-shore current system.

Of the major types of ocean pollution—solid wastes, thermal energy, chemicals, and radioisotopes—oil pollution is perhaps the most familiar. Considerable efforts are being made to obtain information on the natural input of oil to the ocean by seepage and the background level of concentration. The amount of oil seeping into the ocean from natural sources is estimated at about 0.6 million metric tons per year. Roughly 1 million tons per year are thought to enter the ocean from leaks and spillage of crude oil caused by man.

WOLFGANG H. BERGER
Scripps Institution of Oceanography

UPI

Reconstructing the 1970 shootings at Kent State University for the grand jury, a Justice Department staff member fires a blank round from an M-1 rifle.

OHIO

Legislative actions and elections highlighted events in Ohio in 1974.

Legislative Concerns. On January 1, a new criminal code became effective, the first comprehensive revision in 159 years. Sexual acts between two consenting adults behind closed doors and not resulting in physical harm to either party were no longer illegal. The new code also sought to reestablish capital punishment where circumstances seemed to justify it, although the U. S. Supreme Court had ruled against such a penalty being generally applied.

In February the state legislature ratified the proposed 27th amendment to the U. S. Constitution, extending equal rights to women. Ohio was the 33rd state to take such action.

Effective in May was a limited no-fault divorce law that allows a couple living apart for two years to be granted a divorce without one proving that the other was at fault. The new statute also removed the use of the doctrine of incrimination, which prevents a divorce if both parties are to blame.

A law prohibiting welfare payments to poor women seeking abortions was declared void by U. S. District Court Judge Robert M. Duncan. Appointed by President Nixon in July, Duncan is Ohio's first black federal judge.

Funds in the state treasury derived from the state income tax and anticipated state lottery profits resulted in pay raises for state and local employees and teachers, and for such persons on pensions. Additional support was provided to aid local schools and higher education; to finance the first year's payments of the Vietnam-era veterans' bonus; to provide a transportation subsidy for elderly bus riders; to establish family practice medical departments in the medical schools of the state; and to give aid to local governments of southwestern Ohio to help rebuild tornado-damaged public facilities.

Elections. In the May primaries Democratic incumbent John J. Gilligan won the party's nomination for governor, as did former governor

OHIO • Information Highlights

Area: 41,222 square miles (106,765 sq km).
Population (1973 est.): 10,731,000. *Density:* 263 per sq mi.
Chief Cities (1970 census): Columbus, the capital, 540,025; Cleveland, 750,879; Cincinnati, 452,524.
Government (1974): *Chief Officers*—governor, John J. Gilligan (D); lt. gov., John W. Brown (R). *General Assembly*—Senate, 33 members (17 R, 16 D); House of Representatives, 99 members (58 D, 41 R).
Education (1973–74): *Enrollment:* public elementary schools, 1,420,972 pupils; public secondary, 949,460; nonpublic, 306,500; colleges and universities, 394,200 students. *Public school expenditures,* $2,200,000,000 ($1,009 per pupil).
State Finances (fiscal year 1973): *Revenues,* $5,624,679,000; *expenditures,* $4,997,249,000.
Personal Income (1973): $53,788,000,000; per capita, $5,012.
Labor Force (July 1974): *Nonagricultural wage and salary earners,* 4,193,600; *insured unemployed,* 65,100 (1.9%).

James A. Rhodes that of the Republican party. Mayor Ralph J. Perk of Cleveland became the Republican party's choice for senator. Former astronaut John Glenn secured the Democratic senatorial nomination over Howard Metzembaum of Cleveland. Also, a proposal providing for a state Ballot Board to simplify language on issues on the ballot was passed.

In November, three state constitutional amendments were approved. One would permit the General Assembly to reduce the homestead value in the case of permanently and totally disabled persons, thereby reducing their taxes.

Glenn easily secured the U. S. senator post. Rhodes won the governorship by a narrow margin, being one of the few Republicans in the nation to win a governorship from an incumbent Democrat. Democrats gained control of both houses of the legislature and key statehouse posts except that of secretary of state and the governorship. Republicans won 15 of the state's 23 congressional seats.

Disaster. Early in April a devastating tornado hit the city of Xenia, resulting in more than a score of deaths, injuries to hundreds, and tremendous property damages.

Kent State Case. In Cleveland the chief judge of the U. S. District Court acquitted eight former Ohio National Guardsmen in the 1970 Kent State shootings that killed four.

FRANCIS P. WEISENBURGER
The Ohio State University

OKLAHOMA

David Boren, a young Rhodes scholar and college professor, scored an upset victory in the Democratic primary and then captured the governorship in the November 1974 balloting.

Elections. Boren, at 33 the state's youngest chief executive, defeated Clem McSpadden in a runoff vote for the Democratic nomination in September. Earlier, in the first primary, Gov. David Hall was beaten in his bid for reelection. In November, Boren, a political science professor at Oklahoma Baptist University who ran on a clean government slate, won handily over Jim Inhofe, his Republican opponent.

In the race for a U. S. Senate seat, incumbent Republican Henry L. Bellmon won a narrow victory over Ed Edmondson, his Democratic challenger. For the first time since 1948, the voters elected all Democrats to the six-member state delegation in the House of Representatives.

Government Scandals. A maze of lawsuits and investigations plagued Governor Hall during the year and led to Boren's victory. Amid allegations of corruption in his administration, he endured two grand jury probes, legislative investigations, Internal Revenue Service probes, and an impeachment inquiry.

Amid his trial on nine counts of mail fraud and extortion, Democratic State Treasurer Leo Winters announced his candidacy for reelection. In May, a federal grand jury acquitted him of four of the charges against him. Although mail fraud counts were still pending due to a mistrial, the popular Winters easily won reelection.

State and federal probes implicated legislators and the administrator of the Oklahoma Securities Commission in the collapse of related firms trading in commodity options within the state. In Oklahoma City, charges of corruption in the electrical inspection, water distribution, and utilities service divisions faced Howard McMahon when he took office in January as the city's new manager.

Natural Disasters. Tornadoes on the night of June 8 took 15 lives and damaged property in 12 counties. Sections of Oklahoma City and Drumright suffered severe storm damage, while Tulsa experienced the worst storm in that city's history.

The drought that covered the Southwest hit hard at the farmers and ranchers of Oklahoma, who subsequently faced flooding from torrential August rains that broke the drought. In early November the state again suffered severe losses from rains that flooded eight central and eastern counties where damage was estimated at $10 million.

Education. In May, a federal judge accused the Oklahoma City school board of not implementing court-ordered integration. Further integration proceeded there as two black principals in predominantly black high schools exchanged jobs with white principals in two predominantly white high schools.

In Tulsa, the U. S. Court of Appeals remanded the school system's desegregation plan to Tulsa courts for further action. A federal court had ordered four schools desegregated in 1972–73 and found de facto segregation in five other schools, but did not require them to desegregate. The U. S. Justice Department and the NAACP then sued the school board over the five de facto schools, and the case was pending in U. S. District Court.

C. B. CLARK
University of Oklahoma

OKLAHOMA • Information Highlights

Area: 69,919 square miles (181,090 sq km).
Population (1973 est.): 2,663,000. *Density:* 38 per sq mi.
Chief Cities (1970 census): Oklahoma City, the capital, 368,856; Tulsa, 330,350; Lawton, 74,470; Norman, 52,117.
Government (1974): *Chief Officers*—governor, David Hall (D); lt. gov., George Nigh (D). *Legislature*—Senate, 48 members (38 D, 10 R); House of Representatives, 101 members (74 D, 27 R).
Education (1973–74): *Enrollment*—public elementary schools, 324,000 pupils; public secondary, 272,000; nonpublic, 12,000; colleges and universities, 125,740 students. *Public school expenditures,* $465,000,000 ($835 per pupil).
State Finances (fiscal year 1973): *Revenues,* $1,442,-432,000; *expenditures,* $1,416,147,000.
Personal Income (1973): $11,156,000,000; per capita, $4,189.
Labor Force (July 1974): *Nonagricultural wage and salary earners,* 872,700; *insured unemployed,* 14,400 (2.1%).

OLDER POPULATION

In 1974 continuing inflation caused particular hardships for the more than 21.8 million Americans aged 65 and older because most older people live on relatively fixed incomes.

In January, 19,453,027 persons aged 65 and older were receiving social security benefits, and many of these beneficiaries were eligible for supplemental security income because their social security benefits were so low.

The Supplemental Security Income Program, enacted in 1972, replaced the former state-federal program of Old-Age Assistance, Aid to the Blind, and Aid to the Permanently and Totally Disabled. The Social Security Administration program began on Jan. 1, 1974.

Legislation. On Jan. 3, 1974, an act increased social security benefits by 11% during the year, 7% in March and 4% in June. The act provided for the first automatic cost-of-living increases to take effect in June 1975. It also provided increases in supplemental security income payments for individuals from \$130 to \$140 a month. For couples, the increase was from \$195 to \$210 a month. Both increases were retroactive to January 1. The increases were raised to \$146 and \$219 a month in July 1974. (See SOCIAL WELFARE—*Social Security*.)

Another measure that will affect the incomes of many older people is a landmark pension reform bill enacted in September. Among other things, the act provides that retirement benefits will be earned even by those who serve less than a full career with one employer.

The Housing and Community Development bill, passed in August, revived the program of direct loan housing for the elderly, which produced 45,000 housing units before it was phased out. The new law also authorized construction of senior centers and the financing of services not available through other federal programs.

A National Institute on Aging was established as one of the National Institutes of Health in 1974. It will fund aging research and training in the medical, biological, and behavioral sciences.

Community Planning and Services. In 1974 older people were beginning to benefit from the Older Americans Comprehensive Services Amendments of 1973. In 1973–74, state agencies on aging divided the country into 600 planning and service areas and established agencies on aging in more than 400 of them. Each area agency acts as an advocate for older people and works to establish a comprehensive coordinated system of services. This will help them remain in their homes or places of residence as long as they wish and are able to do so. The area agencies are identifying existing services and working to coordinate them, identifying and pooling untapped resources, and requesting funds from state agencies to initiate or strengthen services that no other agency can or will provide.

Nutrition for the Elderly. Among the resources that area agencies may draw on in establishing service systems is the \$100 million Nutrition Program for the Elderly. By 1974, 665 nutrition projects were operating. In September, projects were serving 220,000 hot meals a day five days a week, 31% of them to minority individuals and an estimated 66% to persons with incomes below the poverty threshold. Each of the projects was providing outreach services to find people who needed the meals, transportation to meal sites, and social services. In June, Congress extended the program for three more years.

Federal Coordination. To assist state and area agencies on aging, the Department of Health, Education, and Welfare's Administration on Aging began negotiating a series of policy agreements with other agencies at the federal level under which federal funds would be made available for local programs.

Under the first of these, the U. S. Department of Transportation made money available to states for the purchase of vehicles and equipment for the elderly and handicapped. Other agreements were being negotiated on a variety of services as well as the use of certain public facilities.

Employment. During the year the U. S. Department of Labor continued to press age discrimination suits against companies proved in violation of the law. The largest suit initiated to date—for approximately \$2 million to 160 former employees—was settled in July. A second, even larger suit was instituted for more than \$200 million to some 300 present and former employees of two companies.

The Labor Department also received a \$10 million 1974 appropriation for the Older American Community Service Employment Program. Most of the federal money was awarded for new projects.

Older Americans Month. President Nixon changed the designation of May from Senior Citizens Month to Older Americans Month in 1974. In his proclamation, he called for a new declaration of rights and responsibilities of older Americans to be developed by May 1975 "as a rallying point" during the nation's bicentennial year in 1976.

International Developments. In June in Madrid, the International Center for Social Gerontology sponsored an international course on preparation for retirement.

The second conference of the International Federation on Aging was held in Kenya in July. Representatives from 17 organizations in 12 countries are members of the federation.

(See also a special feature, THE SEARCH FOR A "YOUTHFUL" OLD AGE, on page 55.)

CLARK TIBBITTS
Director, National Clearinghouse on Aging Administration on Aging, U. S. Department of Health, Education, and Welfare

ONTARIO

The Conservative government of Premier William Davis in 1974 tried to counter the effects of inflation while continuing with its established policies on transportation, the environment, and welfare.

Budget and Fiscal Affairs. The provincial budget of April 19, which increased spending by 14.2% to $8,341,000,000, touched all these areas but aimed primarily at restoring the purchasing power of the consumers' dollar. The 7% sales tax was removed from a wide range of personal items, including soap, toilet articles, and shoes costing less than $30. A guaranteed annual income of $2,600 was established for the elderly, blind, and disabled, and free prescription drugs were provided for the elderly and those on welfare.

To keep municipal property taxes from rising sharply, an additional $124 million was made available to municipalities as well as an additional $115 million in grants, bringing total provincial aid to municipalities to $2.1 billion in 1974–75. In keeping with the established policy of encouraging public transit and discouraging expressways, grants were increased to municipal transit authorities on condition they agree to freeze fares.

In an attempt to discourage land speculation and keep the price of building land down, the major innovation of the budget was a land speculation tax of 50% on the profits of the sale of unimproved land. A 20% tax was also imposed on the transfer of land by non-Canadian residents in an attempt, in the words of Treasurer John White, to "maximize Canadian ownership of our real estate."

The major items of provincial expenditure continue to be health and education. But just as educational spending was restrained several years ago, Health Minister Frank Miller has made it clear that health costs, which now comprise about one quarter of the budget ($2.2 billion), have been increasing at an alarming rate and must be brought under control. Housing remains scarce and expensive, and in addition to trying to stabilize prices by the land speculation tax, Housing Minister Sidney Handleman initiated a new policy in May to create 13,000 new units.

Among welfare measures introduced during the summer, a new policy on day-care centers was announced. Spending was to be increased by $15 million to $29 million. However, since this increase was coupled with a relaxation of regulations and a rise in the ratio of children to staff, there was much criticism, especially from women's groups. To meet the increasing cost of living, the minimum wage was raised to $2.25 an hour, and general welfare and family benefits were boosted 13%.

Rapid Transit. The Ontario government's attempt to develop new forms of urban rapid transit received support in September when the McDonnell-Douglas Corporation indicated it was investing $20 million in the magnetic levitation system being developed by the Ontario Urban Transport Development Corporation in connection with the German firm of Kraus-Maffei, in return for exclusive U. S. marketing rights for the system. This agreement was also expected to help the Douglas Aircraft plant at Malton. The test track for the new rapid transit system was expected to be completed by the summer of 1975. The provincial government was embarrassed in November, however, when the German firm announced it was stopping the venture.

Political Affairs. Commentators believe the Conservative government's popularity is slipping, and a series of by-election losses of former Conservative seats to opposition parties would indicate that there is some substance to the claim. Especially noteworthy was the loss of former Labor Minister Fern Guindon's seat in Eastern Ontario to the New Democratic party—the first that party has captured in the area.

In September, Premier Davis undertook a two-week tour of Italy. There seems little doubt that the trip was essentially motivated by domestic political considerations. Ontario now has a very large Italian immigrant population, mainly concentrated in the Toronto region. Traditionally, this group has not been associated with the Conservative party. Premier Davis seems to be attempting to widen his support, which is weak in the metropolitan Toronto area.

Other Developments. Ontario made history in 1974 when Pauline McGibbon was installed as lieutenant governor of the province, succeeding Ross MacDonald. This is the first time that a woman has held a viceregal position in Canada.

In the area of environmental protection, a major controversy raged around the continuation of logging activities in Algonquin Provincial Park. The environmentalists wish to see the work totally excluded, while others have stressed the need to provide jobs in the area. In October, the government announced that limited logging will be permitted.

PETER J. KING, *Carleton University*

ONTARIO • Information Highlights

Area: 412,582 square miles (1,068,587 sq km).
Population (1974 est.): 8,067,000.
Chief Cities (1971 census): Toronto, the provincial capital, 712,786; Hamilton, 309,173; Ottawa, the federal capital, 302,341.
Government (1974): *Chief Officers*—lt. gov., Pauline McGibbon; premier, William G. Davis (Progressive Conservative); atty. gen., Dalton A. Bales (PC); min. of educ., Thomas L. Wells (PC); chief justice, George A. Gale. *Legislature*—Legislative Assembly, 117 members.
Education (1972–73): *Enrollment:* public elementary and secondary schools, 2,081,462 pupils; private schools, 44,826; Indian (federal) schools, 7,106; colleges and universities, 135,024 students.
Public Finance (fiscal year 1974–75 est.): *Revenues,* $8,376,000,000; *Expenditures,* $8,341,000,000.
Personal Income (1972): $33,835,000,000; average annual income per person, $4,366.
(All monetary figures given in Canadian dollars.)

OREGON

Elections in Oregon generated a surprising amount of interest in 1974.

Elections. U. S. Sen. Robert Packwood, in gaining reelection by 55% to 45%, was the only Republican to win a major office. For the first time in Oregon's history, four Democrats were returned to the U. S. House of Representatives. Victories went to Les AuCoin, 56% to 44%, and Al Ullman, with 77% of the vote. Robert Duncan tallied 70% of his district's vote, and James Weaver, a virtual political unknown, scored a surprise victory over incumbent John Dellenback.

For the governor's seat, Robert W. Straub (D) won over Victor Atiyeh, 58% to 42%. Republican Gov. Tom McCall, who had had sharp differences with Atiyeh over the years, was clearly not displeased with the results. Straub, a former state treasurer, will be Oregon's first Democratic governor in 16 years and the first elected to a full four-year term in 40 years.

Democrats increased their control of the state legislature, won in 1972. For the first time in at least 50 years, the governor's seat and both houses of the legislature will be controlled by Democrats. The legislature's composition portends a more urban-oriented body than previously.

Oregon voters passed by a slim majority a controversial ballot measure prohibiting the display or distribution of obscene material, very broadly defined, or of live sex shows. The voters also passed a referendum requiring state candidates and officials to file statements of property and financial interests. A measure to prohibit the sale of steelhead trout from the Columbia River, sponsored by sport fishermen, received a 63% affirmative vote.

The general election saw a voter turnout of about 65%. President Ford's last-minute campaign visit to the state did not deter Oregon's going firmly Democratic.

Earlier, Wayne Morse, who had served 24 years in the U. S. Senate until January 1969, easily won the Democratic nomination to challenge incumbent Senator Packwood, who was unopposed in his party. But Morse's vigorous campaign was cut short by his untimely death on July 22 at the age of 73. Four contenders sought his position. The state Democratic central committee conferred it on Betty Roberts, a 51-year-old Portland lawyer and an outstanding state senator.

A number of hopefuls sought the positions of retiring U. S. Representatives Edith Green and Wendell Wyatt. For Wyatt's seat, nominations were won by Diarmuid O'Scannlain (R), 37, former state public official, and Les AuCoin, 31, Oregon House majority leader. For Edith Green's seat, former U. S. Rep. Robert Duncan (D) and John Piacentini (R), a Portland businessman, were nominated.

OREGON • Information Highlights

Area: 96,981 square miles (251,181 sq km).
Population (1973 est.): 2,225,000. *Density:* 23 per sq mi.
Chief Cities (1970 census): Salem, the capital, 68,856; Portland, 380,555; Eugene, 78,389.
Government (1974): *Chief Officers*—governor, Tom McCall (R); secy. of state, Clay Myers (R). *Legislative Assembly*—Senate, 30 members; House of Representatives, 60 members.
Education (1973–74): *Enrollment*—public elementary schools, 277,998 pupils; public secondary schools, 198,842; nonpublic schools, 24,700; colleges and universities, 131,281 students. *Public school expenditures,* $453,300,000 ($1,058 per pupil).
State Finances (fiscal year 1973): *Revenues,* $1,513,-963,000; *expenditures,* $1,302,693,000.
Personal Income (1973): $10,451,000,000; per capita, $4,697.
Labor Force (July 1974): *Nonagricultural wage and salary earners,* 850,200; *insured unemployed,* 26,700 (4.0%).

In a surprising upset, conservative state Senator Atiyeh won the Republican nomination for governor by nearly a two-to-one margin over Secretary of State Clay Myers, usually assumed to be McCall's heir apparent. The popular Governor McCall was constitutionally ineligible to succeed himself.

Primary voters defeated measures to shift the school tax burden from local property taxes to state income and corporation taxes and to fund mass transit from the gasoline tax.

Economy. Unemployment in Oregon in 1974 exceeded national figures, especially in the lumber, plywood, and other wood products industries. November unemployment was 7.5%, compared with a national figure of 6.5%, and was expected to go higher by the end of the year. Major blame was placed on the sharp fall in housing starts. There was also much controversy over log exports to Japan, depriving Oregon wood-processing mills of work.

Legislation. A special session of the state legislature, February 11–24, was motivated in part by the severe gasoline shortage. The voluntary alternate-day digital license plate purchase plan, so widely copied in the nation, ceased to be effective, and long lines returned at gasoline stations. The governor was given a 30-day authority to act in a critical energy or gasoline shortage. On March 6, Governor McCall made mandatory the odd-even purchase day plan and imposed regulations on service stations. In December, McCall gave state agencies new orders to conserve fuel and gasoline.

The special legislative session extended Oregon's offshore fishing limit to 50 miles, a reaction to foreign trawlers sighted within that limit, despite the measure's questionable enforceability.

Environment. Continuing the state's pioneering role in pollution control, Oregon's Environmental Quality Commission in July set decible limits on permissible vehicular noise, followed in September by restrictions on the amount of industrial noise.

JOANNE AMSPOKER
Oregon College of Education

OTTAWA

The quality of life emerged as a dominant issue in 1974 in Ottawa, Canada's national capital.

Limits to Growth. Local citizens groups were active in programs to halt traditional development schemes and to preserve local neighborhoods by opposing trunk highways, by rerouting traffic, and by closing many streets to through traffic. The idea of continuous growth for Ottawa has been increasingly challenged, and many have urged that further growth in the federal civil service take place elsewhere in the nation.

Decentralized Government. In a special report to the federal government, Douglas Fullerton, former chairman of the National Capital Commission, recommended the creation of a greatly enlarged national capital that would formally incorporate Ottawa and Hull, Quebec, the city across the Ottawa River. He also proposed the creation of a super regional council with strong power to administer both the Ontario and Quebec parts of the region. The council would consist of 50% elected members, 25% appointed by the federal government, and 25% appointed by the provinces of Ontario and Quebec. Municipal councils would exist under the regional council, and both the provinces and the federal government would relinquish many of their present powers. These proposals, opposed by many local politicians, especially in Quebec, would require a constitutional amendment for full implementation.

Mayor. In October, Mayor Pierre Benoit announced he would not seek reelection in December 1974. He was succeeded by Lorry Greenberg, who defeated fellow Controller Tom Macdougall in the mayoralty election.

Municipal Finance. The city of Ottawa budgeted a gross operating expenditure of $68,527,-900 for 1974, an increase of 3.4% over 1973. Of this, 33% was to be provided by federal and provincial grants and 39% by taxation on an assessment of $818,000,000. Capital expenditure jumped by 58% to $45.2 million, almost half of which was for the Civic Hospital.

The Regional Municipality proposed to spend $65.5 million, of which $24.9 million was to be raised by levies on regional municipalities and $24.8 million was to come from provincial grants. The largest item of expenditure remained social services at $16.9 million. Police and fire protection remained the responsibility of local municipalities.

The federal government planned capital expenditure of almost $72 million on office building and land acquisition in the city of Ottawa during 1974.

Education. Overall school enrollment in the suburbs of Ottawa continued to grow, while the total number of pupils in the city continued to decline.

PETER J. KING, *Carleton University*

PAKISTAN

The year 1974 saw an improving economy and a slight lessening of political separatism, but some religious strife. It also saw strides in reestablishing normal relations with Bangladesh and to a lesser extent with India.

Foreign Affairs. The normalization of affairs with India and Bangladesh continued in 1974. A world conference of Muslim leaders, held in Lahore in late February, was chosen as the occasion for Prime Minister Zulfikar Ali Bhutto to extend formal recognition to Bangladesh.

The next step was a meeting of foreign ministers of Pakistan, India, and Bangladesh (the first such meeting) in New Delhi in April. On April 10 an agreement on certain key points was announced. As part of this agreement, Bhutto apologized for the violence done to Bangladesh in the 1971 civil war. He asked the people of Bangladesh to "forgive and forget," and his words were echoed by Prime Minister Sheikh Mujibur Rahman of Bangladesh. As a *quid pro quo* for this apology, Bangladesh agreed to drop all charges and plans for trials with respect to 195 Pakistani prisoners of war who allegedly were guilty of atrocities in the 1971 fighting.

The other important issue on which some agreement was reached related to the plight of the Biharis, a pro-Pakistani Muslim refugee group originally from Bihar state in India (prior to independence in 1947). Numbering more than a half-million, they present problems for both Bangladesh (where they are not wanted because of their alleged disloyalty) and Pakistan (where their immigration would present the usual problems of employment opportunities, ethnic rivalries, and so on). Pakistan was reported to be willing to take up to 140,000 Biharis, but the deliberately vague wording of the agreement failed to set any limit on those accepted.

Still another step in these negotiations occurred when Prime Minister Bhutto visited Bangladesh, arriving in Dacca on June 27. He came, he said, on "a mission of peace and reconciliation." He apologized once more for the

PAKISTAN • Information Highlights

Official Name: Islamic Republic of Pakistan.
Location: South Asia.
Area: 310,403 square miles (803,943 sq km).
Population (1973 est. census): 68,300,000.
Chief Cities (1972 census): Islamabad, the capital, 77,-000; Karachi, 2,850,000; Lahore, 2,050,000.
Government: *Head of state,* Chaudhri Fazal Elahi, president (took office Aug. 1973). *Head of government,* Zulfikar Ali Bhutto, prime minister (took office Aug. 1973). *Legislature*—Parliament: Senate and National Assembly.
Monetary Unit: Rupee (9.931 rupees equal U. S.$1, July 1974).
Gross National Product (1972 est.): $6,230,000,000.
Manufacturing (major products): Textiles, processed foods, cement, petroleum products.
Major Agricultural Products: Wheat, cotton, rice, sugarcane, corn, millet, chickpeas, rapeseed, livestock.
Foreign Trade (1973): *Exports,* $958,000,000; *imports,* $981,000,000.

Col. Muammar el-Qaddafi (*lower right*), president of Libya, receives an enthusiastic response from the thousands who packed a Lahore, Pakistan, stadium for an Islamic "summit" conference.

UPI

1971 activities of the Pakistani Army, and stated that Pakistan and Bangladesh were natural trading and political partners. He also derived what benefits he could from the growing anti-Indian feeling in Bangladesh.

Relations with India continued their uncertain course during the year. Although the New Delhi meeting of foreign ministers in April was devoted largely to Bangladesh, it was also another step in normalizing Indian-Pakistani relations. On May 18, when India exploded a nuclear device, Pakistan reacted strongly to what it considered a grave threat. In late May, Pakistan asked the United States and other major countries for some kind of guarantee against Indian nuclear agression. Although at first insisting that Pakistan would not use its own reactors to make weapons, the government quickly added that it might be compelled to develop such weapons. On June 1, Pakistan cancelled a meeting scheduled for June 10 to normalize relations between India and Pakistan; and on June 7, in the United Nations, Pakistan charged that India was perfecting a nuclear delivery system. At the same time, Bhutto pledged that Pakistan's nuclear developments would be restricted to peaceful uses.

The talks originally scheduled for June 10 began on September 12, and two days later the two countries agreed to restore postal, travel, and telecommunications facilities that had been severed in 1971. In late November the two nations agreed to end their ban on trade.

Relations with the United States were generally friendly, as they were with China. On July 8, Bhutto reminded the United States that it was obligated to resume arms shipments to Pakistan. He followed this up with even more forceful words in October, when he said that unless Pakistan received reasonable conventional military equipment it would be compelled to develop nuclear weapons (even if it preferred not to do so). On October 31, U. S. Secretary of State Kissinger met with Bhutto in Rawalpindi and promised continued U. S. support of Pakistan's "integrity and territorial sovereignty."

Domestic Affairs. There was much about the economic picture in Pakistan that was encouraging. A record wheat crop for 1974—perhaps 8.5 million tons—was being harvested, and much of this was to be exported. Exports were expected to reach $1 billion. In January, all remaining private banks in Pakistan were nationalized; the government now virtually controls all shipping, banking, and petroleum industries. Pakistan, like other countries, was hurt by the increase in oil prices during the year. In April, Pakistan sought the consolidation and refinancing of some of its nearly $2 billion of debts to the United States.

Religious and communal strife continued in 1974. In May, clashes between Muslims and the heretical—but tolerated—Ahmadis (or Qadianis) in the Punjab resulted in at least 50 deaths. The Baluchi and Pathan separatist movements, although not dead, were more quiescent. There continued to be bombings in Peshawar. On April 14, Bhutto declared a political amnesty and an end to government military operations against the tribal revolt in Baluchistan. In September, Bhutto announced that the semiautonomous state of Hunza, bordering on China in the mountains to the north (and sometimes called Shangri-La), was being taken over by the central government.

Prime Minister Bhutto announced a considerable revision of his cabinet on October 22, including the appointment of four new members and the dropping of Finance Minister Mubashir Hasan. Bhutto retained the foreign affairs and defense portfolios.

In December a devastating earthquake destroyed several northern towns. Some 5,200 persons were killed.

CARL LEIDEN
The University of Texas at Austin

UPI

Juan Antonio Tack, Panamanian foreign minister, signs a declaration of intent in the negotiations for a new Panama Canal treaty, in Panama City on February 7.

PANAMA

There was more unrest in Panama during 1974 than at any other period in the rule of Gen. Omar Torrijos. Political opposition became more open, and the economic boom appeared at an end. Gains were made with the United States in canal treaty negotiations, but the "Banana war" produced no victories.

Treaty Negotiations. Early in the year, Panama and the United States reached an eight-point agreement on principles to guide the negotiation of a new Panama Canal treaty. U. S. Secretary of State Henry Kissinger was in Panama on February 7 to formally sign the joint declaration of principles worked out by Ambassador at Large Ellsworth Bunker and Panama's Foreign Minister Juan A. Tack. The principles included an acknowledgement of ultimate Panamanian sovereignty over the canal, Panamanian participation in the defense of the waterway, a "just and equitable" share of the benefits derived from the use of the canal by Panama, and a gradual assumption by Panama of jurisdiction over the Canal Zone.

The joint declaration was attacked by lawyers in Panama and by many U. S. senators. Talks continued throughout the year, but a new treaty was not expected until 1975. Support for Panama in its negotiations with the United States came from the presidents of Peru and Argentina, whom Torrijos visited in January.

Internal Unrest. Panamanians became increasingly restive under the prolonged Torrijos dictatorship. Some 35 business and professional groups banded together in January to demand a relaxation of authoritarian rule.

Charged with subversion and denied any right of appeal, five leaders of the banned Liberal and Panameñista parties were given one- and two-year prison terms in March. A proposed daily newspaper was closed down in January prior to publication; the government explained that it could not risk an opposition daily when groups were "conspiring against the government."

"Banana War." Panama initiated an international Union of Banana Exporting Countries (UPEB) in March. Formalized in September, the purpose of the cartel was to hike revenue from exports by adding a $1 tax per box of bananas shipped after April 1. The new levy caused United Brands, the only fruit company operating in Panama, to close down its operations at the end of July. By September 4 the workers were back on the job, and the tax was retained, at least temporarily.

Economic Uncertainty. Adverse reaction to a 1973 rent law, freezing rents at 1972 levels, caused a reconsideration of about $125 million in building projects, and also a flight of capital. Because of a decline in private construction, the government authorized a 38% increase in funds for public works in 1974. The $315 million allocation included low-cost housing, as well as airport and water-system construction. The public-works projects were financed in part by foreign loans.

The new loans pushed the public debt beyond $550 million, among the highest per capita in Latin America. The economic growth rate, estimated at between 7% and 8% in 1973, declined to 6% in 1974. Agricultural production continued its downward trend.

Relations with Castro. Terming Cuba an "objective reality," Panama reestablished diplomatic ties with the island nation in August. Relations had been severed in 1962.

LARRY L. PIPPIN, *Elbert Covell College University of the Pacific*

PANAMA • Information Highlights

Official Name: Republic of Panama.
Location: On the isthmus of Panama which links Central America and South America.
Area: 29,209 square miles (75,650 sq km).
Population (1973 est.): 1,600,000.
Chief City (1970 census): Panama, the capital, 348,704.
Government: *Military junta,* led by Gen. Omar Torrijos Herrera (took power Oct. 1972). *Head of state,* Demetrio Lakas Bahas, president (took office Dec. 1969). *Legislature* (unicameral)—People's Assembly.
Monetary Unit: Balboa (1 balboa equals U. S.$1, July 1974).
Gross National Product (1973 est.): $1,360,000,000.
Manufacturing (major products): Processed foods, petroleum products, textiles, wood products.
Major Agricultural Products: Bananas, vegetables, rice, forest products, fish.
Foreign Trade (1973): *Exports,* $133,000,000; *imports,* $489,000,000.

PARAGUAY

With the political atmosphere relatively quiet, economic matters were the foremost concern of the government of Paraguay in 1974. Gen. Alfredo Stroessner, Latin America's most durable dictator-president, completed his 20th year in power.

Economic Developments. Like many other countries of Latin America and the world, Paraguay was in the grip of inflation in 1974. The Central Bank of Paraguay announced that the cost of living had risen 60% during the last eight months of 1973. The trend continued in 1974 as the government increased public transportation prices by 50% and gasoline prices by 100%. To meet its fuel needs the government imposed a strict fuel ration system.

Faced with soaring prices the Paraguayan Labor Federation asked the government for a 50% salary and wage increase. The rise in cost of living also sparked student demonstrations in which over 100 persons were arrested. Fifteen student leaders were charged with fomenting disorder and riots among students and peasants. The agitators also called for the release of political prisoners, three of whom are leaders of the outlawed Communist party.

To meet its domestic fuel needs, Paraguay, which had spent $10 million on oil imports in 1973, had concluded an agreement with Bolivia in late 1973. Under the pact, Bolivia will supply Paraguay with 50% of its annual oil requirements, 3,000 barrels daily at a cost of $18 a barrel. Hoping to find oil of its own, the government granted Texaco 40-year oil exploration rights on 7.6 million acres in northwest Paraguay. The company will spend an initial $2 million for exploration.

Construction. A variety of construction projects were under way in 1974. A $17.2 million improvement of the Asunción airport was begun in March with a $15.4 million loan from Argentina. The state railway company announced plans to electrify and modernize the 93 miles (150 km) of rail between Asunción and Villarica at a cost of $40 million.

PARAGUAY • Information Highlights

Official Name: Republic of Paraguay.
Location: Central South America.
Area: 157,047 square miles (406,752 sq km).
Population (1973 est.): 2,700,000.
Chief City (1972): Asunción, the capital, 387,676 (federal district).
Government: *Head of state and government,* Gen. Alfredo Stroessner, president (took office Aug. 1954). *Legislature*—Congress: Senate and Chamber of Deputies.
Monetary Unit: Guaraní (126 guaranies equal U. S.$1, Aug. 1974).
Gross National Product (1973 est.): $798,000,000.
Manufacturing (major products): Meats, leather, wood products, quebracho extract, vegetable oil.
Major Agricultural Products: Cassava, bananas, tobacco, cotton, soybeans, oilseeds, citrus fruits, cattle, forest products.
Foreign Trade (1973): *Exports,* $127,000,000; *imports,* $105,000,000.

Foreign Affairs. Victor Paz Estenssoro, the former president of Bolivia, was granted asylum in Paraguay. President Juan D. Perón of Argentina paid a state visit to Paraguay one month before his death. While in Paraguay he stressed the need for economic development of the area. President Stroessner attended Perón's funeral in early July.

Stroessner also visited the Republic of South Africa for five days and signed agreements calling for economic, cultural, and scientific cooperation.

LEO B. LOTT
University of Montana

PENNSYLVANIA

Pennsylvania's electorate, unlike that of most of the states around it and in the Northeast, reelected its federal officeholders in the November general election, in spite of any aftereffects of the Watergate scandal in Washington. Aside from a few "local" incidents, the state also went through 1974 with little significant change from the year before.

Elections. The voters on November 5 reelected Republican U. S. Sen. Richard Schweiker, who had staked out key differences earlier in his voting record with the national Republican administration, and who had won continued support from labor, farmers, business, and ethnic groups. He defeated Democrat Peter F. Flaherty, mayor of Pittsburgh. Also reelected were all incumbent members of the U. S. House of Representatives and the Democratic state administration of Gov. Milton Shapp and Lt. Gov. Ernest Kline. Governor Shapp defeated Republican Andrew L. Lewis, Jr., and became the first governor in a century to win reelection.

Earlier, on February 5, Democratic State Rep. John Murtha won the special election in the 12th Congressional District to fill the vacancy caused by the death of Republican John P. Saylor in October 1973.

Energy Crisis. As 1974 opened, the nation and the state were in the midst of a crippling gasoline and heating fuel crisis. Pennsylvania was reported to be one of the three states most seriously hurt, the others being New York and New Jersey. As the national energy-crisis situation began to ease somewhat, independent truck drivers objected that some of the constraints aimed at conserving gasoline were unfair to them. They protested by stopping their trucks on the roads; and because two main east-west arteries go directly through Pennsylvania (Interstate 80, from New York to Chicago and west, and the famous Pennsylvania Turnpike, from Philadelphia west through Pittsburgh), the state had the largest number of halted trucks.

In this situation, Governor Shapp initiated action by going to Washington as personal spokesman for the truckers. There he arranged a 96-hour-long negotiating session with federal

PENNSYLVANIA • Information Highlights

Area: 45,333 square miles (117,412 sq km).
Population (1973 est.): 11,902,000. *Density,* 265 per sq mi.
Chief Cities (1970 census): Harrisburg, the capital, 68,061; Philadelphia, 1,950,098; Pittsburgh, 520,117.
Government (1974): *Chief Officers*—governor, Milton J. Shapp (D); lt. gov., Ernest P. Kline (D). *General Assembly*—Senate, 50 members; House of Representatives, 203 members.
Education (1973–74): *Enrollment*—public elementary schools, 1,197,800 pupils; public secondary, 1,145,200; nonpublic, 478,900; colleges and universities, 440,321 students. *Public school expenditures,* $2,709,140,000 ($1,247 per pupil).
State Finances (fiscal year 1973): *Revenues,* $7,486,296,000; *expenditures,* $7,380,319,000.
Personal Income (1973): $58,252,000,000; per capita, $4,894.
Labor Force (Aug. 1974): *Nonagricultural wage and salary earners,* 4,511,500.

administrators, resulting in an agreement which eased the trucking stoppage in Pennsylvania and elsewhere. Governor Shapp gained national attention, in-state political support, and a letter of praise from Philadelphia Mayor Rizzo for taking the initiative.

Other Events. The last ferryboat to travel from Pennsylvania to New Jersey and return across the Delaware River from Chester, Pa., ended service in 1974 as traffic used instead the new Commodore Barry Bridge at Chester.

The 30-year-long practice of using private lawyers to collect state debts also came to an end in 1974 by order of Attorney General Israel Packel. Under the old practice, a "fee attorney" would get 20% of the first $750 collected and 15% of the balance. There had been 64 such attorneys in 36 counties; they had handled 169 cases as of 1974.

On March 1, Governor Shapp vetoed a bill which would have clamped strict controls on pornographic books, magazines, and movies, calling it "unfair, unworkable, and unconstitutional." On March 23 the governor vetoed a bill that would have restored capital punishment in the state.

In July, two islands in the Delaware River south of Easton, in Northampton county—Shoemaker's (or Maxwell's) Island, and Groundhog (or Raub's) Island—were donated to the state by Mr. and Mrs. Russell Calvin.

JOHN F. FOLTZ
Pennsylvania State University

PERU

For Peru the most significant events of 1974 were the signing of an agreement with the United States which awarded compensation to 11 companies whose properties were nationalized, two reorganizations of the government, which strengthened President Juan Velasco Alvarado, and the reappearance of anchovies in coastal waters.

Relations with the United States. Under the February 19 settlement, Peru agreed to pay the U. S. government $76 million for distribution to the 11 companies whose properties in Peru had been nationalized. The terms were to be arranged by the U. S. State Department.

On November 17 the U. S. Peace Corps was asked to leave Peru because of alleged revelations of U. S. involvement in the 1973 overthrow of Chile's President Salvador Allende.

PERU • Information Highlights

Official Name: Republic of Peru.
Location: West coast of South America.
Area: 496,223 square miles (1,285,216 sq km).
Population (1973 est.): 14,900,000.
Chief City (1972 census): Lima, the capital, 3,350,000 (met. area).
Government: *Head of state,* Gen. Juan Velasco Alvarado, president (took office 1968). *Head of government,* Edgardo Mercado Jarrin, prime minister (took office 1973). National Congress suspended Oct. 1968).
Monetary Unit: Sol (38.70 soles equal U. S.$1, July 1974).
Gross National Product (1973 est.): $7,885,000,000.
Manufacturing (major products): Processed foods, textiles, chemicals, metal products, automobiles, fish meal, fish oil.
Major Agricultural Products: Cotton, sugar, rice, coffee, sheep, potatoes, fish.
Foreign Trade (1972): *Exports,* $943,000,000; *imports,* $792,000,000.

Velasco Solidifies Power. On January 4 it was announced that Gen. Francisco Morales Bermúdez had been promoted to army chief of staff, placing him in direct line to succeed Gen. Edgardo Mercado Jarrin as minister of defense and prime minister. A conservative, Morales had opposed the proposed nationalization in 1973 of *El Comercio,* the Lima newspaper owned by the Miró Quesada family. In addition, Gen. Rudecindo Zavaleta Rivera took over the National Social Mobilization Agency (SINAMOS), whose outgoing chief, Gen. Leonidas Rodríguez, assumed command of the second military district, based in Lima.

On May 30, Vice Adm. Luis E. Vargas Caballero, who had also opposed expropriation of *El Comercio,* was forced to resign as Navy minister after calling for greater freedom of expression and more political activity. Two other admirals also resigned their cabinet posts. After announcing its support for Admiral Vargas, Acción Popular (AP) was banned as a legal party on May 31 and several AP leaders were exiled.

Major Newspapers Expropriated. On July 27, the government expropriated the country's major newspapers, including *El Comercio* and *La Prensa.*

Economic Developments. The 1974 anchovy catch was estimated to be 4 million tons, the same as in 1973, but down from the 10 million tons of 1969–70. Prices remained high, however.

Construction was started on the 530-mile (853-km) North Peruvian oil pipeline, financed in 1973 through a $350 million Japanese loan.

In February 1974, the Ministry of Agriculture announced that 10.8 million acres (over 4 million hectares) of land had been distributed to 175,561 families since 1963.

NEALE J. PEARSON
Texas Tech University

Stanley Cup, 1974: Bill Barber of the Philadelphia Flyers raises his hockey stick in jubilation after Rick MacLeish scores goal against the Bruins. The Flyers won the Cup, 4 games to 2.

UPI

PHILADELPHIA

The "City of Brotherly Love" received pledges from gang leaders on New Year's Day to stop killings and to sign peace pacts, and the news of the year 1974 as it unfolded revealed that killings and gang fights did, in fact, decrease. Also, certain hopeful steps were taken in the impacted parts of the city to improve the school system, the living accommodations for the poor, and the police department. However, some problems still remained.

Urban Improvements. Under sponsorship of a community group, the gang leaders met with about 200 persons at a "summit conference" as the year began to iron out differences and seek to avoid bloodshed. The total number of incidents and killings in late 1974 was significantly lower than in 1973. In 1973, for example, 44 persons were killed in gang fights.

In 1974, too, the city saw the beginning of a network of 50 learning centers for gifted elementary children begun by the city school system. The $1 million project represented an effort to stem the exodus of middle-class families from the public school system. School Superintendent Matthew Costanzo said that for the first time in the city's history the public school system was serving more poverty students (as defined by federal standards) than nonpoverty students. Hope was expressed that the new learning centers would keep many families in the middle of the urban area.

The city also received a $2 million federal grant to help rehabilitate in-city dilapidated homes and offer them anew for sale or for rent to low-income families. Another $10.5 million from local money was put into the program. From 500 to 600 old homes were to be rebuilt.

Mayor Rizzo's veto of the City Council's decision to increase real estate taxes was overridden by the Council, 12–5, on June 6.

The state gave the city $90,000 of the total $500,000 allocated for rat-control programs.

Police. On the debit side, the Pennsylvania Crime Commission concluded an 18-month-long study in 1974 with a report that police corruption was widespread in Philadelphia and that the city government had tried to interfere with the commission's investigation. The president of the city's Fraternal Order of Police, Charles Gallagher, said that there might have been a few "bad apples" but did not believe the situation was as bad as the report said. Walter M. Phillips, Jr., assistant U. S. attorney in New York, was appointed special prosecutor, and efforts to solve whatever problems might exist were continuing at year's end.

Championship. The Philadelphia Flyers of the National Hockey League became the toast of the city when they captured the Stanley Cup on May 19. The Flyers, led by goalie Bernie Parent, defeated the Boston Bruins in the final round, 4 games to 2. In its seventh season, Philadelphia became the league's first expansion team to win the Stanley Cup. (See also SPORTS—*Hockey*.)

JOHN F. FOLTZ
School of Journalism
The Pennsylvania State University

PHILIPPINES

In the second year of President Marcos' martial law regime, the Philippines made further progress toward the goals of the "New Society." Meanwhile the five-year struggle between government forces and Muslim rebels in Mindanao and the islands of the Sulu chain continued in 1974. In June, President Marcos offered amnesty to all rebels who would lay down their arms and help end the "senseless bloodshed."

On October 4 the leaders of the Communist party of the Philippines called on the president to offer its cooperation in the government's reform movement. President Marcos accepted the offer and assured the Politburo leaders that he would extend amnesty to them and to all their followers.

The Economy. Despite adverse effects of global inflation and recession, the country's economy remained strong and stable in 1974. The gross national product for fiscal year 1973–74 increased 7.4% over that of the previous fiscal year. Government revenue collections increased by 120% over those of 1973. The Central Bank reported a $198 million surplus in balance of payments for the first half of 1974.

Bold steps were taken by the administration to lessen the impact of inflation. Emergency allowances were given to low-income workers in the government and in the private sector. Efforts were intensified to achieve increased food production.

Two significant events marked the country's economic progress in 1974. In July, six of the foreign firms operating in the Export Processing Zone in Bataan began exporting their finished products. On September 7, the multimillion-peso Pantabangan Dam, the initial phase of a multipurpose project in central Luzon, was dedicated 17 months ahead of schedule.

Peace and Order. The progress of the government's campaign for the maintenance of peace and national security was sustained. In the Muslim south, a program of social, economic and cultural development was put into effect aimed at removing the root cause of discontent, dissidence, and dissatisfaction, and strengthening the foundations of national solidarity. The program involved defense, rehabilitation, land reform, education, and economic development.

Tourism. Two major tourist attractions of the year were: the historical pageant presented on July 7 on the inauguration of the Folk Arts Center, a major project of the first lady; and the Miss Universe pageant (July 21). The first, in which representative groups from the country's cultural minorities participated, depicted 10,000 years of Philippine history from the Stone Age to the New Society. The Miss Universe presentation, held in the Folk Arts Center, was climaxed by the proclamation of Amparo Muñoz, Miss Spain, as 1974 Miss Universe, succeeding Margie Moran, Philippine beauty who was the 1973 Miss Universe.

A New Labor Code. Of particular significance to the New Society was the new Labor Code, signed into law by President Marcos on May 1. The president called it "a charter of human rights, as well as a bill of obligations of every workingman." Salient features of the code are: establishment of a permanent National Labor Relations Commission in place of the old Court of Industrial Relations; abolition of the graft-ridden workmen's compensation system; integration of workmen's benefits into the Social Security System for the private sector and the Government Service Insurance System for government workers; creation of an Overseas Employment Board and a National Seamen Board designed to liberate Filipino labor from graft, abuse, and exploitation; and placing all government-controlled corporations under the Civil Service Commission in accordance with a mandate of the new Constitution.

Foreign Relations. In foreign affairs, the Philippines pursued what President Marcos called "a development-motivated foreign policy." Important diplomatic events of the year included expansion of the country's relations with socialist countries in eastern Europe and Asia; forging of ties of friendship with Arab countries; meeting of President Marcos and President Suharto of Indonesia at Menado, Celebes, where problems of regional cooperation among members of the Association of Southeast Nations (ASEAN) were discussed; and a 10-day goodwill visit by Mrs. Imelda R. Marcos to the People's Republic of China.

An important result of the first lady's mission was the signing of a trade agreement under which China would sell oil to the Philippines and buy quantities of Philippine exports. On October 4, President Marcos, on recommendation of the National Security and Foreign Policy Councils, ordered the sending of a mission to Peking to pave the way for the establishment of diplomatic relations with China.

NICOLAS ZAFRA
University of the Philippines

PHILIPPINES • Information Highlights

Official Name: Republic of the Philippines.
Location: Southeast Asia.
Area: 115,830 square miles (300,000 sq km).
Population (1973 est. census): 42,200,000.
Chief Cities (1972 est.): Quezon City, the capital, 848,800; Manila, 1,399,600; Cebu, 372,100.
Government: *Head of state,* Ferdinand E. Marcos, president (took office for 2d term Dec. 1969). *Head of government,* Marcos, prime minister (took office under new constitution Jan. 1973). *Legislature* (unicameral)—National Assembly.
Monetary Unit: Peso (6.78 pesos equal U. S.$1, June 1974).
Gross National Product (1972 est.): $8,245,000,000.
Manufacturing (major products): Petroleum products, processed foods, tobacco products, plywood and veneers, paper.
Major Agricultural Products: Rice, corn, coconuts, sugarcane, abaca, sweet potatoes, lumber.
Foreign Trade (1973): *Exports,* $1,798,000,000; *imports,* $1,773,000,000.

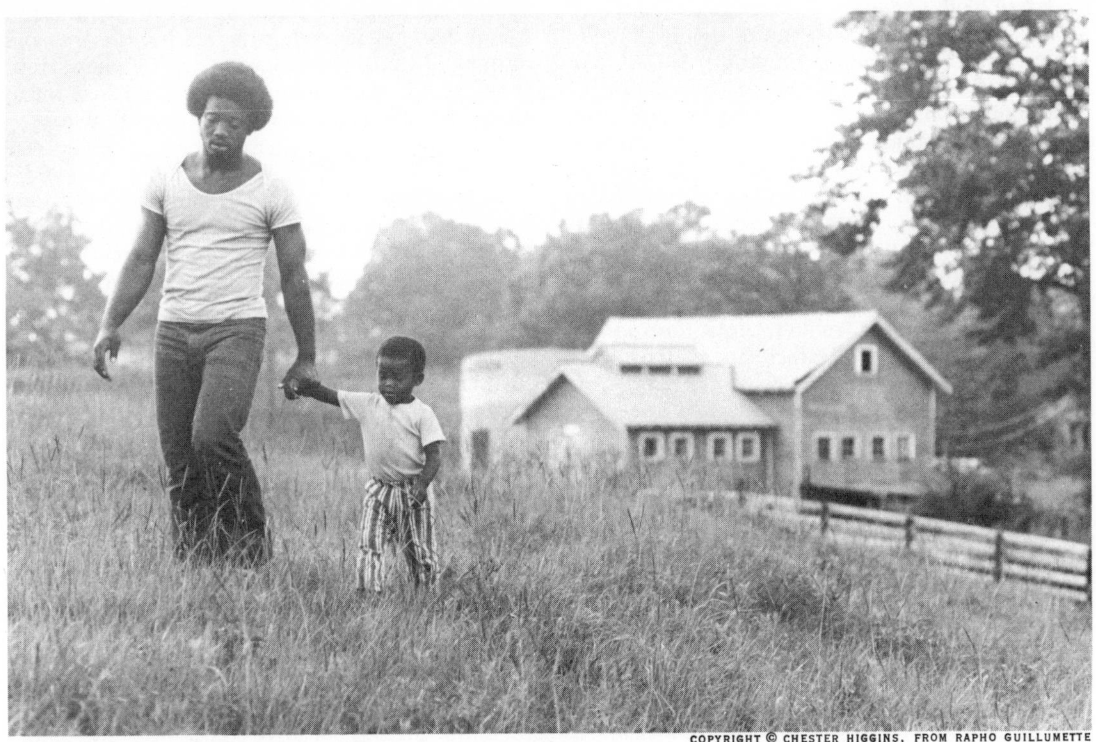

The photographs in the book *Drums of Life: A Photographic Essay on the Black Man in America* are by Chester Higgins, Jr., and the text is by Orde Coombs.

photography

Photokina—the World's Fair of photography held biennially in Cologne, Germany—celebrated its 13th exhibition of products, pictures, and films in the fall of 1974, drawing 825 exhibitors from 27 nations and attracting 98,000 visitors from 117 countries. More than 75 new models of pocket cameras were announced, the bulk of them being fully automatic. In all types of cameras, both amateur and professional, there was a strong trend toward an ever-increasing degree of automation provided by sophisticated electronic devices.

STILL CAMERAS

One example of international cooperation in camera manufacture in 1974 was the Contax RTS, a product of cooperation between Carl Zeiss of West Germany and Yashica of Japan. The camera body is made by Yashica in Japan, and the lenses are supplied and fitted by Carl Zeiss. The Contax RTS is part of a large 35-mm photography system that initially will include an array of lenses ranging in focal length from 15 mm to 200 mm. A motor drive, close-up devices, large-capacity backs, and remote-control devices will be available. The name "Contax" had disappeared from the photographic marketplace when Zeiss ceased production of the classic rangefinder in 1955.

Hasselblad Cameras. Victor Hasselblad AB of Göteborg, Sweden, announced the availability of an automatic diaphragm control for their cameras. This is the first use of a continuously operating diaphragm on a professional still camera. The diaphragm control unit, which utilizes a built-in exposure meter, automatically sets the diaphragm at the correct f stop in relation to the film speed and the shutter speed setting. At the present time the system is available for 80-, 100-, 150-, and 250-mm lenses. Automatic diaphragm control is particularly useful when the camera is used in a remote-control setup for wildlife photography. Hasselblad also offers a discrete FM-radio-control device for triggering the camera. The year 1974 marked the 25th anniversary of the introduction of the first Hasselblad camera.

110 Pocket Cameras. More and more manufacturers are offering 110 pocket cameras. Recent models include units with built-in electronic-flash and date-recording devices. Typically, completely automatic electronic exposure control is standard. Among the new 110 cameras, there is an outstanding ultracompact unit made by Rollei of West Germany. It is the smallest of the 110 pocket cameras, measuring just 3.3 by 0.75 by 1.2 inches and weighing less than 7 ounces.

Sinar View Cameras. The Sinar view cameras, first marketed in the United States several years ago, are the most advanced cameras of the type ever made and may represent the highest development of view-camera design. The addition of a form of particularly sophisticated through-the-lens spot metering system called the Sinarsix, made by Gossen of West Germany, is a natural complement to these cameras. It allows spot metering of individual scene elements, which takes into account the transmission qualities of the lens. It also is adjustable to compensate for reciprocity failure of the films.

MOVIE CAMERAS

The Super-8 film format, introduced as an improved amateur product a decade ago, is finding ever-increasing application in professional areas. Greatly improved emulsions and optics have raised the quality of this product remarkably. The Eastman Kodak Company is now marketing a high-speed Super-8 film processor that will turn out a finished reel of film ready for projection in about 12 minutes. Initially, this product is expected to be used in such places as TV studios where rapid processing is essential. In the future its use may spread to private laboratories or even to department stores, where a customer could have film processed while shopping.

The first macrofocusing Super-8 cameras appeared several years ago. The Noris 6000 M, equipped with a f/1.7 8- to 48-mm zoom lens, can be sharply focused right down to the front lens surface. The appearance of an increasing variety of movie cameras with macrofocusing ability for extreme close-up work parallels a trend that began somewhat earlier in the still 35-mm format. Several years ago, a number of lenses that largely eliminated the need for special close-focusing accessories became available.

EXPOSURE CONTROL

There is a trend toward using light-sensitive silicon cells to replace cadmium sulfide (CdS) cells in both automatic and nonautomatic light-measuring systems. The primary advantage of a silicon cell is that its range of spectral sensitivity more nearly matches that of available films, resulting in more accurate measurements. A further advantage is the substantially faster response time of the silicon cell. In one camera, the new Rollei A 110, this characteristic has a special application. When used with a flashcube, the silicon cell measures the light reflected from the subject instantly and automatically adjusts the aperture and shutter speed. This system is similar to electronic-computer flash systems.

PROJECTORS

Although the bulk of amateur photographs made with 110 pocket cameras are color negatives for making prints, the 110 format also is used for making positive slides for projection. The Eastman Kodak Company introduced a line of very compact projectors for the 110-size slides several years ago. Since then, a number of manufacturers have entered the miniature 110 slide projector market.

The Hanimex Rondette 110, which is manufactured in Australia, holds 110-size slides in clips on a nylon belt instead of having them held in the usual rotary tray. With moving-belt transport, the slides can be moved in and out of the lens plane four times faster than usual. At this speed and with a curved shutter that eliminates light spillage, the Hanimex virtually ends blackout between slides, thereby imparting a close approximation to a slow-motion movie.

Braun of Germany is marketing a dual 35-mm rotary-tray slide projector. Two complete projectors are housed in a single neat package, complete with a lap-dissolve capability that automatically blends one slide into another during projection.

LENSES

A number of remarkable photographic lenses were introduced for special applications or for providing unusual design features. Solid glass catadioptric (combining lenses and mirrors) objectives were introduced for 35-mm photography by Vivitar. This unusual construction and the folding of the light path provides great compactness. For instance, one lens of 1,200-mm focal length has only 1/7th the physical length a conventional lens would have.

The Peri-Apollar 360° Circular Image Lens permits simultaneous image recording in all directions. When mounted facing vertically, it produces a circumferential view with a 60° vertical angle as well as a central image looking straight up.

The Fujinon 85-mm SF f/4 is a variable soft-focus lens that can impart any desired degree of diffusion to the image. It is intended primarily for portraiture.

Shifting and tilting lens movements, formerly available only on large-format view cameras, are now possible on 35-mm single-lens reflex cameras by making use of the new Canon f/2.8 TS lens.

Lenses introduced by Kodak for 35-mm slide projectors are designed to project corner-to-corner sharp images from the slightly bowed surfaces of transparencies in cardboard or plastic mounts.

YASHICA INC.

The Contax RTS, developed by Carl Zeiss of West Germany and Yashica of Japan, is part of a large system for 35-mm photography, which will include an array of lenses of various focal lengths.

SENSITIVE MATERIALS

New films introduced in 1974 included Kodachrome 25 and 64 films. Better color rendition is claimed and, in the case of the 64 films, there is a considerable improvement in image sharpness and graininess.

Dry silver films as well as photographic papers were announced by the 3M Corporation for certain instrumentation applications. The image is developed by the application of heat in a special device, and no liquids are used.

Kodak announced Type G Ektachrome movie film for filmmaking under all types of lighting, natural and artificial, without the use of filters. This property, along with its high speed, makes it valuable for use in available light cameras.

Resin-coated photographic papers continued to increase in popularity and were being offered by more manufacturers. These papers, coated on both sides of their supports with a thin plastic film, do not absorb processing chemicals except in the emulsion layer itself. Washing time is reduced from nearly an hour to only a few minutes, and the prints dry in air quite rapidly without the use of a heated drying machine.

LITERATURE

Many books on photography were published in 1974. They included *Photography: A Practical and Creative Introduction,* by A. E. Woolley; *Dictionary of Contemporary Photography,* by L. Stroebel and H. Todd; *Photo Know-How,* a self-instructing program on the effective control of the view camera, by Carl Koch; and *One Mind's Eye: The Portraits and Other Photographs of Arnold Newman.*

PHILIP L. CONDAX, *Curator, Equipment Archives,* and MARTIN L. SCOTT, *Consultant on Technology, International Museum of Photography at George Eastman House*

New Topcon Super DM, the first 35-mm single-lens reflex camera with a motorized film advance mechanism. It allows the user to take pictures at ½-second intervals, much faster than is possible with a manual camera.

PAILLARD

PHYSICS

The year 1974 was a very good one in physics. In summary, controlled fusion prospects continued to improve; new results indicated a connection between the electromagnetic force and the weak nuclear force; superconductivity was observed at a new record-high temperature; and advocates of quarks had some setbacks. Meanwhile, the manpower surplus in physics appeared to be dwindling rapidly.

Controlled Thermonuclear Fusion. One basic world problem is the development of new energy sources. Present-day fission reactors provide a first step toward a solution, but the ultimate alternative to fission processes is controlled thermonuclear fusion. Although uncontrolled fusion of light elements has been established for 20 years, the practical problems in controlled fusion are monumental.

Basically the problem is to heat the materials so that the fusion reaction will occur and to control the process. The temperatures involved are in the range from 10 million to 100 million degrees Kelvin. At such extremely high temperatures the fusion materials form a plasma (ionized gas). No solid wall can contain the plasma at the required temperatures, so researchers have tried to use electric or magnetic fields that serve as a bottle or container for the plasma.

An alternative approach that has received much attention is the use of high-powered lasers. In a typical scheme, several laser beams strike a target material from many sides, resulting in an implosion. If the material—probably deuterium and tritium—is heated sufficiently, then the desired nuclear fusion reaction will take place. However, the energy must be extracted extremely rapidly before the material disperses.

A newer proposal is to use a hybrid approach in which a laser-induced implosion would be used to trigger the nuclear reaction, and magnetic containment would be used to keep the plasma contained. This would reduce the stringent requirements now placed on the power of the laser and the quality of the containment.

The stated goals of the U. S. Atomic Energy Commission are to establish the feasibility of controlled fusion by 1982, build a test fusion reactor in the late 1980's, and build a demontration fusion power reactor by the mid-1990's. The target date for the last step has been advanced about five years, reflecting both increased technological optimism and increased concern over energy sources.

Unification of Forces. The four types of interaction between matter are called the strong nuclear force, the weak nuclear force, the electromagnetic force, and the gravitational force. The strong force provides the glue to hold the nucleons (and thus the nucleus) together. The weak force governs the lighter particles such as electrons. The electromagnetic and gravitational forces are more familiar, but again are quite distinct.

A recurring dream of physicists has been to unite the four forces (interactions) under one universal law. In the past no one was able to connect any of the four forces, which seem so different.

It now appears that the first step in this unification may be possible. This step is a connection between the weak and electromagnetic interactions, based on the theory of Steven Weinberg of Harvard University. His theory involves an idea called symmetry breaking: although nature's laws have symmetries or simple patterns, these symmetries may be distorted or broken in the world that we observe.

Experimental evidence for Weinberg's theory has come from the Fermi National Acceleratory Laboratory in Illinois, the CERN Laboratory in Switzerland, and the Argonne National Laboratory in Illinois. These new experiments involve interactions of neutrinos. These massless, chargeless particles interact very, very weakly with matter, and then only through the weak interaction.

In weak interaction processes the particles had always exchanged a unit of charge, with charged ones becoming neutral and neutral ones becoming charged. Since the mathematical description of these processes resembled that for currents, these phenomena were called charged weak currents. The new experiments provided evidence for neutrino interactions without charge transfer, and thus the new phenomena are called neutral weak currents. These experiments now appear to have established this new effect, which is considered a striking breakthrough for the new theory.

Superconductivity. Superconductivity is a remarkable physical property that certain materials possess at low temperature. A material in a superconducting state has essentially no resistance—no heat is generated when a current is passed through the material. However, the basic practical problem is that materials do not become superconducting until they reach a very low temperature.

The highest temperature at which superconductivity has been observed has been gradually increasing in recent years. In September 1973, John R. Gavaler of Westinghouse Research Laboratories reported that a compound of niobium and germanium became superconducting at 22.3° Kelvin (—251° C). This record was broken late in 1973 when a group at Bell Laboratories reproduced Gavaler's result and obtained a value of 23.2° K for the critical temperature. Although these temperatures are still quite low by ordinary standards, low-temperature physicists are quite encouraged because the values are several degrees above the boiling point of hydrogen (20.4° K). Thus, liquid hydrogen may be used to make some compounds become super-

LAWRENCE LIVERMORE LABORATORY, UNIVERSITY OF CALIFORNIA

Researcher Suzanne Anderson takes data from a mass spectrometer during a uranium enrichment experiment.

conductors, obviating the need for expensive liquid helium (boiling point 4.2° K).

Elementary Particle Physics. The giant proton accelerator at the National Accelerator Laboratory is in operation while a similar machine, the CERN super proton synchrotron, is being built in Switzerland. Particle physicists are concerned about the next step beyond these machines. Since the cost of larger versions of existing machines verges on the astronomical, more subtle approaches are being proposed.

The key point is to use colliding beams because two colliding particles produce an effective energy many times greater than one particle of the same bombarding energy striking a stationary target. To obtain sufficient intensity the beams are trapped (or stored). Proposals have been submitted to build a storage ring for proton beams at high energies (200 GeV), and also to build a storage ring for electron and positron beams.

Meanwhile, particle physics is in a quandary. The conventional view in recent years has been that hadrons—particles that are affected by the strong nuclear force—are composed of subparticles called quarks or partons. These subparticles have some fascinating characteristics, including charges that are fractions of the unit electronic charge. Although no quark has been observed, experiments have indicated that the proton is a composite particle.

However, recent results at the Stanford Linear Accelerator Center, as well as earlier results at Frascati (Italy) and the Cambridge Electron Accelerator, are not consistent with the quark model. Apparently, too many hadrons are produced at high energies in electron-positron annihilation to be consistent with any quark model. Although partons and quarks are not yet dismissed, they are in trouble.

Element 106. The list of transuranium elements created by man was extended in 1974 when Soviet and American scientists independently reported that they had synthesized element 106.

New Particle. A new particle, called the J or psi particle, was discovered by American physicists late in the year. It has unexpected properties that puzzled physicists.

Manpower. In recent years there has been an oversupply of physicists due to effective reductions in federal research spending, lack of growth in colleges and universities, and changing patterns of industrial research and development. The number of students majoring in physics continued to drop, and the fraction of undergraduate physics majors who continued to graduate school in physics dropped even more sharply. In 1974, predictions on the number of Ph.D. physicists to be produced in the late 1970's were far below previous estimates.

In 1974 the employment situation took a sudden, sharp turn for the better. The energy crisis appeared to trigger a reawakening to the critical practical importance of research and development. The new positions that became available in connection with energy research and development, coupled with the favorable long-term supply outlook, should make physics once again attractive to students.

GARY MITCHELL
North Carolina State University

POLAND

Continuing prosperity, increased diplomatic contacts with the non-Communist world, economic expansion, and internal stability characterized developments in Poland in 1974.

The most significant political change involved the removal of Franciszek Szlachcic from the Secretariat of the ruling United Polish Workers' party (PZPR) on May 31. In the last two years, Szlachcic had been generally considered the party's second most powerful leader behind First Secretary Edward Gierek. His associations with Gen. Mieczyslaw Moczar, onetime rival of Gierek, were believed responsible for his demotion. The regime's treatment of ousted officials, however, remained lenient.

The Economy. Polish production, investment, incomes, and consumption continued to grow at a high rate in 1974. According to the government, economic progress was at its peak in the 30-year history of the Polish People's Republic, with the gross national product expanding at an annual rate of 10%. Great increases in wages and social welfare benefits were decreed during the year. More funds were devoted to housing construction and to a variety of consumer services, as well as to agriculture. As a reward for increasing worker productivity, the regime was reducing the workweek (requiring 6 fewer Saturdays of work in 1974) and promising still higher wages and shorter hours.

Poland's economic gains appeared threatened, however, by an increasing imbalance between imports, aimed at improving and modernizing the Polish economy, and the exports needed to finance them. The situation was aggravated by worldwide inflation and particularly by increased fuel prices. Poland depended on non-Communist sources for about one fourth of its 1974 oil supplies. Soviet help to Poland, in terms of fuel oil, 1.5 million tons of grain, and some 10,000 tractors for the increased mechanization of Polish agriculture, was widely heralded in the official media. While pledging an effort to maintain price stability, the regime nevertheless increased prices significantly on gasoline, alcohol, the services and products of catering establishments, and taxi fares. In deference to pent-up consumer frustrations, plans for increased production and ownership of private automobiles continued unabated, the world energy crisis notwithstanding.

Church-State Relations. The government significantly extended its contacts with the Vatican in 1974. Archbishop Agostino Casaroli, a papal secretary, visited Warsaw in February to explore the issue of diplomatic relations between Poland and the Holy See. In July, Polish Vice Minister of Foreign Affairs Jozef Czyrek held talks at the Vatican. At home, however, a serious rift continued between the Catholic Church, led by the primate, Stefan Cardinal Wyszynski, and the state. There were high-level party attacks on the Polish episcopate. In late March party leader Jan Szydlak called the church the principal institutional structure of opposition to the regime. In May, Kazimierz Kakol, an ideological hardliner, became head of the State Office for Religious Denominations and was subsequently elevated to ministerial rank.

International Affairs. Poland continued to maintain close ties with the USSR. In mid-April, Soviet Communist party leader Leonid Brezhnev and Premier Aleksei Kosygin visited Warsaw. Polish party leaders and the media drew closer to the Soviet attitude toward China, condemning the "Maoists" as splitters and saboteurs of the international Communist movement, and as enemies of détente and the socialist system.

Poland's relations with West Germany deteriorated markedly, ostensibly over Poland's refusal to repatriate nearly 300,000 ethnic Germans to the Federal Republic, and over Polish demands for indemnification for World War II damages and for substantial low-interest credits. Soviet and East German pressures appeared to influence cooling West German-Polish relations. In late January, in the midst of Polish-West German negotiations, some 80 Polish citizens defected to the West from Poland's cruise liner *Batory*, most of them in Hamburg, West Germany.

Poland's relations width the United States and with other non-Communist nations were generally greatly improved. In late May, Vice Premier Jan Mitrega visited Washington, seeking an expansion of Polish-U. S. trade, particularly increased U. S. purchases of Polish coal, and an exchange of mining and oil-drilling technology between the two countries. On October 8, Edward Gierek became the first Polish Communist chief to be received at the White House. He conducted talks with President Ford and concluded an agreement for a doubling of U. S.-Polish trade by 1980. The agreement was accompanied by unprecedented expressions of friendship on both sides.

ALEXANDER J. GROTH
University of California, Davis

POLAND • Information Highlights

Location: Eastern Europe.
Area: 120,724 square miles (312,677 sq km).
Population (1973 est.): 34,000,000.
Chief Cities (1971 est.): Warsaw, the capital, 1,326,200; Łodz, 765,400; Cracow, 595,100.
Government: *President of the Council of State,* Henryk Jabłonski (1972). *Premier,* Piotr Jaroszewicz (1970). *First Secretary, United Polish Workers' party,* Edward Gierek (took office 1970). *Legislature* (unicameral)—Sejm.
Monetary Unit: Zloty (3.20 zlotys equal U. S.$1, July 1974).
Gross National Product (1972 est.): $54,600,000,000.
Manufacturing (major products): Petroleum products, transport equipment, chemicals, machinery.
Major Agricultural Products: Rye, oats, potatoes, sugar beets, wheat, tobacco, livestock.
Foreign Trade (1973): *Exports,* $6,428,000,000; *imports,* $7,856,000,000.

POLAR RESEARCH

Whereas 1974 was a relatively quiet year in the Arctic insofar as research in the exploitation of resources is concerned, it was a very active year in Antarctica. Even this coldest and most remote of the continents felt world pressures to find new sources of food and fuel.

Mineral Resources. Long ignored except for heroic exploration by Amundsen, Scott, Byrd, and others, Antarctica settled in as a huge scientific "laboratory" after vigorous research there by 12 nations during the International Geophysical Year, 1957–58. The 1961 Antarctic Treaty, which reserved the continent for peaceful purposes and suspended territorial claims, was not concerned with the subject of exploitable resources.

Now, after 18 years of continuous research in many scientific disciplines, Antarctica's potential usefulness is a matter of concern. Representatives to the seventh Antarctic Treaty consultative meeting in 1972 noted "the increasing interest in the possibility of there being exploitable minerals." They recommended that their governments study the effect of any mineral exploration and discuss it in 1975 at the eighth meeting, to be held in Oslo.

As part of the U. S. preparation for the Oslo meeting, the Geological Survey studied the available data on Antarctica. It concluded in 1974 that the existence of large mineral deposits is highly probable, but that the chances of finding them are small. Thus far, minerals have been found in great variety but only in small quantities. A problem, of course, is that ice covers 98 percent of the continent. Even if we find the deposits that almost certainly are under the ice somewhere, extraction may be prohibitively expensive. Nevertheless, the study does not rule out completely the possibility of valuable finds.

Though a burden to geologists, the Antarctic ice cover has received special attention at the Rand Corporation. Each year, 1.4 trillion metric tons of ice calve from the Antarctic ice mantle to form icebergs. Rand scientists calculate that some of the icebergs could be towed economically to arid lands for use as fresh water. Southern Hemisphere countries are looking further into this possibility.

In the past, Antarctica has been suggested as a deep freeze for surplus food reserves. With reserves now much depleted, that proposal has evolved into one for using the ice cap as a cold-storage area for radioactive waste from nuclear power plants. The packaged waste would melt its way to bedrock, there to stay forever—perhaps. This idea has generated considerable debate. United States and British scientists, using airborne radar to sound ice thickness, discovered sub-ice lakes that conceivably could drain into the sea, carrying the hot waste with the runoff. The Antarctic Treaty, though subject to change in this regard, forbids dumping of radioactive waste there.

Living Resources. Living resources in Antarctic waters have received attention since the 18th century. Seals were hunted nearly to extinction by the early 19th century. Whales have been hunted continually, with stocks declining drastically in the 20th century. At the bottom of the food chain is phytoplankton, nourished by the cold, nutrient-rich waters. One step up the chain is the shrimplike krill (*Euphausia superba*).

Krill occur in vast quantities around Antarctica. Biologists estimate that up to 100 million tons could be taken annually without disturbing the main stock. (The world marine catch in 1973 was only 67 million tons.) Soviet factory ships have begun harvesting krill experimentally, and the protein-rich animal has found acceptance among Soviet consumers as "ocean paste."

Commercial U. S. interest in krill is low. Unlike the superbly organized Soviet fleet, U. S. fishermen tend to work independently, and thus are ill prepared for distant expeditions requiring expensive factory ships. Recognizing this, a California firm suggested in 1974 that the government subsidize a pilot operation that would include test marketing in the United States. The stakes are high, for krill is the world's largest unexploited protein resource.

Most countries now recognize the danger of overexploitation. In July 1974, UNESCO's Intergovernmental Oceanographic Commission encouraged increased study of Antarctic marine ecosystems. Two months earlier, the Scientific Committee on Antarctic Research had expressed concern about the unknown impact of exploitation on krill and pelagic fish. The purpose of further study is to learn enough about krill to determine proper levels of harvest before exploitation begins in earnest.

With all this talk of resources, the days of Antarctica as just a scientific laboratory may be numbered. Yet, because of its peaceful scientific tradition, Antarctica may become a model for wise international management of resource exploitation. With the Antarctic Treaty as an enabling mechanism, the 12 member nations in 1972 recommended a pact for the conservation of Antarctic seals that severely limits total annual catches. The consultative meeting at Oslo in 1975 may ease the way to a similar agreement regarding mineral resources.

One form of commercial enterprise already is proving to be profitable in Antarctica. For the affluent, a New York travel agent offers comfortable trips to Antarctica aboard a ship strengthened against ice damage. The four or five cruises possible during each short austral summer usually are booked far in advance of sailing dates.

GUY G. GUTHRIDGE, *Office of Polar Programs National Science Foundation*

CAMERA PIX-KEYSTONE

Women in Kenya receive family-planning information as the nation attempts to keep economic growth from being swamped by a rapidly rising population.

POPULATION

The world's population, estimated at 3.9 billion in mid-1974, is increasing at the rate of approximately 2% per year. If this rate of increase continues, another 78 million persons will be added by mid-1975, and the world's population will double in 35 years.

Because of higher fertility rates, the populations of the less-developed nations are growing much more rapidly than are those of the industrial nations. While the population of the world's slowest growing region, western Europe, will double in 175 years, the populations of Asia, Africa, and Latin America will double in 30, 28, and 25 years, respectively, if current trends continue.

WORLD POPULATION

Reliable evidence indicates that a rapid decline in fertility is beginning to occur in some underdeveloped nations due to changing age structures, marriage practices, and reductions in marital fertility. The Population Council lists 15 nations which experienced a "certain" fertility decline during the past decade, including South Korea, Chile, and Egypt, and 8 additional countries where such a change may have happened, including Communist China, Turkey, Brazil, and Colombia.

In spite of these examples, rapid rates of population increase are expected to continue in the less-developed regions of the world for decades, assuming mortality rates are maintained at present low levels. Tomorrow's parents already have been born—they are the children under 15 today—and they greatly outnumber their parents. Due to past high fertility, and to sudden reductions in childhood mortality, most underdeveloped nations have 40% or more of their populations under 15 years of age, compared with 27% for the United States and 24% for western Europe. These children will add massive numbers of new births to their national populations.

World Population Policies. During the past ten years, governments throughout the underdeveloped world have recognized the importance of reducing national fertility rates in order to better achieve economic and social development goals. With certain major exceptions—such as Brazil, Ethiopia, Burma, and North Korea—almost all of the population of the underdeveloped world resides in nations which favor making family planning available, either to explicitly reduce population growth or for humanitarian and health reasons.

A much smaller proportion of the underdeveloped world, however, lives in nations which have actually implemented such family planning policies. In addition to four Asian nations noted for major programs (Hong Kong, Singapore, South Korea, and Taiwan), the Population Council states that favorable developments in family planning have occurred recently in Colombia, Costa Rica, Fiji, Indonesia, Iran, Mauritius, the Philippines, Thailand, and Venezuela.

UN World Population Conference. The fact that family planning programs are only part of the solution to the world population problem was illustrated by the differing opinions of the approximately 2,500 delegates from 135 countries to the UN World Population Conference, held in Bucharest in August 1974.

Generally the discussion was between two broad perspectives. On the one hand, developed nations emphasized the need for massive fertility-control programs to reduce the high birthrates of the poor nations. Delegates from many underdeveloped nations countered that the rich nations should consume less of the world's resources, thereby reducing pressures on supplies of energy, food, and minerals. The rich nations also should give more aid to the poor nations, it was argued, since the best motivation to limit one's fertility is the hope of improved living conditions for oneself and one's children.

The debate was not resolved at the conference, but a World Population Plan of Action was adopted by consensus. The head of the United States delegation, Casper W. Weinberger, secretary of health, education, and welfare, commented that while much public attention was given to controversial issues, the totality of the Plan of Action is most important. The plan's practical sections on information collection and analysis, on research, on training and education, and on the spreading of knowledge are fundamental to nations preparing their own population programs. Since bringing 135 nations together to discuss population was an achievement in itself, Weinberger considers the consensus on the Plan of Action a landmark advance.

Population and Food Supplies. Providing adequate food supplies is one of the most pressing population problems; and following the Bucharest meetings, the United Nations held a World Food Conference in Rome in November 1974. Delegates from 130 nations met with the knowledge that famine already had begun to appear in several nations of central Africa, in Bangladesh, and in parts of India. The famine was expected to continue at least through early 1975 because less than optimum weather conditions in 1974 reduced world supplies of food.

Due to existing famine conditions, a major objective of the conference was to increase international cooperation in maintaining food stocks, and in coordinating food reserve policies. This would be a first step toward what the secretary general of the World Food Conference, Sayed A. Marei, described as "an agreement on more effective measures for providing emergency relief in cases of disaster, including creating international food reserves for use in emergencies."

Given the expected doubling of the populations of most poor nations in the next two to three decades, however, the United States reaction to a large, long-term "world food bank" was mixed. For example, in his speech to the United Nations on Sept. 18, 1974, President Gerald R. Ford expressed a willingness to cooperate but specified a limit to such aid: "From the time of the founding of the United Nations, America volunteered to help nations in need, frequently as the main benefactor. We were able to do it. We were glad to do it. But as new economic forces alter and reshape today's complex world, no nation can be expected to feed all the world's hungry people. . . . America will continue to do more than its share. But there are realistic limits to our capacities." (See also FOOD—*World Food Supply*.)

UNITED STATES POPULATION TRENDS

In August 1974, the total population of the United States was estimated to be 211.5 million. This represented an increase of 31 million persons since the 1960 Census, and an increase of 60 million persons since the 1950 Census.

The rate of population growth continues to slow, as the nation's women have fewer births. The crude birthrate—the total number of births per 1,000 persons—was 14.8 during the 12-month period ending in August 1974. This figure was 3% lower than that for the same period in 1973. About 3.12 million births were registered in the 12-month period ending in August 1974, or 2% fewer than in the corresponding period in 1973.

The declining level of fertility in the United States is primarily due to a reduction in the number of children desired by young women. On the basis of a survey conducted in 1972, the U. S. Bureau of the Census reported that women between 18 and 24 years of age expect to complete childbearing with an average of about 2.3 births.

A fertility level of 2.1 births per woman would result in a United States population of about 263 million in the year 2000, growing at an annual rate of 0.6%. This population projection includes a continued net immigration of 400,000 annually, and makes the general assumptions that there will be no disastrous war, widespread epidemic, major economic depression, or similar catastrophe. Even if women average only 1.8 births each, zero population growth (ZPG) will not be achieved by the year 2000. The population then would be smaller (250 million persons) than in the first projection, but it still would be growing by 0.4%.

CANADIAN POPULATION TRENDS

By mid-1974 the total population of Canada was estimated to have reached 22.4 million persons, assuming a continued 1.2% annual rate of population growth. During 1973 the Canadian crude birthrate continued to decline, and reached a level of 15.8 births per 1,000 persons in the total population.

Assuming a gradual decline from an average of 2.19 births per woman in 1971 to 2.13 by 1985 and the years thereafter, an annual net immigration of 60,000 persons, and improvements in life expectancy, the population of Canada is projected to grow to about 31.4 million persons by the year 2001.

ROBERT E. KENNEDY, JR.
University of Minnesota

UPI

Junta that took power in April 25 coup in Portugal (*seated, l to r*): Gen. Francisco da Costa Gomes; Gen. António de Spinola, first head of the junta; and Navy Captains José Baptista Pinheiro de Azevedo and Antônio Alba Rosa Coutinho.

PORTUGAL

The overthrow of Premier Marcello Caetano in April 1974 ended a Portuguese dictatorship dating from 1926. Though generally overjoyed at their new freedom, Portugal's people soon realized that a change of government did not solve all problems. The excesses committed by an inexperienced public threatened to bring not democracy but a new dictatorship of the left, as Communists made headway.

Political Events. In February, Gen. António de Spinola, deputy chief of staff and former governor of Portuguese Guinea, published *Portugal and the Future,* denouncing the African colonial wars. For this, he and his superior, Gen. Francisco da Costa Gomes, were dismissed, but on April 25 they headed a military coup backed by young officers calling themselves the Armed Forces Movement, many with past tours of duty in Africa and all dissatisfied with pay and working conditions.

Premier Caetano and President Américo Thomaz were arrested and exiled to Madeira, and later to Brazil. Spinola was inaugurated provisional president on May 15 and governed with a 7-man junta, promising free elections in 1975. The cabinet was dismissed on July 11, and a military leftist, Col. Vasco dos Santos Gonçalves, was appointed to head a new military-oriented cabinet that was sworn in on July 18.

Political exiles began returning to Portugal in late April, notably the Communist leader Alvaro Cunhal (on April 30), whom Spinola was obliged to include in his cabinet. The Communists, though a minority, were the only organized party in the country, but many splinter parties now formed, some around trivial issues. Spinola intended the period before elections to be one of giving inexperienced Portugal time to grow accustomed to democracy, but during the spring and summer he found it increasingly hard to govern as leftists made headway and violence erupted in many places. Objects of special hatred were the secret police of the dictatorship —originally trained under the tutelage of Nazi Heinrich Himmler—who were either imprisoned or took refuge in Spain.

Spinola, who planned a Portuguese commonwealth with equality for African possessions, receded from this position and announced immediate or early independence for them all. A scheduled demonstration pledging national support to him and set for September 28 was blocked by young leftist officers who demanded

PORTUGAL • Information Highlights

Official Name: Portuguese Republic.
Location: Southwestern Europe.
Area: 35,553 square miles (92,082 sq km).
Population (1973 est.): 8,600,000.
Chief Cities (1970 census): Lisbon, the capital, 782,266; Oporto, 310,437.
Government: *Head of state,* Gen. Francisco da Costa Gomes, provisional president (took office Sept. 1974). *Head of government,* Vasco dos Santos Gonçalves (took office July 1974). *Legislature* (unicameral)—National Assembly.
Monetary Unit: Escudo (25.37 escudos equal U. S.$1, July 1974).
Gross National Product (1973 est.): $9,300,000,000.
Manufacturing (major products): Wine, canned fish, processed foods, textiles, ships.
Major Agricultural Products: Grapes, tomatoes, potatoes, wheat, figs, olives, fish, forest products.
Foreign Trade (1973): *Exports,* $1,837,000,000; *imports,* $3,016,000,000.

the ouster of three conservative members of his cabinet-junta. Spinola resigned on September 30, saying that Portugal was headed for chaos and "new forms of slavery." Costa Gomes became provisional president with a leftist cabinet again headed by Premier Gonçalves; and while many doubted that he could remain long in office, the announced plan for elections in 1975 remained unchanged.

Nearly all classes reacted happily to Spinola's April revolution. Flowers appearing in many buttonholes caused the movement to be called the "carnation revolution." A people unaccustomed to liberty reveled in the new freedom. Plays by foreign leftist authors, hitherto banned in Portugal, were announced for Lisbon theaters. Most leaders were Communists who, at least momentarily, became champions of law and order, evidently profiting by Communist errors in other countries.

One opinion was that the Communists preferred not to take possession of the country while its economy remained weak, but to let other leaders make the almost-inevitable mistakes. Should Portuguese women be fully enfranchised, as the original revolutionary program stipulated, the illiterate rural people would probably vote as their conservative priests instructed. But, should the voting age be lowered to 18, the literate young people in the industrial cities would probably vote leftist.

Economy. Portugal's economic situation went from bad to worse during Spinola's presidency. His government inherited an inflation rate running to 30% annually, and a balance-of-trade deficit of more than $1 billion in 1973 and now certain to grow worse. Many smaller Portuguese firms suffered bankruptcy; and though money was frozen to prevent a flight of capital, some people of means evaded this law.

Low wages and inflation brought a rash of strikes, and unemployment reached high levels.

UPI

During the bloodless coup, Portuguese troops have almost no trouble keeping order in the streets.

These problems were certain to be aggravated as Portuguese colonials poured in from the liberated African possessions, and as thousands of demobilized soldiers returned from Africa.

Foreign Affairs. Both before and after the downfall of Spinola, the Portuguese government announced that it would respect all international obligations incurred by the previous regime. This applied to the Azores, where the United States maintained an airbase. President Costa Gomes gave this assurance to President Ford during a visit to Washington in October.

CHARLES E. NOWELL
University of Illinois

In September, Lisbon crowd cheers appointment of Costa Gomes to replace Spinola as provisional president.

DEJEAN/BUREAU, FROM SYGMA

U. S. POSTAL SERVICE

Women, who for long have performed many jobs inside U. S. post offices, now make the rounds as letter carriers.

POSTAL SERVICE

The volume of mail handled by the U. S. Postal Service in the fiscal year 1974 totaled 90.1 billion pieces (as compared with 89.7 billion pieces in the previous year), including 430 million parcels. Gross income for fiscal 1974 increased by $900 million to $10.7 billion. The Postal Service suffered a net loss of $400 million despite the increase in gross income and government appropriations. Federal appropriations amounted to $1.6 billion, but were expected to be reduced by $100 million in the fiscal year 1975.

Service. In 1974 the Postal Service continued its efforts to provide better service to customers. A series of national service standards has led to the delivery of 95% of first-class local mail overnight, and 169 self-service postal units were added in fiscal 1974 to bring the total number of units to 1,042. Burglary losses were reduced by 94% to $200,000, from the all-time high of $3.2 million in the fiscal year 1970. Additional savings were anticipated from a new policy effective Nov. 17, 1974, whereby all mail without the correct amount of postage would be returned to the sender.

Mailgrams, a combination of letter-telegram, which are cheaper than telegrams and faster than a letter, now exceed U. S. telegram volume. On Sept. 6, 1974, mailgrams were first transmitted by satellite. Philatelic services were expanded to outlets in 8,000 post offices, where commemorative stamps, mini-albums, stamp collector starter kits, and *Stamps and Stories* are sold to 16 million stamp collectors.

Despite these improvements, the appointment of a postal consumer advocate, trends in mechanization, and decentralization of operations to meet regional and local needs, the Postal Service continues to be criticized for slow and erratic delivery service. This is most notable in parcel post, where deliveries dropped by 45 million pieces in fiscal 1974. Private competitors, including the United Parcel Service (UPS), now handle approximately 60% of the parcel post deliveries. UPS is considered less expensive and more reliable than the Postal Service, with a damage rate reported at 80% less than that of the Postal Service. Private competitors have the advantage of handling a higher volume of the more profitable commercial deliveries, while the Postal Service is required to handle house-to-house parcel delivery.

Selection of Postmasters. Since the establishment of the U. S. Postal Service on July 1, 1971, political patronage as a method for selecting postmasters and rural carriers has been replaced by a merit system through which applicants are evaluated and selected by national and regional management selection boards. Over 60,000 postal employees, including 12,500 postmasters, have been appointed under the system since patronage was abolished. Nineteen women now serve as postal inspectors. Females had been barred from this service since its inception by Benjamin Franklin.

Labor Relations. Labor relations in an otherwise peaceful year were marred in January 1974 at the Bulk and Foreign Mail Center in Secaucus, N. J., where employees disrupted operations for several days in protest over management's unilateral change in the scheduled hours of work. Under pressure from a U. S. district court, the unions and the Postal Service reached an agreement whereby future scheduled changes would be subject to negotiations and, if necessary, to arbitration for a final determination of the issues.

Collective bargaining agreements containing cost-of-living escalator clauses offer protection from inflation to the highly unionized work force. It is estimated that the average employee wage will reach $14,200 in fiscal 1975, an increase from $10,310 in 1971.

A successful and far-reaching plan for the treatment of alcoholic employees has resulted in an increase in productivity and a decrease in absenteeism. More than 4,000 postal employees have enrolled in the Program for Alcoholic Recovery, with 75% of the employees recovering to continue productive careers.

DAVID R. BLOODSWORTH
University of Massachusetts

PRINCE EDWARD ISLAND

Despite declining returns from fishing, the economy of Prince Edward Island showed remarkable strength in 1974. Improvement in the prices of farm produce and the effectiveness of the Island Development Plan, now in its fifth year, were responsible for much of this strength. According to Minister of Finance T. Earle Hickey, the gross provincial product rose 48.8%.

Industrial Development. Expansive lending programs by both federal and provincial governments made it possible for many businesses to expand and update their facilities. A new plant was established to produce factory-built homes and the George Town shipyard was expanded. These developments, combined with special loans to farmers wishing to relocate in urban areas, resulted in a construction boom. The construction boom, in turn, was the occasion of a prolonged strike in which the main issue was a demand for a wage increase from $3.00 to $5.00 per hour for construction workers. They settled for gradual increments to $4.80 per hour by December 1975.

Government. The Liberal government of Premier Alexander B. Campbell was reelected in the face of allegations of corruption in government land dealings. With the exception of the establishment of a Land Use Commission, there was no major new legislation in 1974. The commission was initiated to deal with the sale of island property to nonislanders, but its actual scope includes all aspects of land use.

In October Gordon L. Bennett succeeded the late J. G. MacKay as lieutenant governor.

Fishing and Farming. Agriculture prospered in 1974, with potato prices doubling to $4.00 per hundredweight. Milk subsidies rose, and the cabbage crop marketing plan was implemented over the objections of the National Farmers Union. In the fishing industry, however, the lobster catch fell by 30% and mackerel prices fell so low that fishermen refused to sell and began to organize a union to bargain with the processors.

R. F. NEILL, *Carleton University*

PRINCE EDWARD ISLAND • Information Highlights

Area: 2,184 square miles (5,656 sq km).
Population (1974 est.): 116,000.
Chief Cities (1971 census): Charlottetown, the capital, 19,133; Summerside, 9,439.
Government (1974): *Chief Officers*—lt. gov., Gordon L. Bennett; premier, Alexander B. Campbell (Liberal); min. of justice and prov. secy., Gordon L. Bennett (L); min. of educ., Bennett Campbell (L); chief justice, C. St. Clair Trainor. *Legislature*—Legislative Assembly, 32 members (25 Liberal, 7 Progressive Conservative).
Education (1972–73): *Enrollment:* public elementary and secondary schools, 29,415 pupils; Indian (federal) schools, 65; colleges and universities, 1,581 students. *Public school expenditures* (1972), $26,400,000.
Public Finance (fiscal year 1974–75 est.): *Revenues,* $159,000,000; *expenditures,* $150,000,000.
Personal Income (1972): $276,000,000; average annual income per person, $2,478.
All monetary figures are in Canadian dollars.

PRISONS

The 1974 prison population in the United States was estimated at 425,000. A conservative estimate of the yearly cost for operating the nation's prison systems, federal, state, and local, is more than $1 billion. As a process of rehabilitation, the system is not working effectively. A 1974 U. S. Justice Department survey indicated that one out of three Federal offenders commits a new crime within two years after release from prison. Some experts have estimated the recidivism rate to be as high as 80%.

The nation's prisons remain, in the words of the National Council on Crime and Delinquency, "1) ineffectual, 2) probably incapable of being operated constitutionally, 3) themselves productive of crime and, 4) destructive of the keepers as well as the kept." A House Judiciary Subcommittee, chaired by Representative Robert W. Kastenmeier (D-Wis.) has been studying the nation's prison systems since 1971. In its report, issued in March 1974, the committee argued that if the public were informed of conditions they would insist on improvements. The report noted that "Prison walls serve just as well to keep the public out as they do to keep the inmates in."

Behavior Modification. Many prisons have adopted behavior modification programs. Such programs systematically manipulate the inmates' behavior through the use of punishments and rewards. The programs often met with strong objections from civil libertarians and, in some cases, from the prisoners themselves.

One of the most widely attacked projects, START (Special Treatment And Rehabilitation Training) was conducted at the Medical Center for the Federal prison system in Springfield, Mo. There, prisoners who broke rules were placed in solitary confinement for up to three weeks and denied such ordinary privileges as permission to exercise, access to reading materials, and freedom to attend religious services. They could regain the privileges only by demonstrating systematically improved behavior. Inmates charged in a lawsuit that the program violated their constitutional rights, including due process and the right not to be subjected to cruel and unusual punishment. The courts agreed, and the program was dismantled in February 1974. Prison officials stated that the small number of inmates and the larger number of staff members involved made the program unsound. At the same time, the Federal Law Enforcement Assistance Administration stopped its funding of 400 behavior modification programs in prisons in 20 states.

A more complex program to alter the behavior of convicted child molesters at a maximum security prison in Somers, Conn., was also under heavy attack. Child molesters have a high rate of repeated arrests. In this project a mild electric shock is administered to the inner thigh of the participant when he is shown the slide of a naked child. No shock is applied when the picture of an adult is shown. Through hypnosis and other techniques the inmates are taught to associate objects they fear with their thoughts of children. Nine of the 16 repeated offenders in the program have been paroled and none has been rearrested for any crime. One of the participants, a 50-year-old skilled laborer who had served a total of 16 years in prison since 1952, reported that the program has "definitely been working." Results in the program are still too limited to judge its success. Critics fear that if such programs are successful they could lead to a society in which behavior modification could be used to control social and political dissent. In May 1974 the Connecticut Civil Liberties Union voted to oppose the Somers program by any means possible, and promised to file a lawsuit as soon as a prisoner could be found who would act as a plaintiff in the case.

Attica. On Sept. 13, 1971, in response to the Attica Prison revolt in New York, state police and corrections officers stormed the prison and recaptured yard D, which had been controlled by inmates. In the brief but ferocious storm of bullets, 10 prison employees held as hostages and 29 inmates were killed. A grand jury has handed down 1,400 separate indictments, including indictments for murder, attempted murder, kidnapping, assault, coercion, and robbery against 61 present and former inmates. With several thousand participants and eye witnesses to be questioned and investigated, and with more than 40 separate trials anticipated, court action will probably continue until 1978. Defense lawyers, granted $750,000 by the state in help for the legal assistance, estimate that the state has already spent $4 million for the prosecution.

Some prison systems are distinguishing more systematically between those prisoners they regard as "nondangerous," and who can be assisted, and those regarded as "dangerous," who show a behavior pattern of "persistent assaultiveness." In June, California Corrections Department Director Raymond Procunier announced a new system in which violence-prone convicts would serve their time in virtual isolation, apart from the general prison population.

Released Time. An experimental release program for prison inmates in New York State was expanded and made permanent in 1974. Since the program began in July 1972, 9,501 furloughs and leaves of absence were granted, with only 104 inmates not returning voluntarily. In its expanded version, furloughs may last up to seven days and inmates may be away for up to 14 hours a day for educational and vocational training programs. In addition, with special approval, inmates would be allowed to accept invitations to take part in athletic, religious and social activities in communities outside the prison.

DONALD GOODMAN, *John Jay College of Criminal Justice, City University of New York*

Guards at Huntsville (Texas) State Prison stand watch over shield (*left*) used by inmates in escape attempt in which some inmates and hostages were killed.

UPI

CONSULATE GENERAL OF JAPAN

Eisaku Sato, former Japanese prime minister, is co-winner with Sean MacBride of Ireland of 1974 Nobel Peace Prize.

While several rich new awards were created in 1974, at least one long-established prize committee encountered funding difficulties. In November the National Book Committee, sponsor of the prestigious National Book Awards and the $5,000 National Medal for Literature, announced that it would disband following presentation of the 1975 book awards because of increased costs and reduced income.

The names of those who helped unravel the complex Watergate affair figured importantly in the list of award winners for the second consecutive year. Reporters James R. Polk of the Washington *Star-News* and Jack White of the Providence, R. I., *Journal Bulletin* won Pulitzer Prizes for their disclosures in the case. The Southern Christian Leadership Conference (SCLC) presented its highest honor, the Martin Luther King Award, to Frank Wills, the security guard who discovered the break-in at Democratic party headquarters in June 1972.

A selected list of the most important and newsworthy prizes announced in 1974 follows.

NOBEL PRIZES

Nobel Prizes were awarded in 1974 in peace, economics, literature, physics, chemistry, and physiology or medicine.

The prizes (valued at about $126,000 each) were presented by Sweden's King Carl XVI Gustaf in Stockholm on December 10. At the ceremonies, Soviet writer Aleksandr I. Solzhenitsyn, who had been expelled from the USSR in February, took possession of his 1970 Nobel Prize in literature.

Peace. The 1974 Nobel Peace Prize was shared by Eisaku Sato, a former premier of Japan, and Sean MacBride, the United Nations commissioner for South-West Africa. The 73-year-old Sato was cited for his work to limit the use of nuclear weapons and for his contribution to stabilizing conditions in the Pacific area. The 70-year-old MacBride was honored for his "many years of efforts to build up and protect human rights all over the world."

Economics. The 1974 Nobel Prize in economics was shared by two 75-year-old social economists, Gunnar Myrdal of Sweden and Austrian-born Friedrich August von Hayek. They were cited for "their pioneering work in the theory of money and economic fluctuations and for their pioneering analysis of the interdependence of economic, social, and institutional phenomena."

Literature. The 1974 Nobel Prize in literature was shared by two Swedish writers, Eyvind Johnson and Harry Edmund Martinson. Johnson, 74, a novelist and short-story writer, was cited for "a narrative art, far-seeing in lands and ages, in the service of freedom." Martinson, 70, a poet, novelist, and dramatist, was honored for "writings that catch the dewdrop and reflect the cosmos." None of the works of Johnson and Martinson was in print in the United States.

Physics. The 1974 Nobel Prize in physics was shared by two British radio astronomers, Sir Martin Ryle and Anthony Hewish, who are professors at Cambridge University. Ryle, 56, was honored for devising techniques that enable radio astronomers to build up very finely detailed maps of the sky. Hewish, 50, was honored for his decisive role in the discovery of pulsars, which are distant celestial bodies that regularly emit radio-wave pulses. Their awards marked the first time that the Nobel committee recognized achievements in astronomy.

Chemistry. The 1974 Nobel Prize in chemistry was won by Paul J. Flory, a professor of chemistry at Stanford University. Flory, 64, was cited for his fundamental theoretical and experimental achievements in the physical chemistry of long-chained molecules called polymers. His work has led to thousands of new polymer compounds used in clothing, tires, paints, toys, and many other products.

Physiology or Medicine. The 1974 Nobel Prize in physiology or medicine was shared by cell biologists Albert Claude, Christian René de Duve, and George Emil Palade for their major contributions to the understanding of the inner workings of living cells. Claude, a 75-year-old American, pioneered in the use of the electron microscope and the centrifuge in studies of cells. De Duve, a 57-year-old Belgian, discovered lysosomes, which he says function like "stomachs of the cell." Palade, a 61-year-old American, discovered ribosomes, which work to synthesize proteins inside cells.

PULITZER PRIZES

Winners of the Pulitzer Prizes were announced by the trustees of Columbia University on May 6, 1974. Each prize was worth $1,000 except the public service gold medal. No awards were made in the categories of fiction and drama.

Journalism. Investigative local reporting—William Sherman of the New York *Daily News,* for a series of articles on abuses in the Medicaid program in New York City. Local general reporting—Hugh F. Hough and Arthur M. Petacque of the Chicago *Sun-Times,* for uncovering evidence that led to the reopening of the murder case of Sen. Charles H. Percy's daughter. Editorial writing—F. Gilman Spencer of the Trenton, N. J., *Trentonian,* for editorials attacking scandals in the New Jersey state government. International reporting—Hedrick Smith of the New York *Times,* for coverage of the Soviet Union and Eastern European nations in 1973. National reporting—James R. Polk of the Washington *Star-News,* for disclosing irregularities in the financing of former President Nixon's 1972 re-election campaign, and Jack White of the Providence (R. I.) *Journal-Bulletin,* for disclosing Nixon's 1970 and 1971 tax returns. Spot news photography—Anthony K. Roberts, a freelance photographer, for a series of photographs of a kidnapping attempt in Hollywood, Calif. Feature photography—Slava Veder of the Associated Press, for a photograph of the reunion of a former prisoner of war and his family after repatriation from North Vietnam. Commentary—Edwin A. Roberts, Jr., of the *National Observer,* for his column *Mainstreams.* Criticism—Emily Genauer, art critic for the Newsday Syndicate. Editorial cartooning—Paul Szep of the Boston *Globe.* Meritorious public service—*Newsday* of Garden City, N. Y., for a series of articles tracing heroin traffic from Turkey to France to the New York City metropolitan area.

Letters. History—Daniel J. Boorstin, for *The Americans: The Democratic Experience.* Biography—Louis Sheaffer, for *O'Neill, Son and Artist.* Poetry—Robert Lowell, for *The Dolphin.* General nonfiction—Ernest Becker, for *The Denial of Death.*

Music. Donald Martino, for *Notturno.* Special citation—Roger Sessions, composer, for his life's work.

ARTS

American Institute of Architects awards: honor awards—Richard Meier and Associates for Twin Parks Housing in the Bronx, Mitchell/Giurgola Associates for Foundation Hall of the American College of Life Underwriters, and I. M. Pei and Partners for the Paul Mellon Center for the Arts at Choate School; architectural firm award—Kevin Roche, John Dinkeloo and Associates of Hamden, Conn.; special awards: the New York State Urban Development Corporation and the Olivetti Corporation.

American Institute of Graphic Arts Gold Medal—Robert Raushenburg.

Art Dealers Association of America Award for "outstanding achievement in art history" ($3,000)—Millard Meiss.

Dance Magazine Awards—Gerald Arpino, Maurice Béjart, and Antony Tudor, choreographers.

Edward MacDowell Medal of the MacDowell Colony for "exceptional contributions to the arts"—Walter Piston.

National Academy of Recording Arts and Sciences, Grammy Awards for excellence in phonograph records: record of the year—*Killing Me Softly with His Song,* sung by Roberta Flack; song of the year—Norman Gimbel and Charles Fox, writers, for *Killing Me Softly with His Song;* album of the year—Stevie Wonder for *Innervisions;* male vocal performance—Stevie Wonder for *You Are the Sunshine of My Life;* female vocal performance—Roberta Flack for *Killing Me Softly with His Song;* vocal performance by a group—Gladys Knight and the Pips for *Neither One of Us;* new artist—Bette Midler; male country vocal performance—Charlie Rich for *Behind Closed Doors;* female country vocal performance—Olivia Newton-John for *Let Me Be There;* country music song—*Behind Closed Doors,* by Kenny O'Dell; male rhythm and blues vocal performance—Stevie Wonder for *Superstition;* female rhythm and blues vocal performance—Aretha Franklin for *Master of Eyes;* rhythm and blues song—*Superstition,* by Stevie Wonder; original cast show—Stephen Sondheim for *A Little Night Music;* classical album of the year—Bartók's *Concerto for Orchestra,* performed by the New York Philharmonic; opera recording—Bizet's *Carmen,* performed by the Metropolitan Opera Orchestra.

National Institute of Arts and Letters awards: art ($3,000)—Perle Fine, Richard Fleischner, Marilyn Gelfman-Pereira, George Griffin, Nancy Grossman, Ibram Lassaw, and Charlotte Park; music ($3,000)—Richard Felciano, Raoul Pleskow, Phillip Rhodes, and Olly Wilson; gold medal for graphic art—Saul Steinberg; award for distinguished service to the arts—Walker Evans; Arnold W. Brunner Memorial Prize in Architecture ($1,000)—Hugh Hardy with Malcolm Holzman and Norman Pfeiffer; Charles E. Ives Award ($10,000)—the Charles Ives Society; Richard and Hinda Rosenthal Foundation Awards ($2,000)—Julie Curtis Reed and Alice Walker; Marjorie Peabody Waite Award ($1,500)—Ray Prohaska.

Arthur Rubinstein International Piano Competition awards: first prize ($5,000)—Emanuel Ax; second—Eugen Indjic.

JOURNALISM

Maria Moors Cabot Gold Medals for "distinguished journalistic contributions to the advancement of inter-American understanding ($1,000)—Don Bohning and William D. Montalbano of the Miami *Herald,* and Ferando Pedreira of *O Estado de São Paulo, Brazil.*

Long Island University, George Polk Memorial Awards: foreign reporting—Henry S. Bradsher of the Washington *Star-News;* investigative reporting—Seymour Hersh of the New York *Times;* national reporting—Andrew H. Malcolm of the New York *Times;* metropolitan reporting—James Savage and Mike Baxter of the *Miami Herald;* local reporting—Carol Talley and Joan Hayde of the Dover, N. J., *Daily Advance;* community service—William Sherman of the New York *Daily News;* magazine reporting—John Osborne of the *New Republic* for *The Nixon Watch:* television reporting—the Public Broadcasting Service for coverage of the U. S. Senate Watergate Committee hearings; television news documentary—Jeremy Isaacs of Thames Televison; news photography—George Brich of the Associated Press; book—David Wise for *The Politics of Lying;* special award—Donald L. Barlett and James B. Steele of the Philadelphia (Pa.) *Inquirer.*

Newspaper Guild of New York, Page One Awards: national reporting—Seymour Hersh of the New York *Times;* foreign reporting—Arnaud de Borchgrave of *Newsweek* magazine; crusading journalism—William Sherman of the New York *Daily News;* local reporting—James Ryan of the New York *Daily News.*

Overseas Press Club awards: George Polk Memorial Award—Leon Dash of the Washington *Post;* Capa Gold Medal for still photography—David Burnett, Raymond Depardon, and Charles Gerretsen of Gramma Press Images of France; Ross Award for international reporting in health and welfare—Robert Northshield and Vo Huynh of NBC-TV; daily newspaper or wire-service reporting from abroad—Raymond R. Coffey of the Chicago *Daily News;* newspaper or wire service interpretation of foreign affairs—Al Burt of the Miami *Herald;* newspaper or wire service photographic reporting from abroad—Sydney H. Schanberg of the New York *Times;* photographic reporting from abroad in a magazine—*Life* magazine's special issue on Israel; radio reporting from abroad—Group W Foreign News Service; radio interpretation of foreign affairs—Dan Rather, Marvin Kalb, and Bob Schieffer of CBS News; radio documentary on foreign affairs—CBS News for *A Question of Peace;* television reporting from abroad—CBS News; television interpretation of foreign affairs—NBC News for *Peace Begins;* television documentary on foreign affairs—Harry Reasoner of ABC News; magazine reporting from abroad—Anthony Bailey for an article in the *New Yorker* magazine; book on foreign affairs—C. L. Sulzberger for *An Age of Mediocrity;* reporting on Latin America—Everett G. Martin of the *Wall Street Journal;* reporting on Asia—Donald Kirk of the Chicago *Tribune.*

Drew Pearson Prize for excellence in investigative reporting ($5,000)—Jerry Landauer of the *Wall Street Journal.*

Scripps-Howard Foundation awards: Roy W. Howard Public Service Award ($2,500)—William Blundell of the *Wall Street Journal;* Edward J. Meeman Conservation Award ($2,500)—George F. Neavoll of the Fort Wayne, Ind., *Journal-Gazette.*

LITERATURE

Academy of American Poets awards: Fellowship Award ($10,000)—W. S. Merwin; Lamont Poetry Prize—John Balaban for *After Our War.*

American Library Association (ALA) Awards: Newbery Medal—Paula Fox for *The Slave Dancer;* Caldecott Medal—Margot Zemach, illustrator, for *Duffy and the Devil;* Clarence Day Award—Augusta Baker, former coordinator of Children's Services, New York Public Library; Grolier Award—Regina U. Minudri, director of professional services at the Alemeda County Library, California; Melvil Dewey Award—Robert B. Downs, dean of library administration at the University of Illinois; Margaret Mann Citation—Frederick G. Kilgour, director of the Ohio College Library Center; Joseph W. Lippincott Award—Jerrold Pyne, professor at the School of Library Science, University of North Carolina at Chapel Hill.

Bancroft Prizes of Columbia University for distinguished writing in U. S. history and international relations ($4,000 each)—Ray Allen Billington for *Frederick Jackson Turner: Historian, Scholar, Teacher;* Stephan Thernstrom for *The Other Bostonians;* Townsend Hoopes for *The Devil and John Foster Dulles.*

Booker Prize for fiction ($11,500): Nadine Gordimer for *The Conservationist;* Stanley Middleton for *Holiday.*

Books Abroad International Prize for literature ($10,000)—Francis Ponge, poet.

Carey-Thomas Award for a distinguished project of creative book publishing—Princeton University Press for publication of the Bollingen Series.

Copernicus Society Awards for poetry, sponsored by the Copernicus Society of America and the Academy of American Poets: Copernicus Award ($10,000)—Robert Lowell; Edgar Allan Poe Award ($5,000)—Mark Strand.

Governor General's Awards (Canadian): English fiction—Rudy Wieke for *The Temptations of Big Bear;* English poetry—Miriam Mandel for *Lions at Her Face;* English nonfiction—Michael Bell for *Painters in a New Land;* French fiction—Réjeau Ducharme for *L'Hiver de force;* French poetry—Roland Giguère for *La Main au feu;* French nonfiction—Albert Faucher for *Québec en Amérique au 19ème siècle.*

Mystery Writers of America, Edgar Allan Poe ("Edgar") Awards: mystery novel—Tony Hillerman for *The Dance Hall of the Dead;* true-crime book—Barbara Levy for *Legacy of Death;* juvenile mystery—Jay Bennett for *The Long Black Coat;* Grand Master Award—Ross MacDonald.

National Book Awards ($1,000 each): fiction—Thomas Pynchon for *Gravity's Rainbow* and Isaac Bashevis Singer for *A Crown of Feathers;* arts and letters—Pauline Kael for *Deeper Into Movies;* philosophy and religion—Maurice Natanson for *Edmund Husserl: Philosopher of Infinite Tasks;* biography—Douglas Day for *Malcolm Lowry;* poetry—Allen Ginsberg for *The Fall of America: Poems of These States, 1965–1971;* history—John Clive for *Macaulay;* contemporary affairs—Murray Kempton for *The Briar Patch;* sciences—S. E. Luria for *Life: The Unfinished Experiment;* translation—Karen Brazell for *The Confessions of Lady Nijo,* Helen Lane for *Alternating Current* by Octavio Paz, and Jackson Mathews for *Monsieur Teste* by Paul Valéry; children's book—Eleanor Cameron for *The Court of the Stone Children.*

National Institute of Arts and Letters awards in literature ($3,000)—Ann Cornelison, Stanley Elkin, Elizabeth Hardwick, Josephine Johnson, Donald Justice, David Rabe, Charles Rosen, Sam Shepard, James Tate, Henry Van Dyke, and Lanford Wilson; E. M. Forster Award ($5,000)—Paul Bailey; Loines Award for Poetry ($2,500)—Philip Larkin; award of merit for the novel—Nelson Algren.

Poetry Society of America Awards: Alice Fay di Castagnola Award for a work in progress ($3,500)—Charles Edward Eaton; Shelley Memorial Award ($1,300)—W. S. Merwin; Melville Cane Award ($500)—William Stafford.

PUBLIC SERVICE

American Institute of Public Service Awards for distinguished public service ($5,000 each): Elliot L. Richardson, Ralph Nader, and Maynard Jackson.

Eugene V. Debs Foundation Award in public service—Arthur M. Schlesinger.

Lyndon Baines Johnson Foundation Award ($25,000)—Ivan Allen, Jr., former mayor of Atlanta, and Franklin A. Thomas, president of the Bedford-Stuyvesant Redevelopment Corporation.

Jawaharlal Nehru Prize for furthering international understanding ($15,000)—André Malraux.

Presidential Medals of Freedom—Melvin R. Laird, Charles LeRoy Lowman, and Paul G. Hoffman.

Rockefeller Public Service Awards for outstanding long-term service to the federal government ($10,000)—administration—George M. Low; human resource development and protection—James Bruce Cardwell; professional accomplishment or leadership—George Jaszi; physical resource development and protection—Robert M. White; intergovernmental operations—Maurice J. Williams.

Society for the Family of Man Award, sponsored by the Council of Churches of the City of New York—William R. Tolbert, Jr., president of the republic of Liberia.

Southern Christian Leadership Conference (SCLC), Martin Luther King Award—Frank Wills.

SCIENCE AND TECHNOLOGY

American Cancer Society, National Award—Karl Erik and Ingegerd Hellstrom.

American Chemical Society awards: Irving Langmuir Award in chemical physics ($5,000)—Harry George Drickamer; Nuclear Applications Award ($2,000)—Lawrence E. Glendenin.

American Medical Association awards: Distinguished Service Award—William F. House; Sheen Award—R. Lee Clark; Brookdale Award—Thomas E. Starzl; Goldberger Award—Robert E. Olson; Scientific Achievement Award—Philip H. Abelson.

American Physical Society awards: Oliver E. Buckley Solid State Physics Prize ($1,000)—Michael Tinkham; High Polymer Physics Prize ($1,000)—Frank A. Bovey; Tom W. Bonner Prize in Nuclear Physics ($1,000)—Denys Wilkinson.

Atomic Energy Commission, Ernest O. Laurence Awards ($5,000)—Joseph Cerny III, Harold P. Furth, Henry C. Honeck, Charles A. MacDonald, Jr., and Chester Richmond.

Franklin Institute awards: Franklin Medal—Nikolai Bogolyubov, Russian physicist and mathematician; Potts Medal—Jay Forrester of the Massachusetts Institute of Technology; Michelson Medal—Peter P. Sorokin of I. B. M.

Geological Society of America awards: Penrose Medal—M. King Hubbert; Arthur L. Day Medal—David T. Griggs.

Louisa Gross Horowitz Prize for outstanding research in biology ($25,000)—Boris Ephrussi of the Centre de Génétique Moléculaire du Centre National de la Recherche Scientifique, France.

Albert Lasker Medical Research Awards: clinical research ($10,000)—John Charnley of the University of Manchester, England; basic research ($5,000)—Ludwig Gross of the Bronx Veterans Administration Hospital, Sol Spiegelman of Columbia College of Physicians and Surgeons, Howard M. Temin of the University of Wisconsin, and Howard E. Skipper of the Southern Research Institute.

National Academy of Engineering, Vladimir K. Zworykin Award ($5,000)—Ivar Giaever.

National Aeronautics and Space Administration (NASA) Distinguished Service Medals—Gerald P. Carr, Edward G. Gibson, and William R. Pogue, Skylab III crewmen.

J. Robert Oppenheimer Memorial Prize in theoretical physics ($1,000)—Edwin E. Salpeter of Cornell University.

Proctor Prize in scientific research, administered by Sigma XI ($1,000)—Percy L. Julian of the Julian Research Institute, Chicago.

Vetlesen Prize for achievement in the earth sciences, administered by Columbia University ($25,000)—Chaim Leib Pekeris of the Weizman Institute, Israel.

Robert A. Welch Foundation Award in chemistry ($75,-000)—Albert Eschermoser of the Swiss Federal Institute of Technology.

TELEVISION AND RADIO

Academy of Television Arts and Sciences ("Emmy") Awards: best special program—*The Autobiography of Miss Jane Pittman* (CBS); actor in a special—Hal Holbrook in *Pueblo* (NBC); actress in a special—Cicely Tyson in *The Autobiography of Miss Jane Pittman* (CBS); variety special—*Lily,* starring Lily Tomlin (CBS); dramatic series—*Upstairs, Downstairs* (PBS); variety series—*The Carol Burnett Show* (CBS); comedy series—*M*A*S*H* (NBC); actor in a comedy series—Alan Alda in *M*A*S*H* (NBC); actress in a comedy series—Mary Tyler Moore in *The Mary Tyler Moore Show* (CBS); actor in a dramatic series—Telly Savales in *Kojak* (CBS); actress in a dramatic series—Michael Learned in *The Waltons* (CBS); supporting actor in a comedy series—Bob Reiner in *All in the Family* (CBS); supporting actress in a comedy series—Cloris Leachman in *The Mary Tyler Moore Show* (CBS); supporting actor in a drama—Michael Moriarty in *The Glass Menagerie* (CBS); supporting actress in a drama—Joanna Miles in *The Glass Menagerie* (CBS); director of a series—Robert Butler for *The Blue Knight* (CBS); director of a special—Dwight Hemion for *Barbra Streisand and Other Musical Instruments* (CBS); writer of a series—Treva Silverman for *The Mary Tyler Moore Show* (CBS); writer of a special—Fay Kanin for *Tell Me Where It Hurts* (CBS); children's special—*Marlo Thomas and Friends in Free to Be. . .You and Me* (NBC); sports programming—*ABC's Wide World of Sports* (ABC); cultural documentaries—*Journey to the Outer Limits* (ABC), *The World at War* (PBS), and *The Rockefellers* (CBS); interview programs—*Solzhenitsyn* (CBS) and *Henry Steele Commager* (PBS); religious program—*Gift of Tears,* a segment of the *This Is the Life* series (PBS); news and documentary direction—Pamela Hill for *Fire!* (ABC); magazine-type programs—*First Tuesday* (NBC), *Behind the Lines* (PBS), and *Bill Moyers' Journal* (PBS).

International Radio and Television Society Gold Medal for accomplishments in broadcasting—Walter Cronkite.

THEATER AND MOTION PICTURES

Academy of Motion Picture Arts and Sciences ("Oscar") Awards: best film—*The Sting;* foreign-language film—*Day for Night* (France); best actor—Jack Lemmon in *Save the Tiger;* best actress—Glenda Jackson in *A Touch of Class;* supporting actor—John Houseman in *The Paper Chase;* supporting actress—Tatum O'Neal in *Paper Moon;* director—George Roy Hill for *The Sting;* screenplay based on material from another medium—William Peter Blatty for *The Exorcist;* original screenplay—David S. Ward for *The Sting;* nonmusical score—Marvin Hamlisch for *The Way We Were;* musical score—Marvin Hamlisch for *The Sting;* original song—*The Way We Were* from *The Way We Were,* by Alan and Marilyn Bergman and Marvin Hamlisch; art direction—Henry Rumstead for *The Sting;* set decoration—James Payne for *The Sting;* costume design—Edith Head for *The Sting;* cinematography—Sven Nykvist for *Cries and Whispers;* short subject (live action)—Allan Miller and William Fertik, producers, for *The Bolero;* short subject (cartoon)—Frank Mouris, producer, for *Frank Film;* documentary feature film—Keith Merrill, producer, for *The Great American Cowboy;* documentary short subject—Julian Krainin and DeWitt L. Sage, producers, for *Princeton: A Search for Answers;* Jean Hersholt Humanitarian Award—Alfred Hitchcock; Irving Thalberg Award—Lawrence Weingarten; special citations—the Marx Brothers and Henri Langlois.

American Theater Wing, Antoinette Perry ("Tony") Awards: best drama—*The River Niger,* by Joseph A. Walker; best musical—*Raisin,* based on a play by Lorraine Hansberry; best actor (musical)—Christopher Plummer in *Cyrano;* best actress (musical)—Virginia Capers in *Raisin;* best actor (drama)—Michael Moriarty in *Find Your Way Home;* best actress (drama)—Colleen Dewhurst in *A Moon for the Misbegotten;* dramatic supporting actor—Ed Flanders in *A Moon for the Misbegotten;* dramatic supporting actress—Frances Sternhagen in *The Good Doctor;* musical supporting actor—Tommy Tune in *Seesaw;* musical supporting actress—Janie Sell in *Over Here!;* director (drama)—José Quintero for *A Moon for the Misbegotten;* director (musical)—Harold Prince for *Candide;* costume—Franne Lee for *Candide;* set design—Franne and Eugene Lee for *Candide;* lighting—Jules Fisher for *Ulysses in Nighttown;* score—Frederick Loewe and Alan Jay Lerner for *Gigi;* choreography—Michael Bennett for *Seesaw;* special awards—Peter Cook, Dudley Moore, Liza Minnelli, and Bette Midler.

Cannes International Film Festival Awards: grand prize—*The Conversation* (American); best actor—Jack Nicholson in *The Last Detail* (American); best actress—Marie José Nat in *Les Violons du Bal* (French).

New York Drama Critics' Circle Theater Awards: best drama—*The Contractor* by David Storey; American drama—*Short Eyes* by Miguel Piñero; musical—*Candide,* produced by Ruth Mitchell and Harold Prince.

New York Film Critics Circle Awards: best actor—Jack Nicholson in *The Last Detail* and *Chinatown;* best actress—Liv Ullmann in *Scenes from a Marriage;* best director—Federico Fellini in *Amacord;* best film—*Amacord;* best screenwriting—Ingmar Bergman for *Scenes from a Marriage;* best supporting actor—Charles Boyer in *Stavisky;* best supporting actress—Valerie Perrine in *Lenny;* special citation—Fabiano Canosa.

PUBLISHING

The publishing world and its activities in 1974 are reviewed in this article under three headings—Books, Magazines, and Newspapers.

Books

Rising costs plus continued material shortages were the major problems book publishers had to cope with during 1974.

Cost-Price Squeeze. A highly competitive and fluctuating world market, unfavorable timberland distribution and ownership, escalating costs for new paper mills, and increased demand for paper were cited as the prime reasons for the continuing high cost and shortage of paper. In some instances, the price of paper increased 100%. Cloth, plastic, ink, printing, labor, warehousing, and distribution all rose on the average of 40%. Publishers caught in a cost-price squeeze were forced to raise book prices. With inflation and recession on a collision course, many major firms pruned their title lists and consolidated staffs.

Labor Developments. Macmillan, Inc., in what it called "an overall belt-tightening program," fired 179 persons in mid-October from a total work force of about 1,300 in its corporate headquarters. Many of these cuts were made in its trade publishing division. The company also cut back its new title list by 50%. Since the firings followed closely upon efforts to unionize Macmillan employees, and complaints by women employees of job discrimination by the company, there was much angry talk about company reprisals. Several editors, including heads of the adult trade division and the juvenile division, resigned in protest. An unfair labor charge was filed against Macmillan. The company, however, stressed that the reductions were made because of the bleak national economic picture

The abruptness with which the Macmillan employees were fired buoyed union activity in publishing circles. However, the real catalyst for the increased efforts toward union affiliation was the unprecedented 17-day strike (from June 17 to July 3) against Harper & Row, Inc. by the Association of Harper & Row Employees, which represents about 320 H&R employees in a nonsupervisory level and is the only active house union in book publishing. The strike was called after contract talks with management had broken down. The association received financial and moral support from individual members in other trade publishing houses.

In the wake of the strike, individual members of about 20 trade publishing firms formed an independent committee to organize book publishing, and in the early fall the committee voted for affiliation with District 65, Distributive Workers, an independent union unaffiliated with the AFL-CIO. The Harper & Row Association subsequently affiliated with District 65.

Copyright Legislation. An interim copyright bill was approved by Congress on December 19. It provided for a two-year extension of subsisting copyrights from the end of 1974, when the temporary extension measure runs out; a permanent ban on record piracy, with increased penalties for violations; and the creation of a national commission on new technological uses of copyrighted works.

Meanwhile, the long-pending omnibus copyright revision bill, which has been delayed by the complicated problems presented by library photocopying and reprography, plus other issues, passed the Senate. The Senate bill had been approved by publishers and authors as responsive to their needs by extending copyright and by placing definite limits on photocopying of copyrighted works. House action on the general revision bill was not expected until 1975.

Best Sellers. An allegorical fantasy featuring rabbits (*Watership Down*), the story of a man-eating shark (*Jaws*), and three repeats from 1973 (*Joy of Sex, How to be Your Own Best Friend,* and *Burr*) were among the year's best sellers.

The following, in order of rank, were the best sellers in 1974.

FICTION

Watership Down, Richard Adams
Jaws, Peter Benchley
Tinker, Tailor, Soldier, Spy, John le Carré
Burr, Gore Vidal
The Dogs of War, Frederick Forsyth
Centennial, James A. Michener
The Snare of the Hunter, Helen MacInnes
Come Nineveh, Come Tyre, Allen Drury
The Fan Club, Irving Wallace
Something Happened, Joseph Heller

NONFICTION

You Can Profit from a Monetary Crisis, Harry Browne
All the President's Men, Carl Bernstein and Bob Woodward
Plain Speaking: An Oral Biography of Harry S. Truman, Merle Miller
Alive: The Story of the Andes Survivors, Piers Paul Read
The Memory Book, Harry Lorayne and Jerry Lucas
How to be Your Own Best Friend, Mildred Newman, et al.
The Woman He Loved, Ralph G. Martin
The Gulag Archipelago, Aleksandr Solzhenitsyn
The Joy of Sex, Alex Comfort, ed.
Times to Remember, Rose Fitzgerald Kennedy

Mergers and Acquisitions. W. W. Norton & Company, the oldest and largest U. S. publishing house that is still absolutely independent, acquired Liveright, the publishing house that began in 1917 and had one of the most notable of American literary lists in the 1920's. The 76-year-old Grosset & Dunlap was purchased by Filmways, Inc., a Los Angeles-based company operating in magazine publishing and in TV and motion-picture production. Bantam Books, the leading paperback publishing house, was sold for $70 million to an American subsidiary of IFI, a business conglomerate in Turin, Italy.

DAISY MARYLES
News Editor, "Publishers Weekly"

Magazines

The magazine industry struggled to hold its own in 1974—a year of economic uncertainty, steeply rising production and postal costs, and critical shortages of paper.

In the first six months of the year, the number of general magazine advertising pages declined slightly from the same period of 1973. For the same half year, advertising revenue totaled $653.6 million; the 3% increase over the comparable period of 1973 barely compensated for inflation. Yet, despite scattered reports of financial troubles, the first three quarters of 1974 passed without the collapse of a mass-circulation magazine.

There were several transactions of importance. The 38-year-old Vision group, a New York enterprise publishing Spanish and Portuguese language news and business magazines for an international audience, was acquired for $3 million by Rafael Garcia-Navarro, a London financier who said he planned to move Vision's headquarters to Britain. *The New Republic,* a political weekly founded in 1914, was sold by Gilbert A. Harrison for $380,000 to Martin Peretz, a Harvard teacher who had been a prominent contributor in the 1972 McGovern campaign. *True,* a male monthly, was acquired by Petersen Publishing Company and moved to Los Angeles.

One notable gain in the face of adversity was the recovery of the *Saturday Review,* acquired in 1973 by its former editor, Norman Cousins, after its previous publishers had filed for bankruptcy. As the magazine, now a biweekly called *Saturday Review/World,* celebrated its 50th anniversary, Cousins announced that it was no longer operating at a deficit and had reached a guaranteed circulation of 550,000.

Editorial Developments. Magazines of news and public discussion concentrated attention again on the Watergate scandals, the Nixon impeachment proceedings, and the transition to a new administration. Prepublication excerpts from Watergate-related books were a staple. Notably, the best seller by the Washington *Post* reporters Robert Woodward and Carl Bernstein, *All the President's Men,* made its first appearance in excerpts published by *Playboy.*

The Society of Magazine Writers, a New York-based organization of freelance professionals, established for the first time a schedule of minimum rates of payment: 20 cents a word for trade, regional, and Sunday magazines, and $1 a word for general magazines of more than 3 million circulation. The society had no power to enforce these rates.

New Periodicals. Among magazines started or announced in 1974 were the following:

People, a weekly on personalities, tested by Time Inc. in 1973, published its first regular issue on March 4, 1974. In September the cover price was raised from 35 to 40 cents.

PEOPLE WEEKLY, PHOTO BY STEVE SCHAPIRO

The cover of the first issue of the magazine *People* features Mia Farrow as she appeared in *The Great Gatsby*.

Book Digest, a venture by John J. Veronis and Nicholas H. Charney, former owners of the *Saturday Review,* began bimonthly publication. It features excerpts from current books.

Country Journal, issued monthly from Brattleboro, Vt., by William S. Blair and Richard M. Ketchum, initiated publication with its May issue. Content and circulation are concentrated in New England.

Marriage & Divorce was started in January in Los Angeles as a service magazine for divorced persons.

Atlas World Press Review, which produced its first issue in May, is a revival of a magazine devoted to reprints and summaries from the foreign press. John A. Millington is the publisher; Alfred Balk, formerly of the *Columbia Journalism Review,* is the editor.

JAMES BOYLAN, *Columbia University*

Newspapers

The most newsworthy event of 1974 in American journalism—as in the history of the United States—was the resignation of President Nixon as a result of the Watergate disclosures. While other media, the courts, and the Congress had all figured in the series of exposures that brought about the unprecedented resignation of the President, it was the newspapers that had originated the efforts to uncover the secrets involved in the Watergate cover-up.

Business Conditions. Labor, newsprint, and postage all cost more in 1974 and cut deeply into profit margins. The complaints were universal. German publishers complained of rising prices and falling advertising revenues, and were predicting closings and bankruptcies. Rising costs were eliminating profits for all French newspapers, except *Le Monde* and *Le Figaro* (twelve French dailies have closed in the past decade). Reports indicated that all Italian dailies were operating in the red. In the United Kingdom the government's restrictions on pricing were working serious hardship on newspapers.

In America the situation was not so dire, but a squeeze was being felt. There was one major closing as the year progressed—*Chicago Today,* an afternoon daily of 415,000 circulation, owned by the Chicago Tribune Co. The Tribune picked up its subscribers and became an all-day newspaper.

The cost of newsprint illustrated the kind of pressure that caused newspapers concern. From a price of about $175 a ton in mid-1973, newsprint had jumped to $260 a ton as 1974 ended. The press generally found ways to cope with that steep increase, however. In 1973 the supply of newsprint dwindled because of mill and rail strikes in Canada, and there were serious shortages. In that situation newspapers learned frugality and trimmed margins, cut page sizes, bought lighter stock, and watched wastage. The result, as the year proceeded, despite record circulations, was an overall decline of slightly under 5% in newsprint consumption.

Newspapers were learning other ways to save money. Automation had a big year, with the use of computerized operations, cold-type composition, and scanners showing a steady growth. The proportion of U. S. newspapers now being printed by offset rose to 55.4% (23% in Canada). When the papers in New York City finally signed their contracts with the typographers (after long negotiations and work slowdowns at the *Daily News*) a significant breakthrough was achieved when the union agreed to management's insistence that economies be achieved through automation.

Furthermore the newspapers were increasing their income. In early September the New York *Times* went from 15 to 20 cents for its street-sale price. The *Wall Street Journal,* New York *Post,* and Honolulu *Star-Bulletin* also went to 20 cents, and the Oakland (Calif.) *Tribune* charged 25 cents at the newsstand.

Advertising also was bringing in more cash. Advertising income for the year 1974 was in the range of $7.6 billion, approximately 5.2% greater than for 1973.

Newspaper Statistics. The number of American dailies in 1974 stood at 1,774, a rise of 13 over the year before. Circulation was 63,147,280, up more than half a million. Canadian dailies increased by 1, to a total of 114, but circulations were down. One of the newcomers was a popular weekly journal, the *National Star,* enterprised by an Australian group and said to be circulating 2 million copies.

Groups and Mergers. Group ownership of newspapers continued to increase. In 1971 the halfway point was reached with just over half of U. S. dailies in chains. A further 11% increase in group-owned dailies took place in the next three years. Two mammoths, the Knight Newspapers chain and the Ridder Publications chain, agreed during 1974 to merge—Knight with 16 dailies (Miami, Detroit, Akron, and others) and Ridder with 18 (San Jose, St. Paul, Wichita, and others).

The *Village Voice* (New York) and *New York* magazine also merged. The *Arkansas Democrat* in Little Rock was sold to Palmer Newspapers of Camden, Ark. In late September, Joseph Allbritton, a Texas banker, paid $25 million for 10% ownership and executive management of the Washington *Star-News.* The Washington *Post* bought the Trenton *Times.* Other chains—Scripps-Howard, Freedom, Stauffer, Morris, Ingersoll, and Worrell—also added dailies.

Broadcasting Problems. Also affecting newspaper finances was a steady pressure from the Justice Department via the Federal Communications Commission on newspapers to get rid of their broadcasting outlets in their own circulation areas. Targeted for challenge were WTMJ-TV-AM-FM, owned by the Milwaukee *Journal;* KRNT-TV-AM-FM, owned by the Cowles newspaper interests in Des Moines; the stations in Salt Lake City owned by the Mormon Church; two stations in St. Louis owned by the Pulitzer interests (*Post-Dispatch*) and the Newhouse group (*Globe-Democrat*); WCCO in Minneapolis, owned jointly by the Cowles newspapers there and the St. Paul *Pioneer Press and Dispatch;* and WIBW in Topeka, owned by the Stauffer newspapers.

Miscellaneous. A right-of-reply decision involving a Florida politician and the Miami *Herald* was overruled by the U. S. Supreme Court in June. (See also CIVIL LIBERTIES.)

A disquieting development during the year involved use of the media by terrorist groups. A single man, claiming to represent the so-called American Revolutionary Party, kidnapped J. Reginald Murphy, editor of *The Atlanta Constitution,* on February 20, and the nation's press had to publicize the terrorist's story.

Howard H. Hays, Jr., of Riverside, Calif., became the new president of the American Society of Newspaper Editors. Harold W. Anderson, president of the Omaha World-Herald Co., became chairman of the American Newspaper Publishers Association. And Michael L. Davies, publisher of the Kingston (Ont.) *Whig-Standard,* became president of the Canadian Publishers Association.

RICHARD TERRILL BAKER, *Columbia University*

PUERTO RICO

An advisory commission set up to study political relations between Puerto Rico and the United States and to work out improvements on the present commonwealth status began its work during the year 1974.

Commission on Puerto Rico. The Ad Hoc Advisory Group of seven, appointed by Gov. Rafael Hernández Colón in September 1973, was matched by a similar committee of seven representatives of the federal government, headed by Sen. Marlow W. Cook of Kentucky. The two committees form a joint Ad Hoc Commission on Puerto Rico. Its specific assignment is "further to develop the maximum of self-government and self-determination [of Puerto Rico] within the framework of Commonwealth —a common defense, a common market, a common currency, and the indissoluble link of United States citizenship."

After working out 15 points for discussion, including Puerto Rico's right to participate in federal decisions affecting the island as well as such matters as immigration and minimum wages, now handled by the federal government, the Puerto Rican group went to Washington where the federal committee submitted 28 questions seeking clarification of the Puerto Ricans' points. Following a series of discussions and formal meetings, the commission announced that the next step should be the drafting of a new Federal Relations Statute by the Puerto Rican committee. When completed, the draft will be submitted to the people and legislature of Puerto Rico and later to the U. S. Congress.

The Puerto Ricans' request for control of immigration to their island by noncitizens of the United States was prompted by the fact that an annual average of 5,594 aliens entered Puerto Rico from 1964 to 1973, compared with an average of 1,331 in the preceding decade. Of the 55,366 aliens on the island today, 23,857 are Cubans who fled from Castro and 16,206 are from the Dominican Republic. The Puerto Ricans claim that so large an influx creates hardships for a small island, dramatically poor in natural resources and with a density of population 15 times larger than that of the United States.

Independence Rally. On October 27 advocates of Puerto Rican independence—who insist that their island is still a colony and bitterly oppose all efforts to "improve" commonwealth status —held a well-attended mass meeting in New York's Madison Square Garden to call national attention to their cause. Attended by representatives of Indian tribes, supported by messages from American Indian tribes, Chicanos and Dominican organizations, the meeting indicated that the island's "independentistas," who habitually win fewer than 5% of the total vote in local elections, are joining the general U. S. radical movement.

Telephone, Shipping Acquisitions. On July 24 a contract was signed by which the Puerto Rican government purchased the Puerto Rico Telephone Company from the International Telephone and Telegraph Company. The basic price paid was $125.5 million, plus substantial additional funds for other considerations. The company is now owned and operated by Puerto Rico's Telephone Authority.

With legislative approval obtained early in June, Puerto Rico acquired its own merchant marine by purchasing two container-ship companies which had for some years operated between the mainland and the island. The cost was approximately $300 million. In Chester, Pa., the new ship *Puerto Rico* was launched on November 1. The ship, which cost about $35 million, will be operated by the new Puerto Rican Maritime Shipping Authority.

Other Developments. In midsummer Puerto Rico suffered from a drought so severe that the city of San Juan was in danger of losing its water supply, which was rationed for some two months by being cut off at night. Rains, unusually frequent and heavy, began to fall in October, doing much harm in the coffee regions but aiding the sugar crop. Large parts of eastern Puerto Rico and the Virgin Islands suffered from serious floods. The island appealed to the federal government for flood relief.

Sabotage committed in the course of a strike against the Aqueducts and Sewers Authority resulted in San Juan's being out of water for 30 hours in November. The governor called out National Guard units to protect the installations. The strike ended on December 12.

In November and December, some 20 bombs, eight of which were found and defused, were placed in business properties owned by Americans. Considerable damage was done to property, but no lives were lost. Members of the Puerto Rican Socialist party were widely suspected of responsibility for these activities.

EARL PARKER HANSON
Former Consultant, Department of State
Commonwealth of Puerto Rico

PUERTO RICO • Information Highlights

Area: 3,435 square miles (8,897 sq km).
Population (1973 est.): 2,951,000. *Density:* 790 per sq mi.
Chief Cities (1970 census): San Juan, the capital, 452,749; Bayamon, 147,552; Ponce, 128,233; Carolina, 94,271.
Government (1974): *Chief Officers*—governor, Rafael Hernández Colón (Popular Democratic party); lieutenant governor, Victor M. Pons, Jr. (PDP); secretary of justice, Francisco de Jesús Schuck; secretary of education, Ramón A. Cruz. *Legislature*—Senate, 29 members (PDP); House of Representatives, 54 members.
Education (1973–74): *Enrollment*—public elementary schools, 432,277 pupils; public secondary schools, 280,183; nonpublic schools, 67,700; colleges and universities, 80,475 students.
State Finances (fiscal year 1973): *Revenues*, $1,262,000,000; *expenditures*, $1,430,000,000.
Personal Income (1973): $5,328,000,000; per capita, $1,836.
Insured Unemployed (July 1974): 55,000 (10.3%).

QUEBEC

In July 1974 the Official Languages Act became law. Four months later the Indians and Eskimos of northern Quebec won a $150 million settlement of their land claims against developers of the James Bay hydroelectric project. These two events highlighted news in the province of Quebec in 1974.

The Languages Act. In 1974 the Official Languages Act (known as Bill 22), making French the official language of the province, became law. Immediately the new act was assailed by non-French-speaking minority groups and French-speaking nationalists, especially members of the Parti Québécois. Equally critical were several Anglophone (English-speaking) members of Premier Robert Bourassa's Liberal party. Their criticism was based on the vagueness of the legislation regarding the guarantees of English-speaking rights. For example, all official documents will be printed and distributed in French but will be available in English on specific request.

There was less confusion regarding the education provisions of the act, but nevertheless minority groups expressed concern in this area too. According to the act, there will be a language test for all children entering school and only those claiming English as their mother tongue or clearly proving that English is their better language will be admitted to English schools. The most serious objection to this aspect of the law came from the large number of immigrants, primarily from Europe and Latin America, who speak neither English nor French. The majority of these immigrants, who live in the Montreal region, look upon Montreal as a door to the English-speaking parts of Canada and thus want their children educated in English. From now on potential immigrants will be warned before coming to Quebec that their children will have to be educated in French unless English is their mother tongue.

Montreal is the location of many large companies, especially head offices. The problems these companies encountered in adopting the French language or in moving to another province were often in the news in 1974. However, it appeared that the majority of these corporations were making the effort to comply with the spirit of the law.

James Bay Project. According to the agreement reached in November by the native peoples of the James Bay region—the 6,300 Cree Indians and the 4,000 Inuit—and the federal and provincial governments, the province was given official permission to build the huge hydroelectric project. In return, the Crees and Inuit were to receive $150 million over a period of about ten years, and the Crees and Inuits would retain 2,000 square miles (5,180 sq km) and 3,130 square miles (8,100 sq km), respectively, as their reserves. In addition, the Crees will receive 25,000 square miles (64,750 sq km) and the Inuit 35,000 square miles (90,650 sq km) for their exclusive use for the purposes of fishing, hunting, and trapping.

Other aspects of the hydroelectric project also made news during the year. As a result of labor union conflict at the site, resulting in $35 million in damage, a three-man commission (the Cliche commission) was appointed by the provincial government to investigate Quebec's construction industry. The Cliche commission exposed evidence of violence and corruption in the industry.

At year-end it was estimated that the cost of the James Bay project would total $12 billion and that it would produce 11,400 megawatts of electricity.

Labor Relations and the Environment. In addition to the languages bill, the Bourassa administration had two other problem areas in 1974. One was labor relations, particularly strikes in large industries which have head offices in the United States. On the one hand, the labor unions were criticizing loudly the outside (non-Quebec) control these companies came under; on the other hand, the provincial government was trying to convince financial interests from all parts of the world that Quebec is a sound area for investment.

Another area that continued to be a source of trouble for the government was environmental policy. The provincial administration was criticized not only for its lack of sensitivity regarding the James Bay Project but also for failing to develop new environmental control policies or to strictly enforce existing laws. Pollution of Quebec rivers and lakes as well as of the atmosphere over urban areas remains at a serious level.

Olympic Games. Although preparations for the 1976 Summer Olympic Games, scheduled to be held in Montreal, are primarily a municipal responsibility, some events are planned for other parts of the province. For example, sailing is to be held at Kingston on Lake Ontario (see also MONTREAL).

THEO L. HILLS, *McGill University*

QUEBEC • Information Highlights

Area: 594,860 square miles (1,540,687 sq km).
Population (1974 est.): 6,124,000.
Chief Cities (1971 census): Quebec, the capital, 186,088; Montreal, 1,214,352; Laval, 228,010.
Government (1974): *Chief Officers*—lt. gov., Hughes Lapointe; premier, Robert Bourassa (Liberal); min. of justice, Jérôme Choquette (L); min. of educ., Francis Cloutier (L); chief justice, Lucien Tremblay. *Legislature*—Legislative Assembly, 110 members (102 L, 6 Parti Québécois, 2 Creditiste).
Education (1972–73): *Enrollment:* public elementary and secondary schools, 1,599,601 pupils; private schools, 67,940; Indian (federal) schools, 4,016; colleges and universities, 65,428 students. *Public school expenditures* (1972), $1,350,900,000.
Public Finance (fiscal year 1974–75 est.): *Revenues*, $7,684,000,000; *expenditures*, $7,388,000,000.
Personal Income (1972): $20,350,000,000; average annual income per person, $3,003.
(All monetary figures are in Canadian dollars.)

CBS RECORDS

To mark the 100th anniversary of the birth of the American composer Charles Ives (*above*), RCA released a new recording (*right*) of his masterpiece, the Fourth Symphony.

RCA RECORDS

recordings

A shortage of vinyl, required in the manufacture of recordings discs, led to a decrease in the number of classical records issued in 1974 and slowed down the search for new popular talent. It also resulted in an increased price for some albums. There was no outstanding new personality in popular records, but the music was probably of somewhat higher quality. Ragtime—notably the piano rags of Scott Joplin—dominated jazz recordings. The audio-equipment industry had a quiet year, with slow consumer acceptance of quadraphonic sound.

CLASSICAL RECORDS

The classical record scene during 1974 showed remarkable stability and unusual prosperity compared to the tight budgets and dwindling sales that had plagued the industry over the previous several years. Owing to the shortage of vinyl necessary to produce the discs themselves, there were perhaps fewer releases than there might have been under ordinary circumstances. On the whole, however, classical records enjoyed good commercial health.

The most encouraging sign from the two largest U. S. producers of classical records, Columbia and RCA, was the inception or reactivation of long-term creative projects that promise much in the years to come. Columbia, long a vigorous proponent of contemporary music, revived its Modern American Music series with a collection of important works by some of America's most distinguished composers: Elliott Carter, Aaron Copland, Leonard Bernstein, Leon Kirchner, and George Crumb. In addition, Columbia began a thorough investigation of music by classically oriented black composers. The first releases in this new undertaking included works by the 18th century Chevalier Saint-Georges, Americans William Grant Still and Ulysses Kay, the 19th century English composer Samuel Coleridge-Taylor, and Roque Cordero of Panama.

RCA, whose classical releases had long been dominated by either "Greatest Hits" rereleases (symphonic staples drawn from past issues and repackaged) or "gimmick" discs (classics played by the Moog synthesizer and the like), also took a more active role in the production of newly recorded material by Leopold Stokowski, Eugene Ormandy, Leontyne Price, Eugene Fodor, Placido Domingo, and other notable musicians. RCA also reissued numerous recordings of prime historical importance from its vaults, such as the complete recordings of Sergei Rachmaninoff and a centenary tribute to Enrico Caruso

THE TEN MOST NOTABLE CLASSICAL RELEASES OF 1974:

ALBÉNIZ, *Iberia:* Alica de Larrocha, piano (London)
CARTER, *String Quartets Nos. 2 & 3:* Juilliard Quartet (Columbia)
CHOPIN, *Piano Sonatas Nos. 2 & 3:* Murray Perahia, piano (Columbia)
DEBUSSY and RAVEL, *Complete Works for Piano Duet and Two Pianos:* Alfons and Aloys Kontarsky, pianos (Deutsche Grammophon)
IVES, *Symphony No. 4:* London Philharmonic Orchestra, José Serebrier, conductor (RCA)
MOZART, *Don Giovanni:* Martina Arroyo, Kiri Te Kanawa, Mirella Freni, Ingvar Wixell, Stuart Burrows; Orchestra of the Royal Opera House, Covent Garden, Colin Davis, conductor (Philips)
SCHUBERT, *Symphonies Nos. 5 & 8:* New Philharmonia Orchestra, Dietrich Fischer-Dieskau, conductor (Angel)
SCHUMANN, *Scenes from Goethe's "Faust":* Elizabeth Harwood, Peter Pears, Dietrich Fischer-Dieskau; English Chamber Orchestra, Benjamin Britten, conductor (London)
TIPPETT, *The Knot Garden:* Yvonne Minton, Thomas Hemsley, Raimund Herincx; Orchestra of the Royal Opera House, Covent Garden, Colin Davis, conductor (Philips)
WOLF, *Spanisches Liederbuch* (*Songs from the Spanish Songbook*): Jan DeGaetani, mezzo; Gilbert Kalish, piano (Nonesuch)

that offered several hitherto unissued recordings by the great tenor.

Smaller labels such as Nonesuch, Vox, Genesis, Orion, Vanguard, Delos, CRI, and Desto continued to expand the recorded repertoire by releasing many works, primarily contemporary or from the late Romantic era—fringe areas that the major companies are often reluctant to cultivate. Most of the "prestige" recordings—complete operas with all-star casts as well as discs by renowned European artists—are still made in Europe, particularly in London which must now be regarded as the world's classical record capital. Stars such as Von Karajan, Sutherland, Caballé, Ashkenazy, Solti, and Pavarotti were all amply represented on European labels distributed in the United States.

PETER G. DAVIS
Recordings Editor, "The New York Times"

POPULAR RECORDS

Popular recordings did not do outstanding business in 1974. Several record companies, talking of a vinyl shortage, raised album prices and appeared to curtail the search for new talent; and the last holdouts agreed that the latest rock boom was now but an echo.

The music, however, was as diverse as it had been in the previous two years and probably of a slightly higher quality. No phenomenal new trend or personality took charge—no "next Beatles" appeared, but the actual former Beatles played together again in an album called *Ringo,* ostensibly Ringo Starr's; no "next Dylan" surfaced, either (although several tried to), but the real Bob Dylan created some excitement by touring the United States and releasing two albums with the Band, *Planet Waves* from the studio and *Before the Flood* from live performances on the tour.

No single genre held sway over the others, but the modern incarnations of folk singers, in the year of Dylan's tour, constituted a large minority. Canadians Joni Mitchell and Gordon Lightfoot, with *Court and Spark* and *Sundown,* respectively, scored great commercial and critical successes. Lightfoot, at age 35, became far more popular than ever. John Denver's midsummer album *Back Home Again* was not a sample of his best work, but 1974 was his—if anyone's—year with the public. John Prine, Jackson Browne, Janis Ian, John Stewart, and Jerry Jeff Walker were among the folk-image performer-writers whose recordings won increasing respect. Joan Baez released a lovely album of Spanish-language songs.

"Glitter" rock appeared to be fading fast, although the antics of such as David Bowie and Alice Cooper continued to sell to live and television audiences. Rock on records seemed to be fighting the calendar, as several performers revived—or tried to revive—various tunes from the late 1950's and early 1960's. A number of radio stations adopted an "all fifties" format, but such machinations seemed more involved with nostalgia than music; and some stations scrapped the "fifties" gambit and returned to the 1970's.

Perhaps it all meant there was more room for diversity. Acceptance of the off-beat humor of Jimmy Buffett and Martin Mull and of the strange old songs unearthed and performed by Ry Cooder suggested that. So did the way popular music looked, for spice and condiments, to country music (Tom T. Hall and Waylon Jennings, especially) and, at the same time, to jazz. It was, among other things, the year in which several producers learned how to use horns and fiddles in the same folk-rock arrangement.

It was, in all, a good year for music. But, some feared, it was an interim one.

NOEL COPPAGE
Contributing Editor, "Stereo Review"

SELECTED POPULAR RELEASES IN 1974

JOAN BAEZ: *Gracias a la Vida,* A&M SP 3614
JACKSON BROWNE: *For Everyman,* Asylum SD-5067
JIMMY BUFFETT: *Living and Dying in 3/4 Time,* Dunhill DSD-50132
RY COODER: *Paradise and Lunch,* Reprise MS 2179
JIM CROCE: *I Got a Name,* ABC ABCX-797
BOB DYLAN/THE BAND: *Before the Flood,* Asylum AS 201
TOM T. HALL: *For the People in the Last Hard Town,* Mercury SRM-1-687
THE HOLLIES: *Hollies,* Epic KE 32574
JANIS IAN: *Stars,* Columbia KC 32857
ALBERT KING: *I Wanna Get Funky,* Stax STS-5505
GORDON LIGHTFOOT: *Sundown,* Reprise MS 2177
JONI MITCHELL: *Court and Spark,* Asylum 7E-1001
HARRY NILSSON: *Pussy Cats,* RCA CPL 1-0570
JOHN PRINE: *Sweet Revenge,* Atlantic SD 7274
JAMES TAYLOR: *Walking Man,* Warner Bros. W 2794
LOUDON WAINWRIGHT III: *Attempted Mustache,* Columbia KC 32710
JERRY JEFF WALKER: *Viva Terlingua,* MCA MCA-382
STEVIE WONDER: *Fulfillingness' First Finale,* Tamla T6332S1

JAZZ RECORDS

Spurred by the Academy Award won by the score of the film *The Sting*—which consisted of arrangements of the piano rags of Scott Joplin—ragtime, which had been building an interested following for several years, suddenly burst out in a flood of recordings.

The performers ranged from the pioneer ragtime revivalist, Max Morath (*The World of Scott Joplin, Vanguard* 310) to the New England Conservatory Ragtime Ensemble, conducted by Gunther Schuller (Golden Crest 31031), the hottest "Joplin" group on the concert circuit. The busiest and most adventurous of the recorded ragtimers was Milton Kaye, a pianist who turned his attention to a follower of Joplin (*The Classic Rags of Joseph Lamb,* Golden Crest 4127) as well as a variety of lesser known but no less interesting ragtime composers (*Ragtime at the Rosebud,* Golden Crest 31032).

The death of Duke Ellington (see OBITUARIES) caught the record companies with no memorial albums prepared. By coincidence, a pair of excellent two-disc survey sets came on the market—*The Golden Duke,* Prestige 24029, and

The World of Duke Ellington, Columbia G 32564.

Three young old-timers, who had been waiting 25 years to reach a broad audience with their tradition-rooted music, emerged from relative obscurity—Dick Wellstood, a pianist, and Kenny Davern and Bob Wilber, both of whom play clarinet and soprano saxophone. Wellstood and Davern were paired on *Dick Wellstood and His Famous Orchestra,* Chiaroscuro 129, while Wilber and Davern joined in duets on *Soprano Summit,* World Jazz 5.

Keith Jarrett, a modernist pianist, established himself with a three-disc album of solos, *Solo Concerts,* ECM 1035-37. David Holland, a bassist and cellist, made effective use of some of the devices of avant-garde jazz on *Conference of the Birds,* ECM 1027.

The year also marked the end of the 22-year career of the Modern Jazz Quartet, which broke up after making *Blues on Bach,* Atlantic 1652.

JOHN S. WILSON
"The New York Times" and "High Fidelity" Magazine

AUDIO EQUIPMENT AND TECHNIQUES

The year 1974 was not an innovative one for the audio-equipment industry, although evolutionary progress was made in several areas of design. The Sequerra Company in the United States and Yamaha of Japan both introduced new FM tuners claiming unprecedentedly low levels of audible noise and distortion. Frequency-synthesizing FM tuners, noted for their tuning accuracy and stability, showed signs of growing in popularity, with Kenwood and Scott offering new models.

Four-Channel Stereo. Quadrasonic sound had an indecisive year in 1974, with concern over consumer acceptance still troubling the industry. Most new four-channel products were receivers incorporating logic-assisted matrix decoders of somewhat greater sophistication than in 1973. These developments were spurred by the availability of compact integrated circuits for most four-channel systems, including the RCA CD-4 system, the SQ matrix system of CBS, and Sansui's QS Vario-Matrix.

Various proposals for a true four-channel FM broadcasting system awaited approval by the Federal Communications Commission (FCC), with field trials of many of the techniques scheduled for late in the year, in cooperation with San Francisco's station KIOI.

Amplifiers. The development of vertical-type field-effect transistors (FET's) suitable for high-power applications opened the way for the first FET audio power amplifiers, which were announced by Sony and Yamaha around mid-year. Field-effect transistors have long been admired for their high linearity and other characteristics, but their use in audio has been limited to FM tuners until recently.

REPRISE RECORDS

(Above) Ry Cooder's new album *Paradise and Lunch* blends Country and Western with popular music. (Below) More *Scott Joplin Rags,* one of several new recordings of the music of Joplin, who died in 1917.

GOLDEN CREST RECORDS

Infinity Systems expected to have the first Class-D "switching" audio power amplifier on the market by the end of 1974.

FTC Power Ruling. In 1974 the Federal Trade Commission (FTC) promulgated a regulation that would compel audio-equipment manufacturers to adhere to certain uniform test procedures and standards in their advertised claims for amplifier power. The ruling states that certain minimum information about steady-state power output, distortion, and bandwidth, derived under test conditions detailed by the FTC, must appear prominently in all amplifier advertising that makes specific reference to the power-output capability of the equipment.

RALPH W. HODGES
Associate Technical Editor, "Stereo Review"

UPI

RELIGION

Faculty and students boycotted the Concordia Seminary, St. Louis, to protest suspension of the Lutheran school's president. "Exiled" is scrawled across barricaded entry.

During 1974 an International Congress on Evangelism was held in Switzerland; the Roman Catholic Church prepared for a Holy Year; and the world of Judaism became increasingly concerned over the question of religious freedom. These and other developments are covered under the following headings: (1) General Survey; (2) Protestantism; (3) Roman Catholicism; (4) Holy Year; (5) Judaism; (6) Orthodox Eastern; and (7) Islam.

General Survey

In 1974 adherents of the major religions engaged in debate regarding what is distinctive in each faith, in the light of increased awareness of religious pluralism and intensified interfaith dialogue. They also debated what is viable in any religious world view, in the light of increasing secularization.

Protestantism. In July, 2,500 Evangelical Protestant leaders from 150 countries met in Lausanne, Switzerland, for an International Congress on World Evangelism. They called for renewed affirmation of traditional Evangelical Protestant views of biblical interpretation, and for active evangelization of both nonbelievers and followers of other religions.

The World Council of Churches was criticized by some members for allegedly providing financial aid to some revolutionary political movements in Africa and South America. The council reaffirmed its commitment to justice through social change, and also planned to hold a world conference on the question of evangelism in 1975.

Muslim World. In the Muslim world there were signs of renewed vitality. Thousands of Malaysian tribesmen have converted to Islam as a result of government efforts to unify a culturally diverse nation through an established religion. Mosque construction and attendance were booming in many Muslim countries.

There was also widespread debate about many items of traditional belief and practice. In Cairo, Egypt, women organized to press for new rights, and in many countries groups worked for reform of traditional marriage and inheritance laws.

In India, Pakistan, Turkey, and elsewhere students and others sought to relate Muslim faith to modern science and present-day philosophy, and to bring Muslim ideals to bear on secular political practice. Turkey was represented at an international Muslim conference, in Lahore, Pakistan, for the first time since the Atatürk revolution (1908).

The war in Cyprus exacerbated Muslim-Christian relations there, and also divided member communions of the Eastern Orthodox Church, as Archbishop Makarios was deposed temporarily as president. In the USSR the church remained officially nonpolitical, but there were continuing signs of religiously based criticism of current Russian culture.

Judaism. There was some relaxation of barriers to Jewish emigration from the Soviet Union. Jews in the United States and elsewhere expressed continued concern for religious freedom and for the future of the state of Israel. There was intensified activity aimed at increased awareness of distinctive beliefs and increased observance of traditional practice. In the United States the Lubavitcher Hasidim engaged in campus and street-corner activity. In Israel the question of Jewish identity and of the relation of Judaism to the state continued to evoke intensive debate.

Religious Identity. In India questions of religious identity were involved in conflicts about official languages in various regions, and about university curricula and organization. In Japan several "new religions," claiming Shinto and Buddhist roots, attracted large followings. They promised personal meaning, health, and prosperity. A similar group in Korea, called the Unification Church, claiming Christian origins and suggesting Messianic status for its leader, the Rev. Sun Young Moon, engaged in evangelistic work in the United States.

Roman Catholicism. The Synod of Roman Catholic Bishops, meeting in Rome in the fall, called for further implementation of reforms initiated by the Second Vatican Council, and many questioned the extent of Pope Paul VI's commitment to the principle of collegiality. At the same time, groups of Catholics in the United States and elsewhere called for a return to the Latin Mass and to the reaffirmation of traditional theology.

J. A. MARTIN, JR., *Columbia University*

Protestantism

In 1974 two large Protestant denominations were involved in internal quarrels centering on theological and church law problems.

Lutheran Problems. At its 1973 convention the Lutheran Church–Missouri Synod adopted a conservative creedal position aimed at ridding the church of alleged liberal theology. In January 1974, Dr. John H. Tietjen, president of Concordia Seminary, St. Louis, was suspended for espousing alleged liberal scriptural views. He was fired in October. The entire seminary faculty, with the exception of five professors, and student body walked out in protest and organized a Seminary in Exile (Seminex) with an enrollment of well over 400.

Protests against the synod's conservative actions continued through the year, focused on the newly formed Evangelical Lutherans in Mission (ELIM), which counted some 2,000 clergy within the membership, plus many congregations. The synod was further torn apart when its overseas mission staff resigned in protest against conservative policies. Disciplinary actions have been taken against dissenting clergy, laity, and professors at the church's colleges.

Episcopal Ordinations. The Episcopalian Church's troubles involved the ordination of 11 women to the priesthood in Philadelphia on July 29. Presiding Bishop John M. Allin summoned a special meeting of the House of Bishops in August, and by a 128–9 vote the bishops declared the ordinations invalid. A few weeks later, charges of violations of church law were filed against the four bishops who had participated in the ordination. In October, at the regular meeting of the House of Bishops, the bishops voted overwhelmingly in favor of the ordination of women. However, the house counseled that further action must await the decision of the General Convention in 1976.

Evangelism. A noticeable trend within Protestantism was the increasing interest in evangelism, with several large mass rallies attracting huge crowds. In July, 2,500 church leaders, mostly from conservative denominations, met in Lausanne, Switzerland, for the International Congress on World Evangelism. While there was general agreement on the need to evangelize the world, there was also a consensus that the social aspects of the Gospel needed to be emphasized. The assembly adopted the Lausanne Covenant, which reaffirmed beliefs in conservative biblical interpretation.

Ecumenism. Although many observers felt that the ecumenical movement within Protestantism had fallen on hard times in recent years, nevertheless there were several significant developments in the church unity movement. The Presbyterian Church in the U. S. (Southern)

Women are ordained Episcopal priests in ceremony later ruled invalid by presiding bishop of Episcopal Church.

UPI

First Mormon temple east of the Rockies is in Kensington, Md., near Washington, D. C. A marble hexagon with gold spires, the structure cost $15 million. Spencer W. Kimball (*left*) is the new president of the religious group.

approved formal union talks with the United Presbyterian Church and the Cumberland Presbyterian Church. The three churches will consider *A Plan for Union* at the 1976 assemblies. Australian Presbyterians, Congregationalists, and Methodists agreed to unite in 1976. In Scotland, Methodists and the Church of Scotland (Presbyterian) may unite once approval is obtained from the British Methodist Church.

In the United States the nine denominations involved in the Consultation on Church Union (COCU) marked time in merger discussions. The nine churches—African Methodist Episcopal Zion, African Methodist Episcopal, Christian Church (Disciples of Christ), Christian Methodist Episcopal, Presbyterian Church in the U. S., United Church of Christ, the Episcopal Church, United Methodist Church, and United Presbyterian Church—have for more than ten years considered forming a 25-million member church. In Canada, the merger of the United Church of Canada, the Anglican Church, and the Christian Church (Disciples of Christ) requires the approval of the *Plan for Union* by the Anglicans. This became doubtful in 1974.

Lutheran and Roman Catholic theologians concluded a three-year study on differences, with the Lutherans agreeing that papal primacy "need not be a barrier to reconciliation."

Membership. Membership losses, while not drastic, still caused concern. Lutheran membership dropped for the fifth consecutive year, but several evangelical, conservative, and Pentecostal churches reported gains.

Other Concerns. Protestants and Roman Catholics alike were deeply concerned over the continued harassment and persecution of Christians in South Korea, Chile, and the Philippines, where clergy and laity were frequently arrested on false accusations. Within all churches there was deep concern over the ethical and moral implications of the Watergate episode. Regardless of theological positions, most churches agreed the nation's moral climate needed improvement.

ALFRED P. KLAUSLER
Editorial Coordinator, "Christian Ministry"

Roman Catholicism

The most important event in Roman Catholic life in 1974 was the Synod of Bishops held in Rome from September 27 to October 26.

Synod on Evangelization. This was the fourth synod held since the close of the second Vatican Council in 1965. The purpose of such meetings is to continue the process of collegial collaboration among the bishops of the Church. There were 208 members in the synod, most of them bishops selected to represent local churches. The topic addressed was the task of "evangelization in the modern world." Both during the months of preparation that preceded it, and during the weeks of the actual synod itself, evangelization proved to be a topic so broadly conceived that the expectation of precise doctrinal clarifications or even universally supported pastoral proposals became unrealistic.

The first phase of the synod was an exchange of pastoral experiences. Five bishops, representing five different language groups and continents, reported on the state of the church. Individual bishops could then address the plenary sessions, if they chose. Finally, small group discussions were held, with the groups divided according to language.

The bishops from Third World countries emerged as spokesmen for a different experience of the church than that in Europe or North America. The Asian bishops urged greater attention to the non-Christian religions of the world. The African bishops insisted on the need for an indigenous church, separated from its colonial past. The bishops of Latin America stressed the necessary involvement of Christians in movements of human liberation. Many bishops hailed the growth of small communities of Christians as a sign of vitality.

A turning point in the synod came on October 23 when the bishops voted to reject a draft document prepared for their approval. Instead, a very general final statement was issued, and the bishops presented the Pope as pastoral proposals a list of the topics discussed in their small

ROOTED IN ANCIENT TRADITION

Catholics Observe Holy Year 1975

On Christmas Eve 1974, Pope Paul VI opened one of the doors of St. Peter's Basilica in Rome and solemnly inaugurated the Holy Year of 1975. The door, designated the Holy Door, is normally sealed with bricks. It will remain open until Christmas 1975.

History of the Holy Year. The origins of the holy year go back to the practice of the jubilee year described in the Old Testament (Leviticus 28:8–17; 29–31). Every seventh sabbath year, that is, every 49th or 50th year, was heralded by the blowing of the ram's horn and set aside in recognition of Jahweh's dominion over the land and all of life.

During the jubilee year, slaves were freed, sowing and harvesting of the land were suspended, and, ideally at least, alienated lands were restored to their owners. Between jubilee years, land was considered leased rather than sold. Although there is some question about how strictly the law was observed in practice, it represented the belief that no individual should be allowed to develop any monopoly over the land, since Jahweh intended his creation to be for the benefit of all.

The Christian adoption of the jubilee year has always been associated with the idea of a pilgrimage. In 1220, Pope Honorius III declared a jubilee year and attached indulgences to a pilgrimage to the tomb of Thomas à Becket. In 1300, Boniface VIII confirmed the growing practice of pilgrimages to the basilicas of Saints Peter and Paul in Rome by declaring a Roman jubilee year. This set the pattern for future holy years, which have occurred every 25 years since the 15th century, except when circumstances did not permit. In this century the ordinary holy years have been celebrated in 1900, 1925, and 1950. Pius XI declared 1933 an extraordinary holy year to celebrate the anniversary of the Redemption.

Renewal and Reconciliation. Although the distinctive feature of a holy year is the pilgrimage, its deeper purpose has always been the renewal of the whole life of the church throughout the world. Pope Paul VI announced the 1975 Holy Year on May 9, 1973, at a general audience. He set as the twin themes of the year "renewal and reconciliation," and directed that the Holy Year observances begin in the local dioceses on Pentecost Sunday, 1973.

On May 23, 1974, the papal bull officially proclaiming 1975 a Holy Year was published. As is the custom, the title of the bull was taken from the first two words of the Latin text, *Apostolorum Limina.* Along with the expected function of specifying the conditions of the Holy Year indulgences, the bull also recalled the history of the Holy Year and suggested ways in which the principal themes should be realized. Renewal and reconciliation should take place within the life of each individual, the church, and society.

More specifically, *Apostolorum Limina* encouraged greater efforts in the work of evangelization and the renewal of the liturgy, particularly the sacrament of penance. Congresses and meetings should also be held that would allow for an exchange of viewpoints on many levels in the church.

More attention should be paid, also, to the development of newer forms of community, along with the traditional structures of diocese and parish, among such groups as workers, young people, and intellectuals. Pope Paul also called for social reform as well as personal charity during the Holy Year.

Celebrations Planned. A central committee was established by the Vatican to prepare for the influx of pilgrims to Rome. Estimates ranged from 6 million to 24 million possible pilgrims to one of the four basilicas selected as pilgrimage centers: St. Peter's, St. Paul Outside the Walls, St. John Lateran, and St. Mary Major. Christians throughout the world who are unable to make such a pilgrimage can gain the Holy Year plenary indulgence by spiritually uniting themselves with the pilgrimage and offering their own prayers.

For many modern Catholics, however, the notion of indulgences and pilgrimages seem the expression of an outdated theology. Pope Paul VI admitted some misgivings, in announcing the Holy Year, about whether the institution retained relevance for many today. The importance of the Holy Year themes of renewal and reconciliation were nonetheless universally recognized. The Peace and Justice Commission of the U. S. Catholic Conference published a booklet with suggestions for celebrating the Holy Year by underlining the centrality of justice to any kind of real reconciliation, and linking the Holy Year to such issues as world hunger and women's rights.

Among the ecumenical activities planned for the Holy Year were three study missions to Israel and Rome, in which several hundred Christians and Jews would participate. Cosponsored by the Graymoor Ecumenical Institute and the American Jewish Committee, the missions will attempt to strengthen understanding between Christians and Jews by studying the Jewish roots of the Catholic Holy Year.

JOSEPH A. O'HARE, S. J.

UPI

Pope Paul VI, sitting beneath Michelangelo's *Last Judgment* in the Vatican's Sistine Chapel, addresses the cardinals and bishops of the fourth World Synod of Bishops.

discussion groups. For some this failure to produce a final doctrinal synthesis was a disappointment. The prevailing view, however, was that the independence asserted by the bishops and the candor that characterized their discussions throughout represented a significant advance in the development of the synod as an institution of collegiality in the church.

Political Conflict. In many countries of the Third World—Asia, Africa, and Latin America—Church support for human liberation resulted in conflicts with authoritarian governments. In several instances, bishops came under fire from more conservative church members. On January 20, the six Catholic bishops of Rhodesia issued a pastoral letter denouncing their government's racial policies. Their criticism was repeated later at the synod in Rome and also in collaboration with leaders of other churches in Rhodesia. The bishops, in turn, were criticized by the government and some Rhodesian Catholics.

In Latin America, the Catholic Bishops' conferences of Chile, Brazil, and Bolivia protested their governments' treatment of political prisoners. Government censorship of Catholic publications and broadcasts occurred in all three countries, and some foreign missionaries were expelled. In Asia, Protestant and Catholic churchmen protested the harsh repression policies of South Korean President Park Chung Hee. A Catholic bishop was arrested in August and sentenced to 15 years in prison. The bishops of the predominantly Catholic Philippines urged President Ferdinand Marcos to restore civil liberties and gradually remove martial law.

A quite different kind of political conflict occurred in Italy—a referendum on divorce in May. Despite strong support by Italian bishops for a repeal of a liberalized divorce law, Italians rejected the repeal.

Ecumenism. On March 4 the Lutheran–Roman Catholic Consultation published a common statement on the papacy that concluded that the different attitudes of Lutherans and Catholics toward papal primacy did not necessarily stand in the way of reconciliation.

Prayer and Liturgy. The 1974 International Conference on the Charismatic Renewal in the Catholic Church attracted 30,000 people to Notre Dame University in June. Phenomena associated with the ministry of healing became more prominent in the movement. A number of instances of faith healing were reported at the meeting and there was some criticism of the kind of attention given them. In February the Vatican issued a revised ritual for the sacrament of penance that encouraged greater flexibility in the forms the sacrament could take.

Mother Seton. In December, Pope Paul issued a decree declaring Elizabeth Ann Seton a saint. The founder of the Sisters of Charity is the first native American to be canonized.

Cardinal Mindszenty. In February, Pope Paul VI removed Jozsef Cardinal Mindszenty as honorary primate of the Church in Hungary. The 81-year-old prelate had been living in Vienna since 1971.

JOSEPH A. O'HARE, S. J.
Associate Editor, "America"

Judaism

The shadow of the "Yom Kippur War" cast a pall over world Judaism in 1974. Grief over the heavy loss of lives suffered during the October 1973 war was compounded by shock over subsequent terrorist massacres in Israel, news of Jews murdered in Syria, and the increased persecution of Jews in the USSR.

Aftermath of War. Arab terrorist massacres of women and children inside Israel claimed more lives. Widespread indignation over Arab atrocities in Kiryat Shemona, Maalot, Shamir, and Nahariya prompted mass demonstrations and memorial services the world over. Virtually every major U. S. city was the scene of a protest rally at which statements issued by Jewish and Christian leaders assailed the United Nations for its failure to take effective measures against Arab terrorism.

Harassment of Jews. In Syria, the murder of four young Jewish women and two men, the death sentence of two, and the arrest of several others also caused deep concern. Protests against Syrian harassment of Jews included a plea by Sephardic Chief Rabbi Ovadya Yosef to UN Secretary General Kurt Waldheim and an appeal by cabinet ministers in Paris calling for an end to discrimination. The New York Board of Rabbis called for world pressure on Syria to allow its 4,500 Jews to emigrate.

In Russia, harassment, arrests, and physical attacks on Jews seeking emigration to Israel increased in 1974. Worldwide sympathy for their plight was often expressed during the year. In addition to mass demonstrations, artists and scientists (among them eight Nobel laureates) voiced their condemnation of Soviet persecution of fellow professionals. U. S. pressure in the form of the Jackson Amendment to the Trade Reform Bill held a promise of relief.

West Bank Settlement. In Israel, the religious aspect of the Arab-Israeli conflict became evident in the formation of a militant settlement movement, composed mainly of religious groups. In defiance of government policy, this movement made massive attempts at settling the West Bank to demonstrate its opposition to giving up any territory of "Biblical Israel."

"Who is a Jew?" The National Religious party of Israel, as a condition of its participation in the government coalition, demanded exclusive recognition of Orthodox conversions. The issue created a conflict within the government and stirred religious controversy in world Judaism as Conservative and Reform groups sharply deplored the Orthodox position. As a result, the Union of Orthodox Congregations of America pulled out of the Synagogue Council of America, causing Reform institutions to review their conversion procedures.

Centennial. The Union of American Hebrew Congregations celebrated its centennial in a somber mood of realization that it faces erosion of its strength through intermarriage and an increasing absence of theological commitment on the part of its membership.

LIVIA E. BITTON, *Herbert H. Lehman College, City University of New York*

Orthodox Eastern Church

The exile of Aleksandr Solzhenitsyn from the Soviet Union drew new attention to the plight of Orthodox Christians in the USSR (see BIOGRAPHY). Solzhenitsyn was condemned by Soviet church authorities for being a traitor to his country, while being universally defended by fellow Orthodox churchmen in the free world, including Archbishop Anthony Bloom, the Russian Orthodox bishop who resigned his position as official representative of the Moscow Patriarchate in Western Europe. In the USSR interest in religion continued to grow with increasing alarm to the atheist regime. In March 1974 the Moscow priest Dimitri Dudko was forced to resign from his pastorate for conducting open discussions in his church.

In Greece, following the overthrow of the Papadopoulos government in late 1973, Archbishop Ieronymos of Athens was replaced by Seraphim, former bishop of Ioannina, on Jan. 12, 1974. A number of bishops consecrated during the Ieronymos period were removed from office.

In 1974, Patriarch Demetrios of Constantinople followed a conservative line toward his Orthodox brothers and toward the non-Orthodox. In talks with Roman Catholics he reaffirmed the Orthodox opposition to papal supremacy.

In June 1974 theologians from the Orthodox churches in the Middle East, the USSR, Yugoslavia, Rumania, Bulgaria, Greece, and the United States discussed questions relative to the forthcoming assembly of the World Council of Churches in 1975. The meeting indicated renewed concern among the Orthodox about participation in the WCC, whose policies have continued to be criticized in Orthodox circles.

THOMAS HOPKO
St. Vladimir's Orthodox Theological Seminary

Islam

Muslims began the year on two optimistic notes—a disengagement treaty between Egypt and Israel and the reconciliation of two of Islam's most populous nations, Pakistan and Bangladesh. Later, problems of religious interpretation arose within the Muslim community in Pakistan and tensions developed between various Muslims and their non-Muslim neighbors.

In February, representatives from 38 countries and the Palestine Liberation Organization assembled in Lahore, Pakistan, for a Conference of Islamic States. At the opening session, Pakistan announced that it was granting full recognition to Bangladesh. The resolution of differences between these states had been a major objective of Muslim leaders. The conference reflected a theme of Islamic unity.

Riots erupted in Pakistan in June between adherents of the Ahmadiyya sect, said to number over 300,000, and other Muslims. The Ahmadiyya's claim that their founder, Mirza Ghulam Ahmad, who died in 1908, was a prophet, offended orthodox Muslims who believe prophecy terminated with Muhammad. Dozens died in the fighting, as Ahmadiyya mosques were burned and shops looted before order was restored.

Muslims demonstrated in Addis Ababa, Ethiopia, in the spring. They protested religious discrimination in the predominantly Christian country, demanding equal treatment for Muslims.

The Philippine Islands, plagued for years by a revolt of Muslim tribesmen in the south, attempted to placate the rebels by organizing public projects and appointing Muslims to office. President Marcos announced an amnesty in June, but the Muslims received the news with little enthusiasm.

KENNETH J. PERKINS
University of South Carolina

RHODE ISLAND

Rhode Island, like the rest of the nation, became increasingly preoccupied with Watergate and the state of the economy in 1974. When the year began, the state was in the throes of the oil crisis. There were fears in late 1973 that Rhode Island's heavy dependence on oil for heating and power generation would mean shortages and serious dislocations, but relatively mild winter weather and extra allocations helped avoid such problems.

Economic Developments. Rhode Island continued its efforts in 1974 to cope with the economic problems that had been brought on by the announcement in 1973 that the U. S. Navy was planning to close down most of its important installations in the state. Gov. Philip Noel introduced legislation at the end of February to set up an Economic Development Corporation and to create a new Department of Economic Development. The Economic Development Corporation was to have broad powers to fund and carry out development projects anywhere in the state. Its immediate efforts would be to create new jobs to replace those being lost, by finding industries to locate on the navy land about to be released.

The Governor's proposal provoked much opposition because the corporation would have had the power to take land at will and to override city and town zoning, as well as the jurisdiction of the Coastal Management Council. When finally passed the bill gave considerably less sweeping authority to the corporation, conferring unlimited powers only in relation to the former navy land. Otherwise the corporation must conform to local zoning provisions. Nonetheless, it was described as one of the most important steps in centralizing governmental power in the state that had yet been taken.

Environment. Legislation relating to waste disposal also moved toward greater centralization. A bill was passed to set up a Solid Waste Management Corporation with authority to contract with individual communities and private groups for centralized waste disposal systems.

RHODE ISLAND • Information Highlights

Area: 1,214 square miles (3,144 sq km).
Population (1973 est.): 973,000. *Density:* 923 per sq mi.
Chief Cities (1970 census): Providence, the capital, 179,116; Warwick, 83,694; Pawtucket, 76,984.
Government (1974): *Chief Officers*—governor, Philip W. Noel (D); lt. gov., J. Joseph Garrahy (D). *General Assembly*—Senate, 50 members (37 D, 13 R); House of Representatives, 100 members (72 D, 27 R, 1 independent).
Education (1973–74): *Enrollment*—public elementary schools, 112,292 pupils; public secondary, 72,332; nonpublic, 35,400; colleges and universities, 55,122 students. *Public school expenditures,* $216,472,000 ($1,250 per pupil).
State Finances (fiscal year 1973): *Revenues,* $656,-896,000; *expenditures,* $613,623,000.
Personal Income (1973): $4,651,000,000; per capita, $4,780.
Labor Force (July 1974): *Nonagricultural wage and salary earners,* 355,800; *insured unemployed,* 21,400 (6.6%).

Politics and Government. The year 1974 was an important political year. Following trends prompted by Watergate, the Rhode Island General Assembly passed legislation requiring the reporting of campaign contributions and setting limits on campaign expenditures. An income tax checkoff system had been established in 1973, with the proceeds going to the Democratic and Republican state party chairmen.

Under the new law candidates for governor can spend up to $400,000, candidates for lieutenant governor and attorney general up to $100,000, and candidates for secretary of state and general treasurer, $50,000. All contributions of $200 or more must be reported, as must all expenditures. Primary election spending for state offices was also limited. These provisions and the tax checkoff went into effect for the first time in the 1974 elections.

The Rhode Island election results showed the same Democratic sweep found in the rest of the country. Governor Noel was reelected with a record-breaking 78% of the vote, and the Democratic candidate for attorney general, Julius Michaelson, also won, enabling the party to recapture the one statewide office that had been in the hands of the Republican party.

The General Assembly results showed the full extent of the Republican defeat and of the party's future problems. Prior to the election the GOP had been able to field a smaller than usual number of legislative candidates, and 37 of the 150 seats went to Democrats by default. When the election results were in, the GOP held only 4 instead of its previous 13 out of 50 Senate seats, and only 17 of its previous 27 out of 100 House seats. Thus in both houses, already slender minorities were further weakened almost to the point of impotence. Seemingly, Rhode Island has become virtually a one-party state, at least for the near future.

In the midst of this dismal news for the party, Providence Republicans, to the surprise of many, elected their first mayor since 1940. This apparent anomaly came in the wake of a bitter party split among Democrats and a four-way primary fight. What this means for the future politics of the state's capital city, long overwhelmingly Democratic, remains to be seen. The city council remained Democratic, 24 to 2 seats. The only other significant Republican victory was the reelection of popular Mayor James Taft of Cranston.

Education. The year saw important personnel changes in the state's educational system. The University of Rhode Island acquired a new president—Frank Newman, who had held an administrative position at Stanford University. Dr. Fred G. Burke, the first state commissioner of education under the Regents system enacted in 1969, resigned at midyear. He was succeeded by Dr. Thomas Schmidt.

ELMER E. CORNWELL, JR.
Brown University

RHODESIA

Prime Minister Ian Douglas Smith's election victory, and efforts to introduce black participation in the government headed events in 1974.

Election. Smith's Rhodesian Front party won all 50 parliamentary seats reserved for whites in a general election on July 31. The military and economic threat of Portugal's forthcoming withdrawal from neighboring Mozambique lay behind the white rally to Smith. In his third victory since 1962, Smith received more than 70% of the votes cast. Black Africans elected 8 blacks to the 16 black-reserved seats, and tribal leaders named the other 8.

African Talks. Before Prime Minister Smith had broken with Britain in 1965, Britain had pressed him to reach a constitutional agreement with the 5.6 million blacks, who outnumber the 250,000 whites by more than 20 to 1. More recently, Smith was under pressure from South Africa to reach such an agreement, and in early December 1974, he agreed to negotiate political equality for the majority black population.

On December 8, leaders of three black Rhodesian nationalist organizations that had been banned in Rhodesia, meeting in a conference at Lusaka, Zambia, under leadership of Zambian President Kenneth D. Kaunda, agreed to join an expanded executive group of the African National Council, under the chairmanship of Abel T. Muzorewa of the United Methodist Church of Rhodesia, to prepare for whatever conference might be arranged with Smith to negotiate equal black participation in the Rhodesian government. The Organization of African Unity (OAU) immediately rejected this agreement and demanded nothing short of black rule in Rhodesia.

On December 11, Smith announced that his government and the black nationalists had agreed to a cease-fire on the northern frontier; that detained black leaders would be released; and that black participation in the government would be negotiated at a constitutional convention to be held early in 1975.

Guarded Villages. To prevent aid to guerrillas from Mozambique, the government moved some 60,000 Africans from Chiweshe tribal trust reserves into 21 fortified villages. Inhabitants had to build their own homes; the government supplied schools and clinics.

FRANKLIN PARKER
West Virginia University

RHODESIA • Information Highlights

Area: 150,803 square miles (390,580 sq km).
Population (1973 est.): 5,800,000.
Chief Cities (1969 census, met. areas): Salisbury, the capital, 386,040; Bulawayo, 245,040.
Government: *Head of state,* Clifford Dupont, president (took office 1970). *Head of government,* Ian Smith, prime minister (took office 1964).
Monetary Unit: Rhodesian dollar (0.5348 R. dollar equals U.S.$1, Oct. 1974).
Major Agricultural Products: Tobacco, sugar, tea, groundnuts, cotton, corn, millet and sorghum.
Foreign Trade (1972): *Exports,* $499,000,000; *imports,* $417,000,000.

RUMANIA

In 1974, Rumania continued unchanged its major internal and foreign policies of 1973.

Domestic Affairs. At a plenary meeting of the Central Committee of the Rumanian Communist party on March 25–26, significant governmental and party changes strengthened the position of Secretary General Nicolae Ceauşescu. The party's ruling Presidium was abolished and replaced by a Permanent Bureau, and Ceauşescu's supporters were appointed to posts within the new structure. Premier Ion Gheorghe Maurer, a critic of Ceauşescu, was replaced by Manea Manescu, deputy premier and chairman of the State Planning Committee. Finally, on March 28, Ceauşescu himself was unanimously elected to the newly created post of President of the Socialist Republic, simultaneously becoming commander-in-chief of the armed forces. Late in the year Ceauşescu was reelected to a new five-year term as secretary general.

At another plenum of the Central Committee held at the end of July, the country was presented with the draft directives for its economic development during the coming 5-year plan (1976–80), as well as the following decade (1981–90). It was clear that heavy capital investment and rapid industrial development would continue to take precedence over the production of consumer goods.

The new press law of March 30 abolished preliminary official screening of articles, making editors themselves responsible for censoring their own publications for material deemed injurious to the interests of the state, the party, and the "socialist social order."

Foreign Affairs. In 1974, Rumanian foreign policy continued to search for political and economic alternatives to the Soviet bloc through ties with all other parts of the world. Rumania often adopted the role of spokesman for the Third World.

Following an official visit of King Hussein of Jordan to Rumania in late January, Ceauşescu visited Libya, Lebanon, Syria, and Iraq in February in an apparent effort to better relations with the Arabs. In March, Ceauşescu visited Liberia, Guinea, and Argentina. The visits resulted in the establishment of diplomatic relations with Libya and Liberia and the signing of a number of economic-technical agreements with all of the host countries. In June, Rumania resumed diplomatic relations with Portugal after a break of 25 years.

Rumania's growing importance in world affairs was recognized by the holding of the United Nations World Population Conference in Bucharest on August 19–30, with 130 countries sending delegates. Ceauşescu himself spoke for the Communist and poorer countries, attributing the gap between the rich and poor nations to "the imperialist, colonialist, and neo-colonialist exploitation and oppression of many peoples," and seeing the solution not in limitations on population growth but in a redistribution of the world's wealth.

Rumanian-U. S. relations continued to build on Ceauşescu's successful state visit to the United States in December 1973. In January, the International Telephone and Telegraph Corporation signed a cooperative agreement with Rumania. In April, U. S. Secretary of Commerce Frederick B. Dent and the heads of a large number of U. S. companies attended the first session of the U. S.-Rumanian Economic Commission in Bucharest. In May, a branch of the Manufacturer's Hanover Trust Company was opened in that city. A dispute over the seizure of a Rumanian trawler by the U. S. Coast Guard in March, for allegedly violating U. S. territorial waters off the North Carolina coast, was settled amicably when Rumania paid a fine of $100,000.

In its relations with the Soviet Union and other members of the Communist bloc, Rumania adamantly held to the principles of full national equality, state sovereignty, and noninterference in internal affairs. It continued to oppose the Soviets' desire to expel China officially from the orthodox Communist community. It opted for selective participation in projects of the Council for Mutual Economic Assistance (COMECON) and refused integration in a supranational economic complex. This stance was evident at the meeting of the Political Consultative Committee of the Warsaw Treaty Pact in Warsaw, April 17–18; at a COMECON meeting in Sofia, June 18–21; and at the Rumanian Communist party congress in Bucharest in November.

In mid-summer, there were persistent rumors of a Soviet-Rumanian rift, alleging Soviet pressures on Rumania to allow Soviet troops to pass through Rumania to Bulgaria and covert Soviet involvement in a series of explosions at important industrial sites in Rumania. Although the rumors were publicly denied by both countries, Rumania did appear to draw closer to Yugoslavia, another target of Soviet displeasure, at meetings in July and September.

JOSEPH F. ZACEK
State University of New York at Albany

RUMANIA • Information Highlights

Official Name: Socialist Republic of Rumania.
Location: Southeastern Europe.
Area: 91,700 square miles (237,500 sq km).
Population (1973 est.): 21,000,000.
Chief Cities (1971 est.): Bucharest, the capital, 1,488,300; Cluj, 205,400; Timisoara, 195,500; Iaşi, 188,000.
Government: *Head of state,* Nicolae Ceauşescu, president and secretary general of the Communist party (took office 1965). *Head of government,* Manea Manescu, premier (took office March 1974). *Legislature* (unicameral)—Grand National Assembly.
Monetary Unit: Leu (4.97 lei equal U. S.$1, July 1974).
Gross National Product (1973 est.): $31,000,000,000.
Manufacturing (major products): Construction materials, metals, chemicals, machinery, processed foods, textiles, petroleum products.
Major Agricultural Products: Corn, sugar beets, potatoes, wheat, rye, sunflower seeds.
Foreign Trade (1973): *Exports,* $3,675,000,000; *imports,* $3,447,000,000.

ST. LOUIS

An experiment in public housing ended in May 1974 when the last families moved from the Pruitt-Igoe public housing project, a high-rise complex built in the mid-1950's as a model for housing the poor. The project, which once housed nearly 12,000, fell victim to crime, poor maintenance, too many welfare families, and design errors.

While Pruitt-Igoe was being prepared for demolition, many other buildings were going up downtown. Construction began on a $30 million convention center, a 35-story Mercantile Trust Co. office center, a Boatman's Bank Building, and a 23-story hotel above the long-vacant Spanish Pavilion. In addition, the state began converting Louis Sullivan's Wainwright Building into a state office building.

Referendums. St. Louis voters refused to go along with this rebuilding trend, however. In November, they turned down 9 of 10 proposals in a $109 million bond issue for civic improvements, approving only equipment and buildings for the fire department. One of the projects was to be the renovating of the overcrowded city jail, which was ordered closed by a federal judge because of inhuman treatment of inmates. City officials were appealing this decision, while at the same time making directed improvements. Voters also twice turned down a 66-cent school tax increase.

Politics. The 12-year tenure of St. Louis county (suburban) Supervisor Lawrence K. Roos, Republican, ended with his retirement. But voters sought a continuation of his policies by picking Gene McNary, a Roos protégé, over Democrat Don Anton to replace him. McNary's victory came while Democrats were winning nearly everything else.

Religion. A faculty-student boycott of the Lutheran Church-Missouri Synod's Concordia Seminary followed the suspension of seminary president Rev. John H. Tietjen for alleged heretical teaching. The boycott led to the firing of 43 of 48 faculty members and the establishment of a "seminary in exile" at St. Louis University and Eden Seminary. Most of the school's 520 students joined the dismissed faculty at "seminex." Tietjen was subsequently fired.

City Government. Building Commissioner Kenneth O. Brown was indicted for conflict of interest for alleged business relationship with city contractors. City Judges Richard Brown and Harold Fullwood were suspended temporarily, Brown for presigning bail bonds and Fullwood for berating police officers in court.

Trash Reclamation. A pilot project in which some city trash was burned to generate electricity for Union Electric Co. was declared a success, and the utility announced plans to go into the trash-burning and reclamation business on a full scale.

RONALD D. WILLNOW, *St. Louis "Post Dispatch"*

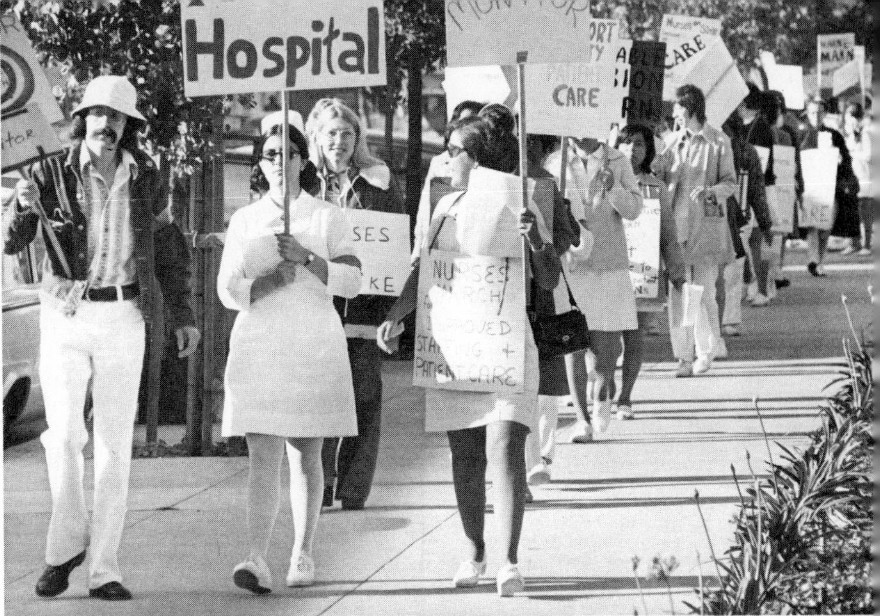

Hospital nurses, including the man at left, picket a San Francisco hospital. Northern California nurses struck for a voice in the staffing of hospital units.

UPI

SAN FRANCISCO

Among noteworthy events of 1974 were the opening to traffic of the 3½-mile BART tunnel, the removal of the last obstacles to the building of the $535 million Yerba Buena Center, and the kidnapping of 19-year-old Patricia Hearst.

BART System. With the opening on September 16 of the tube beneath the bay, the 72-mile Bay Area Rapid Transit (BART) System began operating over its full length. Pending the elimination of defects in the system of automatic control, service was restricted to the hours from 6 A.M. to 8 P.M., but so many persons chose to patronize the fast and comfortable new facility as to significantly reduce the volume of traffic on the San Francisco–Oakland Bay Bridge, particularly during the morning and evening rush hours. This, the first all-new metropolitan transportation system to be built in the United States in more than half a century, was scheduled to begin full operation early in 1975.

Yerba Buena Center. At year-end, final approval was given to the building of the Yerba Buena Center, a much-needed convention facility, the construction of which was delayed for several years until suitable housing could be provided for former residents of the area. Work on the first two units of the project—a convention center and a mall—was expected to begin in the spring of 1975, with the entire complex, which will occupy some 87 acres, scheduled for completion about 1978.

Other New Construction. While during most of 1974 the city shared with the rest of the nation a virtual suspension of residential building, new construction in the downtown area remained active. Among major buildings put up during the year were Liberty House, a department store in the retail shopping district; the Levi Strauss Building in the Embarcadero Center; and a lofty office building for the Standard Oil Company in the 500 block on Market Street. Plans were announced in June for an enormous block-square structure to be built for the Bank of America on Market Street. Designed to serve as a data-processing center for the bank's 500 branches in Northern California, the building will have floor space equal to 44 football fields. The building is being designed by Skidmore, Owings & Merrill, and the work of clearing the site will begin late in 1975.

Labor Problems. For nine days in early March a strike of city employees brought numerous municipal activities—including public transportation and the city hospitals—to a virtual halt. The settlement, effected on March 15, provided for yearly pay raises of $600 for some 15,500 employees, together with substantial payments by the city into employees' pension funds, plus up to $500 per annum for their dental care. At about the same time the San Francisco Federation of Teachers, representing some 2,500 of the district's 4,100 teachers, went on strike, asking a 15% salary increase and other benefits. After prolonged and often bitter negotiations, concessions on both sides brought the crippling strike to an end on March 28.

Budget. The city and county budget for the 1974–75 fiscal year was fixed at $897 million, a record high. Of that sum, 34% will be raised by property taxes, 24% by state and federal subventions, 26% by license fees, etc., and 16% by city-owned facilities. After prolonged argument between the mayor and the board of supervisors over the tax rate on real and personal property, a compromise was reached, fixing the amount at $12.75 per $100 assessed valuation, an increase of 50 cents over that of the previous year.

Election. At the elections on November 5, city voters faced a ballot listing not only nearly 80 candidates for federal, state, and local offices but also 17 state and 14 local propositions.

Approximately 60% of the city's voters turned out and, as is their custom, gave heavy majorities to the Democratic candidates. Of the city measures the most hotly contested were two propositions providing for increases in the pensions of retired policemen and firemen at a cost to the city of San Francisco of from $16 to $20 million annually. Both measures carried, but by narrow margins.

Patricia Hearst Kidnapping. The kidnapping on February 5 of Patricia Hearst, daughter of Randolph Hearst, publisher of the *San Francisco Examiner,* shocked the city and claimed a major share of attention for weeks thereafter. Unusual events of the period included the free distribution to the poor of some $2 million worth of groceries (which the kidnappers had demanded as a condition of her release), her announcement on April 3 that she planned to "stay and fight" with her captors and, 12 days later, her participation in the gang's armed robbery of a San Francisco bank. As the year closed, the mystery of her whereabouts and her behavior remained unresolved.

OSCAR LEWIS
Author of "San Francisco: Mission to Metropolis"

SASKATCHEWAN

Saskatchewan continued its economic buoyancy, with further social, industrial, and agricultural development in 1974. Unemployment continued to be the lowest in Canada.

Floods. Spring flooding was a major problem in 1974, causing damage estimated at $9 million. Hardest hit were the city of Moose Jaw, where 1,400 people were driven from their homes, and the valley town of Lumsden, saved from the rampaging Qu'Appelle River after a week-long struggle to build dikes 30 feet high.

Energy. Measures were taken by Premier Allan Blakeney's New Democratic party government to bring oil and gas reserves in Saskatchewan under the ownership and control of the province. Tough bargaining with the federal government brought a $200 million package to Saskatchewan when crude oil prices were pegged at $6.50 a barrel.

Economy. Although a major effort is being made to diversify the economy by developments in manufacturing, forestry, and mining, agriculture still remained the largest single economic factor in the province, accounting for about half of its gross product.

A late spring, heavy rains in the harvest season, and early, killing frosts drastically reduced yields of cereal crops. Many late-sown crops were only suitable for feed, and frozen flax was burned in the fields. The estimated yield of low-quality spring wheat was about 20 bushels per acre.

Despite the poor growing season, a high cash flow to farmers for grain and livestock continued in 1974. International sales of wheat were high, but labor disputes in the ports of Vancouver and Thunder Bay backed up the movement of the 1973 crop and choked prairie elevators. Livestock sales brought good returns, although cattle prices were weaker.

Mining continued to show an increased rate of expansion. Elimination of restrictions on potash production resulted in shipment of an estimated 7 million tons in 1974. Late in October the government announced a new taxation formula on potash that was expected to bring in an additional $86.8 million in 1975, and moved toward public ownership or control of all new potash mines.

Government and Social Services. A balanced budget of nearly $900 million was brought down for 1974–75.

Advances in the health field included abolition of all premiums for medical care and hospitalization, initiation of universal dental care for children up to 12 years through the school system, and passage of legislation to introduce a major prescription drug program. In other social services, a $2 million program was launched to assist the operation of 4,500 day care spaces. A new Family Income Plan enables working people to supplement their incomes to a level considerably above payments they would receive under social assistance. A new Legal Aid Plan will make essential legal services available to all.

On July 1, 1974, the University of Saskatchewan's Regina branch became the University of Regina, with John H. Archer as president.

Department of Northern Saskatchewan. This unique experiment incorporates all the services of government for a large, sparsely populated area into one department centered at La Ronge. Progress has been slow, but a Northern Municipal Council now involves local people in government, and new air strips, roads, schools, and sanitation facilities are bringing the quality of life in the north closer to the level enjoyed in the south.

DOROTHY HAYDEN
Regina Public Library

SASKATCHEWAN • Information Highlights

Area: 251,700 square miles (651,900 sq km).
Population (1974 est.): 907,000.
Chief Cities (1971 census): Regina, the capital, 139,469; Saskatoon, 126,449; Moose Jaw, 31,854.
Government (1974): *Chief Officers*—lt. gov., Stephen Worobetz; premier, Allan Blakeney (New Democratic party); atty. gen., Roy Romanow (NDP); min. of educ., Gordon MacMurchy (NDP); chief justice, E. M. Culliton. *Legislature*—Legislative Assembly, 60 members (45 NDP, 15 Liberal).
Education (1972–73): *Enrollment:* public elementary and secondary schools, 240,063 pupils; private schools, 1,268; Indian (federal) schools, 4,465; colleges and universities, 13,380 students. *Public school expenditures* (1972), $170,700,000.
Public Finance (fiscal year 1974–75 est.): *Revenues,* $901,000,000; *expenditures,* $983,000,000.
Personal Income (1972): $2,719,000,000; average annual income per person, $2,991.
(All monetary figures are in Canadian dollars.)

SAUDI ARABIA

Saudi Arabia was a major spokesman for the Arab world in 1974. The largest oil-exporting country in the world, it saw its wealth vastly increased by the rise in crude oil prices.

Budget. Saudi Arabia's 1974–75 budget, published in July, revealed officially for the first time the massive effects of the rise in crude oil prices. The country's total income, of which 95% comes from petroleum, was listed at $27.95 billion, and expenditures were budgeted at $12.88 billion, leaving about $15 billion to be added to its reserves. In November, Saudi estimated reserves totaled $11.5 billion.

In the expenditures for the current year 10% was marked for loans and aid to foreign governments. In September it was announced that $2.8 billion was being consigned to the Saudi Arabian Development Fund for loans to developing countries, with the proviso that no loans should be made for more than 50% of the cost of a project. Expenditures in the current budget averaged 100% above 1973; income was up about 330%. In December, Saudi Arabia announced that it would lend the World Bank $750 million for loans to developing countries.

Oil. Just prior to the October 1973 war in the Middle East, Saudi Arabia had been producing about 8 million barrels per day with over 9 million barrels expected to be produced by the end of 1973. But with the outbreak of the war Saudi Arabia cut back production by 10% and in November by 25% and placed an embargo on all oil shipments, direct or indirect, to the Netherlands and the United States. Oil deliveries resumed at regular levels in December 1973 to Britain, France, and Spain, and Saudi Arabia made an arrangement with France to deliver 800 million tons of oil over the next 30 years in exchange for military armaments. At the same time the United States announced it was prepared to discuss the sale of F-4 Phantom jets to Saudi Arabia.

The oil embargo to the United States was lifted on March 18, 1974, and the 8.3 million barrels per day figure for production was restored. Saudi Arabia also announced that it was prepared to lower prices if other OPEC (Organization of Petroleum Exporting Countries) members agreed. In October it lowered the posted price for oil from $11.65 to $11.25 per barrel but increased the taxes on export of oil by $0.40. Actually this meant that the average price of oil in Saudi Arabia moved from $9.40 to $9.76 a barrel, but it also meant that it would be less expensive for governments than for oil companies to purchase oil in Saudi Arabia.

Late in 1972, Aramco, the giant oil producing company in Saudi Arabia (owned jointly by Standard Oil of California, Texaco, Exxon, and Mobil) had agreed to sell 25% ownership to the Saudi government. In June 1974 a new agreement raised the government's ownership to 60%, with the understanding that Aramco would buy the government's share of production at 93% of the posted price. In October negotiations were opened for Saudi Arabia to buy the remaining 40% of Aramco for $800 million, the same rate paid for the first 60%. Also, the Saudi government asked the oil companies to buy back the oil produced at prevailing market prices for guaranteed sales.

Arab Affairs. Since the 1973 war, Saudi Arabia has given strong diplomatic and financial support to Egypt, Jordan, Syria, and the Palestinians. King Faisal gave $300 million to Egypt in August 1974 for reconstruction and current needs. Agreement was reached in May with Sudan over the development of rich mineral deposits in the seabed of the Red Sea. In July, a long-held dispute with Abu Dhabi was settled, and diplomatic relations were restored.

At the Arab Summit meeting in October in Morocco, King Faisal supported the vote to recognize the Palestine Liberation Organization (PLO) as the representative of the Palestinian people. King Faisal has been constant in his statements that there can be no peace in the Middle East until Israel has withdrawn from Arab territories taken in the 1967 war, recognized the Arabism of Jerusalem, and granted self-determination to the Palestinians. He repeated this to President Nixon, who visited him in June.

Defense. A $335 million agreement was signed with the United States in April to provide weapons and training for the Saudi National Guard. In June, Prince Fahd, King Faisal's brother, signed an agreement in Washington establishing a joint military commission to aid Saudi Arabia in maintaining security in the Persian Gulf area. This includes the supplying of Hawk ground-to-air missiles, F-5E jet fighters, C-130 cargo planes, and the construction of two big army bases at Tofuk.

Development. The inflow of money into Saudi Arabia has touched off a gigantic economic boom. New air fields are being built, and a 26-story office building is under construction in Jidda. The Abha Dam was opened in April.

SYDNEY NETTLETON FISHER
The Ohio State University

SAUDI ARABIA • Information Highlights

Official Name: Kingdom of Saudi Arabia.
Location: Arabian Peninsula in southwest Asia.
Area: 830,000 square miles (2,149,690 sq km).
Population (1973 est.): 8,400,000.
Chief Cities (1965 est.): Riyadh, the capital, 225,000; Jidda, 194,000; Mecca, 185,000.
Government: *Head of state,* Faisal ibn Abdul-Aziz, king (acceded Nov. 1964). *Head of government,* Faisal ibn Abdul-Aziz.
Monetary Unit: Riyal (3.55 riyals equal U.S.$1, Aug. 1974).
Gross National Product (1972 est.): $5,250,000,000.
Manufacturing (major products): Petroleum products, cement, fertilizers, iron and steel.
Major Agricultural Products: Dates, vegetables, wheat.
Foreign Trade (1973 est.): *Exports,* $7,200,000,000; *imports,* $1,800,000,000.

SINGAPORE

Singapore's main concern in 1974 was to maintain its high rate of economic growth, while dampening inflation.

Domestic Affairs. Economic prospects for the new year were considerably dimmed by the world energy crisis and attendant price increases for petroleum. The government responded to the inflation problem with a series of sharp tax increases on automobiles, liquor, and tobacco, coupled with selective credit controls. Mid-1974 figures suggested a 6–8% growth in gross domestic product for the year (compared with a recent annual average of 12.5%) and a declining but still substantial rate of inflation. The economy's strength was indicated by its diversification, expectations of a 1974 balance of payments surplus, a currency fully backed by gold and foreign assets, and the highest per capita income in Asia excepting Japan.

Internal security became an issue in January when Palestinian and Japanese terrorists attacked a Singapore oil refinery, inflicting minor damage. In June, over 30 alleged members of an underground arm of the Malayan Communist party were arrested. The government strengthened its already formidable capability for controlling the press, the presumed target being two major Chinese-language dailies.

Foreign Relations. The Commonwealth Five-Power Defense Agreement was weakened by a scheduled withdrawal of Australian forces from Singapore at the end of the year. It was further eroded by indications that Britain's new Labour government planned to withdraw the 2,250 British troops stationed in the republic.

Strained relations with Malaysia, the other Asian signatory of the agreement, gradually improved during the year, despite various irritants. These included Malaysian efforts to build direct trade links with its export markets, bypassing Singapore's entrepot facilities. In addition, Malaysia's decision to establish diplomatic ties with Peking was seen in Singapore as potentially aggravating internal security problems within the republic.

MARVIN C. OTT, *Mount Holyoke College*

SINGAPORE • Information Highlights

Official Name: Republic of Singapore.
Location: Southeast Asia.
Area: 224 square miles (581 sq km).
Population (1973 est.): 2,300,000.
Chief City (1970 census): Singapore, the capital, 2,122,466.
Government: *Head of state,* Benjamin H. Sheares, president (took office 1971). *Head of government,* Lee Kuan Yew, prime minister (took office 1959). *Legislature* (unicameral)—Parliament.
Monetary Unit: Singapore dollar (2.46 S. dollars equal U. S.$1, July 1974).
Gross National Product (1972 est.): $3,110,000,000.
Manufacturing (major products): Petroleum products, steel, textiles, tires, wood products, processed foods, electronics, ships, assembled automobiles, electrical appliances, precision instruments.
Foreign Trade (1973): *Exports,* $3,610,000,000; *imports,* $5,070,000,000.

SOCIAL WELFARE

New developments in the field of social welfare during 1974 are reviewed in this article under the following headings: (1) General Survey; (2) Child Welfare; (3) Health Care; (4) U. S. Health Insurance; and (5) U. S. Social Security.

General Survey

There was famine in Africa and Bangladesh and widespread hunger elsewhere in the world in 1974. Such disasters could be only partly compensated for by national and international social welfare programs. In the United States, mounting unemployment and inflation were dislocating the economy. As a consequence public service employment and a guaranteed minimum income were considered increasingly as ways for the country to help its own poor and economically disadvantaged people.

WORLD DEVELOPMENTS

International agricultural, industrial, and population policies were recommended at the World Population Conference in Bucharest in August and at the World Food Conference in Rome in November. Their worldwide impact on social welfare institutions and programs will be felt gradually over a period of years.

National Programs. Gradual development of social welfare programs was indicated in the U. S. Department of Health, Education, and Welfare (HEW) publication *Social Security Programs Throughout the World, 1973.* It showed that 127 countries had one or more welfare programs in 1973, whereas only 58 countries had one or more programs in 1949. One hundred and twenty five countries have some sort of work-injury program, and 105 countries have some form of old-age, invalid, or survivor's benefits. A smaller number of countries have sickness and maternity, family allowance, or unemployment programs, and 15 countries have only one program.

From 1970 to 1972, 40 countries made changes or additions to their programs. Iceland, Mexico, Norway, Spain, and Yugoslavia changed many programs, while Denmark, France, and Ghana changed at least two during that period.

National Policies. The XVIIth International Conference on Social Welfare was held in Nairobi, Kenya, in July. It elicited a widespread concensus that governmental policies should be shifted to place greater emphasis on social balance sheets as against strictly economic and political goals. While many developed countries arrive at national social welfare decisions with only informal and irregular input from citizens, some developing countries have well-organized systems for encouraging grass-roots participation. They make use of local suggestions and reactions for needed national projects.

Developing countries recognize that work is an essential part of the national life. For instance, Tanzania has a slogan: "Freedom is Work." Also recognized is the government's part in the stimulation and support of socially important projects. In Ghana, villages that undertake such projects as building schools receive government help, perhaps in the form of a roof, after they have exhausted their own resources.

Child Welfare Needs. In May, Henry R. Labouisse, executive director of the United Nations Children's Fund (UNICEF), warned that severe malnutrition or starvation faces 400 million to 500 million children in the poorer countries of the world. Labouisse said that living conditions in the poorest and most populated countries may slip from the barely tolerable to the desperate.

UNICEF has approved a $138 million assistance program, and Executive Director Labouisse has said he would seek about $45 million more a year to help Asian and African countries that are under economic stresses.

U. S. DEVELOPMENTS

In the United States in 1974, there was a lull in the legislative fight over social welfare, but administrative consolidation and redirection continued. Early in President Ford's administration there were signs that the 1973 stalemate between the administration and Congress over social welfare matters might be broken. However, it was not clear how much Congressional initiative the new president would accept.

Public Service Employment. There was increased funding for public service employment, and there were indications that President Ford would recommend expansion of this program, probably along lines advocated by Sen. Jacob Javits (R-N. Y.) and Arthur F. Burns, chairman of the Federal Reserve Board.

Such a plan was outlined by the National Planning Association in July. It proposed: (1) A permanent national program to provide public service jobs for handicapped or other persons for whom such employment would be appropriate or essential; (2) doubling of this basic program when national unemployment reaches 4%, with further increases with each additional percent of unemployment; and (3) additional funds to be channeled into localities at any time they have heavy unemployment with no immediate prospect of improvement.

The basic program would be financed by an allocation of 0.5% of the annual federal budget. As projected, the cost of the program would be about $6 billion in a period when there is over 6% unemployment and the annual federal budget is $300 billion.

If passed by Congress, such a program would help traditional social welfare agencies avoid inflated caseloads where the basic need is employment; tend to reduce the social problems frequently associated with financial stresses; and produce needed community services. Such a program might assist in providing manpower for state and local public employment, which is expected to increase more rapidly than private employment during the next decade. Just before adjournment, Congress passed a less comprehensive measure to put 550,000 persons to work.

DEPT. OF HEALTH, EDUCATION, AND WELFARE

A mentally handicapped child is helped along the road to a normal life by the genuine sympathy and individual attention he receives from this young nurse.

Guaranteed Income Plan. Reportedly, HEW was preparing a new guaranteed income plan that not only would replace all existing public assistance programs but also would be available to low-income workers. The new proposal reportedly will call for a minimum income of $3,600. Thereafter, benefits would be reduced by $1.00 for every $2.00 of income, permitting a family of four to receive some benefits until its income exceeds $7,200. This is not far below the figure of $1,000 per person for which Sen. George McGovern was strongly criticized during the presidential campaign of 1972. Whether it will be high enough to satisfy those who opposed previous proposals as totally inadequate remains to be seen.

Previous opposition also came from persons who thought the expenditures would be too great and would destroy the incentive to work. Inclusion of low-income persons would elevate the cost. However, this would be a way to provide adequate income to the aged, handicapped, and children, without it being argued that relief recipients were getting more than those who were working. Research in recent years indicates little if any lessening of motivation to work when an assured income is provided. Numerous studies made for the Joint Economic Committee of Congress point to political problems related to cost as the major area of difficulty rather than work motivation.

Starting a new program involves a multitude of details. A guaranteed minimum income program with 25 million or more recipients might well have to be implemented in steps, with each step requiring formulation and testing of guidelines, regulations, and procedures at both federal and state levels. Experience has been gained in the Supplemental Security Program (SSI), which was inaugurated Jan. 1, 1974. This supposed program simplification was a tangled skein at the start, but by the end of 1974 it was in a fairly stable, if complicated, operating pattern.

Work Opportunities and Work Incentives. The discussion about public service employment and guaranteed income indicates an increasing willingness to expect the government to assume some responsibility for work opportunities and work incentives. In a decade when the "normal expectation" of unemployment has gone from one worker in 25 to one worker in 16, and when inflation is eroding the resources of nearly everyone, it is difficult to sustain the traditional attitude that both incentives and work opportunities have to be generated by the worker. Work training programs have failed, not because of an unwillingness to work but because there were no jobs to be had after training.

State Welfare Programs. During 1974 the federal administration put increasing pressure on the states to adopt business management and antifraud techniques in public welfare programs. "Accountability," "goal directed performance," and "error ratios" became commonly used terms.

RALPH PUMPHREY
Washington University, St. Louis

Child Welfare

In 1974 child welfare needs rose as the economic situation worsened, inflation greatly increased the cost of services, while federal funding declined. In consequence, services in many states deteriorated.

Social Security Act Regulations. A bill signed by the President in January mandated the suspension until 1975 of social service regulations proposed by the Department of Health, Education, and Welfare (HEW). These rules would have narrowed eligibility, limited funds, and removed the requirement that child day-care services comply with federal standards.

In December 1974 the passage of a new Title XX of the Social Security Act replaced the program of federal financial aid to states for social services. Effective July 1, 1975, the legislation mandated that eligibility for services, including child welfare and day care, be based on family income rather than welfare status, at considerably higher levels. The Federal Interagency Day Care Requirements of 1968 were retained, with some weakening modifications.

The Supplemental Security Income Program (SSI) went into effect in January 1974, with the federal government assuming the cost of cash assistance for the aged, blind, and disabled program. Handicapped children could become eligible for SSI benefits.

Child Abuse. On Jan. 30, 1974, the Child Abuse, Prevention, and Treatment Act became law, creating in HEW a National Center on Child Abuse and Neglect. Its functions include the compilation and dissemination of research and program information; development of training materials; technical assistance; and research.

Juvenile Delinquency. In September 1974, the Juvenile Justice and Delinquency Act was signed into law, authorizing $380 million over three years to combat juvenile delinquency.

Guaranteed Family Income. By the end of 1974, the possibility of family income legislation had again come to the fore. With poverty still afflicting 15% of the nation's children, this had important child-welfare implications. The administration completed a proposal to assure a jobless family of four a basic income of $3,600 a year, adjusted for family size.

MARY D. KEYSERLING, *Economic Consultant President, National Child Day Care Association*

Health Care

In 1974 government and health industry leaders in the United States were preoccupied by the rising costs of health care and its adverse effect on improving the availability of health care generally.

Cost Controls. A determined attempt by the Nixon administration to continue wage-price controls over health care was defeated by Congress in April. Convinced by provider organizations such as the American Medical Association (AMA) and the American Hospital Association that controls were not necessary, Congress let the controls die on April 30.

The following month, the cost of health-care services rose sharply, causing Caspar Weinberger, Secretary of Health, Education, and Welfare (HEW), to warn that failure of providers to police themselves could result in reinstitution of controls. After three months, the increases moderated somewhat, but Ford administration economists warned that a continued leveling off would be necessary.

Legislative Battles. In a continuation of a trend that had been intensifying since passage of the Medicare law in 1965, the health-care industry became increasingly involved in federal government affairs. For instance, attempts by Congress to write new laws governing federal aid to education of health professionals and to mandate improved planning of health-care facility construction encountered controversy in 1974.

The AMA and the Association of American Medical Colleges successfully opposed attempts by Congress to require that students, particularly those attending medical schools, "pay back" the taxpayers for federal aid to the schools by serving for a specified time in rural and urban areas where physicians and dentists are in short supply.

The objective of the Congress and the Nixon-Ford administrations in supporting comprehensive health-planning legislation was to restrict building of unneeded hospital bed space. Health economists pointed out that the maintenance of empty beds must be supported by patients in filled beds, a situation that tends to raise the cost of health care for the sick and their insurers. The controversy lay in the resistance of hospitals and localities to strengthened federal controls, but a compromise bill was passed.

Cooperation with PSROs. After an intense internal debate, delegates to the AMA convention in June acceded to the association's leadership and agreed to recommend that physicians cooperate with the Professional Standards Review Organizations (PSROs). The PSROs were mandated by the 1972 Social Security Amendments to ensure that professional services delivered under federally funded programs are necessary and of adequate quality.

Blood Program. A major step toward the establishment of a national voluntary blood-collection system was taken by HEW in September. After consultation with health and consumer organizations, HEW appointed an ad hoc committee to set up an American Blood Commission. The goal is to lower the cost of donor blood and to eliminate hepatitis as a hazard in blood transfusions.

Foreign Medical Graduates. Reliance on physicians educated in medical schools outside the United States, or foreign medical graduates (FMGs), was criticized by the Association of American Medical Colleges (AAMC) and several congressional committees. The AAMC noted that the number of FMGs practicing in the United States is approaching 20%. Congressional leaders called for laws restricting the use of FMGs, particularly in hospitals.

Health Care Abroad. In 1974, Great Britain's National Health Service was threatened with the greatest crisis since its inception in 1948 when physicians threatened to pull out wholesale in protest against proposed restrictions on private practice by doctors employed in the service.

Argentina began planning a vast new state-controlled health-care system as the government attempted to assure better distribution of services. Mexico announced plans to finance a new national health service; and Italy began making plans for a total overhaul of its health service.

JEROME F. BRAZDA
Editor, "Washington Report on Medicine & Health"

U. S. Health Insurance

The Nixon administration and the House Ways and Means Committee attempted to win enactment of National Health Insurance (NHI) legislation during 1974. The attempt failed, but several congressional Democratic leaders made statements interpreting their impressive gains at the polls in November as an indication that the people want NHI, and promising renewed attempts to enact a law in the 94th Congress.

President Nixon's submission of a liberalized version of his health insurance proposal of the previous year was interpreted in some quarters as an attempt to divert public attention from the Watergate scandals. And the sudden scheduling of NHI hearings by Chairman Wilbur Mills (D-Ark.) of the House Ways and Means Committee in July was interpreted by some political observers as a means of diverting the attention of committee members from a tax reform bill. Although the committee failed to agree on an NHI bill, the extensive hearings and an unprecedented open session brought the issues to public attention and underscored the intense controversy that surrounds National Health Insurance.

Chairman Mills announced early in the hearings that his committee would not vote on any single one of the many NHI bills before it but would strive to work out a compromise measure, building on the basic principles contained in the various bills.

Before the hearings began, Mills sought to come up with the basis for compromise. He introduced, in conjunction with Sen. Edward M. Kennedy (D-Mass.), an NHI bill that the two felt drew on the best and most popular features of such proposals as the Nixon administration's "Comprehensive Health Insurance Plan," the American Hospital Association's "Ameriplan," the American Medical Association's "Medicredit," the health insurance industry's "Healthcare" bill, and a measure introduced by Senators Russell Long (D-La.), chairman of the Senate Finance Committee, and Abraham Ribicoff (D-Conn.).

When a general lack of support for the Kennedy-Mills bill developed during the committee hearings, Chairman Mills drew up a new compromise proposal with the cooperation of Secretary Caspar Weinberger of the Department of Health, Education, and Welfare. The Mills-Weinberger bill, implicitly backed by the Nixon administration and later by the Ford administration, included so-called catastrophic protection for major illnesses, a requirement that employers offer their employees health insurance with the employers paying a substantial portion of the premiums, and a federal-state insurance plan for low-income families to replace the Medicaid program.

Much broader coverage would have been offered by the Mills-Kennedy plan. There was strong opposition to both bills, with intensive

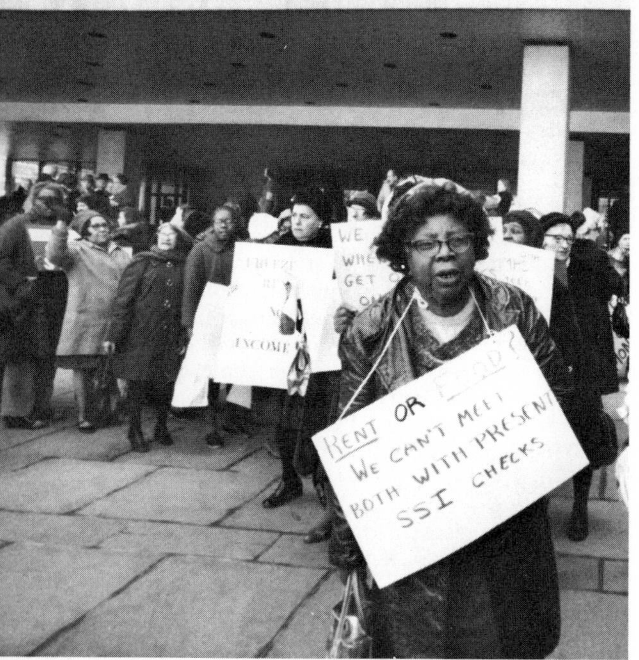

JACK MANNING/THE NEW YORK TIMES

Elderly people demonstrate for reform of the new federal welfare system, which has been plagued with long delays in payments resulting partly from computer malfunction.

lobbying by the insurance industry and American Medical Association. A majority of members of the Ways and Means Committee objected to a provision in the Mills-Weinberger bill that would have placed administration of the catastrophic protection plan in the Social Security Administration, financed by a payroll tax.

President Ford, who had taken office by the time the committee advanced to the voting stage, sent word that he favored approval of a bill along the lines of the Mills-Weinberger measure. However, seeing that the votes were not forthcoming for the basic principles he favored, Chairman Mills recessed the committee session indefinitely.

Later, President Ford sent Congress a post-election message saying he would "continue to seek agreement with the Congress on legislation" along the lines of the original Nixon administration bill if Congress would "join with me in cutting federal expenditures before we can afford this program." Congressional leaders interpreted the message as meaning that the President's enthusiasm for NHI had waned out of concern for inflation.

After the abortive Ways and Means attempt to write a NHI bill, Chairman Long of the Senate Finance Committee met with President Ford to discuss possible action by the Senate panel in 1975 on a health insurance compromise.

JEROME F. BRAZDA
Editor, "Washington Report on Medicine & Health"

U. S. Social Security

Laws enacted in July and August 1974 amended the supplemental security income program to provide for automatic cost-of-living increases in payment levels whenever such increases occur in social security monthly benefits, with the same percentage increase applying to both programs.

The 11% "cost-of-living" increase in social security benefits in 1974 triggered a determination relating to the maximum earnings base and to the exempt amount a beneficiary can earn without loss of benefits. Under this determination, beginning Jan. 1, 1975, the maximum amount of earnings taxable and creditable for benefits is $14,100. The most that a beneficiary can earn in 1975 without losing some of his benefits is $2,520, except that he can get his full benefit for any month in which he does not earn more than $210 and does not perform substantial self-employment services.

Late in 1974 the Secretary of Health, Education, and Welfare set new deductible and coinsurance rates for the hospital insurance part of Medicare: $92 for the hospital deductible; $23 for the daily hospital coinsurance rate after 60 days and $46 after 90 days; and $11.50 for the daily coinsurance rate in skilled-nursing facilities after 20 days.

Financing. In 1974, employers and employees each paid contributions of 5.85% on the first $13,200 of a worker's earnings. The rate for the self-employed was 7.9%. For all, 0.9% was earmarked for hospital insurance.

Coverage. In June 1974, about 79,000,000 persons were in employment covered by the Social Security Act. About 9 out of 10 gainfully employed persons have social security protection for themselves and their families against the risks of prolonged disability, old age, and death of the family earner. Medicare protection against the costs of hospital care is provided for social security and railroad retirement beneficiaries aged 65 and over, for persons eligible to receive a benefit because of disability, and for certain other persons.

Cash Benefits. In the 12 months ended June 30, 1974, monthly cash benefits for retired and disabled workers and their dependents and for the survivors of deceased insured workers totaled $53.7 billion, and lump-sum death payments amounted to $316 million. For November 1974, monthly benefits of $5.0 billion went to 30,744,000 persons. For a retired worker, the average November benefit was $188; it was $205 for a disabled worker.

Supplemental Security Income Operations. In January 1974 operations began under the supplemental security income program that was set up to replace federal grants to states for aid to the aged, blind, and disabled.

ARTHUR E. HESS
Deputy Commissioner of Social Security

SOUTH AFRICA

South Africa had a disquieting year in 1974, marked by a dramatic intensification of external pressures on its apartheid regime. As anticipated, a general election held in April resulted in yet one more overwhelming victory for the National party, which has been in power since 1948. But domestic affairs were overshadowed by the military coup in Portugal and subsequent developments in Mozambique and Angola, and by the move toward the creation of independent black states in Africa.

At the United Nations, South Africa came under the strongest attack yet, and was saved from expulsion from the organization only by the veto action of France, Great Britain, and the United States.

Mood of Uncertainty. As the year drew to a close in an atmosphere increasingly charged with talks of impending social change, public concerns were dominated by a new sense of urgency, if not crisis, and a considerable uncertainty. In large measure this uncertainty reflected the more general uncertainty concerning the future dispensation in southern Africa as a whole.

It also stemmed from the absence of any clear picture of what the government's various responses to the new situation on its frontiers and at the United Nations really meant. There was Ambassador Roslof Botha's statement in the General Assembly: "We will move away from discrimination." There was the remarkable speech of Prime Minister B. J. Vorster during the first week of November: "All I ask them is to give South Africa a chance of about six months . . . if South Africa is given the chance they will be surprised at where the country will stand in 6 to 12 months." In the same week, the leader of the opposition spoke of "changes so vast that they amount to nothing less than the destruction of a way of life or its rebirth by adaptation."

Whether such intimations of major policy changes referred only to external affairs—for example, the issues of Namibia/South West Africa, Rhodesia, and South Africa's role in Africa—or to the internal policies of apartheid, or both, were questions which remained to be answered.

UN Relations. The campaign against South Africa's apartheid policies continued to build up in the United Nations in 1974. On September 30 the General Assembly voted, as it had in previous years, to reject the credentials of the South African delegation. It requested the Security Council to review the relationship between the country and the United Nations. On October 30 the Security Council voted 10–3, with 2 abstentions, on a resolution to expel South Africa from the United Nations. The use of the veto by three permanent Security Council members—Britain, France, and the United States—kept South Africa in. On November 13 the majority in the Assembly voted 91–22, with 19 abstentions, to suspend South Africa's participation in the current session of the Assembly. Prime Minister Vorster's government responded by withdrawing its ambassador and freezing its annual contribution to the organization but maintaining its mission in New York. For the first time South Africa had included three nonwhite members in its delegation to the United Nations.

With regard to Namibia/South West Africa, Prime Minister Vorster stated in March that the people of South West Africa would decide their own future and that South Africa would neither dictate to the various groups nor allow the United Nations to do so.

Politics. At the general election held in April, the ruling National party increased its already overwhelming majority at the expense of the United party, the official opposition. At the same time the Progressive party succeeded in winning five more seats, thus for the first time providing parliamentary party support for Mrs. Helen Suzman. The parliamentary results were: National party, 124; United party, 41; and Progressive party, 6. The losses were sustained by the official opposition. The breakaway Herstige Nasionale party was rejected. Later, at a by-election, the Progressive party won a seventh seat from the United party.

Domestic Affairs. The year 1974 saw growing emphasis on the need for the removal of "petty" apartheid discrimination, but the main lines of government policy remained unchanged. Confronted with the Coloured Persons Representative Council's vote of no confidence in both the council and "separate development," Prime Minister Vorster told the council in September that government policy would not permit direct participation in Parliament for the Coloured peoples. A month later the leader of the opposition offered party support to the government for any political formula acceptable to the Coloured peoples.

RONALD B. BALLINGER
Rhode Island College

SOUTH AFRICA • Information Highlights

Official Name: Republic of South Africa.
Location: Southern tip of Africa.
Area: 471,444 square miles (1,221,037 sq km).
Population (1973 est.): 23,700,000.
Chief Cities (1970 census): Pretoria, the administrative capital, 543,950; Cape Town, the legislative capital, 691,296; Johannesburg, 642,967; Durban, 495,458.
Government: *Head of state,* Jacobus Johannes Fouché, president (took office 1968). *Head of government,* Balthazar John Vorster, prime minister (took office 1966). *Legislature*—Parliament: Senate and House of Assembly.
Monetary Unit: Rand (0.6729 rand equals U. S.$1, 1974).
Gross National Product (1972 est.): $21,060,000,000.
Manufacturing (major products): Textiles, iron and steel, chemicals, fertilizers, assembled automobiles, metals, machinery and equipment.
Major Agricultural Products: Sugarcane, tobacco, corn, fruits, wheat, dairy products, sheep, wool.
Foreign Trade (1973): *Exports,* $3,435,000,000; *Imports,* $5,020,000,000.

James Edwards (with wife Ann) is the first Republican in a century to be elected governor of South Carolina. The Democratic party's first choice was declared ineligible.

SOUTH CAROLINA

The year 1974 was an exciting one politically for South Carolina, with an unusual turn of events in the race for the governorship.

The Elections. State Senator James B. Edwards was elected the first Republican governor in a century, following a hectic year for the Democrats. A newcomer to politics, Charles D. Ravenel, had won the Democratic primary on July 30, defeating Congressman William Jennings Bryan Dorn. The state Supreme Court, however, ruled on September 23 that Mr. Ravenel did not meet the five-year residence requirement to be eligible for the governorship, having lived outside the state until March 1972. By convention, the Democratic party then selected Mr. Dorn as its candidate. Out of the confusion and the disillusionment of the Ravenel forces, Dr. Edwards won the election by carrying the heavily populated counties.

The Democrats otherwise had a good year. U. S. Sen. E. F. Hollings was reelected, as were six constitutional officers. A Democrat was elected lieutenant governor, and Democrats captured 5 of the 6 congressional seats, a gain of 1. Republican Floyd Spence retained his congressional seat by defeating Matthew J. Perry, the first black nominated for Congress.

Under the single-member district plan, Democrats won 107 of the 124 House seats, including 13 blacks. For the first time in history a black woman was elected. A number of key members in the House, however, failed to win reelection.

Legislation. The state had its longest legislative session in history, prolonged by a Justice Department order requiring the House to have single-member districts rather than a membership based on counties. Major legislation included an abortion law, a limited no-fault insurance plan, merger of programs on alcohol and drug abuse, a three-year automobile license, provision for funds for recreation lands and low-rent housing, and reenactment (over the governor's veto) of the death penalty.

Education and Social Services. The state continued to upgrade its public education through providing a substantial salary increase and health-insurance plan for teachers, expansion of kindergarten programs, improving vocational education, and adopting 12-month terms in several districts.

The Veterans Administration made a $20 million grant to the University of South Carolina to establish a second medical school. The university also established a School of Public Health and a graduate program in criminal justice.

Mental health institutions and the Medical University were reaccredited. State funds for mental health were materially increased. Substantial improvements were authorized in the correctional system.

Economy. The state economy remained sound, even though in the last quarter many textile plants reduced the workweek. Unemployment in South Carolina remained below the national average. Industrial expansion equaled the growth of previous years, and the state had a substantial surplus of revenues. Although hampered by spring rains and insects, more acres were planted, and it was a good agricultural year. Plans were approved for major port expansion, especially at Charleston. Continued improvements were made in the tourist areas by the completion of major facilities on the coast and the mountain foothills highway.

ROBERT H. STOUDEMIRE
University of South Carolina

— SOUTH CAROLINA • Information Highlights —

Area: 31,055 square miles (80,432 sq km).
Population (1973 est.): 2,726,000. *Density:* 88 per sq mi.
Chief Cities (1970 census): Columbia, the capital, 113,542; Charleston, 66,945; Greenville, 61,436; Spartanburg, 44,546.
Government (1974): *Chief Officers*—governor, John C. West (D); lt. gov., Earle E. Morris, Jr. (D). *General Assembly*—Senate, 46 members (43 D, 3 R); House of Representatives, 124 members (103 D, 21 R).
Education (1973–74): *Enrollment*—public elementary schools, 384,928 pupils; public secondary, 236,260; nonpublic, 29,300; colleges and universities, 94,699 students. *Public school expenditures,* $493,107,000 ($856 per pupil).
State Finances (fiscal year 1973): *Revenues,* $1,489,-575,000; *expenditures,* $1,332,133,000.
Personal Income (1973): $10,406,000; per capita, $3,817.
Labor Force (July 1974): *Nonagricultural wage and salary earners,* 1,054,600; *insured unemployed,* 17,-600 (2.2%).

SOUTH DAKOTA

Democrats and Republicans divided major offices about equally in the 1974 elections as 71.8% of the state's registered voters went to the polls. The year brought financial losses to agriculture and tourism because of inflation and adverse weather conditions.

Election. Democrats nominated George McGovern and Richard Kneip as candidates for third terms in the U. S. Senate and the governorship, respectively. Through personal popularity and a campaign commitment to correct "injustices of the economic system," McGovern won with relative ease over war hero Leo Thorsness, although Thorsness enjoyed strong support because of his admirable record as a prisoner in North Vietnam, and his political conservatism. Largely as a reward for achievement in the reorganization of state government, Kneip also won with a substantial percentage of votes over former state Highway Department Director John Olson, and became the first governor in the state's history to be elected to a third term.

Despite the satisfaction of reelecting McGovern and Kneip, Democrats could not claim a complete victory. Republican U. S. Congressman James Abnor won reelection in the 2d Congressional District, and 32-year-old Republican Larry Pressler unseated incumbent Democrat Frank Denholm in the 1st District. Republicans also won about half of the important constitutional offices in state government, and gained a slight majority in the state Legislature.

Legislation. In the 1974 legislative session, attention centered on a bill introduced to enlarge the University of South Dakota's two-year medical school into a four-year institution. The medical school had served since 1907 as a "half-school," offering the science courses required for entry into third-year classes in medical schools outside the state. The bill passed with limited opposition, and the medical school announced its intention to admit four-year candidates beginning in the fall of 1975.

An appropriations bill established the state budget for 1974–75 at approximately $130 million—$18 million more than the budget for 1973–74. Increases resulted from needs in education, youth programs, and social welfare.

Economy. Despite a 3% increase in the labor force, and improvements in business trends, most South Dakotans experienced serious economic problems during 1974. Livestock producers paid more for feed, but were paid as much as 25% less for their animals than they had received in 1973. Farmers faced higher production costs but limited production due to drought during the growing season and frosts before harvest time. Corn growers expected to produce only 80 million bushels in 1974—a reduction of 43% from production levels in 1973—and stated that the increase in corn prices would not compensate for the decline in yield.

SOUTH DAKOTA • Information Highlights

Area: 77,047 square miles (199,552 sq km).
Population (1973 est.): 685,000. *Density:* 9 per sq mi.
Chief Cities (1970 census): Pierre, the capital, 9,699; Sioux Falls, 72,488; Rapid City, 43,836.
Government (1974): *Chief Officers*—governor, Richard F. Kneip (D); lt. gov., William Dougherty (D). *Legislature*—Senate, 35 members; House of Representatives, 70 members.
Education (1973–74): *Enrollment*—public elementary schools, 106,400 pupils; public secondary, 51,400; nonpublic, 11,600; colleges and universities, 26,530 students. *Public school expenditures,* $138,600,000 ($921 per pupil).
State Finances (fiscal year 1973): *Revenues,* $356,583,000; *expenditures,* $346,758,000.
Personal Income (1973): $2,943,000,000; per capita, $4,296.
Labor Force (July 1974): *Nonagricultural wage and salary earners,* 214,000; *insured unemployed,* 2,100 (1.5%).

Businessmen involved in tourist industries experienced even greater losses. Motels and campgrounds were seldom filled to capacity, and filling stations could not sell their quotas of gasoline. The owners reported that fewer tourists entered the state than in any year in memory.

American Indians. The American Indian Movement (AIM), led by Russell Means, was no less active than it had been in 1973, when its members occupied Wounded Knee, but showed a greater tendency to "work within the system." In February, Means campaigned to unseat Oglala Sioux President Richard Wilson in a tribal election at Pine Ridge Reservation. He came close to victory with strong support among young and elder members of the tribe, due to his promise to promote greater self-determination for Indians, more economic opportunities on the reservation, and a general revival of Indian culture. Wilson won the election by a small margin because he had support from voters between 25 and 55 years of age—many of whom had not voted in a presidential election for many years but turned out because the president promised to prevent another militant protest like the one at Wounded Knee in 1973.

During April and May, Means' AIM followers became more militant as many of them congregated outside the court house at Sioux Falls. At one point they broke windows and battled the police, as several AIM members were tried and sentenced for crimes they allegedly committed in western South Dakota a year earlier. When the protesters failed to bring the release of all of those accused, Means and other leaders declared South Dakota to be a "war zone," and threatened serious reprisals.

Except for a few incidents, the reprisals did not materialize. Governor Kneip denounced the "war zone" declaration as an "inflammatory" outburst designed to "fan the flame of racism." The voters expressed approval for the governor's strong position by electing William Janklow, leading prosecuting attorney in the trials at Sioux Falls, to the office of attorney general.

HERBERT T. HOOVER
University of South Dakota

NASA

NASA

(*Above*) Russian cosmonauts and U. S. astronauts of projected Apollo-Soyuz mission meet President Ford at White House. (*Left*) Astronaut Vance Brand and cosmonaut A. S. Ivanchenko in docking module trainer at Johnson Space Center, Houston.

space exploration

Achievements in manned space flight in 1974 were highlighted by a new living-in-space record set by the Skylab-3 crew and by good progress toward a joint U. S.-USSR mission set for 1975. Exploration of the planets continued, notably by a Mercury-Venus probe and a Jupiter-Saturn probe. Advances in space technology were focused on the development of a space shuttle.

MANNED SPACE FLIGHT

The highly successful U. S. Skylab program to determine man's ability to live and work in space for extended periods of time came to an end early in 1974 with the return of the Skylab-3 crew. No manned U. S. missions were launched in 1974. However, American and Soviet preparations were proceeding on schedule for a historic joint mission in 1975 when a manned Apollo spacecraft and a manned Soviet spacecraft will rendezvous and dock in orbit.

Mission of Skylab-3 Crew. Astronauts Gerald Carr, Edward Gibson, and William Pogue—the Skylab-3 crew—left the Skylab space station and returned to earth in their Apollo spacecraft on Feb. 8, 1974, setting a record of 84 days of living in earth orbit in a weightless environment. Doctors found them wobbly-legged but apparently even in better shape than the two previous Skylab crews, whose 28-day and 59-day missions also broke endurance records.

The Skylab-3 crew was given credit for an exceptional performance. While living on board Skylab, they maintained an intense level of exercise, performed new medical tests, photographed comet Kohoutek, and repaired an air cooling system. In addition, they returned to earth with thousands of photographs of the sun and earth and 100,000 feet (30,500 meters) of tapes that recorded scans of the earth's surface on different wavelengths of light.

Salyut 3. On June 25, the USSR launched Salyut 3, the third in their series of Salyut unmanned space stations. After a series of maneuvers, the space station was put in a circular orbit awaiting the arrival of a manned Soyuz spacecraft. In July the crew of Soyuz 14 lived and worked aboard the space station. After the departure of the cosmonauts, Salyut 3 continued unmanned operations and data collection. The space station ejected a data capsule that was recovered in the USSR on September 23, thus ending the mission of Salyut 3. It was the most successful Soviet space station thus far.

Soyuz-14 Mission. Soyuz 14 was launched on July 3, carrying cosmonauts Pavel Popovich and Yuri Artyukhin. They proceeded to rendezvous and dock with the Salyut-3 space station on July 4 and commenced to activate the station and perform experiments. During their stay of almost 15 days, the cosmonauts photographed the earth's surface and conducted medical and biological experiments. Other experiments were conducted to study the polarization of the solar light and the atmosphere.

After placing Salyut 3 in an automatic mode in preparation for the next rendezvous mission, the crew of Soyuz 14 returned to earth on July 19, landing in Kazakhstan.

Soyuz-15 Mission. Soyuz 15 was launched on August 26 with rookie cosmonauts Lt. Col. Gennady Sarafanov and Col. Lev Demin on board. A rendezvous with Salyut 3 was to have occurred on the 16th orbit of the spacecraft, but Soyuz 15 missed Salyut 3 completely. The cosmonauts rendezvoused with and made repeated approaches to Salyut 3 on August 27, but no hard docking was achieved. Repeated docking attempts were made during the next day but with no apparent success.

The unsuccessful docking attempts began to place the cosmonauts in serious danger of running out of power and dictated a return to earth in darkness on August 29 after spending only three days in orbit. Soyuz 15 landed at night in Kazakhstan in difficult weather conditions. Previously, only Soyuz 10 had been recovered by the Soviets at night.

According to Maj. Gen. Vladimir Shatalov, chief of cosmonaut training, the three-day duration of the mission was according to plan, and the landing at night was one of the major objectives of the mission.

Soyuz-16 Mission. The Soviet Union rocketed Soyuz 16 into earth orbit on Dec. 2, 1974. It carried a two-man crew, Air Force Col. Anatoly Filipchenko, 46, and Nikolai Rukavishnikov, a 42-year-old civilian. The spacecraft and its crew returned safely to earth on the snow-blanketed steppes of central Kazakhstan on December 8, completing a six-day mission.

The Soviet press said that the Soyuz-16 flight was specifically intended to prepare for the 1975 rendezvous of Apollo and Soyuz spacecraft. Tass, the official press agency, described the Soyuz 16 as identical to the Soyuz-type spacecraft that will be used for the 1975 rendezvous and docking missions. Maj. Gen. Shatalov declared that Soviet cosmonauts now were "fully prepared for staging the joint Soyuz-Apollo flight."

EARTH SATELLITES AND SPACE PROBES

Venus-Mercury Probe. Mariner 10, a 1,160-pound (525-kg) spacecraft launched on Nov. 3, 1973, obtained pictures of the Venusian clouds on Feb. 5, 1974, as it flew by Venus en route to an encounter with Mercury. The spacecraft's twin television cameras took the first close-up high-resolution pictures of the Venusian cloud cover, showing that it has at least three major layers and distinct convection currents resembling atmospheric patterns on earth. The velocity of the clouds in the equatorial region was estimated to be greater than 328 feet (100 meters) per second. Mariner 10's other experiments recorded significant data on Venus' atmosphere and magnetosphere.

A month and a half later Mariner 10 reached the vicinity of Mercury and passed within 460 miles (740 km) of its surface on March 29. Television pictures of the planet showed an incredibly rough terrain. A wide variety of impact craters, valleys, and features that resemble the mare regions on the moon were recorded at resolutions as fine as 500 feet (152 meters). Other pictures showed deep rills, valleys, and fault lines, possibly tracing breaks in Mercury's crust or outlining lava flow patterns.

A weak magnetic field was detected around the planet, and the presence of a bow shock wave indicated that the magnetic field deflects the solar wind around the planet. A radio experiment found no evidence of an ionosphere or atmosphere. An infrared radiometer on board the spacecraft recorded temperatures ranging from 370° F (188° C) on Mercury's dayside to a low of —300 °F (—185 °C) on the nightside.

As the spacecraft flew by Mercury, it was in an orbit about the sun with a period of 176 days, twice the orbital period of Mercury. Therefore, Mariner 10 was able to complete a second flyby of the planet on September 21, obtaining additional data on the planet.

Mars Probes. Four Soviet probes that were launched in the summer of 1973 arrived in the vicinity of Mars in early 1974. Mars 4 failed in its mission to orbit Mars and shot past the planet on February 10 with its TV cameras operating. Mars 5, a companion spacecraft, arrived at the planet on February 12 and was successfully inserted into a highly elliptical orbit with a closest approach of 1,095 miles (1,760 km) above the Martian surface. Shortly thereafter, the spacecraft began sending pictures of the Martian surface to earth. Mars 6 and Mars 7 failed in their attempts to soft-land capsules on the surface of Mars. However, during entry into the Martian atmosphere, Mars 6 detected variations in the atmospheric water content, tending to indicate an air-to-ground cycling of water on the planet.

Jupiter-Saturn Probe. Pioneer 11, launched on April 5, 1973, flew within 26,600 miles (42,800 km) of Jupiter on Dec. 2, 1974, bettering the record of Pioneer 10, the first Jupiter

ROCKWELL INTERNATIONAL SPACE DIVISION

(*Above*) Mock-up of Space Shuttle orbiter being developed for NASA in Downey, Calif. (*Left*) Artist's conception of the orbiter in flight, showing solid rocket boosters that will be used to augment the orbiter's main engines during the initial phase of the vehicle's launch from earth.

ROCKWELL INTERNATIONAL SPACE DIVISION

probe, which flew within 81,000 miles (13,350 km) of the planet on Dec. 3, 1973. Pioneer 11 obtained the first pictures of Jupiter's polar regions and sent back data on the most intense part of the planet's radiation belts.

Lunar Probes. The USSR launched Luna 22 on May 29 and placed the spacecraft in an orbit around the moon on June 3. Its mission was to photograph the lunar surface and obtain altimeter readings and measurements of the gamma radiation from the surface.

Luna 23, launched by the USSR on October 23, was placed in a lunar orbit for a quick flight down to the surface. However, the Soviets reported that the moon probe was so badly damaged in landing on the moon's Sea of Crises that it could only carry out a limited investigation.

Solar Probes. The first of two Helios satellites was launched on December 8 in a West German-U. S. program to gather scientific information about the sun's influence on earth. Scientists hoped the craft would make three orbits of the sun, coming to within 28 million miles (46.8 million km) of our star.

Communications Satellites. Two Western Union communications satellites were launched by the United States during 1974—Westar A on April 13 and Westar B on October 10. These 660-pound (300-kg) satellites were the first in a series of domestic communications satellites designed to provide transmission of television, voice, and digital data throughout the continental United States, Alaska, Hawaii, and Puerto Rico. Each satellite has 12 transponders, each of which has the capacity to relay 600 two-way voice channels, or one color television program with audio, or digital data at a rate of 50 million bits per second.

On May 30, the United States launched the ATS-6, the sixth and most sophisticated of the series of applications technology satellites. The 1,860-pound (1,270 kg) spacecraft, which has a large antenna and powerful transmitters, will be used for transmitting educational and medical television programs to remote areas in the United States and India. In addition, the first successful microwave transmission from ship to shore was accomplished via the ATS-6 on August 20. Further operational systems of this type for maritime and aeronautical applications could save millions of dollars by speeding up day-to-day operations.

On November 21 the U. S. launched the Intelsat IV F-8 satellite for providing international communication across the Pacific. This was followed by the U. S. launch of the Symphonie communications satellite. The 886-pound (399-kg) spacecraft, built by France and West Germany, will be used for experimental communications between Europe, Africa, and South America.

The USSR launched six communications satellites in 1974—two in the Molniya-1 class (Molniya 1-27, 1-28) on April 20 and October 24; three in the Molniya-2 class (Molniya 2-9, 2-10, 2-11) on April 27, July 23, and December 21; and a new geostationary communications satellite, Molniya 1-S, on July 29. The Soviet-sponsored intersputnik satellite communication system was inaugurated in February with regular relays between Cuba and Russia via Molniya 2.

Weather Satellites. On May 17 the United States launched SMS-1, the first of a new class of weather satellites designed to provide continuous pictures of cloud cover over the United States and the Atlantic Ocean, both day and night. This synchronous meteorological satellite also will be very valuable for locating, tracking, and predicting severe storms such as hurricanes.

The fifth in a series of U. S. polar-orbiting weather satellites, NOAA 4, was launched on November 15. This satellite carries sensors that permit observations of the global cloud cover on a daily basis. It also measures the earth's atmospheric radiants, and this data can be used to determine vertical temperature profiles of the atmosphere over every part of the earth's surface at least twice daily. This information is important in improving the accuracy of long-range weather forecasts.

The USSR launched five meteorological satellites in its Meteor series in 1974. Meteor 16, 17, 18, 19, and 20 were launched on March 5, April 24, July 9, October 29, and December 17.

Cooperative Satellite Programs. On July 16 the United States launched a West German satellite, Aeros B, as part of a cooperative program between the two countries. It will study the state and behavior of the upper atmosphere.

The Netherlands Astronomical Satellite (ANS A), the first U. S.-Netherlands cooperative satellite, was launched on August 30 by the United States. The primary objective of ANS A is to study stellar ultraviolet and X-ray sources.

On October 15, the UK-5 spacecraft was launched off the coast of Africa in a U. S.-United Kingdom cooperative program. The satellite's six scientific instruments are to increase knowledge of galactic and extragalactic X rays.

The USSR launched Intercosmos 11 and 12 on May 17 and October 31, respectively. These satellites are cooperative efforts of Bulgaria, Czechoslovakia, East Germany, Hungary, Rumania, and the USSR. The spacecraft are designed to study radiation density, the upper atmosphere, and the flow of micrometeorites.

PITT G. THOME
National Aeronautics and Space Administration

ADVANCES IN SPACE TECHNOLOGY

During 1974 space technology was increasingly focused on the development of the space shuttle, a hybrid spacecraft and delta-wing airplane that can enter earth orbit and then return to earth to land like an airplane.

Space-Shuttle Program. In 1974 the National Aeronautics and Space Administration (NASA), its contractors, and its European associates developed plans and programs leading to a final configuration of the space shuttle. Its purpose would be to place U. S. and European satellites into orbits for later retrieval or to make repairs to satellites or space stations already in orbit.

Rockwell International developed a plan that NASA will follow during the next decade in shuttle development and deployment. This plan calls for a four-man flight crew to operate the space shuttle. The crew will have the option of manually overriding automatic controls and will

NASA

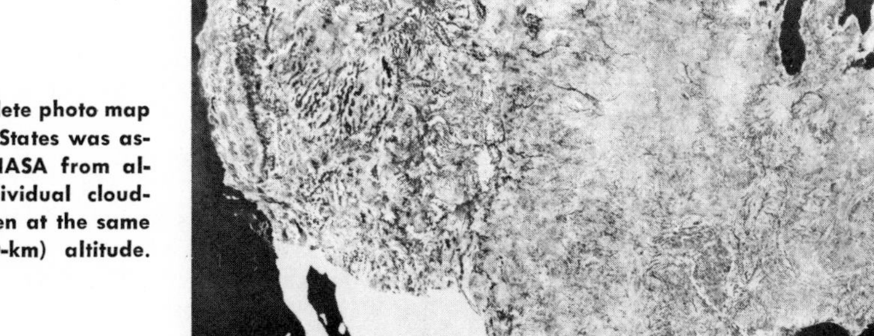

This first complete photo map of the United States was assembled by NASA from almost 600 individual cloud-free shots taken at the same 560-mile (900-km) altitude.

have full responsibility for primary control while the shuttle is in orbit. Lift-off of the shuttle will be automatic after countdown, with the flight crew monitoring the functioning of all major subsystems. At lift-off, the space shuttle will be riding piggyback on two recoverable solid-fuel booster rockets and a disposable liquid-fuel tank. The gross lift-off weight will be 4.16 million pounds (1.89 million kgs).

The space shuttle will weigh 150,000 pounds (68,000 kgs) and will carry payloads from 32,000 to 65,000 pounds (14,500 to 29,500 kgs) in its payload bay, which will be 60 feet (18 meters) long and have a diameter of 15 feet (4.6 meters).

The shuttle will have three liquid hydrogen-oxygen main rocket engines, each having a 375,000-pound (170-000-kg) thrust at takeoff. A tank strapped on the underside of the shuttle will carry liquid hydrogen and oxygen for the three main rocket engines. The tank will be 150 feet (46 meters) long, 28 feet (8.5 meters) in diameter, and weigh 1.6 million pounds (0.73 million kgs) when loaded with propellants.

Two solid-fuel rocket booster engines strapped on the underside of the shuttle will provide a 5-million-pound (2.3-million-kg) thrust in the early phases of launch. Thiokol Chemical Corp. is building these engines. Each solid-fuel booster rocket will be 145 feet (44 meters) long, 11 feet (3.4 meters) in diameter, and weigh 1.2 million pounds (0.54 million kgs).

The solid-fuel boosters will be jettisoned as the space shuttle approaches near orbit. Various small liquid-propellant rocket engines for maneuvering are mounted at different points on the space shuttle to permit correct attitude control as the shuttle flies into low earth orbit. The large fuel tank that powers the three liquid-fuel rocket engines will be jettisoned shortly after the solid-fuel rockets have been discarded.

Space experts inspect Hawkeye, a satellite built at the University of Iowa to examine earth's magnetic field. The craft was launched successfully in June.

UNIVERSITY OF IOWA NEWS SERVICE

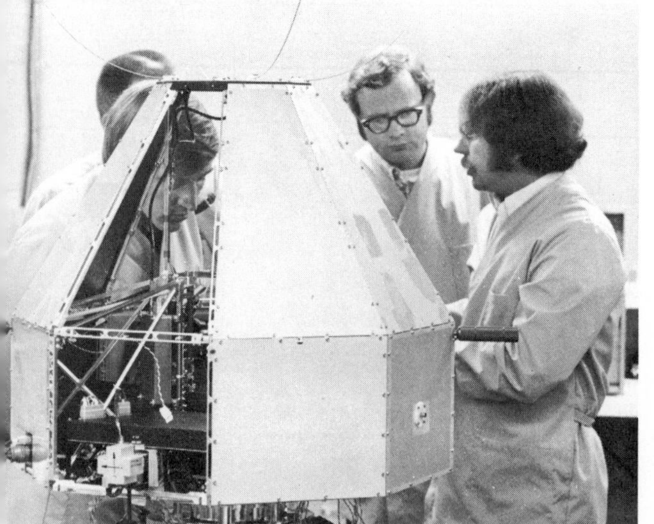

The shuttle, then in a low earth orbit, will eject its payload into its own or a higher orbit. The shuttle then will depart from orbit by using retrofiring liquid-fuel rocket engines that will slow the vehicle down to a maneuverable speed in the atmosphere. At this point the shuttle becomes a large metal glider with only small thrusters for maneuvering to a landing.

The crew will approach the runway of an airport near the Kennedy Space Center in Florida and land there. Then the shuttle will be towed from the runway to a maintenance hangar where it will be refurbished for another flight. Each shuttle vehicle will need about 40 reaction-control rocket engines with a planned lifetime of 10 years or 100 flights.

Environmental Tests in the Atmosphere. The Department of Transportation Climatic Assessment Program, NASA, and the military are conducting environmental tests in the upper atmosphere with the Titan 3D launch vehicle. These tests, begun in March, will continue for several years. Each flight of a Titan will be monitored by a weather reconnaissance aircraft.

The Titan 3D uses large strap-on solid-fuel rockets whose exhaust is similar to that of the space shuttle. It is expected that the test flights will reveal a great deal about ozone changes, nucleation, and other atmospheric disturbances that could be traced to exhaust pollution of the upper atmosphere. If such tests show that the exhaust depletes the ozone layer shielding the earth's surface from lethal ultraviolet radiation or produces other harmful effects, then new rockets with nonpolluting exhausts may have to be developed by scientists for the shuttle.

Air-Launched Missiles. The U. S. Air Force is studying the possibilities of launching intercontinental ballistic missiles from aircraft in level flight. The purpose of this program is to ensure that a fraction of the U. S. missile force is reasonably secure from first-strike enemy action. (See also DEFENSE.)

Solar Energy. Aerospace companies are on the verge of breakthroughs for cheaper silicon solar cells, which convert sunlight directly into electrical energy. If solar cells costing $100 per watt of power can be reduced to $1 per watt, an era of cheap and plentiful solar energy may be at hand.

Mars Rover. NASA is studying a rover vehicle for exploration on Mars. In the 1979 Viking mission a spacecraft may land on Mars carrying a four-wheel vehicle smaller but similar to the lunar rover. The Mars rover will cruise in a programmed path, gathering data by video scanning, soil samplers, and other tools. Its data will be telemetered to the Viking spacecraft and then back to earth.

KURT R. STEHLING
U. S. Government Aerospace Consultant

SPAIN

The year 1974 was a difficult one for the regime of Generalissimo Francisco Franco. The Spanish church moved steadily away from its liaison with the government, and the economy, flourishing in 1973, took a sharp drop in 1974. No visible progress was made toward settling Spain's foreign disputes over the future of Gibraltar and Spanish Sahara.

Politics. Premier Carlos Arias Navarro, who took office after the assassination of Premier Luis Carrero Blanco in December 1973, was considered less of a "strong man" than his predecessor. He was heard from less often and conducted his duties quietly.

The overthrow of the dictatorship in Portugal by the armed forces in April produced repercussions in Spain. The authorities sought to insure against a similar coup in Spain, and plans were formulated, although with seeming reluctance, for some liberalization. One such plan, announced in August, provided for establishment of "political associations"—right-wing, center-right, center, and left—with the expectation that they would develop into political parties. Communist groups would continue to be outlawed.

Spanish Chief-of-Staff Gen. Manuel Diez-Alegria, considered a liberal among military figures, was ousted in June because of fear that he might be planning to lead a military coup against the government. He was replaced by Gen. Carlos Fernández Vallespin, a conservative. At the same time, and also in reaction to Portuguese events, the Spanish government seized four newspapers within a week, two for printing editorials approving the Portuguese coup and two for attacks on the regime.

Franco, approaching 82, was hospitalized on July 9 for phlebitis and blood clots in a thigh. Bulletins by doctors were uniformly optimistic. But Prince Juan Carlos de Borbón, 36, since 1969 king-designate of Spain, temporarily took Franco's place as head of state. Juan Carlos presided over two cabinet meetings and signed many decrees, but did nothing on his own initiative. Liberal monarchists and Spanish liberals in general were known to prefer his father, Prince Juan de Borbón, 61, who has never renounced his claim to the throne. The senior prince remained silent, however, during the weeks when Juan Carlos nominally exercised an authority really wielded by Premier Arias.

SPAIN • Information Highlights

Official Name: Spanish State.
Location: Iberian Peninsula in southwestern Europe.
Area: 194,897 square miles (504,782 sq km).
Population (1973 est.): 34,200,000.
Chief Cities (1970 census): Madrid, the capital, 3,146,071; Barcelona, 1,745,142; Valencia, 653,690.
Government: *Head of state,* Francisco Franco, caudillo (leader) (officially assumed power Aug. 1939). *Head of government,* Carlos Arias Navarro, premier (took office Jan. 1974). *Legislature* (unicameral)—Las Cortes Españolas.
Monetary Unit: Peseta (57.30 pesetas equal U. S.$1, May 1974).
Gross National Product (1973 est.): $55,000,000,000.
Manufacturing (major products): Iron and steel, electrical machinery, automobiles, textiles, chemicals, ships, processed foods, leather.
Major Agricultural Products: Wheat, rye, barley, corn, citrus fruits, vegetables, almonds, olives, potatoes, fish, forest products, sheep.
Foreign Trade (1973): *Exports,* $5,162,000,000; *imports,* $9,538,000,000.

UPI

Prince Juan Carlos, Spain's acting chief of state during Francisco Franco's illness, signs a Spanish-United States defense pledge. U. S. Ambassador Horacio Rivero looks on.

Franco's health was reported "fully recovered" on July 23, and after a vacation in his native Galicia he resumed his powers as head of state on September 2. The resignation on October 1 of Gen. António de Spínola, who had led the Portuguese government since the April coup, and the growing possibility of a Communist instead of a liberal regime in Portugal unquestionably strengthened Spanish conservative sentiment and shook even the moderates.

The Church. The Spanish church continued to move away from its once close relationship with the government. Friction was especially acute in the Basque area. The authorities tried unsuccessfully in March to force Bishop Antonio Añoveros Ataún into exile because, in a sermon, he advocated cultural autonomy for the Basque minority. The government desisted when the permanent commission of the Spanish Episcopal Council fully supported the bishop. The Spanish clergy increasingly tended to side with laborers in industrial disputes, and 48 priests were jailed during the first half of 1974 for critical sermons.

The concordat of 1953 between the Spanish government and the Vatican was scheduled to be revised as a series of separate agreements. Important to the discussions will be the tax privileges enjoyed by the church and the $18 million annual subsidy paid it by the state. While the negotiations will take place between the government and the papacy, the wishes of the Spanish bishops will be important in the decisions. One major question involved the selection of bishops, hitherto resting mainly with Franco but with some papal participation. The Vatican, having recently come to dislike the arrangement, had refused cooperation, thus leaving eight Spanish dioceses vacant. The government wished to change a situation that gave priests special status and sometimes placed them above the law, holding that they had used their positions to undermine the regime.

Economy. The Spanish economy, flourishing despite agricultural recession in 1973, experienced reverses in 1974. Increased costs of travel and of Spanish accommodations caused tourism and the revenue it brought to fall off substantially. Remittances from Spanish workers abroad were severely curtailed by European price rises and general recession.

One of the consequences of Spain's rapidly expanding industrialism has been a great increase in energy imports. Spain, though classed as a friendly nation by Arab oil exporters, was charged the same price for crude oil as other customers. Having very little petroleum, natural gas, uranium, and high-grade coal of its own, Spain found its bill for combustible liquids mounting from 63 billion pesetas ($1,100,000,000) in 1972 to an estimated 200 billion ($3,500,000,000) in 1974. Increased energy costs were passed on to the domestic consumer, and rates for electricity, gasoline, butane gas, and transportation rose, in some cases, as much as 70% above recent levels.

Generalissimo Francisco Franco escorts his 21-year-old granddaughter Mariola Martinez Bordiu to the altar for her wedding in the chapel of El Pardo Palace, Madrid.

UPI

Rising prices imposed hardships on the Spanish working class. The minimum legal wage was only 186 pesetas (about $3.30) per day, which was utterly insufficient to support a family of four on any scale. Average wages fluctuated between 12,000 ($210) and 18,000 ($315) pesetas per month, but many workers earned less, and laborers often either took two jobs or worked long overtime. While strikes continued to be legally forbidden, the government seemed to be losing control of the labor unions, and 1974 saw severe strikes with more threatened. The Arias government limited annual pay increases to 14.5%, but wage demands were expected to run to about 20%. Multinational firms that in the past had found Spain a profitable place to invest or start new industries, were hard hit by strikes and began to find the prospect less inviting.

Foreign Affairs. The perennial question of Gibraltar arose again with Great Britain. Exploratory talks about its return to Spain were held in Madrid in May, but there was no agreement on terms. The British asked immediate easement of Spanish restrictions regarding the air approach to the "Rock," and the Spaniards refused a concession that would "consolidate" the British presence there. The Gibraltarians had voted overwhelmingly in 1967 against incorporation in Spain, and Britain's representative in the United Nations General Assembly stated in October 1974 that his country would never turn them over against their wishes.

A dispute of mounting importance continued over Spanish Sahara, claimed for several years by Morocco, which said that it must be "integrated with the motherland." Although the claim had doubtful historicity, Spain took it seriously enough to promise the Saharans a referendum on their future in 1975. Morocco spurned such a solution, insisting that the approximately 60,000 migratory native tribesmen would not vote in a referendum, thus leaving the decision to the few townsmen of largely Spanish stock. An apparent weakening of Spain's claim was seen in October when Foreign Minister Pedro Cortina Mauri spoke of eventual independence for Spanish Sahara, which he called "Western" Sahara. The real issue was economic because of the valuable offshore fisheries and rich phosphate deposits of the territory. Spain expected to ship 10 million tons of phosphate in 1974, offering serious competition to Morocco, the world's largest phosphate exporter.

CHARLES E. NOWELL, *University of Illinois*

WIDE WORLD

SPORTS

(*Above*) Muhammad Ali knocks out George Foreman in the 8th round of their heavyweight title fight, held in Kinshasa, Zaire, October 30. (*Below*) Gene Tenace (*top*) and Ray Fosse leap on reliever Rollie Fingers after Oakland beat the Dodgers for third straight World Series win.

UPI

By Bill Braddock
"The New York Times"

Any bewildered citizen who turned to sports in 1974 as an escape from inflation, the energy crisis, or the political upheavals was likely to become more befuddled instead by the confusion among owners, players, and fans.

Pro football was in turmoil because of a player strike in the established league and the plans of a number of its stars to jump to a new group. The American Basketball Association, unable to effect a merger with the National Basketball Association, switched franchises, coaches, players, and commissioners. Hockey was still trying to settle differences between the older National Hockey League and the young World Hockey Association as each expanded. Tennis continued its bickering among player groups as well as nations, which prevented play of the final Davis Cup round. The Amateur Athletic Union and various groups of athletes had not solved their differences.

Baseball finally came up with a black manager, Frank Robinson at Cleveland, but Henry Aaron, ready to retire after breaking Babe Ruth's home run record, found there was no place for him in the Atlanta Braves' front office (so he signed with Milwaukee). Charles O. Finley,

UPI

Jimmy Connors and Chris Evert, top-ranked American tennis stars, hold trophies of their Wimbledon victories. The couple later called off their planned wedding.

owner of the Oakland A's, winner of the World Series for a third straight year, was taken to arbitration by Jim Hunter, star pitcher, over pay. After being declared a free agent, Hunter signed with the Yankees in a $3.75 million deal.

Sports, of course, was much concerned with the economic problems. The energy crisis affected all groups. Auto racing units, in defense of their sport as gas wasters, released figures designed to show that more fuel was used by fans motoring to other sports than was burned up in racing. However, Nascar cut its early races by 10 percent and the United States Auto Club reduced the number of trials for the Indy-500, in which cars burn an alcohol derivative. However, all auto racing was being hurt by the loss of sponsors in a tight economy.

Inflation was hurting attendance at all events, and promoters fell back on TV, especially closed-circuit, for additional revenue. They paid attention to Shakespeare's words that "All the world's a stage" by booking title fights between George Foreman and Ken Norton in Caracas, Venezuela, and Foreman and Muhammad Ali in Zaire. The Zaire government promoted the fight there for publicity, and it was scheduled for 4 o'clock in the morning in Kinshasa so that it could be seen live at the usual hour in the United States (10 P. M., Eastern standard time). Closed-circuit viewings were arranged at high prices.

Ali, who knocked out Foreman and regained the title, applauded the method by which he and the former champion each received $5 million. "Governments want me now, not promoters. Governments want me to put them on the map," said Ali in discussing his plans. However, it cost Zaire about $4 million as tourist fans failed to show up for the bout in expected numbers.

A worldwide audience of at least 800,000 saw the World Cup soccer action from West Germany in June, most of them on live TV but on closed-circuit in America at high prices that were condemned by the fans. The spectacle was held in nine cities, with the final in Munich. The tournament was such a success that it made $2 million for the sponsors.

In the United States, the World Football League was trying to provide more stages for followers of the game. Right in the midst of a strike by veteran players of the National Football League, the new group began play among 12 teams. Before the season was half over, though, two clubs had dropped out and two others had changed cities, and most of the others were in bad financial straits, with unpaid players. Meanwhile, the NFL strike fizzled out as the fans indicated disapproval of it. During the league season attendance fell, leaving confusion over the cause: inflation, the relaxation of the TV blackouts, a drop in interest—or boredom.

Basketball was paying salaries that averaged $85,000 a year, and the strain forced changes in the ABA. The Charlotte Cougars became the Spirits of St. Louis. Memphis changed hands and was renamed the Sounds; Mike Storen, the league commissioner, quit to become the club president. Tedd Munchak, the former Cougar owner, was named commissioner.

In hockey the leagues were trying to curb an increase in brawling, which was the mark of the Philadelphia Flyers, who won the Stanley Cup. The NHL added the Washington Capitals and Kansas City Scouts and redivided its 18 clubs into four divisions. The WHA put clubs in Indianapolis and Phoenix, with three divisions for its 14 franchises.

Tennis began the year with controversy as France barred World Team Tennis players from its championship tourney. This kept out Evonne Goolagong and Jimmy Connors, the Australian Open champions who sued because they could not be eligible for a special prize for winning the big four tournaments. Connors did take the other titles, winning at Wimbledon as his sweetheart, Chris Evert, captured the women's singles, and at Forest Hills. A year-end controversy involved the women, led by Billie Jean King, who demanded higher prize money at Wimbledon. But the British women said they would play there in 1975 even if the others did not.

America's women swimmers also were involved in a decision of international importance. In 1973 they were beaten by the East Germans, who not only had great ability but wore swimsuits of new material and design. Similar skin-tight, revealing suits were made available to the U. S. women, who decided to wear them. They then broke 15 records in the indoor nationals, and two world marks and five American marks in the outdoors. They lost by only 5 points in a dual meet with the East Germans.

AUTO RACING

Three of the better-known drivers were not held back by the forces that were braking auto racing and sped to titles again. The most consistent of these was Richard Petty, who took the Nascar Grand National championship for the fifth time. Next was Bobby Unser, who won the California 500, finished second at Indianapolis, and fifth in the third big race at Pocono in regaining the United States Auto Club national title he first won in 1968. Emerson Fittipaldi of Brazil took the world championship again, winning three grand prix races.

Johnny Rutherford greets fans after taking the Indianapolis 500 auto racing classic. He won about $375,000 in 1974.

UPI

Auto Racing Highlights

World Championship Grand Prix Races

Argentina (Buenos Aires, Jan. 13)—Denis Hulme, New Zealand, driving a McLaren; distance 199.5 miles; time: 1 hour, 41 minutes, 2 seconds; average speed: 116.7 miles per hour

Brazil (São Paulo, Jan. 27)—Emerson Fittipaldi, Brazil; McLaren; race cut to 158.7 miles by rain; 1:24:57.06

South Africa (Johannesburg, March 30)—Carlos Reutemann, Argentina; Brabham; 195 miles; 1:42:40.96; 116.2 mph

Spain (Madrid, April 28)—Niki Lauda, Austria; Ferrari; race cut to 177.7 miles by rain; 2:29:57; 88.99 mph

Belgium (Nivelles, May 12)—Fittipaldi; 196.69 miles; 1:44:20.57

Monaco (Monte Carlo, May 26)—Ronnie Peterson, Sweden; Lotus-Ford; 158.87 miles; 1:58:03.7; 80.4 mph

Sweden (Anderstorp, June 9)—Jody Scheckter, South Africa; Tyrrell-Ford; 199.2 miles; 1:58:31.39; 100.7 mph

Netherlands (Zandvoort, June 23)—Lauda; 196.6 miles; 1:43:00.35; 114.72 mph

France (Dijon, July 7)—Peterson; 163.13 miles; 1:21:55.02; 119.50 mph

Britain (Brands Hatch, July 20)—Scheckter; 198.75 miles; 1:43:02.2; 115.73 mph

Germany (Neuerburgring, Aug. 4)—Clay Regazzoni, Switzerland; 198.8 miles; Ferrari; 1:41:35; 117.37 mph

Austria (Zeltweg, Aug. 18)—Reutemann; 198.3 miles; 1:28:44.72; 134.8 mph

Italy (Monza, Sept. 8)—Peterson; 186.34 miles; 1:22:56.6; 134.54 mph

Canada (Mosport, Ont., Sept. 22)—Fittipaldi; 196.72 miles; 1:40:26.13; 117.52 mph

United States (Watkins Glen, N. Y., Oct. 6)—Reutemann; 199.2 miles; 1:50:21.43; 119.12 mph

United States Auto Club Championship Trail

Indianapolis 500 (Indianapolis Motor Speedway, May 26)—Johnny Rutherford, Fort Worth, Texas, driving McLaren-Offy; 500 miles (200 laps); 3 hours, 9 minutes, 10.06 seconds; average speed: 158.589 mph; winner's purse: $245.032

California 500 (Ontario, Calif., Motor Speedway, March 10)—Bobby Unser, Albuquerque, N. Mex.; Eagle-Offy; 200 laps; 3:11:03.71; 157.017 mph; $88,758

Schaefer 500 (Pocono International Speedway, Long Pond, Pa., June 30)—Rutherford; 200 laps; 3:11:26.81; 156.701 mph; $92,200

Phoenix 150 (Phoenix, Ariz., March 17)—Mike Mosley, Brownsburg, Ind.; Eagle-Offy; 1:17:08; 116.663 mph; $7,556

Trenton 200 (Trenton, N. J., April 7)—Bobby Unser; 1:33:42.04; 125.615 mph; $7,556

Rex Mays 150 (Milwaukee, June 9)—Rutherford; 1:21:39.04; 110.225 mph; $17,209

Michigan Twin 200's (Cambridge Junction, July 21)—Bobby Unser; 1:14:40.53; 160.695 mph; $16,402. Stock car race: A. J. Foyt, Houston; Chevrolet; 1:32:35; 129.940 mph; $6,698

Bettenhausen 200 (Milwaukee, Aug. 11)—Gordon Johncock, Phoenix; Eagle-Offy; 1:41:03.04; 118.752 mph; $12,829

Norton 250 (Cambridge Junction, Mich., Sept. 15)—Al Unser, Albuquerque, N. Mex.; Eagle-Offy; 1:45:31.76; 142.141 mph; $18,950

Trenton 300 (Trenton, N. J., Sept. 22)—First race (150 miles): Foyt; 1:06:29; 135.372 mph; $8,457; Second race (150 miles): Bobby Unser; 0:57:40; 155.799 mph; $8,457

Phoenix 150 (Phoenix, Ariz., Nov. 2)—Johncock; 1:12:27.77; 124.202 mph; $9,620

National Association for Stock Car Auto Racing

Winston Western 500 (Riverside, Calif., Jan. 26)—Cale Yarborough, Timmonsville, S. C.; Chevrolet; 4 hours, 56 minutes, 52 seconds; average speed: 101.140 miles per hour; winner's purse: $16,325

(The following races were reduced by 10 percent because of fuel shortage: 500 to 450; 400 to 340; 600 to 540)

Daytona 500 (Daytona Beach, Fla., Feb. 17)—Richard Petty, Randleman, N. C.; Dodge; 3:11:38; 140.894 mph; $34,100

Carolina 500 (Rockingham, N. C., March 3)—Petty; 3:42:50; 121.622 mph; $15,025

Atlanta 500 (Hampton, Ga., March 24)—Yarborough; 3:01:26; 136.910 mph; $15,650

Rebel 500 (Darlington, S. C., April 7)—David Pearson, Spartanburg, S. C.; Mercury; 3:50:06; 117.543 mph; $16,525

Winston 500 (Talladega, Ala., May 5)—Pearson; 3:28:09; 130.220 mph; $20,285

Mason Dixon 500 (Dover, Del., May 19)—Yarborough; 3:54:40; 119.99 mph; $15,300

World 600 (Charlotte, N. C., May 26)—Pearson; 3:58:21; 135.720 mph; $25,900

Tuborg 400 (Riverside, Calif., June 9)—Yarborough; 3:31:40; 102.489 mph; $14,925

Motor State 400 (Irish Hills, Mich., June 16)—Petty; 2:48:46; 127.098 mph; $14,190.

(Remainder of races were run at regular stated distances)

Firecracker 400 (Daytona Beach, Fla., July 4)—Pearson; 2:53:32; 138.301 mph; $16,850

Dixie 500 (Atlanta, July 28)—Petty; 3:42:31; 131.1 mph; $16,350

Purolator 500 (Pocono Raceway, Aug. 4; cut to 480 miles by rain)—Petty; 4:09:09; 115.593 mph; $14,000

Talladega 500 (Talladega, Ala., Aug. 11)—Petty; 3:21:52; 148.637 mph; $21,465

Yankee 400 (Brooklyn, Mich., Aug. 25)—Pearson; 3:23; 133.045 mph; $15,265

Southern 500 (Darlington, S. C., Sept. 2)—Yarborough; 3:30:48; 111.075 mph; $25,000

Delaware 500 (Dover, Sept. 15)—Petty; 4:23:59; 113.64 mph; $15,175

National 500 (Charlotte, N. C., Oct. 6)—Pearson; 4:10:41; 119.912 mph; $22,075

American 500 (Rockingham, N. C., Oct. 20)—Pearson; 4:13:21; 118.493 mph; $15,850

Times 500 (Ontario, Calif., Nov. 24)—Bobby Allison, Hueytown, Ala.; 3:42:17; 134.963 mph; $15,125

Other Major Sports Car Races

Monza 1,000 Kilometers (625 miles, April 25)—Mario Andretti, Nazareth, Pa., and Arturo Merzario, Italy; Alpha Romeo; 4 hours, 45 minutes, 57.4 seconds; average speed: 130.607 miles per hour

Neuerburgring 1,000 (Adenau, West Germany, May 19)—Jean-Pierre Beltoise and Jean-Pierre Jarier, France; Matra-Simca; 4:08; 113.5 mph

Imola 1,000 (Imola, Italy, June 2)—Henri Pescarolo and Gerard Larrousse, France; Matra-Simca; 6:13:36; 99.979 mph

Auto Racing Highlights (continued)

Targa Florio (Cerda, Sicily, 312.46 miles, June 9)—Larrousse and Amilcare Ballestrieri; Lancia-Stratos; 4:35:76; 81.167 mph
24 Hours of Le Mans (Le Mans, France, June 15–16)—Pescarolo and Larrousse; Matra-Simca; 2,862.35 miles; 119.166 mph
Six Hours of Watkins Glen (Watkins Glen, N. Y., July 13)—Beltoise and Jarier; Matra-Simca; 651 miles; 108.61 mph
Brands Hatch 1,000 Kilometers (Brands Hatch, England, Sept. 29)—Beltoise and Jarier, 107.51 mph

Individual Champions

World Grand Prix—Emerson Fittipaldi, Brazil (55 pts)
United States Auto Club—Championship Trail: Bobby Unser, Albuquerque, N. Mex. (4,870 pts; $275,000); leading money winner: Johnny Rutherford, Fort Worth, Texas ($375,000); stock car: Butch Hartman, South Zanesville, Ohio; Dodge (3,270 pts); dirt track: Mario Andretti, Nazareth, Pa.; Viceroy-Ford; (900 pts); sprint car: Duane Carter, Jr., Huntington Beach, Calif. (922 pts); Midget Division: Mel Kenyon, Lebanon, Ind. (602 pts)
Nascar—Grand National: Richard Petty, Randleman, N. C. (record fifth title); Dodge (4,827 pts; $265,000); Grand National West: Ray Elder, Caruthers Calif.; Dodge (1,939.75 pts; $13,545)
International Motor Sports Association—Camel GT Challenge Series (10 races): Peter Gregg, Jacksonville, Fla.; Porsche Carrera (101 pts); Goodrich Radial Challenge Series (8 races): George Alderman, Newark, Del.; Gremlin (79 pts)

Sports Car Club of America Champions

Canadian-American Challenge Cup (5 races)—Jackie Oliver, England; UOP Shadow (82 pts; $68,900)
Formula 5,000 (also sponsored by United States Auto Club, 7 races)—Brian Redman, England; Lola-Chevrolet (105 pts; $81,150)
Trans-America (3 races)—Over 2 liters: Peter Gregg, Jacksonville, Fla.; Porsche Carrera (60 pts); under 2 liters: Richard Weiss, Phillipsburg, N. J.; Porsche (35 pts); Manufacturer: Porsche (36 pts)
VW Gold Cup (also sponsored by International Motor Sports Association; 13 races)—Elliott-Forbes Robinson 2d, La Crescenta, Calif.; Lynn (175 pts)

Other Sports Car Winners

Tasman Cup (Australia and New Zealand, 8 races)—Peter Gethin, England; Chevron (41 pts)
International Race of Champions (series of four races in Camaros at three tracks; final to be run at Daytona Beach, Fla., Feb. 14, 1975)—Point leaders after third race: Emerson Fittipaldi 41, Bobby Unser 38, George Follmer 36, Bobby Allison 33, A. J. Foyt 32, David Pearson 30, Cale Yarborough 29, Ronnie Peterson 23, Johnny Rutherford 21. Winners of 1973–74 series (final at Daytona Beach, Feb. 15, in Porsche Carreras)—Mark Donohue 93.94 miles at 114.979 mph; $41,000

Sports Car Club of America Road Racing Classic
(Road Atlanta, Flowery Branch, Ga., Nov. 1–3)

A Production—J. Marshall Robbins, Troy, Mich. (Corvette) 96.01 mph
B Production—Bill Jobe, Dallas (Corvette) 96.32 mph
C Production—Walt Maas, Mountain View, Calif. (Datsun) 95.21 mph
D Production—Lee Mueller, Lynwood, Calif. (Healey) 90.38 mph
E Production—Bill Schmid, Wilton, Conn. (Porsche) 89.84 mph
F Production—Rick Cline, Gainesville, Fla. (Triumph) 88.35 mph
G Production—Joe Hauser, Odenton, Md. (Sprite) 89.66 mph
H Production—John McCue, Marion, Ohio (Sprite) 82.87 mph
A Sports Racing—Warren Tope, Troy, Mich. (McLaren-Chevy) 106.11 mph
B Sports Racing—Jerry Hansen, Wayzata, Minn. (Lola-Ford) 108.78 mph
C Sports Racing—Sam Gilliland, Fairfield, Conn. (Arachnid-Ford) 94.02 mph
D Sports Racing—Bob Marshall, Edmond, Okla. (Quasar) 91.38 mph
A Sedan—Joe Chamberlain, Tigard, Oreg. (Camaro) 92.97 mph
B Sedan—Dave Frellsen, Evanston, Ill. (Datsun) 90.65 mph
C Sedan—Don Devendorf, Los Angeles (Datsun) 86.75 mph
D Sedan—Formula A—Jerry Hansen, Wayzata, Minn. (Lola) 111.17 mph
Formula B—Ken Duclos, Boxborough, Mass. (Brabham) 105.37 mph
Formula C—Bill Anspach, North Palm Beach, Fla. (Laminaire) 94.81 mph
Formula F—Eddie Miller, Lakewood, Colo. (Lola) 97.35 mph
Formula Vee—Harry MacDonald, Southfield, Mich. (Lynx) 86.01 mph
Formula Super Vee—Fred Phillips, Shreveport, La. (Elden) 102.17 mph

Petty began his rush to the title by winning the Daytona 500. He finished first in five more of the bigger stock car races for 10 victories altogether and a total of $278,175 in purses. He had already won more Nascar titles than any driver, with victories in 1964–1967, 1971, and 1972. He had a battle through the season with Cale Yarborough, who also won 10 races and $232,885.

Unser's closest competitor was Johnny Rutherford, the winner at Indianapolis and of the 500-mile race at Pocono. His luck changed after three straight triumphs, but he got enough points to finish in second place and to win about $375,000.

Fittipaldi beat out Clay Regazzoni of Switzerland by three points for the world title.

There were two deaths in grand prix racing. Peter Revson, 35, one of America's best road-racers, was killed in a practice run for the South African event at Johannesburg, March 28. He was one of four Americans who had won a grand prix race. In the finale at Watkins Glen, N. Y., Helmuth Koinigg, an Austrian in his second grand prix, was killed in a crash on the 10th lap.

BASEBALL

Henry Aaron got the 1974 season off to a historic start by bettering Babe Ruth's career home run record in what was supposed to be the Atlanta player's final year of play. But by October he had decided to add another chapter to his illustrious career by shifting from the National League to the American. After the World Series he signed a two-year contract as a designated hitter with the Milwaukee Brewers.

In the meantime, the Oakland A's took their third straight World Series, defeating the Los Angeles Dodgers, 4 games to 1; Frank Robinson became the first black manager, being chosen by Cleveland for 1975; Lou Brock stole 118 bases, breaking Maury Wills' season mark of 104; St. Louis edged the Mets, 4–3, in 26 innings in the longest night game; Nolan Ryan hurled his third no-hitter and Steve Busby his second; and Gaylord Perry won 15 straight but missed tying the American League record by one game.

Aaron, who had sat through the winter just one homer short of Ruth's mark with 713, did not waste any time in hitting No. 714. In the opening game at Cincinnati, April 4, he drove a fast ball pitched by Jack Bellingham over the left-field fence on his first swing of the season. He broke the record in Atlanta, April 8, in a nationally televised night game. Again it was on his first swing of the game. Al Downing, a Dodger left-hander, had walked him in the first inning on five pitches, one a called strike. In the fourth inning, after an inside pitch, Downing came in with a fast ball that made history as Aaron hit it over the left-

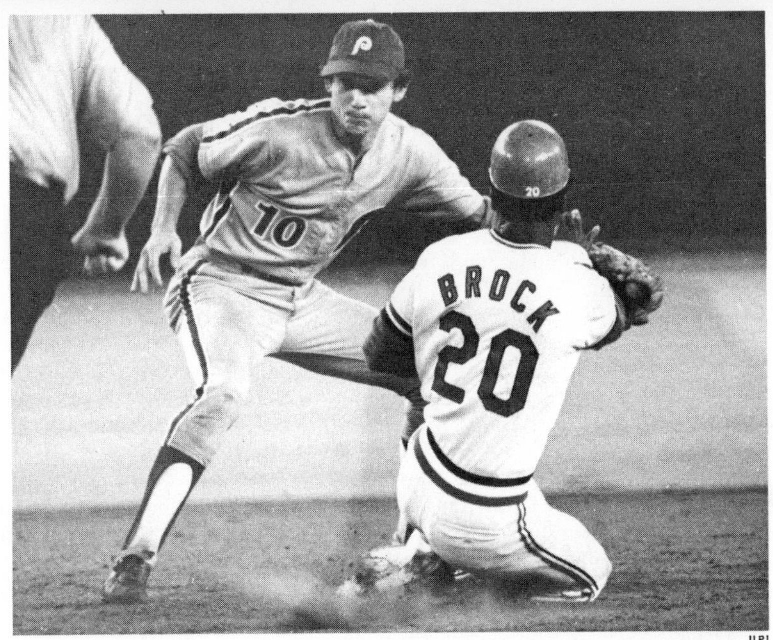

Lou Brock of St. Louis beats throw to Phillies' Larry Bowa and registers his 105th stolen base of the season for a new major league record. He wound up with 118 steals for the year.

UPI

center field fence. Aaron hit 18 more and ended the season with 733.

The fact that Aaron was piling up other records was usually overlooked. The 40-year-old outfielder–first baseman has established these marks, among others: major league records: most games: 3,076; most times at bat: 11,628; most extra-base hits: 1,429; most total bases: 6,591; most plate appearances: 13,058; most intentional bases on balls: 289. National League records: runs: 2,107; runs batted in: 2,202; grand slam homers: 16.

Neither the Dodgers nor the A's had much trouble winning the Western Division titles in their leagues. The Dodgers, a good all-round team, roared off to a fine start, wavered some on a late road trip, and then coasted. The A's started slowly for a championship team and for a while trailed the Texas Rangers, one of the most exciting and improved clubs in the league. Oakland's talent and experience were too much for their rivals. The Rangers, with Billy Martin as manager, were sparked by Jeff Burroughs, a 23-year-old outfielder who was named the American League's most valuable player, and a pitching staff headed by Ferguson Jenkins, acquired from the Cubs. Jenkins won 25 games and lost 12, and Jim Bibby won 19 and lost 19. Burroughs batted .301, hit 25 homers, and led the league in runs batted in with 118. Texas won 84 games, 27 more than in 1973 when it had the worst record in the majors.

Jeff Burroughs, young Texas Rangers outfielder, was named MVP in the American League.

TEXAS RANGERS

The other surprising AL team was the Yankees, who came alive in the latter part of the campaign. They were fourth in the Eastern Division, trailing Boston, Cleveland, and Baltimore on August 19, seven games back. With much juggling by Manager Bill Virdon of players gained in trades, New York won 11 of 12 games in one span. The Yankees moved into first place on September 4 and were in and out of the lead. They finally lost out to resurgent Baltimore Orioles the day before the season ended.

The Orioles' hitting and pitching became coordinated in early September, and they won 10 straight. They shut out their foes in an AL record string of five games and 54 consecutive innings. The Red Sox, caught in that streak, were scoreless through 34 innings while losing eight straight and failing to win for their top pitcher, Luis Tiant, who won 22 games. The Cleveland Indians had faded gradually.

In the National League East, Pittsburgh came on strongest at the finish and beat out St. Louis. The Cards were paced by Lou Brock and

Reggie Smith. Brock was the main spark with his base stealing and hitting. He batted .306, had 194 hits, and scored 105 runs.

In the playoffs, the Dodgers won two games before Bruce Kison stopped them. But they romped through the fourth, 12–1, for the third victory that put them in the World Series. Steve Garvey, first baseman who was chosen the NL's most valuable player, Bill Buckner, and Jim Wynn led the offense. Mike Marshall set a major league record by appearing in 106 games and became the first relief pitcher to win the Cy Young Award. The other top Dodger hurlers were Don Sutton and Andy Messersmith.

The A's were substantially the same as the team that had won the series the preceding two years, except that Al Dark was the manager, not Dick Williams. In the playoffs they took three in a row from the Orioles after losing the first. Rollie Fingers, a relief man; Ken Holtzman; Vida Blue; and Jim (Catfish) Hunter, the AL Cy Young Award winner, kept Baltimore from scoring for 33 straight innings. Hunter won 25 and lost 12, as did the Rangers' Jenkins.

The A's won the first game of the first West Coast World Series, 3–2, in Los Angeles, with Fingers getting the victory after relieving Holtzman in the fifth and beating Messersmith. The Dodgers, behind Sutton and with help from Marshall, who pitched in all five games, took the second game, 3–2. In Oakland, the A's won again, 3–2, as Hunter, aided by Fingers, beat Al Downing. In the fourth game, the 3–2 scoring pattern was changed to 5–2 by the A's, who tallied four runs in the seventh inning in routing Messersmith. Holtzman was the winner, aided, of course, by Fingers. In the final, Oakland reverted to 3–2, getting the deciding run in the seventh on Joe Rudi's homer. This time Marshall got beaten and "Blue Moon" Odom won. The most valuable player award went to Fingers, who pitched 9⅓ innings in four games.

Baseball Highlights

Professional—Major Leagues

AMERICAN LEAGUE (Final Standings, 1974)

EASTERN DIVISION

	W	L	Pct.
Baltimore	91	71	.562
New York	89	73	.549
Boston	84	78	.519
Cleveland	77	85	.475
Milwaukee	76	86	.469
Detroit	72	90	.444

WESTERN DIVISION

	W	L	Pct.
Oakland	90	72	.556
Texas	84	76	.525
Minnesota	82	80	.506
Chicago	80	80	.500
Kansas City	77	85	.475
California	68	94	.420

NATIONAL LEAGUE (Final Standings, 1974)

EASTERN DIVISION

	W	L	Pct.
Pittsburgh	88	74	.543
St. Louis	86	75	.534
Philadelphia	80	82	.494
Montreal	79	82	.491
New York	71	91	.438
Chicago	66	96	.407

WESTERN DIVISION

	W	L	Pct.
Los Angeles	102	60	.630
Cincinnati	98	64	.605
Atlanta	88	74	.543
Houston	81	81	.500
San Francisco	72	90	.444
San Diego	60	102	.370

Playoffs—American League: Oakland defeated Baltimore, 3 games to 1; Los Angeles defeated Pittsburgh, 3 games to 1

World Series—Oakland defeated Los Angeles, 4 games to 1; paid attendance, 5 games, 260,004; total receipts, $3,007,194 ($4,760,787 including playoffs); commissioner's office share, $451,077; individual club and league shares, $324,388; players' share of playoffs and series, $2,045,443 ($1,258,562 from the series and $786,880 from the playoffs), including full shares of $22,219 for each Oakland player and $15,703 for each Dodger player

First Game (Dodger Stadium, Los Angeles, Oct. 12): Oakland 3, Los Angeles 2; *second game* (Los Angeles, Oct. 13): Los Angeles 3, Oakland 2; *third game* (Oakland–Almeda County Coliseum, Oct. 15): Oakland 3, Los Angeles 2; *fourth game* (Oakland, Oct. 16): Oakland 5, Los Angeles 2; *fifth game* (Oakland, Oct. 17): Oakland 3, Los Angeles 2

All-Star Game (Pittsburgh, July 23)—National League 7, American League 2

Most Valuable Players—*American League:* Jeff Burroughs, Texas outfielder; *National League:* Steve Garvey, Los Angeles first baseman

Cy Young Memorial Awards (outstanding pitchers)—*American League:* Jim (Catfish) Hunter, Oakland; *National League:* Mike Marshall, Los Angeles

Rookie of the Year—*American:* Mike Hargrove, Texas first baseman; *National:* Bake McBride, St. Louis outfielder

Leading Batters—Percentage: *American:* Rod Carew, Minnesota, .364; *National:* Ralph Garr, Atlanta, .353. Runs Batted In: *American:* Jeff Burroughs, Texas, 118; *National:* Johnny Bench, Cincinnati, 129. Home Runs: *American:* Dick Allen, Chicago, 32; *National:* Mike Schmidt, Philadelphia, 36

Leading Pitchers—Earned Run Averages: *American:* Jim (Catfish) Hunter, Oakland, 2.49; *National:* Buzz Capra, Atlanta, 2.28. Victories: *American:* Hunter and Ferguson Jenkins, Texas, 25; *National:* Andy Messersmith, Los Angeles, and Phil Niekro, Atlanta, 20. Strikeouts: *American:* Nolan Ryan, California, 367; *National:* Steve Carlton, Philadelphia, 240

No-Hit Games Pitched—Steve Busby, Kansas City (AL) vs. Milwaukee, 2–0; Dick Bosman, California (AL) vs. Oakland, 4–0; Nolan Ryan, California (AL) vs. Minnesota, 4–0.

Hall of Fame Inductees—James (Cool Papa) Bell, James L. (Sunny Jim) Bottomley, John (Jocko) Conlan, Edward C. (Whitey) Ford, Mickey Charles Mantle, Samuel L. Thompson

Professional—Minor Leagues

American Association (AAA)—Indianapolis, East Division; Tulsa, West Division and playoff

International League (AAA)—Rochester, North Division and playoff; Memphis, South Division

Pacific Coast League (AAA)—Albuquerque, East Division; Spokane, West Division and playoff

Mexican League (AAA)—Mexico City Reds, Southeastern and playoff; Jalisco, Southwest; Tampico, Northeast; Saltillo, Northwest

Eastern League (AA)—American Division: Bristol; National Division: Quebec City; playoff: Thetford Mines

Southern League (AA)—Jacksonville, Eastern Division; Knoxville, Western Division and playoff

Texas League (AA)—Victoria, Eastern Division and playoff; El Paso, Western Division

California League (A)—Fresno, first half and playoff; San Jose, second half

Carolina League (A)—Salem

Florida State League (A)—Tampa, Northern Division; Fort Lauderdale, Southern; West Palm Beach, playoff

Midwest League (A)—Appleton, Northern Division; Danville, Southern Division and playoff

New York–Pennsylvania (A)—Oneonta

Northwest League (A)—Bellingham, Western Division; Eugene, Eastern Division and playoff

Western Carolina League (A)—Gastonia

Intercollegiate Champions

NCAA—University Division: Univ. of Southern California (defeated Miami of Florida, 7–3, in final); Division II: Univ. of California at Irvine (defeated New Orleans, 14–1, in final)

NAIA—Lewis Univ. of Illinois (defeated Sam Houston State, 3–2, in final)

Amateur Champions

American Legion—Rio Piedras, Puerto Rico
Babe Ruth League—Sugar Creek, Mo.
Bronco League—Lake Worth, Texas
Colt League—Cayce, West Columbia, S. C.
Connie Mack League—Jim Smith Carpets, Flint, Mich.
Dixie Youth World Series—Pensacola, Fla.
Little League—Taiwan (defeated Red Bluff, Calif., 12–1, in final)
Mickey Mantle League—Duke's Office Supply, Tulsa, Okla.
National Amateur Baseball Federation—Castro Valley, Calif.
National Amateur Baseball Federation Senior—Tonawanda, N. Y.
National Baseball Congress—Fairbanks, Alaska
Pee Wee Reese League—Kronk Cubs, Detroit
Pony League—West Covina, Calif.
Sandy Koufax League—Power Rental, Denver
Stan Musial League—Larco's Inn, Detroit

Professional Basketball Highlights

National Basketball Association
(Final Standings, 1973–74)
Eastern Conference
Atlantic Division

	W	L	Pct.	Scoring Avg. For	Agst.
Boston Celtics	56	26	.683	109.0	105.1
New York Knicks	49	33	.598	101.3	98.5
Buffalo Braves	42	40	.512	111.6	111.8
Philadelphia 76ers	25	57	.305	101.2	107.5
Central Division					
*Capital Bullets	47	35	.573	101.9	100.4
Atlanta Hawks	35	47	.427	108.6	110.0
Houston Rockets	32	50	.390	107.4	107.6
Cleveland Cavaliers	29	53	.354	100.3	104.6
Western Conference					
Midwest Division					
Milwaukee Bucks	59	23	.720	107.1	99.0
Chicago Bulls	54	28	.659	102.0	98.7
Detroit Pistons	52	30	.634	104.4	100.3
Kansas City–Omaha Kings	33	49	.402	102.0	105.8
Pacific Division					
Los Angeles Lakers	47	35	.573	109.2	108.3
Golden State Warriors	44	38	.537	109.9	107.3
Seattle SuperSonics	36	46	.439	107.0	109.5
Phoenix Suns	30	52	.366	107.9	111.5
Portland Trail Blazers	27	55	.329	106.8	111.6

* Now Washington Bullets

Eastern Conference playoffs—final: Boston defeated New York, 4 games to 1; Western Conference: Milwaukee defeated Chicago, 4 games to 0. NBA championship: Boston defeated Milwaukee, 4 games to 3.
Most Valuable Player—Kareem Abdul-Jabbar, Milwaukee
Rookie of the Year—Ernie DiGregorio, Buffalo
Leading Scorer—Bob McAdoo, Buffalo; 2,261 points; 30.6 average per game

American Basketball Association
(Final Standings, 1973–74)
Eastern Division

	W	L	Pct.	Scoring Avg. For	Agst.
New York Nets	55	29	.655	109.4	104.0
Kentucky Colonels	53	31	.631	107.4	103.3
Carolina Cougars	47	37	.560	110.5	107.0
Virginia Squires	28	56	.333	106.4	111.3
Memphis Tams	21	68	.250	101.2	108.2
Western Division					
Utah Stars	51	33	.607	105.1	104.7
Indiana Pacers	46	38	.548	105.8	105.0
San Antonio Spurs	45	39	.536	97.6	96.7
Denver Rockets	37	47	.440	107.0	107.5
San Diego Conquistadors	37	47	.440	113.2	115.7

Eastern Division playoffs—final: New York defeated Kentucky, 4 games to 0; Western Division: Utah defeated Indiana, 4 games to 3. ABA championship: New York defeated Utah, 4 games to 1
Most Valuable Player—Julius Erving, New York
Rookie of the Year—Swen Nater, San Antonio
Leading Scorer—Erving; 2,299 points; 27.4 average per game

BASKETBALL

Professional

John Havlicek stayed healthy in the playoffs and the Boston Celtics regained the National Basketball League championship in 1974. Havlicek was so healthy, in fact, that he was named the outstanding player of the postseason games. To achieve that, he had to do better than Kareem Abdul-Jabbar, the star Milwaukee center and the regular-season most valuable player. Havlicek, whose injuries in 1973 blunted Boston's chances against the Knicks in the final series, led the Celtics to victory over the Bucks, 4 games to 3. The series almost proved that the home court was a disadvantage.

The Buffalo Braves, the best offensive team in the league, gave Boston some trouble. Led by Bob McAdoo, the scoring champion, and Ernie DiGregorio, the rookie of the year, Buffalo won two games before being eliminated. The Bucks beat Los Angeles and Chicago to reach the final.

In the American Basketball Association, the young New York Nets, with Julius Erving as the star, took the title. Dr. J, who was obtained from Virginia just before the start of the season, led the league in scoring and was named the most valuable player. His play in the final against the Utah Stars was sensational, and the Nets won, 4 games to 1. Larry Kenon, Billy Paultz, and Brian Taylor were other Net stars.

College

UCLA did not win the championship in 1974. The Bruins' string of 7 straight championships and 38 tournament games in a row ended on March 25 in an 80–77 loss to North Carolina State in a double-overtime, semifinal game. North Carolina State, two days later, took the title by beating Marquette, 76–64, at Greensboro, N. C. Oddly, the Wolfpack was beaten only once in 31 games and that was by UCLA, 84–66, on December 15.

The tournament loss was not the first of the season for the Bruins. Notre Dame had beaten

The Boston Celtics defeated the Milwaukee Bucks, 4 games to 3, in the NBA title series. Here, Boston's John Havlicek scores against Bucks' Bob Dandridge.

UPI

UPI

Bill Walton received the Sullivan Award in February, but his UCLA basketball team's record winning streak was finally stopped.

the team led by 6-11 Bill Walton, 71–70, on January 19, ending the record winning streak of 88 games over three seasons. A week later the Bruins evened the count with the Irish with a 94–75 triumph in Los Angeles. Then, in one weekend, UCLA lost two games in a row for the first time since 1966, falling before Oregon State and Oregon. The Bruins had another close tournament game in Tucson, going into three overtime periods before downing Dayton, 111–110.

North Carolina State was led by Dave Thompson, 6–4, and Tom Burleson, 7–4. The Wolfpack, unbeaten in 27 games the previous season, was ineligible for NCAA play in 1973. Marquette reached the final by ousting Kansas, 64–51, and UCLA beat the Jayhawks, 64–51, for third place.

Morgan State, paced by Marvin Webster, defeated Southwest Missouri, 67–52, for the Division II championship. West Georgia upset Alcorn State, 97–79, for the National Association of Intercollegiate Athletics title, with Clarence (Foots) Walker in the star role. The women's collegiate crown was won again by Immaculata (Pa.). The Macs beat Mississippi College, Clinton, 68–53, for their third title. The Jacksonville Stars won the AAU championship, and the women's AAU title was taken by the Hutcherson Flying Queens of Plainview, Texas.

Amateur Basketball Highlights

Major Tournaments

NCAA (Greensboro, N. C., March 25)—North Carolina State (defeated Marquette, 76–64); Division II: (Evansville, Ind., March 15): Morgan State (defeated Southwest Missouri, 67–52)
National Intercollegiate (NAIA, Kansas City, March 16)—West Georgia (defeated Alcorn State, 97–79)
National Invitation Tournament (New York, March 24)—Purdue (defeated Utah, 87–81)
Association for Intercollegiate Athletics for Women (Manhattan, Kan., March 23)—Immaculata (Pa.) College (defeated Mississippi College, Clinton, 68–53)
Men's AAU (Baton Rouge, La., March 24)—Jacksonville (Fla.) Stars (defeated Baton Rouge Hawks, 98–97)
Women's AAU (Gallup, N. Mex., March 31)—Hutcherson Flying Queens, Plainview, Texas (defeated John F. Kennedy College, Wahoo, Neb., 54–51)
National Junior College (Hutchinson, Kan., March 23)—Mercer County (N. J.) C. C. (defeated Chipola, Marianna, Fla., 60–58)

College Conference Champions

(Figures in parentheses indicate victories and losses in conference games only.)

Atlantic Coast—North Carolina State (12–0); won championship tournament
Big Eight—Kansas (13–1)
Big Ten—Indiana and Michigan (12–2)
Big Sky—Idaho State and Montana (11–3)
Ivy League—Pennsylvania (13–1)
Mid-American—Ohio University (9–3)
Middle Atlantic—Eastern: St. Joseph's (6–1); Western: Rider (8–2); St. Joseph's won championship tournament
Missouri Valley—Louisville (11–1)
Ohio Valley—Austin Peay and Morehead State (10–4)
Pacific 8—University of California, Los Angeles (12–2)
Southeastern—Alabama and Vanderbilt (15–3)
Southern—Furman (11–1); won championship tournament
Southwest—Texas (11–3)
Pacific Coast Athletic—Long Beach State (12–0); Los Angeles State (8–4) played in NCAA
West Coast Athletic—San Francisco (12–2)
Western Athletic—New Mexico (10–4)
Yankee—Massachusetts (11–1)

Leading Major Independents

East—Providence (28–4); Pittsburgh (24–4); St. John's (20–7)
South—North Carolina, Charlotte (22–4); South Carolina (22–5); South Alabama (22–6)
Midwest—Notre Dame (26–3); Marquette (26–5); Creighton (23–7)
Southwest—Oral Roberts (23–6); Pan American (13–9)
Far West—Hawaii (19–9); Utah State (16–10)

BOXING

Muhammad Ali finally regained the world heavyweight championship in 1974. In a bizarre setting in Zaire at 4 o'clock in the morning, October 30, Ali knocked out George Foreman in the eighth round. Ali had won the title the first time as Cassius Clay in 1964, but various commissions had stripped him of it in 1967 when he refused induction into the armed services. After four years of battling in and out of the ring once he had again been licensed to fight, Ali caught the right foe at the right time.

The bout was originally scheduled for September 25 but was postponed when Foreman suffered a bad cut over his right eye in a sparring session. At a weigh-in carnival three days before the fight, Foreman weighed 220 and Ali seemed heavy at 216½. Once they were in the ring, Ali took control. Staying on the ropes, he had Foreman bewildered and swinging wildly. The defender, who was a 3–1 favorite, ran out of punch, and Ali nailed him and regained the crown as Floyd Patterson had done in 1960.

Earlier, Ali had outpointed Joe Frazier in a 12-round rematch at Madison Square Garden, January 28. But this time Frazier was not the champion. The chagrined Frazier stopped Jerry Quarry in his "comeback" in the fifth round,

Boxing Highlights

World Professional Champions

Flyweight—Susumu Hanagata, Japan, World Boxing Association; Shoji Oguma, World Boxing Council
Bantamweight—Rafael Herrera, Mexico
Featherweight—Alexis Arguello, Nicaragua, WBA; Bobby Chacon, Sylmar, Calif., WBC
Junior Lightweight—Ben Villaflor, Philippines, WBA; Kuniaka Shibata, Japan, WBC
Lightweight—Roberto Duran, Panama, WBA; Gattu Ishinatsu, Japan, WBC
Junior Welterweight—Antonio Cervantes, Colombia, WBA; Perico Fernandez, Spain, WBC
Welterweight—Jose Napoles, Mexico
Junior Middleweight—Oscar Alvarado, Houston, Texas
Middleweight—Carlos Monzon, Argentina, WBA; Rodrigo Valdez, Colombia, WBC
Light Heavyweight—John Conteh, WBC; Victor Galindez, Argentina, WBA
Heavyweight—Muhammad Ali, Cherry Hills, N. J.

National AAU Champions
(Knoxville, Tenn., June 13–15)

106 Pounds—Claudell Atkins, St. Louis
112 Pounds—Gregory Richardson, Cleveland
119 Pounds—Mike Ayala, San Antonio, Texas
125 Pounds—Mike Hess, Albany, Oreg.
132 Pounds—James Kenty, Columbus, Ohio
139 Pounds—Ray Leonard, Washington, D. C.
147 Pounds—Clinton Jackson, Las Vegas, Nev.
156 Pounds—Jerome Bennett, U. S. Air Force
165 Pounds—Vonzell Johnson, Columbus, Ohio
178 Pounds—Leon Spinks, U. S. Marines
Heavyweight—Dwain Bonds, Detroit

June 17, at the Garden. Meanwhile, Foreman, in the second defense of the title he had won from Frazier, knocked out Ken Norton of San Diego, Calif., in the second round at Caracas, Venezuela, in March.

There was a change at the light heavyweight level, too. Bob Foster of Albuquerque, N. Mex., retired on September 16. He had fought a draw with Jorge Ahumada, June 17, and kept the title. John Conteh of England outpointed Ahumada, October 1, for the vacant crown.

Bobby Chacon of Sylmar, Calif., won the World Boxing Council featherweight championship by stopping Alfredo Marcano of Venezuela in the ninth round at Los Angeles, September 7. Alexis Arguello became Nicaragua's first world champion by knocking out Ruben Olivares of Mexico City in the 13th round at Inglewood, Calif., November 23, for the WBA title.

FOOTBALL

Professional

Pittsburgh, making its first appearance in the Super Bowl, took on Minnesota, playing for the second straight year, in Super Bowl IX on Jan. 12, 1975. The Steelers won, 16–6.

Earlier, the Steelers had surprised a powerful Oakland team, 24–13, to win the AFC title. The Raiders had stopped Miami in the playoff, 28–26, and thwarted the Dolphins' bid for a third straight Super Bowl title. The Vikings had gained a bowl berth and the NFC crown by beating Los Angeles, 14–10.

For a while in midsummer it appeared that there might not be an NFL season in 1974 because of a strike by the Players Association that carried into the exhibition game season. The players, in addition to a higher minimum salary and extra pay for preseason and postseason games, were concerned with "freedoms"—freedom to play for the team of their choice, freedom from discipline, and freedom from having disputes settled by Commissioner Pete Rozelle rather than by an impartial arbitrator.

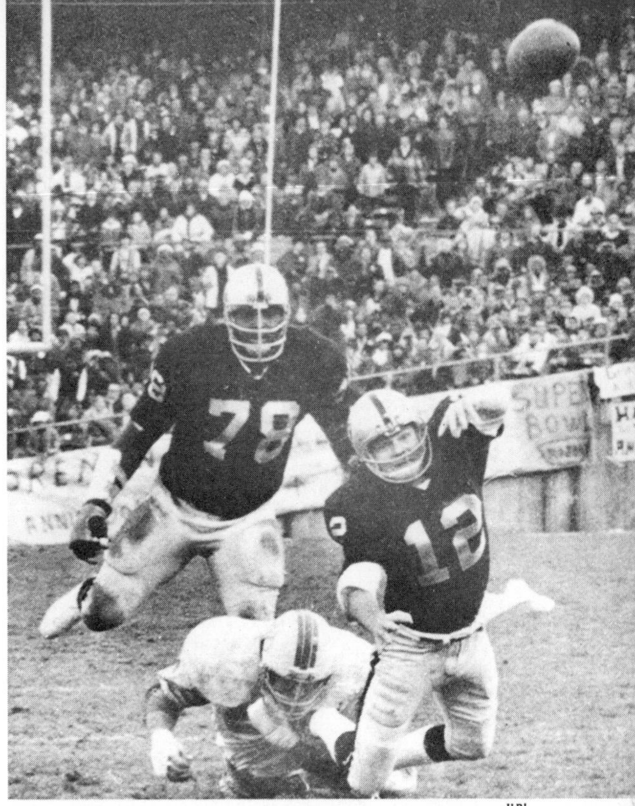

UPI

Oakland's Ken Stabler, being tackled, gets off pass in final seconds to beat Miami, 28–26, in playoffs and foil Dolphins' hopes for a third straight Super Bowl crown.

By mid-August the veterans agreed to report to training camps for a 14-day cooling-off period, which ended on August 27 with the players rejecting a new proposal by the National Football League Management Council, 25–1. But they decided to stay in camp, and the longest labor dispute in pro sports just sort of evaporated.

There had been concern, too, that stars such as Larry Csonka, Jim Kiick, and Paul Warfield of the Miami Dolphins would not be at their best because they had signed contracts for 1975 with teams in the new World Football League, which began play July 11. The new group seemed to have instant acceptance of its 12 teams until it was learned that many attendance figures were inflated and padded by free tickets. By the time Birmingham won the championship in November, two clubs had moved, two had folded, and most had unpaid players.

The Dolphins did start badly, losing two of their first five games, then played like champions and won their division. The Dallas Cowboys failed to qualify for the first time in eight years. Their place was taken by the St. Louis Cardinals,

Pro Football Highlights

NATIONAL FOOTBALL LEAGUE
(Final Standings, 1974)

American Conference

Eastern Division

	Won	Lost	Tied	Pct.	Pts.	Opp.
Miami	11	3	0	.786	327	216
*Buffalo	9	5	0	.643	264	244
N. Y. Jets	7	7	0	.500	279	300
New England	7	7	0	.500	348	289
Baltimore	2	12	0	.143	190	329

Central Division

	Won	Lost	Tied	Pct.	Pts.	Opp.
Pittsburgh	10	3	1	.750	305	189
Cincinnati	7	7	0	.500	283	259
Houston	7	7	0	.500	236	282
Cleveland	4	10	0	.286	251	344

Western Division

	Won	Lost	Tied	Pct.	Pts.	Opp.
Oakland	12	2	0	.857	355	228
Denver	7	6	1	.536	302	294
Kansas City	5	9	0	.357	233	293
San Diego	5	9	0	.357	212	285

* Fourth, or wild card, qualifier for playoffs

Playoffs—Oakland defeated Miami, 28–26, Dec. 21; Pittsburgh defeated Buffalo, 32–14, Dec. 22

Conference Championship—Pittsburgh (defeated Oakland, 24–13, at Oakland, Dec. 29)

League Champion (Super Bowl)—Pittsburgh (defeated Minnesota, 16–6, at New Orleans, Jan. 12, 1975)

National Conference

Eastern Division

	Won	Lost	Tied	Pct.	Pts.	Opp.
St. Louis	10	4	0	.714	285	218
*Washington	10	4	0	.714	320	196
Dallas	8	6	0	.571	297	235
Philadelphia	7	7	0	.500	242	217
N. Y. Giants	2	12	0	.143	195	299

Central Division

	Won	Lost	Tied	Pct.	Pts.	Opp.
Minnesota	10	4	0	.714	310	195
Detroit	7	7	0	.500	256	270
Green Bay	6	8	0	.429	210	206
Chicago	4	10	0	.286	152	279

Western Division

	Won	Lost	Tied	Pct.	Pts.	Opp.
Los Angeles	10	4	0	.714	263	181
San Francisco	6	8	0	.429	226	236
New Orleans	5	9	0	.357	166	263
Atlanta	3	11	0	.214	111	271

* Fourth, or wild card, qualifier for playoffs

Playoffs—Minnesota defeated St. Louis, 30–14, Dec. 21; Los Angeles defeated Washington, 19–10, Dec. 22

Conference Championship—Minnesota (defeated Los Angeles, 14–10, at Bloomington, Minn., Dec. 29)

National Football League Leaders

National Conference

Scoring—Chester Marcol, Green Bay (25 field goals, 19 extra points, 94 points)

Scoring (nonkickers)—Chuck Foreman, Minnesota (90 pts)

Passing—Sonny Jurgensen, Washington (107 of 167 for 1,185 yards and 11 touchdowns; 64.1% completions)

Receiving—Charles Young, Philadelphia (63 for 696 yards)

Interceptions—Ray Brown, Atlanta (8)

Rushing—Lawrence McCutcheon, Los Angeles (236 for 1,109 yards)

Punting—Tom Blanchard, New Orleans (42.1-yard average)

Punt Returns—Dick Jauron, Detroit (16.8-yard average)

Kickoff Returns—Terry Metcalf, St. Louis (31.2-yard average)

American Conference

Scoring—Roy Gerela, Pittsburgh (20 field goals, 33 extra points, 93 points)

Scoring (nonkickers)—Cliff Branch, Oakland (78 pts)

Passing—Ken Anderson, Cincinnati (213 of 328 for 2,667 yards and 18 touchdowns; 64.9% completions)

Receiving—Lydell Mitchell, Baltimore (72 for 544 yards)

Interceptions—Emmitt Thomas, Kansas City (12)

Rushing—Otis Armstrong, Denver (263 for 1,407 yards)

Punting—Ray Guy, Oakland (42.2-yard average)

Punt Returns—Lemar Parrish, Cincinnati (18.8-yard avg.)

Kickoff Returns—Greg Pruitt, Cleveland (27.5-yard avg.)

WORLD FOOTBALL LEAGUE

Division Champions—*Eastern:* Florida Blazers; *Central:* Memphis Southmen; *Western:* Southern California Sun.

Playoffs—Hawaiians defeated Sun, 34–14; Blazers defeated Philadelphia Bell, 18–3. *Semifinals:* Birmingham defeated Hawaiians, 22–19; Blazers defeated Southmen, 18–15.

Championship (World Bowl, Birmingham, Dec. 9)—Birmingham Americans 22, Florida Blazers 21.

Canada

Grey Cup (Vancouver, Nov. 24)—Montreal Alouettes 20, Edmonton Eskimos 7

who after seven games were the only unbeaten club. They fell back in the late stages.

Rule changes instituted in 1974 included moving the goalposts back 10 yards; starting play on missed field goals from the line of scrimmage if over 20 yards from the goal line; and one sudden-death overtime period for tied games.

College

Two big upsets in the New Year's Day bowl games scrambled the race for the national collegiate football championship in 1974. Southern California was named No. 1 in the UPI Board of Coaches poll following the Trojans' 18–17 win over Ohio State and Notre Dame's 13–11 victory over unbeaten Alabama, which had held the top ranking at the end of the regular season. But the Associated Press writers and broadcasters poll voted top honors to undefeated Oklahoma. The Sooners were ineligible for consideration in the coaches' poll because of a two-year probation for recruiting violations. Notre Dame's victory, following a 24–23 win over Alabama in the Sugar Bowl the previous year, came in Ara Parseghian's final game as coach of the Irish. He had announced his resignation in December.

A lapse by Texas, one of the bowl-game regulars, let an outsider into the post-season competition. The Longhorns, the hosts in the Cotton Bowl the preceding six years, were beaten out by Baylor. But the Bears, who had not taken the Southwest Conference title since 1924, needed and received help from Texas. The Longhorns routed Texas A&M (which had downed Baylor, 20–0) in the season finale, and Baylor won the title and its first Cotton Bowl berth against Penn State.

The Orange Bowl signed up Alabama and Notre Dame before the scheduled time for post-season pairings. The Irish had been upset early by Purdue, 31–20, but their flair and drawing power were more than acceptable. The Irish skinned past Navy and Pittsburgh and then took one of their worst beatings in their 11th game—the annual drama with Southern California. Notre Dame, guided by Tom Clements, led 24–0 until Anthony Davis scored for USC with 10 seconds remaining in the second quarter. With the score 24–6, Davis took the second-half kickoff in the end zone and raced the length of the field for a touchdown. Within 6½ minutes of the third quarter he scored his third and fourth touchdowns, and the Trojans won, 55–24.

USC's Anthony Davis (28) returns second-half kickoff 100 yards to spark the Trojans to a come-from-behind 55–24 victory over Notre Dame. His team went on to defeat Ohio State in the Rose Bowl and gain No. 1 ranking in the UPI poll.

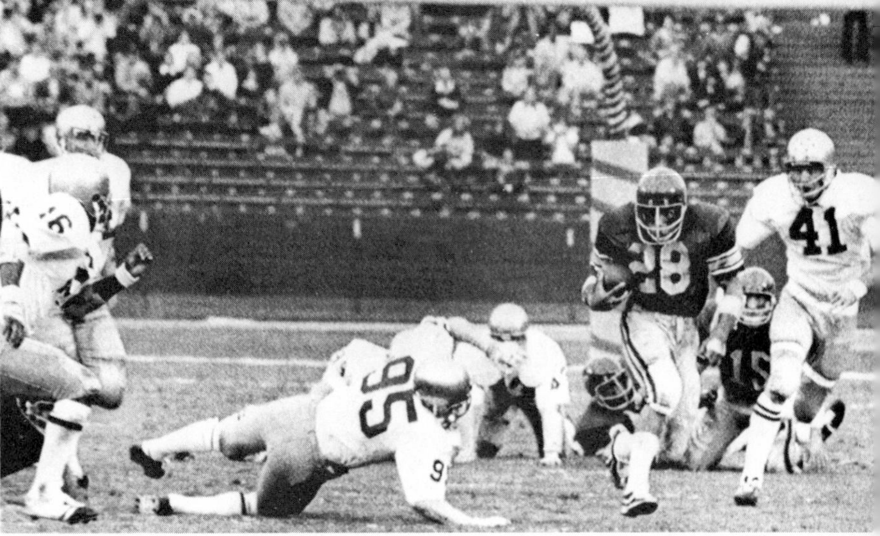

UPI

USC was thus prepared for the Rose Bowl game with Ohio State, which had won the annual ruckus with Michigan over the Big Ten Berth. A vote of athletic directors named the Buckeyes, who edged previously unbeaten Michigan, 12–10, with four field goals. Ohio State had lost to Michigan State and thus tied Michigan for the title. The loss to Michigan State was a source of acrimony. Ohio State thought it had gone in for a touchdown as the game ended, but the officials ruled that time had run out and that, even if it had not, the Buckeyes had lined up improperly. Woody Hayes, the Ohio State coach, was reprimanded by the league for his remarks about the officials, but he felt better when he took his team to Pasadena for the third straight year.

Ohio State's attack was led by Archie Griffin, who was awarded the Heisman Trophy as the nation's top collegiate football player. He gained 1,620 yards rushing. Davis of USC was second in the voting for the trophy.

College Football Highlights

Intercollegiate and Conference Champions

National Press Polls—AP (writers and broadcasters): Oklahoma; UPI (coaches): Southern California (Oklahoma, on probation, was not eligible in this poll)
Heisman Trophy—Archie Griffin, Ohio State back
Eastern (Lambert Trophy)—Penn State
Eastern Small College—Lambert Cup: Delaware; Lambert Bowl: Ithaca
Atlantic Coast—Maryland (6–0)
Big Eight—Oklahoma (7–0)
Big Sky—Boise State (6–0)
Big Ten—Tie between Michigan and Ohio State (7–1)
Ivy League—Tie between Harvard and Yale (6–1)
Mid-American—Miami (5–0)
Missouri Valley—Tulsa (6–0)
Ohio Valley—Eastern Kentucky (6–1)
Pacific-8—University of Southern California (6–0)
Pacific Coast A. A.—San Jose State (4–0)
Southeastern—Alabama (6–0)
Southern—Virginia Military (5–1)
Southwest—Baylor (6–1)
Western Athletic—Brigham Young (6–0)
Yankee—Tie between Maine and Massachusetts (4–2)

Leading Independents

East—Penn State (9–2), Boston College (8–3), Temple (8–2), Rutgers (7–3)
Midwest—Notre Dame (9–2), Pittsburgh (7–4), Cincinnati (7–4)
South—Memphis State (7–4)
Southwest—Houston (8–3)
Far West—Utah State (7–4), Hawaii (6–4)

NCAA Playoff Bowls

Division II Semifinals

Grantland Rice Bowl (Baton Rouge, La., Dec. 7)—Delaware 49, Nevada-Las Vegas 11
Pioneer Bowl (Wichita Falls, Texas, Dec. 7)—Central Michigan 35, Louisiana Tech 14

Division II Final

Camellia Bowl (Sacramento, Calif., Dec. 14)—Central Michigan 54, Delaware 14

Division III

Semifinals—Central Iowa defeated Evansville, 17–16; Ithaca defeated Slippery Rock, 27–14
Final—Central Iowa defeated Ithaca, 10–8

NAIA Championships

Division I

Semifinals—Henderson State defeated Elon, 21–7; Texas A. & I. defeated Cameron State, 21–19
Final—(Champion Bowl, Kingsville, Texas, Dec. 14)—Texas A. & I. defeated Henderson State, 34–23

Division II

Championship (Sequin, Texas, Dec. 7)—Texas Lutheran defeated Missouri Valley, 42–0

Major Bowl Games
(December 1974 and Jan. 1, 1975)

Pelican Bowl (New Orleans, Dec. 7)—Grambling 28, South Carolina State 7
Orange Blossom Classic (Miami, Dec. 7)—Florida A&M 17, Howard University 13
Liberty Bowl (Memphis, Tenn., Dec. 16)—Tennessee 7, Maryland 3
Tangerine Bowl (Orlando, Fla., Dec. 21)—Miami (Ohio) 21, Georgia 10
Gate City Bowl (Atlanta, Dec. 21)—Tuskegee 15, Norfolk State 14
Astro-Bluebonnet Bowl (Houston, Dec. 23)—Houston 31, North Carolina State 31
Fiesta Bowl (Tempe, Ariz., Dec. 28)—Oklahoma State 16, Brigham Young 6
Peach Bowl (Atlanta, Dec. 28)—Texas Tech 6, Vanderbilt 6
Sun Bowl (El Paso, Texas, Dec. 28)—Mississippi State 26, North Carolina 24
Gator Bowl (Jacksonville, Fla., Dec. 30)—Auburn 27, Texas 3
Sugar Bowl (New Orleans, Dec. 31)—Nebraska 13, Florida 10
Cotton Bowl (Dallas, Jan. 1)—Penn State 41, Baylor 20
Orange Bowl (Miami, Fla., Jan. 1)—Notre Dame 13, Alabama 11
Rose Bowl (Pasadena, Calif., Jan. 1)—Southern California 18, Ohio State 17

TYRONE DUKES, THE NEW YORK TIMES

Johnny Miller lines up a putt in the Westchester Classic as Jack Nicklaus waits his turn. It was one of eight tournaments won by Miller during the year.

GOLF

Johnny Miller won eight tournaments. Hale Irwin and Lee Elder took only one apiece, but it was a tournament of special significance to each. Irwin's victory gave him the U. S. Open championship, while Elder's opened a door that had long remained closed. He became the first black golfer eligible to play in the Masters, thus putting an end to the controversy over the tournament played in Augusta, Ga., each April. Irwin and Elder joined the tour in 1968, and Irwin had won two tourneys previously.

Doors opened for eight other players who managed to win one of the tourneys that Johnny Miller did not. Another Miller, Allen, was one who got on the list of those who did not have to qualify each Monday for the next tourney. The others were Leonard Thompson, Rod Curl, Bob Menne, Richie Karl, Vic Regalado, Forrest Fezler, and Terry Diehl.

Johnny Miller won the first three events and $87,750 before taking time out because of illness. His fifth victory came in the Tournament of Champions when he defeated all the other winners. After a summer of limited play he won three more titles and, with a total of $353,021, eclipsed the season earnings record of Jack Nicklaus.

None of the major titles was included in Miller's list. Two of those, the Masters and British Open, were taken by Gary Player. After winning the Masters for the second time, the South African announced his aim of taking the big four. He was stopped quickly when he failed to solve the intricacies of the Winged Foot course in Mamaroneck, N. Y., in the U. S. Open. Irwin finished the four rounds with 287, seven over par, and still won from Fezler by two shots. Player went sour with a 41 on the incoming nine the third day and finished in a tie for ninth at 293.

Player recovered, though, in the British Open, led all the way, and triumphed by four strokes. The Professional Golfers' Association tourney went to Lee Trevino, with Nicklaus one shot back.

Sandra Haynie scored a double in the women's ranks for the first time since Mickey Wright in 1961 by taking the LPGA tourney and the U. S. Open. In the Open she rolled in long putts for birdies on the 17th and 18th holes and won by a stroke from Carol Mann and Beth Stone. Like Irwin, her total of 295 was seven over par for the LaGrange, Ill., Country Club course. In the LPGA, Miss Haynie beat JoAnne Carner by two strokes—and Mrs. Carner was not beaten often. She had won six tourneys by November 15 and earned $89,447.

Jerry Pate of Pensacola, Fla., and the University of Alabama won the U. S. Amateur, beating John Grace of Fort Worth, Texas, in the final after eliminating Curtis Strange, the National Collegiate champion, in the semifinals. Cynthia Hill, of Colorado Springs, turned back the bid of Carol Semple of Sewickley, Pa., to retain the U. S. women's amateur title with a 7 and 5 victory in the final. Pate and Miss Hill led respective U. S. teams to world championships. A United States women's team previously had defeated Britain in Curtis Cup competition, 13–5.

Golf Highlights

Men's Individual Champions

U. S. Open—Hale Irwin, Kirkwood, Mo. (287)
British Open—Gary Player, South Africa (282)
Masters—Gary Player (278)
PGA Tourney—Lee Trevino, El Paso, Texas (276)
Canadian Open—Bobby Nichols, Akron, Ohio (270)
Tournament of Champions—Johnny Miller (280)
PGA Senior—Roberto deVicenzo, Argentina (273)
PGA Club Pro—Roger Watson, Cary, N. C. (284)
Vardon Trophy—Lee Trevino
World Senior Pro—Roberto deVicenzo (defeated Eric Leser, Britain, 5 and 4)
World Series of Golf—Lee Trevino (139)

Pro Team

World Cup—South Africa; *individual:* Bobby Cole, South Africa (271)
PGA National—Hubert Green, Mac McLendon (255)

PGA Tournament Winners

Bing Crosby Pro-Am—Johnny Miller (208)
Phoenix Open—Johnny Miller (271)
Tucson Open—Johnny Miller (272)
San Diego Open—Bobby Nichols (275)
Hawaiian Open—Jack Nicklaus (271)
Hope Desert Classic—Hubert Green (341)
Los Angeles Open—Dave Stockton (276)
Inverrary Classic—Leonard Thompson (278)
Citrus Open—Jerry Heard (273)
Doral Open—Brian Allin (272)
Jacksonville Open—Hubert Green (276)
Heritage Classic—Johnny Miller (276)
New Orleans Open—Lee Trevino (267)
Greensboro Open—Bob Charles (270)
Monsanto Open—Lee Elder (274); won playoff
Tallahassee Open—Allen Miller (274)
Nelson Classic—Brian Allin (269)
Houston Open—Dave Hill (276)
Colonial National—Rod Curl (276)
Memphis Classic—Gary Player (273)
Kemper Open—Bob Menne (270); won playoff
Philadelphia Classic—Hubert Green (271)
American Classic—Jim Colbert (281); won playoff
Western Open—Tom Watson (287)
Milwaukee Open—Ed Sneed (276)
Quad Cities Open—Dave Stockton (271)
B. C. Open—Richie Karl (273); won playoff
Pleasant Valley Open—Victor Regalado (278)
Hartford Open—Dave Stockton (268)
Westchester Classic—Johnny Miller (269)
Tournament Players Championship—Jack Nicklaus (272)
Southern Open—Forrest Fezler (271)
World Open—Johnny Miller (281); won playoff
Kings Island Open—Miller Barber (277)
Kaiser Open—Johnny Miller (271)
Sahara Invitation—Al Geiberger (273)
San Antonio-Texas Open—Terry Diehl (269)

Men's Individual Amateur Champions

U. S. Amateur—Jerry Pate, Pensacola, Fla. (defeated John Grace, Fort Worth, Texas, 2 and 1, in final)
British Amateur—Trevor Homer, England (defeated Jim Gabrielson, Atlanta, Ga., 2 up in 35 holes, in final)
Canadian Amateur—Doug Roxburgh, Vancouver, B. C.
U. S. Public Links—Charlie Barenaba, Laie, Hawaii (290)
U. S. Junior—Dave Nevatt, Merced, Calif. (defeated Mark Tinder, Pebble Beach, Calif., 4 and 3, in final)
National Collegiate (NCAA)—Curtis Strange, Wake Forest (282); Division II: Matt Bloom, Riverside (294)
National Intercollegiate (NAIA)—Dan Frickey, Washburn (294)
Junior College—Mike Donald, Broward, Fla. (282)
USGA Senior—Dale Morey, High Point, N. C. (defeated Lew Oehmig, Lookout Mountain, Tenn., 4 and 2, in final)
U. S. Senior G. A.—James B. Knowles, Londonderry, Vt. (143)

Other Amateur Tournaments

Amputee—Dave DeHebread, Indianapolis (301)
Eastern—Andy Bean, Lakeland, Fla. (272)
Left-handers—Bob Michael, Gainesville, Fla. (297)
New England—Bob Caprera, Southbridge, Mass. (284)
North and South—George Burns, Port Washington, N. Y.
Northeast—Bill Hyndman 3d, Huntingdon Valley, Pa.
Pacific Coast—Mark Pfeil, Redondo Beach, Calif. (284)
Porter Cup—George Burns (276)
Southern—Danny Yate, Atlanta, Ga. (281)
Southeastern—Bo Trotter, Columbus, Ga.
Southwestern—Stan Lee, Baton Rouge, La. (283)
Trans-Mississippi—Tom Jones, Tulsa, Okla.
Western—Curtis Strange
American Senior—Ray Palmer
International Senior—Bill Zimmerman, Green Island, Ga. (297)
World Junior—Nicky Price, Rhodesia (287)

Amateur Team Champions

World (Eisenhower Cup; LaRomana, Dominican Republic, Oct. 30–Nov. 2)—United States (888); Japan (898)
NCAA—Wake Forest (1,158); Division II: University of California, Fullerton (1,205)
NAIA—U. S. International (1,212)
Junior College—Broward, Fla. (1,162)

Women's Individual Pro Champions

U. S. Open—Sandra Haynie, Dallas, Texas (295)
LPGA Tourney—Sandra Haynie (288)
Vare Trophy—JoAnne Carner
Player of the Year—JoAnne Carner

Other LPGA Tour Winners

Burdine's—Sandra Palmer (215); won playoff
Sears Classic—Gail Denenberg (71)
Lely Classic—Carol Mann (209)
Orange Blossom—Kathy Whitworth (209)
Houston S & H—Carol Mann (219)
San Isidro—Jane Blalock (215)
Colgate-Dinah Shore—JoAnn Prentice; won playoff
Birmingham—Jane Blalock (211)
Lady Tara—Sandra Spuzich (219); won playoff
Raleigh Classic—JoAnn Prentice (137)
Bluegrass—JoAnne Carner (215); won playoff
Hoosier Classic—JoAnne Carner (213)
Baltimore Championship—Judy Rankin (144)
Desert Inn Classic—JoAnne Carner (284)
Medina Open—Sandra Haynie (215); won playoff
Peter Jackson, Canada—Carole Jo Skala (208)
Niagara Frontier—Sue Roberts (213)
Borden Classic—Sharon Miller (211)
Wheeling Classic—Carole Jo Skala (212)
George Washington—Sandra Haynie (213)
Colgate European—Judy Rankin (218)
St. Paul Open—JoAnne Carner (212)
Jewish Hospital, Denver—Sandra Haynie (213)
Southgate—Jane Blalock and Sue Robert (142)
Dallas Civitan—JoAnne Carner (210)
Charity Classic—Sandra Haynie (208)
Portland Classic—JoAnne Carner (211)
Sacramento Union—Carole Jo Skala (213)
Cubic Classic—Sandra Palmer (215)
Bill Branch Classic—Bonnie Bryant (209)
Lady Errol Classic—Jane Blalock (215)

Women's Individual Amateur Champions

U. S. Amateur—Cynthia Hill, Colorado Springs (defeated Carol Semple, Sewickly, Pa., 5 and 4, in final)
USGA Girls—Nancy Lopez, Roswell, N. Mex. (defeated Lauren Howe, Colorado Springs, 7 and 5, in final)
British Amateur—Carol Semple
Canadian Amateur—Debbie Massey, Bethlehem, Pa.
Intercollegiate—Mary Budke, Oregon State
World Junior—Lori Nelson, West Chester, Pa.
USGA Senior—Mrs. Justine Cushing, New York (231)

Team

World (Espiritu Santo Trophy, La Romana, Dominican Republic, Oct. 23–26)—United States
Curtis Cup—United States 13, Britain 5
Intercollegiate—Rollins College (1,281)

Leading Money Winners in 1974

Men's PGA

Johnny Miller	$353,021	Dave Hill	$133,674
Jack Nicklaus	238,178	Bruce Crampton	131,356
Hubert Green	211,709	Tom Weiskopf	127,529
Lee Trevino	203,422	Bobby Nichols	124,747
J. C. Snead	164,486	Leonard Thompson	122,349
Dave Stockton	155,105	John Mahaffey	122,189
Hale Irwin	152,529	Rod Curl	120,154
Jerry Heard	145,788	Ray Floyd	119,385
Brian Allin	137,950	Gary Player	108,372
Tom Watson	135,474	Gene Littler	102,822

Career Earnings

Jack Nicklaus	$2,243,623	Miller Barber	$912,875
Arnold Palmer	1,664,096	Bobby Nichols	856,441
Billy Casper	1,479,330	Dave Hill	841,700
Lee Trevino	1,264,445	George Archer	800,243
Bruce Crampton	1,190,867	Doug Sanders	760,003
Gary Player	1,089,210	Dan Sikes	751,381
Gene Littler	1,020,658	Dave Stockton	741,598
Tom Weiskopf	1,005,714	Johnny Miller	721,034
Julius Boros	957,445	Tommy Aaron	716,095
Frank Beard	929,163	Gay Brewer	688,589

Women's PGA

JoAnne Carner	$87,094	Carole Jo Skala	$47,692
Jane Blalock	86,442	Judy Rankin	45,882
Sandra Haynie	74,560	Donna C. Young	38,075
JoAnn Prentice	67,228	Murle Breer	37,789
Sandra Palmer	54,874	Laura Baugh	36,564
Kathy Whitworth	52,025	Gail Denenberg	35,749
Carol Mann	47,721	Sandra Spuzich	33,645

Career Earnings

Kathy Whitworth	$540,344	JoAnn Prentice	$263,969
Sandra Haynie	387,389	Sandra Palmer	254,919
Carol Mann	348,575	Jane Blalock	231,478
Mickey Wright	329,793	Mary Mills	214,913
Betsy Rawls	301,002	Louise Suggs	188,938
Marlene Hagge	289,597	Patty Berg	188,890
Marilynn Smith	278,053	Clifford Ann Creed	186,199
Judy Rankin	276,991	Donna C. Young	182,672

Harness Racing Highlights

U. S. Trotting Association Champions

Trotters

2-Year-Old—Bonefish
3-Year-Old—Dream of Glory
4-Year-Old—Colonial Charm
Aged—Delmonica Hanover
Trotter of the Year—Delmonica Hanover

Pacers

2-Year-Old—Alert Bret
3-Year-Old—Armbro Omaha
4-Year-Old—Armbro Nesbit
Aged—Invincible Shadow
Pacer of the Year—Armbro Nesbit

Harness Horse of the Year

Delmonica Hanover (48 votes), Armbro Nesbit (32), Handle With Care (30)

Major Stakes Winners

Trotting

American Championship (Roosevelt)—Savoir
American Classic (Hollywood)—Savoir
American National (Sportsman's Park)—Nevele Diamond
Challenge Cup (Roosevelt)—Dosson, Italy
Colonial (Liberty Bell)—Keystone Gabriel
Dexter Cup (Roosevelt)—Surge Hanover
Hambletonian (Du Quoin, Ill.)—Christopher T.
Hambletonian Filly Stake (Du Quoin)—Berna Hanover
Hoosier Futurity (Indianapolis)—Ways to Win
Kentucky Futurity (Lexington)—Waymaker
Old Oaken Bucket (Delaware, Ohio)—Dream of Glory
Prix d'Amerique (Paris)—Delmonica Hanover
Realization (Roosevelt)—Wayne Eden
Roosevelt International—Delmonica Hanover
Westbury Futurity (Roosevelt)—Noble Rogue
Yonkers Trot—Spitfire Hanover

Pacing

Adios (Meadows)—Armbro Omaha
American Classic (Hollywood)—Keystone Smartie
American-National Maturity (Sportsman's Park)—Otaro Hanover
Canada Derby (Toronto)—Otaro Hanover
Cane (Yonkers)—Boyden Hanover
Fox (Indianapolis)—Alert Bret
Gaines (Vernon Downs)—Boyden Hanover
Hoosier Futurity (Indianapolis)—Steady Ellie T.
Little Brown Jug (Delaware, Ohio)—Armbro Omaha
Messenger (Roosevelt)—Armbro Omaha
Prix d'Ete (Montreal)—Armbro Hanover
Realization (Roosevelt)—Otaro Hanover
Reynolds (Buffalo)—Boyden Hanover
Roosevelt Futurity—Shirley's Beau
U. S. Pacing Series (3 races)—Sir Dalrae

HARNESS RACING

Three weeks after Delmonica Hanover, the leader of the international harness racing set, was sold for $300,000, she was named horse of the year. The 5-year-old trotting mare took the award by a wide margin over Armbro Nesbit, the top pacer. Delmonica Hanover, in July, won the Roosevelt International for the second straight year after capturing the Prix d' Amerique in France in January, achievements not realized before by an American trotter.

Delmonica Hanover's earnings for the year were $252,165 for a total of $709,799 in a career that included 45 victories. She built up quite a profit for Del Miller of Meadow Lands, Pa., and Arnold Hanger of Lexington, Ky., who bought her as a yearling for $5,000 in a 1970 auction. She was purchased in November by Mrs. Ed Ryan and Mrs. Joseph Hardy of Pittsburgh.

Dream of Glory, a 3-year-old who won 19 of 26 races, was second in the voting for trotter of the year. Armbro Nesbit, a 4-year-old winner of 16 of 20 races, was named pacer of the year by a narrow edge over Handle With Care and Armbro Omaha, the 3-year-old champion who won the Little Brown Jug, the Adios, the Messenger, and Prix d'Ete for a total of $334,207 by mid-November. Handle With Care posted a world record for trotting fillies of 1:54⅘ at the Hollywood track in November. Colonial Charm won at Lexington in 1:56⅕, a record for a trotting mare. Sir Dalrae, the top 1973 horse, had a bad season and received only one vote for pacer of the year.

HOCKEY

The bad guys from across the tracks ran off with the National Hockey League's Stanley Cup in 1974, and a dissatisfied "old man" led his team to the World Hockey Association championship. The bad guys were the rough but talented Philadelphia Flyers, the first of the newer, or expansion, clubs to take the title away from the established teams. The "old man" was Gordie Howe, 46, who became unhappy as a retired front-office man in Detroit and accepted a challenge from Houston. Playing with his

Hockey Highlights

National Hockey League
(Final Standings, 1973–74)

East Division

	W	L	T	Goals For	Goals Agst.	Pts.
Boston Bruins	52	17	9	349	221	113
Montreal Canadiens	45	24	9	293	240	99
New York Rangers	40	24	14	300	251	94
Toronto Maple Leafs	35	27	16	274	230	86
Buffalo Sabres	32	34	12	242	250	76
Detroit Red Wings	29	39	10	255	319	68
Vancouver Canucks	24	43	11	224	296	59
New York Islanders	19	41	18	182	247	56

West Division

	W	L	T	Goals For	Goals Agst.	Pts.
Philadelphia Flyers	50	16	12	273	164	112
Chicago Black Hawks	41	14	23	272	164	105
Los Angeles Kings	33	33	12	233	231	78
Atlanta Flames	30	34	14	214	238	74
Pittsburgh Penguins	28	41	9	242	273	65
St. Louis Blues	26	40	12	206	248	64
Minnesota North Stars	23	38	17	235	275	63
California Golden Seals	13	55	10	195	342	36

Stanley Cup Playoffs

Preliminary Series—East Division: Boston defeated Toronto, 4 games to 0; New York Rangers defeated Montreal, 4 games to 2. West Division: Philadelphia defeated Atlanta, 4 games to 0; Chicago defeated Los Angeles, 4 games to 1
Semifinals—Boston defeated Chicago, 4 games to 2; Philadelphia defeated New York Rangers, 4 games to 3
Final—Philadelphia defeated Boston, 4 games to 2

Individual National Hockey League Awards
(Trophy winners receive $1,500 each from league)

Hart Trophy (most valuable)—Phil Esposito, Boston
Ross Trophy (leading scorer)—Phil Esposito
Norris Trophy (best defenseman)—Bobby Orr, Boston
Calder Trophy (rookie of year)—Denis Potvin, N. Y. Islanders
Lady Byng (sportsmanship)—John Bucyk, Boston
Vezina (goalie)—Tie between Bernie Parent, Philadelphia, and Tony Esposito, Chicago
Conn Smythe Trophy (most valuable in playoffs)—Bernie Parent, Philadelphia
Masterton (courage)—Henri Richard, Montreal

NHL All-Star Teams

	First Team	Second Team
Goal	Bernie Parent, Phila.	Tony Esposito, Chicago
Defense	Bobby Orr, Boston	Bill White, Chicago
Defense	Brad Park, Rangers	Barry Ashbee, Phila.
Center	Phil Esposito, Boston	Bobby Clarke, Phila.
Right Wing	Ken Hodge, Boston	Mickey Redmond, Detroit
Left Wing	Rick Martin, Buffalo	Wayne Cashman, Boston

two sons, he not only led the Aeros to the championship but also won the most valuable player award. That wasn't new to him. He had done it six times in the NHL.

The Flyers, who had finished second in 1973 as Bobby Clarke, a diabetic center, was named most valuable player, got Bernie Parent, goalie, back from the WHA. His work was outstanding, and, with Clarke again leading a group of fast skaters, the Flyers won the West Division honors. In fashioning their victory, they had another active ingredient and one psychological. The active one was a corps of fighters led by Dave Schultz and Bob Kelly who leveled their opponents, with Shultz setting a record of 348 minutes in penalties. The psychological one was a Kate Smith recording of "God Bless America." Of 40 games at which the recording was played, the Flyers won 36.

In the playoffs, the Flyers battled past the New York Rangers, 4 games to 3, but not until they had been warned by the league president to cut down on the fighting and concentrate on playing hockey. Then they upended the former big, bad Bruins, 4 games to 2, for the title and cup. Parent was named the outstanding player of the playoffs. He tied with Tony Esposito of Chicago for the Vezina Trophy.

The Bruins took the East Division title. They were led by Phil Esposito, the season's leading scorer for the fourth straight year, and Bobby Orr, named the outstanding defenseman for the seventh straight year.

Houston signed the Howe family, including Mrs. Howe as a consultant, to a 4-year, $1 million contract. The team, with Don McLeod as goalie, jelled quickly. It won 12 of 14 playoff games, sweeping the surprising Chicago Cougars, paced by Pat Stapleton, in the final. Gordie Howe showed he had lost none of his all-round ability, finishing third in season scoring, 8 points behind Mike Walton of Minnesota, the leader. Gordie's son, Mark Howe, was named the outstanding rookie.

Hockey Highlights (continued)

World Hockey Association
(Final Standings, 1973–74)

East Division

	W	L	T	Goals For	Goals Agst.	Pts.
New England Whalers	43	31	4	291	260	90
Toronto Toros	41	33	4	304	272	86
Cleveland Crusaders	37	32	9	266	264	83
Chicago Cougars	38	35	5	271	273	81
Quebec Nordiques	38	36	4	306	280	80
New Jersey Knights	32	42	4	268	313	68

West Division

	W	L	T	Goals For	Goals Agst.	Pts.
Houston Aeros	48	25	5	318	219	101
Minnesota Fighting Saints	44	32	2	332	275	90
Edmonton Oilers	38	37	3	268	269	79
Winnipeg Jets	34	39	5	264	296	73
Vancouver Blazers	27	50	1	278	345	55
Los Angeles Sharks	25	53	0	239	339	50

Avco Cup Playoffs

Preliminary Series—East: Toronto defeated Cleveland, 4 games to 1; Chicago defeated New England, 4 games to 3. West: Houston defeated Winnipeg, 4 games to 0; Minnesota defeated Edmonton, 4 games to 1
Semifinals—Houston defeated Minnesota, 4 games to 2; Chicago defeated Toronto, 4 games to 3
Final—Houston defeated Chicago, 4 games to 0

Individual WHA Awards

Most Valuable Player—Gordie Howe, Houston
Defenseman of Year—Pat Stapleton, Chicago
Most Sportsmanlike—Ralph Backstrom, Chicago
Rookie of Year—Mark Howe, Houston
Leading Scorer—Mike Walton, Minnesota (117 pts)

WHA All-Star Teams

	First Team	Second Team
Goal	Don McLeod, Houston	Gerry Cheevers, Cleveland
Defense	Pat Stapleton, Chicago	J. C. Tremblay, Quebec
Defense	Paul Shmyr, Cleveland	Al Hamilton, Edmonton
Center	Andre Lacroix, Jersey	Wayne Carleton, Toronto
Left Wing	Bobby Hull, Winnipeg	Mark Howe, Houston
Right Wing	Gordie Howe, Houston	Mike Walton, Minnesota

Other Professional Champions

American League—North: Rochester Americans; South: Baltimore Clippers; playoffs: Hershey Bears defeated Providence Reds, 4 games to 1
Western League—Regular season and playoffs: Phoenix Roadrunners
Central League—Regular season: Oklahoma City Blazers; playoffs: Dallas Black Hawks

Amateur Champions

International League—North: Muskegon; South: Des Moines; playoffs: Des Moines
North American League—Regular season and playoffs: Syracuse
Southern League—Regular season and playoffs: Roanoke
United States League—Northern Division: Thunder Bay; Southern: Madison; playoffs: Thunder Bay
World—USSR; Class B: United States
Memorial Cup (Canadian junior)—Regina Pats
Allan Cup (Canadian senior)—Orillia Terriers
Amateur Hockey Association of the United States—Squirt: Brownstown, Mich.; PeeWee: Detroit; Bantam: Roseville, Minn.; Midget: Detroit; Junior: St. Paul Vulcans; Intermediate: St. Paul

Intercollegiate Champions

NCAA—Minnesota (defeated Michigan Tech, 4–2, in final)
NAIA—Lake Superior State (defeated Bemidji State, 4–1, in final)
ECAC—Division I: Boston University; Division II: Vermont; Division III: Worcester State
WCHA—Michigan Tech and Minnesota
Canadian—University of Waterloo (defeated Sir George Williams, 6–5, in overtime, in final)

Old pro Gordie Howe, former NHL star, led the Houston Aeros of the WHA to the league title. Mark (*right*), one of his two sons with the Aeros, was named top rookie.

UPI

COURTESY CHURCHILL DOWNS

Cannonade, with jockey Angel Cordero in the saddle, won the 1974 Kentucky Derby at Churchill Downs. The two other races in the Triple Crown went to Little Current.

HORSE RACING

A long-legged filly drew much of the attention of the horsemen during the summer. The 2-year-old with the unladylike name of Ruffian displayed such speed that it appeared she was better suited to race against the colts. However she was kept in her own class and won all five of her races. Only an ankle injury and the design of her trainer, Frank H. Whitely, Jr., to campaign her sparingly ended her season at that point. She set stakes and track records, earned $134,052 and had her admirers saying, "Wait 'til next year."

Ruffian's credentials may not have been good enough for horse-of-the-year honors, but those of Forego certainly were. The 4-year-old gelding finished his season with a victory in the 2-mile Jockey Club Gold Cup after triumphs in the 1½-mile Woodward and a 7-furlong sprint handicap. Forego won 8 of 13 races and finished second twice and third twice for earnings of $545,086. His career totals are 17 victories in 31 races and winnings of $733,995.

In the Triple Crown races, Little Current won the Preakness and Belmont Stakes, each by seven lengths, after Cannonade triumphed in the Kentucky Derby. Other American horses of distinction were Foolish Pleasure, a 2-year-old colt who won his first five races; and Chris Evert, a 3-year-old who won the triple crown for fillies and a $350,000 match race. Dahlia, an American bred, with victories in five countries, became the first filly to win over $1 million. She was named British racehorse of the year.

Horse Racing Highlights

Champions of the Year
Eclipse Awards

(Consolidation of polls of the Thoroughbred Racing Association, the Daily Racing Form, and the National Turf Writers Association)
Horse of the Year—Lazy F. Ranch's Forego
2-Year-Old Filly—Locust Hill Farm's Ruffian
2-Year-Old Colt—J. L. Greer's Foolish Pleasure
3-Year-Old Filly—Carl Rosen's Chris Evert
3-Year-Old Colt—Darby Dan Farm's Little Current
Older Filly or Mare—H. T. Mangurian, Jr.'s Desert Vixen
Older Colt or Gelding—Forego
Sprinter—Forego
Turf—Nelson Bunker Hunt's Dahlia
Steeplechase—Mrs. F. Ambrose Clarke's Gran Kan

Major Stakes Winners
(Purses over $100,000)

American Derby (Arlington)—Determined King
Arkansas Derby (Oaklawn)—J. R.'s Pet
Arlington Handicap—Buffalo Lark
Arlington-Washington Park Futurity—Greek Answer
Beldame (Belmont)—Desert Vixen
Belmont Stakes—Little Current
Brooklyn Handicap (Aqueduct)—Forego
California Derby (Golden Gate)—Agitate
Californian (Hollywood)—Quack
Campbell Handicap (Bowie)—True Knight
Century Handicap (Hollywood)—Big Whippendeal
Champagne Stakes (Belmont)—Foolish Pleasure
Coaching Club American Oaks (Belmont)—Chris Evert
Del Mar Futurity—Diabolo
Del Mar Handicap—Red Top III
Fantasy Stakes (Oaklawn)—Miss Musket
Flamingo (Hialeah)—Bushongo
Florida Derby (Gulfstream)—Judger
Futurity (Belmont)—Just the Times
Governor (Belmont)—Big Spruce
Gulfstream Park Handicap—Forego
Haskell Handicap (Monmouth)—True Knight
Hawthorne Gold Cup—Group Plan
Hialeah Turf Cup—Big Whippendeal
Hobson Handicap (Liberty Bell)—Infuriator
Hollywood Derby—Agitate
Hollywood Gold Cup—Tree of Knowledge
Hollywood Juvenile—DiMaggio
Hollywood Lassie—Hot n Nasty
Illinois Derby (Sportsman's Park)—Sharp Gary
Jersey Derby (Garden State)—Better Arbitor
Jockey Club Gold Cup (Aqueduct)—Forego
Kentucky Derby (Churchill Downs)—Cannonade
Kindergarten Stakes (Liberty Bell)—Master Derby
Laurel Futurity—L'Enjolier
Man o' War Handicap (Belmont)—Dahlia
Marlboro Cup (Belmont)—Big Spruce
Metropolitan Handicap (Belmont)—Arbees Boy
Michigan 1⅛ Mile (Detroit)—Tom Tulle
Monmouth Invitational—Holding Pattern
Oak Leaf (Oak Tree at Santa Anita)—Cut Glass
Oak Tree Invitational (Santa Anita)—Tallahto
Ohio Derby (Thistledown)—Stonewalk
Pan-American Turf (Gulfstream)—London Company
Preakness (Pimlico)—Little Current
Santa Anita Derby—Destroyer
Santa Anita Handicap—Prince Dantan
San Juan Capistrano (Santa Anita)—Astray
San Luis Rey (Santa Anita)—Astray
Santa Margarita (Santa Anita)—Tizna
Sapling (Monmouth)—Foolish Pleasure
Secretariat Stakes (Arlington)—Glossary
Selima (Laurel)—Aunt J
Sorority (Monmouth)—Ruffian
Strub (Santa Anita)—Ancient Title
Suburban Handicap (Aqueduct)—True Knight
Sunset Handicap (Hollywood)—Greco II
Swaps Stakes (Hollywood)—Agitate
Travers (Saratoga)—Holding Pattern
Trenton Handicap (Garden State)—True Knight
United Nations Handicap (Atlantic City)—Halo
Vanity Handicap (Hollywood)—Tallahto
Washington, D. C. International (Laurel)—Admetus (France)
Widener (Hialeah)—Forego
Woodward Stakes (Belmont)—Forego

Match Race

Hollywood Park, July 20—Chris Evert defeated Miss Musket by 50 lengths

Other Races

Ascot Gold Cup (England)—Ragstone
Canadian International (Woodbine)—Dahlia (France)
Epsom Derby (England)—Snow Knight
Epsom Oaks (England)—Polygamy
Grand National Steeplechase (England)—Red Rum
Irish Sweeps Derby (Dublin)—English Prince
King George VI and Queen Elizabeth (England)—Dahlia
Melbourne Derby (Australia)—Think Big
1,000 Guineas (England)—Highclere
2,000 Guineas (England)—Nonoalco
Prix de l'Arc de Triomphe (France)—Allez France
Queens Plate (Canada)—Amber Herod

Quarter Horse
(Ruidoso Downs, N. Mex., Sept. 2)

All-American Futurity (purse, $1 million)—Easy Date (Don Knight, jockey; winner's purse, $330,000)

SOCCER

The most prestigious championship in team sports returned to West Germany on July 7, 1974, with the defeat of the Netherlands, 2–1, in the World Cup soccer final before 62,000 fans in Munich. West Germany had previously won the quadriennial competition in 1954.

The match in Munich was the conclusion of quarter-final and semifinal round-robin play among 16 teams remaining from 62 in eliminations that began three years previously. Quarter-final play at nine sites in West Germany began on June 23. The two top teams in each of four groups went into the semifinal round. The top teams of each of two groups met in the final. The standings after the semifinal round were: Group A: Netherlands, 6 points; Brazil, 4; Argentina and East Germany, 1 each. Group B: West Germany, 6; Poland, 4; Sweden, 2; Yugoslavia, 0.

In a match for third place, Poland beat Brazil, 1–0.

West Germany, one of the strong favorites, had to come up with a brilliant defense to defeat the Dutch, who scored in the first minute of play. Gerd Mueller, the highest scorer in Cup play, booted the deciding goal, his 14th in the world matches and fourth of the 1974 games. Johan Neeskens had scored for the Dutch on a penalty when Johan Cruyff, considered the best active player, was tackled from behind on a rush toward the goal. Paul Breitner, also on a penalty, had evened the score for the Germans.

The surprises were—in addition to the Dutch, who went into the final with five victories and one draw—Sweden, Scotland, and Poland. The disappointments were Brazil and Italy, which went out in the semi-finals. (See also *Miscellaneous Sports Summaries.*)

SWIMMING

World marks were made so fast in three great meets during an August fortnight in 1974 that some were submerged before being recorded. The wave of record-breaking was led by the United States and East Germany. The onslaught began in the European championships, continued in the National AAU meet at Concord, Calif., and was regenerated in the U. S.-East German dual meet, also held in the fast, freshwater Concord pool.

In the Vienna meet 17 world and 23 European marks were bettered; in the AAU carnival 11 world and 18 American records went under; and at the dual meet 8 world marks were broken and 2 tied. The United States won the dual meet with an overall score of 198–145, but the American women lost by 5 points.

After the final race on September 1 there were only nine records left unchanged by the three meets. One, the 800-meter freestyle mark of 8:15.88, was set by Tim Holland of Australia on January 31. Of the 22 records broken, 14 were by women, mainly the East German group of Cornelia Ender, Renate Vogel, Rosemarie Kother, Ulrike Richter, and Ulrike Tauber. In the AAU meet, Shirley Babashoff of Mission Viejo, Calif., set two freestyle marks, and Joe Harshbarger of Bellevue, Wash., and Jenny Turrall of Australia set one each. In the dual meet the U. S. 400-meter relay team won in world-record time.

Tim Shaw, a Long Beach, Calif., high school student, set men's records in the 200, 400, and 1,500-meter freestyle AAU events. John Hencken of Santa Clara, Calif., bettered two breaststroke marks against the Germans. David Wilkie of England in the 200 medley and Andras Hargitay of Hungary in the 400 medley broke the East Germany monopoly at Vienna. Steve Furniss of Long Beach tied Wilkie's mark at Concord. Christel Justen of West Germany also beat the East Germans at Vienna, but her 100-meter breaststroke mark lasted only until Miss Vogel dived into the pool at Concord.

John Naber, 18, of Ladera Oaks, Calif., defeated Roland Matthes of East Germany in both backstroke events in the dual meet. The losses were the first for the 23-year-old world record-holder since 1967.

WIDE WORLD

West Germany's Gerd Mueller (*left*) boots home the winning goal in 2–1 victory over the Netherlands in World Cup soccer final, July 7. Arie Van Haan tries in vain to stop the kick.

Swimming Highlights

National AAU Indoor Championships
(Dallas, Texas, April 10–13)

Men

100-Yard Freestyle—Joe Bottom, So. Calif. (0:44.84)
200-Yard Freestyle—Kurt Krumpholz, Santa Clara (Calif.) S. C. (1:39.47)
500-Yard Freestyle—Tim Shaw, Long Beach (Calif.) S. C. (4:23.50)
1,650-Yard Freestyle—Mike Bruner, Stockton, Calif. (15:15.33)
100-Yard Backstroke—John Naber, So. Calif. (0:50.41)
200-Yard Backstroke—Naber (1:49.70)
100-Yard Breaststroke—John Hencken, Santa Clara S. C. (0:55.50)
200-Yard Breaststroke—Rick Colella, Totem Lake S. C., Seattle (2:01.43)
100-Yard Butterfly—Steven Baxter, Santa Clara S. C. (0:49.51)
200-Yard Butterfly—Robin Backhaus, U. of Wash. (1:47.27)
200-Yard Medley—Lee Engstrand, U. of Tenn. (1:51.28)
400-Yard Medley—Colella (3:57.19)
400-Yard Freestyle Relay—So. Calif. (Steve Furniss, Bruce Kocsis, Kim Tutt, Joe Bottom; 3:02.16)
400-Yard Medley Relay—So. Calif. (John Naber, Mark Chatfield, Allen Poucher, Joe Bottom; 3:20.87)
800-Yard Freestyle Relay—So. Calif. (John Naber, Jack Tingley, Rod Strachan, Steve Furniss; 6:41.24)
Team—University of Southern California (564 pts)

Women

100-Yard Freestyle—Kathy Heddy, Jersey A. C., Trenton (0:50.89)
200-Yard Freestyle—Shirley Babashoff, Mission Viejo, (Calif.) S. C. (1:48.79)
500-Yard Freestyle—Shirley Babashoff (4:47.34)
1,650-Yard Freestyle—Karen Hazen, Arden Hills (Calif.) S. C. (16:28.37)
100-Yard Backstroke—Linda Stimpson, Lakewood (Calif.) S. C. (0:57.30)
200-Yard Backstroke—Wendy Cook, Vancouver, B. C. (2:04)
100-Yard Breaststroke—Marcia Morey, Decatur, Ill. (1:05.53)
200-Yard Breaststroke—Lynn Colella, Totem Lake S. C., Seattle (2:19.77)
100-Yard Butterfly—Peggy Tosdal, Mission Viejo, Calif. (0:55.9)
200-Yard Butterfly—Valerie Lee, Mission Viejo (2:00.84)
200-Yard Medley—Kathy Heddy (2:05.06)
400-Yard Medley—Jenni Franks, Wilmington (Del.) A. C. (4:26.22)
400-Yard Freestyle Relay—Mission Viejo (Peggy Tosdal, Kelly Hamill, Valerie Lee, Shirley Babashoff; 3:29.22)
400-Yard Medley Relay—Santa Clara S. C. (Nancy Fitzpatrick, Amy Bettencourt, Meg Gerken, Kelly Rowell; 3:54.21)
800-Yard Freestyle Relay—Mission Viejo (Peggy Tosdal, Kathy Howe, Valerie Lee, Shirley Babashoff; 7:30.73)
Team—Santa Clara (Calif.) S. C. (323 pts)

National AAU Outdoor Championships
(Concord, Calif., Aug. 22–25)

Men

100-Meter Freestyle—Tom Hickcox, Phoenix, Ariz. (0:52.16)
200-Meter Freestyle—Tim Shaw, Long Beach S. C. (1:51.66*)
400-Meter Freestyle—Shaw (3:54.69*)
1,500-Meter Freestyle—Shaw (15:31.75*)
100-Meter Backstroke—John Naber, Ladera Oaks, Calif. (0:58.12)
200-Meter Backstroke—Naber (2:03.53)
100-Meter Breaststroke—John Hencken, Santa Clara (Calif.) S. C. (1:04.38)
200-Meter Breaststroke—Hencken (2:18.93*)
100-Meter Butterfly—Mike Bottom, Santa Clara S. C. (0:55.50)
200-Meter Butterfly—Mike Bruner, Stockton, Calif. (2:01.69)
200-Meter Medley—Steve Furniss, Long Beach, Calif. (2:08.26). (Furniss bettered listed world record with 2:06.65 in trials)
400-Meter Medley—Furniss (4:30.56)
400-Meter Freestyle Relay—Gatorade S. C., Bloomington, Ind. (Mel Nash, Tom Hickcox, Ken Knox, John Murphy; 3:30.46)
400-Meter Medley Relay—Santa Clara S. C. (Mike Bottom, John Hencken, Steve Baxter, Joe Bottom; 3:50.23)
800-Meter Freestyle Relay—Long Beach (Calif.) S. C. (Steve Furniss, Peter Spurzem, Tim Shaw, Bruce Furniss; 7:32.62)
Team—Santa Clara (Calif.) S. C. (297 pts)
* Bettered listed world record

Women

100-Meter Freestyle—Kim Peyton, David Douglas S. C., Portland, Oreg. (0:58.224)
200-Meter Freestyle—Shirley Babashoff, Mission Viejo, Calif. S. C. (2:02.94*)
400-Meter Freestyle—Shirley Babashoff (4:15.77*)
1,500-Meter Freestyle—Jenny Turrall, Australia (16:33.947*) (Jo Harshbarger, Bellevue, Wash., bettered world record for 800 meters in 8:47.66 during race)
100-Meter Backstroke—Margie Moffitt, Silver Spring, Md. (1:04.68)
200-Meter Backstroke—Wendy Cook, Vancouver, B. C. (2:18.81*)
100-Meter Breaststroke—Marcia Morey, Decatur, Ill. (1:14.192)
200-Meter Breaststroke—Marcia Morey (2:39.90)
100-Meter Butterfly—Deena Deardurff, Cincinnati (1:02.776)
200-Meter Butterfly—Valerie Lee, Mission Viejo (2:16.52)
200-Meter Medley—Kathy Heddy, Milltown, N. J. (2:22.477)
400-Meter Medley—Jenni Franks, Wilmington, Del. (5:00.51)
400-Meter Freestyle Relay—Mission Viejo Nadadores (Peggy Tosdal, Kelly Hamill, Valerie Lee, Shirley Babashoff; 3:58.10)
400-Meter Medley Relay—Lakewood (Calif.) Aquatic Club (Linda Stimpson, Anna Jean Burge, Shari Ramage, Lelei Fonoimoana; 4:24.76)
800-Meter Freestyle Relay—Mission Viejo (Peggy Tosdal, Kathy Howe, Valerie Lee, Shirley Babashoff; 8:30.232)
Team—Mission Viejo (Calif.) Nadadores (236 pts)
Combined team (men and women)—Santa Clara S. C. (531 pts)
* Bettered listed world record

Diving (Indoor)
(Dallas, Texas, April 3–7)

Men

1-Meter—Tim Moore, Ohio State (517.65 pts)
3-Meter—Lt. Phil Boggs, Air Force (547.20 pts)
Platform—Steve McFarland, Miami Univ. (486.21 pts)

Women

1-Meter—Christine Loock, Southern Methodist (459.09 pts)
3-Meter—Jenni Chandler, Birmingham, Ala. (459.33 pts)
Platform—Janet Ely, Dallas (327.75 pts)

Diving (Outdoor)
(Decatur, Ala., Aug. 13–17)

Men

1-Meter—Tim Moore, Columbus, Ohio (555.36 pts)
3-Meter—Keith Russell, Mesa, Ariz. (625.05 pts)
Platform—Russell (546.84 pts)

Women

1-Meter—Cynthia Potter, Houston (491.34 pts)
3-Meter—Christine Loock, Fort Worth (522.99 pts)
Platform—Teri York, Vancouver, B. C. (362.19 pts)

National Collegiate (NCAA) Championships
(Long Beach, Calif., March 27–30)

50-Yard Freestyle—John Trembley, Tennessee (0:20.23)
100-Yard Freestyle—Joe Bottom, So. California (0:45.06)
200-Yard Freestyle—Jim Montgomery, Indiana (1:39.18)
500-Yard Freestyle—John Naber, So. California (4:26.85)
1,650-Yard Freestyle—Jack Tingley, So. California (15:29.28)
100-Yard Backstroke—Naber (0:50.51)
200-Yard Backstroke—Naber (1:48.95)
100-Yard Butterfly—Trembley (0:48.71)
200-Yard Butterfly—Robin Backhaus, Washington (1:47.0)
100-Yard Breaststroke—David Wilkie, Miami (0:56.72)
200-Yard Breaststroke—John Hencken, Stanford (2:01.74)
200-Yard Medley—Steve Furniss, So. California (1:51.52)
400-Yard Medley—Furniss (3:57.80)
400-Yard Medley Relay—Tennessee (Kevin Priestley, Rick Seywert, John Trembley, Tom Lutz; 3:22.78)
400-Yard Freestyle Relay—Indiana (Mel Nash, Bill Hickcox, Jim Montgomery, John Murphy; 3:00.35)
800-Yard Freestyle Relay—Indiana (Jim Montgomery, John Kinsella, Fred Tyler, Bill Hickcox; 6:40.32)
1-Meter Dive—Tim Moore, Ohio State (494.25 pts)
3-Meter Dive—Rick McAllister, Air Force Academy (526.41 pts)
Team—University of Southern California (339 pts); Indiana, second (338 pts)

Association for Intercollegiate Athletics for Women Championships
(University Park, Pa., March 14–16)

50-Yard Freestyle—Debbie Renz, Monmouth (0:26.58)
100-Yard Freestyle—Sally Tuttle, Arizona State (0:53.30)
200-Yard Freestyle—Sharon Berg, Miami (1:55.67)
400-Yard Freestyle—Sharon Berg (4:03.93)
50-Yard Backstroke—Laura Pasternak, Florida (0:28.72)
100-Yard Backstroke—Libby Tullis, Arizona State (0:59.74)
50-Yard Butterfly—Camille Wright, Virginia (0:26.69)
100-Yard Butterfly—Camille Wright (0:57.87)
50-Yard Breaststroke—Vicki Hays, Stanford (0:30.90)
100-Yard Breaststroke—Cathy Carr, New Mexico (1:06.36)
100-Yard Medley—Cathy Corcione, Princeton (1:00.54)
200-Yard Medley—Cathy Corcione (2:10.10)
200-Yard Freestyle Relay—Arizona State (Maryanne Graham, Debbie Hudson, Cyd Horsley, Libby Tullis; 1:41.54)
200-Yard Medley Relay—Arizona State (Carol Pflugheber, Debbie Hudson, Cappi Siefarth, Sally Tuttle; 1:51.40)
400-Yard Freestyle Relay—Florida (Barb Thomas, Laura Pasternak, Karen Stottlemeyer, Sue Halfacre; 3:39.15)
400-Meter Medley Relay—Arizona State (Libby Tullis, Pinkie Collins, Cappi Siefarth, Sally Tuttle; 4:07.20)
1-Meter Dive—Jane Manchester, Michigan State (421.56 pts)
3-Meter Dive—Jane Manchester (430.23 pts)
Team—Arizona State (242 pts)

TENNIS

Love has always been an integral part of the game of tennis, but at Wimbledon in 1974 rather than meaning "nothing" it became something very positive. In fact, it almost became the theme of the venerable competition as the singles championships were won by Chris Evert and Jimmy Connors. Earlier in the year the young Americans had announced their plans to wed, and after their triumphs they danced the first dance at the traditional ball. Miss Evert defeated Olga Morozova of the Soviet Union, 6–0, 6–4, 6–4, in the final, then watched Jimmy crush Ken Rosewall of Australia, 6–1, 6–1, 6–4.

Each had brought a fine record to Wimbledon. Jimmy had won the Australian Open and the U. S. Indoor. Chris, the runner-up in Australia to Evonne Goolagong, had taken the Italian and French titles and was in the midst of a

Tennis Highlights

Major Tournaments

Davis Cup—Semifinals: India defeated USSR, 3–1; South Africa defeated Italy, 4–1. Cup was awarded to South Africa when India refused to play in final because of apartheid policy of South Africa.
Wightman Cup (Deeside, Wales, Oct. 24–26)—Britain defeated United States, 6–1
Federation Cup (Naples, Italy, May 13–19)—Australia defeated United States in final, 2–1
Bon Belle Cup (Cleveland)—United States defeated Australia, 5–4
Stevens Cup (senior men, Kiamesha Lake, N. Y., Aug. 26–28)—United States defeated Australia, 2–1
U. S. Open (Forest Hills, N. Y., Aug. 28–Sept. 9)—*Men's singles:* Jimmy Connors, Belleville, Ill.; *women's singles:* Billie Jean King, Hilton Head, S. C.; *men's doubles:* Bob Lutz, San Clemente, Calif., and Stan Smith, Sea Pines, S. C.; *women's doubles:* Billie Jean King and Rosemary Casals, San Francisco; *mixed doubles:* Pam Teeguarden, Los Angeles, and Geoff Masters, Australia; *men's 35 singles:* Gene Scott, New York; *Grand Masters singles:* Richard (Pancho) Gonzalez, Las Vegas, Nev.; *junior men's singles:* Billy Martin, Palos Verdes, Calif.; *junior women's singles:* Ilana Kloss, South Africa
National Men's Indoor Open (Salisbury, Md., Feb. 19–24)—*Singles:* Jimmy Connors, Belleville, Ill.; *doubles:* Connors and Frew McMillan, South Africa
National Women's Indoor (New York, March 26–31)—*Singles:* Billie Jean King (defeated Chris Evert, 6–3, 3–6, 6–2, in final)
National Clay Court (Indianapolis, Aug. 5–12)—*Men's singles:* Jimmy Connors; *women's singles:* Chris Evert; *men's doubles:* Connors and Ilie Nastase, Romania; *women's doubles:* Gail Chanfreau, France, and Julie Heldman, Houston
National Amateur Grass Court (Newport, R. I., Aug. 19–25)—*Men's singles:* Chico Hagey, La Jolla, Calif.; *men's doubles:* DeArmond Briggs and Rand Evett, Rock Island, Ill.
National Senior Clay Courts (Charlottesville, Va., July 21–28)—*Men's singles:* Bob Barker, Manhasset, N. Y.; *men's doubles:* Homer Richards, Charlottesville, Va., and Leonard Brose, Southfield, Mich.
National Men's 35 (Manhasset, N. Y., July 29–Aug. 4)—*Singles:* Gene Scott, New York; *doubles:* Ned Weld, Weston, Mass., and Michael Green, Yardley, Pa.
National Amateur Clay Courts (Chattanooga, Tenn., July 1–7)—*Men's singles:* Victor Amaya, Holland, Mich.; *women's singles:* Lynn Epstein, Miami, Fla.; *men's doubles:* Nick Saviano, Los Altos Hills, Calif., and Peter Fleming, Chatham, N. J.; *women's doubles:* Lindsay Morse, Pasadena, Calif., and Sue Boyle, San Diego, Calif.
National Women's Clay Courts (Pensacola, Fla., July 24–28)—*Singles:* Nancy Reed, Winter Park, Fla.; *doubles:* Jane Crofford, Nashville, Tenn., and Betty Gray, Knoxville, Tenn.
National Junior (Kalamazoo, Mich.)—*Singles:* Ferdie Taygan, Framingham, Mass.; *doubles:* Francisco Gonzalez, Puerto Rico, and Rocky Maguire, Woodside, Calif.
National Girls 18 (Philadelphia)—*Singles:* Rayni Fox, North Miami Beach, Fla.; *doubles:* Barbara Hallquist, Arcadia, Calif., and Anne Bruning, La Jolla, Calif.

Other U. S. Championships

NCAA—*Singles:* John Whitlinger, Stanford; *doubles:* Whitlinger–Jim Delaney, Stanford; *team:* Stanford. Division II: *singles:* Andy Rae, University of San Diego; *doubles:* Rae–Russell Watts, Univ. of San Diego; *team:* Univ. of San Diego
NAIA—*Singles:* Stan Franker, Texas Southern; *doubles:* John Blomberg–Bengt Anthin, California Baptist; *team:* Univ. of Redlands
Women's Intercollegiate—*Singles:* Carrie Meyer, Marymount; *doubles:* Ann Lebedeff–Karen Reinke, San Diego State; *team:* Arizona State
Junior College—*Singles:* Fernando Maynetto, Wingate (N. C.); *doubles:* Martin Vasquez–Paul Fineman, Odessa; *team:* Central Texas
National Interscholastic—*Singles:* Chris Delaney, Georgetown Prep; *doubles:* Jim Hodges–Tim Jenkins, Landon Prep; *team:* Landon Prep

Other Countries

Wimbledon (Wimbledon, England, June 24–July 7)—*Men's singles:* Jimmy Connors, Belleville, Ill.; *women's singles:* Chris Evert, Fort Lauderdale, Fla.; *men's doubles:* John Newcombe and Tony Roche, Australia; *women's doubles:* Evonne Goolagong, Australia, and Peggy Michel, Pacific Palisades, Calif.; *mixed doubles:* Billie Jean King, Hilton Head, S. C., and Owen Davidson, Australia; *junior singles:* Billy Martin, Palos Verdes, Calif.; *junior women:* Mima Jousovas, Yugoslavia; *senior doubles:* Ron Dunes and Gardnar Mulloy, Coral Gables, Fla.
Australian Open (Melbourne, finals, Jan. 1)—*Men's singles:* Jimmy Connors; *women's singles:* Evonne Goolagong; *men's doubles:* Ross Case and Geoff Masters, Australia; *women's doubles:* Evonne Goolagong and Peggy Michel
French Open (Paris, June 3–16)—*Men's singles:* Bjorn Borg, Sweden; *women's singles:* Chris Evert; *men's doubles:* Dick Crealy, Australia, and Onny Parun, New Zealand; *women's doubles:* Chris Evert and Olga Morozova, USSR; *mixed doubles:* Martina Navratilova, Czechoslovakia, and Ivan Molina, Colombia
Italian Open (Rome, May 26–June 3)—*Men's singles:* Bjorn Borg; *women's singles:* Chris Evert; *men's doubles:* Raul Ramirez, Mexico, and Brian Gottfried, Fort Lauderdale, Fla.; *women's doubles:* Chris Evert and Olga Morozova
Canadian Open (Toronto, Aug. 12–19)—*Men's singles:* Guillermo Vilas, Argentina; *women's singles:* Chris Evert; *men's doubles:* Vilas and Manuel Orantes, Spain; *women's doubles:* Julie Heldman and Gail Chanfreau, France

Professional Champions

U. S. Championship (Brookline, Mass.)—*Singles:* Bjorn Borg; *doubles:* Stan Smith, Sea Pines, S. C., and Bob Lutz, San Clemente, Calif.
World Championship Tennis tour final (Dallas, May 12)—John Newcombe, Australia (defeated Borg, 4–6, 6–3, 6–3, 6–2)
Virginia Slims tour final (Los Angeles, Oct. 27)—Evonne Goolagong (defeated Chris Evert, 6–3, 6–4)
World Doubles Championship (Montreal, May 5)—Bob Hewitt and Frew McMillan, South Africa
Team Tennis Championship (Philadelphia, Aug. 26)—Denver Racquets (defeated Philadelphia Freedoms, 28–24)

LEADING MONEY WINNERS IN 1974

World Championship Tennis Tour
(Contract Professionals)

John Newcombe	$174,085	Tom Okker	$47,750
Arthur Ashe	79,175	Frew McMillan	42,725
Bjorn Borg	76,645	Roscoe Tanner	39,401
Rod Laver	70,600	Bob Hewitt	32,975
Stan Smith	61,900	Cliff Drysdale	29,560
Ilie Nastase	57,135	John Alexander	29,170

Virginia Slims-USLTA
(Contract Professionals)

Chris Evert	$149,985	Kerry Melville	$42,940
Billie Jean King	129,950	Betty Stove	39,233
Evonne Goolagong	73,480	Julie Heldman	27,468
Virginia Wade	55,993	Martina Navratilova	26,963
Rosemary Casals	62,375	Lesley Hunt	26,675
Françoise Durr	40,008	Olga Morozova	25,775

Commercial Union Grand Prix
Men

Guillermo Vilas	$100,000*	Ilie Nastase	$19,750
Jimmy Connors	55,000	Onny Parun	17,750
Manuel Orantes	37,500	Harold Solomon	16,000
Bjorn Borg	27,500	Arthur Ashe	15,000
Raul Ramirez	22,500	Stan Smith	14,000

* Also won masters tournament and $40,000

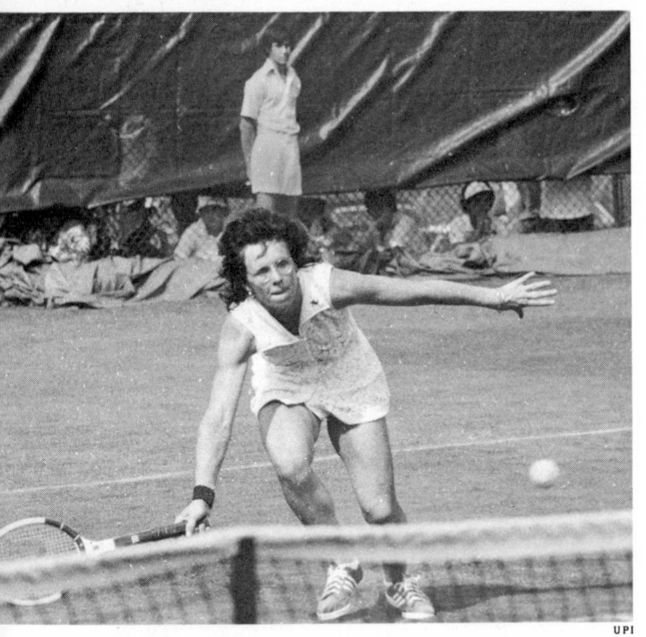

UPI

Billie Jean King rushes to make return during play in the U. S. Open championship at Forest Hills. She beat Evonne Goolagong in the final for her fifth U. S. title.

long winning streak. After the British tourney, each won the title in the U. S. clay courts, and Chris took the Canadian crown at Toronto.

In the U. S. Open, Connors gained his second major championship again by beating Rosewall in the final, 6–1, 6–0, 6–1. Miss Evert, though, was stopped in the semifinals, again by Miss Goolagong. Billie Jean King then defeated the Australian champion with a splendid rally, 3–6, 6–3, 7–5, for her fifth U. S. title.

Aside from Mrs. King, Rosewall, and John Newcombe, who led the World Championship Tennis tour winners with $174,085, the year belonged to the young players. In addition to Connors, 22, who won $285,490, Miss Evert, 19, and Miss Goolagong, 23, the young stars included Bjorn Borg, 18, of Sweden; Guillermo Vilas, 22, of Argentina; Vijay Amritraj, 20, and his brother, Anand, 22, of India; and Martina Navratilova, 17, of Czechoslovakia.

Borg won the French, Canadian, and Italian opens and the U. S. pro title but was beaten in the WCT final by Newcombe. Vilas took the overall grand prix of $140,000.

The Amritraj brothers led India to the final round of the Davis Cup against South Africa. But because of South Africa's racial policies, India refused to play, and the Cup went to South Africa by default.

Miss Goolagong again beat Miss Evert in the USLTA-Virginia Slims final, winning $32,000 for a total of $73,480. But Miss Evert, by winning $14,500, broke Margaret Court's record for a season's earnings with $194,157. Mrs. Court had won $191,495 in 1973.

TRACK AND FIELD

Filbert Bayi and Tony Waldrop kept up a steady attack against Jim Ryun's world records in 1974 and left him with only one—that for the outdoor one-mile run. Bayi took off with the record for the 1,500-meter run, or metric mile, at the Commonwealth Games in Christchurch, New Zealand. He won in 3 minutes, 32.2 seconds, bettering Ryun's 6½-year-old record of 3:33.1 by almost one second.

Waldrop posted a series of times under 4 minutes during the winter, hitting 3:55 in San Diego, February 17, a world best for the indoor mile since there are no official indoor records. Tom O'Hara had done 3:56.4 in 1964 for the previous best, and Ryun had equaled it in 1971. Waldrop then became the third-fastest miler, with 3:52.3 at the Penn Relays on April 27. Only Ryun with his record of 3:51.1 and a 3:51.3 and Ben Jipcho with 3:52 have run the mile faster.

Rick Wohlhuter of Chicago, who had taken another of Ryun's marks, the half-mile, from him in 1973, lowered the time again. He hit 1:44.1 at Eugene, Oreg., June 8, breaking his mark by five-tenths of a second. Ryun's record had been 1:44.9. Wohlhuter also ran 1,000 meters at Oslo, Norway, on July 30 in 2:13.9, breaking Daniel Malan's world record of 2:16.

The world record fell also in another of track's glamour events: the 100-yard dash. Ivory Crockett ran it in 9 seconds, May 11, at Knoxville, Tenn., bettering by one-tenth of a second a mark shared by five famous dashmen. Steve Williams of San Diego won the AAU 100-meter dash, June 21, at Los Angeles in 9.9 seconds, tying the world mark held by six others. Jim Bolding of Oklahoma City lowered the mark for the 440 hurdles to 48.7 from 48.8 at Turin, Italy, July 24.

Record-breaking was not confined to men's competition. In a three-week span three women's marks were broken and one tied. Irena Szewinski of Poland ran 400 meters in 49.9 seconds at Warsaw, June 22, and 200 meters in 22 seconds at Potsdam, July 13. At the AAU meet, Debra Sapenter of Prairie View, Texas, equaled the record of 52.2 seconds for the 440 and Ludmilla Bragina of the USSR set a record for 3,000 meters at Durham, N. C., July 6, in a meet with the United States. She did 8:52.74. In walking, Susan Brodock of Rialto, Calif., set a world mark for 5,000 meters of 24:54.8 at Stockholm for the world title.

George Woods created an odd situation in an indoor meet at Inglewood, Calif., by putting the shot 72 feet 2¾ inches. That is the farthest the 16-pound weight has been propelled, but the record still stands at 71-7, the mark made by Al Feuerbach in 1973 in an outdoor meet. Since there are no accepted official world indoor records, Woods' performance can only be listed as a world best and an American record.

Track and Field Highlights

National AAU Indoor Championships
(Madison Square Garden, N. Y., Feb. 22)

Men

60 Yards—Herb Washington, Ann Arbor, Mich. (0:06)
60-Yard Hurdles—Tom Hill, U. S. Army (0:06.9)
600 Yards—Wesley Williams, San Diego T. C. (1:11.3)
1,000 Yards—Rick Wohlhuter, Univ. of Chicago T. C. (2:06.8)
Mile—John Walker, New Zealand (4:01.6)
3 Miles—Dick Tayler, New Zealand (13:08.6)
2-Mile Walk—Larry Walker, Beverly Hills Striders (13:24)
Sprint Medley Relay—Adelphi University (Ray Lee, William Henderson, Keith Davis, Richard Hardware; 2:05.1)
Mile Relay—Philadelphia Pioneers (Ed Roberts, Vic McKenley, Curtis Mills, Herman Frazier; 3:17)
2-Mile Relay—Univ. of Chicago T. C. (Tom Bach, Ken Sparks, Rick Wohlhuter, Lowell Paul; 7:32.6)
Shot Put—Terry Albritton, Palo Alto, Calif. (69 ft 3/4 in)
Pole Vault—Vic Diaz, Beverly Hills Striders (17 ft 8 in)
Long Jump—Jerry Proctor, Beverly Hills Striders (25 ft 10 in)
High Jump—Tom Woods, Oregon State (7 ft 2 in)
Triple Jump—Milan Tiff, Beverly Hills Striders (54 ft)
35-Pound Weight Throw—Jacques Accambray, Kent State (70 ft 6 in)

Women

60 Yards—Theresa Montgomery, Tennessee State (0:06.7)
60-Yard Hurdles—Patty Johnson, La Jolla (Calif.) T. C. (0:07.7)
220 Yards—Tie between Linda Cordy, Atoms T. C., Brooklyn, N. Y., and Theresa Montgomery (0:25)
440 Yards—Brenda Nichols, Atoms T. C. (0:56.1)
880 Yards—Mary Decker, Blue Angels (2:07.1)
Mile—Robin Campbell, Sports International, Washington (4:50.7)
Mile Walk—Susan Brodock, Rialto (Calif.) Road Runners (7:28.6)
640-Yard Relay—Mayor Daley Y. F., Chicago (Roselyn Bryant, Valerie Milan, Celeste Johnson, Terry Hopkins; 1:12.4)
Mile Relay—Atoms T. C., Brooklyn, N. Y. (Michele McMillan, Renee Desadies, Gale Fitzgerald, Brenda Nichols; 3:48.3)
Shot Put—Maren Seidler, Mayor Daley Y. F. (54 ft 4 in)
High Jump—Joni Huntley, Oregon T. C. (6 ft)
Long Jump—Martha Watson, Lakewood (Calif.) Int. (20 ft 9½ in)
Team—Atoms T. C., Brooklyn, N. Y. (24 pts)

National AAU Outdoor Championships

Men
(Los Angeles, June 21–22)

100 Meters—Steve Williams, San Diego (0:09.9)
200 Meters—Don Quarrie, Beverly Hills Striders (0:20.5)
400 Meters—Maurice Peoples, D. C. Striders (0:45.2)
800 Meters—Rick Wohlhuter, Univ. of Chicago T. C. (1:43.9)
1,500 Meters—Rod Dixon, New Zealand (3:37.5)
3,000-Meter Steeplechase—Jim Johnson, Club NW (8:28.8)
5,000 Meters—Dick Buerkle, New York A. C. (13:33.4)
10,000 Meters—Frank Shorter, Florida T. C., Gainesville (28:16)
5,000-Meter Walk—John Knifton, New York A. C. (22:23)
110-Meter Hurdles—Charles Foster, N. Carolina Central (0:13.4)
400-Meter Hurdles—Jim Bolding, Oklahoma City (0:48.9)
Long Jump—Bouncy Moore, Pomona, Calif. (26 ft 5¾ in)
Triple Jump—John Craft, Univ. of Chicago T. C. (54 ft 4¾ in)
High Jump—Dwight Stones, Pacific Coast Club (7 ft 3¼ in)
Pole Vault—Dave Roberts, Gulf Coast T. C. (17 ft 6 in)
Shot Put—Al Feuerbach, Pacific Coast T. C. (70 ft 9¾ in)
Javelin—Sam Colson, Lawrence, Kans. (280 ft 8 in)
Discus—John Powell, San Jose, Calif. (214 ft 11 in)
Hammer—Steve DeAutremont, Beverly Hills Striders (226 ft 6 in)

Women
(Bakersfield, Calif., June 28–29)

100 Yards—Renaye Bowen, Lakewood (Calif.) Int. (0:10.4)
220 Yards—Alice Annum, Sports Int., Washington (0:23.1)
440 Yards—Debra Sapenter, Prairie View A. & M. (0:52.2)
880 Yards—Mary Decker, Garden Grove, Calif. (2:05.2)
Mile—Julie Brown, Los Angeles T. C. (4:45.1)
2 Miles—Lynn Bjorklund, Duke City Dashers, Albuquerque, N. Mex. (10:11.1)
Mile Walk—Susan Brodock, Rialto (Calif.) Road Runners (7:29.7)
110-Meter Hurdles—Patty Johnson, La Jolla (Calif.) T. C. (0:13.2)
400-Meter Hurdles—Andrea Bruce, Prairie View A. & M. (0:59.7)
440-Yard Relay—Texas Women's University (Janet Brown, Lucy Vaamonde, Rochelle Davis, Audrey Reid; 0:45.6)
880-Yard Medley Relay—Sports International, Washington (Alice Annum, Rose Allwood, Gwen Norman, Debbie Pastel; 1:38.5)
Mile Relay—Sports International (Sherry James, Gwen Norman, Robin Campbell, Debbie Pastel; 3:39.6)
2-Mile Relay—San Jose Cinderbelles (Kathy Haughey, Judy Graham, Amy Haberman, Cyndy Poor; 8:49.1)
Long Jump—Martha Watson, Lakewood (Calif.) Int. (21 ft 3½ in)
High Jump—Joni Huntley, Oregon T. C. (6 ft)
Discus—Joan Pavelich, La Jolla (Calif.) T. C. (173 ft 11 in)
Shot Put—Maren Seidler, Mayor Daley Y. F., Chicago (54 ft 3 in)
Javelin—Kathy Schmidt, Los Angeles T. C. (203 ft 2 in)
Team—Sports International, Washington (56 pts)

Other AAU Events

56-Pound Weight Throw—Albert Hall, Backus H. C. (44 ft)

Relays
(New York, July 13)

440 Yards—Philadelphia Pioneer Club (0:40.3)
880 Yards—Philadelphia Pioneer Club (1:23.4)
One Mile—Philadelphia Pioneer Club (3:09.6)
Two Miles—University of Chicago T. C. (7:31.4)
Four Miles—New York Athletic Club (16:58.6)
Distance Medley—University of Chicago T. C. (9:53.8)

Distance Runs

20 Kilometers—Gary Tuttle, Ventura, Calif. (1:02:16)
30 Kilometers—Reid Harter, Santa Monica (Calif.) T. C. (1:38:30)
20 Kilometers (Junior)—Lionel Ortega, New Mexico T. C. (1:04:57)

Walks

5 Kilometers (Junior)—Jim Bentley, Sierra Race Walkers (24:28)
15 Kilometers—Larry Walker, Beverly Hills Striders (1:10:08)
15 Kilometers (Junior)—Bentley (1:16:34)
20 Kilometers—Jerry Brown, Colorado T. C., Boulder (1:33:33)
25 Kilometers—John Knifton, New York A. C. (1:56:03)
25 Kilometers (Junior)—James Mutchie, Long Island A. C. (2:11:12)
35 Kilometers—Floyd Godwin, Colorado T. C. (2:55:28)
50 Kilometers (Women)—Esther Marquez, Rialto (Calif.) Road Runners (26:27.4)

Decathlon Champions

AAU—Bruce Jenner, San Jose, Calif. (8,245 pts)
USTFF—Rick Wanamaker, Des Moines (7,543 pts)
NAIA—James Herron, Cameron State (6,939 pts)
NCAA—Runald Backman, Brigham Young (7,874 pts)
NCAA Division II—Paul Fink, Calif. State, Fullerton (7,067 pts)
Penn Relays—Fred Samara, New York A. C. (7,864 pts)

Pentathlon Champions

AAU—Jack Carter, New York A. C. (3,403 pts)
AAU Women—Mitzi McMillian, Seattle (4,051 pts)
AAU Women (Junior)—Lisa Chiavario, Albuquerque, N. Mex. (3,653 pts)

Marathons

AAU—Ron Wayne, Oregon T. C., Eugene (2:18.52)
AAU Masters—Pat Esrick, Westport, Conn. (2:31:21.6)
Boston—Neil Cusack, Ireland (2:13.39); first woman finisher: Mrs. Mickiko Gorman, Los Angeles (2:47.11)
USTFF—John Lesch, University of Chicago T. C. (2:26:03.2)
USTFF (meet)—Roberto Rosales, Salina T. C. (2:36.01)
NAIA—Lucian Rosa, Wisconsin-Parkside (2:22.54)
Junior College—Terry Baker, Hagerstown (Md.) C. C. (2:28.48)
Women—Judy Ikenberry, Rialto (Calif.) Road Runners (2:55.17)
World Masters—Bob Kurrie, Beverly Hills Striders (2:28.48)

Other Team Champions

NCAA Division II—Tie between Eastern Illinois (51 pts) and Norfolk State (51 pts)
NCAA Division III—Eastern Illinois (61 pts)
NAIA—Outdoor: Eastern New Mexico (67 pts); indoor: Texas Southern (45 pts)
Women's Intercollegiate—Prairie View A. & M. (84 pts)

International Competitions

At Moscow (March 2, indoor)—*Men:* United States 89, USSR 72; *women:* USSR 69, United States 52
At Durham, N. C. (July 5–6)—*Men:* United States 117, USSR 102; *women:* USSR 90, United States 67
At Austin, Texas (June 28–29, junior)—*Men:* United States 133, USSR 99; *women:* USSR 82, United States 64

National Collegiate (NCAA) Outdoor Championships
(Austin, Texas, June 4–8)

100 Yards—Reggie Jones, Tennessee (0:09.2)
220 Yards—James Gilkes, Fisk (0:19.9)
440 Yards—Larance Jones, Northeast Missouri (0:45.5)
880 Yards—Willie Thomas, Tennessee (1:49)
Mile—Paul Cummings, Brigham Young (4:01.1)
3 Miles—Paul Geis, Oregon (13:39)
6 Miles—John Ngeno, Washington State (28:14.6)
3,000-Meter Steeplechase—Doug Brown, Tennessee (8:36)
120-Yard Hurdles—Charles Foster, N. Carolina Central (13:36)

Track and Field Highlights (continued)

440-Yard Hurdles—Bruce Collins, Penn (0:50.3)
440-Yard Relay—Kansas (Tom Scavuzzo, Eddie Lewis, Mark Lutz, Emmett Edwards; 0:39.5)
Mile Relay—UCLA (Lynnsey Guerrero, Benny Brown, Jerome Walters, Maxie Parks; 3:06.6)
High Jump—Randy Smith, Kansas (7 ft 2 in)
Long Jump—Jerry Herndon, UCLA (26 ft 6¼ in)
Triple Jump—Charlton Ehizuelen, Illinois (54 ft 8 in)
Pole Vault—Ed Lipscomb, Oregon State (17 ft 3 in)
Hammer—Peter Farmer, Texas–El Paso (230 ft 6 in)
Shot Put—Jesse Stuart, Western Kentucky (66 ft 5¼ in)
Discus—Zdravko Pecar, Brigham Young (190 ft 2 in)
Javelin—Jim Judd, Oregon State (271 ft 3 in)
Team—Tennessee (60 pts)

NCAA Indoor Championships
(Detroit, March 8–9)

60 Yards—Cliff Outlin, Auburn (0:06)
60-Yard Hurdles—Danny Smith, Florida State (0:07)
440 Yards—Larance Jones, Northeast Missouri (0:48.6)
600 Yards—Stan Vinson, Eastern Michigan (1:10.1)
880 Yards—Reggie Clark, William & Mary (1:52.2)
1,000 Yards—Wesley Maiyo, Wyoming (2:08.1)
Mile—Tony Waldrop, North Carolina (3:59.5)
3 Miles—John Ngeno, Washington State (13:20.8)
Mile Relay—Seton Hall (Al Daley, Charles Joseph, Art Cooper, Howard Brock; 3:14)
2-Mile Relay—South Carolina (Don Brown, Mike Shelley, John Brown, Jim Schaper; 7:27.4)
Distance Medley Relay—Missouri (Mike Rabuse, Jim Crawford, Dave Rogles, Charles McMullen; 9:45)
Pole Vault—Larry Jessee, Texas–El Paso (16 ft 6 in)
Triple Jump—Tommy Haynes, Middle Tennessee (54 ft 6¾ in)
Long Jump—Kingsley Adams, Colorado (25 ft 3¾ in)
High Jump—Mike Fleer, Oregon State (7 ft 2 in)
Shot Put—Hans Hoglund, Texas–El Paso (67 ft 7¼ in)
35-Pound Weight Throw—Jacques Accambray, Kent State (71 ft 10¾ in)
Team—Texas–El Paso (19 pts)

U. S. Track and Field Federation Outdoor Championships
(Wichita, Kans., May 31–June 1)

Men

100 Yards—Dean Williams, Kansas State (0:09.5)
220 Yards—Bill Collins, Texas Christian (0:21)
440 Yards—Stan Vinson, Eastern Michigan (0:46.7)
880 Yards—Jim Hinchliffe, Kansas State (1:48.3)
Mile—Rick Wohlhuter, Univ. of Chicago Track Club (3:55.1)
3 Miles—John Halberstadt, Pacific Coast T. C., Long Beach, Calif. (13:22.8)
3,000-Meter Steeplechase—Randy Lussenden, Univ. of Chicago T. C. (8:38.2)
120-Yard Hurdles—Efren Gipson, Lamar (0:13.6)
440-Yard Hurdles—Jim Bolding, Pacific Coast Track Club (0:50)
440-Yard Relay—Southern Methodist (Mike Rideau, Joe Pouncy, Rufus Shaw, Gene Pouncy; 0:40)
Mile Relay—Texas (Glen Goss, Ed Wright, Craig Brooks, Don Sturgal; 3:08.2)
Pole Vault—Casey Carrigan, Pacific Coast T. C. (17 ft 6 in)
High Jump—Randy Smith, Kansas (7 ft 2 in)
Long Jump—Theodeus Hamilton, Kansas (25 ft 11½ in)
Triple Jump—Tommy Haynes, Middle Tennessee State (53 ft 6½ in)
Shot Put—Al Feuerbach, Pacific Coast Track Club (70 ft 10½ in)
Discus—Jim McGoldrick, Texas (191 ft)
Javelin—Van Holloway, unattached (248 ft 8 in)
Hammer—Peter Galle, Beverly Hills Striders (199 ft 4 in)
Team—Pacific Coast Club, Long Beach, Calif. (78 pts)

Women

100 Yards—Audrey Reid, Texas Women's Univ. (0:10.7)
220 Yards—Debra Sapenter, Prairie View A. & M. (0:23.9)
440 Yards—Debra Sapenter (0:55.2)
880 Yards—Tecla Chemabwai, Chicago State (2:11.1)
Mile—Peg Neppel, Iowa State (4:59.4)
100-Meter Hurdles—Debbie Esser, Woodbine T. C. (0:14.3)
330-Yard Hurdles—Marilyn Linsenmeyer, Texas T. C. (0:44.9)
440-Yard Relay—Texas Women's Univ. (0:45.9)
880-Yard Medley Relay—Prairie View A. & M. (1:44.7)
Mile Relay—Prairie View A. & M. (3:47)
Long Jump—Cathy Newman, Iowa State (19 ft 3 in)
High Jump—Louise Ritter, Texas T. C. (5 ft 6 in)
Discus—Linda Montgomery, Texas T. C. (136 ft 8 in)
Javelin—Susie Norton, Kansas State (129 ft 6 in)
Shot Put—Mary Jacobson, unattached (44 ft 8½ in)
Team—Texas Women's Univ. (80 pts)

Mary Decker breaks the tape to win the women's 440-yard dash in the Kennedy Games at Berkeley, Calif. She also took the 880 in the National AAU outdoor and indoor meets.

WIDE WORLD

YACHTING

Australia's fourth attempt to win the America's Cup foundered quickly. *Courageous,* the United States yacht in the 22d defense of the trophy, won four of the five races from *Southern Cross,* Sept. 10–17, 1974, off Newport, R. I. The other race was no contest as neither boat finished within the time limit because of lack of wind.

Yachting Highlights

North American Yacht Racing Union Champions

Men (Mallory Cup)—Vann Wilson, San Anselmo, Calif.
Women (Adams Cup)—Deborah Freeman, Beachwood, N. J.
Single-handed, Men (O'Day Trophy)—Carl Buchan, Seattle
Single-handed, Women (Mertz Trophy)—Jane Pegel, Lake Geneva, Wis.
Juniors (Sears Cup)—Tom Burton, Deep Haven, Minn.
Junior single-handed (Smythe Trophy)—Richard C. Lyons, Huron, Mich.
Interclub (Prince of Wales Trophy)—Noroton (Conn.) Y. C.; Bill Cox, skipper
National Explorers (Sea Scout)—Van Wesley, Chattanooga, Tenn.

Ocean and Long-Distance Racing

Bayview–Mackinac (295 miles)—Dora IV, Lynn A. Williams, Chicago; 49:19:45
Chicago–Mackinac (330 miles)—Class I: Dora IV; 37:76; Class II: No Go, Eliot Siegel and Grant Crowley; 46:75
Newport–Bermuda (635 miles, start June 21)—Overall: Scaramouche, Class B; Charles E. Kirsch, Sturgeon Bay, Mich., and Chicago Y. C.; elapsed time: 3 days, 3 hours, 5 minutes, 14 seconds; corrected time: 2:15:59:56. First to finish: Ondine, Sumner A. Long, New York; 2:19:52:22. Other class winners: Class A: Dora IV, L. A. Williams; Class C: Recluta III, C. A. Corna; Class D: Diane, J. Mattingly; Class E: Cayenne, D. Tate; Class F: Hot Canary, J. Rubenzahl.
Trans-Pacific (Los Angeles–Tahiti, 3,571 miles)—Sorcery, Jacob D. Wood, Salem, Oreg.; elapsed time: 18 days, 11 hours, 14 minutes, 32 seconds)
Trans-Pacific (Victoria, B. C.–Hawaii, 2,310 miles)—Tinsley Light, Henry Grandin, San Francisco. First to finish: Joli, William Niemi, Seattle; in record time of 12 days, 17 hours, 53 minutes, 26 seconds
San Diego–Acapulco (1,430 miles)—Standfast, John MacAllister, San Diego; 8:21:33:28. First to finish: Swiftsure, Nick Frazee in record time of 10:02:39:33
World (27,120 miles; start from Portsmouth, England, Sept. 8, 1973)—Sayula II, Ramon Carlin, Mexico; elapsed time: 152 days; corrected time: 134 days. First to finish: Great Britain, Chay Blyth, Britain; 144 days)

Major Trophy Winners

Bacardi Cup (Star Class)—Ding Schoonmaker–Jerry Ford, Miami
Congressional Cup—Bill Ficker, New York Yacht Club
Gold Cup (Finn Class)—Henry Sprague 3d, Newport Harbor, Calif.
One-Ton Cup—Gumboots, Jeremy Rogers, Britain
Southern Ocean Racing Conference—*Overall:* Robin Too II, Ted Hood, Marblehead, Mass. (1,939 pts). *Race winners:* St. Petersburg–Anclote Key (105 miles): The Magic Twanger (Martin Field, 16.9570); St. Petersburg–Fort Lauderdale (403 miles): Robin Too II (50.2796); Ocean Triangle (132 miles): Scaramouche (Chuck Kirsch, 15.9550); Lipton Cup (38 miles): Robin Too II (4.1461); Miami–Nassau (176 miles): Osprey (Alan Gurney, skipper; 13.5229). (Osprey rescued crew of sinking Winoweh and was awarded 1:23 for time spent and 37 minutes for weight of extra 18 people of rescued crew.) Nassau Cup: Terrorist (Al Cassell, 4.4190)

Collegiate

North American Collegiate Championship (Boston Harbor)—Tuthill Trophy (overall team): Tulane (Augie Diaz, Doug Ball, Toby Darden); Morse Trophy (paired dinghies): Harvard (Terry Neff); Foster Trophy (single-handed): Diaz, Tulane; Shields Trophy (sloops): Darden, Tulane.
Admiral Moore Trophy—New York Maritime College (Dick Sadler and Tom Galligher)
Owen Trophy—Harvard (Terry Neff and Chris Middendorf)
Sweet Series—University of Hawaii (Dennis Durgan, John Daigh, Lewie Wake)

UPI

The U. S. yacht *Courageous* (*right*) takes an early lead in the fourth race of the America's Cup series. She turned back Australia's *Southern Cross* with four straight wins.

Probably the best contested portion of the summer-long series of trials was that between *Courageous* and *Intrepid,* the craft that had successfully defended the Cup in 1967 and 1970. The old wooden-hull, *Intrepid,* which was backed by over 1,000 West Coast contributors, almost got the call again. Only after winning for the fifth time in a series of nine races was the new aluminum boat, *Courageous,* given the assignment. She was 5,000 pounds lighter than *Intrepid* although two feet longer. Before the Cup competition began, the Americans were fully confident of victory because *Intrepid*'s great effort had taught the crewmen of *Courageous* how to get the most out of their boat.

Southern Cross had been built specifically to go for the Cup at a cost of $5 million, including trial expenses. In her first official test, she eliminated the French contender in four straight races. *Southern Cross,* under the burgee of the Royal Perth Y. C., had James Hardy as her skipper.

Under Ted Hood, a sailmaker who was put in charge at the close of the trials, *Courageous* swept to victory in the first race by 4 minutes, 34 seconds. In the second race, the Aussie boat lost by only 1:10. After a day's rest came the windless race. On September 16, *Courageous* proved much faster to windward and raced to a 5:27 triumph over the 24.3-mile course. The Aussies never got close in the fourth race, losing by 7:19. The total time difference for the four races was 18 minutes 51 seconds, as *Southern Cross* was found not equal to the acceleration and power of *Courageous* or to the seamanship of the American crew.

MISCELLANEOUS SPORTS SUMMARIES

ARCHERY—National Archery Association: *Men:* Darrell Pace, Reading, Ohio; *women:* Doreen Wilber, Jefferson, Iowa. **National Field Archery Association:** *Freestyle: Open:* Tim Moyer, Glendora, Calif.; *women's open:* Barbara Morris, Frankfort, Ky.; *amateur:* Terry Ragsdale, White Oak, Texas; *women's amateur:* Kathy Cramberg, Dallas City, Ill.; *Barebow: Open:* David Hughes, Irving, Texas; *women's open:* Janis Beverly, Americus, Ga.; *amateur:* Mike Flier, Pekin, Ill.; *women's amateur:* Betty Selkirk, Canton, Ill.

BADMINTON—U. S. Championships: *Singles:* Chris Kinard, Pasadena, Calif.; *women's singles:* Cindy Baker, Salt Lake City; *doubles:* Don Paup, Washington, and Jim Poole, Northridge, Calif.; *women's doubles:* Pam Bristol, Flint, Mich., and Diane Hales, Claremont, Calif.; *mixed doubles:* Mike Walker, Alhambra, Calif., and Judiann Kelly, Norwalk, Calif.; *senior singles:* Poole

BOWLING—American Bowling Congress: *Regular Division: singles:* Gene Krause, Cleveland (773); *doubles:* Chuck Sunseri and Bob Hart, Detroit (1,419); *all-events:* Hart (2,087); *team:* Olympic Beer, Omaha (3,186). *Classic Division: singles:* Ed Ditolla, Hackensack, N. J. (747); *doubles:* Bob Perry, Paterson, N. J., and Tye Critchlow, Claremont, Calif. (1,359); *all-events:* Jim Godman, Vero Beach, Fla. (2,184); *team:* Ebonite Corp., Hopkinsville, Ky. (3,117). *Booster Division:* Elliott's Jeaters, Peoria, Ill. (2,839). *Masters:* Paul Colwell, Tucson, Ariz. Bowling Proprietor's Assn. of America Open Championship: *Men:* Larry Laub, San Francisco (defeated Dave Davis, Atlanta, Ga., in final); *women:* Pat Costello, Carrolltown, Md. (defeated Betty Morris, Stockton, Calif., in final). **Women's International Bowling Congress**—*Open Division: singles:* Shirley Garms, Leland Lake, Ill. (702); *doubles:* Carol Miller and Janie Leszczynski, Milwaukee (1,313); *all-events:* Judy Cook Soutar, Grandview, Mo. (1,944); *team:* Kalicak Int. Construction, St. Louis (2,973); *Queens Tournament:* Judy Soutar. **Duckpins**—*Singles:* Smith Greene, Providence, R. I. (489); *doubles:* Bob Burchard and Bob Devine, Providence, R. I. (925); *all-events:* Basil Boone, Annapolis, Md. (1,337); *team:* Marchone's Italian Deli, Wheaton, Md. (2,093). *Women: singles:* Lori Cabral, Providence, R. I. (432); *doubles:* Nancy Gawor and Jean Stewart, Baltimore (844); *all-events:* Phyllis Rapso, Manchester, Conn. (1,239); *team:* Scallop's, Pope's Creek, Md. (1,899)

BRIDGE—World Team (Bermuda Bowl): Italy (defeated Dallas Aces, North America, 195–166). **World Bridge Federation:** *Open pairs:* Bob Hamman and Bob Wolff, Dallas; *women's pairs:* Rixi Markus and Fritzi Gordon, Britain; *mixed pairs:* Tony Trad and Lula Gordon, Switzerland; *mixed team:* Jo Morse, Steve Robinson, Steve Parker, Bob and Peggy Lipsitz, Washington

CANOEING—Kayak: *singles: 500 and 1,000 meters:* Steve Kelly, New York; *10,000 meters:* Bill Leach, Newport Beach, Calif.; *500-meter tandem:* Leach and Mike Johnson, Newport Beach, Calif.; *1,000-meter tandem:* Bruce Barton, Niles, Mich., and Phil Rogosheske, Washington; *10,000-meter tandem:* Barton and Rogosheske. *Women: 500 meters:* Lind Murray, Washington; *5,000 meters:* Sperry Rademaker, Floral City, Fla.; *500-meter tandem:* Candy Clark, Niles, Mich., and Sperry Rademaker; *5,000-meter tandem:* Patience Vanderbush and Carol Fisher, Niles, Mich. **Canoe:** *500 and 1,000 meters:* Roland Muhlen, Cincinnati; *10,000 meters:* Andy Weigand, Balboa Island, Calif.; *500- and 10,000-meter tandem:* Weigand and Muhlen. **Whitewater:** *kayak slalom:* Eric Evans, Hanover, N. H.; *canoe slalom:* Angus Morrison, Wayzata, Minn.; *women's kayak slalom:* Candy Clark, Lafayette, Calif.

CHESS—World competition (winner to challenge Bobby Fischer of Los Angeles for title in 1975)—*Quarterfinals:* Boris Spassky, USSR, defeated Robert Byrne, New York; Viktor Korchnoi, USSR, defeated Henrique Meching, Brazil; Anatoly Karpov, USSR, defeated Lev Polugaevsky, USSR, Tigran Petrosian, USSR, defeated Lajos Portisch, Hungary; *semifinals:* Korchnoi defeated Petrosian; Karpov defeated Spassky; *final:* Karpov defeated Korchnoi, 3 games to 2, in 24 games. (Fischer had resigned in June in protest of rules for match, but resignation was not immediately accepted.)

CROSS-COUNTRY—NCAA (6 miles)—Nick Rose, Western Kentucky (29:22); Oregon (77 pts); *Division II:* (5 miles): Garry Bentley, South Dakota State (23:33.8); Southwest Missouri (112 pts); *Division III* (5 miles): David Moller, Rochester (24:39); Mount Union (105 pts); **NAIA** (5 miles) —Mike Boit, Eastern New Mexico (23:45); Eastern New Mexico (28 pts). **AAU** (10,000 meters): John Ngeno, Washington State, Kenya (29:58.8); *team:* Colorado T. C. (89 pts); *women* (3 miles): Lynn Bjorklund, Los Alamos, N. Mex. (17:31.7); *team:* UCLA (68)

CURLING—World: United States (defeated Sweden, 11–4, in final). **U. S. Championships:** *Men:* Superior, Wis., skipped by Bud Somerville; *women:* Virginia, Minn., skipped by Mrs. Newton G. Hahne. **Canada:** Alberta, skipped by Hec Gervais

CYCLING—World championships: *Sprint:* Anton Tkac, Czechoslovakia; *pursuit:* Hans Lutz, West Germany; *tandem:* Vladimir Vackar and Miroslav Vymazal, Czechoslovakia; *road* (172 km): Janusz Kowalski, Poland (4:43.10); *time trials:* Sweden. *Women: sprint:* Tamara Piltsikova, USSR; *pursuit:* Tamara Garkushina, USSR; *road* (60 km): Genevieve Gambillon, France (1:47:36). **U. S. Championships:** *Road: senior* (115 miles): John Allis, Cambridge, Mass. (4:29.57); *junior* (50 miles): David Mayer-Oakes, Lubbock, Texas (2:00); *veterans* (46 miles): Jim Mayers, Costa Mesa, Calif. (1:54.2); *women* (34.5 miles): Jane Robinson, Seattle (1:53.30). *Track: sprint:* Steve Woznick, Ridgewood, N. J.; *10 miles:* Ralph Therrio, Torrance, Calif. (20:17.87); *4,000-meter pursuit:* Therrio (5:09:03); *1,000-meter time trials:* Woznick (1:09.83); *team pursuit:* So. California. *Women: sprint:* Sue Novarra, Flint, Mich.; *3,000-meter pursuit:* Mary Jane Reoch, Philadelphia (4:12.1); *junior overall:* Gilbert Hatton, El Monte, Calif.

DOG SHOWS—Westminster (New York): *Best:* Ch. Gretchenhof Columbia River, German short-haired pointer, owned by Richard F. Smith, Hayward, Calif. **International** (Chicago): *Best:* Ch. Salilyn's Classic, English springer spaniel, owned by Mrs. Julie Gasow and Barbara Gates, Troy, Mich.

FENCING—World championships: *foil:* Alex Romankov, USSR; *team:* USSR; *épée:* Rolf Edling, Sweden; *team:* Sweden; *saber:* Aldo Montano, Italy; *team:* USSR; *women's foil:* Ildeko Bobis, Hungary; *team:* USSR. **U. S. championships** —*Foil:* Heik Hambarzumian, San Francisco; *team:* U. S. Marine Corps; *épée:* Dan Cantillon, Detroit; *team:* Salli Mori, Los Angeles; *saber:* Peter Westbrook, New York; *team:* New York A. C.; *women's foil:* Gaye Jacobsen, San Francisco; *team:* Salle Santelli, New York. **NCAA**—*Foil:* Greg Benko, Wayne State; *épée:* Risto Hurme, New York Univ.; *saber:* Steve Danosi, Wayne State; *team:* New York Univ. **Women's Collegiate:** Peggy Walbridge, Cornell; *team:* University of California, Fullerton

GYMNASTICS—World: *Men: Overall:* Shigeru Katsamatsu, Japan; *team:* Japan; *women: overall:* Ludmila Turischeva, USSR; *team:* USSR. **NCAA**—*All-around:* Steve Hug, Stanford; *team:* Iowa State. **AAU**—*all-around:* Yoshi Hayasaki, Chicago; *team:* New York A. C.; *women: all-around:* Joan M. Rice, Philadelphia; *team:* Philadelphia Manettes

HANDBALL—United States Handball Association champions: *4-wall: singles:* Fred Lewis, Cleveland; *doubles:* Ray Neveau, Oshkosh, Wis., and Simie Fein, Milwaukee; *Masters: singles:* Joey Maher, Ireland; *doubles:* Arnold Aguilar and Gabe Enriquez, Los Angeles. *3-wall: singles:* Fred Lewis, Cleveland; *doubles:* Paul Haber, San Diego, and Steve Decatur, New York; *masters doubles:* Joe and Charlie Danilcyzk, New York. *One-wall: singles:* Al Torres, New York; *doubles:* Wally Ulbrich and Joel Wisotsky, New York; *junior:* David Garcia; *masters doubles:* Danilcyzk and Artie Reyer, New York. **AAU Champions** —*Singles:* Steve Sandler, New York; *doubles:* Mike Dikman and Artie Reyer, New York; *masters doubles:* Reyer and Joe Rispoli, New York. **YMCA Champions**—*Singles:* Tom Kopaytic, Milwaukee; *doubles:* Simie Fein, Milwaukee, and Ray Neveau, Oshkosh, Wis.; *masters doubles:* Tom Schoendorf and Jim Cronin, Milwaukee

HORSE SHOWS—American Horse Show Association Medals: *Dressage:* Cyndy Miller, Bloomfield Hills, Mich.; *Hunter Seat:* Robin Rost, Branchville, N. J.; *Saddle Seat:* Mary DeNure, Albany, N. Y.; *Stock Seat:* Kim Andersen, Napa, Calif. *Combined Training Trophy:* Andrew J. Mouw, Leesburg, Va.; *Senior Dressage:* Kitty Ireland, Los Angeles. **National Horse Show Medals:** *Saddle Seat (Good Hands):* Linda Lowary, Tulsa, Okla. **ASPCA (Maclay):** Alexandra Dunaif, Ossining, N. Y. **World:** *3-day:* United States

ICE SKATING, FIGURE—World: *Men:* Jan Hoffman, East Germany; *women:* Christine Errath, East Germany; *pairs:* Irina Rodnina and Alexander Zeitsev, USSR; *dance:* Ludmila Pachonova and Alexander Gorshkov, USSR. **U. S. Champions:** *Men:* Gordon McKellen, Lake Placid, N. Y.; *women:* Dorothy Hamill, Riverside, Conn.; *pairs:* Melissa Militano, Dix Hill, N. Y., and Johnny Johns, Bloomfield Hills, Mich.; *dance:* Coleen O'Connor, Chicago, and Jim Milnes, Addison, Ill.

ICE SKATING, SPEED—World Champions: *Men: all-around:* Sten Stensen, Norway; *women:* Atje Keulen-Deelstra, Netherlands; *sprints: all-around: men:* Per Bjorang, Norway; *women:* Leah Poulos, Northbrook, Ill. **U. S. Champions:** *National Outdoor: men: all-around:* tie between Leigh Barczewski, West Allis, Wis., and Mike Pasarella, Chicago; *women:* Kris Garbe, West Allis, Wis. **National Indoor:** *men:* Allan Rattray, Los Angeles; *women:* Peggy Hartrich, St. Louis

LACROSSE—NCAA champions: *Division I:* Johns Hopkins (defeated Maryland, 17–12, in final); *Division II:* Towson State (defeated Hobart, 18–17, in overtime in final); **ECAC:** *New England:* Bowdoin; *Upstate New York:* Geneseo; *Met. New York:* Fairleigh-Dickinson. **Club champions:** Long Island A. C. **World:** United States

MOTORBOATING—Unlimited Hydroplanes: *champion:* Pride of Pay 'N Pak, George Henley, driver, Eatonville, Wash.; **Distance Races:** *Griffith Memorial:* Sammy James, Miami; *Bahamas 500:* Carlo Bonomi, Italy; *Hennessy Grand Prix:* Art Norris, Detroit; *Hennessy California:* Billy Martin, Clark, N. J.; *San Francisco Tognoli Memorial:* Paul Cook, Atherton, Calif. **U. S. inboard champion:** Norris; **World offshore:** Bonomi

POLO—National: *Open:* Milwaukee; *20-goal:* Milwaukee; *16-goal:* Boca Raton, Fla.; *8-goal:* Oak Brook, Ill.; *intercollegiate:* University of Connecticut

ROLLER SKATING—World: *Singles:* Michael Obrecht, West Germany; *women's singles:* Sigrid Mullenbach, West Germany; *dance:* Christina Henke and Udo Donsdorf, West Germany; *mixed pairs:* Sue McDonald, Steubenville, Ohio, and Ron Sabo, Painesville, Ohio. **United States:** *Singles:* Darryl Bayles, Delanco, N. J.; *women's singles:* Natalie Dunn, Bakersfield, Calif.; *figures:* Keith King, East Meadow, N. Y.; *women's figures:* Debbie Palm, East Meadow, N. Y.; *mixed pairs:* Mark Rever and Darlene Waters, Pontiac, Mich.; *dance:* Debra Coyne and John Briola, Whittier, Calif.; *speed:* Chris Snyder, Springfield, Mo.; *women's speed:* Robin Wilcock, Thousand Oaks, Calif.

ROWING—World: *Singles:* Wolfgang Honig, East Germany; *eights:* U. S. National Crew; *lightweights: singles:* Bill Belden, King of Prussia, Pa.; *eights:* U. S. National Crew. **U. S. Champions:** *Singles:* Sean Drea, Undine, Philadelphia; *dash:* Jim Dietz, New York A. C.; *doubles:* Dietz and Larry Klecatsky, New York A. C.; *pairs:* John Campbell and Kurt Kaufman, Vesper B. C., Philadelphia; *pairs with coxswain:* Bill Miller and Bill Jurgens, with Ken Dreyfus, coxswain, Vesper; *eights:* National Assn. of Amateur Oarsmen crew; *155 pounds: singles:* Larry Klecatsky, New York A. C.; *dash:* Bill Belden, Undine; *doubles:* Belden and Fred Duling, Undine; *pairs:* John Sonberg and Joe Caminiti, New York A. C.; *eights:* New York A. C. **Intercollegiate Champions:** *I. R. A.: Varsity:* Wisconsin; *second varsity:* Wisconsin; *freshmen:* Cornell; *Pairs:* Penn; *pairs with coxswain:* Santa Clara; *fours:* Coast Guard Academy; *team* (Jim Ten Eyck Trophy): Wisconsin. *Dad Vail Trophy: eights:* Massachusetts; *overall:* Massachusetts; *Eastern Sprints: Varsity:* Harvard; *second varsity:* Harvard; *freshmen:* Cornell; *team* (Rowe Cup): Harvard; *lightweight team* (Jope Cup): Harvard; *Mid-America Regatta:* Marietta. *Mid-Western:* Wisconsin. *Western Sprints: Varsity, junior varsity,* and *freshmen:* Washington; *team* (Ebright Trophy): Washington. *Dual regattas:* Harvard defeated Yale; Oxford defeated Cambridge; Harvard defeated Wisconsin. **British Royal Henley**—*Diamond sculls:* Sean Drea, Ireland; *Wyfold Cup* (fours): Porcellian Club, Harvard; *Princess Elizabeth Cup* (schoolboy eights); Holy Spirit H. S., Absecon, N. J.; *Grand Challenge Cup* (eights): Trud Kolomna, USSR

SHOOTING—Trapshooting: Grand American, Vandalia, Ohio: *G. A. Handicap: Men:* John Steffen, Minnetonka, Minn. (24 yds, 99); *women:* Mrs. Georgie McCown (20 yds, 99); *junior:* Randy Voss, Le Sueur, Minn. (26 yds, 98); *veterans:* A. J. Meyer, Elbe, N. Y. (23 yds, 96). **Skeet**—National Skeet Shooting Assn. champions: *Men:* Noel Winters, Baltimore (548); *women:* Karla Roberts, Bridgeton, Mo. (542); *veterans:* George Vicknair, Baton Rouge, La. (533); *senior:* Paul Dublin, Jacksonville, Texas (534); *junior:* Mike Schmidt, Prior Lake, Minn. (544)

SKIING—World Championships: *Alpine: Downhill:* David Zwilling, Austria; *slalom:* Gustavo Thoeni, Italy; *giant slalom:* Thoeni; *combined:* Franz Klammer, Austria. *Women: downhill:* Annemarie Proell, Austria; *slalom:* Hanny Wenzel, Liechtenstein; *giant slalom:* Fabienne Serrat, France; *combined:* Fabienne Serrat. *Nordic: Jumping: 70 meters:* Hans-Georg Aschenbach, East Germany; *90 meters:* Aschenbach; *combined:* Stefan Hula, Poland. *Cross-Country: 15 kilometers:* Magne Myrmo, Norway; *30 kilometers:* Thomas Magnusson, Sweden; *50 kilometers:* Gerhard Grimmer, East Germany; *women: 5 and 10 kilometers:* Galina Kulakova, USSR. **World Cup**—Men: Piero Gros, Italy; *women:* Annemarie Proell, Austria. **United States Champions:** *Alpine: Slalom:* Cary Adgate, Boyne City, Mich.; *giant slalom:* Bob Cochran, Richmond, Vt.; *women: slalom:* Susie Patterson, Sun Valley, Idaho; *giant slalom:* Marilyn Cochran, Richmond, Vt. *Nordic: jumping:* Ron Steele, Leavenworth, Wash. (315 and 302 ft); *veteran:* Olav Ulland, Seattle; *junior:* Jim Denney, Duluth, Minn. *Combined:* Bruce Cunningham, Mexico, Maine. *Cross-country: 15 kilometers:* Larry Martin, Durango, Colo.; *30 kilometers:* Mike Devecka, Bend, Oreg.; *50 kilometers:* Ron Yeager, Durango, Colo.; *junior, 10 kilometers:* Bill Koch, Guilford, Vt. *Women: 5, 10, and 15 kilometers:* Martha Rockwell, Poultney, Vt. **National Collegiate A. A.**—*Downhill:* Larry Kennison, Wyoming; *cross-country:* Steinar Hybertsen, Wyoming; *slalom:* Bill Shaw, Boise State; *Alpine combined:* Peil Christensen, Denver; *jumping:* Didrik Ellefsen, Colorado; *Nordic combined:* Stig Hallingbye, Wyoming; *team:* University of Colorado

SOCCER—World Cup: *Champion:* West Germany (defeated Netherlands, 2–1, in final); *third place:* Poland (defeated Brazil, 1–0). **United States Champions:** *Challenge Cup:* New York Greek-Americans; *Amateur Cup:* Philadelphia Inter; *junior:* Florrissant Celtics, St. Louis. **North American Soccer League:** Los Angeles Aztecs. **NCAA:** Howard University; *Division II:* Adelphi; *Division III:* Brookport State. **NAIA:** Quincy College. **Other Champions**—*English Association Cup:* Liverpool; *English League Cup:* Wolverhampton; *Scottish Association Cup:* Glasgow Celtic; *Scottish League Cup:* Dundee; *European Cup:* Bayern Munich, West Germany; *Cup Winners Cup:* Magdeburg, East Germany

SOFTBALL—World Champions: *Women:* United States. **Amateur Softball Assn:** *Fast pitch:* Santa Rosa, Calif.; *women:* Raybestos Brakettes, Stratford, Conn.; *slow pitch:* Howard Furniture, Denver, N. C.; *women:* North Miami Dots; *industrial:* Aetna L. & C., Charlotte, N. C.; *16-inch:* Chicago Strikers

SQUASH RACQUETS—*Singles:* Victor Niederhoffer, New York; *doubles:* Niederhoffer and Colin Adair, Montreal; *veterans' singles:* Charles Ufford, New York; *veterans' doubles:* Don Leggett, Hamilton, Ont., and Chuck Wright, Toronto; *senior singles:* Floyd Svensson, San Francisco; *senior doubles:* William Ketchum, New York, and Newton Meade, Philadelphia. *Women: singles:* Mrs. Gretchen Spruance, Greenville, Del.

SURFING—World: Reno Abellira, Haleiwa, Hawaii; **United States:** Rick Rasmussen, Westhampton Beach, N. Y.; *women:* Isabel McLaughlin, New Smyrna Beach, Fla.

TABLE TENNIS—U. S. champions: *Singles:* Kjell Johansson, Sweden; *women's singles:* Yukie Ohzeki, Japan; *doubles:* Stellan Bengtsson, Sweden, and Johansson; *women's doubles:* Ann-Christine Hellman and Birgitta Olsson, Sweden; *senior singles:* Tim Boggan, Merrick, N. Y.; *senior doubles:* Bill Sharpe and George Rocker, Philadelphia

VOLLEYBALL—U. S. Volleyball Assn. champions: *Open:* University of California, Santa Barbara; *women:* Los Angeles Renegades; *senior:* Balboa Bay (Calif.) Masters; *collegiate:* California at Santa Barbara. **Other champions:** *AAU:* Michiana A. C. Chicago; *AAU women:* Dallas A. C.; *YMCA;* Hollywood (Calif.) YMCA; *NCAA:* UCLA; *NAIA:* George Williams College

WATER SKIING—U. S. champions: *Overall:* Ricky McCormick, Hialeah, Fla.; *slalom:* Kris LaPoint, Castro Valley, Calif.; *tricks:* Russ Stiffler, Upland, Calif.; *jumping:* Mike Suyderhoud, Petaluma, Calif. *Women: Overall:* Liz Allan Shetter, Groveland, Fla.; *slalom, tricks, jumping:* Liz Shetter

WEIGHT LIFTING—U. S. champions: *114 pounds:* Joel Widdel, Dewar, Iowa; *123:* Sal Dominguez, York, Pa.; *132:* Roman Mielec, York, Pa.; *148:* Dan Cantore, San Francisco; *165:* Fred Lowe, York, Pa.; *181:* Tom Hirtz, York, Pa.; *198:* Phil Grippaldi, York, Pa.; *242:* Al Feuerbach, San Jose, Calif.; *superheavyweight:* James Gargano, Los Angeles

WRESTLING—AAU: *105.5 pounds:* Dave Range, Garfield Heights, Ohio; *114.5:* Sergio Gonzales, Venice, Calif.; *125.5:* Rich Sofman, New York A. C.; *136.5:* Don Beam, East Lansing, Mich.; *149.5:* Gene Davis, Lakewood, Calif.; *168:* Stan Deziedzic, New York A. C.; *180.5:* Greg Hicks, Lancaster, Pa.; *220:* Greg Wojciechowski, Toledo, Ohio; *unlimited:* Mike McCready, Watsonville, Calif.; *team:* New York A. C. **NCAA champions**—*118 pounds:* Gary Breece, Oklahoma; *126:* Pat Milkovich, Michigan State; *134:* Tom Sculley, Lehigh; *142:* Rick Lawinger, Wisconsin; *150:* Jarrett Hubbard, Michigan; *158:* Rod Kilgore, Oklahoma; *167:* Doug Wyn, Western Michigan; *177:* Floyd Hitchcock, Bloomsburg State; *190:* Greg Strobel, Oregon State; *heavyweight:* Jim Woods, Western Illinois; *team:* Oklahoma

SRI LANKA (Ceylon)

For Sri Lanka the year 1974 was marked by a serious food shortage, galloping inflation, a worsening foreign exchange situation, internal dissensions, a new judicial system, and increased controls by the United Front government over the press and opposition groups and movements.

Economy. The food shortage was so serious that the government was compelled to allocate two thirds of Sri Lanka's foreign exchange earnings for the import of rice and flour. Expenditures for oil imports rose from $50 million in 1973 to $150 million in 1974. The increase in foreign indebtedness (to $2 billion), the heavy costs of food and fuel imports and the social welfare programs, and the food shortage led to heavy budget deficits.

Politics. In the face of widespread internal dissensions and protests the government imposed further controls over opposition groups, the press, foreign companies, film producers, education, and large landowners. In late April it banned political demonstrations planned by opposition groups, imposed a curfew, and ordered police to occupy the offices of the Independent Newspapers Group. In July it obtained approval of the National State Assembly to buy up all the shares of the Associated Newspapers of Ceylon, the largest newspaper group in the country.

Foreign Policy. In January, during a visit by Mrs. Sirimavo Bandaranaike, the prime minister, to India, the two governments reached agreement on the status of some 150,000 persons of Indian origin in Sri Lanka whose future had not been settled in the 1964 Sirimavo-Shastri agreement. About half of these persons would be allowed to emigrate to India and would be given Indian citizenship, and the other half would be permitted to become citizens of Sri Lanka. In June, following a visit by Indian Prime Minister Mrs. Indira Gandhi to Sri Lanka, the two women agreed to draw the boundary between their countries in the waters from the Palk Strait to Adam's Bridge, giving the long-disputed island of Kachchativu to Sri Lanka.

NORMAN D. PALMER
University of Pennsylvania

SRI LANKA • Information Highlights

Official Name: Republic of Sri Lanka.
Location: Island off the southeastern coast of India.
Area: 25,332 square miles (65,610 sq km).
Population (1973 est. census): 13,500,000.
Chief City (1971 census): Colombo, the capital, 562,160.
Government: *Head of state,* William Gopallawa, president (took office May 1972). *Head of government,* Mrs. Sirimavo Bandaranaike, prime minister (May 1972).
Monetary Unit: Rupee (6.533 rupees equal U. S.$1, June 1974).
Gross National Product (1972 est.): $2,127,000,000.
Manufacturing (major products): Milled rice, chemicals, cement, petroleum products, paper.
Major Agricultural Products: Tea, rubber, coconuts.
Foreign Trade (1973): *Exports,* $389,000,000; *Imports,* $421,000,000.

U. S. COMMEMORATIVE STAMPS OF 1974

Subject	Denomination	Date of issue
Mt. Rushmore	26¢	Jan. 2
Elizabeth Blackwell	18¢	Jan. 3
Zip Code (Seattle Fair)	10¢	Jan. 4
Bicentennial aerogramme	18¢	Jan. 4
Bicentennial postal card	12¢	Jan. 4
Statue of Liberty	18¢	Jan. 11
Veterans of Foreign Wars	10¢	March 11
Robert Frost	10¢	March 26
NATO aerogramme	18¢	April 4
Preserve Environment	10¢	April 18
Kentucky Derby centenary	10¢	May 4
Skylab	10¢	May 14
Universal Postal Union centenary	8x10¢	June 6
Mineral Heritage	4x10¢	June 13
Kentucky Settlement bicentennial	10¢	June 15
Continental Congress bicentennial	4x10¢	July 4
Chautauqua Movement centenary	10¢	Aug. 6
Kansas Wheat centenary	10¢	Aug. 16
Lawn Tennis centenary	10¢	Aug. 31
Energy Conservation	10¢	Sept. 23
Sleepy Hollow	10¢	Oct. 10
Retarded Children	10¢	Oct. 12
Christmas	3x10¢	Oct. 23

STAMP COLLECTING

The U. S. Postal Service vigorously promoted its stamp business in 1974 in an effort to reduce its deficits. In an unprecedented action, it retained Madison Avenue advertising experts to spend $5 million for spot commercials on TV programs and full-page advertisements in the largest national magazines. These advertisements urged Americans to buy new domestic stamps and begin the philatelic hobby for fun, education, and future profits.

In addition, the Postal Service spent millions of dollars to produce and distribute motion pictures and filmstrips that were shown in schools all over the country.

The American Philatelic Society gave its "black blot" to eight different 10-cent stamps issued to mark the centenary of the Universal Postal Union. Its black blot is given to stamps that are issued to exploit collectors rather than meet postal requirements.

An innovation came on June 13 when a block of four diamond-shaped stamps was released "to honor our mineral heritage." A second novelty, which appeared on November 15, was the nation's first stamp to have a self-stick adhesive rather than normal gum. Only the protective wax-paper backing is perforated, not the die-cut stamp itself. Another innovation was introduced on October 10 when panes of 50 Sleepy Hollow stamps were imprinted with two plate numbers rather than one so that collectors had to buy eight blocks instead of four if they wanted a complete matched set of numbers.

The U. S. Postal Service also went after foreign collectors' money by renting booths at international stamp exhibitions in Switzerland and Sweden where U. S. stamps, packets, and quasi-philatelic materials were offered for sale.

On the international scene, the Universal Postal Union marked the centenary of its successful operation in handling international mails without interruption by holding a seven-week

NEW STAMPS

Among U. S. 1974 Commemorative stamps are (*clockwise*) reminders of the nation's retarded children, mineral heritage (four stamps), and literature, and a precanceled Christmas stamp.

U. S. POSTAL SERVICE

congress in Lausanne, Switzerland. To mark the event, every member nation in the world issued special stamps. Some were issued early in 1974, others during the congress, but most on the actual anniversary date, October 9. More than 1,000 different items were produced, and they were eagerly sought by collectors.

Because of strong inflationary trends in the United States and abroad, almost every rare stamp offered at auction brought record-high prices. Most notable was a $47,000 price for a 24-cent U. S. airmail stamp issued in 1918 with an inverted center. Almost all of these stamps were purchased by investors.

ERNEST A. KEHR, *Stamp News Bureau*

STOCKS AND BONDS

An already beleaguered stock market in the United States took another stiff drubbing in 1974, extending the decline that began in January 1973. The two-year downturn ranks as one of the most severe in modern stock market history. Stock prices, as measured by the broad-based Standard & Poor's 500-stock index, retreated to a 12-year low.

The stock market had ended 1973 with a slight upswing, but almost at once stock prices began to erode. The list perked up briefly in March, in anticipation of a lifting of the Arab oil embargo, then turned downward again. While the decline was punctuated by occasional and sometimes brisk rallies, the bear market atmosphere prevailed throughout the year.

The array of problems with which Wall Street had to contend in 1974 was staggering. These included the energy crisis, a deepening recession, double-digit inflation, soaring interest rates, faltering leadership in Washington, shortages in many sectors of the economy, and rising unemployment. Thus, it was no surprise that stock prices plummeted.

Stock Prices. The stock market entered 1974 on a modestly optimistic note, after appearing to have found a footing a bit above the early December 1973 low. The early surge was prompted by efforts by President Nixon to foster cooperation between oil producers and consumers, hopes for an end to the Arab oil embargo, and two Federal Reserve moves to facilitate a flow of money into the securities markets: a reduction from 65% to 50% in the margin requirements on stocks bought on credit, and a lowering in the reserve requirements on large certificates of deposit. But stock prices quickly suffered a sharp setback. It was difficult for the list to find a footing, grounded as it was in the shifting sands of the Middle East. The ebb and flow of hopes for progress toward an end to the oil embargo would continue to be a predominant stock market influence for the first three months of 1974.

The problem was that nothing like this embargo had ever before happened. Ample and cheap supplies of energy had been taken for granted, but now that shortfalls were evident, there were uncertainties over the impact of an energy squeeze. Then too, inflation, propelled by the surge in oil prices, was accelerating, and the administration's program of economic controls was clearly not working to contain the price spiral. Hence, the decision to allow remaining wage and price controls (except for the health care and petroleum industries) to expire on April 30. By mid-February, the market had plunged through its December 1973 low.

Evidence that the oil embargo was not fully effective, combined with an easing of interest rates and the end of the truckers' strike, prompted a worthwhile surge in March. How-

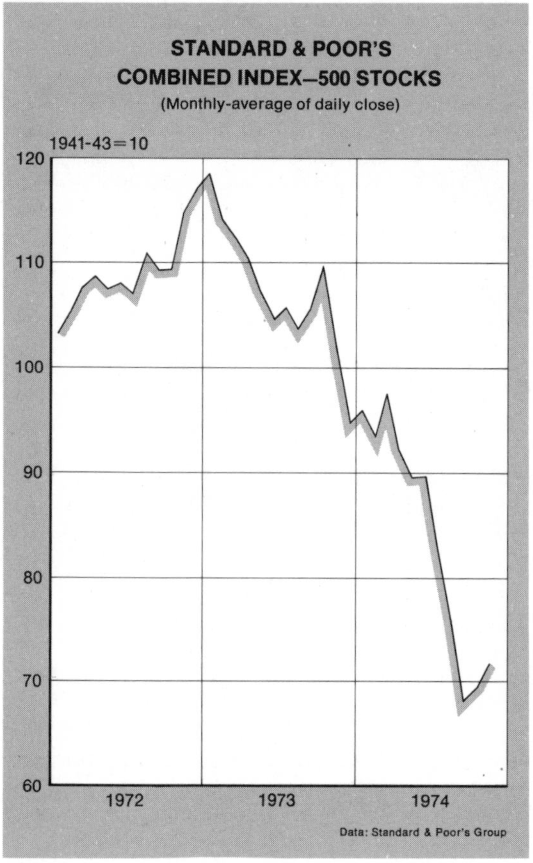

ever, stock prices turned weaker again after the middle of the month. The decline, though interrupted by rallies from time to time, continued unabated until October.

The devastating downturn which decimated stock prices reflected an extension of earlier problems, compounded by others. Interest rates skyrocketed, with the highly visible prime bank lending rate reaching a peak 12% by July. Inflation was a pervasive force, with prices soaring practically unchecked, while the "real" (after factoring out inflation) gross national product continued to head downward. Then came the liquidity crisis. First, Consolidated Edison, a well-known giant utility, omitted its quarterly dividend. Then a crisis of confidence in the entire banking system was narrowly averted by the Federal Reserve's massive infusion of funds to Franklin National Corp. (a bank holding company) and the subsequent orderly takeover of this bank's operations.

The stock market during these months was dominated by the large institutions, and its performance was characterized by massive reflex responses to developments, sometimes without the benefit of convincing evidence. The institutional influence, then, accounted for the severity of the market decline, for its occasional breathtaking drops, and for the sporadic, abortive rallies.

Overhanging all of this, of course, were the Watergate developments in Washington. With pressures mounting, President Nixon resigned on August 9. Anticipation of his resignation gave a short-lived lift to stock prices, but despite hopes for better times under a new administration, selling pressure resumed. The weakness was aggravated by concern over the Ford administration's willingness or ability to deal with the economic problems.

In early October a sharp rally developed in the oversold market, aided by a break in the 12% prime interest rate. The recovery, which lifted stock prices 20% in less than a month, continued through early November, despite evidence of a deepening recession. Stock prices subsequently retreated as 1974 ended; but there was some firming in the final sessions.

Earnings and Dividends. For most companies, a substantial earnings improvement occurred in 1974. In terms of Standard & Poor's industrial stock price index, net income (partly estimated) rose to $10.15 a share, from $8.90 in 1973. Dividends, which also moved higher, averaged $3.87 (indicated) a share on Standard & Poor's 425-stock index, as against $3.46 in 1973. These stocks sold at an average price of 10.5 times earnings and had an average return of 4.1%, compared with a 1973 multiple of 12.8 and a yield of 3.2%.

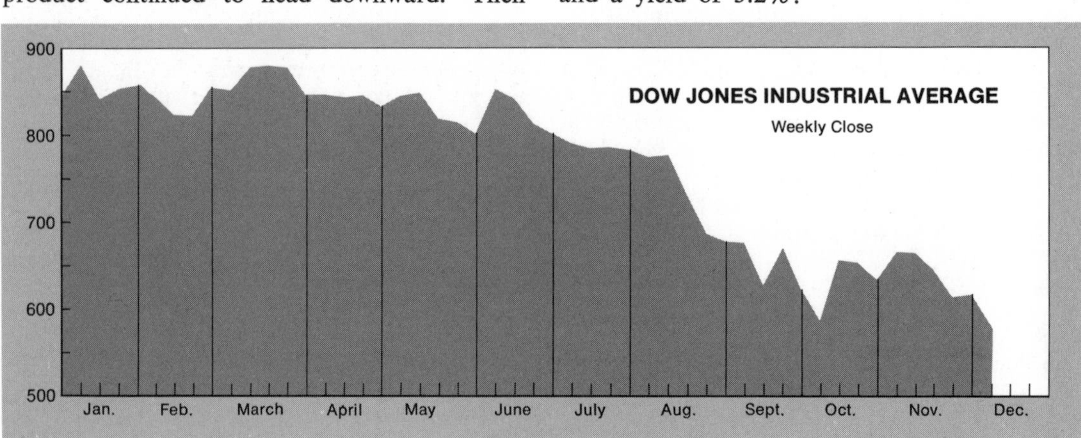

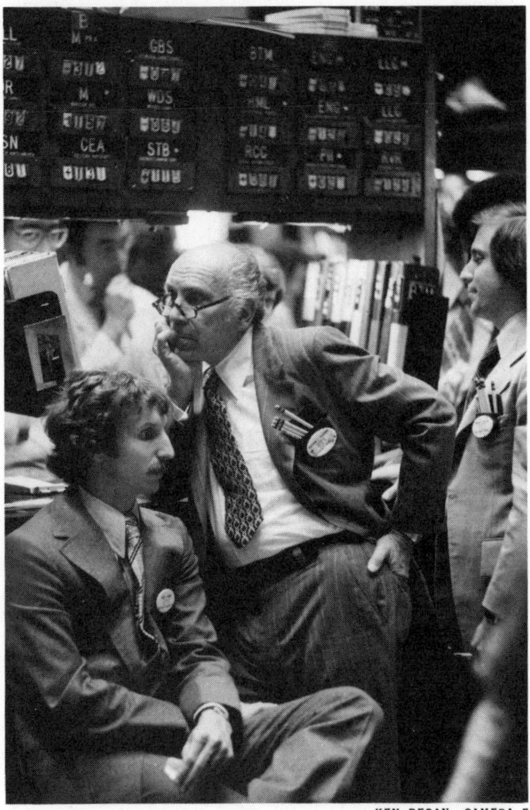

KEN REGAN, CAMERA 5

With little to occupy them, stockbrokers on the floor of the New York Stock Exchange look glum as the Dow Jones industrial average hits a 12-year low in October.

Volume. Trading on the New York Stock Exchange in 1974 totaled 3.518 billion shares, down from the 4.053 billion shares traded in 1973.

Bond Prices. The bond market came under many of the pressures that affected stock prices in 1974. The combined impact of the deteriorating economy, soaring inflation, and spiraling interest rates was reflected in soaring yields on these fixed-income investment instruments, and in a concomitant dip in bond prices. Companies coming to the bond market for financing had to pay record coupons for their funds. Yields on highest-grade industrials were at a low 7.51% on January 3, and reached a high of 8.50% on October 10.

Corporate bond offerings advanced sharply in 1974. Public offerings of corporate bonds, including convertible issues, were $25.7 billion (partly estimated), up from $14.7 billion in 1973. The substantial gain may be traced to robust corporate financing plans, which placed heavy demands on credit markets. Due to the interest-rate situation, corporations, which normally came to the short-term money market for their cash needs, found it necessary to issue long-term debt instruments.

CAROLYN J. COLE
Paine, Webber, Jackson & Curtis, Inc.

SUDAN

In 1974, Sudan continued its recovery from 17 years of devastating civil war between the Muslim north and the non-Muslim south. In fact, some termed the reconciliation as nothing short of "miraculous." Internationally, however, Sudan found itself in less tranquil waters as it became the first Arab nation to bring Arab terrorists to trial.

Reconciliation. More than one million people displaced during the war, which ended in 1972, continued to return from the bush or from exile, mostly in neighboring Uganda, and were the focus of a massive and highly successful international aid effort. Troops of the Anyanya (the southern rebels) were absorbed into the army, police, and prison services. Symbolic of the reconciliation was the fact that in October, Joseph Lagu, former Anyanya commander, was named general of the Sudanese army in the south and is now considered a close friend of Gen. Jaafar al-Numeiry, Sudan's president. Economic advancement in the battle-scarred south was proceeding at a slower pace, but Numeiry continued to enjoy the prestige that accrued to him from having settled the conflict.

Foreign Relations. Sudan found itself under intense pressure from both the Arab world and the West when it tried and convicted eight Black September terrorists who a year earlier had slain two American diplomats and a Belgian foreign service officer in Khartoum.

A life sentence meted out by the courts was commuted to seven years by President Numeiry, and the eight prisoners were turned over to the Palestinian Liberation Organization and were reportedly jailed in Egypt. Upset by what it considered unwarranted leniency, the United States withdrew its ambassador and assistance projects.

Meanwhile, Sudanese-Egyptian relations improved with new economic ties. Bonds with Libya, recently tense, deteriorated early in 1974, Numeiry charging Libya with aiding a coup attempt. However, tensions eased by May, and in November Numeiry met with Qaddafi of Libya.

ROBERT L. DENERSTEIN and NANCY MCKEON
The African-American Institute

SUDAN • Information Highlights

Official Name: Democratic Republic of the Sudan.
Location: Northeast Africa.
Area: 967,497 square miles (2,505,813 sq km).
Population (1973 est.): 17,400,000.
Chief Cities (1970 est.): Khartoum, the capital, 261,840; Omdurman, 258,532.
Government: *Head of state,* Gen. Jaafar Mohammed al-Numeiry, president (took office Oct. 1971). *Legislature* (unicameral)—People's Assembly.
Monetary Unit: Pound (0.3482 pound equals U. S.$1, July 1974).
Gross National Product (1972 est.): $1,875,000,000.
Manufacturing (major products): Vegetable oil, processed foods, textiles, shoes, pharmaceuticals.
Major Agricultural Products: Cotton, oilseeds, gum arabic, sorghum, sesame seeds, groundnuts, wheat, livestock.
Foreign Trade (1973): *Exports,* $434,000,000; *imports,* $436,000,000.

SWEDEN

Sweden in 1974 was concerned primarily with the adoption of a new constitution, the wedding of Princess Christina, and the government's measures to abate inflation. Parliament passed a series of important acts, mainly in the fields of social legislation.

The Constitution. The oldest written constitution in Europe ceased to be valid on Jan. 1, 1975. Sweden's new constitution, adopted on Feb. 27, 1974, by 321 votes to 19 after 20 years in the making, removes all power from the king. It provides that "the Government guides the kingdom" but is responsible to the Riksdag (Parliament), the seats of which are reduced from 350 to 349. The king also loses the right to name new governments, to participate in cabinet meetings, and to command the armed forces. He no longer will open the Riksdag session, and all centuries-old ceremonies will be abolished, including the king's traditional speech from the throne. The king shall pay taxes on his capital and must pay customs duties. King Carl XVI Gustaf thus on Jan. 11, 1974, opened the annual Riksdag session for the first and the last time in his reign.

Social Legislation. A wide range of reforms went into effect as 1974 began, some being changes effecting compensation for sickness and unemployment, pension fees, and family and other social benefits. A dental program, reducing dentists' bills by at least 50%, went into full operation. Patients will pay only half the bill to the dentist, who receives the other half from insurance funds.

The Economy. Health and social programs as usual accounted for the largest single budget item in the 1974–75 budget. The value-added tax of 17.65% on practically all goods and services was lowered to 12% during the period April 1–September 15 in order to stimulate private consumption, check price increases, and further building and construction work.

According to a government proposal, unanimously approved by Parliament in May, $1 billion will be needed to finance the construction of Steelworks 80, the government's largest and most extensive industrial investment. The new plant will be built in Luleå, northern Sweden, and is projected to go into operation in 1980.

Sweden's gross national product showed a growth rate of 4.5% in 1974, as compared with 3% the year before. At the end of July, Sweden showed the second-lowest inflation rate among the 24 OECD nations, West Germany reporting the lowest rate.

Princess Christina. Sweden's wedding of the year was the marriage of Princess Christina, sister of King Carl XVI Gustaf, to Tord Magnusson, a company director, on June 15. The wedding took place in the chapel of the Royal Palace. Under the name of Princess Christina, Mrs. Magnusson, the princess will continue to assist the king in representing Sweden.

Swedish-American Relations. Sweden and the United States in late March announced agreement on the exchange of ambassadors, ending a 15-month lack of top-level diplomatic representation between the two countries after Sweden's condemnation of U. S. bombing of North Vietnam. Count Wilhelm Wachtmeister, head of the political department at the Ministry for Foreign Affairs, was appointed the new envoy to Washington at a cabinet meeting on March 21. The announcement was simultaneously made from Washington that U. S. Ambassador to Belgium Robert Strausz-Hupé was nominated to fill the post in Sweden; he arrived in Stockholm on May 22. In a statement presented to President Nixon, Sweden's new ambassador recalled the long history of friendship between Sweden and the United States.

Relations with Other Countries. The expulsion from the USSR on February 13 of the Russian novelist Aleksandr Solzhenitsyn generated indignant reaction in Sweden. Prime Minister Olof Palme stated: "The Soviet move is even more regrettable since it is taken at a time when the East as well as the West is striving for détente and an intensified exchange of views and information across borders."

A ten-year agreement between the Swedish and Libyan governments, ensuring a flow of 2 million tons of crude oil toward Sweden's annual needs, was signed on March 6. A ten-year program on economic, industrial, technical, and scientific cooperation between Sweden and Poland was signed during a visit by Prime Minister Palme to Poland, April 1–4. King Carl XVI Gustaf made an official state visit to Norway in October.

Cultural Events. Pär Lagerkvist, Swedish poet, dramatist, and novelist recognized as one of the country's ranking literary figures, died on July 11 at the age of 83. He received the Nobel Prize in 1951. Swedish authors Eyvind Johnson and Harry Martinson were named to share the 1974 Nobel Prize in literature.

MAC LINDAHL
Reporter, Writer, and Translator

SWEDEN • Information Highlights

Official Name: Kingdom of Sweden.
Location: Northern Europe.
Area: 173,649 square miles (449,750 sq km).
Population (1973 est.): 8,200,000.
Chief Cities (1971 est.): Stockholm, the capital, 723,680; Göteborg, 450,420; Malmö, 263,830.
Government: *Head of state,* Carl XVI Gustaf, king (acceded Sept. 19, 1973). *Head of government,* Olof Palme, prime minister (took office Oct. 1969). *Legislature* (unicameral)—Riksdag.
Monetary Unit: Krona (4.377 kronor equal U. S.$1, July 1974).
Gross National Product (1973 est.): $45,400,000,000.
Manufacturing (major products): Pulp and paper, iron and steel, machinery and equipment, ships.
Major Agricultural Products: Oats, sugar beets, potatoes, wheat, livestock, forest products.
Foreign Trade (1973): Exports, $12,171,000,000; imports, $10,625,000,000.

SWITZERLAND

The status of foreign workers, right to abortion, inflation, and the creation of a new canton were dominant issues in Switzerland in 1974.

Aliens Bill. One sixth of the population and 37% of the work force in Switzerland are foreigners. A proposed aliens exclusion act, subject of an October 20 referendum, stipulated a 12% limit on each canton's foreign population, except for a 25% allowance to Geneva. Implementation would have necessitated deporting 1,100,000 foreigners by the end of 1977.

To a great extent, support for this measure resulted from deep cultural prejudices, especially against the Italians who constitute more than 50% of the immigrants. Fearful government, religious, business and labor organizations mounted a massive campaign against the bill. They argued that in Switzerland's full-employment economy its passage would be "economic suicide" for the hotel, restaurant, construction, and textile industries, as well as leaving no one to fill low-paying service jobs. In the October voting, 1,689,870 (66%) opposed the bill and 878,739 (34%) supported it.

Abortion. On October 5 the Swiss cabinet recommended to parliament that women be allowed abortions either for medical reasons (currently permissible) or on the recommendation of a social worker. In a country divided evenly between Protestants and Catholics, abortion is a highly emotional issue. Feminist groups have obtained the necessary 50,000 signatures to ensure a national referendum on a bill proposing individual freedom of choice for all women.

Jura Independence. On Dec. 18, 1973, the government of Berne canton announced that it would allow seven Jura districts to decide on the creation of a 23d canton. In a June 23 referendum, the three northern, most heavily French-speaking districts voted affirmatively; the other four plus certain communes will have an opportunity to vote again on joining the new canton or remaining part of German-speaking Berne. Although a constitutional amendment allowing a new canton must be approved by parliament and in a national referendum, the long-standing and often violent Jurassian issue finally appeared to be near permanent resolution.

SWITZERLAND • Information Highlights

Official Name: Swiss Confederation.
Location: Central Europe.
Area: 15,941 square miles (41,288 sq km).
Population (1973 est.): 6,500,000.
Government: *Head of state,* Pierre Graber, president (took office Jan. 1975). *Legislature*—Federal Assembly: Council of States and National Council.
Monetary Unit: Franc (3.008 francs equal U. S.$1, Aug. 1974).
Gross National Product (1973 est.): $38,800,000,000.
Manufacturing (major products): Machinery, chemicals, textiles, watches, clocks, clock parts.
Major Agricultural Products: Potatoes, sugar beets, wheat, barley, dairy products, forest products.
Foreign Trade (1973): *Exports,* $9,482,000,000; *imports,* $10,626,000,000.

Economic Problems. Despite annual figures that in July 1974 indicated a 2% decline from the 1973 inflation rate of 11.9%, parliament extended the Emergency Powers Law to September 1977. This law grants the government and the National Bank special powers designed to slow down inflationary growth.

PAUL C. HELMREICH, *Wheaton College, Mass.*

SYRIA

The aftermath of the October 1973 Arab-Israeli war dominated the concerns of Syrian President Hafez al-Assad and his government in 1974. Demanding the return of all Arab lands occupied by Israel since 1967 and the recognition of the rights of the Palestinians, President Assad engaged in difficult talks with U. S. Secretary of State Henry Kissinger and the Israeli government until May 1974, when a disengagement agreement for the separation of Syrian and Israeli troops in the bitterly contested Golan Heights region was finally negotiated. Faced with $2.5 billion in war damages and the challenge of rebuilding the damaged industrial sector, Assad was fortunate to receive massive financial assistance from the Arab world in recognition of Syria's war effort as well as substantial loans and technical aid from industrialized states. However, as the year came to a close, the apparent failure of efforts to bring about an overall peace settlement to the Middle East led Assad, buoyed by major arms shipments from the Soviet Union, to support political decisions within the Arab League that threatened another war in the region.

Negotiations with Israel. Although President Assad had accepted a UN ceasefire resolution in late October 1973, fighting continued between Syrian and Israeli troops in the Golan Heights. Assad's position that negotiations for a separation of forces could not begin until Israel pledged to withdraw from all occupied Arab lands was met by the equally firm Israeli position not to start talks until Syria released the names of Israeli prisoners of war held in Syria. Given this bargaining situation, diplomatic activity was curtailed until January 17, when Egypt announced its disengagement agreement with Israel on the Sinai front.

The good offices of U. S. Secretary of State Kissinger were relied upon to transmit the negotiating positions of the belligerents to each other. By February, Assad had shifted his stance: he declared that he would release the names of the Israelis as soon as Israel agreed to allow the return of an estimated 170,000 Syrian refugees to their homes in the Golan Heights. Through March and April the negotiations foundered many times.

However, the efforts of Kissinger finally bore fruit in May. After Kissinger had shuttled proposals and counter-proposals between the two countries in May, a disengagement

Y. NAGATA/UNITED NATIONS

UN Secretary General Waldheim is greeted in Damascus by Syrian Foreign Minister Abdul Halim Khaddam, June 4.

agreement was announced on May 29 and signed formally in Geneva two days later. The agreement called for both sides to withdraw to lines on either side of the 1967 ceasefire line and for the key Golan town of Quneitra to be returned to Syria. That the agreement was reached when it was surprised most observers, since Israel had called for a ten-day delay in the talks on May 16, due to a hopeless deadlock.

Although the agreement had achieved a separation of forces by June 26, preliminary talks for an overall settlement remained deadlocked on the issue of Israel's withdrawal from the Golan Heights, a part of Syria prior to 1967. In speeches in June and July, the Israeli head of state declared that the Golan could not be returned to Syria even in "the context of a final settlement," thus dooming in advance any talks of a permanent peace in the region. Adding to the tension was the fact that Soviet arms shipments to Syria had restored Syria to its pre-October 1973 strength.

SYRIA • Information Highlights

Official Name: Syrian Arab Republic.
Location: Southwest Asia.
Area: 71,586 square miles (185,408 sq km).
Population (1973 est.): 6,900,000.
Chief Cities (1970 census): Damascus, the capital, 836,179; Aleppo, 639,361; Homs, 215,526.
Government: *Head of state,* Lt. Gen. Hafez al-Assad, president (took office March 1971). *Head of government,* Mahmoud al-Ayubi, premier (took office Nov. 1972). *Legislature* (unicameral)—People's Council.
Monetary Unit: Pound (3.70 pounds equal U. S.$1, June 1974).
Gross National Product (1972 est.): $2,244,000,000.
Manufacturing (major products): Petroleum products, textiles, cement, glass, soap.
Major Agricultural Products: Wheat, barley, sugar beets.
Foreign Trade (1973): *Exports,* $339,000,000; *imports,* $593,000,000.

Assad, more militant than many other Arab leaders, took a decidedly radical position with respect to the Israelis. He publicly made the negotiating position of the Palestinian Liberation Organization (PLO) his own and led the diplomatic fight to have the PLO recognized as the sole spokesman for the Palestinian people at the October Arab summit conference in Rabat, Morocco. This decision increased the possibility of another major round of fighting and by mid-November war fears caused the mobilization of Syrian and Israeli troops two weeks prior to the scheduled lapse of the UN Observer Force's mandate.

Economy. On February 6, Syria announced that the damage inflicted during the October war amounted to at least $2.5 billion. This, however, was a conservative estimate, as the full effects of the destruction of Syria's vital power stations had not been calculated. However, by the end of February, financial contributions from the Arab World had already compensated for a quarter of Syria's losses.

On March 21, Prime Minister Mahmoud al-Ayubi announced that the 1973 Development Plan had been altered upward to $950 million to counterbalance war damages. To stimulate the economy, restrictions on the private sector were lifted the following day, allowing private industry to contract with foreign investors. Laws on hard currency were liberalized. Major development projects were announced in August. On August 23, Czechoslovakia agreed to supply $35 million for rebuilding the Homs oil refinery and on August 27, England was awarded a $30 million contract for a textile mill in Latakia. (See also feature article on page 36.)

F. NICHOLAS WILLARD, *Georgetown University*

TANZANIA

Mainland Tanzania's ruling and only political party, the Tanganyika African National Union (TANU), celebrated its 20th anniversary in 1974. The day of the party's founding, July 7, has become the country's most important national holiday.

Party Anniversary. The annual celebration of TANU's founding was attended by President Kenneth Kaunda of Zambia and Samora Machel, president of Frelimo, the nationalist movement in neighboring Mozambique.

TANU has continued to advocate socialism (*ujamaa*) and gradual nationalization. However, President Julius Nyerere reported that the establishment of *ujamaa* villages was moving slowly. Since 1967, only 15% of the population has moved into the *ujamaa* villages. Of those moving, 80% were concentrated in 7 of the country's 18 regions, most of which were in the poorer areas where land was more readily available.

In keeping with its policy of rural development, Tanzania began the process of moving its capital from the coastal city of Dar es Salaam to Dodoma, 250 miles (400 km) inland.

Pan-African Congress. The sixth Pan-African Congress—the first since 1945 and the first on African soil—was held in Dar es Salaam on June 19–27. The conference was attended by 500 delegates from 29 countries in Africa and the Caribbean, the United States, Canada, and Britain, along with representatives from eight liberation movements fighting in Africa.

Zanzibar Trial. At the end of a year-long trial, 34 people in Zanzibar were sentenced to death by a three-man people's tribunal for a 1972 plot that led to the assassination of the island's leader, Sheikh Abeid Karume. Tanzanian authorities had refused to return to Zanzibar 18 others accused in the plot, because they said they had not received assurances that the accused would be allowed defense lawyers.

Relations with Britain. Britain and Tanzania agreed on a program settling many of their outstanding disputes, ending nine years of strain.

JAY E. HAKES, *University of New Orleans*

TANZANIA • Information Highlights

Official Name: United Republic of Tanzania.
Location: East Africa.
Area: 364,899 square miles (945,087 sq km).
Population (1973 est.): 14,400,000.
Chief City (1970 est.): Dar es Salaam, the capital, 344,000.
Government: *Head of State,* Julius K. Nyerere, president (took office 1964). *Chief minister,* Rashidi Kawawa, premier (took office 1972). *Legislature* (unicameral)—National Assembly.
Monetary Unit: Shilling (7.143 shillings equal U.S.$1, July 1974).
Gross National Product (1972 est.): $1,583,000,000.
Manufacturing (major products): Textiles, cement, petroleum products, refined sugar, aluminum.
Major Agricultural Products: Cloves, sisal, cotton, coffee, oilseeds, groundnuts, tea, tobacco, sugarcane.
Foreign Trade (1973): *Exports,* $321,000,000; *imports,* $448,000,000.

TAXATION

Any government finds itself in a fiscal dilemma during an inflationary period such as that experienced in 1974. Families that are hard hit by the increase in the cost of living, particularly those in lower income brackets, are entitled to tax relief. Those who have profited by inflation are presumably fit subjects for heavier taxation. At the same time, inflation control calls for general tax increases to reduce the level of demand.

Congressional Action. The actions of the administration and the Congress during 1974 reflected these multiple objectives. The House Ways and Means Committee held many hearings on the "Tax Reform Act of 1974." In some of its versions this was a most complicated piece of legislation, with as many as 117 provisions, some of which would have closed loopholes, others of which would have extended them.

The committee considered four or five major revisions. One of these would increase the minimum standard deduction from $2,000 to $2,300. This would lower average taxes on income below $7,000 by an estimated $53 annually and on incomes between $7,000 and $15,000 by $56 annually.

The measure under consideration by the committee also provided for an increase in the investment tax credit for utilities from 4% to 7%, and a reduction in the controversial percentage depletion allowance for oil and gas producers from 22% to 14% for 1974, with elimination by 1979. The combination of these tax increases and reductions would add about $1 billion to federal revenue. In addition, the committee seriously considered a provision that would exempt from personal income tax the first $1,000 of interest on savings accounts. If adopted, this would result in a revenue loss of $2 billion.

After some seven years of sporadic committee hearings the Congress adopted the Pension Reform Act in September. The act alters the status of private pension schemes. Individuals who are not covered by qualified plans can establish their own retirement accounts for liberalized tax treatment, while those in upper income brackets who are now covered by corporate retirement plans will be limited in their use for purposes of "tax shelter." A revenue loss of $460 million is expected as a result of these alterations.

In October, President Ford proposed a 5% anti-inflation surtax on all family incomes above $15,000, but this proposal was not taken seriously by Congress. As the unemployment rate increased, the administration reversed course and appeared to favor a major revenue reduction of $10 to $20 billion. A sharp increase in the gasoline tax was also under consideration.

Social Security. Both taxes and benefits for social security, including Medicare, have continued to increase more rapidly than federal revenues and expenditures as a whole. In fiscal

1974, social insurance receipts increased by 19%, from $60.2 billion to $72.0 billion, while other federal revenue increased by 11%, from $187.6 billion to $209.0 billion.

The additional social security taxes have come through increases in the amount of income subject to tax, not by rate increases. The tax base moved from $10,800 to $13,200 in 1974 and will increase further to $14,100 in 1975. In 1975 the maximum social security tax, paid by employers and employees alike, will rise to $824.85. (See also SOCIAL WELFARE.)

State and Local Revenue. Federal aid to states and local governments has been increasing in recent years at a 20–25% annual rate. In fiscal 1974 the increase was only $1.7 billion, or 4%. The rate of increase in state and local taxes also declined. In 1973 it was 12.7%, and in 1974 it was 9.0%. In dollar amounts the increase was $18.9 billion in fiscal 1973 and $15.2 billion in 1974. Part of this leveling off was attributable to the decline in state gasoline tax receipts during the energy crisis of the spring, and part was due to the continuing move to limit property taxes at the local level, especially for elderly homeowners. In addition, changes in state tax laws focused on tax relief, with 14 states reducing levies and only 9 states increasing them, for an estimated net annual reduction of $350 million.

Reforms in financing patterns for public elementary and secondary education continued unabated in 1974. In states where taxes were increased in 1974, the revenues were typically applied to local school property tax reduction. Nine states were under court order to revamp their school-finance patterns to equalize taxable resources per pupil.

Supreme Court Decisions. No landmark decisions involving taxation were handed down by the Supreme Court in 1974. In *Alexander* v. *Americans United, Inc.* and in *Bob Jones University* v. *William E. Simon* the court upheld the authority of the commissioner of internal revenue to revoke the tax-exempt status of nonprofit organizations. In the Alexander case a nonprofit organization was declared by the commissioner to be involved in lobbying activities. In the Bob Jones case the university's tax-exempt status was revoked due to racial discrimination in admissions and hiring.

In an important corporation case, *Commissioner of Internal Revenue* v. *National Alfalfa Dehydrating and Milling Company,* the court ruled that a capital loss resulting from an exchange of stock for corporate bonds could not be utilized as an income tax deduction.

The court also decided three cases involving state and local taxes. In *Kahn* v. *Shevin* the court ruled that a Florida state property tax exemption for widows was constitutional. The plaintiff, a widower, contended the statute violated the equal protection clause of the 14th Amendment. In *Pittsburgh* v. *Alco Parking Corporation* a 20% tax on gross receipts of off-street parking facilities was determined to be constitutional. In *Kosydar* v. *National Cash Register Co.,* an Ohio personal property tax was held to be valid when assessed against property intended for shipment to foreign customers, but not yet en route to such customers.

Canada. Canada was one of the first countries to link personal income tax exemptions with the cost of living. This 1973 legislation raised personal exemptions in 1974 and 1975.

Other Countries. Western European countries grappled with double-digit inflation in various ways. In some countries, such as the Netherlands, the major concern was to lessen the impact of inflation on low-income families. This was accomplished by increasing low-bracket deductions and offsetting this by an increase in the rate of net worth tax from 0.7% to 0.8%. Belgium linked allowable deductions under the personal income tax to the rate of inflation. In West Germany there was an increase in exemptions and childrens' allowances, and also an increase in the corporate tax rate. In Spain the basic income tax rate was lowered from 14% to 12%, and in the lowest income brackets the rate was dropped to 9%. In Italy corporation and personal income tax rates were increased, as was the rate of value added tax (VAT), with no offsetting concessions to lower-income groups.

There were major tax changes in France. The structure of local taxation was simplified; the rates of personal income tax were increased from 10% to 15%, and a special levy on corporations of 1,000 francs ($215) was adopted. France plans to extend withholding for personal income taxes in 1978.

The United Kingdom moved in the direction of greater progressivity in its income tax structure, with the basic rate increased from 30% to 33%, and the maximum rate from 75% to 83%, combined with an increase in personal exemptions and a 10% surtax. A gift tax was enacted, and a wealth tax was proposed. The low-income tax relief, however, was substantially offset by increased excise tax rates on spirits, beer, and tobacco.

Japan followed the western European pattern, with reductions in personal income taxes and more generous low-income deductions, coupled with increases in corporate taxes on both distributed and undistributed profits. In the Philippines, tax reform continued, with a further minimization of tax concessions and a reform in collection procedures. However, the tax on intercorporate dividends was reduced.

In India, the highest top-income tax rates were reduced (in an effort to minimize evasion) from 97.95% to 77%, with corresponding reductions in lower brackets. A surtax on company profits was introduced, and the net wealth tax was increased.

JESSE BURKHEAD
Syracuse University

TELECOMMUNICATIONS

Despite energy and materials shortages, telecommunications equipment and service markets continued to grow impressively in 1974. U. S. telephone industry observers estimated that $12.5 billion was spent on telephone system construction in 1974, and this was but a small fraction of the total investment in private telecommunications systems and services.

There were several controversial developments during the year, including some regulatory battles waged between certain segments of the telecommunications industry and the Federal Communications Commission (FCC).

Hi-Lo Tariff. The Bell System's so-called Hi-Lo tariff, approved by the FCC in April 1974, supposedly made its rates more competitive with the relatively new and aggressive specialized common carriers. However, several hearings were held later in the year to discuss continuing complaints from Bell System competitors, business and trade organizations, and five major news wire services. The Hi-Lo tariff eliminated Bell's long-standing uniform nationwide mileage charge on private lines used exclusively by business. The old rates were replaced by a two-tier system that lowered rates for high-density routes between 370 major cities and raised rates for low-density routes to small cities and towns. The FCC is expected to reconsider its approval and come to a formal decision on Hi-Lo early in 1975.

Resale of Circuits. In June the FCC opened a major inquiry into the resale and sharing of the common-carrier circuits leased from American Telephone & Telegraph Co. (AT&T) and Western Union Telegraph Co. AT&T, for instance, has allowed certain very large users of its private-line services, such as the stock exchanges and the airlines, to buy blocks of circuits and resell them to their own customers. Since AT&T has not made this arrangement available to all of its major users, the FCC inquiry is expected to consider whether to allow AT&T to continue these arrangements.

Meanwhile, there were indications that the airlines, the largest users of private-line telephone service outside the federal government, were beginning to look outside AT&T for service. By midyear, MCI Telecommunications, a specialized common carrier, already was providing service for 17 major U. S. airlines.

Domestic Communications Satellites. The FCC ruled that AT&T and its Bell System companies must provide interconnection facilities to domestic-satellite carriers. The commission's action states that it is the commission's "intention to ensure full interconnection for all authorized services provided by the satellite carrier to their customers."

There are now two communications satellite systems serving North America—Telesat Canada's Anik-series satellites and Western Union's Westar I and Westar II. RCA Global Communications, which leased communications channels on the Telesat system during 1974, expects to launch its own domestic satellite in 1975. Similarly, American Satellite Corp. has leased channels on Westar I while developing its own satellite system.

Land Mobile Systems. In May the FCC opened 115 megahertz (MHz) of the frequency spectrum for land mobile radio services, giving 40 MHz to the wire-line common carriers, 30 MHz to private users, and holding the remaining 45 MHz in reserve. The radio common carriers (RCC's), which offer paging and radiotelephone services at lower land mobile frequencies, complained that they were "left out in the cold." Their main objection was that the equipment suppliers will be able to offer services in competition with the RCC's but will be unregulated under the rules. The FCC was expected to take another look at its ruling.

Waveguide. The Bell System began installing a 20-mile (32-km) underground test link of cylindrical millimeter waveguide in northern New Jersey. The waveguide, a copper-lined steel pipe, eventually will carry up to 500,000 simultaneous telephone conversations. By comparison, the newest high-capacity coaxial cable carries 108,000 simultaneous conversations.

AT&T Suit. In November the U. S. government filed an antitrust suit to break up AT&T, to make it divest itself of the Western Electric Company and alter its arrangements with local phone companies it owns wholly or in part.

RONALD A. SCHNEIDERMAN
"Electronics" Magazine

TELEPHONES IN MAJOR COUNTRIES

Country	Telephones Jan. 1, 1973	% increase over 1972	No. per 100 population
Argentina	1,952,109	6.9	8.10
Australia[1]	4,399,782	6.0	33.95
Austria	1,694,194	9.5	22.72
Belgium	2,305,218	6.6	23.75
Brazil	2,190,000	6.1	2.17
Bulgaria	581,657	8.9	6.77
Canada	10,987,141	7.0	49.98
China, Rep. of	596,663	21.2	3.90
Colombia	1,009,791	0.4	4.49
Czechoslovakia	2,232,481	5.7	15.37
Denmark	1,912,449	6.6	37.93
Finland	1,412,067	9.5	30.47
France	10,338,000	8.3	19.91
Germany, East	2,232,069	3.1	13.10
Germany, West	16,521,149	8.4	26.79
Greece	1,437,578	16.9	16.32
Hong Kong	795,167	15.0	19.38
Hungary	923,966	5.8	8.87
India	1,479,475	9.5	0.27
Israel	619,709	10.0	19.37
Italy	11,345,497	9.9	20.76
Japan[1]	34,021,155	14.1	31.50
Mexico	1,957,972	14.2	3.79
Netherlands, The	4,003,455	7.6	29.91
New Zealand[1]	1,327,134	3.6	44.61
Norway	1,262,254	4.8	32.00
Poland	2,087,032	5.9	6.29
Portugal	873,339	7.9	9.89
South Africa, Republic of[1]	1,706,794	5.1	7.30
Spain	5,712,549	11.4	16.45
Sweden	4,829,047	3.2	59.29
Switzerland	3,404,427	6.0	53.95
Turkey	728,358	11.3	1.94
United Kingdom[1]	17,570,904	8.8	31.39
USSR	13,198,700	10.2	5.31
United States	131,606,000	5.2	62.75
Yugoslavia	910,695	10.9	4.38

[1] 1972 data. Source: AT&T

CBS TELEVISION NETWORK

Cicely Tyson (*left*) in her Emmy Award performance as a 110-year-old former slave in the two-hour special *The Autobiography of Miss Jane Pittman*.

television and radio

The extremes of television broadcasting in 1974 may well be illustrated by two important events: the televising of the House Judiciary Committee hearings on the impeachment of President Richard M. Nixon, and the one-time broadcast of *The Godfather,* the movies' most lucrative film. Both events had repercussions.

TELEVISION

The Impeachment Hearings. The networks, as they had in the case of the Senate Watergate hearings, rotated coverage of the House Judiciary Committee impeachment hearings. The broadcasts fully revealed the dignity, the deliberateness, and, for many, the anguish brought by the committee members to an event of awesome historical significance. The total lack of any circus atmosphere, in conjunction with the increasing public demand for fuller information about and control over our political process, has led Congress seriously to reconsider its ban on the televising of regular sessions.

Legal Curbs. Violence and sexual frankness in television have long been matters of congressional concern, heightened in 1974 by the broadcast of *The Godfather* (NBC, November 16 and 18) and the TV movie *Born Innocent* (NBC, September 10). *The Godfather* (reported to

Rhoda, a new situation comedy starring Valerie Harper, is a "spin-off" from the _Mary Tyler Moore Show_.

CBS TELEVISION NETWORK

have cost NBC $6.6 million for the one showing) is by any standard a violent film. *Born Innocent* contained a scene in which a 14-year-old girl is sexually violated. In the latter case, part of the congressional criticism lay in the fact it was shown at the early hour of 8 P. M. Both the House and Senate Appropriations committees directed the Federal Communications Commission (FCC) to report by year's end means by which violence and sexual frankness could be curbed in future TV programs. The FCC, enjoined by law from censoring programs, can only express the hope that "jawboning" will produce results. Chairman Richard E. Wiley has observed that if broadcasters "won't serve as public trustees . . . then inevitably the call will be for governmental action and governmental redress."

Mexico has taken just such action, banning 37 imported series, mostly American and including *Ironside* (not normally violent) and the *FBI,* on the ground that their violence is a harmful influence on Mexican youth.

Federal Communications Commission. Through no fault of its own, the FCC entered the year in some disarray. It began the year with five members, but was reduced to four when Chairman Dean Burch was named in February as a counsel to President Nixon, and arrived at full strength on July 11, its 40th birthday.

In part at the request of the chairman of the House and Senate Commerce committees, the FCC made no major moves while it was at low ebb. In January it modified its prime-time access rule, cutting in half those hours in which network programs were prohibited, and doing away entirely with access time on Sundays. The National Association of Independent TV Producers and Distributors took the matter to court; in June a U. S. court of appeals in New York ordered the FCC to stay the change in rules until September 1975 or later, suggesting that there be further study of the access question.

Interpretation of the fairness doctrine continued to plague both the FCC and the courts. In September the U. S. court of appeals in Washington ruled in favor of NBC in a fairness doctrine dispute with the FCC over the 1972 documentary *Pensions: The Broken Promise.* In June the FCC adopted a staff report on the doctrine. In the hope of limiting areas to which the doctrine might apply, it did away with the 1967 ruling requiring stations to accept anti-cigarette spots to balance cigarette advertising, thereby removing counteradvertising from the doctrine. It rejected the idea of hard and fast rules governing the public's right of access to the media, believing it better to leave access to "the licensee's journalistic discretion."

NOTABLE U. S. TELEVISION PROGRAMS OF 1974

After the Fall—Adaptation of Arthur Miller's play, produced by Gilbert Cates; featuring Christopher Plummer, Faye Dunaway, and Bibi Andersson. NBC, Dec. 10.

The Ambassador—First of four plays about Benjamin Franklin, by Howard Fast, concerning Franklin's protection of American colonial interests while serving in Paris during the Revolution; with Eddie Albert, Gig Young, Alexis Smith, and Rene Auberjonois. CBS, Nov. 21.

The Autobiography of Miss Jane Pittman—Story of a black woman and the tragedies in her life through more than 100 years of U. S. history; from the novel by Ernest J. Gaines, adapted by Tracy Keenan Wynn; starring Cicely Tyson. CBS, Jan. 31.

A Case of Rape—Drama by Robert E. Thompson, directed by Boris Sagal; featuring Elizabeth Montgomery and Cliff Potts. NBC, Feb. 20.

Clarence Darrow—Adaptation of the stage play by David W. Rintels, based on Irving Stone's book; starring Henry Fonda. NBC, Sept. 4.

The Country Girl—Hallmark Hall of Fame production of Clifford Odets' play, featuring Jason Robards, Shirley Knight Hopkins, and George Grizzard. NBC, Feb. 5.

Crown Matrimonial—Hallmark Hall of Fame presentation of Royce Ryton's play about events leading to King Edward VIII's abdication; with Greer Garson, Peter Barkworth, Andrew Ray, and Amanda Reiss. NBC, April 3.

The Energy Crisis: American Solutions—Two-part documentary on oil and the U. S. economy. NBC, March 21 and 28.

The Execution of Private Slovik—Dramatic adaptation of William Bradford Huie's book about the first U. S. soldier executed in 1945 for desertion. NBC, March 13.

The Gathering Storm—British Broadcasting Corporation's dramatization of vol. 1 of Winston Churchill's World War II memoirs, covering the years 1936–40; starring Richard Burton as Churchill and Virginia McKenna as Mrs. Churchill. NBC, Nov. 29.

The Godfather—Slightly edited version of the 1972 movie, starring Marlon Brando, Al Pacino, and Robert Duvall. NBC, in two parts, Nov. 16 and 18.

Great Expectations—Dramatization of the Dickens novel by Sherman Yellin; with Michael York, Sarah Miles, James Mason, Robert Morley, Margaret Leighton, Anthony Quayle, Rachel Roberts, and Heather Sears. NBC, Nov. 22.

The Last of the Belles—Film biography of F. Scott Fitzgerald, played by Richard Chamberlain. ABC, Jan. 7.

Lincoln: Trial by Fire—American Heritage series documentary-style film story of the conflict between Lincoln and Gen. George B. McClellan. ABC, Jan. 20.

The Man from Independence—Portrait series story of Harry S Truman, with Robert Vaughn, June Dayton, Martha Scott, and Arthur Kennedy. ABC, March 11.

Marlo Thomas and Friends in Free to Be. . .You and Me—Musical variety, featuring Marlo Thomas with several guests. ABC, March 11.

Mass—A Theater Piece for Singers, Players and Dancers—Leonard Bernstein's musical composition, staged by John Mauceri at Yale University and recorded at the Vienna Konzerthaus. PBS, Feb. 27.

The Merchant of Venice—British National Theatre production of the Shakespeare play, with Sir Laurence Olivier, Joan Plowright, Jeremy Brett, Antony Nicholls, and Michael Jayston. ABC, March 16.

The Migrants—Playhouse 90 drama of poor farm laborers moving from South to North in search of work; by Lanford Wilson, from an idea of Tennessee Williams; starring Cloris Leachman and Ron Howard. CBS, Feb. 3.

The Missiles of October—Dramatization of the Cuban missile crisis of 1962; script by Stanley R. Greenburg; with William Devane, Martin Sheen, Howard Da Silva, Ralph Bellamy, Larry Gates, Dana Elcar. ABC, Dec. 18.

Murder and the Right to Bear Arms—Documentary study of gun-control laws, narrated by John Hart. CBS, July 7.

Oil: The Policy Crisis—Documentary on background of the energy crisis. ABC, March 20.

The Palestinians—Documentary by Howard Stringer, narrated by Bill McLaughlin, showing the history and nature of the Palestine guerrilla movement. CBS, June 15.

Primal Man: Struggle for Survival—Documentary dramatization of the evolutionary process; narrated by Alexander Scourby; produced by David L. Wolper. ABC, June 21.

6 Rms Riv Vu—Adaptation of the play by Bob Randall, starring Carol Burnett and Alan Alda. CBS, March 17.

The Whirlwind—Second play in series about Franklin, by Loring Mandel; with Lloyd and Beau Bridges, Sheree North, Susan Sarandon. CBS, Dec. 17.

The World You Never See—Microphotographic study of tiny living things, narrated by Hugh Downs. NBC, March 14.

PBS

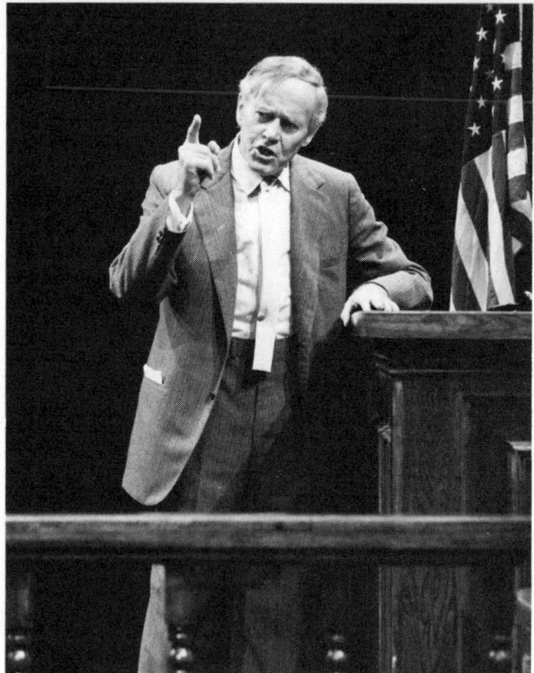

NBC-TV

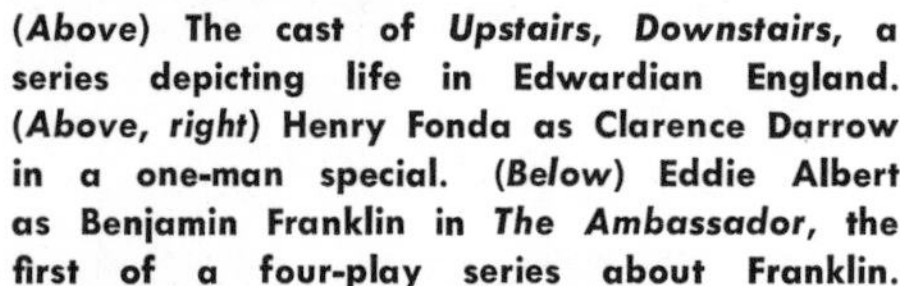

(*Above*) The cast of *Upstairs, Downstairs,* a series depicting life in Edwardian England. (*Above, right*) Henry Fonda as Clarence Darrow in a one-man special. (*Below*) Eddie Albert as Benjamin Franklin in *The Ambassador,* the first of a four-play series about Franklin.

CBS TELEVISION NETWORK

News and Public Affairs. Polls over the past several years have shown that television news programs are the major source of news for the American people; they are also good business. According to a 1974 Arbitron study, in 41 of the top 50 markets, news programs, local and network, ranked among the top 25 programs. Many local stations have extended their evening news programs to an hour, and NBC's New York flagship station to two hours.

Death claimed three gifted figures in television journalism in 1974: Fred Freed, NBC News executive producer (March 31); Frank McGee, host of NBC's *Today* (April 17); and Chet Huntley, from 1957 to 1970 with *The Huntley-Brinkley Report* (March 20). Freed and McGee last collaborated on *NBC Reports: The Energy Crisis,* broadcast in September 1973. On March 14 the crash of a chartered airplane near Bishop, Calif., killed 31 members of a Wolper Productions crew on its way to shoot scenes for an ABC program, *The Primal Man.*

Children's Programs. One of the persisting problems for the industry has been the kind and quality of children's programs, notably those offered on Saturday mornings. After more than four years—it was in February 1970 that Action for Children's Television (ACT) made its original petition—the FCC issued a policy statement meant to clarify broadcasters' responsibilities in both content and amount of advertising in children's programs. In brief, the statement urged broadcasters to spread programs throughout the week, to make a "significant" amount of their programs educational or informational, and to accept the limits on advertising recommended by television's code board. The advertising limits call for nonprogram time ranging between 10 and 14 minutes per hour in 1975, 9½ and 12 minutes in 1976, the lower amounts for weekends, the higher for Monday-through-Friday programs. ACT found this distinction "absurd" and the statement "disappointing and disturbing."

Earlier in the year Canada's Radio-Television Commission (CRTC) went the whole way, proposing a complete ban on advertising aimed at children, to go into effect on Jan. 1, 1975. It also suggested pegging the renewal of licenses for CBC's 50 AM and FM stations on their giving up virtually all advertising as of the same date. The CBC's television stations, now carrying about 10 minutes of advertising per hour, would be required to reduce that amount over a period of five years to five minutes per hour. The purpose, in the words of CRTC Chairman Pierre Juneau, is to free Canadian broadcasting from the "North American mold." In matters such as these, Parliament has the final say.

Prime-Time Entertainment. Four of the six new shows presented in January's "second season" failed to make the grade when the "new season" (beginning in September) was announced by the networks in late April. CBS announced that seven shows would be dropped, among them *The Lucy Show, The Dick Van Dyke Show,* and *The Sonny and Cher Show.* NBC gave the ax to a whopping 14, including *Heck Ramsey, Banacek,* and the *Flip Wilson, Dean Martin,* and *Brian Keith* shows. ABC discontinued 10, including the long-running *The Brady Bunch, The Partridge Family, Owen Marshall,* and *The FBI.* And, to cap the disaster news, "Miss Kitty" (Amanda Blake) left the Long Branch Saloon after 19 years in *Gunsmoke.*

The new 1974 season got under way in September with 23 new program offerings and high network hopes for such shows as *Rhoda, Planet of the Apes,* and *Friends and Lovers* on CBS; *Little House on the Prairie, Lucas Tanner, Chico and the Man, Movin' On,* and *The Rockford Files* on NBC; and *Paper Moon, Harry O,* and *The Texas Wheelers* on ABC. By November it had become apparent that there would be many changes, involving at least 12 programs, in January 1975, among them the long-running *Mannix, Gunsmoke,* and *Ironside,* which seemed to have been fatally wounded by the release for rerun of the early episodes of the series under the title *The Raymond Burr Show.* Despite these program deaths and the enormous waste of money in poor program choices or poor scheduling, however, network business was at an all-time high. One odd note: in the new season there were only two variety (song-and-dance-and-snappy-patter) programs—the perennial *Carol Burnett Show* and *The Sonny Comedy Revue,* the latter marked to be dropped in January.

Specials added some luster to the year, among them variety shows with Barbra Streisand, Bing Crosby, Ann Bancroft, Shirley MacLaine, Frank Sinatra, and others; and dramas, notably *The Autobiography of Miss Jane Pittman* (starring Cicely Tyson and winner of four Emmy awards), Henry Fonda as Clarence Darrow, and several dramatizations of aspects of American history, as a prelude to the country's bicentennial.

Motion pictures, both the theatrical and the made-for-television kind, accounted for some 16 hours a week of prime time, not always with distinction. There is reason to believe that lower ratings and higher costs may diminish the amount of movie fare on television in the next year or so.

Public Broadcasting. Money, or the lack of it, and organizational problems continued to plague public broadcasting, with considerable tension between the Corporation for Public Broadcasting (CPB) and Public Broadcasting Service (PBS) over allocations to the stations from governmental funding. A group was formed to iron out or compromise the differences. The desperately desired long-range funding bill for CPB at least cleared the Senate Commerce Committee during 1974 and was praised by President Ford, but further action awaited the new Congress in 1975.

Public television received a jolt when it became known that the FCC was likely to deny license renewal to the eight stations of the Alabama Educational Television Commission. The grounds for the action are the stations' refusal to carry such PBS programs as *Black Journal* and *Soul!* and their discrimination against the hiring of blacks.

The FCC's action, were it to become final, would be historic: the FCC has never questioned the license renewal of any public station, nor ever taken away the licenses of any network of stations. The decision was not expected for several months.

Congress and Broadcasting. Both the House and Senate have labored long over the writing of new laws governing copyrights, a difficult task at best in an age when the duplication of printed and recorded material is no technical problem. The Senate finally voted a copyright bill, but the House took no final action, which meant that the whole question would continue on into the new Congress in 1975.

A bill governing license renewal for stations was a different matter. Both the House of Representatives and the Senate passed bills, and both houses agreed on at least one major change in present law: the substitution of a five-year license term as opposed to the present three years.

Cable TV. The struggle between cable and on-air broadcasting intensified during the year, with particular attention being given to pay-cable—that form of cable service charging for specific programs rather than an overall fee for a monthly service. Over-the-air broadcasters consider the threat of pay-cable so serious that the president of CBS, Inc., Arthur R. Taylor, wrote a book titled *Does the American Family Need Another Mouth to Feed?* The FCC in

NBC-TV

Newcomer Freddie Prinze (*left*) as Chico and veteran actor Jack Albertson as Ed Brown, a garage owner, star in the new hit comedy series *Chico and the Man*.

mid-November completed the outline of a new policy governing pay-TV, or pay-cable, generally loosening restrictions on the use of films and sports events but still basically protecting on-air broadcasting against what a National Association of Broadcasters official called "wholesale siphoning."

Cable interests organized to fight the copyright bill adopted by the Senate, on the ground that it could scuttle their entire industry. Cable-TV's greatest objection to the bill is that it establishes the principle that cable owes fees for all the on-air television programs it carries. The fear is that the networks could at some time in the future force copyright fees to prohibitive heights. Reconciliation between the two forms of the legislation, as approved by the House and the Senate, as well as important changes to come, await the new Congress in 1975.

Radio drama is revived in 1974 via the nightly CBS Radio Mystery Theater, with E. G. Marshall as the host. Here Tammy Grimes and Paul Hecht emote in *A Drop of Poison*.

CBS RADIO

RADIO

Congressional Action. The radio industry was no happier over some of the terms of the Senate-passed copyright bill than were cable interests. The bill, as it went from the Senate Copyright Subcommittee to the parent Judiciary Committee, contained a provision requiring broadcasters to pay a royalty of roughly 2% of their net revenues into a fund to be evenly divided between record companies and artists. The Senate passed the bill on September 9, with an amendment by Sen. Sam Ervin (D-N. C.) deleting the royalty section, but with Sen. Hugh Scott (R-Pa.), its major proponent, vowing to fight for the provision in 1975.

Congress gave time to considering an all-channel radio bill that would require set manufacturers to make only AM-FM receivers. Many Senate Commerce Subcommittee members felt the bill was necessary to keep the FM band commercially viable. Despite stout opposition, the bill passed the Senate on a 44–42 vote. The later House version confined the requirement only to radios for use in automobiles. A House-Senate conference would be needed to resolve the differences.

Miscellaneous. The radio year was marked by the increasing nationwide acceptance of country and western music. Nashville's Grand Ol' Opry, which has shaped the country music tradition and made Nashville a major center of recording production, moved into a new home. President Nixon attended the opening festivities and telecast.

In May the Associated Press announced a new radio news service to compete with those already provided by United Press International and the several offered to stations by the networks. AP claimed a "firm commitment" from 100 stations and set a starting date in the fall.

During the year, Motorola, Inc., completed arrangements to sell its television home receiver manufacturing business to Matsushita Electric Industrial Co. of Japan, manufacturers of Panasonic products. Motorola retains its land-mobile business, far and away its major source of profit. It is estimated that Motorola controls about 85% of the manufacture of equipment for the land-mobile field.

JOHN M. GUNN
State University of New York at Albany

TELEVISION AND RADIO ENGINEERING

There was little growth in the number of U. S. commercial or public TV broadcasting stations in 1974, although TV broadcasting continued to expand abroad and cable TV expanded both in the United States and abroad. The first regular TV transmissions from an earth-orbiting satellite intended for home reception took place during the year.

TV Broadcasting. The number of TV broadcasting stations on the air in the United States

SUMMARY OF WORLD TELEVISION STATIONS AND SETS
(As of March 1974)

Country	Stations	Number of TV sets	Country	Stations	Number of TV sets	Country	Stations	Number of TV sets
Albania	1	3,000	Honduras	5	45,000	Paraguay	1	50,000
Algeria	6	260,000	Hong Kong	5	706,000	Peru	18	450,000
Antigua	1	8,500	Hungary	18	2,200,000	Philippines	17	450,000
Argentina	34	4,000,000	Iceland	7	47,000	Poland	36	5,695,300
Australia	137	3,535,700	India	5	150,000	Portugal	12	598,000
Austria	195	1,762,000	Indonesia	16	300,000	Puerto Rico	[1]	655,000
Bangladesh	1	20,000	Iran	16	250,000	Qatar	1	25,000
Barbados	1	32,000	Iraq	5	500,000	Rhodesia	2	58,000
Belgium	15	2,288,000	Ireland	23	585,000	Rumania	17	1,946,000
Bermuda	2	21,400	Israel	12	430,000	Samoa (American)	6	5,000
Bolivia	1	24,000	Italy	89	12,455,000	Saudi Arabia	8	300,000
Brazil	52	8,700,000	Ivory Coast	6	85,500	Singapore	2	180,000
Bulgaria	8	1,368,650	Jamaica	9	100,000	Spain	35	5,625,000
Cambodia	2	30,000	Japan	208	25,000,000	Sudan	2	65,000
Canada	500	9,150,000	Jordan	2	110,000	Surinam	1	33,000
Chile	31	1,000,000	Kenya	4	35,000	Sweden	240	3,985,000
China (Mainland)	36	2,650,000	Korea (South)	12	1,140,000	Switzerland	203	1,912,000
Colombia	18	1,200,000	Kuwait	3	130,000	Syria	5	160,000
Costa Rica	4	154,000	Lebanon	9	320,000	Thailand	5	400,000
Cuba	25	555,000	Liberia	1	9,000	Trinidad & Tobago	3	82,000
Cyprus	2	82,000	Libya	2	3,000	Tunisia	9	131,000
Czechoslovakia	28	3,250,000	Luxembourg	2	86,000	Turkey	14	270,000
Denmark	30	1,645,000	Malaysia	30	737,500	Uganda	6	30,000
Dominican Republic	6	150,000	Malta	1	70,000	United Arab Emirates	2	15,000
Ecuador	12	250,000	Martinique	1	15,000	United Kingdom	264	17,800,000
Egypt	23	550,000	Mauritius	1	31,500	United States[2]	940	117,000,000
El Salvador	5	109,300	Mexico	92	5,471,000	Upper Volta	1	7,700
Ethiopia	1	22,000	Monaco	1	17,000	Uruguay	15	350,000
Finland	72	1,237,000	Morocco	9	330,000	USSR	167	42,000,000
France	197	14,820,000	Netherlands	20	4,020,000	Venezuela	31	1,145,000
Germany (East)	28	4,810,000	Netherlands Antilles	3	35,000	Vietnam (South)	1	500,000
Germany (West)	180	17,100,000	New Zealand	27	775,000	Virgin Islands	[1]	33,000
Ghana	4	30,000	Nicaragua	2	68,000	Yemen	3	30,000
Greece	17	800,000	Nigeria	8	80,000	Yugoslavia	35	2,561,000
Guadeloupe	2	11,500	Norway	82	1,000,000	Zaire	2	7,500
Guam	[1]	40,000	Okinawa	2	230,000	Zambia	3	19,500
Guatemala	3	119,000	Pakistan	7	185,000			
Haiti	3	11,000	Panama	11	193,000	Total[3]	18,271	344,396,710

[1] Stations included in U. S. count. [2] Preliminary estimate. [3] Includes 13,671 satellites and repeaters, and some small places not listed. (Source: Television Factbook, 1974-75.)

at the end of 1974 was 947, compared with 938 at the end of 1973. Of these 947 stations, 709 were commercial and 238 were public (noncommercial) stations; 609 operated in the VHF band (channels 2–13) and 338 in the UHF band (channels 16–69). TV broadcasting outside the United States continued a steady growth, as reflected in the accompanying table.

Cable TV. According to the National Cable Television Association (NCTA), the number of cable TV (CATV) subscribers in the United States increased from 8.25 million to 9.25 million in 1974, representing approximately 13% of the nation's 68.8 million TV homes.

Cable TV lagged in the large metropolitan areas as cable system operators and franchise holders continued their search for sources of popular programming. Most of the new cable TV connections added in 1974 reflected an expansion of existing cable systems.

Satellite-to-Home Broadcasting. Regular TV broadcast transmissions from an earth satellite were initiated in 1974. The NASA Applications Technology Satellite No. 6 (ATS-6) conducted a variety of regular television transmissions, including educational programs intended both for general and specialized audiences, and interactive (two-way) transmissions permitting such things as medical diagnoses in remote areas. Most of the transmissions were directed to selected receiving locations in the Appalachian area, the Rocky Mountain area, and Alaska.

The ATS-6 satellite is positioned in a synchronous equatorial orbit (22,300 miles, or 35,890 km, above the earth's surface) generally over the Galápagos Islands. The satellite transmissions do not take place in the regular television broadcast band and cannot be received directly by viewers without specialized expensive receiving equipment. For these demonstrations, use is being made of cable systems, which receive the satellite transmissions, convert them to signals in the regular TV broadcast band, and distribute them to homes and schools for regular reception.

Following a year's demonstrations in the United States, ATS-6 is to be drifted to a location over Africa, where it will be used in connection with the planned U. S.-USSR Apollo-Soyuz docking, following which it will be moved to a location over India. From there, demonstration transmissions to India are planned, similar to those now taking place in the United States.

TV Receivers. Sales of both black-and-white and color TV receivers declined sharply in 1974 as part of the worsening economic picture in the United States. Total U. S. sales in 1974 were approximately 14 million sets (of which approximately 8 million were color sets).

AM and FM Radio. Both AM and FM radio broadcasting enjoyed a modest expansion in the United States. The number of AM stations increased in 1974 from 4,395 to 4,427, and the number of FM stations from 3,135 to 3,350 (including 729 noncommercial educational stations).

The proportion of home and portable radio receivers capable of receiving both AM and FM increased sharply in 1974, with a substantial decline in sales of AM-only receivers.

HOWARD T. HEAD, *A. D. Ring & Associates*

WIDE WORLD

Gunmen (*in dark glasses*) take three hostages during a bank robbery in Memphis, Tenn. Two of the holdup men were captured; the third killed himself rather than surrender to police.

TENNESSEE

The Democratic party regained control of the state in the 1974 election after four years of Republican domination. As was true throughout the nation, Watergate and a depressed economy were the main reasons for the sweeping Democratic victories. Humanistic legislators turned to reforms and a record high budget, while businessmen and the public in general talked of inflation and recession.

The Elections. The Democrats regained control of the state government on November 5 when former Congressman Ray Blanton defeated a young attorney and former associate of President Nixon, Lamar Alexander. Although Republicans retained both U. S. Senate seats, Democrats elected two new congressmen and now hold five of the eight seats. Democrat Harold Ford of Memphis was elected from the 8th Congressional District and became the first Negro congressman in the state's history. Mrs. Mort Lloyd, of Chattanooga, defeated veteran Republican Congressman Lamar Baker of the 3d District, and became the first woman elected to a full term.

Four new Democratic justices were chosen to the five-man Supreme Court, and incumbent Republican William Fones was returned to his seat on the court.

TENNESSEE • Information Highlights

Area: 42,244 square miles (109,412 sq km).
Population (1973 est.): 4,126,000. *Density:* 98 per sq mi
Chief Cities (1970 census): Nashville, the capital, 447,877; Memphis, 623,530; Knoxville, 174,587.
Government (1974): *Chief Officers*—governor, Winfield Dunn (R); lt. gov., John S. Wilder (D). *General Assembly*—Senate, 33 members; House of Representatives, 99 members.
Education (1973–74): *Enrollment*—public elementary schools, 531,397 pupils; public secondary, 344,307; nonpublic, 33,600; colleges and universities, 154,410 students. *Public school expenditures,* $664,759,000 ($804 per pupil).
State Finances (fiscal year 1973): *Revenues,* $1,882,304,000; *expenditures,* $1,675,600,000.
Personal Income (1973): $16,279,000,000; per capita, $3,946.
Labor Force (July 1974): *Nonagricultural wage and salary earners,* 1,575,200; *insured unemployed,* 30,100 (2.4%).

Legislation. The General Assembly approved a $2 billion operational budget, which was 72% larger than that of four years earlier when Gov. Winfield Dunn took office. Legislators turned their attention to reform measures and enacted a law requiring full disclosure of campaign financing, a "Sunshine Law" which bans closed-door meetings of governmental agencies, and a provision for more committee time for full discussion of proposed legislation. They also passed, over the governor's veto, a measure which would establish a medical school at Johnson City.

Economy. Economists painted a dismal picture of economic slowdown in 1974. Statistics indicated substantial decline during the year in both commercial and residential construction. State tax collections showed gains of only 8.9%, as compared with gains of 13% in 1973. Prospects of rising TVA rates and higher coal prices were not encouraging. High gasoline prices and fuel shortages helped to curtail tourism by nearly 30%. Farmers fared a little better, but the price of livestock continued to be depressed.

Education. Enrollment in public schools in 1974 reached an all-time high. The Department of Education continued to urge counties with small and inadequate high schools—particularly in Giles and Rutherford counties—to consolidate.

In higher education, the major state universities also increased enrollments. Tennessee State University president Andrew Torrence resigned during the year to accept a position at Tuskegee, and was replaced by Frederick S. Humphries of Washington. Dr. Arliss Roaden, formerly of The Ohio State University, succeeded Dr. Everett Derryberry as president of Tennessee Technology University.

Transition. The year marked the death of the state's foremost historian, Emeritus Professor Stanley J. Folmsbee at the University of Tennessee; of Dr. Earl W. Sutherland, former Vanderbilt University professor and Nobel laureate, whose studies of the human cell had brought him worldwide renown; and of Andrew Doyle, respected general sessions judge, of Nashville.

ROBERT E. CORLEW
Middle Tennessee State University

TEXAS

An unsuccessful constitutional convention and the actions of several desperate convicts were among the most memorable events of 1974 in the state of Texas.

Constitutional Convention. Hopes for a new state constitution died in the last minutes of July 31, when the statutory time allotted for a constitutional convention ran out. A labor provision on which many delegates would not compromise aborted two years' efforts to replace the much-amended 1876 charter. Their point of disagreement was the so-called right-to-work provision—an amendment to the present constitution that forbids union membership as a condition of employment.

Work on the proposed new constitution began with approval of a 1972 referendum calling for both houses of the legislature to sit as a convention and work out a charter to be ratified by Texas voters. Preliminary work was done by a citizens revision committee, which prepared the preliminary draft for the legislator-delegates when they met in Austin in January 1974.

The convention earned the dubious distinction of being the first constitutional convention in modern American times to fail to produce a charter. The final compromise package failed 118–62, missing the required two-thirds majority by three votes.

After the convention's failure, talk of any future efforts appeared to favor a convention made up of citizen-delegates, who might not have the loyalties to special interest groups that are sometimes political necessities for state legislators.

Election. In the November 5 election, Gov. Dolph Briscoe (Democrat) won reelection to a second term, defeating Jim Granberry (Republican). In a U. S. House of Representatives contest, Robert Price (R) was defeated for reelection by Jack Hightower (D), giving the Democrats 21 of the 24 House seats.

Labor. Labor claimed a victory of sorts when it blocked the right-to-work proposal, but it claimed a more definite victory in February when the Farah Manufacturing Company, Inc., of El Paso recognized the Amalgamated Clothing Workers of America as official bargaining agent, thus ending a 22-month dispute that had resulted in a boycott of Farah products and shut down three Farah plants. The company, one of the nation's largest manufacturers of men's pants, is El Paso's largest employer. Ninety percent of Farah's work force is Mexican-American, and the company's eventual acceptance of the union was seen as a sign of the growing power of traditionally low-paid border workers.

Crime. In July, Texas prison officials had to deal with a life-or-death crisis. Fred Gomez Carrasco, a reputed South Texas narcotics figure sentenced to life imprisonment, shattered the summer stillness at the Huntsville headquarters unit of the Texas prison system on July 24 when he and two other convicts used smuggled pistols to take 15 hostages in the prison library. Eleven days of terror—the longest prison siege in American history—followed as Carrasco and his two comrades, Rudolpho Dominguez and Ignacio Cuevas, bargained the lives of the hostages for their freedom.

The siege ended on August 3 when the three armed inmates thought they had arranged a deal with prison authorities. Walking out of the library surrounded by the hostages and a makeshift shield crafted from chalkboards and books, the desperate trio were met by an armed force of prison guards and other law-enforcement officers. In the ensuing gunfire, Carrasco, Dominguez, and two hostages (prison librarian Julia Standley and prison teacher Elizabeth Beseda) were killed, and Rev. Joseph O'Brien, the prison priest, was seriously wounded.

In Amarillo, a 36-hour jail siege, in which four inmates held a guard hostage, ended on August 21 when the guard was rescued, and an inmate was killed. Three days later, three convicts escaped from a Colorado penitentiary and left a trail of terror across New Mexico and west Texas before one was killed and the other two captured near Stephenville, Texas.

An infamous criminal case left over from 1973 came nearer to a close in July when a San Antonio jury found 18-year-old Elmer Wayne Henley, Jr., guilty of six murders in what has come to be known as the Houston mass murders of 27 young men.

Education. In November, Gov. Dolph Briscoe, shortly after his reelection, unveiled a new plan for funding public schools in Texas. State officials had been faced with developing a new funding system since a three-judge federal panel had declared the present system inequitable because it puts a heavier tax burden on residents of poorer districts. However, the legislature would have to pass a new plan, an item expected to get top priority in 1975.

ADREN ETHERIDGE
The Houston "Post"

TEXAS • Information Highlights

Area: 267,338 square miles (692,405 sq km).
Population (1973 est.): 11,794,000. *Density:* 44 per sq mi.
Chief Cities (1970 census): Austin, the capital, 251,808; Houston, 1,232,802; Dallas, 844,401; San Antonio, 654,153.
Government (1974): *Chief Officers*—governor, Dolph Briscoe (D); lt. gov., William P. Hobby (D). *Legislature*—Senate, 31 members; House of Representatives, 150 members.
Education (1973–74): *Enrollment*—public elementary schools, 1,594,559 pupils; public secondary, 1,305,-245; nonpublic, 117,200; colleges and universities, 503,612 students. *Public school expenditures,* $2,-261,707,000 ($898 per pupil).
State Finances (fiscal year 1973): *Revenues,* $5,254,-353,000; *expenditures,* $4,498,120,000.
Personal Income (1973): $51,144,000,000; per capita, $4,336.
Labor Force (July 1974): *Nonagricultural wage and salary earners,* 4,350,100; *insured unemployed,* 1%.

THAILAND

In the year following the overthrow of the Kittikachorn government, Thailand experienced some political unrest at home and a withdrawal of some of the U. S. Air Force units stationed there on six bases.

Foreign Relations. The year 1974 began on a turbulent note. On January 5, the United States admitted that an official of the Central Intelligence Agency (CIA) had sent a false offer of a cease-fire, purportedly from the Thai Communist insurgents, to the Thai government. The U. S. ambassador, William R. Kinter, expressed embarrassment and promised categorically that such instances would not recur. Demonstrating students, who consider themselves to be the ombudsmen of Thai politics, demanded Kinter's ouster. Although the Thai government on January 17 officially expressed dissatisfaction with the United States, relations between the two countries did not seriously deteriorate.

American military forces in Thailand were being cut as the year began. In March 1974 the United States agreed to withdraw about one third of its Air Force units in Thailand. In May some of the B-52 bombers began to leave, and a squadron of F-4 jets was transferred to South Korea. It was also announced in June that Air America (the CIA-supported airline) would no longer fly in and out of Thailand. By the end of the year it was expected that only four American airbases and about 25,000 U. S. servicemen would remain.

A Thai policeman guards a temple in the Chinese section of Bangkok during an outbreak of anti-Chinese violence.

UPI

Thailand seemed not unwilling to loosen the intimate bonds that have characterized its relations with the United States, in an attempt to improve those with her neighbors. Prominent Thais, including Thanat Khoman, former foreign minister, have urged that the United States withdraw its military forces from Thailand.

In January, Thailand urged the Soviet Union to play a bigger role in obtaining peace in Southeast Asia; in February, the Thais reported that they had received assurances that Communist China was no longer supporting Thai insurgency.

Also in January, Premier Tanaka of Japan visited Bangkok and in a most unusual move met with student leaders who had led demonstrations against him and his government. In general, his visit seemed inconclusive.

New Constitution. On January 28 the drafting committee completed its work on a new constitution. The new version, the ninth Thai constitution, is more liberal and democratic than its predecessors. It was approved by the Cabinet in February and by the National Assembly in September, and was promulgated by the King on October 7.

Political Events. On May 21 the government of Premier Sanya Dharmasakti resigned and a military alert was proclaimed. Sanya expressed the wish to enter a Buddhist monastery; his fall was the result of a variety of political pressures. However, the Thai National Assembly appealed unanimously to Sanya to reconsider his resignation. Sanya, known as Thailand's "most gentle premier," agreed to remain in office, and by May 27 his new government, more youthful and less military, was formed.

Other Events. In July, violence erupted in the Chinese district of Bangkok. Triggered by a trivial incident, the result was three days of rioting in which about 150 were wounded and possibly 25 were killed. The police and army troops were called in, and after a show of force the disturbance subsided.

CARL LEIDEN
The University of Texas at Austin

THAILAND • Information Highlights

Official Name: Kingdom of Thailand.
Location: Southeast Asia.
Area: 198,456 square miles (514,000 sq km).
Population (1973 est.): 39,900,000.
Chief Cities (1967 est.): Bangkok, the capital, 2,008,000; Thonburi, 606,300.
Government: *Head of state,* Bhumibol Aduladej, king (acceded June 1946). *Head of government,* Sanya Dharmasakti, premier (took office Oct. 1973). *Legislature*—National Assembly: Senate; House of Representatives.
Monetary Unit: Baht (20.45 baht equal U. S.$1, July 1974).
Gross National Product (1972 est.): $7,684,000,000.
Manufacturing (major products): Processed foods, textiles, clothing.
Major Agricultural Products: Rice, rubber, tapioca, corn, tobacco, fruits, sugarcane, kenaf and jute, forest products, fish.
Foreign Trade (1973): *Exports,* $1,531,000,000; *imports,* $2,046,000,000.

FRIEDMAN-ABELES

One of the most successful Broadway musicals of 1974 was *Candide*, by Hugh Wheeler, Stephen Sondheim, and Richard Wilbur. The sparkling score was written by Leonard Bernstein.

theater

The most curious tendency of the theater in 1974 was the virtual return of the American theater to British colonial status. In the first half of the year, not much notice was taken of this phenomenon, although some significant omens were visible. But by the end of 1974, British domination of the American stage could no longer be overlooked; theatrical pundits spoke of nothing else.

Why had the British taken over? Many attributed this development to the good use made of the government subsidies which enabled the National Theater and the Royal Shakespeare Company to maintain strong permanent acting rosters and to commission new plays. The subsidies are adequate but not lavish, and so it was a good idea for the National and the Royal Shakespeare to supplement their incomes by sending visiting productions overseas. However, many of the British plays in New York had begun in London as purely commercial ventures, without benefit of subsidy. One had to assume, finally, that the secret of British success was not subsidy alone and that the atmosphere and organization of the London theater, even in the commercial West End, was somehow more encouraging to producers, playwrights, and actors.

Broadway Plays. The Royal Shakespeare Company contributed two of its recent hits in genuine Royal Shakespeare productions—*Sherlock Holmes* (a play of 1899 written in collaboration by an American and an Englishman) and *London Assurance* (a play of 1841 by an Irishman who became an American). *Sherlock Holmes* was a creaky thriller and *London Assurance* a comedy of manners born some years past its proper time, but both productions won support for the bravura playing of their stars and the ensemble acting of their supporting casts.

The National Theater's principal offering was *Equus,* by Peter Shaffer, about a teen-age stable boy whose frustrations lead him to blind some horses. All of the cast was American except for the leading actors, Peter Firth as the boy and Anthony Hopkins as a psychiatrist who, weighing his own unsatisfying existence, comes to envy the boy's unbalanced life of the mind. John Dexter repeated his imaginative London production, without which this play would have been unthinkable on any stage.

Two other productions less legitimately raised the banner of the National Theater and came to a speedy end. Clifford Williams' all-male version of *As You Like It* was an all-British version of a National Theater experiment of a few years ago. But it was not the real thing, because it did not have a National Theater cast, and it certainly was not the Elizabethan real thing, because the men impersonating women were older than the Elizabethan boy-actors. Eduardo de Filippo's *Saturday Sunday Monday,* giving credit to the National Theater and employing the National Theater's translation, was interpreted by the same director-designer who had made a success of it in London, Franco Zeffirelli, but this comedy of Italian family life failed with an American cast.

On the other hand, another American cast won a mainly favorable reception at the Circle in the Square on Broadway for a limited engagement of Peter Nichols' *The National Health,* a grisly comedy of hospital life which the National had staged a few years before. Tom Stoppard's *Jumpers,* another play which had premiered at the National, arrived on Broadway from the Kennedy Center in Washington, with Britain's Brian Bedford heading an American cast. The Broadway public was cool to Stoppard's witty comedy of mental and physical gymnastics.

The enterprising Brooklyn Academy of Music imported three productions from London's Young Vic, a company associated with the National Theater. One of the three, Molière's *Scapino,* owed much of its unusually warm reception to Jim Dale's spirited performance as the rogue of the title. *Scapino* transferred first to the Circle in the Square and then to a larger Broadway theater. In the Brooklyn Academy of Music's British season, the Young Vic had been preceded by two other British companies—the Royal Shakespeare (with *Richard II* and a staged reading based on the works of the poet Sylvia Plath) and the new Actors Company (with four productions, of which Chekhov's *The Wood Demon* proved to be a revelation).

British plays originally presented by commercial managements also found their way to New York. Alan Ayckbourn's *Absurd Person Singular,* a comedy that contrasts three married couples representing different social classes, was a popular hit with a mostly American cast. Charles Laurence's comedy *My Fat Friend,* with Lynn Redgrave as a girl trying to lose weight so that she can win a young man who is not worthy of her, had a long run. John Hopkins' *Find Your Way Home,* a solemn drama about male homosexual lovers, owed its popularity mostly to Michael Moriarty's sensitive playing.

Noel Coward in Two Keys, a program of two plays by Noel Coward, originated in London a few years before. These plays attracted praise primarily for the expert acting of Hume Cronyn. Terence Rattigan's *In Praise of Love,* in which a wife tries to keep her husband from knowing of her impending death, won its best effects from the star appeal of Rex Harrison and Julie Harris. As he had done in 1967, Roy Dotrice came to Broadway with *Brief Lives,* a fascinating one-man show based on the writings of the 17th century biographer John Aubrey. History repeated itself; Dotrice got, and richly deserved, the critics' warmest praise, but his show quickly closed. Perhaps encouraged by the British invasion of Broadway, Peter Ustinov became the only British dramatist who had a world premiere on Broadway in 1974. His *Who's Who in Hell* was not up to the high level of Ustinov's sparkling conversation on television talk shows.

Sizwe Banzi Is Dead and *The Island,* two plays devised by the white South African dramatist Athol Fugard in collaboration with the two black actors who appeared in them, originated in South Africa and then earned attention in London. Both plays movingly interpret the tragedy of black life in South Africa.

Foreign importations which happened not to be British generally had a short life—the Irish Brian Friel's *The Freedom of the City,* in which three innocents are taken to be terrorists; the French-Canadian Michel Tremblay's *Hosanna,* about two male homosexuals; and the French Jean-Claude Grumberg's *Dreyfus in Rehearsal,* in which Polish-Jewish actors of the pre-Hitler period rehearse a play about Alfred Dreyfus.

Joseph Papp's new regime at Lincoln Center continued to be controversial. The Vivian Beaumont Theater won its best critical notices with a play that had originated elsewhere—Miguel Piñero's *Short Eyes,* a searing picture of prison life. Ron Milner's *What the Wine-Sellers Buy* was an interesting portrait of a black boy rejecting the pimp's way of life, glamorously embodied by Dick Williams. A revival of Strindberg's *The Dance of Death* blunted that classic play's sharp edges. In the fall, Papp found himself in the midst of a new controversy when he contested the critics' general disapproval of Anne Burr's *Mert and Phil,* the drama of a woman who has had a mastectomy—comedy-drama, one should say, because the play kept getting laughs at the expense of the pitiful protagonists. At the smaller Mitzi E. Newhouse Theater (formerly the Forum), a passable version of *The Tempest* was followed by an unreviewed production of *Macbeth.* In the fall Michael Moriarty starred in *Richard III.*

And where were the American dramatists? For the most part, not on Broadway. Elizabeth Ashley distinguished herself in a revival of Tennessee Williams' *Cat on a Hot Tin Roof* (which had originated at the Shakespeare Festival of Stratford, Conn.). An interesting off-Broadway production of Williams' *Battle of Angels* (the original version of *Orpheus Descending*), coupled with a dismal off-Broadway rendition of Arthur Miller's early *All My Sons,* gave support to the view that Williams and not Miller is our foremost living dramatist.

But where were the new American plays? Not much can be said for Broadway's new American plays, except for *Short Eyes* and Terrence McNally's *Bad Habits,* a program of two one-act plays, each set at an eccentric sanatorium. Neil Simon's *God's Favorite,* an evening of one-line jokes about a modern Job (explosively

GIFFORD/WALLACE INC.

***The Magic Show,* a musical popular with children as well as adults, starred Doug Henning, an outstanding Canadian illusionist.**

played by Vincent Gardenia), took neither Job nor its modern characters seriously.

My Sister, My Sister, by Ray Aranha, was a sympathetic study of a black woman's life. Herb Gardner's *Thieves,* a comedy of New York life, probably owed its long run to the public's interest in seeing a television favorite, Marlo Thomas, in person. One-man shows included Henry Fonda as Clarence Darrow and James Whitmore as Will Rogers.

Among the other revivals on Broadway were the New Phoenix Company's versions of Congreve's *Love for Love* and Pirandello's *The Rules of the Game,* the latter of which seemed to work better. Some plays of earlier seasons were revived—*Ulysses in Nighttown,* adapted by Marjorie Barkentin from James Joyce's *Ulysses,* with Zero Mostel repeating his extraordinary performance as Leopold Bloom; and John Steinbeck's *Of Mice and Men,* with one of the migratory workers played by James Earl Jones.

Broadway Musicals. Broadway musicals were less numerous. Revivals were prominent, and nostalgia was often the keynote. *Lorelei,* which was set in the 1920's, reused materials from *Gentlemen Prefer Blondes* (1949) and featured the amazing star of that show, Carol Channing. *Over Here!* recalled the home front of World War II and utilized the two surviving Andrews Sisters. *Candide,* a tremendous success which transferred from the Brooklyn home of the Chelsea Theater Center, set its action in the midst of the audience. It employed the songs of the 1956 *Candide* but substituted a new book, adapted from Voltaire by Hugh Wheeler.

Gypsy, a revival of the Saga of Gypsy Rose Lee, had Angela Lansbury repeating her London success as the stripteaser's mother. *Mack and Mabel* recalled the early filmmaker Mack Sennett and his star Mabel Normand. *Where's Charley?* was revived at the Circle in the Square. *Good News,* a college musical of 1927, had former film stars in the leading roles.

A surprise popular hit of the season was *The Magic Show,* whose star, illusionist Doug Henning, drew rave reviews. Although the musical itself was anemic, critics and audiences alike were taken with Henning's magic.

Off-Broadway. If we may exclude those plays that went on to Broadway, the most promising off-Broadway plays were contributed by the Circle Repertory Company (which also revived Williams' *Battle of Angels*). These were *The Sea Horse,* about the mating of an unlikely couple, credited to James Irwin, which was revealed to be the pen name of one of the performers, Edward J. Moore; and *The Wager,* a brittle comedy of university life by Mark Medoff. Marshall Mason staged *The Sea Horse* and *Battle of Angels* with loving care. *The Wager* had the benefit of a lively production by the film actor Anthony Perkins.

Off-Off-Broadway. The off-off-Broadway theater created two notable experiments. One was a series of three classical plays at the new Annex of the La Mama Experimental Theater Club, normally performed two to an evening and spoken in ancient languages—*Medea, Electra,* and *The Trojan Women.* Directed by a young Rumanian, Andrei Serban, with an unusual musical score by Elizabeth Swados, these dramas employed a large playing area in which the audience sometimes wandered at will. The other curious experiment was Robert Wilson's production of *The Life and Times of Joseph Stalin,* presented at the Brooklyn Academy of Music, lasting through the night for 12 hours and offering an astonishing variety of scenes.

Outside New York. Regional theaters continued to present new plays—or plays new to America—for which New York was not ready. Early in the year, Washington's Arena Stage offered Elie Wiesel's *Zalmen, or the Madness of God,* dealing with the plight of Jews in the Soviet Union; *Horatio,* an original musical about Horatio Alger, with book and lyrics by Ron Whyte; *Leonce and Lena,* a rarely performed 19th century play by Georg Büchner, inventively staged by a Rumanian director, Liviu Ciulei;

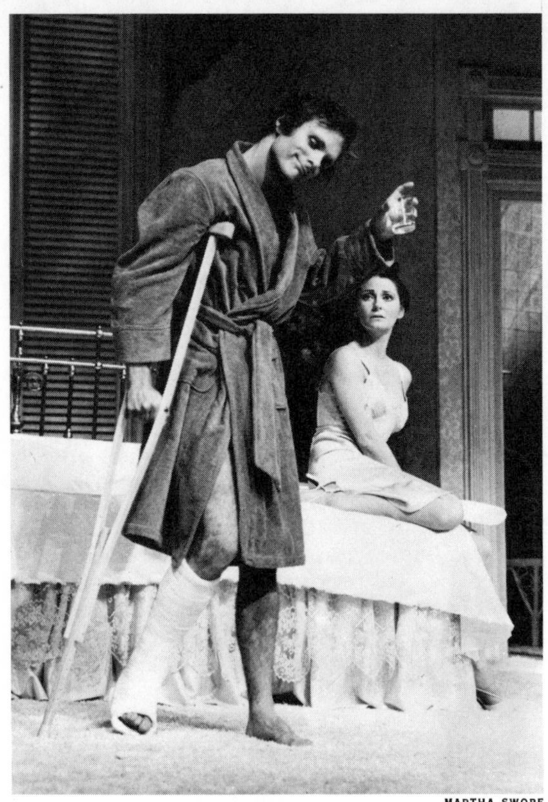

MARTHA SWOPE

Keir Dullea and Elizabeth Ashley were featured in the Broadway revival of *Cat on a Hot Tin Roof* by Tennessee Williams.

MICHAEL ALPERT

The Royal Shakespeare Company's *Sherlock Holmes* starred John Wood as Holmes and Nicholas Selby (*R*) as Larrabee.

One of the most widely discussed plays of 1974 was the electrifying work *Equus* by the British dramatist Peter Shaffer.

VAN WILLIAMS

The versatile performer Jim Dale enchanted audiences of all ages in the Young Vic production of *Scapino*.

MARTHA SWOPE

BROADWAY OPENINGS IN 1974

PLAYS

Absurd Person Singular, by Alan Ayckbourn; directed by Eric Thompson; with Carole Shelley, Richard Kiley, Geraldine Page, and Sandy Dennis; Oct. 8—.

All over Town, by Murray Schisgal; directed by Dustin Hoffman; with Cleavon Little; December 29—.

An American Millionaire, by Murray Schisgal; directed by Theodore Mann; with Paul Sorvino; April 20–May 5.

As You Like It, by William Shakespeare; directed by Clifford Williams; December 3–7.

Bad Habits, by Terrence McNally; directed by Robert Drivas; with Cynthia Harris and Michael Lombard; May 5–October 5.

Brief Lives, adapted and directed by Patrick Garland; with Roy Dotrice; October 16–December 1.

Cat on a Hot Tin Roof, by Tennessee Williams; directed by Michael Kahn; with Elizabeth Ashley and Keir Dullea; September 24—.

Clarence Darrow, by David W. Rintels; with Henry Fonda; March 26–April 23.

The Dance of Death, by August Strindberg, adapted by A. J. Antoon from Elizabeth Sprigge's translation; with Zoe Caldwell and Robert Shaw; April 4–May 5.

Dreyfus in Rehearsal, by Jean-Claude Grumberg; adapted and directed by Garson Kanin; with Sam Levene and Ruth Gordon; October 17–26.

Equus, by Peter Shaffer; directed by John Dexter; with Anthony Hopkins and Peter Firth; October 24—.

Fame, written and directed by Anthony J. Ingrassia; November 18 (one performance).

Find Your Way Home, by John Hopkins; directed by Edwin Sherin; with Michael Moriarty, Jane Alexander, Lee Richardson, and John Ramsey; January 2–April 28.

The Freedom of the City, by Brian Friel; directed by William Woodman; with Kate Reid; February 17–23.

God's Favorite, by Neil Simon; directed by Michael Bennett; with Vincent Gardenia and Charles Nelson Reilly; December 11—.

Hosanna, by Michel Tremblay; directed by Bill Glassco; with Richard Monette; October 14–November 3.

In Praise of Love, by Terence Rattigan; with Rex Harrison and Julie Harris; December 10—.

The Island, devised by Athol Fugard, John Kani, and Winston Ntshona (in repertory with *Sizwe Banzi is Dead*); directed by Fugard; with Kani and Ntshona; November 19—.

Jumpers, by Tom Stoppard; directed by Peter Wood; with Brian Bedford; April 22–June 1.

London Assurance, by Dion Boucicault, adapted and directed by Ronald Eyre; with Donald Sinden and Elizabeth Spriggs; December 5—.

Love for Love, by William Congreve; directed by Harold Prince; with John McMartin; November 11–30.

Medea and Jason, adapted (from Robinson Jeffers' version of Euripides' *Medea*) and directed by Eugenie Leontovich; October 2 (one performance).

Mert and Phil, by Anne Burr; directed by Joseph Papp; with Estelle Parsons; October 30–December 8.

Mourning Pictures, by Honor Moore; with Kathryn Walker; November 10 (one performance).

My Fat Friend, by Charles Laurence; directed by Robert Moore; with Lynn Redgrave and George Rose; March 31–December 8.

My Sister, My Sister, by Ray Aranha; directed by Paul Weidner; April 30–August 11.

The National Health, by Peter Nichols; with Leonard Frey; October 10–November 24.

Noel Coward in Two Keys, by Noel Coward; directed by Vivian Matalon; with Hume Cronyn, Jessica Tandy, and Anne Baxter; February 28–June 29.

Of Mice and Men, by John Steinbeck; directed by Edwin Sherin; with James Earl Jones and Kevin Conway; December 18—.

The Rules of the Game, by Luigi Pirandello; directed by Stephen Porter; with John McMartin and Joan van Ark; December 12–21.

Saturday Sunday Monday, by Eduardo de Filippo; directed by Franco Zeffirelli; with Sada Thompson and Eli Wallach; November 21–30.

Scapino, by Molière; directed by Frank Dunlop; with Jim Dale; May 18—.

Sherlock Holmes, by Arthur Conan Doyle and William Gillette; directed by Frank Dunlop; with John Wood and Philip Locke; November 12—.

Short Eyes, by Miguel Piñero; directed by Marvin Felix Camillo; May 23–August 4.

Sizwe Banzi is Dead, devised by Athol Fugard, John Kani, and Winston Ntshona (after November 19, in repertory with *The Island*); directed by Fugard; with Kani and Ntshona; November 13—.

Thieves, by Herb Gardner; directed by Charles Grodin; with Marlo Thomas and Richard Mulligan; April 7—.

Tubstrip, by A. J. Kronengold; directed by Jerry Douglas; with Calvin Culver; October 31–November 17.

Ulysses in Nighttown, adapted by Marjorie Barkentin from James Joyce's *Ulysses;* directed by Burgess Meredith; with Zero Mostel; March 10–May 11.

What the Wine-Sellers Buy, by Ron Milner; with Dick A. Williams; February 14–March 17.

Who's Who in Hell, by Peter Ustinov; directed by Ellis Rabb; with Ustinov, George S. Irving, and Beau Bridges; December 9–14.

Will Rogers' U. S. A., adapted and directed by Paul Shyre; with James Whitmore; May 6–11.

MUSICALS

Candide, book by Hugh Wheeler, adapted from Voltaire; music by Leonard Bernstein; lyrics by Richard Wilbur, Stephen Sondheim, and John Latouche; directed by Harold Prince; with Lewis J. Stadlen; March 10—.

Flowers, devised, designed, and directed by Lindsay Kemp; sound composed by Andrew Wilson; with Kemp; October 7–26.

Good News, book by Laurence Schwab, B. G. De Sylva, and Frank Mandel, words and music by De Sylva, Lew Brown, and Ray Henderson, adapted by Garry Marshall; directed by Michael Kidd; with Alice Faye, Gene Nelson, and Stubby Kaye; December 23—.

Gypsy, book by Arthur Laurents, music by Jule Styne, lyrics by Stephen Sondheim; directed by Laurents; with Angela Lansbury; September 23—.

Lorelei, based on *Gentlemen Prefer Blondes* (book by Anita Loos and Joseph Fields, music by Jules Styne, lyrics by Lee Robin, based on Miss Loos' stories); new book by Kenny Solms and Gail Parent, new music by Styne, new lyrics by Betty Comden and Adolph Green; directed by Robert Moore; with Carol Channing; January 27–November 3.

Mack and Mabel, book by Michael Stewart, music and lyrics by Jerry Herman; directed by Gower Champion; with Robert Preston and Bernadette Peters; October 6–November 30.

The Magic Show, book by Bob Randall, music and lyrics by Doug Henning; directed by Grover Dale; with Henning; May 28—.

Music! Music!, cavalcade of American music with footnotes by Alan Jay Lerner; with Gene Nelson and Larry Kert; April 11–May 12.

Over Here!, book by Will Holt, music and lyrics by Richard M. Sherman and Robert B. Sherman; directed by Tom Moore; with the Andrews Sisters; March 6—.

Ride the Winds, book, music, and lyrics by John Driver; directed by Lee D. Sankowich; May 16–18.

Sextet, with book by Harvey Perr and Lee Goldsmith, music by Lawrence Hurwit, lyrics by Goldsmith; directed by Jered Barclay; March 3–10.

Where's Charley?, book by George Abbott (based on *Charley's Aunt,* by Brandon Thomas); music and lyrics by Frank Loesser; directed by Theodore Mann; with Raul Julia; December 19—.

Words and Music, by Sammy Cahn, lyrics by Sammy Cahn, music by various composers; directed by Jerry Adler; with Sammy Cahn; April 16–August 3.

and British plays by David Storey and Alan Ayckbourn.

The Yale Repertory Theater's selection included the second play by a distinguished novelist, Isaac Bashevis Singer's *Shlemiel the First;* Albert Camus' *The Possessed* (based on Dostoevski's novel), dazzlingly directed by Andrzej Wajda, whose Polish production of this play had won praise in Europe; and elaborate versions of Brecht's *Mahagonny* and Aristophanes' *The Frogs.*

Fresh from his Broadway success in *A Little Night Music,* Len Cariou played the lead in *King Lear* at the Guthrie Theater of Minneapolis. Venturing far afield, the Trinity Square Theater of Providence found a friendly reception for Robert Lord's *Well Hung,* a New Zealand farce set in a police station.

International Theater. The upsurge in Canadian playwriting continued, and, as before, Toronto's Tarragon Theater led the way with David Freeman's comedy of a family excessively attached to its television set, *You're Gonna Be Alright, Jamie Boy;* the second part of James Reaney's trilogy on a bloody incident in Canadian history, *The Donnellys, Part Two;* and a Québecois play in English, *Hosanna* (which moved to Broadway). In Montreal, Tremblay's newest play, *Goodbye, There, Goodbye,* had incest for its theme.

In London, too, the dramatists were at work: David Storey, Tom Stoppard, Edward Bond, Peter Nichols, Peter Barnes, Alan Ayckbourn, and David Mercer all had new plays. If one particular event captured attention in the London theater scene, it was the final shift of authority in the National Theater from Laurence Olivier, its founder, to Peter Hall, the former head of the Royal Shakespeare Company. But nothing Hall did in his first year stirred quite the excitement of *Equus,* which belonged to the Olivier administration and the previous year. Hall's own production of *The Tempest,* with John Gielgud as Prospero, was adequate but conventional.

Frank Wedekind's *Spring Awakening* got a fine revival, and John Hopkins' *Next of Kin,* a play of family life, was an occasionally engaging curiosity. However, anyone desiring to see new life breathed into an old play was well advised to go to the commercial sector and view Alec McCowen and Diana Rigg in Shaw's *Pygmalion,* directed by John Dexter. These three truants from the National had fashioned what many considered to be the revival of the season.

As for plays, especially new plays in repertory, it was hard to beat the Royal Shakespeare's combination of *Sherlock Holmes;* Peter Barnes' *The Bewitched,* the most controversial play in town; and Tom Stoppard's *Travesties,* an ingenious exploration of the simultaneous presence in Zurich in World War I of James Joyce, Lenin, and Tristan Tzara.

Two dramatic curiosities deserve to be mentioned in this review. In Edward Bond's *Bingo,* John Gielgud played an embittered Shakespeare in retirement at Stratford. Alan Ayckbourn's *The Norman Conquests* was an enormously successful trio of comedies taking contrasting views of the same events.

The theater year in Paris belonged to the directors. One piece of negative evidence: the most acclaimed new play was Grumberg's *Dreyfus,* which had no more substance in Paris than it did when it was retitled *Dreyfus in Rehearsal* and presented on Broadway. The big events of the spring were the visit of Roger Planchon's company from the provinces with *Tartuffe* (elaborated but not improved over Planchon's earlier version); Planchon's own play *The Black Pig* (which proved him a better director than he is a dramatist); and his colleague Patrice Chéreau's production of Tankred Dorst's drama of a post-World War I uprising in Bavaria, *Toller.* The sensation of the fall season was Peter Brook's French-language version of *Timon of Athens.* Another director, Jean-Louis Barrault, organized his company on a commercial basis and, by year's end, was presenting a dramatic version of *Thus Spake Zarathustra.*

As usual, the West Berlin Theater Festival in the spring, representing, presumably, the best German-language productions of the past season, was dominated by Peter Stein's left-wing Schaubühne am Halleschen Ufer, of West Berlin. The Schaubühne's entries were Labiche's 19th century French farce *The Piggy Bank* and *The Antiquity Project* in two evenings—the first, *Exercises for Actors* (directed, like the Labiche, by Peter Stein himself), constituting an introduction to the second, Euripides' *The Bacchae.*

Might the continental theater be said to belong to its directors? One could come to that conclusion by considering the place of Planchon, Chéreau, Barrault, and Brook in France and of Stein in Germany. Also, the principal event of the Scandinavian theater season is usually the annual production by Ingmar Bergman; in 1974, Bergman did Strindberg's *To Damascus* in Stockholm in a staging more visually elaborate than is usual with him.

The great man of the Italian theater is still Giorgio Strehler of the Piccolo Teatro of Milan. His fascinating four-hour-long *King Lear* was playing at the European festivals in 1974.

In Moscow the most important event in the theater is always the latest production by Yuri Lyubimov at the Taganka. At midyear, his latest was *Wooden Horses,* a pair of bitter dramas of peasant life adapted from his own fiction by Fyodor Abramov and directed with more austerity than usual by Lyubimov. No question about it: the continental theater is definitely a directors' medium.

HENRY POPKIN
State University of New York at Buffalo; Drama Critic, Westchester-Rockland Newspapers

TORONTO

The municipal elections of December 1974, in which only 30% of the voters turned out (partly because of bad weather), returned Mayor David Crombie for a second term and made almost no changes in the reform-oriented City Council. Other events of 1974 included a break in the rising cost of housing after enactment of new provincial legislation, a visit by Queen Mother Elizabeth in June, and a series of strikes highlighted by the first strike of the Toronto Transit Commission in 22 years.

Government. Toronto comprises the city proper and five boroughs, within a metro framework. Paul Godfrey became metro chairman in 1973. In 1974 the provincial government overhauled the Metro Toronto Act to allow the boroughs to become cities within metro, and to extend the size of the Metro Council and allow it to assume planning board functions.

Transportation. The 2.73-mile (4.4-km) extension of the Yonge Street Subway to Finch Avenue was opened in March 1974; a fare increase was prevented by a provincial subsidy; the GO railway transit began to experiment with double-decker trains; and the Toronto Transit Commission decided to order 200 new street cars. The maximum charge was removed in city-owned car parks, and the two-year project to straighten the Queen Elizabeth Way was completed.

Development. In May 1974, work began on the $250 million Eaton Centre, with the clearing of the ground and the moving of two historical houses. Controversy continued over the 200-acre Metro Centre, which finally received Ontario Municipal Board approval, but there was still disagreement on the fate of the Union Station. In September, work began on the superstructure of the 72-story Bank of Montreal building, which will be Toronto's highest office tower. The 45-foot (14-meter) height limit imposed by the city in 1973 for the downtown core area ran into continuous opposition. Construction continued on the 1,805-foot (550-meter) CN Tower, to be the world's tallest self-supporting structure when completed in 1975.

Education. The long legal battles involving once-educational Rochdale College, which was $5.8 million behind in mortgage payments, appeared to be drawing to an end, as the receivers got permission to evict the tenants. At the university of Toronto in March, interruption of a speech by Prof. Edward Banfield led to hearings which eventually brought in new rules for orderly assemblies, the calling of the police on campus, and the expulsion of two students.

Strikes. The York Region high schools north of the city were closed down for nearly two months by a teacher strike, which left 14,000 students without classes. The Post Office was closed for nine days in May, and 11 hospitals had nonprofessional workers walk out on an

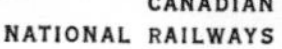
CANADIAN NATIONAL RAILWAYS

PANDA ASSOCIATES, PHOTOGRAPHERS, TORONTO

CN Tower, a communications and observation tower under construction in Toronto. When completed (*model, left*), it will have a "sky pod" with broadcasting facilities and revolving restaurant. Over 1,800 feet (550 meters) high, it will be the tallest self-supporting structure in world.

illegal strike. The nearly month-long strike of the Toronto Transit employees in mid-August tied up the city until it was stopped by provincial legislation.

Miscellaneous. Andrew Davis became the new conductor of the Toronto Symphony Orchestra, and H. Ian Macdonald became president of York University. James Cardinal McGuigan, archbishop of Toronto for nearly 40 years, died on April 8 at age 79.

The new Metro Toronto Zoo opened on 700 acres of Scarborough in August. The Royal Ontario Museum completed a $200,000 dinosaur gallery, and in the autumn was host to a display of Chinese art.

The International Building at the Canadian National Exhibition was hit by a bad fire in August, destroying the Spanish display, for a total loss of $1.5 million. The refurbished Art Gallery of Ontario was reopened on October 26 with its new Henry Moore Sculpture Center, containing over 300 works by the famous British sculptor.

FREDERICK H. ARMSTRONG
University of Western Ontario

BOEING VERTOL COMPANY

PERT DIAL-A-BUS, ROCHESTER, N. Y.

(*Above*) Chicago's new trolley cars have stainless steel bodies, molded fiberglass seats, and air conditioning. (*Left*) In Rochester, N. Y., the first dial-a-bus system brings doorstep public transit to a limited area.

transportation

The year's most important news in transportation is discussed in the following surveys. Additional developments in the field are reviewed under the headings AUTOMOBILES; ENGINEERING, CIVIL.

General Survey

Despite the problems of inflation and recession, increases were noted in 1974 in virtually all areas of the transportation industry.

Railroads. The rate of return for the nation's railroads was 3.71% for the 12 months ended Sept. 30, 1974. For the third quarter of 1974, operating revenue climbed $757 million to $4.4 billion, while operating income was up from $163.6 million to $308.3 million during the year. Efficiency of the railroads also has been improved, as indicated by the fact that the net ton-mile per serviceable car-day was up 8% over the prior year. At midyear 1974, a total of 541,211 persons were on Class I railroad payrolls, an increase of 2.2% over the prior year's figure. At that time, the backlog of orders for new freight cars reached 95,131.

Internationally, Kampsax, a large Danish engineering firm announced that it will build a 550-mile railroad in Iran linking Bandar Abbas, a port city on the Persian Gulf, with the existing rail network terminal at Barq in the interior.

Water Transport. The total number of ocean-going ships calling at 11 major U. S. ports during 1973 was 48,129, an increase of 1,270 over 1972. The most frequently used port was New York, with 9,093 callings, or 18.8% of the total. Philadelphia, Los Angeles, and New Orleans each had over 10% of the total. Boston was the least-used port with only 1,629 ships. Total sea passengers arriving or departing from the U. S. in 1973 amounted to only 1,964,438, as against 26,659,179 who used air service.

Through Sept. 7, 1974, the number of ocean-going vessels using the Great Lakes numbered only 327 for the year, as compared with 691 in 1973. Only 1,150 lake freighters used the Welland Canal, down from 1,469 in 1973. Grain shipping was down from 14.6 million tons to 9.5 million tons.

The World Bank reported loans amounting to $900 million to 42 nations in 1973–74 for purposes of port development. France, for example, is constructing a 700,000-DWT repair drydock at Marseille, and a tanker terminal north of Le Havre to accommodate vessels of 540,000 DWT. At the port of Kobe in Japan a 46.9 million-square-foot (4.4 million-square-meter) island is being constructed. It will have wharves capable of berthing 30 large vessels.

Vehicle Registration. The U. S. Federal Highway Administration estimates that at the end of 1974 there were 105,287,000 automobiles registered, an increase of 3.5% over the 101.8 million registered in 1973. Truck and bus registrations were expected to increase 7.6% to 25,464,000. This combined increase of 5,330,-

124 to a total registration of 130,751,000 motor vehicles represents a 4.2% rise in the year but a decrease from the 5.6% growth rate in 1973. California is again the leading state with 13.8 million motor vehicles registered. Texas, New York, Ohio, Pennsylvania, Illinois, Florida, and Michigan all have registrations of more than 5 million vehicles. The 10 leading states account for 52.5% of the national total.

Motorcycle registrations were expected to increase by about 615,000, or 19.5%, in 1974.

Bikeways and Walkways. The Federal Aid Highway Act of 1973, for the first time, provided for the use of highway monies to be used for the construction of cyclist and pedestrian facilities on a funding basis of 70% federal and 30% state appropriations. The Federal Highway Administration approved requests by 23 states and the District of Columbia to use $24,100,275 in federal funds for such purposes.

Trans-Alaska Pipeline. On April 29, 1974, approximately 1,200 construction workers began construction of the 800-mile Trans-Alaska pipeline from the oil field at Prudhoe Bay on the Arctic coast to a marine tanker terminal at Valdez, in south-central Alaska. The first work undertaken was the construction of a 360-mile-long road from the Yukon River to Prudhoe Bay, to be used later during pipeline construction.

Safety. The National Transportation Safety Board announced that in 1973 transportation-related accidents dropped 1%, to 60,118 from 60,765 in 1972. Highway fatalities dropped 2%, to 55,600 from 56,700.

JAMES R. ROMAN, JR.
The George Washington University

Air Transportation

Shortages of fuel for jet airliners and a dramatic increase in the price of fuel thrust most of the world's airlines into turmoil in 1974. A serious financial squeeze caused by higher fuel costs was aggravated by a slump in travel on many routes. The decline was caused by worldwide inflation and a steep increase in the price of airline tickets, which was supposed to help offset higher fuel bills. U. S. domestic airlines were less affected by the fuel crisis than international airlines, and some logged record profits.

Airlines responded to the fuel crisis by reducing flights, grounding jets, consolidating operations, and taking the first moves toward a restructuring of the world civil air transport system.

Fuel Crisis. Early in 1974, after the full weight of the Arab oil embargo was felt, the airlines' principal problem was a shortage of kerosene, the fuel burned by jetliners. U. S. airlines grounded more than 80 planes and cancelled an average of 15% of their 14,000 daily departures. Similar cutbacks were made by most airlines abroad.

By spring, fuel prices had become the main concern. Before the embargo, world airlines paid about 11 cents per gallon for jet fuel. By mid-summer, they were paying more than 35 cents a gallon, and in some countries they were paying more than $1 a gallon. Increases were not nearly so severe in the United States, where the airlines had access to price-controlled fuel refined from domestic crude oil. Even so, prices shot up to more than 23 cents a gallon.

Knut Hammarskjöld, director-general of the International Air Transport Association, a group of 111 world airlines, estimated that by mid-summer, despite several fare increases, the hard-hit international airlines had had to absorb more than $600 million in additional fuel costs.

Passenger Traffic. In the United States during the first half of the year, many airlines saw their passenger volume go up 5% to 10% or more. Gains went as high as 20% among smaller regional airlines that specialized in short-haul flights.

Much of the increase was attributed to the people who switched to airliners rather than risk uncertain gasoline supplies. Later in the year, however, as gasoline became more plentiful, this phenomenon eased. And, by fall, many U. S. airlines were experiencing no traffic gains or were carrying fewer people than in the previous year.

Internationally, air travel declined. On the important routes between North America and Europe over the North Atlantic—where travel had grown by an average of 15% annually since 1958—many airlines experienced a 10% to 20% dip in passenger travel during 1974.

A major impetus behind previous gains had been the relative buying power of the dollar abroad. Middle-income Americans could tour Europe and spend much less for hotels, meals, and sightseeing than they did at home. But by mid-1974, two dollar devaluations and relentless inflation had taken a European vacation out of the reach of many middle-class Americans. A curious reversal of historical patterns became evident—even with America's own inflation, many European and Japanese tourists began to discover that a U. S. vacation was a bargain.

Fares. Soaring prices at airline ticket counters accelerated the drop in travel. Between the United States and Europe, fares were increased by more than 25% during the year—more than in the previous four years combined.

For travel to Europe and within the United States, an era of cheap trips for young people ended. The Civil Aeronautics Board (CAB), calling them "discriminary" to older people, ended youth discount fares that since 1966 had permitted young people to fly for up to 50% less than regular fares.

The CAB, which was accused by several consumer groups of being too sympathetic to airline profit-making interests and too unsympathetic to consumers, also ended discount family fares and several other discount plans. These

LOCKHEED-CALIFORNIA DIVISION OF LOCKHEED AIRCRAFT

A Lockheed TriStar, the first wide-bodied aircraft to land in the Soviet Union, is shown to Soviet aircraft and airline officials in a bid for a major order.

moves and other decisions caused domestic fares to go up more than 16% during 1974.

Profits. The high price of fuel on the international market created heavy losses for major airlines in Italy, Belgium, Britain, and other countries that were dependent on a fuel whose price was not regulated.

At the same time, many U. S. domestic airlines appeared to benefit from some aspects of the fuel crisis. Besides gaining some passengers because of gas shortages, the airlines found the government particularly compliant in their efforts to reduce flights, especially money-losing flights to smaller cities.

Because of their wholesale flight reductions, domestic airlines lifted their load factor—a key element of profitability—from an average of about 50% of the seats being filled with paying passengers to 60% in many cases.

Reduced operating costs and personnel cutbacks, coupled with more revenue from fare increases, resulted in record profits in 1974 for some airlines. At year-end industry economists said a decline in travel and the uncertain economic picture made it difficult to predict how long such profits would continue.

Pan Am Crisis. Pan American World Airways, one of the major international airlines, was hit hardest by the industry's two major problems—the soaring cost of fuel not subject to U. S. price regulation and the sharp slump in trans-Atlantic travel. Pan Am had lost more than $170 million between 1969 and 1974, largely due to its premature decision to order the costly Boeing 747 jumbo jet in 1966 and to increased competition on many routes.

Under a new management team led by chairman William T. Seawell, Pan Am had appeared to be pulling out of its nosedive until the oil embargo in 1974 added more than $200 million annually to its fuel bill.

During the spring, Pan Am and a second major international carrier, Trans World Airlines (TWA), applied for federal subsidies to offset the increased fuel bill. In August, Pan Am said its need was urgent and sought a $10.2 million monthly emergency subsidy.

However, President Ford, seeing little chance of the measure being approved in Congress and unconvinced Pan Am had done enough to solve its problems, turned down the request, as did the CAB. Instead, the Ford administration announced a seven-point program designed to help the airline. The plan included efforts to reduce excess competition on some highly saturated routes by means of flight consolidations, mergers, and steps to end what Pan Am had claimed was discriminatory treatment by some foreign countries.

For the third time since 1961 Pan Am began merger negotiations with TWA. Aviation industry experts expected the decline in international travel and inflationary costs to bring about a widespread restructuring and consolidation of airline operations in the future, possibly through several mergers.

Safety. On March 3, a Turkish Airlines DC-10 trijet crashed near Paris, killing 346 persons. It was the worst tragedy in the history of aviation. Investigators traced the accident to the opening of a faulty cargo compartment door during flight. Failure of the door caused an explosive decompression that damaged the plane's controls.

Among other air tragedies during the year were two landing accidents involving Pan Am Boeing 707's on Pacific islands. On Jan. 31, 97 persons died in a crash at Pago Pago, American Samoa; on April 22, 107 were killed in a crash on the island of Bali in Indonesia.

Other Developments. The rising cost of jet fuel and the airlines' collective economic headaches deterred additional orders for the $50 million, 1,400-mile-per-hour (2,250-km-per-hour) Concorde built jointly by Britain and France. Nevertheless, under direction of their governments, Air France and British Airways went ahead with plans to put the new plane into regular service over the Atlantic in late 1975 or in 1976, at rates 10% to 25% above regular first-class fares.

In a series of demonstration flights in 1974, the Concorde demonstrated that it was nearly ready for flying passengers. In the most dramatic example, a Concorde with 32 passengers flew across the Atlantic twice in one day—leaving Boston in the morning, flying to Paris for refueling, and landing at Boston in late afternoon. The total elapsed flying time for the round-trip was 6 hours and 18 minutes, and the plane's average speed was 1,000 miles (1,600 km) per hour.

ROBERT H. LINDSEY
Transportation Reporter, "The New York Times"

Shipping

The year 1974 was the first of a new world order dominated by the oil-producing nations rather than the military and industrial nations. The year began with an Arab oil boycott followed by oil-price increases, and it ended with uncontrolled inflation in Europe, Japan, and North America. The first two are heavily dependent on shipments of Middle East oil, while the United States requires increasing imports of oil and ores.

The Arab-Israel war and the ensuing Arab oil embargo resulted in a sharply decreased demand for shipping. But with the lifting of the oil embargo in March 1974, shipping again became prosperous. Over the long run this prosperity may continue because the world depends not only on overseas shipment of oil, ore, and grain but processed goods as well. The merchant ship remains essential in international relations.

Shipbuilding. In the shipbuilding industry, 1974 brought an end to the plans for the 500,000-deadweight-ton (DWT) supertanker and dreams of the million-tonner. The workable size for very large crude carriers (VLCC) is now about 285,000 DWT. Of the 539 crude carriers under construction, 173 will be Liberian registered for nonnational companies. Japan has 46 under construction; Norway, 56; Britain, 41; and the United States, 6. Russia leads in building conventional ships, accounting for 210 of the 1,071 world total on order. Russia also leads in building container ships, accounting for 29 of the 163 world total on order. Greece has the second-largest order, 52 conventional vessels and 27 container vessels. Communist countries usually construct their types smaller than do the rest of the world.

Ship Crews. The permanent crisis in shipping stems from personnel. There are too few and their competence is too low. As a result, collisions and groundings increase yearly. One fourth of the world's tonnage is registered in countries without sea traditions.

There is little provision or power to regulate these ships, which are manned by nondescript crews. The traditional maritime nations suffer from lack of men and large turnovers. Thus, the task of a supertanker master now is almost superhuman.

This sad sea story is told in a foremost book of 1974, *Supership,* by Noel Mostert. His somber conclusion is that transport over the world seas cannot survive if large ships continue to be built and operated under the low standards now prevailing. If such management is practiced with the growing number of chemical cargo vessels, the outlook is even bleaker.

Sea Law. Existing anarchy in sea transport is a product of anarchy in international law. The 3d United Nations Conference on the Law of the Sea was held in Caracas in 1974. It focused on territorial limits, reduction of pollution, and mining of sea resources. These issues have little to do with shipping, which urgently needs policing, traffic control, and shipboard supervision and inspection. (See also LAW—INTERNATIONAL.)

Ports. On every continent, ports are being built or modernized to adjust to new trends in trade and shipping. Three types prevail—the oil port, the ore port, and the container port. The oil terminals include Shannon in Ireland, Rotterdam's Europoort, and the man-made island of Kobe, Japan. There is no comparable U. S. terminal.

The ore ports usually are located in undeveloped areas. The world's largest is near Vitoria, Espirito Santo, Brazil. The major container ports have been increasing in size and decreasing in number. Shippers now bypass other ports by rail. Port authorities now realize what road planners have long known: building in advance of demand creates it.

JOHN D. HAYES
Rear Admiral, U. S. Navy (Retired)

Railroads

Despite a faltering national economy, 1974 was a year of growth and relative prosperity for both freight and passenger railroads in the United States. The energy crisis of the winter of 1973–74 and the heightened national consciousness of the efficiency of railroads compared with most other forms of transportation were in large measure responsible.

Passengers. While accounting for less than 5% of total revenues, passenger trains continued to be the most visible part of railroad operations. The National Railroad Passenger Corp.—Amtrak—at midyear reported a 25% increase in train travel. With the blessings of a friendly Congress, Amtrak placed orders for 200 new coaches to beef up its existing fleet of 2,000 and ordered 11 more French-designed Turbotrains following the successful testing of two of these trains in Chicago-St. Louis service. Late in the year, Congress passed the Amtrak Improvement Act of 1974, authorizing a $200 million subsidy to cover the corporation's operating losses in the current fiscal year and raising its ceiling on borrowing (for new equipment and other improvements) from $500 million to $900 million.

Freight. The freight railroads measured their success not only in record traffic levels but also in bigger payrolls and sharply higher earnings. A 30-year decline in employment was reversed: in mid-1974, railroads employed 541,200 persons, a 2% increase over the previous year. In the first three quarters of 1974 alone, railroad net income amounted to $593 million, exceeding earnings for any entire calendar year since 1966.

Under mandate from the Interstate Commerce Commission to spend the proceeds of a 10% freight-rate increase (about $1.25 billion a year) on roadway and rolling stock improvements, the railroads raised capital expenditures in 1974 to a record $2.4 billion.

For the second year in a row orders were placed for more than 100,000 new freight cars. But industry leaders, noting that a 3.7% rate of return was a long way from the 10% which they estimate is needed to modernize the railroad plant, applied in November for an additional 7% freight-rate hike.

The Northeast. Due to lawsuits questioning the constitutionality of the Regional Rail Reorganization Act of 1973, the United States Railway Association moved more slowly than expected toward the creation of the new railroad system which Congress ordered to be evolved out of the bankrupt northeastern carriers—Penn Central, Reading, Lehigh Valley, Lehigh & Hudson River, Boston & Maine, and the Ann Arbor. Deadline for submission of a preliminary plan was moved from October 1974 to February 1975. It will be 1976 before the new Consolidated Rail Corp. (Conrail) can come into being.

Mergers. After 11 years of hearings and 200,000 pages of testimony, the ICC in November approved the merger application of the Union Pacific and the Rock Island; but the decision was so complex, and the conditions of the merger partners had changed so drastically over the years (the Rock Island in 1974 was close to bankruptcy), that there was considerable doubt as to when, or even if, the merger would be consummated. The ICC ordered the Union Pacific to sell those parts of the Rock Island south of Kansas City to the Southern Pacific and the Santa Fe. It authorized the Denver & Rio Grande Western to acquire the Rock Island line between Denver/Colorado Springs and Omaha, Neb.

The year's only other major merger action came when shareholders of the Missouri Pacific, Texas & Pacific, and Chicago & Eastern Illinois authorized their directors to apply to the ICC for merger of T&P and C&EI into the MP.

Legislation. Stalled in the 93d Congress, the Surface Transportation Act of 1974—authorizing federal guarantee of $2 billion in loans for railroad improvements—appeared likely to be reintroduced in the 94th. Meanwhile, talk about setting up a government-controlled pool of freight cars to help relieve persistent car shortages subsided when the railroads decided to create a free-running ("next load, any road") pool of box cars under the aegis of the new American Rail Box Car Co.

LUTHER S. MILLER, *Editor, "Railway Age"*

Highways

The Federal Highway Administration announced that there are 3,786,713 miles (6,093,-957 km) of roads and streets in the United States under the jurisdiction of all levels of government. Municipal mileage composes 16% of the total, or 613,426 miles (987,214 km). The federal aid highway fund, obtained from federal highway user taxes, support 25% of the total road and street mileage, 26% of rural, and 17% of urban mileage.

About 20%, or 792,210 miles (1,274,938 km), are under state control. Over 209,000 miles (336,353 km) of roads in national parks and forests are under federal control, accounting for 6% of the total United States mileage.

Interstate Highway System. A total of 36,021 miles, or 84.8%, of the 42,500-mile Interstate Highway System in the United States are now in use (1 mile equals 1.6093 km). Another 2,889 miles, or 6.8%, are under construction. Work is under way or completed on 99% of the system. In 1974, 85% (28,952 miles) of the 34,072 miles of rural highways and 83.9% (7,069 miles) of the 8,428 miles of urban highway were open. Engineering or right-of-way acquisition was under way on another 2,764 miles.

Appalachian Region. Through June 30, 1974, over $2.409 billion in federal and state funds was obligated for development of highway and local access roads in the 13-state Appalachian region, including $1.329 billion of federal funds. A total of 1,834 miles of highways and access roads were completed or under construction at the end of June, while engineering and right-of-way acquisition were under way on an additional 445 miles, design approval or hearings were held on 82 miles, and locations had been approved on 271 miles.

The Appalachian development highway system created by Congress in 1965 authorized a total of $2.090 billion for the construction of up to 2,700 miles of development highway and 1,600 miles of local access roads.

Receipts and Expenditures. State highway departments had 2% higher total receipts ($18.9 billion) for 1973, including $11.2 billion in borrowed funds and $4.6 billion in federal aid. State road user taxes provided $11.2 billion, and $1.0 billion came from tolls. Federal aid accounted for 48% of the $9.5 billion of total capital expenditures for highways, including $3.9 billion spent on the Interstate Highway System. Total expenditures of $17.9 billion in 1973 were 3% higher than in 1972. Maintenance expenditures totaled $2.5 billion; administration, highway safety, law enforcement, and interest on debt totaled $2.9 billion; and grants-in-aid to local government for highway purposes totaled $3.0 billion.

JAMES R. ROMAN, JR.
The George Washington University

Mass Transit

Although mass transit was much in the news in 1974, the year's most important development occurred on November 26 when President Ford signed the National Mass Transportation Bill of 1974. The legislation approves $11.8 billion in federal aid for the states and the nation's cities to meet transit needs for a six-year period. A total of $7.8 billion will be available over six years toward constructing and equipping transit systems. The federal government will pay 80% of any project it approves. The balance of the funds will be available for either capital outlays at 80% federal share or operating subsidies at 50% federal share.

UMTA Grants. Grants by the U. S. Department of Transportation's Urban Mass Transportation Administration (UMTA) generally fall into three categories: assistance for transit planning, assistance to purchase new equipment and construction, and assistance to cities or transit authorities to help them acquire private companies. Planning grants are usually quite small (for example, there was a grant of $31,640 to Mankato, Minn.), but larger grants are made, such as $2.7 million to New York City and $1.3 million to Washington, D. C.

Individual equipment/construction grants may vary from the $101,760 grant to New Castle, Pa., to the $70 million grant to Chicago. Sometimes a series of grants during a year can raise the total substantially, such as the $155 million granted to New York City. Grants to aid in purchasing private companies ranged from $261,120 to the Transportation Authority of Northern Kentucky to $2,872,800 to Detroit's Southeastern Michigan Transportation Authority.

Special Projects. Grants are made also to try to improve transit in the future. Such a grant of $1 million to the Florida Department of Transportation will permit an experiment with special equipment to be installed in buses and traffic signals. The traffic signals then will electronically sense approaching buses and turn the light green, thereby improving bus speed and hence service to customers. Another such grant of $703,000 will permit a demonstration and evaluation of both British and German double-decker buses in daily revenue service in both Los Angeles and New York.

Market Research. The first major federal commitment to develop comprehensive marketing techniques for transit operators came when the UMTA awarded a contract for $465,000 to develop a methodology for measuring the effectiveness of a transit marketing program that includes market research, planning, revision of fares and schedules, and promotion.

Highway Funds Diverted. The Federal Aid Highway Act of 1973 made it possible for urban highway system funds to be used for mass-transit purposes. Among the first diversions granted was $1.5 million to St. Louis, Mo.

Energy Efficiency. With the current emphasis on making efficient use of energy, it is important to consider the efficiency of mass-transit modes. A current study by Alan M. Voorhees and Associates, Inc., developed the following average energy-efficiency rates, measured in terms of passenger miles per gallon of fuel: express bus, 54.2; rail transit (New York City), 51.2; commuter rail, 43.6; bus transit, 34.9; passenger car, 26.4; dial-a-bus, 10.4; and taxi, 9.0. Perhaps more people would use mass transit if they realized that it costs 15.89 cents per mile to operate the average standard-size car and 12.88 cents to operate a compact car.

BART. On Sept. 16, 1974, San Francisco's 71-mile, $1.5 billion Bay Area Rapid Transit system was finally in full revenue operation. BART was expecting a daily passenger count of 140,000 to 160,000 on completion of the system, but in October the count was averaging only 115,000. It was hoped that by spring 1975, service would be improved with shorter headways and longer hours of operation with the completion of a permanent automatic traffic-control system called Sequential Occupancy Release, using 26 mini-computers to provide automatic check-in and check-out of trains in subsequent blocks. When the system has its full complement of 450 cars, it will be able to handle 250,000 passengers per day.

JAMES R. ROMAN, JR.
The George Washington University

UPI

Passengers, among the 1,648 transferred to a rescue ship, wave goodbye to the *Queen Elizabeth II.* Luxury liner's boiler system broke down in April, 270 miles from Bermuda.

TRAVEL

During the first months of 1974 it appeared that the acute fuel shortage would prevent most Americans from driving to domestic summer vacation sites, and the outlook for vacations in Europe was made bleak by dollar devaluation, rampant inflation, and a fuel shortage worse than that at home. Although fuel was plentiful by summer, millions of people vacationed close to home, making it a banner year for resorts near cities. Tourism in most of Europe was much reduced in 1974.

As 1976 approached, U. S. Bicentennial plans took shape. Transatlantic passenger ship service suffered the loss of the *France,* but cruises were increasingly popular. Scheduled airlines reduced schedules to save fuel, and raised transatlantic ticket prices five times during the year. Cycling, hiking, cross-country skiing, sailing, canoeing, rafting, and other nonfueled means of travel became more popular than ever. As Europe became more expensive, Caribbean islands by comparison seemed less expensive than before; many of them started intensive training of personnel serving tourists and tried to impress on their populations the value of tourism, in anticipation of vastly increased numbers of visitors.

Energy Crisis. During long waits in line to buy high-priced gasoline in January and February 1974, millions of people who customarily spend much of their annual vacation on the road decided to play safe by renting a cottage or visiting a resort within one gas tank of home and passing their entire vacation in one place.

Many resorts and state tourist organizations cut out national advertising (seriously affecting travel publications). Florida suffered a 25 percent loss in its 1973–74 winter season, and mounted a massive campaign in late spring to save the summer season.

Some ski resorts chartered buses to bring skiers from the cities. Resort operators began meeting trains, planes, and buses of all visitors. Bus and train travel increased enormously.

In Europe, the fuel shortage plus inflation raised the cost of gasoline to as much as $2.50 per gallon in some countries; other costs also rose steeply.

National Parks. To save fuel and cut pollution, free busing began at Grand Canyon, operating from April 1 to September 15. A dozen small buses, burning low-polluting propane, handled up to 6,000 persons daily. West Rim Drive was closed to private cars; hikers and cyclists were encouraged to use it, and bicycles were available for rent. Mass transit also was in use at Yosemite, Mt. McKinley, Everglades, Mesa Verde, Point Reyes, and National Capital parks, and at Dinosaur National Monument.

Congress authorized seven new parks on Oct. 1, 1974. A new type was Big Thicket National Preserve in southeast Texas, a "biological crossroads" noted for its variety of animal and plant life. Landmarks of the American Revolution in Boston, Mass., will be preserved as part of Boston National Historical Park, started with seven sites and with a possible seven more sites to be added.

At the end of 1974 there were 308 units and over 30 million acres in the National Park System. If land in Alaska marked for possible inclusion is taken, the size will be doubled.

Cycling. Automobiles sold poorly in 1974, but bicycle manufacturers could not keep up with the demand. Federal Energy Administrator John C. Sawhill estimated that 5 million more bicycles than autos would be bought in 1974, and he applauded this saving of energy.

Special cycling routes were being established, but not fast enough. Maryland opened many "Class II bikeways"—highway shoulders adapted to cycling. Palm Springs, Calif., opened a 10-mile cycling trail. A 15-mile bike path from Washington, D. C., to George Washington's home, Mount Vernon, attracted as many as 5,500 riders each weekend.

More than 1,000 local cycle clubs were active in 1974, many of them holding weekend bike tours of 15 to 100 miles. Tours and rallies were being organized by three national organizations: American Youth Hostels, the League of American Wheelmen, and the International Bicycle Tours Society.

Unfortunately, the U. S. Consumer Safety Product Commission estimated that in 1973 nearly 419,000 persons suffered bicycle accidents severe enough to require hospital emergency room treatment. The commission issued regulations to ban hazardous bicycles and establish mechanical safety requirements, to become effective Jan. 1, 1975.

Air Travel. A Gallup survey showed that 55% of all American adults have flown on a scheduled airline—up from 33% in 1962.

Fuel shortages caused elimination of 2,000 daily scheduled flights and a consequent rise in load factor (filled seats) from 52% in the first nine months of 1973 to 56.8% in 1974. International air traffic dropped 10.5% in the first nine months of 1974, while domestic traffic rose 4.3%.

The fifth transatlantic airline fare increase of 1974, on November 1, placed the cheapest New York–Paris round-trip winter fare at $412, and summer economy New York–London round-trip fare at $764.

The U. S. Civil Aeronautics Board acted to raise transatlantic charter fares by agreement among airlines and to eliminate cheap affinity charters by March 31, 1975.

Sea Travel. A new passenger-ship terminal opened in New York City on Nov. 23, 1974, designed to increase the port's cruise business, which was only half that of Miami plus Port Everglades, Fla. It was hoped that the 24 ships cruising from New York would increase to 30 in 1975. As fuel soared in price, economy required sailing more slowly, spending more time in cruise ports, and reducing table luxuries and steward staffs. The *France,* losing $20 million annually, was retired immediately when the crew struck at Le Havre in September. The USSR, bidding for cruise trade, based the *Maxim Gorki* in New York.

Rail Travel. Because of the automobile fuel shortage, Amtrak's trains were filled, and hundreds of retired passenger cars were pressed into service. Full trains and the obvious need for efficient passenger service lent substance to Amtrak's expansion plans submitted to Congress, in expectation of doubling the number of riders (19 million in 1974) within five years. Amtrak and Greyhound agreed to sell each other's tickets, beginning Jan. 1, 1975, so passengers could make trips using a combination of rail and bus.

Bicentennial. Firm plans for 1976 gradually evolved. A World Theater Festival will bring noted theatrical companies from many countries to perform in U. S. cities. The National Endowment for the Arts will fund the composition of 15 new symphonies, to be played by 31 orchestras in 320 performances. Operation Sail '76 will bring 150 sailing ships to New York and other ports, with activities centered at New York's antique South Street Seaport. (See also UNITED STATES—*Bicentennial.*)

Passports. The U. S. passport will be superseded in three years by a machine-readable document that will permit computerization of passport processing. The Passport Office warned that a U. S. passport brings as much as $2,000 among smugglers, and 3,500 are stolen annually.

The Society of American Travel Writers, meeting in Rio de Janeiro in September, asked Congress to abolish visa requirements for citizens of countries that accept U. S. visitors without visas, and urged establishment of a national tourist policy under the U. S. Travel Service.

ROBERT SCOTT MILNE
Coauthor, "Around the World with the Experts"

Instead of using a traditional room key, a guest inserts a coded plastic card in a "station keyport" in a new electronic system providing greater security in hotels.

ADT

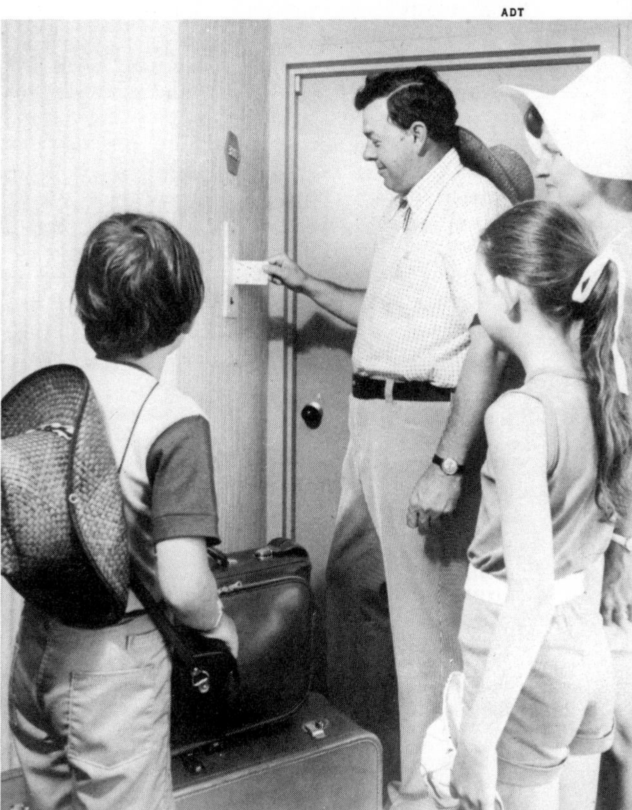

TUNISIA

For Tunisia, the tiny, relatively resource-poor neighbor of the North African oil giants, 1974 began in political and diplomatic embarrassment and ended in economic triumph.

Merger with Libya. Plans were outstripped by events in January, when Tunisian President Habib Bourguiba emerged from secret talks with Libya's Col. Muammar el-Qaddafi on the Tunisian resort island of Djerba and announced the agreement in principle to a federation between the two countries.

Although they are neighbors on the Mediterranean and both members of the Arab League, it was difficult for observers to imagine two partners who are less suited to a political match. Although Tunisia was one of the first Arab nations actively to aid Egypt in the October 1973 war against Israel, the Maghreb nation has always been most realistic about Israel's existence and has urged other Arab states to recognize it as a state. Libya's Qaddafi, on the other hand, has been hostile toward the state of Israel—only slightly more hostile than he has been toward Arab states who preach moderation.

In deciding to found the "Arab Islamic Republic," Libya also chose to ignore, at least for the time being, the moderately pro-West stances taken by the conservative President Bourguiba, as well as the liberated attitude toward women in Tunisia that runs counter to Qaddafi's strict Islamic world view. In a purely economic sense, some observers thought the merger might be mutually advantageous. Tunisia had a foreign debt exceeding $1 billion, over 5 million inhabitants, and few natural resources. Oil-rich Libya was starved for labor and had surplus revenues. Tunisia might also have considered the merger in order to protect its new offshore oil field, which was located near the Libyan border.

But the planned merger lasted less than a week, and when it was all over it was clear that the 71-year-old Bourguiba was as much in control of his country as ever. Viewing the machinations of Foreign Minister Muhammad Masmoudi in arranging the merger as an attempt to move to the head of the line of succession to Bourguiba, the president dismissed the foreign minister on January 14—two days after the merger was announced. Saying that a popular referendum on the question had to wait until changes were made in the Tunisian constitution, Bourguiba quietly shelved the federation pact, to the relief of most Tunisians. In so doing, Tunisia joined Egypt in silently but effectively turning a cold shoulder to the advances of revolutionary Libya.

Economic Boom. For the first time since independence from the French in 1956, Tunisia expected the value of exports to exceed that of imports. Petroleum exports played a large role in this turnaround, with offshore oil concessions run by French, Italian, and American companies—in full operation since April—turning out high-quality crude oil at an annual rate of 14 million barrels, twice the rate experts had predicted. Total income from petroleum exports in 1974 was expected to exceed $460 million, compared with $120 million in 1973.

With world prices soaring, Tunisia's phosphate exports also increased in value, triple that of 1973 and anticipated to reach $160 million by the end of the year. Olive oil production rebounded from a poor 1973 harvest and was thought capable of equaling the 1972 record of $100 million.

After a disappointing 1973, Tunisia's tourism industry benefited from unrest on Cyprus as Europeans headed instead for Tunisia's sunny coast. Seeing tourism as a major foreign-exchange earner, Tunisia is busy building hotels, creating 7,000 to 8,000 rooms a year, with a goal of 90,000 rooms by 1975.

President for Life. It was in this atmosphere of unprecedented prosperity that Bourguiba, who had been ailing, came back to center stage in Tunisia, proving that, although there is dissension in the country—especially among the students—none would make a lasting impression for some time to come. While the aging president has not faced a serious challenge to his authority within the nation's one-party system in 20 years, he has several times refused the ultimate accolade of being named president for life. He finally relented in September, when, having filled out the maximum three terms permitted by the constitution, he was acclaimed president for life of the ruling Destour Socialist party, which was purged of its peskier liberals at the latest party congress. Election results on November 2 confirmed Bourguiba as Tunisia's life president.

After avoiding the question for a long time, amid jokes that he planned to live to be 100, Bourguiba named as his eventual successor Prime Minister Hedi Nouira, the mastermind of Tunisia's current economic boom.

ROBERT L. DENERSTEIN and NANCY MCKEON
The African-American Institute

TUNISIA • Information Highlights

Official Name: Republic of Tunisia.
Location: North Africa.
Area: 63,170 square miles (164,150 sq km).
Population (1973 est.): 5,600,000.
Chief City (1966 est.): Tunis, the capital, 468,997.
Government: *Head of state,* Habib Bourguiba, president (took office 1957). *Chief minister,* Hedi Nouira, premier (took office Nov. 1970). *Legislature* (unicameral)—National Assembly.
Monetary Unit: Dinar (0.435 dinar equals U. S.$1, July 1974).
Gross National Product (1972 est.): $2,312,000,000.
Manufacturing (major products): Processed foods, wines, petroleum products, olive oil, pulp and wood products.
Major Agricultural Products: Wheat, olives, vegetables, grapes, citrus fruits, forest products.
Foreign Trade (1973): *Exports,* $386,000,000; *imports,* $606,000,000.

TURKEY

In 1974, Turkey invaded the island of Cyprus when the Cypriot president was overthrown in a coup backed by the Greek junta, thus intensifying the bitterness between Greece and Turkey that had already been exacerbated by their conflicting claims to oil deposits in the Aegean. The invasion also brought denunciations from the U. S. Congress, as did Turkey's decision to resume opium cultivation. Although Turkey's military successes in Cyprus redounded to Premier Bulent Ecevit's credit, the country's political instability led to his downfall in September. On the economic front, Turkey suffered from serious inflationary pressures, with wholesale prices rising more than 30% in 1974.

War on Cyprus. In July and August Turkey and Greece came close to war over developments in Cyprus. On July 15 the Greek Cypriot national guard, with the encouragement of the Greek military junta, overthrew Archbishop Makarios as president of Cyprus. Invoking its right to intervene in Cyprus, should the terms of the London and Zürich agreements of 1959 be broken, Turkey invaded the island on July 20. The invasion involved some 40,000 troops. Turkey's declared purpose was to prevent *enosis* (union) with Greece and to achieve a political solution along federal lines that would secure the rights of the Turkish Cypriot minority. The Turkish Cypriots number about 125,000, or 18% of the population. (For further details on the war in Cyprus, see the feature article on Cyprus, page 62.)

As a result of the invasion, severe strains developed in Turkey's relations with the United States and with NATO, of which both Turkey and Greece were members. The U. S. Congress threatened to cut off all aid to Turkey unless substantial progress toward a settlement had been made by December 10. President Gerald Ford accepted congressional approval (October 17) of continued military aid to Turkey until December 10, if Turkey refrained from using U. S. "implements of war" on Cyprus. Ultimately the cut-off date for aid was set at Feb. 5, 1975.

TURKEY • Information Highlights

Official Name: Republic of Turkey.
Location: Southeastern Europe and southwestern Asia.
Area: 301,381 square miles (780,576 sq km).
Population (1973 est.): 38,000,000.
Chief Cities (1970 census): Ankara, the capital, 1,208,791; Istanbul, 2,247,630; Izmir, 520,686.
Government: *Head of state,* Fahri Korutürk, president (took office April 1973). *Head of government,* Sadi Irmak, caretaker premier (took office Nov. 1974). *Legislature*—Grand National Assembly: Senate and National Assembly.
Monetary Unit: Lira (14 liras equal U. S.$1, April 1974).
Gross National Product (1973 est.): $18,100,000,000.
Manufacturing (major products): Textiles, petroleum products, cement, iron and steel, fertilizers, processed foods.
Major Agricultural Products: Raisins, wheat, cotton, rye, sugar beets, barley, fruits, tobacco, hazelnuts, sheep, cattle.
Foreign Trade (1973): *Exports,* $1,317,000,000; *imports,* $2,049,000,000.

WIDE WORLD

Although the Cyprus crisis had made Turkish Premier Bulent Ecevit a national hero, he resigned the post because he had not accomplished his domestic goals.

Though the Cypriot problem remained unresolved, quiet negotiations were begun in the autumn. Wiser counsels seemed to prevail in both Greece and Turkey, but a final solution continued to evade the negotiators' grasp.

Oil Claims. Before the invasion of Cyprus, relations with Greece had been roiled by the conflicting claims of the two countries to the continental shelf in the Aegean, where oil deposits had been discovered. In response to repeated Greek claims to sole rights over the area, the Turkish foreign minister declared on May 9 that Turkey would never agree to moves that would turn the Aegean "into a Greek sea or lake."

Opium Poppy Production. Turkey decided to resume opium poppy production in July, thereby creating difficulties with the United States. This production had been banned by agreement with the United States in May 1971. At that time, the United States contended that 80% of the heroin reaching the United States was refined from Turkish opium. The United States had pledged to compensate Turkish farmers over a four-year period to the amount of $35,000,000.

As a result of Turkey's decision to resume production, bills were introduced in the U. S. Congress to cut off some $180,000,000 in military aid and $27,000,000 in economic assistance. In September it appeared that a reasonably satisfactory solution had been reached, providing for inspection and controls.

Politics. On the volatile 1974 political scene, Bulent Ecevit, leader of the Kemalist Republican People's Party (RPP), which is somewhat leftist, appeared to emerge as the man of the hour, although his party commanded only 185 seats in an Assembly of 450. In an unlikely coalition with the right-wing National Salvation Party, Ecevit came to office on January 25 and was confirmed on February 7. His program called for basic reforms within a democratic framework, a more equitable distribution of wealth, rural development, reform of state enterprises, free university education, and a general amnesty for political prisoners. While Ecevit became something of a national hero because of his actions in the Cyprus crisis, he was unable to achieve his domestic program, and he resigned on September 18.

On November 17, President Fahri Korutürk approved the formation of a largely nonpolitical cabinet, with only four party politicians, all from the Republican Reliance party. Sen. Sadi Irmak was designated as premier. The Irmak cabinet was unable to win parliamentary approval and continued only as a caretaker government, pending elections in 1975.

HARRY N. HOWARD, *The American University*

UGANDA

Uganda continued in 1974 under the turbulent rule of President Idi Amin, who was swept to power by a military coup in January 1971.

International Criticism. The Amin regime came under sustained international criticism in 1974. Most notably, the International Commission of Jurists accused President Amin's government of creating a reign of terror in Uganda, "from which thousands of people from all walks of life, Africans as well as Asians, have sought refuge in voluntary exile."

Former Foreign Minister Wanume Kibedi, living in exile, called on Amin to resign. Kibedi said that liquidations of innocent Ugandan civilians, which reached a peak in 1972, were continuing to the present.

The bullet-riddled body of Michael Ondoga, former foreign minister, was found in the Nile, soon after his dismissal from the cabinet. Elizabeth Bagaya, Princess of Toro, was named foreign minister, but in November she too was dismissed and her future was in doubt.

Military Clashes. Fighting within the military broke out on March 23–24. The shooting stemmed from ethnic animosities and a desire on the part of some officers to replace Amin. Brigadier Charles Arube was killed in the fighting. In the aftermath, President Amin purged at least 50 army officers.

Economic Conditions. Uganda was still adjusting to its expulsion of Asian businessmen and professionals on 90-days notice in 1972. Many businesses have been taken over by private individuals, often soldiers and supporters of Amin.

SYGMA

In 1974 Idi Amin, president of Uganda since 1971, not only sustained severe international criticism but also survived clashes within his nation's military ranks.

The major industrial plants and corporations have been taken over by the parastatal Uganda Development Corporation.

Relations with Tanzania. Several times during the year, President Amin accused neighboring Tanzania of plotting against Uganda. Relations between Tanzania and Uganda have been erratic since Tanzania granted asylum in 1971 to Milton Obote, deposed president of Uganda. Despite some signs of reconciliation after bilateral talks in Kampala, Amin threatened to invade Tanzania and annex its territory as far as the Kagera River.

JAY E. HAKES, *University of New Orleans*

UGANDA • Information Highlights

Official Name: Republic of Uganda.
Location: East Africa.
Area: 91,134 square miles (236,036 sq km).
Population (1973 est.): 10,800,000.
Chief City (1969 census): Kampala, the capital, 330,700.
Government: *Head of state,* Gen. Idi Amin, president (took office Feb. 1971). *Head of government,* Gen. Idi Amin. *Legislature* (unicameral)—National Assembly (dissolved Feb. 1971).
Monetary Unit: Shilling (7.143 shillings equal U.S.$1, July 1974).
Gross National Product (1972 est.): $1,450,000,000.
Manufacturing (major products): Processed agricultural products.
Major Agricultural Products: Coffee, millet, cotton, sisal, groundnuts, tobacco, sweet potatoes, cassava.
Foreign Trade (1973): *Exports,* $325,000,000; *imports,* $161,000,000.

UPI

In Moscow, as Kremlin and American officials look on, U. S. President Nixon and Soviet Communist Party Chairman Brezhnev sign agreements worked out during a week's conference.

USSR

For the first year in world history two different United States Presidents, Richard M. Nixon and Gerald R. Ford, both visited the USSR in 1974 and concluded important agreements with Leonid I. Brezhnev, secretary general of the Soviet Communist party. Nixon's summer visit resulted in eight pacts for scientific cooperation, trade, new consulates, and arms limitation. Ford's two-day winter stay produced a treaty pledging each country to limit intercontinental missiles, submarine-based missiles, and long-range bombers to equal totals for 10 years. Thus U. S.-USSR détente continued, despite many minor incidents, a difference in viewpoints on Near East problems, and President Ford's abrupt halt of a huge U. S. grain sale to the Soviets.

Soviet oil output in 1974 exceeded that of the United States, with the USSR thus becoming the world's largest producer of petroleum. Because of bad weather, Soviet grain, potato, and sugar beet harvests slumped, requiring further imports of both grain and sugar.

Though dissident Soviet intellectuals continued to be harassed, demoted, or imprisoned, the USSR government in 1974 rid itself of many leading dissidents by simply exiling them abroad.

FOREIGN AFFAIRS

United States. The visit to the USSR by U. S. President Nixon from June 27 to July 3 resulted in the signing of additional U. S.-Soviet pacts for: five-year cooperation in housing construction research; five-year cooperation in energy studies; three-year cooperation in artificial heart research (all signed on June 28); and economic, industrial, and technical cooperation for ten years (June 29).

More important were three arms-limitation agreements signed on July 3. The first modified the 1972 perpetual treaty limiting anti-ballistic missiles so that in the future the United States and the USSR will each deploy only one cluster of 100 ABM's instead of two, with the cluster either located around the capital city or protecting intercontinental rocket sites. The second stated that for five years, commencing on March 31, 1976, neither country will conduct underground test-explosions of nuclear weapons exceeding 150 kilotons in explosive power, though larger nuclear underground blasts would be permitted for peaceful purposes. The third provided that both countries would exchange detailed data on the location and geology of their nuclear test sites, so each could detect the other's tests from long distance. Along with these formal written pacts, the two leaders agreed informally that a U. S. consulate-general will be opened in Kiev in the Ukraine and a Soviet consulate-general in New York City.

When Richard Nixon resigned from the U. S. presidency on August 9, the new president, Gerald R. Ford, immediately promised to continue détente and quickly received a Soviet governmental message congratulating him.

The USSR was displeased, however, when on October 5, President Ford ordered two American companies to cancel their sale of 3,400,000 tons of corn and wheat to the Soviet government. After hasty negotiations the U. S. government permitted the USSR to purchase only 2,200,000 tons, with shipments to be spread over the remainder of 1974 and the first six months of 1975.

In December the Soviet government angrily denied ever having concluded an informal U. S.-USSR agreement that the Soviet Union would permit greater Jewish emigration after the United States granted most-favored-nation status to Soviet imports.

Despite these tensions during the early months of the new presidency, Soviet leader Brezhnev and President Ford met on November 23–24 in a suburb of the East Siberian city of Vladivostok and concluded an agreement empowering their respective representatives in the Strategic Arms Limitation Talks (SALT) to negotiate in 1975 a 10-year treaty limiting the United States and USSR each to a total of 2,400 intercontinental rockets (ICBM's), submarine-based missiles (SLBM's), and intercontinental bombers, with 1,320 of the missiles permitted to have multiple hydrogen-bomb warheads (MIRV's). The 2,400 ceiling was little more than the total long-range offensive vehicles that each country already possessed. Ignored by the Vladivostok agreement were medium missiles, medium bombers, and fighter-bombers, all of which can also carry hydrogen bombs. At the time the pact was signed, the USSR was superior in number of ICBM's, SLBM's, medium missiles, and medium bombers, while the United States held a lead in MIRV's, intercontinental bombers, and fighter-bombers.

Walter J. Stoessel, a Russian-speaking career diplomat, arrived in Moscow in March as the new U. S. ambassador to the USSR.

Europe. In 1974, Soviet relations with Europe were marked by little tension and many new pacts of cooperation. Trade agreements were concluded with Austria, Belgium, Luxembourg, France, Finland, Britain, Italy, and West Germany in non-Communist Europe, and with the Communist countries of Czechoslovakia, Hungary, Rumania, and Yugoslavia. Bulgaria and East Germany started operating their first atomic power stations, both built with Soviet assistance. After completion of long-distance pipelines, Soviet natural gas began arriving in Bulgaria, Finland, and Italy.

During 1974, 70% of the food and raw material imports of Bulgaria, Czechoslovakia, East Germany, Hungary, Poland, and Rumania were provided by the USSR. All these eastern European Communist countries both received and rendered technical aid from and to the Soviet Union, which also exchanged technical aid with Finland and Yugoslavia. Among NATO countries, Iceland was the only nation obtaining USSR technical assistance.

The only semi-serious crisis in Soviet relations with western Europe during 1974 occurred in August, when transit routes from West Germany into West Berlin were harassed because the West German government opened a local environmental office of West Germany in West Berlin. The harassment ended when the United States delayed diplomatic recognition of East Germany until the routes were free from obstruction.

Near East. Although the USSR continued to arm Syria and Egypt against Israel during 1974, the chief crisis during the year was the Cyprus civil war in July, in which Turkey intervened by military invasion. From the start, Soviet propaganda and diplomatic maneuvers in the United Nations opposed annexation of Cyprus by Greece. At first the USSR condoned Turkish military intervention, but later urged that all foreign troops—Greek, Turkish, and NATO—be withdrawn from Cyprus, allowing the Cypriots to determine their own fate.

During the year Soviet trawlers helped clear the Suez Canal of underwater mines. The USSR concluded trade, cultural exchange, and technical aid pacts with Syria and a new aid agreement with Southern Yemen.

Far East. The year 1974 was noteworthy for closer Soviet relations with Japan and continuing hostility toward Communist China. During the summer the USSR received $1.5 billion worth of Japanese credits to be spent in Japanese aid in developing East Siberian coal, gas, and timber resources, including construction of railways and pipelines, with long-term repayment to Japan from East Siberian coal, gas, and wood.

Relations with Communist China began badly in January, when China expelled two Soviet embassy officials, their wives, and an embassy translator for alleged espionage. The USSR expelled a Chinese embassy official in retaliation. Then in March a Soviet helicopter made an emergency landing in the Chinese province of Sinkiang, and China seized both the plane and

USSR • Information Highlights

Official Name: Union of Soviet Socialist Republics.
Area: 8,649,412 square miles (22,402,000 sq km).
Population (1974 est.): 252,000,000.
Chief Cities (1973 est.): Moscow, the capital, 7,410,000; Leningrad, 4,066,000; Kiev, 1,827,000.
Government: *Head of state,* Nikolai V. Podgorny, president (took office Dec. 1965). *Head of government,* Aleksei N. Kosygin, premier (took office Oct. 1964). *Secretary general of the Communist party,* Leonid I. Brezhnev (took office 1964). *Legislature*—Supreme Soviet: Soviet of the Union, Soviet of Nationalities.
Monetary Unit: Ruble (0.776 ruble equals U. S.$1, Sept. 1974).
Gross National Product (1973 est.): $615,000,000,000.
Manufacturing (major products): Steel, cement, chemical fertilizer, machine tools, electric power.
Major Agricultural Products: Grain, sugar beets, sunflower seeds, potatoes, cotton.
Foreign Trade (1973): *Exports,* $21,463,000,000; *imports,* $21,108,000,000.

UPI

Jewish ballet star Valery Panov and his ballerina wife, Galina, in London after being allowed to emigrate from the Soviet Union. They planned to live in Israel.

the crew as an alleged spy mission. Despite repeated Soviet requests for the release of the plane and crew, on the grounds that the landing in China was accidental, China refused to return them.

Meanwhile, according to Soviet émigrés, border skirmishes occurred between the two Communist countries throughout the year, though neither nation saw fit to publicize them. In the autumn, China offered a nonaggression pact to the USSR, providing both sides withdrew their troops from the mutual frontier. The USSR, which had originally suggested such a pact, ignored this peace proposal. Western newspapermen traveling in Soviet Central Asia near the Chinese frontier reported that nuclear bomb shelters were being built and mass air raid drills were regularly enforced.

Africa. Soviet interest in Africa in 1974 remained minor, although technical aid pacts were concluded with Algeria, Libya, and Mauritania and a friendship treaty with Somalia. Except for Egypt, Soviet technical assistance was small but covered many countries: Congo, Guinea, Malagasy, Mali, Morocco, Nigeria, Senegal, Sierra Leone, Somalia, Sudan, Tanzania, Uganda, and Upper Volta.

Latin America. The USSR displayed little interest in Latin America during 1974, although trade and technical aid pacts were concluded in February with Argentina and Soviet diplomatic recognition was extended during June to Tobago and Trinidad. During the year Soviet technical aid was rendered to Argentina, Peru, and Cuba, with the latter being the main Latin American recipient by receiving $2 million worth of Soviet supplies per day.

DEFENSE AND SPACE

Armed Forces. The Soviet armed forces in 1974 totaled about 3,400,000 men. Their impressive equipment included the world's largest totals of tanks (36,000), submarines (285), medium bombers (800), medium missiles (600), submarine-based missiles (700), and intercontinental ballistic missiles (1,600).

Showing their ability to operate far from home waters, Soviet naval ships during the year paid official visits to Algeria, Cuba, and Tunisia. In 1974 the USSR maintained a fleet of about 50 ships in the Mediterranean Sea and 20 in the Indian Ocean. Soviet-Polish-East German joint naval maneuvers were held in September in the Baltic Sea.

Marshal Georgi K. Zhukov, the greatest Soviet army commander of World War II, died in Moscow on June 18 at the age of 77.

Space Program. During 1974 the USSR successfully launched at least 46 earth satellites, including 35 unmanned Cosmos research rockets, 4 Molniya communications satellites, and 4 Meteor meteorological satellites. In addition, the orbital scientific station Salyut 3 was launched in June, and the Soyuz 14 with a two-man crew docked with it in July. However, the Soyuz 15 in August was unable to dock with an orbiting Salyut, and the Soyuz 16 in December did not try, although their two-man crews both returned safely to earth. Another unmanned orbital research station, Salyut 4, was launched successfully in December, and two cosmonauts aboard Soyuz 17 linked up with it on Jan. 12, 1975. Early in the year four space probes reached the vicinity of Mars. (See also SPACE EXPLORATION.)

GOVERNMENT AND POLITICS

New Supreme Soviet. On June 16 a new Supreme Soviet (parliament) was elected, consisting of 1,517 deputies, of whom 72% were members of the USSR Communist party. This newly elected legislature held its first meeting on July 25–26, reappointing Nikolai V. Podgorny as USSR president, Aleksei N. Kosygin as premier, and all ministers of the previous cabinet. Four former party Politburo members were dismissed from the Supreme Soviet Presidium (rump parliament): Anastas I. Mikoyan, who at age 78 was honorably retired; Pyotr Y. Shelest and Gennadi I. Voronov, both of whom opposed U. S.-USSR détente; and Yekaterina A. Furtseva, who was in disgrace because of her lavish living. Miss Furtseva died at age 63 on October 24 and was replaced as governmental minister of culture by Pyotr N. Demichev, a Communist party secretary who openly opposed any freedom for the arts.

TASS, FROM SOVFOTO

Red Square in Moscow undergoes extensive repairs and restoration.

On September 2 a marble monument replaced the simple tombstone over the grave of the late Soviet Premier Nikita S. Khrushchev. Part of the funds for the monument were provided by his relatives and part by the Soviet government.

Communist Party. Statistics released in 1974 indicated that the Soviet Communist party had 15 million members, of whom 40% were workers; 15%, collective farmers; 30%, middle class; and 15%, government or party officials. Two fifths of all Soviet Communist party members had no more than a grade school education, and only 23% were women.

Ecology. Safeguarding of human lives seemed to interest the Soviet government in 1974 more than environmental improvement. The Soviet press complained that cancer and heart failure were the two greatest killer-diseases in the country. A law in April provided 5 to 15 years of imprisonment for stealing narcotics and also decreed severe penalties for illegally manufacturing, growing, supplying, or possessing dangerous drugs.

The main Soviet environmental measure in 1974 was a joint treaty with Finland, Denmark, Sweden, Poland, and East and West Germany to lessen pollution of the Baltic Sea.

Minority Problems. In 1974 the Soviet press complained about widespread instances of anti-Russian nationalism in the Armenian, Azerbaidzhan, Georgian, Lithuanian, and Ukrainian Soviet republics. Several Armenians were arrested for forming an anti-Russian revolutionary group, as were several Lithuanians for starting an anti-Soviet underground magazine and many Ukrainian intellectuals for various anti-Russian activities.

CULTURE AND SOCIETY

Religion. In 1974, Soviet authorities harassed the Baptist, Georgian Orthodox, Jehovah's Witness, Pentecostal, Roman Catholic, and Uniate churches by arresting clergy and lay officials and sometimes taking children away from religious parents. Other faiths were less harassed. In May, Father Dmitri Dudko, a Russian Orthodox priest in Moscow, resigned from the priesthood after the Moscow Patriarch forbade him to continue holding popular question-and-answer meetings about religion.

The number of Soviet Jews permitted to emigrate from the USSR in 1974 was one third less than the 33,500 who left in 1973. Jews expressing a desire to emigrate often were dismissed from their jobs, heavily interrogated by the police, and sometimes arrested.

Intellectual Unrest. Soviet police made a strong attempt to suppress the illegal underground literature called *samizdat,* which publishes the reformist views of civil rights advocates, humanitarian Marxists, and isolationist Slavophiles. Among the many intellectuals imprisoned were Viktor Khaustov, for sending abroad a Soviet prison-camp diary; Gabriel Superfin, for having been author Aleksandr Solzhenitsyn's researcher; and psychologist Eduard Naumov, for maintaining contacts with foreign scientists.

In September an unofficial display of modern art in a vacant lot in Moscow was stopped by police using bulldozers and trucks, with four artists arrested. The U. S. government protested that police had roughed up three American newspaper correspondents at this gathering. The embarrassed Soviet government later allowed the same artists to hold a second, unrestricted art show in a Moscow park.

A new Soviet tactic in combating intellectual dissent became obvious during the year when many prominent dissenters were forced or permitted to leave the USSR, with little hope of return. Among those thus exiled were the Nobel Prize-winning author Solzhenitsyn (see BIOGRAPHY), the scientist Pavel Litvinov, the writers Vladimir E. Maksimov and Viktor Nekrasov, the poet Aleksandr Galich, the ballet star Valery Panov and his ballerina wife, Galina Ragozina, and the religious historian Anatoli Levitin-Krasnov.

Education. The Soviet press indicated in 1974 that one third of all Soviet workers and half of the collective farmers have no more than a grade school education. A decree in May ordered that more high school students work during their summer vacations. Another, in June, demanded improvement of college instruction in Marxism-Leninism by increasing the number of ideological courses.

Athletics. The Soviet government was delighted by the decision of the International Olympic Committee that Moscow would be the site for the 1980 summer Olympic Games.

ECONOMY

Industry. Soviet industrial growth in 1974 was about 8%, which was well above the 6.8% that had been planned for the year and the 7.4% actually achieved in 1973. The USSR continued to be a world leader in output of coal, iron ore, cement, and chemical fertilizer, and for the first time outproduced the United States in petroleum.

Despite these successes, the Soviet press complained that most factories were idle 10% of their working time because of interruptions of supplies, and that industry suffered from shortages of fuel, electricity, cement, stone, leather, chemical fibers, plastics, paper, and machinery for the woodworking, sugar refining, chemical, and aircraft plants. (See also INDUSTRIAL REVIEW.)

Agriculture. Because of bad weather conditions, the 1974 grain harvest was admitted to be only 195.5 million metric tons, compared with the record crop of 222.5 million tons in 1973. The smaller grain harvest explains why grain imports continued and Soviet citizens were urged to conserve bread. Potato and sugar-beet crops also slumped, although the Soviet press gave no precise statistics on the admitted decline. In contrast, the cotton crop of 8.4 million tons was the largest in history.

A landmark decree of April 3 provided for immense governmental investment during 1976–80 for agricultural development of the partially wooded farmlands of north-central European USSR, where production has declined in comparison with Czarist and early Soviet times.

Transport. In 1974, by purchasing ships from 13 foreign countries, the Soviet merchant marine was the fifth largest in the world, with 2,000 vessels. This merchant fleet had one third of the world's passenger-carrying capacity, and in 1974 transported 45 million people, mostly on short coastal trips.

Aeroflot, the official Soviet airline, claimed in 1974 to be the world's largest airline, transporting 90 million passengers. In October, Aeroflot opened the world's first supersonic air route, from Moscow to Central Asia.

Trade. The USSR increased its foreign trade by 20% in 1974, with much of the increase being with Western capitalist countries. The chief capitalist trading partners were West Germany, Japan, and the United States. Soviet financial status for foreign trade greatly increased —first, by the rise in the price of gold, which increased the value of Soviet gold stocks to $8 billion, and second, by the higher oil prices, which earned the USSR at least $1 billion from oil exports.

Standard of Living. The Soviet standard of living remained mediocre in 1974, the average urban monthly wage being 139.5 rubles ($187). The Soviet press complained about store shortages of eggs, meat, milk, fruit, potatoes, vegetables, canned fish, butter, salad greens, beer, furs, rubber footwear, metal dishes, rugs, and door locks. Many provincial cities admittedly had insufficient paved streets, running water, buses, non-food shops, service establishments, gasoline stations, and children's nurseries. Almost absent in rural villages were cooking gas, steam heat, running water, and sewers. Urban housing, as before, remained overcrowded, with long waiting lists for new apartments.

ELLSWORTH RAYMOND, *New York University*

Puzzled Muscovites look at an abstract painting in an exhibit of abstract art. The show was granted official permission after police had broken up an earlier one.

UPI

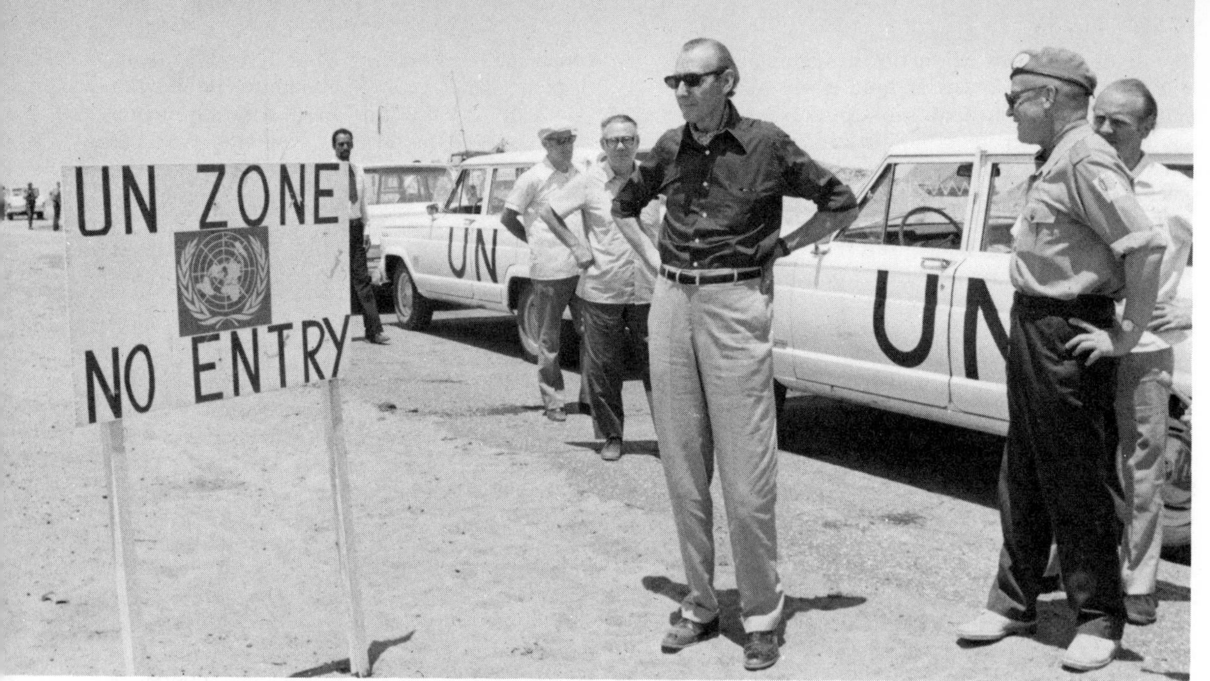

Y. NAGATA/UNITED NATIONS

UNITED NATIONS

UN Secretary General Kurt Waldheim (*center*), while on an extended tour of the Middle East in June, inspects a UN Emergency Force (UNEF) position in the UN buffer zone in Sinai, manned by members of the UNEF Nepalese Battalion.

Events at the United Nations in 1974, particularly during the 29th session of the General Assembly, increasingly demonstrated the changes in the composition of the organization since its founding in 1945. No longer are the original members able to influence the course of debate decisively, or the resolutions adopted, in the way that they once did. National liberation movements and regional organizations have produced a Third World of emerging nations, each of which, in the General Assembly and in all other UN bodies except the Security Council, has a vote equally as effective as those of the powers that created the UN. The extent of the change was epitomized by the election of Abdelaziz Bouteflika, the Algerian foreign minister, as president of the Assembly's 29th session, not so much because he was elected but because he was elected unanimously.

This new domination of the world body by the developing countries, many of them very small, was the subject of a strongly worded address by John A. Scali, chief U. S. delegate, on December 6. Warning against what he termed the "tyranny of the majority," he declared that the United Nations was losing the support of the American people. He charged that the organization was adopting "one-sided, unrealistic resolutions that cannot be implemented," some of which ignore its own Charter. His speech, which reflected similar criticism by Britain, France, and West Germany, was promptly denounced by spokesmen for the nonaligned countries.

Notable during the year was the approval of a draft definition of aggression, approved by the drafting committee on April 12 and by the Legal Committee in November, some 24 years after the original Soviet draft was submitted in 1950. Hardly less important was the work of the third Law of the Sea conference in Caracas from June 21 to August 29. (See also ENVIRONMENT; LAW—*International Law*.)

A UN World Food Conference held in Rome from November 2 to 16 ended with a call for the creation of a World Food Council to coordinate food production. The conference also recommended an international fund for agricultural development and a food aid program for developing countries. (See also FOOD.)

The principal activities of the United Nations in its 29th year are summarized below under the following headings: (1) General Assembly; (2) Security Council; (3) Economic and Social Council; (4) Trusteeship and Decolonization; and (5) International Court of Justice.

GENERAL ASSEMBLY

The 6th special session of the General Assembly, called to study problems of raw materials and development, opened on April 9. Leopoldo Benites of Ecuador was elected president by acclamation.

Two important resolutions were adopted on

May 1, one a Declaration on the Establishment of a new Economic Order, and the other containing a program of action for achieving the new order. The new economic order was to be based on equity, sovereign equality, interdependence, common interest, and cooperation among all states. The program of action covered such subjects as raw materials, food, general trade, transportation, insurance, and reform of the international monetary system.

The General Assembly opened its 29th session on September 17. In an acceptance speech more political in tone than those of his predecessors, the new president, Bouteflika, opened up the question of self-determination for the Palestinians, thus foreshadowing what became the most remarkable part of the Assembly's deliberations. Three new members—Bangladesh, Grenada, and Guinea-Bissau—were admitted on the opening day, bringing the total membership to 138.

South Africa. The credentials of the South African delegation were rejected by the Assembly on September 27 by a vote of 98 to 23, with 14 abstentions. A request for a Security Council review of the relationship between the UN and South Africa was approved by a vote of 125 in favor, with only South Africa against, and 9 abstentions. Three vetoes in the Security Council in October prevented South Africa's expulsion from the UN (see *Security Council,* below). South Africa was, however, suspended from participation in the work of the current session of the Assembly by the Assembly itself in mid-November.

Cambodia. At its meeting on November 28, the Assembly called on all the powers influencing the parties to the Cambodian conflict to use their good offices for conciliation in order to restore peace. The action was taken by a margin of two votes—56 in favor, 54 against, and 24 abstentions. The resolution was a compromise draft, thereby precluding a vote on a 37-nation draft that proposed that the Assembly acknowledge the government of Prince Sihanouk as the legitimate Cambodian government and seat its representatives in the UN.

Palestinian Liberation Organization. The General Assembly, in an unprecedented move, invited the leader of the Palestine Liberation Organization, Yasir Arafat, to take part in its debate on Palestine. Amid extraordinary security precautions, Arafat appeared before the Assembly on November 13.

The debate continued until November 22, when two resolutions were approved, the first of which asserted the Palestinian people's right to self-determination, national independence, and sovereignty, and identified the PLO as "the representative of the people of Palestine." The resolution was adopted by a vote of 89 to 8, with 37 abstentions. The second resolution, adopted by a vote of 95 to 17, with 19 abstentions, granted the PLO permanent observer status in the General Assembly and gave the movement the right to participate in international conferences under UN auspices. In statements before and after the votes, a number of countries made it clear that their votes did not question the statehood of Israel, which was strongly opposed to the Assembly's action.

Cyprus. A compromise resolution on Cyprus was adopted on November 1 by a unanimous vote. It called on all states to respect the sovereignty, territorial integrity, independence, and nonalignment of Cyprus, and called on the Greek and Turkish Cypriots to negotiate a "mutually acceptable political settlement."

New Economic Charter. A Charter of Economic Rights and Duties of States was adopted by a vote of 120 to 6, with 10 abstentions, on December 12. The declaration, which is not legally binding, would grant every nation full sovereignty over its resources, wealth, and economy and provide for the regulation of foreign investment and multinational firms. The controversial document was sponsored by Third World countries, supported by Communist members, but was strongly opposed by the big industrial nations which argued that its provisions would discourage foreign investment in the developing countries.

SECURITY COUNCIL

The two major problems with which the Security Council was concerned were the continuing question of a settlement in the Middle East and the reestablishment in Cyprus of a stable situation acceptable to all the parties concerned following the events of July and August.

The Council decided to include Chinese as one of its working languages in a resolution adopted on January 17.

Middle East. The Security Council was informed by UN Secretary General Kurt Waldheim on January 18 that an Egyptian-Israeli Agreement on Disengagement of Forces had been signed that day. A similar agreement between Israel and Syria was signed on May 31, following which the Council approved a resolution setting up a UN Disengagement Force to serve as a buffer between Syrian and Israeli troops in the Golan Heights area.

The Council met four times during April in response to a request contained in a letter from Lebanon, dated April 13, protesting Israeli raids against six Lebanese villages in reprisal for an Arab guerrilla attack on the Israeli village of Kiryat Shemona. A resolution condemning Israel's violation of Lebanon's territorial integrity and sovereignty was passed on April 24 by a vote of 13 to 0, with China and Iraq abstaining.

A complaint by Iraq concerning incidents on its frontier with Iran was discussed by the Council at meetings in February. A consensus, adopted on the 28th, found that the cause of the incidents lay in the fact that the legal basis of the frontier was contested. The secretary

ORGANIZATION OF THE UNITED NATIONS

THE SECRETARIAT

Secretary General: Kurt Waldheim (until Dec. 31, 1976)

THE GENERAL ASSEMBLY (1974)

President: Abdelaziz Bouteflika (Algeria). The 138 member-nations were as follows:

Afghanistan
Albania
Algeria
Argentina
Australia
Austria
Bahamas
Bahrain
Bangladesh
Barbados
Belgium
Belorussian SSR
Bhutan
Bolivia
Botswana
Brazil
Bulgaria
Burma
Burundi
Cambodia (Khmer Republic)
Cameroon
Canada
Central African Republic
Chad
Chile
China, People's Republic of
Colombia
Congo
Costa Rica
Cuba
Cyprus
Czechoslovakia
Dahomey
Denmark
Dominican Republic
Ecuador
Egypt
El Salvador
Equatorial Guinea
Ethiopia
Fiji
Finland
France
Gabon
Gambia
German Democratic Republic
Germany, Federal Republic of
Ghana
Greece
Grenada
Guatemala
Guinea
Guinea-Bissau
Guyana
Haiti
Honduras
Hungary
Iceland
India
Indonesia
Iran
Iraq
Ireland
Israel
Italy
Ivory Coast
Jamaica
Japan
Jordan
Kenya
Kuwait
Laos
Lebanon
Lesotho
Liberia
Libyan Arab Republic
Luxembourg
Madagascar (Malagasy Republic)
Malawi
Malaysia (Malaya)
Maldives
Mali
Malta
Mauritania
Mauritius
Mexico
Mongolia
Morocco
Nepal
Netherlands
New Zealand
Nicaragua
Niger
Nigeria
Norway
Oman
Pakistan
Panama
Paraguay
Peru
Philippines
Poland
Portugal
Qatar
Rumania
Rwanda
Saudi Arabia
Senegal
Sierra Leone
Singapore
Somalia
South Africa
Spain
Sri Lanka (Ceylon)
Sudan
Swaziland
Sweden
Syrian Arab Republic
Tanzania, United Republic of
Thailand
Togo
Trinidad and Tobago
Tunisia
Turkey
Uganda
Ukrainian SSR
USSR
United Arab Emirates
United Kingdom
United States
Upper Volta
Uruguay
Venezuela
Yemen
Yemen, Democratic
Yugoslavia
Zaire
Zambia

COMMITTEES

General: Composed of 25 members as follows: The General Assembly president; the 17 General Assembly vice presidents (heads of delegations or their deputies of Austria, Central African Republic, China, France, Federal Republic of Germany, Haiti, Ivory Coast, Lebanon, Mexico, Nepal, Nicaragua, Philippines, Rumania, USSR, United Kingdom, United States, Zambia); and the chairmen of the following main committees, which are composed of all 138 member countries:

First (Political and Security): Carlos Ortiz de Rozas (Argentina).

Special Political: Per Lind (Sweden).

Second (Economic and Financial): Jihad Karam (Iraq).

Third (Social, Humanitarian and Cultural): Mrs. Aminata Marico (Mali).

Fourth (Trust and Non-Self-Governing Territories): Butantyn Dashtseren (Mongolia).

Fifth (Administrative and Budgetary): Costa P. Caranicas (Greece).

Sixth (Legal): Milan Sahovic (Yugoslavia).

THE SECURITY COUNCIL (1975)

(Membership ends on December 31 of the year noted: asterisks indicate permanent membership)

Belorussian SSR (1975)
Cameroon (1975)
China*
Costa Rica (1975)
France*
Guyana (1976)
Iraq (1975)
Italy (1976)
Japan (1976)
Mauritania (1975)
Sweden (1976)
Tanzania (1976)
USSR*
United Kingdom*
United States*

Military Staff Committee: Representatives of chiefs of staffs of permanent members.

Disarmament Commission: Representatives of all UN members.

THE ECONOMIC AND SOCIAL COUNCIL (1974)

President: Aarno Karhilo (Finland), 56th and 57th sessions (1974). (Membership ends on December 31 of the year noted; asterisks indicate the 27 additional members elected for terms beginning Jan. 1, 1974)

Algeria (1975)
Argentina (1974)*
Australia (1976)
Belgium (1976)*
Bolivia (1974)
Brazil (1975)
Burundi (1974)
Canada (1974)*
Chile (1974)
China (1974)
Colombia (1976)*
Congo (1976)
Czechoslovakia (1974)*
Democratic Yemen (1976)
Egypt (1976)*
Ethiopia (1974)*
Fiji (1975)*
Finland (1974)
France (1975)
German Democratic Republic (1976)*
Germany, Federal Republic of (1975)*
Guatemala (1975)*
Guinea (1975)*
India (1974)*
Indonesia (1975)*
Iran (1976)*
Italy (1976)*
Ivory Coast (1976)*
Jamaica (1976)*
Japan (1974)
Jordan (1976)*
Kenya (1974)*
Liberia (1976)
Mali (1975)
Mexico (1976)
Mongolia (1975)
Netherlands (1975)
Pakistan (1974)*
Poland (1974)
Rumania (1976)
Senegal (1975)*
Spain (1975)
Sweden (1974)*
Thailand (1976)
Trinidad and Tobago (1975)
Turkey (1975)*
Uganda (1975)
USSR (1974)
United Kingdom (1974)
United States (1976)
Venezuela (1975)*
Yugoslavia (1975)*
Zaire (1974)*
Zambia (1976)

THE TRUSTEESHIP COUNCIL (1973–74)

President: Sir Laurence McIntyre (Australia), 41st session (1974).

Australia[1]
China[2]
France[2]
USSR[2]
United Kingdom[2]
United States[1]

[1] Administers Trust Territory. [2] Permanent member of Security Council not administering Trust Territory.

THE INTERNATIONAL COURT OF JUSTICE

(Membership ends on February 5 of the year noted)

President: Manfred Lechs (Poland, 1976)
Vice President: Fouad Ammoun (Lebanon, 1976)

Isaac Forster (Senegal, 1982)
André Gros (France, 1982)
César Bengzon (Philippines, 1976)
Sture Petren (Sweden, 1976)
Charles D. Onyeama (Nigeria, 1976)
Hardy C. Dillard (U. S., 1979)
Louis Ignacio-Pinto (Dahomey, 1979)
Federico de Castro (Spain, 1979)
Platon Morozov (USSR, 1979)
Eduardo Jiménez de Aréchaga (Uruguay, 1979)
Sir Humphrey Waldock (United Kingdom, 1982)
Nagendra Singh (India, 1982)
José María Ruda (Argentina, 1982)

SPECIALIZED AGENCIES

Food and Agriculture Organization (FAO); Intergovernmental Maritime Consultative Organization (IMCO); International Atomic Energy Agency (IAEA); International Bank for Reconstruction and Development (World Bank, IBRD); International Civil Aviation Organization (ICAO); International Development Association (IDA); International Finance Corporation (IFC); International Labor Organization (ILO); International Monetary Fund (IMF); International Telecommunication Union (ITU); United Nations Educational, Scientific and Cultural Organization (UNESCO); Universal Postal Union (UPU); United Nations International Children's Emergency Fund (UNICEF); World Health Organization (WHO); World Meteorological Organization (WMO).

general was requested to appoint a special representative to investigate and report within three months. A four-point agreement between Iraq and Iran, aimed at de-escalating the situation, was endorsed by the Council on May 28.

Already scheduled to meet on July 20 to consider a resolution calling for the withdrawal of Greek army officers serving with the Cyprus National Guard, the Council was confronted with the outbreak of hostilities in Cyprus that began July 15. It then passed the first of a series of eight resolutions on the crisis which it adopted between July 20 and August 30. Passed unanimously, it called for a cease-fire, demanded the end of foreign military intervention, and called on Greece, Turkey, and the United Kingdom to enter into negotiations for the restoration of peace. The subsequent resolutions were designed to achieve the same end. Two resolutions were adopted on August 15, one insisting on the implementation of the previous resolutions, and the other demanding that all parties respect the international status of the UN forces in Cyprus and cooperate with them. The seventh resolution, adopted on August 16, recorded the Council's formal disapproval of the unilateral military action taken in Cyprus. The final resolution, on August 30, requested the secretary general to submit a report on the refugees and to continue to provide emergency UN humanitarian assistance.

South Vietnam Complaint against China. On January 20, South Vietnam charged China with violating its territorial sovereignty by attempting to seize three islands in the Paracels group in the South China Sea on January 19–20. Five days later, however, the attempt to have the complaint considered was abandoned because of China's veto in the Council.

Rhodesia. Rhodesia was only of minor concern to the Security Council in 1974. The 6th report of the Council's committee, issued on January 3, showed no progress toward a solution of the problem. Its sanctions committee issued a communiqué on May 24 expressing concern over U. S. imports of Rhodesian chrome ore and other materials which it wished to see stopped; the Council expressed similar concern again during the month of October.

South Africa. Following the General Assembly's rejection of the credentials of the South African representatives, the Security Council undertook a review of the relationship between the UN and South Africa on October 18–30. A resolution to expel South Africa from the United Nations was blocked only by vetoes on the part of the United States, the United Kingdom, and France.

ECONOMIC AND SOCIAL COUNCIL

Organizational meetings of the 56th session of the Economic and Social Council took place in New York on January 7–10, when Aarno Karhilo (Finland) was elected president for 1974 by acclamation. The substantive part of the session took place in New York from April 9 to May 10, while the 57th session was held at Geneva from July 3 to August 2.

The 56th session in April–May called for the creation of an international fertilizer pool and a greater volume of assistance to the drought-stricken countries of the Sahelian region of the continent of Africa. The session also acted on human rights issues, on narcotic drugs, and on plans to improve the status of women by convening an international conference on women. At Geneva, in July–August, the 57th session adopted an omnibus resolution on the Program of Action on the Establishment of a New Economic Order. Other resolutions adopted covered multinational corporations, operational activities for development, international environmental cooperation, and assistance in cases of natural disasters.

A World Population Conference was held in Bucharest, Rumania, on August 19–30. It adopted a world population plan containing recommendations and guidelines for a better quality of life and rapid socio-economic development for all peoples. (See POPULATION.)

TRUSTEESHIP AND DECOLONIZATION

The Trusteeship Council met for its 41st session on June 3–14, when it adopted a report on the Trust Territories of the Pacific Islands administered by the United States. In October it recommended to the General Assembly that it agree to the termination of the trusteeship agreement for Papua-New Guinea, administered by Australia, as of the date of the territory's independence, which is to take place following the enactment of a constitution.

The Special Committee on the Situation with Regard to the Implementation of the Declaration on the Granting of Independence to Colonial Countries and Peoples (the Special Committee on Decolonization) met frequently during the year. Salim A. Salim of Tanzania was elected chairman unanimously for the third year in succession. The committee's main concern during the year was the situation in the Portuguese territories in Africa.

INTERNATIONAL COURT OF JUSTICE

At the beginning of 1974, the International Court of Justice had under consideration the nuclear tests case against France, brought by Australia and New Zealand, and the fisheries jurisdiction cases brought by the United Kingdom and West Germany against Iceland.

In an unusual step, the court adopted a resolution on March 21 expressing strong disapproval of "the making, circulation, or publication of all statements anticipating or purporting to anticipate the manner in which the Judges of the Court will cast their votes in a pending case." This was occasioned by press reports in Australia and the Netherlands, and a statement by the Australian prime minister, that the court was expected to decide in Australia's favor in the nuclear tests case. Open hearings on the case were held between July 4 and July 11, but no decision was handed down.

Judgment in the fisheries jurisdiction cases was rendered on July 25. The judgments were identical in both cases, as was the 10-to-4 vote of the judges. The court held that Iceland could not keep United Kingdom or West German vessels from areas between the 12- and 50-mile limits. The court further held that the United Kingdom and Iceland, and West Germany and Iceland, were under a mutual obligation to undertake negotiations to find an equitable solution to their differences. (See also LAW—*International Law.*)

RICHARD E. WEBB
Former Director, Reference and Library Division
British Information Services, New York

WIDE WORLD

Following the change in the U. S. presidency, a portrait of President Ford replaces one of former President Nixon at the U. S. Embassy in Bonn, West Germany.

UNITED STATES

For Americans 1974 was a year in which their country seemed to plunge from one crisis into another. First there was Watergate, climaxed by Richard Nixon's resignation as president under the threat of impeachment. A brief period of relief followed, but then the new president, Gerald Ford, found himself involved with difficulties of his own.

Critics complained of a vacuum of leadership, and never was leadership more badly needed. The shortage of energy posed a critical problem. Most troublesome of all was the economy, whose complex weaknesses produced soaring inflation and deepening recession at the same time.

A study of public attitudes, *State of the Nation 1974*, by William Watts and Lloyd A. Free, reported that as Americans looked around them "they were saying in no uncertain terms that there was indeed something 'deeply wrong' with their country."

DOMESTIC AFFAIRS

The Presidency. Underlying much of the difficulty were the problems of the presidency, the institution upon which the nation has come almost solely to depend for its fundamental direction and purpose.

During his seven months in office in 1974, Nixon sought to carry on with his normal responsibilities as chief executive. In his State of the Union address on January 30 he outlined ten ambitious goals for 1974, covering a broad gamut of national concerns ranging from energy, the economy, and health care to tax reform, urban transit, and personal privacy.

But the threat of impeachment preoccupied Nixon and his close advisers until the day he quit. And meanwhile his sinking prestige robbed him of the leverage with Congress he needed to reach his goals.

His successor, Gerald Ford, arrived in the White House on August 9 like a breath of fresh air. As the first president who had never stood for office in a national election, he acknowledged the limitations of his mandate. "I am acutely aware that you have not elected me as your President by your ballots," he told the country in his brief inaugural address. "So I ask you to confirm me as your President with your prayers."

Ford proclaimed the end of the Watergate "nightmare," asserted his belief that "truth is the glue that holds governments together," and vowed to make "openness and candor" the hallmarks of his administration.

The country found Ford's direct and modest style refreshing, and in his first 30 days in office he won widespread public support.

Then, on September 8, came his unconditional pardon of Nixon. His startling decision abruptly ended the presidential honeymoon with

—— UNITED STATES • Information Highlights ——

Official Name: United States of America.
Area: 3,615,123 square miles (9,363,169 sq km).
Population (Jan. 1, 1975 est.): 213,203,059.
Chief Cities (1970 census): Washington, D. C., the capital, 756,510; New York, 7,895,563; Chicago, 3,369,359; Los Angeles, 2,816,061; Philadelphia, 1,950,098.
Government: *Head of state and government*, Gerald R. Ford, president (took office Aug. 1974). *Legislature*—Congress: Senate and House of Representatives.
Monetary Unit: Dollar.
Gross National Product (3d quarter 1974 est.): $1,411,-600,000,000.
Manufacturing (major products): Motor vehicles, aircraft, ships and railroad equipment, industrial machinery, processed foods, chemicals, electrical equipment and supplies, fabricated metals.
Major Agricultural Products: Wheat, rye, corn, barley, oats, soybeans, tobacco, cotton, sorghum.
Foreign Trade (1973): *Exports*, $71,314,000,000; *imports*, $69,121,000,000.

Congress, the press, and the country. Ford sought to defend and justify his action in a press conference and even in an unprecedented appearance before a House judiciary subcommittee. He said that he had acted "for the purpose of trying to heal the wounds throughout the country between Americans on one side of the issue or the other," and he denied that there had been any secret bargain or "deal" struck between him and Nixon.

Yet many Americans remained puzzled and disturbed by the President's intervention in the legal process. The pardon revived Watergate as a political issue, to the detriment of the Republicans. More than that, Ford's action, because it seemed to belie the atmosphere of cooperation and candor he had sought to foster, made him vulnerable to attack on other issues. It soon became difficult for the President to take any step of consequence without drawing criticism from one side or another, and sometimes from all sides.

One example was his program of clemency for the 28,000 or more Vietnam War draft evaders and deserters, which he announced on September 16. The requirements for clemency are swearing an oath of allegiance to the United States and performing up to 24 months of public service. A nine-member clemency board was established to review cases of those already convicted. His purpose, Ford said, was to "do everything in my power to bind up the nation's wounds." House Republican leader John Rhodes called the program "practical and fair." But both the American Legion and the Veterans of Foreign Wars denounced the proposal.

UNITED STATES CABINET MEMBERS
(as of Dec. 31, 1974)

Secretary of State—Henry A. Kissinger
Secretary of the Treasury—William E. Simon
Secretary of Defense—James R. Schlesinger
Attorney General—William B. Saxbe*
Secretary of the Interior—Rogers C. B. Morton
Secretary of Agriculture—Earl L. Butz
Secretary of Commerce—Frederick B. Dent
Secretary of Labor—Peter J. Brennan
Secretary of Health, Education, and Welfare—Caspar W. Weinberger
Secretary of Housing and Urban Development—James T. Lynn*
Secretary of Transportation—Claude S. Brinegar*

* Announced plans to resign.

For their part, draft evaders and deserters, living in exile in Canada and Sweden, also attacked the Ford plan. They charged that it was too punitive, and that accepting its conditions amounted to an admission of guilt.

Ford was also criticized by some for failing to move swiftly enough to replace Nixon appointees in his administration. But when he did pick his own men, he sometimes ran into difficulty. Andrew E. Gibson, whom Ford nominated to be head of the new Federal Energy Administration, asked to be withdrawn from consideration when it was learned that he would also be receiving $88,000 a year in severance benefits from an oil transportation firm. Ford had to withdraw the nomination of former top Nixon aide Peter M. Flanigan as ambassador to Spain because of allegations that Flanigan had

In Pittsburgh, Pa., demonstrators protest President Ford's pardon of Richard Nixon for all crimes he "committed" or took part in as president.

WALLY MCNAMEE, NEWSWEEK

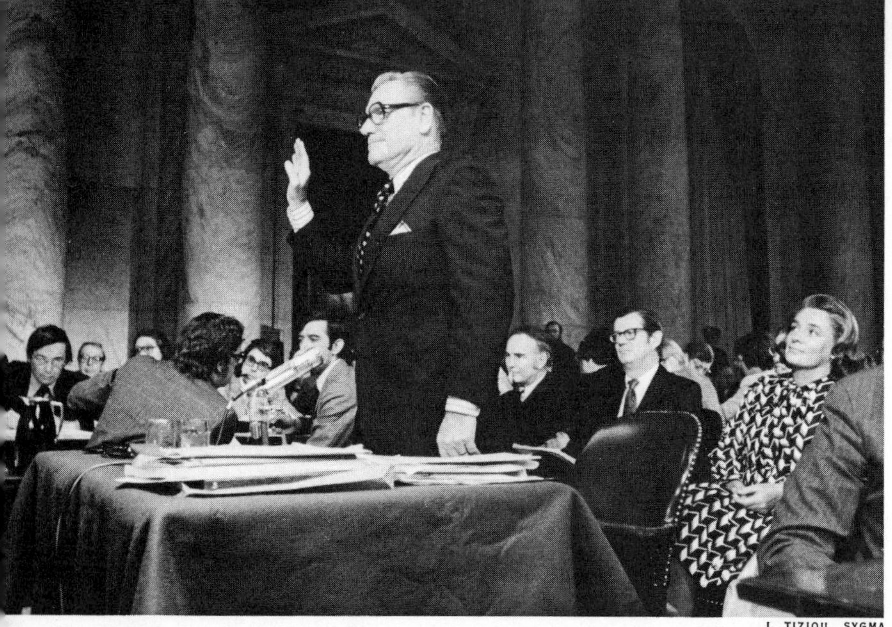

J. TIZIOU, SYGMA

With Mrs. Rockefeller at his side, Vice President-designate Nelson A. Rockefeller takes oath prior to testifying before Senate Rules Committee. Following extensive hearings, Congress approved the Rockefeller appointment on December 19.

sought ambassadorial appointments for big contributors to the Nixon campaign.

The Vice Presidency. It was Ford's most significant nomination that caused the most controversy. This was his choice, under the 25th Amendment to the Constitution, of former New York Gov. Nelson A. Rockefeller to replace him as vice president. The nomination, announced August 20, at first drew wide acclaim because of Rockefeller's experience both in the federal government and in New York state.

But then it was disclosed that Rockefeller had made substantial gifts, totaling about $2 million, either outright or in the form of forgiven loans, to a number of associates prominent in public affairs. Among them were Secretary of State Henry Kissinger, former New York Republican Chairman Judson Morhouse, and New York Port Authority Chairman William J. Ronan.

The controversy over the propriety of these actions was compounded when it was disclosed that Rockefeller had arranged financing, through his brother Laurance, of a derogatory biography of former U. S. Supreme Court Justice Arthur Goldberg in 1970, when Goldberg ran unsuccessfully against Rockefeller for governor of New York.

Recalled to testify before the Senate Rules Committee, Rockefeller denied that his generosity to these officials was "intended to influence or reward their official conduct." He insisted instead that he had merely tried to relieve the personal problems or family "tragedies" of loyal associates. As for his role in getting backing for the book on Goldberg, Rockefeller said: "Let's face it, I made a mistake." Later, appearing before the House Judiciary Committee, Rockefeller promised to put his vast financial holdings in a blind trust when he became vice president, to avoid any conflict of interest.

Rockefeller finally was confirmed by Congress, and he took the oath of office on December 19. But opinion polls indicated that public support for his nomination had declined, suggesting that his political future, and his usefulness to the Ford administration, might have been damaged by the revelations over the uses of his wealth.

Congress. If Watergate cast a shadow over the executive branch, it also intruded on the lawmakers on Capitol Hill. The lengthy impeachment inquiry by the House Judiciary Committee and preparations for the expected impeachment debate on the House floor were serious distractions from the legislative routine. Moreover, the struggle over impeachment colored the overall legislative process during the Nixon administration, adding to the normal tensions between a Republican president and a Democratic-controlled Congress.

Ford's succession to the presidency, after his 25 years of service in the House of Representatives, at first appeared to improve the situation considerably. In his first address to both houses of Congress, on August 12, the new chief executive promised "communication, conciliation, compromise, and cooperation." He added: "I do not want a honeymoon with you. I want a good marriage."

But this harmonious atmosphere was soon marred by discord. The general negative reaction to the Nixon pardon affected Ford's relationship with Capitol Hill. Many lawmakers also became irritated at what they considered ill-considered presidential vetoes.

Three of Ford's first 13 vetoes were overridden into law by more than two-thirds majorities of both houses. The first override was in October, on Ford's veto of a railroad retirement bill. In November both houses also overrode presidential vetoes of a proposal to broaden the

Freedom of Information Act—to ease access to government files by press and public—and of a measure to reorder federal vocational rehabilitation programs. On the latter proposal, the vote in the Senate was 90 to 1 against the President. Contributing to the rebellious mood in the Congress was the fact that the information act and the vocational rehabilitation bill had met with almost no opposition from either party when they originally were approved by Congress.

Despite the friction with the executive branch, Congress did carve out some major lawmaking achievements. Spurred on by the excesses of Watergate fund-raising and spending, it approved a long-debated campaign reform law, which the President signed on October 15. The new law, taking effect in 1975, will probably revolutionize campaign financing. It provides for spending ceilings and public funding of presidential campaigns, drawing on the $1 income tax check-off fund established in 1971. Major party nominees for the White House will be able to receive $20 million each from the check-off fund, which will be the ceiling on what they can spend.

Candidates for a presidential nomination can spend up to $10 million, plus a 20 percent allowance for fund-raising expenses. Qualified candidates can receive up to $5 million in government grants, which are available for matching individual contributions up to $250. Spending ceilings also were set for House and Senate races, although candidates for these offices will not receive federal funding.

Individual contributions are limited to $25,000 to all federal candidates in any election

MICHAEL BUDRYS, CHICAGO TRIBUNE

As a protest against high feed prices, calves are shot to death by farmers in the Midwest.

A cartoonist's view of the Ford button campaign against inflation. WIN is an acronym for Whip Inflation Now. Despite much campaigning by the President, Democrats scored major gains in November elections.

EDITORIAL CARTOON BY PAT OLIPHANT © THE DENVER POST; REPRINTED WITH PERMISSION OF LOS ANGELES TIMES SYNDICATE

94th CONGRESS OF THE U.S.

SENATE MEMBERSHIP

(As of January 1975: 61 Democrats, 38 Republicans, 1 vacancy—election in doubt)

Letters after senators' names refer to party affiliation—D for Democrat, R for Republican. Single asterisk (*) denotes term expiring in January 1977; double asterisk (**), term expiring in January 1979; triple asterisk (***), term expiring in January 1981.

ALABAMA
**J. Sparkman, D
***J. B. Allen, D

ALASKA
**T. Stevens, R
***M. Gravel, D

ARIZONA
*P. J. Fannin, R
***B. Goldwater, R

ARKANSAS
**J. L. McClellan, D
***Dale Bumpers, D

CALIFORNIA
***A. Cranston, D
*J. V. Tunney, D

COLORADO
**F. K. Haskell, D
***Gary Hart, D

CONNECTICUT
***A. A. Ribicoff, D
*L. P. Weicker, Jr., R

DELAWARE
*W. V. Roth, Jr., R
**J. R. Biden, Jr., D

FLORIDA
*L. Chiles, D
***Richard Stone, D

GEORGIA
***H. E. Talmadge, D
**S. A. Nunn, D

HAWAII
*H. L. Fong, R
***D. K. Inouye, D

IDAHO
***F. Church, D
**J. A. McClure, R

ILLINOIS
**C. H. Percy, R
***A. E. Stevenson III, D

INDIANA
*V. Hartke, D
***B. Bayh, D

IOWA
**R. Clark, D
***J. C. Culver, D

KANSAS
**J. B. Pearson, R
***R. Dole, R

KENTUCKY
**W. Huddleston, D
***W. H. Ford, D

LOUISIANA
***R. B. Long, D
**J. B. Johnston, Jr., D

MAINE
*E. S. Muskie, D
**W. D. Hathaway, D

MARYLAND
***C. McC. Mathias, Jr., R
*J. G. Beall, Jr., R

MASSACHUSETTS
*E. M. Kennedy, D
**E. W. Brooke, R

MICHIGAN
*P. A. Hart, D
**R. P. Griffin, R

MINNESOTA
**W. F. Mondale, D
*H. H. Humphrey, D

MISSISSIPPI
**J. O. Eastland, D
*J. C. Stennis, D

MISSOURI
*S. Symington, D
***T. F. Eagleton, D

MONTANA
*M. Mansfield, D
**L. Metcalf, D

NEBRASKA
*R. L. Hruska, R
**C. T. Curtis, R

NEVADA
*H. W. Cannon, D
***Paul Laxalt, R

NEW HAMPSHIRE
**T. J. McIntyre, D
***Vacant

NEW JERSEY
**C. P. Case, Jr., R
*H. A. Williams, Jr., D

NEW MEXICO
*J. M. Montoya, D
**P. V. Domenici, R

NEW YORK
***J. K. Javits, R
*J. L. Buckley, R[1]

NORTH CAROLINA
**J. Helms, R
***Robert Morgan, D

NORTH DAKOTA
***M. R. Young, R
*Q. N. Burdick, D

OHIO
*R. Taft, Jr., R
***J. H. Glenn, Jr., D

OKLAHOMA
***H. Bellmon, R
**D. F. Bartlett, R

OREGON
**M. O. Hatfield, R
***B. Packwood, R

PENNSYLVANIA
*H. Scott, R
***R. S. Schweiker, R

RHODE ISLAND
*J. O. Pastore, D
**C. Pell, D

SOUTH CAROLINA
**S. Thurmond, R
***E. F. Hollings, D

SOUTH DAKOTA
***G. S. McGovern, D
**J. G. Abourezk, D

TENNESSEE
**H. H. Baker, Jr., R
*W. E. Brock 3d, R

TEXAS
**J. G. Tower, R
*L. M. Bentsen, D

UTAH
*F. E. Moss, D
***Jake Garn, R

VERMONT
*R. T. Stafford, R
***P. J. Leahy, D

VIRGINIA
*H. F. Byrd, Jr., D[2]
**W. L. Scott, R

WASHINGTON
***W. G. Magnuson, D
*H. M. Jackson, D

WEST VIRGINIA
**J. Randolph, D
*R. C. Byrd, D

WISCONSIN
*W. Proxmire, D
***G. Nelson, D

WYOMING
*G. W. McGee, D
**C. P. Hansen, R

[1] Ran as a Conservative. [2] Ran as an Independent.

HOUSE MEMBERSHIP

(As of January 1975: 291 Democrats, 144 Republicans)

"At-L." in place of congressional district number means "representative at large." Asterisk (*) before name indicates elected Nov. 5, 1974; all others were reelected.

ALABAMA
1. J. Edwards, R
2. W. L. Dickinson, R
3. W. Nichols, D
4. T. Bevill, D
5. R. E. Jones, D
6. J. H. Buchanan, Jr., R
7. W. Flowers, D

ALASKA
At-L. D. Young, R

ARIZONA
1. J. J. Rhodes, R
2. M. K. Udall, D
3. S. Steiger, R
4. J. B. Conlan, R

ARKANSAS
1. W. V. Alexander, Jr., D
2. W. D. Mills, D
3. J. P. Hammerschmidt, R
4. R. H. Thornton, Jr., D

CALIFORNIA
1. H. T. Johnson, D
2. D. H. Clausen, R
3. J. E. Moss, D
4. R. L. Leggett, D
5. J. Burton, D
6. P. Burton, D
7. *George Miller, D
8. R. V. Dellums, D
9. F. H. Stark, D
10. D. Edwards, D
11. L. J. Ryan, D
12. P. N. McCloskey, Jr., R
13. *N. Y. Mineta, D
14. J. J. McFall, D
15. B. F. Sisk, D
16. B. L. Talcott, R
17. J. Krebs, D
18. W. M. Ketchum, R
19. R. J. Lagomarsino, R
20. B. M. Goldwater, Jr., R
21. J. C. Corman, D
22. C. J. Moorhead, R
23. T. M. Rees, D
24. *H. A. Waxman, D
25. E. R. Roybal, D
26. J. H. Rousselot, R
27. A. Bell, R
28. Y. B. Burke, D
29. A. F. Hawkins, D
30. G. E. Danielson, D
31. C. H. Wilson, D
32. G. M. Anderson, D
33. Del Clawson, R
34. *M. W. Hannaford, D
35. *J. Lloyd, D
36. G. E. Brown, Jr., D
37. J. L. Pettis, R
38. *J. M. Patterson, D
39. C. E. Wiggins, R
40. A. J. Hinshaw, R
41. B. Wilson, R
42. L. Van Deerlin, D
43. C. W. Burgener, R

COLORADO
1. P. Schroeder, D
2. *T. E. Wirth, D
3. F. E. Evans, D
4. J. P. Johnson, R
5. W. L. Armstrong, R

CONNECTICUT
1. W. R. Cotter, D
2. *C. J. Dodd, D
3. R. N. Giaimo, D
4. S. B. McKinney, R
5. R. A. Sarasin, R
6. *A. T. Moffett, D

DELAWARE
At-L. P. S. duPont 4th, R

FLORIDA
1. R. L. F. Sikes, D
2. Don Fuqua, D
3. C. E. Bennett, D
4. W. V. Chappell, Jr., D
5. *R. Kelly, R
6. C. W. Young, R
7. S. M. Gibbons, D
8. J. A. Haley, D
9. L. Frey, Jr., R
10. L. A. Bafalis, R
11. P. G. Rogers, D
12. J. H. Burke, R
13. W. Lehman, D
14. Claude Pepper, D
15. Dante B. Fascell, D

GEORGIA
1. R. B. Ginn, D
2. M. D. Mathis, D
3. J. Brinkley, D
4. *E. H. Levitas, D
5. A. Young, D
6. J. J. Flynt, Jr., D
7. *L. McDonald, D
8. W. S. Stuckey, Jr., D
9. P. M. Landrum, D
10. R. G. Stephens, Jr., D

HAWAII
1. S. M. Matsunaga, D
2. P. T. Mink, D

IDAHO
1. S. D. Symms, R
2. *G. Hansen, R

ILLINOIS
1. R. H. Metcalfe, D
2. M. F. Murphy, D
3. *M. A. Russo, D
4. E. J. Derwinski, R
5. J. C. Kluczynski, D
6. *H. J. Hyde, D
7. C. Collins, D
8. D. Rostenkowski, D
9. S. R. Yates, D
10. *A. J. Mikva, D
11. F. Annunzio, D
12. P. M. Crane, R
13. R. McClory, R
14. J. N. Erlenborn, R
15. *T. L. Hall, D
16. J. B. Anderson, R
17. G. M. O'Brien, R
18. R. H. Michel, R
19. T. Railsback, R
20. P. Findley, R
21. E. R. Madigan, R
22. G. E. Shipley, D
23. C. M. Price, D
24. *P. Simon, D

INDIANA
1. R. J. Madden, D
2. *F. J. Fithian, D
3. J. Brademas, D
4. J. E. Roush, D
5. E. H. Hillis, R
6. *D. W. Evans, D
7. J. T. Myers, R
8. *P. H. Hayes, D
9. L. H. Hamilton, D
10. *P. R. Sharp, D
11. *A. Jacobs, Jr., D

IOWA
1. E. Mezvinsky, D
2. *M. T. Blouin, D
3. *C. E. Grassley, R
4. N. Smith, D
5. *T. Harkin, D
6. *B. Bedell, D

KANSAS
1. K. G. Sebelius, R
2. *M. Keys, D
3. L. Winn, Jr., R
4. G. E. Shriver, R
5. J. Skubitz, R

KENTUCKY
1. *C. Hubbard, Jr., D
2. W. H. Natcher, D
3. R. L. Mazzoli, D
4. M. G. Snyder, R
5. T. L. Carter, R
6. J. B. Breckinridge, D
7. C. D. Perkins, D

LOUISIANA
1. F. E. Hébert, D
2. C. C. Boggs, D
3. D. C. Treen, R
4. J. D. Waggonner, Jr., D
5. O. E. Passman, D
6. Henson Moore, R[1]
7. J. B. Breaux, D
8. G. W. Long, D

MAINE
1. *D. F. Emery, R
2. W. S. Cohen, R

MARYLAND
1. R. E. Bauman, R
2. C. D. Long, D
3. P. S. Sarbanes, D
4. M. S. Holt, R
5. G. N. Spellman, D
6. G. E. Byron, D
7. P. J. Mitchell, D
8. G. Gude, R

MASSACHUSETTS
1. S. O. Conte, R
2. E. P. Boland, D
3. *J. D. Early, D
4. R. F. Drinan, D
5. *P. E. Tsongas, D
6. M. J. Harrington, D
7. T. H. Macdonald, D
8. T. P. O'Neill, Jr., D
9. J. J. Moakley, D
10. M. M. Heckler, R
11. J. A. Burke, D
12. G. E. Studds, D

MICHIGAN
1. J. Conyers, Jr., D
2. M. L. Esch, R
3. G. Brown, R
4. E. Hutchinson, R
5. R. F. Vander Veen, D
6. *B. Carr, D
7. D. W. Riegle, Jr., D
8. B. Traxler, D
9. G. A. Vander Jagt, R
10. E. A. Cederberg, R
11. P. E. Ruppe, R
12. J. G. O'Hara, D
13. C. C. Diggs, Jr., D
14. L. N. Nedzi, D
15. W. D. Ford, D
16. J. D. Dingell, D
17. *W. M. Brodhead, D
18. *J. J. Blanchard, D
19. W. S. Broomfield, R

MINNESOTA
1. A. H. Quie, R
2. *T. Hagedorn, D
3. B. Frenzel, R
4. J. E. Karth, D
5. D. M. Fraser, D
6. *R. Nolan, D
7. B. S. Bergland, D
8. *J. L. Oberstar, D

MISSISSIPPI
1. J. L. Whitten, D
2. D. R. Bowen, D
3. G. V. Montgomery, D
4. W. T. Cochran, R
5. T. Lott, R

MISSOURI
1. W. L. Clay, D
2. J. W. Symington, D
3. L. K. Sullivan, D
4. W. J. Randall, D
5. R. Bolling, D
6. J. L. Litton, D
7. G. Taylor, R
8. R. H. Ichord, D
9. W. L. Hungate, D
10. B. D. Burlison, D

MONTANA
1. *M. S. Baucus, D
2. J. Melcher, D

NEBRASKA
1. C. Thone, R
2. J. Y. McCollister, R
3. *V. Smith, R

NEVADA
At-L. *J. Santini, D

NEW HAMPSHIRE
1. *N. E. D'Amours, D
2. J. C. Cleveland, R

NEW JERSEY
1. *J. J. Florio, D
2. *W. J. Hughes, D
3. J. J. Howard, D
4. F. Thompson, Jr., D
5. *M. Fenwick, R
6. E. B. Forsythe, R
7. *A. Maguire, D
8. R. A. Roe, D
9. H. Helstoski, D
10. P. W. Rodino, D
11. J. G. Minish, D
12. M. J. Rinaldo, R
13. *H. S. Meyner, D
14. D. V. Daniels, D
15. E. J. Patten, D

NEW MEXICO
1. M. Lujan, Jr., R
2. H. Runnels, D

NEW YORK
1. O. G. Pike, D
2. *T. J. Downey, D
3. *J. Ambro, Jr., D
4. N. F. Lent, R
5. J. W. Wydler, R
6. L. L. Wolff, D
7. J. P. Addabbo, D
8. B. S. Rosenthal, D
9. J. J. Delaney, D
10. M. Biaggi, D
11. *J. H. Scheuer, D
12. S. A. Chisholm, D
13. *S. J. Solarz, D
14. *F. W. Richmond, D
15. *L. C. Zeferetti, D
16. E. Holtzman, D
17. J. M. Murphy, D
18. E. I. Koch, D
19. C. B. Rangel, D
20. B. S. Abzug, D
21. H. Badillo, D
22. J. B. Bingham, D
23. P. A. Peyser, R
24. *R. L. Ottinger, D
25. H. Fish, Jr., R
26. B. A. Gilman, R
27. *M. F. McHugh, D
28. S. S. Stratton, D
29. E. W. Pattison, D
30. R. C. McEwen, R
31. D. J. Mitchell, R
32. J. M. Hanley, D
33. W. F. Walsh, R
34. F. Horton, R
35. B. B. Conable, Jr., R
36. *J. J. LaFalce, D
37. *H. J. Nowak, D
38. J. F. Kemp, R
39. J. F. Hastings, R

NORTH CAROLINA
1. W. B. Jones, D
2. L. H. Fountain, D
3. D. N. Henderson, D
4. I. F. Andrews, D
5. *S. L. Neal, D
6. L. R. Preyer, D
7. C. G. Rose, D
8. *W. G. Hefner, D
9. J. G. Martin, R
10. J. T. Broyhill, R
11. R. A. Taylor, D

NORTH DAKOTA
At-L. M. Andrews, R

OHIO
1. *W. D. Gradison, Jr., R
2. D. D. Clancy, R
3. C. W. Whalen, Jr., R
4. T. Guyer, R
5. D. L. Latta, R
6. W. H. Harsha, R
7. C. J. Brown, R
8. *T. N. Kindness, R
9. T. L. Ashley, D
10. C. E. Miller, R
11. J. W. Stanton, R
12. S. L. Devine, R
13. C. A. Mosher, R
14. J. F. Seiberling, D
15. C. P. Wylie, R
16. R. S. Regula, R
17. J. M. Ashbrook, R
18. W. L. Hays, D
19. C. J. Carney, D
20. J. V. Stanton, D
21. L. Stokes, D
22. C. A. Vanik, D
23. *R. M. Mottl, D

OKLAHOMA
1. J. R. Jones, D
2. *T. M. Risenhoover, D
3. C. B. Albert, D
4. T. Steed, D
5. J. Jarman, D
6. *G. English, D

OREGON
1. *Les AuCoin, D
2. A. Ullman, D
3. *R. Duncan, D
4. *J. Weaver, D

PENNSYLVANIA
1. W. A. Barrett, D
2. R. N. C. Nix, D
3. W. J. Green, D
4. J. Eilberg, D
5. *R. T. Schulze, R
6. G. Yatron, D
7. *R. W. Edgar, D
8. E. G. Biester, Jr., R
9. E. G. Shuster, R
10. J. M. McDade, R
11. D. J. Flood, D
12. J. P. Murtha, D
13. L. Coughlin, R
14. W. S. Moorhead, D
15. F. B. Rooney, D
16. E. D. Eshleman, R
17. H. T. Schneebeli, R
18. H. J. Heinz III, R
19. *W. F. Goodling, R
20. J. M. Gaydos, D
21. J. H. Dent, D
22. T. E. Morgan, D
23. A. W. Johnson, R
24. J. P. Vigorito, D
25. *G. A. Myers, R

RHODE ISLAND
1. F. J. St Germain, D
2. *E. P. Beard, D

SOUTH CAROLINA
1. M. J. Davis, D
2. F. D. Spence, R
3. *B. Derrick, Jr., D
4. J. R. Mann, D
5. *K. L. Holland, D
6. *J. W. Jenrette, Jr., D

SOUTH DAKOTA
1. *L. Pressler, R
2. J. Abdnor, R

TENNESSEE
1. J. H. Quillen, R
2. J. J. Duncan, R
3. *M. Lloyd, D
4. J. L. Evins, D
5. R. H. Fulton, D
6. R. L. Beard, Jr., R
7. E. Jones, D
8. *H. E. Ford, D

TEXAS
1. W. Patman, D
2. C. Wilson, D
3. J. M. Collins, R
4. R. Roberts, D
5. A. W. Steelman, R
6. O. E. Teague, D
7. B. Archer, R
8. B. Eckhardt, D
9. J. Brooks, D
10. J. J. Pickle, D
11. W. R. Poage, D
12. J. C. Wright, Jr., D
13. *J. Hightower, D
14. J. Young, D
15. E. de la Garza, D
16. R. C. White, D
17. O. Burleson, D
18. B. C. Jordan, D
19. G. H. Mahon, D
20. H. B. Gonzalez, D
21. *R. Krueger, D
22. R. R. Casey, D
23. A. Kazen, Jr., D
24. D. Milford, D

UTAH
1. G. McKay, D
2. *A. T. Howe, D

VERMONT
At-L. *J. M. Jeffords, R

VIRGINIA
1. T. N. Downing, D
2. G. W. Whitehurst, R
3. D. E. Satterfield III, D
4. R. W. Daniel, Jr., R
5. W. C. Daniel, D
6. M. C. Butler, R
7. J. K. Robinson, R
8. *H. E. Harris II, D
9. W. C. Wampler, R
10. *J. L. Fisher, D

WASHINGTON
1. J. M. Pritchard, R
2. L. Meeds, D
3. *D. Bunker, D
4. M. McCormack, D
5. T. S. Foley, D
6. F. V. Hicks, D
7. B. Adams, D

WEST VIRGINIA
1. R. H. Mollohan, D
2. H. O. Staggers, D
3. J. Slack, D
4. K. Hechler, D

WISCONSIN
1. L. Aspin, D
2. R. W. Kastenmeier, D
3. *A. Baldus, D
4. C. J. Zablocki, D
5. H. S. Reuss, D
6. W. A. Steiger, R
7. D. R. Obey, D
8. *R. J. Cornell, D
9. *R. W. Kasten, Jr., R

WYOMING
At-L. T. Roncalio, D

PUERTO RICO
Resident Commissioner
J. Benitez

DISTRICT OF COLUMBIA
Delegate
W. E. Fauntroy, D

[1] Elected Jan. 7, 1975

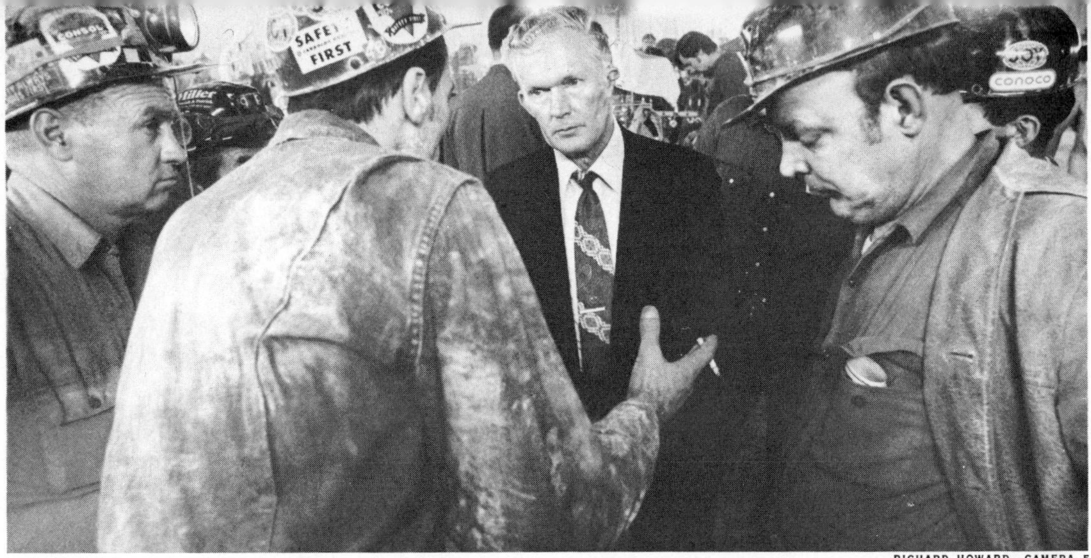

RICHARD HOWARD, CAMERA 5

Striking U. S. coal miners and union leader Arnold Miller discuss the miner's demands. The strike ended in December.

year—up to $1,000 to any candidate for president and up to $3,000 to a congressional candidate. Candidates, too, are limited on what they can spend on their own behalf—$50,000 for a candidate for the presidency, $35,000 for the Senate, and $25,000 for the House.

Congress also broke new ground on the urban front when it approved a mass transit program providing $11.8 billion in federal subsidies over six years to aid capital improvement and help meet operating expenses of local transit systems.

A long, bitter controversy centering on school busing was compromised when Congress approved a measure granting $25.2 billion in federal aid to primary and secondary schools. The law prohibits busing a student beyond the school next closest to his home—except where federal courts decree that a longer ride is required to protect a student's constitutional right against segregation.

Other major legislation included a foreign trade bill that opens the way to trading negotiations with other countries; an antirecession measure appropriating more than $2 billion to extend unemployment compensation and $1 billion to create public service jobs; and a pension reform bill that aims to protect the private pension rights of 30 million workers. In the field of foreign affairs, Congress adopted legislation limiting the president's power to commit troops to foreign combat without its approval.

Congress also raised the minimum wage to $2.30 an hour by 1976, extending coverage to more than 7 million workers. And it revamped its handling of the federal budget and restricted impoundment of congressionally mandated funds by the executive branch.

The Economy. In his economic message to Congress in February, President Nixon conceded that the economic outlook was "highly uncertain." But he argued that inflation could be curbed through monetary and budgetary policies rather than wage and price controls, and that budgetary measures could relieve any downturn in economic activity. And in a later economic report in May, Nixon said: "The worst is behind us."

But in August the Commerce Department reported that the gross national product had declined for the second straight quarter, a situation which fit the classic definition of a recession accepted by most economists. And by December the jobless rate had increased to 7.1 percent, the highest figure since 1961 and an increase of 1.9 percent since January. In November a spokesman for President Ford officially conceded that the United States was in a recession.

Meanwhile, inflation was running rampant. The wholesale price index and consumer prices rose steadily during the year.

In September the President held an economic summit conference in Washington, attended by some 800 representatives of different sectors of the economy. He promised a "coherent and consistent" policy to combat inflation and recession.

Ford laid out his anti-inflation program before a joint session of Congress on national television on October 8. He proposed a 5 percent surtax on families earning more than $15,000 a year, which would provide funds for extending unemployment insurance and for a public works project. He created a board to formulate national energy policy and urged a million-barrel-a-day cut in foreign oil imports. Aside from the surtax, Ford's program relied heavily on voluntary action in dealing with such problems as conservation of food and energy.

The surtax proposal received little support in Congress from either party, and critics contended that Ford's proposals were too weak and too limited to meet the crisis. (See also ECONOMY OF THE U. S.)

Politics. From the start of the year Republican prospects were not very bright for the fall elections. Apart from the general maxim that the party in power generally loses ground at midterm, the Republicans had to face the special problems of Watergate and inflation.

The first hard evidence of the extent of the Republican handicap came early in the year when Democrats won four special congressional elections in districts that had long been GOP strongholds. Among the Republican losses was the House of Representatives seat in Grand Rapids, Mich., that Gerald Ford had held for 25 years before his elevation to the vice presidency in December 1973.

Nixon's resignation in August, followed by Ford's early success in the presidency, gave Republicans some hope. But the Nixon pardon cost them much of the ground they had regained. President Ford campaigned vigorously around the country, but he was more successful in raising funds than he was in changing votes.

On election day the Democrats gained at least 43 seats in the House and at least 3 in the Senate, strengthening their control of both houses. The Democrats also scored a net gain of four governorships, among them the two largest states in the union, New York and California. (See also ELECTIONS.)

Social Protest. Although the radical violence that marred the 1960's seemed to have subsided, one bizarre episode made nationwide headlines during the year. In February, Patricia Hearst, 19, daughter of San Francisco publisher Randolph A. Hearst, was kidnapped by the Symbionese Liberation Army, a radical terrorist organization. In response to demands from the SLA for his daughter's release, Hearst under-

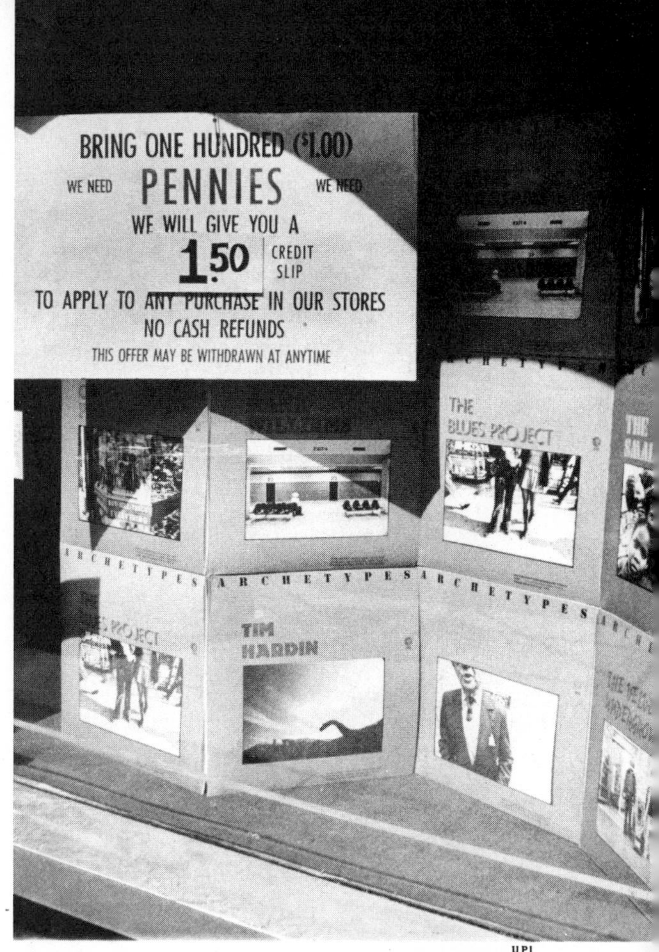

UPI

With the U. S. penny in short supply, many stores and banks across the nation offered bonuses to customers who brought in a certain amount of the scarce coin.

On the U. S. college scene, the newest fad of 1974 was "streaking," or brief public appearances in the nude. The craze was relatively short-lived.

UPI

took to finance and organize a massive food giveaway program to the poor, beginning on February 22.

But then in April, in a tape-recorded message, Miss Hearst labeled the food program a sham and announced that she had joined the SLA. Later the FBI claimed to have photographic evidence that she was involved in a bank robbery in San Francisco, and she was subsequently indicted on the charge.

Meanwhile, in Los Angeles, six SLA members were killed in a shootout when police attacked a hideout there. Miss Hearst was not present at the shootout and remained a fugitive at year's end.

In a painful reminder of past violence, the Justice Department indicted and put on trial eight members of the Ohio National Guard for their role in the slaying of four students at Kent State University in 1970. But the trial ended in a directed verdict of acquittal when the judge ruled that the government had failed to prove that the guardsmen had intentionally set out to violate the civil rights of the students, who had been protesting the U. S. invasion of Cambodia.

ROBERT SHOGAN
Washington Bureau, "Los Angeles Times"

In September the government outlined a clemency program for Vietnam-era draft evaders and military deserters. Below, James Bjerkan is greeted by his wife after being released on furlough from a Minnesota prison where he was serving an 18-month sentence for draft violations.

WIDE WORLD

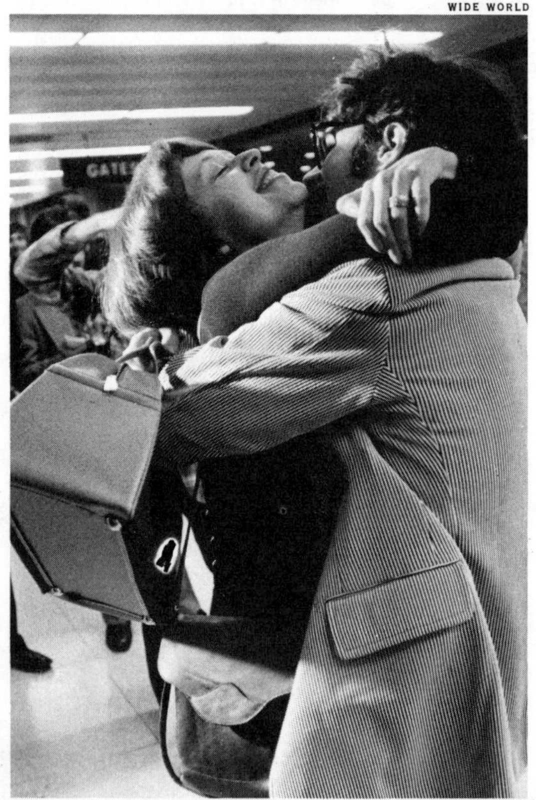

FOREIGN AFFAIRS

The year 1974 was one of several important new starts but few historic consummations in the realm of foreign affairs. Mainly it was a period of reaffirming policy and continuing negotiations. The principal broad questions dealt with involved détente, disarmament, and alliance matters, whereas the main functional issues included the seas, population, food, and energy. Aside from residual affairs in Southeast Asia, the territorial crises concerned the Middle East and Cyprus.

The United States launched diplomatic relations with East Germany, Grenada (Caribbean), and Guinea-Bissau (Africa), and restored severed relations with Egypt, Syria, and Algeria—increasing the American diplomatic community to nearly 140 countries.

When Gerald Ford became president, he retained Henry Kissinger as both his special assistant and secretary of state, and he promised continuance of the basic U. S. policy that had been followed by Kissinger under President Nixon.

Détente, the Soviet Union, and China. As defined by Secretary Kissinger, détente is neither simply an American policy nor an explicit permanent achievement but rather a continuing process of coexistence. It presumes restraint, minimizing conflict and maximizing negotiation, and, as Kissinger put it, both sides must "reconcile the reality of competition with the imperative of cooperation."

East-West negotiations continued at Moscow, Peking, Washington, and elsewhere. The exchange of diplomatic liaison offices with Peking, commenced in 1973, remained unchanged in 1974. Following a visit to Peking by Secretary Kissinger in November, it was announced that President Ford would visit China in the last half of 1975.

From June 27 to July 3, President Nixon visited Moscow, where the leaders, in addition to deciding to open additional consulates, signed a treaty on the limitation of underground weapons tests (of 150 kilotons, beginning March 31, 1976); a protocol to the treaty of 1972 limiting antiballistic missile systems; and five agreements on energy, housing, health, and trade. On November 23–24, President Ford met with Soviet party chairman Leonid Brezhnev at Vladivostok, where they achieved a "breakthrough" in agreeing on new instructions to Soviet-American negotiators at Geneva to conclude an agreement on the limitation of strategic offensive weapons for 10 years, to 1985. The two leaders set a ceiling of 2,400 long-range offensive missiles and bombers for each side. Of the total, each side would be permitted to place multiple independently targetable warheads, known as MIRV's, on 1,320 land- and sea-based missiles.

Thus progress was made respecting limited aspects of nuclear weaponry and certain less sensitive matters. While the Geneva SALT talks,

WIDE WORLD

U. S. foreign relations in 1974 were highlighted by a tentative agreement with the USSR to limit offensive nuclear weapons and the reestablishment of diplomatic relations with Egypt. (*Above*) President Ford and Soviet party chairman Brezhnev sign communiqué in Vladivostok. (*Right*) Secretary of State Henry Kissinger confers with Egyptian President Sadat.

ALAIN DEJEAN, SYGMA

the negotiations on mutual force reductions in central Europe, the conference on European security and cooperation, and the 25-nation Geneva disarmament conference continued, they failed to produce the basic treaties desired. (See also DISARMAMENT.)

Europe. When, in April 1973, Kissinger proposed a new charter to nudge the Atlantic alliance off dead center, he believed the matter was noncontroversial and could rapidly result in a general policy agreement. But it took 14 months to produce an insipid NATO declaration. The United States hoped to strengthen alliance relations and fuse security, political, and economic matters, as well as to assure the European powers that the United States was not concerned solely with its adversaries.

At its Ottawa session on June 19, the NATO foreign ministers adopted a Declaration on Atlantic Relations, which was signed at a summit meeting in Brussels a week later. In it the signatories reaffirmed that the North Atlantic Treaty constitutes the indispensable basis for their mutual security and that their ties must continue. They also reiterated that their common defense "is one and indivisible" and that U. S. forces must remain in Europe.

In December, President Ford met French President Giscard d'Estaing on the island of Martinique. The chief topic on their agenda was energy.

Western Hemisphere. U. S. policy in the Western Hemisphere advanced along several fronts in 1974. Early in the year Kissinger signed a joint statement of eight principles for negotiating a new Panama Canal treaty to replace the one dating from 1903. It was framed to clarify the parameters for negotiation, specifying that the United States will abandon continuing sovereignty in exchange for rights to control and defend the canal during a specified period, increase its compensation to Panama, and assist in Panamanian assumption of particular jurisdictional functions in the Canal Zone.

Founded on Kissinger's proposal of October 1973 for a "new dialogue" among American foreign ministers, meetings were convened at Bogotá, Tlatelolco (Mexico City), and Washington. These were designed to offset the criticism that the United States neglects Latin America and to infuse new spirit into inter-Americanism.

Another issue concerned the proposed termination of the diplomatic-commercial quarantine of Cuba, established under the Rio Pact ten years earlier. While the United States previously supported the embargo, it assumed a passive role at a foreign ministers conference in Quito, November 8–12. The final tally fell two votes short of the necessary two-thirds majority, with the United States abstaining.

Middle East. Secretary Kissinger played a central mediatory role in seeking resolution of the Arab-Israeli conflict of October 1973 and the negotiation of a permanent peace settlement. Working individually with each of the principal parties, he helped to produce a cease-fire (late 1973) and a disengagement agreement (January 1974) for Egyptian and Israeli forces, as well as a Syrian-Israeli agreement to withdraw troops from the Golan Heights (May 1974). In June, President Nixon visited Egypt, Syria, Israel, and Jordan, at the conclusion of which he reported the deferral of Arab-Israeli peace negotiations at Geneva until late fall in order to enable the parties to resolve their differences as to Palestinian participation in the negotiations.

Pursuing his phased diplomacy, Kissinger returned to the Middle East in October, hoping to formulate the most negotiable components of the conflict. The main issues involved territorial settlements, security, seagoing communications, Jerusalem, and the status of the Palestinians—

As 1975 began, former Attorney General Elliot L. Richardson was named U. S. ambassador to Britain.

DENNIS BRACK, BLACK STAR

of which the last was among the most formidable. But the Arab powers met at Rabat and decided to let the terrorist Palestine Liberation Organization represent the Palestinians in Mideast negotiations, thus forcing the matter of priorities. During a trip to the Mideast in November, Kissinger succeeded only in preventing the collapse of negotiations and in continuing to probe for areas of negotiability, while encouraging the parties to resume their direct diplomacy. (See special article on page 36.)

Cyprus. When the crisis broke out in Cyprus in mid-July and Greek and Turkish forces intervened, the UN Security Council called for the cessation of hostilities. The guarantors of the treaty of 1960 signed a cease-fire declaration at Geneva on July 30. American policy supported implementation of the truce, negotiation of a settlement by the principal parties directly involved, phased withdrawal of Greek and Turkish forces, and a constitutional solution worked out by the Cypriots themselves. The United States offered mediatory assistance but avoided assuming initiatives, preferring to back the diplomatic efforts of Britain. (See special article on page 62.)

Seas, Population, Food, and Energy. The United States played a leading role at international conferences dealing with a number of major substantive issues. At Caracas, June 20 to August 29, delegates of 148 states met to negotiate a multilateral convention to replace the rudimentary 17th century sea code. American policy was liberalized to accept an outer territorial limit of 12 miles (19.3 km) and a 200-mile (322-km) economic zone in which riparian states possess exclusive rights over resources, including fisheries. While progress was made respecting some conference documentation, no treaty was consummated.

The UN designated 1974 as World Population Year, and at a conference of 135 states at Bucharest in August, a "World Population Plan of Action" was approved by acclamation. It calls on governments to incorporate population measures into comprehensive social and economic projects and to adopt population management programs by 1985. A World Food Conference was held in Rome in November, attended by 130 nations. It established a World Food Council to deal with the struggle against hunger, but left most matters—even emergency stockpiling—to further negotiations.

In response to the position taken by the petroleum-producing nations late in 1973—embargoing exports and quadrupling prices—the United States assumed leadership among the major industrial powers to formulate an international action plan. The means of implementation proved to be more difficult than the framing of objectives and national policy, however. Aside from working out an emergency oil-sharing pact, little was achieved.

ELMER PLISCHKE, *University of Maryland*

BICENTENNIAL

Local Observances To Mark Anniversary

UPI

Pennsylvania Gov. Milton Shapp and President Ford view the Liberty Bell in Philadelphia as they begin America's Bicentennial celebration slightly ahead of schedule.

The U. S. Bicentennial, the commemoration of the 200th anniversary of the birth of the United States beginning officially in March 1975, is a time for all Americans to review what the country accomplished in its first 200 years, what the country means to them now, and how they see the nation's future. As Americans observe the Bicentennial, they should ask: In terms of freedom and wise government, have the republic's founding documents—the Declaration of Independence, the U. S. Constitution, and the Bill of Rights—been a success? Indeed, the Bicentennial offers every American an excellent opportunity to rekindle the spirit that built 13 weak colonies into one of the strongest nations in the world.

The Bicentennial has three basic themes: (1) America's heritage, a survey of past achievements and history; (2) Festival, community celebrations plus a personal examination of the richness of American arts and crafts; and (3) Horizons, a look to the future.

Unlike the U. S. Centennial, which was marked in Philadelphia in 1876, the Bicentennial will not be concentrated in a single city or community. The location of the celebrations for the 200th anniversary is "throughout America." Every part of the nation and all of its overseas territories are involved.

The Bicentennial is to be celebrated according to the wishes of the people of each community. Local tastes and needs are to be observed. The signing up of communities for local celebration was vigorously under way by the American Revolution Bicentennial Administration in 1974.

The Bicentennial Community. The Bicentennial Administration encourages every U. S. city, town, village, county, and Indian tribe to qualify as a Bicentennial Community. The advantages of being such a community are manifold. The community not only becomes an active part of a great national commemoration but also its social and economic lives are refreshed. Long-range improvements result. Most importantly, people from all sectors of the community work together for the common good.

To qualify as a Bicentennial Community, a community must:

(1) Organize a special Bicentennial planning and coordinating committee that is representative of all segments of the community.

(2) Plan a Bicentennial program that will have at least one lasting reminder—one permanent result—of the special effort the community undertook for the commemoration.

(3) Obtain the approval of the executive officer or governing body of the community.

(4) Submit an application to the national Bicentennial Administration through the appropriate state Bicentennial agency.

(5) Notify local members of Congress that the application has been submitted.

As 1974 ended, numerous programs had been approved. Examples of such programs include:

Montgomery, Ala., is building a civic center on the Alabama River scheduled for dedication in 1976. The city is also developing a series of riverfront parks.

Austin, Texas, is restoring Symphony Square, moving several century-old buildings to the square. A new arts center will lend encouragement to the Austin Symphony Orchestra.

Charleston, S. C., has projects involving one out of every 12 citizens. One project includes the construction of a naval museum with an aircraft carrier, and the development of a Bicentennial park.

The people of Sparks, Nev., are restoring the city center to its original character.

Thus, across the United States, individuals are building a varied Bicentennial.

JOHN W. WARNER, *Administrator, American Revolution Bicentennial Administration*

URUGUAY

The constitutional-democratic civilian system for which Uruguay has long been noted disappeared definitively in 1974. Political arrests, closings of media, pressure to reorganize political parties, and the arrest and trial of university administrators and faculty all pointed to increasing control by the military. The 1966 constitution, abrogated in 1973, was to be replaced. President Juan María Bordaberry raised doubts that the elections scheduled for November 1976 will occur on time.

Political Developments. Tension caused by relative national bankruptcy, severe inflation, clashes between the military and the Tupamaro urban guerrillas, and ineffectual leadership by the traditional Colorado and Nacional parties facilitated the ever-increasing entry of the military into partisan politics. In February 1973 a military coup established a National Security Council (COSENA) to push for a 19-point national recovery program. Bordaberry, who took office in 1972 for a 5-year term, responded in June 1973 with his own "self coup," which dissolved the General Assembly and created a Council of State of 25 civilians.

The Council of State was organized on Dec. 14, 1973. Its duties were to legitimize the acts of government and to write a constitution. Bordaberry had much trouble finding participants, however, and settled largely for ultrarightists and personal friends. Through the first half of 1974 he negotiated with COSENA for details of the 19-point program's application in a series of meetings.

On May 22, Bordaberry's principal military supporter, Gen. Hugo Chiappe, was forced to resign as commander in chief of the army by hard-line officers led by Gen. Esteban Cristi. Bordaberry also was forced to move against his most intimate long-term support group, the Rural Federation, composed of small and medium farmers. In July, however, he demonstrated unexpected manipulative skill by downgrading COSENA to largely security matters, while organizing a mixed Economic and Social Advisory Commission as the new principal policy body. Its organic law recognizes the military as "the essential support of the power of the government," however. At year-end, Bordaberry seemed to be fighting for both his own political life and the remnants of constitutionalist practice.

Economy. Under heightened military control, marked improvement in the economy seemed possible until the sharp increases in oil prices disrupted matters. Consumer price inflation of 95% in 1972 was reduced to 77% in 1973, and seemed likely to fall in 1974. Substantial reduction of short-term small foreign debts had begun, due to a trade surplus of $24.2 million in 1973. Although in 1972 and 1973 there had been zero growth of GNP, projected growth of 4% in 1974 seemed possible.

About 50% of Uruguay's energy usage is based on imported fuel. Although prospects for offshore deposits of oil were being pursued in 1974, the country has no domestic sources at this time. Historically about 20% of all foreign exchange has gone for fuel, but in 1974 it was expected to cost 40% or more. The government terminated all foreign company contracts to import oil in June 1974, and sharply raised domestic prices at that time. It withstood heavy explicit Arab pressure to change its diplomatic attitudes toward Israel as the price for assured supplies, but entered into close cooperative arrangements with Argentina to obtain oil (since Argentina made the compromises with the Arabs).

Energy needs accelerated negotiations among Brazil, Argentina, Paraguay, and Uruguay concerning eight massive hydroelectric projects in the river system of the region; the most advanced, Salto Grande, involving Argentina and Uruguay, is expected to be in service in 1979 at a cost of $591 million. In January the Inter-American Development Bank loaned $79 million to begin the project.

Oil prices reduced Uruguayan exports of wool and beef to western Europe and Japan, as those customers diverted funds to oil. Uruguay made investments in citrus and soya for export, however, and useful capabilities are expected as a result.

International Relations. Greatly improved relations with Argentina, at the relative expense of Brazil, were the principal change of the year. President Juan Perón and his widow-successor to the presidency, Isabel (María Estela), thus scored political successes, while President Bordaberry and ultrarightist generals, who had supported Brazil, were the losers in influence. Agreements with Argentina included plans for construction of a major supertanker unloading facility and a major new port in Uruguayan waters to serve both countries; enlargement of the joint national highway network through construction of long-delayed bridges; and early mutual elimination of tariffs.

PHILIP B. TAYLOR, JR., *University of Houston*

URUGUAY • Information Highlights

Official Name: Eastern Republic of Uruguay.
Location: Southeastern coast of South America.
Area: 68,536 square miles (177,508 sq km).
Population (1973 est.): 3,000,000.
Chief City (1963 census): Montevideo, the capital, 1,202,757.
Government: *Head of state,* Juan M. Bordaberry, president (took office March 1972). *Head of government,* Juan M. Bordaberry. *Legislature*—General Assembly (suspended June 1973).
Monetary Unit: Peso (1,290 pesos equal U. S.$1, May 1974).
Gross National Product (1973 est.): $1,848,000,000.
Manufacturing (major products): Meat products, textiles, construction and building materials, beverages, chemicals.
Major Agricultural Products: Wheat, corn, rice, livestock, wool.
Foreign Trade (1973): *Exports,* $322,000,000; *imports,* $285,000,000.

UTAH

As is often the case in Utah, religion and politics dominated the scene in 1974.

Religion. President Harold B. Lee of the Church of Jesus Christ of Latter Day Saints died on Dec. 26, 1973. Spencer W. Kimball, of the church's Council of the Twelve Apostles, was selected and ordained as the new president. President Kimball gained the highest office of the church at 78 years of age. He comes from a pioneer church family; his grandfather, Heber C. Kimball, was a member of the first Council of the Twelve, appointed by the Prophet Joseph Smith in 1835. President Kimball is known throughout the church for his world travels, his great concern for American Indians, and his leadership in the church's worldwide missionary program.

In his first official statement, President Kimball referred to his own efforts in working with the Indian people and stressed that the church would continue to carry special programs to its minority members. Further, he stated, "We are especially interested in the family and the home, and we hope to encourage and increase the effectiveness of this great work." He also emphasized support for U. S. political leaders, saying, "We believe in our country and in honoring and obeying the law. We believe in supporting our leaders in their righteous endeavors."

As counselors in the First Presidency, Kimball selected President N. Eldon Tanner as first counselor and President Marion G. Romney as second counselor. Elder Ezra Taft Benson, former secretary of agriculture during the Eisenhower administration, was named president of the Council of the Twelve.

Politics. The U. S. senatorial campaign to select a successor to retiring Sen. Wallace F. Bennett, a Republican veteran of 24 years, dominated the Utah general election in 1974. Salt Lake City Republican Mayor Jake Garn defeated the freshman Democratic Congressman Wayne Owens by a substantial margin in the midst of a national swing to the Democrats. Senator-elect Garn at age 42 is the youngest popularly elected senator in the state's history.

The hotly contested race to fill Representative Owens' seat in the 2d Congressional District resulted in the election of Democrat Allan Howe over Republican Salt Lake City Commissioner Stephen M. Harmsen. In the 1st Congressional District, incumbent Representative Gunn McKay, a Democrat, overwhelmed his Republican opponent, Ron Inckley.

In statewide elections, Democrats took over organizational control of the House from Republicans by a 40-to-35 margin and will hold a 15-to-14 margin in the state Senate.

Three of four constitutional propositions on the 1974 ballot were rejected by Utah voters. Proposals to establish a lieutenant governor, create a uniform tax on transportation property, and lending state credit to private industry were defeated by substantial margins. The lone proposition to gain support was one which will allow counties and municipalities to establish special service districts under certain conditions.

A deeply divisive Utah Land-Use Act was decisively rejected by referendum. It was defeated by overwhelming majorities in many counties. Major sources of opposition to the act were identified as the John Birch Society, the American party, and other right-wing organizations active in Utah, such as Friends of the Utah Constitution and the Libertarian party.

LORENZO K. KIMBALL, *University of Utah*

UTAH • Information Highlights

Area: 84,916 square miles (219,932 sq km).
Population (1973 est.): 1,157,000. *Density:* 14 per sq mi.
Chief Cities (1970 census): Salt Lake City, the capital, 175,885; Ogden, 69,478; Provo, 53,131; Bountiful, 27,956.
Government (1974): *Chief officers*—governor, Calvin L. Rampton (D); secy. of state, Clyde L. Miller (D). *Legislature*—Senate, 29 members; House of Representatives, 75 members.
Education (1973–74): *Enrollment*—public elementary schools, 161,355 pupils; public secondary schools, 144,445; nonpublic schools, 4,500; colleges and universities, 80,465 students. *Public school expenditures,* $235,000,000 ($816 per pupil).
State Finances (fiscal year 1973): *Revenues,* $783,581,000; *expenditures,* $687,347,000.
Personal Income (1973): $4,634,000,000; per capita, $4,005.
Labor Force (July 1974): *Nonagricultural wage and salary earners,* 437,600; *insured unemployed,* 8,300 (2.6%).

VANCOUVER

Mayor Art Phillips was easily elected to his second two-year term when voters in British Columbia's largest city went to the polls on November 20. But his party's representation on the ten-member council, which takes office January 1, dropped to five aldermen from eight. A five-year, $65.7 million capital spending program was narrowly rejected, but Mayor Phillips said the plan, to cover streets, parks, housing, and civic property, would likely be resubmitted to voters in the spring.

In September the city council voted to raise the salaries of aldermen elected on November 20 by 65 percent—to $13,200 a year from $7,900. The raise had to be approved by the new council. In June proposals were outlined for a downtown residential-commercial community on two miles of waterfront. The plan emphasizes recreational activity related to the area.

Canada's third-largest metropolitan center had the lowest rental accommodation vacancy rate in the country—three in 1,000—and housing starts declined. The value of building permits issued also dropped, due partly to a two-month strike in the British Columbia construction industry. In October the regional government rejected provincial government suggestions for a $140 million rapid transit system and drew up its own proposals with an eye to encouraging the growth of regional centers. The six-block downtown Granville Mall opened at the end of the summer, with pedestrians and buses sharing the $2.9 million concrete facilities.

Port Developments. Activity at the Port of Vancouver, second-largest in North America, was reduced in late August when grain export shipments were crippled by a shutdown at the terminals. The federal government ordered a return to work in mid-October, ending the lengthy contract dispute involving five grain elevator companies and 550 grain handlers. Grain shipments were tied up again a month later when federal grain inspectors went on strike for higher pay across Canada.

Meanwhile, work continued on a $30 million container terminal, to be completed in 1975, designed to try to win back some of the Canadian cargo that was going through Seattle because of inadequate container facilities in Vancouver. Bill Rathie, the often-criticized local head of the port, resigned on October 4, and Mayor Phillips said his resignation would mean the port's reorganization under the direction of port manager Fred Spoke.

Sports. The city officially withdrew its bid for the 1980 Winter Olympics in October after the provincial government refused to support it, claiming the bid was financially risky and environmentally hazardous.

DEBRA CRAINE
"The Canadian Press," Vancouver

VENEZUELA

Venezuela remained in the ranks of the democratic nations of Latin America during 1974. For the fourth successive time since 1959, power was transferred peacefully to a new president after free elections. Carlos Andrés Pérez of the Democratic Action party (AD) took office on March 12, 1974, succeeding Rafael Caldera of the Christian Social party (COPEI). The AD also controlled both houses of Congress.

Urgent economic problems faced the new president. These included an 11% annual rate of inflation, chronic unemployment of 10% of the working force, a need to find jobs and housing for a population of which 56% is less than 21 years old, heavy reliance on imports for essential items, and inadequate productivity in the agrarian and industrial sectors.

Economic Policy. In a pre-election statement, Andrés Pérez said that his oil policy would be the most important of his economic programs. Great wealth was flowing into Venezuela because of world energy shortages. The third-largest oil exporter, Venezuela was producing more than 3 million barrels a day, over half of which went to the United States. President Pérez responded vigorously to President Ford's admonition to oil-producing nations against maintaining high prices for petroleum. In full-page advertisements appearing in several U. S. newspapers, he defended Venezuela's sovereign rights to its oil resources. The position of President Pérez was warmly applauded by all segments of Venezuela society.

VENEZUELA • Information Highlights

Official Name: Republic of Venezuela.
Location: Northwestern South America.
Area: 352,143 square miles (912,050 sq km).
Population (1973 est.): 11,900,000.
Chief Cities (1971 census): Caracas, the capital, 1,625,000; Maracaibo, 650,002; Barquisimeto, 334,333.
Government: *Head of state,* Carlos Andrés Pérez, president (took office March 1974). *Head of government,* Carlos Andrés Pérez. *Legislature*—Congress: Senate and Chamber of Deputies.
Monetary Unit: Bolívar (4.30 bolívares equal U. S.$1, Aug. 1974).
Gross National Product (1973 est.): $14,330,000,000.
Manufacturing (major products): Processed foods, paper and paperboard, petroleum products, beverages, metal products, furniture, clothing.
Major Agricultural Products: Coffee, cacao, bananas, sugarcane, cotton, rice, corn, dairy products.
Foreign Trade (1972): *Exports,* $3,130,000,000; *imports,* $2,277,000,000.

Nationalization of foreign enterprises appeared to have become a cardinal feature of Venezuela's economic planning. President Caldera nationalized the milk and electricity-producing industries before he left office. President Pérez warned that the oil industry would pass to state control long before the target date of 1983 set by the previous administration. He also announced that the government would nationalize the iron-ore industry on Jan. 1, 1975, by which U. S. Steel and Bethlehem Steel would lose concessions that were to have run until 2000 A. D. Many other foreign enterprises were given three years in which to sell 80% of their stock to Venezuelan nationals.

The new government planned to use 50% of its oil revenues in projects designed to stimulate agriculture and livestock productivity as well as diversification of industry as a whole. In other moves to strengthen the economy and to fulfill his pledge to enhance the economic and social well-being of Venezuelans, the President asked for and received special powers from Congress. Using these, he decreed wage increases ranging from 25% for those earning 1,000 bolívares ($233) or less a month, to 5% for those earning up to 5,000 bolívares ($1,163).

Other Economic Developments. More than 100,000 apartments and houses for small- and medium-income families were completed in 1973–74. The Labor Bank of Venezuela claimed to have built 190,000 units for 800,000 people during the past five years. A new cement factory was under construction in Anzoátegui state. When finished, the $45 million plant would produce 1.8 million tons of cement a year. The government agency CADAFE completed the General José Antonio Páez dam. It has a generating capacity of 240,000 kilowatt-hours. In September, Venezuela launched an oil tanker, purchased from Italy. The first of a projected fleet, the vessel has a capacity of 37,000 cubic meters. Venezuela will need at least 100 ships of 60,000 tons each to enable it to transport its oil to buyers.

The ten commercial banks of Venezuela purchased $23 million in Inter-American Development Bank (IDB) bonds with a 7% interest rate and a maturity date of 13 years. The first such purchase in Latin America, it will channel Venezuelan resources to less developed countries in the Western Hemisphere.

The 1974 budget reached an all-time high of 19.5 billion bolívares ($4.5 billion). The departments of the interior, public works, and agriculture each received 3 billion bolívares ($700 million), while education was granted 2.8 billion bolívares ($650 million).

Education. The University of Simón Bolívar, founded in Caracas in 1970, expanded from 500 to 3,000 students in four years. The curriculum concentrates on scientific and technological courses. The university was expected to build 16 more buildings with aid from the IDB.

UN Conference. Caracas was host to the second session of the Third United Nations Conference on the Law of the Sea. Some 5,000 delegates from 148 countries attended. The delegates reached no agreement on any of the more than 100 items on the agenda. Venezuela sought international recognition of a 200-mile patrimonial sea and a 12-mile territorial sea.

LEO B. LOTT
University of Montana

VERMONT

The Watergate scandals in Washington overshadowed Vermont's political campaigns and the November elections in 1974. Meanwhile the Democratic governor was confronted by a Republican legislature whose leaders seemed determined to prevent the Democrats from getting credit for any legislation, and which therefore had one of the least productive sessions in years.

The Elections. The surprise announcement by Sen. George D. Aiken that he would not stand for reelection in November brought quick announcements for a game of musical chairs in higher state offices.

In March, disillusionment of Vermont voters with the Watergate scandals resulted in several town meetings voting for President Nixon's impeachment. There was intensive preprimary election activity, followed by a strenuous and somewhat hectic campaign by all statewide candidates. The Watergate influence was evident in the apparent apathy of the voters, in an almost pathological concern with campaign financing and expenditures by the candidates, and in the election results.

Democratic Gov. Thomas Salmon was an easy victor, as were Republicans James Jeffords and Richard Thomas for the U. S. House of Representatives and secretary of state, respectively. Other statewide candidates were unable to command a majority vote. The state Constitution and statutes provide that, if there is no majority, the General Assembly is to elect from the three candidates for each office who received the highest number of votes. In each case the two leading candidates received from 47 to 49 percent of the votes. The Liberty Union party made a surprising showing of 6 percent or more votes for each office, and thus is now to be counted as a major party in future campaigns. This party's votes have led to the impasse.

Patrick Leahy, Democrat, who received 69,694 votes to his two competitors' combined 71,383, will succeed George D. Aiken, the Republican dean of the Senate. Representative Richard Mallary received only 65,630 votes in a surprising upset. Leahy will be the first Democratic senator from Vermont since 1856.

In the state Senate, the Republicans retained a majority of 19 to 11, but in the House their majority was reduced to less than 10. Many hail this as a return to a two-party system in Vermont but speculate as to the legislative outcome of the voting.

Legislation. The legislature fully debated the prohibition of "skinny-dipping" or nude bathing in rural streams. It finally passed a $208 million budget in the last hours of a third overtime period, with little debate. A bill aiding children in need was enacted, and bankers got higher interest rates on mortgages. By not acting, it frustrated lobbying efforts to repeal the nonreturnable bottle bill.

Effective land-use planning was rejected, tax reforms were emasculated, lobbying regulations were defeated by the lobbyists, and a long-discussed reduction of highway department powers and budget was defeated.

Weather. A relatively warm winter with lighter than normal snowfall dealt a deadly blow to the ski industry in the state, only partially compensated by abnormally heavy snowfalls in March. It also plagued maple syrup producers, who reported reduced gallonage, but saved Vermonters, whose fuel oil and electric energy quotas were reduced.

ANDREW E. NUQUIST
University of Vermont

VERMONT • Information Highlights

Area: 9,609 square miles (24,887 sq km).
Population (1973 est.): 464,000. *Density:* 50 per sq mi.
Chief Cities (1970 census): Montpelier, the capital, 8,609; Burlington, 38,633; Rutland, 19,293; Bennington, 14,586.
Government (1974): *Chief Officers*—governor, Thomas P. Salmon (D); lt. gov., John S. Burgess (R). *General Assembly*—Senate, 30 members; House of Representatives, 150 members.
Education (1973–74): *Enrollment*—public elementary schools, 64,631 pupils; public secondary schools, 41,645; nonpublic schools, 12,000; colleges and universities, 27,705 students. *Public school expenditures,* $127,846,000 ($1,308 per pupil).
State Finances (fiscal year 1973): *Revenues,* $394,176,000; *expenditures,* $400,381,000.
Personal Income (1973): $1,861,000,000; per capita, $4,011.
Labor Force (July 1974): *Nonagricultural wage and salary earners,* 167,500; *insured unemployed,* 5,500 (4.2%).

UPI

Nguyen Van Thieu (*center*), president of South Vietnam, wears traditional red robe and black hat at ceremonies marking founding of Vietnamese kingdom.

VIETNAM

Neither the Communist nor the anti-Communist sides made major gains in Vietnam's continuing war in 1974, although both Hanoi and Saigon continued their prosecution of the two-decade-old conflict. Disillusion with the "peace" that came in 1973 was evident in both capitals, and war weariness visibly increased in each of the two Vietnams. The three major powers involved in the war over the last 20 years—the United States, the Soviet Union, and China—significantly decreased their aid to their allies in the struggle for supremacy in the once-united country.

SOUTH VIETNAM

Reduction of American military aid to the Saigon government of President Nguyen Van Thieu had two major effects: it restricted the military capabilities of the South Vietnamese regime and forced it to curtail some of its operations, and it signaled critics of the Thieu administration that the Saigon leader was no longer as much a political favorite of the United States as he once had been. The political and economic difficulties of the Thieu regime increased in the second half of 1974, as a wide range of opposition elements took to the streets in demonstrations—partly in reaction to the war's persistence and partly to protest the consequences of continuing inflation.

The War. South Vietnam's army gave a good account of itself, not least of all in adapting to the new circumstances of increasingly limited American military aid. The cut in U. S. assistance forced Saigon's armed forces to reduce their use of ammunition, fuel, helicopters, and fighter-bombers and even to abandon outposts in August because of their decreased capability to defend them. The worldwide price squeeze and energy shortage further restricted operations of Thieu's government.

The long struggle for control of the country remained a stalemate, with no signs of any steps toward the kind of political accommodation envisaged in the January 1973 pact that ended direct U. S. combat participation in the conflict. North Vietnam and the Vietcong, indeed, suspended their participation in the two commissions set up following the 1973 "cease-fire": the Joint Military Commission (to work out terms of the armistice) and the Joint Military Team (to search for the various combatants missing in action).

Politics. A largely Catholic protest movement, originally aimed at eliminating corruption, grew during the year, and Buddhist, student, labor, and press elements increasingly rallied to its support. By midyear there were open demands for President Thieu's resignation. While his removal did not appear imminent at year's end, there was growing agreement that Thieu would probably not stand for a third presidential term in 1975, for which South Vietnam's constitution had been appropriately altered in January 1974.

The anti-Thieu movement was led by a 59-year-old anti-Communist Catholic priest, the Rev. Tran Huu Thanh. Thieu called it Communist-inspired, but Hanoi claimed that the United States was behind it. Neither charge was true, and the movement's widespread appeal was demonstrated in mid-1974 when the powerful An Quang Buddhist faction announced its backing for the "People's Anti-Corruption Movement." Thieu tried to placate the opposition by having the National Assembly pass somewhat liberalized laws controlling the press and political parties, but to no avail. In late October police and the anti-corruption, anti-Thieu demonstrators clashed on the streets of Saigon in the most violent encounter between Thieu and his anti-Communist opponents in his eight years in power.

The basis for the growing discontent with Thieu's leadership was variously rooted: disillusionment with the 1973 "peace," inflation and other economic problems, and the persisting and costly war with the Communists (which many non-Communists apparently believed could be ended under a leader other than Thieu). Thieu had offered to resume the Paris talks, broken off by the Communists, but Hanoi had no desire to help out the South Vietnamese leader politically. The beleaguered president was not without support, however: the all-important army still backed him, and in provincial and city council elections in July pro-Thieu candidates won 300 of 478 seats (compared with 240 in the previous voting).

Economy. There were several bright spots in the economy, but these were offset by the problem of simultaneously occurring inflation and recession, the worldwide increase in commodity prices, and the impact of declining U. S. financial support. Serious question was raised as to the economic ability of Saigon to continue the war with the Communists.

The 1973–74 rice crop was a record one for South Vietnam—approximately 6.6 million tons—but additional amounts of the grain still had to be imported from the United States. Inflation moderated somewhat but was still at the rate of 80% a year. Exports were considerably higher than in 1972, but the war severely limited rubber and timber production. Oil discoveries suggested appreciable quantities of the resource in the adjacent South China Sea, and the rising world price for sugar came as a pleasant economic surprise.

Industrial production declined, however, and unemployment grew dramatically, partly as a result of the American withdrawal. Unemployment reached nearly one million (in a work force of seven million).

Foreign Relations. In April, U. S. Secretary of State Henry Kissinger stated that Washington was committed to provide South Vietnam whatever it needed for its self-defense, but Congress subsequently slashed American military aid to Saigon. The forced resignation of President Nixon particularly concerned the Thieu government, in light of Nixon's past backing of the anti-Communist cause in Vietnam and successor President Ford's inexperience in foreign affairs. American aid accounted for 65% of the support for combined military and civilian resources committed to prosecution of the war (compared with 78% the previous year). U. S. military assistance for the year totaled about $700 million, half the level of a year earlier.

— SOUTH VIETNAM • Information Highlights —

Official Name: Republic of Vietnam.
Location: Southeast Asia.
Area: 67,108 square miles (173,809 sq km).
Population (1973 est. census): 19,400,000.
Chief Cities (1971 est.): Saigon, the capital, 1,804,880; Da Nang, 437,668; Hue, 199,893.
Government: *Head of state,* Nguyen Van Thieu, president (reelected Oct. 1971). *Head of government,* Gen. Tran Thien Khiem, prime minister (took office Sept. 1969). *Legislature*—National Assembly: Senate and House of Representatives.
Monetary Unit: Piastre (670 piastres equal U. S.$1, Sept. 1974).
Gross National Product (1972 est.): $2,900,000,000.
Manufacturing (major products): Processed foods, textiles, chemicals, rubber products.
Major Agricultural Products: Rice, rubber, corn, sweet potatoes, fruits, poultry, fish.
Foreign Trade (1972): *Exports,* $13,000,000; *imports,* $707,000,000.

NORTH VIETNAM

North Vietnam, preoccupied with political and economic problems internally and receiving much-reduced military supplies from its Soviet and Chinese allies, did not make a major offensive effort during the year. Statements of the leadership, however, left no doubt that North Vietnam intended to continue to use military means to reunite the divided land under its control, although this might take longer than once anticipated.

The War. About 200,000 North Vietnamese regular troops remained south of the demilitarized zone, in addition to the Vietcong force of 60,000 fighting against the South Vietnamese government. North Vietnam probably had more than 60 tanks in the south as well as substantial amounts of sophisticated weaponry. Part of the explanation for the absence of a major offensive by these elements may have been a shakeup of top Communist commanders in the south, which probably restricted the anti-Saigon military effort in various ways.

The Hanoi press repeatedly suggested that domestic political opposition, economic dislocation, and lessened American military aid might bring about the downfall of the South Vietnamese regime. This belief could have been another reason for the absence of any major military thrust.

Politics. There was evidence of serious jockeying for political power among the North Vietnamese leaders during the year. Hanoi

— NORTH VIETNAM • Information Highlights —

Official Name: Democratic Republic of Vietnam.
Location: Southeast Asia.
Area: 61,294 square miles (158,750 sq km).
Population (1973 est.): 22,500,000.
Chief Cities (1960 census): Hanoi, the capital, 414,620.
Government: *Head of state,* Ton Duc Thang, president (took office 1969). *Head of government,* Pham Van Dong, premier (took office 1954). *First secretary of Vietnam Workers' (Communist) party,* Le Duan. Legislature (unicameral)—National Assembly.
Monetary Unit: Dong (2.35 dong equal U. S.$1, July 1974).
Gross National Product (1972 est.): $1,800,000,000.
Manufacturing (major products): Processed foods, cement.
Major Agricultural Products: Rice, sugarcane, tea, sweet potatoes.

newspapers offered strong criticism of the Standing Committee of the National Assembly—chaired by the No. 2 man on the 12-member politburo, Truong Chinh—which was really an attack on the latter leader, whose influence appeared to decline. Defense Minister Vo Nguyen Giap, long known to be suffering from cancer, was also the object of a persisting whisper campaign of criticism, according to foreign diplomats in Hanoi. Giap, who publicly endorsed the unsuccessful 1972 North Vietnamese offensive despite his opposition to it within the politburo, was succeeded in the performance of various of his duties by 57-year-old Gen. Van Tien Dung.

The eclipse of the influence of both Chinh and Giap was a reflection of the increased power of top North Vietnamese leader Le Duan (who strongly supported the still-controversial 1972 offensive). Le Duan was probably stronger than at any time since Ho Chi Minh's death in September 1969.

Economy. The preoccupation of North Vietnam with economic reconstruction was reflected in the overwhelming emphasis in Hanoi newspapers on economic matters (as contrasted with war drumbeating). There was evidence of increased peasant resistance, however, to reorganization of the north's collective farming setup—much of which had been hastily implemented during the difficult wartime years up to the 1973 "settlement." Farmers had given greater effort to their "private" plots in the early 1970's, and the Hanoi government sought to rectify the situation.

Foreign Relations. Both the Soviet Union and the People's Republic of China substantially increased their economic assistance to North Vietnam during the year, but the Communist "big powers" also cut their military help to Hanoi in half. As a consequence, external Communist military aid to the North Vietnamese in 1974 was estimated to be somewhere between one third and one half of the level of American military assistance to South Vietnam (even in its own reduced amount).

RICHARD BUTWELL
State University of New York
College at Fredonia

South Vietnamese mother and baby wait to cross a river as they flee fighting between government and rebel forces.

UPI

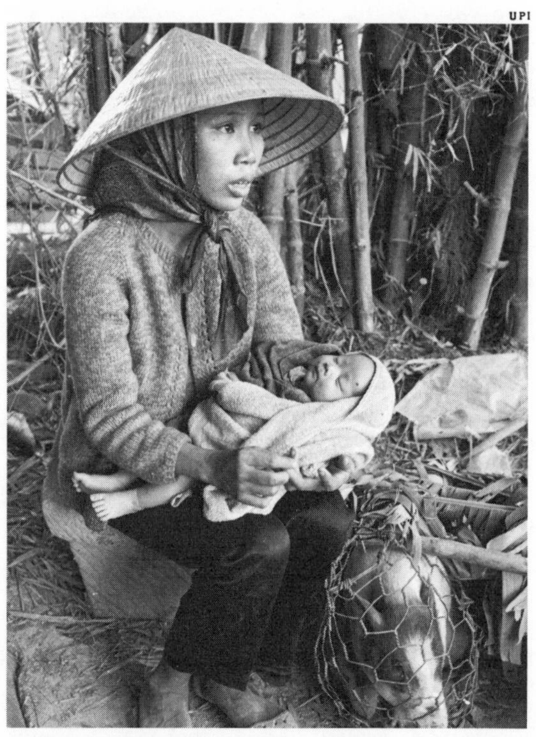

Sen. Vu Van Mau has his head shaved in protest against a third term for South Vietnam's President Thieu.

WIDE WORLD

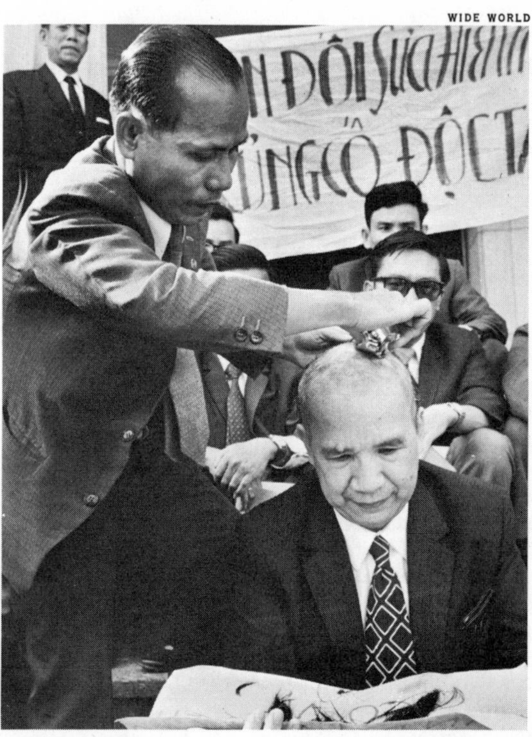

VIRGIN ISLANDS, U. S.

The incidence of violence which had plagued the Virgin Islands during the past two years declined sharply in 1974, particularly toward the end of the year. A strict weapons-control law and increased professional police surveillance undoubtedly contributed to the drop in violent crimes. As a result, tourism made a rapid recovery, particularly on St. Croix.

Economy. A much higher rate of inflation has affected the consumer in the Virgin Islands than in the continental United States. A report early in 1974 indicated that food prices had risen over 30% in the previous 12-month period. The government was fairly successful in securing substantial federal grants for the creation of new jobs, housing, road repair and construction, education, and support for small businesses.

Industrial development of St. Croix continued with the delayed start of construction of the island's second oil refinery. Residential and business groups demanded that the new construction be carried out in such a way as to keep pollution at a minimum and not disfigure the island's scenery. The other refinery, one of the largest in the world, expanded its capacity by almost 50% in 1974, to about 600,000 barrels of crude petroleum a day. An offshore mooring terminal, to be located two miles from the south coast of St. Croix, is being constructed to accommodate supertankers.

Election. A wet election day, coming after almost two weeks of rain, managed to dampen only the spirits of the Republicans in the traditionally Democratic island communities. Dr. Melvin Evans, the Republican candidate, who in 1972 had become the first elected governor of the Virgin Islands, failed in his bid to return to office. However, since neither of the two front-runners received 50% of the vote, a runoff election had to be held.

In an upset victory, the Independent Citizens' Movement candidate, Cyril King, narrowly defeated the Democratic candidate, lawyer Alexander Farrelly, in the runoff election held on November 19. King, who had broken away from the local Democratic party in 1969, polled 10,388 votes to Farrelly's 9,154.

Ron DeLugo, the nonvoting representative from the Virgin Islands in the U. S. House of Representatives, was unopposed in his bid for reelection. The Democratic party elected nine members to the 15-seat unicameral legislature of the Virgin Islands, while the Independent Citizens' Movement placed five members, and the Republicans one.

Floods. After three weeks of rain, severe flooding struck the islands on November 12, temporarily closing the two international airports, cutting off electricity, and causing damage estimated at millions of dollars.

THOMAS MATHEWS
University of Puerto Rico

VIRGINIA

The dominant political and economic mood in Virginia during 1974 was one of caution and disillusionment. Because of Watergate and its damage to the Republican party, Virginia voters reelected only five of seven Republican incumbents to the U. S. House of Representatives. On the state level, Republican Gov. Mills Godwin cooperated with a Democratic General Assembly to maintain a general governmental posture of conservatism and retrenchment.

Legislature. The General Assembly met early in the year. It killed or postponed such headline items as the women's equal rights amendment, pari-mutuel betting, no-fault auto insurance, collective bargaining between local governments and public employees, and a proposed $84,000,000 bond issue to finance a major expansion of state parks. On the other hand, it gave a major thrust to mass transit by allotting $23,000,000 from highway funds for bus and rail public transport in major metropolitan areas. The assembly passed a bill tightening up the state's blue laws—but also permitting localities to vote to escape coverage by the new law, and it established the state's first minimum wage at $1.60 an hour for employees in small stores and motels not covered by the national minimum.

Education. Governor Godwin, a former Democrat and a former governor who earned a reputation in the 1960's as a progressive advocate of better education, assumed a more conservative stance under his new party label. Faced with a tightening economic situation caused by inflation and lower-than-expected revenues, Governor Godwin twice during the year brought pressure on state agencies to prune operating expenditures by 5%. The governor specifically recommended to the General Assembly that all capital outlay requests from colleges and universities be deferred. The Assembly concurred.

A consulting firm's report to a legislative study commission contributed to the general atmosphere of retrenchment in higher education. The report contended that Virginia's higher edu-

VIRGINIA • Information Highlights

Area: 40,817 square miles (105,716 sq km).
Population (1973 est.): 4,811,000. *Density,* 120 per sq mi.
Chief Cities (1970 census): Richmond, the capital, 249,430; Norfolk, 307,951; Virginia Beach, 172,106.
Government (1974): *Chief Officers*—governor, Mills E. Godwin (R); lt. gov., John N. Dalton (R). *General Assembly*—Senate, 40 members; House of Delegates, 100 members.
Education (1973–74): *Enrollment*—public elementary schools, 678,000 pupils; public secondary schools, 407,000; nonpublic schools, 63,300; colleges and universities, 193,277 students. *Public school expenditures,* $1,018,000,000 ($1,010 per pupil).
State Finances (fiscal year 1973): Revenues, $2,619,679,000; expenditures, $2,446,379,000.
Personal Income (1973): $22,683,000,000; per capita, $4,715.
Labor Force (July 1974): *Nonagricultural wage and salary earners,* 1,769,400; *insured unemployed,* 11,200 (0.8%).

cational institutions were overbuilt. However, one of its specific proposals, a study of a merger of Virginia Polytechnic Institute and Radford College, was defeated in the General Assembly. A far-ranging proposal to give greater power of coordination to the State Council of Higher Education was adopted by the legislature, and the council ordered the elimination of various graduate programs deemed nonproductive.

Utilities. The state's two major electrical utilities, Virginia Electric and Power and Appalachian Power, came under consumer fire in 1974 after they appealed to the State Corporation Commission for large emergency rate increases. The firms contended the increases were necessary to maintain their construction projects. The commission granted Virginia Electric an increase, but denied the application from Appalachian Power.

Prison System. Virginia's prison system received major attention during the year. A Richmond grand jury indicted six top-level panel administrators for alleged misconduct in office. At trial, however, the charges were dismissed for lack of evidence. Also, Governor Godwin resolved the long-simmering Green Springs dispute. Under his predecessor, Governor Holton, plans had been made to construct a diagnostic receiving center for prisoners at Green Springs in Louisa county, but the center was opposed by local residents, who unsuccessfully attempted to block the project through court proceedings. After reviewing the situation, Godwin decided to halt construction and seek an alternate site.

Watergate. In national politics, Virginians shared the nation's obsession with the Watergate debacle. The spotlight was on Sixth District Congressman Caldwell Butler, Virginia's only member on the House Judiciary Committee, which handled the impeachment inquiry. Butler won national attention when, as a Republican, he announced he could not condone the President's actions and would vote for several articles of impeachment.

Because of Watergate, two incumbent Republican congressmen, veteran Joel Broyhill and freshman Stanford Parris, were defeated. Five Republican and three Democratic incumbents were reelected.

State Politics. The continued domination of the state Republican party by conservatives was demonstrated by the selection of George McMath, a member of the House of Delegates, to replace Richard Obenshain as state chairman. Obenshain, a conservative, was selected by President Ford to serve as cochairman of the Republican National Committee. To replace Obenshain, Governor Godwin took the lead in picking McMath, a former Democrat like Godwin and also a conservative. McMath was accepted by the Republican state committee over protests of the formerly dominant moderate wing of the party.

WILLIAM LARSEN, *Radford College*

WASHINGTON

A highly successful world's fair—Expo '74 in Spokane—and the November elections attracted attention in Washington in 1974.

World's Fair. Spokane's Expo '74, the first world's fair dedicated to the environment and the nation's first major Bicentennial event, closed its six-month run on November 3 after having received 5,187,826 visitors. Sponsors of the exposition were confident that the fair would more than break even financially. The fair's theme was "Celebrating Tomorrow's Fresh, New Environment." The theme triggered a few demonstrations against the Japanese and Soviet exhibits in protest against the whaling practices of those countries. Eleven nations and 37 commercial exhibitors participated in the fair, which was officially sanctioned by the Bureau of International Expositions in Paris.

The fair, which spurred a $300 million building spree in the core of the city near the 100-acre Spokane River fair site, left a legacy to Spokane of a new opera house and convention center and several permanent exhibition and meeting halls. More importantly, what was once a blighted railroad switchyard, industrial jumble, and skid-row area on the edge of the central business district will become a city riverfront park and convention center.

Elections. U. S. Sen. Warren G. Magnuson, a Democrat, easily won his bid for a sixth term. He defeated state Sen. Jack Metcalf, a conservative Republican who had also lost to Magnuson in the 1968 race. In the congressional races, four Democratic incumbents and one Republican incumbent were returned to the House. The one new member of the delegation is Don Bonker, a Vancouver Democrat, who won over Secretary of State Ludlow Kramer.

Referendums. The citizens of Washington had voted overwhelmingly in 1972 to change the state constitution to permit limited forms of gambling and to remove the prohibition against a state lottery. The following session of the Legislature passed several measures to provide for a state lottery, but Gov. Daniel J. Evans

WASHINGTON • Information Highlights

Area: 68,192 square miles (176,617 sq km).
Population (1973 est.): 3,429,000. *Density:* 52 per sq mi.
Chief Cities (1970 census): Olympia, the capital, 23,111; Seattle, 530,831; Spokane, 170,516; Tacoma, 154,581.
Government (1974): *Chief Officers*—governor, Daniel J. Evans (R); lt. gov., John A. Cherberg (D). *Legislature*—Senate, 49 members; House of Representatives, 98 members.
Education (1973–74): *Enrollment*—public elementary schools, 405,711 pupils; public secondary, 382,613; nonpublic, 44,100; colleges and universities, 199,478 students. *Public school expenditures,* $708,057,000 ($974 per pupil).
State Finances (fiscal year 1973): *Revenues,* $2,790,206,000; *expenditures,* $2,622,737,000.
Personal Income (1973): $17,106,000,000; per capita, $4,989.
Labor Force (July 1974): *Nonagricultural wage and salary earners,* 1,188,500; *insured unemployed,* 58,600 (6.3%).

WALTER HODGES, EXPO '74 WORLD'S FAIR

EXPO '74

WALTER HODGES, EXPO '74 WORLD'S FAIR

(*Above*) Opening-day ceremonies of Expo '74, a mini-World's Fair that was held from May 4 to November 3 in Spokane, Wash., and was attended by 5.2 million people. It was the first exposition with an environmental theme, and the once-blighted area on which it was built will be transformed into a downtown park after the pavilions are removed. (*Right*) A ski-lift type of overhead tramway carries its passengers past the Soviet Restaurant and the U. S. Pavilion. (*Below*) The popular British Columbia exhibit.

WALTER HODGES, EXPO '74 WORLD'S FAIR

vetoed each one. The Legislature then referred the matter to the voters in 1974. While a majority voted their approval of a state lottery, the measure failed to achieve the 60% affirmative vote required.

The Legislature also proposed to the voters an amendment to the state constitution that would limit the previous item veto power of the governor to appropriation bills only and to authorize the Legislature, on the petition of two thirds of the members of each house, to reconvene the Legislature for a limited time to reconsider any bills or items vetoed by the governor. The proposed amendment was approved by approximately 55% of the voters.

Indian Fishing Rights. Uncertainty regarding the rights of Indians to fish in commercial waters of Washington was thought to be resolved on February 12 when U. S. District Court Judge George Boldt ruled that the Indians, who are members of 14 tribes covered by federal treaties signed in the 1850's, are guaranteed the right to catch 50% of the harvestable salmon in waters classified as "usual and accustomed" fishing places. But the reaction of the Puget Sound commercial fisheries industry was immediate, and an appeal was filed by the state fisheries and game departments. When late in the year no decision had been rendered on the appeal, most of the state's congressional delegation appealed to President Ford to declare the Puget Sound non-Indian commercial fishery eligible for federal disaster relief, but the plea was denied on the basis that no natural disaster was involved.

New Stadium. Construction of King county's domed stadium in Seattle—plagued and delayed for six years by hearings regarding its location, lawsuits, accidents, and strikes—continued through the year, with the first ribs of its unique roof being put in place near year's end. But its troubles were not over because the contractor served notice in October that claims would be submitted for approximately $10.5 million to cover additional costs caused by delays and changes in the design of the stadium. The stadium had been approved in 1968 by the voters of King county, who authorized a $40 million bond issue for its construction. The county executive remained under heavy pressure to keep the cost of the stadium within the $40 million spending limit in the face of severe inflation in construction costs.

Transit Strike. The first transit employees' strike since 1956 idled more than 1,000 transit workers in Seattle, November 9–24. More than 90,000 commuters experienced confusion, minor traffic jams, and frayed nerves as they sought other means of transportation. Transit employees, who were protesting wages and working conditions, rejected a proposed 21.5% wage increase before going on strike.

WARREN W. ETCHESON
University of Washington

WASHINGTON, D. C.

A new period in the history of the District of Columbia began in 1974. On May 7, 83% of those voting in a special election approved the home rule charter written by Congress. The charter established an elected mayor-council form of government. Under home rule, the elected city officials have increased financial and rule-making powers, although Congress retains authority over the District's budget and can repeal legislation passed by the City Council.

The voters also approved, by a three-to-one margin, the charter provision to establish advisory neighborhood councils. Residents who want to establish a neighborhood council can submit petitions to the City Council signed by at least 5% of the registered neighborhood voters. In a nonpartisan election, those voters would select five to ten council members. The councils will be charged with ascertaining and transmitting public sentiment to the legislators about bills pertinent to the neighborhood's interests.

Elections. District residents voted to select the city's mayor and council for the first time in over 100 years. Eighty-nine candidates ran for 14 offices in the primary election held on September 10.

At the general election on November 5, the nominees of the Democratic and Republican parties faced Statehood party, D. C. Socialist Workers' party, U. S. Labor party, and independent candidates. The Democrats won overwhelming majorities. Walter E. Fauntroy was reelected as nonvoting delegate to Congress, incumbent Walter E. Washington was elected mayor, and Sterling Tucker was elected chairman of the City Council. The home rule charter prohibits more than two at-large councilpersons to be from the same party, thus enabling one Republican and one Statehood party candidate to attain councilmanic positions. Democrats also won the eight ward seats in the Council.

Federal Legislation. Congress passed a stringent campaign finance law that set limits on the amount of donations to and expenditures of candidates in primary and general elections in the District of Columbia. In addition, the law prohibits conflict of interests, requires personal and detailed financial disclosure statements from candidates and elected and high-ranking appointed officials.

Congress appropriated $1,073,642,900 to the District for fiscal 1975. While the appropriation was over $100 million more than for fiscal 1974, it was $40.5 million less than requested.

Congress repealed the rarely used powers granted District police in the 1970 D. C. Crime Act, to enter and search dwellings without knocking and identifying themselves.

Education. Federal City College, the first urban land-grant college, was granted accreditation in its sixth year of operation.

Barbara A. Sizemore's first year as school superintendent was marked by a deteriorating relationship with the 11-member D. C. School Board. She claimed that the board was meddling in administrative affairs, and the board contended that the superintendent was trying to subvert its policymaking role. Despite the dispute, the School Board gave Mrs. Sizemore a unanimous mandate to restructure the grade and placement system of student assignments, develop new curriculum approaches, and decentralize the school system into six regions.

Transportation. A five-day Metrobus drivers strike, a $1.8 million deficit, and slow expansion progress marked Metro's year. The awarding of construction contracts to complete four Metrorail stations was stalled for two months until the District of Columbia members on the Metro Board obtained a board policy which insures that contracts for 10% of structural work and 20% of the finishing work would be awarded to minority firms.

New Museum. The Hirshhorn Museum and Sculpture Garden opened in October. The $17 million cylindrical structure with its sunken outdoor garden will exhibit from its collection of the 4,000 paintings and 2,000 sculptures donated by Joseph H. Hirshhorn. (See also ART.)

ELEANOR G. FELDBAUM
University of Maryland

SMITHSONIAN INSTITUTION

Aerial view of the new Hirshhorn Museum and Sculpture Garden in Washington, D. C., the city's first important museum devoted exclusively to exhibiting modern art.

WEST VIRGINIA

A Democratic sweep at the polls, a bitter struggle between a Republican governor and a Democratic Legislature, and an explosive textbook controversy dominated the news in 1974.

Elections. The state returned all four Democratic members of the House of Representatives. Democratic gains in both houses of the state Legislature confronted Gov. Arch A. Moore, Jr., with a veto-proof majority of 86 to 14 in the House of Delegates and 28 to 6 in the Senate. The electorate also approved a judicial reform amendment.

Legislation. The governor and Legislature maneuvered all year on fiscal matters, preventing the passage of a budget until after the beginning of the fiscal year. From January 9 through adjournment of the regular session on March 14, there was little agreement on budgetary priorities.

A special session in April again failed to produce much agreement. It was not until a second special session on July 3 that the budget was passed. Governor Moore accepted the bill, but vetoed 10 specific items. The Legislature recessed to await the results of an appeal to the state Supreme Court on those vetoes. The court upheld the governor on 8 of the 10 items.

Textbook Controversy. A dispute in Kanawha county simmered throughout the summer and exploded in the fall over textbooks which parents and fundamentalist ministers objected to as "unchristian," "un-American," and "immoral." Opponents of the books moved from demands for the removal of the texts to boycotts, strikes, arson, dynamiting, and sniper firing at school buses. Miners in Kanawha and adjoining counties struck in sympathy with the protest. The school board at first removed the controversial textbooks pending a review by a citizens committee, but in November it returned most of the books with the provision that a student objecting to a book would not have to read it.

Coal Strikes. Numerous wildcat strikes, especially in the southern coal fields, centered on a gubernatorial ban in May on tire studs (on election eve, Governor Moore rescinded the order). The economy sagged as the nationwide coal strike (November 12–December 5) neared.

W. REYNOLDS MCLEOD
West Virginia University

WEST VIRGINIA • Information Highlights

Area: 24,181 square miles (62,629 sq km).
Population (1973 est.): 1,794,000. *Density:* 74 per sq mi.
Chief Cities (1970 census): Charleston, the capital, 71,505; Huntington, 74,315; Wheeling, 48,188; Parkersburg, 44,208.
Government (1974): *Chief Officers*—governor, Arch A. Moore, Jr. (R); secy. of state, Edgar Heiskell III (R). *Legislature*—Senate, 34 members; House of Delegates, 100 members.
Education (1973–74): *Enrollment*—public elementary schools, 229,605 pupils; public secondary, 179,863; nonpublic, 11,300; colleges and universities, 68,074 students. *Public school expenditures,* $331,682,000 ($871 per pupil).
State Finances (fiscal year 1973): *Revenues,* $1,256,169,000; *expenditures,* $1,206,980,000.
Personal Income (1973): $6,867,000,000; per capita, $3,828.
Labor Force (July 1974): *Nonagricultural wage and salary earners,* 563,000; *insured unemployed,* 13,000 (2.9%).

WISCONSIN

Government and politics received much attention in Wisconsin during 1974, but farm problems also concerned the public in this agricultural state.

Elections. The Republican party's national problems were evident in the fall election campaign in Wisconsin as the Democrats scored sweeping victories.

Gov. Patrick J. Lucey won his second four-year term by defeating William D. Dyke, former mayor of Madison, 628,639 to 497,189. The outcome was never in doubt, since Governor Lucey had not only built a solid base in his own party but had won a number of friends among Republican businessmen with a newly enacted tax relief measure for industry. Dyke, on the other hand, faced party dissension and lacked financial support. His campaign budget of about $100,000 contrasted with the governor's $370,000.

The Democrats won all the other state offices, with Martin J. Schreiber returned as lieutenant governor and Charles Smith as treasurer. The La Follette name showed that it still had political clout. Bronson La Follette, a direct heir to the famous old Progressive family, was elected attorney general, a position he held from 1965 to 1969. Douglas LaFollette, a distant relative, was elected secretary of state, the first member of the Democratic party to hold that position since 1892.

Also for the first time since 1892, Democrats won control of the state Senate, 19 to 14, and they increased their margin in the Assembly, 63 to 36. In other Democratic victories, Sen. Gaylord Nelson won his third term, and two more congressional districts were captured, leaving only two of the nine to Republicans. Among the Democratic winners was the Rev. Robert Cornell, a political science teacher at St. Norbert College in De Pere, who will become the second Roman Catholic priest in the House of Representatives.

Legislative Sessions. The state Legislature met twice in 1974. It acted on so few of Governor Lucey's list of major legislative proposals in the first session that he called it into special session, in which five of his nine proposals were enacted.

The major item was a campaign finance reform measure, which imposes campaign spending and contribution limits, allows only limited entry by corporations into campaigns, requires continuing reports of contributors, and establishes a state board to oversee elections.

Other legislation completed the merger of the University of Wisconsin and the Wisconsin State Universities systems; provided pensions for teachers and government employees who retired before 1973; budgeted an additional $37.7 million for state programs; and banned the use of studded tires in the state.

Farm Problems. Wisconsin farmers were hit by drought during the summer, then suffered disastrous losses from early frosts in the fall. Damage because of the weather was estimated at almost $400 million, and the corn crop was the smallest in 10 years. Dairy farmers, meanwhile, were devastated by the cost-price squeeze, and members of the National Farmers Organization received considerable criticism when they slaughtered 636 calves on October 15 in an attempt to dramatize their problems.

Tornadoes. A series of tornadoes on April 21 brought havoc to east-central Wisconsin, killing two persons. The greatest damage was at Oshkosh, where 300 homes were damaged or destroyed at a loss of more than $3 million. By fall, however, most homes were rebuilt.

School Unrest. The little village of Hortonville, west of Appleton, became a national symbol for teachers in the spring after members of the teachers' union there went on strike on March 18. On April 3 the school board fired all of the teachers on the ground that strikes by public employees are banned under Wisconsin law. The teachers received support on their picket lines from throughout the state, with violence sometimes resulting, but the school board was upheld in two court suits. In the fall, the school opened with a nearly all-new teaching staff.

In Milwaukee, Washington High School, on the edge of the inner city, was disrupted for weeks in the fall by members of the Nazi party who attempted to capitalize on racial tensions in the school. The Nazis, whose membership is believed to be small, announced a recruitment campaign in the schools, but a Milwaukee judge restricted their activities.

Economy. Wisconsin's economy outperformed that of the nation in such measures as employment and income in 1974. Net farm income was down, but the demand for machinery and other Wisconsin-produced capital goods was strong. It was questionable whether the trend could continue in 1975 unless there was a recovery on the national level.

PAUL SALSINI
The Milwaukee "Journal"

WISCONSIN • Information Highlights

Area: 56,154 square miles (145,439 sq km).
Population (1973 est.): 4,569,000. *Density:* 83 per sq mi.
Chief Cities (1970 census): Madison, the capital, 172,007; Milwaukee, 717,372; Racine, 95,162.
Government (1974): *Chief Officers*—governor, Patrick J. Lucey (D); lt. gov., Martin J. Schreiber (D). *Legislature*—Senate, 33 members (18 R, 15 D); Assembly, 99 members (62 D, 37 R).
Education (1973–74): *Enrollment*—public elementary schools, 564,255 pupils; public secondary schools, 422,767; nonpublic schools, 181,000; colleges and universities, 221,256 students. *Public school expenditures,* $1,075,000,000 ($1,200 per pupil).
State Finances (fiscal year 1973): *Revenues,* $3,107,175,000; *expenditures,* $2,789,544,000.
Personal Income (1973): $21,173,000,000; per capita, $4,634.
Labor Force (July 1974): *Nonagricultural wage and salary earners,* 1,701,300; *insured unemployed,* 31,200 (2.2%).

UPI

Alix, nine-month-old daughter of Phyllis Langer (*right*), has accompanied her mother to work in the offices of *Ms.* magazine since she was five weeks old.

WOMEN'S RIGHTS

Three additional states ratified the Equal Rights Amendment in 1974. The U. S. Congress passed measures prohibiting discrimination against women in mortgage credit and also outlawing discrimination on the basis of sex or marital status in credit generally. President Ford named Mary Louise Smith of Iowa chairman of the Republican National Committee. Nearly twice as many women as in 1972 sought election to state and congressional offices, many successfully (see ELECTIONS). Preparations began for observance in 1975 of "International Women's Year" by members of the United Nations. A summer conference in Mexico City will be the focal event.

Equal Rights Amendment. Legislatures of Maine, Montana, and Ohio approved the 27th Amendment which provides that "equality of rights under the law shall not be denied or abridged by the United States or any state on account of sex." The actions brought the number of adopting states to 33, though there were efforts to rescind the earlier approvals of Nebraska and Tennessee.

The American Bar Association endorsed the amendment in 1974. The National Federation of Business and Professional Women's Clubs, the National Organization for Women, the League of Women Voters, Common Cause, and other proponents of the amendment stepped up efforts to gain the required approval of 38 states by 1979.

Legal Actions. The American Telephone and Telegraph Company agreed to pay 25,000 managerial employees, mostly women, an estimated $30 million in back pay and future salary raises in a U. S. District Court consent decree settling further discrimination complaints against the nation's largest private employer by the Equal Employment Opportunity Commission and the Departments of Labor and Justice.

In the largest such settlement in an American university to date, Rutgers University agreed to give 210 women and minority group faculty members $375,000 in back pay and salary adjustments. The case grew out of a complaint in 1971 by eight women. These received retroactive awards from $3,000 to nearly $20,000. Settlements also were disclosed involving Duke University, Northwest Airlines, Montgomery Ward & Co., and several other companies.

The U. S. Supreme Court dealt a serious blow to efforts of women to establish rights to disability benefits for normal pregnancy. The court upheld, 6–3, the constitutionality of California's disability insurance program which excludes maternity-related benefits.

In another decision, the Supreme Court ruled, 7–2, that public schools cannot force women teachers to take maternity leave months before they expect to give birth. The court also

UPI

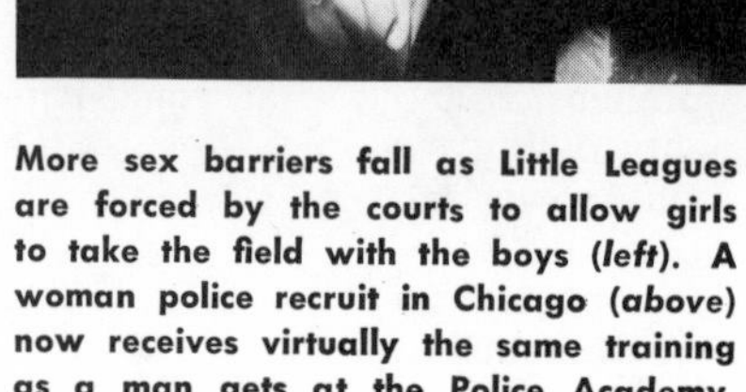

UPI

More sex barriers fall as Little Leagues are forced by the courts to allow girls to take the field with the boys (*left*). A woman police recruit in Chicago (*above*) now receives virtually the same training as a man gets at the Police Academy.

upheld the constitutionality of a 10-year-old law entitling women employees to the same wages as men for the same work.

The Movement. The National Organization for Women (NOW) in a hotly contested election chose Karen DeCrow, a 36-year-old lawyer from Syracuse, N. Y., as president. Ms. DeCrow, the author of *The Young Woman's Guide to Liberation* and *Sexist Justice,* defeated Mary Jean Collins-Robson of Chicago.

The 700-chapter, 36,000-member organization adopted a resolution to work "to raise the status of homemaking" by obtaining social security credits for full or part-time housework. Rep. Bella Abzug (D-N. Y.) proposed such legislation in Congress.

NOW also embarked on a campaign to require companies to make public their affirmative action programs and to publish their employment figures. Sears, Roebuck and Co., the world's largest retailer, was singled out for special attention.

The U. S. Merchant Marine Academy at Kings Point, N. Y., admitted women for the first time in 1974, heralding, some believe, eventual entry of women to other military academies.

Change. Dr. Virginia Y. Trotter of the University of Nebraska became the first woman to be named assistant secretary for education. Dr. Margaret Mead was elected president of the American Association for the Advancement of Science. Mrs. Hanna Holborn Gray became Yale provost. Barbara Allen of Long Beach, Calif., and Judith Neuffer of Wooster, Ohio, became the first women to qualify as Navy pilots. They joined the Hurricane Hunters squadron at Jacksonville, Fla. Col. Mary E. Bane became the first woman Marine to command a unit of men—2,000 at Camp Pendleton in California.

Four bishops ordained 11 women as Episcopal priests in Philadelphia but their superiors nullified the action (see RELIGION). The National Little League opened its teams to girls after losing a suit filed in New Jersey by NOW. The American Kennel Club allowed women to serve as delegates. Civitan International, the service organization, and Phi Delta Kappa, education fraternity, admitted women.

International. In France, President Válery Giscard d'Estaing appointed Françoise Giroud, a 58-year-old journalist and leading feminist, to the new post of secretary of state for the condition of women. It is believed to be the first such post in the world. She planned a bureau with "special delegates" who will rate schools, businesses, and government bureaus on the way they treat women.

In Canada, the Royal Canadian Mounted Police opened its ranks to women. The first group of 32 women recruits began training in Regina, Saskatchewan.

CAROLINE BIRD, *Author of "Everything a Woman Needs to Know to Get Paid What She's Worth" and "The Case Against College"*

WYOMING

The energy crisis in 1974 attracted interest in minerals-rich Wyoming, but the impact of the crisis was suspected to become more severe in the next few years. Meanwhile, unemployment remained below 4% because expansion in the minerals industry more than made up for weakness in tourism. Low cattle prices and drought in the east hurt ranchers and farmers.

Minerals. Strip mining of coal caused greatest concern. Production of coal in the state, almost all of it by strip mining, exceeded 18 million tons, and was expected to exceed 100 million tons by 1980. Unit trains carried most of the coal to electric power plants in the Midwest, although some of it was used in recently built Wyoming plants. The anticipated expansion stirred apprehension about what would happen to the quality of life when coal gasification plants, additional power plants, and other industrial developments arrived. Already there were painfully impacted areas, particularly in Sweetwater and Campbell counties.

Wyoming ranked ninth among the 50 states in coal production, first in uranium and soda ash, and fifth in oil. While minerals other than coal caused less argument, they contributed considerably to population growth and social problems. High prices brought record crude-oil production, although it was only slightly above the 142 million barrels marked up in 1973. Some 120 drilling rigs were active. No great oil or gas discoveries occurred, but there was continuous development of smaller fields, especially in the Powder River Basin. There was much deep drilling, up to 20,000 feet, particularly in Sweetwater County.

Legislature. The legislature met in a 20-day "budget" session in January. The minerals severance tax, which had stood at 1% since first enacted in 1969, was increased to 3%. A coal-slurry pipeline project, to deliver Powder River Basin coal to Arkansas, received approval. When it was learned, after adjournment, that water from the deep Madison formation, which was to be used in the pipeline, was potable and not brackish as had been thought when approval was granted, much protest erupted since good water is so scarce in Wyoming.

Elections. In the November 5 election, incumbent Congressman Teno Roncalio (D) defeated independent oilman Tom Stroock of Casper, 69,610 to 57,315. The normally Republican state elected a Democrat governor for the first time since 1958. Ed Herschler, Kemmerer lawyer-rancher and state representative who had opposed the coal-slurry pipeline, won easily, 71,899 to 56,743, over former state Senator Dick Jones (R).

For the other four state elective offices the electors chose Republicans over Democrats. Thyra Thomson, incumbent secretary of state, won a third term, defeating Charles Carroll.

WYOMING • Information Highlights

Area: 97,914 square miles (253,597 sq km).
Population (1973 est.): 353,000. *Density:* 4 per sq km.
Chief Cities (1970 census): Cheyenne, the capital, 40,914; Casper, 39,361; Laramie, 23,143; Rock Springs, 11,657.
Government (1974): *Chief Officers*—governor, Stanley K. Hathaway (R); secy. of state, Mrs. Thyra Thomson (R). *Legislature*—Senate, 30 members; House of Representatives, 62 members.
Education (1973–74): *Enrollment*—public elementary schools, 45,025 pupils; public secondary schools, 40,992; nonpublic schools, 2,100; colleges and universities, 17,922 students. *Public school expenditures,* $78,950,000 ($999 per pupil).
State Finances (fiscal year 1973): *Revenues,* $282,146,000; *expenditures,* $257,924,000.
Personal Income (1973): $1,699,000,000; per capita, $4,813.
Labor Force (July 1974): *Nonagricultural wage and salary earners,* 136,400; *insured unemployed,* 700 (0.8%).

Since the Constitution bars the treasurer from succeeding himself, incumbent Jim Griffith exchanged positions with incumbent Auditor Ed Witzenburger. Griffith defeated Bob Adams, while Witzenburger defeated Elizabeth Phelan. Incumbent State Superintendent of Public Instruction Robert Schrader defeated Sydney Spiegel.

More Democrats than usual, however, won seats in the Legislature. Fifteen members of each party won places in the state Senate. Elected to the U. S. House of Representatives were 32 Republicans, 29 Democrats, and one independent.

T. A. LARSON, *University of Wyoming*

YUGOSLAVIA

A new Yugoslav constitution, the fourth since World War II, was promulgated on Feb. 21, 1974. It contains three main changes: (1) All remnants of a representative parliamentary system were replaced by a complex "delegational system" in which delegates to federal legislative bodies will be selected by lower-level assemblies and will be bound by imperative mandates. (2) Instead of the previous five chambers, the new Assembly will have two: the Federal Chamber and the Chamber of Republics and Provinces. (3) Membership in the collective state Presidency was reduced from 23 to 9.

Politics. On May 16, the federal Assembly reelected the 82-year-old Tito (Josip Broz) president of Yugoslavia for an unlimited term and elected the new collective Presidency. The Assembly also approved the new cabinet (Federal Executive Council) headed by Džemal Bijedić. Two army generals assumed high governmental functions: Franjo Herljević, as secretary for internal affairs, and Vuko Goce-Gučetić, as public prosecutor.

The 10th congress of the League of Communists of Yugoslavia (LCY), held in May, reinstated the central committee, with 166 members, which in turn elected a 39-member presidium. The latter selected a 12-member executive committee. Tito was reelected president

UPI

President Tito of Yugoslavia poses with a 550-pound (250-kg) bear he shot during a two-day hunting trip in the central Yugoslavian republic of Bosnia Hercegovina.

of the LCY for an unlimited term, and Stane Dolanc was named secretary of the executive committee. While the new constitution emphasized strengthening of the workers' self-management system, congress aimed to restore LCY unity and its overall centralized controls.

Economy. Economic performance in 1974 was uneven. Industrial production for the first nine months rose 9.6% over the same period in 1973. Bumper harvests of wheat and maize recorded a gain of 10% over the previous year. Domestic employment was up 4.2%. On the other hand, accelerating inflation and higher prices (rising 26.1% in January–September over the same period in 1973), nonliquidity of enterprises, low labor productivity, and energy shortages contributed to the failure of economic stabilization. During the first eight months, exports rose 45%, imports 78%.

Foreign Affairs. In June, President Tito paid his first official visit to West Germany, confirming good relations between the two countries, especially in the economic field. Earlier, the Bonn government agreed to extend to Belgrade $300 million in credits with 2% interest over 30 years.

Relations between Yugoslavia and the USSR remained close. After an absence of almost two decades, high-level representatives of the LCY attended the consultative meeting of European Communist parties in Warsaw in October. Tito's visit to Hungary in April marked the improvement of relations between the two countries. In July, Tito was in Rumania for talks with Nicolae Ceauşescu. But friendly Yugoslav-Rumanian relations paralleled persisting Yugoslav-Bulgarian tensions over the Macedonian issue.

In other developments, the dispute with Italy over sovereignty in the Trieste "Zone B" was rekindled in March. NATO naval maneuvers in the Adriatic Sea in April were denounced as "anti-Yugoslav." U. S. Secretary of State Kissinger visited Belgrade in November. Westinghouse Electric Corp. signed a contract to construct Yugoslavia's first nuclear power plant.

MILORAD M. DRACHKOVITCH, *Stanford University*

YUGOSLAVIA • Information Highlights

Official Name: Socialist Federal Republic of Yugoslavia.
Location: Southeastern Europe.
Area: 98,766 square miles (255,804 sq km).
Population (1973 est.): 21,200,000.
Chief Cities (1971 census): Belgrade, the capital, 741,613; Zagreb, 566,084; Skopje, 312,091.
Government: *Head of state,* Tito (Josip Broz), president (took office 1953). *Head of government,* Džemal Bijedic, prime minister (took office 1971). *Legislature*—Federal Assembly: Federal Chamber and Chamber of Republics and Provinces.
Monetary Unit: Dinar (17.28 dinars equal U. S.$1, Nov. 1974).
Gross National Product (1973 est.): $18,400,000,000.
Manufacturing (major products): Iron and steel, processed foods, chemicals, machinery, textiles.
Major Agricultural Products: Corn, wheat, fruits, potatoes, sugar beets, forest products, fish, livestock.
Foreign Trade (1973): *Exports,* $2,853,000,000; *imports,* $4,511,000,000.

YUKON TERRITORY

The issues of responsible government and provincial status for the territory influenced political and legislative events in 1974.

Government and Politics. In the July 8 federal election, Yukon returned the incumbent Progressive Conservative commissioner, Erik Nielsen. Through an amendment to the Yukon Act, the Territorial Council was increased from 7 to 12 members. On November 18, 10 independents and 2 New Democrats were elected to the Council.

Native land-claims negotiations remained static, but Minister of Indian Affairs and Northern Development Judd Buchanan indicated that he would not negotiate at the end of a gun.

Minerals. Mineral production in 1974 was expected to have a value of $160 million, up $15 million over 1973. A copper deposit near Minto appears able to support a new mine.

W. BRIAN SPEIRS, *Territorial Archivist*

YUKON TERRITORY • Information Highlights

Area: 207,076 square miles (536,327 sq km).
Population (1974 est.): 19,000.
Chief Cities (1971 census): Whitehorse, the capital, 11,600.
Government (1974): *Chief Officers*—commissioner, James Smith; asst. commissioner, J. B. Fingland. *Legislature*—Territorial Council, 12 members.
Education (1972–73): *Enrollment:* public elementary and secondary schools, 4,749 pupils. *Public school expenditures* (1972), $6,742,000.
Public Finance (fiscal year 1974–75 est.): *Revenues,* $44,000,000; *expenditures,* $55,000,000.

ZAIRE

For many Westerners, Zaire—the former Belgian Congo—was put on the map in 1974 by the heavyweight boxing contest between Muhammad Ali and George Foreman. The staging of the world championship bout in Zaire's capital, Kinshasa, on October 30 symbolized both the country's growing stature in African and Third World affairs and its increasingly successful management of its domestic problems.

Assassination Attempt. A potentially serious threat against President Mobutu's life was easily thwarted in October 1973 when former rebel leader Gaston Soumialot and five associates reportedly surfaced in Bujumbura, Burundi, for the purpose of murdering the Zairese head of state during a projected summit conference. Forewarned by local informers, Zaire security police nabbed five conspirators on Burundi soil and carried them off to Zaire, but Soumialot himself managed to escape arrest.

Domestic Politics. In mid-July the 1967 constitution was amended to give increased power to the leaders of Zaire's single political party, the Mouvement Populaire de la Révolution (MPR). Under the 1967 constitution voters directly elected the president, who then automatically became the chairman of the MPR. Under the amended constitution, however, voters will elect the party chairman, who will then automatically become the head of state. The significance of this change stems from the fact that the single candidate for the office of party chairman is nominated by the MPR's political bureau, whose importance in the process of an orderly succession will therefore be greatly increased. However, this reform does not apply to President Mobutu, who was thus handed a de facto life presidency, in addition to being formally made head of the Political Bureau, of the party congress, and of all three branches of the national government. The politically crucial directorship of the MPR's Political Bureau had been given in March to Nguza Karl I Bond, currently regarded as Zaire's number two man.

Foreign Relations. Relations with Belgium deteriorated rapidly following the publication in March of *L'Ascension de Mobutu,* a vitriolic attack of the regime written by the leftist Belgian lawyer Jules Chomé. By the end of the year, however, relations between Belgium and Zaire showed signs of a return to normalcy.

In April the overthrow of Premier Marcello Caetano's regime in Portugal indirectly propelled Zaire into the midst of an intricate diplomatic game involving Angola and its oil-rich Cabinda enclave. Among Angola's three competing nationalist movements, Mobutu has consistently backed Holden Roberto's FNLA, whose area of support is limited to the Northwest but which is regarded favorably by the Western powers and has paradoxically begun to receive some support from China. Its chief rival, the MPLA, enjoys wider recognition but has been internally divided into three rival factions. In June, the Organization of African Unity summit conference set up a conciliation committee headed by Mobutu to settle internal rifts among African freedom fighter groups. However, Mobutu continued to back the FNLA by helping them mount token military operations in several areas of Angola adjacent to Zaire, including some in the MPLA's sphere of influence. He also welcomed in Kinshasa Fernando Falcao, leader of the Frente Unido de Angola (FUA), a white settler group.

Economic Developments. As copper prices reached record highs in 1973, Zaire's balance of trade registered a comfortable surplus, but throughout 1974 the price of copper fell significantly, opening the prospect of reduced earnings. Food imports were on the rise during the year, partly as a result of natural conditions, but also because of the government's continuing neglect of agriculture, which received only 2% of the recurrent budget for 1974, compared with 14.7% for the military. Emphasis on mining was reflected in the continuing growth of copper production, which topped the 500,000-ton mark in 1974, and in the opening of new areas to prospecting.

The trend toward economic nationalism, which has been evident in Zaire for several years, continued to manifest itself throughout the year. Following the November 1973 decision to terminate all rights over land held by nonnationals, the government took over total control of a Belgian diamond-mining firm and ordered all other mining concerns to sell half of their shares to Zaire. Real estate operations, construction, and the distribution of petroleum products were also placed under public control. The decision to gradually eliminate all foreigners from the retail sector, however, raised several complex problems. For example, it soon became apparent that only a handful of wealthy Africans were likely to be in a position to profit from this measure. Thus the measure can be expected to reinforce the country's incipient class stratification.

EDOUARD BUSTIN, *Boston University*

ZAIRE • Information Highlights

Official Name: Republic of Zaire.
Location: Central equatorial Africa.
Area: 905,565 square miles (2,345,409 sq km).
Population (1973 est.): 23,600,000.
Chief Cities (1972 est.): Kinshasa, the capital, 1,623,760; Luluabourg, 506,000.
Government: *Head of state,* Mobutu Sese Seko, president (took office Nov. 1965). *Head of government,* Mobutu Sese Seko. *Legislature* (unicameral)—National Legislative Council.
Monetary Unit: Zaire (0.50 zaire equals U. S.$1, Aug. 1974).
Gross National Product (1972 est.): $2,262,000,000.
Manufacturing (major products): Processed foods, clothing, textiles, soap.
Major Agricultural Products: Palm oil and kernels, coffee, rubber, tea, cacao, groundnuts, bananas, cassava.
Foreign Trade (1972): *Exports,* $623,000,000; *imports,* $669,000,000.

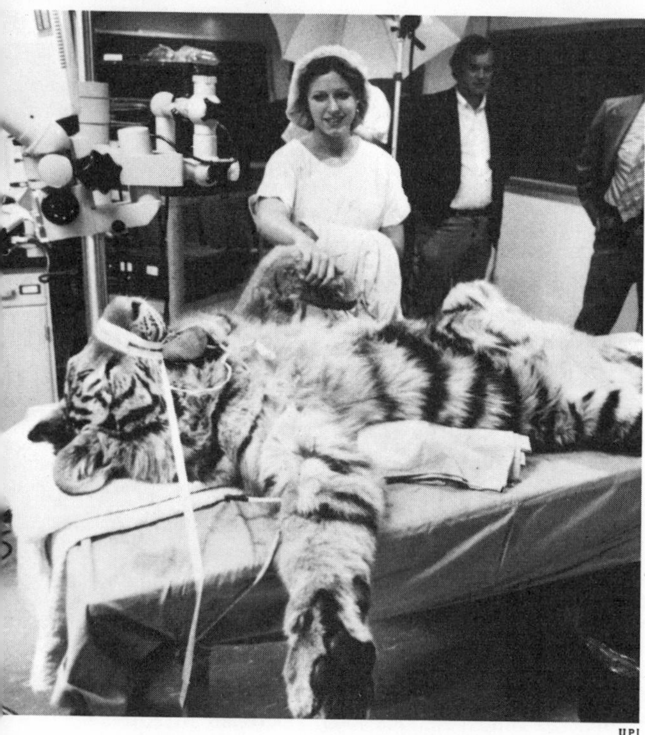

UPI

A nurse at the University of Illinois Eye and Ear Infirmary in Chicago makes sure that Brutus, a Siberian tiger, is ready to have cataracts removed from his eyes.

ZOOLOGY

One of the major events of 1974 in zoology was the recognition that ecology has "come of age."

Ecology Studies. Early ecologists were almost always descriptive in their approach. Their studies were centered on the factors influencing either a single species (autecology) or all of the inhabitants of a given region (synecology, or community ecology). Theoretical ecology, using computer models of entire ecosystems and mathematical models of specific situations, is being used to predict probable effects on man-made and other changes in ecosystems. For example, a small area set aside as a nature preserve or national park essentially becomes an island when the surrounding regions are converted into agricultural ecosystems or cities, or undergo other major shifts. Even though the park ("island") is protected, many species in it, especially the rare ones, will soon become extinct. This island effect results from the fact that most such areas are not large enough to maintain populations of many species over long periods.

Ecosystem fragility, especially in desert, subdesert, and arctic-alpine situations, is being recognized and quantified. In such situations land misuse by overgrazing or similar activities can destroy the existing system in a short time. Even if the area is then abandoned and protected from further misuse, several thousands of years may be required to restore the original balance.

A number of the studies in ecology have been focused on the various problems ensuing from the increased human populations having ever-increasing impacts on their environment. Some examples of these activities follow.

Coyote Control. The outlawing of coyote poisoning by the Environmental Protection Act has led many cattle and sheep growers to complain of increased losses of animals to coyote predation. Carl R. Gustavson and associates of the department of psychology at the University of Utah have studied the possibility of coyote predation control by conditioning the animals to avoid eating domestic animals. Their experiments show that coyotes fed sheep and cattle meat treated with poison that makes them ill, but does not kill, soon learn to avoid all such meat, whether poisoned or not. They suggest that this be utilized to control coyote predation on ranchlands.

Pesticides. Attempts to find alternatives to pesticides for controlling insect pests in forest and agricultural systems have continued.

E. A. Donforce of California State Polytechnic University reported on the ecology of insect host-parasitoid communities. He dealt with some of the problems associated with using natural parasites to control the various insect populations.

Further effects of DDT and other organochloride pollutants were documented when Robert L. Long and his associates of the National Marine Fisheries Service reported premature births in California sea lions associated with high pollutant levels. Although the premature young are not dead at birth, they die within a few hours.

Nicholas Wade of *Science* magazine summarized the known material on insect viruses as pesticides. A virus that kills the cotton bollworm is now ready to be used commercially.

Other Research. Interesting reports from other fields of zoology include the discovery of an early Paleocene fossil primate in Montana. This find, reported by William A. Clements of the University of California at Berkeley, sheds light on the origin of all living primates.

James C. Hickman of Swarthmore College reported that ants are not always villains in their interactions with plants, and gave details of a small plant in the Cascades of Oregon that depends entirely on a species of ant for pollination (see BOTANY).

C. E. Wickstrom and R. W. Castenholz of the University of Oregon reported that certain ostracods (tiny crustaceans) living in thermal hot springs are the metazoans with the highest known temperature tolerances. They thrive at temperatures of 40–45° C (104–113° F) and survive for up to an hour at temperatures in excess of 50° C (122° F).

E. LENDELL COCKRUM
University of Arizona

index

Main article headings appear in this index as bold-faced capitals; subjects within articles appear as lower-case entries. Main article page numbers and general references are listed first under each entry; the subentries which follow them on separate lines direct the reader to related topics appearing elsewhere. Both the general references and the subentries should be consulted for maximum usefulness of this index. Illustrations are indexed herein. Cross references are to the entries in this index.

A

B

C

H

I

J

K

L

M

T

U

V

W

X, Y, Z